D1484137

A Book about the Film
Monty Python and the Holy Grail

A Book about the Film
Monty Python and the Holy Grail

All the References from African Swallows to Zoot

Darl Larsen

Rowman & Littlefield
Lanham • Boulder • New York • London

Published by Rowman & Littlefield
A wholly owned subsidiary of The Rowman & Littlefield Publishing Group, Inc.
4501 Forbes Boulevard, Suite 200, Lanham, Maryland 20706
www.rowman.com

Unit A, Whitacre Mews, 26-34 Stannary Street, London SE11 4AB

British Library Cataloguing in Publication Information Available

Library of Congress Cataloging-in-Publication Data
Larsen, Darl, 1963–
  A book about the film Monty Python and the Holy Grail : all the references from African swallows
to Zoot / Darl Larsen.
      pages cm
  Includes bibliographical references and index.
  ISBN 978-1-4422-4553-2 (hardback : alk. paper) — ISBN 978-1-4422-4554-9 (ebook) 1. Monty
Python and the Holy Grail (Motion picture) I. Title.
  PN1997.M68L38 2015
  791.43'72—dc23   2014036215

∞™ The paper used in this publication meets the minimum requirements of
American National Standard for Information Sciences—Permanence of Paper
for Printed Library Materials, ANSI/NISO Z39.48-1992.

Printed in the United States of America

To
my family; my sister, Stacey Larsen Feigel;
and my friend Andrew John Black

CONTENTS

CONTENTS

ACKNOWLEDGMENTS

There are many thanks to be handed out.

Stephen Ryan of Rowman & Littlefield, for first asking for the book, and then waiting patiently for it to be finished; Dr. William Proctor Williams, who puts up with my silliness while he accomplishes all sorts of more important things; and the gracious Julian Doyle—who wore many hats on the *Holy Grail* shoot—he answered as many questions as I threw at him.

Closer to home, Drew Duncan and Kelyn Ikegami provided tireless editing work, Dean Duncan read many pages and made helpful comments, while Amy Jensen and Rodger Sorensen offered unflagging department and college support. My Theatre and Media Arts colleagues Sharon Swenson, Kelly Loosli, Megan Sanborn-Jones, Wade Hollingshaus, Brad Barber, Ben Thevenin, Tom Russell, Tom Lefler, Jeff Parkin, Mary Farahnakian; Elizabeth Funk and the TMA Department office; and my university colleagues Daryl Lee, Roger Macfarlane, and Chip Oscarson all contributed.

This research would have been impossible without the invaluable collections at BYU's Harold B. Lee Library, and especially the hardworking staff of HBLL Interlibrary Loan, who managed to find every obscure item I asked for.

Jennifer Nicol at Stirling helped get the word out to extras who worked on the film shoot, and thanks to a handful of former Stirling students who responded with their own memories, including Alastair Scott, Jim McIver, and Nick Rowe.

Thanks also to my friend and colleague Randy Malamud, for being very supportive.

Finally, my wonderful family—Nycole, Emrys, Brynmor, Eamonn, Dathyl, Ransom, Culainn, Keir, Misti and Hayden, and Mom and Dad. Thank you.

INTRODUCTION

His triumph was the last victory of western Rome; his short-lived empire created the future nations of the English and the Welsh; and it was during his reign and under his authority that the Scots first came to Scotland. His victory and his defeat turned Roman Britain into Great Britain.

—John Morris[1]

We come, last in the fifth century and first in the sixth, to Arthur, a man without position or ancestry in pre-Geoffrey Welsh sources. I think we can dispose of him quite briefly.

—David Dumville[2]

In 1973, the warrior-king Arthur is the father and maker of Great Britain, thanks to the prodigious and emphatic historian John Morris. But Arthur's meteoric elevation was as short-lived as his alleged empire. With David Dumville's brusque and assured promise in 1977 the scholarly mandarins closed the book on the historical King Arthur. Less than two years after the release of *Monty Python and the Holy Grail*, where Arthur found himself being hustled into a police van as the film came to a forced and perhaps inevitable conclusion, Arthur's role in history was also arrested.

This book isn't just about the real or imagined Arthur, it's about a smallish British film that became a cultural phenomenon, especially outside Britain. More precisely, this book is a study of the worlds that could produce such a film—an annotation of the Arthurian legends, of the Middle Ages, and of the twentieth century, in many respects. For this study we will focus on two major sources. The first is the 1975 film *Monty Python and the Holy Grail* itself—natch. The second, complementary source is the "book of the film," *Monty Python and the Holy Grail (Book)* released in 1977,[3] the same year Dumville interred Arthur and Arthurian "scholarship." This printed source contains copies of the initial, thrown-together script created as the Pythons tossed their desk drawers looking for unused sketch ideas that might fit into a feature film.[4] It also offers a nearly final draft of the script as eventually shot,[5] with major changes (some very recognizable, as they've become part of our cultural lexicon) penciled in after the fact. There are also many pages of production photos, film frame captures, and notes and drawings from codirector Terry Jones, but especially codirector, animator, and production designer Terry Gilliam. The bulk of these annotations and discussions are included in the appendices, as laid out in the table of contents.

The heft of this work, however, is given over to a kind of *vade mecum* of the film *Monty Python and the Holy Grail* and its historical, literary, political, and sociocultural milieu. The Pythons drew on Arthuriana, the Middle Ages, and their own histories—including the *Geistesgeschichte* of the postwar years and into the Great Britain of 1975, the same ore they mined for *Flying Circus*—to cobble together the story of a legendary, itinerant knight questing through an England not of Arthur's time but of all time(s). Like Bede's *Ecclesiastical History of the English People*, Chaucer's *Canterbury Tales,* or Spenser's *Faerie Queene*, *Monty Python and the Holy Grail* is "a revealing document of its world";[6] it is a film that is tugged along behind the crest of the various New Waves in world cinema, and, importantly, it is as much about the 1970s as it is about the 930s. Roman Polanski's 1971 version of *Macbeth* is a helpful genesis: "[Polanski] proceeds by transmogrifying the Christian text of Shakespeare's own time into the contemporary 1972 world of unredeemed sin, suffering, and death" (Rothwell, 1973, 71). The Pythons demand that their Arthur undertake a similarly ruthful journey. *Monty Python and the Holy Grail* is an artifact informed by the history of film and filmmaking, reflexive enough to acknowledge its pastiche nature as a shifting, postmodern construct, but aware, also, that it is a paeanic elegy to a dimming and diminished Great Britain.

Again, there are at least three distinct spheres that troupe members Graham Chapman, John Cleese, Terry Gilliam, Eric Idle, Terry Jones, Michael Palin and *Monty Python and the Holy Grail* will navigate: the worlds of King Arthur and his exploits, of the Middle Ages, and of the Pythons' contemporary Britain. Since the first of these is almost entirely mythical, the second is obscured by the shadows of the past, and the third still so close as to be softly focused, teasing out this wool can be a challenge. As will be demonstrated, there is conflict in and between these separate but more or less equal diegetic influences throughout the film. The fairy tale or legendary world of King Arthur is impacted by the "realities" of an imagined Middle Ages, and both are intruded upon by not only more modern ideas and values, but also the extradiegetic liminality involving the physical production of the film. The tensions and faulting between these worlds—and the fact that there are no omniscient characters who "see" everything (narrators are as prone to "influence" as any character we see)—have kept the film from settling neatly into any particular genre; it's become a transmissible cultural artifact, a culturgen, especially in the United States—and likely accounts for its continuing popularity some forty years after its release in May 1975.[7]

The seeds for this project were planted in a Northern Illinois University doctoral seminar in 1995. After class one evening Dr. Williams[8] and I were discussing the lively, sometimes scatological verbal exchanges in Jonson's *Volpone* and Shakespeare's *Much Ado*, and we agreed that the Oxford and Cambridge-educated Pythons were certainly aware of these works as they created their own colorful dialogues of silly insult and well-crafted invective. The discussion happily became a term paper, then a series of papers, then a dissertation, and finally a published book: *Monty Python, Shakespeare and English Renaissance Drama* (2003).[9] Work on that project pushed me inexorably toward my next: a close annotation of the forty-five-episode *Monty Python's Flying Circus* television series, which became the single-volume mouthful *Monty Python's Flying Circus: An Utterly Complete, Thoroughly Unillustrated, Absolutely Unauthorized Guide to Possibly All the References from Arthur "Two Sheds" Jackson to Zambesi* (2008), followed by an expanded two-volume edition in 2013.[10] And why? Honestly, it's the same reason annotations and glosses continue to be essential when students study Spenser or Shakespeare or Dryden—the increasing impenetrability of language and especially meaning as epochs pass into history. The cultural legibility of the television scripts and episodes of *Flying Circus* becomes hazy and then indecipherable to subsequent viewers, as is always the case with especially the topicalities that create and then re-create popular culture from show to show, year to year, and then age to age. The detailed annotations attempt a reclaiming of these fading referents, reinvigorating and resuscitating the world as experienced and then sent up by Monty Python in the late 1960s and early 1970s.

Stepping out of the wayback machine, we arrive at the current project—yet another study of the Monty Python *oeuvre*. Given that most of even my culturally literate students only know Monty Python in connection to the troupe's feature films, and especially *Holy Grail* (and, yes, some wonder which troupe member was named "Monty"), it seemed natural to add the third panel to the diptych. After all, *Holy Grail* is one of the most oft-quoted and misquoted films in all of cinematic history; it can appear on "best of all time" movie lists;[11] and the film was even part of a much-promoted "cultural exchange" between Great Britain and Brezhnev's Soviet Union in 1976, at the height of the Cold War.[12] In short, the Pythons have contributed to film history and cultural criticism in ways they couldn't possibly have anticipated, creating phenomena that are worthy of close study.

My goal, then, is to situate this film both in the Python canon and the broader world, much as I attempted for *Flying Circus*—examining how the feature film elaborates familiar themes, mines history—in this case Arthuriana and the Middle Ages—reflects itself and its production-ness, and most significantly, how completely this erstwhile medieval film is a product of its more modern genesis. It is as much a film of the new waves and the post-Vietnam era as any currently canonized; it manages to be sardonic and festal. To accomplish our goals we must thoughtfully examine the state of both Arthurian and medieval studies in the early 1970s—the two intersect often during this period; we must look closely at miscommunication, at social unrest and violence, at the eruptions of films and film meaning in the postwar period; and we must agnize how important the falling, diminishing status of Great Britain and the Empire must be to Arthur's ultimately circumscribed quest.

Of Medievalists and Methodologies—

This is as good a time as any to make my first apologies, and it's to medievalists for playing in their yard. I am not a medievalist, and I'm not going to pretend to be one. I have done the honest legwork, though—I've read and appreciated many of the medievalists' books, and especially those that would have been available and even required reading for Oxbridge-types like the Pythons studying in the 1960s. Troupe member Terry Jones read poetry and history at Oxford,[13] and as I've gathered and pored over source materials, I've imagined a syllabus of the seminal texts on the medieval period he might have been assigned. My list includes important titles from Frank Stenton, Christopher Brooke, G. G. Coulton, Maurice Powicke, George Holmes, May McKisack, David Dumville, and A. L. Poole, et al.; these act as foundational material herein, along with a number of the Middle Ages authors and their texts, from Bede to Gildas and through Chrétien, Malory, and beyond. Seeing the lists just provided, it should be obvious to the reader looking for a *Monty Python and the Holy Grail* trivia book that this isn't the book for them (no apologies here). As for the state of Arthurian studies, I have tried to puzzle together the zeitgeist of the immediate years leading up to the Pythons' writing and production of the film in 1973–1975. Several of the noteworthy "Age of Arthur" scholarly books released between 1968 and 1973—by Alcock and Ashe and Morris—along with very new archaeological evidences germane to life in the fifth and sixth centuries in Britain, made for an exciting reinvigoration of the glorious age of Arthur in the late 1960s and early 1970s, just when the sagging, flagging Empire seemed to need that fabled figure most.

As for a methodology, I try and look at the world informing the film *wie es wirklich war*, or "how it really was." I don't as much interview the film (though treating it, still, somewhat as a character for a biography) as interrogate it. In this quasi-biography of *Monty Python and the Holy Grail*, then, what am I teasing out? Where are the informing sources? *Where* and *what* and *when* are its social, political, and cultural influences? And against what acculturating landscape can or should the film be set? I will illuminate what allowed the creation of this particular film at this particular time—Great Britain, c. 1973–1975. Period newspapers, television shows and advertisements, recent domestic and international films, and the pages of *Private Eye* are helpful, for example, in determining alternately what was very serious and what was being laughed at, and, often, what serious things were being laughed at. It's crucial to look at other literatures, including pessimistic novels about Britain's slide into a new fascism like *The Lost Diaries of Albert Smith* (1965), as well as nonfiction works that sailed off bookstore racks. These popular and fiery Penguin paperbacks sold in the thousands—including more obvious titles like *The Stagnant Society*, *The Other England*, and *What's Wrong with British Industry?*[14]—and attest to waves of pessimism, even nihilism, and to a divide in the 1960s between "progressive" London and the Home Counties (O'Hara, 6). The overall malaise of the late 1960s and certainly the early 1970s is critical—when the promises of the 1950s gave way to the realities of an era of continual war, both hot and cold. In *Dr. Strangelove*, Ambassador Sadeski (Peter Bull) speaks for the Soviet people, certainly, but British folk could nod along as he decries the unforeseen expenses of "the arms race, the space race, and the peace race"—annual expenditures that kept struggling welfare countries with prehistoric labor practices like Britain from flourishing even as her former ally and enemy (the United States and West Germany, respectively) raced pell-mell into economic prosperity.

The whole of the Pythons' work on *Monty Python's Flying Circus* is key resource material, as they reference themselves and betray their hobbyhorses over and over again.[15] In their treatment of upperclass figures and commoners, of women as sexual objects, in their quarrying of history for period characters who can live in the now, and in their general disregard for the unities, the Pythons' work in *Flying Circus* set the table for *Holy Grail*. As the Dumville quote at the start indicates, any 1970s "Age of Arthur" celebrations were short-lived—energy embargoes, strikes, and governments without mandate had settled in, and Britain's miserable 1978–1979 Winter of Discontent was still on the sooty gray horizon.

Is This the Middle Ages Which I See Before Me?—

Monty Python and the Holy Grail is a film set in the Middle Ages and written by well-read, thoughtful university wits; but is it a medieval film, by genre, if there is such a thing? In Arthur Lindley's "The Ahistoricism of Medieval Film," that question is treated, and the significance of the *now* is clear:

> In any case, the subject is the present, not the past. "History," Pierre Sorlin[16] has written, "is a society's memory of its past, and the functioning of this memory depends on the situation in which the society finds itself. . . . That is to say, *our* priorities order the selection that mythologizes the past. . . . We get the past we need." (10, 12)

In *Monty Python and the Holy Grail* we are presented with a tenth-century setting, thirteenth-century knights, fourteenth-century castles, as well as peasants and kings, plagues and squalor, and witch burnings and superstition, but what is missing? Most of the Middle Ages, as it turns out. There aren't fields full of grazing sheep, or sheep being shorn for their valuable wool; there are no sacks of this industry standard wool ready for export, or any sign of textile works.[17] There are no cathedrals, abbeys, or shrines awaiting pilgrims. There are no town markets or fairs.[18] There is no scutage, tallage or Danegeld, or taxes of any kind. There are no dynastic struggles or endless wars with and on the Continent. There are no invasions by Picts, Scots, or Vikings from the north, or the Welsh from the west. (Maybe this is why there are no taxes.) There are no married couples. There are no families. There is a mother and son, yes (Dennis and his mother), but we only know their relationship thanks to the *printed* script. There are no children.[19] There is no industry—no iron-mongers or charcoal-burners, no mercers, drapers, or needle makers; there are no visible wind- or watermills, though Domesday Book counts more than 5,600 of the latter.[20] There are no roads or navigable waterways, no plowed or planted fields, no remains of Roman, Saxon, Danish, or even Norman civilization; there are no cities, no towns, no nobles, and no bishops. As will be demonstrated, the Middle Ages setting is employed by the Pythons where it's useful, and then shrugged off when the narrative moves toward things "Arthurian"—meaning legendary or mythological, even fairy tale settings and events. Chaucer connects these as well, through his Wife of Bath as she begins her tale: "In th'olde dayes of the Kyng Arthour, / Of which that Britons speken greet honour, / Al was this land fulfild of fayerye" (lines 857–59). Fantastical characters and creatures—the Knights Who Say Ni, the Three-Headed Knight, Tim the Enchanter, the Killer Rabbit, the Legendary Beast—occupy their specific environs but can be left behind quite easily as the quest moves forward or sideways. The Wife of Bath also admits that time has changed Britain, and that Arthur's fairyland of magic and mystery has been displaced by "matyns" and "hooly thynges"—by religion and the modern world:

> The elf-queene, with hir joly compaignye,
> Daunced ful ofte in many a grene mede.
> This was the olde opinion, as I rede;
> I speke of manye hundred yeres ago.
> But now kan no man se none elves mo,
> For now the grete charitee and prayeres
> Of lymytours and othere hooly freres,
> That serchen every lond and every streem,
> As thikke as motes in the sonne-beem,
> Blessynge halles, chambres, kichenes, boures,
> Citees, burghes, castels, hye toures,
> Thropes, bernes, shipnes, dayeryes—
> This maketh that ther ben no fayeryes.
> For ther as wont to walken was an elf,
> Ther walketh now the lymytour hymself. (lines 860–74)[21]

Toward the end of the film Brother Maynard will replace the helpful but ineffective Tim the Enchanter, for example—men of the Church (with explosives) supersede superstition— and the Grail quest can move on to its inconclusive conclusion. Such dislocations occur often in *Holy Grail*, as the magical world gives way to the crushing reality of the grimy Middle Ages, which in turn can be stanched by a policeman's hand covering a camera lens. In the end, however, the reason most of the fairy tale and medieval elements mentioned above are missing is simple—there was no budget to reproduce on film the rather busy England of the Middle Ages. The Python version of the England of the Middle Ages would have to do.[22]

It's no surprise that the Pythons chose, then, to reproduce the Middle Ages as described by contemporary chronicler Thomas Walsingham,[23] evoking "days of wrath and anguish, days of calamity and misery" (Tuchman, 377). In this choice they were writing of the past they needed, to paraphrase Lindley and Sorlin, corresponding to views from their own windows as much as of the distant medieval world. *Time* magazine's correspondent in London wrote of Britain's dreary, somber visage in early 1972:

> Britain labored under a Dickensian midwinter gloom last week. Off went the garish neons of Piccadilly Circus. After twilight, Big Ben could be heard but not seen. Buckingham Palace was lit by candles and hand torches. Millions of Londoners went to and from work beneath dimmed streetlights. Thirty crews of firemen helped rescue people who were trapped in stalled elevators. Dramatizing the nation's power shortage, one BBC newscaster had to read his bulletin by candlelight.[24]

Both 1973 and 1974 would provide similar privations, as Britain's economy sputtered under the weight of its balance of payments, worker unrest, spiraling energy costs, and the much-cooled "white heat"[25] of technological advancement pushing other countries ahead and into the future. The dislocative years 1973–1974 ring like the plague years 1348–1350, when much of Britain changed utterly, and much of life was dismal. The seminal British punk band the Sex Pistols[26] were fronted by Johnny Rotten (John Lydon), who remembered these darker days:

> Early Seventies Britain was a very depressing place. It was completely run-down, there was trash on the streets, total unemployment—just about everybody was on strike. Everybody was brought up with an education system that told you point blank that if you came from the wrong side of the tracks . . . then you had no hope in hell and no career prospects at all. (Robb, 97)

Writing in 1977, when the wounds were still fresh, C. J. Bartlett is admirably circumspect about the period's eventual heritage, but clear:

> With the passage of time it will become possible to see more clearly just how great a divide the years 1973–4 were in British history—whether or not they represent a significant break in the course of events since 1945 and the real end of the postwar era. At the very least the dramatic developments of 1973–4 ushered in an unexpected election, the fall of a government, a period of acute political uncertainty, and the worst recession since that which followed the Wall Street crash of 1929. (*A History of Postwar Britain*, 315)

The answer is likely clear by now. The events of 1973–1974 ushered in a tired Labour government headed by an equally tired prime minister; two years later Wilson resigns unexpectedly, Callaghan steps in, is quickly overwhelmed by events of the day, and the table is set for the revolution of Margaret Thatcher and the Tories in 1979.

The 1970s were seen as dark and dreary, especially in newspaper columns and surveys penned immediately as 1979 turned to 1980.[27] During the 1970s "full employment" had become even more of a fantasy; fewer "school-leaver" students were passing fewer "A levels"[28]; price rises were experienced across the board for food, energy, and housing; regular church attendance continued its decline; and forecasts for economic growth had been more optimistic than accurate.[29] Add the seemingly inexhaustible number of crises both domestic and foreign discussed in later sections, and you have the makings of a doozy of a decade. The penultimate chapter of Christopher Booker's *The Seventies* (1980) is titled "Cultural Collapse," and it begins rather drearily: "In the past ten years, our culture in the widest sense—architectural, artistic, scientific, philosophical—has reached the most dramatic dead end in the entire history of mankind" (253). What has been lost and how society has managed to cope are of particular concern to Booker, and will be to us as we see how Monty Python reanimates the medieval genre from lifelessness to, well, a higher form of lifelessness. Booker continues:

But suddenly, standing at the end of that great adventure [the advances of post-Renaissance Western culture], we can see with appalling clarity where it was all leading—to the eventual complete loss of *meaning*. . . . [O]n the one hand, the scientists have accumulated more and more facts and "knowledge," the philosophers have subjected language to ever more minute and rigorous examination; on the other, artists have more and more pursued effects, sensations, illusion; and as that gap has opened ever wider, so, almost without our noticing it, has meaning gently been sliding further and further out of view—to the point where, confronted with the gaping void, the cosmic despair that lies at the heart of our contemporary culture in all directions (except where we can paper it over by rushing back for consolation into those embodiments of meaning which survive from the past), we do not even recognize the fact. (254)

So by the end of the 1970s we have lost "meaning," accumulated stuff (become hoarders of cultural, scientific, and artistic bric-a-brac), glimpsed "despair," and tried to caulk the gaps with nostalgia, according to Booker.[30] How does this apply to our film? Arthur searches for the Grail at God's command, giving "meaning" to the "sad times" in England; various Grails are promised and even seen, found and put together in versions of the script and film; but every "successful" transition/transaction in the film leads to another *cul de sac*, another dead end, before the external forces of reality overcome nostalgia, and the film is abruptly stopped.

It may be just a coincidence that in summer 1973, a few months before the first draft of the script for *Holy Grail* is completed (by Palin and Jones), the "Ely Cathedral Goblet" is being flogged for sale in major English newspapers.[31] There will also be similar goblets on sale commemorating the cathedrals of Lincoln, St. Paul's, Chichester, Hereford, et al., during this same period—all limited editions, all going fast. More importantly, the cups are being sold as "truly unique investment(s)," each "signed personally" by various Deans. These "embodiments of meaning" are semi-valuable curios destined for English front room mantles, not quite what the God of *Holy Grail* intended for His Grail.[32] In the first draft of the printed script, it turns out there are multiple grails found or cobbled together, and eventually they're all presented to God in the coffee shop at Harrods (*MPHGB*, 46). God isn't pleased, and tells Arthur and mates to go and find the *true* Grail "somewhere in Italy" (46). Just one page later, the questers steal a chalice from a church in Italy, race outside to where God waits in a VW "getaway van," and they speed off, militarized clergy on their tail. Their van plunges into the sea as God promises to "part this lot" (the sea)—the van sinks, and the credits roll (47). The ending of the original draft would have likely brought the reproach their next film invited, but this shirty God who dies with his holy accomplices never made it off the typed page. God, the ultimate authority figure, can expect the same treatment as an Upperclass Twit or a "King of the Britons" in the Pythons' carnivalesque, topsy-turvy world.[33]

This collective dis-ease is generational, as Booker[34] describes his own memories of Britain's mighty struggles during World War II, and especially the role foreigners played in that struggle. He and his friends told stories about plucky Brits doing the dirty or precise work that the Americans couldn't manage, but the caveat was there:

Looking back, I suppose that we used to tell these stories at least partly just as a salve to our national pride, to console ourselves for the way we had come to look on the Americans—these hugely rich and powerful cousins from across the Atlantic—as our protectors. We relied on them completely. . . . [F]or the people of a country who had been through the Battle of Britain, which was still in theory the center of a worldwide empire, covering a quarter of mankind, it was quite a blow to find out just how much we had suddenly become the weak, dependent junior partner. (*The Seventies*, 69)

And these disappointments wouldn't end with the war. As we'll discuss later, there were plenty of upstart inferiors asking for or more likely demanding their "rights" in the post-colonial era. From about 1900 the great British Empire would get smaller and smaller, its managers less and less internationally effectual, in the years after a war the British had ostensibly won. Colors on the global map were changing[35] as Britain ceded the "jewel" of India, dismantled Mandatory Palestine, and surrendered influence in Suez and Aden. Meanwhile the United States took the front seat in the nuclear arms race, as well as the race to the moon, and Britain had to watch Rhodesia and then Malaysia slip away, and on. We will discuss later the effects of colonial diminishment, where the ruled become rulers, and see that it's really no surprise that King Arthur's epic becomes mock; if he *were* to succeed, the film becomes a blinkered, wish-fulfillment story, and less a reflection of the period, which Booker describes as a time "most brutally anarchic" (45). In such a merciless world there is no possibility for a legendary Arthur to achieve his legendary goals.

And just what are the Pythons doing with their historical baubles, the nuggets they quarry from history's mine? Amusing themselves with them, of course. During the first episode of *Flying Circus* they gave Mozart his own television show, setting the tone for the rest of the series:

> Python's use of historical figures and settings will become essential to the structure and humor of *FC*. In this case, the incongruity of an eighteenth-century composer hosting a television show provides the jumping-off point for the sketch's humor. In most cases, there is no attempt to explain or account for the presence of long-dead figures, or characters separated by geography, time, or culture, as they interact or just appear in modern settings. This . . . reflects the significant influence that seminal Modernist works like Eliot's *The Waste Land*—where class and accent, the past and present, and even cultures and languages interact in a sort of ever-present, decaying London—exhibited in the works of Monty Python. (*MPFC: UC*, 1.6)

In this they are doing what many in the scholarly world have done with Arthur and his milieu over the years, though the Pythons' end result is admittedly comedic, not academic. N. J. Higham describes the process: "In practice, most, if not all, of the academic community prefer to explore the so-called 'Arthurian' texts of the central Middle Ages within a contemporary intellectual, political and cultural context, rather than as a quarry for 'Dark Ages facts'" (*King Arthur: Myth-Making and History*, 37). The Pythons have decided to explore the Malorian version of Arthur, primarily, and they are forcefully pulling the characters forward into their "contemporary intellectual, political and cultural context"—1970s Britain. This is why "Constitutional Peasant" Dennis is able to stand toe-to-toe with King Arthur, espousing fringe twentieth-century political models, without worrying about losing his head—the worst that will happen is a mild throttling. In *Flying Circus*, this freedom allows Sir Philip Sidney to be both an Elizabethan courtier as well as a twentieth-century "porn merchant," for example. The Sidney character (played by Palin) begins the episode as Superintendent Gaskell, a modern-day police inspector on the hunt for illegal pornography sold through the Tudor Jobs Agency, but crosses a temporal threshold (represented by a backroom dirty bookshop) into the sixteenth century, becoming, for everyone in that time, Sir Philip Sidney, "fighter against filth."[36] When he finally crosses back over into the modern world, he's placed under arrest by former police mates as Sir Philip Sidney, porn merchant, though he vehemently claims he's still Gaskell of the Vice Squad. In *Holy Grail*, Arthur will also be faced with very contemporary problems, including obstinate workers, societal indolence and ignorance, and "French persons" who are both rude foreigners *and* the looming embodiment of the great *"non"* of Charles de Gaulle.[37] (Arthur must confront legendary and mythological challenges, too; the film world provides no prompts for discerning which is which.) Malory employed this standard, as well, according to Helen Cooper, as he wrote his *magnum opus* from his fifteenth-century jail cell:

> Malory's work may ostensibly be set in a legendary age in which chivalric behavior was lived most fully, but not the least interesting thing about his own redaction of his Arthurian material is the way it intersects with the conditions of his own era . . . [his] awareness of the connections between the story he is recounting and his own times becomes on occasion explicit . . . . Malory's *Morte Darthur*[38] is not an exercise in nostalgia for a golden age: it is an account of the destruction of an ideal.[39] (*LMD-WM*, xii)

And rather than patiently waiting for moments in their tale where such "intersections" could organically occur, as Malory does, the Pythons often force the issue by tossing about terms like "gay" and "anarchosyndicalist" as if they belonged to the Middle Ages, and by including images and eventually influences of modern authority figures who stop both the quest and the film.

"And Now for Something Completely the Same"

Part of what sets this medieval film apart from others (and from other genre films, as well) is the looming presence throughout of the Pythons' favored writing structures, biases, hobbyhorses, narrative styles, and the like. They have favorite targets, of course. As through the run of *Flying Circus*, the Pythons poke fun at attempts to communicate, at the challenges inherent in simple transactions, at village life, at "others" including homosexuals and women and toffs and foreigners, and at the cozy and eccentric "Middle England" of Luton, Bradford, Esher, et al. As young liberals coming of age in the heady days of the Kennedy and Johnson administrations, followed by the homegrown version of socially conscious leadership in Wilson's Labour Party after 1965, the Pythons naturally, joyfully jabbed at conservative thought and the Tories, fustigating both know-it-alls and know-nothings along the way. Bowler-hatted and brolly-armed men of the city appear often in this series, and are universally displayed in their moral, ethical, spiritual, and intellectual bankruptcy. These Upperclass Twits tend to favor apartheid policies, capital punishment, eugenics, and profit, and are also sexually suspect. The everyday Englishman and (mannish) woman are also fair game, their accents, dress, and rusticity betraying both salt-of-the-earth and simpleton qualities—these oddities are the backbone of "this green and pleasant land."[40] For their first narrative feature film, the Pythons wanted to move beyond the scatteredness of the *MPFC* sketch/interstitial/sketch structure. They learned from and leaned on the semi-consistent "*Njorl's Saga*" of Ep. 27 and the episode-long "The Cycling Tour" of Ep. 34, where a single central character could be followed along a fairly stable narrative trajectory—with digressions and asides and silliness intact. The first draft of their "second" film was much closer to *MPFC* in both tone and construction; when Jones and Palin finally settled on Arthur and Patsy as their guides, the film's through lines became visible.

Thanks in part to this flimsy narrative and structural cohesiveness, *Monty Python and the Holy Grail* has become the best-known and most oft-quoted work in the Python *oeuvre*, and for many is the essence of what is Monty Python. The film is polymorphic and heteroglossic: it is an example of its subgenre as well as a genre-transgressing work that threatens the integrity of the medieval film. It can operate as an authentic-looking film set in the Dark Ages, and by virtue of its authenticity (its authentic "look" thanks to careful production design) it effectively parodies that same genre, hoisting the historical epic with its own petard, so to speak. This film that is both send-up and celebration opened at the London Casino on Thursday, 3 April 1975, to no real fanfare or expectations, since the film had to that point only pre-screened significantly in the United States. New episodes of the television show *Flying Circus* had been off the air since December 1974, after an abbreviated (and to many, unsatisfactory) final half-season run. It had gone out with a whimper in Britain, but the "bang" was just beginning in the United States.

In 1975 *Flying Circus* began appearing in syndication on various public television channels in the United States,[41] running late at night, and gathering a sizable and committed college-age following. In the "club notes" section of the 1975 Lehigh University yearbook, for example, one of the year's celebrated events is listed as "Monty Python at 10:30"; in 1976 one Peter Templeton is a member of the Monty Python Fan Club and "wants to find the Holy Grail" at Guilderland Central High School;[42] John Ewert mentions his love for Monty Python in the *Chronicle 1976* yearbook of Lewis High School in Southington, Connecticut; and students at the Abington Friends School in Jenkintown, Pennsylvania were devoted "Monty Python fans" as early as 1976. Other American high school and college yearbooks rate the Pythons as the leading comedy group of the day, or list *Flying Circus* as one of their "must see" programs, along with *Kojak* and *Baretta*.[43] By 1977, there are images of students wearing their Monty Python T-shirts in many U.S. high school and college yearbook photos, and the phenomenon has gained its own life.[44]

The Art Film: *"Un film trouvé á la ferraille"*

We'll get to the French lesson momentarily. Let's begin with *Monty Python and the Holy Grail* and the art film—that's one precipice on which we teeter. Even admitting that the film was conceived, written, and produced within and into the same social, historical, and cultural mélange that produced some of the most acclaimed films of "arthouse" directors like Bergman, Antonioni, and Buñuel (and with Das Neue Kino just finding its legs), most critics have seen *Holy Grail* as a clever parody and little more.[45] Most paying audiences just think it's funny. It is both parodic and humorous, of course, and more complex and revealing than most parodies or historical epics. So let's start with a snippet from a contemporary film reviewer, writing for the *Times*:

> [The film] succeeds to a remarkable degree in awakening these dismal echoes from the past, but the story is so episodic and bizarre that at times it becomes unintelligible. However, a thread of continuity is given to the narrative by the two central characters, a knight and his squire.[46]

This *could* have been a thoughtful reviewer describing Arthur and Patsy as they wandered a filthy medieval England, certainly, but it's not. Still ignoring the French subtitle, since it's purposely misleading, the art film precedent that likely comes to mind when considering the paternity of *Holy Grail* isn't from Godard or Truffaut's La Nouvelle Vague, but rather Ingmar Bergman's Swedish-language masterpiece *The Seventh Seal* (1957).[47] The review article quoted above—"Swedish Film of Medieval Fatalism"[48]—is a critical examination of the then newly released, Cannes-blessed Swedish arthouse film. Consider the obvious semantic elements: a medieval-era knight wandering across a plague-ravaged land, saucy page in tow; his encounters with fellow sufferers and legendary beings; and a quest for some certain proof of God's existence and even His grace in a time of great uncertainty, in "these dark times." The parade of players in this crisply photographed *Totentanz* includes rotting corpses and accused witches, also actors, brigands, flagellants, bored housewives, spiritually cauterized peasants, and even grim Death himself. Norman Holland, writing about what he calls "puzzling movies" of the late 1950s, notes that *The Seventh Seal* is "a strange and wonderful paradox: a singularly modern medium treated in a singularly unmodern style—a medieval film" (71). And though *The Seventh Seal* seems the ideal for such atavistic influence, it will become evident that this high-art cinema totem is as much an object of the Pythons' jabs as it is their genie.[49] And if, as Derek Elley writes, "the chief feature of the historical epic film is not imitation but reinterpretation . . . works which have carefully respected the legacy received from other art-forms, and adapted and built on it in a thoroughly filmic way, which are the true historical epics of cinema" (*The Epic Film*, 1), then the Pythons are also having a go at "serious," big-budget Hollywood films like *The Vikings*[50] as well as "serious" art cinema.

"*Un film trouvé á la ferraille*" (A film found on a scrap heap) boasts the title card in Jean-Luc Godard's acerbic, meandering, bourgeois-baiting New Wave classic *Week End* (1967). It's not a medieval film, except perhaps in its regressive depictions of human behavior and the savagery of the allegedly civilized countryside. It is, instead, a film featuring bloody accident scenes, sexual flippancy, banality and excess, Third World anticapitalist types, and nasty bourgeois characters and nihilistic jargon; it's also a sort of hopelessly lost quest scenario sidetracked by the ambivalent, crushing modern world. It's at times both horrifying and funny.[51] This little list should read familiar to those who have seen *Holy Grail* more than once—the Pythons are playing in the same sandbox. *Monty Python and the Holy Grail* owes as much to not only Godard's *Week End*, but also Pasolini's *Canterbury Tales* and *The Decameron*, Herzog's *Aguirre: The Wrath of God*, and Wenders's *Goalie's Anxiety at the Penalty Kick*—even Resnais's mesmeric *Last Year at Marienbad*, Ken Russell's *The Devils*[52] and, yes, Bergman's *Seventh Seal*—as it does to any Arthurian or quest or historical epic film it may be parodying. *Holy Grail* is a film seed that was clearly fertilized by the dung (often literally) of the various New Waves, and even though *Holy Grail* is sending up those sometimes oh-so-serious art-house films, it does so by acknowledging and consistently employing art cinema's very own semantic elements and connecting syntax.

In "The Art Cinema as a Mode of Film Practice" David Bordwell writes that an art film mode is one of "production/consumption," as well as shared "formal traits and viewing conventions" (56–57). Succinctly, Bordwell (writing in 1978–1979, as the art film period gave way to the Hollywood "blockbuster" era) strives to

> show that whereas stylistic devices and thematic motifs may differ from director to director, the overall *functions* of style and theme remain remarkably constant in the art cinema as a whole. The narrative and stylistic principles of the films constitute a logically coherent mode of cinematic discourse. (57)

The "classical narrative cinema" tends to be recognizable by what it shares with most traditional narrative films produced over the history of cinema, traits that audiences have come to recognize and expect. Bordwell describes this classical cinema well, and it's worth quoting him at some length to see the pattern the Pythons knowingly work with and against in producing *Holy Grail*:

> We can say that in the classical cinema, narrative form motivates cinematic representation. Specifically, cause-effect logic and narrative parallelism generate a narrative which projects its action through psychologically-defined, goal-oriented characters. Narrative time and space are constructed to represent the cause-effect chain. To this end, cinematic representation has recourse to fixed figures of cutting (e.g., 180 continuity, crosscutting, "montage sequences"), mise-en-scene (e.g., three-point lighting, perspective sets), cinematography (e.g., a particular range of camera distances and lens lengths), and sound (e.g., modulation, voice-over narration).

More important than these devices themselves are their functions in advancing the narrative. The viewer makes sense of the classical film through criteria of verisimilitude (is x plausible?), of generic appropriateness (is x characteristic of this sort of film?) and of compositional unity (does x advance the story?). Given this background set, we can start to mark off some salient features of the art cinema. (57)

It's easy to see where and how the Pythons could push back against these givens, acknowledging their anti-status credentials, but also their intimate knowledge of both classical and art film aesthetics. Is a living, de-limbed Black Knight plausible? Is an in-your-face peasant characteristic of this sort of film? Does the search for a shrubbery or assaulting a narrator advance the story? In *MPFC* Ep. 23, they lampoon the "French Subtitled Film," a particularly clumsy and self-conscious French New Wave film interested in garbage tips, Webb's Wonder lettuce, and self-proclaimed revolutionaries. There are a number of pertinent entries for this scene in *MPFC: UC* (2013), including one that discusses the appearance of a boom mic in a shot:

New Wave filmmakers drew attention to the formal elements of cinema, in this case acknowledging the cinematographic frame, its existence and role as "divider" of photographed space. The fact that the boom mic drops into the shot is also a comment on the movement's inattention to some of the "finished" details of film, more interested in the visceral experience of the cinematic moment. Also, lower-budget films tend to suffer more continuity problems, as reshoots are more expensive than can be justified. (1.352)

In this same sketch the Pythons will send up the New Wave's use of jerky, handheld cameras, aimless, ambiguous narratives and mysterious character motives, and the ennui-laden, distracted talkiness of many New Wave denizens. They'd clearly watched a number of Godard, Chabrol, and Resnais-type films prior to writing and staging these episodes. In Ep. 29, it's the Italian New Wave artists Michelangelo Antonioni and Luchino Visconti who pay for their anguished or eroticized puffery; in Ep. 33 a still from *Bonnie and Clyde*[53] (of the American New Wave) is used. It's clear that not only are the Pythons aware of the look and sound of the New Waves, they are certain that their audience is also familiar with these more obscure filmmakers and movements, and can be fruitfully part of the in-joke.[54] In Ep. 29, for example, the scene changes from an Elizabethan drawing room featuring Elizabeth I and courtiers, all astride mopeds, to the realization that this is a film set run by a Japanese man pretending to be Italian writer/director Visconti, thence to a raid by the Foreign Film Squad looking specifically for film director impersonators. The episode ends with the introduction of multiple Flying Squad detectives who can ably tick off Italian New Wave directors, writers, films, and even significant moments in Italian history (the "Risorgimento") as they justify more arrests; this episode's causal relationships are convoluted, where they exist at all, like the films the scene is lampooning. And by Ep. 39, the Pythons are satirizing Pasolini's alleged latest film, *The Third Test Match*, with scenes on the cricket pitch that feature cackling skeletons, hooded monks, a nude batsman, onanism, a tittering woman, a naked couple in a grassy embrace, and a laughing bishop. A panel of actual cricketers hate the movie, wondering why popular cricketers Geoff Boycott, Fred Titmus, and Ray Illingworth don't appear (*MPFC: UC*, 2.150–57). Pasolini is also mentioned in Ep. 36, and discussed (by the author) in relation to Mrs. Long Name's purposeful walk in Ep. 45, very reminiscent of a scene in Pasolini's 1968 film *Teorema* (*MPFC: UC*, 2.124 and 2.209). In short, the troupe is somewhat fixated on these New Wave film figures, so it's no surprise they'd want to make a film in their art film vein. From an entry in *MPFC: UC*, Ep. 39:

Italian New Wave film director Pasolini (1922–1975) had recently directed *Teorema* (1968), *Porcile* (1969), and *The Decameron* (1971), all "experimental" in their approaches to classical filmmaking. Pasolini may have faced this kind of interpretive scrutiny as he created his version of an English treasure, Chaucer's *The Canterbury Tales* in 1972, where he would drift away from Chaucer with his own written material and characterizations. *The Third Test Match* sketch is probably satirizing Pasolini's raucous *Decameron* . . . but there are also images (tight close-ups, crash zooms, face offs) borrowed from at least two other Pasolini films, *Oedipus Rex* (1967) and his most recent, *Canterbury Tales*. . . . It's abundantly clear, for example, that at least some of the Pythons had watched Pasolini's *Oedipus* adaptation before embarking on the *Holy Grail* film project.[55] (2.155)

Still in the art film mode, Bordwell sees the *loosening* of causal relations, meaning "this" doesn't inevitably have to lead to "therefore that," and beginnings, middles, and ends in the traditional story structure are more mutable. Arthur's quest could have fixed points along a predetermined path, the ultimate point being a Grail Castle where he secures his providential prize. Not so. Art cinema's narrative motivation, according to Bordwell, tends to come from realism and authorial expressivity (real locations, real and psychologically complex characters): "Characters of the art cinema lack defined desires and goals," and "events become pared down toward a picaresque successivity," Bordwell writes[56]—Arthur has a goal, but it is unreachable and we know it; in fact the audience may even expect it, given what we know about Monty Python's *oeuvre*. Supernatural forces larger than the characters or the text can control legendary or fairy-tale narratives; real-world forces of angst, oppression, and simple human failings (and crushing, inexorable fate) often push the art film's narrative, and to inconclusive conclusions, as in Truffaut's *400 Blows*, Pasolini's *Porcile*,[57] or Antonioni's *L'Avventura*. In the art film, action becomes reaction, and the characters can "tell" us much as "the forward flow of causation is braked and characters pause to seek the aetiology of their feelings," while spatial and temporal construction is also affected, including plot/time manipulations that can include the flashback, flash-forward, and the *temps mort* (Bordwell, 58). The moment in *Holy Grail* where Dingo, Zoot's sister, turns to the camera for an assessment of the film so far—and she's upbraided by other characters from both earlier and later in the film—will be just such a break/brake. Like Launcelot, Galahad, and Robin, the "hero" of the art film tends to wander rather than progress forward. In *Holy Grail* Arthur stands at the balancing point between classical and art cinema, as he moves aggressively toward what he thinks is his goal, the Grail Castle, only to be disappointed along the way and when he finally gets there. In the art film, Bordwell continues,

> choices are vague or nonexistent. Hence a certain drifting episodic quality to the art film's narrative. Characters may wander out and never reappear; events may lead to nothing. The Hollywood protagonist speeds directly toward the target; lacking a goal, the art-film character slides passively from one situation to another. (58)

Again, Arthur is forced to try to navigate both cinematic worlds. He nobly pushes forward, but the world he's in shifts and changes around him, from mythical to medieval to modern, from art film to classical narrative cinema, and so he's most often simply encountering new episodes (the "Coconuts and Swallows" sentries, the Black Knight, Camelot as a "silly place"), or catapulted animals or cascading ordure, without learning anything or making any real progress. His successful tribute of a shrubbery to the Knights Who Say Ni yields him nothing except leave to continue struggling on; though these magical knights promised nothing else, anyway. Finally, the art film tends to promote "the author as a structure in the film's system," Bordwell writes.

"The author becomes a formal component, the overriding intelligence organizing the film for our comprehension" (59). This is true for everyone from Antonioni through Bergman, Pasolini and Visconti—their films tend to be seen as "theirs." So imagine Monty Python as writers/creators, with all attendant expectations and suppositions, and their version of the art film comes into plainer view. Theirs is the art film that would make fun of art films while making a kind of funny art film.

The 1970s was also the decade of the film parody, when the genre film structures had become innately understood and their original "intents" and "meanings" emptied out (as culture changed, matured, or became sophomoric), making parody possible across film genres. Mel Brooks's *Blazing Saddles* premiered in London cinemas in June 1974, parodying the western, followed by his *Young Frankenstein* less than a year later,[58] as did the homegrown *The Rocky Horror Picture Show*—which was being shot in fall 1974[59]—a sci-fi/horror/musical parody. Throw into this brew the earlier Bond spoof *Casino Royale* (1967), all the *Carry On* films, as well as 1974's *Flesh Gordon*, *The Groove Tube*, and *Dark Star*, all available in British cinemas before *Monty Python and the Holy Grail* made its debut, and the parodic furrow has been tilled. Classic genre forms were under assault from all sides in the 1960s and 1970s, their innards laid open as Hollywood scrambled to compete with television and foreign film influences, figuring out what the paying audience of the 1970s might want to see. Audiences had embraced *The Sound of Music* in 1965, for example, catapulting it to record box office receipts, but follow-up musicals including *Doctor Doolittle* (1967), *Star!* (1968), and *Hello, Dolly!* (1969) all flopped. This uncertainty was something of a blessing in that American "auteurs" like Altman, Penn, Hill, and Peckinpah were able to be funded, and each made individualistic films that tapped into the navel-gazing mood of the period, and the film-school-brat blockbuster epoch—starting with *The Godfather* (1972) and *Jaws* (1975) and cemented by *Star Wars* in 1977—waited just on the horizon. Genre-bending films included the low-budget *Dark Star* by John Carpenter—really a student film—and the glossier *Young Frankenstein* and Richard Lester's *Three Musketeers* (1974). Winking at a genre's hidebound expectations and quaint semantics became standard practice—acknowledging the genre baby as they threw out the bathwater. Similar challenges also came from admittedly fringe films like Paul Morrisey's *Flesh for Frankenstein*, which English critic J. R. Taylor celebrates for its "unselfconscious gusto," and for the fact that it "plunges gleefully in, up to the elbows in blood and guts";[60] and Brian de Palma's *Phantom of the Paradise* (1974), described by David Robinson as both "a medley of horror themes" and "as camp as they come": "*The Phantom of the Opera* is muddled together with *Faust*, *Mystery of the Wax Museum*, *The Picture of Dorian Gray*, and a touch of the *Rocky Horrors* for good measure.[61] In short, there were plenty of generically unstable films from which the Pythons could draw inspiration, though *most* of those stopped short of winking (or smirking) at the audience directly, or stopping themselves with a hand over the camera lens. More importantly, these same films had proven their box office legitimacy, meaning an odd film like *Monty Python and the Holy Grail* could get picked up by a company like Cinema 5 for U.S. distribution with the reasonable expectation that money could be made.[62]

Parodying the genre and subverting films in the corpus of that genre—whether the art film (as a sort of meta-genre) or the medieval or historical film—is the task of *Holy Grail*. Here we are presented with the antithesis of events depicted in *The Seventh Seal*: rather than Death visiting the mundivagant knight and accepting a challenge, God (in the form of W. G. Grace) visits the medieval hero Arthur and issues his own challenge. Bergman's knight is to perform a single, significant act and keep playing a game of chess with Death; Arthur's "purpose" is to turn aside from the gathering of knights in Camelot and find instead the Holy

Grail. Neither challenge is accomplishable, of course, and both knights are fated to lose their respective games. After all, this is the Sartrean era, where life and death are "absurd," and "freedom" the only consideration, and these are not Hollywood epic films, where good guys and good causes win. Norman Holland suggests that *The Seventh Seal* is more than "merely a necroterpsichorean parable for modern times,"[63] and that seems to apply to *Holy Grail*, as well, though both are concerned with plague, the specter of death, personal salvation, and even the existence of God, they are both "more" than those parts. Is *Holy Grail* a version of "metatheater," an equally baffling "metafilm"? According to Holland, the "meta" term

> seems to suggest not only the original Greek that meta-X is X moving toward more-than-X, but also, in modern usage, that meta-X plays, toys, flirts with being X alone. Thus we tend to assume (in our mimetic tradition) that theater portrays reality. Metatheater takes off from this portrayal-theater and plays against it in the tradition of Pirandello. Because metatheater, insofar as it is successful, destroys its own foundation, the audience's "set" toward a mimetic theater, those troubled by it can take comfort: metatheater should be an unusually short-lived genre. (Holland, "Puzzling Movies," 83)

So *Holy Grail* is playing, toying, flirting with being a generically pure medieval quest film, all the while subverting, denying, shunting aside those assays *and* embracing the art film aesthetic. It wants to have its cake and eat it, too. It does "destroy," or at least undercut, "its own foundation," as well, especially as the film comes to its abrupt end. It is more than a medieval film, and more than a comedy film. *Holy Grail*'s art film ambitions are also, of course, subverted and denied, as the Pythons and *Holy Grail* flirt with both parody and mimicry of the more "serious" art film indulgences, the goal being mirth, not introspection or political change. The real difference, of course, is just that—seriousness. The art film tends to be deadly serious (or tragically comical) about its content, motives, and political or cultural points of view, and the Pythons are not.

So what kind of art film is it, if it is a kind of art film indeed? It's not the detached, formal art film, like Antonioni's *L'Avventura*, *Red Desert*, or *L'Eclisse*, or experimental like many from Brakhage, Deren, Warhol, Lye, or McLaren,[64] or aloof like Resnais's and Robbe-Grillet's excruciating but hypnotic *Last Year at Marienbad*.[65] It's not the very autobiographical, personal films of Truffaut, where his doppelgangers act out bits of the auteur's remembered life, nor the politically charged and often purposely confrontational "Children of Marx and Coca-Cola" direct-address ilk of Godard's political films (or films politically made). There are snatches, though, of all these in *Holy Grail* (and earlier in *Flying Circus*), along with some of the monstrous body horror of Borowczyk's *The Beast*, or the dismembering and re-membering found in the cartoons of Stan Vanderbeek and Jan Lenica,[66] along with the ribald humor of Makavejev's *WR: The Mysteries of the Organism* (1971) and virtually everything Pasolini committed to film.[67] The Pythons have taken what they need from myriad genres, and many international films. If Antonioni's films are about an inability to communicate, for example, which they are, then *Holy Grail* is inspired there, as was *Flying Circus*. And if Godard's films feature politically astute and vocal characters prepared to argue their beliefs with all comers, then our favorite peasant Dennis is no lumpen proletariat, he's Godardian. But with all this talk of important art films as fertile ground for the Pythons, we must remember *Carry On Cleo* (1964). This silly, bawdy farce—which Palin pointedly mentioned as the kind of film the Pythons *did not* want to make—is also a significant stepping-stone toward *Holy Grail*. *Carry On Cleo* inherited fabulous, expensive costumes and sets from the Hollywood star-vehicle *Cleopatra*,[68] and used those "authentic" costumes and sets to create a very real-looking world where funny things could happen. That should sound familiar . . . .

Stepping on the Brass Tacks

As for our structure in this book, the annotations are laid out chronologically, meaning as they occur in the film. Rather than chapters, individual scenes will act as dividers; we'll begin with the "Title and Credit Sequence," thence to the "Coconuts and Swallows" scene, the "Bring Out Your Dead" scene, etc. Scenes that are either included as part of the printed script and do not appear in the film, or are included in the film and only suggested in the script are also annotated, though to varying degrees. Some missing animated sequences are just mentioned as being absent, while others that are included are examined much more thoroughly. Also, an excised, ten-page "King Brian the Wild" scene was completely written by the troupe and is still a part of the script as printed, but due to budget and time considerations was never filmed—tossed overboard before the cast and crew reached Scotland. We spend some little time with this missing portion, just as we will look only briefly at the "complete" first draft of the script, much of which was either *written out* of the finished version, or saved for the fourth season of *Flying Circus*. That rough first draft is referenced throughout the main portion of these annotations as necessary, and occupies the first pages of the *Monty Python and the Holy Grail (Book)*.[69] The endnotes throughout contain useful additional information—explanations, elaborations, nods to related areas—as well as a handful of *complete* citations, especially for period newspaper references.[70] The bibliography and index will point the interested reader in proper and accurate directions for reference and further study.

The animated title and interstitial sequences are discussed and annotated as we encounter them in the running sequence of the film. Connected to these animated sequences are the dozens of sketches and notes penned by both Jones and Gilliam, and included on the pages opposite the printed script pages in *MPHGB*. These sketches give us an idea of the types of creatures, characters, and scenes Gilliam envisioned as he prepared for his cartoon contributions to this medieval film, and act as a guide to his Gothic manuscript source material, as well. These "facing pages" annotations are compiled separate from the body of the work, in appendix A, and are ordered by page number (e.g., "Facing Page 33").[71] Otherwise, appendix B is given over to the handful of personal recollections from Stirling University extras; the following bibliography and index are meant to be as helpful as possible.

The type of entry in the main body of this book is easily discernible. Those entries referring to scene directions are given in *italics*, and with the original capitalization of names throughout, as they appear in the script (e.g., *The GIRL and the duck swing slightly but balance perfectly*). Those entries referring to dialogue begin with the name of the character, followed by the spoken line (e.g., ARTHUR: "Well . . . I am King"), and these are also reproduced just as they appear in the script. Lastly, those entries that refer to the printed script only, and not the film as eventually produced, are labeled with a "PSC," meaning "Printed Script Commentary" (e.g., *DENNIS winks at the OLD Woman*—PSC).

Monty Python and the Holy Grail is the scion of a mixed, rich paternity, and a "revealing document of its world." It is influenced by the "look" and "feel" of period films such as Polanski's *Macbeth*, Kurosawa's *Throne of Blood*, Pasolini's *Canterbury Tales* and *The Decameron*, and by contemporary films such as Godard's *Le mepris*, *Pierrot le feu*, and *Week End*. It shares some of the existential aimlessness of Das Neue Kino, including Wenders's *Alice in the Cities* and *Goalie's Anxiety*; also the historical richness and reflexivity of Herzog's *Aguirre*; and even the existential ambiguity and angst of period novels like Frisch's *Homo Faber*. It is intimately connected to Pythons' own history, liberally referencing and borrowing from *Monty Python's Flying Circus*. We will examine this rich text by looking closely at the "mirror"-ness of the film, settings, and characters, the moments that reflect current events—topicalities, essentially; we will look at British history, ancient and modern, legendary and factual, their inter-sections and divergences toward Morris's Arthur of history and Dumville's Arthur of legend; we will speak of the remnants of colonialism and the Commonwealth, and the shrinking of the British Empire; and also of body horror, where the inner self is fractured by the modern world, and the Vietnam conflict offers images of broken bodies on the nightly news. There are medieval literatures from Gildas and Bede and Malory to be referenced, and the critical work of academics looking at Arthur, Arthuriana, and the Middle Ages.

This medieval film—or is it a film made medievally?—is also about 1970s Great Britain, meaning we will discuss the effects of recession, inflation, "stagflation," energy shortages, weak governments and strong trade unions, IRA bombings, racial unrest, the sinking Brit-ish economy, epic films and mock-epic films, Hollywood and the British film industry, the state of British television, and the grimly painted scenery of a cultural dis-ease identified by so many pundits of the period—and that still managed to engender a little comedy film that has stood the test of time.

Notes

1. From Morris, *The Age of Arthur*, xiii.

2. From Dumville, "Sub-Roman Britain." See also Kirby and Caerwyn Williams, "Review of *The Age of Arthur*." These important articles, the books and scholarly articles (an Arthurian cottage industry) they snuff out, and the whole question of the historical Arthur will be discussed in detail as we move forward.

3. Designed by Derek Birdsall (New York: Methuen, 1977).

4. Most of these ideas were *not* used in *MPHG*. Instead, several ended up in the abbreviated fourth season of *Monty Python's Flying Circus*, recorded (without John Cleese) in October–November 1974.

5. This is not a "shooting script," per se—meaning the script used on the set as the film was being shot. The *MPHGB* version includes several scenes not shot for the finished film and several others, penciled in after the fact, that do appear in the film. More on those as we move along.

6. Brooke, *The Twelfth Century Renaissance*, 22. Christopher Brooke's very helpful works on the Middle Ages will be referenced throughout.

7. References to the film began appearing in American high school and college yearbooks as early as 1976, as will be discussed below.

8. William Proctor Williams, NIU professor of English emeritus, author of *An Introduction to Bibli-ographical and Textual Studies*, editor of myriad Shakespeare editions, and a treasured friend and mentor.

9. The term paper only exists now as a reworked chapter of the finished dissertation, "*It's . . .*" *Shakespeare : English Renaissance Drama and Monty Python* (2000).

10. The 2008 edition is from Scarecrow Press; the 2013 edition from Taylor Trade/Scarecrow.

11. *MPHG* currently sits at number eighty-eight on IMDb's "Top 250" lists, as voted by IMDb us-ers, and number fifty-four on *Time Out*, London's list of best British films, for example. It's nowhere to be found on the American Film Institute's best films listings, however.

12. See Gosling, "Two-Year Agreement Boosts Cultural Exchanges," *Times*, 21 October 1976: VII. The film obviously didn't change the world overnight, though—when British film critic David Rob-inson is surveying what he calls "a funny sort of year" (1975) in cinema, *MPHG* isn't even mentioned. See the *Times*, 2 January 1976: 5.

13. And has notably published and presented in the area since, primarily in Chauce-rian studies, which will be mentioned later. Jones studied English and history at St. Edmund's.

14. Michael Shanks, 1961, and Geoffrey Moorhouse and Rex Malik, both 1964, respectively.

15. For these annotations the completed *Circus: An Utterly Complete . . .*(2013 edition)—abbreviated throughout as *MPFC: UC*—will be cited as often as necessary. The Pythons quote and reflect their own work extensively.

16. Lindley is quoting Pierre Sorlin from *The Film in History: Restaging the Past*, 16.

17. There are two sheep in Gilliam's animations—seen twice—both quite as lifeless as the sheepskin hurled onto Arthur and Bedevere at the Grail Castle. See appendix A, the "Facing Pages" section, for more on these animations.

18. The Pythons' more ambitious (more expensive, more historically faithful) *Life of Brian* is much better populated with period details, starting with period-accurate locations. *Holy Grail* has to make do with what it can—certainly part of its enduring charm.

19. In the "Dennis the Peasant" scene, the background peasants milling about or digging in the filth include production manager Doyle's father, mother, and daughter. In the finished film they are simply shapeless figures scuttling about the green field. From a 21 November 2013 e-mail correspondence with the author.

20. Rowley, *The High Middle Ages*, 142.

21. Text from *The Riverside Chaucer* third edition, 1987.

22. In this the Pythons could find ample inspiration in the recent production of Norman Jewison's film *Jesus Christ Superstar*, shot on location in Israel but with a more spare, theatrical-type approach to sets and costuming.

23. Walsingham (c. 1340–1422) was a monk at St. Albans and virulent foe of John of Gaunt. We know much about Richard II's reign, including the Peasants' Revolt, thanks to Walsingham. See Taylor's entry for Walsingham in *Oxford Dictionary of National Biography*.

24. "Forecast: Cold and Dark," *Time*, 21 February 1972: 47.

25. A leftover from the Wilson years, the "white heat" future had seemed very bright in 1963, when at a party conference Labour leader Harold Wilson promised a sparkling new day thanks to science and technology:

> In all our plans for the future, we are re-defining and we are re-stating our Socialism in terms of the scientific revolution. But that revolution cannot become a reality unless we are prepared to make far-reaching changes in economic and social attitudes which permeate our whole system of society. *The Britain that is going to be forged in the white heat of this revolution will be no place for restrictive practices or for outdated methods on either side of industry.* (Wilson, *Report of the 62nd Annual Conf. of The Labour Party*, 139–40; italics added)

It was just such "restrictive practices" and "outdated methods" that kept Britain in the throes of the energy and employment crisis through the 1970s—ushering in the Thatcherites—and just the kind of changes Dennis will "be on about" as he harangues Arthur. See the "Dennis the Peasant" section for more on Britain's economic and political conditions in the 1970s.

26. Formed in 1975 in London.

27. Part of this may have been attributable to the expected Lib-Lab depression following the Conservative rush to power, and part may have been an attempt to purge the bad taste left by the decade via pointed identifications of the decade's special weaknesses. Most contemporary critics were happy to see the 1970s in the rearview mirror.

28. "Fall in Number of A Level Passes This Decade," *Times*, 3 December 1979: 4.

29. These worse-than-expected forecasts hit most developed countries during the decade. Britain forecast 3.2 percent annual growth, and achieved 2.1 percent, for example, while France, the United States, Japan, and Germany all experienced similar or even worse drops. See Rothman's "How Predictions Fared 10 Years On," *Times*, 4 December 1979: ii.

30. To be fair, by 2007 journalist Andy Beckett, in a look at the resurgence of the 1970s in British TV, films, and everyday life, is calling Booker a "fogeyish British journalist," one too quick to judge the decade that offered "a bit of something for everyone."

31. Find the original ad in the classified advertising section of the *Times* on 23 June 1973, page 8. There are just 673 goblets available, celebrating the religious foundation's thirteen-hundredth anniversary. NB: Most citations from the *Times of London* can be found through the *Times* Digital Archive 1785–1985.

32. The Ely goblets, which sold for £96 in the 1970s, can be had today on eBay and at various auction houses for around £300.

33. The depictions of Jesus in the Pythons' next film, *Life of Brian*, are quiet and even reverent; it's the lot in the back at the Sermon on the Mount disturbing the serene preaching moment.

34. Booker was born in 1937, just two years earlier than any of the Pythons; he experienced the same Britain they did, in essence. He also attended Shrewsbury School—he was a Salopian—like Palin, and Corpus Christi College at Cambridge. (The printed script for *Holy Grail*—typed up by Jones and Palin—even mentions "Salopian slang" on page 43. See entries in the "Knights Who Say Ni" section below.)

35. World maps of the *fin de siècle* period display in pink or light green the international territories of the Empire, which stretched from Canada to parts of South America, Africa, the Middle East, South and Southeast Asia, and Australasia. Before the middle of the century most of those colors would be changed.

36. See the entries in Ep. 36 of the second volume of *MPFC: UC* for much more on this episode.

37. De Gaulle twice vetoed England's entry into the Common Market. See the "Taunting by Frenchmen" section below for much more on this Gallic thorn in Britain's side.

38. There are versions of Malory's work available, and their differences are significant, especially in relation to language and description of events. Principally, we will cite from Cooper's edition *Le Morte Darthur: The Winchester Manuscript* (Oxford: Oxford University Press, 2008 [orig. 1998]; abbreviated as *LMD-WM*), as well as Cowen's *Le Morte D'Arthur, Volumes I & II* (London: Penguin Books, 2004 [orig. 1969]), abbreviated as *LMD'A*, and followed by the volume (1 or 2) and a page number.

39. Cf. Dante and Cervantes for similar topical literary excursions.

40. From the re-recorded Cleese voiceover narration found in the one-off *Euroshow 71—May Day Special*. See the many entries in *MPFC: UC* in the index under "television shows," then "*Euroshow 71—May Day Special*" for more.

41. Making its debut on KERA-TV in Dallas, Texas. The Pythons were interviewed on KERA as part of the promotional trip for the Los Angeles festival premier of *MPHG*.

42. From *Tawasenthan 1976*, the Guilderland Central High School yearbook. All of these yearbook citations can be found through database searches at ancestry.com, "U.S. School Yearbooks."

43. The first from page 153 in *The Garnet and Black*, University of South Carolina; and the latter from Bridgewater State College's yearbook (*As We Were? As We Are*), page 107. *Kojak* (CBS) aired 1973–1978, while *Baretta* (ABC) aired 1975–1978. Both were very popular network police dramas.

44. From the Southwest High School yearbook, Fort Worth, TX. At many of these schools, the Pythons' 1971 compilation film *And Now for Something Completely Different* was being screened as a regular and successful fundraiser in 1976 and 1977.

45. A contemporary review of the film in the *Times* is fairly typical, calling it a "risky" parody that can deliver—"all hit-and-miss; but the hits are often rich fun" (Robinson, *Axel's Lonely Castle*, 4 April 1975: 9).

46. *Times*, 10 March 1958: 5.

47. The film made its European debut at the Cannes Film Festival in May 1957. It appeared on British movie screens in March 1958, making its debut at the Academy Cinema in London.

48. *Times*, 10 March 1958: 5.

49. *The Seventh Seal* played in London at the Berkeley Cinema (Tottenham Court Road) beginning in 1958. The film made regular reappearances in London cinemas through the early 1970s.

50. A 1958 Kirk Douglas–Tony Curtis epic, directed by Richard Fleischer.

51. The film couldn't (or wouldn't) make it past British censors, so *Week End* was screened in London for the first time in July 1968 at the Institute of Contemporary Arts Cinema (members only), and without a ratings certificate. The *Times* reviewer John Russell Taylor calls the film Godard's "most complex and subtle," and "one great, savage central metaphor of the human condition" (4 July 1968: 13).

52. See frequent mentions of prolific British film director Russell (1927–2011) in *MPFC: UC* (e.g., 2.34, 44, 65).

53. Directed by Arthur Penn; it made its London debut in September 1967 at the Warner.

54. Film societies ("civic cinemas") were fairly active during this period (and had been since about 1925), and these New Wave films were most commonly shown to larger audiences on English college campuses, as part of cinema studies classes and film society gatherings. For more see *MPFC: UC*, 1.145–46.

55. Both *Teorema* and *Oedipus Rex* were playing in London in April 1969, as the Pythons created *MPFC*.

56. Bordwell, "The Art Cinema as a Mode of Film Practice," 58.

57. *400 Blows* appeared at the Curzon in March 1960, while *Porcile* debuted in January 1970 at the Cameo Poly.

58. *Young Frankenstein* was released in December 1974 in the United States, and in March 1975 in London theaters, premiering at the ABC 1.

59. The stage musical *The Rocky Horror Show* had graced London theaters beginning 21 June 1973.

60. "Hollywood Opens Its Doors to the World," *Times*, 1 May 1974: 12.

61. "The Dazzling Style of High Camp," *Times*, 9 May 1975: 13.

62. Cinema 5 had also distributed *Z* (Costa-Gavras 1969), *Gimme Shelter* (Maysles 1970), and *The Garden of the Finzi-Continis* (Vittorio de Sica 1971). Cinema 5 tended to distribute the types of art films the Pythons are aping and lampooning, with titles from Bergman to Paul Morrisey, of de Sica and Ken Loach.

63. Holland, "Puzzling Movies," 72 ("necroterpsichore" is essentially a dance of death).

64. Titles I'm thinking of here include Stan Brakhage's *Mothlight* (1963), Maya Deren's *Meshes in the Afternoon* (1943), Andy Warhol's *Empire* (1964), Len Lye's *Colour Box* (1935), and McLaren's *Begone Dull Care* (1949).

65. *L'Avventura* played at the National Film Theatre in November 1960, and garnered a rave review from the *Times* (2 November 1960: 2); the Golden Lion-winning *Red Desert* made it to British cinemas by March 1965; *L'Eclisse* screened from February 1963; and *Last Year at Marienbad* from December 1972.

66. Stop-motion animators Vanderbeek and Lenica were clearly influential to not only Gilliam (like them, he employs cut-outs quite often) but to the Pythons as they depicted the fragile, parsable nature of the human body throughout the run of *MPFC* and on into *MPHG*. The Black Knight's final condition is comical, cartoony, as he "stands" on stumps, armless, as well, not only refusing to die but to submit, either. He is Daffy Duck with his beak blown off, essentially. The speed and violence found in the WWII-era Warner Bros. cartoons (Klein, 186–89) are also clearly inspirational to both the Goons and the Pythons, as discussed in *MPFC: UC*, 1.19–20. Cartoony violence (giant hammers, anarchist's bombs, catapulted wooden rabbits) is a big part of the Pythons' metier.

67. *WR: Mysteries of the Organism* (Yugoslavia) made its debut in London in November 1971 to strong reviews (and a surprise that the censor passed it). See "Dusan Makavejev: Expert Bubble Pricker," *Times*, 19 November 1971: 10. Borowczyk's controversial *The Beast* (as part of *Immoral Tales*) premiered at the London Film Festival in 1973.

68. The big budget *Cleopatra* starred Richard Burton and Elizabeth Taylor, ran longer than three hours, cost more than $44 million, and nearly bankrupted Twentieth-Century Fox.

69. Example: In the first draft there are multiple grails either found or created. This multiplicity becomes significant in certain moments of the finished film where a misleading "grail-shaped beacon" is glimpsed, or someone claims to already have a grail, etc.—in these moments the first draft becomes germane, and will be discussed.

70. If the reference is *fully* cited in the endnote, it will likely not be included in the bibliography.

71. The myriad illuminated manuscripts discussed (most from Randall, *Images in the Margins of Gothic Manuscripts*) are cited in the text and endnotes, not the bibliography.

ABBREVIATIONS

AO	*The Axe and the Oath*, R. Fossier
BBC	British Broadcasting Corporation
BCA	British Cartoon Archive
BLCIM	British Library Catalogue of Illuminated Manuscripts
BN	Bibliotheque Nationale
CE	*Catholic Encyclopedia*
DBMC	*From Domesday Book to Magna Carta*, A. L. Poole
EBO	*Encyclopedia Britannica Online*
EEC	European Economic Community (aka the Common Market)
FAH	*From Alfred to Henry III: 871–1272*, C. Brooke
FMA	*The Flowering of the Middle Ages*
HB	*Historia Brittonum*
HBI	*History of Britain and Ireland*, R. G. Grant, et al.
HBMA	*The Horizon Book of the Middle Ages*, M. Bishop
HKB	*History of the Kings of Britain*, Geoffrey of Monmouth
HW	*A History of Warfare*, B. Montgomery
IMDb	Internet Movie Database
IMGM	*Images in the Margins of Gothic Manuscripts*, L. Randall
JTW	*Monty Python's Flying Circus: Just the Words*, Vols. 1 and 2
KAMH	*King Arthur: Myth-Making and History*, N. J. Higham
LMA	*The Later Middle Ages: 1272–1485*, G. Holmes
LMD'A	*Le Morte D'Arthur*
LMD-WM	*Le Morte Darthur (Winchester Manuscript)*
LHE	*A Literary History of England*
MM	*Malleus Maleficarum (The Hammer of Witches)*
MMA	Museum of Modern Art
MPFC	*Monty Python's Flying Circus* (BBC TV, 1969–1974, episodes 1–45)
MPFC: UC	*Monty Python's Flying Circus: An Utterly Complete, Thoroughly Unillustrated, Absolutely Unauthorized Guide to Possibly All the References: From Arthur "Two-Sheds" Jackson to Zambesi* (2013)

ABBREVIATIONS

MPFZ	*Monty Python's Fliegender Zirkus*
MPHG	*Monty Python and the Holy Grail*
MPHGB	*Monty Python and the Holy Grail (Book)*
MPSERD	*Monty Python, Shakespeare and English Renaissance Drama*
NG	National Gallery
NPG	National Portrait Gallery
PSC	Printed Script Commentary, *Monty Python and the Holy Grail (Book)*
ODNB	*Oxford Dictionary of National Biography*
OED	*Oxford English Dictionary*
QAB	*The Quest for Arthur's Britain*, Ashe
SNK	*The Saxon and Norman Kings*, C. Brooke
THG	*The Holy Grail: Imagination and Belief*, R. Barber

SCENE ONE

TITLE AND CREDIT SEQUENCE

Author's Note: The titles sequence is a mixture of straight-ahead credits for the film (as required by organizations like the BBC and the BFI) and Pythonesque silliness. Where possible, the names and roles of the cast and crew have been annotated in this section. For some participants, especially actors playing bit parts, *Monty Python and the Holy Grail* is their only significant film credit, and they are listed in groups if this is the case.[1] More important are the silly bits—the famous names, the subtitles—that make the credits what they are, and we spend most of our energies there.

    TITLE: *Monty Python and the Holy Grail*—Already trading on their valuable and recognizable brand name, the Pythons went with the simplest, most effective title. This was likely a conscious decision after the modest success of their first film, *And Now for Something Completely Different* (1971), where on advertising material the troupe's name was generally much smaller than the film's title and especially the famous "foot" imagery. That, or the poster, postcard, or lobby card was *so* graphically busy that "Monty Python" couldn't possibly stand out in competition with Gilliam's panoply of characters and images. Plus, rather than being "different" at all, the film offered somewhat lifeless restagings of a handful of the more popular sketches from the television series, the interiors of which were shot on film in a decidedly unintimate milk warehouse—the A1 Dairy, Whetstone High Street—creating not only murky sound but more leaden performances when compared to the original, more edgy BBC studio tapings (Palin, *Diaries* 43).[2] *Holy Grail* and the following two feature films depicted the "Monty Python" title much more prominently.

    The structure of title is likely multi-influenced, beginning with the names of popular medieval "Robin Hood" ballads, including *Robin Hood and the Monk*, *Robin Hood and the Potter*, and *Robin Hood and the Sheriff of Nottingham*, all circa fifteenth-century. These were gathered by editor Francis James Child and published in volume five of *English and Scottish Ballads* in 1858, with a number being republished in the 1960s, as well.[3] The title may also be a borrow from the very popular *Biggles* book series (1932–), to which the Pythons refer in Ep. 33 of *Flying Circus*. These W. E. Johns titles include *Biggles and the Leopards of Zinn* (1960) and *Biggles and the Black Raider* (1953). This is also a nod to the success of the *Carry On* films, which had begun in 1958 with *Carry On Sergeant* and continued apace through *Carry On Cleo* (1968), *Carry On Henry VIII* (1971), and *Carry On Christmas* (1973), eventually totaling thirty-one films over a span of thirty-four years. The name *Carry On* became shorthand for a pun-laden, broad, anachronistic, and bawdy farce comedy style that made as many people

1

cringe as chortle, but their popularity was undeniable. More below on how the Pythons managed (consciously and unconsciously) to both acknowledge and then move beyond the *Carry On* "genre" of farcical historical pillaging.[4]

Lastly, the film isn't actually about the Grail search until Arthur and his retinue receive a visit from God partway into the film.[5] Prior to that divine moment, Arthur is gathering knights to join his legendary Round Table at Camelot; the Grail is a nonissue, as is any evidence of the supernatural. Even when the Grail quest is initiated, of course, it is a series of missteps and misadventures, full of Fielding-like or *Tristram Shandy*-esque digressions and misdirections, rather than a through-line journey. In this the film mimics not only the Sterne novel and *Tom Jones* but some of the earliest Grail sources, including Chrétien de Troyes's *The Story of the Grail* (c. 1160), where, as Barber writes, "the title [Chrétien] chooses . . . does not necessarily indicate the topic of the story, but simply the object on which the plot hinges—Hitchcock's MacGuffin, in effect" (*The Holy Grail*, 14). According to Barber, Arthur and his knights are at the center of this picaresque, an "unfinished masterpiece" of Grail literature (27). In the *Lancelot-Grail*, Barber continues, the purity of Galahad allows for his success, while others have no such promise, leading to many trials but few quest-worthy moments:

> Gawain, the most sinful of the knights, is dismayed to find that nothing happens to him for months on end, "having expected the Quest of the Holy Grail to furnish a prompter crop of strange and arduous adventures than any other emprise"; and what happens to him and the other knights who are not destined to achieve the quest is often misadventure rather than adventure . . . even for the chosen knights, the Grail is notably absent from the account of what befalls them, and makes only one appearance before the final apotheosis.(59)

For our Arthur, an image of the Grail is provided by God, and Galahad sees a "Grail-shaped beacon" thanks to the maidens of the Castle Anthrax—beyond that, it's all talk. As for Gawain, he is mentioned in the *MPHG* script and in the film, but is essentially an afterthought. He and other of Arthur's identifiable knights—Tristram, Hector, Gans, Bors—were obviously in the Pythons' minds as they wrote the script initially, but the closer they came to the final draft, the more limited their appearances became. As will be seen, some of them remain just to be mauled to death later by the Killer Rabbit.[6]

Final Draft 20.3.74—(PSC) According to Palin's 15 March 1974 diary entry the final draft was completed on that day (15 March), with the lengthy "King Brian the Wild" story thread excised completely (*Diaries* 158).[7] There's no mention in Palin's journals of a specific 20 March deadline date, though that's likely a "finished" date agreed upon by all the Pythons and those producing the film, when the script was "locked," turned in, and copied. Palin notes that he and Jones performed the bulk of the rewriting work (159). Filming would begin at the end of April 1974, in the Glencoe[8] area, for the Bridge of Death sequence. The first "complete" draft of the script (to which all the Pythons contributed) had been completed just four months earlier, in December 1973.

title music—(PSC) In his audio comments for the 2012 Blu-ray edition of the film codirector Jones mentions that they'd commissioned friend and collaborator Neil Innes to compose music for the film. When it came time to view the scenes with the "finished" music soundtrack, they found the music too "quaint" and even too *appropriate*, which undercut the Pythons' attempts at undercutting the medieval world they were trying to depict.[9] They then fell back to the position they'd occupied so successfully during the run of *Flying Circus*— canned music. The title music and most of the film's score are all borrowed from existing music stock (see "DeWolfe" below), and in this case includes music used in other feature films, as well.[10] Page 63 of *MPHGB* is a copy of the first page of the music "cue sheet"—notes for the editors (visual and sound) as to what music is to be inserted and where/when, a crude timing sheet, essentially. For the beginning titles sequence there are four bits of music called for: "Wide Horizons," "Ice Flow," Countrywide," and "Mexican Busker." Of these, only "Ice Flow," "Countrywide," and "Mexican Busker" are actually used in the credit sequence. The first—"Ice Flow"—is the more strident, percussive score as the credits start seriously, then devolve into pseudo-Nordic silliness. This music starts and stops again, when titlers get the sack. "Countrywide" (by Anthony Mawer) flows in gently under the new and more serious credits, only to be cut off by silly credits yet again. The "flashing" credits are finished over the "Mexican Busker" tune.[11]

Mawer's incidental music was earlier chosen for use in *MPFC*, and can be heard in Ep. 28 during the "Trim-Jeans Theatre" advertisement sketch (*MPFC: UC*, 2.28). "Wide Horizon(s)" and "Ice Flow" are Pierre Arvay compositions, on the Hudson Music Company label, from the *Empty Horizons* album, released in 1974.

Python (Monty) Pictures Ltd—This was the company formed in 1973 to manage the Pythons' own film projects, separate from the BBC or other controlling entities. It was this company, in association with Forstater's and Doyle's Chippenham Films that eventually produced the film.[12] This is also the company later sued by producer Mark Forstater, who alleged he'd been given reduced royalties from the film, ancillary products, and even *Spamalot*, advertised as "lovingly ripped off" from *Holy Grail*. The Pythons' letterhead in 1974 lists this company's registered address as 20 Fitzroy Square, London. In the 1974 London area phonebook they're listed (as "Film Producers") at 17 The Mall Stus, Tasker Rd SW3, phone number 01-485-6159.[13]

Michael White—Born in Scotland in 1936, White had already produced the theatrical hits *Sleuth*, *Oh! Calcutta!*, and *The Rocky Horror Show* before agreeing to produce *Holy Grail*. The whole *Grail* experience, though, only rates a fleeting mention in White's 1984 autobiography, *Empty Seats* (171–72).

Mønti Pythøn ik den Hølie Gräilen—(PSC) This title appears in the printed script, but *not* in the finished film. The "silly" subtitles and credits begin immediately, though these won't be obvious until, instead of identifying the camera crew, a title asks in Pythonesque Jabberwock Swedish "Wi nøt trei a høliday in Sweden this yër?" (More precisely, this may be Jabberwock Norwegian or even Danish, since the Swedes don't use the slash-o letter.) London-area and college-age audiences would have been more accustomed to seeing subtitled Nordic films, including Ingmar Bergman's *The Seventh Seal*, the movie most obviously referenced by *Holy Grail*, and more recent and adult New Wave–era films from Mai Zetterling,[14] as well as erotica like *Seventeen* (1967), *I Am Curious (Yellow)* (1967), and *I Am Curious (Blue)* (1968).[15] Bergman's films had been appearing in British cinemas since 1949, with *Seventh Seal* making its post-Cannes debut at the Berkeley Cinema, Tottenham Court Road, in March 1958.[16] This dark tale of the game between a Knight and Death would resurface regularly in British cinemas through the early 1970s. The foreign "art film" tradition had a significant effect on the Pythons, and the fact that British audiences were accustomed to "reading" foreign films is a given. The more erotic content of many of these Nordic titles, Bergman's work included (e.g., the rape scene in *The Virgin Spring* [1960] caused quite a stir[17]), likely made most Swedish, Danish, and Norwegian films a guilty pleasure for London-area viewers.

The more precise translations for these few bowdlerized titles are as follows:

Monty Python and the Holy Grail—Better translated as *Monty Python och den Heliga Graalen*, though the film title as released in Sweden was actually *Monty Pythons galna värld*

(*Monty Python's Crazy World*). Again, for some reason the translated version of the title appears in the printed script only, and not in the film itself.

SUBTITLE: "Røten nik Akten Di"—This is structured "more like phonetic English" with a Danish flair then actual Danish—as if it were to read "written 'n' acted by"[18]—which is a typical farrago for the Pythons of English and whatever language they're pretending to speak. In Ep. 40 of *MPFC*, a representative of the Norwegian Party (Eric Idle) asks for British votes using lilting, mellifluous fake Norwegian: "In Norge we hatta svinska offikiose buinni a gogik in Europa" and "Sti glikka in Norge tijik dinstianna gikloosi stijioska kary."[19] Listening carefully, it's often possible to pick out the Anglicized Nordic words Idle is creating. In the *Euroshow 71—May Day Special* created by the Pythons as the BBC's Euroshow entry in 1971, the Pythons look at distinctly English village rituals associated with May Day. In one short sequence, a spectacled Swedish intellectual, played by Graham Chapman, stares down into the camera in a static black and white shot, commenting, *sans* subtitles, in a Swedish-sounding language. The only recognizable word is "Svenska," while five other words are "bleeped" by the censor. The dreary monochrome of this shot is in full contrast to the bright colors of the rest of this short film, a clear comment on the somber seriousness of many Swedish and Danish films from this period.

"With" (meaning "starring")—"Med."

"Also appearing"—"Också med."

"Also also appearing"—"Också också med."

SUBTITLE: "*Wik*"—The principal "Wik" sub-players here are both known and new, four of the six having appeared in the *Flying Circus* series:

Connie Booth—Booth (b. 1944), an American by birth, had been John Cleese's wife since 1968, and appeared on *MPFC* a number of times, most notably as the disappointed "rebel maid" in the "I'm a Lumberjack" sketch from Ep. 9 (*MPFC: UC* 1.146, 281). She would go on to perform and contribute to the very popular *Fawlty Towers* (1975–1979) series, also with Cleese, and, just as soon as Cleese was finished with his production work on *Holy Grail*, would leave with him to shoot *Romance with a Double Bass*, a short film. In *MPHG* she will appear as the accused witch, who in the script is named "Miss Islington."

Carol Cleveland—An original Python, very nearly, though only in performance, not in conceptualization or writing. Cleveland (b. 1942) was featured in early publicity photos with all the boys, and appears first just as a real (and anatomical) girl but eventually as a comic contributor through all four seasons of *MPFC*.[20] In *Holy Grail* Cleveland plays both Dingo and Zoot, twin sisters living at Castle Anthrax.

Neil Innes—A Python associate from pre-*Flying Circus* days, Innes had been a member of the musical group The Bonzo Dog Doo-Dah Band, appearing on the children's television show *Do Not Adjust Your Set* (Rediffusion, Thames; 1967). That show's cast and writers included Idle, Palin, and Jones. Innes will contribute music and some sketch writing to the abbreviated fourth series of *Flying Circus*, helping to fill in for John Cleese after he left the show.[21] Innes will be mentioned again below for his minor musical contributions to *MPHG*. In the film Innes plays the lead headbanging, chanting monk, Robin's most pesky minstrel, the page crushed by the giant rabbit, and the "owner of a duck."[22]

Bee Duffell—Veteran Irish actress Duffell (1914–1974) had appeared on memorable shows including *Z Cars* (1962–1973), *The Prisoner* (1967–1968), and *Dr. Finlay's Casebook* (1962–1971), though she was also a respected stage actress. Both *Z Cars* and *Dr. Finlay* were regular stops for extras also appearing on *Flying Circus*.[23] In *MPHG* Duffell plays the crone who won't answer questions regarding shrubbery. Sadly, Duffell died in December 1974, before the film was finished or screened.

John Young—Another veteran actor, Scottish-born Young (1916–1996) also appeared in several episodes of *Dr. Finlay's Casebook*, then in feature films including the cult hit *The Wicker Man* (1973), *Life of Brian* (1979), and Gilliam's *Time Bandits* (1981). In *MPHG* Young plays both the Famous Historian who is hacked to death, and the plague victim who isn't quite dead (yet). In the "Cast List" included as part of the printed script in *MPHGB*, Young's characters are described as "The Dead Body That Claims It Isn't," and "The Historian Who Isn't A.J.P. Taylor At All" (90). Historian and academic A. J. P. Taylor is mentioned in *MPFC*, Ep. 11 as

> the Oxfordian author of *English History 1914–1945* (1965), the final volume from the *Oxford History of England*, as well as the very controversial *The Origins of the Second World War* (1961), where Germany was blamed for the war, but where both France and England also came under fire for "vacillation" and appeasement policies. The reception of the book's thesis led to "a mixture of international obloquy and acclaim" for Taylor . . . .
>
> Also, for an example of perhaps some kind of shared mindset between Taylor and the Pythons, note just the title of Taylor's 1956 work: *Englishmen and Others*. Taylor's painting of all Conservatives and any conservative thought or policy with a negative, socially regressive brush betrays his own politics, and may actually be quite in line with those of the Pythons. (*MPFC: UC*, 1.181–82)

Taylor was also a well-known and recognizable presenter of political and historical programs, especially in the 1950–1977 years.

Rita Davies—A recognizable name and face from *MPFC*, Davies appeared in Eps. 8, 19, 27, and 29.[24] She had also appeared in *Dr. Finlay's* in 1967. Davies plays the Famous Historian's wife, and is named in the end credits list as "The Historian Who Isn't A.J.P. Taylor At All (Honestly)'s Wife" (*MPHGB* 90). Taylor had been married three times, incidentally.

SUBTITLE: "Also appearing"—The featured "Alsø wik" supporting cast include the following—these are *featured* extras likely because they have (or were scheduled to have) small speaking parts:

Avril Stewart—Stewart has only two roles to her name after *MPHG*, and seems to have retired from film and TV acting by about 1976. She plays Dr. Winston in the film.

Sally Kinghorn—Kinghorn continued acting after *Holy Grail*, appearing a decade later, for example, in *A Passage to India* (1984), then taking many voice-over roles, most recently as a voice actor in Disney's *Brave* (2012). Kinghorn plays Dr. Piglet, and along with Dr. Winston "examines" Sir Galahad (Palin) at Castle Anthrax.[25] She has been married to fellow actor Alex Norton since 2001.

SUBTITLE: "Also also appearing"—These are the "Alsø alsø wik" performers who played bit parts scattered throughout the film, including one-off featured extras, wedding guests, and Castle Anthrax maidens, etc. Many of these were culled locally:

Mark Zycon—He memorably plays the seemingly happy prisoner hanging from a Camelot wall, glimpsed during the "Knights of the Round Table" song-and-dance sequence. Gilliam mentions him by name in his DVD comments. Zycon had somehow heard about the filming and had "driven [in a taxicab] all the way up from Birmingham."[26] Gilliam remembers Zycon doubling for Idle throughout, and then they used him in various stunts, including a sentry falling over barrels at Swamp Castle (after being hacked by Launcelot), as well as the hanging prisoner at Camelot. As a testament to the dangers of relying on the memories of the Pythons to reconstruct the nuances of the shoot, as Jones and Palin tour Doune Castle for *The Quest for the Holy Grail Locations* (2001), they both mangle Zycon's name into "Zack Matalon," and Jones goes on to talk about "Zack"[27] doing impressive stunts in the Swamp Castle sequence.

Mitsuko Forstater—Doyle doesn't remember Mitsuko playing one of the "lovelies" in the Castle Anthrax, but one of the French sentries in the French castle scenes, instead. She was known as "Suko," and was married to producer Mark Forstater.[28]

Sandy Rose—A Castle Anthrax maiden, along with Joni Flynn, Fiona Gordon, Elspeth Cameron, Loraine Ward, Sally Coombe, Yvonne Dick, Judy Lams, Sylvia Taylor, Alison Walker, Anna Lanski, Vivienne Macdonald, Daphne Darling, Gloria Graham, Tracy Sneddon, Joyce Pollner, and Mary Allen. Most of these actresses have a handful or no other verifiable film or television credits. A number of these ladies were brought from Glasgow by coach, according to Idle and Cleese, and they only stayed in the shooting area one night, and only had to shoot on one cold evening at Doune, Doyle remembers.[29]

Sandy Johnson—Johnson (b. 1953) was not one of the Castle Anthrax girls, *he* was instead one of the Knights Who Say Ni, a villager, a musician, and a knight in battle, according to IMDb.com. He went on to direct episodes of *The Play On One* (1989), *Roughnecks* (1994), and *Benidorm* (2008–2011), among many other titles.

Romilly Squire—Mr. Squire appeared as a musician at Prince Herbert's wedding, as well as a villager at the weighing of the witch. He has since become a well-known heraldic artist living in Edinburgh.

SUBTITLE: "Wi nøt trei a høliday in Sweden this yër?"—In Ep. 27 of *MPFC* the town of North Malden manages to hijack a BBC Icelandic saga, and uses the saga to promote tourism and business investment in North Malden. In the first draft of the *Holy Grail* script this setup is echoed. There, groups of Camelot townsfolk wait for the knights to return with the Grail, some carrying banners, with one reading "North Camelot Welcomes the Grail-Finders and So Does South Camelot" (*MPHGB*, 25). In the *MPFC* episode, the "dukes of the land of Bjornsstrand" carry swords, shields, and signs like "Invest in Malden" and "Malden: Gateway to Industry" (*JTW*, 2.49–50).

The production credits on this title page are as follows:

Camera Operator—Howard Atherton—Atherton moved from camera crew to cinematographer, and from the UK to Hollywood, performing second unit work on *Alien* (1979) and *The Empire Strikes Back* (1980), then lensing Adrian Lyne's *Fatal Attraction* in 1987 and later Michael Bay's *Bad Boys* (1995). See the entry for Roger Pratt below for another prolific *MPHG* camera crew alum.

Camera Focus—John Wellard—Wellard has only one additional credit at IMDb.com, as a camera assistant for *Message to Love: The Isle of Wight Festival* in 1997. By definition a camera assistant could well be the focus puller; Wellard was likely part of the crew on the scorpion dolly mentioned by Doyle in the "Cave of Caerbannog" section below.

Camera Assistant—Roger Pratt—Pratt has become a very active and in-demand cinematographer since his *MPHG* work, lensing Gilliam's *Crimson Permanent Assurance* (1983), *Batman* (1989), *Chocolat* (2000), and two Harry Potter films. Pratt found his way onto the team as *MPHG* was in preproduction, via Chippenham Films.[30]

Camera Grip—Ray Hall—Hall has also been busy as part of myriad camera crews, working on Ridley Scott's *The Duellists* (1977), Sydney Pollack's *Out of Africa* (1985), and the three Brosnan Bond films.

Chargehand Electrician—Terry Hunt—Hunt had worked on a couple of *Flying Circus* episodes in the early second season, then after his *MPHG* work there seems to be a twenty-year hiatus (credit-wise) before he returns to electrical work on film and television projects. A "chargehand" is a foreman or supervisor of a particular job, in this case over the electrical crew on the film set.

Lighting—Telefilm Lighting Service Ltd.—There is a Telefilm truck in the photograph of shoot extras provided by Stirling extra Russell Walker.[31] Graham Chapman—in costume but sans helmet—is standing just behind the truck, and the scene they're prepping is the final gathering and assault sequence, shot on Sheriffmuir. In 1974 the company was located at 133 Oxford Gardens W10. **Andrew Ritchie and Sons Ltd.** have no other verified credits, likely because they were an electrical engineering firm (309 W. George St. G2, Glasgow[32]), rather than electricians generally working in filmed media.

Technicolor—A proprietary three-strip color film process from the Hollywood studios' heyday, the British Technicolor labs were one of the few labs left utilizing the expensive dye technology by the mid-1970s.

Rostrum Cameraman—Kent Houston—Houston had worked with Gilliam photographing animation sequences during the *MPFC* days, and continued to assist now-director Gilliam as a visual effects consultant on *Life of Brian*, *Time Bandits*, and *The Fisher King* (1991), among many others. The rostrum camera is essentially an animation camera setup that allows for single frame advancement photography. See *MPFC: UC*, 1.427.

SUBTITLE: "See the løveli lakes"—Perhaps not surprisingly, there were similar print ads promoting Swedish tourism in English newspapers during this period. Torline offered a "Summer Playground Paradise" in Sweden, with, yes, the promise of camping on the shores of "one of Sweden's 96,000 lakes," as well as sunshine, clean air, and clear roads.[33] The ad accompanies a March 1971 special series in *The Times* devoted to Sweden.

The production credits for this title page are as follows:

Sound Recordist—Garth Marshall—Marshall continued his sound career long after *Holy Grail*, working on documentaries like *The Song Remains the Same* (1976), both later Python films, as well as *Prospero's Books* (1991) and *Outlanders* (2007).

Sound Mixer—Hugh Strain—Strain has worked on dozens of sound projects since *MPHG*, including Lindsay Anderson's *Britannia Hospital* (1982), *Withnail & I* (1987), and episodes of the popular *Monarch of the Glen* (2001) and *Ballykissangel* (1997–2001). Doyle remembers Strain leading the second dubbing run on the film at World Wide, following the first dubbing session at Twickenham.[34]

Boom Swinger—Godfrey Kirby—Kirby has worked sound in films and TV, spending significant time on shows like *Jeeves and Wooster* (1992), and cooking shows with Jamie Oliver. The boom swinger operates the fishpole microphone, and assists the sound mixer on the set.

Sound Maintenance—Philip Chubb—Chubb has credits on *LB*, *Time Bandits*, and *ML*.

Sound Assistant—Robert Doyle—Doyle's credits include virtually all Python and post-Python film projects, as well as *Lord of the Rings* work. Bob is Julian Doyle's brother, and assisted on the Kidwelly location footage completed after principal photography (without sound, credit, or pay). On *MPHG*, Bob transferred sound onto 35 mm film mag, and would later become a boom swinger and then a mixer, according to Julian.[35] Bob Doyle is mentioned again later in notes to the "Coconuts and Swallows" scene.

Dubbing Editor—John Foster—Foster worked sound on *Superman* (1978) and *LB*, and was part of the principal editing team for *MPHG* that included Hackney, Doyle, Gilliam, and Jones.[36]

Assistant Editors—John Mister has been a film editor, cutting *The Leader, His Driver and the Driver's Wife* (1991), an *Omnibus* episode (2001), and *McQueen and I* (2011); **Nick Gaster** has become a busy editor, including titles *The Whales of August* (1987), *Mirror Mask* (2005), and *Moon* (2009); **Alexander Campbell Askew** has sound edited in several areas, and worked on *Dark Crystal* (1982), *Henry V* (1989), and *Harry Potter and the Order of the Phoenix* (2007);

Brian Peachey has been associate and assistant editor on *Reds* (1981) and *Someone to Watch Over Me* (1987). **Danielle Kochavi**'s only published credit seems to be *MPHG*.

Sound Effects—Ian Crafford—Crafford has had an impressive move to straight-ahead editing, working on *Hope and Glory* (1987), *Field of Dreams* (1989), and *Walker Payne* (2006).

SUBTITLE: "The wønderful telephøne system"—Certainly a bit of silliness, but according to Ericsson's own history, Sweden in the early 1970s was "second only to the United States in terms of telephone penetration."[37] Ericsson's agreement with Swedish Telecom likely became newsworthy, since in 1965

> the data communications service was introduced in Sweden. In April 1970 Swedish Telecom consolidated its strong relationship with LM Ericsson by signing agreements to set up . . . Ellemtel, which would develop advanced electronic communications systems and products. One of the first such projects was the development of electronic switching systems—the AXE system— together with equipment for data networks, electronic private exchanges, telephone systems based on the integrated system technique, and advanced electronic telephone instruments. The last manual exchange was taken out of service in 1972. ("Swedish Telecom")

By way of comparison, the *Times* would report that in April 1965 England's first "fully electronic telephone exchange" for a *village* was installed at Ambergate, Derbyshire, with Ericsson being the principal manufacturer.[38] The *Times* also announced in 1965 Ericsson's planned installation of a state-of-the-art electronic exchange (outside Stockholm) by 1967,[39] as well as many mentions of Ericsson winning UK bids for new telephone exchanges. In short, advancing Swedish phone companies and technologies were mentioned regularly in British newspapers during this period.

The *concern* about these increasing Swedish imports would be played out in the newspapers, as well, with political cartoonists taking up the cause. In the 11 January 1975 *Daily Express* edition, Michael Cummings depicts PM Harold Wilson (1916–1995) and Secretary of State for Employment Michael Foot (1913–2010) wondering whether they'll have to begin importing new prefabricated unemployment centers from Sweden to handle the multiplying English workers made redundant.[40]

The credits on this title card include the following:

Continuity—Penny Eyles—Continuity has become "script supervisor," generally, and Eyles worked on many films, including pre-*Grail* work *Kes* (1969), and the later *Brimstone and Treacle* (1982), *Gosford Park* (2001), and *The Queen* (2006). More recently, Eyles has been tutoring others in her craft at the Skillset Screen Academy at the London College of Communication and Ealing Institute of Media.

Accountant—Brian Brockwell—Brockwell has been a production accountant on earlier films including Lindsay Anderson's *If . . .* (that the Pythons send up in *MPFC* Eps. 6, 19, and 36), *Gumshoe* (1971), as well as Palin's *A Private Function* (1984).

Production Secretary—Christine Watt—Working as a production assistant and production secretary, Watt participated in the films *The Jewel in the Crown* (1984) and *The Return of Sherlock Holmes* (1988).

Property Buyer—Brian Winterborn—As a production buyer Winterborn worked on *Carry On Columbus* (1992) and *Lucky Break* (2001). He is listed as a set dresser on *Amy Foster: Swept from the Sea* (1997).

Property Master—Tom Raeburn—Raeburn had worked on *Steptoe and Son Ride Again* (1973) as well as *The Man Who Fell to Earth* (1976). Raeburn also appeared in *MPHG* as the first sentry killed by Lancelot at Swamp Castle.[41] Jones remembers Raeburn being given the unpleasant job of gutting the dead sheep found by Doyle for use in a Castle Stalker scene.[42]

Property Men—Roy Cannon—Cannon is also listed as working on *2001: A Space Odyssey* (1968), and *The Young Americans* (1993); **Charlie Torbett—**Torbett contributed his prop craft to *The Empire Strikes Back* (1980), *Return of the Jedi* (1982), Gilliam's *The Adventures of Baron Munchausen* (1988), *Batman*, and *Carry On Columbus* (1992); **Mike Kennedy—**No other credit.

Catering—Ron Hellard Ltd—*MPHG* appears to be this company's only significant film or television credit.

Vehicles—Budget Rent-A-Car Ltd—For whatever reason these rented cars and vans (lorries) are mentioned a number of times by the Pythons, both in the interviews for the *BBC Film Night* documentary, and in Palin's *Diaries*. In one of the production photos included in *MPHGB*, the Budget Van can be glimpsed and is listed as being rented from Hornsey, meaning they drove it up from London, probably loaded with props and equipment (opposite page 26). Doyle remembers that a man accompanying these vehicles actually took a small role in the film—"bashing" the stream in the lead up to the "Rude Frenchman" scene—and they managed to damage all the vehicles over the course of the shoot, as well.[43]

SUBTITLE: "And mani interesting furry animals"—The credits listed on this title page include the following:

Assistant Art Director—Philip Cowlam—Cowlam had worked on *Carry On Again Doctor* (1969) as well as *Steptoe and Son Ride Again* (1973), both sequels to popular original projects. Cowlam would go on to become both an art director and design consultant.

Construction Manager—Bill Harman—Harman has been construction coordinator on dozens of major films, including *Jabberwocky*, *A Christmas Story* (1983), *Tommy Boy* (1995), *X-Men* (2000), and *Cold Creek Manor* (2003).

Carpenters—Nobby Clark—Clark is a special effects and art department craftsman and has worked on *A Bridge Too Far* (1977), *The French Lieutenant's Woman* (1981), *Gladiator* (2000), and *Judge John Deed* (2005); **Bob Devine—**Devine has worked in art department roles on *Time Bandits*, *The Last Temptation of Christ* (1988), and *Sheltering Sky* (1990).

Painter—Graham Bullock—Bullock worked painting and construction on both *LB* and *Time Bandits*; **Stagehand, Jim N. Savery,** and **Rigger, Ed Sullivan,** have no other film or television credits.

CAPTION: "With special extra thanks to"

Charlie Knode—Knode designed costumes for the *BBC Play of the Month* (1969–1970) and *War and Peace* (1972–1973), and later worked on *Blade Runner* (1982) and *Braveheart* (1995). Knode also willingly donned costumes and participated on camera. He plays one of the guards at the gates of Swamp Castle (the one on the right *not* eating the orange), and he is also one of Robin's minstrels (the taller one prancing at the back). He also later plays a bit part alongside Palin in the "Ex-Leper" scene in *Life of Brian*.

Brian McNulty—As either a production assistant or floor manager McNulty also worked on *Knots* (1975), and the *Taggart* TV series. Palin notes that McNulty read lines for the Pythons to read/act against during shooting of *MPHG*, and he was especially impressed by McNulty's "rich Glaswegian" accent spouting Cleese's "outrageous" French lines (*Diaries* 175). McNulty can be heard quite clearly reading these and other prompts during the *BBC Film Night* documentary made during production, and now available on the 1999 DVD edition of *MPHG*.

John Gledhill—An electrician and gaffer for *The Biederbecke Affair* (1985), and *Emmerdale Farm* (2007).

Peter Thomson—His last name may actually be spelled "Thompson," and he worked in the public relations and press areas on subsequent films including *LB*, *Henry V*, and *The Madness of King George* (1994).

Sue Cable—She stayed connected to the Pythons, becoming the costume maker for *Jabberwocky* and *LB*, as well.

Valerie Charlton—A visual effects artist, Charlton built, for example, the dragon prow on the boat used to reach the Grail Castle, and would contribute to later Python projects including Gilliam's *Baron Munchausen*, as well as *Who Framed Roger Rabbit*. Valerie also happened to be Julian Doyle's girlfriend, and performed significant postproduction work on *Holy Grail*, primarily *gratis*, including making the tents for the Black Knight scene (shot by Julian) and a model Trojan Rabbit for an effects shot, etc., *after* principal photography had been completed.[44]

Drew Mara—Mara was a still photographer on the *Holy Grail* set, and is given photographic credit (with Derek Birdsall designing) for the *MPHGB* project.

Charlie Coulter—Likely a sound crewmember, maybe even the crew sound chief, working for TFA Electrosound in 1974.

Steve Bennell—Perhaps Steve *Bannell*, mentioned by extra Jim McIver as a Stirling student who worked longer on the film shoot than others. See appendix B.

Alpini McAlpine—Likely local labor, working with MacInnes on the Bridge of Death construction and throwing dummies into the Gorge of Eternal Peril. Idle will borrow the word/name "McAlpine" as part of a nonsense dialogue intro for the first show of his *Rutland Weekend Television* series for BBC 2 (1975–1976).

Hugh Boyle—As a floor manager or production manager, he also worked on *Eastenders* (1985) and *Taggart*.

Dave Taylor—Part of the smallish camera crew, Taylor also worked on *The Goodies*.

Gary Cooper—Not *the* Gary Cooper, but likely another similarly named production accountant. There is also a "Kate Hepburn" associated with the film (one of Gilliam's assistants). These serendipitous famous names (attached to normal people) render the Pythons' practice of including famous names as part of the humor a bit more problematic.[45]

Peter Saunders—An art department member who would later work in animation and modeling, including the films *Cockleshell Bay* (1980) and *Wind in the Willows* (1984–88).[46]

Hamish MacInnes—A rock climbing practitioner, guide, and safety expert (for the Glencoe area), MacInnes would later work on *The Eiger Sanction* (1975), *The Mission* (1986), and *The Living Daylights*. MacInnes (b. 1930) is also the author or coauthor of climbing and guide books. Jones also credits MacInnes with "putting up" a safe (steel cable) version of the Bridge of Death used toward the end of the film. MacInnes is interviewed near his home by Jones, Palin, and production manager Doyle as part of *The Quest for the Holy Grail Locations*.

Terry Mosaic—Mosaic accompanied BBFC representative Tony Kerpel to an early screening of *Holy Grail* at Twickenham on Friday, 2 August 1974, then wrote a memo on Python (Monty) Pictures Ltd. letterhead conveying the censor's reactions, along with suggestions for proposed edits. The letter is included in the front matter of *MPHGB*, and is discussed below.

Bawn O'Beirne Ranelagh—Born in 1948, Bawn is an interesting participant. She attended St. Austin's house, Cheltenham Ladies' College, and was then at Vassar College by 1969. Bawn later contributed a kind of reuse it column to the *Independent* newspaper in the mid-1990s, and also wrote short fiction. But for *MPHG*, Bawn came on as a secretary for Chippenham Films in 1974 as fundraising and preproduction got underway.[47]

Made entirely on location . . . —The credit sequence includes a listing of filming locations and local/regional organizations that contributed to the successful filming of *Holy Grail*, and those are listed below, beginning with Doune Castle. To be honest, *most* of the film was shot "entirely on location" in Scotland, but pickup shots were both scheduled and shot nearer London and elsewhere.[48] For example, the scene where Launcelot runs (and runs and runs) toward Swamp Castle was a pickup shot filmed after principal photography was completed, on Hampstead Heath, in Greater London.[49]

At some point in the pre- or postproduction phase of the film the Pythons had obviously also considered shooting some exteriors (or were planning pickup or promotional shots) much closer to London. In *MPHGB* there is a handwritten note included in the assorted (and unpaginated) material between the first draft of the script and the finished script (approximately page 58). The note lists locations primarily south and east of London in Kent and the Greater London area (as well as page numbers for the production team's reference) including: "Knowle Park" and "Seven Oaks" (no page number), "Castlewoods—near Blackheath" (page "83"), "Chislehurst" in "Kent" (page "113"), the "Shoreham Valley area" (no page number), the "Petts Wood" area of "Orpington" (page "113"), "Shooters Hill" and the "Oxleas Woods" (page "83"), and the "Bostall" [*sic*] and "Lesnes (Abbey) Woods" (page "84/85"). The page numbers, as it turns out, refer to specific map images in the 1968 *Geographers' A to Z* book. All these proposed locations were either heavily forested (Petts Wood) or open areas (Blackheath), and lacking modern structures.

As for filming on Scottish locations, Scotland is described unflatteringly by Geoffrey of Monmouth in *The History of the Kings of Britain*, one of the primary sources (along with Malory and the romances) for things Arthurian: "For that country had never missed an opportunity of making matters worse whenever the Britons were in distress. It was a land frightful to live in, more or less uninhabited, and it offered a safe lurking-place for foreigners."[50] The French had also struggled with Scotland's "rusticity" as early as 1385, when French forces and materiel arrived to equip the Scots for an invasion southward, into England:

> The Scottish envoys had indeed asked the French to bring equipment to arm a thousand Scots, which should have been a warning, but the realities of Scotland proved an unpleasant surprise. Castles were bare and gloomy with primitive conditions and few comforts in a miserable climate. The damp stone huts of clan chieftains were worse, lacking windows or chimneys, filled with peat smoke and the smell of manure. Their inhabitants engaged in prolonged vendettas of organized cattle-raiding, wife-stealing, betrayal, and murder. (Tuchman, *A Distant Mirror*, 420)

This planned invasion did not come off, though Gilliam characterizes the film crew's stay in the Doune area as an "invasion" in his audio track commentary.

Doune Castle—This castle had to serve as multiple locations during the film, since it was the only castle the Pythons could get permission to enter and shoot for any period of time. According to Jones, as many as ten Scottish castles had been identified as adequate for location shooting, but just days before filming was to start, the Scottish trust authorities decided to not grant access to the Pythons.[51] A surviving fourteenth-century castle in the Stirling District, it served as a setting for multiple scenes, including "Coconuts and Swallows" early in the film, the Camelot dance sequence, and interiors of both Swamp Castle and Castle Anthrax. Doune Castle continues to be an *MPHG* pilgrimage destination, and one study noted a significant increase in tourist visits to Doune in relation to other Scottish castle sites, crediting the Pythons (Connell and Meyer, 31).[52]

Castle Stalker—A castle near Port Appin, Argyll, Scotland, and not far from Glencoe and Oban, where the Pythons shot some exteriors for *MPFC* in October 1971 for season three (*MPFC: UC*, 2.9). Stalker is a fifteenth-century castle on an island at the mouth of Loch Laich, and is privately owned, like Doune.[53] And even though this castle is the setting for the final scenes of the film, they were some of the earliest shot. See the entries in "The Wonderful Barge and the Grail Castle."

Killin—A village also in the Stirling district. Parts of the ill-famed *Casino Royale* were shot in this area, including the picturesque bridge seen in a traveling shot featuring Sir James Bond (David Niven). Jones and Palin also pass through this town as they visit various filming sites in *The Quest for the Holy Grail Locations*.

Glen Coe—These credits were likely typed up by someone other than a Python troupe member, as they invariably spell the word "Glencoe" throughout the *Flying Circus* files and in the *Holy Grail* script itself. Glencoe is the area in Argyll where portions of "*Njorl's Saga*" (Ep. 27) were shot in October–November 1971. Part of the reason the Pythons would have likely chosen Scotland was their previous knowledge of the rugged area, as well as the success they'd had securing filming permissions earlier. Some of those written permissions—including one for filming at the Hospital Loch above Glencoe Hospital, thanks to the Forestry Commission—are part of the *MPFC* files at the BBC Written Archives Collection in Caversham Park, Reading. See the author's *MPFC: UC* for more on the invaluable archival collection.

Arnhall Castle—Near Stirling, this early seventeenth-century castle is a ruin in front of which the Famous Historian (John Young) lectures, then loses his life.

Bracklinn Falls—Also near Stirling, this setting is used when Launcelot and Concorde are making their way across a stream, and Concorde is shot. The Pythons had used a waterfall near Glencoe as a backdrop for a portion of the earlier *MPFC* Ep. 27.

Sheriffmuir—Lonely hills near Stirling, and north of the University of Stirling campus. This is the area, according to extras like students Alastair Scott, Jim McIver, and Nick Rowe, where the Pythons shot the final massed battle scenes. These group images were then intercut with those shot on the shore near Castle Stalker, and made to seem as if the locations were contiguous. Comments from these three extras comprise appendix B.

Twickenham Film Studios—Twickenham has been an active film studio since 1913, and dozens of films, including *A Hard Day's Night* and *Help!* were filmed/completed in the facilities there. Other films being completed here at about the same time as *Holy Grail* included Stuart Cooper's *Overlord* (1975), and Lester's *Royal Flash* (1975). Julian Doyle remembers being treated like "the poor relatives" at Twickenham since the "bigger" film, *Royal Flash*, was also in postproduction (dubbing), and was evidently given more perks. Wrote Doyle: "[N]obody thought much of the Pythons doing a cheap film. . . . It shows you never know which film is going to be the most long lasting—and it is not who has the most money."[54] *Royal Flash*, starring Malcolm McDowell, would go on to be yawned at by most reviewers.

"Forestry Commission . . . help in the making of this film"—As mentioned above the Forestry Commission had been very helpful a few years earlier when the Pythons were in Scotland shooting exteriors for *MPFC*. Various permissions had been asked and granted to shoot on or near lakes, fields, and even public utility sites, as needed for sketches like "*Njorl's Saga*," "Lifeboat" and "Trim Jeans Theatre" (both Ep. 33), and "Rival Documentaries" (Ep. 38). See *MPFC: UC* for more.

Doune Admissions Ltd—The company charged with giving access to Doune Castle, and with whom the Pythons would have worked closely.

Keir and Cawdor Estates—The Keir Estate (and Keir Home) had been the ancestral home of the Stirlings since the fourteenth century. Doune Castle is visible from the estate. The Cawder Estate was also controlled by the Stirlings. The Keir and Cawder Estate is west of Dunblane in Perthshire.

Stirling University—A nearby "new" university—it opened as part of the government's expansion of higher education in the 1960s—Stirling provided willing students (both undergraduate and graduate) as extras, including Iain Banks (1954–2013),[55] Jim McIver, Alastair Scott, Nicholas Rowe, Steve Bannell,[56] Duncan MacAulay, and Russell Walker. The Robbins Report, released in 1963, called for immediate construction of new universities, in part to expand access to higher education beyond the Pythons' own Cambridge and Oxford. Lord Robbins (1898–1984) would become chancellor of Stirling in 1968.[57]

"people of Doune"—The Pythons and crew stayed in Doune for the duration of the shoot, and likely ate there, shopped there, relaxed there, etc.

"Signed Richard M. Nixon"—A consistent target of the Pythons,[58] this conservative American politician (congressman, vice president, then president) had endured a prolonged ethical-cum-criminal investigation—and then resigned from office—all during the production and postproduction of *Holy Grail* (and portions of *MPFC*). Diarist Palin writes of the Watergate crisis and Nixon a number of times, and exults as he pens an entry on 8 August 1974, certain that a presidential resignation is in the offing (*Diaries*, 186–87). The *Times* also ran a very long, timeline-type story detailing the entire Watergate fiasco the day after Nixon resigned, 9 August 1974. Nixon signed his letter of resignation that same day.[59] The news was front page in papers of the right and left, and as the Pythons showed during the run of *Flying Circus*, topicalities were of great interest to them (following in the footsteps of *Private Eye* and *That Was The Week That Was*)—i.e., parliamentary antics, Cold War saber rattling, Northern Ireland troubles, even American presidents—topicalities found new life on their weekly show.

Incidentally, on the back cover of *Monty Python and the Holy Grail (Book)*—published in 1977—there are more than twenty "suggested advertising slogans" from prominent individuals—including the Queen, Andy Warhol, Reginald Maudling, Margaret Thatcher, and Ted Heath[60]—praising *MPHG*. Fittingly, there are also a handful of alleged quotes from prominent Nixon administration members, those names and their secret acts capturing the headlines of newspapers between 1974 (when Watergate fully came to light) and 1977, when the book was being produced. Richard Nixon, Jeb Magruder, Charles Colson, John Dean III, John Mitchell, Maurice Stans, Richard Kleindienst, and Dwight Chapin[61] are all "quoted" or mentioned in these made-up blurbs. The Watergate affair had returned to world headlines in May 1977 with the release of previously secret and then much-talked-about White House tapes, some featuring recordings of special counsel Colson and the president discussing the need to "stonewall" investigations into the Watergate burglary. For the Pythons and many political pundits of the day, Nixon and his administration represented everything that could be wrong with the conservative right, a barbed comedic gift that kept on giving.

Neil Innes—See the "Neil Innes" entry above.

DeWolfe—A "canned" music operation, DeWolfe was and is in the business of providing incidental music for films and TV shows whose budgets might have precluded hiring a composer, or paying for rights for well-known music and songs. (Music heard in *MPFC* and *MPHG*, for example, can also be heard in myriad Hong Kong films of the 1970s.) A number of DeWolfe titles had been used during the *Flying Circus* run, featuring British light composers like Jack Trombey, Jack Shaindlin, and Trevor Duncan.[62] After deciding to *not* use Innes's original compositions for the score, Jones remembers poring through hundreds of DeWolfe "grams" (gramophone records) over a couple of weeks as the *pasticcio* music editing process moved forward.[63]

Hazel Pethig—A costume designer who had worked on *Flying Circus*, she would later assist on Gilliam's *Jabberwocky*, the Pythons' *LB* and *Live at the Hollywood Bowl* (1982), and

Cleese's *A Fish Called Wanda* (1988). Most of the Pythons mention Pethig's contributions as inestimable—*MPHG* couldn't have been accomplished without her. Doyle remembers, for example, that after a full day's shooting at the Castle Stalker location (first days of the shoot) they were all supposed to drive one hundred miles to Killin to the hotel. (They had shot all the Grail Castle footage in that long day.) Doyle refused, staying in the Appin-Argyll area overnight, while Pethig made the drive, but barely: "Costumes are one of the last[;] Hazel set off late and kept falling asleep driving."[64]

SUBTITLE: "Norwegian møvies"—Though Swedish film (and by association, Scandinavian film) had become somewhat notorious during this period—especially following the release of the *I Am Curious* titles, along with scores of lesser-known softcore exploitation films—Norway itself was not known for its pornographic films, or maybe even for its dentists. In fact, the opinion at the time seems to have been that if anything Norway was more "puritanical" than its sexually profligate cousins to the east and south. One Mr. Anders Lange (1904–1974), leader of a nascent, eponymous right-wing political party in Norway, described the contemporary product of Norwegian broadcast television as "the worst pornography imaginable."[65] As for the notorious Swedish title *I Am Curious (Yellow)*, it finally made it to British cinemas in March 1969,[66] though only after the most explicit images had been cut from the film, rendering it "a very tedious film-within-a-film," according to film critic John Russell Taylor, and a "peculiarly uninspired and uninformative piece of would-be *cinema verité* about Sweden today."[67] Given this flaccid review (pun intended), it's easy to see how the Pythons could give the nod to Norwegian dentists for more erotic film stimuli potential. (The unedited versions of these films appeared in select British cinemas in 1971, to similarly disinterested reviews.) The Pythons have poked fun at teeth and the dental profession before, in *MPFC*. In "Secret Service Dentists" (Ep. 4), dentists and hygienists are Cold War-era Fleming-type characters constantly getting the drop on one another; in Ep. 24 a film director and his major characters all have enormous front teeth; and in the "Dentists" sketch in Ep. 43, home dentistry is on the rise.

SUBTITLE: "Fillings of Passion"—Perhaps a play on the fairly recent Bergman film *The Passion of Anna* (1969), though there were also dozens of Swedish softcore films available for interested viewers in the London area. Relatedly, in Ep. 2 of *Flying Circus*, the "Mouse Problem" sketch, "perverts" dress up as mice and watch suggestive "blue cheese" films (*MPFC: UC*, 1.28).

SUBTITLE: "The Huge Mølars of Horst Nordfink"—The Nordfink is a snow finch (or northern finch), perhaps building off of the swallow discussion found in the first dialogue scene of the film. These subtitles were written (by Palin) well after the film was shot, and even after a handful of screenings had been undertaken, and were a bit of a pleasant surprise to Chapman, Cleese, and Idle when they screened the film for the first time.[68] Most of the Pythons mention the subtitles in their individual audio commentary tracks. They all agree the main reason the titles were accomplished in this manner was there was no budget left for anything else.

The attempts to "stem the tide" of Swedish pornography exported to the UK were well underway by the late 1960s, when sex education films (some legitimate, some not) and straight-ahead softcore pornography (often known as "blue films" in Britain's newspapers) had become more and more available. The British government had urged the Swedish government to enact more stringent laws, all "relating to the exporting of pornography. This should enable [the Swedish government] to cooperate with the police forces of other nations and prosecute the rising number of dealers sending pornography abroad to people who have not asked for it."[69] The Pythons have already sent up this somewhat sanctimonious public reaction to "naughty" magazines in Ep. 36, where the Elizabethan-era Philip Sidney fights against Spanish "porn merchants," not Swedes, before being arrested in a modern-day sting operation (*MPFC: UC*, 2.121–29). The juxtaposition of period characters and action with modern interlopers (and their attendant narrative authority) will of course be revisited in the culminating scene of this film.

During this period it wasn't the Norwegians or even the Swedes,[70] however, being singled out as the most prolific *printed* "porn merchants," but the Germans. In covering the Frankfurt Book Fair for 1970 the *Times* reported a "pornoffensive" available on West German booksellers' displays, as opposed to no offensive titles on Eastern Bloc display stands (Poland, Russia, East Germany). Even Sweden was given a miss at this fair, with the correspondent pointing out "the Swedes are noted chiefly for the excellence of their children's books."[71] In 1971 there were almost 2,900 "blue films"—most produced "particularly" in Scandinavia"—seized by British authorities.[72] The Danes are also credited with helping reduce the stigma of nudity and sexuality in media during this period, including the "removal of all censorship on pornography" in the late 1960s and the rise of "sensationalist" papers like *Ekstrabladet*, featuring sex ads and abundant nudity.[73]

In 1969 *Times* critic J. R. Taylor surveyed the explosion of sex in cinema upon his return from the Cannes Film Festival, noting that northernmost Europe seemed to be setting the bar for new levels of sexual explicitness:

> Let me make out a little tally. Bo Widerberg's *Adalen Riots* [*Sweden*], a highly respectable and serious film, contains one very explicit nude scene and another in which certain obvious manifestations of the sex urge are discussed with unusual frankness. Jarl Kulle's *The Bookseller Who Gave Up Bathing* [also Sweden] has a lot of male nudity (front view, that is) and a very convincing pornographic photograph (which plays an important role in the plot) showing the heroine in the midst of a somewhat unconventional sex act. Male nudity crops up again in Susan Sontag's *Duet for Cannibals* and just about every other Swedish film, *Without a Stitch On* and just about every other Danish film, [and] the Finnish *Sixtynine*, the latest work of Jorn Donner. (Taylor, "A Camera in the Bed," 19)

In short, it seems to have been well known which Scandinavian countries were producing erotic films in the late 1960s and early 1970s, and the Pythons were simply poking fun at the less-than-prolific Norwegians.

Lastly, there was a fairly popular 1971 Danish softcore film known as *Bedside Dentist* (*Tandlæge på sengekanten*) starring Birte Tove, one of many that would have been available on 8 mm or 16 mm film through Soho "porn merchants."

SUBTITLE: "We apologise for the fault in the subtitles"—Purposely bad subtitles don't happen often—especially in feature films—though inelegant, approximate, or *accidentally* funny subtitling would have been regularly found in the recent wave of imported "grindhouse" films from Hong Kong, for example. The breakthrough martial arts film, *King Boxer* (aka *Five Fingers of Death*), appeared in London-area cinemas in March 1973.[74] Later the *MPHG* printed script (the "Killer Rabbit" scene) will call for specific camera shots that "[rely] *heavily also on the Kung-fu and karate type films*"—the Pythons were obviously just as aware of these frantic, high-octane and rough-around-the-edges chop socky films as they were of the more erudite New Wave imports. In *King Boxer* the subtitles aren't so much mistranslated (or rendered in fractured English, as is often the case) as they are "loose"—the spoken dialogue is often not even close to what's being printed below. A number of these Hong Kong features—most receiving "X" ratings—played at the Warner West End Cinema in Leicester Square.

Characteristically bad subtitling is cousinly to another film's flaws from this period, the creative but purposeful dubbing inflicted on a pulpy Japanese gangster film by Woody Allen and friends, eventually known as *What's Up, Tiger Lily?* (1966). The comedic Japanese spy film *International Secret Police* (1965) served as the "serious" original, and, after removing the Japanese soundtrack, the film was redubbed (and re-edited) entirely, undercutting every thrilling moment with inane dialogue or out-of-place sound effects. The film wouldn't appear in Britain's cinemas until well later, in 1976, but most of the Pythons—including Cleese and Gilliam—were working in the United States at the time of the film's release. Jonathan Rosenbaum's review of the film appeared in *Monthly Film Bulletin* (March 1976), and reads as if he's describing the Pythons' approach to medieval history:

> [T]his 1966 *jeu d'esprit* avoids the chauvinistic possibilities inherent in a reverse procedure, post-dubbing live-action Japanese actors with American voices, many of them evocative of cartoon animals—by beginning with material that is already reeking with American influence, and by taking care to remind audiences of what is being done every step of the way. Indeed, without being too solemn about it, one might propose this movie as an exemplary demonstration of the sort of things that sound and image can do to one another, a principle which figures as the basis for many of the best gags. (65–66)

Production Manager—Julian Doyle—Doyle wore many hats—editor, visual effects, writer, director, even actor—and he worked with most of the Pythons on most Python-related films (*Life of Brian*, *Time Bandits*, *Meaning of Life*, *Brazil*, and on). Doyle is now also known for teaching master classes at the London Film Academy. According to Jones and Doyle himself, Doyle played a policeman seen in later portions of the film, and it's his hand famously bringing the film to a close. Doyle also accompanies (and directs) Jones and Palin as they created *The Quest for the Holy Grail Locations*, a special feature on recent DVD and Blu-ray versions of *MPHG*.

Assistant Director—Gerry Harrison—Harrison has credits on *The Wednesday Play* (1965) and *Knots* (1975).

Special Effects—John Horton—Horton had performed significant effects work on *MPFC*, specifically in the fourth series. These added effects were likely part of the reason the episodes' budgets were so much higher than in previous seasons, when low production value was a hallmark of the Pythons' outsider-ness.[75] He'd also worked on *2001: A Space Odyssey*, *Ripping Yarns*, and *Doctor Who*.

Choreography—Leo Kharibian—Kharibian (1927–2001) worked as both a choreographer and an actor on *Wednesday Play* (1965) and *Don't Raise the Bridge, Lower the River* (1968). Kharibian has extensive stage credits, choreographing in London and the universities, and for television, as in *Lyrics by Shakespeare* (1964). His obituary can be found in the *Guardian*, 12 November 2001.

Fight Director & Period Consultant—John Waller—A fight and stunt arranger, Waller also contributed to *Black Arrow* (1973–1974) and *Doctor Who*.

Make-up Artists—Pearl Rashbass—As a makeup artist, Rashbass also participated in the later iterations of *Benny Hill*, and *Rumpole of the Bailey* (1992); **Pam Luke**—Luke had worked earlier on *Charles Dickens' World of Christmas* (1974).

Special Effects Photography—Julian Doyle—Double-cited in these credits (see "Production Manager" above), Doyle would also help create Gilliam's visually stunning worlds in *Time Bandits* and *Brazil*, and he is on familiar terms with the Pythons to this day.[76] In 2012, as the profit divisions for properties associated with and including *Monty Python and the Holy Grail* were being tested in court, Doyle gave depositions to document his participation in the film, and his credits list is actually much longer than the two he's given in the finished film. (This is typical of the low-budget, independent feature film, of course—everyone does everything.) Doyle testified that he wore many hats: production supervisor, second unit director, cameraman, set dresser, special fx director, props maker,[77] actor, location manager, sound recordist, editor, wardrobe, makeup, spark,[78] lorry driver,[79] grip, caterer, dead sheep stealer,[80] and INVESTOR—"I seeded 5% of the budget."[81] As will be seen, Doyle was key to completing *Holy Grail*.

Animation Assistance—Lucinda Cowell—Cowell also assisted with Gilliam's art book *Animations of Mortality*, and illustrated *Bertie: The Life after Death of H. G. Wells* (1974). Cowell also illustrated for movie posters (*Mona Lisa*, 1986), magazine features (*Mother Jones*), album covers, and multiple pulp science fiction novels; and **Kate Hepburn**—not the Hollywood actress, but an assistant to Gilliam actually named Kate Hepburn. Gilliam mentions her in his portion of the DVD commentary track, crediting her with all the hard work, essentially. Cowell and Hepburn cut out the images selected by Gilliam from copies of the pages of Gothic illuminated manuscripts and books on the Middle Ages, including Randall's *Images in the Margins of Gothic Manuscripts* and Evans's *The Flowering of the Middle Ages*, among others. These are the images and notes discussed at length in appendix A.

Møøse trained by—Tutte Hermsgevørdenbrøtbørda—"Tutte" is likely a reference to the popular and much-employed dancer and actor Tutte Lemkow (1918–1991), an Oslo, Norway–born performer who appeared in small roles in dozens of films and television shows, including TV episodes of *Doctor Who* (with William Hartnell) and Blake Edwards's *A Shot in the Dark* (1964).

Special Møøse Effects—Olaf Prot—This makes sense if the film has an animatronic or trained moose to deal with, which it doesn't. Relatedly, Pasolini's *Medea* (1969) features a fully realized centaur character, where an actor is combined with a half-horse prop, and to good effect. He doesn't move much, at least in a full shot, but careful editing and camera placement help sell the fantastical character.

Møøse Costumes—Siggi Churchill—A short list of political and newsworthy figures begins here, including Douglas-Home, Wigg, Slater-Walker, Benn, and Thatcher—a Python list of usual suspects:

First, Sir Winston Churchill (1874–1965) would have been a larger-than-life figure for the Pythons, having led the country through the dark days of the Blitz and World War II, and inescapably in the public eye from 1940 through 1955, when he retired. He was also the epitome of the "Establishment" to younger Britain in the Pythons' school days, representing the aristocracy, old money and influence, and business as usual in the corridors of power. Churchill's lifespan had also witnessed both the full power and then collapse of the British Empire, a rich vein of sardonic comedy for the Pythons. Churchill's image is used several times in *MPFC*, and he is necessarily discussed often, thanks to his high-profile stature during the Pythons' formative years. See "Churchill, Winston" in the *MPFC: UC* index for more.

Designer—Roy Smith—Designer Smith also worked on *The Last Valley* (1971) and *The Hound of the Baskervilles* (1978).

Møøse Choreographed by—Horst Prot III—It's uncertain whether Horst is related to Olaf Prot mentioned above, though since they're both working with moose, it wouldn't be a surprise. "Horst Prot" is likely another fictional name made to sound Norwegian. In the run of *Flying Circus*, the Pythons had created such lists before, significantly for Ep. 19 and the "Timmy Williams" sketch's faux-credits. There, they made up names, borrowed and mangled

17

names from history and pop culture, as well as friends' names, then rigged the caption machine to scroll them quite quickly. Names on that list (there are sixty to choose from) included: "Burt Ancaster" and "Kirk Ouglas"; dead poet Ralph Emerson and living British actor Geoffrey Hughes; Jonathan Ashmore, a child actor and later flatmate of Idle's friends; Humphrey Barclay, a TV producer the Pythons had worked with; Soho nudie publisher Paul Raymond and *Times* film critic David Robinson; and Adrian Beamish, a Christ's College grad (there are a number of Cambridge alums on the list, likely thanks to Idle) who went on to become ambassador to Mexico. See *MPFC: UC*, 1.289–310 for more of and on these names.

Møøse trained to mix concrete and sign complicated insurance forms by—Hengt Douglas-Home—Sir Alec Douglas-Home (1903–1995) has already been lampooned by the Pythons in *MPFC* Ep. 30, where he is listed as a producer, along with the deceased King Haakon of Norway, of *The Pantomime Horse Is a Secret Agent* film (*MPFC: UC*, 2.54, 56). Douglas-Home had been PM for a short time after Macmillan resigned for health reasons and before Labour and Harold Wilson won the 1964 General Election. See the *MPFC: UC* index for the many Douglas-Home mentions.

Jurgen Wigg—A reference to George Wigg (1900–1983), later Baron Wigg, a high-profile Labour politician (under Harold Wilson) who had pushed for the Profumo[82] affair to be put on the record in Parliament a decade earlier. The fact that the Pythons give their Jurgen Wigg two jobs—training a moose to both "mix concrete and sign complicated insurance forms"—may be connected to George Wigg's sort of *Johannes factotum* role in Wilson's government (he served as Paymaster General, then Chairman of the Horserace Betting Levy Board, etc.) Not a real hero to either Conservatives or Labour, George Wigg is called "that industrious garbage collector" by Anthony West in a contemporary article in the *Spectator*.[83]

A very different opinion comes from a "Personal View" penned in late November 1973 as the *Holy Grail* script was being conceptualized.[84] Richard Crossman (1907–1974) had recently served in the Wilson cabinet[85] and was a fixture of the left wing of the party, but is perhaps best known for coauthoring the progressive *Keep Left* pamphlet with Michael Foot[86] and Ian Mikardo in 1947. Just five months before his death Crossman wrote an opinion of the loud and essentially bootless public/private combat between PM Heath and Opposition Leader Wilson, calling them "aging and nearly blind sea lions roaring up in their separate pools and flapping and baying at each other from a distance."[87] In this same article Crossman characterizes Wigg as a man of principle and stature, perhaps offering a reason for his inclusion by the Pythons:

> [Military] experience gave George Wigg an undying contempt for most of those who conduct our affairs and turned him into the militant socialist who captured Dudley for Labour in 1945. In the House of Commons he became a great master of parliamentary procedure, which enabled him first to conduct brilliant guerrilla activities from the backbenches against the Government and later to become the closest confidant of a Labour Prime Minister. (18)

This type of man would clearly have intrigued Jones and Palin (who were cowriting the more "medieval" version of the film), Jones later opining about another left-of-Labour MP, Tony Benn, as good PM material. See the "Large Møøse" entry below for more on Benn and his effect on the more moderate (or perhaps, just more cynical) Cleese.

Editor—John Hackney—Hackney would also edit a number of documentaries including *Warriors of the Deep* (1982) and *The Year without Summer* (2004). He performed sound editing work on the horror film *Raw Meat* (1973). Hackney and his assistant John Foster began the editing work in the Tasker Road studio space, according to Doyle, before moving to Twickenham for the music and dubbing editing work. Doyle also mentions that the editing "team" included, for the most part, Hackney and Foster (and assistants), as well as Doyle, Jones, and Gilliam.

Møøses' noses wiped by—Bjorn Irkestrom-Slater Walker—The heartless Merchant Banker (Cleese) featured in *MPFC* Ep. 33 works for the firm "Slater-Nazi." From the "Slater-Nazi" entry in *MPFC: UC*:

> Slater Walker Securities (a secondary bank) turned £2,000 to £200 million in just eight years (1965–1973), only to see it all crumble by 1974. The "Walker" was Peter Walker [1932–2010], the oft-satirized (in *Private Eye*) Conservative MP and Cabinet member at this time. Walker is credited with creating the PEG, or "price earnings to growth ratio," a formula which looks at projected prices and expected earnings, and is based significantly in speculation. (2.59, 109)

A contemporary described them in a way that makes it clear how the more left-leaning Pythons would have viewed/loathed this "irksome" duo: "Slater is (like Walker) the very paragon of the new Heath-type Tory—self-made, hard-working, unsentimental, competitive" (Whitehead, 93). They are types who felt it better "to make money than to make things" (92).[88] Palin mentions Slater-Walker in passing—but judgmentally—in his *Diaries* in May 1974 (118). It may be appropriate to note that here in the *MPHG* credits Palin gives the Moose nose-wiping job to these speculating venture capitalists—asset-strippers, essentially—who were financial world darlings until their schemes fell to pieces, threatening thousands of pensions. These ruthless capitalist types would take it on the chin in Gilliam's pirate featurette *The Crimson Permanent Assurance*, part of the Pythons' last feature film, *Meaning of Life*.

Large møøse on the left half side of the screen in the third scene from the end, given a thorough grounding in Latin, French and "O" Level Geography by—Bo Benn—Anthony Neil Wedgwood Benn—Tony Benn (1925–2014)—was a prominent Labour politician and Cabinet minister.

When Benn's father (William Wedgwood Benn, First Viscount Stansgate) died the Viscountcy automatically passed to his son, Anthony, a sitting minister (for Bristol Southeast). He was promptly disqualified from a seat in the Commons, as was the law of the time. Benn lobbied for and was instrumental in enacting the Peerage Act of 1963, which allowed for the renunciation of peerages. See *MPFC: UC* for more on Benn and the Peerage Act.

Benn was always something of a bogeyman to the Tories, of course, being a leftist, but became so even to his own party as he moved further and further toward democratic socialism in the 1970s, becoming, as will be argued later, a Dennis the Peasant prototype, that is, a spokesperson for the benefits of syndicalism and co-operatives. In a later conversation recorded by Michael Palin in his *Diaries*, Terry Jones is said to have opined for a Benn-led Labour government, after which Cleese was seen to "twitch uncontrollably" (602). This is the only mention of Benn in Palin's long work (inveterate diarists both). See the "Dennis the Peasant" scene below for much more on Benn.

The "'O' Level" is the Ordinary Level qualification needed to receive the General Certificate of Education, which the Pythons would remember from their school days, and is mentioned twice in *Flying Circus* (*MPFC: UC*, 1.199, 368). In J. G. Ballard's[89] semi-autobiographical novel *Empire of the Sun*, young Jim is assigned science, French, and Latin—"*Amatus sum, amatus es, amatus est*"—by Dr. Ransome, an attempt to continue the boy's education in the privations of a Japanese POW camp in China (149).

Suggestive poses for the Møøse suggested by—Vic Rotter—Likely another reference to noted psychologist Julian Rotter (1916–2014), whose "Locus of Control" theories were currently popular. For more on Rotter, see Ep. 27 (*MPFC: UC*, 2.16). That, or his name describes him—a rotter is a morally corrupt person, a scoundrel. It shouldn't come as a surprise to Python fans that noted political figures—Churchill, Douglas-Home, Wigg, Walker, Benn, and (below) Thatcher—are included in this rogues' gallery.

Antler-care by—Liv Thatcher—A portmanteau reference, Liv Ullman (b. 1938) was at this time a favorite *Norwegian* actress for Swedish director Bergman. The "Thatcher" is undoubtedly yet another quick swipe at former Finchley MP, Minister of Education and Science, and Tory pillar (and eventual PM) Margaret Thatcher (1925–2013), whose Conservative-ness in the front and backbenches of government had earned her the Pythons' opprobrium. See the entries on Thatcher and Thatcherism in *MPFC: UC*.

. . . *in an entirely different style at great expense and at the last minute*—The budget for the film had been a point of contention from the start. It was originally thought that the film should be completed for no more than £165,000,[90] a negligible amount for a feature film even in 1974, and the money would come from multiple sources. Gilliam mentions that wealthy bands like Led Zeppelin and Pink Floyd, as well as friend and fan George Harrison were keen to lay off some of their potentially hefty UK tax burdens by investing in the film.[91] Julian Doyle also "seeded" the film (buying equipment, etc.) with his own money.[92] The production budget for the film eventually exceeded £229,500, which is still a fairly small investment for a feature-length film. By the time these credits were being prepared, there was nothing left in the production budget, and Palin took the austerity route to great effect. The "Cost of Production" paperwork is included at the back of *MPHGB*, and dated 17 September 1975.

John Goldstone—Executive Producer—Goldstone (b. 1943) would go on to produce *Rocky Horror Picture Show* (1975), *all* Python films, *Wind in the Willows* (1996) and *Déjà Vu* (1997).

Ralph the Wonder Llama—Perhaps a nod to Rex the Wonder Dog, a DC Comics character (1952–1959) drawn by Alex Toth (1928–2006). The Pythons had included a Superman-like cartoon character (penned by Gilliam) in an animated link in *MPFC* Ep. 6, and earlier a live-action sketch in Ep. 3 ("Bicycle Repair Man").

Mark Forstater—Producer—An American living in the UK for many years, Forstater would continue producing and executive producing into the mid-1990s. He's also authored and lectures on philosophy and spirituality. Forstater was on hand for the entire postproduction process, including the initial editing run. He would successfully sue the Pythons many years later for his share of the profits from all *MPHG*-related projects, including *Spamalot*. As Julian Doyle's one-time partner in Chippenham Films, Forstater would also try to reduce Doyle's profit participation as Forstater sued the Pythons. (Doyle's full profit participation was reinstated after a flurry of legal actions.)

Assisted by Earl J. Llama . . . —In *MPFC* Ep. 6 the Pythons had "worried" about the exorbitant cost of captions in the titles sequences, leading, of course, to higher costs as the silly credits continues to roll (*MPFC: UC*, 1.95). On (the unpaginated) page 59 of *MPHGB* are notes for proposed changes made after a run-through of the draft credit sequence and film trailer, reading "Check costs of alterations?" The Pythons worried about expense, clearly, but not at the cost of the funny bits, meaning the silly credits would continue, giving producer credit to "Mike Q. Llama III, Sy Llama, and Merle Z. Llama IX," who sound like typical Hollywood producers. The last might be a reference to Samuel Z. Arkoff (1918–2001), a lawyer and producer of such memorable films as *Teenage Cave Man* (1958), *How to Stuff a Wild Bikini*, and *Planet of Vampires* (both 1965). These were extremely low-budget but popular exploitation films, most aimed at the emerging youth audience of the 1950s and 1960s. In 1968 the Edinburgh Film Festival had honored Arkoff's partner and exploitation director Roger

Corman (b. 1926), along with their prolific and profitable company, American International Pictures (AIP). In the 1969 iteration of the festival, Arkoff himself was invited to participate, on the same bill as director Samuel Fuller (1912–1997).[93]

Ecuadorian Mountain Llamas . . . 14 North Chilean Guanacos—Previously mentioned in *MPFC* Ep. 9—where the llama is a "quadruped which lives in big rivers like the Amazon . . . has two ears, a heart, a forehead, and a beak for eating honey . . . [and] is provided with fins for swimming"—the creature is a danger and warnings must be shouted when it is spotted (*JTW*, 1.109). A guanaco is of the same genus as the llama—the minutiae here will be revisited when arguments about types of swallows (and in the original draft of the script, of ants and termites) are encountered.

Reg Llama of Brixton—Certainly a reference to Reg Kray (1933–2000), who, along with his twin Ronnie (1933–1995), had been notorious criminals in London's East End before a spectacular trial and subsequent imprisonment in the late 1960s. The Pythons devoted much of Ep. 14 to the Kray-like "Piranha Brothers," Doug and Dinsdale, and their reign of terror in East London and Luton, where they detonated a nuclear device (*MPFC: UC*, 1.221–39). In 1968 Reggie had been incarcerated in Her Majesty's Prison in Brixton, hence "Reg of Brixton."

Notes

1. Much of this information is available on websites like IMDb.com and through the BFI Film Database and the BFI National Archive.

2. Just the fact that a number of the scenes for this film were recorded on film—as opposed to shot in the studio on videotape—likely affected audience response to the scenes in a negative way.

3. The popular series of Robin Hood comic books will be discussed later. There are a number of Robin Hood (and Prince Valiant) comic book set pieces, characters, and bits of dialogue that lean very close to those found in *Holy Grail*.

4. Palin writes in his *Diaries* that he and Jones wanted to avoid just repeating *Carry On*, aiming for a more subtle film (*Diaries*, 146). The *Carry On* series was popular television programming during this period (1972–1974), with *Carry On Sergeant*, *Carry On Cruising*, *Carry On Nurse*, and *Carry On Constable* appearing on Thames TV on Tuesday evenings throughout January 1972, for example.

5. God appears to the knights at about 23:52 into the film.

6. Gawain makes it all the way to the Bridge of Death before succumbing. His lines are divvied up to other cast members of the smaller, more manageable quest.

7. The fact that the "King Brian the Wild" sequence was removed at this early date means that the script copy that made it into *MPHGB* in 1977 was *not* the final version of the script—it was a final but one (or two or . . .). Production Manager Julian Doyle remembers wanting to keep the scene, but choices had to be made: "We had to drop something in Scotland for scheduling reasons: The choice was Ni or Brian." From a 6 December 2013 e-mail correspondence with the author. See the "King Brian the Wild" entries for more on this long, violent scene that would eventually appear, in shifting guises, in *Jabberwocky* and *Yellowbeard*, for example.

8. Glencoe is mentioned in the script at the beginning of the Bridge of Death scene (*MPHGB*, 79). The Pythons had spent a good deal of time in the Glencoe region as they readied inserts and scenes for the third series, and especially the "*Njorl's Saga*" story of Ep. 27. See *MPFC: UC*, 2.9, 11, 18, 56, and 80.

9. Audio comments from all surviving troupe members can be found in the special features section of the 2012 Blu-ray edition of *MPHG*. Jones and Gilliam are included in one track; Palin, Cleese, and Idle's comments comprise the second track.

10. "Ice Flow" can be heard in the energetic Shaw Brothers film *Five Deadly Venoms* (1978), for example, an early Hong Kong martial arts classic from director Chang Cheh. In the scenic description for the battle sequence with the Killer Rabbit much later in the film, the shots are described as resembling "kung-fu and karate-type films."

11. These postproduction music choices would have been primarily made by Jones and Gilliam, since Cleese was already off working (shooting in Wiltshire in October 1974) on his pet project *Romance with a Double Bass*, starring his then-wife Connie Booth.

12. In the "Approved Judgment" paperwork acknowledging Mark Forstater's rights to a larger share of the film's (and *Spamalot's*) profits, the genesis of these companies and their original structures and intents are carefully outlined. Chippenham Films gets no screen credit in the opening titles.

13. British Telephone Records, London Postal Area, London Surnames L–R, 1974, page 707. This had been Mary Moore's studio (daughter of sculptor Henry Moore) prior to the Pythons' occupancy. The initial (picture) editing run-through was performed here, according to Doyle, along with Gilliam's "heart attack" sequence, with the dubbing and music editing accomplished later at Twickenham. Information from a 17 December 2013 e-mail to the author.

14. As an actress, Mai Zetterling (1925–1994) had been appearing in Danish films since about 1944; as a director, her short film *War Game* made a splash in 1962. Her next two films—*Älskande par* (1964) and *Nattlek* (1966)—were banned by film festivals. The films made appearances in British cinemas in 1965 and 1966 respectively, and were well received.

15. The "*Curious*" films wouldn't appear in British cinemas in their original, uncut versions until 1971, by which time, reviewers noted, the available sex education films screened in British schools were much more "explicit," and often more interesting ("Skolimowski's Baroque Bath House," *Times*, 26 March 1971: 11).

16. *Times*, 10 March 1958.

17. One review of the film as shown at the Edinburgh Film Festival characterized the film well: "If Mr. Bergman has abandoned much of his symbolism he has never put more brutal passages on the screen, and the one in which the girl is attacked is most unlikely to pass the censor. Yet whether this vast, fundamental work causes affront or not, it remains one of his most important films" ("New Bergman Film," *Times*, 26 August 1960: 5). The film began its run in British cinemas in June 1961.

18. Thanks to Dr. Chip Oscarson, BYU Scandinavian Studies, for the Swedish/Danish/Norwegian translations, and for helpful comments in relation to the Pythons' creative Nordic language.

19. "Gibberish, but again vaguely English" (in its syntax word-forming) according to Dr. Oscarson. The *MPFC* Ep. 40 scene can be found in *Monty Python's Flying Circus: Just the Words*, 2.253–54; see also *MPFC: UC*, 2.164.

20. See *MPFC: UC*, 2.251 for the many Carol Cleveland entries.

21. This fourth series of *MPFC* will be recorded in October and November 1974, well after the Pythons have returned from Scotland, but before *Holy Grail* is finished and distributed.

22. See the semi-official cast list at the end of *MPHGB* for a listing of actors and their roles. This cast list was likely meant to crawl at the end of the film, but the hand-over-the-lens ending changed that.

23. See the various "Episode" entries in each section of *MPFC: UC*, as well as in the *MPFC: UC* index under "*MPFC* extras and walk-ons (as scheduled)" for a complete listing of these crossover actors.

24. See the *MPFC: UC* index (1.454–56; 2.270–72), "*MPFC* extras and walk-ons (as scheduled)."

25. In the "Cast List" (*MPHGB*, 90) Kinghorn and Stewart are listed as "Either Winston or Piglet" and "Either Piglet or Winston," respectively. Kinghorn and Stewart, along with Duffell, Young, Innes, Davies, Booth, and Cleveland are the non-Pythons allowed speaking parts in the film. They are grouped together here in the opening credits, as well as in the "Cast List." In their scene, incidentally, only "Piglet" (Kinghorn) is given lines.

26. Listen to Gilliam's and Jones' audio commentary track on either a DVD or Blu-ray version of the film.

27. Zack Matalon (1928–2005) was a working actor, director, and singer of the 1950s and 1960s.

28. Mitsuko's name comes up when producer/husband Forstater successfully sued the Pythons in 2012 for his full one-seventh cut of profits from *Spamalot*, the musical "lovingly ripped-off" from *MPHG*. The Pythons had been sending Forstater royalties worth one-fourteenth of the adjusted gross to that point. In 2002 Mark Forstater had assigned 0.6875 percent of his 3.1875 percent profit participation to Mitsuko, according to the "Approved Judgment" heard by Mr. Justice Morris in 2012–2013. See *Forstater v Python (Monty) Pictures Ltd.* for more.

29. E-mail correspondence with the author dated 10 December 2013.

30. From an 11 December 2013 e-mail correspondence with Doyle.

31. Walker was one of the extras coaxed onto the shoot from Stirling for £2 plus meals. Extras correspondence with the author is included in appendix B.

32. British Telephone Archives, Central Scotland, 1978 (www.ancestry.com).

33. *Times*, 30 March 1971: V.

34. From a 17 December 2013 e-mail correspondence with the author. World Wide were located in St. Anne's Court, Soho, according to Doyle.

35. Doyle, 20 December 2013 e-mail.

36. Doyle, 18 December 2013 e-mail.

37. See "The History of Ericsson."

38. *Times*, 21 April 1965: 12.

39. *Times*, 3 December 1965: 21.

40. See the Cummings cartoon at the British Cartoon Archive.

41. Raeburn is the guard on the left, eating, as Launcelot approaches. The other guard—who says "Hey"—is Charles Knode, also a minstrel for Robin.

42. See the latter portion of *The Quest for the Holy Grail Locations*—Jones and Palin remember Knode and Raeburn.

43. Doyle, 26 November 2013 e-mail correspondence.

44. Information from e-mail correspondences with the author, as well as High Court of Justice, Chancery Division documents, 2012.

45. See *MPFC: UC* (2013) for much more on naming in the Python world ("naming/power of names," 1.456).

46. Les Shepherd, Vaughn Millard, Sue Smith, Iain Monaghan, and Bernard Belenger are also listed on this page, but unaccounted for.

47. Gleaned from Doyle's "Witness Statement" to the High Court of Justice, Chancery Division, in the case of *Forstater v. the Pythons* (2012). Copies of these statements were provided to the author by Doyle.

48. Other pickups not named here include a single shot of a castle in Wales—Kidwelly Castle—seen later in the "Swallows" scene, and later filmed footage of Bodiam Castle for the Swamp Castle exterior. See notes to those scenes for more.

49. This repeated shot was actually first recorded on location in Scotland, but the image wasn't deemed acceptable (Cleese's run is a bit more "silly" in the discarded footage). This unused footage can be seen in the "outtakes" section of the Blu-ray edition.

50. *HKB*, VIII.3, Thorpe, 1966, 189 (quoted in Gidlow, 198); also Dunn's *HKB*, 156.

51. Listen to Jones's and Gilliam's audio commentary track on either the DVD or Blu-ray editions for more on this imbroglio. Being privately owned, Doune was not under government control, and was accessible at the last minute. A slightly different version of events is offered by Doyle, whose testimony in the 2012 Forstater case mentions that the Pythons began shooting in or near some of these other castles (including Hermitage) before realizing the multiple camera setups would not only take forever, but were very costly. After about two days of this—and heeding Doyle's advice—the codirectors decided to scale back to just two castles, Doune and Stalker, creatively shoot at those locations, and pick up exteriors from other castles (including Kidwelly and Bodiam) as needed. Doyle's testimony to the National Film Trustee Company was made available to the author. Doyle mentions Hermitage Castle—another verboten Historic Scotland holding—in a 27 November 2013 e-mail correspondence to the author.

52. Doune and some of the following settings are visited by Palin for a 2001 documentary, *Pythonland*, and by Jones, Palin, and Doyle for *The Quest for the Holy Grail Locations*.

53. Stalker was purchased in 1965 by the Allward family, as a ruin, and restored before the Pythons found it in 1974.

54. From an 18 December 2013 e-mail correspondence with the author.

55. Banks would go on to become a prolific author of both fiction and science fiction.

56. See McIver's comments in appendix B for more on Bannell's significant role in the film.

57. See *MPFC: UC*, 1.291, 322, 324.

58. Perhaps especially Gilliam, since *images* of Nixon tend to appear most often in *MPFC* in relation to his animated sequences. The mentions in Palin's *Diaries* of Nixon are also completely unfavorable, while Jones, favoring a more radical Tony Benn-like Britain, would have been a natural Nixon antagonist.

59. Three days later Palin learns that PBS has agreed to broadcast *MPFC* on American television for the first time, leaving him "speechless," and certain that new American president Gerald Ford should be credited (*Diaries*, 187). These film credits were written and completed—primarily by Palin—well after the film's production, and even well into the postproduction process, meaning events surrounding Nixon would have been front page news.

60. All these are at least mentioned (and most seen, as well) during *MPFC*, with Tory politicians receiving plenty of attention. See the index in *MPFC: UC* for more. Also mentioned on the "suggested advertising slogans" back jacket are tennis players Virginia Wade and Rosemary Casals; singer Frank Sinatra; *Goon Show* bandleader Ray Ellington; and Tory politician and Cabinet member Maurice Macmillan (son of former PM Harold Macmillan). Tennis players, the Goons, and contemporary political figures populate and flavor *MPFC* from start to finish.

61. Magruder was deputy director of Nixon's reelection committee, and was sentenced to prison in May 1974; Colson was Nixon's special counsel—sentenced to prison in June 1974; Dean was White House counsel—sentenced to minimum security confinement in August 1974; former attorney general John Mitchell was sentenced to prison in February 1975; Stans—Nixon's reelection finance chair—was indicted in 1973 but later acquitted; A. G. Kleindienst was never indicted for Watergate crimes; and appointments secretary Chapin was jailed in May 1974. Seeing how prominent the Nixon and Watergate fiasco played in international headlines from May 1974, it's easy to see why the Pythons would have referenced him.

62. See the "Recorded and Live Music Cues" section in *MPFC: UC*, 2.215–20 for a complete listing of these artists and titles requested for *Flying Circus*.

63. Listen to Jones's portion of the Gilliam-Jones audio commentary track on either the DVD or Blu-ray versions of the film. Innes's period-accurate compositions sounded too "quaint," and were replaced with more dramatic, on-the-nose music cues.

64. From a 28 November 2013 e-mail communication with the author.

65. "Cultural Relations a Success," *Times*, 26 February 1974: III. The correspondent, Geoffrey Dodd, is comparing Norwegian television offerings to the more racy selections on Danish, Swedish, and even Finnish televisions.

66. The film had been "seized by [British] customs because it portrayed the sexual act graphically," according to the *Times* film correspondent, and was still unseen in British cinemas in late 1968 ("Czechs and Sex," 18 September 1968: 11). The sex depicted in the film was all simulated, of course, so distributors could avoid the "pornography" label. The film premiered in 1969 at the Cameo Victoria, Victoria Street.

67. *Times*, 6 March 1969: 13.

68. Except for participating when necessary in ADR sessions, Chapman, Cleese, and Idle had little to do with the postproduction process, leaving that to codirectors Jones and Gilliam, Julian Doyle, and producer Forstater.

69. Peter Evans, *Times*, 8 October 1970: 8.

70. It was well known that a flood of pornographic material washed in regularly from Denmark, to profiteers like "Big Jeff" Phillips, a Surrey-based importer. Phillips and another "Home Counties wholesaler," Gerald Citron, had been enriching themselves in the early 1970s thanks to tons of imported, illegal material. Both men were in the news for their sensational crimes and extravagant lifestyles beginning in 1972 and culminating, coincidentally, in May 1974, just as Palin was contemplating writing these silly subtitles ("Pornography in the Cowshed," *Times*, 22 May 1974: 6). See Sandbrook, *State of Emergency*, 440–41 for more. Citron and associates, for example, were initially arrested in January 1973 and charged with "possessing pornographic material for gain" ("Woman and 10 Men Are Remanded After Raids by Crime Squad," *Times*, 31 January 1973: 3).

71. "Pornoffensive," *Times*, 28 September 1970: 8.

72. "2,846 Pornographic Films Seized in a Year," *Times*, 8 June 1972: 5.

73. Geoffrey Dodd, "Scandinavia," *Times*, 17 December 1970: IX.

74. *King Boxer* appeared at the Warner in Leicester Square from 23 March 1973 (*Times*, 23 March 1973: 16). *Times* film critic David Robinson profiles Bruce Lee and the success of the imported martial arts film in "Life and Death of the Little Dragon," when Lee's *Enter the Dragon*, *The Big Boss*, and *Fist of Fury* were all appearing in London cinemas (*Times*, 18 January 1974: 7).

75. See entries including "*décor of a rather exclusive restaurant*" in Ep. 44 (*MPFC: UC*, 2.197). Much of the location shooting for the third series, for example, had been performed on the Island of Jersey, increasing the transportation budget significantly.

76. And he was *very* helpful on this book. Thanks Julian.

77. Doyle listed this twice, for some reason; I've removed one.

78. A "spark" is an electrician-type on the set.

79. A lorry is a larger truck, for which, Doyle admits, he did not have the requisite HV (heavy vehicle) license at the time. From an e-mail correspondence with the author dated 28 November 2013.

80. For the Grail Castle scene at the end of the film; the scene was filmed in the first few days of the shoot at Castle Stalker. See notes for the "Grail Castle" scenes for more.

81. From "Julian Doyle—My Work" document submitted to the court in October 2012, as well as the undated *Witness Statement*.

82. In 1963, Secretary of War John Profumo admitted to lying to Parliament in regard to a sexual relationship with Christine Keeler, who also happened to share her affections with a Soviet naval attaché. Though no pillow talk secrets were divulged, the Cold War made the scandal bigger than it might have been, with Profumo's deceit leading to censure. The Pythons had created an entire sketch, "The Mouse Problem," to satirize a scandal that involved role-playing, orgies, sadomasochism, etc. See *MPFC: UC* entries for "Profumo."

83. "McCarthy in Westminster" 8; quoted in Gilmour 21.

84. In *Diaries*, Palin notes that it was about November 1973 when he and Jones settled on Arthur and the Grail tales for a medieval film script they were contemplating. They knew they wanted a Middle Ages setting, and Palin wrote of their desire to emulate the visual style of the recent *Canterbury Tales*, while avoiding a slouch toward a *Carry On King Arthur*-type film (146).

85. Crossman was secretary of state for health and social services in 1968–1970.

86. Foot, Mikardo, and Wigg were more democratic-socialist than most of the Labour faithful. See *MPFC: UC*, 1.134.

87. "The Battle of Aging, Shortsighted Sealions," *Times*, 21 November 1973: 18.

88. See also Booker's discussion of "paper tiger" Slater and his impact in *The Seventies*, 135–40.

89. James Graham Ballard, 1930–2009.

90. From Doyle's *Witness Testimony* in the case *Forstater v. Python (Monty) Productions*.

91. Listen to Gilliam's audio commentary on either the DVD or Blu-ray editions of the film. The Pythons together and separately would go on to work with Harrison's Handmade Films on *LB*, *Time Bandits*, *Monty Python Live at the Hollywood Bowl*, *A Private Function*, etc.

92. From Doyle's *My Work* testimony.

93. See J. R. Taylor's "Cinema," *Times*, 23 August 1969: V.

SCENE TWO
COCONUTS AND SWALLOWS

EXTERIOR—CASTLE WALLS—DAY—Already reeling from the silly opening credits, the screenplay and film proper begin with a bit of an anachronism, which is probably fitting. Whether set in 787 or 932 (see below), the kinds of castles utilized throughout are well out of their depicted time. In fact, as Christopher Brooke points out:

> There were few castles in England before the Conquest, and the English fortresses were usually *burhs*, i.e. walled towns . . . [even] the early Norman castles were mostly very primitive . . . the significant development was the stone keep—an extreme rarity even in Normandy before 1066."[1]

The castle the Pythons are thinking of when they think "castle" is "Bodium" [*sic*] (referenced and misspelled in the screenplay), a fourteenth-century structure, and of the castles they actually used as settings in the film, none were built (in their present form) before the fourteenth century (e.g., Doune, Stalker), and some were still new in the seventeenth century (Arnhall). This particular castle, however, is none of these. This extreme long shot, an establishing shot, is Kidwelly Castle in Wales, a thirteenth- to fifteenth-century structure, one of the "Welsh castles" filmed by Doyle for just such pick-up needs. Doyle mentions that he captured the image with an Arri 2c movie camera "kept . . . in the back of the car." Doyle's brother Robert (Bob) assisted on this shot—helping with the necessary smoke—remaining uncredited until now. The *Bodiam* footage mentioned later was recorded on the way back from an Isle of Wight trip.[2]

It would have been quite a challenge in the 1970s to employ a usable Anglo-Saxon–era stronghold, since most would have long moldered or been destroyed and newer castles built on their bones, while others were simple or more elaborate hill forts (e.g., Cadbury Castle, Somerset) many of which had been in continual usage, militarily, since the Bronze Age. Antiquarian John Leland (writing in the sixteenth century) had recorded that the Cadbury Castle site was actually Arthur's Camelot, while a 1966–1970 excavation there revealed a "Great Hall" that was the center of trade and even a Saxon mint for a period (see Alcock, 1972). The *Times* even trumpeted the discoveries as an "Arthurian Find at Camelot Dig."[3]

So the site—a "multivallate hillfort of Iron Age date, subsequently refortified and reoccupied in the post-Roman and late Saxon periods"—would have been the state-of-the-art eighth- to tenth-century British (or even Saxon) "castle," but clearly not what the Pythons envisioned as Arthur's milieu, as not being "castle enough."[4] Audiences would have likely expected Arthur's environs to be more romantic and Camelot-ish, like those depicted by Gustave Doré for Tennyson's *Idylls of the King* (1868)—the looming, turreted spires of the castle set on a hillock—or even the production design for the recent Hollywood film *Camelot* (1967). These, or perhaps the castles and sets seen in the recent *Macbeth* production helmed by Roman Polanski, including Bamburgh, Harlech, and Lindisfarne castles in Northumberland and Wales, would have met audience expectations.

This creative geography wasn't anything new for the troupe. In preproduction for *MPFC* Ep. 38 they'd asked and been denied access to Edinburgh Castle—where they'd planned to shoot scenes for "Kamikaze Highlanders" in November 1971. Part of the scene involved throwing a dummy made up as a Scotsman from the highest parapet. They opted instead for Norwich Castle[5]—which was much closer to home and where the cast and crew were welcomed—and just called it Edinburgh Castle (*MPFC: UC*, 2.142, 148).

Mist. Several seconds of it swirling about—(PSC) There is little description here as to what the audience is supposed to be seeing, excepting the mist, but there is a hilltop in sight as well as what appears to be a corpse on a raised cart wheel. Gilliam describes it as a "Catherine wheel"[6] in his commentary, a nod to the breaking wheel on which St. Catherine was martyred in about 305.

It's apt that the Pythons have decided to begin their tale of the Dark Ages with a clear hint at its cold, gray barbarity—this displayed victim would have been executed, then posted on the wheel for the birds to feed on and peasants to see—but it's also a clue to the troupe's visual inspiration for this world. In the Bruegel painting *The Triumph of Death*, which they'll cite in the script for the transition to the "Bring Out Your Dead" sequence (and which they've used earlier in *MPFC*), there are six such wheel structures, four of which are festooned with corpses, the other two ready and waiting. The raised cartwheel complete with corpse will reappear at the beginning of the "Dennis the Peasant" scene later.[7] Historian Barbara Tuchman mentions not only the prevalence of violence and cruelty in medieval life (and art), but the *acceptance* of both: "Accustomed in their own lives to physical hardship and injury, medieval men and women were not necessarily repelled by the spectacle of pain, but rather enjoyed it" (135). The heads, limbs, and bodies of especially traitorous criminals were regularly put on display; sometimes parts of a single criminal or traitor were sent to different corners of the kingdom for display. The film itself accepts and enjoys this violence, as well.

Gilliam and Doyle note that this initial scene was shot well after principal photography had been completed, on Hampstead Heath and not far from Gilliam's home at that time.[8] It was a "pickup" shot, one that demanded fewer participants and could be completed once they'd come back from the filming locations; it is a much cheaper shot.

SUPERIMPOSE "England AD 787"—(PSC) This is from the final printed script, a date that would be changed (to 932) by the time the film was completed, and was likely one of at least three (and perhaps even five) different setting dates the Pythons considered. As will be discussed, the Pythons and producers posited the years 787, 932, 1167, and 1282 as possible time settings, and codirector Jones always had the thirteenth and fourteenth centuries in mind as he and Palin wrote the initial drafts.

. . . out of the mist comes KING ARTHUR—(PSC) This atmospheric moodiness is reminiscent of the very popular Kurosawa *Macbeth* adaptation *Throne of Blood*, reviewed in the *Times* in 1957:

> Mr. Kurosawa might be criticized for abusing the effects of rolling mists and whistling gales on bleak mountain sides, of heavily contrasted scenes of light and darkness, of the rhythmic beat of war drums to create atmosphere. Certainly there is something a little superficially dramatic in the gloom-enveloped Cobweb Castle . . . the sun never seems to shine upon the scene.[9]

To wit: The opening shot of *Throne of Blood* is a slightly low-angle view of low hills and hillsides, with substantial mist (or, likely, mist and added production smoke) wafting over the barren landscape. The sound of wind rustling across the expanse breaks the silence. A horseman appears out of the mists, and approaches the castle walls, which have also materialized from the gloom. In other words, the Pythons copied the haunting introduction of Kurosawa's masterpiece almost completely, simply undercutting its totality of despair with visual gaggery—coconuts instead of horses, and impertinent rather than hostile sentries at the castle. They will borrow similarly from other classics, including *The Seventh Seal*, Polanski's *Macbeth*,[10] Borowczyk's *Blanche* (1971), and *Canterbury Tales*. More on those titles later. *Throne of Blood* would premier at the Curzon cinema in London in April 1958, and then reappear regularly in London theaters in retrospectives in 1960, 1963, and 1970, and on BBC2 as recently as November 1972.

Though not described at all in the script, the clothing that Arthur wears, and that the other knights will also wear, is both suitable *and* anachronistic, at least for the date captioned below. The kitted-out Knight of the Round Table as envisioned by the Pythons is a borrow from many sources. There is, for example, a very useful chapter illustration in Howard Pyle's *The Story of the Champions of the Round Table* (a children's book republished in 1942) featuring Launcelot dressing himself in Kay's armor (86). With the exception of the heraldic device (the Pyle Launcelot wears a dragon insignia; our Launcelot wears a griffin) the costuming is almost precisely the same: long white gown, chain mail hauberk, gloves, thick belt and scabbard, and (nearby) a helm and shield. The armed and armigerous Knights of the Round Table will wear this same outfit throughout *MPHG*, and their pages wear slightly diminished versions of the same (minus armor or weaponry), complete with matching heraldic devices. Shields with heraldic decorations won't appear until about 1150, while the white "gowns" Arthur and knights wear (also even later inscribed with his heraldic insignia) came into use shortly thereafter. Poole notes that "between 1200 and 1250 the normal heraldic principle that every knight's shield-bearing should be distinct became generally established" (*Medieval England*, 1.350). The mail shirts they all wear (actually wool painted with silver paint[11]) had been part of the Norman soldiers' armor of the eleventh century. The riveted gauntlets that Arthur wears (the other knights simply wear gloves) are of an even later design, emerging about 1330–1340.[12] Most of what the Pythons wear, then, comes from the later centuries mentioned by Jones as the source for the "look" of the film, and have very little to do with "932 A.D."

Arthur does wear a very obvious crown, and not a helmet like the other knights. The crown is emblematic of his kingship, of course, but as Brooke reminds us in relation to Anglo-Saxon kings: "We do not know when a crown was first worn" (*SNK*, 66). The first images we have are coins featuring a crowned King Æthelstan, who would have been the most powerful king during the period depicted by the film; he ruled 925–939. Patsy even carries a spare crown on his backpack, just in case. The recognizable orb and scepter wouldn't appear until later in the tenth century in Britain, and then only as a borrow from Otto the Great's example on the continent (66). Brooke also notes that the Anglo-Saxon period kings didn't necessarily have a singular home or dwelling where their things were kept; these kings traveled a great deal, and the people and the material of government and finance, including the crown jewels and treasures, traveled with them (67). Patsy is obviously tasked with carrying on his back everything of importance in the matters of state.

"England 932 A.D."—The final draft of the script actually calls for this superimposed title to read "England AD 787," and there is no indication why or when the setting date was ultimately changed. (See below for a note mentioning two other dates, 1167 and 1282, as possible settings.) Either date—787[13] or 932—sets the action firmly in Anglo-Saxon Britain, the period beginning toward the end of Roman domination sometime in the early fifth century and ending with the Norman invasion of 1066. The credit sequence would have been completed well *after* principal photography, and likely even after a rough or maybe a fine cut of the film had been assembled, so there was plenty of time to make such changes. (There are mentions in the *Holy Grail* DVD commentaries that screenings of the film were undertaken before the film was "finished," and a number of changes were made based on audience reactions.[14]) The initial eighth-century setting would have been only slightly more accurate for an alleged historical Arthur figure (*fl.* late fifth to early sixth centuries), though *avoiding* anachronisms hasn't been a Python concern in the past.

The jury is still out for many, of course, as to the actual existence of an Arthur separate from the demands of mythology and nation building, which will be much discussed throughout these pages. The "many" mentioned above are primarily peddlers of Arthuriana as opposed to medieval scholars—scholarship has decided the issue for itself, as Dumville's quote earlier affirms. There just isn't much "evidence for 'King Arthur' that survives from within five centuries of his supposed existence around AD 500," according to the most recent scholarship.[15] Even preeminent historians like Sir Frank Stenton (1880–1967) couched his arguments carefully when the subject of Arthur was broached, as indicated by this section on Gildas from his groundbreaking 1943 work *Anglo-Saxon England*:

> It is remarkable that Gildas ignores the British leader whose legendary fame was to carry the struggle between Saxons and Britons into the current of European literature. Gildas has nothing to say of Arthur, whose claim to an historic existence rests upon the ninth-century compilation of the Welsh scholar Nennius, and upon the observation of an earlier Welsh poet that a certain warrior, though brave, "was no Arthur." The silence of Gildas may suggest that the Arthur of history was a less imposing figure than the Arthur of legend. But it should not be allowed to remove him from the sphere of history, for Gildas was curiously reluctant to introduce personal names into his writing.[16]

(Both Arthur *and* Nennius were relocated from history to legend during this period, as we'll see.) In 1969, as the Pythons were gearing up for their first go at *Flying Circus*, there was a much-touted international Arthurian Congress held in Cardiff and featuring a field trip to Glastonbury (one of Arthur's purported burial sites). There, Arthurian scholar Professor Jean Frappier (of the Sorbonne) sniffed rather famously: "I do not believe in Arthur, therefore I do not believe in Arthur's tomb."[17] *Quot homines, tot sententiae*, certainly. This was the thirty-ninth year of the congress, by the way, meaning the urn of scholarly/mythological Arthurian endeavors had been publicly churning away since before any of the Pythons were born, and there were plenty of scholars and even more enthusiasts who had no trouble believing in the historical King Arthur. The early 1970s would be coincidentally fecund for Arthurian surmising and scholarship, as will be seen, coincidences probably not lost on the Pythons as they cast about for suitable feature film material.[18] For our purposes, 1960s–1970s Arthurian scholar Leslie Alcock's determination of "Arthurian fact" will serve as a jumping-off point, where Alcock (who arranged and attended the Arthurian Congress, and was "contemporary" in that he published *Arthur's Britain* in 1971), asks

> the question: if the whole weight of reasoning and reasonable scepticism is brought to bear on Arthur, what remains as the irreducible minimum of historical fact? The answer is that we are left with a single entry in the Welsh Easter Annals: "*An[nus xciii]. Guieth camlann in qua arthur et medraut corruerant.*" "Year 93. Strife of Camlann in which Arthur and Medraut perished." (*Arthur's Britain*, 88)

Alcock took pains to show that the Easter Tables tended to be as or more factual than other surviving period documents, and he trusts this single, unadorned entry because it

> assure(s) us that Arthur was an authentic person; one important enough to be deemed worthy of an entry in an Easter Annal; most probably a king or prince, but if not that, then emphatically a great warrior. And even if we cannot calculate a reliable date for the battle, we can at least be sure that Arthur died in the first half of the sixth century. (88)

Much more recently it seems that scholars have moved well away from Ashe (1968), Alcock (1971), and Morris (1973), et al.—more from them throughout—and healthy skepticism has changed to outright certainty: the kingly Arthur was no more real, for example, than the fantastical Fionn, or even Hengest and Horsa, the fabled progenitors of the Kentish royal house.[19] Two years after the release of *Holy Grail*, David Dumville penned that now famous and pointed response to the tomes of Morris and Alcock, neatly and effectively undercutting every bit of Arthurian foundational material erected by the two eminent historians—literary and archaeological, respectively—setting the table for a more skeptical approach to any historical Arthur still with us today. Most recently (2013), Guy Halsall notes that Morris's primary source material—"later medieval Welsh and Breton saints' lives"—cannot be trusted since those sources can't be "projected back into the fifth and sixth centuries" (*Worlds of Arthur*, 83). The unreliable sources, then, undermine Morris's sweeping, fascinating work. Halsall does appreciate Morris, writing that *The Age of Arthur* is "a marvellous, inspiring read" that, unfortunately, "cannot be relied upon" (8). (James Campbell earlier [1986] also praised the scholar and damned the work.) Halsall concludes: "If Morris's intention was to be deliberately provocative and, by proposing an intentionally outrageous theory of post-imperial British history, make people think hard about the problems of the sources for this period, he certainly succeeded" (8). The Pythons' approach to the histories of Arthur and the Grail and the Middle Ages are also "deliberately provocative," and this book is a direct result of that playful provocation. Thomas Green (2007) also works through every bit of available "Arthurian" proof (i.e., *Y Gododdin*, the *Historia Brittonum, Annales Cambriae*, and a handful of the occurrences of the name "Arthur" in sixth- and seventh-century literature), in *Concepts of Arthur*. He concludes the following as he's about to examine in detail these "sources":

> Given the above conclusions drawn by previous surveys of the early Arthurian legend, there would seem to be only one possible conclusion. The weight of the non-Galfridian [*not* derived from Geoffrey of Monmouth's work] material (early and late) provides, it has frequently been asserted, a very clear and consistent picture of Arthur as a thoroughly legendary figure of folklore and myth not associated in any way with either the Saxons or Badon, and with this figure resembling in many of its characteristics the Gaelic Fionn who was a mythical figure—originally a god—later historicized with battles against foreign invaders. If we can accept this judgment, then we can eliminate most of the uncertainties in our original conclusion . . . the "historical" Arthur must be seen as a secondary development of an originally legendary, folkloric or mythical figure. (43)

This Arthur is the kind of figure that a Soldier could call out ("Pull the other one!"), or peasants might fail to recognize ("I didn't vote for you"), and upon whom nasty Frenchmen might heap opprobria ("you so-called Arthur King"). Two hundred pages later (a very compelling read, by the way), Green concludes that "Arthur was primarily a folkloric and mythical Protector of Britain, who may have always been such a folkloric hero or who might, just possibly, have developed from a Brittonic protective deity of some sort" (246). Arthur is "a composite figure," Green writes, built from the demands of folkloric pan-Brittonism, gifted with victories in battles likely actually fought by the contemporary Ambrosius Aurelianus (more on him below), and ultimately historicized in the ninth century and beyond as the man who led the fifth- to sixth-century "counterattack against the *Saxones*" (245–46). Subsequent compilers and authors would build on and expand both the historicization and mythologizing of Arthur, all the way through the Pythons and *Holy Grail*.

Additionally, there are two more dates to consider. A scribbled note (by either Gilliam or Jones) alongside rough storyboards for the first scene (Arthur and Patsy "riding" toward the "Coconuts and Swallows" castle) included in *MPHGB* reads simply: "*1167 AD*."[20] This means at some point during or prior to production the Pythons were thinking of pulling the film's setting forward into the twelfth century, and out of the eighth or tenth centuries. A twelfth-century setting would have accurately allowed for the inclusion of castles like Hedingham in Essex (c. 1130–1140), and a little later Orford Castle in Suffolk (1165–1173), both of which featured significant keep structures, great halls, and so forth.[21] There is no indication as to when the final setting decision was made—in favor of 787, 932, or 1167—or why. This 1167 date would also have set the film in the period when grail romance author Chrétien de Troyes was alive and writing, his unfinished Arthurian opus *The Story of the Grail* appearing about 1160 (*THG*, 10). As will be seen, the Pythons were clearly envisioning a later set of influences (twelfth to fourteenth centuries[22]) for at least the visual elements of their Arthur, his deeds and situations emerging from later romance writers, especially Malory, but including Chrétien. Gilliam's choices for animated material come primarily from twelfth- to fourteenth-century Gothic illuminated manuscripts, as well. See appendix A, "Facing Pages," for those annotations.

Secondly, in an interview conducted and published as the film was in production in Scotland (May 1974), producer Forstater mentioned that the film could be subtitled "Where were you in 1282?"[23] If this was actually the case at some point during preproduction, neither the date nor the alleged subtitle appear anywhere in the available production material or in any other interview; it was likely simply Forstater's attempt to pun on the marketing slogan for the recent American cult hit *American Graffiti*: "Where were you in '62?" This slogan was featured prominently on the lobby posters for the nostalgic film, amid drawings by *Mad* artist Mort Drucker (b. 1929).[24] Significantly, just the day before this story appeared in print George Lucas's *American Graffiti* had opened in London at the Ritz in Leicester Square, after a successful run in American cinemas from 11 August 1973. The thirteenth-century date still fits for the period Jones said he envisioned as they created the film, costumed the characters, etc.

The stated date for the film's action and the almost immediate depiction of an anachronism—the fifth-century Arthur "riding" through the tenth-century mists—sets up a tension that happily problematizes the rest of the film.[25] Here the Pythons are propagating the British nineteenth-century trope of adapting Dark Ages figures and stories into more recognizable, even palatable Renaissance times and settings, for example.[26] Artist William Dyce (1806–1864) created "Arthurian frescoes" for the House of Lords (following a destructive fire and subsequent remodel), painting large panels with Arthurian characters and symbolizing various virtues. Dyce had to avoid the Malorian adulteries and violence and hew close to the chivalrous, of course, as Barber points out, though the choice to "anachronize" the stories and characters sounds quite Pythonesque:

> Dyce's style also removed the image [featuring Galahad, Bors and Perceval] from its medieval context; his models were from the Renaissance, as was usual for the period. So the Grail itself is carefully absent . . . [as] the story of the Grail pose[s] difficulties for official artists. (*THG*, 266–67)

These tensions include Arthur as a historically shadowy figure, as well. An Arthur may have existed but precisely when and where and doing what remain elusive, even today, and he is likely to remain unfound—the dearth of sub-Roman written material is well known, and the fifth century is particularly dark. Arthur, however, is *more* than any real man could be or could have been—he can be claimed by many places and cultures in British and northern European folklore, as will be evidenced. Historians and folklorists who see Arthur as a viable person of history agree that he lived in the late fifth and possibly the early sixth centuries, that he may have been a tribal leader, at least, perhaps even a leader among "an alliance of British rulers," and that he likely engaged in significant battles against the invading Saxons, including the battle of Badon Hill (Gidlow, 232). Again, these are the arguments of those who treat Arthur as historically real, not an amalgamation of folklores serving the national interests of an emerging, unifying England. Gidlow tries to summarize the "legendary" Arthur as separate from the historical record, and gives credit where credit is due:

> Some of the Arthurian legends are revealed by their absence from either Geoffrey [of Monmouth] or the earlier material, as being unlikely to preserve historical truths. That Arthur has to demonstrate his title to rule against rival British kings, that Merlin was "his" magician and Morgan Le Fay an enemy enchantress, that his famous knights sat together at a round table or that questing for the Holy Grail was their chief activity, the sources not only do not say, but in some cases flatly contradict. However appealing these motifs are, we have to conclude that they are products of the imaginations of twelfth- and thirteenth-century writers. (*The Reign of Arthur*, 230)

Beyond that, as we will find, hundreds of years of British chest-thumping (beginning in the ninth century with *Historia Brittonum*) have elevated Arthur to mythic, even messianic status (including reports that he was only injured at his final battle, went away to be healed, and would return again), and an actual Arthur—whomever he was or might have been—is likely forever lost in time.

What's important to remember here is the state of Arthurian studies as the Pythons—on hiatus from *Monty Python's Flying Circus*, which finished taping season three in May 1972—determined the subject of their first original feature film.[27] The most recent and popular versions of Arthuriana had turned *toward* the historical and *away from* the mythological in the late 1960s and early 1970s—coincidentally, as the British economy sputtered and the Empire constricted—and the English hero Arthur was writ large, and into better focus, but against a very troubled world backdrop.[28] The Pythons' titular king wanders back and forth between various Arthurs—from unifying monarch to nation builder to tool of the Almighty to a character in a medieval tale to a kind of picaresque malefactor—*all* recorded and substantive versions of the historical, literary, and legendary Arthur available to the Pythons in 1974.

...followed by a SERVANT... —(PSC) Patsy here is making horse sounds but he's not really pretending to be a horse[29]—he can speak, he has opinions and feelings—and he's actually a *liveried* retainer, meaning he wears his lord's colors and his lord's heraldic device or badge. He's likely the Python version of the "gesith" (OE *gesíþ*), an Anglo-Saxon term for a king's companion. Most likely he's simply meant to be this film's version of Jöns, the surly squire to doomed knight Antonius Block in Bergman's *The Seventh Seal*.[30] Patsy wears the same golden sun heraldic device his master wears, and by his dress he is meant to be identifiable as Arthur's servant. McKisack notes that for the Middle Ages, at least, Patsy's fake-horseness isn't the only diminishment here, since "even a plain knight would normally travel with a retinue of at least half a dozen servants" (263). More important men and especially kings like Arthur were expected to employ dozens of liveried servants, and when they traveled, there could be

hundreds of household members in the train. As the quest expands in size, the other invited knights appear with their individual liveried servants, as well.

. . . *banging two half coconuts together*—(PSC) This revealing, deflating image is the first in the film proper (after the silly credits) to create a rupture in the film's perceived narrative world—it undercuts not only the purported early medieval setting but draws attention to itself as an incongruity and an anachronism, as well. In this the image acts very much like many of those found in the Gothic illuminated manuscripts, where hares tree dogs and men dance to apes playing musical instruments—the world can be turned about and made to comment on itself by the juxtaposition. In the *Rutland Psalter* there is a marvelous image that manages to capture much of the Pythonesque of *Holy Grail* seven hundred years before the film existed: a rabbit playing cymbals, which look very much like coconuts (f. 54r, *bas-de-page*). Gilliam would use figures, trees, and hillocks from this mid-thirteenth-century English psalter throughout his sketchings and the film itself. Into this unstable world an ironic or cynical modern ethoi can intrude, forcing the audience to adopt a skeptical eye. Viewers of the *Flying Circus* television show would have expected this structure, and had likely learned to take every "serious" moment presented by the Pythons as a setup for a subversive payoff. The Pythons will regularly expose such narrative ruptures or fissures, reminding the audience that even though this is a period film, it is a constructed, artificial world that is being presented—a hallmark of various New Waves.

As will be seen throughout this book, BBC radio's *Goon Show* of the 1950s also led the Pythons to this trough of reflexivity. In "Ye Bandit of Sherwood Forest," the artificial sound effects track is outed:

Friar Balsam (Sellers): Oh, Robin, we can't keep this up much longer, will they never arrive?

Robin Hood (Secombe): Who?

Friar Balsam: Those blasted sound-effects men. (*Sounds of fighting*) Blunge! Thoglog!

Robin Hood: Let me help. (*Sound of fighting*) Blat! (28 December 1955)

Earlier in that same episode Maid Marion (Charlotte Mitchell) is being imprisoned by the evil Sheriff, and she points out the source of the sounds we're hearing:

Maid Marion: Sheriff of Nottingham, take your hands off me! If they are not off in the next three hours I'll write to the police.

The Sheriff (Sellers): Little Spitfire!

Maid Marion: Oh fie, oh fie! You see, my fiancé, Mr. R. Hood will come and fisticuff you. He'll hit thee! Splat, thun, blat, zowee, zocko. blam, thud, biff! He learnt all his boxing from comic strips. Have you ever seen a comic strip?

The Sheriff: Only in a Turkish Bath. (28 December 1955)

In "The Plasticine Man," a character asks for a sound effect to be fried and saved for breakfast, and in "The Emperor of the Universe," after Neddie stops and announces "this looks like the place in the script," not only is the necessary sound effect acknowledged, but its mode of delivery, as well:

Neddie (Secombe): There you are, living proof that he's Chinese.

Chinese Man (Milligan): (*Chinese-sounding gibberish*) Yes indeed, he lar . . . he are Chinese. And now, please, to follow me, please.

SCENE TWO

Sound Effect: A few pairs of footsteps on pavement—it goes on seemingly forever.

Neddie: (*After footsteps stop, pause*) We can't stand here all day listening to a record of footsteps!

Chinese Man: Please, please, sir, that record . . . are number one on Chinese hit parade. (3 January 1957)

The Goons acknowledge the use of practical sound effects, the repetition of jokes and gags from previous episodes or even from other comic sources, and that actors take on more than one part in each episode, etc. The audience is acknowledged often, as well, especially when a joke falls flat (often purposely) or the show's silliness or incongruity has reached a level of absurdity. At one point a cast member is warned to keep clear of the audience: "You don't know where they've been." Given the chance, the Pythons will not let any of Arthur's recognized set pieces—facing the Black Knight, receiving a calling from God, encountering Camelot, etc.— pass without undercutting the moment or somehow drawing attention to the scene's silliness.

ARTHUR: "Whoa there!"—The script here calls for the servant (Patsy) to make "*noises of horses halting, with a flourish*" (*MPHGB*, 1[31]). A knight just isn't a knight—or a king a king, for that matter—without a horse under him, especially during the medieval period when knightly codes flourished. From Tuchman:

> The horse was the seat of the noble, the mount that lifted him above other men. In every language except English, the word for knight—*chevalier* in French—meant the man on horseback. "A brave man mounted on a good horse," it was acknowledged, "can do more in an hour of fighting than ten or maybe one hundred could do afoot." . . . In fulfilling military service, horse and knight were considered inseparable; without a mount the knight was a mere man. (15–16)

Arthur must know this, so he brings along Patsy to be his horse; he upholds the ideals of knighthood this way. This inseparability—the certainty of a horse and a rider—is likely why the Pythons would incongruously unseat Arthur, bring him down to the Third Estate's level, and let characters like Dennis look him in the eye.

CUT TO shot from over his shoulder: castle (e.g. Bodium) . . . —(PSC) The Pythons are thinking of a particular National Trust[32] castle when setting up Arthur's first encounter with potential new adherents, going so far as to mention the (misspelled) name of a potential setting, "Bodium." The only problem with choosing a *stone* castle is that, according to Brooke, "[t]he stone castle was the characteristic novelty of the Normans," not the Anglo-Saxons (*SNK*, 66). Kings during the times of Alfred and Æthelstan built and rebuilt wooden structures—great, long halls with peaked roofs and a propensity for burning down. To underscore his own longevity William I would institute the building of a number of first wood and then stone castles—like the Tower of London (c. 1078)—often for defensive (or repressive) but also domestic purposes, after the Conquest. Stone construction would become the preferred method through the twelfth and thirteenth centuries for kings and barons.[33] As discussed elsewhere in this book, no Anglo-Saxon fortifications would have been available to the Pythons, anyway, and the "look" of the film leans forward to the later Middle Ages, so a "Bodium"-type castle is suitable.

A fourteenth-century moated castle in East Sussex, *Bodiam* was built in 1385 by Sir Edward Dalyngrigge (c. 1346–1395)—a former knight of Edward III (1312–1377)—and with the blessing of Richard II (1367–1400). Specifically (and for the film's purposes, fittingly) Bodiam was fortified to stem a presumed invasion by the French, who had attacked nearby Rye and Winchelsea just a few years before, partly in retaliation for earlier English pillaging raids on the continent as the Hundred Years War dragged on.[34] The castle was likely chosen by the Pythons for its proximity to London—Bodiam is about forty-four miles southeast of the capitol, near Robertsbridge, Sussex.[35] As the film was in preproduction, the Pythons hoped to shoot in the Kent and Sussex areas, at the furthest, and then in and around the green belts of Greater London (*MPHGB*, 58). They would eventually have to move far north, to Scotland, shooting only a handful of postproduction "pickup" shots in green acres of the London area, like Hampstead Heath. See the entry for "Made entirely on location" for more.

On the castle battlements a SOLDIER is dimly seen—This is Palin, who in the Cast List included at the end of the printed script is known as "1st Soldier With a Keen Interest in Birds" (*MPHGB*, 90).[36]

ARTHUR: "It is I, Arthur"—Or maybe it isn't. There is no mention of Arthur by any *historical* writer between 400 and 820,[37] not including hagiographical works such as the *Life of Saint Columba* (*Vita S Columbae*, seventh century), where an Arthur is mentioned:[38] "*Illo se respondente nescire quis esset de tribus filius suis regnatures, Arturius, an Echodius Find, an Domingartus*" (Adamnani and Fowler, 25). The Pythons' Arthur is clearly relying on the later institutional knowledge the sentries and the viewers should possess, knowledge that posits Arthur as "King of the Britons." As we'll find later, however, there are many occasions in the various Arthurian romance tales where a knight is misrecognized, especially in relation to some enchantment or the armor and shield he may or may not be wearing.

Cultural historian Geoffrey Ashe (1968)—one of the three major voices in the historical Arthur discussion during this period—notes that during the age of Malory, Arthur is almost always depicted wearing not a sun (as the Pythons present him) but the images of three crowns; in the thirteenth century an image of the Madonna and Son are on his shield (this from the *Annales Cambriae*, late tenth century); and later, "in the late thirteenth and part of the fourteenth centuries, attempts were made to devise arms for Arthur and his knights, and in these rolls of arms Arthur is often depicted with ten to thirteen crowns on a blue shield" (*The Quest for Arthur's Britain* 4n5, 23n). The number of crowns often stood for the number of "haughty" princes Arthur had allegedly unseated (23n). The casebound version of Ashe's 1968 book even features Arthur's three crowns on its otherwise undecorated cover.

It's equally clear that an emblazoned shield was the standard—in the Grail romances, at least—for knightly identification.[39] Knowing this—in *A Noble Tale of Sir Lancelot du Lake* from the Winchester version of *Le Morte Darthur*—Lancelot[40] determines to surprise participants in a martial tournament by visual patchery:

> "Sir," said Sir Lancelot, "as I hear say, that the tournament shall be here within these three miles of this abbey. But sir, ye shall send unto me three knights of yours such as ye trust, and look that the three knights have all white shields, and no picture on their shields, and ye shall send me another of the same suit; and we four will come out of a little wood in midst of both parties, and we shall fall on the front of our enemies and grieve them that we may. And thus shall I not be known what manner a knight I am." (*LMD-WM*, 102)

Just a few pages later when Lancelot has overcome Sir Tarquin, they are waiting for Tarquin's prisoners (all knights) to be set free. Each of those so interned can be identified by his shield hanging without the castle, according to Lancelot, speaking to Gaheris:

> I am sure ye shall find there many knights of the Round Table, for I have seen many of their shields that I know hanging on yonder tree. There is Sir Kay's shield, and Sir Galihud's shield, and Sir Brian de Listenoise's shield, and Sir Aliduke's shield, with many more that I am not now advised of; and Sir Marhalt's. (106)

And finally, Lancelot later even purposcly takes up Kay's shield rather than his own before looking for adventure. He knows that would-be opponents will come at him if they mistake him for Kay, but also that Kay (carrying Lancelot's shield) will be able to return to Camelot unmolested, being mistaken for Lancelot (112).

Throughout the illuminated manuscripts of the twelfth to fourteenth centuries are dozens of marginal illustrations featuring knights, most kitted out like Arthur and, later, Bedevere, Launcelot, Robin, and Galahad. It's not unreasonable to assume that codirector and production design maven Gilliam would have taken inspiration for the knights' costumes[41] from the same sources he will employ to create the film's animated sequences, many borrowed from or modeled after those found in Randall's *Images in the Margins of Gothic Manuscripts* (1966). See the animation entries below and the Facing Pages (appendix A) for much more on Randall's book, and codirectors Jones and Gilliam's painstaking research and production work.

ARTHUR: "Arthur, King of the Britons"—Happily, Medieval Britain scholar Christopher Snyder begins his book *The Britons* (2003) by quoting this section of *MPHG*, before moving on to discuss the "truly complex . . . subject of ethnic identity in the Middle Ages" (1). This valiant, battle-tested version of Arthur comes from several sources, from the Dark through the Middle Ages, from high Victorian poetry and right up to the Pythons' own childhoods in the pages of comic books.

In the ninth-century text *Historia Brittonum* (the "oldest reliably dated text to mention Arthur," according to Wiseman), often attributed to Nennius (though Dumville [1977] says that "is a mistake" [176]; and a work that Alcock (1989) wanted to call *British Historical Miscellany* [31–32]),[42] Arthur is described as a worthy local hero, a "dux bellorum," or battle leader in the following oft-cited and unendingly parsed chapter 56:

> Then Arthur fought against them in those days with the kings of the Britons but he himself was leader (Duke) of battles. The first battle was at the mouth of the river which is called *Glein*. The second and third and fourth and fifth upon another river which is called *Dubglas* and is in the district *Linnius*. The sixth battle was in the Caledonian wood, that is, *Cat Coit Celidon*. The eighth battle was in Fort *Guinnion* in which Arthur carried the image of St Mary, ever virgin, on his shoulders and the pagans were turned to flight on that day and a great slaughter was upon them through the virtue of our Lord Jesus Christ and through the virtue of St Mary the Virgin, his mother. The ninth battle was waged in the City of the Legion. The tenth battle he waged on the shore of the river which is called *Tribruit*. The eleventh battle took place on the mountain which is called *Agned*. The twelfth battle was on mount Badon, in which nine hundred and sixty men fell in one day from one charge by Arthur, and no one overthrew them except himself alone. And in all the battles he stood forth as victor. (quoted in *Arthur's Britain*, 55–57)

So Arthur and God are on the same page well prior to the Pythons' writing, and Arthur is already doing God's work. (See the "defeater of the Saxons" entry below for more.) Higham describes *HB* as a Northern Welsh "redemptive narrative" (composed c. 829–830), and was importantly "a defensive review, from a British perspective, of the moral, political and military meaning of the Anglo-Saxon settlement" (*King Arthur: Myth-Making and History*, 6). "The anonymous author," Higham continues (following Dumville away from "Nennius"), "has set about ordering the past for the sake of contemporary authority (and therefore power). . . . This work offers a grandiose historical framework, couched in moral and providential terms" (6). In other words, it's a weighted account in defense of a particular godly people and against a known and likely godless invader group, and historians, medievalists, archaeologists, and hobbyists have for decades argued over its historicity. See chapter 3 of Higham's work for much more on these "contested histories." Dumville is less tactful, generally, or just more pointed. He not only sees *HB* as lacking an attributable author/compiler, but he is certain that the possibly medieval Irish "synchronizing historian" who did put *HB* together "struggled . . . with inadequate source-material, especially for the fifth century," and that under proper historical examination the claims made using the text cannot be supported ("'Nennius' and the *Historia Brittonum*," 176–77). "So much for the so-called 'British Historical Miscellany,'" Dumville concludes (178).

Another somewhat contemporary scholar, Kenneth Jackson (active in the postwar period), would look closely at all these battles' Latin place names—"*ostium fluminis Glein, flumen Dubglas, region Linnuis*," et al.—and conclude that only two were "fairly certainly identifiable," one other "probable," and the balance "conjectural."[43] In fact, more than twenty years before the Pythons gathered for *Flying Circus*, and thirty years before *Holy Grail*, Jackson (1945) is arguing that the author of *HB* likely treated history much like the Pythons would:

> It looks very much as if, in writing about Arthur, Nennius or his source knew only that he had won twelve famous victories. Not having their names by any trustworthy tradition, and not both-ering himself with scruples as to where they were, he searched his memory for any battles of olden time about which he had vaguely heard—so vaguely that one of them was really a British defeat, the battle of Chester about A.D. 616, long after Arthur's time. This would parallel with what he seems to have done with the tradition, learned from Gildas [mentioned below; c. 500–570], that Britain possessed twenty-eight chief cities. (57)

But it's twelfth-century "historians" like Geoffrey of Monmouth (d. 1154) who can be given credit for consolidating Britain—allowing for a "king of the Britons"—according to Christopher Gidlow, when in *The History of the Kings of Britain* (*HKB*) Geoffrey anoints Arthur king of all Britons, ignoring the separate kingdoms of the fifth and sixth centuries in favor of a united Britain under one glorious monarch (*The Reign of Arthur*, 211, 245). Gift-ing Arthur with this marshaling achievement hasn't withstood the test of time, of course, with scholars like Christopher Brooke asserting in 1961 that "true unity was not to come to the English peoples until a Dane sat on Alfred's throne, in 1016" (*FAH*, 52). Brooke is referring to Cnut the Great,[44] not Arthur, and Cnut's time is almost one hundred years after the film is supposedly set, and five hundred years after Arthur's alleged flourishing. As is discussed elsewhere (chapter 3 of the author's *Monty Python, Shakespeare and English Renais-sance Drama*, for example), playing free and easy with history has not only been a Galfridian, French romance or even later a Python staple (and between them The Goons of BBC radio), but has become something of a tradition in Arthuriana before and including T. H. White's Arthurian collection *The Once and Future King*,[45] originally published in 1958. This valiant hero is also an Arthur very much in the vein of the upright, honorable King Arthur featured in Frank Bellamy's *King Arthur and His Knights* (1955) comic strip, which the Pythons would have known as teens.

The Goons, incidentally, paid little attention to Arthur and Camelot. Of the more than 230 recorded radio episodes (many of which do not survive), Arthur is the pseudo-subject of one—"The Spectre of Tintagel," where Neddie is King Arthur Seagoon—and Arthur is mentioned in just one other episode ("The Shifting Sands"). In the latter reference, Neddie is reminded that all "Union Jacks are made from an original set of rare plans left behind by King Arthur in an early British waiting room, circa B.C." The Goons, then, have aligned themselves with Geoffrey, Tennyson, and historians Ashe and Charles Thomas in connecting Arthur or Arthuriana to Cornwall[46] (Tintagel); the Goons join disparate confused scholars and medievalists by dating him wildly, here to before the time of Christ; and finally they anachronize him, making him somehow responsible for the early nineteenth-century flag of the United Kingdom. All in good fun, of course, and a tribute to writer Spike Milligan's omnivorous wit. As for the Pythons they avoid Arthur and Arthuriana completely in *Flying Circus*, while Cleese and the cast of *I'm Sorry I'll Read That Again* dedicated a portion of a single episode to things Arthurian ("Camelot"). In this April 1967 *ISIRTA* sketch, Cleese plays King Arthur, and introduces himself expansively: "I am the good, strong, masculine, virile King Arthur"—to which Sir Prancelot replies, "Well, nobody's perfect."[47]

ARTHUR: " . . . Britons . . . "—The term "Britons" was not recorded in writing, according to the *OED*, until the thirteenth century. See "Who are the Britons?" (spoken by Dennis's mother) below for more on these harried native peoples.

ARTHUR: " . . . Uther Pendragon"—According to Geoffrey of Monmouth (who likely created most of Arthur's ancestry), Uther is Arthur's father (*supp. fl.* late fifth century), Arthur being conceived after a deceptive liaison with Lady Igraine. Uther is the son of Constantine II, and regains the throne after killing Vortigern, who has usurped the throne from Uther's older brother. Arthur's exploits—and those of all other "kings of the Britons" are duly included in Geoffrey's *Historia Regum Britanniae*, or *The History of the Kings of Britain* (c. 1138). This source is mostly fanciful and part (putatively) historical, though as Higham notes,

> writers of the early Middle Ages have now [2002] . . . begun to be read in very different ways, with the construction of histories and chronicles, for example, being viewed as political and ideological action, rather than the passive recording of events. (*KAMH*, 5)

Higham wants to see this work as less "a rather poor attempt to record the past," and more as a polemical tract, purposely "constructed for recoverable, contemporary political, cultural and ideological purposes" (6). For these and additional reasons postwar medieval scholar Kenneth Jackson (1909–1991), writing in 1945, terms Geoffrey a "worthless authority," while Padel (1994) acknowledges Geoffrey's "impressive imaginative powers," but *not* his historicity.[48] Albert C. Baugh (1958) describes the influential work well:

> Geoffrey's *Historia* is a mixture of matter drawn from previous books, the products of his own free invention, and probably a large element of legendary lore. It would not have done to admit that what purported to be a serious history was partly fiction and partly a synthesis of old wives' tales. (*A Literary History of England*, 170)

Geoffrey and his king making is a ripe bunch for the Pythons to pick, as the Galfridian work presents a stately, kingly, larger-than-life Arthur (Padel, 10). The Pythons, of course, have picked through history and culture, reframing and recontextualizing for a more modernist sensibility, with enough narrative fissuring to engage even with the postmodern.

Gidlow notes finally that it is Geoffrey alone who places Uther into the position of Arthur's father, a unique Galfridian attribution: "Of most significance is Geoffrey's idea that Uther is the father of Arthur. Nothing until this point has suggested that there was any tradition of Arthur's father" (*Reign of Arthur*, 200). Uther is the center of the *HKB* narrative in parts four through six, including "The House of Constantine" (both parts), and "The Prophecies of Merlin," pages 149–211 in the 1966 Penguin edition.

The fact that Arthur is an "atheling" ("æðeling") the acknowledged son of *King* Uther who is the acknowledged son of *King* Constantine, and so on, makes a good case for Arthur claiming kingship, according to Higham (*Death of Anglo-Saxon England*, xiii). The fact that many of these figures are likely legendary is moot, given the silliness of the film's plot. If Arthur could then provide to his skeptics proof of Uther's blessing or nomination for his succession, that would also help a great deal, as would word of a coronation ceremony, the backing of "senior churchmen," landed families and councilmen, and plenty of money and estates, and so on, Higham points out (xiii). Unfortunately, officially and demonstrably our Arthur has very little of what could justify his claim of kingship.

ARTHUR: ". . . Castle of Camelot"—The mythical seat of the mythical warrior king, Camelot wouldn't appear in the mythology associated with Arthur until Malory's versions of the French romances. (See "Court at Camelot" below.) The noble castle itself was rendered memorable thanks to Doré's illustrations for Tennyson's *Idylls of the King*.

Camelot was in the news at the time of the film's production, as well. Author Mary Stewart's popular Arthur and Merlin series debuted its second title, *The Hollow Hills* in 1973, after the publication of *The Crystal Cave* in 1970. Philip Norman reviewed *The Hollow Hills* in June 1973, describing the fanciful Arthurian world in a way that the Pythons would work almost directly against:

> Ho—but quietly—for Olde England, for true swords and hearts, candle flame and clean straw, for another Camelot moving lustily, yet with propriety, upon its hygienic course. Mary Stewart is a writer to be admired, a dispenser of blameless dreams and a practitioner in regular, even quickening prose. Her Merlin has the heroism of the Man from the Prudential; her landscape invites a Wurlitzer to arise in front of it.[49]

With the exception of the possible "Wurlitzer" accompaniment,[50] the Pythons chose a very different "hygienic course" for their version of the Camelot countryside, where "propriety" is as evasive as the Grail itself.

Also in late summer 1972 it had been announced that a "Merrie England" theme park would be built in Cannock, Staffordshire, and would include Camelot, "a turreted castle on a hill, disguising a restaurant."[51] By late 1973 no real progress had been made on the project, even though it was still being touted as "the British Disneyland," and promising millions of visitor pounds once EEC tourists could be welcomed.[52] Britain's membership in the EEC[53] was realized on 1 January 1973, but the ambitious park never did come to fruition.

In October 1973 travel packages to be known as "Camelot Country Mini Holidays" were offered by hotel chains, where car owners could drive (or take the train) to the English countryside for a "holidays at home" getaway.[54] These stay-at-home vacations became attractive thanks to the steep rise in oil prices, forcing air travel prices to jump considerably. Now that Britain was part of the EEC (after being rebuffed in 1963 and 1967), it was knotted to the European energy market, even though recent North Sea oil and gas discoveries could have fueled the UK almost independently of OPEC.[55]

Further, these "holidays at home" were directly connected to not only Britain's struggles during the Gulf oil embargo, but the plethora of strike actions affecting especially larger cities' day-to-day activities. Petrol prices rose dramatically before dwindling supplies (of oil and coal) prompted rationing, while strike-impacted trains and buses and shipping hubs sputtered to a stop—meaning travel of almost any kind was greatly complicated and dearly expensive. Palin mentions in his diaries that most petrol stations in his area of Greater London closed for lack of supply, making the city in the winter of 1973–1974 much, much quieter than usual (149). By mid-September 1973, the BBC reported, more than 90 percent of petrol stations in the UK had closed.[56] The Camelot of 1973–1974 was a silly, dreary, and commercially exploitable place, clearly, even before the Pythons' turn at the wheel. See the "What I object to . . . " entry below for more.

ARTHUR: "King of all Britons"—This audacious pronouncement isn't original to the Pythons' Arthur. In the 1955 *Black Knight* comic written by the inimitable Stan Lee (b. 1922), after we are introduced to Lancelot and Galahad, King Arthur is presented thusly: "But overshadowing them all, as sunlight overshadows a candle, was the noble, unforgettable figure of Arthur Pendragon, son of Uther, monarch of the realm, master of the Knights of the Round Table" (May 1955: 4).

Historically, Maglocunus (died c. 547) was known as the "dragon of the island"—"*insularis draco,*" spat out Gildas in *De Excidio*—this tyrant was "*nouissime stilo, prime in malo,*" or "last in my list, but first in evil" (32).[57] The title "Chief Warlord" was appended to the mythical Uther Pendragon, according to Gidlow (199–201); the third-century Roman usurper Carausis (d. 293) was known on period coinage as *restitutor Britanniae*, "restorer of Britain" (Snyder 1998, 5); in the fourth century Constantine (c. 272–337) proclaimed himself "*Britannicus Maximus*" ("The Greatest Briton"); and later the very real Alfred the Great (849–899) could actually claim to be King of the Anglo-Saxons. But an actual "King of all Britons"? In the tenth century this would have been someone else entirely.

If it is indeed 932, then Æthelstan (c. 893–939) was proclaiming himself *Rex Totius Britanniae*, "King of All Britain," as his coinage tells us.[58] The chances of Arthur, Æthelstan, or anyone commanding suzerain-like control over *all* of Britain were remote at the time, however, according to Berthelot:

> The socio-political structure of the country [in the sub-Roman period], does not appear to have favoured the emergence of a supreme commander, still less a king. The Ancient Britons seem to have been divided between a multitude of minor kingdoms ruled by as many petty kings who were more anxious to battle out their differences with immediate neighbours than to unite against a common foe. (19)

The title of a recent book examining the sub-Roman period ("sub-Roman" also being a contested term) is kind of a giveaway—*An Age of Tyrants: Britain and the Britons A.D. 400–600* (Snyder, *An Age of Tyrants*). The fracturing of civil, political, and military authority leading to Honorius's "Rescript" (recorded by Gildas and Zosimus) telling the cities and peoples of Britain they were on their own against the Anglo-Saxons was perhaps inevitable, given the Romans' measured removal to the continent, contributing to the rise of myriad strivers—*tyranni*, or tyrants. These were most often the British "landed elite" making attempts at consolidating and wielding power in this pre-Christian period (17–18). Snyder notes that these tyrants were initially bold "claimants to the western imperial title," though "later [they were] more limited insular authorities" (17–18). Confrontations with ersatz emperors, marauders from northern Europe, Scandinavia, and the barbarian north and west, as well as self-appointed regional leaders—in this light, it's easy to see how Dennis and his mother will be confused confronting this new, clean face claiming authority. For all they knew, this Arthur was no different than Æthelstan, the historical king of this period, or part of the "hotbed of local rivalry"[59] inflorescent in the fifth century, when it was more likely to have been any number of regional warlords vying for dominion.

Æthelstan was the son of Edward the Elder (c. 874–924) and father of Edmund (922–946), and is considered the first king of the "unified kingdom of England," but living well after any historical Arthur's time (Halsall, *Worlds of Arthur*, 74). In his later argument with Dennis and his mother, Arthur will allude to this oneness as he tells them: "We all are, we are all Britons. And I am your king" (*MPHG*, 8).[60] The Welsh writings mentioning Arthur nicely problematize his kingliness and influence, including Caradoc of Llancarfan's life of St.

Gildas, wherein Arthur is called "king of all greater Britain," or "the king of the whole of Britain" and "the King of all Britain" in another translation (Padel, 8; *Medieval Sourcebook*, stanza 5). This text dates from the early part of the twelfth century. He is a king, but he is also prone to mistakes, and to acting rashly before coming to agreements with various saints and churchmen. Writes Padel in an encyclopedic entry[61] for Arthur:

> Overall, the [Welsh] saints' lives show that by about 1100 Arthur was used in south Wales to portray a powerful king when one was needed as a foil for a saint . . . and, unlike most other heroes, he has no particular geographical position but can appear anywhere—Wales, Somerset, and particularly Cornwall in the English legends, and Devon, Scotland, and Brittany in other early references. (9)

Ashe gives significant credit to what he comes to call "the Arthurian Fact"[62] for the Britain that would emerge. The adumbration and evidence of Arthur's fight against the Saxons, specifically, and over a period of time, are key to Ashe:

> [T]he question must be asked again: how should we regard the Arthurian Fact as a portion of history? Was it merely an accident that did no more than delay the inevitable, or had it any lasting effect? Is Arthur a part of what we are today in any more way than a literary sense? (*QAB*, 235)

Again, the purpose of this study is not to argue the existence or nonexistence of Arthur, or any "Arthurian fact"—instead following Thomas Charles-Edwards: "one can only say that there may well have been an historical Arthur; that the historian can as yet say nothing of value about him" (29)—but to tease out the general picture and understanding of King Arthur and things Arthurian in the years leading up to the creation of *Monty Python and the Holy Grail*. For this reason, the controversial, challenged, and often supplanted work of Ashe, Alcock, and especially Morris—work contemporary to the Pythons and representing the most au courant scholarship of their time—are essential for our synchronic and diachronic examinations. In 1974–1975, when the film is being researched, written, and then produced, Arthurian studies stands at a major threshold, according to Halsall:

> Before the 1970s a generally accepted narrative of British history between about 400 and the arrival of Augustine's mission existed, based upon early medieval written sources. From the middle of the 1970s, however, scholars turned their attention to more sophisticated analyses of this evidence, looking at the date, nature and purposes behind the composition of such writings. This led to fundamental reassessment of the reliability of the traditional Arthurian narrative. (*Worlds of Arthur*, 51)

Arthurian studies were being reexamined as the Pythons performed an examination of their own. Morris's work emerged in 1973, and was both spectacularly popular and controversial. The significant backlash to these scholars and their certainties about Arthur is therefore important, and will be discussed where appropriate.[63] It's also worth noting that the *historical* Arthur was very much in the common vernacular in the late 1960s, as evidenced by his presence in Morris Bishop's authoritative *The Horizon Book of the Middle Ages*, published in 1968, a coffee table book offering the latest survey of research on the period.[64] Bishop describes the fight against the Saxons, and manages to twice acknowledge an Arthur "in fact" who is not quite a king:

> The native population, part Briton, part Roman, fought the Saxons long and well through two centuries, and even won a major victory in 571. One of their early leaders was King Arthur—in fact a British chieftain who fought against the invaders, in legend a noble chivalric monarch with his Knights of the Round Table. (17)

And secondly, later, calling him "King Arthur, who was, in fact, a British Christian chief of the fifth century" (284).

Further, this wave of an Arthurian renaissance crests when the Pythons are coming of age, working, and then preparing for both *Flying Circus* and *Holy Grail*—the downside of that wave won't happen until the mid-1970s and beyond. From Higham:

> The idea of a glorious Arthurian age of British achievement against the Saxons passed from the world of literature to that of history, therefore, during the 1960s and had become both extremely popular and widely accepted by the early 1970s. Its removal with extraordinary rapidity from the very edges of history to centre stage implies that it conformed particularly well with the intellectual and cultural context of the period. (*KAMH*, 27–28)

Higham sees Morris's tome *The Age of Arthur* as the culminating publication of this remarkable movement, calling it "a complete restructuring of insular history," while noting the work's limitations, as it takes many contested texts and names, dates, and events at face value (28–29). Higham also sees Morris's biases made apparent as he writes about the fifth and sixth centuries from an identifiable vantage point:

> Another message is also at times discernible in Morris's text . . . which is his palpable rejection of all things German. His refocusing of British Dark Age history away from the Anglo-Saxon immigrants and onto the indigenous population [the Britons] and their legendary history offers a metaphor for the attitudes of his own generation to the two world wars. (*KAMH*, 30)

The Pythons' "message is also at times discernible" as they relate their version of medieval and Arthurian history through the filtering lens of 1960s and 1970s Britain, to the economic unrest and labor fiascoes and government ineffectiveness of that period. James Campbell's reaction to Morris's masterwork is also important—he acknowledges the significance of even overreaching scholarship:

> So difficult, diverse and inadequate are the sources that to seek to write a history of the British Isles from the fourth century to the seventh must be to abandon some of the usual principles of historiography. To permute the innumerable possibilities is to impose more on ordinary prose than it can bear and to carry reasoning to the point of agnostic chaos. Only a learned and imaginative man could, and only an imprudent one would, attempt a comprehensive survey. Mr. Morris fills the bill. His imprudence is marked. He uses to excess the ancient historian's black arts for making objects resembling bricks with odd stalks of fact of what may or may not be straw. Supposition is repeatedly presented as fact. But, however easy experts may find it to use his book for target practice, it is of great importance. It is brave, comprehensive and imaginative. These qualities outweigh the flaws which are inevitable when a powerful and sensitive historical imagination is inadequately controlled and waxes dogmatic, and over-specific on particulars. (*Essays in Anglo-Saxon History*, 121)

Damned with rapturous praise, then, but the work prodded years of subsequent scholars and scholarship. Back to Ashe, who eventually answers his own question, confirming Arthur's lasting effect on the Britain that was on its way, the Britain that was *becoming*:

> The shortest and simplest answer is that even the delay made a difference, because the Anglo-Saxons who finally won were no longer the murderous pirates of the fifth century. They had time to settle, to organise, to study the arts of peace and to absorb something of the culture and moral outlook promoted by Christian missions. Civilisation never entirely perished in Britain. The Celts held out against the Teutonic savages till they had ceased to be savages. (*QAB*, 235)

Interesting then that the civilizing efforts exerted by the Pythons' Arthur in *MPHG*—though they seem fruitless over the course of the film—might actually yield something of his vision of Britain long after he's hustled away in a Black Maria.[65] Ashe continues, pointing out that the "invaders were not quite uninfluenced by that stubborn presence" (the Celts), especially as a number of subsequent rulers (Aelle of Sussex, for example, in the late fifth century) called themselves "Britain-ruler," essentially, seeing Britain as a whole, and not a set of fragmented kingdoms. In short, they adopted "the concept of Britain" (235). And even though over the following 300 years the Anglo-Saxon tribes and families remained fairly separate tribes and families ("[e]ach ruling family turned into a local dynasty"), the tribes put down roots and became farmers, they settled (236). Ashe identifies twelve separate kingdoms "that flourished at various times: Kent, Sussex, Wight, Wessex, Essex, East Anglia, Lindsey, Mercia; Bernicia and Deira, the two parts of Northumbria; and the states of Hwicce and the Magonsaetan" (236).

So when the Pythons' Arthur claims "We are all Britons," he's actually continuing the nation building that the mythological Arthur was constructed to help along, especially Layamon's version of the Arthurian tales. Writing in English, significantly, the late twelfth-century poet Layamon (or Lawman) adapted Arthur to the needs of his contemporary England, updating Wace's c. 1155 (and Norman) version of *Brut* "into alliterative English verse," as Poole notes:

> His work, however, is not a mere translation of Wace. He adds local colour, especially in his use of similes; he also develops the story, possibly from tales picked up from his Welsh neighbours. He tells, for example, of the passing of Arthur, and it is from him that the famous versions of Malory and Tennyson are ultimately derived. Layamon's poem, moreover, is English not only in language but also in spirit. It is patriotic, and the British Arthur becomes in his hands a national hero, the pattern of all that was best in English kingship. (*From Domesday Book to Magna Carta*, 255)

Layamon's is the Arthur more likely to stand before these castle walls and call out his heritage and predestinative acclaim, more so than the Arthur of Geoffrey or Wace, and perhaps more than even Malory's later iteration.

ARTHUR: ". . . defeater of the Saxons"—The Anglo-Saxons had come from the continent (northern Germany and southern Denmark), were noted for their "brutality," and, using the sea and river ways, defeated and occupied large portions of south and east Britain in the fifth and sixth centuries following the Roman exodus (Campbell, 13). Gildas blames the "proud tyrant" Vortigern for inviting the Saxons into Britain as mercenaries, though recently historian Guy Halsall suggests the "proud tyrant" whom Gildas blasts was likely Emperor Magnus Maximus.[66] There is no mention in *Holy Grail* of the other known threatening groups in Britain of the late Roman period and following Dark Ages, the Picts, Scots, and Attacotti (Snyder, *An Age of Tyrants*, 9–10).[67] Likely for narrative efficiency the Pythons settled on the one group the legendary Arthur is seemingly known for defeating, the Saxons, though in the "Attila the Hun" sequence from *MPFC* Ep. 20, they showed they weren't afraid of such lists, mentioning warlords Alaric, Gaiseric, and Theodoric before getting to Attila (*MPFC: UC*, 1.311–312).

The legendary Arthur's battles with the Saxons are trumpeted in Geoffrey's quasi-historical work; they are no more outlandish than the Pythons might later claim; and they are fantastical for a reason, and with precedent, according to Green (2009):

> [T]here is no real reason to think that all of the battles used to historicise Arthur were real historical battles—at least some of the battles used to historicise Fionn seem to have been invented spontaneously for the purposes of historicisation and this would well be the case here (a fact that may well explain some of the problems in identifying the battles in *Historia Brittonum* Chapter 56.). (14)

Arthur is said to have killed 470 men by himself in a single battle; he defeats the Irish and barbarians, then defeats and grants pardons to the Scots and Picts; he defeats and subjugates Ireland and Iceland, Gothland and the Orkneys, as well as Norway, Dacia, Aquitaine, Gaul, et al.[68] This "munificent" Arthur hears of the frantic defensive preparations being made on the continent ("they re-built their towns and the towers in their towns"), and "the fact that he was dreaded by all encouraged him to conceive the idea of conquering the whole of Europe" (*HKB*, 222). This is our same Arthur who can best the Black Knight but be flummoxed by uppity peasants, jeering Frenchmen, and knights who demand shrubberies. Historically, there has been much written about an Arthur who lived and breathed as a defender and defeater, quite useful constructs, recent historians agree, quite purposeful, and likely quite fictitious. N. J. Higham (University of Manchester) says he wrote *King Arthur: Myth-Making and History*

> primarily as an investigation of the nature, role and purposes of Arthur in the pre-Galfridian Latin texts, and the way the different generations of historians, both then and thereafter, have chosen to portray their Arthurs within the intellectual and political perceptions which conditioned their purposes in re-envisioning the sub-Roman past in Britain. (9)

Higham then lays out the very real purpose Arthur served to these early chroniclers, suggesting "that Arthur was initially developed in a 'Dark Age' context as a martial and Christian leader to contest visions of a cowardly and immoral British people, and a race excluded from salvation history" (9).[69]

Popular historian Gidlow concludes that "common sense dictates that somebody coordinated the British military response to the Saxons. He lived, it seems, at the turn of the fifth and sixth centuries and led the Britons in their united defence" (246). This "somebody" hasn't been sufficiently proven to *not* be Arthur, according to Gidlow, so the evidence seems to point in Arthur's direction. Scholars of this period have more recently come to an agreement that such a "no smoke without fire" argument isn't a convincing one, with the paucity of provable Arthurian evidence making a strong case for other figures in history accounting for Arthur's exploits (see Dumville 1977; Higham 2002). Dumville is, again, thoughtfully blunt: "The fact of the matter is that there is no historical evidence about Arthur; we must reject him from our histories and, above all, from the titles of our books" (188). Green (2009) agrees, seeing Arthur as at best a legendary or folkloric figure (like Fionn, Hengest, and Horsa)—and a "Protector of Britain," importantly (15)—who was then co-opted into historical service by Geoffrey and others. Green narrows in on our specific focus here, Arthur as "defeater of the Saxons," popping the "historical" balloon rather effectively:

> In essence, the vast majority of the non-Galfridian material, including the earliest sources, paints a notably consistent picture of Arthur as a pan-Brittonic folkloric hero, a peerless warrior of giant-like stature who leads a band of superhuman heroes that roam the wild places of the landscape, who raids the Otherworld whilst being intimately associated with it, who fights and protects Britain from supernatural enemies, who hunts wondrous animals and who takes part in mythical battles, and hence the "weight" of this evidence indicates not a historical origin for Arthur but rather a legendary one (it is particularly worthy of note that Arthur is *never* associated with either the Saxons or Badon in the vast majority of the material, despite the fact that such an association is usually said to be the reason for his fame, and when this association does appear it is only present in those sources which are directly derivative of *Historia Brittonum* Chapter 56). (11; see also 14)

Finally, Guy Halsall is more succinct: "No sane scholar will now argue that there is definitely a 'King Arthur' figure in fifth- or sixth-century history about whom anything solid can be said, so professional historians now tend to leave the issue alone" (*Worlds of Arthur*, 9). Green begins the following section in his 2009 work by writing: "Whatever else Arthur is, he is a composite figure" (15). The Pythons are clearly using the "composite" Arthur in the film—he encounters magical and supernatural creatures and situations (enchanters, soothsayers, legendary beasts), but he also faces real enemies (the Saxons, French), travels through real kingdoms (Mercia), and strives to create a united Britain.

It is Gildas who writes of the Saxon defeater (and Romanized) Ambrosius Aurelianus, who won several victories culminating with the battle at Badon somewhere near the end of the fifth century (Campbell, 16, 23). There has been some discussion that the exploits of this Ambrosius (and other figures, like Vortigern[70]) might have been ascribed later to the folkloric-cum-historical Arthur, fulfilling a particular nation-building need in later centuries (Green, 246). Vortigern was a fifth-century warlord (meaning he lived when a historical Arthur might have lived) whose existence has been forwarded and also challenged for many years, and about whom Dumville (1977) admits nothing "certain" can be said, except that he was likely a military leader of some sort (185). Vortigern is an unlikely avatar for the Pythons' Arthur, though, especially as Gildas blames him for inviting the "fierce and impious Saxons" into Britain (*The Ruin of Britain*, 26). Magnus Maximus (born c. 335), however, is a particularly interesting figure here as a possible ur-Arthur, even though he died in 388. This "British emperor" coming from the west (Wales) is mentioned significantly by Gildas becoming, for Dumville, "the founding figure of independent post-Roman Britain" (180):

> He appears both as the last Roman emperor in Britain and as the first ruler of an independent Britain, from whom all legitimate power flowed—a pleasing irony, in view of his actual history as a usurper. From his death, therefore, begins the history of the independent Brittonic kingdoms. (180)

By the ninth century, Dumville notes, Maximus's legend has grown, he's been mythologized into British history, and the next step can be guessed. Dumville continues: "It seems to me that Maximus is arguably the literary source of inspiration for Geoffrey of Monmouth's Arthur, who does such great—but ultimately unsuccessful—deeds as a British emperor on the Continent" (181). The Pythons' version of Arthur reflects this possibility. Arthur represents his native people ("King of the Britons"), he has come to power by crushing invaders ("defeater of the Saxons"), and now he rules everyone ("Sovereign of all England). Also, like Maximus, in the end he is unsuccessful in his quest.

Lastly, one of the Pythons' sources, Malory's *Le Morte Darthur*, lists young Arthur's military and political accomplishments just after ascending the throne, including return of lands to his "bereft" lords (thanks to Uther's capriciousness):

> When this was done, that the King had established all the countries about London, then he let make Sir Kay seneschal of England; and Sir Baudwin of Britain was made constable; and Sir Ulfius was made chamberlain; and Sir Brastias was made warden to wait upon the north from Trent forwards, for it was that time the most part the King's enemies. But within few years after, Arthur won all the north, Scotland, and all that were under their obeisance. Also Wales, a part of it, held against Arthur, but he overcame them all, as he did the remnant, through the noble prowess of himself and his knights of the Round Table. (*LMD-WM*, 12)

The Pythons' version of Arthur is clearly a borrowing from both the later, more romantic tales, as well as the earliest (pre- and non-Galfridian) texts, where Arthur is a legendary figure fighting mythological creatures.

ARTHUR: " . . . Sovereign of all England"—Arthur is termed the "sovereign lord" of "England" in Malory's *Le Morte D'Arthur* (1485), which is certainly where the Pythons went for at least some inspiration as they wrote *Holy Grail*. (The name "England" appears thirty-six times in the first book of *LMD'A*, for example.) In *MPHG* Arthur separates the title "King of all Britons" from "Sovereign of all England," which actually suits very early usage of the latter term. Likely for the Pythons and their Arthur, the separation indicates Arthur is of the "Britons" (northern and western peoples), and as defeater of the invading Saxons, he rules them, as well. Likely, then, he is a "king" *de jure*, or by birth, and a "sovereign" by military attrition.

Secondly, "England" is an anachronism, certainly, though one that not unreasonably telescopes history into a more manageable depth of field, a practice shared by the Pythons, Gildas, and Shakespeare, no less. Long after the Saxons had been invited, then stayed, versions of Bede's *Ecclesiastical History* (c. 731) and the *Anglo-Saxon Chronicle* (1014) are still a ways from "England," employing "Engla londe" and "Engla lande," respectively (*OED*). Wildly varying spelling traditions taken into account, it's not until about 1325 that "England" is used in print, and even thereafter, will be spelled a number of ways depending on the writer or typesetter. Also, gifting Arthur with a title he may or may not have enjoyed (and as a figure who may or may not have existed) simply extends the Pythons' penchant for anachronisms and ahistoricities, a practice that finds them in good company. Shakespeare created John Falstaff (out of necessity, not wanting to fight a charge of calumny by the Cobham family) and found himself with a particularly useful, malleable character, as discussed in the author's *MPSERD*. The third chapter—"'Is Not the Truth the Truth?': (Ab)uses of History"—is designed

> to discuss Shakespeare's uses and abuses of historical fact as he created his history plays, and to approach other plays and their various submissions of history to the service of dramatic efficacy. Shakespeare's historiography—his valuation of sources like Hall, Holinshed, popular culture and myth, and the demands of contemporary political influences—is also key as certain histories are used and others ignored in the quest for effective drama. Specifically, Falstaff as a fictional character in historical settings and surrounded by historical characters . . . Shakespeare utilizes Falstaff for the special, "metahistorical" character that he is. Monty Python's appropriation of Shakespeare's frequent disregard for the unities of time and space will also be examined; their ahistorical and textually challenging "unconformities" will become significant as time and space are collapsed into an ever-present; and Python's methods of historiography—the constant assessing and weighing of the relative value of historical texts, whatever those might be—will also be considered as comedy in relation to British history is constructed. And as comedy is constructed by Monty Python, so too is another history. (73)

The Pythons then, are purposely moving beyond the seemingly *wirrwarr* but still self-aware structures of the *MPFC* episodes (which typified the first draft of *Holy Grail*)[71] and closer to a visually and thematically consistent narrative set in the medieval world, but peppered by persistent (and increasingly multipotent) irruptions of modernity. The ultimate intrusion will be modern, uniformed policemen bringing the two strands of parallel narrative timelines together, and the film to an abrupt end.

Finally, "England" and "English" are only used three times in the entire film, and "Britons" only once. The first "English" is heard when Arthur proclaims his sovereignty, then later in the banter between Arthur and Dennis and his mother, and finally when French interlopers remind Arthur he is an "English pig." Like the plague that is seemingly ravaging the land but is only mentioned in one scene, the nationalistic identities of Arthur and his knights are also pointed up, then forgotten, as the next bit of silliness (or sketch) approaches.

SOLDIER: "Get away!"—This line is ultimately changed for "Pull the other one" (see below), but in the script version the Soldier is certainly responding to Arthur's rather brazen claims, calling him on those claims, essentially. "Get away" can mean "go on" or "you don't say," according to the *OED*. Arthur has, in order, claimed to be "King of all Britons, defeater of the Saxons, [and] Sovereign of all England." This seems the proper order, however, a natural progression, and a logical hypothesis. If he is first king of the native population, the Britons, and subsequently manages to defeat the invaders/settlers, the Saxons, then he can rightly say that he is "Sovereign of all England."

This lack of credulity permeates the film, as Arthur and his quest are consistently upbraided by peasants and knights, by fellow countrymen and foreigners, by sorcerers and soothsayers, and finally by the "hand" of the controlling entity known as the real world, bringing the film to a precipitate end. Fossier notes that this particular "manifestation of war"—the "imaginary or aristocratic games" that included knights errant would not have impacted the "common people" (like these soldiers, and later Dennis) much, if at all:

> Errant knights . . . might seek a girl, a duel, or—a sure way to be more admired—the sacred chalice of the Holy Grail. All of the cast-off trappings of "courtesy" disguise these agitations, which delight the historians of literature, but it is difficult to believe that the adventures of Percival and King Arthur's knights or Roland with his sword blows enlivened evenings in the cottage or served as a model for any simple man. (282)

Remember, this is the time (the early 1970s) when public figures had become targets of violence, including the Queen and her family, as the IRA lashed out against the smothering British establishment in Northern Ireland. Bombs were planted in Sydney, Australia, in 1973 in an attempt on Philip's motorcade; later the Queen's cousin, Lord Mountbatten, would be killed by an IRA bomb on board his own boat.[72] PM Ted Heath had also suffered ignominy of a less fatal nature when a young woman threw ink on him as he arrived in Brussels for Britain's Common Market initiation in January 1972.[73] A simple "get away," then, to someone claiming to be a king who rides no horse and has almost no retinue doesn't seem out of place, really.

SOLDIER: "Pull the other one"—According to the *OED*, the phrase is "used as a rejoinder to being told something which makes one suspect that one is being deceived or teased." Arthur's bold answer—"I am"—assures the skeptical soldier (Palin) that he is indeed "Arthur, son of Uther Pendragon, from the Castle of Camelot, King of all Britons, defeater of the Saxons, Sovereign of all England." This cheeky riposte must have been a late emendation, an ad-lib on the set. In the final draft of the script, the soldier retorts with "Get away!" instead.

The specter of seeming lessers not kowtowing to their betters runs through the film, as it had through *MPFC*, as it had in British life since the war.[74] It's not a stretch to mention the significance here, though, of more contemporary influences, specifically the ripple effects of the colonial transition that had been underway worldwide since the mid-1940s, and that affected Britain more than most. The formerly colonized—French Indochina, Chad, Algeria, and, for the British, the Jewel of the Empire, India, in 1947 as well as Palestine, and so on—shrugged off their colonizers, refusing to recognize the foreign, white, minority providential ruling power. In *MPFC*, the Rhodesian independence question, for example, is broached a number of times ("Why is Rhodesia called Rhodesia, mum?"[75]), and the specter of Britain's diminishing, fading empire looms large.[76] Higham (2002) sums up nicely the position Britain found itself in after the Second World War, where imperialism is a key, transitioning factor:

> [T]he war over-extended the British Empire both politically and economically. Exhaustion within the imperial enterprise, as much as external pressures from the US and local demands for independence, led to the British retreat from Empire. In a world in which the ex-colonial race had perforce to deal as equals with ex-subjects as rulers, diplomats, religious leaders, shippers and manufacturers, Anglo-British-centric historical values and perceptions were increasingly exposed as indefensible, and were gradually both undermined and overturned. (22)

This fallen and falling postcolonial world is where novelist Graham Greene (1904–1991), for example, often sets his later novels, the grim emptiness infecting both character and setting, according to Snyder, examining *The Confidential Agent*:

> Far more keenly than any he encounters in an England still basking in Edwardian isolationism, prolonged by Neville Chamberlain's policy of appeasement, D. understands that "It was as if the whole world lay in the shadow of abandonment" (72). The metaphor, of course, is quintessential Greene. Bespeaking his skeptical vision, akin to Thomas Hardy's, of Earth as a blighted planet, it conducts us immediately into *"Greeneland," that familiar milieu of seedy borderlands and far-flung frontiers whose degradation highlights the spiritual bankruptcy of a materialistic West.* ("'Shadow of Abandonment,'" 204; italics added)

If Arthur is to be looked at in a more contemporary light, then he might be the new, eager prime minister Edward Heath who moves into 10 Downing Street in 1970, poised to sweep out the lethargy of Labour with an invigorated, action-ready Tory government. He is straightaway faced, of course, with his own "pull the other one" gainsayers. From the BBC's Andrew Marr: "Heath immediately faced a dock strike, followed by a big pay settlement for local authority dustmen, then a power workers' go-slow which led to power cuts. Then the postal workers struck."[77] The 1970s in Britain are remembered for a "one thing after another" malaise, the piling on of crisis after crisis—economic and political millstones, all—and the general feeling that no government could take a breath deep enough, or get its "finger out and get going in the second half," to borrow a Python phrase.[78] In the Pythons' "Philosophers' Football Match," the announcer is excited by a substitution for the German team of Karl Marx, who seems to herald an "all-out attack" on the Greeks. Marx athletically enters the pitch and immediately pulls out a book and strolls casually, eliciting a "What a shame" from the announcer.[79] Thanks to economic doldrums, the early 1970s especially were a go-slow period for most of Britain, and Arthur cannot escape its influence as he traipses through his own "seedy borderlands and far-flung frontiers" toward further degradation.

ARTHUR: "I am"—This is the first of a long line of instances where Arthur has to justify his kingship, his authority, and even his existence to the skeptical "subjects" he and Patsy will encounter. In this the Pythons echo their English dramatic progenitors, where such misunderstandings abound:

> [The] comic misunderstanding occurs when peasants refuse to recognize kings, in the Python world, or when Thomas Dekker's lower-class characters consort with upper-class characters on the same social level, and without self-consciousness, in *The Shoemaker's Holiday* (1599). The tradition is also carried on in myriad eighteenth-century plays (e.g., Sheridan's *The Rivals*) and novels (Fielding's *Tom Jones*). (*MPFC: UC* 1.12)

And as also argued in the author's *Monty Python, Shakespeare and English Renaissance Drama*, appearances really *do* matter. Arthur will soon be identified as a likely king prosopographi-cally—"he hasn't got shit all over him." But in this first scene of perhaps purposeful misunderstanding—shouting up to the skeptical guards on the rampart—it's likely that if Arthur had actually been astride a horse, and not pretending with clip-clopping coconuts, the sentries might have taken him more seriously, based on his august appearance. In English Renaissance drama the king disguised served a narrative purpose; the Pythons are aware of this, but their Arthurian world is one influenced by history, by legend, and mostly by contemporary skepticality:

> In *Holy Grail*, Arthur is not in disguise. In fact, he is dressed very much like a warrior king might or should be dressed. He wears a sun emblem on his chest and a gold crown on his head, and carries Excalibur, the magical sword. A servant follows him, as well, carrying all of the king's necessaries. The iconography is in place, identifying Arthur as at least kingly, if not king. Arthur . . . makes sure everyone he meets knows just who he is: "I am Arthur, son of Uther Pendragon. King of the Britons, defeater of the Saxons, sovereign of all England." . . . The goal of the disguised Edward [depicted in Heywood's *The First Part of King Edward IV*] and others was to achieve something their regalia wouldn't normally allow: honesty from the peasantry without the complications of inherent class differences. [The Pythons'] Arthur, on the other hand, looks to use his kingly bearing and uniform to recruit to his (soon to be) divine purpose. Python, treating the king as representing the state, turns the "king in disguise" convention on its ear and allows the commoners to meet the king at or above his level, where they almost never recognize his providential authority. Some go so far as to openly deny such an authority exists in Nature, and can only arise from the will of the people. (92)

There are no guarantees, of course, that disguise will either work as the king desires, or that it is even necessary, given a king's *lack* of recognizability during the Middle Ages. His image may have appeared on newly minted coins or later in portraits and miniatures, but it's likely that *the majority of a medieval king's subjects would have never laid eyes on any image of their sovereign*. In the confusion of the London streets during the culmination of the Peasants' Revolt in 1381, for example, the boy king Richard journeyed to Baynard castle (on the banks of the Thames) unmolested: "Richard . . . extraordinary though it seems, apparently had been wandering through the scenes of wild disorder in the city and suburbs" (McKisack, 412). Richard's entourage was likely small and kept a low profile in the dangerous streets, so his unrecognizability became a boon.

There is also the problem of multiple contenders for a somewhat imagined throne of a fractured England. Whether this film is set in 787, 932, 1167, or 1282—or even Arthur's alleged age, c. 500—political instability based on regional influences was the rule of the day following the end of Roman control. Making matters even more challenging was the fact that, as Higham writes, there could be more than one *legitimate* king at one time—the Anglo-Saxon kingship had on occasion been "partible," or treated as a "joint inheritance" or "sub-kingship," as happened in the Kent region after Æthelwulf (*The Death of Anglo-Saxon England*, xii).[80] Writing of Northumbria, Mercia, and Wessex, Sawyer gives more detail, noting that these large kingdoms

> were all, at some time, ruled by more than one king or *dux*, and . . . it is probable that multiple kingship was a more common phenomenon in the seventh century than [Bede's] narrative reveals. Sæbehrt of the East Saxons, who died in 616 or 617, and Wihtred of Kent, who died over a century later, were both succeeded by three sons ruling jointly. (49)

Sawyer goes on to mention two simultaneous kings for the East Angles and the South Saxons, meaning a traveler from one area to another within a single kingdom could have encountered more than one king, both legitimate. Brooke mentions that like the early Frankish kings, early English kings weren't "monarchs," meaning there *could* be more than one:

> [I]t may even be that whole families of sons brothers and even nephews of kings were called "kings." When Edwin of Northumbria invaded Wessex, he killed five West Saxon kings in one battle. In many cases, perhaps in most, the committee had a chairman: the senior king had ultimate authority. (*SNK*, 81)

It was likely as confusing then as it is for the sentries and will be for Dennis and his mother, confronted by a clean man claiming to be a supernaturally appointed king.

Higham reminds us that the semi-official close of the Anglo-Saxon period in Britain (1066) was a tumultuous time, as dynastic or epochal transitions often are:

> At its most fundamental, this year witnessed a succession crisis of unprecedented scale and complexity in English history and it is this aspect which offers the greater insights into this distant epoch. Within a single calendar year, five separate individuals were recognized as at least *de facto* king within England [including Harold Godwinson, Edgar the Ætheling, William the Conqueror, et al.] by some group or other of the indigenous political elite. (*Death of Anglo-Saxon England*, ix)

Both the sentries on the wall here and later Dennis and his good mother ask fair questions about Arthur's legitimacy, and he's unable to offer them anything beyond his supposed lineage and his "chosen" status and election proffered by a "moistened bint." He has no herald,[81] no entourage, and no trappings of power. In the historical era of competing kings, lords, subkings, and overlords, a simple "I am" just won't do. In the end, without at least an army behind him, it's no surprise that the commoners don't take Arthur seriously—they don't really have to.

ARTHUR: "Patsy"—A silly name, like Dennis the Peasant, Tim the Enchanter, or Roger the Shrubber, but also anachronistic, likely, since the "patsy—an innocent victim" meaning is a more modern definition, and Patsy (Gilliam) is dragged along on this quest with little choice and even fewer words. It's also likely that "Patsy" is meant to be an effeminate usage, like the Pythons using the names "Vicky" and "Mitzie" for men in *FC* Ep. 1 (*MPFC: UC*, 1.22, 31, 207). "Patsy" has also been one of the few character names consonant since the earliest iteration of the script.[82] In Jones's audio commentary on the 2001 DVD version of the film, he mentions that it was the Arthur and Patsy relationship and "quest"—apart from everything else tossed into the first draft—that intrigued him and Palin enough to focus on the pair for the feature film that would become *Holy Grail*.

ARTHUR: "We have ridden the length and breadth of the land in search of Knights"[83]— If, first, this is the Arthur of myth and legend, then this is a most traditional journey, as he searches for worthy additions to his Round Table. If, however, this is an Arthur of *history*, and he is king of an ur-England, then this is more a "progress," or an official tour of his lands and people, a tradition that has a long history in Britain. Sawyer points out that between at least the ninth and thirteenth centuries in both English and British cultures there were customary payments (often in kind) from regional nobility to support the kings' progresses, local lords and clergy underwriting, essentially, a king's visit, his hunting and hawking, and so on. (88–89). Henry III, for example, is credited with visiting St. Albans monastic school at least nine separate times, "sometimes for a week at a time" (13). Edward II, Henry's grandson, also visited St. Albans but traveled even more, spending "a week or more at over 150 places" (Hallam, 169). Rowley notes that the thirteenth century saw many, many such trips:

> The royal court had an arduous circuit, visiting palaces, castles and ecclesiastical sites in southern and central England on a regular basis. Such movement was in part to maintain a royal presence, but . . . it . . . also had an underlying practical purpose, which was to feed the retinue that accompanied the king and his peripatetic government. . . . King John, for instance, is recorded as having made 360 moves in 1245, visiting some 145 royal manors, 129 castles, 46 religious houses and 40 other places. Altogether John made 1,378 recorded moves compared with 1,458 by Edward II, but remarkably Edward I made almost 3,000 moves during his reign. (171)

Here at the first castle Arthur is merely asking if the local "lord and master" wants to come along; later, when facing the French-held castle, he asks for "food and shelter," as well as the local lord's companionship (*MPHGB*, 25). Even earlier, the Danish and English king Cnut was a well-traveled monarch, seeking spiritual gifts in Britain and beyond, just as Arthur will: "In 1027 [Cnut] went on pilgrimage to Rome, walking in the footsteps of [earlier kings of Wessex] Cædwalla and Ine and Alfred" (Brooke, *SNK*, 137). Cnut was able to meet and treat with Emperor Conrad II, Pope John XIX, as well as visit myriad holy sites (137).

Arthur's range of influence varies from time to time and teller to teller, positing Arthur as a local, regional, national, and even international figure.[84] If we a priori assume he existed, for a moment, was he a Brittonic warrior who plagued the invading Saxons from the wilds of the north? Was he an "emperor" ruling an intercontinental kingdom as Geoffrey celebrates? Was he a local hero in the southwest, where his name has become associated with Cornwall, including Tintagel, as well as Wales? Was he even able to cross Mercia, as our Arthur claims? Green usefully pores through the favorite theories in her excellent overview of the *soi-disant* Age of Arthur, without committing herself to either side of the "existence of Arthur" issue:

> In order for the following guide to work, the question of whether the search for a historical Arthur is a useful one is ignored. Similarly, the notion of "no smoke without fire"—which is criticised heavily elsewhere—is treated as reasonable, i.e. the analyses below follow the theories they discuss in assuming that there probably was a historical Arthur. ("The Monstrous Regiment of Arthurs," Introduction)

The realities of the Arthurian or Brittonic time period do allow for a traveling monarch,[85] historians and archaeologists have agreed. By the seventh century,[86] parts of Anglo-Saxon England became home to "royal villas" built for the king and his retinue, according to archaeologists, including Yeavering in Northumberland. Of course, our Arthur's quest doesn't seem to include bedding down for the night, or even a meal, frankly, as the film's meager budget allowed for outdoor shooting, primarily, and the only alimentary scene is at Camelot in the dance sequence, which is too "silly" to visit.[87] Martin Welch writes of the royal villa at Yeavering:

> Its function was to provide suitable short-term accommodation for the king and his household. There, perhaps once, or at most twice a year they would briefly reside and doubtless engage in such aristocratic pursuits as hunting during the day. They would feast each evening on the food-rents owed to the king by the farmers of the surrounding region. This primitive form of taxation was essential in an economy which lacked coinage and the ability readily to turn food products into coin or bullion as in a market economy. . . . The king would have as many such centres as he had major estates and he and his household would constantly travel from one royal estate to the next. His visit to any individual villa would therefore be periodic, once or twice a year at most,

and if the king or his queen did not happen to visit a villa in any particular year, we might suppose that the inhabitants of the associated region could keep the livestock and the produce they owed for that year. By such means, the pretence could be maintained that these renders were hospitality willingly offered by the king's men, rather than tribute owed by dependent subjects or a defeated enemy. (*Anglo-Saxon England*, 45)

The Pythons' version of this Arthurian world does have coins, but does not have royal villas, though perhaps a king could have been away so long that subjects like the later visited Dennis and mother have completely forgotten such renders existed. In any case, it looks as if they would only have "lovely filth" to offer their lord, anyway.

Historian Halsall—whose *Worlds of Arthur* is the most recent (and a very thoughtful) survey of the question of Arthur—cautions that the title "king" in the fifth century isn't necessarily synonymous with "sovereign," so this Arthur before them could well be anyone (or no one):

Dozens of petty kings existed in early medieval Ireland, for example, none of whom was ever in any sense sovereign. Similarly, many Anglo-Saxon "kings" or "under-kings" never seem to have been other than subordinate, even if their title and jurisdiction might have been hereditary. . . . Across the former Empire kingship was itself a new, fifth-century institution. Its rules were only slowly being invented in the different areas of western Europe. We should not expect it to have all the connotations of later medieval sovereignty. (273–74)

Later the Old Woman (Jones) won't know how a king becomes a king, and in a fifth-century context her suspicions, and those of these sentries, seem to be quite justified.

ARTHUR: "I must speak with your lord and master"—This request is never fulfilled, neither here nor at the castles taken over by the French. In fact, Arthur meets no "lord and master" anywhere in the film. This first castle features sentries but no mention of anyone in charge; the latter French-occupied castle may be run by one "Guy de Loimbard," but he never appears, and it isn't clear he's at home anyway (his spokesman doesn't seem a trustworthy type, to boot). Swamp Castle is run by Herbert's father, but he's a sort of "northerner on the make," anyway, always looking to move beyond his provincial holdings;[88] the Castle Anthrax is most like one of Malory's fairy castles, where the denizens exist without much contact with or need of the outside world, seeming very nearly to spring into existence just for the duration of an errant knight's happy or unhappy visit. There are none met on Arthur's social level, clearly, but plenty of underlings, strivers, and men of magic and religion.

So this is a failed transaction and a failed communication, certainly, a very Pythonesque situation enacted over and over again in *MPFC*, but it's also likely this way thanks to the ease with which these kinds of requests tend to be granted in the source materials, including a 1955 *Robin Hood* comic book. There, Sir Galant approaches a castle that has been invaded and occupied by Sir Mordaunt; Galant's second issues a challenge, and the sentry on the high wall responds casually: "I'll tell him." Simple as that, the drawbridge comes down and a joust is undertaken.[89] And in the Malorian sources, most challenges thrown before Arthur and his good knights can be met with blunt force; a charge on a horse or a duel on a bridge and the obstacle's overcome. Not so in the historical or contemporary world our legendary Arthur encounters.

SOLDIER: "What? Ridden on a horse?"—The real reason no horses are used for the questers in *Holy Grail* is simple: budget. Adding horses for all five knights would mean paying for the horses, their care and handlers, as well as stunt riders for each. The Pythons had used horses during the run of *MPFC* ("Scotsman on a horse"; "Dennis Moore"; "Show Jumping Musical") and in one of the German episodes, as well, but the costs and production headaches associated with such choices likely made the choice rather easy as they prepped for the feature film.[90] Perhaps the "coconut" gag alone helped tip the scales. It's also worth mentioning that none of the carts or wagons in the film is attached to a horse or any beast of burden. Dennis pulls his own cart, the Cart Driver's filthy associates pull the plague cart, Roger the Shrubber's cart is pulled by two hunched peasants, and Brother Maynard's cart is pulled by two lesser monks.

With this pointed question the sentry jumps back over the most recent portion of the conversation to the obvious fallacy that Arthur and Patsy have been riding horses. This is also a bit of a Python trope—there is often no benefit of the doubt given, especially between the lower and upper classes, and digressions abound. This is a moment where the fictional nature of the presentation is forwarded, the time spent on the digression allowing the audience a span to consider the world before them. The longer the digression stays on screen, and the more anachronistic the characters or their knowledge and/or language become, the more fully the audience appreciates the rupture. In this, then, the Pythons condition their audience to expect such undercuttings, the viewer actually waiting for the "serious" or historically accurate situations to be treated to a similar disassembling (or *dismembering*, as with the Black Knight and through Gilliam's animations).

Secondly, the presence, use, and even knowledge of horses (or cavalry) during the Brittonic period are also of significant dispute among the academic elite. It has been argued that if an Arthur-type was the prolific and mobile battle leader he's often been painted, he and many of his followers would have by necessity been mounted, though the archaeological record for the early sixth-century period isn't salted with such cavalry-type finds. Various historians and archaeologists have approached the problem, and their opinions are varied, too, beginning with Morris (1973):

> The nature of the war compelled an unusual strategy. The early poetry of the Welsh consistently sings of mounted warriors wearing scarlet plumes and using swords, riding well-fed horses, who fought an infantry enemy equipped with spears. Their picture of the English is accurate; Germans nearer to the Mediterranean used cavalry, but further north among the Franks, the kings and their bodyguards alone had horses, while the English had none, and were said not even to know what a horse looked like. Horse gear does not begin to appear among their grave goods until the late sixth century, and then only in the occasional possession of a leader who rode to battle while his men marched. (96)

And then Collingwood (via Ashe, 1985), bolstering the probability of a mounted Arthur:

> In 1936 R.G. Collingwood, coauthor of a standard work on Roman Britain and the English Settlements, presented a theory which held for some years. Accepting all the victories—and hence the mobility—as authentic, he explained Arthur by a guess at the position he really held . . . that Arthur was not a King, but a general who revived the cavalry of the later Empire, an arm developed for mobile defense in depth.
>
> In the last phase of Roman Britain, one of its supreme officers was the *Comes Britanniarum*, "Count of the Britains." . . . He commanded cavalry units and had a roving commission to go anywhere. Warriors on horseback were not so dominant then as in the Middle Ages, because the stirrup had not reached western Europe. However, the Saxons were not horsemen at all. Mounted Britons would have had clear advantages through speed, surprise, psychological impact. . . . Collingwood, at any rate, suggested that Arthur was *Comes Britanniarum*, appointed or self-appointed. He won his battles by the use of mobile horsemen against the pedestrian Saxons, and could move such men rapidly about the country. . . . His theory as a whole yielded to criticism, but the cavalry idea survived, and has stayed popular and plausible. (*The Discovery of King Arthur*, 75–76)

Alcock (1971) seems the most assured of the important role cavalry played in Arthur's world (with Arthur existing a priori, yes):

> The tactical pattern of Arthur's battles is one of open warfare, in which fortified places played little part, and river-crossings were all-important. Most if not all of his troops would have been mounted, and would have fought from horseback with sword, lance and javelin, approaching the enemy in a series of rushes rather than in a coordinated cavalry charge. (*Arthur's Britain*, 360)

And finally Gidlow (2004), who sees the plausibility of a fast-moving Arthur *without* need of a cavalry:

> Other writers have concocted ideas of Arthur as a cavalry leader to explain his "extraordinary mobility." As we have no idea over what period these battles were fought, we have no idea how swift his forces would have to be to reach them. Even if they were fought in rapid succession, armies reliant on infantry, such as those of the Roman Agricola or the Saxon Harold in 1066, show us how easily they could move from one part of the country to another. (38)

Most recently, Halsall is more certain in his position: "One of the most frequently stated ideas is that the reason for Arthur's military success was a force of heavily armed cavalry. *It cannot be said too forcefully that there is absolutely no evidence for this contention*" (*Worlds of Arthur*, 145; italics added). He goes on to say that even though there's no direct evidence for a mounted Arthur-type, that doesn't mean it would have been impossible. It's fair to assume that the often mounted Roman soldiers and officials not only left animals behind as they withdrew from Britain through the second decade of the fifth century, but also instilled an appreciation in the Saxons and Britons for the efficacies of a horse culture, whether as cavalry or as beasts of burden in farming and haulage. The fact that the sentry recognizes that a horse is missing from the Arthur and Patsy story means horses are at least known at the depicted time, a time much more akin to the later romance depictions of Arthur's knightly exploits, where horses are plentiful.

ARTHUR: "Court at Camelot"—This lofty version of Camelot is also a borrow from the Arthurian legend as shaped by Malory in *Le Morte Darthur*, then reimagined for the Victorian age by Tennyson in *Idylls of the King*. Other earlier sources, including some versions of Chrétien's *Lancelot, the Knight of the Cart* and Geoffrey's *HKB*, give little or no attention to Camelot as the center of Arthur's power.

Coincidentally, the Pythons had produced *Flying Circus* during an unusually active Camelot-Arthur period (without mentioning or alluding to anything Arthurian in the actual *Flying Circus* episodes), as the celebrated and press-covered archaeological digs headed by Leslie Alcock at Cadbury commenced in July 1966. Newspapers of the day were eager to immediately make the archaeological connections between Cadbury and Camelot, including the venerable *Times*, which made fine points with the following headlines: "Five-Year Dig for Camelot May Be Announced Today" (28 July 1966: 12) and "Arthurian Find at 'Camelot' Dig" (2 September 1968: 8). Sir Mortimer Wheeler (1890–1976) of the Camelot Research Committee (the name says it all) was also involved, and has already been mentioned by the Pythons in the scene directions for *MPFC* Ep. 20, specifically the "*Archaeology Today*" sketch (*MPFC: UC*, 1.329, 336). By the end of the first main dig in August 1967, Alcock and associates—though unable to make a Camelot discovery announcement—could firmly say that they had found the "largest fortress in Britain during the sixth century," and that digging should continue.[91] The fortress, of course, was not one akin to the locations the Pythons had chosen; the Cadbury site would have been a reinforced hill fort, as described above in the "*EXTERIOR—CASTLE WALLS—DAY*" entry.

By spring 1969 the newsy morsels that kept seeping out of the dig—namely that participants were troweling for proof of the actual Camelot, and finding things "Arthurian" with every turned spade—had attracted the attention and scorn of some fellow academics, including Professor Charles Thomas. For much more on this circus-like development see the entry for "It is a silly place" below.

SOLDIER: "You're using coconuts"[92]—Used and commented upon by the Goons in their long-running radio program, *The Goon Show*, coconut shells had by this time been employed in sound recording for many years. Most of the listening audience would likely have known this already, and accepted the fact that they were listening to a sound effect, and not an actual recording of a horse. The digression becomes the key, then, as Arthur is for the first (and not the last) time nudged aside from his quest by a nit-picking but often well-meaning antagonist—here demanding answers and making observations about coconuts versus horses, temperate versus tropical zones, laden versus unladen swallows, and, later, by stubbornly "constitutional peasants," rude Frenchmen in English castles, additional Grail cups, and so on.[93]

See the entry for "the coconut's tropical" for more below, but for now, examples of the Goons' "coconut" moments:

FX: Coconut shells advancing, getting louder.
   Seagoon (Secombe): Wait. Listen. Look. Here comes a man riding a pair of coconut shells. ("The Lost Year" 13 December 1955)

Bloodnok (Sellers): Hark! I hear horses hooves.

Cardigan (Secombe): It's somebody galloping down the road.

Bloodnok: Who is it?

Cardigan: It's a man with coconut shells strapped to his feet.

Bloodnok: Economical devil! ("The Giant Bombardon" 17 November 1957)

The Goons will draw attention to most aspects of radio production, including the script they may or may not be following, positioning and presence of the microphone, the fact that actors play more than one voice, the mistakes (i.e., beginning a line of dialogue in the wrong character voice, then changing), the source of sound effects, a live audience, etc. In both the Goon and Python worlds, the veneer of verisimilitude is rubbed thin.

ARTHUR: ". . . through the Kingdom of Mercia"—This is one of the few admitted moments of "history" in *Holy Grail*. An Anglo-Saxon kingdom, Mercia occupied the River Trent watershed in what is now called the English Midlands.[94] As there were only three *major* kingdoms by about 850—Mercia, Northumbria, and Wessex—this admission from Arthur narrows the possibilities of this particular encounter to Northumbria or Wessex.

Passing through the kingdom of Mercia in the seventh or eighth centuries would have been quite a journey, as it eventually covered the entire Midlands, east and west.[95] Since Arthur is claiming to be King of the Britons, it likely also excludes the outlying (and un-Romanized, meaning untamed) Celtic areas of Cornwall, Wales, and Scotland. The Mercian-Midlands is an apt choice for the Pythons, actually. Three of the troupe were born or educated in the Midlands: Chapman in Leicester, Idle in Wolverhampton, and Palin, born in Sheffield and schooled in Shrewsbury. The majority of village and region names mentioned during the run of *Flying Circus* are also found in the Midlands—Birmingham, Bromsgrove, Buxton, Coventry, Derby, Droitwich, Kettering, Leamington, and Warwick, among many others.[96]

In the "Travel Agent" sketch, Idle's Tourist rants through a laundry list of West Midlands locations, for example.[97] What Arthur is claiming, essentially, is that he and Patsy have just traveled through the regions that *MPFC* called home, very nearly an intertextuality, even an in-joke for those viewers who had watched the show faithfully.

If considering Arthur's (alleged) historical time—c. 500—what would *become* Mercia was a very young and likely wild region at least partly on the borders between the native Welsh and the Anglo-Saxon invaders, and would have been an ideal time/place for a historical Arthur-type to meet and defeat Saxons. A map featuring boundaries at the end of the fifth and beginning of the sixth centuries, however, looks very different than one just two centuries later, given that the Welsh in 500 would have controlled Strathclyde, Gwynedd, Demetia, Damnonia (the westernmost more-than-half of the country) and most of what comes to be known as the Midlands, all the way to The Wash on the east coast. Again, if this is Arthur walking through the Britain of 500, there's no Mercia to cross; if this is 787, as the *printed* script claims, then Mercia is at its largest and most influential, reaching from the edge of Cornwall all the way to the mouth of the Humber, and from Widnes to Kent. At this point it becomes quite a walk. By 932—the date in the titles of the finished film—Mercia is effectively gone, now part of the larger kingdom of England under Æthelstan after 927;[98] by 1167 or 1282 or later, Mercia is an ancient memory.

But this is also one of the handful of moments in the film where the mythological world of Arthur intersects with the world of British history. Mercia was an actual, identifiable, locatable kingdom, if just to historians (like Jones) in 1974. These moments of collision are throughout somewhat awkward—the fictional Arthur would have just traipsed through a kingdom controlled by a real king, a Creoda or Penda or Offa, and there is no acknowledgment of that existing authority, though the kingdom itself is admitted as a reality. In this Arthur is closer to Shakespeare's Falstaff, an ahistorical character in a historical setting.[99] Also, Mercia doesn't come into existence until the decades *after* any actual Arthur's flourishing, and Mercia is technically gone (subsumed into Wessex and thence the greater kingdom of England) twelve or thirteen years before the film's depicted setting. Mercia is likely mentioned, then, simply because it was the "greatest of the English kingdoms" of the mid-Middle Ages, and one that the typical twenty-something might remember from middle school history class (Brooke, *SNK*, 99).

SOLDIER: " . . . the coconut's tropical"—Portuguese traders likely discovered the coconut (or India nut) and brought it back along a trade route, where it would have found its way to Britain, but it doesn't appear to have been termed a coconut ("coquos") until the late fifteenth century (*OED*). As Mortimer notes, there have been eleven medieval coconut cups found and preserved in England (Eton College has at least one), so though incredibly rare, a Middle Ages find of a rogue coconut shell (or two) in what was Mercia is not impossible.[100] Common use of the term "tropical" is even later, well into the sixteenth century. Again, as will be seen below, Python characters are often given knowledge—especially knowledge that might qualify as minutiae—well beyond their historical capacities.

SOLDIER: " . . . this is a temperate zone"—This is one of those bits of information that Python characters have become known for knowing—especially when they shouldn't know. A temperate zone is simply an area not prone to weather extremes—temperatures tend to stay between 0°C and 32°C—and the *OED* dates its use to the mid-sixteenth century. England does happen to be in a temperate zone, yes. Characters' access to knowledge beyond their ken or even their time is a Python mania, especially for a lower-class "normal" person like a Pepperpot or "ratbag," or the *Flying Circus* character Reg Moss, English cycling champion who also happens to be versed in the footlings of twentieth-century art:

[H]ow and why a sprint cyclist would have such intimate knowledge of the history of modern painting can only be answered by referring to Python's penchant for allowing characters (like the Pepperpots, for instance) access to knowledge well beyond their presented position or social station. Coal miners in Ep. 26 will understand classical architecture and European martial/treaty history, for instance; Pepperpots will argue about the true meanings of "freedom" in Sartre's existential masterworks in Ep. 27; and perhaps most famously, Middle Ages peasants will be given intricate knowledge of anarchosyndicalist political structures. (*MPFC: UC*, 1.12)

ARTHUR: "The swallow may fly south . . . "—The following happy diversion—this time into air speed velocities and weight ratios of swallows—is another Pythonism held over from the *Flying Circus* days: the endless digression. Not unlike the wonderful and chapters-long digression undertaken by Laurence Sterne's characters/narrative in *Tristram Shandy*, or the digressions Fielding employs (and defends) in his novels, the Python world is full of characters and situations that have a very difficult time simply communicating successfully. In this case, Arthur's simple request to speak to the guard's "lord and master" devolves into talk of coconuts, climate zones, and birds, and Arthur is frustrated. It's not made clear whether the sentries feel "safe" being out of Arthur's physical reach atop the wall, and therefore joust with him at their ease, or this world is simply a world where an Arthur-type won't be given any benefit of the doubt—the common man is no respecter of persons (reappearing when Arthur confronts Dennis later). Similar moments in *MPFC* include the "Gestures to Indicate Pauses in Televised Talk" sketch in Ep. 30, where:

> [our host] does a masterful job of precisely stepping back from actually beginning his presentation with every refinement he attempts to communicate. First "we" are going to talk, then he qualifies that to "I," then from the future tense ("I *am* going to . . . ") to the present ("I *am* talking about it . . . "), then to clarify he hasn't begun actually talking about the subject, but he is still talking, and on and on. The structure here is very much like the convoluted, qualifying, clarifying, and even extirpating narrative structure in Sterne's *Tristram Shandy*, which spends page after page attempting to relate the facts surrounding Tristram's birth, but digressions abound and overwhelm the narrative thread—and the novel and characters know it. It is Volume III before we reach the (somewhat) blessed event. (*MPFC: UC*, 2.55–56)

This aggressive digressive will become a hallmark of the Pythons' structure in *Holy Grail*, even though it is a quest film, and as a quest film the characters must move forward, as should the narrative. Not so, however, as will be seen. In the "Dennis Moore" sketch (Ep. 37), Moore's first encounter with his victims goes as badly (or as understandably) as can be expected of any Python transaction, as he boasts of his shooting skills and practice regimen:

> I have two pistols here. I know one of them isn't loaded any more, but the other one is, so that's one of you dead for sure, or just about for sure anyway, it certainly wouldn't be worth your while risking it because I'm a very good shot, I practise every day, well, not absolutely *every* day, but most days in the week . . . I expect I must practise, oh, at least four or five times a week, at least . . . at least four or five, only some weekends, like last weekend there wasn't much time so that moved the average down a bit . . . but I should say it's definitely a solid four days' practice every week . . . at least. I mean, I reckon I could hit that tree over there . . . the one behind that hillock, not the big hillock, the little hillock on the left. *(heads are coming out of the coach and peering)* You see the three trees, the third from the left and back a bit—that one—I reckon I could hit that four times out of five . . . on a good day. Say with this wind . . . say, say, seven times out of ten . . . . (audio transcription)

Moore continues, digressing "from the narrative trajectory, and even after all the verisimilitude of eighteenth-century costumes, props, and overall production design, we're quickly thrust sideways into the world of . . . Uncle Toby and Tristram . . . where diversions, backtracks, and self-conscious narrative hiccoughs keep the story from ever actually progressing" (*MPFC: UC*, 2.135). Mr. Orbiter-5's digression earlier creates "brackets of reference and speech within other brackets":

> In this the Pythons are anticipating their feature film *Holy Grail*, where the grimy reality of the sets and Middle Ages design are consistently undercut by the temporal and spatial narrative transgressions—the appearance of coconuts, argumentative peasants, a film production member's death . . . and the "out of bracket" Historian who attempts to narrate the story, only to be killed by someone "inside the bracket." (*MPFC: UC*, 2.135)

These bracketed digressions can also be aggressively digressed, as the Pythons illustrated in *Flying Circus* Ep. 27, "*Njorl's Saga*," where an Icelandic saga is hijacked multiple times by the North Malden Icelandic Society, by peregrinating Pepperpots, and even by frustrated BBC programming staff. Narrative trajectory ricochets—the unsuccessful Grail quest scenario—will be revisited throughout *Holy Grail*, as it has been a staple throughout the run of *MPFC*, in the form of unsuccessful transactions (*MPFC: UC*, 1.165–66, 254–55, 350).

Perhaps most importantly here, this "swallows" digression is actually one that will *serve* the narrative later—it is a setup for an eventual and well-crafted payoff much later in the film. It is also the very kind of digression that Fielding taunts his "reptilian" critics about in *Tom Jones* (1749):

> First, then, we warn thee not too hastily to condemn any of the incidents in this our history as impertinent and foreign to our main design, *because thou dost not immediately conceive in what manner such incident may conduce to that design*. This work may, indeed, be considered as a great creation of our own; and for a little reptile of a critic to presume to find fault with any of its parts, *without knowing the manner in which the whole is connected*, and before he comes to the final catastrophe, is a most presumptuous absurdity. (X:I 453; italics added)

This "swallows" digression is frustrating to Arthur, of course, since he fails to secure the information he seeks at this first castle wall, but it is *only* thanks to this digression that toward the end of the film he avoids this penultimate catastrophe. With the knowledge gained from this failed transaction, he is able to turn the tables on the Soothsayer and watch him be hurled into the hell-kettle known as the Gorge of Eternal Peril. Still, Arthur is seemingly unaware of the inherent "design" or "connected"-ness mentioned by Fielding; when Bedevere asks him how he "knows so much about swallows," Arthur merely attributes it to his kingly nature.[101]

Lastly, the swallow and the martin are also perhaps significant in that they have held a place in English folk belief for generations. Disturbing a swallow or martin nest has been considered unlucky since at least the sixteenth century, with tales of all manner of calamity (limbs breaking, cows drying up, farms failing) attending such desecrations.[102] One of the earliest recorded offers some specifics:

> To robbe a Swallowes nest built in a fire-house, is from some old belldames Catechismes, held a more fearfull sacrilege, than to steale a chalice from out of a Church. . . . The prime cause of this superstitious feare, or hope of good lucke by their kinde vsage, was that these birds were accounted sacred amongst the Romanes, to their housbold gods, of which number Venus the especiall patronesse of swallowes was one. (Jackson, Originall of Vnbeliefe, 177–78)

Removing a swallow's nest was also widely believed to cause nearby cows to give milk spoiled with blood. This connection between incidents—a nest disturbed leading to a farm suffering—is the very connection used over and over again in the various witch and sorcery trials that would plague England in the sixteenth and seventeenth centuries. This same kind of flimsy connection will be employed by the mob as they bring their alleged witch forward for burning—her appearance ("She looks like one") is connected to a man being turned into a newt.

ARTHUR: " . . . or the house martin"—A martin is a swallow, actually, and this term isn't current until at least the eighteenth century, according to the *OED*. In the earliest draft of this sketch, these guards argue about ants, not birds (*MPHGB*, 25). Parts of the unused ant sequence will find its way into the fourth season of *MPFC*, Ep. 41, an episode known as "Michael Ellis." There, customer Chris (Idle) buys a pet ant to add to his menagerie, then tunes in to a lecture on an Open University-type television program for "formicidiphiles," etc. (*JTW*, 2.267–68).

In a book that obviously influenced the Pythons from their youth, T. H. White's *The Once and Future King*—and specifically the first book in the collection, *The Sword in the Stone* (1938)—Merlyn, Archimedes, and Wart (the young Arthur) have a long, pedantic discussion about birds, and Merlyn even transforms Wart into bird form, thrice. Wart first becomes a friendly merlin (69–81); they later discuss various birds, their quotidian habits and differences (155–61); Wart then becomes an owl to fly with Archimedes (162–66); and finally a goose (166–72), where the ant discussion reappears (172).[103]

SOLDIER: "Are you suggesting coconuts migrate?"—"Migrate" is a seventeenth-century term, so this is a bit of an anachronism, helping set the tone for the balance of the film. This theme will be revisited a bit later in the final and abbreviated series of *MPFC*. In Episode 45, Sir David Attenborough (Palin) will pursue "The Walking Tree of Dahomey," an allegedly peripatetic tree (*MPFC: UC*, 2.202).

SOLDIER: " . . . a five-ounce bird could not carry a one-pound coconut"—This sort of rather thoughtful reasoning won't be exhibited later, as "churches" and "small rocks" are thought to float in water, and a witch is weighed against a duck.

SOLDIER: " . . . swallow needs to beat its wings . . . "—Way too fast, according to style.org, where the popular "Unladen Swallow" page (first posted in 2003) puts the Python-proffered swallow facts and figures to the test. Thumbnail sketch: slower wing speed (maybe eighteen per second, not forty-three per second), much lighter (about 0.7161 ounces, not five ounces), and an air speed of about eleven meters per second.[104] This is one of the *Holy Grail* scenes that found its way into shared cultural memory.

These slightly wrong facts aren't key, of course, except to reiterate that the Pythons used bits of checked facts mixed in with a nimiety of estimations, guesses, and wild exaggerations. In some cases—as in the recitations regarding Frederick William in "Dennis Moore" of Ep. 37—it's possible to find the actual book and edition by the "famous historian" G. M. Trevelyan (1876–1962) the Pythons cribbed for their narrative (*MPFC: UC*, 2.133, 137). In Ep. 26, they also mention Trevelyan and even a page number for their citation—and they are *almost* precisely accurate (1.394). Trevelyan also happens to mention our king—"the half-mythical King Arthur"—in his landmark *History of England*, first published in 1926 (44).

ARTHUR: "I'm not interested"—Arthur cannot or doesn't want to be sidetracked, but those he encounters will more often provide distracting asides than direct answers, directions, etc. Here can be seen demands placed on the medieval Arthur involving his single-minded-ness, but also a more contemporary depiction of an idealistic leader trapped by his own vision, and by the strictures of the modern world. First, the ancient Arthur.

SCENE TWO

In the extant sources for many Arthurian tales of the early to middle ages it is the hermit figure who plays the role of information-giver, contextualizer, and even cautionary. The Pythons include the Soothsayer (Gilliam) as well as Tim the Enchanter (Cleese), both of whom give direction to the quest, with the image of God himself as the ultimate compass. There is no straight-ahead hermit figure in *Holy Grail*.[105] And rather than a "Grail question" setting the various quests on their way as in ancient literature, in *Holy Grail* it is the direct command (the "good idea") from the Lord that turns Arthur away from Camelot in favor of seeking the Grail. Barber describes this development in the sources:

> When Perceval first comes to the Grail castle, he is not looking for the Grail; his quest for it begins when he realizes what he has lost, and what he has failed to do. *The Story of the Grail*, *Perlesvaus*, the *Prose Perceval* and *Parzival* all have this in common: Perceval is in search of a place he has once found, and a situation which he has once experienced. In the *Lancelot-Grail*, the quest is very different. It is external, announced by divine powers, as part of the grander scheme. . . . Arthur's creation of an almost ideal earthly kingdom is recognized by heaven when the Grail appears in his court, but the intrusion of the spiritual world destroys earthly harmony instead of co-existing with it. The quest is a search for the experiences which the Grail offers; the knights treat it as another adventure, but quickly realize that there are spiritual dimensions to it which lie beyond the bounds of earthly chivalry. But it is nonetheless an archetypal quest—a vow to leave the safety of the castle walls and to undertake the search for a physical object or person through whatever hardships may befall. . . . The Grail began as part of the story of a knight's progress to maturity, in Chrétien; it was reinvented as a journey to the achievement of worldly perfection in Wolfram; and in its final avatar, it stands as the symbol of the ultimate spiritual perfection. (*THG*, 110–11)

In its Pythonesque avatar, however, the quest is an exercise in twentieth-century nihilism, where no good deed goes unpunished, cloaking itself darkly and comfortably in the Modernist malaise that is fracturing into postmodernism. This is precisely the way the *Flying Circus* series ended, as well, where in Ep. 44 a Man (reading a *Radio Times* article about the show) promises "appallingly expensive scenes of devastation," only to be cut off for lack of interest and budget. The Man asks for another minute of show to replace the "old rubbish" being shown, to no avail (*MPFC: UC*, 2.196, 199).

The more contemporary shadow of Arthur might also have been the "brilliant" and "desperately serious" PM Harold Wilson, whose fixation with a single issue—the value and symbolic importance of sterling—spelled doom for many of Labour's hoped-for social and economic policies after 1966.[106] Arthur cannot be turned aside from his quest—God has confirmed its importance, and Arthur sets himself on the path and keeps to it, no matter what. Wilson and his 1964 Labour government had been saddled with an enormous balance of payments deficit, and the general consensus around him "favoured an immediate devaluation of the pound to restore Britain's competitive position" (Whitehead, 3). Wilson refused, calling the notion "nonsense" (3). It was argued by Wilson's best economic advisors that the devaluation would not only "restore Britain's competitive position," but could easily be blamed on the Tories, if it were accomplished fast enough (3). Wilson still said no, certain that the problem was a temporary one, and could be waited out:

> The temporary case against devaluation—that Labour had a precarious majority, that import surcharges and an effective prices and incomes policy might restore Britain's competitive position and allow a breakout from "stop-go" economic policies—became a permanent one. Wilson saw sterling, says his Defence Secretary Denis Healey, "as a sort of virility symbol; if sterling went, you had somehow failed the exam." (Whitehead, 3)

Barbara Castle quoted George Brown[107] in 1966, who, after the pound fell below $2.80, tried to talk seriously with the Cabinet about devaluation, but admitted that Wilson's dependence on the United States (and President Johnson) might be unbreakable: "[Wilson] won't budge. He can't budge. Why? Because he is too deeply committed to Johnson. . . ." Castle's quote of Brown continues: "What did he pledge? I don't know; that we wouldn't devalue and full support in [Vietnam]. But both of these have got to go" (Whitehead, 6). This could be a conversation between two of Arthur's more reasonable knights, with Johnson taking God's role, and Wilson the committed quester. Arthur won't budge, and is only stopped when he's hustled in a police van in an ending he couldn't possibly have foreseen. George Brown saw this decision as the one that changed everything:

> We had assured the TUC that the prices and incomes policy which they were required to accept would not be a restraint, would be a policy of controlled growth. . . . The moment we decided to make the value of the pound take precedence over that objective we killed the prices and incomes policy. The moment we did that we also rang the bell as far as private enterprise was concerned—they wouldn't get the resources they needed. . . . We killed all that in the interests of the pound, and that finished the [Department of Economic Affairs]. . . . It was undoubtedly the turning point; the point at which the Labour Party's attitude to life changed. (Whitehead, 7)

Once Arthur is rebuffed, and rebuffed again, the audience if not Arthur understands that this isn't the world of medieval romances—it's the world of balance of payments deficits and a belatedly, devastatingly devalued pound.[108] It's also a benighted view of the West that by the mid-1970s has come to full, sickening flower, described in harsh terms by the former Soviet dissident and gulag prisoner Aleksandr Solzhenitsyn (1918–2008). Speaking at Harvard in 1978,[109] Solzhenitsyn surprised his audience and the nation when he blasted the West's "decline in courage," its acquisitiveness and avarice, its concerns about "rights" rather than "obligations," and its complete lack of a "serious press," meaning a vapid newspaper and television industry (Booker, *The Seventies*, 55–56). Booker describes the period that so dismayed Solzhenitsyn:

> So far it might have been possible to see in Solzhenitsyn's picture of the West as a society full of weak, unhappy, squabbling, self-righteous children, obsessed with conformity and trivia, little more than a grotesque caricature, a string of over-stated clichés—though even here some Westerners might have caught in Solzhenitsyn's words an echo of that profound spiritual sickness which they themselves sense has come over Western civilization in recent decades, and which has given the whole flavor of our public and private life a sickly, strained, superficial quality, as if something terrible has been happening to us all, without our really daring to admit it. (56)

There is no possibility that a straight-ahead quest for God and His glory can succeed given this zeitgeist; the genre has emptied out and become clichéd, and the audience likely wouldn't suspend disbelief to the degree necessary for such fantastical events to exist.

SECOND SOLDIER—To this point, the scene has been structured in a very typical Python way—one character meeting another character, followed by an argument or discussion of some sort. In *Flying Circus*, this same structure can be found when a Rustic meets a City Gent (Ep. 2, "Flying Sheep"), when Mafia thugs meet a military man (Ep. 8, "Army Protection Racket"), or when a butcher's shop customer meets the proprietor (Ep. 18, "The Man Who Is Alternately Rude and Polite"). In fact, these are a handful of the many Python scenes—in *Holy Grail*, *Flying Circus*, and in later feature films—that can be appreciated *without* the accompanying images. There is nothing in the back-and-forth between Arthur and these sentries that demands a filmed reaction shot, actually, or even an establishing shot. In this the Pythons are clearly drawing on *The Goon Show* (and before that, the music hall) tradition of verbal humor.[110] Other influences identified in *MPFC: UC* include earlier British shows like *It's That Man Again*, *Round the Horne*, *Band Waggon*, *Hancock's Half Hour*, and more contemporarily *I'm Sorry I'll Read That Again*; as well as American counterparts *Your Show of Shows* and most recently, *Rowan and Martin's Laugh-In*. See the index in *MPFC: UC* under "radio shows" and "television shows."

The coconuts fit well here, then, since this scene, followed by the static "Stay here and make sure 'e doesn't leave" scene in the tower of Swamp Castle, for example, are essentially radio skits. Little or very little verbal introduction and a few sound effects provide all the fleshing out these types of scenes demand; the verbal parrying does the rest. Additionally, the Pythons were able to produce a number of successful record albums of these and additional sketches, including one for *Holy Grail* (*The Album of the Soundtrack of the Trailer of the Film of Monty Python and the Holy Grail*) attesting to the abundantly aural landscape created in many of their sketches. *MPHG* is, then, a series of connected sketches, the common narrative spine being Arthur's journey.

SECOND SOLDIER: " . . . a gannet . . . or a plover"—(PSC) In the elided end credits, this character played by Cleese is known as "Second Soldier With a Keen Interest in Birds" (*MPHGB*, 90). These bird references are scratched through on the third page of the script, and they are replaced by the handwritten "an African swallow" (3). Both are seabirds, and both inhabit Great Britain, though there is no indication that the name "plover" existed prior to the early fourteenth century (*OED*). The word "gannet," however, has been voiced in English since at least the tenth century ("ganotes"), and likely before, according to the *OED*. The Pythons have already mentioned seabirds in their bestiary, with a cross-dressed Cleese selling albatross at a theater, as well as "gannet on a stick," in Ep. 13 (*MPFC: UC*, 1.201–2). Many of these same birds are mentioned in the lengthy "bird" section of *The Sword in the Stone*, as well.

The First Soldier also brings up the "merlin" (replaced later by "African swallow"), but all these are crossed out of the printed script (*MPHGB*, 3). The merlin is a bit of a stretch for the conversation, since it is a type of falcon, a bird of prey. "Merlyon" is also a fairly old, fourteenth-century word. There's no indication that any pun on the word "merlin" is intended. The Merlin character—so key to myriad iterations of the Arthurian tales, beginning with Geoffrey's twelfth-century *HKB* (see *QAB*, 7–9)—never made it out of the original script pages of what would ultimately become *MPHG*. In that version, Merlin is a kind of grizzled scrap dealer who offers to fashion a grail for them from bits of junk (*MPHGB*, 25–26).

ARTHUR: "Will you go ask your master if he wants to join the Knights of Camelot?"— The Pythons (well, Jones) have already admitted elsewhere that the look of this medieval world is based in the thirteenth and fourteenth centuries, not the tenth century, so their character influences may be later, as well. This version of Arthur has the real-world feel of Edward III (1312–1377), who waxes Arthurian in his reconstruction of chivalry and the continuing importance of knighthood:

> Edward III needed knights to serve as officers and to form the backbone of the men-at-arms whether on foot or when acting as cavalry. He was a gallant and chivalrous king, glorying in battle and martial deeds. His personal example helped to popularise the idea of knighthood and he deliberately fostered it [via feasts, tournaments, and new knightly orders]. The emotional attachment to princes found throughout the Middle Ages was sharpened under such a noble king, and all of gentle blood were proud and eager to serve under him. . . . [Edward's orders] usually consisted of a limited number of close friends to the King, bound together by a special oath, taking part in gorgeous ceremonies and elaborate tournaments, in imitation of what were

thought to have been the customs of the courts of King Arthur and Charlemagne. (Norman and Pottinger, 79–80)

Like Edward III, Arthur attempts to lead by personal example as he gathers a few trusted knights to his noble cause; his orders are those involving the search for the Grail, and the promised rewards are supernal. McKisack notes that this Edward's admitted fascination with Arthuriana seems to have coalesced after the conclusion of a "great tournament held at Windsor" in 1344, when "the king took solemn oath that within a certain time he would follow in the footsteps of King Arthur and create a Round Table for his knights."[111] This Arthur fixation accounts, at least partly, for the copious amounts of money Edward was willing to spend on Windsor Castle's reconstruction and expansion. This new building at Windsor, the House of the Round Table (allegedly round and massive), was never completed.[112]

This encounter sets the tone for the balance of the journey: Arthur is more often treated as a kind of wandering piepowder than divine or kingly quester—greeted with suspicion or ambivalence wherever he goes.

FIRST SOLDIER: " . . . African swallows are non-migratory"—This is true, though it isn't likely that these guards would have had access to this kind of information. Similarly, in the first draft of the script, the sentries tend to argue about families and sub-families of ants, rather than swallows: "You're talking about the Myrmicinae sub-family, and they're made up of harvesters, fungus-growers, slave-makers, thief-ants, guest-ants, grease-ants, orborials . . ." (*MPHGB*, 25).

The Pythons may have reached back to one of Wart's encounters thanks to Merlyn's transformative magic in *The Sword in the Stone* section of *The Once and Future King*, where the boy who would be king spent significant time as a member of an ant colony, and much of the narrative energy was expended on ant communication.[113] During the Wart's final lesson—this with Badger—the discussion comes round to which animal rules the animal kingdom, and Wart confidently avers: "Man is the king of the animals" (196). Badger isn't so certain. He thinks Man is a tyrant, and too warlike to ever be a true leader. Ant facts are in the offing as Badger continues:

"And then again we do have to admit that he has a quantity of vices."
"King Pellinore has not got many."
"He would go to war, if King Uther declared one. Do you know that Homo sapiens is almost the only animal which wages war?"
"Ants do."
"Don't say 'Ants do' in that sweeping way, dear boy. There are more than four thousand different sorts of them, and from all those kinds I can only think of five which are belligerent. There are the five ants, one termite that I know of, and Man. (196)

Wart isn't convinced, and Badger's instructions are completed with the boy all the more certain he wants to be a knight who can go to war and "do great deeds"[114] (197). In the following pages, Wart pulls the sword from the stone, becoming King Arthur. (The Pythons will also borrow directly one of Bedevere's character traits from this influential book, as will be seen later.[115]) In the *MPFC* world, Pepperpots and lowly workers are gifted with this insouciant brilliance. These common types know high art, conversational French, the works of Sartre and existentialist thought, architectural terms and history, mathematics, the history of treaties and European wars, and so on.[116]

Arthur raises his eyes heavenwards . . . —(PSC) This "gestural acting" is used often by the Pythons, and is a holdover from the hoary traditions of the music hall, silent cinema and even cartoons of their collective youth.[117] Later, when it becomes clear that Bedevere has muffed the wooden Trojan rabbit plan, both Arthur and Lancelot shake their heads and cover their faces in equally obvious bits of over-the-top acting. In Ep. 8, the "Buying a Mattress" sketch, the Manager (Cleese) thumps himself in the forehead with the palm of his hand when the Groom (Jones) says "mattress"—after being told not to—forcing Lambert (Chapman) to put his head in a bag; later in Ep. 29, in "The Lost World of Roiurama" sketch, the character "Our Hero" played by Jones is forced to roll his eyes for the camera after the shoddy performance of Hargreaves (Palin), the Explorer's Club desk clerk. The aural version of this type of gestural acting is heard in *The Goon Show* whenever Neddie (Secombe) makes a bad pun or laughs at his own bad joke, stifling his own forced laugh with a very pronounced "A-hem."

SECOND SOLDIER: "... strand of creeper"—This bit of dialogue—fading as Arthur and Patsy move away—is included in the finished film, as is the following mention of "dorsal guiding feathers." These changes are *not* noted in the finished script version printed in *MPHGB*, however.

Notes

1. Brooke, *FAH*, 100. The "Conquest" is, of course, the invasion by the forces of William the Conqueror in 1066 (becoming William I, c. 1028–1087), his decisive victory won at the Battle of Hastings. Much more on the effects of the Norman invasion and the "Frenchifying" that followed in later entries.

2. From a 20 November 2013 Doyle e-mail correspondence. Codirector Jones discusses this additional footage and the need for it in his DVD commentary, though he misremembers Terry Bedford as shooting it, not Doyle.

3. 2 September 1968: 8.

4. See PastScape, www.pastscape.org.uk for a complete breakdown of the site, the various digs, and so on. The typical Norman castle would have been a motte and bailey. The motte was a raised hillock surrounded by a moat and topped with a small, palisade-enclosed tower. The bailey was a larger, flatter area adjoining the motte, surrounded by a palisade and moat. This type of fortification can be seen in the Bayeux Tapestry ("Siege of the Castle of Dinan"). "Many hundreds of these castles must have existed all over the islands: some 900 are still recognisable" (Norman and Pottinger, 29). This is *not* the type of castle the Pythons were imagining when writing the film.

5. The introductory bit for the third series—Cleese in a dinner jacket at a desk with BBC microphone—was shot on the grounds of Norwich Castle. This clip was used in Eps. 27–39. See *MPFC: UC*, 2.21.

6. Doyle built the wheel and shot this scene *after* cinematographer Bedford completed work on the film. Information gathered from evidence given in *Forstater v. Python*, as well as correspondence between the author and Doyle.

7. Another Bruegel work, *The Procession to Calvary* (1564), features a prominent Catherine wheel complete with a perched crow in the right foreground; there are a number of other wheels in the background. See the entry "... *of Bruegel prints*" later for more.

8. From Gilliam's and Jones's audio commentary track. Doyle also discusses this sequence in his e-mail correspondences.

9. "A Japanese Film Based upon 'Macbeth,'" *Times*, 27 February 1957: 3.

10. The *Macbeth* credit sequence (just after the introduction of the Three Witches on the deserted beach) comprises simple atmospheric music, the whistling wind, and smoke blowing across the scene; the mist fades as the credits end and the tidelands battlefield is revealed. The Polanski-type seriousness is leaned upon by the Pythons and almost immediately undercut, setting an uncertain stage for the balance of *MPHG*.

11. From extra Alastair Scott: "I remember thinking how clever the chain mail was as it was just wool sprayed with silver paint, and as light as a feather" (appendix B).

12. See Norman and Pottinger, 87–89.

13. Other significant eighth-century Britain events include the life and work of the Venerable Bede (c. 672–735), the first major Viking invasion and the anointing of Offa's son Ecgfrith (both 787), the building of what has become known as Offa's Dyke (c. 790), and Saxon battles against the Welsh (British) kingdoms to the west. In the tenth century, the rule of Æthelstan might be considered a highlight, including the majesty of his rule and victories over the Vikings. See Stenton, and Brooke's *FAH*.

14. An entire "get on with it" sequence from the midst of the Castle Anthrax scene was removed just before the film premiered at a festival in Los Angeles, according to Jones. That short sequence was restored to the film for more recent DVD and Blu-ray editions.

15. Halsall, "The Story of 'King Arthur,'" in *Worlds of Arthur*, 5.

16. *Anglo-Saxon England*, 3–4. It's interesting to note the Arthurian hobbyhorses still very much in place in the medieval scholarship of 1943, including the credibility of a "Nennius," the importance of *Y Gododdin*, and Gildas's penchant for making names significant by their absence. This section is unchanged through all the editions of the Stenton work, up to and including 2001. Still, it is a fair treatment of the subject without specifically giving in to the Arthur-as-historical temptations. Stenton's summary also encapsulates the general scholarly disposition in regard to Arthur as the Pythons grew to maturity.

17. "Arthurians Hold Court at Glastonbury," *Times*, 15 August 1969: 2.

18. Significant Arthurian works from Alcock, Ashe, and especially Morris—all published between 1968 and 1973—will be discussed in detail as we continue.

19. See Barbara Yorke's entry for "Kings of Kent" in the *ODNB*.

20. See *MPHGB* Facing Page 1. The *MPHGB* is not continuously paginated, but thumbing through it can be rewarding.

21. See PastScape for more on period monuments in the UK.

22. In the commentary track for the Blu-ray edition of the film, Jones (the troupe's *de facto* historian) notes that even though they set the film in the tenth century, the *look* of the film is meant to be from *about* 1350. In separate comments (made at the time the film was being shot) from members of the troupe and the film's producer, the twelfth and thirteenth centuries were also mentioned as the film's time period. See "932 A.D." for more. In a more recent comment made to Doyle (based on a question from the author), Jones mentions that since he wanted the characters to wear "tabards" (short coats), the film's look, at least, would necessarily move into the later centuries. From e-mail correspondence with the author, dated 6 December 2013.

23. "Monty Python Hunts the Holy Grail," *Times*, 10 May 1974: 22. As for significant events attached to the date, the thorn-in-the-side to both England and the prince of Wales, Llywelyn ap Gruffudd, died in 1282. Many in England celebrated his passing, seeing the subjugation of Wales as complete (Hallam, 120).

24. Gilliam has admitted to being significantly influenced by *Mad* magazine. See *Gilliam on Gilliam*.

25. This tension doesn't here include the fact that an Arthur riding an *actual* horse might have been unlikely, given the challenges of maintaining cavalry units in sub-Roman Britain, but more on that later.

26. Middle Ages artists also engaged in this updating, clothing biblical figures in *au courant* attire in frescoes, tapestries, and illuminated manuscript illustrations. To a medieval audience, this wouldn't have been anachronistic; the updating served to bring the ancient stories into currency, their messages applicable across time.

27. The Pythons had produced *And Now for Something Completely Different* for theatrical distribution in 1971. It is a series of unlinked, re-recorded (on film stock) sketches from the first two *MPFC* series. By the mid-1970s it was playing regularly at college campuses across the United States.

28. See especially the works of Alcock, Ashe, and Morris, from the late 1960s and early 1970s, all of which we'll examine as we move forward.

29. In the "Cast List" included at the end of the printed script Gilliam is credited as "Patsy (Arthur's Trusty Steed)" (*MPHGB*, 90). This was originally typed as "Patsy" followed by a comma, then "Arthur's Trusty Steed," meaning when the cast list was printed the parts were separate, with Gilliam playing both Patsy *and* Arthur's horse. The parentheses were penciled in after-the-fact.

30. Jöns is played by Gunnar Björnstrand (1909–1986); Block is played by Max von Sydow (b. 1929).

31. This page number is relative, since *MPHGB* is not continuously paginated. Page numbers for the "first draft" section are continuous (1–47), as are those for the "final draft" (1–88).

32. The National Trust is the UK's organization for protecting and controlling places of national historic interest. Jones mentions that representatives of the Scottish version of the Trust denied the Pythons' request for access to its castles just before filming was to begin, on the grounds that their use of the castles would have been "inconsistent with the dignity of the fabric of the buildings." (Palin and Jones get a good chuckle at this, given the violent pasts of these fortified structures.) See the early part of *The Quest for the Holy Grail Locations*.

33. See Brooke, *From Alfred to Henry III* and *The Saxon and Norman Kings*, as well as Carpenter, *The Struggle for Mastery* for more on this period of castle building.

34. See Ryan, *The National Trust and the National Trust for Scotland*, 50–52. This is the kind of book the Pythons (likely Jones, Palin, and Gilliam) could have used as they searched for appropriate-looking castles for the film shoot.

35. The shoot was eventually completed at Doune Castle—camera at the base of a wall, looking upward—would have been much more challenging at Bodiam, as it is surrounded by a moat.

36. This cast list is part of *MPHGB*, found two pages after the printed script's final page. Much of the book is unpaginated.

37. Higham, *King Arthur: Myth-Making and History*, 10–37.

38. Berthelot, *King Arthur and the Knights of the Round Table*, 28–29.

39. This would not have been true during the period the film is ostensibly set, the tenth century, according to Norman and Pottinger. The shields were longer, yes, especially for use on horseback to protect the left leg, but there was no sign of heraldry, yet: "The surface of the shield was covered with abstract designs, or crosses, or series of dots, and in some cases by winged dragons, but at this time [the late Saxon and early Norman period] no sign of systematic heraldry can be seen" (34). The Pythons are blithely traipsing between the tenth and twentieth centuries, of course, so anachronistic elements are to be expected.

40. Names will be spelled, generally, as they occur in the source material, thus "Lancelot" *and* "Launcelot."

41. There are many possible inspirations for these costumes, of course, one of the obvious being recent films of the same period or genre. The style of helmets chosen (and the omnipresent mud and the mayhem) seem to have been lifted almost completely from Polanski's *Macbeth* of a few years earlier, for example.

42. Guy Halsall (2013) also dismisses *HB* as being "of dubious historical worth," and "a highly political response to a very specific set of circumstances" in Welsh and English politics of the ninth century (*Worlds of Arthur*, 142 and 203, respectively).

43. "Once Again Arthur's Battles," 57.

44. Cnut lived c. 990–1035, and was king of much of Scandinavia, as well.

45. *The Once and Future King* will be discussed later, in relation to the character of Bedevere.

46. Halsall points out that such a connection is fanciful at best and quite recent, since "there is, incidentally, no first-millennium source that associates Arthur with Cornwall" (*Worlds of Arthur*, 153).

47. This swishy riposte is a borrowing from Joe E. Brown in *Some Like It Hot* (1959).

48. From Jackson, "Once Again Arthur's Battles," 56; and Padel, "The Nature of Arthur," 10.

49. *Times*, 7 June 1973: 14.

50. The "Intermission" and closing music for *MPHG* is played on a Hammond organ.

51. "Leisure Site Expects 6M Visitors in 1977," *Times*, 28 July 1973: 3.

52. Ronald Kershaw, "£40M British 'Disneyland' Project Faces Setback," *Times*, 7 June 1972: 19.

53. For more on the significance of Britain's participation in the EEC, and especially why the "French factor" became so important, see entries in the "Taunting by Frenchmen" scene.

54. "New Slant on 'Holidays at Home,'" 11 October 1973: 25.

55. "Why We Must Cut Loose the Tentacles of the EEC," *Times*, 9 January 1974: 14.

56. "Countdown to Crisis: Eight Days That Shook Britain," BBC News.

57. The sixth century's only significant chronicler, Gildas, fails to mention Arthur at all, an omission that has forced later Arthurians into creative literary calisthenics when promoting Arthur's life and in-

fluence. See Dumville, "Sub-Roman Britain"; Higham, *King Arthur: Myth-Making and History*; Green, "The History and Historicisation of Arthur"; and Halsall, *Worlds of Arthur*. These Gildas quotes are drawn from Michael Winterbottom's 1978 edition of *The Ruin of Britain*.

58. Halsall sees this period as the country's most unified, the kingdom "at its apogee between the reigns of Æthelstan (924–39) and his nephew Edgar (954–72)" (*Worlds of Arthur*, 74).

59. Halsall, *Worlds of Arthur*, 80.

60. Brooke points out that there were other such claimants at that time—those calling themselves the ruler of all Britain—including a tenth-century "swashbuckling pirate called Anlaf, the Irish-Norse king of York" (*SNK*, 81).

61. "Arthur," *Oxford Dictionary of National Biography*; see the bibliography under "Padel, Oliver" for the URL.

62. "Arthurian fact" is the very type of nomenclature that Dumville will reject entirely in his 1977 article, as will many historians in the following years.

63. See Dumville, "Sub-Roman Britain"; Green, "The History and Historicisation of Arthur."

64. This is a possible source book for at least Gilliam. There is an image of a nun making confession to a monk on page 143 that Gilliam will use in his animations for "The Tale of Sir Galahad." See appendix A (Facing Pages) for more on that image.

65. The "Black Maria" is mentioned by name in the printed script on page 87, part of the final scene of the film. Not a British term originally, these police vans (and horse-drawn carriages before that) were seen in dozens of American films of the silent comedy era (Keystone Kops, et al.), and later in British films, including Hitchcock's first sound film *Blackmail* (1929).

66. Discussed in Halsall, *Worlds of Arthur*. Magnus Maximus (c. 335–388) was a Roman commander in Britain who usurped Gratian's throne, and could be legitimately termed "*tyrannus*" (Halsall, 192–93). Halsall writes later: "As a result of Maximus' generally positive image, Gildas' vagueness, and later Welsh politics, in some stories the blame for the *adventus saxonum* got shifted, some time before 700, onto the figure of Vortigern" (215). See also pages 218–19.

67. In fact, these omissions of actual history and historical figures—with the rare exception of the mention of "Mercia," for example—set *MPHG* apart from the Pythons' next film, *Life of Brian*, where the ahistorical character Brian can know and interact with people of history like Pontius Pilate in historical locations.

68. *The History of the Kings of Britain*, 221–23.

69. Halsall calls this "interesting" book the "one sustained academic attempt to disprove the existence of 'King Arthur' written in recent years" (*Worlds of Arthur*, 120).

70. Vortigern is as slippery as any in the historical record. Most recently Halsall (2013) suggests that Vortigern might be a "doublet" for Vortimer (often cast as Vortigern's son), and that much of this genealogy was created by Geoffrey and others for then-current political purposes (*Worlds of Arthur*, 210–14).

71. Comments on the first, very rough draft of the script are scattered throughout this work, as needed.

72. Mario Ledwith, *Daily Mail* (online), 10 March 2014.

73. See the entry "*human ordure*" in "The Wonderful Barge and the Grail Castle" scenes below for more.

74. A source for the Pythons and this in-your-face-ness can be found in English Renaissance drama of Shakespeare and Jonson, Webster, Kyd and Ford, and including Thomas Dekker's *Shoemaker's Holiday* and Shakespeare's *Much Ado*; see below and *MPSERD* for more.

75. Ep. 45, "The Most Awful Family in Britain." Rhodesia was named for businessman and politician Cecil Rhodes (1853–1902).

76. See entries for "Rhodesia" in *MPFC: UC*, 2.208–9, and its index for many more references to "British Empire" and "Rhodesia" throughout *MPFC*. Ironically, in the Rhodesian situation—where a white minority held power—the British had to take sides *against* Rhodesian Front leader and PM Ian Smith and the white colonizers, but were still frustratingly ineffective—unable to project British demands or military power into *another* war on the African continent. Smith would effectively thumb his nose at Britain for fifteen years, 1964–1979.

77. "Chaos, Rubbish and Revolution," BBC News (5 June 2007).

78. *MPFC* Ep. 23, "Derby Council v. All Blacks" (*JTW*, 1.319). See also *MPFC: UC*, 1.352–53.

79. Second episode of *MPFZ*, and *Live at the Hollywood Bowl* performance. See *MPFC: UC*, 1.175.

80. See also Brooke, *SNK*, 81–82.

81. One of the signals of a king's approach was the call of trumpets; this note of heraldry won't happen until the quest faces the French-held castle, and then, as blown by Patsy, it's as unheraldic as can be expected. Patsy has been carrying the trumpet as part of his baggage from the beginning.

82. Inside *MPHGB*, the entire first draft of the jerry-built script occupies the first forty-seven pages of the book. The script as shot (essentially) starts eighteen pages later. *MPHGB* isn't continuously paginated.

83. This is also the same poetic phraseology used by early chroniclers when describing the awful progress of plague, including Colgrave's 1969 edition of *Bede's Ecclesiastical History*: "the pestilence which carried off many throughout the length and breadth of the land" (252–53).

84. See Ashe, *The Discovery of King Arthur*, 9–13; C. Green, "The Monstrous Regiment of Arthurs."

85. In later years (1387) chronicler Knighton notes that Richard II took a ten-month "gyration" across the midlands and north, the announced goals being "the recruitment of a private army and the consolidation of the royalist party" in the west countries (McKisack, 447). Richard was trying to gather adherents to his own comfortable version of Camelot. Richard's lavishing of gifts and titles on "favorites" (like Robert de Vere) had been causing much concern amongst the nobles, including Richard's uncle, and leaving London for a long spell (and especially the seat of government, Westminster) was seen as a much-needed cooling-off period (447).

86. Nigel Saul notes that later, c. 1400, the challenges of the English monarchy and governmental system bred an insularity that circumscribed, a bit, the mobile monarch, especially in comparison to the Scottish experience:

> Scottish political life had the advantage of an underlying stability which was lacking in England. In Scotland there was no prolonged civil war and no dynastic rivalry. Scottish kingship was successful because it was informal—much more informal than in England. Kings still itinerated round the realm, allowing their subjects to meet them. And government remained relatively decentralized: so communities could regulate themselves. (43)

In this the Pythons' Arthur would seem more Scottish; Dennis as Scotsman seems a better fit later as he lives apart from and challenges the central government.

87. The "mud-eater" (Palin) mentioned as appearing in the "Bring Out Your Dead" scene doesn't count as anything gustatory—we never do see him properly eating anything.

88. He's also not the sort Arthur would welcome into his quest—he's no knight—and only Launcelot and Concorde meet him anyway.

89. Sir Mordaunt cheats, incidentally, and Galant is imprisoned in a tower (issue 1, November 1955, page 16 of 36).

90. The "Scotsman on a horse" moment comes from Ep. 1; the "Dennis Moore" sketch runs through Ep. 37; and the "Show Jumping Musical" set piece comes from Ep. 42. In all these cases, professional riders are employed.

91. "Biggest Fortress of Arthur's Day," *Times*, 28 August 1967: 3.

92. In the first draft of the script, "coconuts" is spelled "cocoanuts" throughout. In the "final" film script, other variant spellings can be found, including both "Launcelot" and "Lancelot." "Launcelot" is the preferred spelling in most of the Malorian source works the Pythons (or maybe just Jones) might have consulted. There are dozens of such misspellings and typos throughout *MPFC*, some of which, like "Mary Recruitment" instead of "Army Recruitment," have real consequences and are addressed in the episode.

93. In the earliest draft of the script, the subject of discussion here at the wall also went to ant and termite minutiae. The ant trope found its way into the fourth and final season of *Flying Circus*, Ep. 41.

94. This tenth-century Arthur would have been "riding" through recognizable country and across likely familiar borders by this time, writes Brooke: "[A]ll the shires we know, with almost exactly their

modern boundaries, were established by the end of the tenth century, save only the four northern counties and Rutland" (*SNK*, 83).

95. Arthur was also about to continue reporting on his journeys, when the Soldier interrupts him. He starts to say "Through—" again, when he's sidetracked. Even part of the missing word could have told us much about their course.

96. *MPFC: UC*, 1.12, 222, 269, 287. See the index of *MPFC: UC* for dozens more Midlands mentions throughout the run of *MPFC*.

97. *MPFC: UC*, 2.68–69; see all "Travel Agent" sketch entries there in *MPFC: UC*, as well, for more.

98. For the Pythons and perhaps for Jones (the medieval historian) specifically, Arthur may be loosely based on Æthelstan, the king who controlled most of what we know as England in the tenth century, when the film is ostensibly set. If, however, the eighth century is the setting (787), then the strong Mercian king Offa (ruling 757–796) could be the exemplar for Arthur.

99. See the author's *MPSERD*, chapter 3, for more on this. If Arthur interacted with *historical* characters in the film, we'd spend more time discussing these incongruities, these potential ruptures. As it is, he interacts with mostly generic, historically everyday characters (peasants, sentries, plague cart drivers—stock medieval characters—and other mythological characters like himself, including Bedevere), so the possible ruptures tend to be contained rather quickly. If Arthur had happened upon the Famous Historian, for example . . . but *san fairy ann*.

100. From Mortimer, *The Time Traveler's Guide to Medieval England*, 303n.

101. For a very interesting chapter on digressions in Fielding, especially, see Sacks, *Fiction and the Shape of Belief*, chap. 5.

102. Opie and Tatem, eds., *The Oxford Dictionary of Superstitions*.

103. White, *The Once and Future King*.

104. See http://style.org/unladenswallow/.

105. It isn't as if the Pythons were unaware of the narrative possibilities of the hermit, either. In *MPFC* they depict self-chastising cenobitic hermits living their lives in the Dartmoor hills, and later there is a hermit character who has taken a lifelong vow of silence in *Life of Brian*. In *MPHG* the hermit's role has been divvied up to others.

106. See Bartlett's aptly titled chapter 10, "Withdrawal on All Fronts," in *A History of Postwar Britain, 1951–1974* for a concise examination of this tumultuous period.

107. Castle (1910–2002), a Labour MP, was minister for transport in 1966, and would later create the contentious *In Place of Strife* white paper as a means of curtailing trade union strength; Labour MP Brown (1914–1985), was secretary of state and then foreign secretary in 1966, the latter after he "resigned" in disgust over the devaluation imbroglio. The DEA had been his baby, essentially, and the economic situation had rendered it moot.

108. Wilson would finally capitulate in November 1967, when the pound had dropped to $2.40, a 14.3 percent slide. The devaluation was front-page news in every major British newspaper, and in the United States, as well. All this would lead the British economy into further stagnancies—by 1975 the British government was applying for an IMF loan. See Dawnay, "A History of Sterling."

109. This was just four years after his deportation from the Soviet Union, when his Soviet citizenship was revoked. Soviet authorities were reportedly very unhappy about the forthcoming *Gulag Archipelago* book project.

110. In 1968, the year prior to the creation of *MPFC*, Cleese—an established writer and performer prior to becoming a Python—would read Wallace Greenslade's part in a Goon re-enactment (for Thames TV) of "The Tales of Men's Shirts" (originally broadcast 31 December 1959).

111. *The Fourteenth Century*, 251; see also Hallam, *Four Gothic Kings*, 261–62.

112. See Munby, Barber, and Brown, *Edward III's Round Table at Windsor*, an account of the archaeological exploration of the site in August 2006.

113. The discarded ant information won't be wasted, it will be recycled into *Flying Circus* Ep. 41, "Michael Ellis." There, a university course on ant communication is presented (*MPFC: UC*, 2.172, 174–75). Several sketches begun prior to *Flying Circus* were reworked and included in that series,

including a used car version of the "Dead Parrot" sketch, and the *Panorama*-type show "Mouse Problem," which had been written for Peter Sellers's *The Magic Christian*, but not used in the final version of the film. See *MPFC: UC*, 1.38.

114. *Sword in the Stone* was published after the Nazis rose to power in Germany, and after several years of saber-rattling across Europe, but before German tanks crushed Poland. The clouds of war were lowering—Italy into Ethiopia, the Spanish Civil War, Japan invades China, Germany annexes Austria and the Sudetenland—and White seems certain that Britain won't be able (or willing?) to avoid the coming conflagration.

115. White's *Once and Future King* was published as a whole in 1958, but began its life in parts—the first section, *The Sword in the Stone*, was published in 1938. *The Sword in the Stone* was serialized by BBC Radio (along with other literary greats the Pythons referenced in *Flying Circus*: Dickens, Hugo, Bronte, Austen, Hardy, et al.).

116. See Eps. 26 and 37, for example.

117. See some of the older actors, for example, in D. W. Griffiths's short films from his years at Biograph, 1908–1912, including *A Corner in Wheat* (i.e., the performance of William J. Butler, playing the Ruined Wheat Trader) and *The Sealed Room* (Arthur V. Johnson, playing the Count).

SCENE THREE
ANIMATION / LIVE ACTION SEQUENCE

DEATH AND DEVASTATION—(PSC) This is the thumbnail description of this second scene, it was supposed to be at least partly animated, and follows immediately on the heels of the previous "strand of creeper" dialogue. The setting is a tiny medieval village, and it's to be as grotty as possible. In an article examining the role and proliferation of rats during the plague years, McCormick mentions that even near to the center of the Roman Empire, by the fifth century many areas had fallen into a sorry state:

> The unsavory sanitation arrangements of the high Roman empire may have worsened in late antiquity. Excavators have observed that, c. 450, some rooms of an apartment block (*insula*), as well as the contiguous city street, began to serve as garbage dumps in downtown Naples. In the very next stratigraphic sequence, c. 500, black rats appear. As the western empire descended into chaos, could dwindling urban administrations, changing social ethos, or simply the failure to enforce the old legal provisions have eroded such sanitation practices as had existed earlier? ("Rats, Communications, and Plague," 17)

Britain, being on the westernmost edges of the empire, would likely have experienced such decay first, likely answering this question in the affirmative. Sawyer sums up the period this way:

> When the Roman imperial government relinquished its claim to rule, and any responsibility to defend, Britain . . . things were changing, and invasions by the Picts, the Irish and the English accelerated the change. Towns decayed, villas were abandoned, and as Britain became less Roman it became more Celtic. (*From Roman Britain to Norman England*, 83)

The civil wars that followed are those bemoaned by Gildas, and were followed by a devastating outbreak of plague in 549, further diminishing the population.

CUT TO Terry Gilliam's sequence . . . —(PSC) Gilliam was the troupe's animator and go-to man for walk-on parts during the *MPFC* series run. (Gilliam mentions some of the planned and missing animated sequences in his behind-the-scenes commentary track on the film's Blu-ray edition.) For *Holy Grail* he and Jones had agreed to codirect, both being visual artists. This scene—a proposed animated transition between the "Swallow" and "Plague Cart" sequences—is *not* part of the finished film. The description in the printed script is as follows (it's noted as scene two):

> ANIMATION/LIVE ACTION SEQUENCE—DEATH AND DEVASTATION CUT
> TO Terry Gilliam's sequence of Breughel prints. Sounds of strange medieval music. Discordant and sparse. Wailings and groanings. The last picture mixes through into live action. (*MPHGB*, 4)

From there the cut moves to a victim on the plague cart. None of this seems to have been produced. The scene description is likely a call for a sequence similar to the one Gilliam put together for *MPFC* Ep. 15, "The Spanish Inquisition." There, the Pythons asked for a "Breugel[1] [*sic*] drawing of tortures" and "epic film music," and a voiceover (Cleese) intoned the evils of the Spanish Inquisition (*JTW*, 1.197). Portions of the upper-right quadrant of the Bruegel painting were copied and used by Gilliam for that introductory scene.

    . . . *of Bruegel prints*—(PSC) In this case, certainly a call for scenes from Pieter Bruegel the Elder's *Triumph of Death* (c. 1562). Bruegel (1525–1569) was a Flemish Renaissance painter and printmaker; he was mentioned prominently in the "Art Gallery Strike" sketch in *Flying Circus* Ep. 25, and a portion of *Triumph of Death* appears earlier in Ep. 15 (*MPFC: UC*, 1.242, 373–75). The look of the following scene (in the plague-ridden village) is clearly meant to mirror this particular Bruegel print, and draws on his sketches, as well. See entries below for more, as well as the mentions of Bruegel in appendix A, annotating the Facing Pages sections of the *MPHGB*.

    medieval music—(PSC) This music—likely to have been composed by Neil Innes—was to be part of the called-for animated sequence that was not included in the finished film. Innes would compose or help compose the songs for Princess Lucky's wedding and Sir Robin's minstrels, but his score for the film was replaced in favor of programmed music from the DeWolfe library.

Note

1. "Bruegel"—sometimes "Brueghel"—is one of the names spelled somewhat indifferently in the scripts for both *Flying Circus* and *Holy Grail*. Spellings likely depended on who had typed up that portion of the script, week to week. In the script for Ep. 15, it is actually spelled "Breugel" (*JTW*, 1.197). See *MPFC: UC*, 1.242, 373–75.

SCENE FOUR
"BRING OUT YOUR DEAD"

***BIG CLOSE UP** of contorted face upside down*—(PSC) This scene does indeed open on an upside-down face on a plague cart, though the animated "Bruegel prints" are *not* physically used as a lead-in, as they were in Ep. 15 of *Flying Circus*. The "contorted face upside down" image called for in the script is recognizable, however. There are at least five dead and dying figures in the grotesque Bruegel work *Triumph of Death* displaying this precise position and visage. Gilliam and Jones likely blocked the shot to closely resemble the Bruegel work.

   huge pile of bodies on a swaying cart—(PSC) This is not unlike the scrap cart the Pythons used in Ep. 44, village residents bringing out their missiles, rocket launchers, bazookas, etc. (*MPFC: UC*, 2.200). There is also a dead cart in the Bruegel painting mentioned above. Driven by two emaciated figures, the cart is pulled by a cadaverous horse and loaded with skulls (center-left). The figure astride the horse rings a bell with his left hand. As the Pythons have eschewed the use of horses almost entirely, grotty laborers pull the plague cart through the mud.

   Just looking outside in early 1970s London offered the Pythons unforgettable images of uncollected garbage thanks to decupled, often overlapping union strikes. In 1969, a *Time* magazine contributor described the widespread effects of these wildcat strikes:

> Outside the glittering show windows of Mayfair clothing shops, garbage was stacked in six-foot piles. London's loverly squares and parks were turned into unofficial dumps. Grenadier Guards were summoned from their duties at Buckingham Palace to join Royal Engineers troops in clearing away heaps of rotting fruit and putrefying chicken carcasses that had lain uncollected for weeks in London's picturesque Petticoat Lane Market.
>
> As a result of a four-week-old nationwide strike of some 70,000 local government employees, mostly garbage men and sewage workers, large parts of Britain were mired in trash. Because many sewage process plants were closed down, millions of tons of raw sewage were being dumped into Britain's rivers. The Avon, the Thames and other waterways were so befouled that fish were dying by the thousands, their white bellies dotting the riverbanks. Public health officials were worried that seepage from the polluted rivers would contaminate drinking water, possibly causing an outbreak of the cholera epidemic that has already affected the Middle East, Russia and parts of Europe.
>
> The workers, who earn $33 to $42 weekly, demand a flat $6.60 raise. But municipal councils, backed up by Ted Heath's Tory government, have refused to give in to what would amount on the average to a 20% yearly increase. Such a settlement, which would be the highest in the present round of wage negotiations, would spur other unions to demand a similar increase.[1]

This brinkmanship would lead, by the end of the decade (1978–1979), to piles of unburied bodies in municipal cemeteries, but also to a new government led by Margaret Thatcher. See the entry "I can't take him like that" below for more on the squalor in Britain as a result of strike actions.

The plague cart is an obvious and frightening example of the plague's ravages, of course, which is likely why the Pythons focus on it. In period literature the cart and its contents are equally frightening, harbingers of ill-fortune and reminders of the fragility of life. In Alessandro Manzoni's *Betrothed* (published in 1827; set in the early 1630s and around the Milan plague events), the plague cart is employed as a reminder of pestilence's destructiveness, especially to those Milanese who were convinced some less fearsome disease or even a bit of witchcraft stalked the city, instead of the plague:

> There were still many who were not persuaded that it was the plague, because if it were, every one infected would die of it; whereas a few recovered. To dissipate every doubt, the Tribunal of Health made use of an expedient conformable to the necessity of the occasion; they made an address to the eyes, such as the spirit of the times suggested. On one of the days of the feast of Pentecost, the inhabitants of the city were accustomed to go to the burying ground of San Gregorio, beyond the eastern gate, in order to pray for the dead in the last plague. Turning the season of devotion into one of amusement, every one was attired in his best; on that day a whole family, among others, had died of the plague. At the hour in which the concourse was most numerous, the dead bodies of this family were, by order of the Tribunal of Health, drawn naked on a carriage towards this same burying ground; so that the crowd might behold for themselves the manifest traces, the hideous impress of the disease. A cry of alarm and horror arose wherever the car passed; their incredulity was at least shaken, but it is probable that the great concourse tended to spread the infection. (XXXI: 429)

With their filthy and savage village scene, the Pythons also employ "an address to the eyes" that shouts "plague."

ragged, dirty, emaciated WRETCHES—(PSC) Actually a bit brighter than the Bruegel source, since those in the business of transporting the dead or almost-dead in the Bruegel painting are all skeletons, representing Death itself. Looking closely at the painting, it's easy to see the time of humans fighting humans has passed; it is Death fighting to claim the living. Also different from the Bruegel image is the Pythons' inclusion of the noble Arthur (and less so, Patsy) in a position of detachment from the ordure-soaked surroundings. The nobleman (likely a king—he has a crown, scepter, and ermine-trimmed cloak) in the bottom left corner of the Bruegel is suffering as everyone else, his gold and silver scattered useless near him, and Death behind him with an hourglass, marking the king's diminishing time. The church is represented by the cardinal figure just to the right of the king figure—the cardinal appears to be dead already, the cadaver lifting his corpse to its ultimate destruction. In *Holy Grail* the church figures are several but set apart, including the monks who bash their foreheads and Brother Maynard's group at the Cave of Caerbannog. More on the churchmen and the church later.

The squalor in this scene is also clearly influenced by Pasolini's recent films, both *Canterbury Tales* and perhaps especially *The Decameron*, made in 1972 and 1971, respectively. In the latter a young rogue is swindled and falls into ordure; he is then humiliated as he wanders around town nearly naked and covered in excrement. This Italian New Wave retelling of the Boccaccio work (c. 1353) features mud, filth, excrement, sex, Church-bashing, death, plague, etc.—quite Pythonesque, actually. *Decameron* premiered in London at the Prince Charles in late February 1972, and before that in Europe at the Berlin Film Festival in June 1971. *Times* film critic J. R. Taylor reviewed *Decameron*, calling the experience a "splendour in the murk" (1 July 1971: 20). The significance of Pasolini's *Canterbury Tales* will be discussed below; see the entry for "*impoverished plague-ridden village.*"

wears a black hood and looks sinister—(PSC) The plague Cart Driver (Idle) doesn't look terribly "sinister" but his description—"slightly more prosperous, but only on the scale of complete and utter impoverishment"—fits; he isn't walking with a limp or scrounging in the filth. He's also not as dirty as most others. There are literary precedents for this more frightening description, however, including a mention in the story "Old Saint Paul's" in *Ainsworth's Magazine*, when a character shudders as he remembers "the hideous attendant on the dead-cart" (Ainsworth, 27). Also, the Cart Driver speaks, one of only three in the scene who do (the others being the Large Man [Cleese] and the "Body"). The Cart Driver pounds at a metallic triangle as he goes, announcing the cart's passing. The jangling bells of the plague carts were considered by some medical authorities of the period so terrifying that the sound alone could cause hearers to catch the disease (Totaro and Gilman, 139).

CART DRIVER: "Bring out your dead!"—The clarion call during plague outbreaks in the Middle Ages and even later. As the plague cart approached, the appearance of the grisly procession set a series of events in motion in English towns during the 1665 plague in London (which claimed upwards of one hundred thousand lives):

> Leonard . . . then shaped his course through the windings of Little Britain and entered Duck Lane. He was now in a quarter fearfully assailed by the pestilence. Most of the houses had the fatal sign upon their doors—a red cross, of a foot long, with the piteous words above it, "LORD HAVE MERCY UPON US!" in characters so legible that they could easily be distinguished by the moonlight. . . . Leonard quickened his pace. But he met with an unexpected and fearful interruption. Just as he reached the narrow passage leading from Duck Lane to Bartholomew Close, *he heard the ringing of a bell, followed by a hoarse voice, crying, "Bring out your dead—bring out your dead!"* he then perceived that a large, strangely-shaped cart stopped up the further end of the passage, and heard a window open, and a voice call out that all was ready . . . and a coffin was brought out and placed in the cart. (Ainsworth, 22–23; italics added)

Daniel Defoe's novelistic details of the plague in London in 1665 (*A Journal of the Plague Year*, 1722) includes a mention of a "grave-digger" or "bearer of the dead," though his take is quite a bit more salutary than Ainsworth or Manzoni above, or a Florentine account mentioned below (see "ninepence"). Defoe (1660–1731) describes one such individual, John Hayward, who as

> under-sexton [of St. Stephen, Coleman-street] was understood at that time grave-digger, and bearer of the dead. This man carried, or assisted to carry, all the dead to their graves, which were buried in that large parish, and who were carried in that form; and after that form of burying was stopped, *he went with the Deadcart and the Bell, to fetch the dead bodies from the houses where they lay, and fetched many of them out of the chambers and houses.* For the parish was, and is still, remarkable, particularly above all the parishes in London, for a great number of alleys and thoroughfares, very long, into which no carts could come, and *where they were obliged to go and fetch the bodies in a very long way. . . . Here they went with a kind of hand-barrow, and laid the dead bodies on it, and carried them out to the carts.* (123; italics added)

Defoe goes on to say that both Hayward and his wife handled the bodies and treated the afflicted without ever falling prey to the "Distemper," dying in their old age much later. The Pythons' plague cart is more of a flat hand-barrow, as well, pulled by grotty wretches.

impoverished plague-ridden village—(PSC) "*Et pestilentia venit.*" Literally, "And the pestilence came"—was how the Venerable Bede summed up the plague that had struck Britain some sixty-seven years earlier (Shrewsbury, 7). The plague in question for the Pythons would likely have been bubonic and/or pneumonic, though the possibility that this is a version of the later-named "Yellow Plague" detailed by Bede as occurring in 664—the "pestilence which carried off many"—works better for Arthur's actual supposed lifetime.[2] The pestilence was known eventually as the "Poore's Plague" in England since it struck so many peasants and working-class types, and earlier in Scotland it was noted that the plague attacked "especially the meaner sort and common people" (Kohn, 344). The plague had been fairly active in Europe since at least the sixth century, when it crushed what remained of the Roman Empire between 540 and 592 (Orent, 145–46). The later visitations of the disease in the fourteenth century would kill on a much more frightening scale, according to Orent: "In England the next epidemic came in 1360, which killed . . . 22.7 percent of the population. This was followed by the epidemic of 1369, killing 13.7 percent and again in 1375, with a mortality of 12.7 percent" (145). The heap of bodies on the plague cart in *Holy Grail*, then, isn't hyperbole.

And this setting is clearly a village, since the Pythons simply did not have a budget sufficient for either building an urban set or dressing an extant city to bring it back to medieval times. Most of these would have been extant outbuildings, and in ill-repair when they dressed them, not a village proper.[3] The "look" they seem to have been going for is the medieval "street village" layout discussed by Hoskins (drawing on Maitland's pioneering *Domesday Book and Beyond* [1897]), where an identifiable roadway passes between homes and shops ("The English Landscape," 4–6). Admittedly, since this is a "found" and then dressed set—meaning very little new construction would have occurred—the Pythons simply dressed what they found and then set up the camera to capture the necessary angles and images. And since the camera was almost always locked down—meaning attached to a tripod as opposed to a crane or dolly—smaller portions of sets could be dressed, keeping the production budget under control. The other significant *tenth*-century village type would have been the village "grouped around a large green or 'square,'" according to Hoskins and Maitland, but the Pythons clearly wanted to avoid this kind of orderliness in their filth-ridden version of medieval England. Hoskins notes that there were also "formless villages" offering building patterns with no discernible "relationship to each other or to any centre" (6). These are the kinds of details that Jones—who had read history at St. Edmund's, Oxford (1961)—likely brought to the production.

These "roughly nucleated" settlements "may be the result of medieval (or later) 'squatting' on the waste," whether the waste was wild lands, occasional pasturage, or the remains of an earlier established village (Hoskins, 1958, 6). This last seems potentially grubby enough to suit the Pythons. It's also certainly not a sub-Roman town; it lacks "the basic apparatus of civilized life," which would have included at the least "a water-supply, baths, temples, an amphitheatre and a forum or marketplace together with a basilica" (Sawyer, 60). It's more likely the Pythons knew what would have constituted a seventh-century British village with Roman influence, and then looked for a setting with *none* of those features. Fossier describes what a visitor might have encountered as he walked the streets of even a smallish urban neighborhood during the Middle Ages, in the back streets where

the "little people," the *popolo minuto*, the "common" folk, the *armen Leute*, the "poor," and the *simplices*—that is, all the others—lived, they would find narrow streets at best six to ten metres wide and, in northern Europe, rarely paved, with a central gutter to collect rainwater and household debris. . . . Debris and dirty water fell out of gabled windows into the middle of these running sewers. . . . Dogs and even wandering pigs took care of the debris . . . it was not until the fourteenth century that street sweepers (known as *éboueurs*) were hired to remove detritus. (237)

The cluttered squalor—seen as possibly a silly, Pythonesque overkill to underscore the darkness of these ages—wouldn't have been out of place in these same alleyways. In his audio commentary for the DVD and Blu-ray versions of the film some thirty years later, codirector Jones even comments that the Middle Ages depicted by the Pythons was perhaps dirtier than any reality, though historian Fossier's assessment of the period's filth and muddle depicts a medieval mess:

> The street was a place for casks, heaps of wood, obstructions created by those who dwelled in the houses, donkey carts or tip carts pushed by hand, a horseman or two, chains that were stretched from one side to the other at night in a vain hope of protection, feeble lights trembling in a niche in a façade, pollution, smells—all of which were covered by a blanket of useless regulations meant to reassure the repose and the comfort of the city dweller. (237)

And not only a mess, but a disorder made worse by irksome "regulations," just like the Cart Driver avers.

Outside of the crowded city, the state of the rural village—in times of plague, specifically—is described by Boccaccio in *The Decameron*, where he narrates the breaking down of all rules and structures of civilization as the pestilence rages on:

> [O]n no wise therefor was the surrounding country spared, wherein, (letting be the castles, which in their littleness were like unto the city,) throughout the scattered villages and in the fields, the poor and miserable husbandmen and their families, without succour of physician or aid of servitor, died, not like men, but well nigh like beasts, by the ways or in their tillages or about the houses, indifferently by day and night. By reason whereof, growing lax like the townsfolk in their manners and customs, they recked not of any thing or business of theirs. ("Day the First" 7; Payne translation)

The "impoverished plague-ridden village" setting and description here are also noteworthy for their cinematic provenance. For codirector and design maven Gilliam, the Zagreb animated film *Mask of the Red Death* (Stalter and Ranitovic, 1969) may have helped flesh out the dark-hued, messy world of the plague-ridden landscape. Michael Palin had written of seeing a portion of *Canterbury Tales*, the Pasolini film shot primarily in southeast England and based loosely on the Chaucer work, and remembers being very impressed by it (*Diaries*, 146). It's a look the Pythons wanted to capture for their own medieval film, to avoid, as Palin writes, the film becoming just "another *Carry On Arthur*" exercise (146).[4] The *Carry On* films/shows were silly, farcical comedies set amid history's great events and locales, including Pompeii, ancient Egypt, Henry VIII's court, and so on.[5] These silly films are often very funny, but quite precious, prone to bad puns, sexual stereotyping, and the overtly slapstick, and hence haven't aged terribly well. Apropos of this comparison, film critic Penelope Houston reviewed Pasolini's *Decameron*, and described the setting as a world where "[a]vid nuns and lewd priests sprout like weeds—the great, continuing *Carry On Convent* folklore of Catholic Europe, from which Henry VIII, perhaps rather mercifully, contrived to rescue us."[6] Just like *MPHG*, Pasolini's *Canterbury Tales* employs period costumes and settings, was shot in Britain, and uses actors that are generally not professionals—they are everyday folk cast for their medieval "look." (The most authentic performances, for Pasolini, came from the untrained.) *Canterbury Tales* premiered in London theaters in June 1973, appearing first at the Swiss Centre. The film was shot in England in fall 1971, and appeared at festivals thereafter, prior to its 1973 UK theatrical release.

But if there is a "look" that the Pythons were clearly influenced by for *MPHG*, it's the cold grimness of the eleventh-century period accomplished by director Roman Polanski for *Macbeth* (1971). Together with the work of Wilfrid Shingleton (production design), Fred Carter (art director), Bryan Graves (set decorator), and Anthony Mendleson (costume designer), Polanski employed windswept locations in Wales and the Northumberland region for his telling of the Scottish story (not unlike the Pythons choosing Scotland for their very English "Arthur King" story). Film critic Roger Ebert described the film—which he marveled was Polanski's own, and *not* an adaptation—in a familiar way: "Polanski places us in a visual universe of rain and mist, of gray dawns and clammy dusks, and there is menace in the sound of hoofbeats but no cheer in the cry of trumpets."[7] In particular, the visits Macbeth makes to the witches' hovel are visually replicated when Arthur and Bedevere meet the Blind Soothsayer—including the slate rock used to create jumbled piles that stand as crude dwellings. This reliance on a kind of historiophoty—representing history on screen in "*visual* images and filmic discourse," as opposed to historiography, representing history using "*verbal* images and written discourse" (italics added)—characterizes the Pythons' approach to a "real-looking" history that can then sound anachronistically modern (White, 1988, 1193).[8]

Both *Macbeth* and the Pythons' *And Now for Something Completely Different* were executive produced by Victor Lownes, of Playboy Productions, and when the Polanski film project was announced in 1970, London media pundits were highly skeptical of Hugh Hefner, *Playboy*, and a "pint-sized Polish Paganini" triune treating one of Shakespeare's hallowed characters.[9] During production the film was known wryly as *Macbuff*, thanks to hints that there would be salacious nudity in the finished film.[10] The Pythons and treasured English legend was likely a match no less suspect. Polanski would start shooting in November 1970 in Snowdonia[11] (northern Wales), hiring forty locals for regular parts, and five hundred more as extras.[12] *Macbeth* premiered at The Plaza cinema in London on 3 February 1972, and was greeted with generally strong reviews, many seeing it as, for example, Polanski's second-best film, after *Rosemary's Baby*.[13]

Finally, the sparse population of the plague-ridden village in *MPHG* is a result of the Pythons' tiny budget and need to keep costs and production outlays to a minimum, but is also historically more accurate, according to Shrewsbury. "Britons" of the seventh century, for example, tended to live in "small, separate communities, commonly situated on the banks of rivers. . . . [Such a community] varied in size according to its prosperity [and the] prowess of its elected chieftain." None were considered large, and "few contained more than one hundred adults" (9). The transition "from dispersed to nucleated settlements appears to have happened mainly in the ninth and tenth centuries," according to Sawyer, meaning the Pythons' choice of setting (AD 932) lands within the transitional phase (266). For the "impoverished" village described by the Pythons, then, the handful of filthy, violent, indolent villagers may be the entire regional population. Even as late as the fourteenth century it's estimated that only 12 percent of English people lived "in a town of some sort, even if it be a small town of just a hundred families," according to Ian Mortimer (12). In 1377 London could only boast about forty thousand inhabitants (almost half not living within the city walls), while towns like Nottingham to the north might have reached just twenty-four hundred people (11). The impoverished village depicted by the Pythons isn't a city, a market town, or even a village, really—it's too small for any of those appellations.[14]

a few starved mongrels—(PSC) Dogs were often culled out of villages and cities during plague outbreaks, and in the 1665 Great Plague "all cats and dogs in London were ordered to be killed, as they were esteemed capable of conveying the infection," leading to some forty thousand dogs and two hundred thousand cats eventually destroyed (Latham, 48). The

Bruegel painting mentioned earlier features one emaciated dog gorging on a dead infant, and another assisting Death as he hunts victims to ground.

The *Holy Grail* script also calls for a donkey or cow carcass to be on display, though none can be seen in the finished version of the film. This level of death and filth isn't necessarily overstated by the Python production design team—the growing population and its goods and waste were substantial, as indicated by Raban, discussing urban living in thirteenth-century England:

> [U]rban streets were crammed with those making a precarious living doing and selling whatever they could find. Even those who were relatively well established lived in squalid, overcrowded conditions. Pigs [or donkeys or cows] were the least of the hazards to be encountered in the gutter. Medieval towns were not healthy places for rich or poor. When we know about urban death rates in the later Middle Ages, they are horrifying. Monks entering Westminster Abbey or Canterbury Cathedral Priory had a life expectancy of less than thirty years for much of the fifteenth century. Mortality at that period was exceptionally high. The subjects of Edward I and Edward II [fl. 1272–1327] were spared epidemics on the scale that haunted society from the mid-fourteenth century. However, open sewers and the close proximity in which people lived no doubt ensured that many died prematurely. This did not deter people from flocking into towns. (61)

Bishop agrees, acknowledging bluntly: "The medieval streets were unquestionably foul" (*HBMA*, 177). And whether it was the slaughter of animals in butchers' shops, performed in the light of the storefront and the open street, the discarded bits tossed into the gutters, or the fishmonger's cull being thrown into the street for the poor to scuffle over, or the scavenging pigs and dogs and their leavings, or even the swarms of flies covering any dead tissue, it was a filthy scene, but there were few complaints registered, since this was city life in the period (177). These were the kinds of descriptions the Pythons used to build their version of the Middle Ages.[15]

woman is beating a cat against the wall—(PSC) Cats have been significant targets in the Pythons' bestiary since *Flying Circus*—they mope and have to be "cured" in Ep. 5, are thrown into the fire in Ep. 9, flung into buckets in Ep. 11, choke to death on lupins in Ep. 37, and double as a doorbell and get ironed flat in Ep. 45. Also, in the "Dennis the Peasant" scene the finished script called for the Old Woman to be looking for "the cat's front legs" as she digs around in the "lovely filth" (*MPHGB*, 8). The Pythons didn't create this animal animosity, either. A favorite Middle Ages game lays bare the time's fascination with (or inurement to) violence: "In village games, players with hands tied behind them competed to kill a cat nailed to a post by battering it to death with their heads, at the risk of cheeks ripped open or eyes scratched out by the frantic animal's claws. Trumpets enhanced the excitement" (Tuchman, 135). A similarly violent game was played by men armed with clubs, targeting a wild pig in an enclosure (135).

The repetitive image of an animal being banged about comes right from the Goons, of course. In the episode "World War One" (24 February 1958) a series of five individual quacks can be heard (as sound effects), followed by the voice of Major Bloodnok (Sellers): "Oh! Someone knocking on the door with a duck." And later in *MPHG* a character will be seen "fishing" by banging a large stick into a rivulet.[16]

Much of the village scene is so filthy and crowded it's difficult to see all the goings-on, but the cat-banging woman is obvious, as are the "two men fighting in the mud," the man "being hammered to death" (though two monks, not four nuns, wield the muckles there), and the general "impoverishment." Missing (or just not visible) are the various legs and limbs "dangling from the ceiling" and "legs sticking out of windows and doors," as well as the man eating mud and the man "falling into a well" (*MPHGB*, 4). It may be that the image of the man rooting in the basket (see below) has taken his place. The smoke in the scene also hides details, an abundant smoke that the cast comments on during interviews for the *BBC Film Night* documentary, and Cleese mentions in his audio commentary.

Many of these images are borrowed directly from the Bruegel painting *Triumph of Death* already mentioned, and already used in *MPFC* Ep. 15 (*MPFC: UC*, 1.242). Bruegel and his populated work—they make "a terrible bloody din"—are also mentioned by a character in Ep. 25, when characters from famous paintings go on strike for better conditions (1.373–74). Like the painting, the filmed scene is multilayered with actions and characters, demanding a careful viewing to appreciate the crowded world. Specific elements in the Bruegel painting that also appear in *MPHG* include a water-encircled castle under siege—not unlike the Grail Castle—along with: an overloaded death cart, Catherine wheels, smoke from multiple fires, a procession of monks, a pond where the dead and dying are being thrown, an unsoiled but imperiled king, figures being burned at the stake, squalor of all sorts, and so on. In the large and complicated Bruegel work, the artist depicts images of Death torturing humanity: death by stabbing, hanging, drowning; a death cart hauling skulls and being led by a skeleton with a bell; an impaled man crawling into a hollow tree; bodies and body parts all around; culminatively, images of death, destruction and disease can be found in every corner, in the foreground, middle ground, and disappearing into the farthest background.

Two such books that Gilliam may have used for his (non-Bruegel) pre-animation sketches (all examined in appendix A) include Charles de Tolnay's *Hieronymus Bosch* (1965) and Carl Linfert's *Hieronymous Bosch* (1971). Both are coffee table–size books, and both feature complete reproductions of Bosch's works as well as significant details from those works. See the many mentions of Bosch in the appendix A, Facing Pages section of this book. A possible sourcebook for Gilliam's Bruegel explorations may also have been another quarto-size book, *Our Bruegel*, edited by Bob Claessens and Jeanne Rousseau, published in 1969.

One particular image in the "Bring out your dead" scene—the man rooting in the basket—is presaged in the works of Bosch, specifically the central panels of *Hermit Saints* (or *The Altarpiece of the Hermits*) and *Last Judgment*, as well as a prominent Bosch-penned sketch page elsewhere. In the first two instances the character takes the precise position of the Python rooter (up to his waist in a woven basket; Linfert, 27, 89), and in the first he's at the feet of the kneeling Saint Jerome (Linfert, 27, 97). The third depicts a series of sketches titled *Witch and Beehive with Frolicking Figures*, the central figures being the man rooting in the basket (which is likely a beehive; Linfert, 27 and Tolnay, 321) as a man prepares to hit him from behind with a mandolin. This "rooting figure in a beehive" image is used by Bruegel, as well, and can be seen in *The Ass in the School* print and drawing (1556). Gilliam will sketch from Bosch[17] and the later Bruegel works significantly as he preps for the animated sequences. See the various entries in appendix A section for much more, and the index under "Bosch" and "Bruegel."

Two MEN are fighting in the mud . . . [a]nother MAN is on his hands and knees shoveling mud into his mouth—(PSC) These images of medieval depravity are nicely addressed by Bede in his *History of the English Church and People*, where they are characterized as Man's hubris inviting God's wrath, and which include wars, general suffering, and the visitation of a great plague ("*pestis*"):

> After [the Picts'] depredations had ceased, there was so great an abundance of corn in the island as had never been before known. With this affluence came an increase of luxury, followed by every kind of foul crime; in particular, cruelty and hatred of the truth and love of lying increased so that if anyone appeared to be milder than the rest and somewhat more inclined to the truth,

the rest, without consideration, rained execrations and missiles upon him as if he had been an enemy of Britain. Not only were laymen[18] guilty of these offences but even the Lord's own flock and their pastors. They cast off Christ's easy yoke and thrust their necks under the burden of drunkenness, hatred, quarrelling, strife, and envy and other similar crimes. In the meantime a virulent plague suddenly fell upon these corrupt people [*Interea subito corruptae mentis homines acerua pestis corripuit*] which quickly laid low so large a number that there were not enough people left alive to bury the dead. Yet those who survived could not be awakened from the spiritual death which their sins had brought upon them either by the death of their kinsmen or by fear of their own death. (49)

Bede then mentions the "very frequent attacks of the northern nations" as further punishment from an angry God. Those depicted wrestling, eating mud, clubbing, or just looking on, as well as the Cart Driver and the Man carrying the Body—all these seem to be included in Bede's condemnation, since none appear to acknowledge their culpability in relation to their degraded situations. The clean "king" who rides through isn't necessarily blessed by God as an acknowledgment of his righteousness—he's royalty (likely meaning wealthy, too), therefore clean.

Also, the fact that there are so many people in this scene is worth discussing. If, as seems to be the case, there are many dropping dead from effects of the plague, the other caitiff inhabitants of this village don't seem too concerned about their proximity to the dread disease. Even though the population of Britain could have been halved over the second fifty years of the fourteenth century, there doesn't appear to be significant evidence of widespread panic, according to McKisack:

[I]t is noteworthy that the plague of 1348–9 seems to have caused neither general panic, flight from the most badly affected areas, nor more than very temporary dislocation of the wool trade. For the most part, its effects were seen in intensification of tendencies already at work, rather than in cataclysmic dislocation of the existing order. (332–33)

It might not be until the so-called Peasants' Revolt of 1381 that the combination of a wretched economy; protracted, expensive continental wars; and further devastations/visitations of the plague produces a social cataclysm—though even then it is a short-lived rupture.

BODY: "I'm not dead"—The "Body" flung over the shoulder of the "Large Man" (Cleese) isn't dead, clearly, but if he's been exposed to the plague his chances of recovery are quite slim. This echoes a *Goon Show* moment from "The Moriarty Murder Mystery" episode, when another corpse-like man is presumed dead:

Willium (Sellers): 'Ello, 'ello.

Seagoon (Secombe): What is it, O'Shea?

O'Shea (Milligan): I never spoke sir! It must be the . . . the body!

Seagoon: What? Did you speak?

Willium: Yes, mate.

Seagoon: Now, play the game, don't mess about. Either you're a corpse or you're not!

Willium: I was, but I'm much better now, thank you. (20 January 1958)

One of the allegedly cursed peasants in the later "She's a witch" scene (played by Cleese) also "got better" after the witch (Connie Booth) had turned him into a newt. Earlier, in Ep. 22 of *Flying Circus*, Mary, Queen of Scots had also denied her own death, responding to "I

81

think she's dead" with "No, I'm not," followed immediately by more violence (*MPFC: UC*, 1.344–45).

Even more specific to the plague years is a story related by Defoe, in his *Journal of the Plague Year*, of an old man known only as "Piper"—he would play the pipes for food and drink—that reads as if the Pythons cut the scene almost whole from Defoe's cloth:

It is said that he was a blind Piper; but, as John [Hayward] told me, the fellow was not blind, but an ignorant weak poor man, and usually walked his rounds about ten o'clock at night, and went piping along from door to door, and people usually took him in at Public-houses where they knew him, and would give him a drink and victuals, and sometimes farthings; and he, in return, would pipe and sing, and talk simply, which diverted the people; and thus he lived. It was but a very bad time for this diversion, while things were as I have told; yet the poor fellow went about as usual, but was almost starved: and when anybody asked how he did, he would answer,—the Dead-cart had not taken him yet, but that they had promised to call for him next week.

It happened one night, that this poor fellow [ate too much, essentially] having not usually had a bellyful, or, perhaps, not a good while, was laid all along the top of a bulk or stall, and fast asleep, at a door, in the street near London-wall, towards Cripplegate; and that upon the same bulk or stall, the people of some house, in the alley of which the house was a corner, hearing a bell, which they always rung before the cart came, had laid a body really dead of the Plague just by him; thinking, too, that this poor fellow had been a dead body, as the other was, and laid there by some of his neighbours.

Accordingly, when John Hayward, with his bell and the cart, came along, finding two dead bodies lie upon the stall, they took them up with the instrument they used, and threw them into the cart, and all this whilst the Piper slept soundly.

From hence they passed along, and took in other dead bodies, till, as honest John Hayward told me, they almost buried him alive in the cart; yet all this while he slept soundly; at length the cart came to the place where the bodies were to be thrown into the ground . . . ; [when] they were ready to shoot out the melancholy load they had in it, as soon as the cart stopped, the fellow awaked, and struggled a little to get his head out from among the dead bodies, when raising himself up in the cart, he called out,—*"Hey! where am I?"*—This frighted the fellow that attended about the work; but after some pause, John Hayward, recovering himself said,—*"Lord bless us! there is somebody in the cart not quite dead!"* So another called to him and said—*"Who are you?"* The fellow answered—*"I am the poor Piper. Where am I?"* *"Where are you?"* says Hayward; *"why, you are in the Dead-cart, and we are going to bury you."* *"But I an't dead, though, am I?"* says the Piper, which made them laugh a little, though, as John said, they were heartily frighted at first; so they helped the poor fellow down, and he went about his business. (125–26)

CART DRIVER *receives some payment*—(PSC) If it's considered, for example, that during the early years of the fourteenth-century plague in Florence gravediggers weren't actually paid with money, then identification of Arthur as royalty via his clean clothes becomes more compelling. Giulia Calvi writes of the Florentine gravedigger's practice of accepting (or stealing) clothes from the bodies of those transported as part or all of their payment:

The relationship between gravediggers and cadavers' clothes had a long history, which helps to explain why these practices survived. Traditionally the gravediggers' work, which was considered easy, was paid not in currency but with clothes from the bodies they buried. Moreover, since gravediggers had to share their allowance with the officiating priests, selling these clothes provided them with an income. . . . The decimation wrought by the plague, however, compelled the guild consuls to change some of the organization's statutes, especially in order to end the commerce in [flea-infested[19]] clothes. (150)

By 1375, "the state issued an order mandating that 'all those commonly called gravediggers' must submit to the rules and regulations of the guild" (150). Idle's Cart Driver may have had city or guild[20] regulations to deal with, too, and the king's louse- and ordure-free clothing that clip-clopped on past him would certainly have merited a somewhat wistful comment.

CART DRIVER: "Ninepence"—This may be a coin worth nine pennies (or he hands him nine pennies separately), though the ninepence coin itself wouldn't appear until the mid-seventeenth century, even though a royal mint had been established in England as early as 886, and Anglo-Saxon and earlier Roman coins were well circulated (hordes of which continue to be discovered).[21] In the mid-fourteenth century, ninepence would have represented an extreme hardship for most, since the daily wage for a carpenter (a skilled tradesman) was only about four and a half pence, while an unskilled laborer might make just three, and a mason as much as six. Just to be a member of a city guild could cost as much as £3 (Mortimer, 101). Two to three days' wages for disposing of a family member's body has to be multiplied by nine for the Robinsons, of course. Further, a reaper (a grain field worker) in Somerset could expect to make about three pence per day in 1348, and after the devastations of the Great Pestilence he could earn as much as six and a half pence—meaning it comes to one to three days' work just to pay for body removal. Even after the first wave of the plague passed, the Statute of Labourers "established the maximum wage reapers could earn at 2 pence per day and set ceilings for craftsmen such as master carpenters, who were to be paid no more than 3 pence per day." These rates would have to be revised upward again after the next plague outbreak, to four pence per day for master carpenters.[22] That would still demand two-and-a-half days' work for the removal fee, a crushing burden.[23] To the monks at Bury St. Edmunds, however, thirteen pence must have seemed a pittance after King John (with his entire touring household) left them just such an amount after a prolonged and expensive sojourn at the abbey in 1199 (Bishop, *HBMA*, 143). That abbey's chronicler bemoans the king's "meanness."[24]

The bulk of the coins in proper circulation during the High Middle Ages would have been pennies, halfpennies, and farthings, or quarter-pennies (Mortimer, 96). If, however, this is Arthur's purported time, then the availability of coins becomes more problematic, according to Sawyer. "The historical darkness of the fifth and sixth centuries," Sawyer writes, "is lightened a little by other types of evidence," including surviving inscriptions and coins (19). (Inscriptions will be discussed later, in relation to Brother Maynard and the Cave.) Sawyer goes on to note that inscriptions and coins, "which have contributed so much to our understanding of the Roman period in Britain, are of less help for the post-Roman period" (19–20).[25] While monumental inscriptions stopped when the Romans stopped building monumentally (especially funerary monuments) in Britain, coins could continue to circulate and be minted, though the need to financially support the struggling empire on the Continent likely saw much Roman coinage leave the British Isles during the fourth century. The "material culture" of Britain became more British than Roman during the fifth century, according to Sawyer, including what counted as money: "Few coins were imported into Britain after the year 400, twenty years later the supply apparently ceased completely and by 430 coins were no longer used in Britain as currency."[26] Life went on, of course, even in the absence of explicit Roman influences, as Snyder (1999) confirms:

> After 410 a few coins circulated but mostly a barter economy prevailed. This should not imply primitive, however, for there is increasing evidence that the Britons carried on an active trade with Gaul, Spain, and the Eastern Mediterranean in the late fifth and sixth centuries, bringing in such exotic imports as olive oil, wine, fine table wares, and glass drinking vessels.[27]

SCENE FOUR

In *An Age of Tyrants* (1998), Snyder admits that coins clearly continued to be used in Britain for trade through the fifth century and beyond, even after minting ceased, intermixed with bartering, yielding a "hotchpotch" coinage, especially in the western regions (133–36). So if this scene of plague *is* Arthur's putative lifetime[28] (and it almost never is, as far as the film is concerned), *and* the setting is in the greater southeast (another surmising), the Cart Driver would most likely be accepting something other than coins for his payment. But the fact that this is a Python world—where newspapers and popular culture tidbits are gleaned into the mélange of their sketches and filmic mise-en-scène—means "ninepence" is just as likely to be a quipped, purposeful anachronism, given, for instance, that the cost of the weekly edition of the *Times Literary Supplement* in the late 1960s was ubiquitously advertised as "On sale today: ninepence."[29]

During later times of plague in Britain and on the Continent, there was generally a charge for the removal of a dead body, including possessions of the deceased or a simple monetary fee, though that fee could fluctuate as conditions worsened. From Cunningham's *The Bubonic Plague*:

> With so many dead, the authorities in Florence recruited men from the country and the poorer classes to dispose of the bodies. Soon gangs of shovel-wielding grave diggers known as the *becchini* stalked the streets. The becchini demanded high wages to bury loved ones in the cemeteries of their local churches. Often, though, they tossed the bodies into the nearest graveyard. With the high mortality rate, there were fewer people working in jobs such as grave digging, so the becchini could charge more for their services despite their disrespectful behavior. (47)

And from Defoe's *A Journal of the Plague Year*, where the cart men were grimly dependable and opportunistic:

> On the other hand, it is observable that though at first the people would stop as they went along and call to the neighbours to come out on such an occasion [when someone died on the street], yet afterward no notice was taken of them; but that if at any time we found a corpse lying, go across the way and not come near it; or, if in a narrow lane or passage, go back again and seek some other way to go on the business we were upon; and in those cases the corpse was always left till the officers had notice to come and take them away, or till night, when the bearers attending the dead-cart would take them up and carry them away. Nor did those undaunted creatures who performed these offices fail to search their pockets, and sometimes strip off their clothes if they were well dressed, as sometimes they were, and carry off what they could get. (76)

In the Pythons' world, however, the grave digger–type is more an efficient, likely guild-associated functionary, willing to engage in pleasant if perfunctory conversation, and to look the other way in regard to "regulations" when the proper coinage crosses his palm.

LARGE MAN: "He will be soon. He's very ill"—Adapted from several *Flying Circus* and *Goon Show* episodes. In Ep. 3, the witness in the box isn't dead, but "he's not at all well" (though he dies moments later); in Ep. 19, a policeman (Chapman) carries in a Dead Indian (Ian Davidson) who's not quite dead, just dizzy from a "faulty cooker"; and in "Salvation Fuzz" the rabbit fish ("It's got fins") being served is *likely* dead, since it was "coughing up blood" the night before. The clearest precursor of the trope is in Ep. 27, where Mrs. Premise (Cleese) and Mrs. Conclusion (Chapman) talk about a pet cat:

Mrs Conclusion: Busy day?

Mrs Premise: Busy! I've just spend four hours burying the cat.

Mrs. Conclusion: *Four hours* to bury a cat?

Mrs Premise: Yes! It wouldn't keep still, wriggling about howling its head off.

Mrs Conclusion: Oh—it wasn't dead then?

Mrs Premise: Well, no, no, but it's not at all a well cat. (*JTW*, 2.53–54).

Later, Launcelot's horse Concorde is evidently "not quite dead," while Princess Lucky's father, though injured, also isn't "quite dead," and may even recover—until he's killed. The Pythons likely borrowed the theme from The Goons, a particularly rich mine for the troupe. In "The White Box of Great Bardfield" (15 March 1955), Minnie (Milligan) tells Henry (Sellers): "This tiger's not well buddy. He's got flu."

LARGE MAN: " . . . stone dead . . . "—Anachronistic, yes, but actually rather an old phrase, dating back to at least the late thirteenth century, according to the *OED*. Contemporary accounts of various plagues for the fourteenth through seventeenth centuries offer many examples of nearly dead plague victims being helped along toward death ("murthered") by impatient or just properly motivated gravediggers, nurses, attendants, and the like (Defoe 80).

CART DRIVER: "I can't take him like that. It's against regulations"—It may seem silly at a time like this, but regulations certainly did exist in the handling of plague victims. It is also not certain whether the "regulations" the Cart Driver cites are those of the village or town he lives in, or from one of the many extant guilds of the medieval period, one representing all cartage or public health workers, for example. There were guilds for all manner of trades, especially in the larger cities, according to Poole:

> The gild was not, as has been sometimes said, a ring of leading merchants, at least not in its early days. On the contrary, it cast its net astonishingly wide, and embraced traders and artisans, rich and poor, great and small. The gild roles of Leicester, which date from 1196, include a remarkable variety of trades and professions such as weaver, dyer, wool-comber, shearman, tailor, hosier, tanner, leather-worker, shoe-maker, saddler, parchment-maker, soap-maker, leech, preacher, mercer, goldsmith, farrier, turner, cooper, potter, miller, baker, cook, butcher, waterman, mason, carpenter, plumber, porter, carter and ostler. It was obviously, therefore, not exclusive but popular in character, and admitted any honest tradesman (or woman, for that matter) who could pay the entrance fees and could find sureties. (*DBMC*, 74–75)

"Grave-digger" or "Cart-driver" would seem to fit into that list rather easily.[30] Poole notes that even "the lepers tried to imitate their more fortunate contemporaries by forming themselves into a gild" (74). Maybe our Cart Driver won't be admitted since he clearly works "off the books" when the situation requires it.

Victims and their families in the Edinburgh area were often isolated or quarantined (in some cases, comprising entire villages), houses were cleaned or even destroyed after deaths or infections, graves had to be a certain depth, corpses had to be handled properly, etc., and most local authorities imposed stiff penalties for those who either broke the rules or would brook such misprision, including "perpetual banishment, branding, and even death" (Kohn, 93).

There is a particularly chilling (and likely sensationalized) exchange in *Ainsworth's Magazine* between a "black-cloak" (a plague cart driver), whose "features [were] hideous, and stamped with . . . a revolting expression," and a potential customer. "Mother Malmayns" has screamed from her window for the coffin-maker, the dead-cart has stopped, and the woman demands that "old Mike Norborough" be taken away. Turns out old Mike was quite the miser, and the dead-cart driver wonders not only if he's actually dead, but whether there's any money for his final services. The woman tells him he can have anything in the miser's house, but the black-cloak gives it a miss, saying there are plenty of other paying customers, and he wants to get back home to supper anyway. With an "atrocious laugh" the dead-cart driver moves on (Ainsworth, 23).

Vaulting into the contemporary world, the Cart Driver's riposte about "regulations" is also clearly connected to the contemporary and very active labor union movement of pre-Thatcherite Britain. Strike activity during the late Wilson (1968–1969), Heath (1970–1974), and then Wilson/Callaghan (1974–1979) administrations effectively gummed up the gears, with work-to-rule slowdowns and then work stoppages—coal miners, dock, utility, and postal workers, et al.—leading to a scarcity of many goods, reductions in government and public services, and drastically reduced power deliveries (Marr, 308–11, 324–26). Palin writes of the brown- and even blackouts much of the country endured in February 1972, for example (*Diaries*, 69–74). Power shortages were experienced by steel, textile and paper mills, and workers were soon made redundant by the thousands (*Times* 8 February 1972: 15), and then millions (29 February 1972: 17). Power was curtailed to hundreds of hospitals and metropolitan potable water pumps just six days later.[31] By Christmas 1973, things looked even bleaker. Just days before the start of the three-day workweek, the Department of Employment "estimated that 400,000 workers were laid off . . . in England and Wales" on 27 December alone—yes, two days after Christmas—and many more redundancies were anticipated in the coming year.[32] By January 1974, unemployment had reached almost 2.3 million, including about 1.5 million who'd registered unemployed after the implementation of the three-day workweek.[33]

More recently, *Independent* columnist John Rentoul, while writing about the release of Pink Floyd's bestselling album *Dark Side of the Moon*, looks back to 1973, noting the stultifying effects of these work-to-rule inactions:

> They were dark days. No, really, they were dark. The year before, in February 1972, as the National Union of Mineworkers' strike started to bite, we had power cuts, on a rota, lasting from six to nine hours a day between 7am and midnight. Candles and cold food. That was fun while it lasted. Soon after *The Dark Side of the Moon* was released, the NUM began a "work-to-rule." For readers to whom this phrase means as much as "enfeoffment" or "saccage and soccage," this was a way of striking without actually going on strike, which gave the Government more time to plan for what would happen when the coal stocks ran out. So in December 1973 Edward Heath, the Prime Minister, announced that, from 1 January 1974, the country would work a three-day week.[34]

The Pythons have poked fun at organized labor before, sending Welsh coal miners on strike until archaic architectural terms are defined (*MPFC*, Ep. 26), and staffing picket lines with occupants of famous paintings striking for "a little bit of bloody consultation" (Ep. 25). The very powerful demander of "consultation," the Trades Union Congress, had become the face of this labor unrest, and was whispered as "a state within a state . . . putting itself above the government in deciding what a government could and could not do" (Marr, 309). Historian Tony Judt is even more on-the-nose: "Trade unions—and especially their local representatives, the factory shop stewards—were more powerful than ever before or since. Strikes—a symptom of labor militancy and incompetent management alike—were endemic to post-war British industrial life" (358).[35] The Cart Driver, locally representing his fellow plague cart comrades (there are three handling the cart), manages to fulfill his duties, collect his monies, and "assist" an unwilling customer onto the cart with the help of an off-the-books cudgeling—then it's off to the Robinsons. Significantly, it's the Large Man's "do us a favour" that seals the deal—it's one workingman to another here, and the "work-to-rule" slowdown is avoided. More on the labor issue below, when Dennis stands up to Arthur.

LARGE MAN: "Don't be such a baby"—A too-early use of this phrase; the *OED* dates this use of "baby" to the early seventeenth century.

LARGE MAN: "Well, can you hang around a couple of minutes. He won't be long"—The times when plague "dead-carts" were needed in large cities like London coincided with surges in plague infections and deaths, of course, and cart drivers found themselves inundated with customers. Waiting at one house meant disease-ridden corpses grew ever-putrid else-where in the parish (often the bodies were piled in the streets), so long waits weren't frequent, according to Defoe's *Journal*:

[S]oon after, as the fellow said, he stopped the Dead-cart, and then knocked again, but nobody answered: he continued knocking, and the bellman called out several times—*"Bring out your Dead!"*—but nobody answered, till the man that drove the cart being called to other houses, would stay no longer, and drove away. (92)

CART DRIVER: "I promised I'd be at the Robinsons'. They've lost nine today"—This line is delivered a bit differently in the finished film, though not significantly. The name will be discussed in a moment, but this numbering of the recently deceased appears in the work of many chroniclers of the period—and often from monastic settings—including the Rochester monk William of Dene[36] (fl. 1317–1354):

In this year [1349], a plague of a kind which had never been met with before ravaged our land of England. The Bishop of Rochester, who maintained only a small household, lost four priests, five esquires, ten attendants, seven young clerics and six pages, so that nobody was left to serve him in any capacity. At Malling he consecrated two abbesses. Both died almost immediately, leaving only four established nuns and four novices. . . . To our great grief, the plague carried off so vast a multitude of people of both sexes that nobody could be found who would bear the corpses to the grave. (Rowley, 20–21)

"Robinson" is likely just a name pulled out of the air, especially since it is and has been a popular surname in Britain for many years. Prior to 1400, though, the chances of finding a common or poor family with a shared surname in Britain might have presented a challenge, even though the patronymic surname began to become "fixed" in much of Britain during the twelfth century (Bishop, *HBMA*, 229). It wasn't until the depredations of the Great Plague that "peasant" folk moved around Britain with any real frequency, seeking work and homes and even the company of other people as the population thinned (Mortimer, 86–87). Just being known as "Dennis" would have sufficed if that Dennis remained in one small village or even region for his life; moving to the larger centers of population would require, eventually, a surname to differentiate the Dennises.[37]

The Pythons have more pointedly jabbed at specific Robinsons in the past, though. In *MPFC*, Ep. 32, a picture of Robert Robinson (1927–2011) is used during the "Tory Housewives Clean-Up Campaign" film. This Robinson was an erudite and loquacious BBC writer and presenter, who between 1971 and 1974 could be heard most mornings on the Radio 4 show *Today*. Robinson appeared on *BBC 3* (1965–1966), *Points of View* (1961–1968), and the long-running *Call My Bluff* (1967–1988). He may have been more in the public eye at this time owing to his "retirement" from the radio show in April 1974, when, Robinson said, it became "too political."[38] Robinson's name and reputation were clearly known and referenced, as in a newspaper review of Robinson's new BBC 1 radio show—*The Book Programme*—where the columnist lamented the meager forty minutes given over to literary discussion: "It was all over before you could say 'Robert Robinson.'"[39] The *Times* would call him "ingratiatingly smug" in its broadcast announcement for *Ask the Family*;[40] and a clock radio company was even using Robinson's appearances on early morning radio to sell its product: "WAKE UP to the sound of Dittersdorf, Terry Wogan, or Robert Robinson with a digital clock radio from Dixons."[41] (Austrian classical composer Dittersdorf's music could be heard on BBC Proms, and Wogan was a fellow BBC radio and television presenter.) Robinson's elegist might have hit the nail on the head, though, when, describing Robinson's radio hosting challenges in the "dark times" of early 1970s, he reminded viewers and listeners that "[o]n dreary news days, the programme team dubbed Robinson and Timpson the Brothers Grimm as they waded through *a gloomy 1970s swampland of strikes, a decaying economy and plummeting pound*."[42] This Robinson, then, fits very well into the plague-devastated England posited by the Pythons, where nine Robinsons could die in a day.

For more on Robert Robinson and why the Pythons included several other Robinsons in their *Flying Circus* work, see *MPFC: UC*, 2.87, 118, 192. There is also a terrific obituary written for Robert Robinson in the *Telegraph*, dated 14 August 2011.

LARGE MAN: "Isn't there anything you could do?"—The answer during various plagues was, of course, yes. Defoe recounts serendipitous deaths ("hastening their end") by "Nurses and Watchmen" during London's plague, where those paid to care for or just guard the homes of the infected (and perhaps even recovering) simply starved or smothered their charges, called the Dead-cart, and moved on to their next employment (115–16).

. . . *all in the village fall to their knees, touching forelocks, etc.*—(PSC) Actually most in the village show little obeisance at all, and only the Cart Driver and Large Man seem to pay real attention to Arthur and Patsy. (Several in the background kneel, but it's not at all clear they're "touching forelocks" as opposed to just collapsing into the mud.) It could have been that this scene worked better with the clean king figure going nearly unnoticed, especially since Arthur struggles throughout the film to convince anyone that he is significant at all.

CART DRIVER: "I dunno. But they're so clean"—(PSC) This was the Cart Driver's response in the final draft of the script, and was ad-libbed at some point into "I dunno. He hasn't got shit all over him" (*MPHGB*, 6). Rather than cleanliness being next to Godliness, Andrew Dickson White notes, history of the period proves often that "filthiness was akin to holiness":

> The main cause of this immense sacrifice of life is now known to have been the want of hygienic precaution, both in the Eastern centres, where various plagues were developed, and in the European towns through which they spread. And here certain theological reasonings came in to resist the evolution of a proper sanitary theory. Out of the Orient had been poured into the thinking of western Europe the theological idea that the abasement of man adds to the glory of God; that indignity to the body may secure salvation to the soul; hence, that cleanliness betokens pride and filthiness humility. Living in filth was regarded by great numbers of holy men, who set an example to the Church and to society, as an evidence of sanctity. St. Jerome and the Breviary of the Roman Church dwell with unction on the fact that St. Hilarion lived his whole life long in utter physical uncleanliness; St. Athanasius glorifies St. Anthony because he had never washed his feet; St. Abraham's most striking evidence of holiness was that for fifty years he washed neither his hands nor his feet; St. Sylvia never washed any part of her body save her fingers; St. Euphraxia belonged to a convent in which the nuns religiously abstained from bathing. St. Mary of Egypt was eminent for filthiness; St. Simeon Stylites was in this respect unspeakable—the least that can be said is, that he lived in ordure and stench intolerable to his visitors. The *Lives of the Saints* dwell with complacency on the statement that, when sundry Eastern monks showed a disposition to wash themselves, the Almighty manifested his displeasure by drying up a neighbouring stream until the bath which it had supplied was destroyed. (A. D. White, ch. 14)

The sanitation, potable (culinary) water, and public bath systems that the Romans had been building in England since the year 43 fell into disrepair in the fifth century and beyond—mostly due to lack of proper maintenance—with much of the building material pilfered over time by locals for newer, smaller, and less technologically up-to-date structures. Britons in any of the periods either depicted or considered by the Pythons for their Arthurian tale (fifth to sixth centuries, tenth, twelfth, or thirteenth centuries) would have lived in what's known as Sub-Roman Britain; and yes, it's as unflattering as it sounds. Here fresh running water systems had failed, public baths (like those at Aquae Sulis [Bath] and Welwyn) fell into disuse as the Church frowned more and more on display of the naked body and especially the intermingling of the sexes, and sewage disposal systems filled up and streets became sewage and offal drainages into nearby streams and rivers. Personal hygiene changed considerably as the pleasures provided by the Roman Empire's infrastructure disappeared, and the realities of eking out a living—perhaps as a single family or handful of families in a hardscrabble village—forced choices leading to survival as opposed to personal comfort or cleanliness. It wouldn't be until Henry VIII's reign that England's sewage problem began to be addressed officially (meaning enforceable and enforced standards and regulations), until the utter destruction of the Great Fire in 1666 before water delivery systems to the capital were seriously thought out and renovated, and it was the 1860s before sewage disposal became fully and centrally modernized in London (see Hansen; also Sabine, 1934).

CART DRIVER: "He hasn't got shit all over him"[43]—First, "shit" is one of the words *not* allowed on BBC television during the original run of *MPFC*, so the Pythons used replacements including "*merde*" (Ep. 33) and "dung" (Ep. 29). Words like "sod," "masturbation," and even "bunt" (a stand-in for "cunt") were also excised from the series.[44] Also, after seeing an early edit of *MPHG* (at a screening in Twickenham), the British Board of Film Classification (BBFC) representative Tony Kerpel recommended the film "[l]ose as many shits as possible" to get an "A" classification (meaning open to virtually all audiences). A photostat of the letter is included in the introductory material of *MPHGB*. Kerpel[45] did ask for the removal of "Jesus Christ," "oral sex," "fuck off," and the French taunts referring to farting and testicles being made into castanets—if the Pythons wanted to be *assured* of avoiding the "AA" rating. (With a handful of changes the film was able to run with an "A" rating.) Most of the film's references to filth and feces remained.[46]

It's not an exaggeration to note that the Pythons exhibit something of a middle school fascination with bodily fluids and secretions of all kinds—a pre-fifth-form version of the four humors, essentially. In *Flying Circus* they spend significant time referencing saliva, urine, vomit, mucous, fecal matter and bowel movements, as well as buckets and geysers of blood (*MPFC: UC*, 1.160). Characters in this carnivalesque and grotty world (see Ellen Bishop[47]) can cough up blood (Ep. 29, "Salvation Fuzz"), spew aortal geysers of blood (Ep. 33, "Sam Peckinpah's *Salad Days*"), or die dramatically with blood arcing gracefully, even poetically from the chest (Ep. 23, "*Scott of the Sahara*"). In this world of corporeality one can gob at great works of art (Ep. 4, "Art Gallery"), smell the pong at Victorian poetry readings (Ep. 41, "Es schmecken wie ein Scheisshauss!"), take delivery of dung and nearly dead Indians (Ep. 19, "Dead Indian"), and meet families like the Gits who don't exist except to revel in "warm pus" and "vomit and catarrh" (Ep. 21, "Mr. and Mrs. Git"). By Episode 45, the series' final episode, wiping "the cat's doo" on the bread, toxic flatulence, diarrhea ("plop plops"), and monumental bowel movements define the Garibaldi and Jodrell families, both vying for the "Most Awful Family in Britain" award. Most of these situations had nothing to do with medieval times, either, meaning the Pythons were simply fascinated by excremental humor (or "fundamental" humor—humor of the lower parts of the body).[48] In this they were neatly following in the footsteps of their literary predecessors Jonson, Voltaire, Rochester, Swift, Dryden, Smollett, Hogarth, et al., not to mention a number of New Wave filmmakers, including Pasolini, Polanski, Nagisa Oshima (1932–2013), and Walerian Borowczyk.[49] In Pasolini's *Decameron*, a randy young man is tricked into hiding in a cesspool, and ends up both shamed and covered in sewage. This "cesspool" moment is revisited twice in *Holy Grail*—here, where the absence of filth is the sure way to know a king, and in the last castle sequence, where Arthur is drenched in something vile and smelly poured from the castle walls.

Artist and cartoonist Gerald Scarfe (b. 1936) could also be added to this list. Scarfe's scathing pen and ink attacked many of the same targets the Pythons tilted at (Enoch Powell, de Gaulle, the Pope, Nixon), and reveled, too, in the most *fundamental* of humor, according to TV critic Julian Critchley, reviewing Scarfe's *One Pair of Eyes*, airing on BBC 2 in August 1968:

> It was a cry of despair, an excremental view of the human condition, the private nightmare of someone who has looked into the pit and cannot forget what he has seen. It was terrifying, and made with such skill . . . [his drawings] were all corroded by what he sees as a natural wickedness, by the burden of original sin. No one gets the benefit of the doubt from Scarfe.[50]

The sentries on the wall, Dennis and his mother, the French taunters, and so on will also give no consideration, no slack, to Arthur or his quest. Everything is corroded; all is corrupt. For more on Scarfe and his relation to the Pythons see the author's *MPFC: UC*.

It may well be that an Arthur *not* covered in ordure represents an odd sumptuary law moment, as well. Because Arthur is clothed differently, moves differently (he's passing through on a "horse" and with a retinue), and he also isn't covered in feces (presumably, everyone else in such a medieval village would or should be), he then *must be* a king. This also makes sense when considering the approved "social spaces" that the peasant and king, the poor and rich could and did inhabit, especially during this time of pestilence, according to Giulia Calvi in *Histories of a Plague Year*:

> Social behavior, therefore, was displayed within a clearly defined spatial opposition: on one side, under normal circumstances, people fell ill and died in enclosed spaces. Within the city, this spatial opposition alluded to the opposition of social classes. The rich and the noble, as well as the medical personnel administering charity and medicine, operated in the open spaces. The working classes, the poor, and suspected victims of the plague remained in the closed spaces. Within this social grammar, simplified and articulated in a binary structure, infractions were instantaneously evident. (152)

So the working classes are living and dying indoors, hence the Cart Driver's call of "Bring out your dead!" The noble Arthur—both rich, likely, and clean—moves through the devastation without hesitation (he and Patsy don't seem to even notice the death and squalor around them). It's been reported, for example, that later kings of the Britons could be similarly detached from the pestilential suffering: "In the same year the Black Death first appeared in England [1348], and raged until 1349 . . . the horrors which it wrought hardly checked the magnificent revels of Edward's court."[51] The peripatetic Arthur and Patsy are immediately noticed by the Large Man and the Cart Driver, peasants both, and just as quickly identified, Arthur's betraying "infraction" being cleanliness and obvious health. "Outbreaks of plague, or even threats of one," writes George Kohn in the *Encyclopedia of Plague and Pestilence*,

> always accentuated the division between rich and poor. Wealthy citizens, whose lives were not as drastically affected by a temporary cessation of commercial activity, were able to flee a town easily, whereas those without resources were usually trapped within an infected community. (373)

In the tiny village Arthur and Patsy move through there is very nearly mayhem, with death and a trip on the dead cart perhaps the only way out of town. Surprisingly, the plague references in the film will surcease after this scene—Arthur and Patsy manage to move away from the *pestilentia* rather effectively, as does the film's narrative.

And, lastly, if there are Arthur and Patsy avatar-figures in the Bruegel painting the Pythons referenced, then they are likely in the bottom right quadrant. The well-dressed young man is staring, horrified, at the carnage before him, his sword partly unsheathed, as if he's just realized the futility of wielding weapons (or courage or *noblesse oblige*) in the face of such irreversible devastation. At his feet, a cowardly squire-type scurries beneath a draped table, hoping to hide from the hellish judgment. These are two of the very few characters in the painting not yet either dead or engaged by Death's minions in a final struggle.

Notes

1. "Wildcats on the Loose," *Time* (3 October 1969).

2. There are disagreements, however. That epidemic, according to Shrewsbury, was likely smallpox (45), and it reportedly killed a huge proportion of those in monastic pursuits—those who studied, wrote, and published—ushering in the "Dark Ages." Maddicott, however, seems certain it was actually bubonic plague (45), as are many others.

3. Jones mentions these sets briefly in his audio commentaries on the DVD and Blu-ray editions of the film.

4. They did not, however, fall prey to all of *Canterbury Tales*'s charms as realized by the iconoclastic Pasolini. David Robinson's review of the film praises the film's backdoor ingenuity: "[T]he film uses actual locations, selecting with no scholarship about period, but with a flair which gives exciting new aspects to familiar places" (*Times*, "Fox Into Jackal," 15 January 1973: 9). The Pythons, of course, did their homework to create as believable a medieval setting as possible, given their budget restrictions. The review also mentions *Canterbury Tales*'s "Keystone Kops" sequence in "The Cook's Tale," bringing the medieval and the modern into the same shot, which the Pythons will employ as police get closer and closer to the questing knights.

5. See the index in *MPFC: UC* under "*Carry On* films" for more discussion of this series, as well as its significant influences—like the Goons and Benny Hill—on *Flying Circus* and the Pythons.

6. *Times*, 25 February 1972: 11.

7. Roger Ebert, "*Macbeth*," 1 January 1971.

8. Another possible reference for the Pythons is Borowczyk's *Blanche* (1971), a medieval farce and love story. The film features accurate period costuming and prop details, including, like *MPHG*, musicians playing period instruments, period dancing, lonely castles and dark passageways, a king's visit to a "silly" castle, as well as a one-on-one combat in a forested clearing—one knight in a helmet and challenging, the other trying to defuse the situation, etc. The entire film plays quite familiar. *Blanche* debuted at Cannes in 1971, and then appeared in London-area cinemas in May 1973—where it was described as "Bizarre and Beautiful. Humorous yet horrifying"—opening to very strong reviews (*Times*, 13 October 1973: 10).

9. *Times*, 22 August 1970: 10.

10. PHS, "*The Times* Diary," 26 October 1971: 12. There is *some* nudity in the film. The witches are seen naked at one point, and Lady Macbeth (Francesca Annis) wanders across a room nude, as well. From Normand Berlin: "Nudity in a young woman (whether witch or Lady Macbeth) is pleasing to the eye: nudity in old hags, with breasts hanging and shapes distorted, is offensive, grotesque, disgusting" (295–96). The nudity in *Macbeth* doesn't seem nearly as gratuitous, ultimately, as the violence.

11. Coincidentally, Snowdonia is where Jones and Julian Doyle would shoot the trailer for *MPHG*, according to Doyle's deposition. Doyle remembers they chose northern Wales so Jones could visit his father on the same trip (5 December 2013 e-mail correspondence). Jones was raised in Colwyn Bay, Wales.

12. "Thousands Flock for Parts in Macbeth Film," *Times*, 2 November 1970: 3.

13. J. R. Taylor, "Polanski's Success: Keeping Shakespeare in His Place," *Times*, 4 February 1972: 9.

14. In 1377 rural settlement density across England ranged from a high of seventy-three total persons per square mile (in Bedfordshire) all the way down to just thirteen per square mile in Cumberland, with the overall favorability of the land often being a deciding population factor (Mortimer, 33). Poorer soils, inadequate drainage, and challenging transportation meant fewer people tried to live in some areas, mostly in the north and west. The south and east of England—with better soils and improved roadways—supported denser populations.

15. *HBMA* was published in 1968.

16. This "fishing" man is an extra who happened to bring rental vehicles to the set. See the entry "MIX THROUGH . . . " in scene 13, "Taunting by Frenchman," for more.

17. Another odd but fitting appearance of Bosch can be found in the 1967 James Bond spoof *Casino Royale*, codirected by Python acquaintance Joe McGrath. In the bedroom sequence featuring Brigitte Bardot and Peter Sellers, a black-and-white wallpaper image copied from the center panel of Bosch's *Garden of Earthly Delights* covers a good portion of the visible walls. See the "Castle Anthrax" section below for more on this film's influence on the Pythons, first in *MPFC*, then *MPHG*.

18. In other translations this word (*saeculares*) is translated as "pagans," not "laymen."

19. Very recent DNA work on skeletons discovered during London's Crossrail dig suggest it was pneumonic not bubonic plague that swept through England 1348–1350. Fleas infected with *Y. pestis*, hitchhiking on rats and spreading bubonic plague from household to household had been the lesson taught for many years. New information points toward a much faster disease spread; the infecteds' coughing seems to have broadcast the pneumonic version effectively and rapidly. See Thorpe's "Black Death Was Not Spread by Rat Fleas," in the *Observer*, 29 March 2014.

20. See Morris Bishop's discussion of the strength and organization of the medieval guilds, and their penetration into virtually every city-based trade in the thirteenth and fourteenth centuries (*HBMA*, 177–78). The officious Cart Driver acts the guild member, certainly, but can "look the other way" when regulations need to be circumvented, profitably.

21. Mortimer notes that the penny was a popular coin, and "[b]etween Edward I's great recoinage of 1279 and the deposition of Richard II (1399) there are about 160 varying sorts of penny struck . . . [and] there are several mints in operation at once" (97).

22. Grant et al., *History of Britain and Ireland*, 103.

23. By way of comparison, the 1377 poll tax assessed virtually everyone over the age of fourteen, for example, and was set at four pence (or one groat) for even the poorest laborer (*HBI*, 104).

24. (The price for a serving of albatross in Ep. 13 of *MPFC* is also ninepence.) See also "Houses of Benedictine Monks: Abbey of Bury St. Edmunds," at British History Online.

25. For more on coins see Sawyer, 213–19.

26. See also J. P. C. Kent, "From Roman Britain to Saxon England," in *Anglo-Saxon Coins*, ed. R. H. M. Dolley (London, 1961), 1–22.

27. From an unpaginated online version of "The Age of Arthur," *The Heroic Age* 1 (Spring/Summer 1999). http://www.heroicage.org/issues/1/hatoc.htm

28. Which very nearly corresponds with the so-called Justinian Plague of 541–542.

29. *Times*, 16 March 1967: 10. The *Times Educational Supplement* was also priced at ninepence.

30. There's no indication whether the Cart Driver's load would be assessed the standard toll—the price of doing business—so prevalent in medieval towns and on bridges and roads. A late twelfth-century "cart-load" of goods in Yaxley (Northants.) was tolled at two pence, for example (*DBMC*, 75). Our Cart Driver has the cash on hand to pay the toll, if necessary.

31. "Five Hospitals Restrict Admissions as Cuts Lead to Water Fears," *Times*, 14 February 1972: 4.

32. "Midland and North West Worst Affected by Lay-Offs—Total Will Grow in New Year," *Times*, 28 December 1973: 11.

33. "British Economics and Trade Union Politics 1973–1974," the National Archives.

34. "40 Years after Dark Side: Never Underestimate the Power of 'The Dark Side' . . . ," *Independent*, 24 March 2013. In this same article the author goes on to remember Pink Floyd—early and enthusiastic *MPHG* investors—as "the musical equivalent of Monty Python."

35. The delightful 1959 Ealing comedy *I'm All Right Jack* depicts this turbid, miasmic "post-war British industrial life," including the award-winning performance of Peter Sellers as the officious shop steward Mr. Kite. See the entry for "at a bi-weekly meeting" below for more.

36. Little is known of this man, who may have been a sometime chronicler and public notary. See his *ODNB* entry.

37. See Mortimer, *The Time Traveler's Guide to Medieval England*, the section on "Identity" in chapter 4 for more.

38. *Times*, 10 April 1974: 5.

39. See Philippa Toomey, "Books on the Box," *Times*, 5 June 1974: 7.

40. *Times*, 24 September 1974: 23.

41. *Times*, 13 July 1974: 13.

42. *Telegraph*, 14 August 2011, italics added.

43. The Pythons variously remember this particular line, for some reason. Idle remembers ad-libbing the line on the spot, while Palin surmises he must have written it, "maybe," since he and Jones had written the scene. Listen to Palin, Cleese, and Idle's audio track commentary on the DVD and Blu-ray editions.

44. See *MPFC: UC*, 1.50–51, 336, and 2.70, 178 for more on language in *MPFC* and the BBC's censorship practices.

45. Kerpel was a member of the Greater London Young Conservatives (and by 1975 its chairman, where he would argue for a more socially conscious Tory party), and took pains to mention at a gathering of Young Liberals "that not all Young Tories are toffy-nosed twits" ("Woman Succeeds Mr Hain as Young Liberals' Leader," *Times*, 23 April 1973: 2).

46. The "fuck off" would find its way prominently into the next feature film, *Life of Brian*, where Brian tries to convince "disciples" to not follow him. *Life of Brian* accepted an "AA" rating ("R" in the United States)—it featured full frontal nudity (male and female), some violence, and strong language.

47. Bishop, "Bakhtin, Carnival and Comedy."

48. *MPFC: UC*, 1.160–61; *MPSERD*, 137–41.

49. *MPFC: UC*, 1.95, 271–72, 306. Borowczyk's *Blanche* has been discussed above; he is also mentioned in "The Book of the Film" section below.

50. "Scarfe's Cry of Despair," *Times*, 23 August 1968: 12.

51. "Edward III," *1911 Encyclopædia Britannica*, vol. 8: 995.

SCENE FIVE
DENNIS THE PEASANT

ARTHUR and PATSY riding—They are riding across a sloping green field, where ragtag farmers dig for filth. Gilliam mentions that they had initially considered shooting this scene atop a section of Hadrian's Wall, with Arthur and Patsy "riding" along the wall and the mass of unwashed peasantry beneath them.[1] This wall had been built beginning in the early second century by the Romans to essentially keep barbarians like the northern Britons well to the north. The Pythons likely would have had to receive permission to access this national treasure at almost any point, and filming on it might have been more challenging still. They'd also then hoped for a plowed field for the peasants to work in, but the challenges of location shooting obviated that.[2] Even a recognizable "ridge and furrow" field—where the ancient strips of non-demesne land farmed by the medieval working man, a "virgate," can still be identified—was also likely out of the question given the archaeological sensitivity of such locations.[3] The Pythons' eventual Doune and Argyll filming locations were well north of Hadrian's Wall, but the wall was right on the way either up or back from London, so a stop off for pickup shots was at least feasible if they'd deemed the shots critical (and Doyle, with his companion camera, could likely have captured the shots on command). In the end, the Pythons either didn't ask for or didn't receive the necessary permissions—not unlike their experiences with the Scottish castles they'd planned on using as locations—and made alternate shooting plans.

By *not* finding a formerly furrowed or tilled field, or even just a field hemmed in by fencing or hedges, they actually hoved closer to the plight of mid-fourteenth-century England, where most arable land was already in use, forcing many to try their luck on the fringes of fecundity, nearer sodden marshes or on thin-soiled and rocky expanses—marginal lands, agriculturally. The surging population in England of the fourteenth century strained the limits of medieval farming, and was only abated when successive waves of plague shut millions of hungry mouths. The fact that Dennis and his mother and the others in the background are working this non-farming field puts them into the lowest of the peasantry, since they don't even seem to be part of the village system where the strips of more and less productive lands would have been evenly divided amongst the villagers (Holmes, 11–18).

Production manager and effects cameraman Doyle's family (his father, mother, and daughter) can be seen in the background playing the other peasants, though on this shooting day Doyle himself was off in the quarry for the later-seen explosions work.[4] Terry Bedford was shooting this peasants' scene, which was probably just around the hillside (a slightly different angle) from the "Camelot" castle shot seen moments later.

. . . a castle in the distance—(PSC) In the near distance the first structure glimpsed is an-other cart wheel on a tall pole, complete with a body attached. This is likely near the same lo-cation as the "Coconuts and Swallows" scene (so in Scotland, and not on Hampstead Heath), but at a brighter time of day, with little or no added smoke, and from a different angle. The castle in the distance is once again the tall plywood flat[5] built for earlier shots of Camelot, and is of a clever forced perspective design. This same flat falls down in an early trailer for the film.

The forced perspective model—creating sets designed to appear to be larger or smaller than they really are, and actors/props, as well—has been used in filmmaking since the early days, and can be seen in special effects features like *Metropolis* (1927), and Hollywood fare from Murnau's *Sunrise* (1927) to Warner Bros.' *Casablanca* (1942). Murnau, for example, needed to build an entire cityscape within the Fox sound stages, and his effects designer Frank Williams (inventor of the Williams Process travelling matte) designed proportional sets that seemed to fade into the distance, even though they were just made smaller than those in the foreground. In *Casablanca*, the final airport sequence featured a proportionally smaller airplane in the distance with proportionally smaller actors (dwarves) servicing the aircraft, creating the illusion of greater distance. Ambitious "student" films like *Equinox* (Dennis Muren, 1967) also employed these trompe-l'œil special effects shots and sequences.[6] The process became the hallmark of low-budget films where, like *MPHG*, the building of giant sets or the luxury of expensive process shots just weren't options. As a director, Gilliam would go on to use forced perspective setups in *Time Bandits* and *Brazil*—creating the illusion of giant characters and looming buildings.

. . . PEASANT is working away on his knees trying to dig the earth with his bare hands and a twig—(PSC) The peasants aren't actually digging for anything, they're both just using their hands to pick up and stack piles of "filth." At the beginning of the film influential to the feel and look of *Holy Grail*—Polanski's *Macbeth*—the three witches are similarly digging together on a deserted beach, burying a severed hand that clutches a knife, a noose, and other objects. The toiling of the Python peasants could be a reference to the gathering of peat (decayed vegetation). Peat (or turf) had been used as a fuel source for centuries in the British Isles, especially in regions where stands of wood weren't available, but its widespread use waned as coal became king. Special peat shovels and digging and stacking practices aren't being fol-lowed here, so it may be that the peasants are digging in the mud looking for "lovely filth" and nothing else, which might indicate a coprophilic slant not out of character for the Pythons. And since this is not a plowed or furrowed field at all it likely can be classified as a "waste," according to Barbara Harvey:

> "Waste" is the term normally used in the present context to describe rough pasture which had not yet been appropriated for individual use, although it might be cultivated from time to time as an outfield[7] by agreement among all those possessing common rights there. Much of the waste was not only rough but also wet, for, regionally, bog and marsh occurred as frequently in the waste as moorland and heath. (10)

This means that perhaps even accidentally the Pythons continue to site their medieval char-acters into and against appropriate medieval tableaux—e.g., having Dennis and his mother digging in this bog—an accuracy that gives the comedic undercutting all the more bite. As mentioned earlier, one minor complaint about Pasolini's influential version of *Canterbury Tales* was his use of "actual locations" selected "with no scholarship about period"[8]; the Pythons seem to have definite thoughts about period accuracy in *Holy Grail*, meaning the anachronisms and ahistoricities—when presented—can stand out in greater relief.

It's noted that peat use in Scotland and Ireland, for example, continues into even the twenty-first century (especially in rural areas). The Pythons have left Ireland almost completely alone, of course (as did the Goons[9]), but not so the Scots. Scotland is not only where the Pythons are shooting *Holy Grail*, but this filth-mucking could be the source of a joke at the Scots' expense, hinting at their backwardness and rusticity. The Goons enjoyed poking fun at thrifty, easily provoked, and violent Scotsmen, almost as much as Dr. Samuel Johnson (1709–1784), who would have a go at the native Scots traditions, geography, manners, and cuisine. In his entertaining *Dictionary* (1755), a single entry is representative: "Oats: A grain, which in England is generally given to horses, but in Scotland appears to support the people." The insult portion of the definition was excised from some later editions of the work. And, from James Boswell's equally readable *Life of Samuel Johnson* (1791): "Norway, too, has noble wild prospects; and Lapland is remarkable for prodigious noble wild prospects. But, Sir, let me tell you, the noblest prospect which a Scotchman ever sees, is the high road that leads him to England!" (120).

And secondly, these peasants discovered in the fields—with no real connection to the nearby manorial castle—reflect well the cultural and political topography of the fifth and sixth centuries in Britain, where towns themselves (as centers of trade, society, and even living) had virtually disappeared, according to Morris:

> A shrunken town might feed itself from fields outside the walls . . . [but] when the war was over, farmers might live more conveniently among their fields, no longer needing the shelter of walls. Government, and townsmen who did not farm, must depend on what they could wring from small farmers . . . tribute in cattle and corn, honey and beer, from reluctant peasants. In the west, tenants still paid rent. But in much of the lowlands, landlords had emigrated, joined the army, or perished and left no heirs. The old compulsions had been broken too long, and the grandson of a former landlord could not easily coerce the grandson of a former tenant into resuming rent that had lapsed for half a century. Subsistence economy condemned each town and each warband to live on what it could get from its own area. No central government could hope to collect taxes and distribute them to its agents; its income was what it could persuade or force each local ruler to contribute. (*The Age of Arthur*, 139)

This is the kind of Britain Arthur would have traveled through in the early sixth century, moving "from centre to centre, eating his way through his country like a medieval king," Morris concludes (139). And if the king were on the move, so were his household, and even the departments of state. "Government travelled with the king round his many residences," Brooke adds, acknowledging the need for the Anglo-Saxon-era king to keep in touch with his landed magnates, at least, if not his people (*SNK*, 70). It's no surprise that Arthur's peasants couldn't or wouldn't recognize him. See the entry for "lovely filth" below for more.

DENNIS: "You could say: Dennis"—It's clear that this peasant is not truckling before this very clean man, king or no. The cheek of the French peasant class was the stuff of song and story, according to Tuchman:

> A deep grievance of the peasant was the contempt in which he was held by the other classes. Aside from the rare note of compassion, most tales and ballads depict him as aggressive, insolent, greedy, sullen, suspicious, tricky, unshaved, unwashed, ugly, stupid and credulous or sometimes shrewd and witty, incessantly discontented, usually cuckolded. . . . The knights saw him as a person of ignoble instincts who could have no understanding of "honor" and was therefore capable of every kind of deceit and incapable of trust. (174–75)

There is an Italian example of the nontraditional peasant, as well. The "common workmen" known as the *Ciompi* had managed to seize power in Florence, and then "rule with surprising moderation for four years, from 1378 to 1382" (*HBMA*, 373). The short-lived Peasants' Revolt of 1381 was England's version of this temporary social realignment, and will be discussed in some detail below.

ARTHUR: ". . . what knight lives in that castle?"—There are reasons that Dennis and his mother might bristle at these kinds of intrusive questions, especially (depending on the time depicted[10]) if they are remembering the "Great Inquest" undertaken to create what would become known as "Domesday Book" in 1085. William I's "commissions of enquiry" traveled across the land after Christmas 1085 asking questions of sheriffs, nobles, "and even . . . reeves and peasants in villages" to ascertain local and regional disposition of *all* land, goods, and chattel in the kingdom.[11] Contemporary respondents were just as cagey in their replies as Dennis is here, having seen over the past nineteen years the Conqueror take for himself most of England, and then divide as spoils much of Britain and Normandy. But there remained profits to be made, according to Morris Bishop:

> A good and greedy businessman, William ordered a complete census and inventory of his kingdom, not only of every man but of every cow and pig. This extraordinary operation provoked riots and perjuries, for William's new subjects were certain that they would be taxed heavily for all the property that was registered. The disorders were cruelly punished in court sittings that were compared by the populace to Judgment Day. Hence the census report was and is called the Domesday, or Doomsday, Book. (*HBMA*, 46)

The surveyors would have asked or likely already known who lived in a nearby castle, naturally, and would have checked that information against records from Edward the Confessor's time to determine who had been taxed and at what rate, whether stewardships had changed hands, duties had fallen into arrears, etcetera. Other questions included the presence and specific number of valuables—livestock, hides, and so on. One contemporary chronicler praised William's thoroughness, his care for England obvious in that he "searched it out so with his cunning, that there was not a hide of land in England that he didn't know who had it, or what it was worth, and afterward he put it down in writing" (*HBMA*, 212). There doesn't seem to be much of real value in sight here in the "filth" field—Dennis has a two-wheel, hand-drawn cart, and his clothing—but the castle, the land itself and the work-value of these people and their offspring would have been part of Domesday Book's purview.[12] All this intrusion would have irked a so-called "constitutional peasant"[13] like Dennis, who doesn't recognize his own place in the manorial system or Arthur's controlling authority in the first place.

Today, of course, there are dozens of abandoned castles in Great Britain, but it wasn't unheard of in the Anglo-Saxon period, or the later Middle Ages, either. Many such structures, like Llawhaden in Pembrokeshire, fell out of fashion during the later Reformation era. Under new ownership of the new state church Llawhaden was abandoned, stripped of its useful items (including stone), and eventually demolished. Too expensive to maintain privately, the daunting Chepstow Castle, in Monmouthshire, Wales, fell out of use during the eighteenth century after being a prison, lastly, and was allowed to decay, as were Conwy Castle in the seventeenth century, and Balquhain Castle, Aberdeenshire, Scotland in the eighteenth century (after being burned by the forces of Prince William in 1746). Much earlier, a spectacular nonstarter was Beaumaris Castle, in Anglesey, Wales. It was begun in 1295 by Edward I but even after thirty years of work and expense was never finished, and Edward II abandoned the project as being too costly.[14] A castellan never occupied the castle, meaning a local peasant—perhaps from Llanfaes, the inhabitants of which were displaced during construction—could have honestly and somewhat indignantly answered that "no one" had ever lived there.[15] Even Tintagel, in Cornwall, to some the legendary birthplace of Arthur, had fallen to ruin by about

1540, and wouldn't be of use again until the nineteenth century, when Tennyson's *Idylls* and Victorian-era tourism sparked interest anew in things Arthurian.[16]

The fact that "no one lives" in the castle may also be a result of the ongoing struggle for control after the Roman governmental diminishments of the fourth and fifth centuries, a struggle that continued for centuries, and for myriad reasons. The invading Saxons met the divided Britons and were able to push them around, effectively, such that "[g]reat numbers of places, inhabited in the Romano-British period, were deserted."[17] The Norman invasion in the eleventh century would have displaced a good number of folk, as well, poor and rich.[18] The challenges of the natural world also contributed to these dislocations. Calamitous harvest and livestock woes began across England in about 1314. Cool, inclement weather severely impacted grain crops for most of the following seven years, which led to famine and disease—in humans and livestock—as well as a dramatic fall in exports of wool. As profits and surpluses disappeared, contraction followed: "There is evidence that villages began to be abandoned early in the 14th century, as the amount of cultivated land contracted."[19] Historian W. G. Hoskins estimates that about thirteen hundred English villages in existence in the thirteenth century would disappear thanks to these privations, many fading from sight during the calamitous fourteenth century.[20] But the worst is yet to come in the form of the appearance of the Black Death in 1348, creating what McKisack calls "a dislocation of society," spawning removes from inter-village trade and associations, a population shift from rural to urban centers as the job market changed (and the manorial system undercut), and acting as "a harsh reminder of the mutability of human fortunes" (137). Tuchman's *A Distant Mirror: The Calamitous 14th Century* is an apt title for the period. The third and fourth quarters of the fourteenth century would have been particularly nasty, according to Tuchman, writing of both the French and English plague experience, specifically:

> Return of the Black Death in 1374–75 . . . thinned more hearths[21] and reduced the tax yield. The recurring outbreaks were beginning to have a cumulative effect on the population decline as they did on the deepening gloom of the century. In the poll tax of 1379 four villages of Gloucestershire were recorded as making no returns;[22] in Norfolk six centuries later, five small churches within a day's visit of each other still stood in deserted silence on the sites of villages abandoned in the 14th century. (287)

Mortimer estimates that "in total more than a thousand [English] villages have been deserted and are in ruins by the end of the [fourteenth] century" (29). Peasants either died or moved to more favorable economic settlements, abandoning any manorial "bonds of service" and simply looking for a new master who will pay them (29).

And of the earlier major towns of *Roman* Britain, four—Verulam, Silchester, Wroxeter, and Caistor-next-Norwich—were gradually deserted and "remained so until modern times."[23] Some have argued that the Saxon invasion pushed Britons further west, while others note that following the loss of Roman influence and the absence of strong, regional lords, many areas became simply too dangerous to occupy (see Ashe, 1968; Shrewsbury). The vast and intricate construction of Roman civilization that had united the country (well-cared for roads, thriving towns and villages, cleared and fertile agricultural land, drained marshlands, controlled waterways, etc.) began to fall into disrepair not long after Roman oversight began to wane and the English arrived, according to Shrewsbury:

> Coincident with this desertion of the urban centres, the Roman highways were neglected and became overgrown, making travel from one part of the country to another slow, difficult, and

dangerous. Agriculture declined, and the woodlands and marshes encroached upon the cleared lands. Trade and industry stagnated and, in place of a free exchange of crops and manufactures throughout the country, each community tended to revert to a Neolithic state of self-sufficiency and isolation. (8)

In fact, excepting perhaps the motte that a castle like Doune likely stands upon (and where a Flavian fort and road have since been discovered [Keppie, 12, 149]), the Pythons offer *no* glimpses of Roman Britain[24] in *MPHG*—they don't appear to travel on roads,[25] ever, nor do they venture across tilled farmland, nor do they pass through any reasonably-sized population center.[26] Part of the Pythons' avoidance of such locations has to do with the film's meager budget, of course, with the difficulty in securing filming permissions for archaeologically sensitive or National Trust sites, and with their stated desire for a bleak, wild-looking medieval Britain. A good portion of their next film, *Life of Brian*, deals with the exigencies of the Roman occupation of Jerusalem, with Reg (Cleese) reciting the litany of Roman abuses, maugre their civilizing activities:

> Reg: All right, but apart from the sanitation, the medicine, education, wine, public order, irrigation, roads, a fresh water system, and public health—what have the Romans ever done for us?
>
> *A hand is raised in the group.*
>
> Xerxes: Brought peace?
>
> Reg: Oh. Peace? Shut up![27]

By setting the film in Britain in an age where impoverishment, "ruffians," and plague abound, the Pythons are acknowledging the past Roman rule as well as the disruptions caused by centuries of Saxon, Danish, and then Norman rule, where formerly Romanized civilization could deteriorate then invigorate and, likely, where peasants like Dennis could challenge a king.

DENNIS: "I'm not old. I'm thirty-seven"—He *is* quite old by the standards of the period, and in many regions would have actually *exceeded* his life expectancy. Infant mortality was quite high during this Early Middle Age period (as high as 30–35 percent), and later death by disease, famine, accident, neglect, and war greatly reduced life spans, on average. One study—quoted in the article "Ageing through the Ages" from the *Proceedings of the Royal College of Physicians, Edinburgh*—reported the following: "The excavation of two Anglo-Saxon cemeteries in England established that in 65 burials the mean age at death was 36 years, with 48% of the skeletons under the age of 10 years and none over the age of 45" (MacLellan and Sellers, 73). Excavations in a Pictish cemetery (in modern-day Scotland) of the same period revealed very similar life expectancy rates (73). The time period for these burials was the Early Middle Ages (400–1000), according to the authors.

ARTHUR: ". . . but from behind you looked . . ."—According to Mortimer, fashion and clothing technologies in the early part of the fourteenth century dictated that men and women often looked very similar, especially from behind. Prior to the widespread use of something as simple as the button, clothing had to be roomy enough to be pulled over the head and shoulders, meaning both men and women tended to be *draped* in their attire, leading to ambiguities:

> [So] how do you distinguish between male and female dress when it just hangs loosely from the shoulders? Men and women are wearing similar forms of tunics in 1300. There are differences in the neckline and the length of skirt, but the main difference lies in the way the head is presented. (111)

And since it is cold and everyone working this particular field is clothed *cap-à-pie*, there's no telling between genders from any kind of distance. The figures in the far background could be young or old, male or female. It won't be until the end of the century that "similarities in styles of clothing have almost entirely disappeared," and the genders are easily discerned by attire (111–12).

The gender misidentification trope (Arthur had called out "Old woman!" to Dennis) has been a Python favorite since the beginning of *MPFC*. Male characters in *Flying Circus* are often effeminized, being called "Miss" and "Mrs," as well as by female names. In Ep. 1 "Vicky" (Idle) is one of the reporters covering Picasso's bicycling efforts (*MPFC: UC*, 1.22); in Ep. 8 there is a male (but effeminized) "Barbara" (1.127–28); and in Ep. 13 a male waiter is referred to as "Janet" (1.207). In Ep. 9, one of the angry letter writers is "Brig. Gen. Charles Arthur Strong (Mrs)"—the letter is read out quite butchly by Cleese (1.153–54). The fact that Dennis's mother is actually a man in drag complicates the situation, of course, meaning Arthur could've been mistaken in addressing Dennis's mother as "Old woman," as well.[28]

The Pythons followed the Goons here, as elsewhere. In "The Last Tram (from Clapham)" episode (23 November 1954), a male chauffeur character is called "Gladys" throughout the episode (1.22), and in "King Solomon's Mines" the following exchange can be heard:

FX: Door knocker.

Bloodnok (Sellers): Come in. Come in.

FX: Door opens.

Minnie (Milligan): Good morning, sir. I'm, I'm just off the river steamer from England.

Bloodnok: Gad! How strange. A white man.

Minnie: Eh? My name is Miss Minnie Bannister.

Bloodnok: Even stranger, a white man called Miss Minnie Bannister. What's happening back in England?

Minnie: They're doing the bling ba-ding buddie, dum . . .

Bloodnok and Minnie: Bling, blum, etc.

Minnie: It's all the rage you know.

Bloodnok: What?

Minnie: What? Nothing's happening back in England.

Bloodnok: Well there's progress for you. Come in dear sir.

Minnie: Sir? Oh . . . I'm a woman.

Bloodnok: Woman? Woman. That name strikes a chord, you know. Where's me old medical charts?[29]

By the time Ep. 8 of *Flying Circus* is produced, a male customer (Cleese) can greet a male shopkeeper (Palin) by "Miss," and claim to have a cold as the reason for his mistake.[30]

DENNIS: "You didn't bother to find out, did you?"—Dennis is explaining himself to Arthur here, who will "find out" just what kind of man he's encountered, though likely never understand him, since Dennis won't play the part of serf or villein or even voiceless, background peasant. According to Turner in *Crisis? What Crisis: Britain in the 1970s*, this character typified much of what was seen on British television and in novels during this period: "[I]t was still the twin figures of the maverick and the malcontent that dominated much of '70s fiction" (128). Dennis is both maverick and malcontent in one—unhappy with Arthur's status quo authoritarianism, and willing to both embrace and share the good news of a collective, proto-syndicalist nirvana. Note also that he and his mother are two of the very few who are *not* narratively punished—by death, disfigurement, or arrest—in this unsettled, retributive film world. Dennis will be manhandled by Arthur, but will live to appear in a later scene (a transition into the Three-Headed Knight scene), still complaining about "class" and the problems of the world.

It's also possible that this Dennis is based on the real-life Labour firebrand, Denis Healey (b. 1917), the shadow Chancellor of the Exchequer 1972–1974. In the run-up to the 1974 general election, Healey was particularly on point, promising that when Labour took back the government ten days later (February 28), he'd "squeeze property speculators until the pips squeak," as well as "wring the neck of the Housing Finance Act."[31] The first quote was mangled somewhere along the way into "squeeze the rich until the pips squeak," the type of talk that would have encouraged Jones and Palin, particularly, as both tended to be more politically (and vocally) liberal. By December 1974 the feckless government is being depicted as a grim pantomime called "Babes in the Woods."[32] Much of this was just so much political folderol, of course, and when Labour took back No. 10, they found a moribund financial situation and few real options for positive change—there weren't many pips left to squeak. Harold Wilson, prime minister again—but this time in much darker days than the "white heat" years—would resign only two years later, setting the table for the infamous "Winter of Discontent," after which Margaret Thatcher and the Tories reclaimed the government.

DENNIS: "What I object to is that you automatically treat me as an inferior"—Dennis is asserting individual rights here, rights that certainly didn't exist as we know them for a medieval serf or villein. P. H. Sawyer notes that even though the invading Saxons (the English) and the *in situ* Britons of the seventh century were in many cases very different societies, there were also shared bits of culture, including their social hierarchies: "In both there was a fundamental distinction between men who were free and those who were not, and in both there were men of intermediate status, the half free" (51). Dennis clearly assumes he is a free man, able to talk and even disagree with any other man, including this clean man before him who's about to claim his kingship. He also may be tapping into the evolving thirteenth- and fourteenth-century notion of "community of the realm," where the people (not just the barons) of the kingdom came to understand that the monarchy couldn't function properly, and especially couldn't undertake wars, without a population that would give consent by dutifully and regularly paying taxes, for example (Rowley, 15). Evading a tax, or just complaining about and delaying payment of a tax is the kind of "passive resistance" Rowley describes as effectively increasing the need for the king to consult advisors, and eventually a parliament (15–16). In this scene, Arthur won't be able to acquire the information he seeks (the name of the knight occupant of the castle), and beyond that the assistance in his quest (convincing the castle's knight to join him) without Dennis's cooperation—and Dennis is acting like a one-man version of the later Good Parliament.[33] And here, "inferior" is also an economic assignation, according to Barbara Harvey, writing of the twelfth- and thirteenth-century "peasant":

[E]conomic life must always be seen in a social context. The societies which we have to consider were extremely diverse, but alike in believing, with few apparent dissentients, that much of the wealth made at their agrarian base should be passed, by various ways and means, up the social scale, to sustain privileged classes of rulers and lords in the enjoyment of the expensive lifestyles appropriate to their high status. Peasants were caught up to varying degrees in these arrangements, but few escaped their consequences altogether. (*The Twelfth and Thirteenth Centuries*, 5)

Dennis is clearly one of these few "dissentients"—he's not buying into Arthur's hierarchical, class-based system, no matter how historically accurate it might be.

And since this is also a class-based argument (as Dennis mentions later), he is invoking the common good of the masses, the working men and women of Britain and their adversarial relations with management, here represented by a self-proclaimed king. This in-your-face approach does run counter to the historical understanding that those with money and influence would make the rules for those without, especially in the era of manorialism. But if no knight lives in the castle at the center of the land they're working, it's likely that Dennis and his mother aren't or haven't been villeins (essentially serfs with some property rights), and they're looking for filth all on their own, acting essentially as freemen or free tenants.[34] They have no interest (double meaning intended) in the *status quo ante*, and seemingly feel empowered to say so. If they are free tenants, then they may owe their allegiance to a king, and this is their first encounter with that authority, which they of course don't recognize—in more ways than one. Brooke points out that this inability to recognize shouldn't really be a surprise, given the nature of travel and communication for most medieval folk, and things like the English Channel or France or even the next county could be imaginary for all they really knew: "[F]or most of the population even England was a concept too vast to be grappled with. The man from the next village or the next shire was as foreign as a visitor from abroad," he writes. Brooke concludes: "By such folk the existence of 'England' as a country or a nation was scarcely felt at all" (*FAH*, 18).

But there is also the specter of the imminent plague, which is confronted in the following "Bring Out Your Dead" scene, and a question of to what degree the pestilence disrupted life in Dark and Middle Ages Europe, especially for the laborer, or "worker," as Dennis terms himself. Rather than thinning the herd and offering more opportunities for a better income for survivors of the peasant class, some studies (e.g., Farmer, "Prices and Wages, 1350–1500") of "prices, wages and standards of living" indicate that in the quarter-century following the Black Death, the "purchasing power of labour actually [fell]," while their standard of living showed "only modest improvements" (Hatcher, 7–8). This seeming oxymoron wouldn't have been lost on a worker as clever as Dennis, and he's ready to confront the first alleged authority figure he encounters with his grievances. In this Dennis is echoing the figures from paintings on strike in *MPFC* Ep. 25, the indignant "poor" in Ep. 37 to whom Dennis Moore nobly attempts to offer succor,[35] as well as echoing the labor unrest of 1970s Britain, which covered the pages of newspapers. The following entry is from the author's *MPFC: UC* for the "Art Gallery Strike" sketch, specifically the "All we bloody want is a little bloody consultation" entry:

Probably a call for more equitable consultation in the NEDC, the National Economic Development Council, where government, trade unions, and management were supposed to be able to talk amicably. In June 1969, British Airport Authority drivers struck (and performed work-to-rule) for eleven days, claiming that new "self-drive" vehicles had been introduced into the workplace "without proper union consultations" (*Times* 24 June 1969: 2). The return of "reformism" with the new Heath administration in 1970 meant that trade unions had become burdensome throwbacks, a more free market economy (and Thatcherism) was on the horizon, and labor unrest would only escalate with increasing global competition (falling prices, runaway production, etc.). . . . An unattributed Trade Union Congress (TUC) announcement after the Conservatives came to power in 1951 made it clear this crucial "consultation" would continue to be pursued during the Tory years: "The range of consultation between both sides of industry has considerably increased, and the machinery of consultation has enormously improved. We expect of this government that they will maintain the full practice of consultation (*A History of Anarchosyndicalism*, Unit 20)." It seems that by 1970, what workers still wanted (and weren't getting from their union leaders) was just a bit of "bloody consultation." (*MPFC: UC*, 1.371–72)

This antagonistic relationship is as much at home in the Middle Ages as it is in the early 1970s, a duality that will consistently be pointed out as it appears in the film many times, and often fuels the off-beat narrative.[36] Similarly, Helen Cooper notes that "Malory's work may ostensibly be set in a legendary age" but confronts just as well "the conditions of his own era" (Malory, 2008) and Barber discusses the contemporaneity of Grail romance author Wolfram von Eschenbach's thirteenth-century *Parzival*:

> Beneath the flourishes and fantasies lies a powerful vision of the ideals by which society and knighthood should be governed: [von Eschenbach] has built on Chrétien's original concept of a romance, which depicts the development of a knight's mind and character, and made of it a resounding affirmation of the possibilities of the human spirit. (*THG*, 74)

Monty Python is also clearly writing about Arthurian times from a Britain-of-the-1970s perspective—the two eras are intermingled and interdependent. In 1972, the National Union of Mineworkers (NUM) led the first national strike since the 1920s, with demands including an eye-watering 45 percent pay rise. The Heath government was "taken by surprise," and with minimal coal stocks to wait out the strikers—coupled with spiking oil prices—had little preparation for the carnage that quickly followed the closing of 289 National Coal Board coal pits in January (Marr, 2007, 337). Immediate effects included the closing of schools in Shropshire and Barnsley, where coal-fired boilers couldn't be stoked. The miners had also been refusing management's overtime demands since the first of November 1971, meaning coal production had been falling steadily for some time.[37] Prime Minister Heath would describe the events in apocalyptic terms, calling it "the most vivid, direct and terrifying challenge to the rule of law that I could ever recall emerging from within our own country. . . . [W]e were facing civil disorder on a massive scale" (337). Heath also feared "the prospect of the country becoming ungovernable," and tried to settle things judicially, not militarily (337). The judge ruled in favor of the unions, Marr calling it "one of the most clear-cut and overwhelming victories over a government that any British trade union has ever enjoyed" (337–38), and the Heath administration was in real trouble.

Marr calls the moment an "impossible storm," one that had been brewing for many years, and across administrations:

> Much of the country was simply more left-wing than it was later. The unions, having defeated Wilson and Castle, were more self-confident than ever before or since. Many industrial workers, living in still-bleak towns far away from the glossy pop world of the big cities, did seem underpaid and left behind. After the Macmillan, Douglas-Home and Wilson experiences, politicians did not have the automatic level of respect that they had enjoyed when Heath had first entered the Commons [in 1950]. (Marr, 337–38)

An editorial in the *Times* in February 1972 underscored the severity of the situation for all of Britain, concluding:

> Over the next few weeks we shall be reminded again, as we have not been for many years, that miners can challenge a Government, and that if support for them spreads they can be very effective in making life miserable for the country at large. . . . There is no doubt about their unity

now—stubborn and bitter, and about to face the exasperation of comfortable people who are to suffer much more than marginal inconvenience. ("The Talks Break Down," 11 February 1972: 15)

Insert "peasants," "serfs," or "workers" for "miners" above and the sentiment is the same. The "comfortable" Arthur will soon face hurled epithets, animals, and eventually a waterfall of ordure, all from those "oppressed" or simple Others who are supposed to recognize his authority and kingly management.

Unparalleled union/worker gains and power left the country completely unprepared for the next crisis. Following the cessation of the Yom Kippur War—where Egypt and Syria attacked Israeli positions in contested territories in October 1973—the Arab oil-producing countries set out to punish Western nations supporting Israel with an oil embargo that would be keenly felt as the Pythons wrote the screenplay for *MPHG*.[38] Oil prices quadrupled in a very short period, boosting inflation, and on top of these difficulties, miners demanded another rise amounting to "half as much again to many pay-packets," rejected a serious 13 percent offer, and voted for another strike (Marr, 340). Coopey and Woodward note that between 1972 and 1974 crude oil prices jumped 420 percent in the UK, for example, as "oil reserves had passed from the multinational oil corporations to the individual countries" (6), some of whom were quite eager to exercise their newfound power over their former colonizers, including Saudi Arabia's King Faisal.[39] Writing in 1977, C. J. Bartlett describes the period in dismal, end-of-days terms, which likely echoed what actual people were thinking and feeling: "A sellers' market in oil had been developing since 1970. Some movement of the terms of trade in favour of the producing states was long overdue, but in 1973–4 it took place with such violence that it plunged the western world into its greatest postwar economic crisis" (*A History of Postwar Britain*, 317). In Great Britain gasoline was rationed, speed limits were decreased dramatically, a three-day working week was announced in January 1974, and power was being meted out and conserved. The UPI wire service reports from Britain to the world were bleak and curt; this from 14 December, 1973:

> The British government has put its industry on a three-day workweek. The move is to save dwindling fuel stocks in what is regarded as one of the gravest economic crises to hit Britain since the depression. Prime Minister Edward Heath told parliament that industry will be allowed to use electric power for a total of only five days between December 17 and 31, after that he said industrial and commercial plants will be limited to three days of electric power each week. Heath also announced that Britain's two national television networks will close down nightly at 10:30 pm. He also appealed to Britons to use electricity for space heating in only one room in each home. ("World in Brief," *The Scroll*)

Importantly for the Pythons, 14 December 1973 also happens to be the very day that Palin and Jones finished their first draft of the script that would eventually become *MPHG* (Palin, *Diaries*, 148). A baby birthed into squalor, certainly. This was a version that included writing work from the entire troupe. In the run-up to this momentous date, myriad strike actions flavored the year thanks to pay freezes and overtime bans by unionized workers; British military regiments had to step in to run fire stations, collect garbage, operate or protect water treatment plants, etc.

Amid this tangle Heath decided to call an election, with the rather ominous platform question of "Who governs Britain?"—meaning, the elected, sitting government or the increasingly powerful trade unions. (The smug "Not you, mate" riposte flowed from satirists' and pundits' pens in the immediate aftermath, and remained au courant, appearing even in a number of obituaries penned at Heath's passing years later.) Heath seemed certain that the British people had seen and experienced enough to realize that a proper Tory heeling of labor unions, including wage controls, could right the ship; his confidence was as misplaced, his tenuous position as misunderstood, as the Pythons' Arthur. Heath and the Tories didn't get whipped, but they did lose their majority (297 seats to Labour's 301 seats), and had no chance of building a coalition. The Liberals and leader Jeremy Thorpe, who picked up eight seats in the election and 19.3 percent of the vote, refused to go along, which Palin notes with some happiness in his *Diaries*,[40] allowing Harold Wilson, *sans* majority, to form a new Labour government (Marr, 340–41).[41] The election results were a surprise to many, since a narrow Conservative victory for Heath had been expected (though a confident Barnsley voter—a northern mining town voice—had predicted a sixty-seat win by Labour).[42] The election also showed big steps forward by fringe parties, including Scot and Welsh candidates. Because of this more-than-tenuous mandate, Wilson would have to call another election in October 1974.

The new Wilson government would go on to gain a tiny majority in the October 1974 election, and he would govern until April 1976, when Wilson abruptly resigned, leaving the store to James Callaghan, who would lose No. 10 to Margaret Thatcher and the Tories in 1979. By 1979, conditions had flip-flopped crazily, leading one *Times* editorialist to note the British election appeared "back to front": Labour was promising status quo and the Conservatives were the party of a cri de coeur for "radical change."[43] Labour Minister and Secretary of State for Trade Peter Shore (1924–2001) described this economically challenging period well, in a 1976 interview: "The greatest crisis that hit the western world had occurred on Boxing Day 1973 in Tehran, when the OPEC cartel quadrupled the price of oil, and the whole postwar world, in a sense, came to an end."[44] This is the environment in which the Pythons wrote the characters of their uppity peasants, Dennis and mother, complete with their filth, cheek, and a Saltley Gate[45] picket-line walkers' inability or unwillingness to recognize the authority figure standing right before them.

DENNIS: "social and economic differences . . ."—The Black Death actually helped improve the lives of the Third Estate, including serfs, villeins, and peasants, according to Hatcher, but "it did not bring a swift end to villeinage," and it did not break down the traditional class barriers, or sweepingly change the structure of society (33). Hatcher notes that scarcity of laborers did increase the value of a healthy workingman, and strengthened his position vis-à-vis the landowners, his potential employers. There were more opportunities for land ownership and the taking up of trades in the cities. There were likely many Dennis types, according to Hatcher: "The competition for their labor as well as the improvement in their living standards enhanced their self-esteem and *encouraged them to question authority and tradition*" (33). Nigel Saul concurs, seeing changes toward the end of the fourteenth century:

> Because labour was scarce, wages shot up. By the early 1380s skilled labourers who had once earned 5s or 6s a year were earning twice that amount. At the same time, the fall in population led to a drop in the price of food. A quarter of wheat, which in the 1320s had cost 8s or 9s, cost no more than half that fifty years later. Among the lower orders there was a general process of betterment, and inevitably, in its wake, came a rise in expectations. The unfree peasants, chafing under seigniorial oppression, longed for freedom—freedom from villeinage and freedom to take advantage of the new economic opportunities. ("Britain 1400," 40)

By the mid-1370s and certainly by 1381, the peasants' tolerance for villeinage had grown thin, especially after they'd earned higher wages, eaten better food, dressed more colorfully and comfortably, and experienced a morsel of the first estate's lives. Tuchman writes of the beginnings of a peasant uprising: "Although the poll tax [to finance foreign wars] was the igniting spark, the fundamental grievance was the bonds of villeinage and the lack of legal and political rights" (373), a complaint Dennis would have shared. The Peasants' Revolt of 1381 displayed the third estate's willingness to break with tradition and demand more from their government, and some (like leader Wat Tyler) called for an end to government entirely. Around this same time the diet of normal Englishmen began to change as well, according to Saul, thanks to a changing economy and the rise in "pastoral husbandry":

> The shift to animal husbandry is to be numbered among the most striking phenomena of the period. The background to it lay in the general improvement in diet. Whereas in earlier times the peasantry had eaten a mainly bread-based diet, in the fifteenth century they were consuming more meat: higher incomes led to a diversity of consumption patterns. (41)

More than 400 years later, Charles Dickens's character Mr. Bumble in *Oliver Twist* noted the significance of a simple thing like rich food, and its deleterious effect on the poor:

> "It's not Madness, ma'am," replied Mr. Bumble, after a few moments of deep meditation. "It's Meat."
> "What?" exclaimed Mrs. Sowerberry.
> "Meat, ma'am, meat," replied Bumble, with stern emphasis. "You've over-fed him, ma'am. You've raised a artificial soul and spirit in him, ma'am unbecoming a person of his condition: as the board, Mrs. Sowerberry, who are practical philosophers, will tell you. What have paupers to do with soul or spirit? It's quite enough that we let 'em have live bodies. If you had kept the boy on gruel, ma'am, this would never have happened." (108)

The Pythons mention Dickens and his work as well as the Victorian world many times in *MPFC*.

DENNIS: "If there's ever going to be any progress . . ."—The clarion call of the New Left, this coupling of political/social change with "moving forward" is peppered throughout newspapers and pamphlets of 1960s–1970s Britain. In a response to a slightly negative review of the *New Left Review* book *Towards Socialism*, editors of *NLR* laid out the book's major arguments in a Letter to the Editor, using the same buzzwords as Dennis:

1. Our society remains essentially a class society with all the human loss and division this entails.

2. The distribution both of wealth and income remains extremely unequal. The present Welfare State redistributes income not *between* classes but *within* them, moreover it has failed so far to eliminate primary poverty.

3. Work relations remain oppressive and authoritarian. Ken Coates, Raymond Williams and Andre Gorz seek to document this fact and to outline concrete suggestions for the trade unions and the Labour Party—for example that the future nationalized steel industry should not repeat the depressing monolithic structure of the first nationalization Bill, but instead incorporate the principle of workers' control.[46]

The Pythons are clearly tapping into the news of the day when they endow Dennis and his mother with the umbrage of the New Left, challenging medieval authority and the status quo in very up-to-date ways.

As early as 1970 the ill winds of the future were being felt, as *Times* economics editor Peter Jay noted in his editorial "Britain in a Threadbare Political Wonderland," where he describes what should be to us a familiar world of "ungovernable social and political turmoil."[47] The article itself looks at Professor J. Kenneth Galbraith's book *The New Industrial State*, wherein Galbraith outlined big industry's hold on and control of "social purpose," painting a dismal picture of corporate freedoms versus individual restrictions in the coming years. It's the blinkered Brit Jay finds frightening—blindness at all levels of society in the face of economic and social malaise, or even catastrophe:

> In Britain alone one finds no recognition of the problem at all. Government dedicates itself (though without more than purely nominal success) to rolling back the tide of collective responsibility for collective problems in a congested and complex society. Business talks only of the pork barrel and is then scandalized at the disaffection and indiscipline of its workers.
>
> Too many trade unionists bend their energies to resisting a trifling and irrelevant piece of industrial legislation, while doing nothing to further their members' real social needs. And our politicians continue to traffic happily in the depleted store of threadbare political ideas which they inherited from their great-grandfathers.[48] (11)

The traditions espoused by Arthur and the reactions of Dennis are both apparent here—neither willing to yield ground, neither really benefiting from their encounter. And if Dennis is at least a reflection of Labour-left icon Tony Benn, as argued below, the "progress" Dennis demands would not only be frightening to a king like Arthur, but to the 1974 British political world, as well, both Right and Left.[49] In the weeks leading up to the hastily called 1974 general election—the election where Heath hoped to put an end to the major unions' influences, as well as his opponents' sniping and by-election attrition, at least for a few years—Benn spoke and wrote excitedly about the "progress" he glimpsed on the immediate horizon, progress that could only be enacted by the spread of government control over industry, prices, and wages. This struck fear into many hearts:

> To all but those on the far left, talk of "emergency powers" was potentially terrifying stuff. Even Benn's own mentors often shuddered at his radical intransigence. Stuart Holland, the intellectual godfather of the state holding company scheme, wrote later of his horror at Benn's "dogmatic" and wildly unrealistic vision of a socialist Little England sealed off from the world economy. And on the right, where Benn had once been seen as an amusing, eccentric but ultimately harmless figure, he now loomed as the incarnation of socialist devilry, the Red Menace made flesh.[50]

But the election wasn't nearly as defining as anyone could have hoped. The Tories "won" but couldn't command a parliamentary majority,[51] and since the Liberals refused to play ball, Heath was forced to resign and Labour, without a mandate, stepped sideways into a position of governing without much authority.[52] Benn's radical changes lost their luster with time and a dose of economic reality—an election in October 1974 increased Labour's strength, but not the country's appetite for wholesale political and economic change. Later we'll see Dennis and mother moving through another Sir Robin scene, Dennis still prattling about anarcho-syndicalism preserving freedom, while almost out of earshot his mother tells him it'd be better if he kept his mind on the mud. The oppressed themselves were not and are not of one mind, then. Sandbrook notes that for all the ebullience over the Tories' fall and the Working Man's ascension in 1974, there certainly wasn't anything close to consensus in regard to Labour's radical manifesto and the future of Britain:

> Quite apart from the problem of finding the money to pay for more nationalization, the obvious problem with the Labour manifesto was that not even its own supporters believed in it. Although

committed activists loved Tony Benn's proposals, the great mass of relatively apathetic Labour voters did not. . . . And on top of that, almost none of the party's senior figures believed in their own commitments. (*State of Emergency*, 622)

Arthur, of course, will eventually go into the police van still pursuing the rigid ideals of his quest, ignoring the realities of even the ordure covering his clothing. The filth and disorder of this world win out.

An OLD WOMAN appears—(PSC) Though not described in the printed script, Dennis and his mother (the Old Woman) are dressed appropriately for country folk (or villeins) of the fourteenth century, according to Mortimer, especially those who labor for a living:

> The clothes worn in the country are practical and plain, made of coarse woollen cloth collectively described as russet—mainly grey, green, murrey (dark brown), brown, reddish brown, and undyed. In the early part of the century a farm woman wears a full-length tunic over her linen smock, with a linen headdress and wimple all in one. . . . Sometimes she will wear a hood instead of a headdress. If working outdoors she may well wear a thick woollen mantle and hat, as well as the wimple. (117)

Dennis's clothes seem to be less defined than his mother's; they are just draped over him. Additionally, she's a bit scabrous, with warts or pustules on her face; she's the "rat-bag" of *MPFC* episodes,[53] also often played by Jones. (Jones will also play Brian's mother in their next feature film, *Life of Brian*.) See the "but from behind you looked" entry earlier for more on appearances and dress.

OLD WOMAN: "There's some lovely filth down here"—In the printed script, the Old Woman is in the process of asking Dennis whether he's "seen the cat's front legs" as she digs through the bog (*MPHGB*, 8). This is changed in the film for the "filth" line above, but it would have carried on the "abuse of cats" motif employed often in the Python *oeuvre*. This "body mutilation" fascination is seen throughout *MPFC*, as well, where, for example, after a few modifications a terrier can be remade into a cat, a parrot, or even a fish (*JTW*, 2.129–30):

> What's actually being proposed here is nothing more than what Gilliam does on a regular basis with his polymorphous animations—taking bits and pieces of figures and creating new, often monstrous beings. The earliest iterations of the opening credits feature a wheeled Cardinal Richelieu and a part-man-part-chicken, for example. (*MPFC: UC*, 1.167)

The dismembering and re-membering of the body, human and animal, is a well-used cartoony trope for the Pythons.

It's also not made clear whether Dennis and his mother hold this land in demesne, whether their "lord" Arthur can claim *droit de suite* or the like, or the castle is part of the king's or a more local lord's *messuage*,[54] though they (and the others peasants around them) do seem to think they have the right to work the lands, likely because they don't have a lord and, by extension, no king. The principles of the collective likely apply, as well, meaning they consider ownership as a group endeavor, without rank or class.

As for the filth, there is actually a significance to these places, to fen-like expanses where nothing sightly lives. St. Guthlac (673–714) had found spiritual refuge in such a place, near Grantchester, an "uncultivated spot of the wide wilderness," where he found "immense marshes, now a black pool of water, now foul running streams, and also many islands, and reeds, and hillocks, and thickets."[55] As late as Middle Ages England these natural quagmires obstructed travel and commerce between villages,[56] meaning small communities just a handful of miles apart could be very nearly strangers to each other, creating an insularity that bred suspicion of newcomers, of anything out of the ordinary—in other words, a perfect setting for the coming witch hunts.[57] In *Anatomy of Disgust*, Miller describes these sites as places where "primitive plant and primitive animal merge into slime, ooze, and murky quagmire . . . [where] we are still wedded to folk belief that such vegetable muck spontaneously generates the worms, slugs, frogs, newts, mudpuppies, leeches, and eels we associate with it" (40–41). This is the kind of environment that can be home to a monster, as described in *Beowulf*: "[T]his horrible stranger / Was Grendel entitled, the march-stepper famous / Who dwelt in the moor-fens, the marsh and the fastness, the land of the giant-race" (II.49–51). See the entries for "Swamp Castle" later for more on this phenomenon.

ARTHUR: "Well . . . I am King"—The lives of these working people in the Middle Ages, according to Hatcher, and especially in the aftermath of the Black Plague, were often defined by historians based on "governmental, judicial and seigneurial records," sources that tended to favor the opinions and views of the upper class, meaning the picture painted was often an unflattering one:

> The élites whose views are represented in surviving records tell us that those whose allotted role was to toil in order to provide them with sustenance have become selfish and greedy; they are demanding extremely high wages and extravagant fringe benefits, including fine clothes and the best food and drink. They are lazy; they refuse to work unless they are hungry, and when they do accept employment they labour far less assiduously than in past times. Most workmen prefer to be hired by the day, refusing to serve by the year, or indeed by any term of reasonable length. They break their contracts and wander from place to place and from employer to employer. They engage in unbecoming leisure pursuits, including excessive drinking, poaching and hunting, and their enhanced incomes enable them to buy clothes and other commodities which are unbefitting their lowly status. (14)

The examples of the "commoner" met in *MPHG* do fairly bear this supposition out—the sentries won't come down off their wall to give proper respect to a king; Dennis and mother are in-your-face Bennites; the Black Knight not only doesn't triumph, he doesn't admit when he's de-limbed; the village peasants are superstitious witch-burners; and those in Camelot are "silly," frolicking wastrels, and so on.

The perhaps apocryphal story told of a peasant woman failing to recognize her king is worth mentioning here. According to the twelfth-century *Chronicle of St. Neot's*, Alfred, in pursuing the Danish forces in winter, had been hiding in a cowherd's home, and while there was tasked by the cowherd's wife with keeping watch on loaves of bread as they baked:

> [A]nd the king was sitting by the fire preparing bows and arrows and other weapons. Presently the unfortunate woman saw the loaves set by the fire and burning; she rushed up and removed them, upbraiding the most unconquered king, and saying: "You wretch, you're only too fond of them when they're nicely done; why can't you turn them when you see them burning?" The unfortunate woman had no idea that he was King Alfred, who fought so many battles, won so many victories against the heathen. (quoted in *SNK*, 108–9)

These are reproving moments in the early life of a promising king, tales told to admonish Alfred's "tyrannical behaviour," behavior that our Arthur seems to take on rather easily as this scene moves forward (109).

DENNIS: "By exploiting the workers . . . economic differences in our society"—This is the jargon of the newsreel sound bite and newspaper quote heard and read since at least post–World War I in Great Britain, flowing from the mouths of stumping Labour and even Liberal candidates, trade union leaders at the bullhorn, and workers standing on the walkout queue. Angry but working miners at the Seafield colliery in Fife, Scotland (not far east of the Stirling area), voiced similar sentiments. One miner said: "The Government tries to blame us but it's bloody deception. They will pay the Arabs what they ask, but not the miners, and we really work for our money."[58] Whitehead reports that in a meeting with the NUM executive in late November 1973, Heath was posed this question—"Why can't you pay us for coal what you are willing to pay the Arabs for oil?"—but "the Prime Minister really had no answer" (104). So this government exploits its workers by acknowledging the "economic differences" between its own miners and the petronations, but the miners are found wanting, clearly, according to these Dennis-types of the coal face.

The Pythons' Dennis is firmly pointing out Arthur's complicity with the impediments of "progress," and is suggesting that Arthur both willingly acknowledge the system's destructiveness and ultimately denounce that system. (In this case it's the medieval manorial system, of course, as well as the more contemporary, adversarial labor-management relationship "inherent" in the capitalist system.) It's interesting that nowhere in Dennis's platform for change is there any threat of revolt—he isn't promising an uprising or even civil disobedience (tools of organized labor for many years)—he simply means to educate this clean man and win him over to the people's cause. This isn't a "do it or else" kind of moment; the pleasantly contumacious Dennis doesn't seem to have even the underlying motive of fattening pay packets for the worker or demanding a forty-hour work week—he's more an idealist.

Scanning period newspapers reveals the depth and breadth of this kind of argument during especially the Cold War period, when the Pythons were in school and then just beginning their careers. The specter of the Communist Bloc as the antithesis of the capitalist West looms large, the fear being that two such contradictory ideologies supported by nuclear arsenals couldn't circle forever—an obliterative clash was inevitable. These competing versions of imperialism fueled much rhetoric, including a hundred-thousand-word article from Mao Tse-Tung (1893–1976) much discussed in British newspapers in spring 1963.[59] In fact it was Chinese leadership who tended to use the "imperialist dogma" terminology in regular attacks on both the West and the Soviets. Mao and the PRC are referenced a number of times in *Flying Circus*, illustrating China's threatening irruption into global politics during the Cold War, even as the bigger, more immediate threat should have been a nuclear Soviet Union.[60] China was likely the inscrutable, unpredictable wild card, though.

At the more local level, charges of "imperialism" were thrown about by trade unions, management, and government figures whenever boundaries appeared to have been overstepped, which meant constantly. It's no surprise to find the sentiment in a Labour Party missive, this one a background paper to the Labour Party Conference in October 1973. In the second paragraph of the introduction Labour sets itself apart from the Conservatives rather decisively: "[T]here are two ways to make policy. The Tory way is to hand down from the top decisions made behind closed doors by its born leaders. The Labour way is through the democratic development of policy in the rank and file of the Party."[61] The imperialist Tories wallowing in hierarchical structures, secrecy, and Old Etonianism is clearly party-speak, as is Labour's self-description of harmless rusticity and the common good, but the message is clear and voters responded, giving Labour the edge in seats in 1974.

Earlier at the Labour Party conference convened in Morecambe in 1952, recently retired Labour MP Hugh Dalton (1887–1962) spoke in optimistic, Dennis-like terms, congratulating Britain and her people for moving past the past:

[British subjects] should be proud and never forget that only Britain and a Britain under a Labour Government, of all the imperialistic powers through the ages, voluntarily surrendered without the use of force her rule over great nations previously subject to her. (Cheers). ("Labour Conference," *Times*, 2 October 1952: 2)

Arthur will not, of course, surrender his authority over his subjects, and moves to (limited) forceful means rather naturally, exposing "the violence inherent in the system."

The "exploiting the workers" factor would seem to have been even more significant during the early Middle Ages, and especially in the wake of pestilential outbreaks, but recent studies haven't underscored this assumption. In "England in the Aftermath of the Black Death," Hatcher looks at the late part of the fourteenth century, finding a surprising balance of power in labor relations:

> The market for labour was clearly far from being a perfect one, but the impression which emerges strongly from the judicial records of the third quarter of the century is that, despite the statutes and the seigneurial authority which landlords possessed over their men, it was very frequently a seller's market. There were very many workmen who drove extremely hard bargains with those who sought their labor. (24)

In other words, after 1348–1349, 1360–1362, and 1390 the peasant often found himself in a position to exploit the nobility, and he obviously used that leverage. Dennis may be in that same position, but he's much more interested in arguing his anarcho-syndicalist political message than entering into a working relationship with this representative of the nobility; this purposeful unemployment would have set him at odds with the moralists of the period. In the time of plagues and rebuilding, it was the able-bodied worker who would *not* work that drew the second and third estates' ire, including the author of *Piers Plowman*, William Langland (c. 1331–1386), according to Hatcher:

> Indeed the harshness with which Langland castigates the sturdy beggars and idlers of his day should alert us to the significance of the new emphasis which society was placing upon the necessity of discriminating between the deserving and the undeserving poor. The indigent able-bodied, personal misfortune aside, were deemed by the affluent classes to be more in need of punishment than of charity, for the simple reasons that gainful employment seemed to be available for everyone capable of working. (Hatcher, 32)

Langland (1992) describes the surly workingman, a man well aware of the fruits of the upper estates, and, like Dennis, they know what they want:

> Landless labourers, with nothing to live on but their hands . . . and if a man of this class wasn't paid a lordly wage, he'd be heard bemoaning the time he was born to be "a lousy bloody labourer." One of these lads doesn't give a twopenny damn for that adage of Cato's—"You were born poor; bear your poverty with patience." (73–74)

DENNIS: ". . . outdated imperialist dogma"—Dennis is clearly a man out of his time, as he's able to reference more modern political structures, and so he is a purposefully anachronistic element. (He also has knowledge beyond his station—another Python favorite.[62]) Dennis isn't alone in marrying the past and present in political terms, however. The medieval historian often telescoped events and mixed fact with fiction to present the proper lessons that history should teach, often without malice or guile toward either the events or characters themselves, or toward his audience. But reproving was history's duty, oft-times. "In the Middle Ages, as now," Bishop writes, "it was a fine and often arbitrary line that divided historical writing or reporting from mere gossip. . . . Historians did not hesitate to judge their subjects" (*HBMA*, 212).

More contemporarily, in a letter to the editor responding to another letter penned by Roman Catholic Archbishops on the eve of the 1974 general election, respondents quote Archbishop Hélder Câmara, who wrote in 1967: "In this way we will stop confusing God and religion with the oppressors of the poor and of the workers, which is what the feudal, capital-ist and imperialist systems are."[63] Arthur has and will continue to align the will of God with his role as both king and seeker of the Grail, so he fits into the first clause of the Archbishop's charge; Dennis lives in the feudal and manorial systems, but raises a splenetic against both capitalism and imperialism. For more on Câmara's influence in this (1970s) period in Britain, see the "violence" entry below.

Finally, Dennis might as well have just stepped out of the hall where the 1974 Trades Union Congress had been meeting in October 1974, where eight points were presented as a means of pulling Britain out of its years-long slump. Dennis would have still been on the fringes of this party, since he is arguing for worker control of the means of production, but his Bennite voice would have at least been heard. The Kenneth Gill article "Socialist Economics as a Way to Preserve Democracy" (published two days before the October 1974 general elec-tion) sums up these radical points, which include:

> a large-scale redistribution of income and wealth; a massive increase in housebuilding with the emphasis on homes for those in need and those on lower incomes; municipalization of rented property; public ownership of the land required for the housing programme; a wider-ranging and permanent system of price control; vastly improved social services by the injection of the necessary resources; substantial increases in public ownership and public enterprise coupled with public supervision of the investment policies of large private corporations; and substantial cuts in defence expenditure in order to release resources to help carry through this programme.[64]

Bigger, more intrusive government, taking from the rich and giving to the poor, and a promised pullback from the international stage? None of those policies had much traction with middle England, especially when food and fuel prices and pay packets were the main concerns. Dennis wouldn't have liked the specter of a larger government, either—it's work-ers' control for him. Needless to say, most of these demands were soft-pedaled into oblivion in the realities of the mid-1970s, as Labour met the economic crisis with less radical, more palatable action, pushing the idealistic, militant minorities like Gill, Benn, and Dennis off to the sidelines.

OLD WOMAN: "Who are the Britons?"—The filthy peasant woman clearly has no nation-concept in 932, which isn't a complete surprise given that Æthelstan's reign (from September 925) began when he took over for his father as ruler of only Wessex and Mercia (the latter mentioned earlier by Arthur). Other neighboring kingdoms, including those of the Scots, Strathclyde, and York, maintained their own sovereignty even after Æthelstan was proclaimed "King of All England," and it wouldn't be until 937 that the Battle of Brunanburh consolidated Æthelstan's kingdom. The battle is recounted in the *Anglo-Saxon Chronicle*, in the pages for the year 937.

Higham notes too that terms such as "Britons" could have easily existed without most folk living in Britain of the early Middle Ages having any concept of the moniker, since it was an external imposition. "As terms, both 'Britain' and 'British' derive ultimately from a precolo-nial, classical context, when both terms were used by Greek authors writing about geography and ethnography" (writings that Dennis and mother weren't exposed to). Higham continues: "The idea of a single 'British' people was constructed outside Britain, therefore, and may well have had little if any insular meaning outside of the geographical locale prior to the Roman conquest" (*KAMH*, 40). And for these members of the third estate, it may have had no real meaning (or use) at all.

The old woman's confusion can also be attributed to the film's own temporal (and likely purposeful) confusion. Is this Arthur's alleged historical time, the late fifth to early sixth century? Is it the middle third of the tenth century, as the title card ultimately indicates? Is it the much later twelfth-century date scribbled in the film's production notes? Or, even more befuddling, is this the thirteenth to fourteenth centuries mentioned by Jones in his DVD commentary? Each time period offers a different set of challenges for Arthur as king, Arthur and Patsy as travelers across what would become Great Britain, and any concept of a united Britain. If it is the late fifth century, the "Britons" would have been natives fighting the Saxon armies (including at the Battle of Mons Badonicus), where some feel Arthur's legend may have some firm historical footing. Britain would have been a wild and fairly lawless place, caught between warring parties in succeeding generations, and "we are all Britons" would have been fairly meaningless. If this is the tenth century, then by about 927 Æthelstan is consolidating his power (uniting Anglo-Saxons and defeating the Welsh) to create the Kingdom of England. Æthelstan's coinage proclaiming "King of all Britain" should be a clue to Dennis's mother, unless they are so distanced from regulated commerce that coins are meaningless to her, too.[65] If, however, this is closer to 1167, then there is much less a chance the peasant woman doesn't know who the Britons are, since the various regions have by this period coalesced into England, Scotland, and Wales. (See the entry "932 A.D." above for more.) By the late Middle Ages, (thirteenth to fourteenth centuries), there should be no misunderstanding as to what constitutes a Briton.

When Arthur's supposed *floruit* is considered, those who might be called "Britons" were geographically isolated, even from each other, and were more likely Welsh, for example. A map illustrating the geographical boundaries of the political entities of Britain in the period places the Britons in what are now Cornwall, Wales, and western Scotland, shouldered into the western wilds by Anglo-Saxon incursions (Shrewsbury, 11; also Morris, 209). Those in Cornwall are cut off from the rest of Britain by the South and West Saxons; those in Wales by the Middle Angles; those in Scotland by both the Picts (to the north) and Northumbrians to the east. Shrewsbury notes the fact that England was both "much boggier and damper at this time" (seventh century) then later, and, as a result,

> the forest areas in seventh century England . . . must have seriously impeded free communication between north and south and, to a lesser degree, between east and west, especially as they were almost certainly the haunts of fugitive and desperate men. The political situation [outlined in the previous paragraph] . . . also militated against free and easy travel from one part of the land to another. Apart from those who had accepted service under, and been enslaved by, the Saxons and their allies, the Britons seem to have had little peaceful intercourse with the invaders, and these were engaged in their respective kingdoms in internecine strife for the hegemony of England. (Shrewsbury, 9)

It should also be noted that the celebrated Roman road network had been allowed to fall into disrepair as early as the fourth century, when bigger problems elsewhere in the empire drained away Romano-British garrisons and domestic spending. Given these inhospitable conditions—where extensive or even regional travel through hostile lands was likely inadvisable if not impossible—the peasant woman's confusion is understandable.

ARTHUR: "All of us are . . . we are all Britons"—Arthur is on the right track here, if it's 932, as the earlier title stated. According to Christopher Brooke, it took quite a long while for the idea of a cohesive "Britain" to form: "It was between the accession of Alfred in 871 and the twelfth century that England achieved political unity and something like its present frontiers with Wales and Scotland" (*FAH*, 17). So invasions and conquerings by and interminglings with the Saxons, Danes, and Normans helped draw the various kingdoms into nationhood by the eleventh and twelfth centuries. But it wouldn't be until the late thirteenth century that this *term* gains any currency, at least in written sources, according to the *OED*, where a "Briton" is defined as: "A member of one of the Brittonic-speaking peoples originally inhabiting all of Britain south of the Firth of Forth, and in later times *spec*. Strathclyde, Wales, Cornwall, and Brittany, before and during the Roman occupation."[66] So the term may have been unknown or at least in fluctuation for many generations, a large number of locals likely living and dying without ever hearing the term. It won't be until the thirteenth century that a "growing feeling of Englishness" begins to emerge, specifically in reaction to Henry III's seeming favoritism toward his Continental cousins and customs (Hallam, 105).

DENNIS *winks at the OLD Woman*—(PSC) This isn't made obvious in the finished film, but it does indicate that the peasantry aren't behaving as Arthur (or we) might expect them to behave. There is no deference here—not to Arthur's lineage or royalty or power—which a number of medieval chroniclers attributed to the disorder and fatalism of both "these dark times" and the harrowing by disease and civil wars of the period. Alfred the Great's biographer Asser mentions that even this greatest of kings suffered similarly in the ninth century:

> His illness apart, his worst trouble was the obstructiveness of his own people, who would not willingly submit to any, or very little, toil for the common need of the kingdom. But he stood alone, dependent on divine assistance. . . . He took every pains gently to teach, flatter, exhort, command, finally, after long patience, sharply to punish the disobedient. . . . Sometimes through the people's laziness royal commands were not carried out; or tasks were begun late were not finished and so of no use. (quoted in Brooke, *SNK*, 105–6)

Asser waxes a bit hagiographical, likely, but the elements of truth are certainly there, as supported by other descriptions we've seen of unwilling commoners in both England and France. Dennis and his mother aren't playing their parts in a sort of *sancta rusticitas* set piece—they're not idealized, happy peasant folk in a bucolic pastoral scene. Theirs is likely the opposite of the *otium ruris*, the rural leisure. (Elsewhere is discussed additional obviates to deference—fluctuations in populations [thanks to war, famine, plague] and distant or just unknown local lords—these would have certainly at least confused the peasantry as to whom they might owe allegiance, if any.) Defoe notes the particularly ill-mannered gravediggers of the seventeenth-century London plague years, who seemed to completely understand their crucial role in pestilential times, and take full advantage of these churlish freedoms. Two such "gentlemen" were heard by the narrator railing at a disconsolate man, his family having recently succumbed to the plague:

> They were at this vile work when I came back to the house, and, as far as I could see, though the man sat still, mute and disconsolate, and their affronts could not divert his sorrow, yet he was both grieved and offended at their discourse. Upon this I gently reproved them, being well enough acquainted with their characters, and not unknown in person to two of them. They immediately fell upon me with ill language and oaths, asked me what I did out of my grave at such a time when so many honester men were carried into the churchyard, and why I was not at home saying my prayers against the dead-cart came for me, and the like. I was indeed astonished at the impudence of the men, though not at all discomposed at their treatment of me. (*A Journal of the Plague Year*, 63)

And it wasn't just gravediggers and cart drivers who entertained notions of social motility in the wake of such destruction, as Hatcher points out, especially from the point of view of the elite:

> The survivors of the Great Plague of 1348–9 were in no doubt that the fortunes and demeanour of the lower orders of society had been transformed. In the experience of the upper strata of society, the trauma of successive waves of devastating pestilence was followed by the prolonged discomfort inflicted by obstreperous tenants and truculent workmen who, conscious of the prospects for betterment which the massive mortality had placed within their grasp, would not be coerced into placidly accepting their time-honoured subservient roles as the meek providers of ample rents and cheap labour. (10)

Hatcher continues, noting that the *traditional* powers (landed gentry, merchants, the church, etc.) shared a "vested interest" in keeping these peasants and laborers at their *traditional* social level, deploying

> a battery of religious, ideological and legal weaponry . . . directed towards the perpetuation and justification of the lowly economic and social status of labour, and towards reconciling and rationalizing the incongruities which existed between the significance of manual toil for the well-being of the community at large and the meagre rewards received by those who performed it. (10)

McKisack notes that the later fourteenth century, particularly the years leading up to the Peasants' Revolt in 1381, were rife with social disturbances, and especially those that were essentially metaphoric nose-thumbings at the betters in society. Tenants harvested their own crops on days they were to be harvesting the lord's demesne, for example, while other tenants "disturbed those who were performing their proper boon-work" (agitating, essentially); one flooded a nobleman's wheat, while another lord's crop was spoiled because the harvesting villein refused to appear for work; other commoners blasted court proceedings against themselves and "would not be prevailed upon by the steward to behave . . . responsibly"; still others refused to appear for annual crop work until what were considered to be exorbitant wage demands were met, and so on (337–38). The fourteenth century saw the tide turn on the villein system, with the differences between a freeman and a bondman becoming much diminished, and the future "demarcation of the agricultural population into three main strata—freeholders, tenant-farmers, and landless, or nearly landless, labourers—which was to form the characteristic pattern of English rural society until the end of the eighteenth century, is already clearly foreshadowed."[67]

And to bring the argument back to the Pythons' contemporary world, in 1972—when the sitting Conservative government was beset on all sides by trade unions and Northern Ireland and a doleful economy—the voices clamoring for government *by* the people were being raised to a fever pitch. In an editorial contributed to the *Times* by Tony Benn, a noted syndicalist sympathizer, he sees the writing on the wall for a "devolution" away from top-down hierarchical control in Britain, and the need for and promise of "power at the grass roots level, including the demand for workers' self-management" (12 April 1972: 16). Benn argues for the governed to in turn take the role of government and rule by informed and common, collective consent, a very Dennisean desire. Benn concludes this speech (delivered to a trade union gathering in West Germany) with a dire warning:

> Unless we can bridge this gulf [between government and the governed] in a meaningful way, the fears of the leaders about ungovernability [the "bloody peasant"], and the frustration of the public about remoteness ["I didn't vote for you"], may both become self-fulfilling prophecies that actually do carry us on to disorder, or back to authoritarianism, or both in turn, in rapid sequence. (16)

Arthur and Dennis never do see eye to eye, nor did the landless peasant and his nervous bondlord of the fourteenth century, and the Western world's tension between governed and government continues, more than forty years on from their filmed encounter.

OLD WOMAN: "I didn't know we had a king"—First, as Higham points out, the Anglo-Saxon-to-Middle Ages peasant might have lived a long while without knowing, for example, a new king had been proclaimed:

> Such men and women lived through a time of considerable change, certainly, but their own perceptions will have contained profound continuities, as did the organizational world of estate, parish, shire and diocese which they inhabited. . . . A farmer who regularly sold his produce in the markets of, for example, Huntingdon during the early 1060s could well have been still doing the same during the latter part of the decade [after the Battle of Hastings]. (*The Death of Anglo-Saxon England*, xviii)

In short, much of the English countryside and peoples felt little immediate effect of the Norman Conquest, and—for those who remained happily outside officialdom—might well have lived and died without encountering Norman French or Latin texts, the "wholesale replacement of the English elite—both lay and clerical—by [Norman] immigrants," and the like (xvi). A couple like Dennis and his mother would have likely been part of a tiny community, living somewhere between or adjacent to crumbling Roman ruins, well off good roads and away from larger towns.[68] The fact that they're part of an "autonomous collective" means they're freemen and not in or near established cities or towns or within a lord's demesne, where—as *villein regardants*—their boasted freedoms would have been significantly curtailed.

Secondly, Dennis's mother may simply be living in an early workers' paradise, at least in her mind, but she is also perhaps confused by the abundance of stories surrounding the man before her, and the changes those stories had undergone. Again, the "Arthur" or even an Arthurian warrior tribal leader changed between the fifth and thirteenth centuries—depending on who was writing the "history" or romance and for what purpose (see Bromwich, Higham, et al.)—and the Pythons are clearly mining this historical quarry at different levels of strata. Berthelot mentions the cyclical romances of the thirteenth century involving Arthur and how those stories "drew on the Arthurian legend and fleshed it out in great detail," modifying the tales significantly (59). Importantly, it's the influence on "all Britons" that has been changed: "Suppressing references to the conflict with Rome [Arthur challenging the authority of the church], they place the emphasis instead on individual adventures, and a national perspective based on warfare and conquest is lacking in the majority of the prose texts" (59–60). This emphasis on the individual might well mean Dennis and his mother would not have heard of Arthur's exploits as *providential* leader of Britain, and, therefore, the best he could hope for would be recognition by the likes of these peasants as a "sovereign *primus inter pares*," or a first among equals. This would mean that these peasants would have to be hearing tales about Arthur from Geoffrey (c. 1136), and Wace's *Roman de Brut* (c. 1155), and not the romances (Berthelot, 68). (Of course, if this *is* 932 as the film's titles aver, and not 1167 or 1282 as other film-related sources mention, they would have no access to these earlier texts. Anachronisms, of course, have been and will continue to be embraced by the Pythons.) In fact, Berthelot also points out that many of the romances featuring revolt against the young Arthur are ones where the noblemen are unaware of his lineage, of his "right" to govern, to pull the sword from the stone, etc. (68). Our Arthur clearly sees himself as the former type of leader, one called by God, and is consistently nonplussed by any reaction counter to that assumption.

OLD WOMAN: ". . . an autonomous collective"—In "Workers' Control," Syndicalist Tom Brown mentions the contemporary Israeli *Kibbutzim* as an example of a long-term, working collective operating in an otherwise capitalist country (and region):

> [T]he Kibbutz movement has revolutionised the economy of this tiny Middle East country. The use of modern farming techniques has transformed arid deserts into arable land. Equally important, however, this has been done through the principle of voluntary collectivisation and Workers' Control. There is no uniformity in the internal administration and day-to-day management of the Israeli communities, but most are organised on the basis that members contribute their labour power to the common pool and live on a basis of social equality. Decisions of policy are taken by general assemblies of all members and those who handle the administrative work are elected and mandated by such meetings.[69]

It's a bit of an afterthought in the pamphlet, but Brown uses it as an example of successful collectivization where there is a collective will.

The sort of worker's paradise opined by Dennis and his mother can be directly connected to Tony Benn and 1973–1974 Britain. Prime Minister Wilson himself was presented with Benn's epiphany on collectives, as was most of the sitting Cabinet. Benn told the story of witnessing Bristol shop stewards passing "a resolution saying they should have the right to sack the whole of management at a week's notice" (Whitehead, 141). Benn agreed, of course, and wanted the rest of the Labour government to come along into this new "wonderful experience," the world of workers' control (141). Benn's belief in the power of the cooperative is the most Dennis-like of his characteristics, echoing Dennis himself, who clearly sees the value of "sacking" this exploitative man before him.

As early as March 1974 and before the new Labour government could even unpack following Heath's departure, it was reported that the new secretary of state for industry, Benn, was already being asked to push substantial public money into the failing motorcycle company Meriden.[70] A year earlier the Conservative government had approved a similar funding meant to shore up this British-based motorcycle concern in the face of canny international manufacturing and sales competition. This competition was coming primarily from Japanese assembly-line motorcycles, the success of which cut deeply into British motorcycle sales at home and abroad, forcing Meriden (affiliated with Triumph) into hard times. The infusion of capital helped, but really just propped up the more expensive, less efficient craftsmen-heavy process of building these British motorcycles the old-fashioned way, and the factory continued to suffer, with ownership inching toward closing the plant outright and consolidating production into more efficient factories elsewhere. Eventually, the idea of a workers' cooperative emerged, with local unions and Meriden employees attempting to convince Norton Villiers Triumph's (NVT) owner, Denis Poore, to sell the troubled Meriden factory to them. With significant capitalization from the government and political arm twisting from No. 10 on down, by July 1974 the factory site was in fact "owned" by Meriden workers. These workers would produce and sell motorcycles to Poore, who would market them, and their future was ostensibly in their own hands.

It didn't take long, of course, for the realities of a competitive marketplace to take hold. As Whitehead notes: "Co-operatives needed the same mix of skills, investment and market research as any other new industrial enterprise. They did not get it" (142). Also, the "dire climate of the recession" offered no leg up (142). Young and idealistic Labour politician Leslie Huckfield—who helped orchestrate the worker takeover of the Meriden plant—would write in July 1974 of the "near-guaranteed market" for these British-built motorcycles, touting local "craftsmanship" over the "gadget-ridden sophistication of the Japanese" bikes.[71] In fact, attempts to prop up the failing venture already included £4.8 million in public money to form the NVT group, followed by another £4.95 million from Benn and the new Labour government. Assessing the failure of this and the two other similarly funded workers' investments in 1981, Christopher Hird in the *New Internationalist* concluded that the projects were doomed from the start for three main reasons: They were underfunded, they were failing and risky business ventures to begin with, and they had no structure for resolving "the *conflict between management and workers*—which is so effectively institutionalised in the industrial relations set-up of conventional companies."[72] Dennis's arguments can be heard loud and clear in this *post mortem* of the cooperatives' failures. Hird goes on:

> The three workers' co-operatives set up under the aegis of Tony Benn, then Britain's Industry Minister, are not the only examples of co-operative enterprise in the country. Their failure—only one survives [Meriden], and with difficulty—should not therefore be taken as a judgment on the co-operative ideal. However these co-operatives attract and deserve special attention they are the only recent examples of attempts to establish large enterprises on a co-operative basis. So long as workers' self-management is part of a political programme in any country, the experience of these co-operatives is important. For those who oppose the idea of workers controlling the direction of enterprises the co-operatives are valuable ammunition; for those who support such ideas, they are an embarrassing inconvenience. (19)

NVT would fold in 1977, and the remainder of the industrial concern would go under in late 1983, partially a victim of the strong British pound against the dollar.

Lastly, Benn's certainty that the trade unions and the Labour government could rule together, co-equally, was clearly revolutionary, at least to the middle-right. Dennis is touting a revolutionary change, as well, from monarchic rule and manorialism to democracy and collective syndicalism, all in one go, sounding like a true Bennite, since by 1972 Benn was

> a man setting himself perhaps the biggest task ever undertaken by a senior peacetime politician: nothing less than a democratic revolution that would bring accountability to education, to the media, to the machinery of the state and, above all, to the workplace. By the mid-1970s Benn's program for change embraced virtually every institution that made up public life in Britain; had it ever been implemented, it would have transformed the nation forever. (Turner, 41)

From the furthest left Benn was demanding that "the very principles of the parliamentary system as currently constituted should be remade and remodeled" (41–42); equally leftist, Dennis is suggesting a similarly vast leap of faith, and to the face of a king. Both Benn and Dennis get throttled for their efforts.[73]

DENNIS: "We're living in a dictatorship . . ."—"Dictatorship" is a sixteenth-century term, while "dictator" had been in usage since Roman times to identify "a chief magistrate with absolute power, appointed for a limited period or for the duration of an emergency" (*OED*), which could be Dennis's meaning.

The Pythons wouldn't have to cast back even that far for examples of totalitarian rule—they'd referenced such governments a number of times during *MPFC*. In Spain, Franco had been ruling with an iron fist since 1936 (*MPFC: UC*, 2.73), while in Bolivia the seat of government had violently shifted multiple times during the Pythons' lifetimes (2.99). Many South and Central American countries were ruled by fascistic governments during this period, Left and Right, including Chile,[74] Paraguay, Uruguay, and others (2.36); Pol Pot (1925–1988) and the Khmer Rouge (Cambodia) had been making news in British newspapers since 1970; and Kim Il-Sung (1912–1994) had been in absolute control of the North

Korean dictatorship since 1948. This was an era of rightist and leftist dictatorships (usually via military junta) in Asia, Africa, and the Americas, as well as Middle Eastern states controlled by wealthy oil families and/or theocratic governments, each supported by either the United States or the Soviet Union and allies as the two superpowers dueled for supremacy during the Cold War.

But the term also had currency in the domestic political diatribe of the day, with each party calling out the other, and even elements within parties decrying others' "dictatorships." In separate incidents, Tony Benn's call for increased government control of broadcasting and programming was so described in a letter to the editor;[75] Opposition Chief Whip Bob Mellish (1913–1998) denied seeking dictatorial control in regard to parliamentary procedure, should Labour win the 1974 election;[76] a Tory chairman of the Greater London Council is a "dictator" to Labour MPs when he clears the gallery during a raucous meeting;[77] and trade unions' control of the Labour party was often shrilly described as "dictatorial"—that charge often going both ways.[78]

It's likely that Dennis is *not* offering a *double entente*, talking about the "dictatorship of the proletariat" espoused by Trotsky in his writings on "Permanent Revolution" (and referenced by the Pythons in *MPFC* Ep. 34), though given his knowledge of syndicalism, it's not out of the question (*MPFC: UC*, 2.107). Lenin, writing in a "draft of RCP reply to the Independent Social-Democratic Party of Germany," also paints a Dennisean image of the phrase:

> The dictatorship of the proletariat means the overthrow of the bourgeoisie by a single class, the proletariat, and by its revolutionary vanguard at that. To demand that this vanguard should first ensure the support of the majority of the people through elections to bourgeois parliaments, bourgeois constituent assemblies etc., i.e. by elections held, while wages slavery still exists, while the exploiters exist and exercise their oppression, and while the means of production are privately owned—to demand this or to assume it, is actually abandoning the dictatorship of the proletariat and going over to the stand-point of bourgeois democracy. (quoted in Hallas, "Reforming the Labour Party?")

This kind of dictatorship is still a straightjacket (no matter what Lenin or Mao opined), as George Bernard Shaw[79] reminded an American audience in a speech given in April 1933, at the height of the Great Depression and just months into the National Socialist's ascension in Germany: "In your dread of dictators you established a state of society in which every ward boss is a dictator, every financier a dictator, every private employer a dictator, all with the livelihood of the workers at their mercy, and no public responsibility."[80] The threat of the dictator would have been more keenly felt in Europe, of course, as a remilitarized Germany seemed a simmering but present threat. Dennis and mother and their adherence to the "autonomous collective" shibboleth actually tease this double meaning into possibility.

DENNIS: ". . . a self-perpetuating autocracy"—Dennis is clearly meant to represent not only Tony Benn, the far-left Labour minister, but period union leaders like Arthur Scargill, Richard Briginshaw,[81] Jack Jones, Jimmy Reid,[82] Hugh Scanlon, or even Jack Dash (1907–1989), the militant, Communist labor firebrand.[83] In 1969, Dash addressed a conference of the Mossford Young Conservatives, and made the following prescient comparison: "There are more knights around the T.U.C. table than there ever were at King Arthur's," he said. "If I'd had my way they wouldn't be knighted but neutered."[84] Dash's mind-set and singularity of purpose is described by another *Times* correspondent in very Dennis-like terms: "The cause of the workers, an almost mystical obsession with proletarian solidarity, enables him to shrug off distasteful facts quite casually."[85] Through the 1960s Dash led a number of unofficial strikes—some for pay, some for principles alone—representing the Royal Dock Group, often holding "dockgate" meetings with his workers at the gates of the docks just as shifts ended, not unlike Dennis meeting Arthur in his field of "lovely filth."

The *Times* labor editor Paul Routledge noted in 1973 that the then-current breed of union leaders were formed in a different crucible, with men like Jones and Scanlon receiving "their political education in the slump of the 1930s, in left-wing (usually communist) movements of the day, and in the wider struggle against fascism," Routledge writes. "The political experience they underwent left an ineradicable mark, which has coloured their attitudes ever since."[86] Dennis would clearly fit as a man formed in the crucible of sub-Roman Britain, fighting against a fascism he sees in this unilateral authority before him or an absent lord, and ready to stand toe-to-toe with his "management" and demand a better life, like the modern union leaders.

Jack Jones (1913–2009) was known as the "bogy-man of the trade unions" when the new and controversial Industrial Relations Bill was being gutted by angry unions and nervous MPs in 1970.[87] Jones was the General Secretary of the powerful Transport and General Workers' Union (TGWU), and seen by many as Scanlon's "terrible twin" (both often labeled "militants" in the press), while Scargill—though younger than these other union leaders (b. 1938)—represented the Yorkshire area for the NUM during this period, leading the crippling miner's strike in 1972, which effectively harried Heath out of office by 1974. Scargill was the face of the strike for many, appearing in TV sound bites for weeks (including at the "Battle of Saltley Gate" in February 1972) as the country ground to a halt (Turner, 13). Incidentally, Scargill was becoming such a celebrity for the militant unionists—profiled by both the *Times* and the *Illustrated London News*, for example—that fellow union leaders became jealous, calling him "King Arthur . . . whose Camelot is Barnsley," according to Paul Routledge (*Times*, 4 January 1974: 12).

Scanlon (1913–2004), who died Baron Scanlon, worked at an engineering firm and joined the Amalgamated Engineering Union (AEU) as an energetic British Communist and admitted Marxist in 1937. In August 1973, writing for the AEU journal he waxed quite Dennisean as he described the impossibility of workers' achieving their ultimate ends while still part of the current political system:

> All the proposals on industrial democracy being put forward are made within the context of a capitalist society and appear to envisage its constitution.
>
> Trade unions obviously have the task of always attempting to improve the position of workers within the existing economic framework, but they must never lose sight of the long-term objective, *which is to create a completely different form of society altogether* (my italics). This is an objective which can only be secured through political action and, therefore, even proposals from the TUC for greater industrial democracy are no more than means towards an end.
>
> Trade unions naturally demand on behalf of workers an ever growing control over working conditions but this must be achieved without compromising our long-term objectives. Only through full public ownership can we secure effective national planning, and an effective system of industrial democracy to supplement the shell of political democracy. (quoted in Routledge, *Times*, 23 August 1973: 14)

Scanlon had been writing and speaking for workers' control for years, publishing, for example, *The Way Forward for Workers' Control* in 1968 (from the Institute for Workers' Control in Nottingham).[88] And as early as 1967, in an interview with the *New Left Review*, Scanlon describes the trade unions as a vehicle for the ultimate change, the kind of change Dennis espouses: "Undoubtedly, the final role of the trade unions must be to change society itself, not merely to get the best out of existing society."[89] So Scanlon, Kenneth Gill, Tony Benn, Dennis, and his mother seem to be on the same syndicalist page.

The term "self-perpetuating autocracy" was part of the cultural lexicon available to the Pythons, as was the rising indignation of the ruled toward the ruling class in the postwar period. In 1961 the annual meeting of the Royal Society for the Prevention of Cruelty to Animals (*MPFC: UC*, 1.387) became an entertaining palaver when anti-blood sport members (i.e., those against fox hunting) harangued the council leadership for its soft position on such perceived cruelty. Police were summoned at one point, and protestors flung themselves to the floor near the rostrum. Environmentalist Mr. Edward Whitley—who would become a new council member elected by postal vote the following year, and who was opposed to fox hunting—was quoted loudly describing the council as moving toward "a self-perpetuating autocracy," after which the meeting eventually "collapsed in uproar" according to a *Times* correspondent.[90] And in 1964 it was the Communists' turn to take a bashing, when ex-Labour candidate John H. Bloom resigned from the Communist Party with this farewell broadside: "The party leadership—the political committee—is a *self-perpetuating autocracy* whose power is so absolute that it determines and controls every phase of party life to the detriment of all other tendencies."[91] Lastly, in June 1973 it was NHS regional hospital boards taking it on the chin from opinionated former minister of health Richard Crossman (1907–1974), calling them "the most *autocratic, self-perpetuating* oligarchies since the Persian Empire."[92]

OLD WOMAN: "There you go, bringing class into it again"—This sounds like a neat bit from a Hegelian dialectic, or even a Marxian one that stretches across time—here by Dennis adroitly compressed into a single moment of interaction with Arthur. Primitive communism (where Dennis and his collective might locate themselves), followed across time by slavery, then feudalism/manorialism, then capitalism, and an ultimate Communism—it's a dizzying proposition, and clearly Arthur doesn't "see," as he says he does. The feudal and manorial system is in place, with Arthur representing the nobility, ruling lords and their demesnes; capitalism is what Dennis is "on about"—a new slavery where the working class eke out a living by the leave of the oppressive bourgeois system that also owns the means of production; while the *ne plus ultra* is a nationwide series of "autonomous collectives" (and *not* self-defeating bureaucratic Communism) that can be independent but interactive as needed—a proletarian paradise.

This diatribe locates Dennis far away from tenth-century Britain, of course, and much closer to the Pythons' lifetimes. More precisely Dennis seems to be aping the eager but misguided modern historian, as described in McKisack's *The Fourteenth Century*, in a section where the changing role of serf and bondman between the outbreak of the Black Death in 1348 and the Revolt of 1381 is being discussed:

> Yet the impression conveyed by some modern writers of a population of agricultural slaves ruthlessly exploited alike by Church and State, by landlords and by their more prosperous brethren, accords better with Marxist preconceptions than with the facts of English history. (342)

"In the fourteenth, as in every subsequent century before our own, many country people were all too well acquainted with poverty," McKisack continues, "but few of them could be equated with slaves, either ancient or modern, and unrelieved misery can hardly have been general" (342–43). McKisack goes on to tick off the often unremarked (and unremarkable, to some writers of history) "spiritual consolation" the clergy could and did provide—the benefits of the sacraments, and the overall "Christian framework" of the age—all very much in place in medieval Britain and likely significant to the common man (343). She also notes that there were many landlords who exhibited humaneness and Christian humility in regard to their lessers, perhaps because they were simply goodhearted, and perhaps because they understood how God's justice works. Piers Plowman does, as he talks with a knight:

"And mysbede nougt thi bonde-men · the better may thow spede;
Thowgh he be thyn vnderlynge here · wel may happe in heuene,
That he worth worthier sette · and with more blisse,
Than thow, bot thou do bette · and lyue as thow shulde;
For in charnel ate chirche · cherles ben yuel to knowe,
Or a knigte fram a knaue there · knowe this in thin herte." (*Piers Plowman* B vi. 46–51)[93]

Just the way Dennis speaks to Arthur tells us that he already sees little difference between knight and knave. Dennis is the voice of the postwar trade union leader and the left wing of the Labour party—both personas that can only confuse the generically restricted Arthur—but he may also be standing in for the Middle Ages historians Jones and the other Pythons encountered in their university studies, those that prescribed the evils of acquisitiveness to every medieval social malady. The fact that the Pythons chose to include the figure of "A Famous Historian"—and then kill him violently—lends more credence to the latter identification, as well.

But as editorials of the period point out, it wasn't the Soviets or indeed any member of the Eastern Bloc or inchoate Communist governments in Africa or Southeast Asia or Latin America where Dennis's utopia *might* be forming—it was in a shadowy, semi-closed country that the Pythons had already, in *MPFC*, highlighted as the world's next threatening superpower—China.[94] The People's Republic of China had been moving away from the "Russian pattern . . . based on the nineteenth century concepts of Marx and Engels" so connected to Europe and even Lenin,[95] prior to 1949 when Mao consolidated his power, and moved in a different—and for many a more frightening direction:

> It was the Chinese and only the Chinese who completely severed these connexions. For the urban base of party activity they substituted the rural; from the workers they turned to the peasants; for union agitation and strikes as a source of power they substituted the armed group of peasant guerrillas; for the *coup d'Etat* in a revolutionary situation as a means to victory they developed the alternative of "liberated areas" ruled by semi-autonomous commands united in a long civil war. This was the road that brought Chinese Communism to power in 1949 and it is the leaders of this astonishing deviation who are still in power today.[96]

Dennis can decry Arthur's "outdated imperialist dogma" and his revolutionary worldview can be cherry-picked out of the above description, but he possesses in spades something that Mao seemed to find the most threatening in a subject: singular wit and intelligence. McKisack's examination of mid- to late-fourteenth-century manor petitions reveals much about the peasant petitioners, "not only as keenly aware of their rights and of their common interest, but also as well able to defend them. For, in their formal protest to the prior against an over-zealous steward, these peasants plead the Great Charter and common and statute law as well as the custom of the manor" (345). In his audio commentary Palin identifies Dennis as a typically brusque Englishman who can shout "I know my rights!" with unselfconscious enthusiasm—clearly more contemporary freedoms afforded citizens of the modern Britain, but *not* Mao's revolutionary China. The subsequent and regrettable disasters of the Great Leap Forward and the Cultural Revolution make this clear.[97]

Closer to home, the problems of and attention to the working class were alive and well in 1973–1974 in the Pythons' Britain. The most local examples include the thousands of striking workers who essentially paralyzed the country in 1973—working-class people (and their shop stewards and union representatives) with a collective axe to grind and a forum to grind it upon.[98] Unemployment figures for this period also sent blood pressures rising in Westminster, especially around election time. The meaningless but still frightening one million mark was reached in January 1972, giving Labour backbenchers something very catchy to shout about in the Commons, and keeping Heath back on his heels.[99] The daily papers offer myriad working-class battlegrounds (always carefully separated from "middle-class" issues) beyond unemployment, from the films of Ken Loach to the challenges of educating poor children to the pulling down of affordable council housing to make way for retail or upscale homes. Class has been an issue for the Pythons throughout *MPFC*, where both upper-class twits and working-class layabouts are regularly lampooned.

Finally, Engels discussed class this way, employing the buzzwords Dennis and his mother seem to know:

> The state arose from the need to keep class antagonisms in check, but also arose in the thick of the fight between the classes; it is normally the state of the most powerful, economically ruling class, which by its means becomes also the politically ruling class, and so acquires new means of holding down and exploiting the oppressed class. . . . Civilization is founded on the exploitation of one class by another class as in the example of slave labor as the dominant form of production. The society which organizes production anew on the basis of free and equal association of the producers will put the whole state machinery where it will then belong—into the museum of antiquities, next to the spinning wheel and the bronze ax.[100]

As recently as 1964 in Britain, just months before the end of Tory rule and the beginning of the "white heat" of a Labour-led Britain, the Young Socialists staged a debate wherein Moderates and Leftists sniped it out. The Moderates, ostensibly looking forward, called for a move away from the "Marxist clichés and the old fashioned ideas" of the Left, and an end to "the claptrap of the class war."[101] The "There you go bringing class into it again" complaint can be heard loud and clear. Tony Benn was present at this conference, attempting to bridge the gap between factions, and it was reported nothing of value actually got done.[102] As late as spring 1972, with the country reeling from union work stoppages, unemployment, the Belfast and Derry debacles, and a badly handled economy, "class" distinctions continued to jaundice the general public's view of modern life, according to Sandbrook:

> [E]xisting political and social differences [were given] a sharper edge: it was telling that according to Gallup, three out of five people . . . believed that there was a class struggle in Britain, the highest proportion for decades. In the rhetoric of parliamentary debates, as well as on the shop floors, on picket lines and in university classrooms, the language of class warfare came increasingly naturally to the tongue, partly because of the popularity of pseudo-Marxist ideas in the late 1960s and early 1970s, but also because a stuttering economy lent a new bitterness to old divisions. (*State of Emergency*, 311)

Given the current environment, it would have been unusual if Dennis had *not* brought "class into it again," since he seems to be speaking for many in the Britain of 1973–1974.

OLD WOMAN: "No one lives there"— In the two centuries following the Norman conquest there were a number of what were known as *honours* arrangements granted by the conqueror William and his successors. In rural England one knight could have been granted several manors (with or without castles) in separate counties, for example, and would have visited these holdings as needed. In these cases the knight often employed a local reeve to manage each estate.[103] The *honours* arrangement meant that, technically, "no one" lived at a particular castle for months at a time,[104] and, as Mortimer confirms of the later fourteenth century: "Most castles are almost empty when the lord is not in residence" (162).

Continuing on the vein of the *abandoned* castle theme started earlier, the various plagues that swept across Britain between the sixth and fourteenth centuries also forced the abandonment of many villages and individual structures, as noted by contemporary chronicler Robert of Avesbury (d. 1359):

> After the foresaid pestilence [the Great Plague of 1349], many buildings, great and small, fell into ruins in every city, borough, and village for lack of inhabitants, likewise many villages and hamlets became desolate, not a house being left in them, all having died who dwelt there; and it was probable that many such villages would never be inhabited. (Ashley, *Edward III and His Wars*, 126)

And it wasn't just famine and pestilence that decreased town or village populations across Britain, of course, but the inexorable reductions in Roman influence beginning sometime in the later fourth century.[105] Archaeologists and historians have found significant "gaps" between Roman occupation (and farming, industry, etc.) and Anglo-Saxon resettlement in most areas, and that "all towns in Roman Britain seem to have been in decline in terms of their habitation area and population size from the third century onwards" (Welch 104).[106] Mirroring what Arthur and Patsy encounter in the way of "civilization," Welch continues:

> It is not clear that any of them really deserved to be called a town after the first decade of the fifth century. Deposits of black earth, partly derived from accumulated wind-blown rubbish built up within the walls of many towns between the late third and seventh centuries. These deposits surely reflect neglect and abandonment. (104)

Also, Gidlow notes the abundance of abandoned Roman or even pre-Roman sites in the fifth and sixth centuries, and their understandably fading identification: "Archaeological evidence shows that the refortified hillforts of the period had usually stood without residential or military use for centuries. They might no longer have had names of their own" (57). Too expensive or cumbersome to maintain, many Roman and then Anglo-Saxon buildings and fortifications simply mouldered into disrepair between the fifth and tenth centuries across Britain.[107]

There is a third possibility for a castle with no lord, and for a failure to recognize same. The Crusades drew away many noblemen and others into foreign service, some for years at a time.[108] Chronicler William of Malmesbury (1095–1143) employs "pious exaggeration" when he describes the peoples' answer to Urban's call, according to Halsall: "The Welshman left his hunting, the Scot his fellowship with vermin, the Dane his drinking party, the Norwegian his raw fish. Lands were deserted of their husbandmen, houses of their inhabitants; even whole cities migrated" (*Worlds of Arthur*, 94). Neat stereotyping aside, many noblemen and those others with the wherewithal to make the journey did take up the gauntlet and leave for the Holy Lands.

In the first issue of Frank Bolle's 1955 comic book *Robin Hood*, Robin—the rightful lord of Huntingdon Manor—tells of following King Richard to the Holy Land, then being asked by Richard to return to England to "guard [his] interests and protect the welfare of [his] people." When Robin returns, he finds that his lands and castle have been given to Gui of Glamore by the usurper Prince John. As he rides "disconsolately" through Sherwood Forest he is set upon by brigands, who are ready to relieve Robin of his gold and his horse. Robin overcomes their leader, proclaiming: "Back, you fools! Don't any of you fools recognize me?"

Coincidentally, of course, he's been attacked by his own retainers—they were evicted from the manor when Gui took over. So not only does the rightful lord not live in the manor, the lord's vassals no longer recognize their lord. (At least when Dennis doesn't recognize Arthur, it's partly because he's *never* seen him before.) And like Bedevere later—who recognizes his "liege" and promptly swears to that allegiance—the men of Sherwood Forest swear to follow Robin and King Richard from that day.

OLD WOMAN: "We don't have a Lord"—This would have been impossible in medieval France, for example, where feudal French law dictated: "No lord without land; no land without a lord."[109] These peasants or *villeins* would have been answerable to some higher authority, some landlord or nobleman, or some reeve or seneschal[110] representing a lord or the king, even during times of pestilence or civil unrest. Even in England, Arthur's confusion is understandable, given the political and social situation of the late fifth and early sixth centuries. Though it seems as convenient as pitting invading Saxons (actually Angles, Jutes, and Saxons, according to Bede[111])—the "English"—against defending natives, the British, Morris points out that as early as Vortigern's tenure the alliances reportedly purchased between local leader Vortigern (who was British) and invited Saxon mercenaries against other British led to confusion all around:

> [F]or a short period in Hengest's[112] later years, his success turned it into a clear conflict between the English and the British; but ended with a more complicated pattern of local variation. The little evidence that shows Saxon sundered from Saxon, British at odds with British, warns that such divisions are likely to have been more numerous than we know. (*Age of Arthur*, 110)

Morris notes that the frontiers between, for example, Haslingfield and the middle Thames, or Surrey and Kent were obviously protected, since trade during this period did not occur between these peoples. The Cambridge settlement is much nearer to Haslingfield (in fact, it is in sight from a nearby ridge) than the middle Thames, but grave contents in Haslingfield for the fifth century indicate no trade between Haslingfield and Cambridge, and

> only in the sixth century did these people acquire Anglian jewelry from Cambridge as well. They were at first as sundered from Cambridge as were the men of Surrey from Kent. But they were nearer the town, in sight from the top of the ridge, and their differences argues a firm, unfriendly frontier that admitted no intermarriage and no exchange. (110)

Other scholars, including Dumville, are more circumspect about Vortigern (or Gwrtheyrn) and his place in history versus legend, and Morris's dependence on sources that aren't sufficiently reliable. Dumville concludes:

> [W]e can place no reliance on the detail of the legends reported by Bede and the Anglo-Saxon Chronicle; and I, at least, am not prepared to write fifth-century British history on the basis of legends retold from Anglo-Saxon sources by a Welshman in the ninth century. ("Sub-Roman Britain: History and Legend," 185)

Vortigern's contributions aside, Dennis and his mother (and the other peasants in view in the background) could have easily scratched out an existence in the lands *between* British and English strongholds, or even British and British settlements, having no direct interaction with any of them, happy to gather filth in their relative freedom.

Tuchman notes another possibility, though, mentioning that in France, by the onset of the first appearance of the Black Death, "free peasants were already in the majority" (232). It may be that Dennis and his mother could have been serfs, but, away from their lord (thanks to his death or their escape), they were "regarded as free" after a year (232).

DENNIS: ". . . an anarcho-syndicalist commune . . ."—The anarcho-syndicalist movement had been active in the UK for many years by this time, culminating in the formation of the Syndicalist Workers Federation in 1950 in Manchester.[113] Not to be confused with the SWP (the Socialist Workers Party), the SWF strove to better working conditions for the working class both nationally and internationally.[114] The movement was especially motivated after the events of 1968, when thousands of youths took to the streets of Paris, and sympathetic demonstrations popped up in British cities, as well. Not coincidentally, Rudolf Rocker's seminal *Anarcho-Syndicalism: Theory and Practice*, originally appearing in 1938 as Fascist powers gripped Europe, was reprinted in 1968, and again in 1972. Rocker suggests replacement of the existing "state-organizations" (which Arthur clearly represents), his reasonable desire for Anarchists being the Dennisean "federation of free communities which shall be bound to one another by their common economic and social interest and shall arrange their affairs by mutual agreement and free contracts" (2). They are collective; they are co-operative; they are anticapitalist and antifascist. Rocker goes on to discuss the fatal drawbacks of both economic and political dictatorships, where the sacrifices of the general interests of human society are made to private interests, leading toward

> every country [divided] into hostile classes internally. . . . [E]xternally it has broken the common cultural circle up into hostile nations; and both classes and nations confront one another ["the violence inherent in the system!"] with open antagonism and by their ceaseless warfare keep the communal social life in continual convulsions. (3)

Rocker and his followers, including Tom Brown and the SWF (see below), provide Dennis with the language of his "autonomous collectives," and share Dennis's perhaps misplaced optimism that such changes are, actually, inevitable.

Closer to the Pythons' home, in February 1968, Tom Brown (retired Labour MP, Ince; 1886–1970) wrote a short "Story of the Syndicalist Workers' Federation," and closed with the following appraisal, where Rocker's fundamentals can be glimpsed:

> The term Syndicalism is more acceptable to the British worker than is the theological-sounding mouthful, Anarcho-Syndicalism, and the Syndicalist ethos is to workers, and even historians, a good ethos in Britain. Some complain that the SWF has not changed its principles. That, in a world where Socialist politicians change their principles far more often than their raincoats, ought to be welcome. But the principles of capitalism have not changed: *we live in a society which is still founded on rich and poor, war and class war still go on, men's lives are still governed by property relations.* What has happened to all those fabulous developments which made Syndicalism and Revolution "irrelevant"—the H-Bomb, Affluent Society, Automation? . . . The old problems are still with us. Capitalism has no answer. The case for Syndicalism remains unanswered.[115] It is no answer to go looking for a new butterfly to chase.[116]

Espoused over and over again in anarcho-syndicalist literature is that anarcho-syndicalism, at its most complete, would be a total *replacement* for capitalism and the state that supports capitalism. Dennis is opining about workers like he and his mother controlling production, distribution, and even consumption of the goods and services they produce—no politicians, mine and mill owners, or even shop stewards in between to skim off the cream. This radical concept had been much-discussed in Britain in the 1910s and 1920s, then inspired by workers taking control of factories in Italy prior to Mussolini's rise to power, as well as militant labor movements in France, and later in 1936 in Spain before Franco took control. The *Times* explained the proposed *syndicalist* changes to French labor in a series of articles printed in April 1909:

> *Syndicalisme* is the distinctive mark of the present labour movement in France and a matter of great interest, which every student of social affairs who wishes to be well-informed ought to understand. It is a new thing and a genuine product of that section of the population which we call, inappropriately, the working classes. Like trade unionism and co-operation, it has developed within the ranks and has not been imposed from without, like Socialism, which is from first to last a "bourgeois" conception. Perhaps the essential character of *Syndicalisme* is best expressed by saying that it is a purely trade union version of Socialism, definitely and even violently opposed to Collectivism and more nearly allied to anarchism, yet distinct from it. . . . The object of *Syndicalisme* is revolution, sudden and complete, in which the State and all the apparatus of government, is to disappear, and the possession and control of material means—which alone count—is to pass from the hands of its present owners, whether private or public, into those of organized labour. This original idea is Socialistic or Collectivist insofar as it is directed against capitalism; it is anarchistic insofar as it contemplates the disappearance of the State; but, above all, it is trade unionist, for the *syndicat* is posited as the unit or cell of the future social organism. ("The Labour Movement in France," 20 April 1909: 4)

And just as those espousing syndicalism looked askance at Socialism as a "bourgeois conception," Socialists saw Syndicalism as just another great fraud, an "importation" from the Continent, and thus untrustworthy. In a *Socialist Standard* review of the 1912 book *Syndicalism and the Great Strike* (Arthur D. Lewis) by A. Kohn (d. 1956), Kohn denounces all forms of Anarchism (including anarcho-syndicalism) as being anti-Socialist, reminding his readers (members of the Socialist Party of Great Britain) that

> Syndicalism thrives on ignorance. Only mis-educated, non Socialist workers would ever trust the Labour Party, would ever expect them to look after the toilers' interests; and when the failure of their political inaction is realised, it is not the political method itself that has been found wanting, but it is the lack of sound knowledge on the workers' part that is demonstrated. Because the political machine has been used in a capitalist direction the Syndicalist and his dupes proclaim the failure of politics! . . . The general strike of miners and other strikes in England bring home the lessons of the Socialist. Whilst the strike, local or industrial, may effect improvement for the time, slavery remains. Whilst the threat of a general strike may induce concessions, it cannot bring a solution. The best results of economic unity can only be effected by class-conscious toilers who recognise the need for class action, class union, for working class ends; who realise that, as the road to emancipation lies in control of political power, political action is a vital necessity. The cure for Syndicalism is education in the Socialist principles and policy. There is no substitute for a Socialist working class seeking its salvation through the political struggle. When the toilers understand Socialism they will have no room in their minds for the sophisms and fallacies of Syndicalism. (25–26)

So Dennis might be on the outs not only with Arthur—a representative of the monarchy, the wealthy, government, and management—but also estranged from both Socialists and Anarchists, since Dennis is clearly making the case for a collective on a small, community basis separate from the masses of the workers and separate from *any* union or political control or leadership. The Soviets were actively denouncing such movements in the Soviet Bloc in the late 1960s, for different but obvious reasons. In a story filed by Dessa Trevisan on 4 March 1969, it was reported that "[t]he Soviet Union . . . condemned moves in eastern Europe towards trade union independence and the establishment of worker control of factories as 'anarcho-syndicalism' which would lead to a return of capitalism."[117] The *Times* article goes on to quote at length from another article appearing in *Pravda* (by Dr. Sergei Titarenko) outlining the pitfalls of this way of thinking:

> The aim of the enemies of socialism is to undermine the authority of the Communist Parties and to remove them from the control of society. . . . Quite natural this would bring about a revival of private ownership psychology and morality. Anarcho-syndicalism is a step to corporationalism and fractionalism, towards degeneration to capitalism in a socialist economy. (6)

Again, Dennis's version of the movement as constituted in his village sounds even more dangerous—to all parties—as it denies the need for the usual bodies of power and authority, none of which, historically, volunteer to surrender their control.[118] (Arthur won't give in, either.) This danger is being experienced in Britain of the 1970s, as well. In an article looking at the "irrelevant" Liberal Party (following the 1970 General Election, when the party lost six seats, and Labour lost the government), the party's disarray was made evident:

> Its annual assembly meets with the party as disunited about its objectives and its *raison d'être* as it is argumentative over its tactics. The Young Liberals, described the other day by one of their own M.P.s, Mr. Emlyn Hooson, as "anarcho-syndicalist youngsters," regard the party only as a convenient means of furthering their own ideas of community politics and pressures. Essentially contemptuous of the whole concept of parliamentary and party government, they are consequently alien to the tradition cherished by most of the people who have worked to keep the Liberal Party in the business of practical politics since the war.[119]

These "youngsters" sound very much like descendants of Dennis.[120]

There is clearly no place for a king like Arthur in any of the anarcho-syndicalist worlds. Gone dormant thanks to World War I and then the rise of fascism across Europe, the syndicalist idea had coincidentally come back in full force in September 1969 and much closer to home—coinciding with the Pythons' recording of the first series of *MPFC*—when workers took over Merseyside factories and announced that managers were no longer needed.[121] The anarcho-syndicalist ideal was, certainly, to "argue for independent industry-wide unions to both co-ordinate day to day struggle and pursue the long term aim of replacing capitalism with a society based on direct democracy and workers' control of the work."[122]

The confusing jargon comes right from the picket lines and newspapers of the day, including workers' cooperative proponent Leslie Huckfield's[123] serious but still linguistically amusing description of just how the new Triumph Motorcycles Meriden Limited works would run its business with its worker/owners in full control:

> [The] scheme represents a half-way house between the original two phases. There will be a professional executive management, responsible to a 12-man supervisory board, representing each of the unions involved. A board of trustees will be responsible for the overall assets and surpluses. Although this represents a slight departure from the proposals for 50 per cent workers' representation on two-tier-boards recently advocated by the Labour Party and the TUC, the essential "trade union connexion" is preserved.[124]

Ken Coates (1930–2010), of the Institute for Workers' Control (IWC), described the situation similarly:

> It signifies a struggle by workers and their organizations to encroach upon the prerogative of management, and to put back managerial authority in the enterprise, and the power of capital

in the economy. It begins with simple trade union demands for control of hiring and firing, tea-breaks, hours, speeds of work, allocation of jobs and so on. It mounts through a whole series of demands (open the books, for example) to a point where, ultimately, over the whole society, capitalist society meets impasse. At this point, which in its general political correlative is described as "dual power", one reaches a revolutionary solution.[125]

It may be worth remembering here that "anarchy" also actually means a state or existence where individuals have complete control of themselves, "without implication of disorder"[126]—not the way the term is often used today. Arthur likely wouldn't have seen Dennis's request this way, however, angry and frustrated as he was with this "Bloody peasant," nor do most members of political parties who can see anarchists only for their disruptive and destructive potential to existing power structures.

DENNIS: ". . . we take it in turns to act as a sort of executive officer for the week"—The syndicalist movement in Britain ascribed to this organizational structure, as well, according to Tom Brown, of the Syndicalist Workers' Federation:

> While Syndicalists look to the elemental mass meeting of the workers at their place of work as the foundation of organisation and the greatest source of labour's strength, there are, nevertheless, certain functions that cannot be carried out by a mass meeting—certain details and arrangements where delegation of function is necessary. So the meeting elects delegates to carry out its wishes and general resolutions.
>
> But these men and women are nothing *but* delegates. They are elected for certain limited functions, to carry out certain general instructions, and always subject to recall. This right of recall is fundamental to Syndicalism, though it is somewhat strange to the orthodox labour movement and completely foreign to the Communist belief.[127]

It is also new to King Arthur, clearly.

DENNIS: ". . . at a bi-weekly meeting by a simple majority" . . .—This minutiae is borrowed from worker-controlled associations, where laundry lists of rules designed to fairly represent and support every member and every possible labor situation mean approved decisions and actions can take an eternity (satirized in the People's Front of Judea meeting scenes in *Life of Brian*). There are also medieval precedents for such orderliness. Sawyer notes that by as early as the middle of the tenth century "royal ordinance required that hundreds [county divisions] were to meet every four weeks," and that "justice" was to be done to all at these monthly meetings (198). Dennis may be simply repeating what some local lord or reeve had decreed earlier from some other king, essentially "emphasizing the function of the local community," especially in terms of public order issues that did not or should not require the king's direct attention (198). It may also be that those peasants we see gathering around Dennis constitute at least part of his "tithing," which was "a group of ten or twelve men who were mutually responsible for their good behaviour and, if necessary, for accusing, arresting and producing any of their number found guilty of a crime" (198). This participation in the tithing was known south of the Humber as a "frank-pledge," which may account for the Old Woman asking after "Frank" for his input. This helpful and watchful tithing could also, likely, serve nicely as Dennis's seconds or jury members to testify against Arthur if this manhandling moment comes before the local court.

Dennis's list (and Dennis himself, to an extent) is reminiscent of the nitpicking silliness of the character Fred Kite (Peter Sellers), the finicky, work-to-rule Communist shop steward in the 1959 satirical film *I'm All Right, Jack*. In one particular scene, the Works Committee, led by the fussy Mr. Kite, enter the factory manager's office with the express purpose of having a new, non-union, and incompetent employee immediately sacked or a work stoppage will be called. By the time the confrontation with the manager (Terry-Thomas) is over, the Committee and Mr. Kite are instead arguing for the inalienable rights of this new man, that "incompetence [never] justifies dismissal," and that firing him would be an act of "victimization"—which would spark an immediate strike.[128] The Committee leaves full of righteous workers' indignation, determined to keep this new "brother" safe from the vicissitudes of their oppressive management.

Away from trade unions but no further from organizational-speak is the Co-Operative Party, a mutualist bastion. A recent version of *The Rule Book* for regional sections of the Co-Operative Party (allied with Labour since 1927 and standing no candidates of its own) reads in a familiarly convoluted way:

> No Rule shall be altered, or new Rule adopted, unless written notice is given to the Secretary at least 28 days prior to the meeting of the Regional Party at which it is to be discussed and circulated at least seven days prior to this date. The proposal must be supported by two-thirds of the members voting. No such Rule shall become operative until it is approved and registered by the NEC of the Party.[129]

The Co-Operative Party has (and has had) a General Secretary but not a "party chairman" who leads, a recent article points out—the difference being, it seems, that the General Secretary "leads with" while the party chairman "leads at the head of"—separating them significantly from any of the three major UK political parties.[130] Historically, since the party itself came about after a rancorous to-do with the Conservative Party during World War I, an Arthur-versus-Dennis scenario fits well, if Dennis could have belonged to or supported a political party. The Co-Op Party sounds, after all, like a place where Dennis could be comfortable:

> It was the Co-operative party, not the Conservatives, which first advocated mutualising (rather than nationalising or privatising) public services (the Co-operative party persuaded Labour to pledge the mutualisation of the life assurance industry in the Labour manifesto for the 1950 election). Locally, it was the Co-operative party that, during the 1960s, pioneered "people power": democratically controlled, mutually-owned co-operative social housing schemes, and persuaded the Labour governments to back them, against the prejudices of Whitehall and council officials. Co-operative party MPs and ministers were also responsible for introducing Britain's framework of consumer rights legislation in the 1960s. ("Co-Op Politics")

The Co-Operative Party and movement were much in the news in the period 1970–1974, with various congresses voting on major changes in membership (perhaps outlawing Communists), support of or opposition to EEC membership, increasing or decreasing mergers, and wrangling with elements of modernization in the business structures to better compete with capitalist enterprises.[131]

ARTHUR: "Be quiet! I order you to be quiet"—In the printed script, Arthur actually orders her to "shut up" (*MPHGB*, 9). More important is the forcefulness employed here by Arthur as rightful sovereign. This is also a Malory conceit, found in the early part of *Le Morte Darthur*, when young, "beardless" Arthur is being opposed by the more surly and time-tested lords of the land, and Merlin counsels him to "fear not, but come out boldly and speak with them, and spare them not, but answer them as their king and chieftain" (*LMD-WM*, 13). Merlin goes on to assure Arthur that he "shall overcome them all, whether they will or nill" (13). Our Arthur has this same certainty of destiny and purpose, and eventually, the doubling assurance of God's permission and support.

Clearly here, too, Arthur does not and cannot appreciate that one of his subjects lives a life separate from the king's pleasure. There are two narrative threads here. Arthur is pursuing the quest model, meaning every stop is merely a rest and a chance to gather adherents or fight any who would attempt to shunt aside the providential journey. This isn't a pilgrimage like *Canterbury Tales*, for example, where stories are told along the way, the stopping points or even the destination becoming secondary. There is no place for a Dennis, who has his own narrative trajectory, separate from Arthur's; his is a life given over to subsistence farming and workers' rights. This encounter is also significant in that no useful knowledge is gained, no secrets or directions found, no new companion met and embraced. This scene follows immediately both the "Coconuts and Swallows" and "Bring Out Your Dead" scenes, neither of which held any information for Arthur that would lead him closer to his goal—at this point, like-minded knights wishing to join him at Camelot. It's simply another funny sketch where expectations are upset. It won't be until the "She's a Witch" scene that Arthur finally finds an acolyte in Sir Bedevere; before that he simply maims the Black Knight after watching the Green Knight die. (A few of the encounters in the film are useful or informational, as will be seen, but not most.)

This is all part of the film's anti-heroic structure, a borrow from much Modernist literature as well as New Wave films that revisit and revise classical or traditional tropes, often emptying those tropes of meaning and significance before trotting them out and revealing their inadequacies (i.e., Buñuel's *The Milky Way*, which sends up the pilgrimage scenario). But it's also, at its heart, just a funny sketch, one that doesn't have to be connected intrinsically to anything else in the film—it's just funny, like the "Make Sure 'e Doesn't Leave" sketch later. The structure of *MPFC* allowed for asides, intrusions, *non sequiturs*, etc., and a Python audience would have expected a feature film to at least nod to this magpie structure. These fruitless encounters—or "unsuccessful transactions," as they are described in *MPFC: UC*—fly in the face of the traditional quest structure, rendering the journey futile and frustrating, which is why Arthur tries to choke Dennis. This inability to communicate or transact successfully in the modern world—or in a Dark Ages world inflected by the fantastic and the modern—has been a Python staple since the first episode of *MPFC*, and continued through the entire series.

OLD WOMAN: "Order, eh? Who does he think he is?"—Dennis and his mother still haven't appreciated just who is standing before them, of course, though even if they knew he was a king it doesn't seem likely that they'd just give him a pass. But Arthur isn't alone in this case of misunderstood identity. Even the fifty-year reign of Edward III couldn't guarantee that his subjects would know him as anything more than a "pasteboard figure," and a king that historians tend to treat badly (McKisack, 269). His recognizability was such that he was rather easily able to dress as a merchant and make a 1331 trip to France for a clandestine meeting with Philip VI, his thin disguise more than enough protection; early in his reign he would don disguises to march in celebrations and fight in tournaments (McKisack, 112; Ormrod, 601). This was a king who might have been accustomed to going unrecognized to most of his subjects; our Arthur clearly isn't such a king. Edward spent much of his life in England, as opposed to earlier English kings who'd valued the continental lifestyle, but he also *spent* almost recklessly, and has been labeled "ambitious, extravagant, ostentatious, and unscrupulous" (McKisack, 269).[132] McKisack's more tempered description of Edward sounds enticingly Arthurian, as if Edward found himself between worlds and competing demands, just as the Pythons' Arthur encountered: "But Edward of Windsor, who conformed to his age as he found it and accepted its standards, has merged into the vanished age of chivalry and now partakes of its unreality" (270). Arthur is playing the part of the questing acolyte on

God's mission—partaking of an unreality, yes—and yet he still has to put up with hectoring peasants, obnoxious Frenchmen, silly knights, and traditional romance settings that don't tend to work out in traditional ways. Arthur is able to win and hold the admiration and un-questioning service of his fellow questers, just as Edward with his subjects and magnates, but Arthur isn't allowed to win over his own subjects, lending a silly, defeated air to the mock-epic nature of his ambitious but historically indifferent quest. It seems that the views of a king's subjects hold significant weight in the final assessment of his kingliness; Edward was able to win and hold "the loyalty of his people and the affection of his magnates, even in the years of his decline" (270). Like Arthur, Edward "accepted the chivalric and militant ambi-tions of his age and used them . . . in the service of his dynasty"; unlike Arthur, Edward was also able to raise his "dynasty from unexampled depths of degradation to a place of renown in western Christendom" (270–71). Arthur's dynasty—no consort, no offspring, no fiefdoms, and no Grail—peters out as he is escorted into a police van. Perhaps the ultimate difference is again one of perception. Despite Edward's flaws and the horrors of the period, Edward's subjects "saw him as the pattern of chivalry and the maker of England's fame" (271). The Py-thons' Arthur is sketched such that he casts *himself* into these roles, and his subjects—perhaps unwilling to surrender their collective historical judgment—are simply not buying it.

Still, the change evident in Britain after the end of the Attlee administration (1945–1951) and through the following thirteen years of Tory rule and the tumultuous 1960s is clear: au-tomatic deference for a leader is no longer automatic. Writing of Harold Wilson—who led the Labour opposition in 1973 before nipping back into No. 10 in 1974—in the appropriately titled article "Britain's Forgotten Prime Minister," Geoffrey Heptonstall pointed up the chal-lenges for even admired leaders:

> A lack of respect may be said to have characterized the Wilson premiership. After the initial enthusiasm Wilson's image underwent a sharp reversal so that he was often portrayed as a mere collection of mannerisms. To become a caricature in the public mind is the fate of all politicians, but it was acute in the case of Wilson. Others have aroused anger and hatred, but Wilson faced contemptuous attrition from left and right almost from the beginning. He aroused in social ide-alists accusations of betrayal. Conservatives thought him provincial and small-minded. After a long succession of patricians noted for their ease of manner and sense of leisurely culture Harold Wilson had the air of a clever and studious meritocrat. (187)

It's easy to see a Dennisean view of Arthur in this description. Arthur's "mannerisms" include his reliance on pedigree and supernatural mumbo-jumbo, on ladies in lakes and mystical swords, and his recourse to violence when the encounter doesn't go his way—he is a caricature of a kingly figure, at least to Dennis and mother, and not a king, and certainly no meritocrat. His fixedness on the quest, his singleness of purpose, will also come to define him even as he is as-saulted with animals and ordure and *verba contumeliosa*. This is one of those moments where the friction between worlds becomes apparent, between the legendary world of King Arthur, the Grail and the Knights of the Round Table, and the real world of an Anglo-Saxon or even Nor-man kingdom. In the romance world, Arthur's chivalric requests and desires would be answered with like responses—eager knights, helpful peasants, willing sub-lords. Arthur's pedigree, no-bility, divine calling, and his sword could bring order to *that* world, as is evidenced often in *Le Morte D'Arthur* and others of the romance sources. But the real world of Norman England is a world of confusion, of disorder, and only the strongest kings can manage that world.

Brooke notes how the "king between the two Henrys," Stephen (ruled 1135–1141), struggled to keep order in his kingdom: "In 1139 and the years which followed there was real anarchy: towns and fields were burned, castles were built without any control, and churches converted to fortresses; local feuds were freely pursued under cover of the civil war" (*SNK*, 188). The equilibrium point, the natural resting state during this period doesn't seem to have been peace, but rather disorder, and stronger kings were up to the task: "It shows how powerful were the forces of disorder which the other Norman kings had held in check" (188–89). An Arthur with one Patsy and a handful of marginally effective knights isn't this kind of Norman king. The successful king depended on personal loyalty, Brooke continues, the one thing Arthur can expect from his committed knights but never finds anywhere else in *MPHG*. This is what's missing, the cooperation of his subjects, and what will prevent Arthur from accomplishing his quest:

> It shows how much kingship owed to personal loyalty. It was the tight bond between king and barons—and between the king and the people at large—which kept England normally peaceful. This bond depended on the feudal oath, on the respect which his followers had for the king, above all on their admiration of his strength and fear of his anger. To all this was added the supernatural aura of monarchy—the "divinity." . . . But without personal loyalty and the fear the bond was easily broken, the divinity quickly forgotten. (*SNK*, 189)

Arthur has strength but he doesn't want to inspire fear; he is respected by his knights but the "people at large" are indifferent, at best, and hostile otherwise. Like Launcelot, Arthur is trapped by his idiom, and even more so by the Pythons' version of that idiom. As Brooke concludes, "The Arthur of Geoffrey's *History* and the legends of the Round Table was a feudal overlord, who took counsel with his barons, and was condemned if he ignored their advice" (193). The Pythons take away Arthur's barons, his loyal vassals and their influence (as well as his Camelot and Round Table), leaving him with no recourse in a world where someone he encounters might doubt, or worse, say "no."

Fittingly, the Tory Heath, like his opposite number Wilson, was also described as tough and fixed, this as he and the Conservatives took the reins of government in June 1970, surprising just about everyone: "[H]e was able to come into government . . . knowing absolutely what he wanted to do, and being prepared to push it through very toughly indeed." Whitehead notes that "this toughness had its bad side: an abrasive manner which could easily be mistaken for stubborn inflexibility" (51). Heath is inflexible and stubborn; Wilson refused devaluation until it was too late to matter, politically; and Arthur pushes on, no matter what is tossed at him. This type of physical assault is also mirrored cleverly from outside the world of the film—meaning the film is alive to its contemporaneity—with PM Heath "inked" by a protestor in January 1972 in Brussels, and Labourite Tony Benn flour-bombed in 1975, the year *Holy Grail* was released.

OLD WOMAN: "Well, I didn't vote for you"—There wouldn't be voting as we know it for many years, but some kind of "common consent" to rule was already understood, even by medieval kings. In Anglo-Saxon Britain, kings were "elected," yes, Brooke describes, but those elections were often set in motion by the previous king who would forward his son, for example, and, upon the old king's death, the magnates of the kingdom (not the peasantry) were tasked with gathering and acknowledging that election with their presumed assent (*FAH*, 79–81). Whether Anglo-Saxon or Dane, Brooke notes, "the English monarchy was never elective in the modern sense of the word" (81). During and after the celebrated visit of the Holy Roman Emperor to Paris in 1377–1378, King Charles of France made clear his case for war against the English, noting especially the claims on French soil the English continued to make—Charles was essentially bringing his case to the people, according to Tuchman:

> Although royal powers were undefined, and the Council's authority unformulated, and the institutions of royal government always in flux, Charles V's sense of the crown's role was firm: kingship

depended on the King's will. The sovereign was not above the law; rather, his duty was to maintain the law, for God denied Paradise to tyrants. Sanction derived in theory from the consent of the governed, for kings and princes, as a great theologian, Jean Gerson, was to remind Charles' successor, "were created in the beginning by the common consent of all." As Charles knew well, the cult of monarchy was the basis of the people's consent. He deliberately fed the cult while at the same time he was first to show that rulership could be exercised "from the chamber" independent of personal leadership in battle. (315)

Arthur is clearly not modeled on Charles, since he assumes the royal prerogative (a divine one at that) from the outset, comfortable in the knowledge that his is a pedigreed, providential rule and quest. These assumptions will be turned back on him time and time again.

The simple impracticality of each subject acknowledging, swearing fealty to, voting for, or perhaps even knowing of their king is also significant, as Fossier discusses. Charlemagne may have wanted to have each of his sovereign subjects "swear obedience to him," but as emperor over scores of thousands such a conceit would have strained the limits of both credulity and practicality in the world of the early ninth century:

> It was a magnificent idea, but close to inapplicable, like almost all ideas of the time. If we can believe the annals, the decision [to document sworn allegiances across the empire] was taken and applied, but given the means of communication of the ninth century, we have every reason to doubt the latter. (*AO*, 274–75)

It's unlikely that even if Arthur had access to a well-spread civil authority under his control—which did not exist until much later in most of Europe—the likelihood of notifying every peasant in every field of filth of their new responsibilities vis-à-vis a distant monarch was a remote one, at best.

ARTHUR: "You don't vote for kings"—True, you don't generally vote for kings. In the Dark to early Middle Ages governance tended to come by royal prerogative, meaning by birth and/or force, and fealty was expected, not asked for. Force of arms, money, and distributed properties kept loyalties and kingdoms intact, and the protection afforded by a noble's guard or armies was likely appreciated by the "oppressed" like Dennis when marauding forces appeared. A "vote" implies some kind of an election, however, and things can get a bit gray there, according to Christopher Brooke. In the 1867 *History of the Norman Conquest of England*, the eminent E. A. Freeman, in arguing against the Tory hobbyhorse of the "Divine Right of Kings," pushed the notion that the Witenagemot (the Anglo-Saxon royal council) was so powerful it could not only "depose the king" but almost certainly "elect the king," and he concluded: "The ancient English Kingship was elective."[133] Brooke (1963) calls this idea "preposterous," since "custom and tradition" have carried the most weight over the centuries, especially when kings and kingship are considered (23):

> There were, indeed, no precise rules; but the succession to the thrones of the Anglo-Saxon kingdoms and the English kingdom was hedged around with a series of conventions, customs and assumptions; and out of the dialectic between these conventions each succession was settled—sometimes peacefully, sometimes by violence. Frequently a "strong man armed" seized the throne; and in later centuries at least he often felt bound to justify his action, and from the way in which he justified it we can tell what rules he was pretending to have followed. If at all possible he showed that he was related to his predecessor—that he had a hereditary claim; he argued that the people had accepted his rule in due form—that he had been "elected," whatever that meant; and he asserted that his predecessor had declared that he was to succeed—he had been designated by a reigning king. (24)

Brooke concludes: "Our investigation of king-making must be woven out of these three threads, inheritance, election and designation; in some way or another these three entered into most acts of king-making in western Europe in the Middle Ages" (24). William was eventually accepted by the Witan not because he was the next in line for the throne, he wasn't,[134] but because he was able to outmaneuver or conquer other aspirants (28). Conquerors and usurpers, then, could also be "elected." Brooke also concludes that an "election" as we know it—one with more than a single candidate, etc.—just wasn't part of the political or dynastic system of the time: "Between 450 and 1154, so far as we know, no election of this kind took place in Europe" (32). So Dennis's mother likely knows that there is no "vote" or elective process in her alleged time, but Arthur only knows his own romance stories paradigm, which Dennis and his mother know to be a fantasy. Our Arthur is caught in between worlds. He has cited his inheritance—he is the son of Uther, the previous king; he does cite his election—the Lady of the Lake offers him the sword, one offered to no other candidate; and he does cite his designation, in his case he is designated by "Divine Providence," or God himself, directly. The challenge is that the Arthur of mythology is talking to the Old Woman of the Middle Ages somehow steeped in twentieth-century political theory. Arthur is hopelessly trapped between these worlds. His citations—his credentials, essentially—are things of myth and legend and the supernatural. Perhaps if he'd led with his story as told in Geoffrey's favorable work—where "he is represented as a great warrior, conquering all the better known parts of the world, rather than as a fairy king holding sway over a realm not too clearly defined"[135]—he'd make better headway here. But the Pythons are selectively harvesting bits of history and legend, and their Arthur who is "defeater of the Saxons" must also face a cursing, de-limbed Black Knight and for some reason be mortally afraid of the word "Ni." The Old Woman and Dennis *might* recognize if Arthur cited a Constantine III or Vortigern, an Alfred or Æthelstan, an Edward or even a Henry—all leaders found in some version of British "history" over the decades. But he has access to only the *fabular* Arthur's history, one that involves romance rituals, chivalry, and miraculous events—the "fairy king" world Baugh mentions above. One doesn't *vote* for a King Arthur. This is a big part of the reason this Arthur can never navigate the world of *Holy Grail* successfully—he's been taken out of Arthur's Britain and dropped into the Middle Ages, where, as a mythological figure, he just doesn't belong.

Dennis's mother didn't vote for Arthur, and likely, as a female, wouldn't have had the right to such freedoms no matter (almost) where she happened to be in 932. However, the merely coincidental date of the first part of the 930s includes a peculiar Viking practice in Iceland beginning in 930. The first "national parliament" or "Alþing" convened at Þingvellir to pass common laws, by vote, and means to amend laws. The Alþing meetings were held in summer, and courts were also set up in quarters of the country. This system would remain in place for centuries, until Icelandic sovereignty was surrendered to Norway, and later Denmark.[136] By the end of the eighth century Vikings were trading, pillaging, and (later) even colonizing in the British Isles and Europe, and eventually could claim significant political control over large areas of Britain, meaning the Icelanders' version of a democratic process could have reached the ears of someone like Dennis's mother.[137] The Pythons had spent a good deal of time and effort with the Icelandic Sagas for the third series of *Flying Circus*, creating the halting and "terribly violent" *Njorl's Saga* for Ep. 27.[138]

ARTHUR: "The Lady of the Lake . . ."—In Malory's *Le Morte Darthur*, the Lady in the Lake is a great help to Arthur and the Grail quest, including giving Arthur the sword Excalibur. The following imagery (and even accompanying music) of fantastical ladies and God's blessings fairly leap from the pages of Bellamy's heroic comic strip, *King Arthur and His Knights* (1955–1956), along with *The Story of King Arthur and His Knights* (1903–1910) by Howard Pyle (1853–1911), both popular titles when the Pythons were growing up.

This would have been a fairly familiar recitation[139] to the great British public, thanks to myriad "Arthurian" entertainment opportunities available across the years. Just a handful include: Henry Purcell's *King Arthur* (a 1691 opera; libretto by John Dryden), often performed by university groups;[140] there were Arthurian Christmas and Easter plays, and Christmas pantos; and *Camelot* based loosely on T. H. White's work, which hit Broadway in 1960, and then the West End in 1964. Perhaps most significantly, the original and newly adapted "King Arthur and his knights" pantomimes played (and still play) across the country in civic and regional theaters, meaning the Pythons grew up in a splendiferous, bigger-than-life Arthurian age.[141]

ARTHUR: ". . . her arm clad in shimmering samite . . ."—Samite is a rich, heavy silk fabric. The euphuistic language here is borrowed from a few sources, including Tennyson and Malory. In Tennyson's *Idylls of the King*, the Holy Vessel is "hung with folds of pure / White samite" ("The Last Tournament" 295–296), and in Arthur's last hours he rehearses to Bedevere how he came to the sword Excalibur:

> For thou rememberest how
> In those old days, one summer noon, an arm
> Rose up from out the bosom of the lake,
> Clothed in white samite, mystic, wonderful,
> Holding the sword ("The Passing of Arthur," 347[142])

And much earlier, from Malory's *Le Morte Darthur*, just after Merlin saves Arthur from Sir Pellinore, and Arthur has broken his sword:

> And as they rode, King Arthur said, "I have no sword."
> "No force," said Merlin, "hereby is a sword that shall be yours, and I may."
> So they rode till they came to a lake that was a fair water and broad. And in the midst Arthur was ware of an arm clothed in white samite, that held a fair sword in that hand.
> "Lo," said Merlin, "yonder is the sword that I spoke of."
> So with that they saw a damosel going upon the lake.
> "What damosel is that?" said Arthur.
> "That is the Lady of the Lake," said Merlin. (*LMD-WM*, 29)

"Samite" as an indicator of the necessary richness of fabrics to underlay the Holy Grail (on alabaster tables) appears in most of the grail legends, including those penned by Chrétien, Robert de Boron, and Wolfram von Eschenbach, as well as *The High Book of the Grail* and the *Lancelot-Grail* (see *THG*). In the *Lancelot-Grail*, for instance, the Holy Grail is first glimpsed "upon the silver table . . . covered with a piece of white samite" (*THG*, 98). And in Percival's tale in *Le Morte Darthur*, a mysterious sailing ship is covered completely, "within and without," by white samite (*LMD-WM*, 340); Bors[143] boards the same samite-bedecked ship after leaving his violent brother Lionel, there greeting Percival (371); and Gawain and Ector are later blessed to see "a hand showing unto the elbow . . . covered with red samite" (352). Throughout Malory's work, samite is associated with both the Grail and Christ.

This same Tennyson line discussed above was included as part of a clue in the *Times* crossword puzzle at least five times between 1943 and 1975, meaning the poem was still part of the education curriculum for many.

ARTHUR: ". . . held Excalibur aloft . . ."—This is the only mention of the name of Arthur's storied sword in the film; its magical properties aren't stressed at all. Geoffrey of Monmouth mentions Arthur's sword "Caliburn" in *HKB*, noting that it was forged "in the Isle of

Avalon" (217). Malory is given credit for conflating various French sources into the following recognizable tale, from *Le Morte Darthur*, the early portion of which was cited above:

> "Lo," said Merlin, "yonder is the sword that I spoke of."
> So with that they saw a damosel going upon the lake.
> "What damosel is that?" said Arthur.
> "That is the Lady of the Lake," said Merlin. "And within that lake there is a great rock, and therein is as fair a place as any on earth, and richly beseen. And this damosel will come to you anon; and then speak ye fair to her that she may give you that sword."
> So anon came this damosel unto Arthur and saluted him, and he her again.
> "Damosel," said Arthur, "what sword is that yonder that the arm holdeth above the water? I would it were mine, for I have no sword."
> "Sir Arthur[144]," said the damosel, "that sword is mine. And if ye will give me a gift when I ask it you, ye shall have it."
> "By my faith," said Arthur, "I will give you what gift that ye will ask."
> "Well," said the damosel. "Go ye into yonder barge and row yourself to the sword, and take it and the scabbard with you; and I will ask my gift when I see my time."
> So King[145] Arthur and Merlin alit and tied their horses unto two trees, and so they went into the barge; and when they came to the sword that the hand held, King Arthur took it up by the handles and bore it with him, and the arm and the hand went under the water. (*LMD-WM*, 29–30)

In Malory's version Arthur rather quickly forgets the name of his sword, though it's not been named previously except in the chapter heading for book 1, chapter 25 (*LMD'A*, 1.55), and the Lady of the Lake appears again, asking for the gift Arthur promised her upon receipt of the sword and rehearsing to Arthur both the sword's name and the name's meaning (*LMD-WM*, 36). Thereafter the sword's name is most often mentioned in relation to its enchanted scabbard, which protects the wearer from blood loss (*LMD-WM*, 41).

The Pythons' version, especially its phraseology, closely resembles Howard Pyle's classic retelling in *The Story of King Arthur and His Knights* (1903), a very popular version that seems to have been in print ever since its publication (reprinted 1933, 1954, 1965, etc.). In the third chapter Merlin describes to young Arthur the enchanted sword and its environs:

> And that is a very wonderful land, for there is in it a wide and considerable lake, which is also of enchantment. And in the centre of that lake there hath for some time been seen the appearance as of a woman's arm—exceedingly beautiful and clad in white samite, and the hand of this arm holdeth a sword of such exceeding excellence and beauty that no eye hath ever beheld its like. And the name of this sword is Excalibur. (66)

And just a bit later, when Arthur and Merlin are standing on "the margin of the lake," Arthur

> beheld there the miracle that Merlin had told him of aforetime. For, lo! in the midst of the expanse of water there was the appearance of a fair and beautiful arm, as of a woman, clad all in white samite. And the arm was encircled with several bracelets of wrought gold; and the hand held a sword of marvelous workmanship aloft in the air above the surface of the water; and neither the arm nor the sword moved so much as a hair's-breadth, but were motionless like to a carven image upon the surface of the lake. (68)

The Pythons' version of Arthur and his Lyly-like language isn't an anomaly, then, and had been consistently florid since at least the fifteenth century. Pyle's books were and are available at the local libraries where the Pythons grew up, including Weston-Super-Mare (North Somerset), Sheffield, north Wales, Leicester, and so on.

Finally, the practice of naming special swords (or that swords were special in the first place) isn't reserved for the Arthurian romances. Norman and Pottinger note that in *Beowulf* the prized sword was named *Naegling*, "while many later blades [in the real world] are signed by their actual makers, such as Ingelrii and Ulfbehrt" (16). Swords in the Anglo-Saxon period were "prized . . . very highly . . . often handed down from father to son, and especially mentioned in the will of a dead man" (16). Poets sung of these swords, and kings gave them as rewards for fealty and valor on the battlefield (16–17). In *MPHG*, Excalibur isn't particularly lucky or magical; it's a named prop. Not only that, but with it Arthur only manages to defend himself from catapulted animals and a killer rabbit, as well as to de-limb a fellow knight—nothing too noble.

ARTHUR: ". . . by Divine Providence . . ."—This is the film's first conflation of both mythological *and* spiritual elements of the Arthur story (and the first mention of God),[146] though these elements have been harnessed before, in the romance source material. As Barber describes the Grail knights in these sources, he points up the contradictions that combine to make the successful Grail-questing knight:

> [W]e find contrasting references to the ways in which the Grail may be won: "whoever aspired to the Grail had to approach fame with the sword"; "no one, indeed, can gain the Grail except he who is known in Heaven to be appointed to the Grail"; "with God's favour I have inherited the Grail." Two of these concerns are the paramount driving forces of feudal society—warlike skills and inheritance of status; the third, divine election, is what sets apart the Grail knights from all other romance heroes. (*THG*, 160)

The Pythons' Arthur uses his sword whenever necessary (as does Launcelot, *in extremis*), he cites his noble lineage as proof of his chosen-ness ("son of Uther"), and now brings his election by God into the mix to complete the questing trifecta.

This matches the clumsy, start-and-stop transitions from the "old religions" to Christianity in the fifth and sixth centuries and beyond, when paganism and Christianity coexisted in the British Isles:

> Christianity, rescued from persecution by the protection of the emperor Constantine, was now the ascendant faith of the Roman world. It had been practised in Britain for many years. Its strength came from the educated class and their dependents. The peasants in the villages remained pagan. (Ashe, 42, 48)

If Ashe is correct and villagers like Dennis "remained pagan" during these transitional decades, that's actually a fair reason for his inability or unwillingness to recognize the Arthur before him, especially if Arthur is called by a new and unfamiliar Christian god.

Historically, according to Gildas's account *The Ruin of Britain*, it was also the fifth-century Romano-Briton leader Ambrosius (Aurelianus) who won his battles over the Saxons by the Lord's assent (26). Arthur gets his providential nod, as well, in a Welsh poem detailing the Battle of Portsmouth (c. 480) and the death of Geraint, "Arthur's / Heroes who cut with steel" battled the invading English (Saxons), and "Heaven's gate stood open; / Christ granted all our prayer; / Lovely to behold, the glory of Britain" (quoted in *Age of Arthur*, 104–5). The mid-tenth-century *Annales Cambriae* also attaches providential and sacred (but not fantastical) assistance to Arthur's efforts, for in the "battle of Badon . . . Arthur carried the cross of Our Lord Jesus Christ, for three days and three nights, on his shoulders, and the Britons were victorious" (*QAB*, 58).

The age-old claim is, of course, that God has chosen the monarch or ruling family, and therefore supporting the monarch means supporting God. It also asserts that no earthly authority can or should have any claim on the divinely appointed king,[147] allowing Arthur to plunge headfirst into every encounter, ever certain of the action's rectitude. He is sure in his divine right; in the last assault on the Grail Castle (where the "Frogs" are in situ, jeering), Arthur swears "by God" that His will must be done. In this Arthur is not cursed (or blessed?) with the romances' fatal flaw or wound that forces those knights to step aside and wait for a certain question to be asked or a wound to be healed or a sin forgiven—the Pythons' Arthur has no such penetrating, inward-looking sight, and resolutely pushes on toward his goal, as commanded by God Himself.

ARTHUR: "I, Arthur . . ."—Once again Arthur is attempting to present his calling card as rightful king, and his subjects are rejecting him. It may be that he's not the only "Arthur" the peasantry might know. Oddly, Thomas of Lancaster (1278–1322), who at the height of his influence controlled a good portion of the north—"the richest landowner in England, after the king"—referred to himself as "King Arthur" in his correspondence with Robert Bruce of Scotland, for example (McKisack, 68). After his execution for treason (he had hated Edward's favorite, Gaveston,[148] earning the enmity of the king), Thomas was mourned by the people and the church as a martyr: "For the unhappy subjects of Edward II, Earl Thomas thus became a symbol of resistance to the powers of darkness, the upholder of ancient liberties against new-fangled tyranny" (70).

ARTHUR: ". . . that is why I am your king"—After all this mythology and preternaturalism, Arthur has arrived back where most Anglo-Saxon kings found themselves when defending their kingships: the kingship needs to be acknowledged to be effective. Whether they assumed power by force or by right of succession or some other machinations, in the end there is a rather perfunctory "this is why" moment that hinges on some kind of public acknowledgment. Early on this "public" meant the wise and wealthy (the Witan); later, as with Edmund (c. 1016), the better citizens of London and their adherents had become the "public" (Brooke, *SNK*, 33). Our Arthur assumes that his divine and mythical right trumps everything; Dennis and the Old Woman haven't heard a compelling argument yet.

OLD WOMAN: "Is Frank in? He'd be able to deal with this one"—One of the lines in the final script but crossed through at some point, it's spoken by Dennis's mother. The inclusion of the name "Frank" (from "Franklin") is likely incidental, but the fact that as early as the tenth century it was understood to connote "free man" in Latin, it seems a fitting name for someone in this collective.

It could be, though, one of two other things. It could be that the Old Woman is asking for Frank since he's the "executive officer" in charge of the "anarcho-syndicalist commune" doings this week; that, or he's a pre-Conquest bastion of local juridical knowledge, someone versed in the institutionalized implementation of the law in this particular shire, hundred, or village. In late Anglo-Saxon Britain[149] it was people like Dennis and Frank—as well as custom—that would have been the law, according to Brooke:

> The people at large were the repositories of law; they were the judges in the public courts. Law represented custom, of which any man with a good memory might be the repository, and local opinion; it was the one quasi-democratic thing about our early society. The judgments of the "hundred" court, says Sir Frank Stenton, "represented the deliberations of peasants learned in the law, who might be guided but could never be controlled by the intervention of the king's reeve, their president."[150] Guidance was often very important in medieval deliberations. But it was never forgotten that these courts were popular courts. (*FAH*, 69)

So Dennis may be not only the collective juridical memory but also the most vocal proponent of the "peoples" law in his hundred, a man Arthur and Patsy just happen to happily stumble upon. "Chance would be a fine thing," indeed.[151]

DENNIS: ". . . strange women lying on their backs in ponds handing over swords . . ."— This is where Arthur goes off the rails as far as Dennis is concerned, and enters the realm of the imaginary, where, according to Fossier, the medieval mind wasn't keen to wander:

> The people of the Middle Ages were not indifferent to productions of the imaginary, but they condemned them when they were told of them. In the [eleventh] century, Burchard of Worms saw in them pagan roots to be extirpated; in the thirteenth century, the Dominicans discerned hetero-dox deviations in them. The imaginary was common to all orders, estates, sexes, and ages. (299)

Dennis the Constitutional Peasant has no use for such flights of fancy, preferring real, identifiable institutions and their effects on the class system he sees around him.

DENNIS: ". . . that's no basis for a system of government"—Dennis is employing a logical argument here, based on foundations of fact, not fancy or the supernatural. The Aristotelian dialectic model was "rediscovered" (via Boethius) and invigorated during the early Middle Ages, partly thanks to the increase in the numbers of students, as well as university settings distinct from churches (Oxford, Bologna, etc.), and partly as an answer to an increasingly confounding world, according to R. W. Southern:

> [The student] learned to classify the types of valid argument, to detect the causes of error and to unmask the process of deception. Once more he found that, instead of the bewildering variety which met the casual inquirer, the types of valid argument are strictly limited in number and can be classified on a simple principle. . . . Logic was an instrument of order in a chaotic world. . . . The world of nature was chaotic—a playground of supernatural forces, demoniac and otherwise, over which the mind had no control. . . . But logic, however obscurely at first, opened a window on to an orderly and systematic view of the world and of man's mind. (*The Making of the Middle Ages*, 179–80; quoted in *HBMA*, 272)

Not much later Bedevere will attempt just such a logical exercise to determine the "witchness" of an accused, reaching a satisfactory, neat, but skewed logical conclusion.

Arthur's "system of government" is one basic tenet on which these peasants and Arthur can never agree, where the traditions of the past fly headfirst into the realities of the "modern" world, which will be ultimately realized when Black Marias sweep across the moors and police make arrests, bringing both the quest and the film to an end. As he strives to fulfill the full measure of his Arthurian legendariness, Arthur the divine king is the missionary spreading the gospel of the mythic. He seeks adherents as the Arthur of the romances should, and he is genuinely at a nonplus ("You make me sad") when those offered the chance at Camelot's riches, God's blessings, and chivalry's rewards do anything but agree and join up. Arthur is pestered from the wall of the first castle he encounters, but sets off immediately for the next wall, the next encounter, the next inevitable miracle or voice from the sky. As will become evident, though, Arthur stubbornly *believes* through all sorts of misadventures and through the puncturings of his worldview—he isn't a consistently self-aware character who utilizes even the most minimal benefits of Patsy's "It's only a model" level of healthy skepticism.[152] Arthur holds to the old order, the traditions of his fathers (including the announcement of lineage), even as the world seems to discount those traditions.

As the violent Peasants' Revolt of 1381 swelled into motion in Kent and Essex, the pent-up frustrations of England's lowest and largest class began to erupt, generally as a response to unrighteous dominion:

> Wyclif's spirit, which had dared deny the most pervasive authority of the time, was abroad. What had happened in the last thirty years, as a result of plague, war, oppression, and incompetence, was a weakened acceptance of the system, a mistrust of government and governors, lay and ecclesiastical, an awakening sense that authority could be challenged—that change was in fact possible. Moral authority can be no stronger than its acknowledgment. When officials were venal—as even the poor could see they were in the bribing of tax commissioners—and warriors a curse and the Church oppressive, the push for change gained strength. (Tuchman, 374)

So Dennis and the English peasantry of the fourteenth century are reacting to being exploited, though with Dennis we have to take him at his word—Arthur seems clueless to any wrongs needing to be righted. Dennis and Wat Tyler are fed up with the same things, however.

Beyond this—at a distance where more of the spectrum can be appreciated—it's easier to realize that the period when the Pythons came of age, 1958–1968, was truly an era of radical change—change that would inevitably find its way into their work. Medieval England was being "re-done" during this period, more than having a wall "knocked through" in various castles, but a wholesale change from the past to an exciting but uncertain future. The ravages of wartime bombing forced the razing of blocks and neighborhoods of eighteenth- and nineteenth-century homes and businesses, replacing them with more up-to-date, even pre-fab architecture, as the country scrambled to re-house itself and deal with an inevitable baby boom. Requisitioning and repurposing of many stately homes by the government and military during the war also damaged many beyond repair. And even before war could have its say on the English countryside, it was the pell-mell move away from the past toward the future as stately, often ancient homes and castles disappeared over the previous century. Booker identifies the beginnings of this wholesale change earlier, noting that "the great keyword of Victorian culture" was "improvement": "What was old might be good. But what was new was still without question better" (*The Seventies*, 262). And the buildings came down. In 1983, the change described by Webbe in the *Christian Science Monitor* amounted to a list of threats to the Britain's heritage: "The deathwatch beetle, dry rot, Draconian taxation, and the wrecking ball have all grievously mauled this nation's historic houses over the past century and a quarter. A sluggish economy now threatens them with further ruin."[153] The article goes on to note that between 1875 and 1975 as many as fifteen hundred stately homes were "destroyed, partially destroyed or severely altered," and more than seven hundred of those during the Pythons' lifetimes following World War II. (We will return to this later as Herbert's father discusses changes he's making to Swamp Castle.) The destruction had peaked in the mid-1950s, but as recently as 1969 it was still fairly easy to justify tearing down an aging ancestral home that had become an economic burden. After 1969, government permission had to be acquired before any demolitions or retrofits could be undertaken; but the double albatross of death duties and upkeep often tolled the bell for these buildings.

As Andrew Marr (2007) points out, the late 1950s and then 1960s saw the emergence of a counterculture that not only questioned everything even remotely traditional or atavistic, but steamrolled over those everythings without waiting for answers to the questions; it was a "new culture . . . far from being elitist: it was shaped by working-class and lower-middle-class people who had never enjoyed this level of cultural power before" (264–65). These are people who can treat Arthur as just another toff who should answer for his entire generation (and class); they don't have lords, they don't bow to the *ancien regime* or its traditions, and they don't remember voting for a king. The changes had been ushered in by the lightning advances of technology and globalism and upended hierarchies in the postwar years; the changes had included efficient "advances" in architecture, such that the new face of public housing was often tall and gray and bleakly concrete, or, as in the case of the various "New Towns," devastatingly over-planned. Booker describes the image "fixed somewhere in our minds of the incredible transformation which has come over the life of mankind in the past 30 years"—between 1947 and 1977, the period of the Pythons' flourishing—"and of which," Booker continues, "the fate of so many cities of the world has seemed to be only one of the more dramatic outward reflections" (*The Seventies*, 84). Cities and towns had changed utterly, and with them England. The Pythons themselves were a part of this change, as they were born of working-class folk, too, and into working-class environments. Marr continues:

> It is hard to recall now, but the Beatles' voices, and the Geordie accents of the Animals, sounded almost shocking to the metropolitan and Home Counties listeners of the mid-sixties. The children of lorry drivers and dock workers, cleaners and shop assistants, found themselves being lionized in expensive new nightclubs and standing in line to be introduced to the Queen. (265)

So Dennis and his mother can stand toe-to-toe with Arthur, King of the Britons, and not recognize his Divine Providence, their "insolence" such that they can and will "destroy much about traditional Britain" (265). The Britain Arthur might represent here (across the ages), the "older Britain with its military traditions, its thousands of slow industrial and village backwaters, its racism, its clear divisions of class and geography," was being nosed out (265). And far from being the "anarcho-socialist paradise" many in the 1960s hoped for, the new Britain was one that might seem alien to both Left and Right, to the old order or the new. Home Secretary Roy Jenkins's Britain was a place where the "State's powers over individual freedoms" were dramatically reduced, and termed "social reform" (251–52). The laundry list of reforms is especially compelling when it's remembered how quickly the changes were implemented, and how far-reaching their effects would be. State executions (by hanging), judicial flogging, the persecution and prosecution of homosexuals, the censoring of plays, the forbidding of abortions, and repressive divorce and immigration laws were all tinkered with or thrown out entirely, and all between 1965 and 1968 (Marr, 251–56).

Lastly, Cecil King's column on pending changes in the House of Lords (importantly, in 1968), reads like a manual for what's wrong or long gone about Arthur's version of a great Great Britain, and why cosmetic changes to the House of Lords or the monarchy or the Lord Mayors of London merely scratch the surface:

> But this is really only part of a larger problem—that of equating appearance with reality in our institutions. At one time important people looked important by their dress, their houses and their style of living. When I was a boy[154] "toffs" dressed differently than others. But nowadays everyone dresses alike and to the ordinary citizen it is quite impossible to judge who is important and who is not. This was particularly conspicuous at the Coronation [in 1953]. This was originally a very solemn and important occasion when the sovereign was dedicated to the service of his country. Endowed with a very great power and made to feel his very great responsibility, after which all the most important people knelt at his feet and swore to behave themselves. Now the whole thing is a charming medieval romance. None of the people taking part matter very much. The most important men in the country do not participate and in many cases were not even present in the congregation. The Duke of Norfolk and the Marquess of Huntly swore fealty to the Queen—all very traditional and charming, but meaningless. The only glimpse of reality was when the Com-

monwealth Prime Ministers appeared briefly. They had no part to play, but were a reminder, I suppose, that the whole ceremony was not pure charade.[155]

In a world where so many institutions had changed irrevocably just in the Pythons' lifetimes, it was likely impossible to posit a classical Arthur without inviting mockery and laughter from the more "with it" modern audience. The Pythons decided to let the film itself poke and prod the earnest king, inviting the audience to go along with the reflexive fun—undercutting the institution was where their humor could be found.

DENNIS: "... supreme executive power derives from a mandate of the masses ..."—A nearly textbook definition of a working representative democracy. Dennis is not asking for Communism, where ideally there would be no class, no money, and no state apparatus (thus no "supreme executive power"). His worldview sounds much more like *anarcho*-communism, where ownership in common and direct democracy would carry the day. But he's also not in the same boat as the postwar British Syndicalists, at least as Tom Brown defines that movement's aims. Their common, guiding principles would never allow any "supreme executive power," even that arising from a "mandate." Brown lays out the sameness of other political systems when compared to the "other" of Syndicalism, and it all comes down to the direction of the flow of power:

> All parties, capitalist or "labour," and all social relationships except Syndicalism, are at one in opposing the principles of control from below. All are willing to fight to the last ditch to preserve the principle of control from above, the relation of master and servant. Communism, Conservatism, Labourism, capitalism, business (big or small)—all are bound and rooted in the master principle, as were the previous systems of feudalism and chattel slavery.
>
> The Syndicalist principle of control from below, then, is truly revolutionary and, as such, is repulsive to the political parties and excites the anger of groups and individuals who wish to appear revolutionary while, at the same time, they retain the principles of a conservative society.
>
> Control from below runs through all Syndicalist manifestations—its organization, its activity and its idea of a future society.[156]

This Arthur feels he is the supreme executive power, of course, and that power has been flowing as it should—from God to King, thence to bless the obedient, helpful rabble like Dennis and his mother.

Part of the inspiration for this discussion of various governments might have been the persistent editorial whinging in British newspapers in regard to contemporary electoral strictures, and the seeming impossibility of a minority party ever coming to power. From at least the early 1950s and through the 1974 general election, there appeared dozens of letters to the editor and articles either bashing or supporting the version of representative democracy (or Parliamentary democracy) as practiced in Britain, and especially the "wasted vote" for the Liberal party, Britain's "third party" during most of the twentieth century. Following the 1951 general election (where the Conservatives and Churchill won with a majority of sixteen seats but lost the popular tally by more than two hundred thousand votes) one letter to the editor contributor (Frank Byers, 1915–1984) identified the choice that presented itself to Britain as that between "Socialism and chaos," since at least 1929. In this back-and-forth the Socialist (or Labour) government would take office and actively nationalize industries like iron and steel, then another election cycle would usher in a more conservative government that would attempt to undo what had been done, and then back again: "If . . . this is to be the future policy it means that we shall have full-blooded Socialism by rapid stages—Socialists nationalizing when in office; non-Socialists unable to de-nationalize except for a short time. In other words, Socialism and chaos."[157] Byers continued, noting that electoral reform was the only way to change this self-defeating, unbalanced system, truly allowing a "mandate from the masses":

> This will happen because we are working under an electoral system which does not give us true representative democracy. If there were an electoral system which provided representation in Parliament in accordance with the views held in the country [meaning, by popular vote], we should not only have a representative democracy but we should have a bulwark against extremism. Under such a system most of the 14 million who voted Conservative [in the 1951 GE] would presumably vote Conservative again. The remainder, I think, would vote Liberal because the Liberals would have a chance. Of the 14 million who voted Socialist [in the 1951 GE], the vast majority would probably vote Socialist again, but many Liberals who voted Socialist because they were anti-Tory would under such a system vote Liberal. The three to five million Liberals who have so far been largely disfranchised would once again be represented in terms of seats. (5)

There were many responses to this call for change, most arguing against Mr. Byers and his version of fairness, of course.[158]

This either/or conundrum (Conservative or Labour) remained in place through the 1974 general election, where the third party Liberals were finally able to act the king maker (or un-maker) in deciding to withhold support for Heath's Conservatives, forcing Heath to cede power to the minority government of Harold Wilson. For the "three to five million" people who felt the way Byers did, however, this continued to be "no basis for a system of government."[159]

DENNIS: "... watery tart ..."—Watery because she's emerging from the enchanted lake, of course. "Tart" is a nineteenth-century term often used *affectionately* for a pretty or well made-up girl. By the late 1940s, though, when the Pythons are growing up, a "tart" can be a promiscuous girl—"[T]hey'd all been with little tarts who'd get behind a back fence with any boy."[160] The term "bint" is often used pejoratively, and was in common usage in the Middle East (by British troops) from World War I, and seems to have come into its own as meaning a "very pretty girlfriend" during World War II. The term was officially defined in a list of servicemen slang printed in *The New Statesman* on 30 August 1941.[161]

The Pythons had created a World War I–themed sketch in Ep. 25, complete with contemporary terms like "Blighty" (meaning England); the sketch never could get going, as it was continuously interrupted and then, as in *Holy Grail*, one of the principal characters was removed via lorry (ambulance).[162] As for World War II, the Pythons all grew up during and just after the war (birth years 1939–1944), and their parents and neighbors were fighting or involved somehow throughout. It's no surprise that the references to World War II—including wartime rationing, the Blitz, the Axis powers, Chamberlain and Churchill, Dunkirk, and so forth can be found throughout *MPFC*, from the very first episode—when an Allied deadly joke turns the tide of the war—through Ep. 45, when it's announced that "The Second World War has entered a sentimental phase."[163]

Also, in most versions of this Lady of the Lake scenario the only time the sword gets tossed is when Bedevere—after hesitations—throws it back *into* the lake just before Arthur's death (and/or departure to Avalon), with the sword being caught by the same arm and hand seen earlier:

> Then Sir Bedevere departed, and went to the sword, and lightly took it up, and went to the water side; and there he bound the girdle about the hilts, and then he threw the sword as far into the water as he might; and there came an arm and an hand above the water and met it, and caught

it, and so shook it thrice and brandished, and then vanished away the hand with the sword in the water. (*LMD'A*, 2.517)

DENNIS: ". . . Emperor . . ."—In at least one medieval Welsh tale, *The Dream of Rhonabwy* (c. 600), Arthur is called "*amberawdyr*, the Latin *imperator*, or emperor" (*QAB*, 60). Historian John Morris, however, is certain that Arthur was indeed an emperor, and was known as such in his lifetime:[164]

> But the traditions of the highlands are emphatic, and are agreed upon one chief essential of Arthur's rule. He was the emperor, the all-powerful ruler of the whole of Britain, and the seat of his power was in the lowlands; in the western and northern highlands he was a foreigner whose authority was accepted resentfully, and asserted by superior force. . . . The government of a lowland emperor is an earlier and more credible tradition than medieval folk-tales told of a western king in Wales and Cornwall. The men who followed Ambrosius and Arthur had fought to preserve and restore the Roman civilization of their fathers; when they won the war, they could not do any other than try to restore its political institutions, and "emperor" is the natural title for the head of those institutions. (*The Age of Arthur*, 132)

If Dennis and his mother happen to be living in the western or northern highlands, then their acknowledgment of Arthur would historically be based on his "superior force," and treated "resentfully," using Morris's terms. They do seem to respond this way, though without acknowledging that they know him at all. The well-known challenges to Morris's conclusions throughout his massive (and quite readable) book are herein acknowledged (Kirby and Williams; Dumville, 1977), but Morris's certainty and the scope of the work is at the very least impressive.[165] What makes this all significant for our study is that at the time of the production of *MPHG*, Morris's *The Age of Arthur* (1973) and Alcock's *Arthur's Britain* (1971) represented the pinnacle of generally accessible Arthurian and ancient British history scholarship, and were much discussed. Whatever, the emperor/king Arthur is clearly the kind of Arthur that our Arthur seems to think himself, "at once the last Roman emperor in the west, and the first medieval king of the country now called England"[166]—just the type that Dennis and his mother fear will tread on their more proletarian desires.

Higham (2002), commenting on the *Historia Brittonum*'s construction of Arthur, sees emperor status as an obvious conclusion for period writers and audiences:

> The *Historia*'s claim that Arthur invariably led the kings of the Britons in battle was naturally read by later audiences as indicative of a great king ruling over other kings. Arthur necessarily emerged, therefore, as an "overking" and as an emperor—and the role was in a sense pre-ordained by reference to the British emperors within the Roman period in the *Historia*. (219)

Dennis could also be referring to the volatile political situation during the later Roman and sub-Roman era in Britain, where a rebellious naval commander like Carausius in the year 286, a barbarian like Magnentius in 350, or, in 383, the above-mentioned Magnus Maximus could seize power in Britain and style themselves "emperor," even if just for a short time (Sawyer, 64–65).[167] While discussing Æthelstan, Brooke notes that there were very few Anglo-Saxon kings who could call themselves "true kings of a united England," with Æthelstan perhaps reaching that zenith:

> But Æthelstan's title was not pure fantasy. Scottish and Welsh kings admitted his overlordship; he was widely respected outside the mainland of Britain. There is some reason to think that he

used the title "emperor," as did the kings of Leon in northern Spain in the tenth century, on account of the many peoples he ruled over or might claim to rule. (*SNK*, 82)

Brooke also mentions that some years after Æthelstan's death his brother-in-law, Otto the Great, "was crowned 'Roman' emperor in Rome" (82). So the actual king during the period the film allegedly depicts was as close to being an emperor as likely could have been imagined—quite a few qualifiers there, but it is Dennis, after all, making the comparison.

The most recent emperor in Great Britain was George VI (1895–1952), whom the Pythons would have grown up with as their sovereign (fl. 1936–1952). His signature reads "George R.I.," or "George, *Rex Imperator*" ("George, King and Emperor"). With the essential diminishment of the empire leading up to and including World War II, and culminating with the loss of India,[168] the title "Head of the Commonwealth" was created, a title maintained by Queen Elizabeth today.

Lastly, Dennis isn't actually calling Arthur an emperor here, he's engaged in the favorite Python trope of excess, a thesaurus moment, so multiple iterations of "king" and "Lady" and "sword" will flow naturally from this wellspring.

DENNIS: ". . . moistened bint had lobbed a scimitar . . ."—This is now a scaled-down version of one the Pythons' favorite diversions, the thesaurus sketch. Seen many times during the run of *MPFC*, a thesaurus sketch is a sketch (initially provided by the writing team of Chapman and Cleese) where multiple versions of a word or concept are tossed off, often escalating toward some deflating punch line, or an act of violence (as in the culmination of "The Cheese Shop" sketch in Ep. 33). For example, the "Dead Parrot" sketch riffs on ways to describe a parrot's death, including "demised," "passed on," "no more," "ceased to be," "expired" and "late" (Ep. 8).[169] This is partly due to the shopkeeper's inability or unwillingness to admit or acknowledge that he's sold a dead parrot. There are also some perhaps accidental regional connections in this phrase, as both "bint" and "scimitar" are terms from the Middle East, where British colonial forces served into the 1960s.

(grabbing him by the collar)—(PSC) This is a parenthetical inclusion from *MPHGB*, 10. This physical assault mightn't have been without recrimination for the oppressor, interestingly. The typical villein during the twelfth century couldn't really have protected himself here (he would have been unarmed), but there were certain protections built into the system:

> The villein was not trusted to carry weapons; there is no hint before 1225 that he was sworn to arms. On the other hand he was not entirely without rights. The lord . . . could not slay or maim his villein; he could not even thrash him without the risk of trouble; an Essex lord in Henry I's time was fined 40*s*. for this offense. (Poole, *DBMC*, 40–41)

Though he is ostensibly the king, Arthur is risking his reputation to and relationship with his subjects by manhandling Dennis here.

The more contemporary 1969 Merseyside conflict between worker and manager mentioned earlier—where three thousand factory workers faced with redundancy considered taking management by the collar in assuming control over Liverpool G.E.C. (English Electric) factories, and running them *sans* managers—lasted only days, the end result being a reminder that unprofitable factories tend to be unprofitable no matter who owns them, the state or a private concern, and can remain unprofitable no matter who runs them, workers or managers. In the film conflict, Dennis is misguggled a bit, but quickly free to continue, like a good shop steward, to argue his case to his fellow oppressed workers, who have gathered to see what's happening.

The rough handling points up Arthur's frustration with this almost ahistorical peasant before him who, not unlike Falstaff—an ahistorical character in historical plays—doesn't have to conform to the demands of either history or genre, and can operate on levels that history-bound characters cannot. Dennis isn't likely worried about the king's wrath or loss of his livelihood—he doesn't recognize Arthur's authority anyway. Falstaff is an interesting character type between the seemingly free Dennis and any actual historical character. Scholar David Bergeron describes Falstaff as "the special artifice of Shakespeare's construction of history, the one who brings narrative history and narrative fiction face to face"; Dennis performs a similar function here, and it can only serve to frustrate Arthur, who is hidebound by his genre.[170] The Pythons don't explore too deeply the possibilities of the mythological (and therefore textually—potentially—more free) Arthur moving through the historical Mercia/England; he isn't allowed to interact with any historical characters (a King Offa or Bede), potentially disrupting or even fulfilling (sideways) the flow of history. The Pythons will spend more time and creative energy in their next film, *Life of Brian*, doing just that. There, the fictional Brian is woven into a historical tapestry that includes both Pontius Pilate and even Jesus, as Brian attends the Sermon on the Mount.

Hewing closer to this medieval world, and to history, the vagaries of justice during this period would have rankled Dennis plenty, since "[r]oyal authority and justice were limited and corruptible," according to Holmes, and especially as enforced by a lord's representatives (30). But this was the world a family *like* Dennis and his mother would have lived in and mutely understood; it's the extrovert reaction in the face of a king that sets Dennis apart from most of his fellows and even his time.[171] The Dennis of medieval history would have accepted that the sometimes brutish retinue of his lord and the lord himself were sui generis—there were no other options: "Retinues and lordly influence were not necessarily as vicious as this," Holmes concludes, "but for good or ill, they were as essential as the open fields to medieval society; neither the magnate nor the commoner could imagine a world without them" (30). Arthur, adhering to his generic demands, must shake this petulant peasant; Dennis, free to access twentieth-century labor paradigms, must shout back, calling for his bruvvers' help.

DENNIS: ". . . the violence inherent in the system . . ."—Certainly a reference to the frequency of violent, oppressive actions either instigated or allowed for in top-down political and economic structured systems, whether medieval or modern—the ruling classes forcing the subordinate classes to remain where and who they are. The headline-grabbing 1973–1974 coup in Chile—where a democratically elected Marxist president (Allende) was ousted by a fascistic military dictatorship, leading to the Pinochet years—is just such a repressive system that Dennis is "on about."[172] But there is also the violence of the oppressed against their oppressors, of course. First, the top-down consideration.

England has a long history of such sentiment, forged against the guarantees of Magna Carta after 1215—"No free man shall be seized or imprisoned, or stripped of his rights or possessions, or outlawed or exiled . . . except by the lawful judgement of his equals"—to the Peasants' Revolt and then at least the Levellers' movement of the 1640s (German and Rees, 48).[173] Dennis here is being "seized" and manhandled by his better, not his equal, meaning both the spirit and the letter of the law are being violated. During the tempestuous reign of Richard II (1377–1399), the monarch's vindictiveness of spirit and extravagant court alienated him from the nobles, merchants, and the common man, bringing his ability to rule into question, according to fourteenth-century scholar Nicholas of Oresme: "[W]henever kingship approaches tyranny it is near its end, for by this it becomes ripe for division, change of dynasty, or total destruction, especially in a temperate climate . . . where men are habitually, morally and naturally free."[174] Arthur's manhandling and repression of the "free" Dennis likely qualifies him as a proto-tyrant. The short-lived Diggers movement in seventeenth-century England, for example, saw working peasants begin to gather together and declare that un-planted, non-freehold land could and should be made available to any who would work it profitably; and if not given over freely, then taken via squatting, manuring, planting, and harvesting, with all area commoners invited to share in the communal experience. Several such man-free-in-nature experiments popped up in the Cobham, Surrey area in 1649–1651, but were soon broken up by local landowners and the New Model Army. This squatter movement would reappear in postwar Britain as a grassroots answer to the desperate housing shortage being felt as late as the 1960s (*MPFC: UC*, 1.203–4).

Closer to the time of *Flying Circus* and *Holy Grail*, the relationship between the oppressed and the oppressor continued to create friction, with some wondering where it could all be leading, and whether violence was inevitable. The editors of the *Freedom–Anarchist Weekly*, John Rety and P. G. Turner, asked just how long the sparks could fly before flames erupted: "In other countries the inflexibility of the state apparatus has produced a violent situation. Here a peaceful revolution is, of course, desirable. But can you envisage the establishment giving up its 'privilege' voluntarily?"[175] And from Leeds University-educated Brian MacArthur, writing in 1971:

> At Oxford, Chris Hitchins[176] [*sic*] described I.S. [International Socialists] as an expression of or-thodox Marxism, which saw no path to power other than winning mass support, starting among workers, with the aim of establishing workers' control. Although he was against violence, he pointed to the need for an empirical attitude. "One has got to give a lot of weight to the possibil-ity that people in power will resist you by force and put the responsibility for it on themselves." He cites three fronts for the world revolution: an end to the exploitation of the underdeveloped world; the need for workers' control and an end to monopoly capitalism; and sympathy and sup-port for revolutionary movements in East Europe and the Soviet Union.[177]

Just over a year later in an invited speech at the House of Commons in June 1972, the Arch-bishop of Olinda and Recife (Brazil), Dom Hélder Câmara,[178] offered a condensed version of his 1971 pamphlet, *Spiral of Violence*. The pamphlet is essentially a look at the continuing repression, often via technology, of the Third World in the postcolonial era, an identification of the violence that exists to keep the oppression in place, and possible solutions for moving forward (viz., loving another's liberty as much as your own). The Archbishop's description of the spiraling "violence inherent in the system" rings quite familiar:

> Why doesn't your political expertise help to show that the primary violence is the injustice that we see everywhere—which isn't the monopoly of any one nation? Why don't you show that the reaction of the oppressed—or of young people in the name of the oppressed—is a secondary violence, itself followed by violence number three, the reaction of governments; and show that governments, within this logic of violence, and the escalating spiral of violence, can, with great facility, adopt arbitrary measures, torture and even dictatorship?[179]

Dennis's concern that he is experiencing institutionalized violence is clearly an echo of the Archbishop; Dennis represents the Third World in its expected submission to a potential colonizer, but he manages to put up enough resistance that the oppressor must move on (though their relative societal positions are unchanged).

This violence as part of the system must also include the very recent levels of intimidation and physicality seen domestically in relation to the miner's strike of 1972–1973. There, at flashpoints like Scunthorpe, Handley,[180] and Saltley Gate, injuries occurred as police tried to maintain separation between the strikers and those attempting to make deliveries at collieries, coke plants, and the like. The strikers and their unions blamed the police, management, and the (Tory) government for strong-arm tactics, while the police and government warned of anarchy and revolution as trade unions attempted to wrest control of the means of production and distribution by force of numbers. Margaret Thatcher, then education secretary, would characterize the government's eventual complete capitulation to the unions' demands as a "victory for violence," the same kind of language that was being used to describe government concessions being made in the bloody streets of Belfast (Turner, 13). This linking of trade unions with intimidation and violence would resonate with voters, it seems, as the Tories were able to ride the horses of law and order and the promised hobbling of the trade unions to a sweeping victory in 1979.

ARTHUR: "Bloody peasant!" *(pushes DENNIS over into mud . . .)*—There is a contemporary and a Middle Ages referent here. Arthur is clearly surprised at this turn of events, at the peasant's cheek, and was expecting a response and then activity that represents the commoner's agreed-upon place in manorial society—remember Langland's citing of Cato and the place of the poor: if you're born poor, bear it. Dennis is part of the largest of the three medieval estates—the other two being the clergy and the nobility (cf. Gower's "clerus," "miles," and "cultor")—but he has transgressed that level of society, that level of decorum (Olsson, 136). Moralist John Gower (a fourteenth-century Roger the Shrubber, but also colleague to Chaucer) would write of his dismay at the behavior of the commoner's estate after the Peasants' Revolt in 1381. In *Vox Clamantis*, Gower lays out the three estates just mentioned: "*Sunt clerus, miles, cultor, tres trina gerentes, / Hic docet, hic pugnat, alter et arua colit*" ("The cleric, knight and ploughman have three tasks, / As teacher, fighter, tiller of the soil").[181] Dennis, his mother, and those in this field are clearly part of the third and last/least/largest group—we see them mucking in the filth as the scene begins. Gower found these to be "sluggish," "scarce" (when hard work was to be done), and overly demanding:

> [A] short time ago one performed more service than three do now, as those maintain who are well-acquainted with the facts. . . . They desire the leisures of great men, but they have nothing to feed themselves with, nor will they be servants. . . . [E]veryone owning land complains about these people; each stands in need of them and none has control over them. The peasants of old did not scorn God with impunity or usurp a noble worldly rank. (208–9)

Arthur and Gower share the surprise that these newer peasants haven't been inculcated into the proper order of estates, clearly remembering the more manageable "peasants of old."[182]

Secondly, the term "peasant" itself isn't heard from Dennis or his mother or anyone else in the world of the film, excepting Arthur himself. The script describes Dennis as a "peasant" twice, before he speaks, thereafter he's known as "Dennis";[183] when Arthur is manhandling Dennis other "*Peasants*" gather to watch the confrontation. Mortimer notes that the term is more early modern than medieval, and that a fourteenth-century "clerk [would] refer to [Dennis] and his companions as *rustici* (countrymen), *nativi* (those born to servitude), or *villani* (villeins)"; "peasant" would have had no meaning, and would likely have been too general in its application to make any sense (48–49). It's Arthur that first uses the term anyway, pejoratively, and Dennis is able to recognize Arthur's class-based *parti pris* immediately.

On a more contemporary note, this physical confrontation is one that the labor movement of the 1970s would have recognized and even embraced—the image of a repressive and violent manager/owner assaulting a defenseless and inoffensive worker. Note that Dennis doesn't fight back in the least, showing his idealized labor credentials as a simple worker wanting a living wage, nothing more. It also points up the intractability of the government-labor situation in the weeks leading up to the beginning of production on *MPHG*. Ronald Faux, reporting for *The Times* at the Seafield colliery, notes that the Scottish mineworker faced low wages, inadequate rest and prep periods, harsh conditions to, from, and at the coal-face, and the necessity of working straight through the early signs of diseases like pneumoconiosis, all "to 'qualify' for an inadequate pension." Faux concludes his sober assessment: "The Government believes this is a confrontation it must win, while the Scottish miners are clearly determined that they cannot afford to lose." He concludes, presciently: "The irresistible force has classically struck the immovable object."[184] Arthur and Dennis reach this same impasse, neither winning, though the writing is on the wall as to Arthur's chances of success in the "sad times" through which he quests.

DENNIS: "I'm being repressed!"—Once again, Arthur's subjects fail to recognize themselves as such, and Dennis even dares to call out for help from others he clearly sees as his comrades in this struggle (they are a collective, after all).

There is a historical precedent for this depiction, for the legendary Arthur's nonexistent or just lowered reputation at a time or place when others are hailing his greatness. The Welsh monastic tradition of Arthurian exploits features some less-than-flattering portrayals of Arthur and his knights.[185] After detailing several alleged incidents recorded by monks in about the twelfth century—including one where Arthur idly plays dice and "takes an unwelcome interest" in the betrothed of another, and one where he is termed "a certain *tyrannus* by the name of Arthur" for his machinations—Ashe posits the image of Arthur as perhaps "a military despot who tries to plunder the monks," which is the reason that, like Charles Martel, "[a]lthough he saved western Christendom, ecclesiastical authors treat him as a villain" (*QAB*, 62–63). Morris notes that these dualistic, opposing traditions—Arthur as hero or Arthur as tyrant—emerge even earlier, and from understandable perceptions (especially in relation to the peasantry), from

> tradition[s] that preserve the highland view of Arthur, a tyrant who came to conquer, and came from foreign parts. . . . The tradition of an alien Arthur, an enemy who ruled the lands that became England, is not a medieval invention. It conflicts with the legend of the hero Arthur, but it is not the product of a different age; it stems from a different social class. The concept of the warrior Arthur was popular with princes. . . . The stories of the detestable Arthur, the national enemy, reflect the outlook of humbler folk, who had no love for kings and lords, warriors and rulers. They are preserved only in the Saints' Lives, for the early monastic leaders also quarreled with kings, and many of the monks themselves came from humble homes. . . . The monastic traditions picked up and perpetuated a viewpoint that it found in the world around it, a plebeian tradition of deep-rooted local resentment against the suzerainty that Arthur powerfully and successfully asserted over the peoples of the highlands of Britain. (*The Age of Arthur*, 122–23)

There are also some *historically* substantive hints to support this antagonism—Church property was often "requisitioned" for maintenance of troops, for example, and any Arthur-type as a successful campaigner simply had to be a successful pillager, too (Ashe, 63–64).[186]

In the world of 1970s Great Britain the specter of repression took on a not dissimilar tone, though without the religious dressing. Instead, it was simply the haves dictating choices for the have-nots, a power relationship Dennis clearly sees operating in this exchange. At the start of this encounter (in the printed script) Dennis has listed Arthur's kingly possessions—"I expect you've got a palace and fine clothes and courtiers and plenty of food"[187]—examples of the top-down repression in this "dictatorship." The word itself ("repressed") was thrown around in the media of the day, of course, like other buzzwords ("imperialist," "capitalist," "socialist," "Marxist," "Communist," etc.), most often to try and describe the *other guy* in a political or economic disagreement (or party manifesto). In Gibraltar, trade unionists are being "rigorously repressed" in February 1973, while in Spain the following year it's the Franco government's eerily euphemistic "controlled expression" of "political forces that have been repressed for so long."[188] For the perennial third-party Liberals such words were a way of delineating between either larger party and what they saw as a clear third, better choice: voting Liberal. In the Liberal Manifesto published prior to the 1974 general election, leader Jeremy Thorpe paints Tories and Labourites as two sides of the same old coin, both bad choices, both sustaining status quo and regressive ideologies.[189] The Liberals, however, in addressing the labor issue and especially lost working days thanks to strike actions, sound more Dennisean, promising to spread the good things around:

> But we must also reform the wage bargaining free for all in which the poorest inevitably come off worst. To do this effectively we must reconstruct our framework of industrial relations to spread the monopoly power now vested in a few very powerful unions.
>
> Britain lost more than 24 million working days last year—more than any other European country and almost double the amount lost in Italy, our nearest rival. Yet what have our opponents to offer as an antidote to industrial chaos? The Industrial Relations Act and the impotent Industrial Relations Court stand as monuments to attempted Tory repression, and a perpetual reminder to the Labour Party of its capitulation to union pressure while in Government. (*Times*, 13 February 1974: 6)

The Liberals would take power away from repressive unions, putting them at odds with Labour; Labour would take power away from ownership and government, upsetting the Tories. In this they are singing a more Bennite tune than even the far left wing of the Labour Party during this period—another reason the Liberals remained in the minority.[190]

ARTHUR: "Bloody peasant!"—There is no record of "bloody" being used as an intensifier prior to the sixteenth century, so Arthur is well ahead of his time, as is Herbert's father in Swamp Castle, who will use "Bloody hell" later. The Pythons had used both "bloody" and "bleeding" many times in *MPFC*, without much censor fuss, according to official records.[191] It was, however, one of the words the BBC had forbidden its shows and personnel to use in a policy guide distributed in 1948 (*MPFC: UC*, 1.50).

The "giveaway" here is Arthur's resorting to a put-down, revealing his aristocratic heart, his sense of entitlement, and his distance from the working class of England—all traits Dennis has already identified in the figurehead before him, and which Arthur has now unwittingly confirmed. Arthur's giveaway puts him in the same class, literally and figuratively, as the *haut monde* master of Blenheim, the Duke of Marlborough. Critic Irving Wardle (b. 1929) mentions the Duke's "reaction on observing some wretched peasant hobbling along a right-of-way and spoiling the Blenheim sky line: 'There go the people, damn them, the people!'"[192]

DENNIS: "Do you see him repressing me?"—The scene directions don't mention it but there are other filth muckers shuffling into the shot in the foreground, and it's to this motley crew Dennis is speaking. It may be that he is claiming his right to a trial by jury, by his peers, essentially, part of the common law implemented by Henry II (1133–1189), the first of the Angevin or Plantagenet kings. These "responsible citizens" could be "assembled and put on oath to tell the truth" (Bishop, *HBMA*, 46). Better than the older trial by ordeal or combat, this new system allowed "jurymen [to reach] their decisions on the basis of common local knowledge, not on evidence produced in court; but their verdict decided the case" (46). Since he seems to be the salt-of-the-earth Englishman who "knows his rights," Dennis is appealing for a jury decision from his fellow laborers as "the violence inherent in the system" is visited upon his collar.

SCENE FIVE

Notes

1. Gilliam's audio commentary track on the Blu-ray and DVD editions of the film.

2. Gilliam's and Jones's audio commentaries on the DVD and Blu-ray versions of the film.

3. For more on these manorial situations see Brooke, *From Alfred to Henry III: 871–1272*, 114–27, as well as Holmes, *The Later Middle Ages: 1272–1485*.

4. From e-mail correspondence between the author and Julian Doyle. In a deposition given by Doyle in 2012 as part of producer Forstater's lawsuit against the Pythons, Doyle lays out his significant contributions to the film's completion, doing everything from shooting second unit and special effects scenes to prop maker and actor to "stealer of dead sheep" (for the Grail Castle sequence), and even caterer.

5. Gilliam remembers the castle flat as being about twelve feet tall, which can also be heard on the Gilliam-voiced audio track.

6. This was a $6,000 film that, with a few additional minutes of footage, was distributed to theaters in 1970. Muren (b. 1946) would go on create practical special effects for *Star Wars*, *Close Encounters*, and others.

7. The outlying lands of a farm, likely rough pasturage or occasionally planted. See the *OED*.

8. From David Robinson's review of the film (15 June 1973); see the "*impoverished plague-ridden village*" entry above. There were other *major* complaints about the Pasolini film, from viewers in Britain and France. One saw the film as testing the "limits of the pornographic and the scatological" (*Times*, 30 May 1973: 19), while three others defended the use of portions of the Wells and Canterbury properties given the assurances of the filmmakers, and another cleverly rendered the complaints moot: "Sir, Your correspondents may not have seen Pasolini's film but I imagine that they must have read Chaucer?" (*Times*, 7 June 1973: 19). Pasolini and the film were acquitted in July 1973 of charges of obscenity in Italy, as well.

9. See *MPFC: UC*, 2.11, 64–65, 83. The political situation in Northern Ireland, which would erupt into widespread violence in the late 1960s, had been turbulent for most of the century. Scotland was a much safer target for derision.

10. Remember, even though the stated date on the film stock itself says "932" (and the script reads "787"), Jones references the thirteenth and fourteenth centuries for the designs in the film's production, the castles used are generally fourteenth to fifteenth century, notes in the printed script mention 1167, one producer mentions the year "1282," and any actual Arthur-type would have lived somewhere at the turn of the fifth to sixth centuries. Timewise, *MPHG* is all over the place.

11. *HBI*, 75.

12. For more on Domesday Book see Sawyer, *From Roman Britain to Norman England*.

13. This is how Palin characterizes Dennis in his DVD and Blu-ray audio commentaries.

14. As will be discussed in the "Swamp Castle" sections, costs, royal finances, and tax-weary subjects were particularly influential factors when state decisions were being made.

15. See McNeill for images of these British castles.

16. See Ashe, *The Discovery of King Arthur*, 88, for more. The Tintagel, Cornwall, region was regularly described in newspapers of the 1960s and 1970s as "King Arthur country." The Goons had created an entire episode centered on the ghostly history of the place, "The Spectre of Tintagel" (1 November 1956). Secombe (1921–2001) plays "King Arthur Seagoon," named so because his parents owned a round table, and says he is a descendant of "King Morte D'Arthur."

17. From Collingwood and Myres, *Roman Britain and the English Settlements*, as quoted in Shrewsbury, "The Yellow Plague," 7.

18. William immediately set about replacing Anglo-Saxon leadership and influence with his own countrymen and organizations. Across Britain, the French had arrived, and would remain. See entries in the "Taunting by Frenchmen" scene below for much more on the French-English situation of the thirteenth and fourteenth centuries.

19. *HBI*, 89. The "Great Famine of 1315–1317" stretched across Europe and Russia, and wouldn't begin to ease until about 1322. See also Raban, 18–19, McKisack, 49–50, and Le Goff, 154–59.

20. *English Landscape*, 93; cited in McKisack, 313. See also Beresford, *The Lost Villages of England*.

21. French authorities calculated taxes based on how many hearths (meaning homes) were in a particular village. See Tuchman, 363–64.

22. These poll tax figures can also be misleading, as many potential, living respondents simply refused to be found—going into hiding when the taxman approached—they didn't want to be taxed anew. See McKisack, 312–13 for more on the unreliability of poll tax rolls.

23. Collingwood and Myres, quoted in Shrewsbury, "The Yellow Plague," 7–8.

24. The Pythons had considered shooting portions of Arthur and Patsy's early wanderings through working Britain from atop a stretch of Hadrian's Wall, but that never came to fruition. Eventually everything (excepting a handful of effects insert shots) was shot either on location in Scotland or later on Hampstead Heath, with J. Doyle running the camera crew.

25. The Gough Map—likely created in the 1370s—depicts an impressive network of roads throughout much of Britain, and especially the southeast. Commerce would have demanded passage from place to place in Britain, even if it were arduous, and if the Pythons are thinking thirteenth and fourteenth century for much of the "look" of the film, then there would have been roads to be had. McKisack concludes: "At all events . . . the roads proved not inadequate for the needs of the age, administrative as well as economic" (314).

26. The Roman fort at Doune—northwest of the castle overlooking the Tieth—wasn't located until a decade after the filming of *MPHG*, and then only thanks to aerial mapping. See Maxwell, 98–100, and the Royal Commission on the Ancient and Historical Monuments of Scotland website.

27. *Life of Brian*, audio transcription.

28. In fact, she is only known as "Old Woman" in portions of the finished printed script; Dennis never refers to her as "Old Woman" or his mother (or his wife or sister), nor does she bring it up, while Arthur simply calls her "Good Lady." Many viewers might have assumed this was a husband and wife couple, a staple throughout *MPFC*, as well as later in *LB* and *ML*. It's not until the closing credits (only appearing in *MPHGB*) that it's made clear Jones played "Dennis's Mother" (90). In the DVD commentary she's just called a "rat-bag."

29. *The Goon Show*, 2 December 1957; audio transcription.

30. See the "Dead Parrot" sketch (*JTW*, 1.104; *MPFC: UC*, 1.135).

31. "Mr Healey Promises . . . ," *Times*, 19 February 1974: 4.

32. "Babes in the Wood or Great Britain on Ice," *Times*, 24 December 1974: 16.

33. This parliament convened in 1376 from late April through July, and in the face of antagonism from John of Gaunt and Edward III, attempted to force reforms on the court and government. See Holmes, *The Later Middle Ages*, 183–84.

34. Holmes notes that there were areas of Britain, often fringes of large counties or in agricultural areas that were marginal (in location and quality), where "many of the peasantry had only a tenuous connection with the manor" (*LMA*, 14). Dennis and mother might, then, actually *not* know their nominal lord. Remoteness notwithstanding, since the "legal maxim" avowed that "All men are either freemen or serfs," it is safe to assume that "most countrymen were subject to some kind of manorial jurisdiction" (14).

35. The poor are fed up with Moore's charity of "bloody silver" and sixteen-carat candlesticks. They want proper charity—"Venetian silver" and a "Velasquez for the loo" (*JTW*, 2.207).

36. Polanski's 1971 adaptation of *Macbeth* is identified in many reviews and essays as also reflecting and commenting on the world, and on Polanski's own history. For example: "He [Polanski] proceeds by transmogrifying the Christian context of Shakespeare's time into the contemporary 1972 world of unredeemed sin, suffering, and death" (Rothwell, 72).

37. "TUC Refusal to Enlist Support for the Pit Strike Upsets Miners," *Times*, 11 January 1972: 1.

38. Palin describes Christmas-time London as eerily quiet during this embargo period; most petrol stations were closed across the city and country (*Diaries*, 149).

39. Faisal's government was able to convince the United States to begin deliveries of jet fighters in mid-November 1973, as well as secure a contract with the British government for "defence services and expertise for the Saudi Air Force." This as the oil embargo was really heating up—an indication of how important future relations with "petronations" were to the United States and UK. See "America Will Supply Jet Fighters to Saudis," *Times*, 15 November 1973: 10. In the article the American dealings are covered first (and they are alone in the headline), followed by Britain's complicity—kind of an afterthought.

40. Palin, *Diaries*, 158.

41. See also *Times* articles "A Ruinous Dispute," 3 January 1974: 13; "Poll Where Winners May Envy Losers," 20 February 1974: 4; and "British Politicians in a Fantasy World," 22 February 1974: 5.

42. *Times*, 12 February 1974: 5.

43. Fred Emery, *Times*, 30 April 1979: 8.

44. "Harold Wilson Resigns," *Eyewitness 1970–1979*; audio transcription.

45. See "self-perpetuating autocracy" above for more on the Saltley Gate incidents and the power of organized demonstration.

46. "WHO Would Benefit?" *Times*, 7 June 1965: 9.

47. *Times*, 6 November 1970: 11.

48. Jay was himself a Labourite and Keynesian—unfettered big business a likely threat, then—writing during the early months of the new (1970) Tory administration.

49. In this Dennis is also the fourteenth-century priest John Ball (1338–1381), who preached of true "commons" in England—"there be no villeins or gentlemen, but that we may be all united together and that the lords be no greater masters than we be" (*HBMA*, 373). Ball, Wat Tyler, and Jack Straw would severally lead the ill-fated Peasants' Revolt in 1381. All three men would be killed as the rebellion failed, and all three would have their heads mounted on pikes on London Bridge—they discovered "the violence inherent in the system" for themselves.

50. Sandbrook, *State of Emergency*, 619.

51. Labour won more seats (301–297), but Conservatives took the popular vote. The Liberal haul of fourteen seats (up from six) spelled the difference between a more certain victory for either Labour or the Tories.

52. Wilson would retire without warning just two years later. See Sandbrook, *State of Emergency*, 633–43 for more on the confusing 1974 election results.

53. See *MPFC: UC*, 1.335. The character appears in *MPFC* episodes 9, 16, 21, 27, and 37.

54. This can be land or a dwelling that is or could be occupied—it's not clear in this scene if the peasants even know who might claim ownership of the castle beyond.

55. *The Anglo-Saxon Version of the Life of St. Guthlac, Hermit of Crowland*. Trans. and Notes by Charles W. Goodwin. London: John Russell Smith, 1848.

56. Most Roman-era roads had fallen into disrepair, if there were roads in a particular area to begin with. Rowley also reminds us, however, that a road during this period might have looked a bit different than we would expect today: "The medieval concept of a road was more of a right of way than an actual physical trackway" (*The High Middle Ages*, 170). A "way" cleared of significant obstacles, then. So Arthur, Patsy, and the quest may actually be following acknowledged "roads," even if we see no obvious road.

57. See the entries for the "She's a witch!" scene below for more.

58. *Times*, 10 January 1974: 14.

59. "Peking Defends 'Paper Tigers' Taunt by Mr. Mao," *Times*, 4 March 1963: 8.

60. *MPFC: UC*, 1.293–94, 296, and 358.

61. *Paying for Labour's Programme*.

62. Cf., for example, *MPFC: UC*, 1.11–12 ("*Guernica* . . ."), 1.13 ("Kandinsky"), 1.43 ("Sartre"), 1.386 ("binomial theorem"), and on.

63. "Issues Behind the Election: Views of Roman Catholics," *Times*, 27 February 1974: 19.

64. Gill (1927–2009) was the general secretary of the technical and supervisory staffs section of the Amalgamated Union of Engineering Unions, who also happened to be an admitted and unapologetic Communist (*Times*, 8 October 1974: 16).

65. Coins have already appeared, however, in a more urban setting in the previous scene, when Arthur and Patsy ride through the plague-ridden village, and we see the Cart Driver paid "ninepence."

66. See the *OED* for more examples of the name's usage.

67. McKisack, 341. See McKisack and Tuchman for more on this gradual transition.

68. There are *no* glimpses of Roman structures, actual medieval-aged towns, or even remains of Roman roadways in *MPHG* though, as Hoskins points out, "remains of some Roman buildings were still

clearly visible in the countryside as late as the 10th century" (Poole, 1.3). It was much easier and cheaper to film in less culturally and archaeologically sensitive locations.

69. "Workers' Control." *Direct Action Pamphlet No. 4*. London: SWF, 1962: 17. Brown admits that it's not likely such successful collectivization could survive in other capitalist countries, the Israeli example—and the Zionist state—being unique.

70. Two other failing businesses earmarked for potential workers' paradises included a Scottish newspaper and a manufacturing concern, both of which received significant government support for reorganization and worker control.

71. "How the Meriden Workers Fought to Keep Going," 30 July 1974: 19.

72. From "The Crippled Giants," *New Internationalist*, December 1981: 18–19; italics added.

73. Benn is earlier mentioned and depicted in Ep. 5 of *Flying Circus* (*MPFC: UC*, 1.87).

74. The 1973–1974 Chilean coup will be mentioned in more detail later in relation to this same scene.

75. "Politicians and TV," *Times*, 24 October 1968: 11.

76. "Labour's Bills Will Have to be Guillotined," *Times*, 2 October 1973: 3.

77. "GLC Halted after Walkout," *Times*, 8 May 1968: 5.

78. *Times*, 18 July 1969: 14.

79. Shaw is featured in *MPFC* Ep. 39 in a battle of witty ripostes with Wilde and Whistler; "Shaw-y" ends up flustered and losing (*MPFC: UC*, 2.152–56).

80. From *The Future of Political Science in America* (11 April 1933): 7–8.

81. Briginshaw (1908–1992) was the general secretary of the National Society of Operative Printers and Assistants during this period, and was outspoken in his stance against government income policies and the EEC.

82. Jimmy Reid (1932–2010) was the public face of the Upper Clyde Shipyard workers who responded with a work-in when the Heath government refused to grant loans, not long after Rolls Royce had been similarly saved from closure by government intervention.

83. That scribes Palin and Jones could offer up medieval versions of real-life people and current events isn't unique, of course. The Pythons had addressed the Profumo scandal in the second episode of *MPFC* ("The Mouse Problem") without putting a fine point on the reference. Elsewhere, the *Doctor Who* series in December 1974 had parodied new PM Heath's Central Policy Review Staff—dubbed the "Think Tank"—in its "Robot" episode, where the organization meant to "hold the world to ransom" (Sandbrook, *State of Emergency*, 68–69).

84. "Tories' Turn to Listen to Jack Dash," *Times*, 24 September 1969: 2.

85. "The Dynamic Docker of Stepney," 29 April 1961: 5.

86. "The Error in Seeing Unions as No More Than Wage Negotiators," 23 August 1973: 14.

87. "Cloudy Outlook for Mrs Castle's Bill," *Times*, 19 January 1970: 22.

88. For more on these firebrand union leaders and their influence on contemporary British society (and even their high visibility during this period) see Sandbrook, *State of Emergency*, 101–5.

89. Quoted in Ferris, *The New Militants*, 9.

90. "Uproar Ends RSPCA Meeting After Police Are Called," *Times*, 15 June 1961: 6; also "Hunting Clash at RSPCA Meeting," *Times*, 15 June 1962: 8.

91. "Ex-Labour Candidate Quits Communists," *Times*, 14 September 1964: 6; italics added.

92. "Crossman Criticism of Hospitals 'Autocracy,'" *Times*, 1 June 1973: 4; italics added.

93. The balance of the section from *Piers Plowman*:

> "Mishandle not bondmen · the better may thou speed.
> Though he be underling here · well may happen in heaven
> That he'll be worthier set · more blissful than thou,
> Unless thou do better · and live as thou shouldest:
> In the charnel at church · churls are hard to pick out,
> Or a knight from a knave · know this in thine heart."

This more modern translation is based on the B text and can be found at Harvard's "The Geoffrey Chaucer Page," under "William Langland."

94. China had been appearing in Gilliam's animations, where its exploding population threatened to overrun the world. See *MPFC: UC*, 1.284, 293–94, 296, and 301, for example. Eps. 19, 24, and 34 feature significant Chinese references.

95. This split led to the troubled and sometimes violent era of Sino-Soviet relations that lasted through the 1970s, ratcheting up the Cold War fears of a nuclear exchange.

96. "The Triumph of Peasant Marxism: Eighth Chinese Party Congress," *The Times*, 17 Sep. 1956: 9.

97. See Priscilla Roberts's section in Friedman, et al. "Forum: Mao, Krushchev, and China's Split with the USSR." As early as 1927, when Mao toured the countryside "documenting" the peasant revolt as the Kuomintang, the Chinese Communist Party and the warlords battled for supremacy, he witnessed and applauded the necessarily violent rise of the peasant, echoing Dennis:

> The patriarchal-feudal class of local tyrants, evil gentry and lawless landlords has formed the basis of autocratic government for thousands of years and is the cornerstone of imperialism, warlordism and corrupt officialdom. To overthrow these feudal forces is the real objective of the national revolution. (*Report on an Investigation of the Peasant Movement in Hunan*, March 1927)

98. It was this level of industrial inertia and the compounded results that would lead to Heath's ousting, a lackluster Labour win in 1974, a torpid mid-1970s that included supplication to the IMF, and the staggering Tory victory in 1979, led by Margaret Thatcher as an organized labor-crusher. As early as October 1970 (just after Labour somehow lost the GE) one former Labour minister opined about the stop-and-go (-and-stop) policies of the party tied inextricably to the labour unions; these policies were "the perfect prescription for keeping Labour out of power through all eternity" (David Wood, "Mr. Wilson Fails to Smother Vote," *Times*, 1 October 1970: 1).

99. "Mr Heath to Answer Censure Call," *Times*, 21 January 1972: 1. See also Sandbrook's *State of Emergency* for more on the "apocalyptic fear" from the perfect storm of rising unemployment, civil unrest thanks to marching and fighting demonstrators, Northern Ireland violence, and the staggering miners' strike (86–91).

100. Engels, "The Origin of the Family, Private Property, and the State," §§3–4.

101. "Young Socialist Moderates Hit Back at Leftists," *Times*, 31 March 1964: 6.

102. "Young Socialist Moderates," 6.

103. *HBI*, 89.

104. In discussing the aftermath of the execution of Thomas, 2nd Earl of Lancaster, McKisack mentions that Lancaster's vast holdings had been administered effectively by local reeves who gathered rents and payments, sending them on to at least two auditors, and thence to the earl's council, where decisions were made for taxation and disbursement (67–68). So even though the earl couldn't be everywhere at once, his estates were administered smoothly.

105. Halsall notes that there is *no* evidence to support the long-held supposition of significant Roman garrison withdrawals from Britain to the Continent after 407. And this final transfer of troops was made to help Romans fight other Romans, not barbarian hordes (*Worlds of Arthur*, 179–81).

106. Reece supports this assertion as well: "[I]n cruder terms . . . the towns of Roman Britain had gone by 350" (77). See Reece, "Town and Country: The End of Roman Britain." Even as early as Arthur's alleged *floruit*, Roman Britain would have been generations old and described by ruins and overgrown roadways.

107. Halsall's *Worlds of Arthur* supports this conclusion in its close look at all the "Arthurian world" evidence.

108. Godfrey of Bouillon (1060–1100), for example, spent the final four years of his life in the Holy Lands.

109. From *Feudal Society* by Marc Bloch (1961), quoted in Bishop, *HBMA*, 96.

110. The "seneschal" (or "steward") might be a gentleman or an elevated commoner, but one who can "know the size and needs of every manor . . . [i]n short, he must be as all-knowing as he is all-powerful" (H. S. Bennett, quoted in Bishop, *HBMA*, 227). The seneschal is in charge when the lord's away, or if the manor is so vast it demands a steward's constant diligence. Here there is a castle with no occupants, and poor people working in a filth field—and no one seemingly above or in between.

111. *Ecclesiastical History*, 1.15.55–56.

112. The nagging question of whether Hengest and brother Horsa were historical or legendary can be noted here, especially when citing Morris as a period scholar. Thomas Green is certain, calling them "Kentish totemic horse-gods historicised by the eighth century with an important role in the fifth-century Anglo-Saxon conquest of eastern Britain" ("The Historicity and Historicisation of Arthur," 1).

113. The movement had emigrated from the Continent, having been much more active in France, Spain, and Italy for many years. Rudolf Rocker's *Anarcho-Syndicalism: Theory and Practice* offers a rundown of continental movements over the years, and Britain is not significantly addressed in any of the editions (1938, 1968, 1972).

114. From the SWF's "Aims and Principles": "The Syndicalist Workers' Federation seeks to establish a free society, which will render impossible the growth of a privileged class and the exploitation of man by man." The organ goes on to offer a Dennisean list, calling for "common ownership and workers' control," the abolition of the "wage system," an acknowledgment of "class struggle," the necessity of "direct action," the destruction of the State, and the need for "organisation" *without* trade unions (back page; Brown, "Nationalisation and the New Boss Class").

115. Just two years later a Tory MP would somewhat agree with Brown, but more finally characterizing anarcho-syndicalism (and Maoism) as "non-solutions," and no way to move forward in the world. See Nicholas Scott, "A Strategy for Conservatism," *Times*, 3 October 1970: 19.

116. Found at the libcom.org site. Tom Brown *and* Rudolf Rocker's writings appear in a number of the organization's *Direct Action* pamphlets, which can also be accessed at this site.

117. "Czech Unions Emerge as Independent Force," *Times*, 5 March 1969: 6.

118. This is why the "need" for violence is so pervasive, as Mao wrote (and justified) and critics of the Far Left consistently reminded—the powers that be want to keep that power.

119. Ronald Butt, "Liberals' Brighter Outlook," *Times*, 24 September 1970: 11.

120. But it's amazing what a little time and nationwide penury can do for a fringe party. By late October 1973, cultural critic Raymond Williams will write of a *Liberal* ascendancy, projected increases in the Commons—essentially a Liberal boost—thanks to the major parties' insular, self-damaging politics. See Williams, "The Liberals Move Up Fast." (NB: The ascendancy was short-lived and disappointing.)

121. "Merit of Workers' Control in Industry," *Times*, 19 September 1969: 11.

122. "A History of Anarcho-Syndicalism," Unit 20: 19.

123. Labour MP, Nuneaton; b. 1942.

124. "How the Meriden Worker Fought to Keep Going," *The Times*, 30 Jul. 1974: 19.

125. "Aggressive Strategies for Workers' Control," *Times*, 23 October 1970: 10.

126. *OED*.

127. Brown, "What's Wrong with the Unions?"

128. Audio transcription, *I'm All Right Jack*, dir. John Boulting, a Charter Films/British Lion Films production, 1959.

129. "Party Support Handbook—*The Rule Book*—Section M—Model Rules for a Regional Co-operative Party," September 2010.

130. Ed Rosen, "Co-Op Politics: Introducing the UK's Fourth Largest Political Party," *Guardian*, 22 May 2012.

131. See for example "London Co-Op Fights National Leaders' Move to Tighten Ban on Communists," *Times*, 29 May 1972: 2.

132. Edward's legendary borrowing, taxing, and spending excesses are discussed elsewhere in this book.

133. Quoted in Brooke, *The Saxon and Norman Kings*, 22–23. The "people" weren't voting, of course, but the nobles and "wise men."

134. Harold "had already been 'elected' and crowned" the day after Edward the Confessor passed away, and before William could invade (Brooke, *The Saxon and Norman Kings*, 28). This "election" didn't deter William, who meant to press his right as the successor *designated* by Edward.

135. Baugh, et al., *A Literary History of England*, 169.

136. See the Árni Magnússon Institute for Icelandic Studies for more on Hafliði's Code http://www
.arnastofnun.is/page/althjodlegt_islenskunamskeid_en.

137. Campbell, *The Anglo-Saxons*, 144–47.

138. See *MPFC: UC*, 2.3–19.

139. The overall scene (Arthur vs. the peasants) was penned by Jones and Palin; the "Lady of the Lake" recitation written by Cleese and Chapman. Listen to Cleese's audio commentary.

140. And which featured fantastical characters like Cupid, Venus, Thor, and Woden. The University of Nottingham and Queen Mary's College, London, and others performed the work in 1956; multiple performances were staged in 1959 for Purcell's tercentenary; and BBC Radio offered versions throughout the 1960s.

141. In a neat conflation (at least for us), a review for the August 1964 Drury Lane debut of *Camelot* witheringly called the show a "passable imitation of a repertory company's Christmas pantomime" (*Times*, 20 August 1964: 12).

142. From the Filiquarian version, 2007.

143. Bors will play a small role in the *MPHG* printed script, and an even smaller one in the finished film, where, played by Gilliam, he loses his head to the Killer Rabbit.

144. A bibliographic tidbit here. In the Penguin version of Malory's work (from 1969) this response reads "Sir Arthur, king." The "king" appellation is missing from other versions, including this Winchester version. (See Volume I, Chapter 25, page 56 of *LMD'A*.)

145. Another variation: in the *LMD'A* version it's "Sir Arthur," both here and in the following line.

146. Halsall notes that in postimperial Britain the kings tended to be pagans, with Æthelbert (560–616) the first to be baptized a Christian in 601.

147. This structure would be tested by Magna Carta and beyond, as common law governance and consent (of the nobles, initially) became de rigueur in English polity. Dennis is simply trying to push the process forward.

148. See McKisack for more, as well as Holmes, *The Later Middle Ages: 1272–1485*, 114–18.

149. The time leading up to the Conquest, when Anglo-Saxon and Danish kings ruled Britain.

150. From Stenton's monumental *Anglo-Saxon England* (1943), specifically the reissued Oxford paperback edition of 2001, page 299.

151. Later, just after a horsed knight rides through the shot and strikes him down, the Famous Historian is called "Frank" by his frantic wife. See below for more.

152. In fact, Arthur "shushes" Patsy at the mention of the artificiality of a prop. In a deleted later scene where the Beast chases Arthur and his knights through the Cave of Caerbannog, Gawain mentions that the beast is "only a cartoon," prompting a "shush" from Arthur there, too. In neither case is it made clear whether Arthur is shushing the unknightly outburst or the "reveal" of the "man behind the curtain" elements of the world.

153. Webbe, "What is Happening to the Stately Homes of Britain?"

154. King was born in 1901, the year Queen Victoria died.

155. "Finding Talent for the Lords," *Times*, 21 November 1968:11.

156. See Brown's "What's Wrong with the Unions?: A Syndicalist Response" in *Direct Action Pamphlet No. 1*: 8.

157. "Electoral Reform," *Times*, 20 November 1951: 5.

158. Byers was a one-term Liberal MP who won his seat thanks to Labour standing no candidate; he then lost the seat in 1950 when Labour did stand a candidate. His calls for electoral reform stem from personal experience, clearly. He was made a life peer in 1964.

159. The more recent 2010 General Election went fairly well for the Conservatives, but they fell twenty seats short of a majority, meaning the first hung election since February 1974. The Tories were able to fashion a coalition government with the Liberal Democrats, ending thirteen years of Labour control.

160. *The New Partridge Dictionary of Slang and Unconventional English* cites Ruth Parks, *Poor Man's Orange*, 184. This is an Australia/NZ novel, and if Palin did have an "Auntie Betty in Australia" (*MPFC*, Ep. 31), the reference makes all the more sense.

161. See the *OED* for more, and the entry for "bint" in the *NP Dictionary of Slang and Unconventional English*.

162. *MPFC: UC*, 1.377–78; see the Sketch Index there for "*Ypres 1914*."

163. Episode 43 also features a lengthy sketch looking at "RAF banter" (*MPFC: UC*, 2.178–86). See *MPFC: UC* index under "World War II" for these and many other entries.

164. I continue to cite Morris (1913–1977) even though much of the connective tissue in his monumental work *The Age of Arthur* has been diminished or severed by subsequent scholarship, and as early as 1975–1977 by scholars like Dumville, and D.P Kirby and J.E.C. Williams ("Review of The Age of Arthur" in *Studia Celtica*, 10–11 [1975-6]: 454–86). It's important to remember that in the early 1970s Morris's voice would have been loudest and certainly the most confident—along with Alcock and Ashe—in Arthuriana, and thus most available for and visible to the general public, including the Pythons. Morris and the Arthur-as-historical scholars are very important for understanding the zeitgeist of 1973–1974 Britain.

165. Morris's obituary in the *Times* is far more generous, calling *The Age of Arthur* "bold, fascinating, and underrated" (10 June 1977: 18).

166. Morris, 141.

167. Carausius was assassinated seven years later, and Magnentius's overthrow—though perhaps popular—was eventually unsuccessful. Both events point up the challenges the Romans faced as their sprawling, multiracial empire rebelled. See Sawyer's *From Roman Britain to Norman England* for more.

168. George had been titled the "Emperor of India"; rupees in 1947 carried his profile and the inscription "George VI King Emperor."

169. For more, see *MPFC: UC*, 1.89 and 2.139, and "thesaurus sketch" in the index.

170. Quoted in *MPSERD*, 80. See chapter three of *MPSERD* for much more on this concept. The significant difference between the Arthur and Falstaff situations, though, is that Falstaff interacts with actual figures from history, while Arthur meets only mythical characters like himself, as well as "ordinary" people from the Middle Ages.

171. Remember that Wat Tyler's rebellion in 1381 seemed to have been proceeding apace, with the fourteen-year-old king Richard II agreeing to virtually all the mob's demands, no matter how short-sighted or mean-spirited. It wasn't until Tyler "got in Richard's face," to use a more modern phrase—speaking pugnaciously from his saddle—that the king's men had heard enough. The mayor of London yanked Tyler down from his mount and a squire "finished him off," striking the belligerent rascal down (McKisack, 413). The rebellion began to collapse on itself almost immediately.

172. In the *MPFC* sketch "Storage Jars" (Ep. 33) a correspondent (Jones) reports from "strife-torn Bolivia"; the Pythons were well aware of this war-torn region and its repressive regimes (*MPFC: UC*, 2.99).

173. The Magna Carta citation comes from Clause 59. See also Hatcher and McKisack for more on the Peasants' Revolt, for example. Tony Benn cited the Levellers in a speech at Burford Church, Oxfordshire, where, according to Bearman: "He used the occasion to connect them with 'workers control.'" Said Benn: "The Levellers would immediately see the relevance of industrial democracy, by workers control and self-management, as a natural extension of the political franchise to replace the power of the new industrial feudalism" ("Anatomy of the Bennite Left," 64).

174. From the "Rule and Fall of Richard II" chapter in McKisack, specifically page 497. Nicholas of Oresme lived and worked in France, c. 1320–1382.

175. "Flowers for the Rebels," *Times* Letters to the Editor, 5 June 1968: 9.

176. Christopher Hitchens (1949–2011) would graduate from Oxford and go on to become a celebrated author and journalist, spending the last thirty years of his life living and working in the United States.

177. "Student Militants Return to Their Books: The Revolutionaries Search for a New Morality," *Times*, 17 February 1971: 14. Brian Macarthur was the editor of the *Times Higher Education Supplement* during this period.

178. Cf. the "outdated imperialist dogma" entry above.

179. "Waiting for a Sign from the Egoists," *Times*, 27 June 1972: 16.

180. See "TUC Suggests Government Inquiry," *Times*, 18 January 1972: 2; and "Picketing Miner Killed by Lorry," *Times*, 4 February 1972: 1.

181. Part III, lines 1–2 of *Vox Clamantis* as quoted in Rigg's *A History of Anglo-Latin Literature*, page 288. See also Stockton, *The Major Latin Works of John Gower*, 116. For more on Gower see Baugh's *LHE* (264–65), or Douglas Gray's entry on Gower in *ODNB*.

182. Gower's later work, *Confessio Amantis* (c. 1390), won't be nearly as didactic; he acknowledges that entertainment is needed to make the lesson readable, and then writes of "Love" (Baugh, *LHE*, 265). Arthur really isn't gifted with this kind of maturing over the course of the film; he is just as surprised to be arrested at the end as he is by Dennis's cheek in this scene.

183. *MPHGB*, 7.

184. "They Will Pay Arabs but Not Miners," 10 January 1974: 14. The provocatively titled article looks at the government's willingness to pay ransomous prices for embargoed Middle East oil while working consistently to keep domestic labor prices down.

185. See also Bromwich, Jarman, and Roberts, *The Arthur of the Welsh*.

186. More on this later, when the plundering sorties of English kings and assorted brigands on the continent—the dreaded *chevauchées*—are discussed.

187. This line has been excised from the finished film (*MPHGB*, 8).

188. Both of these come from the *Times*: "Gibraltar," 10 February 1973: 14; and "An Uncertain Future for Spain," 22 July 1974: 15.

189. Incidentally, even though the bogeymen in the Liberal manifestoes tended to be the two larger, more successful parties, the big brothers did not return the favor. In the February 1974 manifesto for Labour, the Liberal Party isn't mentioned at all; in the Conservative version from the same month and year, the Liberals are mentioned once, but only as an ally with Labour on a key issue. The Liberals weren't seen as much more than an annoyance to either party, it seems, until February 1974, when the Tories suddenly needed Liberal support to successfully form a coalition government. (That turned out badly for Heath and the Conservatives.)

190. The Liberals did pick up an additional *eight* seats in the February 1974 election, but their ascendancy was short-lived. They lost one seat in the following October election, and stood at thirteen until 1979.

191. See the BBC's Written Archives Collection for *MPFC*. File numbers and content descriptions can be found in the *MPFC: UC*, appendixes A and B.

192. "The Theatre Sinks into Self-Satisfaction," *Times*, 13 January 1973: 8.

THE BLACK KNIGHT

They pass rune stones—(PSC) In the finished film Arthur and Patsy do not pass any rune-stones on their way to the Black Knight. The script direction was likely included as a thumbnail, visual way to date the setting, to reinforce its Dark Ages periodicity. Gilliam also mentions in his DVD commentary track that this scene was shot in Epping Forest, northeast of London, in Essex, after completion of principal photography in Scotland. According to cameraman Doyle, they simply ran out of time to shoot this lengthy scene on location in Scotland, and decided to pick it up back near London, instead.[1] And since the first part of the scene was written to be shot with only one troupe member—Cleese as the Black Knight—and with Gilliam already there as both codirector and Green Knight, it was easier to schedule.[2] (See the entry "Made entirely on location" above for other *considered* locations.)

There are far fewer such stones in Britain than in Scandinavian countries, and they are located well away from where Arthur and Patsy are supposed to be traveling. Most of the rune-stones on the Isle of Man, for example, date from the late tenth century and beyond, meaning Arthur and Patsy shouldn't be riding by them in 932 anyway. The Pythons may be referring to carvings like the Ruthwell Cross, located in Dumfriesshire, Scotland, which dates from about the eighth century. The Ruthwell Cross features inscriptions in both Latin and runic.[3] There are many such crosses across Britain, as well as Pictish stones in Scotland, so there were plenty of rune-like inscribed stones for Arthur and Patsy to pass—if they'd followed the script. In the end, it would have likely meant yet another demand from the construction crew for set dressing, one either budget or time could not accommodate; that, or an attempt to film in an archaeologically sensitive location, which they'd avoided to date. By the time this scene was shot—well after principal photography was completed—Julian Doyle would have been nearly on his own when it came to props and set construction,[4] so "runestones" obviously fell by the wayside in favor of the tents and Kensington Gore effects, and so on.

This frankly lovely image of the duo "riding" together through the forest is very similar to the early Cobweb Forest scene in *Throne of Blood*, where Washizu (Toshiro Mifune) and Miki (Minoru Chiaki)—Macbeth and Banquo, respectively—approach the fortress after winning battles for their lord. The Pythons' debt to New Wave film will be referenced throughout; one of the trailers for *MPHG* also mentions *Seven Samurai* and *Seventh Seal.*[5]

a rough wooden foot-bridge across a stream—(PSC) The scenic direction here seems fairly straightforward. Again, like the "rune stone" suggestion above, this was likely intended to be an actual bridge over an actual stream. In the quest for maximum silliness, however, the bridge turns out to be a collection of sticks or boards spanning a tiny, dry stream channel, and covered with leaves.[6] The potential bridge crosser could as easily walk around it as over, even leaping—stepping—easily across the intermittent stream. There are examples of such unassuming bridges in the source material. In *Lancelot-Grail*, King Ban's castle exterior features a smaller bridge made of wattle, meaning it was likely woven from tree and plant material and may have floated in the moat (meaning it could easily have been destroyed as invaders approached), and wouldn't have been the seneschal's major entryway.[7] But just like later, when the noble Launcelot cannot act except in his "idiom," Arthur is also *honor-bound* to cross the bridge guarded by the Black Knight, simply because the situation is what it is.

In White's Arthur-tale *The Sword in the Stone*, the young ur-Arthur, Wart, describes his dream of knight errantry to Merlyn:

> I should have had a splendid suit of armour and dozens of spears and a black horse standing eighteen hands, and I should have called myself The Black Knight. And I should have hoved[8] at a well or a ford or something and made all true knights that came that way to joust with me for the honour of their ladies, and I should have spared them all after I had given them a great fall. And I should live out of doors all the year round in a pavilion, and never do anything but joust and go on quests and bear away the prize at tournaments, and I should not ever tell anybody my name. (56)

Everything seems to be in place here—the frightening name, the place of forbidden passage (for no apparent reason), the tilt, the honor, the pavilion—the Black Knight possesses all these.[9]

Not long after this passage in the book, the knights Pellinore and Grummore (who doesn't want to reveal his name), both completely encumbered by their full, heavy armor, engage in a very recognizable battle:

> In the first stage King Pellinore and Sir Grummore stood opposite each other for about half an hour, and walloped each other on the helm. There was only opportunity for one blow at a time, so they more or less took it in turns, King Pellinore striking while Sir Grummore was recovering, and vice versa. At first, if either of them dropped his sword or got it stuck in the ground, the other put in two or three extra blows while he was patiently fumbling for it or trying to tug it out. Later, they fell into the rhythm of the thing more perfectly, like the toy mechanical people who saw wood on Christmas trees. Eventually the exercise and the monotony restored their good humour and they began to get bored.
>
> The second stage was introduced as a change, by common consent. Sir Grummore stumped off to one end of the clearing, while King Pellinore plodded off to the other. Then they turned round and swayed backward and forward once or twice, in order to get their weight on their toes. When they leaned forward they had to run forward, to keep up with their weight, and if they leaned too far backward they fell down. So even walking was complicated. When they had got their weight properly distributed in front of them, so that they were just off their balance, each broke into a trot to keep up with himself. They hurtled together as it had been two boars. (63–64)

The staging of this scene and fight is also quite similar to an illustration in Howard Pyle's influential *The Story of the Champions of the Round Table*, a new edition of which was published in 1942, and which would have made fabulous reading for young boys of the era. The illustration can be found on page 44 of the 1942 edition, and is captioned (in florid script borrowed by Gilliam for his title work) "Sir Launcelot doeth battle with Sir Turquine." There are two helmed, armored knights fighting with swords, as two people watch.

. . . a tremendous fight is going on—(PSC) Violence and coercion are the hallmarks of this world,[10] just as they were in the romance sources when the quests for the Grail came

untracked. In *Perlesvaus*,[11] the weakness of the king has led to civil war and a waste land (the "dolorous blow"), as Barber points out (*THG*, 206). In *The High History of the Holy Graal* (translated by Sebastian Evans), the presence of the Grail, a weakened king, essential questions unasked, and a country plunging into self-destruction converge when a damsel tells Arthur of his lands' ills:

> "Sir," saith the damsel, "I have not yet told you all that I have in charge to deliver. The best King that liveth on earth and the most loyal and the most righteous, sendeth you greeting; of whom is sore sorrow for that he hath fallen into grievous languishment." "Damsel," saith the King, "Sore pity it is and it be so as you say; and I pray you tell me who is the King?" "Sir," saith she, "It is rich King Fisherman, of whom is great grief." "Damsel," saith the King, "You say true; and God grant him his heart's desire!" "Sir," saith she, "know you not wherefore he hath fallen into languishment?" "Nay, I know not at all, but gladly would I learn." "And I will tell you," saith she. "This languishment is come upon him through one that harboured in his hostel, to whom the most Holy Graal appeared. And, for that he would not ask unto whom one served thereof, were all the lands commoved to war thereby, nor never thereafter might knight meet other but he should fight with him in arms without none other occasion. You yourself may well perceive the same, for your well-doing hath greatly slackened, whereof have you had much blame, and all the others barons that by you have taken ensample, for you are the mirror of the world alike in well-doing and in evil-doing." (24)

At this first martial encounter in the film Arthur is confronted with the "languishment" of his kingdom, the senseless challenging and fighting between knights who could and perhaps should be in his service for the greater good, as well as the trope of "instruction" (at this bridge, from the Black Knight; in the story above, from a bald damsel; later from Bedevere and Tim, earlier from Dennis, et al.) that will rarely enlighten him and more often throw up obstacles as he quests for knights and then the Grail. Roger the Shrubber will later bemoan "these sad times," where violence has replaced civility.

Keeping score, the "dolorous" state of Arthur's kingdom after this scene will have included faux-horses, mouthy castle sentries, the plague, politically motivated churls, and meaningless "either/or" fights to not-death. By the end of the Black Knight scene, Arthur is—understandably, given the *Weltschmerz* of the film—still without new acolytes, and thus no closer to gathering his Round Table retinue.[12]

Black Knight—(PSC) Accoutred all in black[13] excepting the red boar's head device on his chest, the Black Knight (here played and voiced by Cleese) is a figure in earlier Grail romance works, actual medieval heraldry[14] and, much later, cartoons and comic books. In *Le Morte Darthur* the character inhabits a "black laund" full of "black hawthorn," and everything about him is, well, *black*:

> and thereon hung a banner, and on the other side there hung a black shield, and by it stood a black spear great and long, and a great black horse covered with silk, and a black stone fast by. Also there sat a knight all armed in black harness, and his name was called the Knight of the Black Launds. (*LMD-WM*, 127–28)

The Black Knight and the "kitchen knave" Beaumains (actually Gareth, brother of Gawain) fight, with the Black Knight taking a spear all the way through him, but he keeps fighting, drawing his sword to smite "many eager strokes of great might, and hurt Beaumains full sore" (128). It takes the Black Knight an hour and a half to fall off his horse and die. In the following pages Beaumains (and the unwilling damosel) meets a Green Knight who happens to be the Black Knight's brother, and Beaumains is able to overcome him, as well. There is even a Red Knight, a third brother, who Beaumains must fight and defeat, and a fourth, the Blue Knight. Beaumains's knightly deeds are later rehearsed by a dwarf (140–41).

The Black Knight also appears as a character in Warner Bros. and Popeye cartoons.[15] There was also a 1955–1956 comic book series *The Black Knight*, featuring "The Greatest Knight of them All!"[16] By the third issue, he is "ALL NEW" and "Greater Than Ever"—he sounds much like the Pythons' version of this invincible knight. There is also a powerful and much feared Black *Hermit* encountered by Gawain in *Perlesvaus*. This hermit (who lives in a castle and is surrounded by warriors) is such a skilled fighter that Gawain puts off their encounter (at the behest of a damosel; II.3), though Perceval is later able to defeat him (XXXV.22).

smaller KNIGHT in green armour—(PSC) Not likely supposed to be the fabled Green Knight encountered by Gawain in *Sir Gawain and the Green Knight* (fourteenth century). In that alliterative poem the Green Knight comes to Arthur's court and challenges all takers, with Gawain taking the challenge in place of his liege, Arthur. Gawain is able to cut the Green Knight's head off, but the Knight simply takes up his head and returns home, waiting for a further portion of the challenge. In the poem the Green Knight is completely green, including his skin. In the *Holy Grail* version (where he is played by Gilliam) his armor and tunic are green—otherwise he looks very much like the Black Knight. As mentioned above, the character of the Green Knight appears in *Le Morte Darthur* as the *brother* of the Black Knight, and he strives for vengeance against Beaumains, the "kitchen knave" who slew his "full noble" brother (*LMD-WM*, 130). More on both Gawain and the Green Knight below, especially in relation to Launcelot's idiomatic experiences in Swamp Castle.

nasty mace or spiked ball and chain—(PSC) This is most accurately a flail, since it is a spiked weapon. These were prevalent in battle in the later Middle Ages, though they were often as dangerous to one's friends as a foe, since the flail had to be swung.[17] Here, the design of the flail hampers its usefulness, as the chain traps the Green Knight in an indefensible position. Still, Dougherty notes that the flail became a particularly favorite weapon of Crusaders, and it seems to have been particularly effective in close combat (91).

ARTHUR narrows his eyes, wondering whether the BLACK KNIGHT will survive— (PSC) And while the romances and heroic poetry offered all manner of knightly blood and gore—*The Song of Roland* (mid-twelfth century) is particularly gruesome[18]—the actual battles on fourteenth-century battlefields were no less blood-besotted. Tuchman describes the wounds received by one valiant knight, Don Pero Niño. Don Niño—who is characterized by a "rashness that would become [one] of his hallmarks"[19]—was struck by an arrow that penetrated his gorget and neck—thereafter as if they were "knit together"—he took a crossbow bolt into the nostrils, leaving him bleeding and dazed, and still he "pressed forward, receiving many sword blows on head and shoulders which 'sometimes hit the bolt embedded in his nose making him suffer great pain'" (63). By the end of the battle his armor and weapons were in tatters, and he was bloody and battered from head to toe, but alive.

Sound FX of fight scene reaching a climax. Four almighty clangs—(PSC) In the printed script, the Pythons' camera tastefully pans away, leaving the ultimate death blows to be heard, and not seen. The actual filmed scene, of course, is quite a bit more graphic in its depiction of combat and eventual bloodshed. The image of the broadsword that pierces the Green Knight's visor (and head) is quite close to a portion of Macbeth's vision of Macduff's death in the Polanski film version. In that vision (brought on by drinking the witches' potion) Macbeth cries "Thou shalt not live!" and thrusts his sword through the image of Macduff's armor and into his throat. The armor then collapses and (via stop-motion photography) plant life grows over it as it moulders. Later in this same film, a man trying to bar the castle door takes a bolt through the forehead, and Macbeth will skewer another man through the throat, then watch him bleed out. The graphic nature of the violence in *MPHG* owes much to American filmmaker Sam Peckinpah,[20] as well, whose influence on the Pythons will be discussed later.[21] Our Green Knight eventually ends up with a sword through his head (as do many in Malory's work), which is precisely how Princess Lucky's father will die at the hands of the "brave but dangerous Sir Launcelot" later.[22] Additionally, in *Le Morte Darthur*, the Green Knight isn't slain, but he is greatly wounded by Beaumains before the damosel agrees that he should be spared—she doesn't want the "kitchen knave" Beaumains given the glory of the kill (*LMD-WM*, 130–31). But the most similar such attack appears in "Sir Tristram de Lyonesse," also in the Winchester version of *Le Morte Darthur*, in a battle between Sir Tristram and Sir Marhalt:

> By then Sir Tristram waxed more fiercer than he did, and Sir Marhalt feebled, and Sir Tristram ever more well-winded and bigger; and with a mighty stroke he smote Sir Marhalt upon the helm such a buffet that it went through his helm[et] and through the coif of steel and through the brain-pan, and the sword stuck so fast in the helm and in his brain-pan that Sir Tristram pulled three times at his sword or ever he might pull it out from his head. And there Sir Marhalt fell down on his knees, and the edge of the sword left in his brain-pan. (177)

Marhalt doesn't die immediately—he lives to leave the field with a sword in his "brain-pan"—but soon succumbs to his wounds (178). A few scenes after this Black Knight encounter, Lancelot's horse Concorde (Idle) will take an arrow to the chest, fall to the ground with a "Message for you, sir" on his lips; he will live on, as well.

The Pythons used this "cartoony" violence bit a number of times in *MPFC* and later films. In Ep. 14, the Piranha brothers (based on the Kray twins) have nailed characters' heads to floors and coffee tables, screwed their pelvises to cake stands, scraped them behind tanks, and used satire to terrorize them.[23] Gilliam's animations dismember and re-member the human body regularly.[24] In Ep. 33, a pleasant Julian Slade "Salad Days" outing becomes a grisly Peckinpah film as guests wearing flannel pants and jolly boaters are dismembered, impaled, and beheaded. In Ep. 38, an actor posing as "Dr. [Stanley] Kramer" takes an arrow to the head. By *Meaning of Life*, characters in the "Zulu Wars" sections are being hacked to pieces (often not fatally), and in "Middle Age" live organ donations are undertaken.

ARTHUR: "You fight with the strength of many men, Sir Knight"—In the 1955 *Black Knight* comic book, issue 3, the Black Knight is described as fighting "like many men" as he overcomes a host of attackers in the lists, fighting in a sanctioned melee.[25]

In the final draft of the script the Black Knight answers: "Who dares to challenge the Black Knight?"—that line and Arthur's rejoinder: "I do not challenge you," have been penciled through. In the *Black Knight* comic book series, the Black Knight does speak, but he will never answer as to his name, his true identity, excepting to Merlin. His unwillingness to divulge his name enrages more than one foe. The Pythons' Black Knight also says "Never" twice to Arthur's requests—both of those are penciled through, as well.

The BLACK KNIGHT remains silent—(PSC) This is actually handwritten into the script, replacing the Black Knight's response of "Never." As the script was originally written, then, the Black Knight was curt, but not silent. This structure—entreaties from Arthur to a noble knight followed by stony silence—has a precedent in the Welsh Arthurian sources. In a story where Trystan is pursuing Eysellt (Iseult/Isolde), Arthur sings four statements (*englyns*) to an angry, silent Trystan before Trystan finally responds. See entries below in the "Three-Headed Knight" scene for more on these Welsh sources.

SCENE SIX

ARTHUR: "Will you join me?"—In this second attempt at gathering associates (his encounter with the sentries up on the wall being the first), Arthur shows that he is already earnestly questing, though not yet for the Grail. This is also his first direct address to a potential Knight of the Round Table, one of only two he'll make. The second will be far more successful as he convinces Bedevere to join. Lancelot, Galahad, and Robin all join thanks to the "Book of the Film" narration—their individual gatherings were part of a montage sequence (that also includes Hector and Gawain) never photographed, according to Doyle, an on-location decision made to find a cheaper way to deliver the information (meaning animation or narration).[26]

Arthur's single-mindedness in this scene is in contrast to some of the Arthurs found in romance sources. In *Perlesvaus*, for example, "we see Arthur fallen into lethargy, failing to hold court for his knights, and recalled to his high purpose by the vision at the chapel of St. Augustine" (Barber, 152). Arthur's belief and energy are redoubled when he sees an image of the Grail, and when he is "charged with introducing the chalice, until then unknown in Britain, into his kingdom" (152). In *Holy Grail*, Arthur is already on a noble quest when he is visited by God for an even more noble quest. As soon as the divine quest is suggested Arthur and the film cease gathering to the Round Table—Bors, Hector, Gawain, and others appear later out of nowhere, and without any introductory comment.[27]

This level of unflagging optimism is one of the key elements missing—or sniggered at—in contemporary Britain. The forward and upward looking political manifestos of all parties, for example, are crumpled almost before their ink has dried, with the realities of a staggering economy and the necessity of higher taxes more fully realized. When in 1972 Heath embarked on his quest for massive industrial expansion, planning to flood industry with millions of pounds so Britain's industries could modernize and improve to meet the coming EEC years more confidently, the enthusiasm and optimism for immediate growth seems to have outpaced (or replaced completely) the realities that an inflation-prone economy presented, according to Sandbrook:

> Thanks to [Chancellor of the Exchequer] Barber's stimulus measures the previous year, unemployment would have come down anyway, but by throwing even more money at the economy Heath was stoking the flames of inflation.[28] At any time it would have been a naïve, irresponsible gamble. But with the world economy in deepening disorder, this was the worst possible time for such an expensive mistake. It was the product not only of good and noble intentions, but of panic and arrogance, and it was a classic example of the disease to which British politics was peculiarly prone in the 1970s: the economics of wishful thinking, based on rosily optimistic predictions that were never, ever vindicated.[29]

Arthur's knights, but Arthur especially, seem to suffer from this malady, as well, going from one frustrating, dissatisfying encounter to the next, until the quest is stopped entirely by policemen. Arthur and Bedevere, however, never give up—pluck, they've got.

Less than one year after *MPHG* was released, and less than two years into Labour's administration, the mood of the country was morose, at best, starting at the top. Whitehead notes that as a result of the 1973 oil embargo the British economy had actually shrunk, but promises and actualizations of public spending from Heath's fiscally *conservative* government were on the *rise*.[30] Labour would swing the vote its way in February and October 1974 with promises of greatly increased public expenditure, and by the early months of 1976 (right around the time Wilson surprised many with his retirement announcement), the government "decided to introduce cash limits and stabilize expenditure programmes from 1977-8 onwards. In theory, government spending would level off in the years after April 1977" (Whitehead, 182). This was a crushing, catastrophic reality for many. Many Labourites complained, since "cuts in future spending betrayed their pledges and their hopes," Whitehead writes. He continues: "If the party was over, the [Labour] Party was finished too" (183). The horse Labour rode in on was dead; by 1979 the Tory ascension was complete, and Thatcherism took hold. This is actually the country Arthur is questing through—one where promises and pledges have been made in good faith, and with earnest prospects of those promises being kept (noble knights for Camelot and camaraderie; a divine quest sanctioned by God) only to have harsh, insurmountable, and sometimes incomprehensible realities (like French antagonists and British policemen) destroy them all. Arthur's eternal optimism is thrown into contrast all the more in this light. Foreign Secretary Anthony Crosland's notes betray the dark mood of the period:

> (a) Demoralisation of decent rank and file: Grimsby LP . . . (b) Strain on TU loyalty . . . (c) breeding of illiterate and reactionary attitude to public expenditure—horrible. (d) collapse of strategy which I proposed last year. . . . Now no sense of direction and no priorities; only pragmatism, empiricism, safety first, £ supreme. (e) and: unemployment, even if politically more wearable = grave loss of welfare, security, choice; very high price to be paid for deflation and negative growth.[31]

Crosland sees nothing that even gives a glimmer of hope toward a brighter future, and his wasn't the only opinion that had soured.

The postwar era of film had been particularly engaged in the reassessment and reappraisal of its own forms, genres, allegiances, biases, and blind spots, with the result being darker, more mature and complicated, and more problematized scenarios and ennui-laden characters than ever before. The heady artistry of the 1960s—as filmmakers played against the styles and mores of the conservative 1950s—eventually gave way to even darker, more squalid films in the 1970s, where it might only be the sadistic killer who ends up smiling. Breakout films from the late 1960s and on, including *Pierrot le feu, Bonnie and Clyde,*[32] *The Honeymoon Killers, The Wild Bunch, Butch Cassidy and the Sundance Kid, The Goalie's Anxiety at the Penalty Kick,* and *Badlands,* were often more stylized, nihilistic, and pessimistic, and offered violent or chary antiheroes who often had no heroic qualities, except that they were fighting against some form of some "Establishment." Revenge-type films became de rigueur, including Peckinpah's *Bring Me the Head of Alfredo Garcia,* Don Siegel's *Dirty Harry,* and Michael Winner's *Death Wish.* The year 1971 alone produced *Clockwork Orange, Dirty Harry, French Connection, Get Carter,* and *Straw Dogs;* the latter, Peckinpah's viscerally controversial rape-and-revenge film, was shot in Cornwall, making it at least partly a British film. Native British filmmakers produced their own somber films, certainly. The black comedy *The Bed-Sitting Room* (1969) featured postapocalyptic settings and a Britain destroyed by a nuclear holocaust that lasted less than three minutes. A handful of survivors live on in the devastation, struggling for food and shelter; mutant babies are born; the BBC is a single man in torn DJ going from telly to telly; and the National Health Service is represented by one morbid male nurse—all this and the Circle Line still runs.[33] Seeing it at the Berlin Film Festival, one reviewer called it a "zany horror."[34] There were also bleakly noirish northern films like *Get Carter* (1971), where director Mike Hughes is credited with creating a film "at once unpleasant and powerfully effective," where he expresses "his own gloomy view [of Newcastle, of life in general] uncompromisingly, and leaves us to take it how we will."[35] In *Get Carter* Michael Caine's character is on his own quest—to find out who killed his brother and why—and to punish those who killed him, and those who get in the way. The city of Newcastle as depicted is one of unemployment, cold gray skies, idled industry, and despair. Oh, and murder.

These films are ages away from the delightful postwar Ealing Studio eccentricities, and too deadly serious to be *Carry On* films. Carter's quest is as unhappy as Arthur's, as it turns out. Happy endings during this period might be found in the odd musical and the forthcoming blockbuster, but not in most of the films of the New Waves, and not in *Holy Grail*. And joining for a cause is *passé*, as well. The uniformed members of Pike's unit in *The Wild Bunch* are there for the gold, the rapine spoils, and for some, just the fun of killing; it won't be until the final scenes that four survivors act in a selfless (or nihilistic) way, a decision they won't survive.

BLACK KNIGHT: "None shall pass"—Not an uncommon gauntlet thrown down in the world of knights, guardians, and chivalric tests. There are at least a dozen versions of this "none shall pass" moment leading to a joust or sword fight in Malory's work alone, but also in more recent entertainments. In the first issue of the comic book *Robin Hood* (November 1955), Robin—just back from the Crusades—meets Little John standing on a narrow log bridge. Little John demands a fight before any can pass; in the "Sir Galant" story, it is the Red Knight who challenges (and quickly loses to) young Galant, this time at a fording joust. By the fifth issue, Galant and the Red Knight fight again, this time the Red Knight labeled a "felon knight" for trying to use magic; the Red Knight is defeated in less than four panels ("I yield! I yield Sir Galant!").[36] Lastly, in the eighth and final issue, Bors is challenged—"None pass this way!"—by a "Ghost Knight" to a similar fight.[37] As in *Holy Grail*, Bors is "undone" rather quickly. See the "Cave of Caerbannog" section for more on Bors. Just two pages later in this same eighth issue, Galant himself defends a stone bridge from a horde of Danish invaders.

In volume one of *Le Morte D'Arthur* the damosel promises to give Beaumains no quarter, and takes every opportunity to belittle him in front of the court: "for were thou as wight as ever was Wade or Launcelot, Tristram, or the good knight Sir Lamorak, thou shalt not pass a pass here that is called the Pass Perilous" (1.247). In volume two of *LMD'A* Sir Bromel, after announcing that he loves Lady Elaine (Launcelot's consort by enchantment and mother of their child, Galahad) and she proclaims her love for only Launcelot, vows to defend her *from* Launcelot's further attentions (even though Launcelot was tricked into lying with Elaine): "I promise you this twelvemonth I shall keep the Pounte [bridge] of Corbin for Sir Launcelot's sake, that he shall neither come ne go unto you, but I shall meet with him" (2.193–94). There is an earlier sequence where a knight on horseback stands ready to joust with anyone "that passeth this passage": "Then they rode forth all together, King Mark, Sir Lamorak, Sir Dinadan, till that they came to a bridge, and at the end thereof stood a fair tower. Then saw they a knight on horseback well armed, brandishing a spear, crying and proffering himself to joust"[38] (2.19). In the following *LMD'A* chapter (2.21) King Mark and Sir Dinadan come to another bridge "where hoved a knight on horseback" waiting for a fight, and in Chapter XII Sir Percival unhorses a bridge-guarding knight up and over the edge of the bridge, such "that had not been a little vessel under the bridge, that knight had been drowned" (2.210).

Other French versions of these romances feature similar set-tos. In *Lancelot-Grail*, Hector, having just met and measured the man Gawain, travels with his new friend to a very familiar setting:

> So they rode on until late afternoon, when they approached a little bridge over a small river they had to cross. When they drew near they saw an armed knight at the head of the bridge, helmet on head, shield at neck, lance in hand, and with him as many as thirty men-at-arms. (307)

Hector is able to rout the soldiers—killing, maiming, and sending many into the water below—while the challenging knight eventually rides away in fear.

This challenge and even the setting are also reminiscent of the classic Warner Bros. cartoon *Robin Hood Daffy* (1958) starring Daffy Duck as Robin Hood and Porky Pig as Friar Tuck, where Daffy's Robin gets bested, of course, by the unassuming Friar. The Pythons have borrowed from and been inspired by Warner Bros. cartoons since their *Flying Circus* days.

ARTHUR: "I command you, as King of the Britons"—This never does work, really. As an announcement, only Bedevere acknowledges Arthur's kingship (kneeling, and saying "My Liege!"), while the other amenable knights follow him and use the right language ("My Lord," etc.). When it is issued as a command, though, it falls flat. And it doesn't seem to matter whether it's a local peasant, a fellow knight, or silly Frenchmen—the lack of respect is the same. In this it is likely a not-so-veiled reference to Britain's waning international power during the Pythons' lifetimes, including but certainly not limited to: The beginnings of IRA bombings in England (1938; escalating in the 1970s), the devastation of the Battle of Britain (1940), and the loss of the empire's "jewel" India to independence (1947), followed quickly by Ceylon and Burma and Ireland (1948–1949). Britain also lost influence in North Africa during the 1950s, followed by the disastrous Suez Crisis in 1956, the secession of South Africa in 1961, the Rhodesia problem after 1965, and then the avalanche of Middle Eastern, African, South Pacific, and Caribbean colonies declaring their independence. The spigots for underpriced oil and gas, precious metals, foodstuffs, and all manner of manufacturing materials—and the ready markets Britain had depended on as Commonwealth partners—were turned off, shut down, or made much more expensive for the home of the former British Empire. The days of being able to command "as King of the Britons," were over by the late 1960s, and this shrinking and somewhat ridiculous notion of empire is addressed a number of times in *MPFC*.[39] More recent examples would include Britain going to Europe and applying several times for entry into the EEC and being rebuffed (essentially by de Gaulle); or Britain's dependence on the United States for a nuclear deterrent, significant military materiel, or the "invasion" by U.S. forces and technicians in the form of U.S. submarine facilities in British ports; or the closing of bases, mothballing of aircraft carriers,[40] and the bringing home of military units deployed in, for example, Arab countries for decades.[41] In the Pythons' lifetimes, things had changed dramatically, as Anthony Nutting, minister of state for foreign affairs, remembers in a 1967 series on the Suez crisis:

> Within the span of that turbulent half-century [from the Boer War to Suez] the world was transformed and the conditions in which Britain had been able to play her former imperial role ceased to exist. British rule was withdrawn from vast areas of the world as the nineteenth-century concept of Empire was swept away in the scalding torrents of twentieth-century nationalism. . . . And the lesson of the decline in Britain's power to control events and dictate to governments which started in South Africa at the turn of the century was to be completed in Egypt 50 years later.[42]

See Judt and Marwick for much more on Britain's postwar self-delusion.

Barber notes that backwards reading of the Grail legend (or works written about that legend) can artificially add to the legends' "meanings," an analysis anachronism that imposes a later sensibility on an earlier time:

> [Tennyson's] *The Holy Grail* is therefore about the role of religion in the life of the individual and its relationship to the social order, as represented by Arthur. To see it as a commentary on the failure of the British Empire or as a reaction to the Indian mutiny and the re-examination of imperial ideals that followed, is to impose a twentieth-century perspective on it. (*THG*, 274)

But for the Pythons such impositions are *purposeful*: the backwards readings are the thing. For the Pythons the Grail itself is tied directly to Britain's fading empire, as evidenced by its appearance in the original script. There isn't one Grail but several, one even fashioned into a table lamp, and one ready to be banged together by a helpful Merlin, from spare parts; these "duff grails" are available for purchase at Harrods,[43] and are equally unappreciated by the angry God depicted in the first draft of the script. See "He's already got one, you see" below for more on the multiple Grail motif.

A furious fight now starts . . .[44]—(PSC) Arthur's list of legendary battles will be mentioned later, but it's worth noting what fighting situations the Pythons decide to allow the martial Arthur (and his knights), and what this list says about their version of the puissant King of the Britons. Here he fights and easily bests a rogue Black Knight, removing all his limbs but receiving no concession. In fact, in defeat the Black Knight is as brazen as the Green Knight of old, who simply picks up his severed head and leaves, ready for a continuation of the duel. Arthur comes away with a "draw"—it's all the Black Knight will concede. The defeated knight even hurls challenges and insults after Arthur and Patsy as they leave the scene.

Later, Arthur and his knights will skirmish with the French in two one-sided battles at a castle wall, withdrawing both times under withering assault, first by invective, then by hurled flora and fauna. Arthur will then parry and riposte, verbally, with odd knights ("Ni!") who guard the way to an enchanter; he will lead "battles" against mythical creatures (the Killer Rabbit and the beast in the Cave); finally he will try and storm another castle full of rude Frenchmen only to be repelled by coarse language and offal, and then be arrested for his troubles. Elsewhere Sir Robin will run from a fight with the Three-Headed Knight, Sir Galahad will defend his chastity at the Castle Anthrax (thanks to Lancelot's helpful deus ex machina appearance), and Sir Lancelot will kill myriad wedding guests to save Prince Herbert from almost certain marriage at Swamp Castle.

This list is meant to diminish, of course, Arthur's carefully cultivated legend as a warrior king. The only encounters Arthur "wins" in this film aren't battles at all—he solves the "duck" issue so a hopelessly flawed witch trial can carry on; he manages to overcome the Knights Who Say Ni, accidentally (by uttering a certain third-person, singular neuter pronoun); and he bests the Bridge of Death trial by recalling avian minutiae he'd rejected in his first "battle." In most of Arthur's battle or confrontational set pieces, however, the bewildered king is forced eventually to pull up stumps and leave the field.

ARTHUR delivers a mighty blow which completely severs the BLACK KNIGHT's left arm at the shoulder—(PSC) This de-arming image is found earlier not only in Malory and the Arthurian romances, but in comics. In Hal Foster's *Prince Valiant's Perilous Voyage* (1954), Val faces the "champion of the Northmen," Thundaar, who is "unarmed" twice:

> Thundaar had one trick which up to now had proved fatal to all rivals. Horsa, watching from the Viking lines and knowing the trick was coming, smiled with his eyes; while King Arthur on the opposite side, frowned.
>
> Thundaar's ax came up as if for a straight downward stroke, and he hesitated, waiting for Val to raise his shield and cover his eyes. For in that instant the great ax would reverse its direction in a staggering underhand swing. But Val sensed the feint. The shield remained low, the [Singing Sword] flicked upward . . . and the ax-handle was neatly sliced. Thundaar stood unarmed, looking foolish. His comrades threw him another ax and the fight was renewed. But in his blind rage Thundaar was easily led into using his now familiar trick. He raised the ax for a mighty blow. This time Val deliberately lifted his shield and decoyed Thundaar into making the furious underhand stroke. But as the arm shot down, the Singing Sword flicked out. Again the battle-ax flew into the air, and Thundaar's hand flew with it, still grasping. (66–67)

Unlike the never-say-quit Black Knight, though, Thundaar's "fighting days were over" (67).[45]

A cousinly real-world medieval punishment was the cutting off of one hand. In 1125 Henry I (1068–1135), after inspecting his moneyers and finding almost all had debased his coinage (clipping bits off, etc.), ordered all ninety-four mint officers to have a hand removed. Those hands were then "nailed to the ex-owners' office doors" (Bishop, *HBMA*, 178).

BLACK KNIGHT: "'Tis just a scratch"—This level of denial is evidenced by many of the WB and MGM cartoon characters who are horribly injured, as well. In Tex Avery's World War II–era retelling of the "Three Little Pigs" story (sending up the Disney version, of course), *Blitz Wolf* (1942), machine gun fire blasts past the cringing wolf as he clings to a cannon barrel. He sing-songs to the enemy: "You missed me, you missed me, you didn't even touch me," with a German accent (and through a Hitler moustache). Standing in front of a lamp, however, light streams through his many bullet holes.

As part of his DVD commentary for this scene on the 2001 DVD edition, Cleese remembers that he and Chapman wrote this scene based on a story of epic Roman wrestlers he was told by his instructor, C.H.R. "Jumper" Gee, while a student at Clifton College in 1957. The gist of the story is that one combatant dies, still locked in the struggle, never saying "uncle."[46]

ARTHUR: "Your arm's off"—This level of violence or body horror isn't new to the Pythons, and it's often more like a cartoon than reality.[47] In *Flying Circus* the "cartoony" treatment of wounds and death (or at least certain death) ran through the series, in both live action and animated segments. In Ep. 23, "Scott of the Antarctic," the lion Scott is fighting dies and a geyser of blood spews from him, *à la Sanjuro* (1962), and in Ep. 33, "Salad Days," characters lose arms, hands, heads, and are severally impaled in a "Peckinpahish" bloodbath, all the while wearing slacks, pretty dresses, and fixed grins. There are stoats, table lamps, and arrows through heads, multiple shootings and stabbings, many bonks on the head by truncheons, rubber chickens, and giant prop hammers, and every once in a while a sixteen-ton weight drops onto someone. The residual influence of the Warner Bros. cartoons is obvious. Later in the printed script the Pythons will cite both Sam Peckinpah and kung fu/karate movies as a reference for the handling of a scene, both giveaways to their take on the depictions of violence. *Times* film critic David Robinson even uses the moniker "Peckinpah fashion" to describe the more absurdly violent scenes of *MPHG*, including this Black Knight sequence, and later, when Launcelot storms Swamp Castle.[48]

Further, consider this description, from film critic Tom Milne: "The sequence is a *tour de force*, a direct assault on the senses all the more effective after the deliberate hesitations of the beginning as the stranger picks his way uncertainly through the hostilities. It is undeniably nasty."[49] Not an in-depth review of Arthur's fight with the Black Knight, of course, but the visceral response of one British critic to the bloody revenge sequence in *Straw Dogs*. Seeing Arthur as the stranger trying to gauge "hostilities" between the Black and Green Knights fits easily. *Straw Dogs* opened to an "X" certificate,[50] since the violence was both realistic and gratuitous, to many; it's precisely the gratuity the Pythons reached for in their film.[51] From Peckinpah: "It's about the violence within all of us . . . [t]he violence which is reflecting on the political condition of the world today."[52] But where Peckinpah actually wanted to teach a moral lesson, he says, "a catharsis through pity and fear,"[53] the Pythons mimicked the dramatic films of their day, sending them up as they did, but responding as well to their own violent, stagnating world. Perhaps the moral lesson from the Pythons is that there is no moral lesson possible from such violent content, only absurdity.

The fact that *Holy Grail* is also very much a film of its time, even though it is a period film, and that the time—the Vietnam War era—is one of screen and real-life violence can't be understated. Critics saw this same indelible connection between artist, artwork, and the world when Polanski's *Macbeth* made its appearance in early 1972, many remarking that such conflations of life and art were inescapable for Polanski, given the tragic loss of his wife in 1969:

> Beginning with Duncan's murder, the film seems to revel in gore, a criticism leveled against it by reviewers and spectators. Polanski does accentuate the blood and brutality. Because his wife, Sharon Tate, was murdered so brutally and senselessly by Manson and his "family," it seems easy to see in the movie's emphasis on bloodshed a working out of Polanski's personal obsession. Whatever truth such a view may have, it should not stop us from investigating Polanski's use of the horror. (Do not many directors and writers transform their private obsessions into art?) If the violence and gore are there for their own sake, merely to arouse, to titillate, to appeal to our basest emotions, then Polanski's art is decadent. If, however, they serve a larger purpose, as I think they do, then their presentation deserves the kind of respect we are willing to give to the blinding of Oedipus or Gloucester or to the horrors found in Webster's *Duchess of Malfi*. There is no denying that Polanski has an imagination that is essentially Gothic. Mystery and horror abound in his work: witness *Repulsion* and *Rosemary's Baby* and *The Fearless Vampire Killers*. But his Gothic sensibility serves artistic purposes. Violence is part of the reality of the world as Polanski sees the world, and in his *Macbeth* Polanski uses Shakespeare's setting to present his personal vision of bloodshed, mutilation, violence and horror—a vision not altogether unfounded in the light of Auschwitz and, we should add, the Manson murders.[54]

It is somewhat ironic to note here that the BBC had originally promoted *Flying Circus* as a "show to subdue the violence in us all" (*MPFC: UC,* 1.207).

ARTHUR: "Victory is mine." (*sinking to his knees*)—Arthur's immediate act of submission (to God) and gratitude isn't out of order, according to Lester in "Chaucer's Knight and the Medieval Tournament," since God's judgment and appeasement are central to the act:

> In fact, the whole form of the duel as detailed in the ordinances, the wording of the second oath in which each combatant was to swear on the massbook to trust "oonly in God and thi body", and the prescription of death (in most cases) for the loser, were designed to emphasize that God regulates the outcome, a principle which had been part of English law since Anglo-Saxon times. (462)

This kind of closeness to God is also part of the war experience described by the French chronicler Jean Froissart (1337–1405), who wrote of battles including Sluys, Crécy, and Poitiers. McKisack describes Froissart's ardor:

> [M]edieval warfare held deeper and subtler allurements. Again and again, in the pages of Froissart, and for all his awareness of its horrors, we catch echoes of what can only be described as the joy of war, its challenge to professional skill, its appeal to the spirit of adventure and to the desire for glory, the aesthetic, almost spiritual satisfaction which it might afford. . . . Men sensitive to beauty must have shared something of Froissart's delight in the pageantry of war, in the "fresh, shining armour, the banners waving in the wind, the companies in good order, riding a soft pace." (249)

Arthur approaches each of his potential battles with a similar reverence and resolve, and for that would have been accounted a good medieval king.

ARTHUR: "I thank thee O Lord that in thy . . ."[55]—Arthur's orisons here aren't unusual at all, given the source material. In *Le Morte Darthur*, Malory notes that his knights begin not only their journeys but often their new days only after hearing Mass, and that long prayers asking for God's guidance are frequent. Knightly travels often stretch not from inn to inn or castle to castle, but from abbey to abbey or one of myriad small chapels, where sacerdotal unctions and oblations as well as moments of personal religiosity can be undertaken. In *The Tale of the Sangrail*, for example, Galahad "rode many journeys in vain" (meaning he was getting nothing accomplished) before coming to an abbey where he could meet with King Mordrains and hear Mass (*LMD-WM*, 395).

The Pythons' Arthur is actually of a Patrician[56] mold, and he embodies the "British war leader and Christian warrior" tradition as developed by the author of *HB* (Higham, *King Arthur: Myth-Making and History*, 137). Higham writes: "The author's treatment of St Patrick and Arthur [in *HB*] therefore represent his final portrayal of a 'British Britain,' before his enforced acknowledgement of Anglo-Saxon domination" (137). By the end of this Black Knight scene Arthur is not only proven a gifted warrior in defeating the Black Knight, and rather easily at that, he also tries to end the fight honorably and compassionately, and remembers to give thanks to God for His blessings. He is still in a British Britain, too, he assumes, not a Gallic Britain; that won't be the case until they meet the French invaders later.[57] Higham goes on, noting that Vortigern's "disastrous reign" demanded much of the author of *HB*, especially after sections 47 and 48 (leading to Arthur's significant chapter, 56). To counter the bad taste left by Vortigern,

> the author sought to people the subsequent historical space with British figures whose reputations could sustain his key message—that the Britons had long been and were still, both a Christian people, doing God's will and beloved by God, and a martial race, capable of preserving themselves against external attack and taking advantage of divine aid when it appeared. (138)

This is why Patrick (fl. fifth century) is featured as the clerical exemplar, and Arthur as the martial one. The Arthur as created by the Pythons fits this mold rather well—he's defeated the Saxons and is attempting to unify Britain; he's following God's direction and acknowledging His influence. And like these sections (50–56) of *HB*—where "a vision of un-sullied British achievement" could be trumpeted—both Arthurs' celebrations will be short-lived; Arthur's Britain will soon be faced with rude in situ Frenchmen (in the film world), invading and occupying Anglo-Saxons and Danes (in the real Middle Ages), and finally, intrusive interlopers, many of them gallingly French, from the EEC (in the 1970s). There is quite a lot at stake here.

BLACK KNIGHT: "What? Just a flesh wound"—During Henry II's reign the Assize of Clarendon (1166) demanded that those found guilty of crimes as a result of failing the "ordeal of cold water" were to have one foot amputated; not much later, the Assize of Northampton called for a foot and a hand to be removed after such an ordeal failure (Poole, *DBMC*, 402). Sheriff's records in the years that followed (later twelfth century) indicate that there were *many* people in Middlesex, Wiltshire, and Northamptonshire who'd lost a foot, or a foot and a hand, and who had obviously managed to live and continue their "normal" lives (402).[58]

This might also be a play on the typical injury that heroes in action films and TV shows often receive, wounds they shake off and fight through; in dozens of period television shows (police and detective dramas, even westerns) characters are shot in the shoulder, for example, and fairly regularly.[59] American imports like *Kojak* and *The Streets of San Francisco*, as well as the homegrown *The Sweeney*, featured many such "flesh wounds."[60] In *MPFC* they've already joked about a John Wayne film titled "*Buckets of Blood Pouring Out of People's Heads*," and in that same episode a young woman is blown up by a Webb's Wonder lettuce[61]—John Wayne's characters almost always survive no matter how many piercing wounds he might receive. The Black Knight survives, as well.

There are also films that feature this *same* level of violence, many from the batch of New Wave directors testing the boundaries of cinematic expression and good taste, including *Yojimbo*. In the film's first real confrontation—where the newly-arrived no-name bodyguard (Mifune) faces a horde of a local crime lord's men—Yojimbo guts two men and hacks off the sword arm of a third: three strokes, three kills. In this world, losing a limb means death, of course, as it can in the real world.[62] In *Throne of Blood*, Washizu is impaled by dozens of arrows before one penetrates his throat and he falls, dead. In *Sanjuro* the geyser of blood at the film's climax follows many acts of violence (one review called it "vulgar and coarse-grained" but "superbly" entertaining[63])—these are clan wars and everyone is armed with sharp weapons. But the macabre humor (or even banality) surrounding certain death isn't just a Python conceit—it can be seen in other period films, including Miklos Jancso's *The Red and the White* (1968), a Hungarian film that depicts civil war violence in calm, unhysterical, and ultimately chilling terms. A commander who coldly executes an enemy soldier one moment can himself be lined up against a wall just moments later as the upper hand in the battlefield changes, before changing again, and again.[64] Werner Herzog's *Aguirre: Der Zorn Gottes*[65] features the murderous, traitorous Aguirre (Klaus Kinski) who, after seizing control of the expedition by force, casually notes that one of his less motivated minions is a head too tall. His second-in-command takes the hint, drawing his sword. The doomed, clueless man is counting through their meager food stores aloud—"acht, neun"—as the fatal stroke is delivered—his head flies off and lands on the ground, and says: "Zehn." Also, in the final minutes of this nightmarish film the starving, delirious crew float in a waterlogged raft down a swollen river, espying what seems to be a rather large ship at the top of a tree. One crewmember—thirst-wracked—is certain he imagines the ship, telling himself: "That is no ship. That is no forest." From out of the dense forest a long arrow then pierces his leg; he mumbles, staring at it: "That is no arrow."

It's no stretch to assume that the Pythons may also be responding to those in the public view who attack the excesses of media, goading them, as it were, with more of what they rail against. During the run of *MPFC* the Pythons had poked fun at the ubiquitous Mary Whitehouse, for example, whose conservative views on sex and violence in all forms of media had sent more than one publisher or network executive running for cover.[66] Whitehouse would later lead a campaign against the Pythons and *Life of Brian*.[67] Another public figure teased in *Flying Circus* was Bryan Forbes, a writer, director, and producer. In 1969 Forbes gave an interview as the new head of the Associated British Picture Film Corporation (owner of Elstree Studios), decrying the "pornography of violence" in film, and promising his studio would do "better" (than the Hollywood imports, or foreign film in general).[68] He would have to write a follow-up two months later—pundits had attacked his puritanism—trying to explain he was not "a saint in sexless armour who would make Mrs. Mary Whitehouse look like The Beast With Five Filthy Fingers," but that he did want to produce British film "which [did] not depend on violence for . . . spurious shock value."[69] This spuriousness, of course, is precisely what the Pythons provide.

The Goons had used this same terminology before, in the "Giant Bombardon" episode (17 November 1957), when messenger Neddie arrives at HQ:

Seagoon (Secombe): Oh groan, groan, groan, groan. Ahhhgggh! Groan, oh groan!

Bloodnok (Sellers): He's wounded, with groans. Quick, the brandy!

Cardigan (Valentine Dyall): Here . . .

FX: *Liquid pouring from bottle.*

Cardigan: Now, steady now. Drink this.

Bloodnok: (*swallowing*) Thank you. I never could stand the sight of blood you know.

Seagoon: I'm all right sir. It's only a flesh wound.

Bloodnok: Oh, it looked like a bullet wound to me. (audio transcription)

Such disdain for seemingly deadly wounds harks back to Al Capp's "Fearless Fosdick," a character mocking the lantern-jawed *Dick Tracy* comic strip toughs. In "The Wedding" series of Fosdick strips from March 1952, at one point Fosdick removes his shirt to show the Chief how many bullets (and bazooka shells) he's taken for the force—revealing nine holes through his torso.[70] Later, in a 10 November 1968 Sunday panel, Fosdick is shot clean through more than six times and—even though he feels the chill of the wind blowing through him—he is able to continue on, since "[f]ortunately, they're flesh wounds."[71] Capp's *Li'l Abner* began its run in London newspapers in April 1966 when it appeared in *The London Magazine*. Al Capp also made a number of popular public appearances in London throughout the 1960s, generally as a witty commentator on contemporary American politics.

BLACK KNIGHT: *(kicking him)* **"Had enough . . . ?"**—Though not in the printed script, the armless Black Knight taunts Arthur as he kicks him, calling him "chicken." This is also a borrow from cartoons of the period. In the Bugs Bunny and Black Knight cartoon *Knighty Knight Bugs* (1958), King Arthur accuses his knights of the Round Table of being "chicken" when they refuse to confront the Black Knight (followed immediately by the sounds of clucking chickens and a puff of feathers).

Arthur chops his leg off—At this point, according to the troupe, a one-legged "actor"—a local silversmith, Richard Burton—replaces Cleese (the double is considerably shorter), and will play the Black Knight as he hops on one leg, and when he is de-limbed completely.[72] Cleese continues to provide the voice of the Black Knight, all dubbed in later. In *Le Morte D'Arthur*, Arthur also de-limbs a foe, in this case a giant:

> But in especial, King Arthur rode in the battle exhorting his knights to do well, and himself did as nobly with his hands as was possible a man to do; he drew out Excalibur his sword, and awaited ever whereas the Romans were thickest and most grieved his people, and anon he addressed him on that part, and hew and slew down right, and rescued his people; and he slew a great giant named Galapas, which was a man of an huge quantity and height; he shorted him and smote off both his legs by the knees, saying, "Now art thou better of a size to deal with than thou were," and after smote off his head. (*LMD'A*, 1.181–82)[73]

This is the third of four "chops" that the Black Knight will receive in this fight, and the film expresses its debt to Polanski and *Macbeth* with each and every hack:

> Murder and violence beget murder and violence. There is no end to the process in Polanski. It is not necessary to pinpoint the brutality that dots the rest of the film. Mutilated bodies, hacked limbs, throats cut, heads lopped off, bloody faces—a parade of horrors. The film is bathed in gore, as life is bathed in gore, according to Polanski's vision of reality. (Berlin, 294)

BLACK KNIGHT: "I am invincible!"—The length of this fight and the claims of invincibility expressed by the Black Knight can be found in many Grail romance tales. This particular scenario—where a combatant takes blow after blow but keeps fighting—is reminiscent of the duel between King Arthur and Sir Accolon as recounted by Malory in *LMD-WM*.

Arthur's sword Excalibur has been given to Accolon by a damosel of the scheming Morgan le Fay (Arthur's half-sister), and Arthur is losing so much blood "that it was marvel he stood on his feet, but he was so full of knighthood that he endured the pain" (66). Their battle rages, Arthur is losing blood fast, and it looks as if the fight will be Accolon's, but neither will give in (*both* just as stubborn as the Black Knight):

> Then Sir Accolon began with words of treason, and said, "Knight, thou art overcome, and mayst not endure, and also thou art weaponless, and lost thou hast much of thy blood; and I am full loath to slay thee. Therefore yield thee to me recreant."[74]
>
> "Nay," said Sir Arthur, "I may not so. For I promised by the faith of my body to do this battle to the uttermost while my life lasteth; and therefore I had liever to die with honour than to live with shame. And if it were possible for me to die a hundred times, I had liever to die so often than yield me to thee, for though I lack weapon, yet I shall lack no worship. And if thou slay me weaponless, that shall be thy shame."
>
> "Well," said Accolon, "as for that shame I will not spare. Now keep thee from me, for thou art but a dead man."
>
> And therewith Accolon gave him such a stroke that he fell nigh to the earth, and would have had Arthur to have cried him mercy. But Sir Arthur pressed unto Accolon with his shield, and gave him with the pommel in his hand such a buffet that he reeled three strides aback.
>
> When the Damosel of the Lake beheld Arthur, how full of prowess his body was, and the false treason that was wrought for him to have had him slain, she had great pity that so good a knight and such a man of worship should so be destroyed. And at the next stroke, Sir Accolon struck at him such a stroke that by the damosel's enchantment the sword Excalibur fell out of Accolon's hand to the earth. And therewith Sir Arthur lightly leapt to it and got it in his hand, and forthwith he knew that it was his sword Excalibur.
>
> "Ah," said Arthur, "thou hast been from me all too long, and much damage hast thou done me"; and therewith he espied the scabbard by his side, and suddenly he started to him and pulled the scabbard from him, and threw it from him as far as he might throw it.
>
> "Ah, sir knight," said King Arthur, "this day hast thou done me great damage with this sword. Now are ye come unto your death, for I shall not warrant you but ye shall be as well rewarded with this sword or ever we depart as ye have rewarded me, for much pain have ye made me to endure and much blood have I lost."
>
> And therewith Sir Arthur rushed on him with all his might and pulled him to the earth, and then rased off his helm and gave him such a buffet on his head that the blood came out at his ears, nose, and mouth.
>
> "Now will I slay thee," said Arthur.
>
> "Slay me ye may well," said Sir Accolon, "and it please you, for ye are the best knight that ever I found, and I see well that God is with you. But for I promised," said Accolon, "to do this battle to the uttermost and never to be recreant while I lived, therefore shall I never yield me with my mouth, but God do with my body what he will." (*LMD-WM*, 67)

Even in defeat, blood coming from his ears, nose, and mouth, Accolon refuses to surrender—a proto-Black Knight, indeed.

Montgomery indicates that such ill-suited bravery in the face of certain defeat (and maiming) isn't reserved for the fantastical narratives alone, or to the Pythons, for that matter. He describes one such army (a loose descriptor, which will become apparent), boasting few "able kings," through the writings of Leo the Wise, the Byzantine Emperor, whose forces "were never defeated by the Franks" (151). The assembled hordes sound very much like the Black and Green knights facing one another:

> The Franks and Lombards are bold and daring to the excess . . . they regard the smallest movement to the rear as a disgrace, and they will fight whenever you offer them battle. When their

knights are hard put to it in a cavalry fight, they will . . . dismount, and stand back to back against very superior numbers rather than fly. . . . You should take advantage of their indiscipline and disorder. (151)

ARTHUR: "You're a looney"—According to the *OED* this is a fairly new term (derived from "lunatic"), first appearing in print in the nineteenth century. The Pythons have made it their own, however, by using it a number of times during the *MPFC* run, and spelling it either "loony" or "looney," likely depending on which Python had the last go at the script. Praline (Cleese) and the Postmaster (Palin) nearly come to blows in Ep. 23 when the Postmaster suggests Marcel Proust might be a "loony";[75] a wildly dressed "looney" waves to the camera in Ep. 31;[76] Chapman's "loony" character recorded in the Glencoe shooting period makes an appearance in Ep. 32 as a non sequitur insert; and finally an entire sketch in Ep. 38, "Spot the Loony," is devoted to the character.

Again, in *Sir Gawain and the Green Knight*, it's the character's bizarre behavior that confuses Gawain, forcing him uncomfortably away from his idiom, as Arthur here is confronted by a knight who doesn't admit when he should give way, forcing Arthur to be more offensive than usual, even cruel, leaving the disfigured but essentially harmless man—he was certainly no danger to Arthur—to the elements. Arthur will be confronted with such unfulfilled expectations throughout this medieval genre picture—he's the straight man (maybe even Zeppo, or a Margaret Dumont) in a Marx Brothers world.

BLACK KNIGHT: "The Black Knight always triumphs!"—Truly, but there's a caveat. In the *Black Knight* comic book series (1955–1956), Merlin tells Percy (who is the Black Knight's alter ego): "Never shall your sword fail you, so long as it strikes for Arthur and England." If this is the case, in *Holy Grail* the Black Knight's failure to recognize Arthur, then raising his sword against him, dooms him. These kinds of misidentifications leading to accidental maimings or killings can be found throughout *Le Morte Darthur*, for example. There, the offender must then undertake some quest or task for penance (though the Black Knight seems to be staying right where he is).

BLACK KNIGHT: "Have at you!"—Likely from multiple sources (movies and books), but also found in its perhaps purest form for the younger Pythons in the panels of the Frank Bellamy (1917–1976) comic strip *King Arthur and His Knights* (July 1955–May 1956), which ran in the magazine *Swift*, as well as the *Robin Hood* comic (also 1955–1956) by Frank Bolle, where it appears as "Have at thee!" over and over again.

The Goons, of course, have always been a ready source of material and inspiration for the Pythons. In "The Plasticine Man," the story wraps up rather abruptly, and announcer Wallace Greenslade steps in:

Greenslade: Well, that's one way to end the story. But for listeners who don't like dull endings here's an exciting finish.

Sound effects: *Chase music* (Dick Barton *theme*)

Jampton (Milligan): Have at you!

Sound effects: *Swords clashing*.

Seagoon (Secombe): I'll have at you!

Omnes: *Quasi-Shakespearean dueling dialogue*.

Seagoon: Ahhhhhhhhhhhhhhhhhhhhhhhhhhhhhhhhh!

Sound effects: *Splash as Seagoon falls into the water* (23 December 1957)

And not only are the "Have at yous" recognizable, but the music[77] from the popular BBC radio/TV show *Dick Barton* appears in *Flying Circus*, most memorably at the culmination of "The Spanish Inquisition" episode.

For the actual Shakespearean version of this challenge, see *Comedy of Errors*, 3.1.674, 676, *Hamlet*, 5.2.3955 ("Have at you, now!" from Laertes, who wounds Hamlet, and then is wounded by Hamlet), *Henry VIII*, 3.2.2209, *Love's Labour's Lost*, 4.3.1634, *Romeo and Juliet*, 4.5 2781, *Taming of the Shrew*, 5.2.2535, and *Troilus and Cressida*, 5.6.3525.

ARTHUR takes his last leg off—This is both ghastly and silly, of course, and is meant to be, but its connections to the violence of the period have to be considered. The parade of literally hundreds of "multiple limb" amputees returning from battle in Vietnam—a war fully played out and in color on the evening news—had been in the American public eye since 1965. Bombing offensives, counterattacks, and casualty lists were a normal feature of most evening newscasts. The Vietnam coverage on the BBC was much more graphic than that available on American networks, as well, with assessments of the progress of the war and the veracity of American military propaganda always darker, always more skeptical.[78] Not surprisingly, the British coverage of the war tended to focus on the civilian suffering, the collateral damage of bombings and napalm and deforestation strategies. One such broadcast day in 1966 featured reporting on a Vietcong ambush on Australian troops, and ticked off the deaths of more than two hundred Vietcong and seventeen Australian troops, all as part of the regular news day.[79]

And as for the *specific* amputation injuries the Pythons depict in this scene—it has been reported more recently that land mines accounted for the bulk of the casualties to American troops in Vietnam, meaning predominately lower-limb injuries.[80]

Also, a particularly disturbing antiwar film had made its appearance in 1971, *Johnny Got His Gun*. The film was directed by the formerly blacklisted Hollywood screenwriter Dalton Trumbo (1905–1976), and was based on his own 1938 book of the same name. The film depicts a soldier waking up after being wounded, only to find he has no arms or legs, or even a face or mouth. He cannot speak, see, or hear, and eventually learns to communicate with his head, in Morse Code. At about this same time[81] the reports of civilian casualties in, for example, Hanoi, North Vietnam, continued to be well reported in at least European newspapers and television newscasts. These regularly reported the multiple amputations and other body horrors the North Vietnamese population—especially children, women, and the elderly—were enduring as B-52 bombing continued.

The Pythons had already celebrated the celebration of all things violent in Ep. 30 of *Flying Circus*, subtitled "Blood, Devastation, Death, War, and Horror," and even earlier in Ep. 23. There, images from the "French Subtitled Film" sketch, where they intercut acts of violence they'd created (hits on the head, kicks, an eye-gouging, a beheading) with newsreel footage of strafing runs, violent demonstrations and military and police actions against crowds (*MPFC: UC*, 2.353–55).

The BLACK KNIGHT's body lands upright—(PSC) This grotesquerie is clearly inspired by the many, many dismembering moments experienced by characters like Daffy Duck, Sylvester the Cat, or Wile E. Coyote in various WB cartoons of the 1940s and especially 1950s. In the three Duck-Rabbit-Hunter cartoons—*Rabbit Fire, Rabbit Seasoning*, and *Duck! Rabbit, Duck!*[82]—Daffy has his beak blown off a number of times, mangled other times, and his body shredded by shotgun blasts. In other cartoons he drinks gasoline and nitroglycerine before exploding or immolating; he is cut into neat slices on several occasions;[83] and he's also electrocuted. This doesn't include the dozens of hammerings, punches, kicks, crashes, smashes, etc., that fueled the WB cartoon world from World War II through about 1957. From *MPFC: UC*, an Ep. 1 entry in regard to the "silly" death of Genghis Khan:

> The Goon Show pioneered this cartoony-ness, an animated awareness that Peter Sellers characterized years later as being key in developing the show and writing the episodes with [Secombe, Bentine, and Milligan]—writers and performers also emerging from collective service in WWII—setting the show apart from anything that had come before. Sellers remembers: "We wanted to express ourselves in a sort of surrealistic form. We thought in cartoons, we thought in blackouts, we thought in sketches. We thought of mad characters. We thought of—take a situation and instead of letting it end normally, let it end the other way—twisted around" (audio transcription, "The Last Goon Show"). . . . This cartoony approach to structure and subject was adopted and adapted to include the visual elements the television medium would allow—the self-conscious signs . . . knowing glances, fourth wall-shattering asides, pratfalls, the character squash and stretch, even, which had previously only been allowed in the cartoon world—as the Pythons created *Flying Circus*. (1.19–20)

Part of the reason for this increase in speed and violence was to cater to the demands (or cathartic needs) of GIs during World War II. Cartoons produced for soldiers (like the "Private Snafu" series from WB) featured more adult language and situations than cartoons destined for cinemas; most WB cartoons in the war years also embraced the "high octane" action, content, and levels of violence that would likely have read more empathetically for a nation fighting a war than, say, Disney's "safer" Mickey or Goofy shorts of the same period.

BLACK KNIGHT: "All right, we'll call it a draw"—In a duel—which this is, rather than any kind of tournament engagement—the only prescribed outcomes are death or submission, with submission bringing levels of ignominy that most wanted to avoid. There are multiple such confrontations within the Arthurian romances, where submission can be efficacious, and examples of many without, in the real world, where submission is often the penultimate step before death. In this case, Arthur is simply trying to cross a bridge that is under the protection—with no reason given[84]—of the Black Knight. Knights, sorcerers, witches, giants, demons of all sorts guard various natural and man-made places in the romances—fords, bridges, chapels, castles—and some kind of confrontation is demanded for passage or entry. Later in *MPHG* it will be three questions to be answered at the Bridge of Death, for example.

In the world of the lived Middle Ages a duel tended to be more proscribed, especially in the decades after the Norman invasion. Medievalist G. A. Lester, in responding to Terry Jones's book[85] on Chaucer's Knight character from *CT*, clears up some misconceptions surrounding combat especially during the fourteenth century, separating the "tourney" fighting, which was ritualistic and more of a sport, from the duel, which had a definite, lethal, and even legal purpose.[86] After laying out the types of tournament encounters possible—the joust, foot combat, and the melee (mock battle)—Lester describes the duel this way:

> [T]here was another form of encounter which was used when treason, felony, or some slight of honour was involved, of which the object was none other than the death of the adversary. This was the duel, for which in its chivalric form we are fortunate to have the detailed evidence of a formulary made in Chaucer's own time by Thomas of Woodstock, Duke of Gloucester and Constable of England in the reign of Richard II. (461)

179

And even though this is an example from life, and not from the romances—where magic and monsters and pure serendipity can contravene—Arthur follows the proper guidelines rather closely as he encounters this "brave Sir Knight." Lester continues:

> After certain preliminaries three oaths are to be sworn by the appellant and defendant; a proclamation is then to be made, after which the two men are to be confined within the lists until one of them is either forced to surrender or is killed, whereupon the victor is considered vindicated. (461)

Arthur's friendly hails to the Black Knight are his preliminaries, his oaths are his actions and statements of purpose ("I have no quarrel with you"; "I must cross this bridge"), capped by yet another command as "king of the Britons" to one of his subjects. He has fulfilled the prescribed actions leading to a duel, and ("So be it") they are engaged, *à outrance*. Even during the duel Arthur is composed and fair, parrying more than offensively striking, giving a blow on the helm[87] with the hilt of his sword, not the blade[88]—a move to stun, not maim or kill. The removal of the left arm follows, and the Black Knight has the opportunity to submit; he does not, and even denies he's been wounded. The right arm comes off next, and Arthur is certain that's he's won the day, taking a knee to thank God for his support. Again, the Black Knight will not play the role of recreant, and Arthur must eventually render him limbless, and therefore harmless (except he may be able to bite). In the Pythons' Arthurian world, an armless and legless character can indeed continue to not only live, but stubbornly refuse to submit, leaving Arthur to move on, idiomatically confused, again, but seemingly content with the "draw." Here, as with his successful negotiation later across the Bridge of Death (confounding and defeating the Soothsayer at his own game), Arthur learns nothing, but secures a passage—such are the successes of his quest in *Holy Grail*.

Legally, though, just leaving the Black Knight there as a wounded loser wasn't so easy. Lester discusses the third oath, which is fairly clear:

> The document goes on to make provision for three degrees of punishment for an unslain loser, two of which involve execution: if the charge is treason he shall be disarmed, and a corner of the lists broken "in the reprove of hym", through which he shall be dragged by a horse to the place of justice, "where he shalbe hedid or hanged aftir the usage of the country"; if the charge is some other crime, the loser shall be led out, not dragged out, but he also shall be beheaded or hanged; finally, "if it be for a deed or action of arms, he who is convicted and discomfited, shall be disarmed as aforesaid and put out of the lists without any other justice inflicted on him". These provisions only applied in cases in which death did not occur in combat or in which the judge did not intervene to reconcile the two parties. Descriptions of actual duels show that death, in combat or by execution, was the most common result. (463)

The Black Knight is defying the king and swearing to kill him, which likely constitutes treasonous behavior and merits a swift beheading or hanging. There's no certainty, given the Black Knight's constitution, that execution will actually work; remember Gawain's experience with the headless Green Knight. Again, if this was a legal fourteenth-century duel, Arthur would have at least needed to remove the loser from within the lists, and at most see to his prompt, humane execution. Even though this is a romance genre confrontation and not a duel in the legal sense, Arthur tries to take the honorable high road, being firm but fair before moving on.

In another sense, in calling a draw the Black Knight could be voicing what Middle Ages historian Henri Pirenne (1862–1935) saw as the accepted lot of many in medieval times: "To security of existence corresponds a moderation of desires" (*HBMA*, 241). As he can no longer wield a sword, kick an opponent, or attack/defend in any way—and yet he lives—the Black Knight makes the best of his delimbed situation.

ARTHUR and PATSY start to cross the bridge—Arthur leaves the Black Knight alive but wounded, sort of an open-ended moment—a rarity in most Arthurian material. But *Holy Grail* isn't "most Arthurian material." In this, though, it echoes the equally unusual separation scene in *Sir Gawain and the Green Knight*, as Besserman notes:

> In his final encounter with Gawain the Green Knight is not killed, disenchanted, or converted and enrolled in the Round Table as he might have been if *Sir Gawain* were a more conventional medieval romance. Instead, he and Gawain embrace, kiss, and commend one another to "the prince of paradise" (11. 2472–73); he then rides off "whiderwarde-so-euer he wolde" (1. 2478), still a "grene gome" (1. 2239) and a knight in "enker-grene" (1. 2477), apparently still subject to Morgan le Fay, and with the tensions in his nature between friend and foe of Gawain and the Round Table still not fully resolved. His identity remains a puzzle. (225–26)

Arthur and Patsy ride off without actually knowing anything about the invective-hurling Black Knight, and their odd quest continues.

BLACK KNIGHT: "You yellow bastard . . ."—A very contemporary term, "yellow" wasn't used in the context of "cowardly" until well into the nineteenth century, and then as a peculiarly American phrase (*OED*). In *Flying Circus* the Pythons weren't afraid to employ Americanisms like "gosh" and "wacky," of course, generally borrowed from American comic and television culture.[89] This sounds much more like an epithet borrowed from war pictures, for example, or one used during at least both the Korean and Vietnam conflicts as a way to describe the Chinese, North Koreans, and Viet Cong. It's been reported that ANZAC troops in World War II who became Japanese POWs used the term when referring to their captors;[90] there are letters from American GIs serving in the South Pacific in 1944 detailing the smell of the dead and bloating "yellow bastards" wafting from every nook and cranny of Peleliu,[91] and on a tape made by General Creighton Abrams (1914–1974) during the Vietnam war, he mentions that one Vietnamese commander referred to another as a "dirty yellow bastard."[92] The Pythons grew up in the age when the phrase had currency, certainly. Illustrating the depth of feeling even one year into World War II (and the fear and loathing of Asians in general), the very traditional *Time* magazine reported the following on 7 December 1942: "When he heard the news from excited Navy Secretary Frank Knox, all that Franklin Roosevelt could utter was an astonished 'No!' In their living rooms, on the golf courses, driving in their cars, tens of thousands of profane Americans said: 'Why, the yellow bastards!'" (24). The Black Knight's usage of the term, then, conflicts with the presented age, but fits neatly into the immediate post-Vietnam era.[93]

Notes

1. Doyle mentions that bookings for local hotel rooms were running out, and flights back to London were firmly booked, so staying on location wasn't an option. From e-mail correspondence dated 9 December 2013. The scene in Epping Forest was put together by Jones, Gilliam, and Doyle with a handful of support crew, including Valerie Charlton, who made the tent in the background.

2. Cleese seems to have been the hardest Python to schedule during the shoot, and the one who wanted to spend the least possible time in Scotland. Stirling extra Jim McIver describes the day spent with the troupe on Sheriffmuir, shooting the final battle sequence and arrest: "[Gilliam] was extremely friendly, as were the other 'Pythons' with whom we spent the day. The only exception was John Cleese, who arrived, went into Make-Up, did his scene in the back of the Police van and promptly left again,

much to everyone's disappointment" (from a 29 June 2011 e-mail correspondence [see appendix B]). Cleese had been the most visible "star" when the Pythons first formed.

3. "Mystic runes" are mentioned later by Tim the Enchanter as the key to the final resting place of the Holy Grail. See entries in that section for reasons such stones might be in the Pythons' collective eye as they wrote.

4. His wife Valerie was working with him, according to Doyle. Information from e-mail correspondence with the author, as well as court testimony.

5. But also *Herbie Rides Again*. The announcer is speaking in Mandarin, and appropriately silly subtitles are provided. (These sound as if they're read by Bert Kwouk [b. 1930].)

6. It's also likely that since this scene was saved for shooting back in the London area, and with a skeleton crew, to boot, tracking down (or building) rune stones and erecting bridges just wasn't in the cards. The scene was perhaps challenge enough with the choreographed fight sequence, the limb prosthetics, stunt double, and "Kensington Gore" effects, as well.

7. See Norris Lacy's edition of *Lancelot-Grail, Parts I and II* (2010): 7.

8. In this case, "waited," though usually it means to swell or lift (*OED*). The term is used many times throughout *Le Morte D'Arthur*, meaning White—who'd written a university thesis on Malory's work—knew his sources well. See Gallix, *Letters to a Friend: The Correspondence Between T. H. White and L. J. Potts* 93–95, 98.

9. The Black Knight's pavilion is a tent in the background, clearly reminiscent of those seen in battlefield scenes of Polanski's *Macbeth*. Valerie Charlton made the tents for this scene; Doyle shot the scene.

10. This Black Knight scene was so violent that producer Michael White—seeing it as part of a "bad" screening of an early cut—voted for its removal from the film. According to Doyle, Cleese seemed to concur, and the scene was removed for a time. Doyle and others (like Gilliam) thought the scene worked very well, and argued relentlessly for it to be reinserted into the film. (From a 5 December 2013 e-mail correspondence.) Also, Gilliam talks up the significance of the scene in his audio commentary on both the DVD and Blu-ray editions.

11. Old French, early thirteenth century.

12. Remember also, by this point, this is not yet a holy quest for the Grail—God won't appear for that plot twist until after they've decided Camelot is a "silly place." At that point, the film's narrative as originally announced—gathering Knights to the Round Table—abruptly ends. The knights are then gathered *offscreen*, as recorded in "The Book of the Film" section.

13. In mid-thirteenth century armor and clothing, including the full helm with eye slits. See Norman and Pottinger (1966) as well as Dougherty (2008) for descriptions and illustrations.

14. The boar's head charge is a symbol on a very early Sir John de Swinton seal, for example, c. 1389.

15. In the Popeye cartoon *Wotta Knight* (1957, Famous Studios), Popeye fights the Black Knight of Brooklyn, Sir Bluto, at a jousting tournament. In the Warner Bros. cartoon, *Knighty Knight Bugs* (1958), Yosemite Sam is the Black Knight.

16. A five-issue series from Atlas Comics, with story and dialogue written by Stan Lee.

17. See Norman and Pottinger, *English Weapons and Warfare, 449–1660*, 69–70, and 94; Dougherty, *The Medieval Warrior*, 46–47, 91, and 121.

18. We will return to discussions of *The Song of Roland* in the "Tale of Sir Robin" section later.

19. From a review of a reprinted edition of Evans, *The Unconquered Knight: A Chronicle of the Deeds of Don Pero Nino, Count of Buelna*.

20. Prominent Hollywood director of tough guys like William Holden, Warren Oates, and Steve McQueen, Peckinpah (1925–1984) was from Fresno, CA. Both Peckinpah and Fresno are mentioned by Idle's "sniffing" film critic character in Ep. 33 of *Flying Circus*.

21. See the "Your arm's off" entry below for more.

22. One of the early British kings, Harold Godwinson, Earl of East Anglia (1022–1066), took an arrow through the eye during the Battle of Hastings.

23. *MPFC: UC*, 1.221–39.

24. *MPFC: UC:* 1.106, 136, 156, 171, 240; 2.92.

25. *Black Knight* #3, Atlas Comics, June 1955.

26. Doyle's information is gleaned from e-mail correspondence with the author in 2013 and 2014, as well as provided court material.

27. In fact, most of these newly arrived knights are killed off almost immediately, most before their names are even mentioned.

28. The average inflation rate in the UK in 1973 was 9.18 percent, and climbed from about 7.7 percent and 10.5 percent during the year. It had averaged more than 7 percent in 1972, then 15.99 percent in 1974, and 24.11 percent in 1975. The budget deficit in February 1974 was twelve times greater than in June 1970 (Whitehead, 113). See also *MPFC: UC*, 1.373, the "British Empire . . . ruins" entry for more.

29. *State of Emergency* 303, italics added.

30. See the chapter "The Road to the IMF" in Whitehead, *The Writing on the Wall*.

31. Whitehead, 187. Crosland (1918–1977) assumed the foreign secretary position after Callaghan became PM. "Grimsby" was Crosland's constituency, and "TU" were the trade unions.

32. *Bonnie and Clyde*'s posters include the catchy boast: "They're young . . . they're in love . . . and they kill people."

33. Based on a stage play by Spike Milligan and John Antrobus, and directed by Richard Lester, the film appeared at the Cinecenta in March 1970.

34. Michael Stone, "Yugoslav Film Gets Berlin Award," *Times*, 14 July 1969: 11.

35. J. R. Taylor, *Times*, 12 March 1971: 12.

36. "Sir Galant of the Round Table" in *Robin Hood* #5 (March 1957): 5, 14 and 24. There are thirty-six pages in most of these comic books, including the covers.

37. *The Adventures of Robin Hood* #8 (November 1957): 19 of 36. The Ghost Knight turns out to be a pretty girl in disguise, making Bors even unhappier at the outcome.

38. This same sequence appears in the Winchester Manuscript, as well, where Arthur hears about a skilled knight—it turns out to be King Pellinore—who waits at a fountain, challenging everyone who passes. Arthur faces the knight after Arthur's young comrade Sir Griflet is injured—the mysterious knight's "truncheon stuck in his body"—and only survives thanks to Merlin's interference (*LMD-WM*, 25–29).

39. Start at *MPFC: UC*,1.373, then consult the index for much more on Britain's shrinking empire.

40. "More Defence Cuts Needed to Reach £2,000M. Target," *Times*, 11 March 1966: 6.

41. In summer 1967, after the Scottish Argylls regiment was recalled from duty in Aden, the regiment was disbanded. A furor followed, and with significant public and ministerial help a smaller version of the unit was saved (*MPFC: UC*, 1.168). This was just one of many reductions in Britain's overseas military commitments confounded by a White Paper in February calling for an 8.5 percent *increase* in defense expenditure—this as industrial production fell dramatically, and tax revenue dropped along a similar curve. Heath called this decision a "flabbergasting increase in Government spending," and fought against it. Heath was on the razor's edge here, as he also wanted to uphold myriad British defence commitments, to "SEATO, Singapore, Malaysia, the Gulf, Kuwait, Bahrain, the Trucial States, Oman, and Libya," along with Aden. See "Budget Gloom as Costs Soar £660M," *Times*, 17 February 1967: 1; and "Tory Clash Ahead on Defence Cuts," *Times*, 30 June 1967: 4.

42. "The Crisis Begins—Eden Resolves to Remove Nasser," *Times* 29 April 1967: 11.

43. In June 1973 the handcrafted "Ely Cathedral Goblet"—looking very much like a Holy Grail-type cup—went up for sale in a limited edition of 673, its advertisement displayed in the Entertainment section of the *Times*. These "superb commemorative pieces" were £96 each, or two for £190. It's not such a stretch, then, from the Grail as the cup of Christ to the Grail found at Harrods.

44. The exciting martial music (from DeWolfe) used here will reappear in Gilliam's film *Brazil*.

45. The image of the Norseman's hand flying off his arm is actually quite graphic—it's not accomplished out of frame—the precedent for non-stylized violence even in children's literature was in place as the Pythons grew up.

46. This audio track is part of the 2001 DVD edition of the film, and features comments from Cleese, Idle, and Palin. The other audio track on this edition features the voices of Jones and Gilliam.

47. A precedent may have been set in the epic poem *Beowulf* where, in the first battle between Beowulf and Grendel, Beowulf tears off Grendel's arm—the monster then creeps home to die. The Pythons evince a significant knowledge of *Beowulf* and Icelandic sagas in their *"Njorl's Saga"* sketch from Ep. 27. See *MPFC: UC*, 2.3–19. Also, there was a fourteenth-century Breton, Olivier de Clisson, who was known as "the Butcher"—he would regularly lop off the arms and/or legs of foes in the heat of battle (Tuchman, 264).

48. "Axel's Lonely Castle," *Times*, 4 April 1975: 9.

49. "How Are You Going to Keep Them Down on the Farm?" *Times*, 26 November 1971: 12.

50. Not an "X" rating from the MPAA, however. It was released both as an edited "R"-rated film and "Unrated."

51. *MPHG* received an "A" certificate in Great Britain, and in the U.S. market, a "PG" rating.

52. Hayes, *Sam Peckinpah: Interviews*: xiii.

53. Hayes, xiii.

54. Berlin, *"Macbeth*: Polanski and Shakespeare," 290–98.

55. This kneeling moment is Arthur's *second* mention or invocation of God.

56. St. Patrick, a Roman Britain cleric, fl. fifth century, Ireland.

57. Ironically, Arthur's temperament and treatment of others renders him more like beloved *French* king Louis IX (1214–1270). Louis was pious, temperate in his eating and drinking, happy to dress in normal clothing, and willing to listen to and help his poor and those with grievances, as well as to fight for a righteous cause (including two disastrous crusades). He also believed firmly in his role as a strong king of a strong France. John, Lord of Joinville wrote Louis's biography, where the king's "honesty, courage and good sense emerge over and over again" (Hallam, 93). Louis was canonized in 1297.

58. For more on this "ordeal" system of jurisprudence see entries below in the "She's a Witch" section.

59. In the *Goon Show* episode "Six Ingots of Leadenhall Street" (1 March 1955), a similar "flesh wound" moment:

FX: *(Pistol shot)*

Harry (Secombe): Oh! I'm dead!

Greenslade: You get the idea? The man was obviously shot, but not as he proclaimed dead. We are unfortunately not allowed to do this and whenever possible we aim for the legs.

All of Bluebottle's "deadings" over the course of the *Goon Show*'s run are temporary—he can be blown up, electrocuted, squashed, or shot, but he is alive enough to complain about the assault after the fact, and hope for better luck the following week. The cartoony nature of the show clearly rubbed off on the young Pythons.

60. *Kojak* appeared on BBC 1; *The Streets of San Francisco* on Yorkshire Television; and *The Sweeney*, a gritty British cop drama, on Thames. A *Mad* magazine obituary for Dick Tracy even noted that comic book character Dick Tracy was shot in the left shoulder so many times he likely died of lead poisoning. Al Capp's version of Tracy, *Fearless Fosdick*, will be discussed below.

61. *MPFC: UC*, 1.358, "Wayne, John" and "Webb's Wonder" entries, both from Ep. 23.

62. *Yojimbo* finally made it to British cinemas in 1970, appearing at the Paris-Pullman.

63. *Times*, 24 October 1962: 14. *Sanjuro* didn't appear in British cinemas until 1970, at the Academy 3.

64. Jancso uses extended, elegant tracking shots rather than kinetic editing to capture these choreographed massacres; film critic Taylor admitted to being "emotionally mystified" by the "fiendishly clever moving-camera shots" ("The Lively Side of Cannes, *Times*, 25 May 1968: 19). *The Red and the White* played at the Academy 2.

65. Opening at the Paris-Pullman in 1974.

66. See the index in *MPFC: UC*, both volumes, for the *many* references in *MPFC* to Mary Whitehouse. See also Sandbrook, *State of Emergency*, 51–52.

67. See Hewison, *Monty Python: The Case Against*.

68. "Film Chief Attacks 'Filth,'" *Times*, 9 April 1969: 2. This interview was given just as the Pythons began work on the first season of *Flying Circus*. See also *MPFC: UC*, 1.325–26, 354; 2.124.

69. "Forbes: Posed to Light a Bonfire," *Times*, 23 June 1969: 1.

70. This particular strip dates to 21 March 1952. See Capp, *The Best of Li'l Abner*, 17.

71. Capp, 148.

72. Listen to Cleese's audio track on the 2012 Blu-ray edition of *MPHG* for more on this scene, including the name of the one-legged blacksmith (if they're remembering correctly).

73. This story is *not* included in the Cooper's 1998 Winchester Ms. edition. This quote is from Cowen's 1969 Penguin edition.

74. "recreant"—meaning craven, cowardly.

75. *MPFC: UC*, 1.179, 355; 2.140–49.

76. *MPFC: UC*, 2.144–45, 147–48. See the index for more on both, and with both spellings.

77. The music is called "Devil's Gallop," and it is also used briefly in *MPFC*, Ep. 13, the "Quiz Programme—*Wishes*" sketch (*MPFC: UC*, 1.204). The Goons also use the music in "The Whistling Spy Enigma" episode.

78. Julian Pettifer (b. 1935) covered the war for the BBC, among others.

79. All three of the major U.S. networks—ABC, CBS, and NBC—covered this incident almost identically, meaning these were "pool" images and stories—none of their reporters were likely in any close proximity to the events.

80. *Congressional Record* 150: 19 (24 October 2001) p. S20595.

81. The U.S. forces had resumed nighttime B-52 bombing of the North Vietnamese capital on 18 December 1972. See "What the American Bombing is Doing to Hanoi Civilians," *The Times*, 30 Dec. 1972: 1. This same kind of "carpet" bombing had been used in the later stages of World War II on German cities like Cologne and Dresden.

82. Dated 1951, 1952, and 1953, respectively. All directed by Chuck Jones and written by Michael Maltese. These and most WB cartoons from this period are edited significantly before appearing on American television. See Beck and Friedwald's *Looney Tunes and Merrie Melodies* (1989). See also *MPFC: UC* index entries for "animation."

83. This gag is copied precisely by the Pythons in the "Zulu Wars" section of *Meaning of Life*.

84. In *Le Morte D'Arthur*, Launcelot is challenged on a bridge to a joust, then a "noble battle" on foot, both of which he easily wins (*LMD'A*, 1.360). The challenger, Sir Nerovens de Lile, gives no reason for his challenge—it's clearly just part of his idiom as a chivalric character in an Arthurian romance. Launcelot (Cleese) will be trapped by his own idiom as he tries to leave Swamp Castle later.

85. *Chaucer's Knight: The Portrait of a Medieval Mercenary*. London: Weidenfeld and Nicolson, 1980.

86. Lester, "Chaucer's Knight and the Medieval Tournament."

87. There are dozens of strokes like this one in the romances, though many of them cave in or split the helmet; at the least, there is often blood from the nose and mouth from the staggering blow. At worst, the sword travels through the unfortunate victim, cleaving him. The Pythons "cleave" a character in *MPFC* Ep. 13, when a sales assistant is cut in half by Ivan the Terrible (*MPFC: UC*, 1.207). Also, Gilliam's animated samurai character bisects several foes, and then himself with his own sword (Ep. 19; *MPFC: UC*, 1.289).

88. Macbeth uses this same strike against the first man who attacks him in the final battle of Polanski's film.

89. *MPFC: UC*, 1.48, 74, 103, 106, 328. This is a bit ironic since the 1948 BBC programming guide that laid out what should not be said on air gave special emphasis to avoiding American argot, particularly.

90. Graham Seal, "Fighting Words," In *The Lingo* (Sydney: UNSW Press, 1999): 52–71.

91. *Rigby Star*, 16 November 1944 (43.1): 5. The unnamed letter writer is quite candid, and the terminology quite straightforward:

> I have a lot of Jap money and several other souvenirs. The pen and ink I am using belongs to a Jap. I picked it up and it serves the purpose when there is nothing else to write with. The living is not so good here now

but we will get by. The flies are thick and you should just smell one of these yellow bastards after about three days out with the flies. Believe me I'm ready to come back to the States. I am truly a peace loving citizen now.

92. Just days earlier in these same recordings Abrams encourages those around him to *not* call the Viet Cong "dirty yellow bastards" or "dinks" since everyone—the people fighting for and against the United States in Vietnam—were Vietnamese, and the same brush tarred them all (316). *Vietnam Chronicles: The Abrams Tapes, 1968–1972*: 319.

93. American *combat* troops had left Vietnam in March 1973.

SCENE SEVEN
FLAGELLANT MONKS AND "SHE'S A WITCH!"

Chanting of a Latin canon—(PSC) "Pie jesu domine, dona eis requiem" is part of the *Dies irae*, a Latin hymn. As this is a thirteenth-century composition, the "Where were you in 1282" comment from Forstater[1] makes its inclusion at least historically possible, as opposed to all other mentioned possible dates (1167, 932, or 787). The use of anachronisms and telescoping of time is a trait the Pythons share with another English institution:

> Shakespeare also telescopes time, creates non-historical characters in his histories, and delivers anachronisms without hesitation or apology, all of which combine as the warp and woof of Shakespeare's very believable and influential history. . . . Python's appropriation of Shakespeare's disregard for the unities of time and space and their ahistorical "unconformities" will become significant as time and space collapse into an ever present; and [the Pythons'] methods of historiography will also be considered as comedy in relation to how British history is constructed. And as comedy is constructed by Monty Python, so too is another history.[2]

Much more on this later as the Famous Historian's death is discussed.

This is also one of only two places in the film where Latin is employed. This same canon will be chanted as Brother Maynard and friends bring the Holy Hand Grenade to Arthur later in the film. Everyone else speaks English, French, or Franglish—Brother Maynard can read Aramaic, it seems—generally employing the idioms of the twentieth century. The Pythons avoid Old English and Middle English, too. Depending on the period depicted (a bricolage of pre- and post-Conquest times), Latin would have been *the* language, according to Kenneth Jackson (1953), in the pre-Conquest era:

> Latin was the language of the governing classes, of civil administration and of the army, of trade, of the Christian religion, and very largely (but perhaps not entirely) of the people of the towns. The rural upper classes were bilingual; the peasantry of the Lowland Zone, who constituted the great bulk of the population, spoke British and probably knew little Latin; and the language of the Highland Zone (apart from the army and its native camp-followers) was to all intents and purposes exclusively British. (105)

The audience will have to wait for the next Python film, *Life of Brian*, for a closer look at the cultural peculiarities of the depicted period, for example, Brian given a lesson at sword point in proper Latin by a stern centurion. In *Holy Grail* the intersections and confrontations between the mythical (Arthur) and the historical (Mercia as a kingdom) overwhelm any direct lampooning of the feudal or manorial systems or the actual life of a knight or a peasant in those systems. The conflicts don't tend to be between mythology and history, per se—except where Arthur struggles when confronted with an unmythologized character or event—but between a proscribed Arthurian mythos as it meets the more cynical, less programmatic modern world. Faced with that world, the mythical Arthur can *only* be confused.

line of MONKS à la Seventh Seal—(PSC) This influential film is here mentioned in the script (and it will be mentioned in one of the film's trailers), and previously in *MPFC*, Ep. 7, the latter where a line of Englishmen who'd been turned into kilted Scotsmen march across the heather-and-gorse border countryside, bound for Caledonia.[3] The principal characters in this scene—flagellants, monks,[4] angry villagers, an accused witch—are also connected to the recurring outbreaks of plague and famine during the seventh through fourteenth centuries, as will be discussed later. There, however, the alleged witch won't be accused of spreading disease, as was common, but for engaging in *maleficia*, or "malignant acts," what Gaskill calls "the real crime of witchcraft for the majority" (*Witchfinders*, 44). A portion of the (translated) *Seventh Seal* film script here describes a change of mood. A somewhat bawdy but lighthearted musical performance is underway, performed by the travelers Jof (Nils Poppe) and Mia (Bibi Andersson), but something approaches, and "a rapid change occurs":

> *People who had been laughing and chattering fall silent. Their faces seem to pale under their sunbrowned skins, the children stop their games and stand with gaping mouths and frightened eyes. . . .*
>
> *The cross-bearers soon come into sight. They are Dominican monks, their hoods pulled down over their faces. More and more of them follow, carrying litters with heavy coffins or clutching holy relics, their hands stretched out spasmodically. The dust wells up around their black hoods; the censers sway and emit a thick, ashen smoke which smells of rancid herbs.*
>
> *After the line of monks comes another procession. It is a column of men, boys, old men, women, girls, children. All of them have steel-edged scourges in their hands with which they whip themselves and each other, howling ecstatically. They twist in pain; their eyes bulge wildly; their lips are gnawed to shreds and dripping with foam. They have been seized by madness. They bite their own hands and arms, whip each other in violent, almost rhythmic outbursts. Throughout it all the shrill song howls from their bursting throats. Many sway and fall, lift themselves up again, support each other and help each other to intensify the scourging.* (Scene description, *The Seventh Seal*)

The look and setting of *The Seventh Seal* are, of course significant for the Pythons and their version of medieval life, but *Holy Grail* is also a send-up of the high tone, the grim seriousness exhibited by both the world- and war-weary Knight and his sardonic, worldly squire Jöns, as they return home from the Crusades to plague and death. Arthur and Patsy are clearly at least modeled after this pair.

Historically, the monastic lifestyle and the culture it created/supported might have been a significant culprit in the spread of disease during these years, according to Maddicott. The interdependency between the monasteries and especially the rural villages and villagers allowed the disease to spread across large tracts of uninhabited land. Monastery graveyards are home to many men, women, and children not directly associated with the monastery; the role of the monastery in the local economy—either producing goods or as a central market-type location for local goods—is also key; and the importance of the monastery as a destination for the pilgrim or penitent meant ample opportunities for the spread of contagion (34–35). Maddicott concludes:

> Of course, not all regions were thickly planted with monasteries and not all monasteries filled all these functions. Nevertheless many monasteries, like the royal vills, were in effect central places, and often designedly so. If, during the plague, they became reservoirs of infection, the exchange between centre and periphery, monastery and locality, salvational in purpose, may have become lethal by result. (35)

So the monks in *Holy Grail* were most certainly imaged after those depicted in *The Seventh Seal*, but their role in the transmission of pestilence in seventh-century England (closer to Arthur's alleged *floruit*) is also historically supportable.

Middle Ages writers were familiar with how both the wages of sin and the emphasis the Church placed on seeking forgiveness weighed on the hearts of many during this period. Chaucer offers characters like the Pardoner, an unctuous seller of papal indulgences and fake relics—as part of a pilgrimage to earn "sterlynges" and "Nobles or pens"[5] for his lot[6] (he would have done very well in the village depicted here in *MPHG*); as well as the final tale-teller, the Parson, who essentially upbraids the actions and motives of almost everyone and everything that's gone before him, though scholars continue to debate his authentic or ironic motivations.[7] Voltaire writes of Candide and Dr. Pangloss being chosen for auto-da-fé (public punishment) to help prevent earthquakes. Candide is flogged, Dr. Pangloss is hanged, and two others are burned to death; an earthquake strikes later that day anyway.[8] Closer to our sources, Chrétien employs penitence-seekers in *The Story of the Grail*, where ten ladies—"their heads hidden in their hoods, all on foot, in hair-shirts and bare-footed"—seek forgiveness from their sins on a Good Friday (*The Story of the Grail*, 457–58).

. . . flagellation scene—(PSC) The lead flagellant—who bangs himself on the forehead—is musician Neil Innes, his character described in the Cast List as "The First Self-Destructive Monk" (*MPHGB*, 90).

The *Catholic Encyclopedia* terms flagellation either a punishment or "voluntary penance," but it wouldn't be until about the thirteenth century—and the appearance across Europe of the plague in a devastating way—that self-flagellation appeared in the streets:

> It is in 1260 that we first hear of the Flagellants at Perugia. The terrible plague of 1259, the long-continued tyranny and anarchy throughout the Italian States, the prophecies concerning Antichrist and the end of the world by Joachim of Flora and his like, had created a mingled state of despair and expectation among the devout lay-folk of the middle and lower classes. Then there appeared a famous hermit of Umbria, Raniero Fasani, who organized a brotherhood of "Disciplinati di Gesù Cristo", which spread rapidly throughout Central and Northern Italy. . . . All ages and conditions were alike subject to this mental epidemic. Clergy and laity, men and women, even children of tender years, scourged themselves in reparation for the sins of the whole world. Great processions, amounting sometimes to 10,000 souls, passed through the cities, beating themselves, and calling the faithful to repentance. With crosses and banners borne before them by the clergy, they marched slowly through the towns. Stripped to the waist and with covered faces, they scourged themselves with leathern thongs till the blood ran, chanting hymns and canticles of the Passion of Christ, entering the churches and prostrating themselves before the altars.[9]

The movement would fade as the plague's wrath receded, but would erupt again in the fourteenth century when the 1348–1350 visitation of the Black Death killed millions, and survivors were certain the world was ending. The Pythons wouldn't use real-looking blood and suffering—that wouldn't be as funny—so having their monks "banging themselves on the foreheads with wooden boards" might have been the next best thing.

The *Catholic Encyclopedia* also notes that even though there was great death and misery in England during the plague years, the responses by everyday English folk to the flagellant movements was mostly impassive:

> By September of that year [the flagellants] had arrived in England, where, however, they met with but little success. The English people watched the fanatics with quiet interest, even expressing pity and sometimes admiration for their devotion; but no one could be induced to join them, and the attempt at proselytism failed utterly.[10]

Contemporary chronicler Robert of Avesbury also mentions flagellants arriving in London near the "feast of S. Michael" (late September 1349). He notes that they came from "Zealand and Holland," and had made the trip from Flanders to London for this show of penitence (Ashley, 1887, 129). He then describes their twice-daily exercise of self-flagellation and mutual flagellation, as well as singing and replying (in Dutch), crawling and prostration, "sometimes in the church of S. Paul, sometimes in other places" (129). There is no mention of his own take on the spectacle, except that it happened, or the reaction of Londoners who may have been watching with him, though he doesn't indicate that there were any English novitiates convinced to join these public sufferers.

... *banging themselves on the foreheads with wooden boards*—(PSC) The ascetic lifestyle of the monkish in (or separate from) medieval society varied from order to order, and "penance and penalty" for holy men were often quite specific.[11] According to Bishop, "Saint Columban, about A.D. 600, prescribed six lashes for a monk who forgot to say *Amen*, ten for one who notched a table with his knife, six for one who sang out of tune" (14). Head-banging monks would have been no more outlandish or out of place than the more typical flagellants, writhers and dancers, or cross-bearers and the self-crucified, especially during times of pestilence and famine.

... *a group of villagers are dragging* ...—(PSC) During the fourteenth century—and especially in smaller villages—since there are no police forces, the villagers themselves would have been charged with raising the hue and cry if a crime were discovered, followed by a search for the perpetrator (Mortimer, 216–17). The communal nature of the English countryside meant that "everyone belongs somewhere . . . free or unfree, villeins and freemen alike," and that these small communities knew each other and were expected to act communally in their own defense (216). All others are "vagabonds, vagrants, and strangers" and, yes, witches, where needed, and the law must be supported as a community, or in this case, by a community-based mob of villagers: "If one man breaks the law, all the others are responsible for reporting his actions and delivering the culprit to the constable of the township. If they do not, they are fined heavily" (217; see also Dyer, 5–11). Sawyer notes the significance of community and "communal action," especially in relation to their Anglo-Saxon sovereign and his effectiveness:

> Kings also emphasized the importance of communal action. At one level this was seen in the responsibility to repair and man fortifications around shire towns, but they also had great success in organizing groups of neighbours to act as hundreds or tithings. Communal action was not new. Joint cultivation is well evidenced in both England and Ireland in the seventh century. What the English kings did was to institutionalize local communities in their own service. (177)

Arthur just happens along as this communal version of an *infangenpeof*[12] action is underway, of course, but he does help it along considerably as he fills a gap—"A duck"—in the relentlessly logical chain Bedevere and the villagers are pursuing. This is another moment in the film where the "real" world of medieval history (the community witch hunt) meets Arthuriana.

The Pythons' mob includes laborers of all sorts, the old and the young, a man being shaved, farmers with implements, and so on, an eclectic grouping but quite accurate, according to Mortimer: "All those in the vicinity. . . are expected to come in from the fields or get up from their beds to view the scene of the crime and to pursue the criminal" (217). The usefulness of the local community—in the form of the hundred or wapentake (county subdivisions)—is legally ordinanced by the middle of the tenth century, by which time the king had come to expect villages to take the reins in the "preservation of peace and prevention of theft" (Sawyer, 198). There are even situations (involving criminal acts, not necessarily heretical acts) that allow the armed "*posse comitatus*" to carry out an execution as soon as the alleged perpetrator is caught. If the offender is a woman, for example, she can be immediately "forcibly drowned for resisting arrest" (Mortimer, 218). These cases tend to involve, again, the criminal as opposed to the spiritual/heretical, and they also must *generally* stop short of meting out punishment (including torture), but Miss Islington is being accused of the crime of being a witch and "harming" a villager, and the mob exhibits a desire for swift justice. Her "rough music" will be more fatal than most (Dyer, 5). There's no indication that the mob knows the accused (they don't call her by name), so it may be that since she is a stranger to them she is even more likely to be treated with suspicion and more readily accused. Mortimer notes that "as many as 30 percent of all suspected murderers and thieves are described as vagrants" in official documentations during this period (Mortimer, 224). As will be seen below with the case of accused witch Elizabeth Clarke, however, familiarity can also breed contempt.

McGlynn is cited later for his mentions of the social significance of torture as a public spectacle,[13] and here it is the importance of *order* in the face of disequilibrium that seems to fuel this mob.[14] A "witch" has disrupted the village life, and things must be set right—a clear crime-and-punishment scenario. In "The Ideology of Punishment in Late Medieval English Towns," Carrel notes the significance of the "crowd" in these public spectacles:

> In addition to participating actively in the punishment, a crowd was an ideologically important aspect of the ritual for the authorities, as the public display of offenders was designed, in the words of contemporary sources, "to the terror of others," highlighting the belief that public punishment was a useful tool in deterring potential criminals from crime with the possibility of similar treatment. (306)

In this case punishment is called for by the gathered mob ("Burn her!"), and all sorts of helpful evidence is offered to make the case. And since a witch's effect on certain members or aspects of a small community could have a more broadly felt effect—for example, one man's ruined crops could starve many; one wet nurse's "paps" made desiccate means milk-siblings die—her case is therefore treated with a more "deterring" punishment—death by fire. The *Malleus Maleficarum*—the fifteenth-century treatise used to defend and encourage witch hunts—notes that the innocent will often be affected by the choices of the evil, "by Divine permission," sometimes because the community isn't as actively seeking out heresy as the Lord would like, sometimes because children are punished for the sins of their fathers, neighbors for neighbors, local clergy for the unassailed sins of their flock, and so on.[15] The onus of responsibility obviously sat heavily on ordinary folk to root out witches and demonic behavior as quickly as possible to avoid God's (and the Church's) collateral wrath. A papal bull of 1484 made the sin of *not* assisting with the search for heretics an excommunicable one, and threw open the door for a full-throated inquisition led by "Our dear sons [Heinrich] Kramer and [Jacob] Sprenger . . . [in] townships, districts, dioceses . . . of 'Northern Germany' and the 'borders of the Rhine.'"[16]

strange house/ruin—(PSC) According to cast members this was an actual abandoned, ruin home or set of homes in the Stirling area, and simply redressed (with moss on roofs, for example) as a medieval ruin.[17] An undressed photo of this location is included on facing page 5 of *MPHGB*.

This is the second village presented in the film, the first featuring the squalor and impoverishment that might seem typical of a medieval, plague-ridden village. This one is cleaner, less cluttered, and stocked with citizens who can seem to stay out of the mud. It's clear that none of these settings—and indeed, none of the film's settings to follow—are meant to represent the great religious houses of the period, which would have appeared quite heavenly in comparison. We see religious folk twice in *Holy Grail*—once at the start of this scene (monks banging their heads), and once toward the end of the film, where Brother Maynard and his brothers join the quest for a short but narratively significant time. The "typical monastery" of the Middle Ages would have had significantly more curb appeal, and therefore less relation to the filth depicted throughout the film.[18] Such a monastery would have been "situated in the open country or in a small town. The founders chose a site by a stream, to provide drinking and washing water, a fishpond and power mill, and also a sewage disposal system, often ingenious and very elaborate" (Bishop, *HBMA*, 138–42). The Benedictine monastery at Canterbury, for example, had a specially constructed "*necessarium*" that appears to be as elaborate and well kept as any of the more sacred buildings on the site, and is larger (at least on the site plan) than either the infirmary or the rectory (139–40). Gilliam's version of the foulness of Middle Ages sanitation will carry over in his next film, *Jabberwocky*, where the poor defecate out their windows directly into streams.[19]

A strange-looking knight stands outside . . .—(PSC) There's no mention in the printed script of why Bedevere looks "strange," though he seems oddly pregnant-shaped and has to keep lifting his visor to see properly. In many of the Arthurian sources Bedevere is Arthur's most trusted help; it is Bedevere who is given the task of returning Excalibur to the Lady of the Lake after Arthur's death, for example.[20]

It's likely that the Pythons have knit this Bedevere character from several sources, including a wise and thoughtful but sometimes addled Merlin-type, medieval English scientists including Robert Grosseteste (1175–1253) and Roger Bacon (1214–1294), but most particularly from an exemplar created by author T. H. White. White's character is initially known as the "ghost," whom Wart meets when he's searching for his "sulky hawk" lost by Kay in the forest:

"Excuse me," [Wart] said, when he was right under the mysterious figure, "but can you tell me the way back to Sir Ector's castle?"

At this the ghost jumped, so that it nearly fell off its horse, and gave out a muffled baaa through its visor, like a sheep.

"Excuse me," began the Wart again, and stopped, terrified, in the middle of his speech. For the *ghost lifted up its visor*, revealing two enormous eyes frosted like ice; exclaimed in an anxious voice, "What, what?"; took off its eyes—which turned out to be hornrimmed spectacles, fogged by being inside the helmet; tried to wipe them on the horse's mane—which only made them worse; lifted both hands above its head and tried to wipe them on its plume; dropped its lance; dropped the spectacles; *got off the horse to search for them—the visor shutting in the process; lifted its visor; bent down for the spectacles; stood up again as the visor shut once more, and exclaimed in a plaintive voice, "Oh, dear!"*

The Wart found the spectacles, wiped them, and gave them to the ghost, who immediately put them on (*the visor shut at once*) and began scrambling back on its horse for dear life. When it was there it held out its hand for the lance, which the Wart handed up, and, feeling all secure, *opened the visor with its left hand, and held it open.* It peered at the boy with one hand up—like a lost mariner searching for land—and exclaimed, "Ah-hah! Whom have we here, what?" (16; italics added)

The Pythons have clearly remembered and then borrowed Pellinore's look and mannerisms from White's *The Once and Future King*, down to the ill-fitting armor and plumed helmet.

Wart meets Pellinore in the forest, where the knight is lost but still vaguely searching for the Questing Beast. The visor gag will run on as often as Pellinore is in view.

In letters to friends Mary and L. J. Potts, White described the soon-to-be-published *Sword in the Stone* as "a preface to Malory," and (probably) jokingly admits that when he'd written his university thesis on "*Morte d'Arthur* . . . [I] did not read Malory," but had managed to do so in the intervening years (Gallix, 93).[21] His reappraisal of the Malorian world of Arthur is useful for us as a way of seeing other's reactions to Arthuriana, and specifically Malory's version of that world, which surprised White to no end, and influenced his version of these same characters and events:

> Then I was thrilled and astonished to find that (a) The thing was a perfect tragedy, with a beginning, a middle and an end implicit in the beginning and (b) the characters were real people with recognizable reactions which could be forecast. Mordred was hateful, Kay a decent chap with an inferiority complex, Gawaine that rarest of literary productions, a swine with a streak of solid decency. He was a sterling fellow to his own clan. Arthur, Lancelot and even Galahad were really glorious people—not pre-raphaelite prigs. (93)

White also admits to having done "a lot of research into the 14th–15th centuries, in a mild way," which some of the Pythons would understand, and that his intention was to be authentic but contemporary, which should ring familiar: "This *Sword in the Stone* . . . is packed with accurate historical knowledge and good allusive criticism of chivalry" (94). White even notes with some glee that he managed to work in a jab at the "fox huntin'" pastime, a very topical moment for a medieval story (94). Kurth Sprague mentions those things that seem to have made *Holy Grail* some kind of *rara avis*; importantly, though, he's speaking of White's work:

> [*The Once and Future King*] is full of anachronisms, allusions, and personal recollection. By envisioning for Arthur's story an idealized century imagined from Malory's fifteenth century, White was opening the door wide for all kinds of anachronisms. However, if one thinks of the time scheme of *TOAFK*—Arthur's story—as a kind of portmanteau into which is packed the trappings of nearly three centuries of history between 1216 and 1485, then the concept is easier to deal with. By a sort of accordion process the low points are dropped from consideration, and the high points are made to seem closer together.[22]

The Pythons have gone the next step, of course, providing "real people with recognizable reactions" (the sentries, Dennis, the Cart Driver) and pitting them against the idealistic, non-prigs like Launcelot, Galahad, and especially Arthur. They are, too, packing "the trappings of . . . centuries of history" into "an hourglass." The result is the portmanteau "once and future" world that has made *Holy Grail* watchable for more than forty years.

BEDEVERE releases a bird tied to a coconut—(PSC) This is *not* part of the printed final script, appearing in the filmed version only. This "strange-looking knight" is releasing a bird attached to a coconut. It's a funny sight gag that connects back to the European-swallow-cannot-carry-a-one-pound-coconut argument minutes earlier, a setup that will ultimately pay off for Arthur and Bedevere at the Bridge of Death; but it's more than that. Bedevere is performing an *experiment*, representing the return of at least the scientific method to Britain, which can start with the smallest but most necessary effort, according to Kantor: "First and foremost is the fact that scientific work consists of the activities of persons who are motivated to satisfy themselves about the nature of things. Accordingly, scientific work begins when permitted or demanded by the life conditions of such persons" (311). Bedevere is clearly motivated to satisfy himself in regard to birds and their coconut-carrying abilities, so he experiments. The eighth-century Persian scientist (or alchemist) Jabir Ibn Hayyan could have been Bedevere's colleague, at least in spirit:

> The first essential in chemistry is that thou shouldst perform practical work and conduct experiments, for he who performs not practical work nor makes experiments will never attain to the least degree of mastery. But thou, O my son, do thou experiments so that thou mayst acquire knowledge.[23]

We aren't told what experiments Bedevere conducted to prove to himself that the earth is "banana-shaped," or how he determined that sheep's bladders have anything to do with earthquakes, but it's clear he's at least satisfying his own scientific pursuits, and Arthur seems just as convinced. With the methodical Roman exodus and the resulting contraction of the Roman Empire in the fourth to fifth century and beyond, the lands on the empire's horizons, like Britain, its westernmost outpost, experienced a rapid diminishment in new learning and technologies. Roman roads and structures of all sorts fell into disrepair and disuse, the civic order that may have been in place under Roman occupation gave way to more local, tribal pursuits, and the keeping of libraries likely took a secondary importance to sustenance and survival. Freely notes that even as Rome's influence waned and Anglo-Saxon domination approached, however, there were still clusters of learning, primarily associated with religious orders, like the Benedictines (49–59). This monastic tradition of scholarship and teaching would last into the twelfth century and through great educators like Anselm, when, thanks to Bernard's influence, secular learning—the university—came to the fore (Poole, *DBMC*, 232–39). The great written works of the classical Greek thinkers began to find their way—via the monastic library and "scriptorium, a room where books needed by the monks were written out by copyists"—into Britain and into vernacular languages (seventh to eighth centuries).[24] Schools were soon to follow:

> Theodore [of Tarsus] and Hadrian [of Tunisia] founded a monastic school in Canterbury that began what has been called the golden age of Anglo-Saxon scholarship. According to the Venerable Bede, Theodore and Hadrian had "attracted a large number of students, into whose minds they poured the waters of wholesome knowledge day by day. In addition to instructing them in the holy Scriptures, they also taught their pupils poetry, astronomy, and the calculation of the church calendar. . . . Never have there been such happy times as these since the English settled Britain. (52)

Arthur and Bedevere might not have appreciated this "English" learning—meaning Anglo-Saxon models and beliefs—preferring "British" learning, which may be why Bedevere is still struggling in the Dark Ages of science with coconuts and birds, fruit-shaped earths, and miraculous sheep organs. But Bedevere's not alone, either, as new learning and old habits mixed in the centuries to come. In 1365 Thomas of Pisano, a doctor of astrology from the University of Bologna (and personal physician to King Charles), kept his patient the king on a regimen of "medicine containing mercury," meaning the king was ill constantly. Additionally, the good doctor performed his own scientific experiments "unique and ineffable," according to Tuchman,

> of which the object was to expel the English from France. Out of lead and tin, he fashioned hollow images of nude men, filled them with earth collected from the four corners of France, inscribed the foreheads with the names of King Edward or one of his captains, and, when the constellations were right, buried them face down while he recited spells to the effects that this was perpetual expulsion, annihilation, and burial of the said King, captains, and all adherents. (227)

This kind of belief system melds well with what the mob might have believed, including the malicious powers of a supposed witch, the efficacy of ordeals by water or fire, and the relative weights of a witch and a duck. Elsewhere, Emperor Frederick II (1194–1250) was well known for conducting his own scientific experiments, and even penned a scholarly book—*On the Art of Hunting with Birds*—that "is a manual of falconry, and at the same time, a scientific study of ornithology, based on direct observation" (Bishop, *HDMA*, 57). Bedevere's in good company, then, even compared to the best science and medicine (and astrology) of the Middle Ages.

FOURTH VILLAGER: ". . . Sir Bedevere . . ."—In Malory's version, as in the Pythons', "the bold Bedevere" is the knight who stands by Arthur the longest—he carries out Arthur's wish that Excalibur be returned to the lake (after feigning to do it once), and physically carries Arthur to his barge to journey to Avalon.[25] Bedevere will die as a hermit, after telling "the hermit that was tofore Bishop of Canterbury" of Arthur's end, according to Malory, and then: "there Sir Bedevere put upon him poor clothes, and served the hermit full lowly in fasting and in prayers."[26]

In a related printed script commentary (PSC), it seems that the Pythons may have decided on Bedevere's name (or his role in this particular scene) somewhat late in the screenplay's life. On *MPHGB*, 18 (the "She's a Witch" scene) the villagers are asking Sir Bedevere if there are ways one can tell if someone's a witch; he says there are, and one of them asks: "What are they, wise Sir Tristram?" That name is crossed out and "Sir Bedevere?" is penned next to it. It looks like "Tristram" had been the name for at least one draft, and a typed copy edit changing the name to "Bedevere" missed this one instance. (This same wholesale change of a character name will be seen later when Launcelot's horse's name is changed from "Lightning" to "Concorde"—each change made by hand on the pages of the final script.) This is the only place where the name "Tristram" appears in the rough draft, final draft, accompanying scribbled notes (in *MPHGB*), or the finished film.

Tristram was a knight who would become a Knight of the Round Table, in Malory, and would even fight Bedevere (in a tournament setting) at one point, the result being Bedevere "smitten to the earth both horse and man" (*LMD'A*, 1.286). Just a few pages later Tristram smites Gawain, as well: "[T]here Sir Gawain had the worse, for he pulled Sir Gawain from his horse, and there he was long upon foot, and defiled" (1.288). Later Tristram will joust and overcome forty knights, and do "marvellous deeds of arms" (1.301–2). Tristram even has his own named "book" in the Winchester version of *Le Morte Darthur*; Bedevere does not.[27]

Bedevere's heraldic symbol is a blasted (leafless), uprooted tree—its leaves on the ground around its bare roots—known as an "eradicated" and "lopped" (or "couped") image, in heraldic parlance. There were a number of tree heralds—many popular English trees—including oak, ash, linden, elm, spruce, beech, birch, chestnut, sycamore, and so on. Bedevere appears to be wearing likely the most popular tree chosen, the oak. Oaks and oak leaves also appear in dozens of illuminated manuscripts as part of the decoration, framing designs and devices, in depictions of forests, and so on, including the *Luttrell Psalter*, for example, from which Gilliam sketched as he prepared for the film's animations.

FIRST VILLAGER: "We have found a witch"—It won't be until 1233 that Pope Gregory IX (d. 1241) will issue a witchcraft-related edict allowing inquisitors to root out all manner of heretical teachings and activities, including sorcery and witchcraft. Ironically, the pope seems to have been acting to *curb* the rise of just these types of local mob "trials" of alleged heretics or those demon-influenced, almost always followed by immolations.[28] The fits of madness of Charles VI in the late fourteenth century led some in his coterie to blame sorcery, which:

> reflected a rising belief in the occult and demonic. Times of anxiety nourish belief in conspiracies of evil, which in the 14th century were seen as the work of persons or groups with access to

diabolical aid. Hence the rising specter of the witch. By the 1390s witchcraft had been officially recognized by the Inquisition as equivalent to heresy. (Tuchman, 515)

It would be well into the fifteenth century before Pope Innocent VIII's *Summis Desideratnes Affectibus* (1484) allegedly gave papal sanction to the pursuit and punishment of witches, and the use of the *Malleus Maleficarum* (*The Hammer of Witches*) as tools of the Inquisition (Cohn, 24–25). The papal bull was local to Germany,[29] but its influence quickly spread into much of Christendom. It would be the middle part of the seventeenth century in England before a witch fervor set in, coincidentally happening around the disturbances leading to the Interregnum, and certainly in response to the Salem Witch Trials in America.

As far as the period chosen by the Pythons (anywhere from the tenth through thirteenth centuries), the *Catholic Encyclopedia* finds little evidence of at least *widespread* "fanaticism."

> Altogether it may be said that in the first thirteen hundred years of the Christian era we find no trace of that fierce denunciation and persecution of supposed sorceresses which characterized the cruel witch hunts of a later age. In these earlier centuries a few individual prosecutions for witchcraft took place. (Thurston, "Witchcraft")

Norman Cohn supports this conclusion to a great extent in his very readable *Europe's Inner Demons*, and it becomes clear that the time period(s) chosen by the Pythons—whether 787, 932, 1167, or 1282 (or even the fourteenth century)—were not periods of *overactive* witch hunts; official retribution of the church tended to be reserved for heresies of thought and radical interpretations of the sacraments, for instance, and of the state for more treasonous behavior.[30] By the last two dates, however, there was considerable concern regarding heretical behaviors *within* the church, especially in northern Europe, and an inquisitorial regime was in place and used.

Also, Merlin is called a "witch" by detractors (grumbling knights) in *Le Morte Darthur*, though it's clear he is not the object of a fanaticism, more likely envy as he helps Arthur to the throne, and protects him thereafter (*LMD-WM*, 13). Gervase of Tilbury (c. 1150–c. 1228) supports this moniker, mentioning in *Otia Imperialia*—in the Creation section, no less—that Merlin is an example of one born of Incubi, "swallow[ing] the fabrications of Geoffrey of Monmouth" (Oman, 3; Gervase of Tilbury, *Otia Imperialia*, 97).

FIRST VILLAGER: "May we burn her?"[31]—We are clearly no longer in the communal, anarcho-syndicalist collective setting that Dennis and his mother describe earlier; Dennis has no lord to go to for permissions, and no action-ready crowd forms even when Dennis can demonstrate he's being repressed. It's also likely important that Dennis and his mother and political belief system were found in a remote, agricultural setting—in the liminal areas where "filth" can be dug—not in an urban area, closer to the traditional seats of hierarchical power. In this witch scene we've moved to a more urban setting, where the villagers are more likely craftsmen and tradesmen than collective, subsistence farmers, but with access, it would seem, to more up-to-date information. These urban villagers do go to a lord, of sorts, though Bedevere's actual authority over them is never explained. And even though these are village dwellers who are ostensibly exposed to the news and learning of the world, they are the ones dragging an alleged witch to her death based on appearance, superstition, and unprovable allegations.

The resort to immolation is likely arising from these peasants' knowledge (via their clergy) of the Bible's interdiction against this kind of evil, found in *Exodus*: "Thou shalt not suffer a witch to live" (22:18). It's interesting that these villagers so confounded bring the woman to a knight, and seemingly a man of science, and *not* to their local clergyman, who was the more likely font of knowledge on things supernatural, or evil.[32]

The female enchantress of the Arthurian tales, Morgan le Fay (Arthur's half-sister) was so feared and hated that "many knights wished her burnt" (*LMD'A*, 1.141). In fact, the vigilantic sequence of events in chapter fifteen leading to this grim wish should read familiar:

Then said Morgan, "Saw ye Arthur, my brother?"

"Yea," said her knights, "right well, and that ye should have found and we might have stirred from one stead, for by his armyvestal countenance he would have caused us to have fled."

"I believe you," said Morgan.

Anon after as she rode she met a knight leading another knight on his horse before him, bound hand and foot, blindfold, to have drowned him in a fountain. When she saw this knight so bound, she asked him, "What will ye do with that knight?"

"Lady," said he, "I will drown him."

"For what cause?" she asked.

"For I found him with my wife, and she shall have the same death anon."

"That were pity," said Morgan le Fay. "Now, what say ye, knight, is it truth that he saith of you?" she said to the knight that should be drowned.

"Nay truly, madam, he saith not right on me."

"Of whence be ye," said Morgan le Fay, "and of what country?"

"I am of the court of King Arthur, and my name is Manassen, cousin unto Accolon of Gaul."

"Ye say well," said she, "and for the love of him ye shall be delivered, and ye shall have your adversary in the same case ye be in."

So Manassen was loosed and the other knight bound. And anon Manassen unarmed him, and armed himself in his harness, and so mounted on horseback, and the knight afore him, and so threw him into the fountain and drowned him.[33]

Morgan then tells Manassen to go to Arthur, tell him of her interference, and that it was for "love of Accolon"[34]—essentially an act of spite and revenge. There is no such villainy here in the village where we encounter Bedevere and the witch is accused, just a host of eager simpletons.

In *The Seventh Seal*, the Knight and Jöns emerge from a church when they encounter an accused woman being similarly manhandled, but the scene is far more bleak than that painted by the Pythons, or even Malory:

Outside the church, four soldiers and a monk are in the process of putting a woman in the stocks. Her face is pale and child-like, her head has been shaved, and her knuckles are bloody and broken. Her eyes are wide open, yet she doesn't appear to be fully conscious.

JÖNS and the KNIGHT stop and watch in silence. The soldiers are working quickly and skillfully, but they seem frightened and dejected. The monk mumbles from a small book. One of the soldiers picks up a wooden bucket and with his hand begins to smear a bloody paste on the wall of the church and around the woman. JÖNS holds his nose.

The paste is a noxious soup meant to keep the devil away, the soldiers say. The woman has been accused of "carnal intercourse with the Evil One," and she is to be burned the following day. The Knight asks her if she's seen the devil—he's wondering about the encounter he's already had with Death—and the monk gives the real reason for her torture: "[S]he is believed to have caused the pestilence with which we are affected." Our young woman ("Miss Islington") accused of being a witch isn't blamed for the plague, but she has, allegedly, turned one man into a newt, albeit briefly. In Malory it is the enchantress Morgan who both frees and condemns, for her own purposes; in *The Seventh Seal* it is the monk—a learned man—who assures that the woman is condemned and then executed; in *Holy Grail*, it is the wise Sir Bedevere, a man of science.

It's also important that the villagers are asking *permission* of anyone—clerical or secular, knight or lord—to burn the witch they've found, as opposed to just carrying out the sentence themselves. As Murray points out in "Medieval Origins of the Witch Hunt," there are few if any records from the early Middle Ages of *official* proceedings against alleged witches, but there are a number of records suggesting that "[l]ynchings and private vengeance for *maleficia*" happened quite regularly, and seemed to be contained within the village where the activities occurred (66). Citing Norman Cohn's[35] scholarly work in the field, Murray points out that the burden of proof could be burdensome indeed, yet another reason why a mob would ask politely to burn a witch:

> While this ambivalence may have been one reason for the paucity of *maleficium* trials before the late middle ages, there was a more material one. It lay in legal procedure. In most times and places in the early and central middle ages, prosecution for this kind of offence depended on accusation by a private citizen. There was a reason why a private citizen should not accuse another before a law court. By the *lex talionis* an unsuccessful accuser changed places with his intended victim,[36] *i.e.*, was in this case drowned or burned. Who would risk that in a matter so uncertain of proof? (67)

So if the villagers want vengeance on this beautiful witch yet don't want to heft the burden of proof individually, they approach the local knight instead of a court, manufacture evidence that seems insurmountable, and then speak as a mob. With some finagling of logic and new science the mob goes happily on its way, their witch-burning officially sanctioned.

This is also a fair question given the three treatment possibilities laid out by the *Malleus Maleficarum* for "Destroying and Curing Witchcraft": "It is submitted that it must be cured either by human power, or by diabolic, or Divine power."[37] The logic is airtight, bodes poorly for the accused, and means a long wait for the afflicted:

> It cannot be by the first ["human power"]; for the lower power cannot counteract the higher, having no control over that which is outside its own natural capacity. Neither can it be by Divine power; for this would be a miracle, which God performs only at His own will, and not at the instance of men. . . . Also it appears that it is very rarely that men are delivered from a bewitchment by calling on God's help or the prayers of the Saints. Therefore it follows that they can only be delivered by the help of devils; and it is unlawful to seek such help. (*MM*, 155–56)

The Villager ("Mr. Newt") who was transformed gets better on his own, and the accused witch will continue to be a witch and suffer the consequences.

Lastly, having started in earnest in 1563 following the passage of a new Witchcraft Act—the first hanging in Essex coming in 1564, and by 1600 more than two hundred trials—witch burning would remain a part of British life until the eighteenth century, after the publication of the Witchcraft Act of 1735.[38] The act acknowledged that witchcraft and witches did not exist, but that the claim to be a witch or to have a witch's powers (to frighten, intimidate, or gain financially from others) was a punishable offense.

SECOND VILLAGER: "I got better"—This was actually the usual occurrence after an enchantment, according to *The Hammer of Witches*—the bewitched had to simply be patient, and the spell just wore off: "No operation of witchcraft has a permanent affect among us."[39] Again, it was "unlawful" for the bewitched to seek a cure from either the witch who cursed him or, as John Rivet[40] would find out, from another cunning woman even with good intentions; also, other men and women were likely no help, and God would only intervene at His desire. There weren't many choices for the patient believer beyond being believing and being patient.

ALL: "A witch! Burn her!"—This knee-jerk response of torture and destruction at the discovery of something new or frightening isn't a Python creation. The Cistercian monk and chronicler Ralph of Coggeshall (d. 1227) reported the story of a wild man who'd been caught in the sea, and was brought to the castle at Orford. The wild man did not speak, Ralph notes matter-of-factly, not even under extreme duress: "He was naked and presented a human appearance in every part of his body. When taken to church he showed no signs of reverence or belief however often he saw holy things. He did not wish to utter a word, even when hung by the feet and subject to dire and frequent torture."[41] Another story reported as factual by Gervase of Tilbury[42] involved a Norfolk church congregation's sighting of an anchor descending from the clouds:

> The anchor was caught on a tombstone, attached to it and leading up into the clouds was a heavy chain. All of a sudden a sailor appeared from the cloud, climbing down the chain hand by hand using the same technique as we do. He was seized by the churchgoers. The otherworld sailor suffocated by the moistness of our denser air and died in their grasp.[43]

In both cases the church-going and clearly superstitious local folk made judgments of their own, followed by at least an assay of judgment from their church leaders. (The banality with which the violence against the strangers is treated is chilling—hung and tortured, seized and suffocated—at least the Pythons are doing it for a larf.) Again, these incidents aren't reported as ephemera, they are as real and historical as any civic event, birth or death, or the like. As Peter Bartlett points out, in the early Middle Ages "the observable world and the world of divine revelation, the natural and the supernatural, coexist quite comfortably."[44]

Lastly, a story from the animal kingdom as evidence that there is order in all things (animals can form mobs, too); this also from Gervase, and cited by Oman:

> Gervase's native Essex provides one of the most entertaining stories which he has recorded from the eastern counties. It is not, he remarks, generally known that birds strive to equal men in punishing adulterers. . . . One day whilst the knights of Richard de Lucy were in a field near his castle of Ongar, a flight of swans descended and began to hold a council. One in the midst, like the prosecutor or his lord, made a long squawking declamation and then the judges on one side commanded the accused to be produced. Two swans sent by the judges led her into the centre. After much further squawking the judges decided that the adulteress should be expelled from the flock whereupon the assembly fell upon her and having plucked out her feathers left her to perish from cold. (Oman, 7–8; *Otia Imperialia*, 749–50)

No sign of the offending *male* swan, of course. It would have been these kinds of homiletic stories told by local clergy, perhaps, which inspired God-fearing locals to not only keep a keen watch for the chattels of sin in their midst, but to root them out when espied.

BEDEVERE: "How do you know she is a witch?"—Bedevere is simply, rightly asking for proof before proceeding. According to Levack,[45] it was the "long tradition of judicial centralization" in England that helped keep the witch frenzy in check (as well as any excesses that *could* have arisen during the Inquisition, had it taken hold in England) as compared to Germany and most of Western Europe; the common law helped attenuate these witch prosecutions, resulting in "conviction and execution rates . . .exceptionally low by continental

European standards" (99–100). Legal courts would have convened twice a year (county as-sizes[46]) where cases could be heard, and by the "later Middle Ages," at least, such hasty trials and executions would have been avoided (100).

It wouldn't be until the unrest of the English Civil War[47] period (1642–1651) and a very cold winter of 1644 that organized witch purges reappeared in England, where the physical torture of the accused had been forbidden, though self-appointed "witchfinders" like Matthew Hopkins and John Stearne managed anyway. Hopkins had been stirred to action by an accusation of witchcraft against a Manningtree neighbor, Elizabeth Clarke, who happened to have one leg, no husband, and the misfortune of being poverty stricken—to many she may have simply "looked like" someone in league with the devil.[48] With the "entire nation [seemingly] in the grip of an incurable malady," according to Gaskill, and the "ideological war" to abolish popery and idolatry a bloody mess, scapegoats were required, and were easily found (2). When a man whose wife had fallen inexplicably ill attended a known "cunning" woman, a folk healer, and this woman diagnosed bewitchment as the cause of his wife's suffering, the man, John Rivet, identified neighbor Clarke as the evil source (2–3). During examination—and after a thorough physical exam by local matrons and the discovery of abnormal "teats"—without torture, excepting involuntary confinement and sleep deprivation, Clarke would admit to being in league with the devil, confess to many acts of *maleficia*, and name five other women, as well.[49] Eventually, fifteen witches in all would be hanged, Clarke included.

ALL: "She looks like one"—Even though the script attributes this to the mob in general, Palin's character—at the front with Idle and Cleese and the accused—actually shouts out the line. In the Cast List[50] he is known as "Mr. Duck (A Village Carpenter Who Is Almost Keener Than Anyone Else to Burn Witches)" (*MPHGB*, 90).

Like Arthur who must be a king thanks to the way he looks, and the peasant who from behind appears to be a woman, it is appearance that matters. As Ian Mortimer points out: "In medieval society, what you wear denotes what you are" (*The Time Traveler's Guide to Medieval England*, 103). This is also a rather sobering declaration, historically, as the flimsiest of proofs of witchcraft and consorting with the devil were quite enough to not only bring charges, but often were sufficient to start a witch hunt, involving dozens of women. In Ireland in the case of Dame Alice Kyteler (b. 1280), the deaths of her four wealthy husbands (coupled with her own increasing wealth) sparked jealousy, at first, and then outright suspicions from neighbors and disinherited family members, which led to charges of poisonings and witchcraft and eventually saw at least one of Dame Alice's "accomplices" tortured and burned. Dame Alice and her associates were charged with

> renouncing Christ, making sacrifices of living chickens to demons, cursing their husbands, and creating unguents from the intestines of the chickens they had sacrificed, "with certain loathly worms and various herbs, and dead men's nails . . . and garments of children that died unbaptised, and many other detestable ingredients, boiled together over an oak-fire in the skull of a beheaded thief." (Mortimer, 76)

And while she *may* have been poisoning husbands—her fourth husband died in agony and quite suspiciously—it's seems clear the *inheritance* issues were far more important to those who denounced Dame Alice. Dame Alice herself escaped from Ireland to England, where such punishments were much less frequent (76).

Later witch hunts had their genesis in the earlier search for "others" in the faith, for interpreters of the sacraments, meaning the search for heretics in the Catholic Church. According to Norman Cohn, two self-appointed but popular (and effective) inquisitors—Conrad Torso and a man known as "Johannes"—"claimed to be able to detect a heretic by his or her appearance; and as they proceeded from town to town and village to village they denounced people on these purely intuitive grounds" (26). Dozens of the Rhineland-area villagers were consigned to the flames before higher authorities stepped in and brought an end to the demonological work of Torso, Johannes, and Conrad of Marburg.[51] An appearance (of difference) may also have been a convenient charge against Anne Boleyn (c. 1501–1536), who is said to have had an extra finger on one hand and very visible mole or goiter on her neck—meaning she could "look like" a disfigured, and thus bewitched, person.

It was also a concern in the Middle Ages, especially after the ravages of the Great Plague thinned the population in cities, and wages and work improved, that "appearances" could be deceptive:

> Moreover, legislation was enacted to curb not only the excessive rewards enjoyed by common people, but the manner in which they spent their ill-gotten gains. A statute in 1363 was directed towards the correction of "the outrageous and excessive apparel of divers people against their estate and degree," and prescribed detailed regulations for the dress of grooms, agricultural workers and those lowly persons who did not have goods to the value of 40s., thereby confirming the exasperation felt by Henry Knighton with "the elation of the inferior people in dress and accoutrements in these days, so that one person cannot be discerned from another, in splendour of dress or belongings." (Hatcher, 18)

Remember that Joan of Arc was also at least partly condemned because of her dress, the way she looked—*difformitate habitus*—she had dressed herself as a man.[52]

And though not necessarily charged as a *criminal* in this scene from *Holy Grail*, the eagerness of the young woman's accusers was often a feature of Middle Ages "justice," as was a diminished burden of proof:

> Fear bred suspicion, the combination sometimes being sufficient for conviction: in early fourteenth-century London, trial witnesses declared that Walter Foyle "commonly leaves the city with arms and a greyhound at the time of vespers, and returns in the morning"; this was taken as a sign that he was up to no good and was enough to land him a lengthy prison sentence. (McGlynn, 54–55)

But as the following "*beautiful YOUNG GIRL*" entry indicates, the Python version of what a witch "looks like" doesn't match up with late Middle Ages contributors:

> Cranky, acerbic and often angry about her plight, she attracted attention, hostility, suspicion and fear. Sometimes, but by no means always, she possessed physical characteristics that made her appear even more different from the norm. For Reginald Scot,[53] witches were "commonly old, lame, blear-eyed, pale, foul and full of wrinkles . . . lean and deformed, showing melancholy in their faces to the horror of all that see them." (Levack, 162)

There is no indication that the young woman Miss Islington has any of the traditional background elements of the medieval witch, either—she isn't old or lame or disfigured, she isn't particularly offensive or an outsider, she's combative, but with reason. She *may* have practiced witchcraft, but we only have the mob's word on that. Ultimately she doesn't fit the *visual* profile for a witch, so the villagers had to dress her to the part. In this they might have been counting on a popular prosecutorial tool of "manifest ill-fame," used so effectively in the first quarter of the fourteenth century against Hugh Despenser the Elder (1261–1326), a method also known as a "conviction by notoriety." In that case Despenser—a longtime supporter of Edward II—had been run to ground in Bristol as Edward's estranged queen Isabella (now dallying with Roger Mortimer[54]) and her loyal followers surrounded him. Without the king's presence, a "conviction by the king's record" was impossible, so magnates were called, evidence was rehearsed, and, "by the clamour of the people,"[55] a "veneer of legality" was brushed over the proceedings, and old Despenser was found guilty in October 1326 (McKisack, 85–87). By the loud voice of the people (as with the mob hustling Miss Islington around) a guilty verdict was quickly reached, and Despenser was hanged and quartered, and his head was set on public display.[56] Despenser's son, also named Hugh (1286–1326), was caught as well, similarly tried, and executed less than a month later. Seventy years later the enthroned but unliked and embattled King Richard II used similar "notoriety" arguments against Gloucester (Thomas of Woodstock), securing a conviction based on the duke having earlier appeared "in warlike array" in Harringay, ready to take London by force; it turns out Gloucester had already been killed, likely by those close to the king (481–482). Again, at Harringay Gloucester "looked like" an enemy, a threat, and he was later convicted of being such, and would have been executed.

. . . *a beautiful YOUNG GIRL (MISS ISLINGTON)* . . .—(PSC) Turns out this is *not* Miss Islington, but Connie Booth (b. 1944). Booth and Cleese had been married since 1968, and would divorce in 1978. She had appeared in *MPFC* as an extra and walk-on a number of times, and would go on to cocreate *Fawlty Towers* with Cleese.[57] On the Cast List page of *MPHGB* she is listed simply as "The Witch" (90).

This "Miss Islington" reference may be another hint toward the well-known "Page Three Girls" featured in Rupert Murdoch's *Sun* newspaper since 1969. The girls were often referred to by their first names and hometown, and are discussed in *MPFC*, Ep. 24.[58] Several former "Page Three Girls" appeared in *Flying Circus* in bit parts, including Flanagan and Mary Millington.[59] A London borough (and home to Python friend and sometime cowriter Douglas Adams), Islington had become a crowded, row house neighborhood in the nineteenth century and was damaged significantly during World War II, leading to clearance and rebuilding, which progressed slowly. It may be that since *Holy Grail* depicts a disease- and filth-ridden medieval world, the blighted nature of Islington prompted this mention, especially apparent since the 1960s:

> Slum clearance [in Islington] was undertaken, but in 1967 of the London boroughs Islington still had the most multi-occupied dwellings, representing 59 per cent of the total, and the most households, 77 per cent of the total number, lacking such basic amenities as their own stove, sink, bath, and W.C.[60] It was London's most densely populated M.B.[61] in 1951, being very short of public open space, and in 1968 its density at 70 persons per acre (including Finsbury) far exceeded its neighbours Hackney at 52 and Camden at 45.[62]

A certain amount of gentrification followed the slum clearing, meaning the area was being "reclaimed" and rehabilitated—things being "knocked through"—by the time *MPHG* was being produced.

The Miss United Kingdom pageant was broadcast on BBC 1 on 15 August 1973, a show the *Times* called a "cheesecake spectacular," but that "was bound to draw the crowds."[63] Also in 1973, a previous participant in the Miss United Kingdom contest representing Islington, Margaret Tuttle, was in the news. This former Miss Islington was demanding Her Majesty's government provide artificial insemination so that her incarcerated husband could impregnate her—he was serving an eighteen-year sentence for armed robbery, and she didn't want to wait through the sentence to have children with him.[64] This was a page-one story in most London newspapers of the day.

WITCH: "I am not a witch. I am not a witch."—This kind of retort wouldn't have been allowed in many courts, religious or lay. It wasn't often that the accused was allowed to speak on his or her own behalf, and most confessions in trials of heresy came after the promise or practice of torture. Like Miss Islington here, Joan of Arc was allowed "no advocate or defender," but she was able to defend herself (she seems to have been quite bright, though illiterate) during five long months of examination. In the end, rather than being condemned through some specious logical torsions involving ducks and floating churches, as Miss Islington suffered, Joan was condemned by the "sway[ing] of public opinion," and the presentation of false evidence (*HBMA*, 392). In secular and parliamentary courts this same judicial malfeasance could also be found, including the infamous Merciless Parliament of 1388. There the favorites of Richard II's court were charged with treason by the Lords Appellant (including magnates Gloucester, Arundel, and Warwick[65]), and long-simmering contentions were finally brought to a boil, causing great destruction:

> Never before in our history, not even in the dark days of Edward II, had legal sanction been claimed for the destruction on such flimsy legal pretexts of so many men of gentle birth. It may readily be conceded that the courtiers, or most of them, were greedy, irresponsible, provocative, and wrong-headed; but none of them was a criminal and none was deserving of murder by act of parliament. (McKisack, 459)

Miss Islington may "look like" a witch, but she likely isn't one; she has her few denials and a tossed-off "It's a fair cop" before she's hustled off to be committed to the pyre. Unlike Joan's trial, where the presiding bishop, Cauchon, was clearly manufacturing evidence and falsifying the record to suit his purposes (convicting Joan and turning her over to the English), Bedevere and the mob seem to be as earnest and even guileless in the face of obvious witchcraft—they simply act accordingly, dealing with the "facts" of her guilt as they truly see them.[66]

And though it may sound odd, denial was likely the *least* effective means of defense in a witch trial. Jeffrey Russell explains the process in the early fifteenth century that an accused could expect:

> If the witch obdured under torture, professing her innocence while urged by the most terrible agonies to do otherwise, her captors assumed that the Devil was assisting her, perhaps through the use of magical amulets or charms concealed upon her body. If the witch's helplessness in captivity seemed to belie the hideous powers ascribed to her, this too was a trick of the Devil's to disarm the Inquisitors, or else a miracle of Christ's enacted to preserve his champions from harm. Once a woman had been arrested for witchcraft, there was very little that could save her from a harsh sentence. (*Witchcraft in the Middle Ages*, 203–4)

And that sentence, as years passed and various popes saw more and more heretical portents, turned fiery. Russell continues: "From the fifteenth century onward, witches were treated even more severely than heretics, being burned upon first conviction rather than upon relapse" (151).

Elizabeth Reis discusses a 1692 case an ocean away in America, where a man, frightened by a black hog that charged him, "threatening to devour him," was certain his neighbor had bewitched the animal, and so accused her:

> What could a woman confronted with "evidence" like this do? Denial was dangerous, as all the women who denied the charges were hanged.[67] They could not successfully prove that they had

had no dealings, however trivial, with the devil; in other words, that they had not sinned in any way. Confession was a more promising strategy to save one's life.[68]

Back in England, the *Malleus Maleficarum* gives ample opportunity for local authorities to wait out a confession from the accused heretic. After the accused has been convicted—in this case "by the evidence of witnesses against whom [s]he can take no legitimate exception"[69]—authorities are encouraged to keep the accused in appropriate restraints ("fettered and chained") and to visit her often, with other authorities and with friends and even witnesses—all to convince the accused to begin the confession process.[70] This can take a full year, if necessary, during which witnesses can change their statements if needed, or the accused can have a change of heart. If none of this happens, and the accused continues in denial, then she will be labeled an "impenitent heretic," sentenced to death, and "abandoned" to the secular courts where "just men zealous for the faith" await to confirm the sentence and carry out execution (259–60). This transfer of corporal authority—from ecclesiastical to judicial courts—was common in the Middle Ages, especially in northern Europe, where "purification" by fire meant "being burned at the stake," according to Fossier, "and it was the Church that decided to use this punishment against the heretic or the witch, although it did not dare light the fire itself" (*The Axe and the Oath*, 270). In Miss Islington's case, of course, she is already in the hands of the "zealous," and the promised sympathy of an ecclesiastical court is moot; it is Bedevere's "new science"—unemotional and coldly rational—that confirms both the woman's status and her sentence, and the mob can happily set things right.

WITCH: "They dressed me up like this"—Again, unlike the accusers in Joan of Arc's trial—who knowingly manufactured and twisted evidence to ensure a conviction—the mob here seems to be following institutional guidelines of some sort for identifying, presenting, and then exterminating a witch. If she's not dressed as one, then she must be dressed. (Joan had chosen boy's clothing herself, for safety in travel and for ease of movement when astride a horse.) The evidences are clear—Miss Islington's physical deformity, her clothing, her malevolent powers—it's all in order, such that when the scale "proves" she weighs as much as a duck, even the accused is convinced (agreeing "It's a fair cop").

WITCH: "This is not my nose. It's a false one"—This rather obvious false type of nose appeared earlier in *MPFC*, Ep. 19, the "Raymond Luxury Yacht" sketch, and was there described as a cry for attention, not a disguise.[71]

The costuming for the witch here (not including the funnel hat) looks to be right off the pages of the plentiful seventeenth-century woodcuts depicting witches with pointed hats and, occasionally, exaggerated features. The sixteenth and seventeenth centuries saw the circulation of many "witch pamphlets"—they offered popular, salacious reading with titles like *The Witch of Edmonton*, *A Certaine Relation of the Hog-faced Gentlewoman called Mistris Tannakin Skinker*, and *The Wonderful Discoverie of the Witchcrafts of Margaret and Phillip Flower*, among many others. As she has been costumed by the villagers, Miss Islington looks very much like the crone on the cover of *A Most Certain, Strange, and True Discovery of a Witch*, which had been printed by John Hammond in 1643.[72] The treatment of the witch in this last pamphlet rings quite familiar. A group of soldiers (attached to the Earl of Essex) spot a woman seemingly walking on water in a river near Newbury, and on closer inspection determine she is riding a plank or board, "too and fro she fleeted on the water," with no apparent means of propulsion. The spooked soldiers decide they have to "ambush" this "divellish woman," and though they are afraid,

> seized on her by the armes, demanding what she was? but the woman no whit replying any words unto them, they brought her to the Commanders, to whom though mightily she was urged she

did reply as little: so consulting with themselues what should be done with her, being it so apparently appeard she was a witch, being loth to let her goe, & as loth to carry her with them, so they resolved with themselves, to make a shot at here, and gave order to a couple of their Souldiers that were approved good marks-men, to charge and shoot her straight, which they prepared to doe: so setting her boult upright against a mud banke or wall; two of the Souldiers according to their command made themselues ready, where having taken aime gave fire and shot at her as thinking sure they had sped her, but with a deriding and loud laughter at them she caught their bullets in her hands and chew'd them, which was a stronger testimony then the water, that she was the same that their imaginations thought her for to be, so resolving with themselves if either fire or sword or halter were sufficient for to make an and of her. (6)

Bullets miss her at point blank range, even ricocheting back at the soldiers, and the woman simply laughs at them "in a most contemptible way of scorn" (7). They then remember hearing somewhere that cutting a witch across the temple area would drain her blood just enough to render her fit for "triall." Hearing this, she knew they could overcome her sorcery and that "the Devill had left her and her power was gone" (7). One of the soldiers then puts a gun to her head, fires, and she dies.

Just as these men had heard somewhere how to debilitate a witch, the mob in *MPHG* know to dress their "witch" properly—including the false nose—before presenting her for summary judgment. See "a fair cop" below for more on this witch, and her connection to Miss Islington.

FIRST VILLAGER: "And the hat. But she is a witch"—The funnel hat is employed by Hieronymus Bosch in many of his works, often to denote a dim, gullible, or untrustworthy character, but sometimes more. In Bosch's rough sketch "Witches," one of his witches rides a barrel pulled by a rooster, and she hefts a large funnel as if it were an umbrella.[73] Bosch scholar Larry Silver writes of the page of witches, and of this character specifically:

> Moreover, she carries the funnel like an umbrella; in Bosch's paintings, this item, too, was associated with either stupidity or deceit (e.g., the demonic messenger in the left wing of the St. Anthony triptych or the surgeon in the Stone of Folly). Folly and sin were closely linked in late-medieval morality. (*Hieronymus Bosch*, 290)

As Silver mentions, the funnel hat also sits on the head of a beaked, two-legged creature on skates in the left panel of Bosch's *The Temptation of St. Anthony*, from which Gilliam will sketch as he prepares for the animated sequences. See appendix A, "Facing Pages," for much more on the Bosch influence on *Holy Grail*.

BEDEVERE: "Did you dress her up like this?"—Bedevere is searching for culpability here, and already sees that these villagers are presenting him with a "witch," according to their idea of what a witch looks like, and based on their own lack of *pro nostro vitio*, of their own faults. A number of contemporary Middle Ages scholars and commentators mention the rampant sin and ungodliness of the time, blaming people for the fallen state of the world, while those same fallen looked to shrug that blame off on someone else. The rector of Dry Drayton near Cambridge, Richard Greenham, had struggled mightily with his flock's lack of faith and personal execration, even in the face of sin, failed crops, and disease. Gaskill writes: "In the end Greenham admitted defeat, blaming rampant superstition and his parishioners' tendency to hold witches responsible for their misfortunes rather than searching their own sinful hearts and praying for guidance."[74]

FIRST VILLAGER: ". . .she has got a wart"—Known as "Devil's Marks" or witches' marks, any physical imperfection or abnormality could be an outward sign of a devilish soul, the leftovers of intercourse with a demon, a teat for suckling imps—basically the devil's imprimatur on one of his own. These marks were generally discovered during a thorough physical search—usually by local matrons, occasionally by a doctor—and were the first hint that the accused had some league with the devil (Gaskill, 107–8). Unusual scars, warts, teats, genital abnormalities, even hemorrhoids could be indications—the marks were not generally as visible as Miss Islington's wart, hence the rigorous physical examinations. In this case, it's more likely that the Pythons are using the wart-on-the-face element in a more cartoony way, borrowing from the WB character Witch Hazel,[75] who looks the classic modern witch—pointy hat, broomstick, crooked nose, and wart. (Elsewhere, Anne Boleyn's mole or goiter and possibly a tiny sixth finger figured into the bevy of charges that included witchcraft, incest, and treason, leading to her execution in 1536.) Here, the villagers seem to know at least the semantic elements necessary to make up the syntax "witch," and they've managed to provide most of these themselves. It remains for the wise Sir Bedevere to inform them of the next steps in not witch-finding, but witch-confirming.

In the end credits provided in the printed script but not part of the finished film, this character (played by Idle) is known as "Mr. Blint (A Village Ne'er Do Well Very Keen on Burning Witches)" (*MPHGB*, 90). And while "Blint" is an actual surname, it can also mean a fool, and is related to "blind." Our Mr. Blint seems all of these.

SECOND VILLAGER: "She turned <u>me</u> into a newt"—The *Malleus Maleficarum* confirms that a witch can indeed *seem* to do this. "Question X" asks and answers "Whether Witches can by some Glamour[76] Change Men into Beasts," while Chapter VIII in part II explains "Of the Manner whereby they Change Men into the Shapes of Beasts."[77] The fact that this man[78] is claiming to have been turned into a newt—an amphibian, a belly crawler and swamp dweller—is also important, and revealing. Since the newt is one of the "imperfect" creatures that can both be created by God and "generated from putrefaction,"[79] it's all the more likely that a witch could or would accomplish or attempt this transformation spell. It's not likely that Mr. Newt knows this, but it isn't impossible, either. If the man actually *believes* he has been turned into a newt, the *Malleus Maleficarum* declares that he has been made "destitute of Divine grace"—for which he must take some responsibility—and undergo a "good confession" and be "reconciled to God" (173). And since the *MM* does not concede that the devil or his minions have the power to *actually* transform man into beast, those who think themselves so transformed are deceived by "glamour," as are those who see the victim as transformed (173–75). The *MM* goes on to say that the beast transformation magic goes on in eastern countries and is not as prevalent in western Europe.

The witch's powers and her appearance are part of the evolving "lore" of unnatural superstition during the later Middle Ages, which would lead to witch trials and burnings, and which were based on manufactured, agreed-upon traits:

> Since confessions in trials for sorcery were extracted by torture, they tended to reflect the accusations of diabolic power drawn up by the prosecutors. . . . The lore developed as much from the minds of the prosecutor as from the hallucinations of the accused [when "confessing" under torture], and together they laid the ground for the rage against witchcraft that was to explode upon the [fifteenth] century. (Tuchman, 318–19)

So the villagers have "proof" of this woman's evil—in her appearance and her malignant powers—but *Candide* illustrates that such cause-and-effect relationships aren't necessary for this kind of public punishment, or auto-da-fé. As mentioned earlier, Candide and Dr. Pangloss are drawn into this symbolic exercise simply for the common good:

After the earthquake, which had destroyed three-quarters of the city of Lisbon, the wise men of that country could think of no means more effectual to preserve the kingdom from utter ruin than to entertain the people with an auto-da-fe, it having been decided by the University of Coimbra, that the sight of several persons being burned alive in great ceremony is an infallible secret for preventing earthquakes. (Ch. 6)

The villagers in *MPHG* have decided that burning a witch "is an infallible secret for preventing" men being temporarily turned into newts, and eventually, when that proposition falls down, it's decided to "burn her anyway." In this, the village is united, and order will be restored.

This also rings familiar to the treatment of the female Neoplatonist scholar Hypatia (c. 350–415), whose gifts for learning mathematics and philosophy were prodigious. She was a woman, unmarried, beautiful, a "pagan," and unafraid to teach of Aristotle and Plato in the streets. She inspired many and angered or threatened many more. After intervening in a conflict between powerful men (representatives of civic and church government), her fate was sealed, according to *Ecclesiastical History* (VII.15):

[S]he fell a victim to the political jealousy which at that time prevailed. For as she had frequent interviews with Orestes, it was calumniously reported among the Christian populace, that it was she who prevented Orestes from being reconciled to the bishop. Some of them therefore, hurried away by a fierce and bigoted zeal, whose ringleader was a reader named Peter, waylaid her returning home, and dragging her from her carriage, they took her to the church called Caesareum, where they completely stripped her, and then murdered her with tiles [oyster shells]. After tearing her body in pieces, they took her mangled limbs to a place called Cinaron, and there burnt them. This affair brought not the least opprobrium, not only upon Cyril, but also upon the whole Alexandrian church. And surely nothing can be farther from the spirit of Christianity than the allowance of massacres, fights, and transactions of that sort.[80]

The Bishop of Nikiu, however, writing for the "believers" in Jesus Christ, laid out all the reasons Hypatia was a threat. She was a

female philosopher, a pagan . . . she was devoted at all times to magic, astrolabes and instruments of music, and she beguiled many people through Satanic wiles. And the governor of the city honoured her exceedingly; for she had beguiled him through her magic. And he ceased attending church as had been his custom. . . . And he not only did this, but he drew many believers to her, and he himself received the unbelievers at his house. . . . And thereafter a multitude of believers in God arose under the guidance of Peter the magistrate—now this Peter was a perfect believer in all respects in Jesus Christ—and they proceeded to seek for the pagan woman who had beguiled the people of the city and the prefect through her enchantments.[81]

So the women's appearance (the witch "looks like one"; Hypatia was beguiling), their actions (the witch uses magic; Hypatia her magic and "wiles"), and their "enchantments" that transform one man "into a newt" and another from noble believer to pagan, rendered both Miss Islington and Hypatia easy targets, and they will suffer the same fate.

Also, it is much later than the period depicted by the Pythons, but the frenzy surrounding satanic influences and witchcraft in particular was rife in the Middle Ages and well beyond:

Already, before the close of the fifteenth century, Pope Innocent VIII had issued the startling bull by which he called on the archbishops, bishops, and other clergy of Germany to join hands with his inquisitors in rooting out these willing bond-servants of Satan, who were said to swarm throughout all that country and to revel in the blackest crimes. Other popes had since reiterated the appeal; and, though none of these documents touched on the blame of witchcraft for diabolic possession, the inquisitors charged with their execution pointed it out most clearly in their fearful handbook, the *Witch-Hammer,* and prescribed the special means by which possession thus caused should be met. These teachings took firm root in religious minds everywhere; and during the great age of witch-burning that followed the Reformation it may well be doubted whether any single cause so often gave rise to an outbreak of the persecution as the alleged bewitchment of some poor mad or foolish or hysterical creature. The persecution, thus once under way, fed itself; for, under the terrible doctrine of "excepted cases," by which in the religious crimes of heresy and witchcraft there was no limit to the use of torture, the witch was forced to confess to accomplices, who in turn accused others, and so on to the end of the chapter.[82]

But as Alexander Murray points out in "Medieval Origins of the Witch Hunt," the various charges hurled against supposed witches in the later Middle Ages—including the ability to turn someone into a newt, a type of "*maleficium* (causing harm by occult means)"—were in fact holdovers from pre-Christian times, and had been and would be applied to many and varied heretical activities or sects outside whatever mainstream existed at a particular time, for example, Paulicians and Waldensians, Jews and Christians (64–65).[83] Interesting, too, is the fact that this alleged witch hasn't been connected to the plague that stalks the land, which might seem a natural allegation for the period, or even the taking of children for devilish purposes, also a very popular charge. As for a natural disaster like the plague (or floods, earthquakes, famine, etc.), the Middle Ages tended to credit God with such retributive events—disasters "widely seen as a divine judgment on mankind's wickedness, in much the same way that God caused the Flood to wash away the sinfulness of Noah's world" (Mortimer, 75). The plague, pestilence, and "sad times" of this era won't be mentioned again until much later in the film, when Roger the Shrubber is first introduced.

ALL: "Burn her anyway!"—Even though the man allegedly transformed into a newt *per maleficium* has recovered, the mob's bloodlust won't be turned aside. This sentence is unusually harsh, given that even the Roman Empire authorities officially only demanded burning when a witch, for example, was determined to have "compass[ed] the death of some obnoxious person."[84] In 1020 the Bishop of Worms published his *Decretum,* and in it attempted to "correct" wrongheaded beliefs about witches and their supposed supernatural powers, including their ability to ride through the air, and "the changing of a person's disposition from love to hate, the control of thunder, rain, and sunshine, the transformation of a man into an animal, [and] the intercourse of incubi and succubi with human beings" (*CE,* "Witchcraft," para. 8). Further, Pope Gregory VII

in 1080 wrote to King Harold of Denmark forbidding witches to be put to death upon *presumption* of their having caused storms or failure of crops or pestilence. Neither were these the only examples of an effort to stem the tide of unjust suspicion to which these poor creatures were exposed. (*CE,* "Witchcraft," para. 8; italics added)

Truly, the fear and suspicion of the devil interacting with (especially) women for dark purposes continued for hundreds of years—the *Malleus Maleficarum* wouldn't be published until 1486; witch hunts occurred sporadically in western Europe and England in the sixteenth and seventeenth centuries; and it would be the eighteenth century in England before the practice was finally, officially outlawed.

Lastly, during the darkest of the Inquisition years (the thirteenth and fourteenth centuries, and generally most visible in western Europe), it was fairly common for the accused who had confessed under torture to face death, even if he or she recanted and renounced heresy:

The system was in more than one way self-perpetuating. A confession made under torture could not safely be retracted. For that was seen (by a deft misreading of canon law used first on a large scale against the Templars, and later responsible for the death of Joan of Arc) as "relapse into heresy," which meant burning. (Murray, "Medieval Origins of the Witch Hunt," 69)

So "Burn her anyway" was likely quite accurate, no matter the trial's outcome.

BEDEVERE: "There are ways of telling whether she is a witch"—Wright notes that it was well into the fourteenth century before heresy—a most serious offense initially confined to members of the clergy—became firmly entwined with the devil and demonism. From Wright's *Heretics: The Creation of Christianity from the Gnostics to the Modern Church:* "There had always been a dozen ways to explain heresy—lunacy, vainglory, political agitation—but from now on there was a new, especially noxious species of heretic: the practitioner of demonic magic" (148). The specter of science and its shadowy relationship with folk magic and superstition during this period is important:

The division between faith and magic had often been blurry. It was not uncommon for medieval Europeans to utilize Christian objects (images, the sacrament, and so forth) in magical endeavors: their power was not to be underestimated. Magic and the occult had not always been dirty words, especially when associated with kindly, disease-curing village mavens or the alchemists and necromancers who had been the darlings of European courts and universities. A veil of suspicion now fell over such practices. This had telling consequences for the future of Western science—an enterprise that, in its medieval incarnation, often mingled with the darker arts—but the real victims were not the wealthy and the learned. For the next three centuries hundreds of innocent people (with women in a sizable majority) would be persecuted as demonic heretics, or witches. (Wright, *Heretics*, 148)

Bedevere's version of logic and science are woven into the same pattern as the accused's evil powers—tug on one loose thread and the fabric unravels completely—but, again, the villagers are clearly satisfied with a "folk-science" solution to their folk magic dilemma. Also, in the era in England when the burden of proof against an accused *could* be determined by deadly combat—the "injured party" proving "by his body" that he had been wronged[85]—offering proof via the weighing of a duck doesn't seem nearly so loony. The end result is the same, of course—the death of the accused.

The social unrest indicated by the villagers' need to coalesce against an identifiable evil is also significant for an understanding of the symbiotic relationship between witchcraft and society, especially in times of distress, according to Russell:

Witchcraft also has an important part in the history of social protest. Toward the end of the Middle Ages, the simultaneous appearance of numerous movements—flagellants, dancers, millenarians, mystics, and others—indicates that powerful currents of social unrest existed in a period of plague, famine, war, and rapid social change. (*Witchcraft in the Middle Ages*, 2)

In *MPHG* we've already seen the tortured dead raised on Catherine wheels, uncooperative commoners, missing or disinterested lords, plague stalking the land, mud and filth and wretchedness, murder, an absence of roads or real civilization, and knights who don't observe the rules of the lists and won't submit (to death) properly. And now, an alleged witch and justice gone awry—all this, along with the Britain of the 1970s discussed throughout, which tinctures everything in the film, is the putrefaction that propagates social unrest.

THIRD VILLAGER: "Do they hurt?"—The Third Villager asks Bedevere whether the ways of telling a witch cause pain. In the thinking of the period, the use of torture was often approved because the acts or alleged sins were committed away from witnesses, and therefore only the accused could answer. This answer could then often only be elicited by "examination," meaning torture "to extort this confession" was "considered necessary and legitimate" in the eyes of both the state *and* the church, often.[86] These specific instances involved Knights Templars who were arrested on orders of Philip the Fair, King of France (1268–1314) and then tortured to discover the extent of their heretical beliefs and actions (c. 1307). The *Catholic Encyclopedia* is quick to point out that the sitting pope (Clement V) had not given "authorization" for the "ferocious torture," which elicited many (and mostly false) confessions.[87]

In England, the process of common law reduced the number of such mob prosecutions, and since torture was also disallowed, by the sixteenth and seventeenth centuries witch finders and examiners were left with imprisonment, incessant questioning, and sleep deprivation as their major tools of confession extraction, at least within the law. As indicated by the success of Stearne and Hopkins, et al., these tools were still quite effective. The use of torture to extract witch confessions played a large part in the perpetuation and expansion of the witch hunts, according to Russell, though it started much earlier, and for different reasons:

> The increasing use of force, involving crusades against both heretics and infidels, and pogroms against the Jews, as well as the legal execution of heretics and witches, was also manifest in the increasing use of torture by both secular and ecclesiastical courts. Torture—the use of coercion to extract confession or the implication of others—played an enormous role in the development of witchcraft from the thirteenth century onward. . . . [I]nnocent men will confess to monstrous crimes once they have been broken by prolonged torture. . . . After days of unrelenting torment, coupled with the despair of knowing how few people ever escaped death by maintaining their innocence, it was rare a defendant who could continue to resist. (*Witchcraft in the Middle Ages*, 151–52)

For a witch, such tests could include pricking of a witch's mark to see if it bled, or, as in some of the cases investigated by Stearne and Hopkins, waiting and watching with a sleep-deprived accused to see if her imps or familiar spirits appeared in the night to suckle (see Russell; Levack).

BEDEVERE: "Tell me . . .what do you do with witches?"—The answer, of course, is "Burn them." But burning wasn't the only method of dealing with demonic creatures. An early sixteenth-century woodcut found in Ulrich Tengler's *Laienspiegel*, titled *In der Streitsache Teufel gegen Menschheit*, or *In the Dispute Between the Devil and Humanity*, all manner of torture and killings are prescribed for the devils' own. These include hanging, flaying, drowning, eye-gouging, pressing, quartering, the Catherine wheel, garroting, and, yes, death by fire. The Pythons manage to employ a fair number of these in *Holy Grail*.

SECOND VILLAGER: ". . . Because they're made of wood"—Many believed that every witch had a "witch's mark" on her body. This was an insensate spot that could be found by poking the accused with needles and pins and the like, until a spot was found where the accused felt no pain. If a witch is made entirely of wood, of course, she would not feel the pricking, and the accusers would have found a witch.

In *MPFC*, Ep. 5, a Scotsman (Palin) announces that he is "made entirely of wood"; later, that changes to "tin" (*MPFC: UC*, 1.92, 107).

ALL: "Throw her in the pond"—A fairly common test in the later Middle Ages to determine whether one was a witch, the examinee was bound and thrown into a body of water—if she sank, she was not a witch. Gaskill mentions that Stearne (and probably Hopkins, his partner) wanted to perform this test on Elizabeth Clarke, the one-legged, suspected witch in Manningtree discussed earlier, but "magistrates [likely] forbade this as a dubious and sinful ordeal" (41). In England, the torturing of individuals suspected of diabolical or maleficent dealings was eventually unlawful, though some of these ordeals "were for many ages a part of English law and usage in the trial of criminal cases," according to Gibson, and weren't amended until the time of Henry III.[88] Anglo-Saxon laws promulgated such ordeals, and they had been carried over from ancient times. The ordeal by water was used to identify the guilty or innocent in various criminal proceedings, but more on that below. In England, clergy were also supposed to be present at any employment of an ordeal.[89] The reasoning behind the water ordeal for witches was no sillier than the logic Bedevere is following in this scene, and came to be known as a "swimming of witches":

> The basis for the ordeal by water was the widely held belief that water, the pure and cleansing element, the instrument of baptism, would refuse to receive those tainted with crime. Added to this was the widespread superstition that those who dabbled in the occult, that is, practiced sorcery or witchcraft, lost their specific gravity. (Zguta, "The Ordeal by Water," 221)

Zguta goes on to say that this so-called "swimming of witches" was fairly common in England, but not until the late sixteenth century (221). Rather than drowning, if the alleged witch was proved pure by sinking to the bottom, a rope or ropes tied to her would be used to hoist her out. (If the examinee died, however, the thought was that at least she died in God's good graces, and not into eternal damnation as a servant of darkness.) For Bedevere and the villagers, however, that test is bypassed in favor of the logic that if Miss Islington weighs as much a duck she must be able to float and therefore must be a witch. The interesting connection between what the Pythons propose and what medieval period minds were thinking is the gravity consideration. By opting to weigh the alleged witch against a duck, the man of science Bedevere is acknowledging both the dunking tradition *and* the loss of "specific gravity" explanations for identifying a witch, and fulfilling *both* as they "use his largest scales" to complete the proofing.

Held over from the Anglo-Saxon era was the *court*-ordered trial by water, where a local or regional court could order the suspect "immersed in blessed, hence purified, water." The guilty man or woman would float, being rejected by the water's purity; the innocent would sink. Most actually passed this test, and it was favored by many courts as it delivered a very quick verdict (McGlynn, 55–56).[90] This test, then, was all about the accused's virtue or vice, and not specific gravities. According to Henry II's Assize of Clarendon (1166), a failure in the cold water ordeal meant the now convicted must lose a foot, and then "abjure the realm," while a later assize (Northampton) added the loss of a hand, as well (Poole, *DBMC*, 402). In some counties the sheriff's lists of the defooted were "often long" (402).

Barrister William Sidney Gibson details the ordeal by water as practiced as a part of English law, where trial by boiling water and trial by fire (or hot stones) were also used.[91] So what might Miss Islington expect after she's hustled off by the mob? In the cold water ordeal

religious solemnities preparatory to the ordeal were observed [certainly connecting the practice back to its roots in heretical trials, and hence to God]; the accused was deprived of clothing, he was sprinkled with holy water; and, a cord knotted at the distance of two ells and a half from the extremity being fastened round his waist, and his hands being bound crosswise to his feet, he was lowered slowly into the pool. If he sank, so as to draw the knot below the surface, he was pronounced innocent, and was liberated; but, if he floated, his guilt was considered manifest, and he was delivered to the officers of justice. The prevailing idea of this mode of ordeal seems to be the old heathen superstition, that the holy element, the pure stream, will receive within it no evildoer. "This," says Fuller, "is the first footstep we find of the swimming of witches, for which there is no law save the custom at this day" (A.D. 1655). *Although the designation "witch" occurs in the Anglo-Saxon Laws, we do not find any trace of a doom of ordeal for witchcraft in those venerable records.* (14–15)

So according to the lawyer Gibson, there is no mention in laws extant during "Arthurian" times or, for example, in Domesday Book, of using the "swimming" statute against witches, which may simply mean that if such trials happened, they happened outside civil *and* ecclesiastical law, as seems to be the case in Bedevere's village. Gibson goes on the mention that this cold water ordeal was employed in England "until the beginning of the [eighteenth] century" to detect witches (15–16). Without the catalysts of the "great medieval heresies" making their way across the Channel or readily available, in situ papal inquisitors, according to Levack, the witch hunting frenzy was never as frenzied in England as it was in northern Europe.[92]

Relatedly, the possibility of having a ready-made pond for such trials wasn't unusual, since most villages and many manors created or cared for ponds. Rectangular depressions were dug and nearby streams were either diverted or dammed—standing water could serve a purpose. The ponds were primarily used defensively, in the case of a fortified house or castle and its moat, but also were very often purpose-built for mill-works, and/or stocked with fish, ducks, and swans (Rowley, 48–52).

ALL: "Tie weights on her"—There doesn't appear to be a history of alleged English witches being weighted down during this dunking process—if she sank it simply "proved" she was not a witch. If the theory being proved was that witches *couldn't* sink—another widely held belief—then weighting her down makes some kind of sense.

There is a report from the continent that around 303, when the Roman Emperor Diocletian (244–311) ordered a suppression of Christians and Christianity, violence to persons and property followed, as reported by Gregory of Tours,[93] with one such attack ringing familiar:

> Quirinus, bishop of the church of Sissek, endured glorious martyrdom in Christ's name. The cruel pagans cast him into a river with a millstone tied to his neck, and when he had fallen into the waters he was long supported on the surface by a divine miracle, and the waters did not suck him down since the weight of crime did not press upon him. And a multitude of people standing around wondered at the thing, and despising the rage of the heathen they hastened to free the bishop. (*History of the Franks*, I.35)

Here, the fact that the accused floats is clearly credited to his innocence and holiness, meaning God is supporting him, and not that his "specific gravity" has been removed, as if he were demonic. Quirinus obviously called this "a fair cop," however, as he asked these concerned people on the shore to leave him in the water, so that he would not be "deprived of martyrdom." He prayed briefly, "gave up the ghost," and was then removed from the water and buried (*History of the Franks*, I.35).

BEDEVERE: "Exactly. So, logically . . ."—Bedevere is painted as sober and earnest but still hopelessly mired in the so-called Dark Ages, which weren't nearly as dark as was once thought. As Lindberg points out in his *The Beginnings of Western Science*:

> The idea of the Middle Ages (or medieval period) first arose in the fourteenth and fifteenth centuries among Italian humanist scholars, who detected a dark middle period between the bright achievements of antiquity and the enlightenment of their own age. This derogatory opinion (captured in the familiar epithet "dark ages") has now been almost totally abandoned by professional historians. (193)

Lindberg goes on to remind us that post-Roman Europe (and Britain) still had access to and usage of the classical texts, that monastic learning and publication increased significantly during this "dark" period, and that the "renewal of scholarly activity" thanks to Charlemagne[94] helped spread learning like almost never before (194). Schools were founded, scholars were employed, and, perhaps most importantly, "books were collected, corrected, and copied":

The importance of the copying of classical texts is demonstrated by the fact that our earliest known copies of most Roman scientific and literary texts (also Latin translations of Greek texts) date from the Carolingian period. The recovery and copying of books, combined with Charlemagne's imperial edict mandating the establishment of cathedral and monastery schools, contributed to a wider dissemination of education than the Latin West had seen for several centuries and laid a foundation for future scholarship. (196)

The only books seen or used in *Holy Grail* are those on shelves as set decoration,[95] the "Book of the Film" pages, and the scriptures from which a monk (Palin) reads out of the Book of Armaments. Splitting hairs, the pages that Gilliam creates as interstitial animations are made to resemble the pages of Gothic illuminated manuscripts, which will be discussed in detail later, and in appendix A. So books aren't a real source of learning in this depicted world; but given Bedevere's logic and recitations, it sounds much more like folk learning than monastic learning that accounts for his approach to witch identification as well as the "new science."

The logical reasoning possible in the ninth to tenth century isn't to be sniffed at, either. When confronted with a question about dog-men—human bodies with dogs' faces—and whether these are men or animals, and do they have souls or not, a monk and scholar from the period, Ratramnus (died c. 870), was actually able to reason quite reasonably, according to Bartlett:

First he asserts that as the dog-heads are descended from Adam they are certainly human. Admittedly, the shape of their heads and their barking are against them. But nevertheless, they show many crucial human attributes. They lived in villages; they farmed the land and kept domesticated animals; moreover, the fact that the dog-heads cover their genitalia is a sign of their decency, which in turn means they have the power of judging between the decent and the indecent. . . . [Ratramnus writes:] "I do not see how this could be if they had an animal and not a rational soul, for no one can blush at indecency unless they have a certain recognition of decency. A group of moral, rational beings living in a society bound by laws—this is humanity, not mere animality."[96] Therefore, he concludes, dog-heads were in essence human beings.[97]

Bartlett concludes:

It's easy to poke fun at this earnest philosophizing about such bizarre creatures as dog-heads and fish-men and people who come down from the sky. But such debates were pursued with keen logic and an impressive spirit of dedication. Logic and observation were the tools whereby things were made to find their place in a worldview that was intensely religious, and the fit was not always a neat one.[98]

Sir Bedevere is clearly *attempting* to follow this established pattern of examination—observation and logic. The balance of the much-hated *Malleus Maleficarum* is also set out in this pattern: a series of questions, logically posed and then answered using scriptural and apocryphal precedent.[99] Oman points out that Gervase, like Ratramnus, was also keen to follow logic, *and* he wasn't afraid to accept the odd or unusual—those things "beside nature"—encountered in the world:

It is well to remember that Gervase would have resented the suggestion that he ever treated of the supernatural. The strange beings and strange things of which he tells us, had been created like everyone and everything else. They were exceptional, the reason for their existence was not obvious, but they fitted somehow into the scheme of nature. It would be unfair to describe Gervase as being more credulous than most of his contemporaries, for he often tries to explain the phenomena which he describes. His inquisitiveness is directed principally towards inanimate objects, his attitude towards all sorts of spirits is one of unquestioning belief.[100]

SCENE SEVEN

He leads them a few yards to a very strange contraption indeed, made of wood and rope and leather—(PSC) We really don't see much of this "contraption," excepting the two bits of the scale where the woman and the duck are to be seated, and the "supports," which are removed with large mallets. Like the catapult heard later (at the French-held castle) and the promised trebuchets and siege towers of the final scene, this prop may have begun life as a hoped-for example of impressive construction, but the realities of the film set scaled back the final product. With sound effects and careful camera work, though, the prop's purpose is amply served.

In Gilliam's later and better-funded *The Adventures of Baron Munchausen* (1988), the Sultan's torture organ (an organ utilizing humans as pipes) is just such an elaborate, fully realized contraption, on which the Sultan can play his composition, "The Torturer's Apprentice."

The GIRL and the duck swing slightly but balance perfectly—(PSC) The physical proof here is compelling, since as we're watching the girl and the duck do appear to weigh the same without anyone fudging the scales, bringing Bedevere's logical hypothesis to an obvious and satisfying conclusion. Based on everything they "know," then, this girl is a witch, and should be burned. Perhaps this is why even the girl admits it's "a fair cop."

And lest we assume that only the untutored and unwashed peasant thought this way, Cohn notes that it was often the best and brightest who were capable of spreading and even believing some of the most wildly improbable theories. Cohn finds example after example of, for instance, descriptions of demonic rituals (i.e., witches' sabbaths, "nocturnal orgies," "Lucifer's kisses") that were perpetuated from learned to learned—sometimes reported as a sort of "these backwards people think this," but after a handful of successive transmissions becoming canonical (21).[101] The belief that the devil "presided over" these orgies in animal appearance "belonged not to the folklore of the illiterate majority, but, on the contrary, to the worldview of the intellectual elite [like Bedevere]; learned clerics who stood at the very centre of affairs were thoroughly convinced of it" (21). Cohn gives as an example the ecclesiastic Walter Map (c. 1140–1210), an Englishman who was a respected "judge and an officer of the court of Henry II," but who also confirmed that lapsed French Catholics perpetuated these heretical beliefs in midnight Satanism. Many other learned men believed and wrote similarly (21–22).

WITCH: "It's a fair cop"—A phrase heard often on British TV, it's one of those idiomatic expressions that's here both anachronistic and patently English. "Fair cop" is used in several *Flying Circus* episodes, as discussed in an *MPFC: UC* entry for Ep. 3, in the "Court Scene":

> The phrase appears in *FC* (Eps. 3, 6, 27, and 29) and the later feature films, and is spoken by characters both historical and fictional. In . . . the "Salvation Fuzz" sketch (Ep. 29) the murderer (Idle) of various bishops is fingered by the hand of God, and replies: "It's a fair cop, but society's to blame." The *OED* indicates that the phrase . . . first appeared [officially] in print in 1891 (from a quote attributed to an apprehended thief), and has since become a part of the British vernacular. It's also heard in films where police work is simply a part of the plot, including Basil Dearden's *Victim* (1961), starring Dirk Bogarde (who's mentioned later in Ep. 29).
>
> The phrase isn't just reserved for homey police shows like *Dixon of Dock Green*, either, or even just bad detective fiction, but can be found in a 16 July 1965 *Time* magazine article examining Tory vote-gerrymandering on a controversial capital gains tax cut amendment. It seems the Conservatives—who were in the minority 1964–1970, but by just three votes—lulled Labour to sleep in the wee hours of a legislative day, then surprised them by calling for a vote and showing up en masse to beat the sitting government, 180–166. Labour moaned and whinged, but eventually termed the successful surprise attack "a fair cop," and the Wilson government took its second parliamentary defeat as the majority party.[102]

The surfing witch described earlier also expressed a "fair cop" sentiment as she realized there was nothing else she could do to save her own life, just like Miss Islington:

> [T]he woman hearing this, knew then the Devill had left her and her power was gone, wherefore she began alowd to cry, and roare, tearing her haire, and making her moan, which in these words expressed were; And is it come to passe, that I must dye indeed? Why then his Excellency the Earle of Essex shall be fortunate and win the field.[103]

The phrase appears quite frequently in the crime sections of London's papers in the late nineteenth century, and in so similar a syntax and setting (a thief essentially giving up and saying the phrase), that it may be that either the arresting constables or the crime beat reporters were actually crafting the dialogue with the evening edition in mind. Just scanning the pages of a century of the *London Times* yields much. By the 1920s the phrase had found its way into more common vernacular, appearing in stories about being bested by wicked bunkers on golf courses; by 1930 it's a consistent crossword puzzle clue; by the mid-1940s (when the Pythons are growing up) it's termed a prisoner's "traditional" answer spoken with "remarkable uniformity"; and in Parliament it's uttered in 1949 (to much laughter). By the mid-1950s the phrase is being discussed in a "Criminal Clichés" editorial, and called "romantic rubbish," which it likely always was, and by the early 1960s it's even a BBC Light Programme series starring Eric Sykes.[104] By the time the Pythons employ the phrase, it can be coming from the mouth of a truncheon-swinging constable who is not the most reliable of public servants:

> Constable (Palin): I clearly saw the defendant . . . doing whatever he's accused of . . . Red-handed. When kicked . . . he said: "It's a fair . . . cop, I done it all . . . Right . . . no doubt about . . . that." Then, bound as he was to the chair, he assaulted myself and three other constables while bouncing around the cell. The end. (*JTW*, 2.52)

In the end it's an evergreen phrase familiar on several levels to most British audiences, and must've sounded quite funny (and as spoken—into the camera) coming from an accused, bemused, and condemned medieval witch.

This admittedly jarring anachronism—taken with the coconuts and elevated discussions of swallows—comprising an obviousness that can't be ignored, have now laid the groundwork for this film's level of verisimilitude. The occasional "wink, wink, nudge, nudge" to a willing audience is promised, and then delivered by Famous Historians and police constables. But this isn't the first or last medieval film to make a jumble of history, as Arthur Lindley demonstrates, painting John Boorman's *Excalibur* (1981) as "a temporal dislocation signified by the film's deliberately pastiche style (sixth-century knights in fifteenth-century armor with twentieth-century chrome plating accompanied by nineteenth-century music, mostly Wagner)" (8). Another, even earlier title the Pythons could have used as inspiration is the film production of *Jesus Christ Superstar* (1973), where a modern play/dance troupe set up for a production of Christ's life among authentic Middle Eastern ruins. The troupe arrive on the scene in a modern bus, put on costumes, and "act" on the ruins and modern steel scaffolding, some armed with automatic weapons.[105] The film was a success, making more than $13 million in the United States alone. So this jumbling, this in-your-face display of anachronisms doesn't have to be off-putting; in fact, quite the opposite, according to medievalist Greta Austin:

> In this way, medieval films can be profoundly useful to the medievalist. Films may not have foot-notes, they may be historically unreliable, and they may be irrevocably modern in their perspective

and sensibilities. Yet, at the end of the day, most are enjoyable, and, if truth be told, they are often more engaging than reading a scholarly monograph.[106]

Finally, in accordance with the spirit of "fair cop" brevity, accused witch Elizabeth Clarke's admission of guilt (she had allowed the devil the use of her body) to witch finders Stearne, Hopkins, and others gathered to examine her was just as curt: "It is true."[107]

ALL: "Burn her!"—The mob here is employing this mode of execution just as intended by the Church during the Inquisition in Europe—the more public the spectacle, the better the "teaching moment." Though not a religious setting here (they've come to Bedevere, not their local clergy), the narrative and denouement are identical:

> Inquisitors took full advantage of the theatrical opportunities afforded them: for example, sentences were often not announced in private, but publicly at large gatherings. . . . The inquisitors' public performance was not the only dramatic element of heretical penance, however, for the punishments themselves also served to enact the religious teaching and social marginalization to the inquisitorial enterprise. (Kolpacoff, 114)

The awfulness of the witch burning as depicted in *Seventh Seal*—where the accused is tortured to the brink of death before being consigned to the flames—attests to the powerful social deterrent authorities hoped such punishments would reinforce. Inserting our performers into this paradigm, Sir Bedevere helps focus and orchestrate to the "large gathering," his "public performance" being the impressive rhetoric of witch identification, culminating in the impressive weighing ceremony (for which he already possesses a purpose-made device). The mob is "taught," Miss Islington is socially marginalized—"She's a witch!"—and the "extreme penalty" is then justified and carried out. This secular or civic event is more like that which often followed an inquisitorial trial and sentence, since the Church did not itself carry out or order executions—the accused was "relaxed" to non-Church authorities for punishment (114). The end result was almost always a death sentence, unless there was a recanting, though that was also no guarantee of survival, just deathbed penance. And the burning itself was a momentous civic event:

> Such executions were perhaps the greatest spectacle in the Church's arsenal, shocking and horrifying events even in a world accustomed to violence and public punishment. The building of the pyre, procession of the condemned, fixing of living human beings to the stake (often friends and family members together), taunting or weeping or praying by onlookers, and the scrutiny of the condemned's conduct for signs of weakness[108] made for a powerful experience. Fire was the chosen means of execution because . . . it annihilated the body so that it could not be resurrected. (115)

The Pythons chose a witch burning and a lay leader for this scene, and not a heretic burning sentenced by a Church court, even though there seem to have been more inquisitorial punishments and death sentences for faith-related aberrations than witches put to death during the medieval period. It wouldn't be until their following film, *Life of Brian*, that the Pythons would run roughshod, to many, over organized religion.[109]

ALL: "Let's make her into a ladder"—This may be just another useful item to be made from someone made of wood, like the bridge mentioned earlier, but it also may be a nod to the ladders that were built/used during many witch (or heretic) burnings. The accused could be strapped to the ladder and the ladder then lowered onto the pyre—as Bergman portrayed in *The Seventh Seal*—or tied to a ladder and then to a post in a heap of flammable material, as depicted in Carl Dreyer's masterwork *Joan of Arc* (1928). A number of late Middle Ages illustrations depicting Joan's execution also place her on a ladder, ready to be lowered face-first onto the burning pile. In *Seventh Seal* particularly, the construction of the ladder—off-screen, with plenty of ominous rasps and scrapes—is unnerving to the bystanders.

Ladders also figure significantly into many of Bosch's more hellish landscapes. See appendix A for more on Gilliam's sketching of these ladders.

The VILLAGERS drag the girl away—(PSC) Again, the mob of villagers gets just what it wants and needs—a conviction that leads to a burning; with this, village life will likely return to normal. The behavior of the public during these times of theological and/or political disease is illustrated by Jonathan Wright:

> They would sometimes gather outside the churches and palaces in which debates raged about the nature of God and the quiddities of mankind. They would cheer their champions and spit out venomous accusations of anathema at those churchmen they despised. When decisions went well at such councils, the local people would escort clerics home to their lodgings with joyful, drunken, torch-lit processions. When decisions went badly they would burn men in effigy and make bonfires of their books. In better moods the crowds would hold placards aloft. In worse moods they would fight bloody battles in the streets. . . . Armed guards would sometimes be drafted in to prevent eruptions of physical violence. (Wright, 68)

Perhaps unwittingly, Bedevere seems to have quelled a potentially destructive civil outburst by tossing the mob a bone, so to speak.

BEDEVERE: ". . . so wise in the ways of science"—The gradual removal of Roman influence from Britain throughout the fourth century followed by the fall of Rome in about 475 meant the availability and influence of classical learning (especially the Greek influences) diminished in western Europe, and certainly more so further west in the British Isles, and anywhere considered the fringe of the former Roman Empire. The transition from classical, academy learning to more monastic learning—the latter being necessarily more closed *and* more theological—also separated the bulk of the population from book learning. But all was not dark in these Dark Ages. As Kantor points out in "Science Reenters European Culture":

> No matter how unfavorable social and economic conditions had been throughout the Dark Ages and the early feudal period for the development of effective scientific work, the intellectual ground has still not been completely forbidden and barren. Changes were taking place unceasingly which gradually facilitated the development of an active scientific tradition. (314)

The "science" of medicine, as depicted in *Le Morte Darthur*, mostly included miraculous healings thanks to the presence of the Grail or Merlin's intervention, or, where necessary, the application of leeches and salves for proper healing; there's not much in between (*LMD-WM*, 26).

Barbara Tuchman notes that in the fourteenth century someone like a Bedevere—part of the "upper level of a lay society"—could have had access to significant scientific knowledge, much of it accurate:

> Long before Columbus, they knew the world was a globe, a knowledge proceeding from familiarity with the movement of the stars, which could be made comprehensible only in terms of a spherical earth. In a vivid image, it was said by the cleric Gautier de Metz in his *Image du Monde*, the most widely read encyclopedia of the time, that a man could go around the earth as a fly makes the tour of an apple. So far was the earth from the stars, according to him, if a stone were dropped from there it would take more than 100 years to reach our globe, while a man traveling 25 leagues a day without stopping would take 7,157½ years to reach the stars. . . . Visually, people pictured the universe held in God's arms with man at its center. It was understood that

the moon was the nearest planet, with no light of its own; that an eclipse was the passage of the moon between the earth and the sun; that rain was moisture drawn by the sun from the earth which condensed into clouds and fell back as rain; that the shorter the time between thunder and lightning, the nearer the source. . . . Faraway lands, however—India, Persia, and beyond—were seen through a gauze of fabulous fairy tales. (57–58)

Lastly, it's not a surprise that Bedevere wouldn't automatically assume that this clean, magisterial man before him is a king, even though he is wearing a crown and carries himself in a kingly manner. Many of the later medieval kings lived lives of functioning illiteracy, and wouldn't have recognized science from magic at arm's length. Brooke notes that after the Conquest, the twelfth-century Anglo-Norman ruler "Henry II was the first English king . . . to be fully literate"; his father Henry I had only managed to "almost sign his name" a generation earlier (*FAH*, 175). Tactical and battlefield skills were far more important than book and charter-reading to these kings. Earlier Anglo-Saxon kings, especially the ninth-century Alfred, had set the literacy bar high, as he himself describes, remembering especially the clergy of his youth:

So completely had learning decayed in England that there were very few men on this side the Humber who could apprehend their [Latin] services in English or even translate a letter from Latin into English, and I think that there were not many beyond the Humber. There were so few of them that I cannot even recollect a single one south of the Thames when I succeeded to the kingdom. (*FAH*, 40)

Alfred would go on to found a court school on the model of Charlemagne, and would further attempt to educate virtually all young men in his kingdom. Frank Stenton notes: "[Alfred's] unique importance in the history of English letters comes from his conviction that a life without knowledge or reflection was unworthy of respect, and his determination to bring the thought of the past within the range of his subjects' understanding" (*Anglo-Saxon England*, 269–70). His thirst for knowledge and his wont to share that ancient knowledge with his people aligns Alfred the Great with our Arthur and Bedevere, clearly, both of whom want to be amazed by the "new learning."

ARTHUR: "I am Arthur, King of the Britons"—*This is the one and only time that this pronouncement of title and authority has the intended effect* (Bedevere immediately drops to one knee, saying "My liege"). Elsewhere, Arthur is misunderstood, unrecognized, or simply ignored. The script mentions that *"ARTHUR looks at PATSY with obvious satisfaction"* after Bedevere recognizes him—finally, someone gets it.

Brooke notes that during the Anglo-Saxon period the king and his subjects wouldn't have necessarily encountered one another at all, especially if a foreign king like Cnut ruled all of Denmark and Norway, parts of Sweden, and parts of Britain—he simply couldn't be everywhere. And even if he was an itinerant king, one who "made the rounds" of his kingdom as often as possible, the peasant shouldn't expect much beyond meeting one of the king's men, perhaps:

Only the great met the king in person, in the great council, "the moot of the wise men" as it was euphemistically called, the Witenagamot or Witan. But every thegn and many freemen had a chance to meet the royal representative in shire and hundred. Before the Conquest this meant much to the king; little to the subject. Later on it came to mean more to both. (*FAH*, 74)

After the Conquest, the Anglo-Norman kings often spent much of their time on the continent seeing to their vacillating duchies of Normandy, Aquitaine, Anjou, and others with Richard I setting perhaps the worst example by spending just a handful of months in England during his regnal years (he preferred his lands in Aquitaine).[110] The "parfit gentil" knight Bedevere recognizes his king, no "royal representative" needed here, and the gathering to Camelot can begin. Dennis can be forgiven not recognizing his liege lord earlier—he's both an isolated peasant as well as a man out of his time, politically; the Black Knight is trapped by the semantic elements of the Grail romances—fights to the death at bridges and with all comers defines his idiom; and the sentries on the wall are simply doing their jobs not only as keepers of the castle's safety, assaying each and every clamorer at the gate, but acting the Pythonesque characters who waylay even the best-intentioned narrative trajectories, as seen throughout the run of *Flying Circus*.

This scene—where Arthur is recognized by Bedevere as who and what he is—stands out in the Python *oeuvre* because it works out just the way it should. This relationship will remain true and unsullied to the last moments of the film, fittingly.

BEDEVERE: "My liege . . . forgive me . . ."—The Grail romances are replete with misidentifications, delayed recognitions—many times Arthur's own knights fail to recognize him and a fight ensues, followed by a reveal and an embrace. Sometimes these misunderstandings are caused by magical obfuscation (knights rendered invisible; visages changed momentarily by Merlin's influence, etc.), other times not. Occasionally, knights will put on the colors and shield of another, as well. When Sir Accolon faces Arthur, Accolon does not recognize his liege lord, likely because he is "helmed"—wearing a helmet and visor—but also perhaps because the fight couldn't happen if they "knew" each other:

> "It is truth," said Accolon, "but now I have told you the truth; wherefore I pray you tell me of whence ye are, and of what court."
>
> "Ah, Accolon," said King Arthur, "now I let thee wit that I am King Arthur that thou hast done great damage to."
>
> When Accolon heard that, he cried aloud, "Fair sweet lord, have mercy on me, for I knew you not." (*LMD-WM*, 68)

Similarly, Arthur somehow fails to see that Accolon is wounding him in this fight with his own sword, Excalibur, until it's almost too late. Elsewhere, Arthur isn't recognized by Sir Lamorak before they fight and Lamorak is "wounded . . . sore with a spear"; much earlier, the great lords of the land "knew not" that young Arthur was Uther Pendragon's son until Merlin announced it.[111] So Arthur as depicted in *MPHG* isn't in his own company simply because he isn't yet recognized by those around him. This recognition will come, and quickly, since all the other knights join the quest offscreen, as revealed by the narrator in the economical "Book of the Film" section. See below for more on that montage-like scene.

ARTHUR: "Then I dub you . . . <u>Sir</u> Bedevere . . . Knight of the Round Table!"—This moment, with Bedevere kneeling humbly and Arthur nobly standing, sword at Bedevere's shoulder, is a visual borrow from many referents, one being the *Robin Hood* comics of 1955–1956. In the first issue, in a story titled "Sir Galant of the Round Table," it is a white-haired, wizened Arthur, wielding Excalibur, who knights Galant in this way. In issue four, Prince John performs this same ritual for "Sir" Robin, tricking him into accepting a Crusade journey by knighting him.[112] Also, in the Stan Lee–penned comic book series *Black Knight*, Arthur knights the Black Knight after the Black Knight helps Arthur escape Modred's sneak attack.[113] Incidentally, Sir Hector features in this comic as well, and in earlier drafts of the *Holy Grail* script he played a much larger role. In a crossed-out section late in the film Hector—described as "northern and helpful"—seems to be eaten by the Legendary Beast, but it's not entirely clear what happens to him.

Borrowing from comic books isn't a surprise for the Pythons,[114] especially given the notoriety these dangerous art forms achieved in the late 1940s and early 1950s on both sides of the Atlantic. A report—an "eagerly awaited report," the *Times* editorial clucked, tongue planted firmly in cheek—from the Cincinnati Committee on the Evaluation of Comic Books[115] announced that "of the 555 comic magazines which were examined by the committee's staff of fifty trained reviewers no less than 70 percent were found to be in one way or another objectionable," including the "picturing of grotesque, fantastic, and unnatural creatures."[116] Such dangerous material seems ideal reading for young delinquents.

Notes

1. See credits notes above, and "932 A.D." entry for more on Forstater and the thirteenth-century date.

2. From the author's "'Is Not the Truth the Truth?' or Rude Frenchmen in English Castles: Shakespeare's and Monty Python's (Ab)Uses of History," in *The Journal of the Utah Academy of Sciences, Arts and Letters* 76 (1999): 201–12.

3. *MPFC: UC*, 1.83, 123, 129, and 145.

4. The monks in this scene are depicted wearing black (their hoods more faded than their robes), which might indicate they are meant to be Dominican friars—that or black was the only color the film's costumers purchased. Franciscan friars tended to wear gray cassocks during the fourteenth century (Mortimer, 115). Carmelites could be seen wearing both white and brown as early as the twelfth century, though both these colors might have soiled and stained very quickly in the soggy conditions of the film shoot.

5. Lines 907 and 930, respectively, in the "The Pardoner's Tale," *Riverside Chaucer* edition (1987), pages 201–2. These are silver and gold pieces, and valuable coins.

6. Tuchman calls the Pardoner "the only really detestable character in Chaucer's company of Canterbury pilgrims" (30).

7. Delasanta, "Penance and Poetry in the Canterbury Tales."

8. Voltaire, *Candide*, 347.

9. *Catholic Encyclopedia*, "Flagellants," http://www.newadvent.org/cathen/06089c.htm

10. *CE*, "Flagellants." In an *MPFC* sketch from Ep. 12, the bemused residents of North Minehead watch and listen to Messrs. Hilter, Bimmler, and Ron Vibbentrop (Cleese, Palin, and Chapman)—in full Nazi regalia—announce their Bocialist agenda, which include "boncentration bamps," through the pleasant and lightly trafficked city streets (*MPFC: UC*, 1.184–200). For more on the plague and resulting flagellant movements, see Hallam, 261–62.

11. The so-called "Rules of Saint Benedict"—reasonable rules for monks that encouraged "asceticism and otherworldliness, without leading to excess"—had been laid down during Arthur's supposed lifetime, early in the sixth century. See Bishop, *HBMA*, 14.

12. The *infangenþeof* ("in-taken-thief") specifically refers to a landowner being able to execute his own man as a thief—caught red-handed, on his land and/or with his goods—and had been part of Anglo-Saxon law for some time, lasting well into the fourteenth century, at least. The proper OE-ME term for our mob's summary actions might be *infangenwicce* ("in-taken-witch"). See Poole, *DBMC*, 57, for more on these manorial court situations.

13. See the "Camelot Is a Silly Place" entry below, and specifically the *"Prisoner hanging on castle wall"* notes. See Tuchman as well.

14. Norman Cohn notes that in Europe, "[t]he (not very numerous) executions of heretics during the eleventh and twelfth centuries were almost all the work of the secular authorities or of the mob," and that the Church instead encouraged renunciation and penance (22). This mob perhaps knows they'll get the result they want from Bedevere, not their clerical leader.

15. Kramer and Sprenger, *Malleus Maleficarum*, 77.

16. Kramer and Sprenger, *Malleus Maleficarum* xliii–xlv.

17. Listen to Jones's and Gilliam's audio commentaries on either of the more recent DVD/Blu-ray editions of the film. These codirectors talk most about the production and production design elements.

18. Perhaps the neatness and cleanliness of Swamp Castle—as wedding preparations are underway— is meant to represent the other side of medieval life, the side of wealth, a surfeit of food and gracious living; it is the picture of medieval *confort moderne*. The scene, of course, ends in a bloodbath.

19. The Pythons' fixation on the body and cleanliness/filth will be revisited soon after this film is finished, in Ep. 40 of the final series of *MPFC*. There, the Montgolfier brothers (Idle and Jones) are obsessed with washing, and the narrator of their story is a plumber working on a lavatory.

20. *LMD-WM*, 514–15.

21. White had graduated from Queens' College, Cambridge in 1928; these correspondences concerning *The Sword in the Stone* are dated to January 1938.

22. From medievalist Kurth Sprague (1934–2007), this short essay (dated 26 Dec. 1996) is titled "A Further Note on the Time-Period and Anachronisms in T. H. White's *The Once and Future King*."

23. Kantor quotes Holmyard quoting Jabir Ibn Hayyan (ca. 720–813); see Kantor, "Science Reenters European Culture," 322.

24. Freely, *Before Galileo*, 52.

25. Perhaps as a nod to this sacred mission entrusted to Bedevere, after the quest has found the Grail (in Africa) in the first draft of the script, they quickly get bored and decide to hide it again and re-find it. Bedevere is given the job of secreting the Grail, and the questers close their eyes and begin to count. Bedevere takes it to the ant counter at the department store eventually seen in Ep. 41 of *Flying Circus*. See *MPHGB*, 41.

26. *LMD'A*, 2.518–19.

27. In other versions of Malory's work, the text is not divided into sections using titles.

28. See the *Catholic Encyclopedia* for more.

29. Germany's first *official* inquisitor had been Conrad of Marburg, appointed by Pope Gregory IX in 1231; his role was to preach and root out heresy, encouraging others inside the faith to identify heretical thought and deed in their midst (Cohn, 25).

30. Murray, "Medieval Origins of the Witch Hunt," 65.

31. This is one of three mentions of burning as a punishment in the film. Robin's minstrel will sing of the timid knight being unafraid of having "his kidneys burnt," and "his body burned away." Also, the Pythons include this type of scene in all three of their major feature films. In *Life of Brian*, it is the stoning scene, where the public is invited to cast stones, as well as the crucifixion scene; in *Meaning of Life*, a man is chased to his death by bare-breasted women (he was able to choose the method of execution).

32. Arthur will turn to the Church in the form of Brother Maynard later for help against the killer rabbit, but only after the magic of Tim the Enchanter fails to help them overcome the creature.

33. *LMD'A*, 1.140–41. This story is not included in the Winchester version.

34. Whom Arthur defeated in chapter ten; Accolon dies in chapter twelve. See Accolon discussions in the "Dennis the Peasant" scene earlier and "She's a Witch" scene later.

35. Cohn, *Europe's Inner Demons*.

36. Cf. what happens to the Bridge of Death Keeper (Soothsayer) at the end of the film, when he is unable to answer a question in relation to his own question.

37. *MM*, 155–56.

38. Gaskill, 28.

39. *MM*, 1.

40. See the "How do you know she's a witch" entry above for more on Rivet.

41. Audio transcription, Bartlett, *Inside the Medieval Mind: Knowledge*.

42. Mentioned above in relation to Merlin.

43. Also from Bartlett, *Inside the Medieval Mind: Knowledge*. (This anecdote is also discussed in Oman, "The English Folklore of Gervase of Tilbury," 7.) The *Oxford DNB* offered this less-than-flattering tidbit of the man Gervase, who obviously saw evil and duplicity everywhere (excepting within himself):

> This was during the time when the archbishop was especially active in persecuting the "publicani" or "paterins," and probably not earlier than 1183 (Robert of Auxerre, *Chronicle of St. Martin's, Chronicle of Anchin*; *Recueil*, xviii, 251, 291, 536). In later life he told Ralph of Coggeshall [mentioned above] how at this time he one day tried to seduce a young woman, and gathered from the answer with which she repelled his advances that she was a "paterin." The archbishop came up while they were talking; Gervase told him of his suspicions, and the girl and her old instructress were condemned and burnt as heretics (Coggeshall, pp. 122–4). (*ODNB 1885–1900*, Vol. 21)

44. Bartlett, *Inside the Medieval Mind*.

45. *The Witch-Hunt in Early Modern Europe*.

46. The Pythons mention these assizes in *MPFC* (see *MPFC: UC*, 1.336, 372).

47. Involving armed forces supporting parliamentary or royalist factions, and leading to the execution of Charles I and the exile of Charles II.

48. See the entry for "She looks like one" below for more. In this case, the fact that everyone knew this woman—she wasn't the always suspicious "vagrant"—did not help her cause.

49. See Gaskill, *Witchfinders*, ch. 2.

50. Included toward the end of *MPHGB*, page 90, approximately. These character names/traits are not included in the film's finished credits.

51. Cohn notes that this zealous triumvirate all met violent ends, as well. Conrad of Marburg was murdered, likely by friends or family members of those accused; Torso was stabbed to death; and Johannes was hanged. Pope Gregory IX was certain they were all doing the Lord's work, calling Marburg a "champion of the Christian faith" (28–31).

52. She was accused by an ecclesiastical court in Rouen of "witchcraft, magic, impurity, wearing men's clothes, and recalcitrance to the church" (*HBMA*, 392).

53. Reginald Scot (1538–1599) was a gentleman, a demonologist, and author of *The Discoverie of Witchcraft* (1584).

54. This Mortimer—whose family had been endowed with English lands and power by William in the aftermath of the Norman invasion—also fancied himself an Arthur-type. In 1328 he held an extravagant "Round Table" tournament in Bedford, "possibly to serve as a reminder of the Mortimer claim to descent from Arthur and Brutus" (McKisack, 97). With the grisly death of Edward II attributed by many to Mortimer's machinations, it wasn't long before he fell out of favor with the young king Edward III, and he was arrested, tried, convicted, then drawn and hanged as a traitor in November 1330. Edward's mother, Isabella, was not executed.

55. In about 1341 one Sir John Willoughby was also accused in this way—by "clamour of the people"—"selling the laws as if they had been oxen or cows" (McKisack, 205).

56. McKisack, 85–87; see also Holmes, 114–18.

57. See the index in *MPFC: UC* for the many mentions of Booth.

58. *MPFC: UC*, 1.369, 384; 2.209–10.

59. *MPFC: UC*, 1.115, 273.

60. "W.C."—Toilet, lavatory.

61. "M.B."—"Metropolitan Borough."

62. See the section "Islington Growth," *A History of the County of Middlesex: Volume 8: Islington and Stoke Newington Parishes*, at British History Online, http://www.british-history.ac.uk/report.aspx?compid=6734.

63. *Times* 15 August 1973: 27.

64. "Artificial Insemination for Prisoner's Wife Refused," *Times* 4 July 1973: 1.

65. The Lords Appellant were: Thomas of Woodstock, Duke of Gloucester (Richard's uncle); Richard FitzAlan, Earl of Arundel and Surrey; and Thomas de Beauchamp, Earl of Warwick. The future Henry IV, Henry Bolingbroke, Earl of Derby (Richard's cousin), and Thomas de Mowbray, Duke of Norfolk and Earl of Nottingham, also figured prominently in the "trial." The goal of these men seems to have been the removal of Richard's closest advisors (e.g., Robert de Vere), as opposed to the king himself. By 1397 Richard had managed to reconsolidate his power, and the three main participants in the Merciless Parliament's antagonisms were arrested, then either murdered or exiled. The appellants had fallen out with each other following the parliament, the prospect of a new king breeding suspicion and calumny. See McKisack for more.

66. For more on Joan, see Bishop, *HBMA* and Tuchman, *A Distant Mirror*.

67. Reis notes that in American witch trials in the northeast of the seventeenth century, *every* suspect who denied witchcraft charges was eventually hanged. Denial was a very poor defense.

68. From the "Confess or Deny: What's a "Witch" to Do?" New Hampshire Public Radio, http://nhpr.org/post/september-1-elizabeth-reis-confess-or-deny-whats-witch-do.

69. Meaning no one can give testimony who may have a grudge against the accused, allegedly.

70. *MM*, 259.

71. *MPFC: UC*, 1.300.

72. More fully, *A MOST Certain, Strange, and true Di*scovery of a WITCH, Being taken by some of the Parliament Forces, as she was standing on a small planck board and sayling on it over the River of Newbury, printed by John Hammond, 1643 (British Library Collection).

73. See also Linfert, *Hieronymous Bosch*, 18.

74. See Gaskill, *Witchfinders*, 16–17.

75. From the cartoon *Bewitched Bunny* (1954), directed by Chuck Jones and written by Michael Maltese.

76. An enchantment, a spell.

77. *MM*, 61 and 122.

78. In the elided end credits kept as part of the script, this character is known as "Mr. Newt (A Village Blacksmith Interested in Burning Witches)" (*MPHGB*, 90).

79. There was a long-held belief that certain lower creatures—"serpents, frogs, mice"—were generated by putrefying swamp and forest areas. Spenser mentions "Huge heapes of mudd" that "breed / Ten thousand kindes of creatures, partly male / And partly female of his fruitful seed; / Such ugly monstrous shapes elsewhere may no man reed" (*Faerie Queene*, 1.1.21). In these cases, the witch isn't godlike in her "creation"—that would be heretical—instead, this witch is simply mimicking the basest of nature's accomplishments.

80. "Hypatia," *Encyclopædia Romana*, online at http://penelope.uchicago.edu/~grout/encyclopaedia_romana/greece/paganism/hypatia.html.

81. From *Chronicle of John, Bishop of Nikiu*, 84.87–88, 100–103. This quote also found at the *Encyclopædia Romana* site.

82. From White, *A History of the Warfare of Science with Theology in Christendom*, ch. 15.

83. In fact, as Cohn additionally points out, many of the persecutions and even the ways to describe/proscribe "others" into otherness—so they can then be group-victimized by the threatened power—were carried over or revived from the earliest days of persecutions against Christians. See Cohn's chapters on "The Demonization of Medieval Heretics" in *Europe's Inner Demons*.

84. *CE*, "Witchcraft," http://www.newadvent.org/cathen/15674a.htm, para. 5. The harsh sentence is part of the reason this scene reads more like a Church-approved secular punishment (the heretic having been "relaxed" from Inquisitorial to civic authority) than a witch trial.

85. Poole, *DBMC*, 396–97.

86. *CE*, "The Knights Templars," http://www.newadvent.org/cathen/14493a.htm.

87. See also McKisack, 291–92, and Tuchman, 42–44, where Clement V's actions (or inactions) are treated more circumspectly.

88. From Gibson, *On Some Ancient Modes of Trial*.

89. Gibson *On Some Ancient Modes of Trial*, 7.

90. See Tuchman, *A Distant Mirror*, McKisack, *The Fourteenth Century*, as well as Fossier, *The Axe and the Oath* and Mortimer, *The Time Traveler's Guide to Medieval England* for much more on just the challenges of life in this era.

91. Gibson notes that the ordeal by fire was generally reserved for a "freeman," and by water for "rustic" folk (10).

92. Though in more Catholic areas, including Scotland, such trials and executions occurred much more regularly; and during the political uncertainty of the Civil War, illegal uses of torture and punishment did erupt (Levack, *The Witch-Hunt in Early Modern Europe*, 218–19).

93. Fl. 538–594. *History of the Franks*, available at Fordham's Medieval Sourcebook, http://www.fordham.edu/halsall/basis/gregory-hist.asp. Gregory will be mentioned later in relation to the "earthquakes" entry.

94. And Charlemagne himself "took as his teacher Alcuin of Britain . . .the most learned man in the entire world," according to biographer Einhard (Lindberg, 194–95). Alcuin lived 735–804, spending time in York and at the Carolingian court on the continent.

95. Since books during this period were of such value (each having been meticulously handmade, and very expensive), it's not likely they'd have been kept on "bedroom" shelves, but rather in a protected study or library. Chaucer, for example, is believed to have owned a significant number of books in his personal library, perhaps as many as sixty. (See Thompson, *The Medieval Library*.) Even most "distinguished" libraries owned by wealthy individuals would have amounted to no more than "a few dozen" titles (*HBMA*, 283).

96. Audio transcription, Bartlett, *Inside the Medieval Mind: Knowledge*. Originally from Epist. de cynocephalis ad Rimbertum presbyterum.

97. Bartlett, *Inside the Medieval Mind: Knowledge*.

98. Bartlett, *Inside the Medieval Mind*.

99. A number of succeeding pamphlets from self-described witch finders and demonologists clearly copied the logical, question-and-answer structure of *MM* to give credibility to their own texts.

100. Oman, "The English Folklore of Gervase of Tilbury," 3.

101. This simply means that by the time witch hunts were more actively pursued in the fifteenth through seventeenth centuries in England, there was sufficient written testimonial along with an ingrained cultural acceptance of both the reality and malevolence of the demonic. The leap from there to punishment was an easy one, then.

102. *MPFC: UC*, 1.53.

103. *A MOST Certain, Strange, and true Dis*covery of a WITCH.

104. Sykes (1923–2012) would work closely with Spike Milligan as early as 1954, co-writing *Goon Show* scripts whenever Milligan's physical and mental exhaustion took their toll.

105. *Jesus Christ Superstar* appeared in London-area cinemas in August 1973 at the Universal.

106. Austin, "Were the Peasants Really So Clean?," 140.

107. Gaskill, 50.

108. The condemned never does ask forgiveness or recant; she admits to the "fair cop," and goes to her death.

109. See Hewison, *Monty Python: The Case Against*, for more on the visceral reaction to *LB*, the slippery financial slope the film trekked, and its eventual distribution and reception. See also *MPFC: UC*, 1.309.

110. Richard's father, Henry II, also spent the bulk of his ruling years away from England. Harvey notes, however, that even though he was away from his English kingdom for more than nine years of his ten-year reign, "England . . . continued to be efficiently governed, and very efficiently taxed," providing for Richard's chosen continental lifestyle (Harvey, *The Twelfth and Thirteenth Centuries*, 217).

111. *LMD-WM*, 67, Arthur retrieves Excalibur; *LMD'A*, 1.405, Lamorak fails to recognize Arthur; and *LMD-WM*, 13, Merlin announces Arthur's parentage, respectively.

112. In an adroit bit of legerdemain pre-echoing Arthur's "tricking" the Bridgekeeper into his own death plunge, Robin's seemingly rash promise made to John—to touch the soil of the Holy Land with his own fingers—is accomplished by Robin visiting Hector, himself just returned from a Crusade, to touch the soil he'd brought back with him. Robin can then appear in the forest to capture John before his Merry Men can be destroyed, and force the evil prince into signing a full pardon (Arthur: "You have to know these things when you're a king, you know"). Neatly done.

113. *Black Knight* #1, Atlas Comics, May 1955. Lee wrote the text; Joe Maneely and Syd Shores created the artwork.

114. In *MPFC* they referenced Billy Bunter, Superman, and Captain Marvel, and Gilliam used an issue of Action Comics (1968) for an animated sequence. See the index entry for "comic books" in *MPFC: UC* for more references.

115. Composed of parents, clergymen, juvenile authorities, librarians, teachers, and others.

116. "Donald Duck and Other Dangers," 17 February 1950: 7. See *MPFC: UC*, 1.107 for more.

VARIOUS MONTAGE—ANIMATION

This scene—Arthur and Bedevere gathering knights Gawain, Hector, Robin, Galahad, and Launcelot, in that order—is present in the printed script, but crossed out and *not* included in the finished film. This may also have been intended to be a completely animated sequence, but in the end was handled by creating the much more cost-effective "Book of the Film" section.

SIR GAWAIN standing outside—(PSC) Gawain is simply "*standing outside*" when Arthur approaches, and they "*shake hands*" (*MPHGB*, 20). The central figure of *Sir Gawain and the Green Knight*, Gawain is Arthur's nephew, and was likely not included in a major way to simply reduce the film's complexity and running time. Also, adding Gawain and Hector to the bunch would have necessitated adding Python troupe members, or double casting for knight roles, both of which presented additional filming problems.[1] Gawain is along for the quest, but isn't seen or referred to again until he's killed—offscreen, the most ignominious kind of death, à la Falstaff—by the Killer Rabbit.

Gawain is only detailed here by the fact that his page "*is weighed down by an enormous quantity of luggage*" in relation to other pages.

SIR HECTOR—(PSC) Also known as Ector, he is typically Arthur's foster father (father of Sir Kay), the part he plays in White's *The Once and Future King*. The Pythons also removed Ector from the bulk of the film's narrative, excepting his death at the Cave. Bors, Urien, and Gorlois also die in that slaughter, though they appear nowhere else in the film. More on these four—all "comprehensively killed"—when we reach the Cave of Caerbannog.

In the script Hector is approached "*down by a stream*," but there are no more details than that. He is also dubbed a knight of Camelot by Arthur (*MPHGB*, 21).

SIR ROBIN—Robin is described as "*being taught the lute by one of his musicians*," and when Arthur calls he hands the lute to his musician and joins the company (21).

SIR GALAHAD surrounded by chickens—(PSC) Galahad is attired in a carpenter's apron and is building a hen house. As Arthur, Gawain, Hector, and pages approach, "*he throws off the apron and puts down the hen-house and goes to join them*" (21). These scenes together are clearly meant to reference Christ's gathering of his followers:

> And Jesus, walking by the sea of Galilee, saw two brethren, Simon called Peter, and Andrew his brother, casting a net into the sea: for they were fishers.
> And he saith unto them, Follow me, and I will make you fishers of men.
> And they straightway left their nets, and followed him.

And going on from thence, he saw other two brethren, James the son of Zebedee, and John his brother, in a ship with Zebedee their father, mending their nets; and he called them.

And they immediately left the ship and their father, and followed him. (Matthew 4:18–22)

The Pythons will go back to the Christ story in a very controversial way in 1979 for *Life of Brian*. In *Holy Grail*, many of the more crude or irreverent moments involving a mean-spirited, argumentative, or forgetful God never make it out of the rough draft of the script.

SIR LAUNCELOT handing a baby to his WIFE—(PSC) In the penultimate bit of this excised section, Launcelot is first encountered living at the castle "*Eilean Donan*," as he "*strides off to join ARTHUR, leaving his castle, WIFE and CHILDREN . . . his washing hanging outside it . . . there are at least six kids*" (*MPHGB*, 21). The castle at Eilean Donan is a rebuilt version of a thirteenth- to sixteenth-century wall and keep structure now connected to the mainland by a tourist-friendly footbridge. It lies well north of Castle Stalker, so even though it was mentioned in the script—like another castle, Bodiam—the full cast and crew never did make it up there.[2] If the married version of Launcelot had remained, then Launcelot later being affianced to Princess Lucky would be even more complicated and uncomfortable than the final edit of the film could suggest. The conceit of a married Launcelot with a horde of children was likely just a complication the Pythons wanted to avoid once shooting began—it fell off by frugal necessity.[3] In history, though, there are examples of such family grouping, one acidly described by Gerald of Wales who, "writing in the early 13th century, assumed, with some disapproval, that village priests would be married, or at least keep a female 'hearth-mate,' 'who kindles his fire but puts out his virtue, filling his wretched house with babies, cradles, nurses and midwives'" (Hallam, 36). Simply put, Launcelot mightn't have been able to come along if he remained married and a father—he becomes, like the others a single, unattached knight who can devote his full attentions and sword to this noble ideal.

The final shot of this excised scene is the entire group, and all their attendants and baggage:

MIX TO *the complete group, i.e. ARTHUR and PATSY, BEDEVERE and PAGE, GAWAIN and PAGE, HECTOR and PAGE, GALAHAD and PAGE, SIR ROBIN and PAGE and SIX MUSICIANS, LAUNCELOT and PAGE.* (*MPHGB*, 21)

A crossed-through line of scenic description offers a suggestion to the eventual casting director for the secondary actors: "*Notes on the pages: some are old, some are young, but all are smaller than the knights*" (21). As this is scratched out along with the preceding gathering section, it's assumed that it may have either been a moot point—since the screenwriters would be in on the casting, anyway—or, since the pages in the finished film are all the same age or younger than the Pythons, getting older people for those rather laborsome roles might have been second-guessed rather early.

Notes

1. The Pythons also, historically, haven't been keen to share the spotlight with non-Pythons. They didn't accept written material from outside the group during *MPFC* (many shows of the period did), and the funny characters—including the ratbag women—they kept for themselves. Even Carol Cleveland's first bit of "acting" (where her breasts weren't the obvious reason she was invited) didn't come until Ep. 5. See *MPFC: UC*, 1.30, 81, and 315.

2. Production Manager Doyle confirms this in an e-mail dated 4 March 2014. The hectic schedule of the first days of the shoot—when director Jones attempted to squeeze multiple locations into a day—meant

that traveling all the way north to Eilean Donan for one shot just wasn't accomplishable. Two castles—Doune and Stalker—would have to do for every castle scene, with Doune used the most. Three other castles are depicted in the film. One is the "model" castle built from plywood as noticed by Patsy; the second is a filmed image of Kidwelly Castle, doubling as the exterior of the "Swallows" castle; and the third is a filmed image of Bodiam, meant to be Swamp Castle. Doyle captured the Kidwelly and Bodiam footage separate from the Pythons, after principal photography was completed.

3. Child actors on a set also tend to complicate any shoot, no matter the size, given the schedules the minors are allowed by law.

THE BOOK OF THE FILM

"The Book of the Film"—(PSC) This section (which is completely handwritten into the script and voiced by Palin) was created after-the-fact as a simple and *inexpensive* way to tie the film together,[1] but it, too, has a connection to the Arthurian romance sources of the Middle Ages, as well as to earlier epic films and the Pythons' own history. In the first instance, "The Book of the Film" operates as a sort of *estoire*, as Barber describes the term:

> Chrétien lends authority to his vivid portrait by appealing to his source: if "the words are true which the book sets out" (*devise*). At other points, he uses the phrase "as the story (*estoire*) says." *Estoire* was frequently used by historians writing in French, and had acquired, in addition to its original meaning of "story" or "narrative," the more precise meaning of a "true narrative," and it implied a specifically historical text. . . . In every case, the appeal to a source occurs when something superlative or beyond belief is introduced. The *estoire* is a fictional device which is used to suspend our disbelief by appealing to a higher authority. (*THG*, 161)

In this case, since the entire film teeters on the precipice of unbelievability and could be toppled at any moment, this interlude of *estoire* dependability—in the form of an illuminated manuscript complete with sonorous, reassuring voiceover narration—fits comfortably between scenes of witch-burnings and the silliness of Camelot, and is followed immediately by God's appearance, who puts his divine imprimatur on the grouping, further underscoring the believability of the *estoire*. This "pages of storybook" conceit is also recognizable to audiences of 1975 thanks to what they've already seen. First, for these children of the Age of Cinema (and Television), as the Disney hits *Snow White*, *Sleeping Beauty* (1959), and *Jungle Book* (1967) all begin with this "storybook" scene, as do the Fleischer Brothers' answer to *Snow White*, *Gulliver's Travels* (1939), the Disney short *Pigs Is Pigs* (1953), and, appropriately, Disney's 1963 animated version of *The Sword in the Stone*.[2] In the second instance, Hollywood epic films often employed stentorian voice-over narration to impress upon the audience the majesty and gravitas of the filmed story. In 1956, director Cecil B. DeMille himself provided the necessary introductory and linking narration for his biblical epic *The Ten Commandments*, after first appearing from behind a curtain to introduce the three-and-a-half-hour film.[3] Three years later in *Ben-Hur*, Scottish actor Finley Currie (1878–1968) doubled as the believer Balthasar and Narrator, where needed, much like Palin does for *Holy Grail*. Thirdly, in the second *Fliegender Zirkus* episode Princess Mitzi Gaynor (Connie Booth) espies a dashing young man whom she hopes is a prince. She takes a book from her pocket and finds therein a photo of the prince opposite his name and personal information. He is Prince Eberhard ("*Eberhard, Prinz*"), and the rest of his description is drawn from bird-spotting categories: "*Caprimulgus europaeus*," "Geschlecht: männlich," "Familie: Schreitvogel," etc. This prince book is a miniature version of the later "Book of the Film."

As for the physical pages of the book, Gilliam and Doyle essentially created an illuminated manuscript, not unlike the ninth-century Irish *Book of the Kells*, various fourteenth- and fifteenth-century Books of Hours, any of myriad period psalters (volumes containing the *Book of Psalms*),[4] like the *Lutrell Psalter*, and perhaps most appropriately for Arthur's and the film's milieu, the c. 700 *Lindisfarne Gospels*. In *Lindisfarne* each of the four major divisions begins with the name of the saint as incipit material—for example, Marcus (Mark)—including the large and elaborate initial letter, "M," followed by the cleverly crafted letters "A-R-C-U-S." Gilliam has performed his own version of Eadfrith's (d. 721) artwork as he introduces Galahad, Launcelot, and Robin, as well as "The Book of the Film" sections, each becoming what might be called the *incipit page* in this filmed illuminated manuscript. The initial letters here are *decorated*, as opposed to *figural* or *zoomorphic*; the latter two will be seen later in the individual introductions of each knight's adventures.[5]

Also available to Gilliam for inspiration were more contemporary illuminated books, made popular thanks to Tennyson's *Idylls*, the Victorian-era fascination with the Arthurian romance and tradition, and the general revival of medieval artforms and notions of romance in the late nineteenth and early twentieth centuries. Evelyn Paul's *Tristram and Isoude* was published in 1913, while her *Clair de Lune and Other Troubadour Romances* appeared in 1921. Paul (1883–1963) created decidedly Pre-Raphaelite characters, though her borders and decorations were meant to directly mimic the late medieval illuminated manuscript designs found in calendars, books of hours, gospels, and psalters. The juxtaposition of thirteenth-century decorations and lettering against the graceful, sensual, nineteenth-century Rosetti-influenced figures is quite striking.

The first page of "The Book of the Film" contains a version of the dragon that Gilliam created, which is based on the many long, sinewy dragons (often winged and feathered) featured in the margins of myriad illuminated manuscripts.[6] In *Maps and Monsters in Medieval England*, Mittman includes an illustration of one such "Monstrous Initial" from the *Junius Psalter*.[7] These careful, intricate drawings weren't for simple adornment, according to Mittman, they were to be studied, pored over, mentally and spiritually chewed even, hence the term, "*ruminatio*," or the "chewing over and over as a cow does with her cud":

> This metaphor, more resonant in an agrarian culture than in our own, not only implies careful consideration, but also suggests the inherent indigestibility of the unprocessed text or image. In this climate, works were designed to sustain the inevitable *ruminatio*. Hence, any text or image that yields all its meaning after a cursory first glance would likely have been considered inadequate. . . . The value of close reading was not only conveyed by images of pious clergymen.[8] The metaphor of *ruminatio* was also enacted through images of monsters, which are found throughout the period gnawing on the texts they help to form.[9] The violent, gnashing beasts of the fabulous *Junius Psalter*, for example, frequently lash out with sharp fangs at the sacred text before them. (2)

This particular dragon (as created by Gilliam) will reappear in the introductory frame for "The Tale of Sir Robin," where it will become the zoomorphic initial letter *R*. See the entry for "The Tale of Sir Robin" below for more, as well as appendix A for more on these illuminated manuscripts. In Randall's *IMGM* there are more than twenty dragons included in the representative illuminated manuscript pages; they most often appear on margins and between lines, and often stretch to the top and bottom of the page, snout to tail.

Book of the Film—(PSC) All handwritten on a formerly blank opposite page (Facing Page 21), the initial "gathering" scene in the finished script, styled after Christ gathering his disciples, is crossed out completely. Also, sometime during the transition from the writing of the gathering sequence to replacing it with the "Book of the Film" sequence, both Gawain and Hector's roles were reduced significantly.

This phrase "Book of the Film" wasn't original to the Pythons. Editorial comic artist "Vicky" (Victor Weisz), for instance, used it in a panel in 1959 wherein a series of British paperbacks are presented in relation to their Russian counterparts, the Brit offerings including "*Around the World with Nothing On* (The Book of the Film): The Frank Memoirs of Selwyn Lloyd, Author of *Our Man in Havana*."[10] Lloyd would be the Speaker of the House of Commons 1971–1976, and is alluded to in *MPFC*, as well.[11] In common parlance, the "book of the film" was considered to be the novel on which a film is based, but also a novelization, meaning the novel was written after the successful film. By 1950, public libraries in Britain were experiencing significant interest in the former—novels that became popular films (which upset more traditional library types, as well as those who disliked public expenditure on such frivolousness).[12]

VOICE OVER: "The wise Sir Bedevere"—As mentioned above, Bedevere's crest is a formerly deep-rooted, barren tree, its leaves on the ground around it, its branches lopped. The image here is a simple still frame—a photo—from the previous "dubbing" scene, pasted into the Book of the Film. This series of images become a sort of portmanteau of this entire, anachronistic film world—Polaroids in a handmade book.

Palin handles all the voice-over duties for the film, and he was available to work on the postproduction process with Jones, Gilliam, and Doyle (contributing the silly subtitles, for example) more significantly than Cleese, Chapman, or Idle. This may have been due to Palin's role as writing partner to codirector Jones, and the fact that together they'd contributed the bulk of the original film script draft. During the run of *MPFC*, all the Pythons had contributed to voice-overs or narration, as needed, even Gilliam.

HAND TURNS PAGE—(PSC) This hand belongs to Maggie Gilliam, Terry's wife, who was also a makeup artist for *Flying Circus*. The "gorilla's hand" that will snatch away the female hand is Gilliam himself.[13] For more on the gorilla hand, see "*A gorilla's hand*" below.

VOICE OVER: "Sir Lancelot the Brave"—Lancelot's name is spelled with and without the medial "u," likely depending on which troupe member had penned that particular portion of the script. In Malory, it is most often spelled "Launcelot." Since Gilliam, his wife, and Doyle are creating this sequence, credit for this spelling must be given to them. Spelling during *Flying Circus* was also here and there—"looney/loony"—and words including "tassels," "mantological," "swapping," and "cannelloni," names like "Philip," "O'Malley," and "DeBakey," and places like "Cincinnati," "Roraima," and "Magdalene" (College) also failing the spelling sniff test.[14] These misspellings crept into captions and title cards throughout the series.

Launcelot's coat of arms is a majestic griffin, signifying his valor and bravery, and his vigilance. This particular idiom *would* make it a challenge to leave a castle by simply walking out the front gate, hence his Errol Flynn–like swing. And as for possible female entanglements given Launcelot's character in the sources—his dalliance with Guinevere, of course—this Launcelot seems to have learned a hard lesson there, and expends a great deal of energy protecting Galahad's chastity later at the Castle Anthrax.

VOICE OVER: "Sir Galahad the Pure"—Spelled "Gallahad" on the pages of the "Book of the Film" here and later, Galahad's purity in several versions of his story (including Malory) allowed him to both successfully retrieve the Grail as well as choose the time of his own death, and he is assumed into heaven. (He is also Launcelot's illegitimate child by some accounts, which isn't broached in the film.)

In the first draft of the screenplay Galahad is so straight and true that often no one can stand to be around him. At the first French-held castle Galahad leads the furious charge against the castle walls while the others try to sneak in "through the tradesmen's entrance," an ignoble entry Galahad has already declined (*MPHGB*, 11). Later, after achieving the Grail, they find they've mislaid it just when they're ready to show it to the eager masses; Arthur has to threaten to cut off Galahad's head if he tells the mob the truth (13). Galahad is also the only knight who complains when the others choose a tatty Grail bunged together and cleaned up by Merlin (26). Galahad tries to sing a little song with gathered children, each line based on the letters of his name, but he stumbles at "G-A-L-L-" and stops, with the children laughing at him (26). He takes a swipe at them. Many moments in the first draft of the script are meaner, nastier, even pettier than those found in the finished version. Galahad does eventually and accidentally find the Grail, though, and just moments after the Grail company has separated in a particularly majestic, inspiring way (37).

Galahad's crest is the red cross (a flory or fleury cross), and generally means one who is faithful and who has served in the Crusades. The Pythons have accoutered him with the proper shield, at least according to Malory's *Of Sir Galahad* section in *The Noble Tale of the Sangrail* (*LMD-WM*). Prior to leaving Arthur and Camelot on his own adventure the young Galahad is sans shield, a fact mentioned often, with the first words of his chapter being "Now rideth Galahad yet without shield" (321). Reaching a white abbey on his fourth day out, Galahad is told of a shield that will kill anyone who attempts to bear it, and Galahad declares he will take it up, as he has no shield. The abbey's monk (monks and hermits being purveyors of essential information, including warnings and histories, throughout the romances) shows Galahad the shield, leading him "behind an altar where the shield hung, as white as any snow, but in the midst was a red cross" (321). The shield had been made for King Evelake after he accepted "the new law" taught by Joseph, son of Joseph of Arimathea. According to Malory, it was Joseph's own blood that made the cross on the shield, and it won't be worn again (safely) until Galahad takes it up many years later (323).

In the first draft of the script, Galahad is depicted as a straighter-than-straight prig, an annoying younger brother Joseph-type (as in Jacob's son) who has God's favor, is always right, and is therefore disliked by most. This overall churlishness disappears by the time they are filming, the knights quite accepting of each other's strengths and weaknesses (even Robin's timidity and incontinence).

VOICE OVER: "Dragon of Angnor"—Located in what is modern-day Sudan, Africa, this region isn't likely to have been reached, even on a crusade, unless the knight became hopelessly lost. It is possible that this could have been a region and a creature spoken of by those who had returned from various Crusades; those itinerant knights and armies encountered all manner of distractions along the way. The first draft of the script does take the quest to "Africa A.D. 1973" (subtitled "23rd February," and "4:33 p.m."), where Sir Perceval is an accountant for Tarzan and is menaced by a "lost tribe of nymphomaniacs," but that section never makes it into production (*MPHGB*, 41).

"Angnor" also could be a typo, since the Pythons generally wrote from collective memory, very seldom double-checking for pinpoint accuracy. In *MPFC*, for example, they wrote "Abu Simnel" for "Abu Simbel" (Ep. 21); cited "Trevelyan, page 468," when the reference they're referring to is on page 486 (Ep. 26); identified planes as "Red Devils," when they were actually the Royal Air Force group "Red Arrows" (Ep. 32); and offered the unhelpful directions and distances given by the Military Man (Idle) in Ep. 34.

The designs around the initial letters "D" and "A" (for "Dragon of Angnor") are made to resemble those found in Royal 17 E.VII (for example, f. 7 and f. 166v), portions of which can be seen in Randall's *IMGM*.[15] The single leaves extending from the top and bottom borders are characteristic of a number of colorful *bas-de-page* images in the Royal 10 E.IV manuscript, which Gilliam also employs in his animation preparation.[16] See the mentions of "Royal 10" below and in appendix A for more.

VOICE OVER: "Chicken of Bristol"—An apt foe, since Sir Robin has a chicken on his shield.[17] The cock ("coq") was a popular figure of medieval heraldry, and is often depicted beak open (singing) and with a foot boldly raised, ready to battle. Robin's chicken is looking back over its shoulder, likely "in surprise and alarm," its foot raised as if ready to flee. Bristol is in southwest England, near Weston-super-Mare, where Cleese was born and raised.

This type of nomenclature abounds in the Pythons' source material, such as Geoffrey's *HKB* where, in Merlin's prophetic utterings, can be found: the "boar of Cornwall,"[18] the "goat of the Venereal Castle," the "serpent of Malvernia," the "dragon of Worcester," the "boar of Totness," the "fox of Kaerdubalem," and the "adder of Lincoln."[19] Robin could have nearly fought any of these.

The designs surrounding the initial letters "C" and "B" (for "Chicken of Bristol") are reflective of the more geometric designs found in Cambrai 87 (f. 30) and Winchester 45 (f. 91v), both of which can be seen in Randall's *IMGM* (plates XXXI.141 and L.242).

Sir Robin, by the way, was obviously a late addition to this Grail quest, as he has no part (by name) in the first draft.

VOICE OVER: "Battle of Badon Hill"—This is one of those landmarks in Arthuriana that has seen more critical skirmishes than just about anywhere else, yet the Pythons treat Arthur's most famous battle rather blithely, mentioning it, in passing, as a part of Sir Robin's knightly skill level—it was a place where he managed to "wet himself."[20] "Mons Badonicus" had for many years been the one battle that most scholars and interested others could very nearly agree was an actual Arthurian accomplishment, if there was an actual Arthur, because the battle itself—with or without Arthur—seems to have been historical.

Arthur's conquests at this early battle (late fifth to early sixth century) aren't mentioned until *Historia Brittonum* (ninth century), though they are echoed later, including Geoffrey's *HKB* (twelfth century). Gildas's sixth-century *De Excidio* mentions the battle (but *not* Arthur, glaringly), and Ashe notes that "an early Welsh source, the *Annales Cumbriae*, dates the 'battle of Badon' with a slight ambiguity in 516 or 518" (*QAB*, 54). Alcock "favour[s] [an] alternative earlier date," 490, a significant difference that points up the challenges of historical accuracy when so few period documents survive (*Arthur's Britain*, 111). The first two of these medieval texts are referenced above, in relation to Arthur and Camelot. Its approximate date also means that a tenth-century Sir Robin would have been hard-pressed to fight (or wet himself) in the battle at all, of course.

Higham in *KAMH* addresses the scholarly "agreements" on Arthur and the Battle of Badon Hill, his own skepticism evident: "If we were to attempt to sum up the debate about an historical Arthur in the late 1960s, Sheppard Frere's recycling of Collingwood's views would arguably have been as widely accepted as any (1967)." And he cites Frere:

> In the later fifth century the leadership [of Vortigern] had passed to Ambrosius Aurelianus and after him to Arthur. Little is known of either. Ambrosius appears in the pages of Gildas, but Arthur does not, and his activities and personality are almost impenetrably overlaid by medieval romance. The evidence is sufficient to allow belief that he had a real existence and that he was probably the victor of Mount Badon. . . Using mounted forces, these leaders were able to strike back at the Saxons, who had little body armour and inferior weapons. (Frere 1967: 1987 edn, p. 374)

Higham adds: "A rather vague but probably historical Arthur, then, canters through the early post-war period, leading heavily-armed cavalry in a quintessentially late-Roman style of warfare, to contest the Anglo-Saxon settlement and give protection to the sub-Roman Britons" (*KAMH*, 26).

Higham then rehearses the Alcock, Ashe, and Camelot Research Committee work in the 1960s, where lots of digging and excitement led to many dubious conclusions,[21] and then the publication of Morris's book (*The Age of Arthur*, wherein Arthur's "battle list [is accepted] as essentially historical"), emerging in 1973, which would have been the last, loudest word on Arthurian scholarship as the Pythons began writing *Holy Grail*.

The designs around the initial letters "B" and "B" and "H" (as in the "Battle of Badon Hill") are influenced by illuminated manuscripts like *Cloisters* 54.1.2. An image of this manuscript page is included in *IMGM* (XXV.120).

VOICE OVER: "Sir Not-Appearing-in-This-Film"—In a sure sign that memory can be most fallible, both of Michael Palin's infant sons, Tom and William, have been identified by the Pythons as the baby in this photo.[22]

A gorilla's hand—It's possible this was inspired by the recent and somewhat infamous *La Bête*, the Walerian Borowczyk film that featured a creature, a maiden, bestiality, and warnings to faint-hearted viewers.[23] One of the well-circulated movie posters depicted the beast, on his back and mostly out-of-frame, reaching its black, hairy hands up toward the nude maiden, she seen only from the waist down. It's also worth mentioning John Landis's first feature film, 1973's horror-comedy *Schlock*, featuring Landis (b. 1950) as a lascivious, cantankerous gorilla running amok in suburban Los Angeles.[24]

Also, Reuben Martin had played a gorilla in several *Carry On* films, including *Carry on Up the Jungle* (1970), which was precisely the kind of film Palin had vowed *not* to make as they created *Holy Grail*. There had also been two appearances by a gorilla in *Flying Circus*. One, in Ep. 10, a man in a gorilla suit is applying for a librarian's job (and he is only turned away when they find out he's not a real gorilla), and Ep. 29, when explorers are attacked by a wild gorilla in a jungle bistro.[25] Gilliam also uses a gorilla picture in an animation in Ep. 18, where the men from "The Society for Putting Things On Top of Other Things" are trying to escape being trapped on film. This same beastly hand—the gorilla glove worn by Gilliam—will appear later to turn the page again, in the "Scene 24" section.

BEDEVERE: ". . . earth to be banana-shaped"—Like most tropical fruit, the banana wouldn't make it to Europe in a commodity kind of way until the fifteenth century, likely brought back by Portuguese ships, though it had been cultivated in Rome much earlier, meaning Roman-occupied Britain may have had access to the fruit in some form.

As for the shape of the Earth, since Pythagoras's time (sixth-century BC) the Earth as a sphere had been an accepted though not necessarily widespread theorem. There were a number of thinkers that believed the Earth to be flat (round or square), yes, or cylindrical (Anaximander, for example [fl. 546 BC]), and to Isidore of Seville (c. 560–636) it was wheel shaped (Freely, 56). To the uninitiated, early maps like the Hereford Map might give the indication that the Earth was a flat, circular expanse with Jerusalem at its center and wildness on its fringes. The British Isles nearly slide off the bottom left of the map—mapmakers understood how far from the center of the world, Jerusalem, they really were.[26]

ARTHUR: ". . . new learning"—The work of men like the Venerable Bede[27] (674–735) fits well here, according to Freely in *Before Galileo*:

Bede's scientific works were remarkable achievements for their time, and for centuries afterward they were Europe's principal source of knowledge concerning history, cosmology, chronology, astronomy, natural science, mathematics, and the calendar. His fame as a scholar led a ninth-century Swiss monk to write that "God, the orderer of natures, who raised the Sun from the East on the fourth day of Creation, on the sixth day of the world has made Bede rise from the West as a new Sun to illuminate the whole Earth. (58)

By the film's stated time of 932 Bedevere could have at least heard of Bede's accomplishments—his work was later carried on by Egbert and Alcuin,[28] and thence into Charlemagne's court on the Continent. And since the Dark Ages weren't as dark as once believed, inquisitive men like Bedevere—men of respect and some means—could have had access, theoretically, to this "new learning," through the monastic culture even after the fall of Rome. Britain sat at the periphery of the former Roman Empire, thousands of miles from "Hellenic culture," and even farther "from the Arabs who had preserved, absorbed, and by their commentaries, especially in medicine and mathematics, developed classical learning" (Poole, *DBMC*, 244). Britain sat at the edge of the known world on period maps, as well (at the bottom left, generally)—which likely meant that expensive and bulky books in private collections were few and far between, especially in times of want. But knowledge could flow along important trade routes, as Poole points out, with Spain, southern Italy, Sicily, and Syria providing myriad, previously unseen translations of eagerly awaited ancient texts: "In England the *new learning* found a receptive field" (244; italics added). The opening of new schools in the eleventh and twelfth centuries—including Oxford, Exeter, and Northampton[29]—some associated with cathedrals and monasteries, some not, meant that education and the classic texts in translation were more and more needed and available (Lindberg, 203–9). Bedevere, though, might be "trapped" in his own time, according to von Ehrenkrook: "still trapped—to borrow a Petrarchian paradigm of historiography—in the regressive dark ages after the intellectual lights of the classical era had long since dimmed."[30] The hostility that these new "universities" often cultivated, especially with the local population of, for example, Oxford, meant that studying for studying's sake could be quite a challenge.[31]

ARTHUR: "Explain again . . ."—Arthur might here be favorably compared to Alfred the Great (849–899), the English king who not only defeated the Viking Danes but, finding himself "[d]istressed at the ignorance of his clergy and the illiteracy of his people," set about to educate them by

> establish[ing] a court school like that of Charlemagne . . . import[ing] teachings from abroad. He was more literate than his great model. He translated works of piety and instruction into Anglo-Saxon. He concluded one of his books with the words: "He seems to me a very foolish man and very wretched, who will not increase his understanding while he is in the world, and ever wish and long to reach that endless life where all shall be made clear." (Bishop, *HBMA*, 30)

According to Tuchman, much learning during the later thirteenth and fourteenth centuries came precisely in this "Explain again" way—orally and aurally. Combined with available texts for reading, much of God's creation could be known:

> The average layman acquired knowledge mainly by ear, through public sermons, mystery plays, and the recital of narrative poems, ballads, and tales, but during [the first half of the fourteenth century], reading by educated nobles and upper bourgeois increased with the increased availability of manuscripts. Books of universal knowledge, mostly dating from the 13th century and written in (or translated from the Latin into) French and other vernaculars for the use of the layman, were literary staples familiar in every country over several centuries. A 14th century man drew also on the Bible, romances, bestiaries, satires, books of astronomy, geography, universal history, church history, rhetoric, law, medicine, alchemy, falconry, hunting, fighting, music, and any number of special subjects. (59–60)

If the Pythons had decided to firmly set the film in the thirteenth and fourteenth centuries, there was plenty of available learning and knowledge for his upper-class knights. Cherry-picking facts or telescoping epochs as the Pythons do, a jumble of folklore and science and anachronisms becomes the order of the day.

ARTHUR: "sheep's bladders . . ."—Sheep's bladders have actually been quite useful over time. One report from 1962 notes that the island of St. Kilda's mail delivery problems—it is a remote, harborless rock well west of Scotland—were addressed in the earliest part of the twentieth century by handmade "mailboats" that could drift to the mainland over a period of months. One such boat was made of hollowed-out driftwood attached to a sheep's bladder float and a flag.[32] Sheep's bladder was also used as a membrane, a sieve, of sorts.

This is the first of only a few occasions in the film where sheep are mentioned or seen. Cartoon sheep will be visible in the animated title sequence, and a sheep is allegedly[33] catapulted from a French-occupied castle; the same cartoon sheep are used in the "Passing Seasons" animated sequence, and finally a sheep is catapulted from another French-occupied castle and onto Arthur and Bedevere. There are no images of sheep in fields grazing, or of any other aspect of the wool industry so crucial to Britain for centuries. In the late twelfth century it's estimated that "England grazed around six million sheep . . . produc[ing] up to 50,000 sacks of wool a year" (Hallam, 146). The best wool (from Welsh abbeys) was valued at almost £19 per sack in the 1290s, roughly ten times what a laborer could expect to make in a year (147). Over the centuries control of the wool trade gave Britain significant economic power, even when its military might was in question.

ARTHUR: ". . . employed to prevent earthquakes"—The *Annals of Ulster*[34] records at least nine earthquakes occurring during the sub-Roman years 448–740, with another in 664 reported elsewhere, and as occurring in Britain, likely Northumbria (Woods, "An 'Earthquake' in Britain in 664," 258). Britain is not and has not historically been earthquake prone, meaning it's likely that when tremors did occur they were quite memorable. From Woods: "Britain suffers relatively little seismic activity by international standards, but minor earthquakes do occur on a regular basis" (261). Bedevere may be mentioning "earthquakes" due to the very significant seismic activity in parts of the world of the Roman Empire (throughout Italy, for example), vivid descriptions of which appeared in many classical texts. Many of these natural catastrophes were also tied directly to plague events—meaning they were doubly memorable. From McCormick, "Rats, Communications, and Plague":

> Severe earthquakes struck the Middle East in the sixth century, and again in 740, on the eve of the final outbreak of the Justinianic pandemic. Constantinople suffered them in 525, 533, 548, 554, 557, and 740; the first and last two seisms were the most destructive. The timing of the earthquake that is known to have struck in December 557 is particularly noteworthy, since it anticipated the plague that is first reported at Constantinople eight months later, in July 558. (19)

The mystery surrounding earthquakes (and deadly hazards of nature in general) led most cultures to create explanations involving angry or petulant gods (and creatures) causing earth movements.[35] In some ancient cultures, human sacrifices were seen as the best way to appease a god and prevent earthquakes.[36] Complicating matters, earthquakes were also often lumped by chroniclers with other portentous events, many natural, and some seemingly supernal or diabolical. From Gregory of Tours' *History of the Franks*[37]:

> In this year again appeared the following portents. The Moon was eclipsed. In the territory of Tours real blood flowed from broken bread. The walls of Soissons fell down. The earth quaked at Angers. Wolves entered the walls of Bordeaux, and without any fear of men, devoured dogs.

A fiery light was seen to traverse the sky. The city of Bazas was burned, so that the churches and the houses belonging to them were destroyed. We learned, however, that all the sacred vessels were saved from the flames. (253)

Banana-shaped planets, witches made of wood, and scientific sheep bladders fit nicely into this catalog of apocalyptic horrors.

In fact, it was well into the twentieth century and the advent of electrical technology—the seismograph—before science could show any kind of real, measurable understanding of these chthonic processes. Prior to about 1880, spotty knowledge and mythology held sway:

Earthquakes thus had the potential to upend the hierarchies of "modern" and "primitive," "civilized" and "savage." The threat that earthquakes posed to European self-confidence was not only a function of physical devastation. It also stemmed from the methods of research that Europeans invented in their attempts at the intellectual mastery of seismic forces. There were, first, no clear limits to the kind of observations that might be relevant to earthquake research. According to theories widely accepted in the nineteenth century, earthquakes might be triggered by volcanoes, barometric fluctuations, atmospheric electricity, geomagnetism, humidity, or the positions of celestial bodies. Equally, studies of the course and impact of earthquakes required a wide variety of data, from the geological to the zoological and psychological. Geographically as well, earthquakes presented no clear limits. Speculation was rife over the apparent coincidence of earthquakes across vast distances and the subterranean channels that might account for such teleconnections. This uncertainty about what constituted seismology's evidence brought the science into precarious contact with such "pseudosciences" as astrology and spiritualism. (Coen, 4)

These "pseudosciences" could clearly include the use of sheep's bladders, if necessary. Coen goes on: "In a medieval and Renaissance framework, earthquakes were to be interpreted either as punishment for sinners or reminders to the faithful. It was theologically essential that earthquakes, as portents, be recognized as deviations from nature's normal course" (2). Fossier notes that the farther Middle Ages peasants lived from the centers of learning—"Oxford, Paris, Montpellier, or Salerno"—the more likely they were to listen to their local religious leaders' explanations of such phenomena:

[T]he Dominicans' sermons prudently kept the faithful reasoning on the level of the fear of God. It was demons who created tornadoes; comets announced the coming of a miracle; when the sirocco blew in red sand, it announced a bath of blood; if lightning struck the church, Satan prevented it from striking the castle. When they could not explain Nature, since that would be flouting God, at least, and obligatorily, men of the time reacted to her aggressions and caprices. (*AO*, 153)

For Bedevere, the goal is prevention, which might mean that he does not subscribe to the theory that such catastrophes are God's inevitable punishments; this isn't a stretch if we see him as he sees himself: a man of rationality and science.

Candide's travail of corporal punishment (and Pangloss's execution) as a deterrent to earthquakes has already been mentioned,[38] but it isn't just pseuds like Bedevere who miss the mark in science. Three of the great Aristotle's theories suffered similar ignominy, according to John Freely:

These three erroneous theories—that the velocity of a falling body is proportional to its weight, that a void is impossible, and the notion of antiperistasis[39]—persisted for more than a millennium, until they were refuted by the new dynamics that was developed by medieval European scholars, culminating in the laws of motion formulated in 1687 by Isaac Newton. (28)

This is all rather risible and wholly "medieval," we'd like to believe, but as recently as 2012 an Italian court sentenced seismic scientists to six years in prison for failing to *predict* (and then properly warn the population about) a deadly 2009 earthquake.[40]

ARTHUR (*with thankful reverence*): "Camelot!"—This reverential moment will be quickly undercut by a silly musical number inside the distant castle, but Arthur is likely seeing his Camelot in the same light as Alfred saw his hall at Cheddar—the center of culture and learning in an otherwise dangerous and inapposite world. As Asser and Brooke point out, Alfred seemingly had the best intentions for his land and his people—by fortifying towns and reorganizing the military he made the country more safe from the Danes; he also attempted to organize monasteries, he created laws and "raised the standards of his legal officers," and he worked ably on the gathering and translation of many learned texts into English (Brooke, *SNK* 60–61). He clearly had a "thankful reverence" for his kingdom, his people, and his home. He wanted to "rule a kingdom of literate men—a dream as hopeless, yet inspiring, as so many of his schemes" (61). Arthur's "hopeless, yet inspiring" dreams populate the balance of the film. Alfred's and Arthur's aspirations are aligned in both their nobility and their ultimate futility; Alfred is at least fighting against a world he can hope to understand.

More contemporarily, the National Union of Mine Workers' building for South Yorkshire in Barnsley had become known as "Camelot," partly because of the ideals to which the unions were wont to aspire, and partly as a nod to union leader Arthur Scargill, a "King Arthur" in the world of trade unions discussed earlier.[41] This "miners' Camelot" was celebrating its centenary in 1974.[42] The building itself has impressive turrets and spires, and still sits proudly at 2 Huddersfield Road.

CUT TO *shot of amazing castle in the distance*—(PSC) This view is likely a visual reference to the famous Doré print included in Tennyson's *Idylls of the King*. Camelot is also introduced this way in the Black Knight and various King Arthur comic books of the period—noble and majestic on a distant hill. In the Doré image, the viewer is placed well below the castle, set on a prominent crag overlooking the valley below; the king figure—wearing a crown very much like Arthur's in *Holy Grail*—sits in the middle distance astride his horse, reflecting on his throne, subjects, and empire.

As for Poet Laureate Tennyson (1809–1892), he figures prominently in *MPFC*, Ep. 41, where he reads out an "ant" version of his *Charge of the Light Brigade* to assembled Victorians (*JTW*, 2.270–71). The ant motif—as opposed to the swallow—was included in the film script's first draft, and then abandoned in the final version of *MPHG*. See the entry in scene 2 on "African swallows."

In the final draft of the script, the castle is also "[i]lluminated in the rays of the setting sun" (*MPHGB*, 22). The cast and crew obviously didn't wait around for this "golden hour" (or "magic hour") shot, time and budget being major constraints.[43] In the days before specialized after-effects shots and computer-assisted work, these kinds of shots had to be well planned.

PATSY: "It's only a model"—This "model" comment is a portmanteau reference, referring to not only the set built on a small hill, but to film's longstanding use of trompe l'oeil special effects. This flat plywood model of a castle is seen in the original trailer for the film, as well, where, in the foreground, Arthur is knighting Dennis, until in the background the forced perspective castle prop falls down, and Arthur kills Dennis. In the final draft of the script, Gawain was given this "It's only a model" line, to be spoken to a page (*MPHGB*, 22).

Since the earliest days of cinema, filmmakers have employed optical tricks to create the illusion of spectacular vistas and cityscapes, when either budgetary or time constraints prohibited erecting full-size sets. Perfectionist filmmakers like D. W. Griffith, Erich von Stroheim, and DeMille usually demanded actual-size sets, and had such built for films like *Broken Blos-*

soms (1919), *Blind Husbands* (1919), and *The Ten Commandments* (1923 and 1956), respectively. Conversely, former Ufa[44] filmmaker F. W. Murnau asked for forced perspective sets for his 1927 tour de force production for William Fox, *Sunrise*. Murnau wanted to create the illusion of a large city in the controlled confines of a sound stage. Fellow German filmmaker (and fellow émigré) Fritz Lang would also employ the tactic in the dystopic science fiction film *Metropolis* (1927). Without much of a budget, the Pythons relied on Lang and Murnau's trompe l'oeil precedents and built a forced-perspective castle made of wood, and then, in a very postmodernist sort of way, immediately drew attention to the artificiality of the illusion.

Also, there is a visually similar moment in Polanski's *Macbeth* where the looming castle is seen perched on a distant hill. This was likely a matte painting, however—where part of the scene has been painted in great detail on a wide glass sheet—as opposed to a model built in perspective. The extant Lindisfarne Castle was used for the hillock and base of the castle in that film, and matte artists added the two jutting turrets. The matte tradition had been part of cinema since the early days of epic cinema, with significant shots accomplished in *The Wizard of Oz* and *Citizen Kane*, for example.

Lastly, this is nearly a Cervantean moment, where the squire attempts to correct his master knight. In *Don Quixote*[45] Sancho is eager to convince his master that the "thirty or forty" giants he sees and readies to attack are actually windmills. Rather than shushing Sancho, Don Quixote tells him to stand aside and pray, and the knight spurs his horse toward the multi-armed foes. The knight will be battered by the windmill, of course, only then certain that a trickster has changed the giants for windmills (58). Arthur learns his lesson in a slightly different way—the goings-on in Camelot are too "silly" for such a noble quest, and so they avoid the mock castle and go to meet God instead. Arthur will endure physical lessons, as well, when they are assaulted by the French forces (twice), and eventually placed under arrest. And while the Pythons are sometimes mean to their characters (the Black Knight loses all limbs, a page is squashed by the Wooden Rabbit, Herbert is slapped around by his father, several knights are mangled by the Killer Rabbit, and Robin is hectored by his well-intending minstrels), they aren't as cruel as Cervantes can be throughout *Don Quixote*. The knight-errant is beaten mercilessly by a muledriver on his first sally, and "saves" a boy from one whipping to the promise of future whippings—in both of these the knight feels as if he's done right and well, and so the cruel tale continues. The Pythons removed more of the nastier bits found in the first draft, including a God who hides and jumps out to startle passersby, then "lames" a poor man "out of spite," for which the man is grateful (*MPHGB*, 14).[46]

ARTHUR (turning sharply) **Sh!**—This is the *only* moment in the film where Arthur comes close to acknowledging the film world's artificiality. Generally, Arthur is the picture of knightly dedication—to his quest, his God, and to the world of the pursuit of the Grail, no matter how silly, absurd, or frustrating it becomes. As a true believer, it is often Arthur's faith that keeps things going, and as a true believer the conceit of the film depends on his continuing belief. If he falters, the entire world likely collapses.[47] Following the French debacle at Mansourah, where the Saracens defeated the French forces and took hundreds of prisoners, including the king, Louis IX, one chronicler described the anguish and national embarrassment of the loss, but there was more: "[T]he worst aspect of all was that people accused the Lord of injustice, and the faith of many began to waver" (Hallam, 70). In Ep. 35 of *MPFC*, residents of a new tower block erected by the hypnotist El Mystico must "believe in" the building at all times, or it will come crashing down. Lack of belief, a changed mind, a sudden realization—in the Python world, these moments can disrupt immediately, tearing the fabric of whatever reality's been constructed. This "shush" could also simply be a moment where Arthur is trying to maintain the dignity of the moment—the gathered appreciation of Camelot—and he is simply shushing the mouthy Patsy, not commenting on the context-shattering "model" revelation. The film doesn't make itself clear on this point. Arthur doesn't look into the camera, for example, nor does Patsy, which would have completed the acknowledgment of a camera, an audience, and a constructed unreality. Just moments earlier, Miss Islington had looked directly into the camera to comment "It's a fair cop" to the only sensible people within earshot—the viewing audience. In the Camelot dance sequence, almost all action is addressed to the camera, though the generic tendencies of the musical *allow* for this gaze—there is no rupture, no context-smashing. Later, Dingo will also look directly at the audience as she asks about the significance of the scene in which she's participating. These are isolated moments that Arthur and his knights do not share. Even when Arthur is later being arrested and hustled into the police van by "modern" figures, he still doesn't "break character"—he is the legendary and/or historical King Arthur, start to finish.[48] Arthur is clearly cousin to the character of Don Quixote, in some respects.

In his introduction to the 2003 Edith Grossman translation of Cervantes's masterwork, Harold Bloom describes the level of identifiable belief and commitment of Sancho, Don Quixote, and even of the author Cervantes, and it sounds as if he could be talking about our Arthur: "Sancho, as Kafka remarked, is a free man, but Don Quixote is *metaphysically and psychologically bound by his dedication to knight errantry*. We can celebrate the knight's endless valour, but not his literalisation of the romance of chivalry."[49] Arthur is dedicated to his version of knight errantry, and follows two single-minded purposes: a gathering to Camelot, then the Quest for the Holy Grail. He only changes horses mid-stream, as it were, at God's request. Arthur isn't a righter of wrongs, he isn't looking for injustices to upend, nor is he necessarily "battling against death," like Cervantes's knight; but Arthur's is a godly task and his dedication is no less. Bloom points out other connections between Cervantes the author and man and his literary creations, commonalities that can serve us well in understanding Arthur's motivations. Bloom comments more than once on the abject, "vicious and humiliating cruelties" Cervantes inflicts on his knight and squire, and asks "how can this bashed and mocked knight errant be, as he is, a universal paradigm?" The answer is that as pain and suffering are universal, so can be standing again after a fall: "Don Quixote and Sancho are victims, but both are extraordinarily resilient" (xxvi). The knight's "endurance" and his squire's "wisdom" continue to fascinate, Bloom argues, "Cervantes plays upon the human need to withstand suffering, which is one reason the knight awes us" (xxvi–xxvii). Our Arthur carries on, and Patsy shrugs and clip-clops on, too. Arthur is put upon in many ways—he is rejected by his subjects, attacked by intransigent knights, manipulated by supernatural means, threatened by charmed knights, physically assaulted by Frenchmen, chased and harried by legendary beasts, and finally arrested by forces of an authority he can't recognize or understand. The Pythons have fashioned a Cervantean world here, where our plucky heroes will be assaulted from all sides and even from all times. For Cervantes it was the "spiritual atmosphere of a [seventeenth-century] Spain already in steep decline," beset with the horrors of Cervantes's own life as a maimed soldier, frustrated artist, prisoner of war, prisoner, and tax collector; for the Pythons it's the existential horrors of 1970s, post-empire Britain, where the unfulfilled promises of the postwar generation have come home to roost. It's clear that the Pythons were aware of this Cervantean influence in their constructed world; the echoes between Arthur's and Don Quixote's milieus fairly leap from Bloom's descriptions:

> Yet Cervantes, although a universal pleasure, is in some respects even more difficult than are Dante and Shakespeare upon their heights. Are we to believe everything Don Quixote says to us? Does he believe it? He (or Cervantes) is the inventor of a mode now common enough, in which figures, within a novel, read prior fictions concerning their own earlier adventures and have to sustain a consequent loss in the sense of reality. This is one of the beautiful enigmas of

Don Quixote: it is simultaneously a work whose authentic subject is literature and a chronicle of a hard, sordid actuality, the declining Spain of 1605–15. The knight is Cervantes's subtle critique of a realm that had given him only harsh measures in return for his own patriotic heroism at Lepanto. Don Quixote cannot be said to have a double consciousness; his is rather the multiple consciousness of Cervantes himself, a writer who knows the cost of confirmation. I do not believe the knight can be said to tell lies, except in the Nietzschean sense of lying against time and time's grim "It was." To ask what it is that Don Quixote himself believes is to enter the visionary centre of his story. (xxxii)

What does Arthur believe? Does he "altogether believe in the reality of his own vision," as Bloom asks of Don Quixote? Arthur is gifted with no quiet, personal moments of introspection seen so often in New Wave films, no self-exposing monologue on a lonely parapet, but his actions speak. I think he believes.

Notes

1. Entire scenes like "King Brian the Wild" were excised, and this gathering scene became "The Book of the Film," to be completed later, in postproduction. Doyle and Gilliam created the scene in Doyle's living room, with Gilliam's wife turning the pages.

2. Author White agreed to allow Disney production rights for this book in late 1938 or early 1939 (Gallix, 98).

3. Charlton Heston would provide the voice of God—a fascinating moment as he calls to himself from the burning bush on Mt. Sinai.

4. These are likely the types of praise and lamentation books that God will complain about in the following scene.

5. Alcock's *Kings and Warriors, Craftsmen and Priests in Northern Britain* is a useful resource for this period.

6. Including one collected in the Viennese Museum für angewandte Kunst, "Cod. Lat. XIV," folios 25, 153, and 173 (see Morgan, *A Survey of Manuscripts Illuminated in the British Isles (II)*, plates 40–42).

7. See this artwork in Mittman, *Maps and Monsters*, 3.

8. This is a reference to the first example Mittman includes, borrowed from Isidore's *De Fide*, part of the British Library collection (Royal 6, B.viii, f. 1v). Here the initial is a human form—two monks forming an initial "S" and inviting the reader to pay close attention. See Mittman, 1.

9. Taking *"ruminatio"* to its Pythonesque extreme, in the "Art Gallery" sketch in *MPFC*, Ep. 4, both visiting women end up eating the paintings they appreciate. See *MPFC: UC*, 1.70.

10. The in-joke here is that Graham Greene (*Our Man in Havana*) and the Tory government, including Foreign Secretary Lloyd (1904–1978), were engaged in an ongoing tiff over aid to Batista's Cuban government even as Castro moved closer to his eventually successful junta.

11. *MPFC: UC*, 1.323; 2.205.

12. "Public Libraries," *Times*, 15 August 1950: 5.

13. Gilliam discusses this sequence and its participants in his audio commentary on both the DVD and Blu-ray editions of the film.

14. These are the correct spellings. The versions the Pythons provided include, as discussed in *MPFC: UC*: "tassles" (2.37), "mantalogical" (2.139), "swopping" (2.151), "cannelloni" (2.196), "Omalley" (2.31-32), "Du-Bakey" (2.42), "Cincinnatti" (1.159), "Roiurama" (2.47), and "Madgalene" (1.255).

15. Part of the British Library's collection.

16. These dangling leaves appear especially after f. 44; which may indicate a different artist. Most of Royal 10 and 17 can be viewed online at the British Library's illuminated manuscripts catalogue website: http://www.bl.uk/catalogues/illuminatedmanuscripts/welcome.htm.

17. According to Doyle, Valerie Charlton painted this particular shield (9 December 2013; e-mail correspondence). In the popular and culturally aware American cartoon series *Rocky and Bullwinkle*,

creators Ward and Scott offer a Richard the Lionheart character who is actually a coward, and who has a chicken on his shield. *The Bullwinkle Show* had been airing on Granada TV in the UK in August 1962. See *MPFC: UC*, 1.122 and 329 for more on the show and its influence on *MPFC*.

18. Often associated with Arthur.

19. *HKB* book VII, chapters 3 and 4 (pp. 138–52).

20. Perhaps also this Robin is the antithesis of the Robin depicted in the very popular *Sir Robin Hood*, a kids' magazine published in 1955–1957, when the Pythons would have been aged between 13 and 17.

21. See the "Court at Camelot" entry above for more.

22. For Tom, listen to Jones's audio commentary on the 2001 DVD edition; for a vote for William, listen to Palin's commentary on the same DVD. In a short film looking at the locations for the film hosted by Jones and Palin, Jones has to remind Palin that he did indeed lean over the top of a Doune Castle wall and shout to Arthur in the "Swallows" argument—Palin had forgotten completely.

23. Promotional material for the film announced that this "explicit" film was not for everyone. *La Bête* was released in France in January 1975, while the Pythons were working in postproduction. *Holy Grail* would be released in April and May 1975 in Britain.

24. This low-budget parody also featured a trailer that played up the epic nature of the film, comparing it to *Birth of a Nation* and *2001: A Space Odyssey*. See the entry *"They pass rune stones"* in the "Black Knight" scene for more.

25. The man in the gorilla suit in Ep. 29 was, coincidentally, Reuben Martin, of *Carry On* fame.

26. See Mittman, *Maps and Monsters in Medieval England*. The Hereford map is dated c. 1285. This map (and others like it) were not meant to give directions, of course—many included the Garden of Eden and the Flood and the Last Judgment details—but were "ruminative" documents meant for monastic study (Mittman, 27). A number of the fantastical creatures included in the horizons of this map also appear in the various illuminated manuscripts Gilliam studied. See appendix A for those entries.

27. Bede lived and worked in the "double-monastery" Monkwearmouth and Jarrow, in Northumbria, not far south and east of where the Pythons filmed most of *Holy Grail*.

28. See the "Exactly. So, logically. . ." entry in scene 7 for more on Alcuin and Charlemagne.

29. See Poole's chapter "Learning, Literature and Art" in *DBMC* for more on this fertile period of new learning.

30. von Ehrenkrook, "Effeminacy in the Shadow of Empire," 145.

31. In 1209 hostilities between the citizenry and students of Oxford over an alleged accidental death led to retaliation by the citizens, including two hangings, and a five-year interruption in the school's operation when most students and scholars had fled. See *DBMC*, 238–39. Sir Bedevere seems to have the respect of these village people, though, his experiments and rhetorical skills not constituting a threat.

32. "Lonely Island's Bottle Mail," *Times*, 24 July 1962: 12.

33. The sheep doesn't land on anyone, if there is one launched at all. It's not clear—beyond the fake cow and several live ducks—what kind of dead animals are in this barrage. Bits of mud and grass are also thrown from off camera.

34. The *Annals of Ulster* is a chronicle of medieval Ireland, spanning AD 431 to 1540.

35. The Greeks, for example, gave Poseidon control over earthquakes, as well as Zeus with his angry thunderbolts.

36. In the classic Italian epic *Cabiria* (1914), a deadly eruption of Mt. Etna prompts a round of fiery human sacrifices to appease the god Moloch. *Cabiria* was screened fairly regularly on BBC television in the 1960s.

37. Gregory of Tours, *History of the Franks*, VI.21 (1927). Gregory was cited in the "Tie weights on her" entry in scene 7.

38. See the entry for *"line of MONKS à la* Seventh Seal" in scene 7.

39. "Antiperstasis," meaning "Opposition or contrast of circumstances; the force of contrast or contrariness; resistance or reaction roused against any action" (*OED*).

40. "L'Aquila quake: Italy scientists guilty of manslaughter," BBC News, 22 October 2012.

41. See the entry for "self-perpetuating autocracy" in scene 5 for more on Scargill and other union firebrands.

42. "Miners' 'Camelot' is a Century Old," *Times*, 9 December 1974: 4.

43. Cleese also mentions in his DVD commentary track that shooting in the evening was almost verboten and always met with grumbling. It was already often miserable—wet and chilly—and a late start back to the hotel meant no hot water for showers.

44. "Universum Film Aktiengesellschaft"; Ufa was *the* major film studio in World War I and Weimar Germany, hugely innovative and influential, before becoming the de facto Nazi film studio.

45. Edith Grossman's 2003 translation.

46. A scene with a similar tenor finds its way into *LB*, where an "ex-leper"—who's been healed by Christ—complains about his loss of livelihood, wishing he were a bit lame, part-time.

47. In Ep. 35 of *MPFC*, for instance, "The Silliest Sketch We've Ever Done" is stopped when all three participants agree to drop the façade and leave the set.

48. The same is true for most of the knights. Launcelot, Galahad, Bedevere, and even Robin share the full-faith belief in this world. Only Miss Islington, Patsy, and Dingo disrupt the narrative solidity, and to differing degrees.

49. Bloom, introduction in Cervantes, *Don Quixote*, xxiv.

SCENE TEN
CAMELOT ("IT IS A SILLY PLACE")

Interior of medieval hall—(PSC) This is the great hall portion of Doune Castle, the primary set for *all* castle interiors on the shoot. Due to budgetary constraints that demanded good planning, most of *MPHG* was shot out of doors, and not on a studio soundstage, even though those would have been available at Twickenham, where the film was finished.[1] The Cave of Caerbannog, for instance, was a smallish, open mining (hard rock) tunnel—not unlike the popular Bronson Caves in Griffith Park in Los Angeles. Those caves had been in the middle of a metropolitan area for many years, yet looked remote—and could be adequately shot from clever angles—to convince the movie viewer that this was indeed a desolated earthscape (*Robot Monster*, 1953), a place to hide from pod people (*Invasion of the Body Snatchers*, 1956), or a western desert hideaway (*The Searchers*, 1956). The *Holy Grail* production team hoisted a curtain wall (seen in production photos) to keep out the light, and their shallow cave opening suddenly appeared to be a dark cavern where a monster could indeed lurk.

well choreographed song-and-dance routine—(PSC) Choreographed by Leo Kharibian, as noted above. The style of the song and the more rambunctious, less refined choreography (likely for non-dancers, primarily) is less like a Verdon/Fosse number and more like the opening and closing numbers from the Marx Brothers' 1933 film *Duck Soup*.[2] That film employs song-and-dance but with a wink toward the audience all along, as discussed below.

The presence of the musicians and dancers after a meal wouldn't have been inaccurate, as the period composer Guillaume de Machaut (1300–1377) observed: "But here come the musicians after eating, without mishap, combed and dressed up! There they made many different harmonies . . . and whatever one can do with finger, and feather, and bow, I have seen and heard on this floor" (Hallam, 285).

"If they could see me now" type—(PSC) The Camelot song and dance number is meant to resemble this song, according to the printed script. "If They Could See Me Now" was a very popular musical number from the stage play *Sweet Charity* (1966), starring Gwen Verdon (1925–2000), with choreography provided by the legendary Bob Fosse (1927–1987). The touring show that reached London in September 1967[3] featured South African Juliet Prowse (1936–1996) in the lead. The film version appeared in London in February 1969,[4] starring Shirley MacLaine (b. 1934) as Charity, with Fosse again directing and choreographing.

During the run of *Flying Circus* the Pythons employed choreographed dancing a number of times. In Ep. 22, the Pythons and a handful of dancers "ponced it up" in the "Camp Square-Bashing" sketch; in Ep. 28 the *Puss in Boots* performance is "well-choreographed";

in Ep. 31 (mentioned below); and in Ep. 38, Cleese's minister character attempts to deliver a policy speech while dancing.[5] In Ep. 35 they also mention active dance troupes like the Younger Generation, the Lionel Blair Troupe, the Irving Davies' Dancers, and Pan's People, as well as dancers George Balanchine and Martha Graham (*MPFC: UC*, 2.119–20).

It's a stretch to go beyond the admitted Hollywood musical inspiration, but worth noting that dancing did play some remarkable part in this medieval period. First, dancing was a regular part of celebrations of the rich and the poor, as Tuchman notes a number of times. Second, it was believed by many that after witches had made their pacts with the devil they would engage in "blasphemous, obscene and heinous rites" that included frenetic dancing (and arse-kissing and cross-stamping, etc.) And third, one of the apocalyptic movements that flourished during the darker periods of the Middle Ages was so-called "dancers." Russell notes that these "dance manias . . . proliferated after the plagues of the [fourteenth] century," but started even earlier, involving young and old (136). Hundreds of children were reported to have danced, many to death, between Erfurt and Armstadt in 1327, and later the "dance of death" found its way

> into art and literature and reached its height in the fifteenth century along with the obsession with grisly *memento mori*. Though the danse macabre was originally a dance of the dead, it soon became a dance of living people who were reminded of the nearness of death and the vanity of the world. (136)

And these "psychic epidemics" only grew worse and more widespread *after* the first round of plague destruction, 1348–1349, according to Russell. Tuchman mentions the "dancing mania" appearing in the Rhineland where those participating were certain they were "possessed by demons," and the frenzy spread north as they "moved in groups from place to place like flagellants" (260). (This kind of "crippling frivolity" is what Arthur wishes to avoid by steering clear of Camelot.) The jump from self-diagnosed demonic possession in these dark times to the Church's intervention then interdiction was an easy one, according to Tuchman:

> The frenzy died out within a year, although it was to reappear on and off over the next two centuries. Whatever its cause, it testified to a growing submission to the supernatural, of which the Pope took notice. In August 1374 he announced the right of the Inquisition to intervene in trials for sorcery, heretofore considered a civil crime. Because sorcery was made to work by the aid of demons, Gregory claimed it lay within Church jurisdiction. (260)

We know that the plague is outside somewhere in the world of *Holy Grail*—the dead cart in an earlier scene betrayed that—so perhaps these knights have holed themselves up in their castle keep, away from the pestilence, and now partake in all manner of recreation—indicating their own "social and cultural maladjustment" to not only the plague and imminent death, but to the knightly demands Arthur would certainly require of them should he take control of his castle.[6] The word "silly" also has early connotations including "deserving of pity, compassion, or sympathy," and "weak, feeble, sickly, ailing"—meaning those in the castle may be in ill health (including mental health) and beyond succor (*OED*). If that's the case, Arthur simply decides it's best to move on. This separation from traditional roles and society is also a borrow from *MPFC*, Ep. 31, where the fire brigade, instead of responding to calls to fight fires, prefer to sew samplers, cook, and be invited to "little parties," which are "much better than fires" (*MPFC: UC*, 2.61–76).

poorer verses are made clearer by CUTTING to a group of knights actually engaged in the described task—(PSC) The dance sequence and song were part of the first draft of the script, with the lyrics surviving almost intact. The mickey mousing (lyrics matching the visuals) isn't terribly pronounced, though they do dance throughout ("We dance whene'er we're able"), they kick over food items and servers ("We dine well here in Camelot"), and they do seem to be "indefatigable," but they don't wear or make "sequin vests" or "impersonate Clark Gable." Likely, the script version of the scenic directions was written long before they hired a gifted choreographer (Leo Kharibian), who came to the set with fun but still identifiable choreography, transforming the scenes into a Hollywood musical style.

The phrase "poorer verse" is a critical term found fairly often in nineteenth and early twentieth century editions of complete poetical works, including R. Warwick Bond's *Complete Works of John Lyly*, published in 1902, where Bond discusses "a group of [Lyly's] 'Early Love-Poems,' mainly of rougher and poorer verse" (440). In the printed scripts for *MPFC*, the Pythons would often include in-jokes and references not intended for filming/taping, but for their own mutual amusement.[7]

KNIGHTS: "We do routines and chorus scenes" (*lyric*)—The Pythons won't go full-throat into the musical genre again until *Meaning of Life*,[8] but their appreciation for and knowledge of the genre is evident throughout *Flying Circus*. There, Inspector Dim (Chapman) can lead a chorus as he gives evidence in court (Ep. 3); in Ep. 8, a showing of *The Sound of Music* can cause old-age pensioners to riot; Canadian Mounties and a wannabe transvestite remind us of the film musical's genesis on the music hall and vaudeville stages, with the "I'm a Lumberjack" song (Ep. 9);[9] a boys' and girls' school will woodenly perform portions of *Seven Brides for Seven Brothers*, badly, before heading off for "prep" (Ep. 18); Mr. Dibley (Jones) will direct an equally bad version of the recent *Finian's Rainbow* "starring the man from the off-licence" in Ep. 19; archaeologists will sing and fight in the epic "*Archaeology Today*" sketch/film *Flaming Star* (Ep. 21); and, again, in "Camp Square Bashing" the military will "swan about" as if they've just stepped off the musical stage (they have, actually, they're mostly dancers), among many other musical mentions.[10]

KNIGHTS: "We dine well here in Camelot . . ." (*lyric*)—This is precisely what any great lord's great hall was all about, as Brooke explains: "In the hall at Cheddar Alfred very probably rested from the chase, and dined with his followers like Hrothgar in Heorot;[11] the great hall is the symbol of a militant and military type of kingship" (*SNK*, 61).

In many filmed quests some of the necessities of life, like sleep or bowel movements—or in this case, food—are undertaken offscreen so as not to interrupt the drama, or perhaps to avoid causing unnecessary viewer distress. Earlier, Arthur has asked for "food and shelter" from the French sentries as a trade for joining the quest, without success. He is asking for a "night's farm" or the "farm of one night" (*firma unius noctis*), a well-known and somewhat expensive obligation that was common by at least the time of Domesday Book[12] (Sawyer, 200; Brooke, *SNK*, 59). The "night's farm"—the "basic unit of royal food-rent"[13]—was essentially the equivalent of what it would take to feed and shelter the traveling royal household for a day (and night), and the king would have expected—just as Arthur expects—the castle's occupant to welcome his visit. No meal is taken in *MPHG*, though such diversions are hinted at here in Camelot.[14] But since Camelot will very quickly be judged a "silly place" and one that should be avoided (wise, because God will be waiting to greet them in the following scene), food and socializing are clearly marked as tertiary activities that serve only to sidetrack questing knights. In medieval times, the meal, it seems, served several purposes, according to Philippa Pullar, which Arthur must clearly understand: "Mealtimes of the rich were not only for the purposes of feeding: they were remedies against ennui, long successions of dishes punctuated with entertainments, parties offering opportunities to meet people. They were vehicles to parade the host's wealth and benevolence."[15] Pullar goes on to note that in the time of Edward III, laws were written to try and counter this profligacy:

Statute 10 . . . chapter 3, records that "through the excessive and over-many costly meats which the people of this realm have used more than elsewhere many mischiefs have happened: for the great men by these excesses have been sore grieved, and the lesser people, who only endeavor to imitate the great ones in such sorts of meat, are much impoverished." (15)

As will be discussed below, Edward III's impecunity seemed to be unrelenting. He suffered what Arthur was able to escape: "The perennial problems of the medieval ruler—maintenance of an efficient administration and of an adequate flow of supplies—inevitably grew more pressing in time of war" (McKisack, 154). Arthur is allowed to be free from the trappings of his court, since it's a "silly place," and in fairy tale fashion his questers live happily without food or drink or sleep or even shelter. Edward is forced to borrow and borrow from his nobles, the City of London, and continental banks, as well as resort to semi-regular taxations (from the clergy; from wool production) just to support his spendthrift court (154). The food and drink and servants and knights seen dancing in our Arthur's Camelot would have all cost money. The law mentioned by Pullar above even lays out how many courses are legal at non-holiday meals. Given these caveats, it's no surprise that Arthur opts to press on, avoiding Camelot and all its temptations.

To underscore the "life imitates art" maxim, another mention must be made of the "Barnsley Camelot" noted above (the NUM headquarters building). In the year of the building's centenary (1974), press coverage of the events mention the building's history, including a short-lived row in 1958 over a celebratory union luncheon held in the ornate structure that cost a staggering £6 per attendee.[16] They do "dine well" in Camelot, even in Barnsley.

KNIGHTS: "We eat ham and jam and Spam a lot" (*lyric*)—Certainly just fun for rhyming purposes, yes, but the inclusion of that "mystery" pork meat harks back to both episodes 20 and 25[17] of *MPFC*, where the pressed food product figured significantly, and to the Pythons' collective childhoods. Spam, then, is a

[p]ressed, canned meat product from Hormel that appeared in 1937. The UK has been the second-leading consumer of SPAM for many years, according to Hormel. The Pythons may have included the reference due to SPAM's very significant presence during the food rationing postwar years in England, when the tinned product would have been much more available than other meats—if it could be found to buy, it could be eaten without worrying about ration restrictions. Interestingly, only two weeks after this episode was first broadcast, on 15 December 1970, *Private Eye* included a short, familiar passage in their 1 January 1971 issue that betrays the almost instantaneous cultural influence of *Flying Circus* by the end of the second series. An article describing the attractions of Neasden includes the "adventure" of eating out:

Try the Fiesta (Tesco Road) just by the station. Specialities: Egg and chipps [*sic*] 3s 9d. Egg, chips and peas 4s 6d. Egg chips sausage and peas 5s 6d. Egg chips sausage bacon and peas 6s 9d. Egg chips sausage bacon tomato and peas 7s 11d. Egg chips sausage bacon tomato beans and peas 8s 9d. Eggs chips sausage bacon tomato beans fried bread and peas 12s 6d.[18]

"Jam" is likely included partly for its rhyme significance, but there are mentions of warmly remembered war and postwar years of scarcity, where "Spam sandwiches, jelly and blancmange" were absolute treats, while on thrifty seaside holidays both Spam and jam could be had from numerous jerry-rigged storefronts.[19] During the war, newspapers announced occasional double-rations of blancmange and jelly powders and jams, which were both announced and greeted happily.[20] The term "spam" became so ubiquitous between 1939 and

1945 it slipped easily into the cultural lexicon, including a description given in 1954 of what constituted a wartime "housewife":

> [She] became the bureaucrats' puppet, the propagandists' punch-ball. If she was not being exhorted she was being thanked, and in between times she was the recipient of innumerable hints on how to make the most of nothing. She exuded an aura of indomitability and produced—in the abstract, of course—the impression of being constructed of Spam. She did not care for the role.[21]

Margaret Thatcher, who worked in her family's grocery store as a youth, remembers Spam and salad as a wartime treat on Boxing Day, 1943.[22] Spam rolls were even on the menu for bivouacked troops in London for the coronation in 1953,[23] and part of fond remembrances in domestic autobiographies of the war years such as *Spam Tomorrow* by Verily Anderson, published in 1956. To this day, British school children in years three and four, for example, study the wartime era and often sample these treats.

KNIGHTS: "Our shows are formidable" (*lyric*)—In the first draft of the screenplay this same song appears, with very similar lyrics, but the performance is to be interrupted by a swishy (modern) director, and then by Arthur who formally announces the Grail quest. Turns out they are planning a performance in two weeks, but the grail quest forces them to go straight to the West End, and cut down previews (*MPHGB*, 8). The moment is similar to the "choreographed minister" section of *MPFC*, Ep. 38, where a choreographer (Idle) and a nervous MP (Cleese) work on the minister's speech/dance (*JTW*, 2.211–12).[24] This intrusion of modern characters (played by the Pythons) into the Arthurian world was where the film started, concept-wise, and from which they eventually departed as the script process moved along. In the end, it is the modern world itself (represented by authority figures, primarily) that not only intrudes but ultimately stops the filmed world.

Prisoner hanging on castle wall—(PSC) This is an insert shot—starring featured extra Mark Zycon[25]—not accounted for in any version of the printed scripts. It's fitting that Camelot—both a place of virtue and camaraderie for knights as well as a "silly place"—would also be a place for corporal punishment, essentially torture. This man, hanging outside the castle, in full view of the general public, couldn't be more noticeable. The high visibility afforded these public sorts of punishments served a social purpose in the Middle Ages, according to Tuchman:

> The tortures and punishments of civil justice customarily cut off hands and ears, racked, burned, flayed and pulled apart people's bodies. In everyday life passersby saw some criminal flogged with a knotted rope or chained upright in an iron collar. They passed corpses hanging on the gibbet and decapitated heads and quartered bodies impaled on stakes on the city walls. (135)

McGlynn continues: "These exhibitions were not always just crude displays of terror; they also frequently promoted reassurance that justice was being served to protect society" (54). In the centers of great medieval towns and cities stood the cathedral or "great church," as well as

> the town hall, the clock, and the market cross, which reminded the citizens that God was watching to punish any malefactor who might disturb the market's peace. *Here too stood often the pillory, stocks, cucking stool for scolding women, gallows, and gibbet.* (The Paris gibbet accommodated twenty-four; when a new occupant arrived, an old skeleton was thrown into a nearby charnel pit.) (Bishop, *HBMA*, 168; italics added)

This man also seems quite happy where he is, clapping along with the faint music inside. The Pythons will revisit this character to an extent in *LB*, where a jailed but cheery old man (Palin) sings the praises of his Roman captors, his lot in life, and the Roman methods of abuse and punishment: "Nail 'em up I say!" Similarly, in *MPFC*, Ep. 14, the Piranha brothers intimidate and assault many in their crime world, but no victim will say an unfair word against them. One man who had his head nailed to the floor, Stig O'Tracy (Idle), denies that "old Dinsey" hurt him at all, even when his head was nailed to the floor: "Well I mean he had to didn't he, I mean, be fair. There was nothing else he could do. . . . I mean he didn't want to nail my head to the floor, I had to insist! He wanted to let me off" (*MPFC: UC*, 1.224–25; *JTW*, 1.187).

two XYLOPHONISTS play parts—In the final version of the film, only one knight plays the xylophone-like arrangement of knights' helmets. This is the moment most directly borrowed from *Duck Soup*, the Marx Brothers' comedy. That film's final number, "This Country's Going to War," features a sequence where all four brothers play the helmets of Freedonia's soldiers as if they were a living xylophone. They even round it off with a "bang," as Harpo hits the last soldier on the head with a drum major's mace. Though the Camelot performers also acknowledge the audience, looking through the fourth wall (unlike most[26] in the rest of the film's world) as they often sing into the camera, this is still a connection to backstage musicals like the *Gold Diggers* films, *42nd Street*, and even the later *Singin' in the Rain*. In these, the camera-as-theatrical-audience is acknowledged. For example, in the opening sequence, as the female cast rehearses the unforgettable "We're in the Money" routine—complete with gold coins shielding their modesty—Ginger Rogers sings directly into the camera, and in pig-Latin, to boot, inviting the viewer into this titillating and voyeuristic look behind the scenes.[27]

KNIGHTS: "Between our quests / We sequin vests" (*lyric*)—The trope of life as performance runs throughout the Python *oeuvre*. In *MPFC*, Ep. 14 police constables are glamming up for their scene (eye shadow, lipstick, flowers from "Binkie"), the "scene" being the walking of their beat and the investigation of crime, while in Ep. 31 ("The Language Laboratory") the language lesson lab turns abruptly into a 1930s-style Warner Bros. backstage musical, à la WB's *42nd Street* or *The Gold Diggers* series, when extradiegetic music breaks out and the characters begin to dance and sing spontaneously.[28]

This representation of authority figures like these knights in Camelot as sexually suspect or just somehow bent is also a longstanding Python conceit. In *Flying Circus*, policemen, for example, speak in various silly voices (Ep. 12), they can wear tutus and carry wands (Ep. 13), they can engage in homosexual liaisons (also Ep. 13), pretend to be airplanes (Ep. 17), sing upbeat show numbers (Ep. 25), and knit, make paper flower arrangements, and attend parties (Ep. 31).

KNIGHTS: "Clark Gable" (*lyric*)—Gable (1901–1960) was an oft-impersonated iconic Hollywood actor, but he wasn't especially known for his appearances in musicals,[29] and he'd been dead for some time. This is also one of the very few moments where the fantasy of the film world is ruptured, with characters mentioning by name a twentieth-century person.[30] But it's a safe place to do so. This type of rupture is *contained* in the musical genre, since the audience has already granted the film and its characters the authority to transgress the fourth wall, and to be self-aware to certain degrees.[31] (Also, Arthur and the other knights can't actually know what's transpiring as this song-and-dance routine goes on—they're outside.) If the musical genre doesn't invite this association with its audience, characters walking down city streets couldn't break into song to sourceless, non-diegetic music, even if they are performers (think of *Seven Brides for Seven Brothers*, *Singin' in the Rain*, or *Top Hat*). In other genres, like a medieval fantasy, such license does not exist, and the rupture would be seen as just that: a major distraction undermining audience expectations.[32] Elsewhere, the influences of the modern, ennui-laden world seep into this medieval world, but aren't addressed specifically; that, or a narrator figure like the Famous Historian can step in and remind us this has become a "Picture for Schools," when it seemed at first to be a self-contained medieval genre picture. But these modern characters are also temporally separated from the main action—the police investigation *follows* the knights' trail; there is no intersection, no shared screen space, until Launcelot is arrested toward the end. As discussed in the introduction, such ruptures are also the hallmark of many New Wave films and filmmakers, including Fellini, Godard, Buñuel, Pasolini, and others.[33]

KNIGHTS: "It's a busy life in Camelot" (*lyric*)—The specter of choreographed dance routines, costume making, and Hollywood impersonations in the hallowed halls of Arthur's Camelot echo the state of many historic British homes in the twentieth century. The expense of maintaining an estate complete with gardens, forest preserves, farmland, a village, servants, and a very old home or castle itself was daunting; add to those the crushing income tax and estate duties (death taxes), and it's no surprise that many dukes and earls found themselves operating tourist and accommodation businesses to help pay the bills. The 12th Duke of Bedford resorted to hiving off the amazing art collection of Woburn Abbey[34] in 1950 and 1951, for example, before turning to other sources of income.[35] Portions of or entire homes were opened to the paying public as bed and breakfasts and for weddings and conferences, and concerts were even staged on the grounds of the formerly closed, guarded family estates. A representative for the Historic Houses Association characterized the new business ably in 1983, describing such owners as "actually [being] in a branch of show business" (Webbe, "Stately Homes," 33). Stephen Webbe continues, describing a very "silly" setting indeed:

> [S]how business is not something that comes easily to most historic-house owners—even though Lord Tavistock's father, the Duke of Bedford, showed what promotional flair could achieve when he opened Woburn in 1954 and proceeded to make it the best-known historic house in Britain.
>
> "He took this business into the 20th century," says his son with pride. In fact, the Duke of Bedford had no choice but to publicize Woburn with a passion: He had to pay off £5 million in estate duty incurred on the death of his father, the 12th duke.
>
> To attract people to what had, in effect, been a long-secluded treasure house, he opened the grounds to a nudist convention; set fire to furniture as a stunt; and invited Marilyn Monroe to spend the weekend and sleep in Queen Victoria's bed. He even appeared on television, singing Noel Coward's "The Stately Homes of England" with Lord Montagu.[36]

The 13th Duke of Bedford started an admission-based safari park on the grounds in January 1970, and allowed for the filming of movies and television shows, including *Coronation Street*. A silly place indeed, but from the mid-1950s (when the Pythons were teens) the duke was paying the bills with such silliness, offending many of his more sober peers, but keeping the family estate in the family. For more on the changing fortunes of the stately home in England, see entries in the "Swamp Castle" section.

KNIGHTS: "I have to push the pram a lot" (lyric)—This hints perhaps that all this time for ancillary activities might lead to a rise in the castle's birthrate, though the absence of females (none are seen during the dance sequence) counters that, as would the rather high infant mortality rate of this period. In *Flying Circus*, a pram can be a dire threat, a misread *double entendre*, and a means of simple conveyance. In Ep. 2, a "carnivorous pram" eats a number of unsuspecting types before turning on its owner in a Gilliam animation; in another episode the pram is involved in criminality (Ep. 6); in Ep. 14, a seedy customer comes to a tobacconist's looking for "a bit of pram," a play on the sexualized "a bit of tail" (*JTW*, 1.182–83); and finally in Ep. 15, in another animation, a pram delivers Reg's head (played by Chapman's head) into a perspective drawing by de Vries.[37]

ARTHUR: "It is a silly place"—What began as a legendary haven for Arthur and his nation-building designs has been outed for what it is—a mare's nest, a "silly place"—and he didn't have to set foot inside to find out. Since the Pythons' Arthur is clearly one inspired, at least, by Galfridian fictions, this assessment of Camelot's suitability might be jaundiced by William I's habit of only wearing the English crown "three times a year as often as he was in England" in great celebrations, according to Brooke (*FAH*, 112). Geoffrey's reworking of the British warrior into something more contemporary, perhaps something more French, heaven forbid, is discussed by Brooke:

> The Arthurian legend only became really active in the second half of the twelfth century, but already in the eleven-thirties Geoffrey of Monmouth had put Arthur on the map in his fabulous history. Arthur appears here in the improbable guise of a twelfth-century Anglo-Norman king. In the central scene of his book Geoffrey makes Arthur wear his crown at a Whitsun festivity. He describes the solemn ceremonial, the music, the festivities, the tournaments, and the business which occupied the court. If one subdues his exuberant detail and knocks a nought or two off his figures for the numbers present, one can accept Geoffrey's account as a picture of the crown-wearing ceremony in the Anglo-Norman court. (112–13)

In this case, since the French will become the specific antagonists to our Arthur's search for the Grail, he would likely avoid any "silly place" sodden by French festivities, and reject his depiction as an Anglo-Norman-type king.

Camelot may have been more silly than usual thanks to the fairly recent film musical version (1967) of the Arthurian story starring Richard Harris (1930–2002) and Vanessa Redgrave (b. 1937), and directed by Joshua Logan (1908–1988). That version followed a record-setting Broadway run for the stage musical, written by Frederick Loewe (1901–1988) and Alan Jay Lerner (1918–1986), which made its debut in 1960. The formerly mythic and sober denizens of Camelot had been singing and dancing for about thirteen years when the Pythons came to write their own version, with perhaps expected results. Mention can also be made of the Honourable Society of the Knights of the Round Table—a charitable organization whose members dressed up and dined together—which celebrated its 250th anniversary in 1971. At these awards three young people were honored for their service to their communities, part of "an Arthurian banquet in the City of London with pomp and oratory out of Mallory [*sic*]."[38] The fact that the society wears "regalia and robes" and keeps "muniments and chattel" might qualify them for this "silly" appellation, in the Pythons' view.

Arthur is also not going to give in to the Camelot as depicted with dancing and cavorting, and will instead cling to the Camelot of his memory and/or of myth.[39] A 2011 column in the *Telegraph* commemorating the Duke of Edinburgh's nonagenarian status lays out well the ups and downs of being a royal person in an age of change, and seems particularly apt for the medieval royal person Arthur, who is struggling to stay in his idiom and on his quest no matter what the world around him presents, or how out-of-fashion his goals might become. Peter Oborne describes the gracious Duke's challenge as the "cult of the short-term," and the skill that has largely gone missing in the modern world is "statesmanship," a trait that the Pythons' Arthur and Prince Philip share:

> [T]hese politicians were doing no more than succumbing to the spirit of our age. While previous generations built for the future, modern Britons are obsessed by novelty and personal gratification. Presentation matters more than substance—indeed, philosophy lecturers today inform students that the two are identical. As a result *we have learnt to dismiss solidity, complexity, tradition, hierarchy and public spirit.*

The colossal importance of the Duke of Edinburgh, who celebrates his 90th birthday next week, is that *he has defied the spirit of his time.* This is why, for most of his adult life, he has been forced to endure such hostility and contempt. In the 1960s, satirists portrayed him as a member of a bankrupt establishment. The state socialists who ran Britain in the 1970s despised the Duke as a symbol of ruling-class domination. The New Right that came to power in the 1980s could not understand him at all. He was not for sale, he was not efficient, and he was not driven by the profit motive, yet he could not really be classified as part of the public sector. He appeared to have no purpose.

The 1990s were most dangerous of all. This decade is still too close in time to be properly assessed, but I guess that historians will come to classify it as one of the nastiest in all British history. It produced a new breed of publicist whose special expertise was presenting greed and self-interest as a form of public virtue: much of the New Labour phenomenon can be explained in this way. During this period British public life was under vicious and sustained attack, and in the front line of this was the Royal family. For those too cautious personally to target the Queen, the Duke of Edinburgh made an admirable proxy. (Oborne, "The Duke of Edinburgh: At 90"; italics added)

The section works well with the insertion of "Arthur" for most mentions of the Duke, interestingly. Arthur leads this same exemplary life throughout *Holy Grail*, as do Bedevere, Galahad, and even Launcelot, which is likely why all four are destined to be dumped on (sometimes literally) by others who don't share their worldview, or arrested, hurled into a gorge, or hooded and hustled into the Black Maria of history.

Lastly, the contemporary archaeological dig at Cadbury, Somerset—where Camelot may or may not have been sited—had reached what the Pythons might have called a "bitchy" stage by mid-1969, relations that in *MPFC* the Pythons would depict in both the television documentary world and an Everest ascent by hairdressers.[40] In an *Antiquity* journal review of Ashe's *The Quest for Arthur's Britain*, Professor Charles Thomas echoes Arthur's "silly" comment. The Cadbury dig was an expensive undertaking, and organizers had reached into nontraditional areas for financial and public support, including television, newspapers, and various nonacademic societies. Thomas—who would himself later publish Arthur-related texts from his Cornwall region[41]—saw the whole thing as just short of a three-ring circus; he would pull no punches in his review of a text arising, in part, from the results of an infamous, sloppy, and academically dubious dig:

> It will unfortunately go a long way towards confirming the fears held by so many students of this period who are not themselves involved in the project, and by some of those who *are* involved: namely that the results (in strict terms of post-Roman Britain, the era which forms the avowed target) are as yet in no way commensurate with either the money or the ballyhoo laid out in the Quest for Camelot, that the limits of legitimate archaeological inference are probably being exceeded as a result of external pressures, and that the prospects of any future appeals for mass support in connexion with other major sites of this era are likely to have been jeopardized. Secondary disquiet . . . centres on the aspects of the administration of this project, on the ill-advised deal for too low a sum with a Sunday newspaper, on the rumoured engagement of an expensive PR firm to project the Camelot image, and on the concept of a controlling committee embracing bodies (Knights of the Round Table and the Pendragon Society) and individuals whose interests may be non-archaeological and, insofar as the eventual interpretation is concerned, certainly not objective. ("Are These the Walls of Camelot?" 27–28)

So this new Camelot is as silly as the one featuring dancing knights, Spam-feasting, and pram-pushing, it seems, and Thomas concludes, looking with "apprehension" at the future of his beloved profession:

> What does this leave us with, as we thumb the pages so ably edited by Mr Ashe, and gaze at the lavish pictures? Surely a verdict of *non-proven* where any connexion with a real Arthur of his-

tory is concerned. A feeling that the purposes of a superficially admirable excavation are become blurred, and that the essential momentum has somehow been lost. A feeling, perhaps, that there lurks a danger that the project might be brought into a shadow of disrepute—because results can be journalistically misrepresented, or *a priori* theories allowed to colour the interpretations given in popular media, in order to satisfy a publicity machine which now seems indispensable to keep so costly a campaign rolling along. For some of us, a feeling of apprehension, lest the very real progress made during the last few decades in the archaeology and history of Early Christian Britain should be vitiated or discounted by any failure at South Cadbury to produce clear-cut "Arthurian" results. For others, possibly a sense of slight distaste; that a world marginally involving current sales (at Tintagel) of spurious "knighthoods" to the gullible, and the televised caperings in Merlin's Cave (in which Mr Ashe was seen to participate), should not only be concerned at all in a major excavation directed by a field-worker of unquestioned skill and originality, but should even appear to have some say in the control. Are these indeed the walls of Camelot? (29)

Clearly this scientific brouhaha was not lost on the Pythons. In Ep. 21 of *MPFC*, specifically the "*Archaeology Today*" sketch (which morphs into "*Flaming Star*"), two eminent archaeologists will fight each other in a musical setting, each gathering acolytes, and eventually will destroy one another.[42]

Notes

1. Other filming locations included Hampstead Heath, Doyle's living room floor and back balcony, and the studio on Tasker Road, according to Doyle's e-mails, and Gilliam's DVD commentaries.

2. Not that it matters for the Pythons themselves, but *Duck Soup* appeared in London-area cinemas in February 1934. As recently as July 1971, *Duck Soup* was showing at the Notting Hall Gate cinema; and in February 1972, the film was running on BBC 1.

3. The play was staged in the Prince of Wales Theatre.

4. At the Odeon, Leicester Square. The *Times* film critic doesn't rave about the adapted choreography, by the way, but found the film "thoroughly enjoyable" anyway (J. R. Taylor, *Times*, 20 February 1969: 15).

5. This "Party Political Broadcast" sketch was accidentally clipped from later VHS and DVD versions of the episode.

6. The nod toward Poe and his Gothic fiction "The Masque of the Red Death" is acknowledged, too.

7. See, for example, *MPFC: UC*, 1.143, 148–49, 287–88, 292, 339, and 2.205. For others see "in-joke" and "reflexivity" in the *MPFC: UC* index.

8. Where they create a rousing *Oliver*-style ("Consider Yourself") number called "Every Sperm is Sacred," and toward the close of the film a lavish "Christmas in Heaven" number is staged. In 1979, the film *LB* had featured a musical number as the film closed, "Always Look on the Bright Side of Life," sung and "danced" by those hanging on crosses. Controversy followed.

9. And the Gumby Crooner (Chapman) will trill "Make Believe" from *Showboat* (1927) as he bashes himself on the head with bricks in this same episode.

10. In *MPFC: UC*, see the index under film genres: musical, for many more references.

11. Cheddar, Somerset, was home to one of Alfred's halls; Hrothgar was the legendary Danish king who would have lived right around the same time as the historical Arthur; and Heorot was Hrothgar's great mead hall described in *Beowulf*. See Brooke's discussions (in *SNK*) of the influence provided by the epic *Beowulf* to kings like Alfred, and to Britain's understanding of kingship in general.

12. Sawyer mentions that at the time of the Conquest this night's farm fee would have come to about £80, a sizable amount of money at which many noble and religious houses balked, but generally accommodated anyway (200).

13. Brooke, *SNK*, 59.

14. The *Luttrell Psalter*—commissioned by or for Geoffrey Luttrell—features food preparation and the beginnings of a celebratory feast on ff. 207v–208. Gilliam will sketch from this psalter as he prepares for the animated sequences.

15. "Medieval Manners and Meals," *Times*, 2 January 1971: 15.

16. "Miners' 'Camelot' is a Century Old," *Times*, 9 December 1974: 4.

17. The "Spam" mentions in the printed scripts can be found in *JTW*, 1.277 and 2.27–29.

18. *MPFC: UC*, 1.323.

19. "The Hopping Shop," *Times*, 20 September 1957: 12.

20. "Jam To-Morrow: A Double Ration Next Winter," *Times*, 22 July 1943: 4; and "Double Ration of Jam: 12 Weeks' Supply from Sep. 19," *Times*, 8 September 1943: 2. The title of the Verily Anderson book *Spam Tomorrow* is likely a play on this oft-seen newspaper headline, as is the Donald Stokes novel *Jam Tomorrow*, published in 1946, both harking back to Lewis Carroll's "jam to-morrow" lament found in *Through the Looking Glass* (1871). After the war, "jam tomorrow" had become a well-known colloquialism, meaning promises not kept, especially those made by the government.

21. "Othello and the Housewives," *Times*, 13 November 1954: 7.

22. Wyman, *Spam: The Biography*, 26.

23. "'Housing' Troops at Coronation," *Times*, 7 May 1953: 4.

24. The missing "Party Political Broadcast" is discussed in *MPFC: UC*, 2.141–44, 146.

25. See his entry above in the "Title and Credit Sequence" section.

26. The accused witch stares into the camera when she calls her trial "a fair cop," and later Dingo will acknowledge the movie audience, asking for support of a particular scene. None of the knights ever break this imaginary but important veil of verisimilitude.

27. *Gold Diggers of 1934* was directed by Mervyn LeRoy, choreographed by Busby Berkeley, and opened in London in October 1933; *42nd Street* (1933) was directed by Lloyd Bacon and also choreographed by Berkeley, and had opened at the Regal, Marble Arch in London in April 1933. Both are Warner Bros.' musical pictures. *Singin' in the Rain* was an homage to these same musicals, produced in 1952 and directed by Gene Kelly and Stanley Donen.

28. See pertinent entries in *MPFC: UC* for more on these sketches.

29. He did appear in the musical *Dancing Lady* (1933) with Joan Crawford, Fred Astaire, Nelson Eddy, and the Three Stooges, as well as the very popular pseudo-musical *San Francisco* (1940).

30. Importantly, the canny Dennis—who seems to be one straddling the past and present—doesn't mention any more modern political thinker or trade unionist in his diatribe with Arthur. Dennis toes the line ("anarcho-syndicalist") without racing across it.

31. See Rick Altman, *The American Film Musical*, for a very thoughtful look at the subject. The audience of Python fans also allow for the "Pythonesque" carried over from their understanding of how the world works in *MPFC*, of course. This audience would be ready for medieval types to have some sort of future knowledge beyond their ken.

32. Unless, of course, the audience has also acknowledged that they are watching a New Wave-type film, where the traditional narrative structures are being interrogated. The Pythons are lucky in that they can have it both ways—this is a comedic, hybridized genre film emerging in the midst of other narratively tortuous foreign films—*MPHG* can play with/on many levels.

33. Direct address moments can be seen, for example, in Godard's *Pierrot le fou* and *Tout va bien*, as well as Herzog's *Aguirre*. The Pythons satirize these and other sometimes pretentious films in Ep. 23. See *MPFC: UC*, 1: 349–59.

34. Woburn, Bedfordshire, is located midway between Oxford and Cambridge.

35. "Paintings From Woburn Abbey," *Times*, 20 January 1951: 8.

36. Webbe, "What Is Happening to the Stately Homes of Britain?"

37. See *MPFC: UC*, 1: 29, 102–3, 223, and 240–41 for these appearances of a pram in *Flying Circus*.

38. "'Knights' Society Picks Three Camelot Winners," *Times*, 1 April 1971: 18.

39. This is another moment where Arthur is more like Don Quixote, his heart and mind fixed on the version of the world he's constructed, as opposed to how the world might really be.

40. See *MPFC: UC*, 2.55, 63; *JTW*, 2.95–96 and 108, respectively.

41. Thomas, *Tintagel, Arthur and Archaeology*.

42. See *MPFC: UC*, 1.327–38 for notes to Ep. 21, as well as *JTW*, 1.279–82 for the script pages.

SCENE ELEVEN
GOD ANNOUNCES THE GRAIL QUEST

They set off again . . .—(PSC) Note that the physical appearance of God here isn't described at all in the script, likely because the Pythons already knew that Gilliam would be managing this divine manifestation.[1] During the run of *Flying Circus*, Gilliam would work well away from the rest of the troupe during the week prior to the show's taping, completing his interstitial animated bits without much assistance from the others, save a hurriedly recorded voice-over or a still photo. The rest of the troupe generally had little or no idea what the animated bits might look like from week to week. From the first *MPFC* episode entries (for the show's titles sequence) in *MPFC: UC*:

> Gilliam's modus operandi for constructing his title and interstitial animations included both "found" images and created images and sequences. The found images included cutouts from art books, magazines, advertisements, newspapers, and even comic books, as well as postcards and unidentified family photos. More Gilliam-penned backgrounds and purpose-drawn characters also appeared as the series progressed. (*MPFC: UC*, 1.5)

In the *MPHG* script, everything around and imbued by God is described—His radiance, the music that accompanies Him, His "*holy voice*," and the "*light which is GOD*"—but the figure of God himself is never described, and, in fact, isn't part of the script at all. This "reverence" isn't unlike many of the Hollywood films depicting (or not depicting) God the Father or Christ, where offscreen light and sound sources and respectful camera angles often take the place of God's actual visage, and, even by the 1960s and films like *King of Kings* and *The Greatest Story Ever Told*, when Christ's face is shown, God is generally kept offscreen and well "above" His people. By 1973 and *Jesus Christ Superstar*, of course, the Christ figure is one of the gathered actors and crew, generally lit and shot no differently.

As for this shot itself, Doyle notes that he recorded the "plate" of windblown treetops and empty sky out on Hampstead Heath after principal photography was completed.[2] Gilliam would then use the shot as his foreground material for the "God and cloud" animation described below. The rest of the scene is comprised of reaction shots from the quest, all looking up at a prescribed point above themselves (a typical practical effects sequence structure, in other words).

. . . suffused in an ethereal radiance and strange heavenly choir music—(PSC) The appearance of God in clouds and glory isn't unprecedented in the annals of medieval (and especially

Crusade) history. Viscount Montgomery's medieval warfare book describes the "conversion" of Constantine (c. 272–337), perhaps inspiring the Pythons for Arthur's vision:

> One afternoon in 312, on his march to Italy [to be installed as Emperor in Rome] somewhere between Colmar and Saxa Rubra, it is said that he saw in the sky a bright cross, and above it the words *Hoc vince*: "Herein conquer."[3] In a dream that night Christ told him to take the sign for his standard. (125)

Also, in *Flying Circus*, Ep. 17, the "Salvation Fuzz" sketch, the "hand of God" (an image borrowed from the ceiling of the Sistine Chapel) appears to identify the man who killed the "dead bishops on the landing" (*MPFC: UC*, 1.301; *JTW*, 2.80). In *ML*, this same hand of God will appear to deliver a well-placed lightning strike.

This image of the head of God appearing in clouds and radiant glory is depicted a number of times in period illuminated manuscripts, including a version of the "Vision of St. Benedict and St. Paul" in the *Omne Bonum* (c. 1360–1375), today part of the British Library collection (Camille, *Glorious Visions*, 127). Gilliam had sketched a number of versions of this appearance as he prepared for the animation.[4] The final image in *MPFC*'s first-season opening credits is also a God figure surveying mankind, and is a borrow from Carlo Crivelli's *The Immaculate Conception* (1492).[5] That image offers a quieter, more reverent God, quite opposite the sometimes mean, curt God the Pythons depicted in the final script, and especially in the first draft of this script. This Crivelli God also "shushes" as the recognizable Bronzino foot crushes the titles, like Arthur to the murmuring Patsy just moments before.

A holy voice booms out—(PSC) In Robert de Boron's grail stories[6] the voice of God booms out, too (*QAB*, 22). In *The History of the Grail* (*Estoire de Saint Graal*), a voice calls out to the narrator, four times, by name—the brightness of the light overwhelming, and the voice difficult to understand—though this deity doesn't get cheesed off when He's not understood. As the vision comes to a close, God hands the man a book that will answer all questions, it is

> "the Way of Life"; and when he had said this, a voice loud as thunder cried out and when it had cried out, there came a noise so great from above that in my opinion the firmament was crumbling and the Earth had collapsed and if the light before had been great, now it was a hundred times more bright for I thought I had lost my sight by it and there I lay on the earth as if in a swoon and when this emptiness of head was passed I opened my eyes and I saw about me nothing of what I had seen before and I was holding it all a dream until I found in my hand the small book just as the Great Master had put it there.[7]

God's voice had also "boomed out" in His appearance for DeMille's *Ten Commandments*, the 1956 blockbuster film. There, it was Charlton Heston providing the voice of the Almighty (telling Moses, also played by Heston, that he was the chosen one). Here, it's Chapman as Arthur talking to God, whose booming voice is also delivered back to him by, yes, Chapman. There is no indication this doubling was done to mimic *The Ten Commandments*, but it's certainly not out of the question.

In the first draft of the *Holy Grail* script, God is crankier, more easily upset, and angrily expects the knights to find the Grail faster than they do. He even tells Arthur to find it or he'll get his face smashed in (*MPHGB*, 6). In the end of the first draft, this more choleric supreme being drowns along with everyone else in the quest, perhaps the Pythons' version of an abrupt *Bonnie and Clyde*–type ending.

W. G. Grace—(PSC) Rather than the God of perhaps the Old Testament, this is the more up-to-date God of cricket, William Gilbert Grace (1848–1915), known by his sobriquet

"W.G.", who played first-class cricket for forty-four years. Grace has already made an appearance—his face, at least, and cast as a music box—in *Flying Circus*, Ep. 13 (*MPFC: UC*, 1.206).[8]

GOD: "Oh, don't grovel . . ."—But there are a number of examples from this period that indicate groveling is precisely what a vengeful, wrathful God expects. From Bede,[9] a "Letter of Cuthbert to Cuthwin": "He used to repeat the saying of the holy Apostle Paul, *It is a fearful thing to fall into the hands of the living God*" (19); and "He often quoted, 'God scourgeth every son that He receiveth,'" (19); in 449 "the fires kindled by the pagans proved to be God's just punishment on the sins of the nation," and included plague, Saxon destructions across the land, butchery, and slavery (1.15.56–57); King Eadbald, the "apostate king[10] did not escape God's punishment and correction, for he was subject to frequent fits of insanity and possessed by an evil spirit" (2.5.107); and:

> *On the death of the King Egfrid and King Lothere*
> In the year of our Lord 684, King Egfrid of the Northumbrians sent an army into Ireland under the command of Beort, who brutally harassed these inoffensive people who always had been so friendly to the English, and in his hatred he spared neither churches nor monasteries. The islanders resisted force by force as well as they could, and implored the merciful aid of God, praying Heaven long and earnestly to avenge them. And although those who curse may not enter the kingdom of God, one may well believe that those who were justly cursed for their wickedness quickly suffered the penalty of their guilt at the hands of God their judge. (4.26.252)

The first draft of the script also hinted at a newer, hipper God, one tired of all the ancient bowing and scraping. After telling Arthur and the knights He wants the groveling to stop, He says: "I've really had that scene." The line is scratched through, meaning it never made it to the later versions of the script, but here it sounds as if this God talks just like the kids of the emerging generation.

ARTHUR: "I'm averting my eyes, Lord"—In Exodus 3, God gives Moses instructions, lays out the plan, much like he does here for Arthur. Moses looked into the burning bush in order to "see" God without self-destruction. Arthur would know to look away thanks to these depictions of God in the Old Testament, including Exodus 19:21: "And the Lord said unto Moses, Go down, charge the people, lest they break through unto the Lord to gaze, and many of them perish."

GOD: "I really don't know where all this got started"—This is yet another moment where the fault line between the *weltanschauung* of the depicted medieval or even Dark Ages and the more nihilistic, fracturedly postmodernist world of the 1970s lurches into life.

God speaks this line in both the first draft of the script as well as the final draft, but the line was somewhere excised—literally penciled through in the final script—from the finished film. As for where the fear of a vengeful God who demands debased toadying began, contemporary critics knew just whom to blame. Writing in the *Socialist Standard*[11] in response to the controversial 1963 publication of *Honest to God*,[11] by the Anglican Bishop of Woolwich (1919–1983), Pieter Lawrence had this to say, naming names:

> The Roman Catholic Church secured subservience by the weapon of tyrannical superstition. Thus its god was a tyrant and a taskmaster; a god who imposed a duty of constant adulation and who threatened wrongdoers with the nightmare penalty of eternal damnation. Beyond this, since the Church itself was the physical embodiment of God on earth, the worship of God had to be the worship of the Church. The Catholic Church's claim was and is to be the only gateway to heaven and its followers were forced to submit to its authority on all aspects of moral and political behaviour. It involved its adherents in the agony of thorns, a hierarchy of sin, the bleeding heart

of Jesus, the pain of eternally stoked hellfire and other frightening fundamentalist accoutrements of primeval religious fervour. And by means of its power over ignorant and bewildered men, it secured their economic subservience.[12]

Dennis would have nodded vigorously to this description. Marxist Lawrence (1932–2007) goes on to exculpate to a certain extent the Protestant reforms made in the face of Roman Catholic Church control of cowering humanity, paving the way for a "radical"[13] rethinking of Man's relationship to God as well as God's position in our lives. In *Honest to God*, Woolwich (John Robinson) wants both the Church (of England) and man to move away from the supernatural, "out there" God of inapproachable omnipotence toward an "idea of God [that] represents all the best aspirations of man towards brotherhood, mutual tolerance and dedication to community interests." Lawrence continues: "God to him is a force for common good inherited by contemporary man from the most obscure beginnings of history" (124).

This sounds much more like the God the Pythons are depicting, at least in the final version of the film[14]—a God who has a noble task for His people, wants no empty displays of obeisance, and is interested in improving the "dark times" on Earth—even if He is a bit short with His servants. For the avowed Marxist Lawrence, "the ideas of the Bishop of Woolwich form the more credible substance of today's radical theology" (125). Lawrence continues, citing the new views and necessarily outward-looking effects of the space age[15] as one of the main reasons the vengeful, controlling God is dying: "Today, even for those who are yet religious, God is not thought of with the same awesome fear and only a few believe seriously that if life on earth is unsatisfactory, there remains the second chance in heaven" (125).[16]

And the Marxists weren't the only ones celebrating a changing God in the 1960s. The *Beyond the Fringe* group (Alan Bennett, Jonathan Miller, Dudley Moore, and Peter Cook)—quite influential for the Pythons as they prepared *MPFC*—had brought God and the Anglican church into this new age in a sketch called "Man Bites God."[17] In a TV religious program made possible "by the Grace of God and Associated-Rediffusion,"[18] the with-it new vicar (Miller) who wants to be called Dick hosts "a program of religion on the move." His goal is to convince the younger generation that church is still the "spiffing" place to be. The vicar first wants to take questions about God: "Who is He, where is He, and above all, why is He—and of course why is He above all?" The only questions he fields include why there's so much violence in the Bible and God's exact age. As for God's age, the Vicar Dick ("Dicker") responds, very nearly parsing God right out of significance:

> Good, good! Good God! Well, Dudley—it isn't so much the age with God. You see, God is age-less. That is to say He's age-old. He's old-aged, if you like. In fact, God is as old as He feels and in that way He's the same as you or I and that's the message I'm trying to get across to you youngsters down at my little dockland parish. . . . You see, *I think we have got to get away from this stuffy old idea of thinking of God as something holy or divine*, and once we do that we'll get you youngsters flooding back into the churches. (*Beyond the Fringe: A Revue*, 10–11; italics added)

And addressing the reports of increased teenage violence, the Dicker continues:

> I think we can use this violence and channel it towards God. It is my aim to get the violence off the streets and into the churches, where it belongs. In the old days people used to think of the saints as pious old milksops—well, they weren't. The saints were rough, toothless—no, I mean tough, ruthless tearaways who knew where they were going. Matthew, Mark, Luke and John went through life with their heads screwed on. That's the little rhyme we all sing—and with these principles firmly in mind, we've now got ourselves a young, vigorous church where

youngsters like yourselves can come in off the streets, pick up a chick, jive in the aisles, and really have yourselves a ball. (12)

It's no wonder Arthur's a bit taken aback by the God before him. This isn't the God of the fiery sermons, scriptures, or even the illuminated manuscripts he may have seen. According to the Marxist Lawrence, the moment committed men like Woolwich deny "God a supernatural existence outside human society and [use] the concept to mean a social force between them, then whether he is aware of it or not, and whether he likes it or not, he has taken a faltering but definite step into the materialist camp" ("The Bishop of Woolwich Squares the Circle," 125). Lawrence sees this positive move toward humanism and away from organized religion as the Bishop's "death wish" for any God at all. The zeitgeist of the period echoes this noirish appraisal, after Nietszche declared "Gott ist tot" in the late nineteenth century, and more recently *Time* magazine asking on its cover, "Is God Dead?"[19] This same "God is Dead" movement reached British bookstores, libraries, and rostra in November 1966, producing the "extheist"—those people raised with God and religion only to abandon it.[20] Myriad books on the subject of God's existence and his significance to the modern world emerged during this period, including three major titles in the UK in 1966 alone: *Dietrich Bonhoeffer: The Way to Freedom* edited by E. H. Robertson, *I Knew Dietrich Bonhoeffer*, edited by W. D. Zimmerman and R. G. Smith, and *The New Theologian* by Ved Mehta.[21] All look at the new movements in theology, and all ask hard questions about a living, accessible God. So the existence of an omnipotent God—loving *or* vengeful—is under withering attack in the years leading up to both *Flying Circus* and *Holy Grail*. The world of *Holy Grail*, then, is a world where even though God himself has demanded a sacred mission to be undertaken—to seek the Grail— His questers can still be sidetracked and then stopped short of their goal, arrested literally and figuratively by the agency of man. *Deus incarnatus, homo divinus*, indeed.

Lastly, the title of Lawrence's article cited above, the odd "The Bishop of Woolwich Squares the Circle," refers to a rather old geometer's challenge of creating a square with the same area as a circle using a prescribed number of steps and an imaginary compass and straightedge. It wasn't until the nineteenth century that the theorem was finally proved impossible. So the idiom essentially means doing the impossible. Interesting that in the opening credits of *ML*, Gilliam offers an image of God "squaring the circle" as He balances a created Earth in each hand—one spherical, one square—weighing each option; then, choosing the square Earth, he tosses away the other.

GOD: "It's like those miserable psalms"—Perhaps this God is lamenting one like Psalm 44:

Though thou hast sore broken us in the place of dragons and covered us with the shadow of death.
If we have forgotten the name of our God, or stretched out our hands to a strange god;
Shall not God search this out? for he knoweth the secrets of the heart.
Yea, for thy sake are we killed all the day long; we are counted as sheep for the slaughter.
Awake, why sleepest thou, O Lord? arise, cast us not off for ever.
Wherefore hidest thou thy face, and forgettest our affliction and our oppression?
For our soul is bowed down to the dust: our belly cleaveth unto the earth. (Ps. 44:19–25, *KJV*)

Or Psalm 120, full of "distress" and "deceit" and falsity, and even a "Woe is me," or any of the "Lament Psalms"? Laments have been sung in *MPFC*, there to try and keep someone about to encounter the "Funniest Joke in the World" from laughing to death.[22] (The laments are unsuccessful, and the reader dies laughing.) In the Pythons' only "religious" film, *Life of Brian*, God isn't heard or seen at all, though there are brief, quiet moments of Christ preaching the

Beatitudes—this scene offered quite straightforwardly, even reverently, until the camera pulls back far enough to find the people at the back who can't quite hear properly—they aren't nearly as reverent ("Speak up!").[23] In *LB* there is no mean-spirited or short-tempered God; the characters in the film world take on those roles, instead. By the time of the release of the fractured *ML*, a chaplain (Palin) at a boys' school leads a hymn that begs the Lord to not "burn," "toast," "grill," or "brase or bake or boil" his cowering flock.[24] God is often a bit of a pill in the Python world, if he has any real role at all.

It's said that those who did the artistic work in many Gothic illuminated manuscripts could labor in dull, repetitive, or even oppressive conditions, and as a result created their often risqué and bawdy illustrations as an answer to boredom or, perhaps, because they simply disliked the pious monks who penned the books. This could be a reason for the myriad unflattering depictions of clergy in the margins of these manuscripts, especially the more dour psalters.[25] The more hip, "with it" God as depicted by the Pythons, then, should appreciate such irreverent illustrations.

GOD: ". . . your knights of the Round Table shall have a task . . ."—Already on a quest of his own, and one fairly noble, Arthur is here sidetracked by the appearance of God. In the script as printed God notes that Arthur's "knights of the Round Table are complete," but the "are complete" phrase has been penciled through. It may be that this bit of finality was removed to leave room for other knights like Gawain, Hector, and Bors to join them—even to just be killed immediately—or even a nod toward the future participation of necessary fellows like Tim the Enchanter and Brother Maynard, without whom the quest would bog down. This heavenly direction has been seen before. In Pasolini's *Gospel According to St. Matthew* (1964), Joseph is twice prompted to travel by the appearance of an angel.[26]

GOD: ". . . these dark times"—This lamentatory and sometimes corrective language sounds very much like the reprovings of Venerable Bede, yes, but more precisely the British monk Gildas's condemnatory assessments of the fallen state of man in Britain up to the end of the fifth century.[27] Bede was writing of the progress of Christianity from what is now the Jarrow area, while Gildas, born in Wales, wrote from the Continent. From Gildas's lamentation, where his countrymen are their own worst enemies:

> Then all the members of the council, together with the proud tyrant, were struck blind; the guard—or rather the method of destruction—they devised for our land was that the ferocious Saxons (name not to be spoken!), hated by man and God, should be let into the island like wolves into the fold, to beat back the peoples of the north. Nothing more destructive, nothing more bitter has ever befallen the land. How utter the blindness of their minds! How desperate and crass the stupidity! Of their own free will they invited under the same roof a people whom they feared worse than death even in their absence.[28]

Gildas bemoans the age he's witnessed, certain that divine retribution is imminent:

> I saw clearly how men of our day have increasingly put care aside, as though there were nothing to fear. . . . I frequently pondered, my mind bewildered, my heart remorseful. For (I said to myself) when they strayed from the right track the Lord did not spare a people that was peculiarly his own among all the nations, a royal stock, a holy race, to whom he had said: "Israel is my first-born son," or its priests, prophets and kings, over so many centuries the apostle, minister and members of the primitive church. What then will he do with this great black blot on *our* generation? It has heinous and appalling sins in common with all the wicked ones of the world; but over and above that, it has as though inborn in it a load of ignorance and folly that cannot be erased or avoided.[29]

Roger the Shrubber will later echo God's description of these days, bemoaning the "sad times" when "passing ruffians" assault innocents with cudgels like "Ni." The monk Gildas gives substance to the Pythons' version of God when he writes of the importance of the "holy martyrs" who have and will yet (like Arthur) stand "firm with lofty nobleness of mind" in the face of the fallen world:

> God therefore, increased his pity for us; for he wishes all men to be saved, and calls sinners no less than those who think themselves just. As a free gift to us, in the time (as I conjecture) of this same persecution, *he acted to save Britain being plunged deep in the thick darkness of black night*, for he lit for us the brilliant lamps of holy martyrs.[30]

These "dark times" have only been known historically as the Dark Ages since about Petrarch's time (fourteenth century), when it was realized that very little written evidence had survived the period, especially in and of Britain. Petrarch writes in support of crusades against the infidels, citing the age of darkness between Christ's and his Apostle's time on the Earth and the present day: "Now is the time to shake the ancient yoke / From off our necks, and rend the veil aside / That long in darkness hath involved our eyes."[31] In a condensed version of the Life of Petrarch, it's even confessed that Petrarch's unwillingness to visit Britain was likely due to its paucity of enlightened writings, its darkness, essentially:

> Petrarch approached the British shores; why were they not fated to have the honour of receiving him? Ah! but who was there, then, in England that was capable of receiving him? Chaucer was but a child. We had the names of some learned men, *but our language had no literature*.[32]

And this was in the fourteenth century, well after the Pythons' Arthur quested through his own "dark" and "sad times."

Suddenly another light glows beside God or possibly within the light. . .—(PSC) As eventually realized by animator Gilliam, God appears within a glowing cloud, as will the grail when God fades away, before the clouds shut like theatrical curtains (but making the sound of shutting doors). (Gilliam sketches this out, with his notes appearing in the "Facing Pages" of *MPHGB*).[33] Gilliam had used the theatrical curtain motif (and safety curtains, too) a number of times in *Flying Circus*, including the "Full Frontal Nudity" animated sequence, which is also the title of an episode.[34]

This image of the cup[35] emerging from darkness and into light is also reminiscent of a line from *The Quest of the Sangraal* (1863) by Tennyson friend R. S. Hawker (1803–1875), who noted that part of his motivation for writing about the holy subject was to pluck "this Sangraal from its cloudy cave" (*THG*, 274).

The "or possibly" in the scene direction indicates that the Pythons were still operating on a *Flying Circus* footing, meaning even though they might know animation was going to be used in a particular scene, they didn't know what it might eventually look like. (In this case, they clearly knew God would be appearing in the sky, so they at least had a gaze reference point as they shot the scene.) For example, in Ep. 5 the cartoon sequence is heralded in the script by announcing a "two-minute extravaganza," while in Ep. 4 it's simply fronted by a "cut-out animation" hint.[36]

GOD: "Behold . . . Arthur . . . this is the Holy Grail . . ."—(PSC) According to Barber, the vessel isn't finally called "The Holy Grail" until Chrétien's *First Continuation*, being termed "the holy thing" or "the rich Grail" to that point (30).

In the shooting script version, God continues this sentence by identifying the Grail specifically: "the Sacred Cup from which Christ drank at the Last Supper." (*MPHGB*, 24). This elision seems yet another attempt to perhaps "take the curse off" both the scene and the film, pulling back from the more caustic, venal God depicted in the original script and to a lesser extent the script as finished for shooting. God is curt with them, but not nasty. Secondly, removing the description of the Cup's original purpose plays into the varying traditions promulgated by the myriad Grail romances, and clearly the Pythons are adding their own variations to the Grail tradition. Some romances mention the Grail as the cup from which Christ drank, others as the receptacle for Christ's shedding blood as/after he died on the cross (including Boron's *Joseph of Arimathea*), others as the keeper of the Host (see Barber's *THG*). The Pythons settled on the chalice—a cup—and not a dish, a tray, or a bowl, all variants of this device in earlier stories.

just discernible as an iridescent chalice—(PSC) This image—the floating Grail emitting heavenly light—is seen earlier in a number of works, many in the Tennyson-influenced era. Two examples: Arthur A. Dixon's drawing "The Holy Vessel Appeared in Their Midst," an illustration from Doris Ashley's *King Arthur and the Knights of the Round Table* (1922); and Maria Louise Kirk's "And Down the Long Beam Stole the Holy Grail" found in Inez N. McFee's *The Story of Idylls of the King Adapted from Tennyson* (1912).

The Arthurian legends are also replete with descriptions of this group vision of the Grail. In several fifteenth-century French manuscripts concerning Launcelot there are images of Arthur and his knights at the Round Table being overawed by the appearance of a shining Grail held aloft by tiny angels.[37] Most versions available appear to be based on the same image.

GOD: "... that is your purpose Arthur ... the Quest for the Holy Grail..."—This is the point where Arthur leaves off gathering knights for his Round Table at Camelot, and takes up God's quest for the Grail. In several Arthurian romances, including *The Story of the Grail*, "we see ... the development of the hero from an almost agnostic state to that of a virtuous, devout but normal Christian knight" (*THG*, 144). The Pythons' Arthur and his men attempt to make this transition, as well.

LAUNCELOT: "A blessing from the Lord"—In the first draft, this line follows God threatening to smash their faces. There is no image of the Grail, no promise of blessings—just find it or else. The Lord disappears as Patsy tries to get an autograph (*MPHGB*, 6–7).

The line "God be praised!" is spoken by Galahad in the finished film, while in the printed script, it's Bedevere who says "Praise be to God!" (*MPHGB*, 24). This last line is penciled through, as is Arthur's last line: "We have a task, we must waste no time! To Camelot!" (24). This was to have been followed by "*Stirring music crescendo. They ride off*" (25). Instead, the scene cuts directly to the animated trumpets raised for the titles animation, discussed below. The animated sequences would have been expected but not laid out during the filming, and certainly not at the time the "finished" shooting script was ready. The inclusion and exclusion of animated bits continued to be in play throughout postproductions, especially as the editing process revealed narrative fissures and clunky transitions—these cried out for suturing animation and helpful voice-over work.

Notes

1. There doesn't seem to be any indication that any on-set version of God or even the *effects* of God (glowing, blinding light, wind, lowering clouds, etc.) were planned. Everything excepting the quest's reaction shots was to be created after-the-fact by Gilliam and Doyle.

2. From a 9 December 2013 e-mail correspondence between Doyle and the author. According to the British Telephone Archives, Gilliam lived at 10 Sandwell Mansions, West End Lane during this period, just a few blocks southwest of Hampstead Heath, as well as at 51 South Hill Park, essentially just across the street from the handy Heath.

3. Other translations read "By this conquer," referring to the cross of Christ directly (Bishop, *HBMA*, 13). Arthur does seem to follow this admonition as he invokes God's will throughout.

4. See the "Facing Page 6" section in appendix A.

5. *MPFC: UC*, 1.5. The Pythons employed many artworks from the National Gallery, London.

6. These include fragments and some that may or may not be Boron's work, and include *The History of the Grail* and, perhaps, the *Adventures of Gawain*.

7. Quoted in Matthews, *Sources of the Grail*, 9.

8. See the *MPFC: UC* index under "cricketers" (1.437, e.g.) for the many mentions of Grace and many other cricketers in *Flying Circus*.

9. Bede, *A History of the English Church and People*. The citations include book, chapter, and page number in the 1964 Penguin version, where necessary.

10. He is an "unbelieving king" and is visited with the "scourge of Divine severity" in the Sellars 1907 translation.

11. See *MPFC: UC* 1: 28 for more on Bishop Robinson and this ongoing religious controversy.

12. Lawrence, "The Bishop of Woolwich Squares the Circle," 124–25.

13. Lawrence, 125.

14. The God of the script's first draft was certainly more mercurial, petty, and easily distracted.

15. By August 1963 the Mercury program was finishing its very successful suborbital and orbital flight sorties, the Gemini program of spaceflight and spacewalks was imminent, the ambitious Apollo program had been announced, and the bright president of the future, John F. Kennedy, was still alive. Forward-looking times indeed. The Pythons had poked fun at the space programs in Eps. 17 and 28. See the index entries under "Apollo" in *MPFC: UC*.

16. The ultimate and most needed step, for Lawrence, is to remove the shackles of even this more enlightened religious hierarchy—which still stands for and abets capitalist oppression—and move on to Socialism, a truly working class institution (125).

17. Bennett, Cook, Miller, and Moore. *Beyond the Fringe: A Revue*.

18. Associated-Rediffusion—an early commercial television venture—produced shows like *This Week*, as well as the ur-*MPFC* shows *At Last the 1948 Show* and *Do Not Adjust Your Set*. The network had been rebranded in the mid-1960s, positioning itself as the "hip" channel for Swinging London.

19. See Nietzsche's *Die fröhliche Wissenschaft* ("Gott ist todt," §108), as well as the *Time*, 8 April 1966 issue, respectively.

20. Hubert Hoskins, "Death of God Theology Crosses the Atlantic," *Times*, 12 November 1966: 10.

21. "Christian Pastor Believed Sense of Sin Has Gone," *Times*, 24 November 1966: 17. Bonhoeffer had been cited significantly in Woolwich's *Honest to God*.

22. *MPFC: UC*, 1:4. The sketch is in Ep. 1.

23. Here at the back, as well, Christ's message is communicated badly, with hearers left to figure out why "cheesemakers" are blessed, or "the Greek" preferred, and just why this Greek will inherit the Earth. Once again, failed communication.

24. "Growth and Learning" scene, *Meaning of Life* (1983).

25. A psalter is an illuminated manuscript containing versions of the Book of Psalms, along with other liturgical work, often. The *Lisle*, *Ormesby*, *Queen Isabella*, and *Luttrell* psalters (among others) are utilized by Gilliam for his animated sequences and sketches, and are therefore mentioned in the Facing Pages notes. See appendix A for much more on this subject.

26. *The Gospel According to St. Matthew* appeared at the Paris-Pullman in London in June 1967.

27. As Frank Stenton has pointed out, Gildas is not attacking his present-day world, but the sinful men and their choices that led to the decisive battle of Mons Badonicus, c. 500. Thereafter, Gildas indicates more than forty years of relative peace and prosperity had been enjoyed—the bulk of Gildas's

lifetime, essentially. In *MPHG*, both God and Roger condemn the "now" of Arthur's Britain ("these" not "those"). See Stenton, *Anglo-Saxon England*, 3.

28. Gildas, *The Ruin of Britain and Other Works*, 26.

29. *The Ruin of Britain*, 15.

30. Gildas, *The Ruin of Britain and Other Works*, sect. 10, p. 19; italics added.

31. Petrarch, "In Support of the Proposed Crusade against the Infidels," canz. 2, st. 5, in *The Sonnets, Triumphs, and Other Poems*.

32. This is from the Gutenberg online version of *The Sonnets, Triumphs, and Other Poems of Petrarch*, wherein the "Life of the Poet" is contributed by Thomas Campbell (original printing: London: George Bell and Sons, 1879). Italics added. Tuchman calls Petrarch an "inveterate complainer," making him seem more like the loquacious Tourist in the "Travel Agent" sketch in *MPFC* Ep. 31.

33. See the Facing Page 24 section in appendix A.

34. Found in *MPFC* Ep. 8.

35. During postproduction, effects cameraman Doyle will borrow this Gilliam-created cup image and include it over a plate shot by Terry Bedford to create Galahad's first view of Castle Anthrax.

36. *MPFC: UC*, 1:79 and 1.66, respectively.

37. There are at least two very similar versions of this scene: see Scherer, *About the Round Table*, 64; and Snyder, *The World of King Arthur*, 6–7; this latter image is used on the cover of Matthews, *Sources of the Grail*.

SCENE TWELVE
TITLE SEQUENCE ANIMATION

This title sequence[1] (not defined in any meaningful way in the printed script) is set up with a hand-penned "*ANIMATION: THE QUEST FOR THE HOLY GRAIL*" written between the typed lines "*Stirring music crescendo. They ride off*" and "*CUT TO TITLES SEQUENCE.*" There is no other indication as to what these titles are to look like, what the style might be, the content, and so on. This mere mentioning of an animated sequence without description was typical for the Pythons by this time. During the run of *Flying Circus* the writing team (everyone except Gilliam) would be together during the week leading up to the taping of the show—reworking the script, blocking out the taped (studio) scenes, rehearsing, finding music and film cues, etc., while Gilliam would be off working on animated linking and titling sequences. Even earlier, as the scripts were being written, the animation would only be a consideration—it would be accomplished much later, and in a shroud of some mystery. See the "*Suddenly another light. . .*" entry in scene 11 for more.

With Gilliam so actively participating in the *production* of this feature film (as codirector and cowriter, as well as likely the shadow grandee production designer), there was clearly no need for the troupe to expend much more energy on any scene description for Gilliam's eventual animated contributions—the *Monty Python and the Holy Grail (Book)* is loaded with drawing after drawing by Gilliam as he thought about the film, individual scenes, characters, and monsters that didn't make the final cut. The annotations for those drawings and sketches found on the facing pages (pages opposite the script text) are included in appendix A, and reveal the impressive breadth of Gilliam's search for suitable period images.

As for the finished film itself, this first significant animated sequence contains the following, in order of appearance:

Trumpets rising into view in a clouded sky and playing a fanfare—(24:55) The stylized, nebulous-like clouds are copied and then enhanced (xeroxed several times, then laid out in more lifelike cloud patterns). They are borrowed from an image of "The Sounding of the Second Trumpet," which is a panel of a tapestry, photos of which Gilliam found in *The Flowering of the Middle Ages* (1966). This is a quarto-sized history and art book that Gilliam will use extensively for both inspiration and clever copying/adaptation. The tapestry clouds are originally from the fourteenth-century *Angers Apocalypse* embroidered hanging, pictured in color on page 251 of *FMA*.[2] Unlike other cutouts he adapted, Gilliam here maintained the original colors for the clouds—various blues and whites. The trumpets and the heralds attached to them are of Gilliam's design, though they resemble the trumpets depicted in the *Cloisters Apocalypse* (see below) in both design and ornamentation.

   New trumpets emerging (downward, towards the earth) from the clouds and blasting an unsuspecting shepherd off a hilltop—(24:58) The clouds are the same type used in the previous shot, though the trumpets are different, and may be borrowed from (or inspired by) the *Winchester Psalter*, specifically the "Hell mouth" illustration (twelfth century; folio 39r), or both the action of the scene *and* the trumpet (modified slightly) may have been drawn from the so-called "*Queen Mary's Apocalypse*," the "Distribution of Trumpets" plate (early fourteenth century; f. 13v), where the seven angel trumpeters blow downward, through clouds, toward earth.

   The sheep in the shepherd's care seem unaffected by the blast. And though presented as a shepherd here, in the original manuscript the figure is actually holding the leash of a straining hound (the dog doesn't seem to have treed anything), and may even have a whistle in his mouth. The original manuscript is found in the (Baltimore) Walters Art Gallery collection (MS. 82). This manuscript is a Flemish "Psalter and Hours" from the early fourteenth century, and a version of the page is seen in Randall's *Images in the Margins of Gothic Manuscripts*[3] (XVIII: 82). To adapt the image Gilliam had to erase the leash, then shorten the left arm to match the right so that both hands could grip the staff. The sheep appear here and later, after Robin's minstrels have been eaten. They are borrowed from the British Library collection, Add. 42130, the *Luttrell Psalter*, c. 1340. These sheep are also found in Randall (LIII: 257). Interestingly, there are two actual shepherds in this last plate (seen in the Randall book) that Gilliam chose not to use in the filmed version, though both are clearly shepherds in an Annunciation scene—viz., standing among sheep, obvious crooks in their hands.

   A line of nude young men bent over and playing trumpets with their arses (all standing on an illuminated manuscript border)—(25:01) There is a very similar image in the *Rutland Psalter* (f. 73r, *bas-de-page*) featuring a contortionist in this same position—but holding two cups, not a trumpet, and he's fully clothed. This image is also included in Randall (XC: 433).[4] Gilliam sketches this contortionist, and labels it "433"; see the entries for Facing Page 32 in appendix A. There is an even more compelling original image in the Rothschild MS, f. 134, where a naked man holds a long trumpet up to his hindquarters (Randall, CXIII: 543).[5] There is also a character in the same position in Bosch's *St. Anthony* triptych, left panel, a work that Gilliam will sketch from in some detail.[6]

   There are hundreds of images of nudity (primarily male) in illuminated manuscripts, including undressing before Peter at the gates of heaven (e.g., Guillaume de Diguleville's *Pèlerinage de vie humaine*, from late fourteenth to early fifteenth century France); images of baptism, and of those being taken up in napkins by Michael or various angels; a naked trumpeter, blowing a hare out of the bell and with a grotesque's beak up his own arse (from *Estoire del Saint Graal, La Queste del Saint Graal, Morte Artu*, France [fourteenth century, f. 89]), as well as naked men doing just about everything imaginable to each other and with creatures of all sorts. See Randall's pages for some of the many, many instances.[7]

   As mentioned above, Bosch was also a significant Gilliam source, and there are dozens of images in Bosch triptychs featuring characters (human, animal, demon) with all sorts of objects inserted into their anuses, including spears, arrows, swords, snouts, tools, harp strings, musical instruments, and so on. In the right panel of Bosch's *Last Judgment*, for example, an arse trumpeter blows his horn atop a tent of damned, burning sinners (Tolnay, 182).

   The border upon which all these arse trumpeters stand is a typical illuminated manuscript border—many fully illustrated manuscript pages included the original text, various human, animal, and hybrid figures, and a border all around—this one is decorated with rosettes, *fleurs de lis*, and even an angel, it seems. On closer inspection it becomes clear that this border is actually at least two borders spliced together by the animator. The portion to the right and all the way to the third *fleur de lis* is lifted from the upper left border of the *Hours* manuscript known as W(alters)104,[8] part of the Walters Museum collection. Rather than use entire images, Gilliam often copies out and crops the portions of what he needs. For this one small image (which isn't even the center of attention in the shot), he has removed outer border images that include a man with a shawm (a medieval woodwind instrument) and a man balancing a basin, so that his arse trumpeters[9] can stand on a level platform. This same folio will be sourced again for decoration in a later animated scene where, among other things, Robin's minstrels are eaten.

Beyond this initial section on the right of the frame, Gilliam has appended more tendriled designs borrowed from another image, Fitz. 298, f. 1, also found in *IMGM* (Randall, 566). Gilliam uses a small portion from the left border of plate CXVIII, a decorative and inhabited section where not an angel but a hybrid man carrying a long spear and holding a shield is fighting another hybrid man (who wields a club and shield). The hybrid man and spear are borrowed by Gilliam as well as a portion of the tendriled border from which the man emerges, both just above the inhabited initial "O." The rest of the border that continues out of frame to the left is also from the Fitz. 298, f. 1 figure in Randall, though it's found further down the illuminated manuscript page, just to the left of (and slightly above) the inhabited initial "U." These are all black and white images (in the Randall book), and would have been colored by Gilliam and his assistants for photography.

Mirrored angels with organs—Two (mirrored) winged angels (identified by Rylands as St. Cecelia) then ascend through the shot, carrying portative organs. The *single* image is from the John Rylands Library collection at Manchester, MS. Fr. 1-2, f. 82r. Gilliam may have found the image in *IMGM* (I:3), where it is fairly large, and reproduced in black and white. In the Rylands collection manuscript, the angel is wearing a faded blue dress with umber lining, its wings are (from top to bottom) white, olive green, faded blue, and faded rose, and its hair is uncolored except for a few touches of dark red. The organ she's carrying is brown (the wood) and blue (the piping). The coloring was likely more vibrant seven hundred years ago. Also, the organ reaches all the way past the edge of the vellum, meaning Gilliam would have had to add the bottom right corner himself to complete the picture. This musical angel will reappear as the title of the film is hoisted upward in the final segment of the title section.

Mirrored Michaels with napkin—A (mirrored) Michael the Archangel image brings a "napkin full of souls"—originally to the Christ figure about to be seen waving at us (see next entry), now just as border activity (adapted from a full-color image, page 223 in *FMA*). Gilliam has changed the colors here, removing some of the dominant purples, greens, and blues and inserting more amber and gold.[10] He has also clothed the souls—all were naked in the original work excepting the caps/cowls they were wearing.

The psalter Christ—The rising psalter-type Christ (also from page 223 in *FMA*) emerges from the clouds as these angels pass, waving his right hand, and his rays of golden glory act as a wipe, a transition; both of these—the waving Christ and the previously mentioned Michael with a napkin of souls—are from a single Psalter painting found in a nunnery in Shaftesbury, Dorset, which is dated to the mid-twelfth century (Lansdowne 383, f. 168v). Gilliam changed colors (from blues and greens to golds and browns) and added the rays of glory, as well as the clouds. The image in the pages of *FMA* would have been quite large enough for Gilliam to have copied and then manipulated for production. This image can also be viewed online as part of the BLCIM.[11] Gilliam includes this complete image in his 1981 book *Animations of Mortality*. It is one of the paintings in his "Hall of Masterworks," along with many of the images he pilfered for animations during the *MPFC* series run.[12]

At 25:10, a phalanx of identical winged angels ascend, blowing trumpets. This is a single (but layered) image xerographed from a version of either the *Cloisters Apocalypse* (fourteenth century) or the *Angers Apocalypse*, and is part of the "[f]irst trumpet sounded: Hail and fire mingled with blood fall upon the earth" panel (f. 12r and f. 20, respectively). The images are nearly identical and appear in both apocalyptic works, and Gilliam may have actually used both as he put together his version of this angel. It looks as if Gilliam has done a careful bit of cleaning up, since the original *Angers* image features a nimbed angel gone "blue in the face"; the angel also features pursed lips from the effort of blowing the trumpet, and both the coloring and grimace have been diminished considerably. Gilliam also "opened" the angel's eyes a bit, darkening the irises against the white background for effect, and removed the nimb. He has also lengthened the trumpets, and decorated the bells. (These are visibly similar to the trumpets he created for the first shot of this title sequence.) Lastly, he has removed the wings, recolored them, and replaced them in the more typical "spread" array as depicted.[13]

At 25:13, finally, two winged angels, one wearing pink, one blue, hand crank the title "The Quest for the Holy Grail" into place, which is hand-lettered and presented like an elaborate illuminated manuscript incipit page. The pink angel has been seen before, carrying the organ just a few seconds earlier, and comes from the *Lancelot du Lac* books in the Rylands collection (fr. 1, f. 82). This angel still has the organ, but now Gilliam's attached a wheel to it and the angel cranks as the titles rise. The "angel" on the other side of the rising title in blue is both nimbed and cowled which is usually reserved for the Virgin (though a number of psalters feature nimbed angels, as do other texts). Both angels are wearing identical wings, and colored pink and blue, respectively. A stylistic inspiration might be the fourteenth-century French illuminated manuscript that features two angels turning the axis of the world in Matfres Eymengau de Beziers, Breviari d'amor (BLCIM). Generally, in these manuscripts when two matched angels are depicted they tend to be (1) holding the family crest between them, (2) carrying a napkin laden with souls bound for heaven, or (3) participating in the Annunciation.

The initials for both "*Holy*" and "*Grail*" are elaborated, the *H* being simply decorative (no figural or zoomorphic elements), while the *G* is an inhabited initial, featuring two angels. The *H* is quite a common design, looking very much like one used in Lansdowne 464, where Henry III is confirming the Magna Carta (f. 32).[14]

The decorative bordering also features a satyr-like drollery, a supernatural figure common to such manuscripts. In this case the upper tendril ends in the head of a fork-tongued satyr-like head wearing an asp or dragon as headdress. This portion is part of the foot of an elaborate decorated initial *R* created as a self-portrait by Brother Rufillus of Weissenau, and a faithful line drawing of the decorated initial is provided in *FMA* (303). The original manuscript is MS 9, f. 244r, and is found in the Hofbibliothek, Sigmaringen (*FMA*, 355). The original colors there include light blue for the creature's beard and hair, and green for the serpent.

However, the *G* is a type not seen often in medieval manuscripts; Gilliam has included the obvious serif feature to make it a very distinguishable *G*—a number of medieval scribes created sans serif *G* initials. The angels in the *G* are borrowed from a version of the Apocalypse (like *Cloisters*, *Angers*, *Queen Mary's*, etc.). In the case of *Cloisters*, the angels are the second and fourth from the left, both holding spears. These angels Gilliam has borrowed are modeled very much like the angels in the *Cloisters* folio fifteen (and likely copied from an image of that folio), "The Sixth Trumpet Sounded: The Angels Bound in the Euphrates Are Released," including the clothing style, posture, gaze, and head and arm positions. Gilliam has given both angels the same wings, however, wings borrowed from the *third* angel in the original image. He has also made the spears look much more like staffs, and he's nimbed both angels. Red and blue here, the angels as they appear in the *Cloisters Apocalypse* are colored as follows: the angel on the left wears a dark blue robe and is draped with a red and orange mantle (with white and green wings), while the angel on the right wears a red robe and is draped by a light brown and green-trimmed mantle (with violet wings). Both angels' feet are standing *on* the water as opposed to being immersed *in* the water, as Gilliam depicts.

See appendix A, "Facing Pages," for all the annotations associated with Gilliam's preparation for the animated sequences.

Notes

1. Gilliam makes no mention of this animated sequence in his DVD commentary track for the film.

2. The author was able to make this connection thanks to Gilliam's jotted "FofMA," which appeared next to a few sketches, then it was simply (a matter of many frustrating weeks in libraries) finding that title, and comparing the drawings by page number. These sketches had been gathered by Derek Birdsall when *MPHGB* was in production, and laid out opposite pages of script text. Gilliam does not mention *FMA* in any of his DVD commentaries. See the notes to Facing Page 68 in appendix A, "Facing Pages" for more.

3. This is the second of three identifiable books Gilliam used as source for period drawing styles, sketches from which are included in the facing pages of *MPHGB*. Gilliam *does* mention this book in his DVD commentary.

4. In a neat and copacetic twist, the version of the *Rutland Psalter* owned by the Museum of Fine Arts, Boston, still has its old checkout card in a sleeve at the back of the book. On that card is a very short record of just who accessed this rare book, including "Randall" (as in Lilian Randall) from 26 November through 10 December 1963, obviously preparing for her own book, *IMGM*, which Gilliam would access as he prepared animations for *Holy Grail*. Small world.

5. Remember, the artists producing these illustrations were most often working with page after page of thousands of lines of careful text. Sometimes, the illustration matched elements in the written word or sermon—illustrating the folly of man, his gullibility, vulnerability, etc.—and sometimes the drawings were simply fantasies of the artists: whether ironic, profound, or profane.

6. Bosch poses many characters in this same position, exposing their nakedness and often inserting some foreign object (arrow, trumpet) into the anus. In this case, the creature appears to be blowing a kind of bagpipe. See the mentions of Bosch and his creature-filled world in appendix A.

7. There are almost five pages of entries for male nudity in Randall's Index of Subjects (*IMGM* 66–70).

8. Franco-Flemish, early fourteenth century, f. 28.

9. In an unpleasant side note, Cohn notes that a portion of the witches' sabbath (or synagogue) included a dance where other witches would form a circle around a "witch standing bent over, her head touching the ground, with a candle stuck in her anus to serve as illumination" (102). The "arse trumpeters" and the witch described by Cohn are evidences of the juvenile but also historically sinister fascination with the body and excremental sacraments, if you will, where anal gasses blow heraldic trumpetings and the purity of light is corrupted. Pasolini will have provided the Pythons' their best and most recent example of this trope. At the end of his *Canterbury Tales*, the devil's arse farts out monks into a hellish devastation—rewards for their fealty and lifelong service.

10. Versions of these same works found online or in art books often feature slightly different colorings, usually due to varying photographic quality.

11. Both of these images are originally part of one page, 168v, from Landsdowne, 383; see the BLCIM.

12. There are no page numbers in the book. The Hall of Masterworks pages are in the second section, titled "The Wonderful World of Animation."

13. Many of the panels of these two apocalyptic renderings—*Cloisters* and *Angers*—are not only thematically similar but are laid out to very similar designs, meaning Gilliam could have used images of both or either as inspiration. There is also a version of this panel in Add. 17333, part of the BLCIM.

14. Lansdowne, 464, f. 32; BLCIM.

SCENE THIRTEEN
TAUNTING BY FRENCHMEN

MIX THROUGH one or two shots of them on their way again—(PSC) The final cut of the film presents five shots, including the last, wherein the castle appears before them. One of these shots features the line of questers passing a man crouching at a stream channel, bashing the stream with a large stick. This is one of the unexplained bits of background material the Pythons employ throughout—like the woman banging the cat against a wall or the man eating mud—which Gilliam characterizes as their "ambitious" attempt to populate the screen with all sorts of visual goodies.[1] In this case, however, the madness has a method, of sorts. Julian Doyle mentions that this man had come to Scotland with a small fleet of Budget rental cars, vans, and lorries for the shoot (all of which the crew "managed to damage"), and was then conscripted into the scene as the fish-basher.[2]

they approach a terrific castle (a little one would do too)—(PSC) This is yet another angle of Doune Castle (featuring the east wall), which the troupe had to use much more than they'd anticipated. All the close-up shots of the French sentries on the wall are shot on a ground level mock-up built for this scene. Initially, the Pythons had fully expected to have access to almost a dozen castles in England, Scotland, and Wales, but both budgetary restrictions and the unwillingness of the National Trust to allow filming in or near their castles (like Bodiam[3]) forced a more creative use of just two castles, both in Scotland, Doune and Stalker. They visited Eileen Donan, as well, but decided against using it, and shot footage of Bodiam and Kidwelly for additional exterior footage.

This measured demand for a castle location points up the challenges the Pythons faced as they created a film about the Middle Ages without the ability to faithfully reproduce this busy period. In "The English Landscape," Hoskins describes the look of rural England in the early fourteenth century, leading up to the privations of the plague years, the time wherein the Pythons set their story:

> There were, too, many more towns, main roads, and bridges. The twelfth century, and the thirteenth, had seen "the fever of borough creation," when the lords of rural manors all over the country had optimistically speculated upon founding market-towns upon their lands, so enhancing their incomes from urban rents, market tolls, and the revenues of fairs. And the creation of hundreds of little market-towns, each serving a radius of three to five miles, perhaps up to ten miles in the remoter parts, brought into existence, or perhaps we should say solidified, a great number of main roads for the first time, and led to the erection of many bridges all over the country. (*Medieval England*, 1.27)

As mentioned in the introduction, none of these roads or towns or bridges are depicted in the film. The visibility of modern England—motorways, power lines, glass and metal buildings—kept the Pythons' camera from panning too far left or right in any one location, predetermining the "wildness" of their version of Middle Ages Britain.

two PAGES step forward—(PSC) Patsy (Gilliam) is the only page who blows a fanfare here, a slight departure from the printed script. This was again likely a change meant to make the shoot as streamlined as possible. One trumpeter is also more diminishing and silly than two.

Also, as they array themselves to announce their presence, it's very clear that there are only five knights and five pages, each page carrying a small flag bearing his master's crest. There's no sign of Bors, Ector, Gawain, no Perceval or Tristram (from the first draft), no Gandharvas or Langar,[4] nor Brother Maynard or any of his religious fellows. Either these others join the quest in progress (and without introduction), they never joined but remained in the script, or the Pythons aren't concerned that the audience will be thrown off by new faces, seemingly from nowhere—the latter is more likely.

A MAN appears on the battlements—This and the earlier image—guards on a battlement above conversing with (or insulting) knights below—is an image borrowed from illuminated manuscripts of the medieval period. Several are similar thematically, as well. In a folio from *Roman de Godefroy de Bouillon*, a fourteenth-century French manuscript depicting the eleventh-century crusade, two Knights Templar stand at the base of a Jerusalem wall entreating Muslim warriors above (BN, Fr 22495). After Urban II had called for a crusade to liberate Jerusalem from the Muslims, the visiting French knights (led by Godfrey) set about to evict the foreign forces from "their" (Christian) city—not unlike Arthur, King of the Britons, determined to remove the French from an English castle.[5] There are at least seven other folios in this manuscript depicting similar battlement assaults. In f. 30, for example, the soldiers on the wall are hurling rocks and shooting arrows down at the attackers, who load a trebuchet.[6]

Secondly, the presence of French persons on English soil wouldn't have been a surprise by the late eleventh century, of course, following the invasion and victory of William the Conqueror in 1066. As will be discussed below, William brought scores of French vassals to Britain, where they took root and eventually intermingled with the English citizenry (who were already a healthy mix of Saxon and Danish and native British ancestry). Before Chaucer's time, even, the specter of both "French persons" and the French language had become commonplace in England.

In the "Cast List" included at the end of the printed script (and not included in the film) this character Cleese plays is known as "A Quite Extraordinarily Rude Frenchman" (*MPHGB*, 90).

MAN: ". . . Guy de Loimbard"—Viscount Montgomery (one of Jones and Palin's acknowledged sources) writes of the Crusader Guy de Lusignan (c. 1150–1194), who may at least nominally be the inspiration for this Frenchified version of Guy Lombardo (1902–1977), noted big band leader. Lusignan was born in Poitou, part of Aquitaine, meaning he was under the rule of Queen Eleanor of England, and was eventually banished from Poitou by Richard I (Lionheart) for the murder of the 1st Earl of Salisbury (*ODNB*).

ARTHUR: ". . .we have been charged by God . . ."—"*Deus vult*" ("*Dieu le veult!*") or "God wills it," was Pope Urban's heartfelt slogan under which the First Crusade (1095–1099) was organized.[7] God's will could be made manifest through others, as well. Prior to becoming Mercian king in 716, Æthelbald (d. 757) had been in exile, "driven hither and thither by King Ceolred and tossed about among diverse peoples," according to Felix's *Life of Guthlac*[8] (Sawyer, 40). In his wilderness, Æthelbald sought divine guidance: "He made several visits to [Guthlac] who prophesied that he would succeed to the Mercian kingship" (40). Guthlac was also a bit nicer, a bit more patient with Æthelbald than the Pythons' peeved God was with Arthur:

> O my child, I am not without knowledge of your hardships, I am not ignorant of the miseries that have been yours from the beginning of your life. Pitying your distress therefore I have prayed the Lord to help you in his compassion, and he has heard me; and he has given you domination over your people, and he has set you as a ruler of nations, and will subdue the necks of your enemies under your heel. . . . Not as pillage or as spoil will a kingdom be given to you, but you will be given it from the hand of the Lord. (quoted in Sawyer, 191)

"When that prophecy was fulfilled Æthelbald set about re-establishing the Mercian supremacy" (Sawyer, 40). Æthelbald would reign for fifty-one years. Arthur seems to be certain he has this same providential affirmation, thanks to his visit from the Almighty.[9]

Here too Arthur aligns the physical needs of the body ("food and shelter") with the successful undertaking of the Lord's directive ("charged by God" and "a sacred quest"), the first example in the film of Arthur's and the Pythons' version of "muscular Christianity." As George Landow notes, the description of the muscular Christian provided by Thomas Hughes in *Tom Brown at Oxford* "is merely the latest Victorian embodiment of the ideal knight or the true gentleman," wherein

> the least of the muscular Christians has hold of the old chivalrous and Christian belief, that a man's body is given him to be trained and brought into subjection, and then used for the protection of the weak, the advancement of all righteous causes, and the subduing of the earth which God has given to the children of men. (129)

Arthur will unsuccessfully attempt to advance the Lord's "righteous causes" throughout the film, using his sword and canniness.[10] See entries in "At the Grail Castle" below for more on muscular Christianity as employed by Arthur, and for the mockery of such empire-building attempts as far back as the Victorian age.

ARTHUR: ". . . if he will give us food and shelter this night he may join us . . ."—The Man on the castle walls doesn't respond well to this offer of a pseudo-enfeoffment, this reciprocity, perhaps because he is French, and doesn't consider himself subject to this English king, anyway, and neither wants nor needs an *entente cordiale*. He does agree to put the question to his master, though, which is as helpful as these French sentries can be in either of these odd exchanges.[11] This is the only time in the narrative that Arthur attempts to use his boon-granting ability as king (here perhaps a version of socage[12] that doesn't involve fighting) to encourage quest participation. "This principle of reciprocity," Sawyer writes, "permeated English society. . . . This relationship is seen most clearly in the households of great men but it existed at all levels of society" (171). Later, Herbert's father is attempting to finagle a beneficial reciprocal agreement with, first, Princess Lucky's father and then, when "he's died," with Princess Lucky herself and Launcelot as his adopted son. Generally, Arthur offers God's grace and blessings as inducement; we don't know what he might have offered Launcelot, Galahad, or Robin, if anything beyond companionship. Bedevere accepts simply because his lord asks. These same French interlopers will be encountered again in the Grail Castle at the end of the film—shot at Castle Stalker at the beginning of the shoot—and will be equally unhelpful there.

MAN: ". . . I don't think he'll be very keen"—Another of those moments where a more modern usage of a word—"keen"—pops up, and this from a gloating Frenchmen, too. Just moments later these same Frenchmen who can speak reasonable (and even colloquial) English will fail to understand one another, in French.

MAN: "He's already got one, you see"—This problem of multiples appears throughout the Dark and Middle Ages, especially where holy relics and rulers are concerned.[13] There were dozens of pilgrimage destinations claiming slivers of the true cross; bones, shrouds, possessions, or ossuaries of various apostles and saints; holy sites where miracles occurred or heavenly beings visited; and even several claiming to have the holy chalice itself or the bones of Arthur (see Barber's *THG* for more). Sidney Heath enumerates the relics claimed, for instance, by Wimborne Minster, East Dorset, and it is an impressive list:

> A piece of the Cross; part of our Lord's robe; a large stone from His sepulcher; a piece of the altar upon which our Lord was lifted up and offered by Simeon; some hairs of our Lord's beard; a piece of the scourging pillar; part of the alabaster box; a shoe of St. William; part of the thigh of the Virgin Agatha; some bones of St. Catherine; part of St. Mary the Egyptian; part of our Lord's manger; a thorn from His crown; one of St. Philip's teeth; some blood of St. Thomas a Becket; and, the hair shirt of St. Francis. (*Pilgrim Life in the Middle Ages*, 59–60)

Heath notes that this list of claimed relics closely follows similar lists from "continental" religious houses, meaning there was likely significant competition for the pilgrims' attentions between these far-flung churches. It was Erasmus who wrote derisively of the plentiful relics of the true cross (number one on Wimborne Minster's list), likely enough to build buildings (Dillenberger, 5). There were also finds of possible grails over the centuries, the Nazis searched fruitlessly for the grail (and Atlantis) in the mid-1930s, and several still occupy special places in churches around the world, including, for example, in Valencia, Spain, while the San Juan de la Peña monastery claims to have had the grail, as well. As recently as March 2014 researchers speaking for the Basilica of San Isidoro in Leon, Spain, claimed to have incontrovertible proof that their jewel-encrusted onyx cup is the actual cup of Christ.[14] Also, just as during the so-called "Western Schism" (1378–1417) more than one pope claimed papal authority; there were also periods during the life of the Holy Roman Empire when competing emperor claimants wrestled for the throne.

This is also a holdover from the first draft of the script, where multiple grails were found, including one cobbled together by Merlin from bits of junk (*MPHGB*, 26). The Pythons may have borrowed this fecundity from a popular book of their youth, *To the Chapel Perilous* by Naomi Mitchison (1955). In it, two intrepid newspaper reporters covering the search for the Grail discover that virtually all the knights on the quest emerge from the Chapel Perilous with a grail in their hands. The challenge becomes obvious only when the reporters are charged with choosing which grail they should claim is the actual holy chalice:

> "But," said Dalyn, "we always supposed—there was only one Grail—"
>
> "Yes, indeed," said the hermit, "and each knight won it." He smiled gently at Dalyn, who felt very stupid. . . .
>
> "But then," said Lienors, "how shall we know? I mean—we have to have a story, haven't we? And it is generally thought, at any rate one never hears anything else in Camelot, that there is only one Grail: the one that the knights of the Round Table saw. We couldn't very well tell our readers—all this. . . ." Her voice died down and she fidgeted her feet and looked away from the hermit.
>
> "It wouldn't be a story if there was more than one," said Dalyn, half apologizing.
>
> "If you feel like that," said the hermit kindly, "you will have to choose. Naturally, the one you decide on will be generally considered to be the Grail winner. So you have a certain responsibility, my children." (15–16)

This one-Grail-per-quester scenario will reemerge in the later stage musical *Spamalot*, where the Lady of the Lake sings that each seeker must find his or her own Grail ("Find Your Grail").[15]

ARTHUR: "Well, what are you then?"—Albert Baugh notes that after William of Normandy conquered Britain, seized the throne, and began to build castles, he tended to populate those new fortifications with Normans and other "foreigners."[16] It was also reported that several new abbots brought their own Norman armed forces, monks, and priests with them as they took their new seats (Baugh, 134). All would have been fluent in French and many in Latin; none would have had much exposure to or interest in English. This repopulation and subsequent integration—though painful and dislocating in the first generation or so—meant that by 1340 "it had become impossible to distinguish an Englishman from a Norman" (McKisack, 163).[17] The presence of and reactions to these "aliens" are also echoes from Edward I's time, when Edward's government moved against the "alien priories" (religious orders and especially land holdings in England controlled particularly by the French). McKisack gives more credit to "suspicion of foreigners and potential enemy agents" than calculated moves against religion and religious organizations, when Edward, "between 1295 and 1303 . . . took into his hands the estates of 'alien religious of the power of the king of France and his allies'" (293). The ensuing years of both Edward II and Edward III's reigns saw similar actions against these alien priories, and in 1377 a petition that made "demands for the expulsion of all aliens, monks included, on the ground that they were spies" was fairly typical (293). McKisack notes that by Richard II's reign these anti-alien sentiments ebbed, likely due to a significant decrease in French monks being allowed into the country in the first place (293).

Hallam notes that as early as 1290 Edward I was claiming that "the king of France in his malice wishe[s] to eradicate the English language" (163). The real challenge, Hallam continues, wasn't the disappearance of English—the colloquial, English peoples' language—but the wildly different regional dialects spoken across the country. A thirteenth-century Suffolk congregation wouldn't have understood Abbot Samson's Norfolk dialect, and, worse, "during the late 14th century, southern sailors shipwrecked on the Northumbrian coast were murdered because, when they asked in English for food, they were thought to be Frenchmen" (163). Northerners couldn't have spoken to southerners, though midlanders likely could communicate with both (163). As Arthur travels he meets fellow Englishmen he can understand—their language, that is—but their motives and worldviews often confuse him. It's probably fitting that the first major *English* text wasn't published until about 1220, in the "West Midlands dialect," and was a rulebook, essentially, for female hermits (163). It won't be until the late fourteenth century when there was anything like an English "common language," according to Hallam.

When the Sentry retorts that he is French, and not English at all, the contemporary topicality of this scene comes into better focus. From *Time* magazine:

> The six continental nations who had allied themselves in the budding Common Market were convinced that Britain, with its free-trade counterproposals, had been trying to destroy unity on the Continent. The suspicions were often exaggerated, but Britain, whose influence on the Continent was once enormous, now finds itself more and more on the outside looking in. (23 November 1959)

The French had also joined the nuclear club in February 1960, just before saying "*Non!*" to Great Britain in its initial app to the EEC. French president De Gaulle was responsible for much of the anti-Anglo sentiment; Britain's "special relationship" with the United States also sent Gallic blood pressures soaring.[18]

MAN: "You are English pigs"—British soldiers serving in Belfast in 1971 reported groups of young girls often screamed "filthy English pigs" as they rode through neighborhoods on patrol.[19] And in yet another slap at "empire," British troops and embassy personnel got to hear the same jibe in demonstrations in Cyprus.[20] But this is more than just a shouted insult.

In this scene the Pythons' magpie approach to the history of what came to be known as England turns in on itself. The French here seem to be using the term "English" in a more modern way, simply pointing out the otherness of these knights who speak without "outrageous [French] accents," as opposed to an earlier meaning of "English," which was used to identify Anglo-Saxon invaders ("Angles," et al.) and their descendants as separate from "those of Celtic, Scandinavian, or Norman descent," who would have been "British" ("English," *OED*). So this is a simple "us and them" dichotomy for both sides, and some pain is taken to identify each side as, first, "English" and the other, indignantly "French." If this is indeed 932, then the Norman invasion has not happened, it's the British versus the invading English, and Arthur would be justly confused by Frenchmen ensconced in an "English" castle. If this is later, of course, as the script and dress of the characters often indicate (perhaps 1167 or even 1282), then a French (Norman) presence would be unwelcome, but not a surprise. The French accents would also be less out of place since French became the language of the nobility and to a great extent the government[21] after 1066, and would remain so for at least two hundred years (Baugh, 135). When William of Normandy took control of, at first, southeast England, he was quick to replace English governmental persons with Normans; the English nobility were soon either dead (many killed at Hastings, others executed thereafter) or on the run, replaced by French nobility; and English clerics were "more gradually" replaced by French clerics, who came in droves thanks to the new opportunities for advancement (Baugh, 132–34). Norman and Pottinger, however, note that William was mindful of the need for continuity. The Witan[22] had acclaimed William, crowning him in Westminster Abbey, and it was Edward's laws William swore to uphold:

> To make himself appear as the true heir of the Saxon kings, not only by conquest but by legal descent, he made every effort to give his succession continuity by employing many Englishmen, such as Archbishop Stigand and Earl Morcar of Northumbria,[23] and by using all that was best of English institutions, such as the shire- and hundred-courts and the excellent Saxon coinage. Apart from anything else, these features of life were much better organized in Saxon England than in Normandy. (27)

The Norman military organization was also key, including the obligation of every freeman to "serve the King in war," the "shire levy" to support a feudal army, and so on. (27). William was not only repaying favors and building a trusted coterie in his new kingdom, he was ensuring the longevity of Continental institutions, thoughts, and speech in England for years to come.

Earlier, Arthur has already proclaimed himself "Sovereign of all England" (*MPHGB*, 1), clearly indicating that he references a united England of British (native), English (northern European invaders), and even Scandinavian subjects, all subject to him. But he also just a few scenes later describes himself and the peasantry as "Britons," perhaps meaning native dwellers, as separate from and in a fight against the Germanic invaders known as the Anglo-Saxons. Again, it's a confusing mish-mash of history that allows all these threads to weave their way through the film.

This is also a moment where the 1970s world could be intruding. As a part of the Common Market, Britain under Heath had to learn to live with both the primacy of the French language and a "common policy" for agriculture, even when considering "English pigs" from "French pigs." The farming issue first. As early as 1960 when Britain was working as an outsider (part of the Outer Seven) trying to deal with the Inner Six, the specter of trade concessions given to the Danish pig farmers and processors meant that Danish bacon could easily undersell British bacon in Britain, running British curers out of business, according to Lord Netherthorpe as he addressed a gathering of the National Farmers Union.[24] Over the years contested products in question included bacons, eggs, cheese, milk, sugar, apples, grains, fish products, and so on. In 1971, it was a treasured member of the Commonwealth and cheese in the crosshairs:

> After Britain had managed to finagle the necessary votes to gain entry into the European Common Market (yes, after de Gaulle was out of the way), an unforeseen hurdle presented itself. According to a *Time* magazine report from 5 April 1971, the whole deal was about to go sour because Commonwealth member New Zealand demanded guarantees that its dairy farmers could continue to sell the bulk of their cheese (and butter) to the UK, by far their biggest market. Other European countries with dairy interests complained that protectionism was just what the Common Market was trying to overcome (with the French saying "sink or swim" to the New Zealand proposal), and it took an eleventh-hour deal to keep both the negotiations and the cheese flowing ("Common Market: Breaking Out the Bubbly," *Time*, 5 July 1971; and "French Attitude Becomes More Relaxed," *Times*, 12 May 1971: 6).[25]

Britain's entry into the Common Market would keep these kinds of concerns about "English pigs" (versus Continental pigs) in the headlines for years to come.

As for the language used when conducting EEC business, Heath—a lover of the Continent from his youth[26]—had agreed early on that his representatives to Europe would all speak French fluently, which of course galled more nationalist or isolationist Englishmen, of which there were many in all political parties. Being forced to conduct business on France's terms ("hat in hand" was a phrase seen often in period newspapers) *and* in French, to boot, was a bridge too far.[27] Hugo Young notes that Heath felt "a moral obligation" to conduct business in Brussels in French, since he'd promised his French opposite Pompidou he would maintain the "old linguistic ascendancy" if Britain were admitted to the Common Market (312). The other new entrants—Denmark and Ireland—"had given no such undertaking, and made clear from the start that they wanted to speak English" (312). Young goes on to say that other countries also began to push back at the language demands—Italy, for example wanting to move away from both English and French, and Denmark favoring Danish, and so on. Britain's Permanent Representative to the EEC, Michael Palliser, characterized the imbroglio this way: "We had the effect, more through the Danes and the Irish, of turning the committee into a Tower of Babel."[28] The confusion of mangled English idioms confronting Arthur and his knights here and later at the Grail Castle is a projection, then, of the then-current Continental dust-up. And when it was Mr. Wilson's turn at wrestling with the EEC (after 1974), Young concludes, the writing was on the wall, and in plain, understandable English:

> [T]he consequence was to erode the supremacy of French. Texts in other languages slid quietly into Euro-practice. By the time Mrs. Thatcher came to power, French was no longer the exclusive first-draft usage. English was on the way to a place of equality, even, in practice, superiority. (312)

Perhaps on the Continent, but not at this French-held castle somewhere in Arthur's England.

MAN: "I'm French. Why do you think I have this outrageous accent . . ."—Since the prospect of a Frenchmen in an English castle, post-1066, would have been a de facto part of Norman occupation, and not outrageous at all, it makes some sense that these newcomers would have to learn at least some English, according to Baugh, just to get by: "The language of the masses remained English, and it is reasonable to assume that a French soldier settled on a manor with a few hundred English peasants would soon learn the language of the people among whom his lot was cast" (135). French would have been the language of the nobility, and English the coarse language of the native peasant. *Historically, then, this French sentry would have likely yelled down in French-accented English.* One just has to imagine an "outrageous [French] accent" and Old English combined, and the stage is set for the next two hundred years of English history (and for this scene).

And in a turnabout-is-fair-play moment that history often provides, in July 1358 it was a group of "English men-at-arms"—brought into the heart of Paris by Charles of Navarre to support the rebellion led by Étienne Marcel[29]—whose presence caused a popular uprising: "[A]rmed Parisians fell upon them with such effect that they had to be locked up in the fortress of the Louvre for protection" (Tuchman, 183). The rebellion was over just a few days later, and Marcel was assassinated.

Even though the French and English aristocracy had been intermarried and cousinly for generations, by the rule of Richard II (1377–1399) and as the Hundred Years War dragged on without noticeable advantage, the Continental French were considered "adversarius permaximus" by the influential Gloucester—Richard's uncle—and a "francophobia" set in (McKisack, 151). In *Piers Plowman* "the devil himself took shape as 'a proude pryker of Fraunce'"[30]—it may well be that Jones's reading of medieval history proffered the conceit of rude Frenchmen in English castles.[31] Hallam also notes that the growing preference for English among the people of fourteenth-century England had real reasons behind it: "The transformation was almost certainly a result of the surge of patriotism and nationalism associated with the Hundred Years War: the French language came to be associated with the enemy" (297). Arthur and friends will make that association, as well.

GALAHAD: "What are you doing in England?"—A fair question, and one being asked by many Englishmen in 1066, in 1216 (see below), in the fourteenth century as well as the 1960s. William's conquest brought many Normans into positions of power and favor, as has been discussed. His sons' reigns in England and on the Continent must have been both confusing and disheartening to many on both sides of the Channel. "The Norman rulers of England," Poole writes, "were disagreeable men, masterful, stern, and cruel" (*DBMC*, 97). That's as complimentary as Poole gets here. With William Rufus on the throne in England, his brothers Robert and Henry were left to grapple over the remains of their father's holdings in France.[32] As it turned out, Robert was a "despicable" ruler as Duke of Normandy, achieving "universal contempt" (97–98). Henry—born after the Conquest, in England, and married to a woman half-English—was still "grasping, cruel, and lascivious" (99). Finally William Rufus (William II), his father's favorite, was singular in his wretchedness: "From the moral standpoint he was probably the worst king that occupied the throne of England" (99). These three exemplars of Norman *noblesse oblige* would have soured anyone's view of Continental people, so it's no surprise Arthur and friends object to these French types occupying sacred English castles.

But there's more. In 1216, when the nine-year-old Henry III came to the English throne, eastern England was actually controlled by the French king Philip II's son Louis (later Louis VIII)—Louis was even "recognized as king by the majority of English barons" (Hallam, 26; also Powicke, 1–2). Maurice Powicke notes that the struggle in England against Louis "had been won"

> at Lincoln and off Sandwich; but the royal power had been maintained in England since 1215 by King John's baronial friends and his picked servants in the castles and the shires. These men naturally expected to be rewarded rather than dismissed after the restoration of peace, and for some time they were left undisturbed. It was obvious, however, that normal and responsible ad-

ministration under the direction of court and exchequer would be impossible *if foreign adventurers acquired a prescriptive right to hold royal castles* and dug themselves into the shires. . . . No very long tenure of a castle was required to blur the distinction between its "royal" and its "private" character. (19–20; italics added)

So after Magna Carta, "foreign adventurers" would have occupied a number of allegedly English castellany and castles, and if our setting meanders into the thirteenth century—as its "look" does—then Arthur and company shouldn't be surprised by these "outrageous" men and accents.[33] If Arthur and friends had happened to visit London at this time, they would have encountered French-speaking sentries, government bureaucrats, and monarchical representatives.[34] Remember that the connections between the royal houses of England and France were intricate, understandably so after William's Frenchifying of England's government, clergy, and nobility after the Conquest. More than 240 years later, Edward II of England was not only the son-in-law of France's Philip IV, but he was brother-in-law to three of the king's sons, all of whom served time as kings of France (McKisack, 107). "French persons" and traditions (and Francophonia) were regularly found in England during this period; concomitantly, there were English persons occupying fortresses and whole duchies in France (Edward III as duke of Aquitaine, for instance).[35] Due to England's continuing presence in and claims on Aquitaine and even more so to the valuable Gascony,[36] the French government demanded *homage* to the French king from the English king if war was to be averted.[37] In 1320, to avoid just such an outbreak of hostilities, Edward II would travel to Amiens cathedral and finally pay homage to the sitting French king, Philip V (108). It would be after the following French king, Charles IV, asked for Edward's homage for Gascony, and Edward demurred, that the French began more aggressive actions to retake Gascony proper (108–9). The Hundred Years War was still seventeen years away, but visible on the horizon. Many historians locate the war's muted inception on 24 May 1337, when Philip V first declares Gascony "confiscate" (115). It wouldn't be until the 1450s that the English were "finally removed"[38] from France (Rowley, 17).

The turnabout-is-fair-play moment for the French had arrived in 1377, when Richard II's accession "coincided with a renewal of French and Castilian raids on England," McKisack writes. She goes on: "Rye and Hastings were burnt in 1377 and there were assaults on the Isle of Wight and on the Yarmouth herring-fisheries; it was now the turn of the English to suffer the terrors of enemy invasion" (145). By 1386, with Philip of Burgundy and French troops securely in situ just across the Channel in Flanders, "England was threatened with mass invasion" by French forces (146). Again, the expense of such an invasion likely kept troops in their places, and a truce was reached in 1396 (147).

And with a little nod to the history of the isles, these English questers would have known that foreign occupation of castles wasn't reserved for the England-France conflict. In the first fifteen or so years of the fourteenth century, English lords and their armies occupied the Scottish castles at Stirling, Edinburgh, Berwick, and Perth before the forces of Bruce expelled them, while after 1284 English allies built and then held many castles throughout the conquered Welsh countryside (McKisack, 97–99). They could also have remembered John of Gaunt, Duke of Aquitaine and Duke of Lancaster, styled king of Castile and Leon for a handful of years—Englishmen holding Aquitaine and Castilian castles. Gaunt's destructive *chevauchée* across Galicia and toward Castile led to a financial settlement that also involved dynastically significant marriages for his family.

More currently for the Pythons, in 1965 the *Times* ran a special eleven-part series on immigration, ominously titled "The Dark Million," identifying not only the vast numbers of immigrants coming to cities like Birmingham and Smethwick but the equally vast cultural and economic differences[39] between those eager new arrivals—primarily West Indians, Indians, Pakistanis, and West Africans and Chinese—and the skittish British population they were encountering. The articles appeared just two months after Labour won the 1964 election.[40] In *White Heat*, Dominic Sandbrook notes that during this period there were wholesale racial and socioeconomic changes in many neighborhoods and even municipalities, as New Towns outside of London proper were built and populated by former city folk, and other areas experienced gentrification in the form of incoming middle-class families and their discretionary income.[41] Neighborhoods and cities were changing in racial makeup, and seemingly overnight.

And it is this working class region to which Tory MP Enoch Powell referred in his now infamous "Rivers of Blood" speech delivered on 20 April 1968, warning of the masses of unassimilated foreigners and their teeming dependents; they are

> for the most part the material of the future growth of the immigrant-descended population. It is like watching a nation busily engaged in heaping up its own funeral pyre . . . [a]s I look ahead, I am filled with foreboding. Like the Roman, I seem to see "the River Tiber foaming with much blood."[42] (quoted in *MPFC: UC*, 1.90)

This anti-immigration sentiment had been simmering for some time in postwar Britain, especially as legal immigration by Commonwealth citizens increased dramatically through the late 1960s, and thousands of eager members of the Commonwealth took advantage of the offer. Labour had made hay calling out the Tories for their anti-immigration policies in the near past, but by 1968 Labour was forced to quietly and significantly reduce swelling immigration numbers, responding to, among other concerns, trade union complaints of wage drops due to hirings of "coloureds."[43]

Popular fiction of the period tackled the issue as well. In Robert Muller's dystopic 1965 novel *The Lost Diaries of Albert Smith*,[44] neighborhood store manager and poltroon Smith has seen *his* England invaded: "Everywhere you look, the English seem to be losing out to the yobs and the morons, the foreigners, the shirkers and slobs, the Jews and coloureds, who dig themselves in deeper and deeper. No wonder there's unemployment. I'm well and truly fed up with it."[45] For the put-upon Smith and many others like him a new, homegrown fascism is the answer, one that will keep the "coloured layabouts" in their place, and "curb the black threat to our economy."[46] Sandbrook also discusses the hugely popular television character Alf Garnett, star of *Till Death Us Do Part* (1966–1975),[47] who spewed his "us against them" views weekly, in a television show

> that was not merely popular but extremely controversial. Alf Garnett's reactionary tirades set new standards for vulgar and aggressive language on television. The "bloody coons," he insists, are undermining the nation's moral fibre and social fabric, and should be sent back "to their own countries." . . . [The show's producers] always insisted that they wanted people to be repelled by Alf Garnett rather than to empathise with him. But he was such a compelling character that often the audience could not help but laugh along with his reactionary flights of fancy. . . . Indeed, as most critics agreed, the series owed much of its appeal to the fact that there were plenty of Alf Garnetts in real life. (625)

Times critic Henry Raynor wrote an article in 1967 asking about the sorry state of television comedy (he specifically misses the wit of Bertie Wooster and Jeeves and the sting of *TW3*), identifying Alf Garnett as "an antisocial disgrace, but . . . indomitable"—hence the pugnacious character's attractiveness to many viewers who might not be racists but found themselves wondering and frustrated about England's welfare state future as a mixed-race melting pot.[48] Just a few months later fellow critic Julian Critchley, writing about "bad taste" and TV, points out the appeal of *Till Death Us Do Part*, especially outside of centers of power: "Alf Garnett may not be popular in N.W.1,[49] but his views are at least those of the real world."[50] Also in 1968, the fact that Alf offered a contrasting voice on the BBC seems to have attracted many adherents:

> Alf Garnett is a monster, created with obvious delight, but *Till Death Us Do Part* is a justifiably angry outcry against the poverty of mind and spirit in which the vast numbers of people spend their lives. Yet so ambivalent is irony and our response to irony that Alf Garnett's preposterous prejudices seemed almost at times a welcome relief from the relentless drip of official liberalism on the B.B.C.[51]

The special 1965 *Times* articles on immigration mentioned above stressed the fact that it was the *local* councils being forced to shoulder the heaviest burdens for these newcomers, as neighborhoods were being transformed practically overnight. The fictitious Mr. Albert Smith is likely speaking for many who grew up in a much more homogeneous England, who are dismayed by the change, and feel as if they have no control over the transformations in their own streets, neighborhoods, schools, shops, and pubs:

> We must protect ourselves against the pernicious influence of the unemployable type of immigrant, who comes here to make slums of our town, who fills our schools with kids who don't even speak the Queen's English (and hold back the progress of English children), who grab jobs which they are not fit to hold, and rightfully belong to born and bred Englishmen, and who despoil the British way of life by bringing into the country primitive sanitary habits, unhealthy sexual perversions, and diseases like TB and V.D. (*Lost Diaries*, 187)[52]

With *de facto* immigration policies in place to try and curry favor and keep good relations with Commonwealth members, concerned British citizens—like Galahad in *Holy Grail*—were essentially being told to mind their own business. The unnamed author of the *Times* series on immigration mentioned the unwillingness local leaders exhibited in talking about their immigrant issues, including denying an interview with "the [Birmingham] council's liaison officer for coloured people"—another "mind your business" moment. In *MPHG*, the French interlopers have not only taken over a castle in the English countryside, but by doing so have taken English jobs—sentries, livestock handlers, catapult launchers—from English men, and seem to be doing those jobs fairly well.

More contemporary interlopers (for Arthur and friends) would have been both the Saxons and the Danes. The Saxons were invited, came, and stayed, of course, while the Danes, visiting and pillaging at first, eventually realized the benefits of settling in:

> The fierce and bloody Danish raiders of the ninth century . . . were only raiders, planning a return to Denmark laden with booty. The great Danish army which ravaged England in the 'sixties and 'seventies was a different matter; it stayed for thirteen years, moving camp frequently, riding across the country at great speed on stolen horses, and capturing even cities like York and London. . . . The Danes held the north-east and strongly influenced the development of the legal and naval future of England . . . they introduced new weapons and caused new developments in English tactics. (Norman and Pottinger, 18–19)

If this is the Anglo-Saxon period being depicted, the non-natives Arthur and company *should* have been finding in occupied castles were Germanic and Scandinavian; if this is the post-Conquest period, then French invaders fit the bill. Since the Pythons force their Arthur to confront settings/characters of both the historical Middle Ages *and* those more fairy-tale-like—the "impoverished plague-ridden village" and the "Black Knight" scenes respectively, and gift no signal to Arthur as to which scene is which type—perhaps the quest members are simply, perpetually, *confused.*

ARTHUR: "If you will not show us the Grail we shall storm your castle"—This immediate lack of rapprochement between the French and English is a nod to French president de Gaulle's lasting mistrust of the English, and his twice personally scuttling Britain's attempts to enter the EEC. As Sandbrook mentions, that street ran both ways:

> British diplomats had for many years been suspicious, even dismissive, of the six Common Market countries.[53] But [by 1966], having taken into account the relative success of the Continental economies, the Foreign Office was on the verge of a Damascene conversion.[54]

There was no love lost between PM Wilson and the French, either (Wilson had "no natural affection for Europe"[55]), but Heath and Pompidou—who followed de Gaulle as president—seemed to get along famously when Heath was campaigning for British membership in the Common Market by 1971. Heath aide Douglas Hurd (b. 1930) called the successful meetings "the greatest single feat of [Heath's] premiership" (Whitehead, 61). Arthur fails, of course, in his own overtures to the French, but the challenges of EEC membership continue to plague Britain—the simmering resentment of forced alliances, imposed rules and taxes, and apparently unbreakable ties to the Continent resonated. According to one observer:

> By October 1971 a vote was being held in Parliament on the principle of entry, commencing a debate that would last into the next century, that would sporadically break into something close to overt hostility and hatred, and that would ruin more political careers than it made. (Whitehead, 169)[56]

Arthur, admittedly, may have gotten off easy compared to the greater British public of the twentieth and twenty-first centuries.

The significance of the English forces presenting a Trojan rabbit to the French will be discussed below.

MAN: "You don't frighten us . . ."—This standoff is very much what had been experienced in London in the late 1960s as the "squatters" movement blossomed. This (French) Man seems to know his rights (as if he's a solid Englishman), as did the hippies living in Mr. Notlob's stomach in *MPFC*, Ep. 13, who won't budge (and the surgeon can't remove them) without a court order:

> In England . . . the London Squatters Campaign of the 1960s was fueled by the critical housing shortage experienced after the end of WWII, and squatting en masse became a familiar practice, especially in London. Each sitting and hopeful government (Labour and Conservative alike) promised more council houses, year after year, but demand far outpaced the government's ability to build affordable (and livable) homes for all qualified citizens. . . .
>
> Andrew Friend characterizes the years 1969–1977 as the high water point in London squatting, a time when the "adroit use of the law by squatters [had] frequently delayed evictions and provided time for organisation and negotiation." . . . According to Friend, the squatter in England benefited from the fact that under English law squatting was trespassing, which was not a criminal act, meaning police found themselves a bit powerless to enforce property rights if the squatters were in situ. The sketch plays on that notion throughout. By 1970 that balance began to shift, and landlord rights were more often upheld. (*MPFC: UC*, 1.214)

The MAN on the battlement is complicating things, as well, as he has already claimed the castle belongs to his Master, Guy de Loimbard, meaning ownership issues would have to be sorted before Arthur could act legally at all.

MAN: ". . . English pig-dog"—This is a fairly common German insult, calling someone "schweinehund," and had gained currency in the prewar and war years as an insult to Jews[57] in German-occupied territory (rendering them animal, and not human). The Frenchmen's insults here call into question the Englishmen's humanity—they are compared to animals thrice ("pig-dog," "empty-headed animal," and son of a "hamster")—and that they are only fit for the most degrading of labor, the "food trough wiper." Their parentage is also derided as being "silly," animal-ish, and odorous. This is grammar school stuff delivered in mangled English. The Pythons have been here before, in Ep. 25, the "Ypres 1914" sketch, where the caption scroll for the World War I–themed sketch reads:

IN 1914, THE BALANCE OF POWER LAY IN RUINS. EUROPE WAS PLUNGED INTO BLOODY CONFLICT. NATION FOUGHT NATION. BUT NO NATION FOUGHT NATION MORELY THAN THE ENGLISH HIP HIP HOORAY! NICE, NICE YAH BOO. PHILLIPS IS A GERMAN AND HE HAVE MY PEN.[58] (*MPFC*, Ep. 25)

In a 1975 article looking at the evolution of language, and especially cursing, Philip Howard quotes the German radical Ulrike Meinhof, of the Baader-Meinhof group,[59] shouting "You imperialist state-pig" at a judge. Howard parses the curious invective, finally arriving at "pig" and its association with authority figures:

But the *pig* is the most incongruous and instructive element in the compound insult. *Schweinhund* is a venerable German insult, as *cochon* is in French. But the usual German pejorative slang for a policeman is *Bulle*, a bull. *Pig* is American of the late 1960s, a hostile or insulting epithet used especially by radicals to describe policemen and sometimes other law-enforcement officers.[60]

Howard goes on to note that the American Black Panthers use the slang to refer to police officers, and that Meinhof has also written "Die Bullen sind Schweine," or "The bulls are pigs," an equally confused epithet. So these medieval French guards are using an Anglicized version of a German swear word (and avoiding a perfectly good French version) to refer to English-speakers in their native land. It's a jabberwock language, certainly, and right along the lines of those found in the "Dirty Hungarian Phrasebook" ("My hovercraft is full of eels"), also from *MPFC*, Ep. 25.

MAN: ". . . k . . . niggets"—The Frenchman is either badly mispronouncing the word "knight" or, equally likely, making fun of the strange English spelling, and pronouncing it as it looks, phonetically. The Frenchman is, however, pronouncing the word as it nearly would have been pronounced in its Old English form, "*cniht*," with the initial "k" sound vocalized—/kniçt/. The pronunciation would have survived well into the Middle English period, including, importantly, Chaucer's "parfit gentil knyght" in *CT*. It's also entirely possible that the Frenchmen (perhaps Norman Frenchmen) are aware of the earlier Anglo-Saxon meaning of *cniht*, a "servant or household retainer," and are not ready to recognize glorious knights in the direct service of the king, and thence God.

In the 1954 *Goon Show* episode "The Phantom Head Shaver," prosecuting council Ropesock (Milligan) pronounces the "k" in "knowledge"—/kuh-nol-ij/"—as well.[61]

MAN: "Your mother was a hamster . . ."—Raban reports that during this thirteenth- to fourteenth-century period there were definite biases held and expressed against "other" peoples: "The English saw the Scots as savages, wild and hairy in dress and person,[62] and the

French as lecherous, cowardly and covetous" (105). Remember Pope Urban's call to the First Crusade mentioned earlier, where the Scot was known for "his fellowship with vermin," the Dane as a drinker, and Norwegians as eaters of "raw fish"—broad, easy stereotypes all.[63] The French had their own opinions, of course, seeing the English as more animal-like—they "had tails" (105). The Frenchman here confirms that prejudicial assessment, calling Arthur and his English knights "pig," "pig-dog," and "empty-headed animal[s]" in quick turns. In his final barrage of insults at the Grail Castle, this same Frenchman will mention ducks and donkeys as he describes his contempt for the English (*MPHGB*, 87).

The margins of illuminated manuscripts and the period maps of the world tend to be populated by wildly imagined creatures of all kinds, their liminal "otherness" better understood by their odd bodies: monopods, dog faces, monkey men, mermen, men with heads in their chests, with enormous ears, with one eye, chimeras—all sorts. Bosch and Bruegel offer variations on these monstrosities in their work, as well, all of which Gilliam will ponder as the animations are created. That the French here would "other" the Englishmen by pointing out and deriding their animal parentage is par for the course, then.[64]

MAN: "... **your father smelled of elderberries**"—Though used medicinally, cooked with and used for juice for centuries, it may be that the Elderberry—which is often associated not only with women but with witches, in folklore—leaves its smell on those men who are either effeminate or who cavort with witches. Both of these would be sufficiently insulting.

MAN: "... **we shall taunt you a second time**"—According to Palin it was Jones who had been researching medieval times from Montgomery, and together they borrowed events like taunting and animal hurling from that text (145–46). Montgomery, discussing the Viking battles from fortified encampments in Louvain in 891, describes the confrontations this way:

> These water-girt camps, strengthened by stakes and a ditch, and defended by the Viking axemen, were immensely difficult to take. The Frankish king, Arnulf, captured the important camp in the marshes at Louvain in 891: a remarkable feat. The Vikings had been ravaging Austrasia and had slaughtered a large number of Franks. Arnulf had been fighting the Slavs on the Bavarian frontier but he immediately returned, bitterly enraged. Regino of Prum describes his victory:
>
>> The Northmen, elated by the previous battle, set out in full strength on a plundering raid, and the king advanced against them with his army. The Northmen seeing him approach in battle array over the river which is known as the Dyle, constructed a fortification of wood and piled up earth in their usual manner, [and] assailed the [Frankish] line of march with jeers and insults.[65]

So foreigners (Vikings) were in France taunting and intimidating the native population. Montgomery mentions a later encounter between French crusaders and Saracen troops in the Holy Lands, where similar actions occurred: "The Saracens continued to subject them [Crusaders under de Lusignan] to volleys of arrows and unnerving taunts" (180).

Proving that the home team could be as game as any jeering visitor, Norman and Pottinger report that early Saxon armies—the English army, by makeup—hurled both missiles and invectives at their Norman foes:

> [The Saxons] would have formed the centre of the army around the King and the dragon banner of Saxon England. Their round shields were held before them to ward off arrows and spears. The flanks of the army would have been formed of the lightly armed forces of the shire. The battle began with the hurling of spear and insults and a shower of arrows. (*English Weapons and Warfare*, 23)

Lastly, Montgomery also mentions the often clever, back-and-forth badinage that could be found as men at a castle's walls—inside or out—verbally jousted with their opposites. During one such night encounter between Germans and Romans, "an enemy soldier rode up to the Romans stockade and promised any deserter a wife, land and money. The Romans indignantly shouted back that they would help themselves to German women and land after the morrow's battle" (*A History of Warfare*, 114).

MAN: "Fetchez la vache!"—These lines ("Get the cow," supposedly) were handwritten into the script after-the-fact.[66] There are very few mentions of cows in the Arthurian tales, except by association. This is likely due to the fact that the tales feature little in the way of day-to-day life anyway, especially if you're not a knight, monster or damosel, meaning for the Pythons an unthreatening cow is a perfect, ironic projectile.[67] One tale in *LMD-WM* tells of a man and his son, a "cowherd." The man asks Arthur, in the name of "Jesu," to make his son a knight. With Merlin's help it is discovered the cowherd is actually the illegitimate son of Pellinore, and the boy is knighted on the same day as Gawain (*LMD-WM*, 52–54). "Kine" is mentioned once, but in this same story. As for cattle or bulls, the latter is referenced at least twice, in both instances metaphorically (men fighting like bulls lashed together). There are a handful of cow references in White's *The Once and Future King*, since Wart's (and Ector's) work is part of a more bucolic, serene setting: "In the pasture field the cows were on the gad, and could be seen galloping about with their tails in the air, which made Sir Ector angry" (6).

Animals in the Arthurian history and legend include horses, of course, but also boars, bears, dragons, dogs, etc. (Gidlow, 197–98). The pages of illuminated manuscripts are filled with animals. Scanning just a handful of pages in Randall's *IMGM* (even just pages that Gilliam sketched from), one can see sheep, pigs, goats, birds, stags, serpents, bears, lions, horses, apes, griffins, lizards, and hybrid animals of all kinds.[68] Another period source, the famous Bayeux tapestry (an elaborate embroidery), features myriad animals, including horses, dogs, birds, ewes, rams—more than five hundred animals in total, indicating their significance in eleventh-century life and art. The more contemporary source for some of the bits in *MPHG*—including the focus on ant and termite minutiae, for example, and Bedevere's irksome face shield—is White's *The Sword in the Stone*. There, as will be discussed in the "Blind Soothsayer" scene below, the Wart must learn about empathy and the larger (and smaller) world by *becoming* several creatures, while Pellinore seeks the Questing Beast throughout.

ARTHUR: "Oh Christ!"—In the finished film he actually says "Jesus Christ!" as the cow hurtles toward them. This is one of the invectives the BBFC[69] had suggested be removed for a less restrictive rating, though it's clear the Pythons kept a handful (and kept the more favorable rating, as well). The scurrilous William Rufus (1056–1100), also known as William II, third son of William the Conqueror, was known by chroniclers to prefer the invective "God's face!" (*SNK*, 167). He is said to have especially enjoyed swearing, and profaning generally in the presence of shocked churchmen. See Brooke's *The Saxon and Norman Kings*, chapter eleven, for more on this "engaging scoundrel" (168).

cow comes flying over the battlements, lowing aggressively—(PSC) Montgomery's book mentions siege and defense engines and projectile machines, indicating that many of the methods and devices used by the Romans earlier were still in use during the Crusades (though *not* "as effective as the Roman versions"):

> They consisted for the most part of battering rams, siege-towers or *beffrois*, scaling-ladders, penthouses and mantlets, and projectile-throwing engines. The projectiles might be stones, darts, poles, fire, or even carrion. The engines ranged in size from the trebuchet, with its beam of a whole tree trunk, to the crossbow. (170)

The Pythons likely couldn't afford to build any of these more complicated machines—and Arthur and Launcelot later admit to having no bows—relying on their mentions and offscreen sound effects. In yet another example of the printed script containing "inside" jokes meant only for the troupe and crew—as in *MPFC*—the cow is described as "lowing aggressively." In the finished scene, the cow sounds alarmed as opposed to aggressive. And as opposed to launching the full-size cow (they hadn't built a working catapult or trebuchet, of course), one of the insert shots photographed after the production was completed was of a toy cow hurled through the air in Julian Doyle's backyard.[70] The hurling of dead or diseased animals into fortified towns and castles *was* a common practice in medieval warfare (Dougherty, 200). The catapulting of dead human bodies—infected with the plague—is also recorded: "The Genoese colony of Caffa, in the Crimea, was besieged by Asiatics who used as weapons the corpses of plague victims, which they tossed over the town walls" (Le Goff, 159).[71] Doyle had bought the toy cow in a "Kentish Town toy shop." This shot was inserted between others shot on location to complete the action. Doyle would shoot a number of such "connecting" shots well after principal photography had been completed—bits and pieces known as "pickup shots"—for other scenes, including the death of the animator, castle shots, the fight with the Killer Rabbit, and the Trojan Rabbit flying through the air.[72]

The Goons hoed this row first, not surprisingly. In "The MacReekie Rising of '74" (25 October 1956), English soldier Fred Nurke (Secombe) is accidentally fired from a cannon at the Scottish invaders—"they're firing Sassenachs at us!"[73]; the Scots respond by firing harmonicist Max Geldray. Later, the Scots load and fire porridge at the English hiding inside the Tower of London, and the English respond with cannonballs filled with "Brown Windsor soup." Earlier, the Goons had catapulted "batter puddings" at unsuspecting strolling targets in the English countryside ("The Dreaded Batter Pudding Hurler," 12 October 1954).

The cow lands on GALAHAD'S PAGE . . .—In the original draft of this scene, the cow actually lands on two characters named "Gandharvas" and "Langar," curious inclusions both. "Gandharva" is a male spirit, a heavenly being in Hinduism and Buddhism, while "Langar" is a place name in Nottinghamshire, Afghanistan, and Iran, as well as a common meal in Sikhism. These never made it from the first draft to the finished film, but there they are on *MPHGB*, 11. Both Gandharvas and Langar are elements of Hinduism—perhaps this represents the extent of the Pythons' own Maharishi Mahesh Yogi period.[74]

This image of a catapulted cow as casus belli isn't terribly out of place, even in British martial history. A nearly decade-long war between Britain and Spain broke out after a British captain had his ear cut off by the captain of a Spanish vessel. Thomas Carlyle (1795–1881) would later call it "the War of Jenkins's Ear,"[75] noting that the incident made banner headlines in 1731, then again in 1738, when Captain Jenkins and his detached ear were summoned to appear before Parliament. War was finally declared with Spain in fall 1739.

ARTHUR leads a charge toward the castle—This is a silly, almost non-lethal attack (there are sheep- and cow-related casualties), very unlike the actual battles fourteenth-century knights and soldiers experienced. Earlier, the Black Knight lost all his limbs in a scene meant to be ludicrous, but funny; such losses were commonplace, however—and much more horrific—in the Battle of Poitiers.[76] In that contest, the forces of the Valois King Jean[77] and the invaders (English troops on French soil) under the Black Prince Edward had already fought for seven straight hours. Jean and his son Philip were surrounded by the king's guard, but were being squeezed into a sort of kill box. Cardinal Talleyrand witnessed the carnage of the king's forces falling around him—he'd unsuccessfully attempted to broker a series of peace deals—and Tuchman quotes him: "Some, eviscerated, tread on their own entrails, others vomit forth their teeth, some still standing have their arms cut off. The dying roll about in the blood of strangers, the fallen bodies groan, and the proud spirits, abandoning their inert bodies, moan horribly" (151)—a Pythonesque level of grotesquery. King Jean would surrender, he would survive, and then be held prisoner in England (with comfortable royal privilege) until he was ransomed in 1360.[78]

squashed by a sheep—(PSC) In the script Arthur calls for a retreat after "*the MAN next to him is squashed by a sheep.*" In the finished film, it appears that sheep, ducks, chickens, goats, and the cow fall from the sky, but no one is specifically squashed by a sheep. And as significant as sheep and wool were to England of the Middle Ages—wool being the most valuable export and source of income for centuries, and in the thirteenth century alone accounting for *half* the country's wealth[79]—they have little significance in *MPHG*.

These catapulted barnyard animals would have been the fairly typical menagerie of meat and dairy animals kept by any larger medieval manor. The *Luttrell Psalter* features many domestic scenes, offering a close look at medieval life and folklore. Folios 166v–172v of the psalter depict farm and farming scenes, for example, including the feeding of animals, ploughing, and a bounteous harvest. Gilliam sketched images found in the *Luttrell Psalter* many times as he prepared for the animated sequences. See entries in appendix A (Facing Pages) for more.

LAUNCELOT: "The sods!"—This is one of the words that the Pythons had been forbidden to use (by the BBC) in the early episodes of *Flying Circus*, but things would change as the show gained popularity. In Ep. 17, the "Architect Sketch," the BBC had asked that "sod" be removed. It was replaced by a "raspberry" (*MPFC: UC*, 1.267). The BBC would let slip "sodding" and "sodding wick" by Eps. 31 and 45, however. "Sod" (short for "sodomite," originally) is a nineteenth-century term, and would have been funny here for its coarseness and, yes, also since it's so out of place and time.

FRENCH SENTRIES peering into the dusk as night falls—(PSC) In the printed version of the final script, the waiting sentries have to sit through the night, with burning braziers or torches on the battlements and distant campfires in the forest beyond (*MPHGB*, 27). The carpentry sounds continue through the night, as well (28). Bishop notes that in the Middle Ages nighttime brought most life to a halt: "Medieval man had to live by the daylight" (*HBMA*, 110). Artificial light (candles, torches, fires) was expensive, smelly, and dangerous, so the daylight hours had to serve for much of the working and leisure activities of the medieval man and woman, meaning the Pythons as filmmakers were actually holding true to the period's history, if only by accident or convenience. It was likely for budgetary reasons they tried to avoid shooting outdoors at night at all—the lighting needs alone would have increased the film's budget significantly. They would shoot in wet, miserable twilight for at least Galahad's struggle into Castle Anthrax.

The proposed but elided shots as described—"*On the battlements a brazier burns or torches on the wall as the sentries peer into the dark*"—are clearly inspired by Polanski's version of *Macbeth*, especially the night before the assault on Dunsinane. If the Pythons had the time or funds to draw out the evening shots as planned, it likely was to increase the incongruity of the eventual visual surprise—not an army carrying trees before them, but a giant wooden rabbit.

Shots of the woodland with fires burning where the English lines are—(PSC) Found on page 27, this is a scene direction that is penciled through and subsequently not used in the finished film. The direction is a call for images reminiscent of those seen in Polanski's *Macbeth* and Kurosawa's *Throne of Blood*, while the smoke and haze in the scenes (to add mystery and atmosphere, or to obscure ahistorical details in the shot) are borrows from numerous samurai-type films of the period, including *Samurai Spy* (1965) and *Samurai Rebellion* (1967). In *Macbeth*, for example, there are a series of shots as Macbeth, having been called to a guard tower, peers into the distant horizon, straining to see a moving forest in the last light of the setting sun.

Notes

1. Listen to Gilliam's audio commentary on either the DVD or Blu-ray versions of the film. Gilliam also admits that the demands of a particular shot often overwhelmed the little details so carefully planned. He talks at greater length and in more detail about the production of the film itself than codirector Jones or any of the others.

2. Throughout, Doyle's comments are drawn from e-mail correspondences with the author. This information is drawn from a 26 November 2013 e-mail.

3. Bodiam had been one of the castles actually mentioned in the script as a possible (hoped for) location. See the entry for "*(e.g. Bodium)*" in the "Swallows" scene above for more.

4. "Gandharvas" and "Langar" are squashed by the catapulted cow in the first draft of the script (*MPHGB*, 11). They will be discussed below.

5. Godfrey (b. 1060) would die in Jerusalem in 1100.

6. Incidentally, many of these manuscripts can be found, at least in parts, in online collections simply by searching for the manuscript name and/or number, or by browsing collections at larger institutions including Bibliotheque Nationale or the British Library.

7. Montgomery, 171; Bishop, *HBMA*, 76.

8. Guthlac has been discussed earlier, in the "Dennis the Peasant" scene.

9. See Stenton's excellent *Anglo-Saxon England* for more on Mercia and her kings.

10. Cleese, as a member of the cast of the radio show *I'm Sorry I'll Read That Again* (1964–1973), had ventured into Hughes's public school world earlier in the sketch "Tim Brown's Schooldays" (*MPFC: UC*, 1: 205, 394). Cleese played the bully, Flashman, in this episode.

11. This moment mimics one in the 1955 Robin Hood comic series where a knight comes to a castle wall, calls for a joust with the master of the castle, and the man on the wall responds with a dutiful "I'll tell him." See the "I must speak with your lord and master" entry earlier. This same moment will happen again in a post-Python film, *Time Bandits*, when the band of little rogues pay a visit to Robin Hood, and are granted an immediate and uncontested audience.

12. "[T]enure of land by certain determinate services other than knight-service" (*OED*).

13. There were competing papal seats, for instance, each claiming divine and earthly authority, during the so-called Avignon Papacy (1309–1378), when the French monarchy and Rome were at odds. It was Clement V who decided to stay in Avignon rather than move to Rome after his election. Later in the century there were also competing popes, Boniface IX (Rome, 1389) and Benedict XIII (Avignon, 1394).

14. Appearing in a rather sensational article by Mia de Graaf in the rather sensational *Daily Mail* (*Mail Online*, 31 March 2014). These "scientific" findings are to appear in a book, not in any peer-reviewed journal, of course.

15. The symbiosis between the film *Holy Grail* and the musical play *Spamalot* is charming and crucial to the play's success. This same umbilical (the court termed the relationship a "spin-off") meant that when *MPHG* producer Mark Forstater eventually asked for a share in the profits of the wildly popular musical (spin-off), a court could easily find the latter couldn't have existed without the former. The case was decided in May 2013.

16. See Baugh, *A History of the English Language*, 134; see also Orderic Vitalis, *The Ecclesiastical History of England and Normandy*, vol. 4.

17. This intermarrying is important for a number of reasons, of course. One Pythonesque reason was the "presentment of Englishry" procedure, wherein if a man was murdered within a particular hundred (shire subdivision), that hundred was responsible for a "murder fine" if the man was proven to be Norman. If he was English, there was no fine. See McKisack, 163. If the time *Holy Grail* is set happens to be after the Norman invasion and if they happen to kill a French interloper, then they might have been subject to such a fine.

18. On the cover of *Private Eye*'s 100th issue (15 October 1965) there is an image of De Gaulle facing Lyndon Johnson and saying an emphatic "*Non!*"

19. "Humour Keeps Up Troops' Morale amid the Nail Bombs," *Times*, 9 August 1971: 2.

20. "Mob Attacks British Embassy," *Times*, 23 July 1974: 5.

21. Baugh notes that William did acknowledge his new subjects and their language by his "use of English alongside of Latin, to the exclusion of French, in his charters" (139). Latin would become the primary language in all official proceedings, and tended to be the language of the Church, as well. Complicating things was the fact that "eleventh-century Britain was a Babel of many tongues," according to Brooke—"various Celtic languages" in the north and west, "Anglo-Saxon dialects" in "England itself," and "Viking language[s]" in the English Danelaw, not to mention the earlier mentioned French and Latin. "There was no 'standard English,'" Brooke concludes (*FAH*, 189–90).

22. The Witenagemot ("Witan") was a Saxon ruling class assembly, active for about five hundred years.

23. The Archbishop died in 1072; Morcar died c. 1087.

24. "Lord Netherthorpe Warns N.F.U. on European Trade Groups," *Times*, 26 January 1960: 7.

25. *MPFC: UC*, 2: 93.

26. Heath was born in Broadstairs, Kent, within sight of the French coast on clear days. In the tumultuous but exciting 1930s Heath spent many months in France, Spain, and Germany. See the sections on Heath and the EEC in Young, *This Blessed Plot*, and Sandbrook, *State of Emergency*, for Heath's love affair with Europe.

27. Just months after the election of Pompidou (June 1969) it was still being made crystal clear that the primacy of the French language in the EEC was a key issue in any talks with Britain, no matter how eager the Brits might be or how attractive the new shared markets might appear to Continental producers. See David Spanier, "Danger of Half-Heartedness in Common Market Talks," *Times*, 16 September 1969: 11.

28. Quoted in Young, *This Blessed Plot*, 312.

29. Charles of Navarre (1332–1387); Étienne Marcel (d. 1358).

30. *Piers Plowman*, B. ix. 8; quoted in McKisack, 151.

31. It wasn't only castles and manors where foreigners, especially Normans, could be found in abundance, according to Sawyer, and thanks to the preferences of Edward the Confessor: "After 1046 there were never fewer than three foreign bishops holding English sees, and for the last five years of Edward's reign the bishop of London was a Norman and four other sees had bishops from Lorraine" (250). The replacement of English churchmen with Normans continued apace after 1066, of course. It was also foreigners in Church offices (bishops and canons) that Henry III's anxious baronial forces sought to oust in their 1263 rebellion in favor of maintaining the Provisions of Oxford (Hallam, 96).

32. The three of them ended up fighting each other over possessions on the Continent (*DBMC*, 107).

33. Waleran the German (d. 1279) would have been one such foreigner removed from his lawfully granted manor in Cornwall in 1232 (Powicke, 40).

34. It's likely that if Henry's father John *had* managed to defeat Louis, many historians agree, Magna Carta would have been "ceremonially buried"—since King John wouldn't have needed baronial support (Hallam, 26–27). *Losing* the struggle for eastern England including the capital city allowed for William Marshal's nationalistic rallying of Henry's barons, and they defeated Louis in 1217. Magna Carta—which, among many other demands, called for "the common counsel of the realm" before a tax could be granted—was then reissued and reaffirmed as the law of the land (Rowley, 16).

35. Thanks to the success of the crusades in opening trade routes, by the thirteenth century there was even an English quarter in Acre (in present-day northern Israel) known as *vicus Anglicorum* (Poole, *DBMC*, 95). Galahad's is likely a more local concern (why are French soldiers in an *English* castle), and therefore not disingenuous. As one of the fabular characters in this quasi-historical setting, Galahad can be excused for not knowing Middle Ages British history.

36. The English claim to Aquitaine was "undisputed," according to settled agreements of the previous century, and there were "rival claims to the Agenais," but Gascony—"which in 1306–07 had yielded a revenue greater than that of the English crown"—was still a major thorn of contention (McKisack, 107, 114). The question posed by Galahad could have come from Frenchmen, then, asking the English what they're doing in France (e.g., Englishmen occupying Calais in early August 1347 and for a further *two hundred years* [137]).

37. The financial state of the English crown was such that a Continental war would have been disastrous (McKisack, 109–11).

38. Excepting Calais, of course. By the 1450s, the English had no real ability to claim the French crown or support their claims on French land. Calais will be ruled by the English for another one hundred years.

39. Today in Manchester, for example, approximately 200 languages are spoken by its population of just 480,000, according to Multicultural Manchester. From the *Daily Mail*, 15 August 2013.

40. The Labour Manifesto for 1964—*Let's GO with Labour for the New Britain*—devoted three small paragraphs to the immigration issue, all rather vague:

> We believe that the Commonwealth has a major part to play in grappling with the terrible inequalities that separate the developed and under developed nations and the white and coloured races. . . . That is why a Labour Government will legislate against racial discrimination and incitement in public places and give special help to local authorities in areas where immigrants have settled. Labour accepts that the number of immigrants entering the United Kingdom must be limited. Until a satisfactory agreement covering this can be negotiated with the Commonwealth a Labour Government will retain immigration control. (19)

(By 1974, the Labour manifesto could only manage three *lines* devoted to immigration.) In fairness, the Tory manifesto featured immigration in just *one* paragraph in their 1964 manifesto.

41. Sandbrook, *White Heat*, 177–82, 624–42.

42. Whitehead points out that Powell actually quoted Virgil's *Aeneid* in the original Latin for this bit, "and thus passed over the heads of most of the local Tories gathered in Birmingham to hear him," but then "helpfully translated the phrase in his press hand-outs" (*The Writing on the Wall*, 29).

43. *MPFC: UC*, 2:18–19, 124.

44. Reprinted in 1968 as *This Is England, After All* by Penguin. One cover of the 1968 Penguin edition features a Himmler-looking nebbish in full Nazi-like regalia (dagger, epaulets) and the "Britain Awake" standard of the fascist British Action Party.

45. "December 21st," 27.

46. The latter quote ("curb") from page 187 of *The Lost Diaries*; the first from page 16.

47. Norman Lear would redevelop the show into the popular and often equally offensive *All in the Family* (1971–1979) for American television.

48. "What Are You Laughing At?" *Times*, 18 November 1967: 19.

49. "N.W.1" is the postcode for central London, including Westminster.

50. "Bad Taste Is Not the Real Sin," *Times*, 10 February 1968: 19.

51. "*Till Death Us Do Part*," *Times*, 17 February 1968: 9.

52. Perhaps not surprisingly, Smith suffers from a sexual dysfunction of his own, his voyeuristic habit the reason he is keeping this odd journal (on doctor's orders).

53. Especially France, yes, but including Belgium, Italy, Luxembourg, the Netherlands, and West Germany.

54. Sandbrook, *White Heat*, 366.

55. Whitehead, *The Writing on the Wall*, 64.

56. Phillip Whitehead (1937–2005) was a Labour MP for Derby North 1970–1983.

57. The Pythons make no direct or even glancing references to Jews or Jewishness in *MPHG*, even though the place and plight of Jews in the medieval period was significant—they were allowed to lend money with interest (their souls were damned anyway, was the prevailing thought), and they suffered horrifically during the many pogroms, especially following the worst of the plagues. See Tuchman for more, as well as the index for *MPFC: UC*. References to Jews can be found in *all* the other Python productions, including *MPFC*, *LB*, of course, and *ML*.

58. *MPFC: UC*, 1:380. This is delivered via roller caption, meaning a studio technician was standing at the ancient roller caption machine—with a camera focused on its "screen"—hand-cranking the titles so they can scroll up (or down). This is the kind of caption the Pythons called for at the start of the first draft of the script (*MPHGB*, 5). In the end they decided to not use this type of captioning anywhere in the film.

59. The Baader-Meinhof group (or faction) was a left-wing terrorist organization operating in West Germany in the 1970s. In their writings and speeches, the term "pigs" was used quite often, generally referring to anyone in power who opposed them.

60. "New Words and New Meanings," *Times*, 3 October 1975: 14.

61. Episode transmitted 15 October 1954.

62. See the later "northern" characteristics embodied by Herbert's father and Tim the Enchanter for more. The Pythons, of course, had expended a great deal of energy ribbing the Scots during the run of *MPFC*.

63. See the "No one lives there" entry in scene 5.

64. See Thimann, "Marginal Beings."

65. Montgomery, *A History of Warfare*, 154.

66. It's the Pythonesque, memorialized version of French, Franglish, or "Franglais." Here an "English 'fetch' is melded with the formal second person plural ending -ez, then the full French noun 'la vache,'" according to Prof. Daryl Lee. In the printed final script, Robin and Bedevere are shocked—not at the sight of a launched cow or even the death of a page, but that the cow "hadn't even been milked" (*MPHGB*, 27).

67. The cow does low "aggressively," according to the script, so there's that (*MPHGB*, 27).

68. For more on Randall's book and Gilliam's reliance on its images, see appendix A, where the "Facing Pages" of *MPHGB* are annotated.

69. The British Board of Film Classification (formerly the British Board of Film *Censorship*).

70. E-mail correspondence between Doyle and the author, 9 December 2013.

71. There is also the story of a siege on Newbury Castle in the mid-twelfth century where the young hostage William Marshal, 1st Earl of Pembroke, was *nearly* loaded into a trebuchet-type device and fired—all to convince his father to surrender. From *L'Histoire de Guillame Marechal*, 11. The passage is in French.

72. Information gathered from December 2013 e-mail correspondences with the author, as well as a depositional statement given by Mr. Doyle during legal proceedings, 1 October 2012.

73. A "Sassenach" is a Gaelic term—derogatory, yes—for a Saxon, an Englishman (*MPFC: UC*, 2.167).

74. Famously, the Beatles had spent time in August 1967 with the Maharishi (1918–2008) in Bangor, Wales, and in 1968 in India, to study Transcendental Meditation. George Harrison would step in (with his own money and Handmade Films) and produce the controversial *LB* when other companies backed off.

75. Discussed in Carlyle's *History of Friedrich II of Prussia, Frederick the Great*, books VIII, X, and XI.

76. Fought in 1356, and part of the Hundred Years War.

77. Also known as John II (1319–1364).

78. In an odd, Pythonesque kind of eventuality, part of the ransom agreement fell through by 1363, and Jean, concerned about his honor as part of the deal, voluntarily returned to English captivity, and would die there in 1364. His advisers and even history have no certain explanation for this chivalric but odd behavior, according to Tuchman.

79. See Hallam, 146.

SCENE FOURTEEN
THE WOODEN RABBIT

Sounds of extensive carpentry—(PSC) This scene is yet another almost direct borrow from the Japanese classic *Throne of Blood*, which the Pythons clearly remembered as they prepared for *MPHG*. In this adaptation of *Macbeth*, as the attacking army prepares for the morning's castle assault, sounds of sawing can be heard from the surrounding forest. The men in Spider's Web Castle are as frightened (especially when they eventually see the forest moving toward them) as the Frenchmen are perplexed and amused in *Holy Grail*. The setup for this scene in Polanski's *Macbeth* is similar, but without the sounds of carpentry.

As this scene was being prepped for shooting, carpentry work was being performed somewhere off camera, and someone on the camera crew calls out to "Nobby" (Nobby Clark, lead carpenter), asking if he couldn't use a "rubber hammer." This exchange was captured by the *BBC Film Night* cameras, and is part of the special features on the Blu-ray edition.

Also, among these sounds are mechanical sounds of pneumatic ratchets and hubcaps hitting concrete, for example, totally out of place but effective in creating confusion for the French sentry. This may be a borrow from another WB cartoon, the Wile E. Coyote title *Zoom and Bored* (1957). There, as the coyote is being dragged along the sandy, rocky desert ground by a harpoon tied to his leg, the incongruous sounds of car horns and cowbells are added to the soundtrack.

CLOSE-UP FRENCH looking very nervous. Dawn breaking—(PSC) This is a more artfully written section of the script, and much more along the lines of "important" foreign films than the Pythons' usual fare, unless they are making fun of important foreign films. During the *Flying Circus* run this kind of transition would have been just that—a transition, like a wipe or dissolve—and not a series of lengthy shots. As shot, the transition is much more succinct than the printed script describes.

Similarly, in one of the many battles making up the Hundred Years War, the night before combat was described as particularly nerve-wracking:

> In the tension . . . Flemish guards reported shouts and clangs of arms from the French camp, as if the enemy were preparing a night attack. Others thought it was "the devils of hell running and dancing about the place where the battle was to be because of the great prey they expected there." (Tuchman, 390)

twenty-foot-high wooden rabbit—(PSC) Deadly, marauding rabbits had appeared in cinemas before this. In French animator Rene Laloux's apocalyptic short *Les Escargots* (1965), first giant snails and then giant rabbits threaten humankind; and in the camp classic *Night of the Lepus* (1972), based on the Russell Braddon novel *The Year of the Angry Rabbit* (1964), genetically mutated rabbits wreak havoc on a desert town.[1]

As for the wooden version, the Pythons' sourcebook (for Jones and Palin) for medieval warfare was Montgomery's *A History of Warfare*, which first appeared in 1968. In a discussion of Crusades-era armaments, Montgomery lists all sorts of siege engines, many of which had been *de rigueur* for fortress assaults since Roman times—not improving in the interim, either—and then concludes: "The best means of taking a castle were still mining, starvation, and treachery" (170). Hallam agrees: "Treachery or blockade, indeed, probably encompassed the downfall of more medieval fortresses than ever fell to siegecraft" (203). And since Arthur had no engineers for mining, no vast army to surround the castle, and starvation would take far too much time, the Python's Trojan rabbit was his *ruse de guerre*, a time-honored way to assault a seemingly impregnable fortification or army in England since William the Conqueror in the 1066 invasion had used "an old Byzantine" ruse to fool the English (Montgomery, 165–66). In the first draft of the script, Arthur's reason (it was his idea) for building a rabbit is explained: "ARTHUR ARRANGES FOR A HUGE WOODEN RABBIT TO BE BUILT—A RABBIT AND NOT A HORSE SO THAT THE FROGGIES WON'T RECOGNIZE THE TRICK" (*MPHGB*, 11).

Proving also that many of the Pythons' references continue to be both historical and contemporary, this "Trojan Horse" moment of attempted perfidy comes right from the editorial pages of French and British newspapers between 1962 and 1971, when Britain's application to the EEC was being bandied about, and France was the primary impediment to British membership. Even before the 1960s, it seems clear, there was a perceived threat from the French as their postwar "economic miracle" rebuilt the country and economy much faster than Britain experienced, while that economic muscle after 1957 translated into "a struggle with de Gaulle, whose 'certain idée de la France' was asserting that country's leadership of the continent" (O'Hara, 16). The French were, in essence, calling the shots in other countries and for France's benefit, at least as seen by the outsider looking in, Britain. This was also one of the grave fears voices from the right like Enoch Powell's expressed—that of the surrender of English sovereignty—as a proviso for EEC membership. But Britain was also seen in Gallic circles as a threat to France's domination of the EEC, perhaps Britain eventually aligning itself with West Germany and acting in concert against France. From *Time* magazine's coverage of the situation:

> Britain is rejected as unfit economically or politically to join this band of continental brothers because it 1) is an offshore island, and 2) has "special ties" with the U.S. and the Commonwealth. To De Gaulle's jaundiced eye, the British attempt to enter the Common Market was simply a *Trojan horse maneuver* (an expression used with suspicious frequency in Parisian editorials and salons last week) staged by Washington to make sure that the U.S. domination of Europe would not be frustrated.[2]

Slightly earlier and from the British side—appearing in the *Times* in January 1963—this phrase is also invoked, specifically in the article "Trojan Horse in the E.E.C.," and subtitled "French Suspicions of Britain":

> M. Alain Peyrefitte, the French Minister of Information, had no doubt after today's Cabinet meeting that General de Gaulle would deal at his press conference on Monday with the flux of diplomatic moves related to Britain's entry into the Common Market. French commentators, without presuming to read the General's mind, do not see him giving ground. Indeed, they detect signs of a stiffening attitude in both London and Paris. (10 January 1963: 9)

The French suspicions aren't just about Britain, of course, but deeper, centering on America's "special relationship" with Britain in the postwar period. The escalating American insistence that the new and complicated Polaris missile system being deployed in Great Britain have continual American surveillance and technical contact—meaning a permanent increase of the American presence in Western Europe—galled the French. De Gaulle and his ministers (and many French newspapers, angry student missives, and elitist salons) saw Britain's entry into the Common Market "as a risk of opening its doors to an 'American Trojan horse,'" and would continue to say "no" to Great Britain (9). The prickly issue wouldn't be resolved until de Gaulle was out, Pompidou was in, and the Europe-friendly Heath administration cajoled their way into the Common Market in 1973.

There are also a number of period political cartoons in British newspapers addressing the issue (about six appearing between 1962 and 1971 as part of the British Cartoon Archive). On 4 June 1962 Michael Cummings published a cartoon in the *Daily Express*, depicting an epicurean, orb-hoisting "Emperor Charle-magne, Lord of Europe," as well as a wooden horse with PM Harold Macmillan's face and American president John F. Kennedy peeking from inside. The horse is labeled with a sign: "This horse wants to go to market." Both Charle-magne (de Gaulle) and Macmillan are saying the same line: "I'm not who you think I am."[3] A later cartoon from Cummings depicted two Trojan horses—one with a de Gaulle face and Khrushchev hiding inside, and the other with a Macmillan face and Kennedy hiding inside— along with the caption (spoken in unison by each horse): "*L'ennui avec vous c'est que vous êtes un dangereux cheval de Troie!*"[4] ("The boring thing about you is that you're a dangerous Trojan Horse!"). There's even a cartoon panel published 14 May 1971 in the *Daily Telegraph* featuring a wooden horse with Ted Heath's face, a castle wall, and new French President (and former PM) Pompidou looking down from the battlements. Former PM Harold Wilson is sneaking away, having pushed the wooden horse into place.[5] There are also period cartoons featuring a Trojan dove (1969), and a Trojan camel (1970)—the trope was well worn, clearly.

Lastly, see the entry for "Facing Page 6" in appendix A for another early mention of a rabbit siege.

large red bow . . . "**Pour votres amis Francais**"—(PSC) The banner says, fracturedly: "For our French friends."[6] The questers at least understand that they need to speak passable French to these castle dwellers if they're going to make any real headway, though the colorful, Anglo-Norman-ish English heard thus far means communication was at least possible. As mentioned earlier, there was a significant though not overwhelming Norman presence in England after 1066, though they were well armed and well organized.[7] (The castle here has a catapult, for instance, and these "Froggies" know how to use it.) The official language of the nobility became French, partly, of course, because so many of the English nobility were deposed or dead, and had been replaced by the invaders. The language of the masses would have continued to be Old English, and those French arrivals needing communication with the peoples they were now overseeing—to trade, organize, announce new rules and institutions, etc.—would have certainly learned at least some English.

This "gift" rabbit is intended to be the quest's version of the Trojan Horse, clearly, but once they realize they needed to be inside the rabbit to make the plan work, the rabbit becomes nothing more than a gift. For some reason, Arthur and the others embarked on the building of this rabbit without knowing Bedevere's plan at all, a seemingly enormous leap of faith or lack of judgment on the king's part.[8] In the anonymous chronicle *Life of Edward II*, the cleric author describes the scheming nature of Edward II, his machinations being somehow particularly "English": "Therefore, *relying on native caution—for the English flatter when they see their strength is insufficient for the task*—he won them over one by one with gifts, promises and blandishments" (Sawyer, 174; italics added). Knowing they can't assault the castle through the stone walls, the Englishmen attempt a ruse, offering a "blandishment"—which worked very well for Edward, as he "bought off" most of his angry barons—but one that comes hurling back at Arthur and friends in a very fatal way.

Froggie—(PSC) A fairly typical Python jibe, the French are lampooned whenever they appear in *Flying Circus*. In Ep. 2 they lecture in Franglish on "sheep aircraft"; in Ep. 17 they can do "Le Marche Futile" (a French "silly walk"); and in Ep. 23 they are ham-handed filmmakers on a rubbish tip suffering Webb's Wonder lettuce ennui.[9] The Concorde, French intellectualism (Bergson, Sartre, Cartesian dualism), even Parisian life are fair game in *MPFC*. In Ep. 37 the Froggies are the subject of prejudice, while earlier, in Ep. 10, the term is used as a bit of a warning: "'bally froggie'—Slang for 'bloody Frenchman,' probably originally from RAF types during World War I. Biggles[10] (Chapman) comes in here as if he's saving the damsel in one of his many adventures" (*MPFC: UC*, 1. 157). The term itself is a nineteenth-century insult, originally, and likely became more common during and between the World Wars. Characters in both Graham Greene and Kingsley Amis novels use the term, as well. Black Lancashire comedian Charlie Williams was using the term in his act (principally about race and prejudice) as late as 1971.[11]

Sandbrook relates how in 1967 the Labour minister George Brown—whose penchant for drink followed by regrettable behavior had been wickedly euphemized in *Private Eye* (Brown wasn't ever "drunk," he was "tired and emotional") was touring the Continent to try and buoy Britain's fledgling Common Market application when he allegedly called Valery Giscard d'Estaing[12] a "Frog" (*White Heat*, 386). Lastly, the term found its way into newspapers of the day, as well, especially the more "popular" organs like the *Express*, where columnist Jean Rook (1931–1991) summed up the specter of Britain's *official* and long-delayed 1973 entry into the Common Market in this appreciably cheeky way:

> Since Boadicea we British have slammed our seas in the faces of invading frogs and wops, who start at Calais. Today, we're slipping our bolts. And, of all that we have to offer Europe, what finer than contact with our short-tongued, stiff-necked, straight-backed, brave, bloody-minded and absolutely beautiful selves? To know the British (it takes about 15 years to get on nodding terms) will be Europe's privilege.[13]

BEDEVERE: ". . .and take the French by surprise"—Montgomery had written of similar "surprises" in ancient battles, ones where a clever ruse or distraction had carried the day. He cites Tacitus (AD 56–117), who notes that German fighters often carried totems into battles, and that "some lost or losing battles have been restored by the women, by the incessance of their prayers and by the baring of their breasts" (113).

BEDEVERE: ". . .a large wooden badger"—Easily a throwaway line, this bit of silliness has its roots in the real world of contemporary Britain. In April 1971 a single dead badger infected with tuberculosis was found in south Gloucestershire, followed by the confirmation in 1972 of a regional (including parts of Cornwall) infection in the badger population. The calls for and against a badger cull graced local and regional newspapers thereafter, though by July 1973, when the *Times* covered the potential outbreak, no decision on a widespread cull had been reached.[14] This consternation over the badger and its significance to the English countryside environment led to the Badgers Act of 1973, which forbade the killing of badgers by "unlicenced persons."[15]

In the wake of this newfound consideration for the badger's existence, it was reported in November 1973 that certain Argyll and Sutherland Highlanders who had traditionally worn badger skins as part of their sporrans should consider updating to "appropriate synthetic material [where] available."[16] The headline was particularly eye-catching, and somewhat Pythonesque: "Highlanders May March with Plastic Badgers."

Also, the influence of White's *The Once and Future King* can be mentioned again, as the last animal character to be in real association with Wart before he becomes the king is Badger, a kindly but concerned professor of the nobility of the animal kingdom in relation to man.

There is a loud twang—(PSC) The weapon that made this sound but is not depicted is likely a catapult, a siege engine that was a game changer on the medieval battlefield. The film's crew and the Pythons likely decided against building a catapult (or trebuchet, as mentioned later) due to time and cost factors—when a sound effect could accomplish the same effect, as the Goons had proven for many years on radio. The first draft of the script describes the device as "A HUGE ELASTIC CATAPULT," though this line is scratched through and "A STRANGE APPARATUS" is handwritten next to it. The camera was also to record the cow being "WINCHED SLOWLY BACKWARDS" into the device, but that was also scratched through (*MPHGB*, 10). In the finished film we see the cow led from the stall, and then hear the launch.

For the medieval army a catapult must have been the equivalent of the more modern "nuclear option"—a powerful weapon for which there is no real answer or deterrent before cannon. The French had proudly joined the exclusive nuclear club in 1960—testing in the deserts of Algeria—and de Gaulle would trumpet the nuclear-tipped *Force de Frappe* as often as he could.

The insert shot featuring the Wooden Rabbit flying through the air was actually a miniature shot made after principal photography was finished. According to postproduction maven Doyle, his wife, Valerie Charlton, built the model rabbit for free (Doyle wasn't being paid after the shoot), and they shot the flying rabbit in their backyard against a cloudy sky. They'd done the same for the flying cow earlier in the scene.[17]

ARTHUR: "Run away!"—This phrase has become one of the most quoted of many in the film, but also acts as a direct connection back to the Romance sources, especially those comprising the "Post-Vulgate Cycle" (c. 1235). The Pythons have created a frustrating Arthurian world, where successful questing accomplishments are few and far between, which is not unlike their approach to unsuccessful communications and transactions throughout the run of *MPFC*.[18] Far from being a postmodern approach to the traditional, the Pythons are reviving the Post-Vulgate Cycle tradition of depicting increasingly "dark and dismal" *individual* adventures, where lone knights seek adventure apart from the safety and even sanctity of the Grail company, according to Barber:

> Where the *Lancelot-Grail* provides symbolic adventures, whose meaning is expounded by the hermits of the wild forest, the Post-Vulgate continues as in its earlier sections, with adventures whose causes and consequences are carefully worked out *but which have no inner significance.* Such sections of the *Lancelot-Grail* as it retains are overpowered by the continuing adventures, and these adventures are dark and dismal—*mescheance*, mishap or mischance, predominates: the same *malheur* which beset Gawain and other knights in the *Prose Tristan*. Knights kill innocent girls by mistake; best friends fight each other to the death; a promise rashly given leads to a knight beheading his sister. (*THG*, 210)

In the Pythons' version, Robin seeks the Grail until he is confronted by mortal danger, and then he's "just passing through"; Lancelot is sidetracked by an individual quest to save a damsel at Swamp Castle, wandering from the Grail path and almost into an arranged marriage; and Galahad seeks the Grail but is clearly ready to at least put off the quest as he deals with the attractive maidens in the Castle Anthrax. All three have to flee their wayward situations to re-find the Grail path. Arthur himself remains on that Grail path, but is buffeted all along the fruitless way, only to be arrested before storming the Grail castle.

Malory offers his share of less than valorous knights, too, and his judgment is often as fatal as the Gorge of Eternal Peril. When young Breunor le Noire comes to Camelot to ask Arthur for knighthood, the seneschal Sir Kay mocks him for his ill-fitting coat. Arthur is impressed by the expensive but damaged coat, and the young man shares his story. His noble father had been wearing the coat while he slept, when an old enemy crept up and killed him. The son now wears the coat until he can have his vengeance. Arthur promises to knight the young man on the morrow. That evening, after Arthur and most of his retinue have left on a hunt, and the young man rests in the castle with the queen and her dozen knights,

> by sudden adventure there was an horrible lion kept in a strong tower of stone, and it happened that he at that time brake loose, and came hurling afore the queen and her knights. *And when the queen saw the lion she cried and fled, and prayed her knights to rescue her. And there was none of them all but twelve that abode, and all the other fled.*
>
> Then said La Cote Male Taile [the "evil-shapen coat"], 'Now I see well that *all coward knights be not dead*'; and therewithal he drew his sword and dressed him afore the lion.
>
> And that lion gaped wide and came upon him ramping to have slain him. And then he smote him in the midst of the head such a mighty stroke that it clave his head in sunder, and dashed to the earth. (*LMD'A*, 1.382; italics added)

Arthur and friends never admit to being "coward knights" in their various hasty retreats, perhaps choosing to live and fight another day. Elsewhere in *LMD'A*, "churls" and Romans and weaker knights flee when chased by Arthur, and if "cowards" flee then it's better to kill them (this last is mentioned so often, it might be Malory himself interjecting). Robin will profess, after scarpering from the Three-Headed Knight, that he's still "looking for the Grail," though his helpful minstrel[19] announces that he's actually "throwing in the sponge." As a complete quest group again, they will leave the Knights Who Until Recently Said Ni, feet set firmly back on the Grail path, they hope.

And finally in the *Robin Hood* comic series, Robin and his men surprise and send the Vikings running away, the Viking leader calling "Flee! Flee!"; this is followed by chasing the Picts away ("Flee, Picts!"), twice, in issues three and four, respectively.[20] In issue six, Galant attacks two knights of the Castle Hazard—"back and back Sir Galant drives the felon knights"—and they turn tail: "Aie! Make a run for it!"[21] Elsewhere in the Black Knight comic book series,[22] the Saracens begin to charge against an army of sick crusaders, many Englishmen, thinking them easy targets. Then someone yells "Plague!": "Like thunder, the dread word rolled through the Mongol ranks! Then, the savage horde turned and raced away!" (14).

GAWAIN (to his PAGE as they run away): "It's only a model"—This is pronounced by Gawain in the final draft of the script—as they're all staring up at the incoming wooden rabbit—and Arthur shushes him, as he did Patsy earlier, when Patsy commented on the faux-Camelot façade. Arthur is still maintaining the dignity (and the fiction) of the world, even as the world grows more absurd; again, it's still not demonstrably clear whether Arthur believes in this world, or whether he's determined to uphold the fiction. Perhaps not wanting to simply repeat the first joke, coupled with the fact that there's no third, payoff joke written into the script, they crossed this out of the script, and out of the finished film (along with Gawain).

And speaking of Gawain, he will be mentioned again in the printed script as he crosses the Bridge of Death, out of eyeshot, with the implication that he's about to be thrown into the chasm after Robin and Galahad.

The rabbit lands on GAWAIN'S PAGE—(PSC) First, in the finished film it's *not* Gawain's page who is crushed, since Gawain has been removed from the rest of the film. There is no sign of Gawain or two of the others—Tristram and Ector—so these knights never made the transition from script pages to film set.[23] Bors (played by Gilliam) will later be decapitated by the Killer Rabbit, of course. In actuality the wooden rabbit lands on what appears to be Galahad's page, since this page (Innes) is also wearing a red fleury cross, similar but not identical to Galahad's. This page is already injured, as well, sporting a head bandage and arm sling, likely from the first unsuccessful assault on the castle. (This page will come back to life, being part of the "Tim the Enchanter" scene later.)

Second, the specter of the furry rabbit as a mortal threat appears in British life now and again, perhaps no more significantly than when the Pythons were young and impressionable. In 1951 a House of Commons committee looking at hunting and cruelty to wild animals (first convened in 1949) released its report, upholding the benefits of protecting (which included humane culling) hares, foxes, deer, and otters. The article noted the lone, dangerous outlier:

> The only creature for which the committee recommend systematic extermination is the rabbit. Although more than thirty-six million rabbits are killed each year for food alone, their speed in breeding and *the damage they do make them a menace . . .* and [the committee recommend] that the agricultural departments should carry out a policy of extermination. Most country folk will agree that on a whole this is the best solution, but skepticism will prevail as to the feasibility of so ambitious an operation against *so determinedly prolific a little beast.*[24]

It may also be more than just a coincidence that the 1950s outbreak in England of the deadly rabbit disease myxomatosis—known colloquially as the "blind death"—was blamed by many Brits on the *French*—France (and Belgium) being the purported initial outbreak point for the epidemic. A special correspondent for the *Times* even fingered the flashpoint for the disease, placing blame squarely on Gallic shoulders:

> The unlucky gentleman who accidentally allowed some rabbits which he had inoculated with the myoxoma virus to escape from his walled-in garden has not gone without severe censure and threats of legal proceedings; for from this small beginning the present epidemic has arisen.[25]

For more on this deadly rabbit theme see the later entries for "Killer Rabbit."

Notes

1. See the entry on Braddock in *MPFC: UC*, 2.131.
2. *Time*, 8 February 1963; italics added.
3. British Cartoon Archive, 4 June 1962.
4. *Paris-Presse-L'intransigeant*, 8 February 1963.
5. From Nicholas Garland at the BCA, 14 May 1971.
6. It's French, yes, but mangled. Remembering that the Pythons created their own version of Jabberwock French in *Flying Circus* whenever necessary, they were fairly close, as ever. "*Pour votre ami français*" or "*Pour vos amis français*" are more precise. Thanks to Prof. Daryl Lee.
7. Estimates of how many Normans came for the gifts of lands and how many more accompanied them have ranged all over, but Sawyer concludes the following: "In fact the number of foreigners who were granted land in William's reign seems to have been less than 2000 and the total immigration is unlikely to have exceeded 10,000" (253).
8. In the first draft of this scene, the rabbit was Arthur's idea completely, and after the rabbit's built and ready to be stocked with knightly invaders, the French appear and drag it into the castle before

Arthur can act. It wasn't Bedevere's idea, they didn't forget to get inside the rabbit, and there is no suggestion for a wooden hedgehog. The wooden rabbit is then vaulted back toward Arthur and company. See the first draft section, *MPHGB*, 11.

9. See the many entries in the *MPFC: UC* index under "French" and "Europe: France" for more.

10. Captain Biggles (and Alvy and Ginger) were very popular characters in youth fiction, created by W. E. Johns, and featured in *MPFC* Ep. 33.

11. "Learning to Laugh at the 'Silly Business' of Race," *Times*, 18 October 1971: 3. Williams died in 2006.

12. French minister of finance, b. 1926. Sandbrook is quoting a biography of Brown, *Tired and Emotional: The Life of Lord George Brown* (1993) by Peter Paterson.

13. Quoted in Sandbrook, *State of Emergency*, 170.

14. *Times*, 11 July 1973: 3.

15. *Times*, 29 October 1973: 21.

16. *Times*, 16 November 1973: 6.

17. Information from e-mail correspondences with the author, as well as a lawsuit deposition from Julian Doyle dated 1 October 2012. Doyle mentions that both of these inserts were shot from their back balcony for a "plain sky" background—free from trees and buildings and the like (9 December 2013).

18. For more on this phenomenon see the author's *MPFC: UC*, especially the many index entries under "communication/miscommunication."

19. In the Cast List this character (played by Neil Innes) is known as "Robin's Least Favourite Minstrel" (*MPHGB*, 90).

20. *Robin Hood*, March and May 1956.

21. *Robin Hood*, June 1957.

22. The version of the first Black Knight issue I'm citing here is an Australian reprint produced by Stanley Horwitz in Sydney. The cover is different from the American original; the pages are black and white. Elsewhere the American version is cited.

23. In the Killer Rabbit scene, "Uther," "Gorlois," and "Urien" are also mentioned as casualties, just after Bors is killed. These three knight names are crossed out of the script.

24. "Lives of the Hunted," *Times*, 27 June 1951: 7; italics added.

25. "Pestilence and Pest," *Times*, 5 November 1953: 9.

SCENE FIFTEEN
A VERY FAMOUS HISTORIAN

MAN in modern dress standing outside a castle—Instead of an obvious castle—and perhaps just to make a change from the oft-used Doune Castle—the Pythons chose to shoot this scene in front of the ruins at a place called Deer Park. The ruins were known as Arnhall Castle (near Keir House), an early seventeenth-century structure fallen to ruin. This Deer Park area is northeast of Stirling.

More significant here is the presence of this contemporary figure in what to this point has been a (visually) medieval world. Given that medieval histories were clearly admixtures of fact and fantasy, of the proven and reproving, and that medieval entertainments could also feature "profane intrusions, with everyday realism[s]" such as Noah's wife played as a "comic scold," the Pythons' leeway here is great. In an earlier work the author went into some detail on this subject:[1]

> Monty Python felt this same confidence [as Shakespeare with his *ahistorical* character Falstaff], and even depended upon the disruption to keep the narrative together, albeit in an oxymoronic sort of way. . . .
>
> . . . Python's presentation of history is consistent with their previous television work—including anachronisms and visual and verbal incongruities—and they use that history to support and create these new histories. Their historical episodes always eventually undercut the history that is being presented. . . . There is a point where Python is obviously aware of the history they are making—full of gaps and breaks, anachronisms and incongruities. . . .
>
> . . . [I]n *Holy Grail* . . . [a] subtitled . . . "Famous Historian" lectures to [us] about Arthur and his knights on their perilous quest. . . . The Historian comments on the unfolding of history in a narrative form. Bergeron [affirms] that "constructing history underscores its fictional quality" (232). . . . The "[Famous] Historian," commenting on what we have just seen within the narrative, is only allowed to speak for a few moments before a knight on horseback . . . [an actual horse this time] rides through the scene and [kills him]. . . .
>
> . . . [H]ere we have an intrusion of a different time ([represented by] the modern professor) into what we had thought were the Middle Ages, but might actually just be a re-creation. Another intrusion occurs as the knight is somehow able to cross the span of time between the past and present, across history, and kill the historian. . . . History will now proceed, or be created, by those who are/have been participating. The rogue knight here is much like Bergeron's description of the character Falstaff in that he seems "impossible to pin down and possessing elusive, ahistorical qualities: a fiction that threatens the making of history" (241). . . .

The film began as a historical tale, and was interrupted by the school film narration provided by the historian; in essence, there is a tension between authors of that history, and the fictional characters took over. The question also remains as to which is the tale being told. Have we been watching a self-sufficient movie about Arthur and his quest, or have we been watching a film as created and controlled by the Famous Historian, and we are only now being made aware of this exerted influence? . . . If this is Arthur's narrative, then his forces have violently repelled a narrative intrusion; if this is the Famous Historian's narrative, then his creation has attempted to shrug off his narrative influence and make the narrative their own. . . .

. . . Louis Mink notes that "historical narratives are capable of displacing each other"—this fact is clear in . . . Python's work where the competing narratives are so forceful that they almost seem to take on lives of their own. One history is offered, then displaced by another, and another, until the text's position within history is constantly in question. Graham Holderness writes of the difference between Shakespeare as "the author" and "'Shakespeare,' the inferred author; [the latter being] a volatile, flexible, changing construction, engendered, and constantly reborn and rewritten, by the plays" (16). Falstaff walked the line between narrative history and narrative fiction; in the Famous Historian scene, history itself is rewritten by the players.[2]

After this point of obvious rupture there is no stable narrative ground, though the two "times"—that of the medieval quest and that of the police investigation—remain separate, meaning they don't share the same diegetic screen, space, or scene, until the narrative threads come together again at the end of the film, and Launcelot is being frisked for arrest. The ultimate collision will be Arthur's arrest, and the hand over the camera,[3] signaling the end of the quest and the film.

He speaks straight to CAMERA in a documentary kind of way—(PSC) British viewers of the period would have recognized this setup from many shows, including *Panorama*, *The World About Us*, and the long-running *Tuesday Documentary*;[4] and the Pythons have already satirized the plight of the helpless presenter a number of times in *MPFC*. In Ep. 8 a peripatetic sociologist (Idle) falls down an open manhole thanks to mischievous pensioners ("Hell's Grannies"); in the first *MPFZ* episode the German TV presenter is dragged into a reedy swamp by frogmen; and in Ep. 37 the Slade Professor of Fine Art is knocked cold in a boxing match. This Oxford don (Chapman) is bashed into submission as he presents on the orderliness of Palladio's villa designs—and he is knocked out, mid-sentence (*MPFC: UC*, 2.136–37). As it turns out, one of the professors holding this position at Oxford as the Pythons went to university was Sir Kenneth Clark (1905–1983), who would present the popular series *Civilisation* on the BBC in 1969. Clark is clearly the model for this "Famous Historian."[5] In the very first episode of the thirteen-part series Clark stands (and then sits, uncomfortably) before a surviving example of a Roman aqueduct, lecturing knowledgably about the challenges of supporting a mighty civilization like Rome's. Modern viewers—spoiled by the Pythons, certainly—might watch this scene and wait in vain for a violent interruption from somewhere offscreen. One of the founders of *Private Eye*, Christopher Booker,[6] discusses the trenchant significance of this popular show, "the most successful series television has ever produced":

A powerful ingredient in the immediate impact of *Civilisation*, particularly in America, was the contrast it struck with the strange times in which it first appeared. There, on television screens which had been purveying nightly images of Vietnam, race riots, protest demonstrations, and pop festivals, was this urbane figure, in his beautifully cut suits, taking us back into a different world—a realm of exquisite paintings, tapestries, cathedrals, palaces, the rich, ordered harvest of a thousand years of European culture. Amid the chaotic nightmare of the present, Clark seemed a symbol of all that sense of permanence and stability we thought we had lost and were beginning again to yearn for. (*The Seventies*, 31–32)

Holy Grail revivifies itself from sketch to sketch by undercutting the very "permanence and stability" Clark and his program attempt to demonstrate, and as we've seen, the Pythons are very aware of the violence and suffering in the world that produces the film. And as Booker keenly points out, it was Clark himself who set the table for those like the Pythons who, armed with university degrees, skewers, cocked eyebrows, and a forum, set about to poke holes in artfully constructed pasts:

> Indeed as he magisterially surveyed the whole sweep of Western civilization since the Middle Ages, not the least appealing thing for many viewers was the way Clark did not conceal his distaste for the way the story had ended up. Apart from the stray asides directed throughout the series at modern architects, playwrights, psychiatrists, "hellish traffic," and "all those forces which threaten to impair our humanity—lies, tanks, tear gas, ideologies, opinion polls, mechanization, planners, computers," *Clark's fear that we were no longer civilized, his suspicion that we were sinking into a new barbarism, constantly intruded on his survey of the glories of the past like a specter at the feast.* (32; italics added)

Clark may have been, at least unconsciously, not only the Famous Historian but also the marauding knight on horseback (just as the Pythons themselves can be both). The Famous Historian attempts to bring an order to the narrative and to the events of *The Quest for the Holy Grail*—what Booker calls Clark's attempts at a "reordered universe" during a time of uncertainty—only to have the blood and guts realities of not only the Middle Ages but the demands of a 1970s viewing audience ride through with a slashing sword. This scene sets the stage for the balance of the film, where no floated balloon, no matter how historically or mythologically accurate or appropriate, is safe from puncture.

SUPERIMPOSE CAPTION: *A Very Famous Historian*—(PSC) Grail romance author and editor Thomas Malory would also draw attention to his sources, acknowledging the artifice of the telling, as well as giving validity to this retelling. In *Sir Tristram de Lyonesse*, Malory notes that Tristram recuperates for "a month and more" after the battle with Sir Marhalt, a duel wherein Marhalt was mortally wounded, and that Tristram's wound was deadly serious due to a poisoned spear: "[F]or *as the French book saith*, the spearhead was envenomed, that Sir Tristram might not be whole," such that "all manner of leeches and surgeons" could not heal him (italics added; *LMD-WM*, 178–79). The Very Famous Historian will, of course, be struck down momentarily by an unidentified participant in the narrative.

OFFSCREEN VOICE: "Picture for Schools—take eight"—(PSC) This bit of voice-over (Palin) and the following slate *do not* appear in the printed script. The slate clapped in front of the Famous Historian is from the *Holy Grail* film shoot itself. It's slate number 306, and take eight for this particular shot. The date is listed as May 24, and it's an "Ext. Day" (exterior, day) shot. The directors Terry Jones and Terry Gilliam are listed, as is cameraman Terry Bedford. Also known as a clapper board, the slate is used to not only designate scene and take (for film editing purposes later), but to assist the sound department as they synchronize sound in postproduction.

Given what was discussed above regarding the film narratives now in competition, this moment just adds to the complexity. The clapper is part of the film being filmed known as *Monty Python and the Holy Grail*, and yet the slate man mentions "Picture for Schools, take eight" as he claps, meaning he, at least, thinks this film is something else entirely, as do the Famous Historian, Mrs. Historian, and whatever other crew might be on hand. This diegesis is bracketed by another diegesis, and so forth, meaning the Pythons are as interested in playing with the formal elements of cinema as was Bergman in *Wild Strawberries*, for instance.

This scene is discussed in appendix A; there is a copy of the "Daily Continuity Report" for 24 May included in *MPHGB*, Facing Page 29.

The "Picture for Schools" moniker would have been quite recognizable to the paying audience in Britain of 1975. Since the late 1960s sex education films like *Growing Up* had been the subject of continuing controversy. The films, created to be shown in schools, caused an uproar thanks to more graphic depictions of sex and talk of variant sexualities, many seeing the films as nothing more than prurient how-to manuals for sex aimed at the pre-teen set. There are dozens of editorial cartoons and letters to the editor in contemporary newspapers coming down on both sides of the contentious issue (*MPFC: UC*, 2.84). The violent but non-sexual "Picture for Schools" provided by the Pythons here might have been much more acceptable to many British parents.

HISTORIAN'S SPEECH: ". . . seems to have utterly disheartened King Arthur"— This disheartening has its sources in the Grail romances, as well. In Malory's *Le Morte Darthur*, in *The Tale of the Sangrail* section, King Arthur and his knights have returned to Camelot, visited the monastery in "evensong," and are then marvelously visited by "the Holy Grail covered with white samite" (*LMD-WM*, 317). No one was worthy to actually see the holy vessel, however, and they feasted richly instead as the Grail passed through and away from their midst. This bothered Gawain, who immediately made a vow to spend the next year and longer laboring "in the quest of the Sangrail," also vowing: "[A]nd never shall I return unto the court again till I have seen it more openly than it hath been showed here. And if I may not speed I shall return again, as he that may not be against the will of God" (317). The "most part" of the other assembled knights then took this same vow. When Arthur heard this, he was "greatly displeased," and laid bare his sorrow, knowing they were to be separated:

> "Alas," said King Arthur unto Sir Gawain, "ye have nigh slain me for the vow that ye have made, for through you ye have bereft me the fairest and the truest of knighthood that ever was seen together in any realm of the world. For when they depart from hence, I am sure they all shall never meet more together in this world, for they shall die many in the quest. And so it forthinketh me not a little, for I have loved them as well as my life. Wherefore it shall grieve me right sore, the departition of this fellowship; for I have had an old custom to have them in my fellowship." And therewith the tears fell in his eyes; and then he said, "Sir Gawain, ye have set me in great sorrow, for I have great doubt that my true fellowship shall never meet here more again." (318)

Guinevere is amazed that Arthur will "suffer" his knights to "depart from him," though Lancelot calls it a "great honour" to perhaps die in this way (318). Arthur is upset, still:

> "Ah, Lancelot," said the King, "the great love that I have had unto you all the days of my life maketh me to say such doleful words; for there was never Christian king that ever had so many worthy men at his table as I have had this day at the Table Round, and that is my great sorrow." (318)

The Pythons have Arthur himself decide that separate quests are the solution to their misfortunes, according to the Famous Historian, and they do manage to eventually reach the Bridge of Death, where they are reunited. Thereafter, the end result is quite similar.

HISTORIAN'S SPEECH: ". . . the ferocity of the French taunting . . ."—The word "taunt" likely comes from the French phrase "*taunt pour taunt*," meaning a "like for like" or "tit for tat" (*OED*), and until quite recently it was the French who had been on the receiving end of these taunts, especially as their own colonial empire diminished. In 1954 the French had been forced to withdraw from Indochina (Cambodia, Laos, Vietnam) after seventy years of colonial occupation and administration, and following an exhausting eight-year war to try and prop up their regional infrastructure.[7] The term (and the shouting) also crops up quite often in early 1960s accounts of the Algerian struggle for independence from France, not only from Algerian nationalists[8] who naturally wanted colonialism to end, but also from the far right factions in France who fumed about an emasculated French government and policy every time there was a concession.[9] By 1962 France would be out of both Indochina and Algeria, finding itself in a similar position as Britain, whose colonies and protectorates were also in flux in the 1960s.

The French had also until very recently kept Great Britain out of the Common Market, with President de Gaulle himself vetoing the application in the early 1960s. De Gaulle had become well known for possessing and deploying "an infinity of Gaullic inflexions" (yes, taunts) ready to jab and prod especially the British (and then the Americans); his speeches were eagerly anticipated by pundits and winced at by his Anglo and American targets.[10]

The editors of *Time* magazine reported on some of this period's "ferocity," in this case, the Commonwealth's loudly negative reaction to Britain's attempts at more economic coziness with the Common Market Six. Commonwealth economic ministers essentially threatened Britain with in-kind retaliation if Britain changed tariffs to favor the Continent at the expense of the Commonwealth: "British Chancellor of the Exchequer Selwyn Lloyd was *startled by the vehemence of the overseas ministers*, [and] hastily assured them that Britain would consult their governments at every step of any future Anglo-European trade negotiations."[11] Arthur and his knights are being taunted by the French in their own land; Britain of the 1960s is being taunted by the French and supposed Commonwealth friends at every turn. Britain didn't have to "run away," however, they just had to outlive de Gaulle.

The baiting and taunting could be most keenly felt closer to home, often, as coverage of parliamentary "discussion" could attest. With Wilson and Labour in power in November 1965, Heath and the Tories were able to stridently cherry-pick issues that might show the chinks in the sitting government's armor. This battle metaphor was forwarded by various parliamentary correspondents, and is especially keen when opposition leader[12] Heath is able get his feet under him at the Commons lectern on the day that Wilson had to present his second prospectus (and yes, the prospects were dour):

> As [Wilson] reviewed past achievements and elaborated on the Queen's Speech the performance was that of an artisan and not an artist.
> This was a pity for when Mr. Wilson got up the whole House was right on its toes after a roistering half-hour of naked polemics from Mr. Heath. Mr. Heath had tried this line before, but in the past his touch has been too heavy, *his weapon too blunt to pierce Mr. Wilson's armour*. This time he had an advantage: *the Prime Minister had left his steel breastplate at home in some copious Whitehall pigeonhole, and Mr. Heath probed the weakness with stylish mockery until the blood ran red*.[13]

Heath was on about the many unfulfilled pledges made by Labour governments to effectively and productively nationalize the steel industry and—like the taunting Frenchman in the castle—he wasn't afraid to name names:

> *As the cheers of his own side mingled with constant heckling from across the floor*, [Heath] rammed each quotation down its author's throat. What would Mr. Michael Foot make of this, he inquired? Mr. Foot sat slumped in glum depression. And what of Mrs. Jeger, who had published an article on the subject that very day? Mrs. Jeger blushed crimson at the recollection.
> Greatly daring, Mr. Heath challenged the Prime Minister to get right up then and declare that nationalization was no longer part of his party's programme, but Mr. Wilson, with a smile that grew thinner as the speech progressed, waved him on with a flap of his hand.

Mr. Heath was delighted. In that case, he cried, the whole country would know that this was just a squalid act of political expediency by a Prime Minister who put political power before his principles and beliefs.

It was not the sort of remark to win friends, but then Mr. Heath was not in that sort of mood. *He taunted the Cabinet as a whole over age, over weight, and over numerous*, and went on to pick out a few Ministers for special treatment.[14]

This is a siege indeed, both sides hurling epithets and wooden rabbits at the other.

This power relationship would turn rather completely just a few years later, when in 1972 the Heath government faced off with the nation's miners in what was initially seen as a no-win (for the miners, that is) strike action. Weeks later—when the miners and sympathetic others had stood firm and the nation was shivering and living by candlelight—the taunts could come from the formerly oppressed, because, according to Sandbrook: "Heath had not just been beaten; he had been annihilated. 'It was a 'grim day,' [Heath] wrote later, 'for the country and for the government'" (*State of Emergency*, 31). Heath's government had to concede a huge pay raise and virtually every demand the miners had made—they certainly would have liked to "run away," if only there had been somewhere to run.

HISTORIAN'S SPEECH: "Arthur . . . decided that they should separate . . ."—This structure is also reminiscent of the twelfth- to fourteenth-century romances for Arthur and his knights, according to Barber, and is first seen in Chrétien de Troyes' *The Story of the Grail*. Gawain and Percival are set on different but ultimately converging paths by Chrétien, "a narrative technique which was to become a commonplace of Arthurian romance, that of interweaving two series of adventures, and moving the focus from one hero to another, until they eventually meet and the story is resolved" (*THG*, 21). In the Pythons' version, we follow separately Galahad, Launcelot, Robin, and Arthur (along with Bedevere), before they ultimately converge, appropriately, at the Bridge of Death.

A KNIGHT rides into shot and hacks him to the ground—(PSC) This is the only horse seen in the film, and since Arthur and company ride no horses, it may be that none of Arthur's retinue had anything to do with the attack. This likely isn't one of the Pythons on horseback, either. During the run of *MPFC* the show hired professional riders for these kinds of shots.[15]

The level of violence depicted here had become standard for both arthouse and mainstream films. The various New Waves had introduced more "realistic" depictions of violence and sexuality, with those influences felt in Hollywood, as well. But it's also important to point up the levels and varieties of violence in the Arthurian source material. In Malory's work alone, foes are run through with swords and spears, arms and legs are hacked off, as are many heads, and gory descriptions—swords slicing through helms or body armor, through flesh and bone, cleaving a man from his head "unto the paps"—occupy page after page. Other epic works like *The Song of Roland* are equally blood soaked, as are the descriptions of *actual* battles fought, for example, during the Hundred Years War. There is blood everywhere in these knightly times.

This is also likely an indirect reference to the ongoing spat in the world of academia—and specifically those buttering their bread in the pre-Christian, sub-Roman, post-Roman, or Arthurian fields—between those who sought proof of the historical Arthur (via archaeological digs, new interpretations of known texts), those who were certain there was no historical Arthur, and those who looked to the available sources for *whatever* they might reveal. Often these tiffs were engaged in the public eye, as when professors Ashe and Alcock conducted and trumpeted "Camelot" digs at South Cadbury Castle in 1966, providing media access and achieving event status as they dug for Arthur's castle. Other professors in the field bristled at the claims emerging from such expeditions. Archaeologist Charles Thomas (Leicester and Exeter), who detested the carnivalesque atmosphere of the entire undertaking, penned a polite, even thoughtful review ("[Ashe] is a writer of skill and fluency") of Ashe's then new book *The Quest for Arthur's Britain*. Thomas went on to identify the mistakes of both the book and the dig, faulty oversights and overreaching conclusions, penning a withering review of the pseudo-scientific dig.[16] See the entries "It is a silly place" (scene 10) and "Court at Camelot" (scene 2) for more.

C & A twinset—(PSC) This is the "look" of the Python Pepperpot—generally a short-sleeved sweater with golfer cardigan (and modest skirt); aka "the inevitable twinset and pearls"[17]—it appears a number of times in *Flying Circus* (*MPFC: UC*, 2.196). The phrase is also used by the Pythons in the scripts for *MPFC* as shorthand, thumbnail descriptions of what a character should look like, a typology that is easily understood by the show's production designers. It is also, of course, a social, political, and economic description, which to the Pythons would have meant a middle-aged Tory housewife who reads the *Daily Telegraph* (aka the *Daily Torygraph*).[18]

MRS HISTORIAN: "Frank!"—It's not likely they're the same person, but earlier Dennis's mother suggested that "Frank" should be found to deal with the alleged King Arthur. That line was crossed out of the final version of the script. In the Cast List included at the end of the printed script (in *MPHGB*, about page 90), this character is known as "THE HISTORIAN WHO ISN'T A.J.P. TAYLOR (HONESTLY)'S WIFE." Taylor was an eminent historian seen by the Pythons, clearly, as one of the predominant "talking heads" in televised academia. See notes to Ep. 11 in *MPFC: UC* for more.

Notes

1. This work was fleshed out in the author's *Monty Python, Shakespeare and English Renaissance Drama* (McFarland, 2003).

2. *MPSERD*, 102–4.

3. Or, even more forcefully at yet another remove, a hand over the *projector*, since the film stock is seen to slip from the film gate.

4. See the entries in *MPFC: UC* for more on these shows.

5. See the many entries under "Clark, Sir Kenneth" in *MPFC: UC*. The show premiered on BBC 2 on 22 February 1969, just weeks before the Pythons gathered to shoot the first series of *Flying Circus*.

6. Booker (b. 1937) cofounded the satirical magazine in 1961 with Willie Rushton (joined soon thereafter by Richard Ingrams). The news and public figures in its pages were regularly reflected in the *MPFC* episodes. See the many mentions of *Private Eye* in *MPFC: UC*.

7. World War II had been over for the French for only a matter of months when troops had to be sent to Indochina.

8. For crowds of anti-French Algerians taunting authorities, see "More Than 70 Deaths in Algerian Disorders," *Times*, 2 November 1961: 12, and "Bitter Scenes at Funerals of Algerian Muslims," *Times*, 3 November 1961: 10.

9. "Minister's Denial on Moscow Treaty with Rebels," *Times*, 1 December 1961: 12. There were disturbing reports of vandalism, rapes, and murders, by lynching, commonly, of Arabs by local "Europeans" in larger cities like Oran during this period, as the in situ foreign population tried to maintain its control. There were even fistfights in the French Assembly between right- and left-leaning ministers.

10. "Gen. De Gaulle on Britain's Part in Europe," *Times*, 16 May 1962: 12.

11. "The Lonely Dreamer," *Time*, 3 October 1960.

12. Heath had been elected over Gerald Maudling, one of the Pythons' favorite targets in *Flying Circus*, just three months earlier.

13. "Mr. Heath in a Taunting Mood," *Times*, 10 November 1965: 12; italics added.

14. "Mr. Heath in a Taunting Mood"; italics added.

15. "Scotsman on a Horse" and "Dennis Moore" feature stunt riders. See *MPFC: UC*, 1.44 and 2.132, respectively.

16. Thomas, "Are These the Walls of Camelot?"

17. Perhaps worn best by the comic-strip character Carol Day (syndicated 1956–1971), produced by David Wright, Jack Wall, and Kenneth Inns.

18. See also *MPFC: UC*, 2.85 and 2.185, but especially Ep. 32, "The Tory Housewives Political Clean-Up Campaign" entries therein.

SCENE SIXTEEN
THE TALE OF SIR ROBIN

CUT TO forest stock footage—(PSC) This shot *is* part of the finished film but is *not* accounted for in the final script. On his DVD commentary track Idle calls this stock footage shot "Cheddar Gorge,"[1] which is in Somerset, and which it does resemble, to a certain extent. Julian Doyle mentions that the "footage" is actually a still photo, and not film stock.[2] Needing an establishing insert shot of a dense forest and, since it was winter during this portion of postproduction and there were no nearby forests with any leaves on the trees, Doyle improvised. He found a library book with a large forest photo, placed it upright on his piano with candles on the keys below to create a "heat haze," and shot the footage using a slow zoom.[3] The photo itself is clearly an image from Australia, and looks like a low angle on one of the mamelon in Central Victoria, perhaps even Hanging Rock.[4]

... animated frame ... "The Tale of Sir Robin" on it—(PSC) The florid "inhabited initial" used here for the "R" in Robin is one seen often in period illuminated manuscripts. This hybrid creature, a bird-like dragon, is also seen in the *Macclesfield Psalter* for Psalm 119 (Panayatova, 70). In Robin's case the *R* is a zoomorph—meaning the dragon takes the shape of the letter. An image of a man fighting such a creature (in a *Q*) can be seen as a frontispiece in book fifteen of St. Gregory's *Moralia* in Job;[5] in book two of the German *Moralia* the zoomorphic initial *S* features a fire-spewing dragon;[6] in a historiated initial *A* with St. Margaret the same kind of dragon forms the letter, while Margaret is emerging from the side of another dragon;[7] the background style is reminiscent of many initials, including a decorated *D* in Arundel 45, f. 1v; as well as an inhabited initial *R* (for "Regu") with a dragon, in Harley 105,[8] a "theological miscellany," made by monks in Canterbury in the mid-twelfth century.

There are also many other decorated initial examples in several of the books known to be Gilliam sources. In Randall's *IMGM*, there are dozens, some decorated with floral patterns, others with beasts and others with men, mostly saints. In *FMA*, Gilliam had several examples to choose from on page 54, including inhabited and zoomorphic initials. On page 58, a nearly full-page image of a page from *Stephen Harding's Bible* (c. 1110)[9] features an elaborate zoomorphic *H* made from a satyr-like hybrid (blowing a trumpet). The page also features St. John in white Cistercian attire, an eagle, and a lion consuming a dragon. On page 72 of this same book, there are two illuminated initials, one an *A* and one a *G*. The *A* is from a Josephus manuscript produced in Canterbury about 1130, and featuring a bird-winged dragon; the *G* is completely formed by a dragon, and is from Augustine's *De Civitate Dei*, c. 1110. Both feature elaborate tendril designs (floral, known as "white-vine stem") as background, just as

Gilliam's *R* does. Gilliam clearly hasn't copied these, but was instead informed and inspired by them. Additional inhabited initials can be seen in *FMA* on pages 110, 142, 182–85, 198, 213, 303, and 307.

VOICE OVER: "So each of the knights went their separate ways"—This voice-over (by Palin) is not included in the printed script, and would have been added in postproduction—along with the simple zoom-in "forest" shot—as a means of creating a more fluid (and cost-effective) transition. Most of the narrated or animated transitions are handled this way to save money.[10]

Most of the Grail romances also employ quite obvious transitions, for example, with the storyteller Malory starting a new paragraph within a larger tale with "Now we turn unto Sir Tristram," having spent the last few paragraphs with Sir Palomides (*LMD-WM*, 200). This physical separation is what the Arthur of Malory's *Le Morte Darthur* most wanted to avoid (it brought him "to sorrow"), but the Grail quest had to continue, and promises had been made. See the entry in scene 15—". . . seems to have utterly disheartened King Arthur"—for more.

VOICE OVER: ". . . through the dark Forest of Ewing"[11]—This sounds very much like the Idle-voiced narration from *"Njorl's Saga"* in Ep. 27 of *MPFC*, narration that helps Erik (Jones) move from the high street of North Malden and into the Icelandic saga proper:

> Narrator: With moist eyes, Erik leaves this happy land to return to the harsh uneconomic realities of life in the land of Ljosa waters. On his way Erik rested a while in the land of Bjornsstrand, the land of dark forces, where Gildor was King.[12] (*JTW*, 2.49)

The structure of this episode—a period tale interrupted by modern realities—certainly influenced the Pythons' approach to *Holy Grail* (*MPFC: UC*, 2.3–19). The *Holy Grail* narrative began as a straight-ahead period film that showed holes in its narrative fabric from time to time, holes through which more modern, perhaps cynical sensibilities could seep. With the abrupt cut to the Famous Historian, however, the fracture was complete.

VOICE OVER: ". . . accompanied by his favorite minstrels"—When Robin was being recruited initially he was depicted being taught the lute by one of his minstrels (*MPHGB*, 21). That scene was not used in the final film, and not shot, either.

Robin's minstrels are performing a valuable and time-honored service here, even if Robin can't appreciate it. "The British maintained an oral tradition, based on bardic poetry and genealogies, which was professional and systematic," Gidlow writes. "This lasted deep into the Middle Ages and certainly was to be found between AD 500 and 800" (65). The goals of this oral tradition were recall and authenticity, the maintenance of "accurate" genealogical lines, and the rehearsing of noble and disastrous deeds and events. By the early fourteenth century, there were already different types of these minstrels, or storytellers (or entertainers), also known as *histriones*, according to Thomas de Chabham, sub-dean of Salisbury: those that strip and dance lewdly, wearing masks (these are damned); those that are "of no fixed abode" and who simply follow courts with scurrilous talk, and are "wandering buffoons" (these are also damned):

> Then there is a third class, those who have musical instruments for the amusement of men; they are of two kinds. Those who frequent drinking-parties and lascivious gatherings where they sing indecent songs. These are also damnable. But there are others called *joculatores* who sing of the deeds of heroes and of the lives of saints. These alone are capable of salvation. This class of entertainment was generally regarded . . . as respectable.[13]

Robin's minstrels would likely categorize themselves into this last area, where respectability can be found, and Robin would have agreed, at least initially, before their songs stubbornly maintain levels of uncomfortable authority and authenticity. Poole mentions that *histriones* were kept by earls, dukes, towns, guilds, and even lords cardinal (607). By the end of the Middle Ages period these minstrels in England could claim "a guild (or fraternity) at London and at one or two other places formed with the object, if possible, of controlling the profession" (607).

lilting sound of medieval music—(PSC) Since "[o]nly about 30 secular English or Anglo-French songs have survived with their music from the 200 years up to 1377,"[14] and this song isn't likely one of them, Neil Innes and perhaps Idle are responsible for this song, though Innes gets the credit in the opening titles. See the entry for Innes above in the opening credit section. Innes and Idle would collaborate successfully on *Rutland Weekend Television* (1975–1976), and in 1978 on *All You Need Is Cash*, a Beatles mockumentary.

"Music," Poole continues, "till the fourteenth century, was chiefly used to accompany the voice and the dance; it then became an entertainment in itself" (*Medieval England*, 2.608). The only real deviation for the Pythons is that Robin, who doesn't seem to be of any significant means, wouldn't likely have been able to afford such a musical retinue. (Even King Arthur has only Patsy, remember.) Poole continues:

> It was a normal practice in the great houses to have music during meals or on festive occasions. No less than eighty named instrumentalists, including players of tabors, kettledrums, harps, gitterns, citoles, trumpets, flutes, pipes, psalteries, organs, and various forms of fiddle, were gathered together at the court of Edward I to celebrate the knighting of his son in 1306. (608)

If Edward I only saw fit to pay for eighty musicians, it's not likely Robin could afford four. Still, of these instruments mentioned by Poole, several are seen in *Holy Grail*, including a tabor, a gittern, a flute, and a type of fiddle. All of these and more can be found in the pages of Randall's *IMGM*, as discussed in appendix A.

As for the *ad infinitum* performance of Robin's minstrels, Mortimer notes that even during the dark days of the fourteenth century there was celebration: "Everyone dances. Everyone sings" (251). Mortimer mentions that from the attendees at a feast or a wedding to carolers dancing in a churchyard, from the clergy singing Mass and the sounds of English descants and motets to the royal families writing and performing music, and from Chaucer's characters to those in *Piers Plowman*: "Everyone sings and dances. In a country of plague, war and suffering, you have to" (251–52). So Robin had better get used to it. His minstrels won't quit until they are consumed during a long winter, dying ignominiously, offstage, like Falstaff.[15] In the longer version of the script there is an entire section ("King Brian the Wild") centered on a fascination with close harmony groups (who are killed as they perform). Those scenes were never shot (*MPHGB*, 68–78).

thirteenth-century courtly costume—(PSC) This is a curious but purposeful anachronism, and one that the audience wouldn't be in on, necessarily. The viewer wouldn't likely be able to discern between neighboring centuries' appropriate costumes, so anything that "looked right"—perhaps those costumes seen in previous "authentic" medieval films?—would suffice. The Pythons were keen to create a believable look and sound for this medieval period, so that their purposeful disruptions would stand out all the more.[16] In *Flying Circus*, that authenticity wasn't such a concern. A ship is sinking and the crew is supposed to be kitting out as women and children, but some have to improvise. An argument about authentic medieval clothing (naturally) ensues:

Cut to third officer who is putting finishing touches to a medieval outfit.

Third Officer (Idle): Well it's a sort of impression of what a kind of Renaissance courtier artist might have looked like at the court of one of the great families like the Medicis or the Borgias . . .

Fourth Officer (Chapman): No it's not, it's more Flemish than Italian.

Fifth Officer: Yes—that's a Flemish merchant of the fifteenth or sixteenth centuries.

Third Officer: What! With these tassels?

Fourth Officer: Yes, yes. They had those fined doublets going tapering down into the full hose you know—exactly like that.

Captain (Jones): (*into the PA*) One moment, please, don't panic. (*puts his hand over the PA*) Now, what is it meant to be? I've got to tell them something . . . is it a Flemish merchant?

Third Officer: No, it is not a Flemish merchant. It's more a sort of idealized version of the complete Renaissance man . . .

Captain: Oh, all right.

Fourth Officer: It's not. (*JTW*, 2.71)

The argument will spill over to the following scene as they continue to argue about just who wore "hand-embroidered chevrons" and who did not.

The earlier announced time period is the tenth century, 932 specifically, and Arthur's *possible* existence even earlier than that—the fifth- to sixth-century period—has already been established. In the DVD commentary track codirector Jones mentions that he was thinking of a thirteenth- and fourteenth-century look for the film all along, as that was his area of interest, having read some history at Oxford. He has since published *Chaucer's Knight: The Portrait of a Medieval Mercenary* (1980) and *Who Murdered Chaucer?: A Medieval Mystery* (2003), demonstrating his passion for the period.[17] This would have also meant that the use of later castles like Doune and Stalker—fourteenth and fifteenth centuries, respectively—wouldn't have been so out-of-time given the already malleable costume and prop decisions.

tambourine . . . tabor . . . pipes—(PSC) The tambourine, the tabor, and the pipes are instruments seen throughout the pages of period illuminated manuscripts; simply browsing through Randall's *IMGM* would've given the Pythons myriad examples of each of these (as well as ideas for accurate period costuming). In these illuminations there are apes, dogs, cats, and hybrids playing tabors, there are men and women and hybrid men playing tambourines, and there are asses, centaurs, devils, mermaids, and goats playing pipes. There are also images of hand organs, vielles, trumpets, and shawms.[18] A portative organ has already appeared in the animated credits for the film.[19] The importance of music and celebration in the illuminated manuscript tradition is obvious just from this sampling. These same kinds of instruments playing "low" music (meant more for quiet entertaining) also appear in the Swamp Castle sequence where the wedding ceremony is being prepared for Herbert and Lucky.

. . . one bangs at a tabor (a small drum O.E.D.)—Yet another "in-joke," a gag meant for the other Pythons and anyone who might be reading the script. The film was produced in the days before scripts were printed for the general public, after the fact, so such comments were truly insular. This might be a jocular veiled insult, as well, if the production team charged with reading the script and then acquiring the necessary prop material weren't Oxbridge types who'd know what a tabor is without having to look it up. Gilliam was teased a few times as being the lone American and somewhat separate from the writing team, week to week, during *Flying Circus* (*MPFC: UC*, 1.129). The troupe also wrote reflexively, referencing earlier shows or characters or even technical elements for the benefit of the production crew (1.286). The Pythons often simply wrote for their own amusement in the *Flying Circus* scripts. In Ep. 9, they call for mood lighting—"*low sexy lighting—ha ha*"—knowing that the studio they have

been assigned doesn't have manipulable lighting capabilities (1.148–49); in Ep. 18 they put a "[sic]" after Thames Ditton even though it's not misspelled (1.287); in Ep. 22 "*a penguin . . .sits contentedly looking at them in a stuffed sort of way*" (1.339); and in Ep. 44, CIA agent Teddy Salad is described in the script as having a "*little tadger tiny as a tapir's tits*" (2.198).[20] They wrote these asides when they were bored or just having fun, likely thinking that only the other troupe members and a handful of production types would ever see them. The *Flying Circus* script continuity and discontinuity laid the groundwork for *MPHG*. In Ep. 39, the final episode of season three, and the final episode where all the Pythons participated, the mix had clearly gelled—in "New Brain from Curry's," a character answers the phone and has to look at her shoe and say "five-and-a-half," and the audience belly-laughs:

> This reflexive moment connects the audience back to the obviously remembered and popular (they applaud and laugh) moments in Ep. 31, the "Our Eamonn" sketch, when characters answering the phone have to give their shoe sizes in a string of "yes" answers. Other reflexivities—Spiny Norman, Cardinal Ximinez, the Nudge Nudge Man, Richard Baker—continue to erase boundaries between episodes and create a sort of everpresent in the *Flying Circus* world. All this being said, the show continues to separate itself from most of its predecessors in that by late in its third season it still does not rely on long-running characters or obvious familiarities—*instead, the framework tropes of miscommunication, absurdity, unsuccessful transactions, and narrative undercutting support the show.* (*MPFC: UC*, 2.152; italics added)

This last sentence should ring quite familiar for the structure of the world of *Holy Grail* thus far.

DENNIS: "Anarchosyndicalism is a way of preserving freedom . . ."—This conversation—a continuation of the Dennis the Peasant and his mother scene from earlier—does not appear in the printed script.

The indelible connection between workers' control and increased freedoms is made over and over by the movement's most thoughtful advocate, Tom Brown. He sees the freedoms syndicalism promises in, for example, workers having the right to strike at any time and for any cause; they are not beholden to a shop steward or trade union or corporate boss to make these decisions for them: "A worker who has not the right to strike is less than a man, he is a slave."[21] Brown points out the advantages of myriad possible actions: "The lightning strike," "work to rule," the "strike at work," the boycott, the sympathetic strike, the guerilla and the stay-in strike "are Syndicalist weapons" (9). In the earlier scene, Dennis voiced both his opposition to the system as it was currently constituted, as well as his opinion as to how an alternative system could work "if there's ever going to be any progress." He displayed civil disobedience—allowing himself to be thrashed a bit by the authority figure, calling attention to that opprobrium, and looking for the sympathetic ear in the fields of filth around him.

The "greater end" these syndicalists are looking for goes well beyond strike actions and is essentially what Dennis has been asking for—"the abolition of the wages system and the creation of a new society" (15). In Tom Brown's writing, he often emphasizes "new" with all caps—"NEW"—he clearly wanted to separate his syndicalist cause from other systems that worked within the *existing* economic and social structures of society.

SONG: "Bravely good Sir Robin . . ."—Robin's *chanson de geste* and "We're Knights of the Round Table" are composed by Neil Innes, and here performed by Innes. By tradition, the *chansons de geste* were epic in nature—like *The Song of Roland*—and designed to "express the noble ideals of heroism, fidelity to honor, feudal loyalty, and love of the homeland" (*HBMA*, 284). Robin's lay includes almost none of these, of course, excepting to mention over and over again that Robin is indeed brave, meaning brave in the face of certain manglement and death. And where the brave Roland's sin is pride—he will not blow the horn for Charlemagne's help—Robin's is likely cowardice, as he scarpers away before the Three-Headed Knight can properly kill him. Roland's punishment is a noble death, of course, while Robin is able to live to "fight" another day.

SONG: "And his limbs all hacked and mangled . . ."—The body horror of the Arthurian romances has been mentioned, but these were still often celebratory works that managed to use graphic examples of violence and gore—the cheery dance tune sung here is not ex nihilo. Arthur and his good knights (and even ladies) could be injured, sometimes horribly, but also could be healed. The bad guys weren't so lucky. The descriptions of mayhem and bodily violence tend to focus on penetration and dismemberment (as in *MPFC*). Citing just a few: Brastias "smote one of them on the helm, that it went to the teeth, and he rode to another and smote him, that the arm flew into the field. Then he went to the third and smote him on the shoulder, that shoulder and arm flew in the field" (*LMD'A*, 1.34); Sir Marhaus cut off the right arm of a giant, chased him into a lake, and then stoned the giant to death (1.161–62); "Arthur felt himself hurt, [and] he smote him again with Excalibur that it cleft his head, from the summit of his head, and stinted not till it came to his breast. And then the emperor fell down dead and there ended his life" (1.182); and finally, "Sir Gareth . . . with his great force he struck down that knight, and voided his helm, and struck off his head [for the second time]. Then he hewed the head in an hundred pieces. And when he had done so he took up all those pieces, and threw them out at a window into the ditches of the castle" (*LMD-WM*, 152–54).

The French epic *The Song of Roland* is also a likely inspiration for the Pythons here, especially if it was truly intended to be performed orally. Dated to the twelfth century, the four-thousand-line song of heroic deeds is an action-packed retelling of the eighth-century Battle of Roncesvalles. The titular hero Roland acts as a valiant rearguard, protecting Charlemagne's army from the Basques in the Pyrenees. The graphic descriptions of the noble deeds as well as the battle injuries likely helped set the standard for later Arthurian tales, as well as being inspiring to the Pythons. Roland's final battle is with a "Saracen" who tries to steal his famous sword:

> Roland has felt his good sword being stol'n;
> Opens his eyes and speaks this word alone:
> "Thou'rt none of ours, in so far as I know."
> He takes his horn, of which he kept fast hold,
> And smites the helm, which was all gemmed with gold;
> He breaks the steel and the scalp and the bone,
> And from his head batters his eyes out both,
> And dead on the ground he lays the villain low;
> Then saith: "False Paynim, and how wast thou so bold,
> Foully or fairly, to seize upon me so?
> A fool he'll think thee who hears this story told." (2284–94)[22]

Throughout the grisly and marvelous *Song of Roland* blood "sprays" and collects in great "pools"; Paynims are ripped "piece from piece" and cut from helm to hauberk to navel; "pates" are sliced through and off; riders *and* horses are cleft in twain; "bodies and limbs [are] sunder hewn"; and "[t]hey lop off wrists, hew ribs and spines to shreds, / They cleave the harness through to the living flesh; / On the green ground the blood runs clear and red" (st. 1663–65). "Wondrous the battle" is the general consensus, even in glorious defeat; even Robin's minstrels couldn't celebrate Roland's possible death any better.

... *ridden past the following signs*—These are reminiscent of the inscription at the entrance to Hell in Dante's *Inferno*:

I AM THE WAY INTO THE CITY OF WOE.
I AM THE WAY TO A FORSAKEN PEOPLE.
I AM THE WAY INTO ETERNAL SORROW.

SACRED JUSTICE MOVED MY ARCHITECT.
I WAS RAISED HERE BY DIVINE OMNIPOTENCE,
PRIMORDIAL LOVE AND ULTIMATE INTELLECT.

ONLY THOSE ELEMENTS TIME CANNOT WEAR
WERE MADE BEFORE ME, AND BEYOND TIME I STAND.
ABANDON ALL HOPE YE WHO ENTER HERE.[23]

The scene is brought to grim life by William Blake in his 1826 painting, for example. These signs are also used often in period cartoons from all the major studios, including Disney, Fleischer, and Warner Bros.

In the *Adventures of Robin Hood* comic book series (1955–1957),[24] shield signs are hung in public places as messages and warnings, sometimes inscribed. In the eighth issue, Prince John has hung his inscribed shield over the Nottingham gallows, the pledge reading: "So long as this shield hangs here, Prince John shall be ruler of all England, and Master of Life and Death in the Land." It is a challenge from the evil usurper to get Robin to come out of hiding, of course. In Prince Valiant there is also a handy sign hanging on an ogre's castle: "Who welcome death enter." Val, of course, obliges.[25] Similar signs are used in cartoons like the Mickey Mouse classic *Haunted House* (1929), Warner Bros.' *Rabbit Seasoning* and *Rabbit Fire*, and in many Fleischer Bros.' Betty Boop titles, including *Snow-White* (1933).

all in triplicate—(PSC) Here begins the "three" theme, probably a nod to the Welsh Triads, *Trioedd Ynys Prydein*, or the *Triads of the Island of Britain*. The threesomes in these stories were likely mnemonic devices to help Welsh taletellers remember the tales, which fits Sir Robin's *histriones* (or performance) milieu. The Pythons might not have planned the references to oral traditions—here and earlier, with *The Song of Roland*—as apt narrative elements for the only knight with a bard and musicians in tow, but the coincidence is noted. King Arthur and stories surrounding him are part of this collection. In Arthur's court, for example, could be found Three Golden-Tongued Knights, Three Virgin Knights, Three Knights of Battle, Three Counsellor Knights, Three Enchanter Knights, Three Just Knights, Three Royal Knights, and Three Offensive Knights, according to Bromwich.[26] There were also Three Unrestrained Ravagings, Three Frivolous Bards, Three Fair Princes, Three Roving Fleets, Three Powerful Swineherds, Three Fortunate Concealments, Three Unfortunate Disclosures (it was Arthur who disclosed one of these), and Three Red Ravagers (Arthur was one of these). By name, Arthur figures into many of these, and members of his court appear in many more.

... three KNIGHTS sitting on the ground with one enormous axe through their skulls—(PSC) There are three scripted setup moments prior to meeting the three-headed knight, structured, of course, like a standard comedic bit—setup, setup, setup, payoff. This second bit of gruesomeness is *not* part of the finished film—likely the cost of another tableaux of knights oozing Kensington gore figured in the bit's disappearance from the finished film. This bit was

not crossed-out of the finished script, meaning the Pythons likely intended to shoot/keep the scene up to the last minute, then made the change. The first setup is the *"KNIGHTS impaled to a tree"* scene, and would have been followed by the axe scene. The axe scene may have been removed simply because the props and set decoration necessary to make it look like one axe was lodged in three separate heads was too complicated. The third image is mentioned below.

These kinds of trophy displays have a basis in the Grail romances, too. In *The Tale of Sir Gareth of Orkney*, Sir Beaumains (Gareth) rides to meet the Red Knight of the Red Launds, passing a grisly gallery of such:

> And when they came near the siege, Sir Beaumains espied on great trees, as he rode, how there hung full goodly armed knights by the neck, and their shields about their necks with their swords, and gilt spurs upon their heels. And so there hung nigh forty knights shamefully with full rich arms. (*LMD-WM*, 141)

Giving Robin the benefit of the doubt here, these tableaux of knightly torture and death seem reason enough for him to take the long way around the forest—to his credit, he doesn't.

They look timorous—(PSC) This is part of the description of the three knights who were to have been killed by the axe of the giant Three-Headed Knight. This scene only appears in the printed script (*MPHGB*, 30), and is not penciled through, meaning they likely intended to shoot it.

The "timorous" comment is silly, certainly—they're dead, not showing signs of nervousness or lack of confidence—but also connects to something Cleese mentions on the DVD commentary track for a later scene. As the "Tim the Enchanter" scene is approaching Cleese mentions the significance of naming in the Python world, and that "Tim"—shortened from "timorous"—seemed appropriate for a character who was not in the least bit timorous.

Then a huge tree is absolutely packed with MAIDENS—(PSC) This is the third of the three visuals meant to frighten Robin prior to his meeting with the Three-Headed Knight. The Maidens aren't dead or even wounded, the script indicates, merely "fed up," and Robin simply greets them cheerfully as he passes (*MPHGB*, 31). The scene does not end up in the final film, though the Daily Continuity Report (portions of which are included in *MPHGB* on the facing pages) mentions that at least one take was shot: "T. 1 Lost sun half way thru— then came out for girls" (*MPHGB*, 31, facing). So they at least attempted to record the scene, and then at some point decided it needed to be removed.

The "bound maiden" trope is a borrow from the Grail romances, of course. In *Sir Tristram de Lyonesse*, Dame Brangwain—who inadvertently delivers the love potion meant for King Mark to Tristram and Isode—is targeted by the angry queen's order:

> And she was sent into the forest for to fetch herbs; and there she was bound hand and foot to a tree, and so she was bound for three days. And by fortune Sir Palomides found Dame Brangwain, and there he delivered her from the death, and brought her to a nunnery therebeside for to be recovered. (*LMD-WM*, 197)

This image will be revisited by director Gilliam (and Palin) in the feature film *Time Bandits* (1981), when Robin Hood's Merry Men tie Vincent (Palin) and Pansy (Shelley Duvall) to a large tree in Sherwood Forest.

. . . enormous THREE-HEADED KNIGHT—In DVD commentaries this scene is described by Cleese as the one that slows the film down; most of the troupe agreed—it never came out quite right. It may be that the scene was allowed to run too long (though it has been cut down significantly from its original length), or that the demands of the costuming construction meant the Three-Headed Knight couldn't move at all, and wasn't a threat to anyone, including Robin, or that the "bitchy" voices and sniping just weren't funny. (The "Knights Who Say Ni" scene was similarly static, and eventually worked rather well, becoming one of the memorialized bits.) Doyle mentions that for the sake of Robin's singing minstrel (Innes and his song) he "pestered" for the scene's inclusion—"I thought the song was so good we had to save it"—and spent a good deal of time cutting and re-cutting the scene to make it work as painlessly as possible.[27]

As for the three-headedness, there are dozens of polycephalic creatures in mythology, from Cerebus to the Hydra, and from Brahma to myriad three-headed trolls in Scandinavia. The seven-headed beast as described in Revelations is depicted in dozens of illuminated apocalypse manuscripts (and the *Angers Apocalypse* tapestry, already mentioned), as well. Gilliam also sketched a *two*-headed man as he prepared for the animations.[28] The Middle Ages fascination with mortality and death is often depicted in threes, as in the macabre "Three Living and Three Dead" theme found throughout medieval art (*FMA*, 241).

The gag as written in the script is also very similar to the actions of the three-headed character in the WB cartoons *Porky in Wackyland* and the later remake *Dough for the Do-Do*.[29] There—in a Lewis Carroll–like, oneiric world full of characters with wheels instead of legs and characters that play their bodies as musical instruments, for example, the three-headed creature—with heads meant to resemble the Three Stooges—pokes, slaps, and whacks itself. This cartoon would have accompanied a Warner Bros. Studio feature film as package showings (called "block bookings") in British cinemas as the Pythons grew up during the 1940s–1950s.

This also may be the Pythons' version of the three witches. In *Macbeth*, the three witches often speak in threes—a magical number, clearly: "Thrice to thine, and thrice to mine / And thrice again, to make up nine" (1.3.35–36); "Thrice the brinded cat hath mew'd" (4.1.1); and "Thrice, and once the hedge-pig whin'd" (4.1.2). Also, the Second Apparition calls out "Macbeth! Macbeth! Macbeth!":

Macbeth: Had I three ears, I'ld hear thee.

Second Apparition: Be bloody, bold, and resolute. . . . (4.1.77–79)

The Three Witches also repeat each other, then speak in unison (see the following entry as well):

First Witch: Show!

Second Witch: Show!

Third Witch: Show!

All: Show his eyes, and grieve his heart;

Come like shadows, so depart! (4.1.107–11)[30]

The three heads of the knight speak in unison—This bit—speaking in unison—is cumbersome, and they don't do it for long, but can also be traced to the Malorian source. In *The Tale of the Sangrail*, Galahad frees the Castle of Maidens from seven knights who held it hostage for seven years. As a priest recounts the story of the hostage taking and the subsequent seven years (with Galahad sitting on a bed, listening), he mentions that the seven knights answered as one when challenged: "Well," said the seven knights, "sithen ye say so" (*LMD-WM*, 325).

315

The source can also be traced to the Pythons growing up in a world of robust pantomime performances (*Aladdin*, *Puss in Boots*, *Treasure Island*), where audiences enthusiastically responded as one to well-known stage prompts (*MPFC: UC*, 1.86, 163–64).[31] In *Life of Brian*, a crowd of disciples appears at Brian's home, and they speak as one both to Brian and his mother, Mandy (Jones), who tries to shoo them away.

SINGERS: "He is brave Sir Robin, brave Sir Robin . . ."—They are singing their answer because they are minstrels, of course, but if Robin's troupe's musicality and the focus on threes are taken into combined account, then this is another Welsh moment, as the minstrels sing their version of an *Englyn*, or a Welsh short poem. Throughout these Welsh sources singing is an accepted form of communication and declaration. In *A Story of Trystan, How He Went with Eysellt, the Wife of March y Meirchion*, Trystan sings to Eysellt, Kae Hir sings to Eysellt, Gwalchmai sings to Trystan, and then Arthur sings *his* englyn:

> "Gwalchmai of faultless manners,
> who wast not wont to conceal thyself on the day of battle;
> [I bid] welcome to Trystan my nephew."

Notwithstanding that, Trystan said nothing; and Arthur sang the second *englyn*:

> "Blessed Trystan, army chieftain,
> Love thy kindred as well as thyself,
> and me as head of the tribe."

And notwithstanding that, Trystan said nothing: and Arthur sang the third *englyn*:

> "Trystan, chief of battles,
> Take as much as the best,
> and love me sincerely."

In spite of that, Trystan said nothing; and Arthur sang the fourth *englyn*:

> "Trystan of exceedingly prudent manners,
> love thy kindred, it will not bring thee loss;
> coldness grows not between one kinsman and another."[32]

After this, Trystan relents and answers Arthur, praising him, and is eventually rewarded Esyllt (who had been March y Meirchion's wife).

ROBIN: "I seek the Holy Grail—stand aside and let me pass"—This bold line has been crossed-out. Robin actually declares he is a "Knight of King Arthur's Round Table," and is momentarily quite knightly, even Launcelot-like. But like the depiction of God transitioning from mercurial and beastly to just mildly stroppy as the script moved forward, Robin's character likely devolved into this puling runaway, too. He'll bugger off to rejoin the other members of the quest as soon as the Three-Headed Knight looks away.

THREE HEADS: "Shit"—The Second Head says this, but it does not survive into the finished film. This was likely one of the curse words the Pythons removed to ensure the "A" (and not the "AA"[33]) rating from BBFC. By the time *Life of Brian* was in production four years later, they would have been satisfied with the more restrictive rating as it was a more mature film.

FIRST HEAD: "In that case I shall have to kill you"—This kind of immediate, martial response crops up again and again in the Grail romances when knights, magicians, or simple ruffians meet up with admitted Knights of the Round Table. Malory writes in *Le Morte Darthur* the following:

> And then Sir Percival departed and rode till the hour of noon. And he met in a valley about twenty men of arms, which bore in a bier a knight deadly slain. And when they saw Sir Percival they asked him of whence he was; and he said, of the court of King Arthur. Then they cried at once, "'Slay him!'" (*LMD-WM*, 337–38)

The attack was so one-sided that Percival had to be saved by the passing Galahad, who slew knight after knight, maimed others, and chased others into the nearby woods. Percival does "scupper off" in this scene, but only to try and catch up with Galahad, and only then because his horse had been slain in the melee.

THIRD HEAD: "What do I think?"—Crossed-out lines. In the final version of the script the tenor of the argument between the heads is slightly different. Whole sections have been crossed out and replaced with new dialogue, as will be seen later with the "King Brian the Wild" sequences (removed completely). For example, the emphasis on "I" as singular or "I" as part of a trinity is expressed in the original draft:

THIRD HEAD (Palin): (*to FIRST*) What do I think?

FIRST HEAD (Jones): I think kill him.

SECOND HEAD (Chapman): I'm still not sure.

THIRD HEAD: All right . . . How many of me think I should kill him?

FIRST HEAD: I do.

THIRD HEAD: One.

SECOND HEAD: That's not a quorum.

FIRST HEAD: It is if I'm the Chairman.

THIRD HEAD: Oo, it's not.

SECOND HEAD: I'm the Chairman this week.

FIRST HEAD: You're not.

SECOND HEAD: Listen, it'll make it much simpler if I vote with me. (*MPHGB*, 32)

All these lines have been crossed through and are not part of the finished film. The "sharing" of leadership in this trio isn't unlike the *Graiae* of Greek mythology, three sisters who share one eye and one tooth.

Two additional pages of dialogue are also crossed through, and replaced by dialogue as delivered in the final cut of the film. In the script the heads argue about who voted for what deadly action, who abstained, and with which giant weapon (an axe, a mace, a sword, or a dagger) they should kill the intruder. Robin is even given a very forward boast that, if it had remained, would have presented a very different version of "Brave Sir Robin." As the heads argue, Robin butts in testily: "Look, hurry up six eyes, or I shall cut your head off." Robin still scarpers off as in the final film, but at least he had a few moments of honor in the printed script.

SECOND HEAD: "He's buggered off"—A phrase used by Joyce in *Ulysses*, so it has some built-in credibility, it simply means to leave hastily. "Scarpered" is an interesting version of the Italian *scappare*, according to the *OED*, but most likely pushed into prominence thanks to the post–World War I Cockney rhyming slang "Scapa Flow," equating to "to go." The Goons use the term in the "What's My Line" episode (5 December 1956).

The inability of the Three-Headed Knight to actually do anything authoritative—as built, the costume was barely moveable, excepting limited flailings of the arms—might be connected in spirit to the position the Heath government found itself in by 1972 following the crippling NUM strikes.[34] Thanks to ill-preparation for a prolonged strike and just the certainty that no union action could wreak such economic havoc in such a short time, the Heath government was mostly unprepared for the effects of the strike. The cascade of power failures and shuttered schools and industry was catastrophic. It led to an eventual capitulation to almost all of the union's demands by the Heath government, even if those concessions were economically unviable and unsustainable, including a 20 percent pay increase and extra benefits, all approved by a judge Heath himself brought into the negotiations (Marr, 337–38). This compromise (which most interpreted as government surrender) came to be known as "tripartism," which Marr describes as "a three-way national agreement on prices and wages, investment and benefits, involving the government, the TUC and the CBI" (338).[35] Turns out this three-headed creation was initially exciting, even promising, but became clumsy and impractical:

> The industry Act of 1972 gave a Tory government unprecedented powers of industrial intervention, gleefully cheered by Tony Benn as "spadework for socialism." There was much earnest wooing of moderate trade union leaders. Money, effort and organization went into Job Centres as unemployment rose steadily towards a million. The industrialists did as much as they could, sitting on yet more committees when in truth they might have been more usefully employed trying to run their companies. The unions, however, had the bit between their teeth. By first refusing to acknowledge Heath's industrial relations court "as really legitimately a law of the land" and then refusing to negotiate seriously until he repealed the Act, they made the breakdown of this last attempt at consensual economics inevitable. (338)

Palin comments on the conclusion of this strike, the ruling of the arbitrating judge, and the capitulation of the government—which he blames directly for the strike—in his diaries for this period (72–73).

In the end, this trinal creature was as cumbersome to any advancement in industrial relations or return to profitability as can be imagined, and the industrial and economic crisis of the mid-1970s only deepened.

THIRD HEAD: "So he has! He's scarpered!"—This simply means Robin's slipped away, as quietly as possible, and he's in good company with this choice. The history of the Middle Ages in Britain is replete with such "tactical retreats." Stephen of Blois (d. 1154), William I's grandson, was trying to solidify his grip on the throne by ridding himself of his cousin, Matilda (1102–1167), who controlled much of the western regions of England in 1142. Stephen sought to trap her in Oxford, where she held her own court. Stephen's forces approached stealthily, but Matilda was able to slip "out of the castle by night, accompanied by only three knights, and went six miles on foot" (Brooke, *SNK*, 187). Acquiring horses, her company continued undetected as far as Wallingford—she, dressed all in white to avoid detection against the snowy landscape—Matilda would eventually retire, essentially, to Normandy (187). Other famous names—including Piers Gaveston, Edward II, and Hugh Despenser, to pick one notable clutch—also found themselves sneaking away as impinging circumstances demanded, though none escaped their ultimate fate. Even those known for their successes in history, like Scottish king Robert the Bruce, found themselves scarpering from time to time, as when Robert and his trusted few had to abandon their families and flee from Edward I's forces, from Strathfillan, in August 1306 (Powicke, 685). Earlier, in 1300 and 1301, Edward's forces tried repeatedly to engage the Scottish forces in pitched battle, but the clever Scots employed guerrilla tactics—striking and pulling back—and refused to be engaged. They "scarpered," costing Edward money and resources, and the Scottish situation dragged on without conclusion. Robin could easily claim that he was making a *tactical* retreat to regroup and fight another day, and not just running away, as his minstrels happily sing. When he and his group rejoin Arthur later, he will try to explain his situation without admitting to cowardice.

The BODY starts laying into itself with sword and mace . . .—(PSC) A crossed-out line. In the original draft of this scene, the action goes likely where it's been aching to go from the beginning: The Three Stooges. The heads shout at each other and the armed arms pound and hack at the body; shouts of anger and pain as the camera pans away. In this the scene goes right back to a reference mentioned above: cartoons. The three-headed, Three-Stooges-like character(s) in *Porky in Wackyland* introduce themselves, begin to argue, and then smack and poke each other.

MAIDEN: "I suppose we're lucky he's only got <u>three</u> heads"—A crossed-out line. This is the Pythons' version of the old-fashioned payoff. During the run of *Flying Circus*, characters that tried to deliver such hoary lines were cautioned, usually with a stern look and a minatory finger; those that did make it to the payoff were usually punished. In "Restaurant Sketch," Ep. 3, after a long kerfuffle over a slightly dirty fork, the man at the table chirps: "Lucky we didn't say anything about the dirty knife" (*JTW*, 1.37). The audience immediately (and on cue) "boo" the cheesy line. The implication of the "three heads" line is likely sexual, meaning the maidens' plight could be much worse than it is.

LOVELY: "Chance would be a fine thing"—(PSC) A crossed-out line, as well. As the scene ends and the camera pans away "gently," the maidens are still tied to the tree, and "still very fed up." This kind of transition is a bit formal, seen in some of the New Wave films of the period, for example. The fact that the cumbersome Three-Headed Knight can't move at all means the camera is going to have to move away, if it moves at all. The Maidens are also stationary. Similarly, Godard's *Week End* features an extended tracking shot that runs alongside a traffic jam. There, the traffic stands still, so Godard follows the main couple's car as it jerks and starts through and around the mess, revealing little social tableaux all along the way. In Jancso's *The Red and the White* the camera often tracks away from one scene to another—pausing, then moving on—highlighting the shifting nature of the battlefield.

The phrase itself is an English colloquialism. The *OED* (which the Pythons admit using earlier [*MPHGB* 29]) provides this definition: "It would be good if something (stated or implied) were true or likely, but it is not; the opportunity is unlikely to arise." The line may have been excised simply because it hewed too close to the earlier "It's a fair cop" rejoinder.

SINGERS: "Brave Sir Robin ran away"—In the *Black Knight* comic book series, the Black Knight's alter ego, Percy of Sandia—a foppish type loath to fight—sings and plays after he and King Arthur have defeated the disguised Modred and his men: "Sir Modred fell and his mount did drag him over ground so rough / But alas the steed was stupid and did not drag him far enough!" In the panel background, Modred is trying to tell his version of the story, sans cowardice.[36]

By the time the fourteenth century was drawing to a close, the cumulative effects of the Hundred Years War, multiple plague waves, and a fed-up peasant class had roiled together—the nobility of chivalry and knights was greatly, fatally diminished, and their "songs" changed as well:

319

> More than soft beds and foppery, the moral failure of chivalry spread dismay. Instead of troubadours glorifying the ideal knight and ideal love in romantic epics, moralists now deplored in satire and allegory and didactic treatise what the knight had become—predator and aggressor rather than champion of justice. (Tuchman, 439)

Robin's minstrels, then, are merely echoing the world around them as respect for knighthood declines.

Notes

1. Since this shot was completed well after principal photography, Idle wouldn't have had any reason to know the whats or wheres of the shot—Gilliam, Jones, and Doyle handled the bulk of post-production work. Idle was involved with his forthcoming *Rutland Weekend Television* series for BBC 2, which made its debut on 12 May 1975.

2. During the run of *MPFC*, the Pythons scavenged through the film, image, and sound libraries at the BBC, Pathé, the Imperial War Museum, and other collections for needed stock footage, music, and sounds, while Gilliam regularly used still photos in his animated sequences. See *MPFC: UC*, appendix A: "Stock Film Clips and Still Images," for a complete list of the stock requests made by the Pythons during the show's three-and-a-half-season run (1.395–98).

3. From a 5 December 2013 e-mail correspondence with the author.

4. Doyle confirms that the book was likely depicting Australia. From an e-mail correspondence dated 6 December 2013.

5. Harley, 3053, f. 45v, BLCIM.

6. Harley 3052, f. 14, BLCIM.

7. Royal 20 D VI, f. 220, BLCIM.

8. Harley 105, f. 138, BLCIM.

9. St. Stephen Harding had been born in Dorset and died in 1134.

10. "The Book of the Film" section, remember, had been filmed on a living room floor, according to Jones's and Gilliam's DVD commentary.

11. According to Palin and Cleese, "Ewing" was a name borrowed from their then manager, Kenneth Ewing (audio commentary, 2001 DVD edition). In 1971 Ewing was a part of the Fraser & Dunlop Scripts Ltd. firm, along with Jill Foster, James Fraser, Peter Dunlop, and Richard Wakeley. Jill Foster had written a letter in August 1971 to BBC programming chief David Attenborough (b. 1926) asking for more money per episode of *MPFC*. Early on, these requests were politely refused. See the BBC Written Archives Collection, T47/216 1969–1971.

12. For annotations on this section see *MPFC: UC*, 2.4 and 2.9–12.

13. From Poole's "Recreations" chapter in his *Medieval England*, vol. II (Oxford: Clarendon Press, 1958): 606.

14. Hallam, 284.

15. And behind a snowy hillock in an animated sequence, no less.

16. The Pythons never do have a character point out the inaccuracies of the historical reproduction in *MPHG*, which they did throughout *MPFC*. See, for example, the "Complaints" and the "Highlands Spokesman" in Ep. 16.

17. Jones's interpretations of Chaucer's knight have since been taken to task by academics, including G. A. Lester, discussed earlier. On a personal note, in the Chaucer course I took during doctoral work the professor *forbade* us from citing Jones's work as "scholarship." That may have been an overreaction.

18. See the Index of Subjects in Randall's *IMGM* for specific entries.

19. See the entry "mirrored angels with organs" in scene 12 for more.

20. In the printed scripts these can be found as follows: *JTW*, 1.117; 1.236; 1.304; and 2.318, respectively.

21. "The Right to Strike," in *What's wrong with the Unions?*, 9.

22. *The Song of Roland*, st. 170, p. 139.

23. Dante Alighieri, *Inferno*, Canto III, lines 1–9, in *The Norton Anthology of World Masterpieces*, 5th ed. (New York: W.W. Norton, 1985), 1:1153–54.

24. At least three of these issues are connected directly to the very popular *The Adventures of Robin Hood* TV show produced by Associated-Rediffusion (British commercial television, which didn't emerge until 1955). The show was also broadcast in the United States on CBS.

25. Foster, "The Ogre," in *Prince Valiant in the Days of King Arthur*.

26. Bromwich, *Trioedd Ynys Prydein*.

27. From a 5 December 2013 e-mail correspondence with the author.

28. Facing Page 51, appendix A, "Facing Pages."

29. Dir. Robert Clampett, 1938, and dir. Friz Freleng, 1949. The surrealistic and context-smashing world of these cartoons was clearly influential for both the Goons and the Pythons. See *MPFC: UC*, 1.19–20, as well as the index in those volumes under "cartoony" for more.

30. Shakespeare, *Macbeth*.

31. See also the index entries for "pantomime" in *MPFC: UC*, for dozens of mentions of this treasured art form throughout *Flying Circus*. In Ep. 28, the BBC studio audience responds to the Principal Boy (Julia Breck) as part of a *Puss in Boots* adaptation (*MPFC: UC*, 2.32).

32. Translated by Tom Peete Cross.

33. After 1970 the BBFC's "AA" rating meant no one under fourteen would be admitted, while the "A" meant ages five and above could be admitted with parents. The decision was likely an understandably financial one, with the Pythons and their producers wanting the largest possible audience for the film.

34. National Union of Mine Workers (est. 1945). See entries in the "Dennis the Peasant" scene above for more on this volatile period, including the active names and organizations.

35. Trades Union Congress (TUC) and Confederation of British Industry CBI).

36. *Black Knight* #3, Atlas Comics, September 1955.

THE TALE OF SIR GALAHAD AND SPRINGBOARD NOVITIATES

ANIMATION—This animated sequence is *not* part of the final draft of the screenplay—*ANIMATION: "The Tale of Sir Galahad"* was penciled in at some later point. In earlier sequences involving promised but missing animation, the animation direction was part of the script, and then for some reason—perhaps time, perhaps money—not produced.[1] It may be that the initial thought was to produce eye-catching animated transitions between every tale or segment, as had been one of the hallmarks of *Flying Circus*, smoothing transitions between disconnected narrative sequences. As the film was photographed and then entered the editing process the more bumpy transitions or unusable scenes (like the Maidens tied to the tree) became apparent—as happens with most feature films—and decisions for bits of animation were reevaluated.

The animated frame here presents us with a *bas-de-page* (across the bottom of the page), here a line of monkish figures on a decorated border.[2] The queued, springboarding figures could be either men or women, given their cowls and hoods, though their dubbed voices sound decidedly masculine. It turns out that the divers are women (nuns), and the "examiner" is a monk, at least as they appeared in their original source material. In his accompanying sketches for this scene, Gilliam himself refers to the divers as "monks," though the figure he eventually employs is actually a nun copied multiple times.[3] Gilliam found a miniature of a monk taking confession from a nun—likely xerographed (photocopied) from *The Horizon Book of the Middle Ages* (1968). On page 143 of *HBMA* the original, more spiritual version of this image can be found. It simply depicts a nun kneeling for confession next to a monk, with the monk in the act of absolution, not rectal examination. This sexual turpitude is decried by many during the medieval period, with the immoralities of or toward the servants of God marking a low point in debasement, according to St. Boniface in a letter to Æthelbald, the new king of Mercia. In this letter Boniface blasts the conduct of Æthelbald's predecessor, Ceolred, as well as Osred of Northumbria, both of whom have passed away in their sins, the holy man hoping that Æthelbald will learn from their damnable mistakes:

> And lingering in these sins, that is in debauchery and adultery with nuns and violation of monasteries, condemned by the just judgment of God, thrown down from the regal summit of this life and overtaken by an early and terrible death, they were deprived of the light eternal and plunged into the depths of hell and abyss of Tartarus. (Sawyer, 192–93)

Addressing Æthelbald's shortcomings (enjoying sexual relations outside of marriage), Boniface notes that taking a lawful wife or accepting chastity as its own reward were both praiseworthy options, and continues his admonition:

> [I]f, as many say—but which God forbid—you have neither taken a lawful spouse nor observed chastity for God's sake but, moved by desire, have defiled your good name before God and man by the crime of adulterous lust, then we are greatly grieved because this is a sin in the sight of God and is the ruin of your fame among men. And now, what is worse, our informants say that these atrocious crimes are committed in convents with holy nuns and virgins consecrated to God and this, beyond all doubt, doubles the offense. (193)

The many warnings or diatribes like this one published during the medieval period attest to the continuing challenges that celibatic oaths presented to the Church and society. The special status enjoyed by these clerical houses was more and more challenged by laymen, understandably angry that tax or land ownership issues favored these privileged (but often alarmingly worldly) organizations.

The original image "kneeling nun" is found in the Stowe Illuminated Manuscript Collection at the British Library, specifically the *Hours* manuscript, or Stowe 17, f. 191. Randall also includes a small version of the image (XXIII: 112)—Gilliam could have easily copied this version of the image, yes—and it's clear that the nun and monk are large enough to occupy most of the lower portion of the recto page of that particular folio (f. 191).[4]

The excretory playfulness (or anal fixation) depicted here seems silly and even profane but it has historical precedent, especially in the margins of illuminated manuscripts of the period, as well as in the works of Hieronymus Bosch, both very important to Gilliam as he prepared these animations. Michael Camille notes that by the thirteenth century monastic artists were more likely to illustrate these texts *after* the verbiage had been completed (rather than the combined scholar/artist of earlier periods), and that many artists enjoyed countering or answering the sacred (and litanous, and maybe dull and high-minded) text with fantastic, often grotesque images:

> It is the artist of the *Rutland Psalter* who has continued the tail of a letter into his figure's anus, perhaps suggesting to the scribe what he can do with his pen. While often undermining the text, drawing attention to its "openness," marginal images never step outside (or inside) certain boundaries. Play has to have a playground, and just as the scribe follows the grid of ruled lines, there were rules governing the playing-fields of the marginal images that keep them firmly in their place.
>
> By the end of the thirteenth century no text was spared the irreverent explosion of marginal mayhem. As well as the traditional tools of liturgy—Bibles, Missals and Pontificals, and books owned by individuals for use in private devotion, mostly Psalters and the increasingly fashionable Books of Hours—secular compilations, such as Romances, and legal works, such as the Decretals, were filled with visual annotations. (*Image on the Edge*, 22)

Gilliam has already given us the arse trumpeters in the title sequence, of course, and by my count there are at least twenty separate examples of anal or excretory imagery in Randall's pages alone (spears, arrows, or beaks entering anuses; arse-kissing; defecation), which is just a small sampling of the available Gothic illustrated work. Bosch, of course, continues this grotesque fascination, featuring all manner of spread-legged, squatting, and penetrated animals, monsters, hybrids, and humans throughout his work.[5]

The florid border on which the nuns queue as they wait for their turn at the springboard is from at least three separate sources, meaning Gilliam wasn't content to just grab the first illuminated manuscript border he found, copy it, color it, and insert it into the animated frame—there was more selectivity and creativity at play here. Moving from screen right to left (following the camera direction), the image is initially drawn from a thirteenth-century Yale manuscript, *Lancelot del Lac* (part 3), specifically f. 169.[6] In the original, there is a depiction of Adam digging at the root of a tree (bottom right of the manuscript page); the upper portion of that tree can just be glimpsed behind and above the nuns as the scene begins. At the bottom of the frame grassy protrusions at the tail end of the existing decoration can just be seen, though most of the far right end of the decoration is offscreen. This moving image[7] is cut into so quickly (perhaps two frames of film, or much less than a full second of screen time) that a freeze frame is necessary to properly see the beginning of the shot. The figure of Adam has been excised from the image (he would have been mostly hidden behind the nuns, anyway).

The design upon which the queue stand connects somewhat seamlessly from the first bit of decoration, with continuation first from Gilliam's own hand (adding length and curve to the border for a longer tracking shot), and thence connecting to a border design from yet another manuscript, one known as N.K.S. 41.8. The portion borrowed by Gilliam is found on f. 105 in Randall (IX: 37). The N.K.S. 41.8 manuscript is housed in the Kongelige Bibliotek (MS. Ny Kgl. Saml. 41.8) in Copenhagen, and is a Flemish Psalter dated to the early fourteenth century. Gilliam also clearly added some flourishes himself—flowers, tendrils, and protuberances—along the underside of the border, and perhaps for footer space reasons Gilliam detached and slightly adjusted the curving tendril that the nuns cross behind.[8] The bottom leg of the decorative border seems to have been drawn from several examples in Douce 6,[9] bottom left corner of the original, and even Douce 5, which is from the same period and place (early fourteenth-century Ghent). The "pool of water" sequence that follows (see below) is also from Douce 6, as are several of the tree illustrations in the later "Passing Seasons" tracked animated sequence (see Randall, XII: 52).[10]

This type of profane or grotesque image—a drollery, or just marginalia, generally—isn't unusual in these illuminated books, even those produced by and for religious orders. In a c. 1425 manuscript known as "The Petworth Manuscript of Grace Dieu," a dreamer dreams of his soul encountering all manner of nasty torturings (hanging from hooks, bloodlettings, immolations, etc.) thanks to his life's sins, until the soul finally reaches celestial spheres.[11] The margins of many illuminated books feature half-men and half-beasts, mythological creatures (griffins, sea monsters, dragons, unicorns, mermaids), and many instances where a decoration somehow finds its way into a man's naked behind. In *The Art of the Middle Ages*, James Snyder explains the appeal of such admittedly earthy illustrations:

> The marginalia of Late Medieval illuminated manuscripts are sometimes decorated with humorous scenes, such as men defending a castle from attacking hares. In these scenes the world is turned upside-down to reveal the dangers of reversing traditional roles. Humor is employed to affirm the status quo. . . . A female illuminator, Jeanne de Monbastón, produced images for a copy of *The Romance of the Rose*. In scenes below prose describing an old woman's intercession concerning the meaning of love, a nun leads a monk by his penis and then he is shown climbing a ladder into her castle. The anticlerical message cannot be missed. Unable to maintain the vow of chastity, the monk is chained by the instrument of his lust. In late medieval France, male adulterers were sometimes humiliated in public by having a rope tied around their exposed genitals. . . . Other marginal scenes include a nun plucking "fruit" from a tree covered with penises, and a nun and monk engaged in sexual intercourse. . . . Although such images may surprise twenty-first-

century viewers, they playfully reinforce the medieval ideals of courtly love and monastic celibacy by poking fun at failures to live up to expected standards of behavior. (405–6)

Petrarch "complained" about the treatment his and other scholars' works received at the hands of such foul-minded men, who were actually paid to reproduce work faithfully, though that clearly wasn't always the outcome:

> Multiple copying of manuscripts was no longer the monopoly of lonely monks in their cells[12] but the occupation of professional scribes who had their own guilds. Licensed in Paris by the University, supposedly to ensure accurate texts, the scribes were the agony of living authors, who complained bitterly of the copyists' delays and errors. The "trouble and discouragement" a writer suffers, wailed Petrarch, was indescribable. Such was the "ignorance, laziness, and arrogance of these fellows" that when a writer has given them his work, he never knows what he will find in it when he gets it back. (Tuchman, 453)

Back in Gilliam's animated world, once the nun lands and spins, the entire "incipit page" can be viewed. The *inhabited* initial letter—as opposed to *historiated*, since there is no narrative suggested here—that the nun and monk occupy is a decorated *C* (from "*communicantes*"; a *Littera Florissa*, or "pen-flourished initial") but with a very odd design. The frame around the letter resembles a backwards *P*,[13] and the orientation of both the letter (in relation to the borders) and the tendrils snaking up the vertical leg are almost identical to a similar design in a Trinity collection manuscript (B.11.22, f. 148), and is in fact borrowed from Randall's *IMGM*, figure number 423.[14] The very minor differences might be explained by an association of the producers of this and other manuscripts known as "The Lancelot Group," which were produced in the early fourteenth century. The designs around the other initial letters (*T* for *The* and *S* for *Sir*) are designed to resemble the pen-flourished initials found in texts like Burney MS 252, f. 4v, Yates Thompson MS 34, f. 169, and Add. MS 69865, f. 13v, all found at the BLCIM. In the printed script (*MPHGB*, facing 13) Gilliam has doodled a possible scene involving this design as one of Arthur's knight-gathering stops. Arthur is to have approached a large initial, *inhabited* letter like this (he and Bedevere and the servants walking along the curving tendrils) to ask the knight depicted to join their quest.[15] In the Trinity manuscript original the letter is inhabited by what appears to be a young man (a monk?) holding a loaf of bread; this image is also included in Randall (see appendix A, Facing Page 13). In Gilliam's sketch he has roughed out the man with the bread inside the letter—the source is easily identifiable.

Part of the earlier animated imagery also involved nuns springboarding into a pool of water. These images are borrowed once again almost entirely from the Douce 6[16] manuscript in the Bodleian Library (f. 153r), and include the woman's face (gazing screen left), the decorative border, and the pool of water. Changes made by Gilliam include redrawing the woman's hood into what appears to be hair, the additional details of the designs on the decorative border, flourishing of the water itself (so it resembles water depicted in Douce 5, 185r, and especially the sea images in "Cantigas de Alfonso el Sabio"), and removing an ape from the water.[17] Gilliam may have found the original image in Randall (XII: 52), but likely he may also have located a larger color plate elsewhere. Gilliam also adds a fish to the water, which came from *Voeux du Paon* by Jacques de Longuyon (24, f. 84r), a mid-fourteenth century Franco-Flemish manuscript (Randall, CLVII: 733).

The balance of annotations regarding Gilliam's preparations for the animated sequences can be found in appendix A.

Notes

1. See the entries for the "Bring Out Your Dead" and "Book of the Film" scenes above for more on announced but missing animated bits.

2. Gilliam makes no mention of this animated section in any of his DVD commentary.

3. See the entry for Facing Pages 36 and 38 in appendix A, "Facing Pages" for more.

4. See the entry for Facing Pages 36 and 38 in appendix A, "Facing Pages," for more on Gilliam's appraisal of this source material.

5. See, for example, the right panel of Bosch's *The Garden of Earthly Delights*. There, characters' arses sprout arrows, flutes, and stakes; one man's buttocks even feature musical stanzas, and others gathered behind him—men and daemon—sing to the tune. In the center panel, where life is sweeter, arses tend to sprout flowers. See the Bosch entries in appendix A, "Facing Pages," for much more.

6. In Randall II: 6; MS 229 253r, according to Yale.

7. In most animation performed on an animation stand, the image moves, not the camera. Gilliam would have been moving the image platen "past" the stationary camera mounted above.

8. The entire Yale manuscript can be accessed online at Yale's Beinecke Rare Book & Manuscript Library, and is listed under "Arthurian Romances." http://beinecke.library.yale.edu/

9. Folios 16v, 118v, 129r, and 135r.

10. The Douce 5 and 6 manuscripts can be accessed online through the Bodleian's LUNA site, http://bodley30.bodley.ox.ac.uk:8180/luna/servlet/ODLodl~1~1.

11. This manuscript can be viewed at the Digital Scriptorium (NYPL, Spencer 019).

12. Like the monkish figure featured in the Sir Launcelot animation, who is disturbed in his work by the "bloody weather." See "The Tale of Sir Launcelot" below for more.

13. Though it looks as if it may have been an inhabited, tendriled *C* to begin with.

14. In fact, many illuminated manuscripts featuring the Gospel of Luke use this design, including the Lindisfarne Gospels. There, the letter is a *Q* (for *Quo*).

15. See the Facing Page 13 entry in appendix A, "Facing Pages."

16. Searchable at the Bodleian LUNA site.

17. Apes are likely the favorite beast depicted in western illuminated manuscripts. Randall's *IMGM* features pages and pages of ape references (dressed as clerics, performing sacerdotal tasks, preaching sermons, etc.).

SCENE EIGHTEEN

CASTLE ANTHRAX

As the storm rages we pick up GALAHAD forcing his way through brambles and over slippery rocks—(PSC) The storm is more cinematic than a beautiful sunny day, and helps cultivate a foreboding look more like many of Kurosawa's films, and also Polanski's *Macbeth*, for example—the latter where a violent, rain-soaked night of thunder and lightning precedes the killing of the king—but the period's chroniclers and the Arthurian source material also mentions such conditions, especially as the Grail is being approached. Chroniclers like the author of the Waverly Annals and others deliver mostly historical details, but these are interspersed with mentions of (likely prophetic or apocalyptic) thunderstorms, single thunderclaps, driving rains, lightning, unusual atmospheric events (like circular rings in the skies), earthquakes, and even times when "the sun . . . darkened over the whole land" (Hallam, 98–100, 116). Inclement weather obviously meant a good deal to people of the Middle Ages—harbingers were to be found in the elements. From Tuchman: "The Monk of St. Denis, never at a loss for omens, reported clouds of crows carrying lighted coals which they deposited on thatched barns, as well as *one of the terrible storms which appear regularly at all dark moments of his chronicle*" (419; italics added). In the *First Continuation* (appended to Chretien's unfinished work), "Gawain approaches the Grail castle by night, [and] encounters a terrifying storm," along with "marvels" too terrible to mention (*THG*, 162). In a *Le Morte D'Arthur* story involving Sir Percivale a gentlewoman dies, and her death is followed by meteorological signs: "Then they drew all to the castle, and so forthwith there fell a sudden tempest and a thunder, lait [flashes of lightning], and rain, as all the earth would have broken. So half the castle turned up-so-down. So it passed evensong or the tempest was ceased" (*LMD'A*, 2.350). Malory also gives Sir Gareth a major storm to slog through, as well:

> And then fell there a thunder and a rain, as heaven and earth should go together. And Sir Gareth was not a little weary, for of all that day he had but little rest, neither his horse nor he. So this Sir Gareth rode so long in that forest until the night came. And ever it lightened and thundered, as it had been wood. At the last by fortune he came to a castle, and there he heard the waits upon the walls.
>
> Then Sir Gareth rode unto the barbican of the castle, and prayed the porter fair to let him into the castle. The porter answered ungoodly again, and said, "Thou gettest no lodging here."
>
> "Fair sir, say not so, for I am a knight of King Arthur's, and pray the lord or the lady of this castle to give me harbour for the love of King Arthur."

> Then the porter went unto the duchess, and told her how there was a knight of King Arthur's would have harbour.
>
> "Let him in," said the duchess, "for I will see that knight, and for King Arthur's sake he shall not be harbourless."
>
> Then she yode up into a tower over the gate, with great torch-light. When Sir Gareth saw that torch-light he cried on high,
>
> "Whether thou be lord or lady, giant or champion I take no force so that I may have harbour this night; and if it so be that I must needs fight, spare me not to-morn when I have rested me, for both I and mine horse be weary."
>
> "Sir knight," said the lady, "thou speakest knightly and boldly; but wit thou well the lord of this castle loveth not King Arthur, nor none of his court, for my lord hath ever been against him; and therefore thou were better not to come within this castle; for an thou come in this night, thou must come in under such form, that wheresomever thou meet my lord, by stigh or by street, thou must yield thee to him as prisoner." (*LMD'A*, 1.291–92)

Gareth eats well, rests well, and spends a pleasant night in the castle—oddly, there is no surprise waiting for him, as is so often the case in Malory's Grail-quest world.

He pauses and at this moment we hear the howling of wolves. GALAHAD turns, then hurries onward even more urgently—(PSC) The fear of wild animals was very real in the Middle Ages, with the wolf generating the most base fears across cultures and ages, according to Fossier, functioning to fully concentrate medieval

> men's terror and hatred. The wolf was courageous, tricky, able to think ahead, and ambiguous. As the "tiger of the West," he was the only mammal capable, when hungry, of directly attacking humans—the traveler who had lost his way, the defenseless shepherd, the wounded soldier, the child or the old man. His misdeeds, exaggerated by human fear, were told from village to village, even if he did not penetrate the city when hunger gnawed at him, for instance in Paris in the early fifteenth century. Wolves encumbered childhood memory, inundated literature, fed scary tales. (*AO*, 189)

Given the wolf's reputation, Galahad is wise to make haste to the castle door, while a simple postproduction sound effect adds layers to the harrowing scene. Fossier concludes that such animal sounds were key to defining the place of the Middle Ages man of God in relation (or, more accurately, opposition) to the fallen animal world:

> Our nervous equilibrium is strictly dependent on the dangers that threaten it. More than the tooth of the wolf or the dog, *it was the wolf's sinister nocturnal howling* or the ceaseless barking of the dog that created a state of tension (today we would call it stress) that was judged harmful to man's activity as an exceptional being. (198; italics added)

The presence of wolves on the Continent would have been a given during the Middle Ages, but not so in England across the same period. Mortimer notes that by the fourteenth century—the period *MPHG* resembles, visually—wolf sightings were few and far between:

> [A traveler] might wonder if whether there are still wolves in medieval England. . . . Rest assured that there are not. Well, probably not. The modern tradition states that the last English wolf was killed in North Lancashire in the fourteenth century but you are very unlikely to meet it. Ralph Higden, writing at Chester in 1340, comments that there are now "few wolves" left in England. The last set of instructions to trap and kill wolves is issued in 1289, so if you want to see an indigenous wild wolf, you will have to go to the Highlands of Scotland. (27)

The Pythons were, of course, shooting in Scotland, but the film itself is clearly set in England.[1]

... a flash of lightning reveals the silhouette of a huge and terrifying castle ...—(PSC) The vision of the shining Grail experienced by Galahad as he crawls closer to Castle Anthrax is not part of the finished script, and was likely included after-the-fact, as a more visible way to entice Galahad toward the foreboding and *"rather derelict"* castle.[2] Doyle remembers shooting Gilliam's version of the Grail (from the earlier God animation) and superimposing it onto the castle footage.[3] This "blazing" image is associated with the Grail in many of the romances, however, according to Barber:

> Perceval encounters the Grail without knowing it when he sees five lights like candles in the forest at the dead of night, "so bright and clear that it seemed that the great, dense forest was lit up and blazing with their light on every side." He learns the next day that this was a sign of the presence of the Grail. (*THG*, 32)

Coincidentally, the planned theme park at Cannock, Staffordshire (mentioned in the "Castle at Camelot" entry earlier), depicting scenes and amusements from "Merrie England," promised "a floodlit Camelot built on a slag heap . . . it would be seen for miles by approaching wayfarers as a beacon of hospitality, good fare and reveling."[4] The attraction was never actually built.

... lovely ZOOT—(PSC) Excepting the color, Zoot's costume is almost precisely what artists Frank Bello creates for Maid Marian in the 1955 *Robin Hood* comic book. There, Marian's dress has hints of crimson, as well as white.

The name isn't made up, of course, being associated first with the stylized "zoot suits," popular in Latino communities during and after World War II, as well as sax player Zoot Sims, who may have been the referent, if perhaps Idle—who hung with the popular music crowd during the *Flying Circus* days—contributed this name to the script. Sims and other American jazz artists had played at the Festival Hall—to strong reviews—in late November 1966; Sims would appear again at Ronnie Scott's club in August 1967.[5] He would also make an appearance on BBC 2 in July 1968.

The most likely namesake, however, was Zoot Money (b. 1942), a popular Hammond organ player very active in the London music circles in the 1960s and 1970s. He was part of the so-called "Soho scene" during this period, and by Christmas 1973—perhaps cementing this connection—he was appearing at the Mermaid Theatre with the band Grimms, with Neil Innes.[6] By the following Christmas, Innes was *not* listed as appearing with the band in holiday shows—he was likely involved in the postproduction process on *Holy Grail*.[7] Finally, Zoot Money is mentioned by Palin himself as a *possible* referent in his section of an audio commentary (though he doesn't seem certain at all).[8]

GIRLIES—(PSC) A castle full of maidens seems an Oxbridge boys' club dream come true, but the Grail sources got there first, followed by a fairly contemporary spoof film. First, in *Le Morte Darthur*, after obtaining his shield Galahad travels to a small chapel and prays. There he receives guidance from God: "Go thou now, thou adventurous knight, to the Castle of Maidens, and there do away the wicked customs" (*LMD-WM*, 324). (In the film, there are promised and abundantly pleasurable "wicked customs" in Castle Anthrax.) Malory's Galahad is not seeking the Grail here, of course, but moving from adventure to adventure, proving his knightly mettle and perfection. As he approaches the castle (though not through a storm in most versions) Galahad is hailed by an old man who warns him that the castle is "cursed," that there is no ruth within the castle, only "hardiness and mischief" (324).

In Chrétien's *The Story of the Grail*, it is Perceval who discovers the ruins of a castle ruled by the beautiful Blancheflor, whom he chastely protects in his own bed overnight before confronting her enemy the following day (*THG*, 15). There is also a miniature of a monk giving Galahad the keys to the Maiden's Castle in *Estoire del Saint Graal, La Queste del Saint Graal, Morte Artu*, France.

In Sir Gawain's tale (which follows immediately after Galahad's, in Malory), the meaning and significance of the castle are offered by a hermit who has admonished Gawain for being less knightly than Galahad:

> Also I may say you that the Castle of Maidens betokeneth the good souls that were in prison before the Incarnation of Our Lord Jesu Christ. And the seven knights betoken the seven deadly sins that reigned that time in the world. And I may liken the good knight Galahad unto the son of the High Father, that alit within a maiden, and bought all the souls out of thrall; so did Sir Galahad deliver all the maidens out of the woeful castle. (*LMD-WM*, 328)

The Python version, of course, offers the chaste Galahad being tempted by the castle's maidens, his purity at stake, only to be "saved" by Launcelot. In *The Noble Tale of Sir Lancelot du Lake*, Lancelot himself has earlier saved a castle full of maidens—who have "worked all manner of silk works . . . and are all great gentlewomen born"—held captive for seven years by two giants (*LMD-WM*, 110).

As for the film reference, the 1967 Bond spoof *Casino Royale* features a very recognizable setup: When the well-known celibate James Bond (David Niven) visits a Scottish castle he is met by a seductive blonde and a host of tartan-knickered beauties hoping to deflower him (they're all evil SMERSH agents, it turns out). The Pythons have already made fun of this epic disaster of a movie and its codirector, Scotsman Joe McGrath, in Ep. 23 of *Flying Circus* (*MPFC: UC*, 1.351–54.)[9]

ZOOT: "Welcome to the Castle Anthrax"—There are similarly foreboding names in the Grail romances, of course, including the "Pass Perilous," the "Castle Dangerous," and the "Castle Perilous," all found in the *Gareth* section of *Le Morte Darthur*; at the same time in book two there is a Castle Adventurous and a Castle Joyous Isle, as well. Most of the castles described have rather dull names, though—the Castle Beale-Valet, the Castle of Maidens, the castles of Tintagil, Arundel, Liones, Lonazep, and so on.

ZOOT: "It's not a very good name, is it?"—"Anthrax" may not be a very good name, but it was much in the news in the UK during the Pythons' lifetimes. Anthrax had been problematic in animals and even humans for years, but with the discovery of penicillin—and more pointedly, Prof. Florey's 1943 discoveries concerning penicillin's effect on certain organisms, including anthrax—in the Pythons' youth this onetime scourge became treatable.[10] The Minister of Agriculture would often report in the Commons on recent disease activity in the UK, news of which made regular appearances in British newspapers. The following appeared in December 1952: "Anthrax.—The outbreaks of anthrax that have occurred during the past six months have been:—June, 31; July, 90; August, 123; September, 170; October, 185; November, 209 (Minister of Agriculture)."[11] Often, when anthrax-infected cat and dog food was discovered, local health officials would drive through smaller cities using portable loudspeakers, warning people to not feed their animals the tainted product. This certainly would have been a memorable experience for a youngster during the early 1950s.

As late as 1971 the United States was still testing and stockpiling chemical and biological agents in places like Fort Detrick, Maryland, Pine Bluff, Arkansas, and Dugway (Tooele), Utah. Anthrax (known as "TR-2") was one of those feared agents. In March 1968 a testing mishap at the Utah proving ground killed more than six thousand nearby sheep.[12] In 1971, by order of President Nixon, these stockpiles (including anthrax) began to be destroyed. Also in 1971, there were natural, spontaneous anthrax outbreaks at places like the Chester Zoo in Cheshire, England, and in dairy cows in Wales north of Cardiff. In 1972 there were human anthrax deaths reported in Spain and Lancashire, and additional cattle outbreaks in Cornwall, and in 1973 (as the Pythons were writing *Holy Grail*[13]) a West German scientist was arrested for threatening to send anthrax-laced letters to those complicit in the killing of Palestinian terrorists during the Munich Olympics.[14] Anthrax, then, was very much in the news in the 1970s.

ZOOT: "**Away varletesses!**"—The term "varlet" meant a boy servant, initially, and later a "rascal." "Varletess" is a minor eighteenth-century derivation, according to the *OED*. The somewhat original (but still a bit anachronistic) version of this archaic term is also used in the 1955–1957 *Robin Hood* comic book series—"We have the varlets!" and "Come on, you varlets!" In total, the mild invective appears at least a dozen times in the series. It is a smidge out of its time, as the "rascal" definition wouldn't appear until the mid-sixteenth century (*OED*).

ZOOT: "**The beds here are warm and soft and very, very big**"—The "varletesses" are clearly not really talking about simple comfort here. In most of the romance sources a Castle Anthrax would have been a trap where an errant knight could get sidetracked from the quest or perhaps even destroyed if he partook of the lair's temptations.[15] More on that below.

Beds do figure into both the historical medieval period and the Malorian source material, as might be expected. Historically, beds were a rather expensive, even *luxury* piece of furniture, and were often mentioned in wills and certainly inventories of valuables. Poorer folk had no "bed" at all, and slept wherever could be made comfortable and kept dry. Starter beds were made of wooden posts and frame, with a straw-stuffed mattress set on latticed rope supports. More expensive mattresses were feather and down-stuffed, with finer and finer linens as bedding, etc. The merchant Hugh le Bever in 1337 claimed to own "one mattress" and "three feather beds," while six of the top eight items on his household inventory list had to do with beds and bedding (Mortimer, 150). The total value of these items came to about thirty-eight shillings (150). Much later, Shakespeare is well known to have left his "second best bed" to his wife, along with whatever furniture accompanied it.

Beds in the Malorian world are for knights to rest and recover from injury, for the losing or protection of one's chastity, and can even be enchanted by Merlin "that there should never man lie therein but he went out of his wit" (*LMD'A*, 1.90). Most of chapter 22 of book 4 is given over to what is essentially an extended sleepover in various open-air pavilions—there are beds, knights, and damosels everywhere (1.155–57). The Castle Anthrax maidens are clearly hoping that Galahad the Chaste, once in their warm bed, will lose "his wit" and give over his purity to them. Thus any maiden's promise of a bed "warm and soft" can be a ruse in *Le Morte D'Arthur*, a honey trap meant to ensnare weary and weak knights. When King Arthur, King Uriens, and Sir Accolon are on a hunt together, they espy a mysterious ship, and, deciding to investigate, find the familiar Castle of Anthrax items of torches, maidens, soft beds, and allurements:

> So they went in all three, and found it richly behanged with cloth of silk. By then it was dark night, and there suddenly were about them an hundred torches set upon all the sides of the ship boards, and it gave great light; and therewithal there came out twelve fair damosels and saluted King Arthur on their knees, and called him by his name, and said he was right welcome, and such cheer as they had he should have of the best. The king thanked them fair. Therewithal they led the king and his two fellows into a fair chamber, and there was a cloth laid richly beseen of

all that longed unto a table, and there were they served of all wines and meats that they could think; of that the king had great marvel, for he fared never better in his life as for one supper.

And so when they had supped at their leisure, King Arthur was led into a chamber, a richer beseen chamber saw he never none, and so was King Uriens served, and led into such another chamber, and Sir Accolon was led into the third chamber passing richly and well beseen; and so were they laid in their beds easily. And anon they fell asleep, and slept marvellously sore all the night.

And on the morrow King Uriens was in Camelot abed in his wife's arms, Morgan le Fay. And when he awoke he had great marvel, how he came there, for on the even afore he was two days' journey from Camelot. And when King Arthur awoke he found himself in a dark prison, hearing about him many complaints of woeful knights. (1.125–26)

Galahad will be saved from such imprisonment or compromise only by the interdiction of Launcelot and other knights; Arthur will have to fight his way out of the dark prison.

GALAHAD: "Sir Galahad . . . the chaste"—Barber gives Tennyson much credit for elevating Galahad's purity beyond the medieval romance depictions—describing it as "a simple, almost simplistic view of Galahad's character"—based on the Poet Laureate's 1834 work *Sir Galahad*, wherein

> Tennyson places the emphasis on Galahad's prowess, and above all on Galahad's chastity. This was crucial to Tennyson's view of Galahad . . . [who] keeps his heart "fair thro' faith and prayer" and is rewarded by visions of "some secret shrine" where invisible hands celebrate Mass. (*THG*, 263–64)

So Palin's Galahad achieves the "grail castle" because of his purity, and—even though the castle turns out to be a place of frustrating *malheur*, and thus quite Pythonesque—though tempted, with Lancelot's help he retains his chastity and continues his quest.

GALAHAD: "Well look, I'm afraid I really ought to be . . ."—Galahad the Chaste knows what he should be doing, and says so several times, but these ladies will have none of it. In this they are classified as they had been by many medieval writers, as distractions from proper goals and moral pursuits for all men. In fourteenth-century comic fabliaux "women are invariably deceivers: inconstant, unscrupulous, quarrelsome, querulous, lecherous, shameless" (Tuchman, 211). She continues:

> Woman was the Church's rival, the temptress, the distraction, the obstacle to holiness, the Devil's decoy. In the *Speculum* of Vincent de Beauvais,[16] greatest of the 13th century encyclopedists and a favorite of St. Louis, woman is "the confusion of man, an insatiable beast, a continuous anxiety, an incessant warfare, a daily ruin, a house of tempest," and—finally, the key—"a hindrance to devotion." (211)

ZOOT: "You would not be so ungallant . . ."—The significance of honor and gallantry, especially toward women, is peppered throughout the romances. The loss of "maidenhead" for most damosels in Malory was fraught with peril and recriminations, and likely here, it would have been equally bad for Galahad to surrender his chastity, no matter how "ungallant" his refusals. In *Le Morte Darthur*, Bors saves a damosel, and she tells him that had she lost her maidenhead to her captor, "five hundred men should have died therefor," but also, the knight who so defiled her would have "died for the sin of his body . . . shamed and dishonoured for ever" (*LMD-WM*, 362). The "girlies" of Castle Anthrax don't seem too worried about such sufferings—for themselves or their object of affection.

ZOOT: "making exciting underwear . . ."—The "dressing" and "undressing" appeal to the boys' adolescent fantasies, of course, while the making of undergarments actually has sources in both Arthuriana and the actual medieval world. As mentioned just above, from *The Noble Tale of Sir Lancelot du Lake*, Lancelot saves a castle full of maidens who "worked all manner of silk works . . . and are all great gentlewomen born." These maidens have been held captive by two giants (*LMD-WM*, 110). This same fascination with things worldly condemned the abbey at Coldingham, a "monastery of virgins"—which burned down in 683—the Venerable Bede seeing God's judgment being played out. The well-thought-of monk Adomnán had seen a vision of the double monastery's[17] destruction, and it was all due to the unholiness of the adherents within:

> I, having just visited every part of this monastery in turn: I have examined their cells and their beds, and found no one except you concerned with his soul's welfare; but all of them, men and women alike, are sunk in slothful slumbers or else they remain awake for the purposes of sin. And the cells that were built for praying and for reading have become haunts of feasting, drinking, gossip, and other delights; *even the virgins who are dedicated to God put aside the respect for their profession and, whenever they have leisure, spend their time weaving elaborate[18] garments, with which to adorn themselves as if they were brides, so imperiling their virginity, or else to make friends with strange men.* (*HE*, 425 27; italics added)

The maidens of the Castle Anthrax, though likely not nuns, are clearly adorning themselves in alluring, bride-like clothing and weaving "fine" garments, the hope being that "strange men" like Galahad and Launcelot might drop by.

The subject of Middle Ages underwear has actually been one of the more troublesome areas of ancient scholarship. Fossier admits as much as he discusses medieval clothing in general: "We know too little about what underclothes were worn in antiquity to judge whether or not the medieval age brought any innovations" (*AO*, 73). Since these clothing articles cover the private parts of the body, underwear isn't much discussed by chroniclers or the writers of jeremiads of the period, and the nature of the fabric—likely thin, soft, and expensive or rare—means that intact examples of underwear have been scarce. In July 2012 a sealed-off area of Lengberg Castle (Austria, c. 1190) was opened for the first time since the fifteenth century and, along with other waste from a fifteenth-century rebuilding of the castle, several bras and a pair of underpants were discovered, all in fairly good condition. It's likely that since some medieval folk wore underpants and some did not—and perhaps there was a social divide on the issue, rich versus poor—the prospect of any undergarment at all *could* be termed "exciting," as Zoot exclaims.

ZOOT: "But you are wounded!"—Malory records that Sir Tristram, after a "great battle" with Sir Marhaus, "was wounded that unnethe he might recover, and lay at a nunnery half a year" (*LMD'A*, 1.166). There is also no indication in the film itself that Galahad has been injured, excepting perhaps his pride as he and others ran away from the animal assault at the French-occupied castle.

She almost forces him to lie on the bed—(PSC) In *Le Morte Darthur*, Galahad does find himself sitting on a bed, just after he blows the horn to alert local knights, and just before the priest comes to relate the story of the castle's tragic history (*LMD-WM*, 325). In this case, however, he is simply resting as he hears the story of the castle and its curse. The priest tells him that seven years before seven knights took the castle, killed the owner and his son, and held his daughter hostage. They also "by great force . . . held all the knights of [the] country under great sevage and truage." The daughter then prophesied that one knight would come and destroy them. The knights responded somewhat haughtily, as evil knights were wont to do:

> "Well," said the seven knights, "sithen ye say so, there shall never lady nor knight pass this castle but they shall abide maugre their heads, or die therefore, till that knight be come by whom we shall lose this castle." And therefore it is called the Maidens' Castle, for they have devoured many maidens. (325–26)

The knights also seemed to be speaking here as one, perhaps even in unison, perhaps akin to the Pythons' Three-Headed Knight seen and heard earlier.

ZOOT: "You must see the doctors immediately"—At this Galahad tries to leap out of bed, which is understandable. Most who treated illnesses during this period weren't doctors at all, they may have been trained by treating animals or by learning various folk remedies, and likely would have treated imbalances of the "sanguine, phlegmatic, choleric, and melancholic," known as the "four humours."[19] The skills of Middle Ages "doctors" could be elevated if they happened to be employed by the wealthy, the court, or the Church. Since the Church frowned on violating the body after death the chances of a doctor understanding human anatomy were slim, though such courses were sometimes available.[20] Most doctors of the fourteenth century would treat symptoms as opposed to the actual disease, hoping that God would enact the cure, but some were much better trained, and more ambitious:

> Notwithstanding all their charts and stars, and medicaments barely short of witches' brews, doctors gave great attention to diet, bodily health, and mental attitude. Nor were they lacking in practical skills. They could set broken bones, extract teeth, remove bladder stones, remove cataracts from the eye with a silver needle, and restore a mutilated face by skin graft from the arm. They understood epilepsy and apoplexy as spasms of the brain. They used urinalysis and pulse beat for diagnosis, knew what substances served as laxatives and diuretics, applied a truss for hernia, a mixture of oil, vinegar and sulfur for toothache, and ground peony root with oil of rose for headache. (Tuchman, 106)

The "doctors" here—Piglet and Winston—"have a basic medical training" (see below), and seem to know the portion of Galahad's anatomy they are interested in examining, and set to work immediately.

PIGLET and WINSTON enter the room—Fun, odd names again ("Midget" and "Crapper" were heard earlier), but both quite recognizable. "Piglet" is both a name for a baby pig as well as that of Pooh's best friend from the A. A. Milne *Winnie the Pooh* stories. "Winston" is likely another direct reference to Winston Churchill, who had died in 1965.[21] Churchill is mentioned a number of times in *Flying Circus*, and pictured once.

It's also entirely possible this is a throwback reference to another childhood memory of the Pythons. Queen Elizabeth's favorite mount (for Trooping the Colour) was named Winston, and British Pathe cameras caught all the action. The horse was also part of Elizabeth's coronation in 1953, and the young Pythons would have seen him (and heard Richard Dimbleby coo about him) in the live broadcast watched by millions.[22]

ZOOT: "They have a basic medical training"—According to popular historian Barbara Tuchman, this is not necessarily a specious claim for the fourteenth century in Europe:

> Women of noble estate were frequently more accomplished in Latin and other school learning than men, for though girls did not leave home at seven like boys, their education was encouraged by the Church so that they might be better instructed in the faith and more fitted for the religious

life in a nunnery, should their parents wish to dedicate them, with suitable endowment, to the Church. Besides reading and writing in French and Latin, they were taught music, astronomy, and some medicine and first aid. (53)

Ian Mortimer notes that there was a noticeable "absence of physicians across England" during the fourteenth century, which wasn't a bad thing given the success rate most doctors could claim (*Time Traveler's Guide to Medieval England*, 193). Mortimer describes the level of knowledge, and specifically medical knowledge, during this same period:

These ideas about causes of illness and diagnosis might be astonishing but they reveal an important point. Medieval people are not ignorant, in the sense of having no knowledge. It is simply that their knowledge is very different from our own. They probably have as much medical "knowledge" as we do, only it is based on astrology, herbology, religion, a little direct experience, philosophy, fundamental misconceptions about how the body works, a lot of hearsay, and a large measure of desperation. (193)

Piglet and Winston's "basic medical training" likely doesn't include much in the way of actual experience (beyond women's health issues), human anatomy, surgery, or the translated works of Galen and Hippocrates, which would have been de rigueur at an English university (193–94).

Then there is a sharp bong from the lower part of his armour—(PSC) Supposedly the sound of Galahad's erection hitting his armour or shield, this sound effect is *not* part of the film's soundtrack, nor is Winston's guided gaze toward his crotch. It may have been removed for the "A" rating.

GALAHAD: "Torment me no longer! I have seen the Grail!"—This line is missing from the finished script, but refers back to the earlier-mentioned dangers of women and their effect on a knight's successful completion of a Grail-related task: his mind is on "divine things," hers always "earthbound" (Tuchman, 211).

This moment reads very much like a scene from the actual youth of St. Thomas Aquinas. The budding theologian and philosopher had decided to avoid the monastery life, where his wealthy family wanted him, and instead to become a Dominican, where he could pursue a university education as well as live a life of poverty and chastity. His family had other ideas:

His aristocratic relations, outraged, had him kidnapped and imprisoned in the family castle. For over a year they tried every means to make him renounce his vows, even smuggling a beautiful prostitute into his bedroom. Thomas immediately chased her out with a flaming brand. From then on he was blessed with permanent freedom from sexual temptation. (Hallam, 115)

Galahad's in good company here as a sort of prisoner in Castle Anthrax, his chastity and Grail-quest eligibility on the line.

PIGLET: "Back to your bed! At once!"—This, and Piglet's "There's no grail here" are almost lost in the muddy sound mix, thanks to the noise of the bed covers and armor, and just the ambient sound, which would have been a challenge in the drafty castle. These scenes were all shot in a hurry, meaning they were scurrying from camera setup to camera setup, looking to just capture a serviceable take. Doyle remembers the maidens' scenes taking one evening, and Zoot's scenes perhaps the following morning.[23] The Pythons clearly didn't bother to rerecord these lines in postproduction—where typically Foley work and ADR (automated dialogue replacement) add sound effects and clean up or replace the wild sound in a looping session.[24] It's likely that since the sound was acceptable, they decided to forgo the added cost of bringing these actresses—many were recruited in the Stirling area—into the studio at Twickenham as they edited and mixed the film.

As he leaves the room we CUT TO the reverse shot to show that he is now in a room full of bathing and romping GIRLIES, all innocent, wide-eyed and beautiful—This shot and even the entire scene are remarkably similar to a scene from Polanski's *Macbeth*. There, Macbeth has returned to the witches for more good augurs, more "sweet bodements." The setting is almost identical: one man in a darkened, stone-walled room full of "romping" ladies. In *Macbeth*, though, the ladies are completely nude—young and old, maid and crone (mostly crone, admittedly)—they are cackling, not tittering, and they tempt their visitor with portents, not titillation. There is even a grail-like cup offered to Macbeth, from which he has to drink to see his future. Costumer Hazel Pethig convinced codirectors Jones and Gilliam to keep the girls in draped gowns, rather than nude, arguing successfully that the erotic nature of the shot would persist if there were only glimpses of modest nudity.[25] Though not mentioned anywhere in the film material, this decision likely allowed the film to retain the coveted "PG" rating in the United States. More nudity (or language, or more *realistic* violence) would have pushed the film toward an "R" rating, meaning a significant drop in audience potential.

Communal bathing was still a feature of the Middle Ages, though not as public as had been the case in Roman Britain. As the church gathered and then spread its influence, public nudity declined, as did public bathing. Privately, though, communal baths could still be "a social occasion, with food and drink to hand," which appears to be the situation here in Castle Anthrax (Hallam, 218–19).

DINGO: "No, I am Zoot's identical twin sister, Dingo"—An odd choice for a name, but, like Zoot, not likely just pulled out of the ether. In 1967 a new play by Charles Woods (b. 1932), *Dingo*, was refused approval by the Lord Chamberlain—even though it had been written for the National Theatre—and opened instead in Bristol. The play is a rather dark, acidic look at British service in World War II: "Basically, the play is an attack upon the idea of the war as a glorious, noble crusade against evil."[26] In February 1966 Lord Annan (1916–2000) had stood in the House of Lords[27] and decried the continuing government censorship of plays, specifically, mentioning *Dingo* by name (along with works by Arthur Miller, Tennessee Williams, and John Osborne[28]), and proposed that the matter be brought before both Houses for discussion. Annan was simply asking that plays—which were subject to direct censorship by the Lord Chamberlain's office—be treated like BBC fare, the music hall stage, and even Soho strip clubs, which were *not* under the LC's purview. The Theatres Act of 1968 abolished such censorship.[29]

DINGO: ". . . our beacon, which—I have just remembered—is Grail-shaped . . ."—The significance of the grail itself continues to diminish as the quest fractures and lumbers on, with Galahad having to endure "almost certain temptation" in bad faith, as it were. It is Galahad himself being tempted, meaning this is a test of his knightly character, and not necessarily a necessary step in the search for the Grail. Barber notes that Chrétien de Troyes employs a similar structure in his work, wherein the titles he chooses ("The Story of the Grail"; "The Knight of the Cart") "[do] not necessarily indicate the topic of the story, but simply the object on which the plot hinges" (*THG*, 14). He continues:

> For Lancelot, it was the cart into which he hesitated to climb, proving himself a less than perfect lover because he put his own honour before his duty to his love. For Perceval, it is the Grail, about which he fails to ask, proving himself an imperfect knight, because he observes the letter of the instruction he has received, but not the spirit, and shows himself lacking in true sympathy. (14)

Galahad fails to get the grail from Castle Anthrax but retains his virtue; Lancelot "rescues" Prince Herbert from Swamp Castle but cannot/will not consummate his courtly love as a prize; and Robin is confronted by the Three-Headed Knight but scampers off as soon as he is able. None are closer to their goal—the Grail—than they were when encountering these tests, and only Galahad has any new, applicable knowledge: that the Grail in Castle Anthrax is actually only a grail-shaped beacon.

DINGO: ". . . wicked wicked Zoot"—If Galahad the Pure had been aware of the Grail legends surrounding him he would have known for a certainty by this time that the Grail could not possibly reside in the Castle Anthrax. Over and over again the purity of both the structures and attendants in proximity to the Grail are reinforced in the various romances. In *Parzival*, for example, "earth's perfection's transcendence"—"the Grail permitted itself to be carried. The Grail was of such a nature that [the maiden's] chastity had to be well guarded, she who ought by rights to tend it. [The maiden who carried the Grail] had to renounce falseness. . . . [She was] devoid of falsity" (*THG*, 77). Zoot's "wickedness," her misleading of Galahad, Dingo's suggestions of "spankings" and sexual favors, and the salacious intent of the castle denizens in general clearly disqualifies both the castle and its maidens from Grail-keeping.

DINGO: "Do you think this scene should have been cut?"—Dingo has turned to face the camera and is addressing the 1975 theatrical audience directly. This is not a "Picture for Schools" moment, but a real bit of direct address inspired by the Nouvelle Vague, but leaning toward Godard and away from Truffaut, perhaps. Dingo is talking about the dramatic scene/performance being displayed, and asking whether the assembled audience feels it's as significant as she seems to think it is. In Buñuel's *The Milky Way* (1969) a priest tells a terrific story, and looks directly into the camera during the telling. In the Buñuel scene, there seems to be no undercutting, no satire, no hint of a nagging self-consciousness that tends to plague most New Wave films featuring direct address. The self-conscious element is displayed here in Castle Anthrax. Dingo is talking about the film itself, directly acknowledging the artificiality, the constructedness of the moment.

The Pythons laid the groundwork for this moment during the third season of *Flying Circus*. In Ep. 29, "The Lost World of Roiurama," when the explorers emerge from the jungle and see a camera crew, they celebrate their good fortune, and the following image is a longer shot revealing the camera, its crew, and the ragged explorers coming together. At that moment, they realize they are still being filmed, and it's revealed there is yet another camera crew filming this first camera crew and the explorers. This turns out to be the film actually being made, directed by a Jamaican pretending to be Luchino Visconti, who is immediately arrested by a member of the Fraud Film Squad, who happens to be well-versed in the filmography of Visconti, and so on:

> An acknowledgment of the artifice that has become more and more prevalent as the shows have progressed. Part of the troupe's dissatisfaction with the third series was this growing dependence on displaying the man behind the curtain, as it were, the postmodern upending of any narrative track, instead of where they began in 1969—strong gag and character writing, and a healthy dose of irreverence for the television medium. The obvious knowledge of international cinema of the period (Visconti, Antonioni, Godard) betrays the troupe's interest in and perhaps influence from the various New Waves sweeping the film world, and those filmmakers' movement away from traditional narrative structures. (*MPFC: UC*, 2.44)

Possibly activated by her own rupture of the fourth wall, characters from both earlier and later in the film's timeline (Dennis; the assembled armies at the Grail Castle) interrupt Dingo and tell her to "Get on with it." She is nudged back into the narrative continuum by the film itself, and the movie can continue.

It's worth pointing out that Galahad (Palin) never breaks character here, staring perplexedly at Dingo as she talks to the camera, and then chiming back in when she restarts their scene. This is one way to move past a rupture caused by an "It's only a model"-type moment—Arthur "shushes" earlier, and here Galahad simply looks on in earnest.

In the Blu-ray comments for *Holy Grail* Jones mentions that this scene was cut out as a last-minute attempt to streamline the film before it debuted at Filmex in Los Angeles in 1975. The scene had been part of the film for other nonpublic screenings—screenings that Jones characterizes as "terrible" (without explanation)—and that the film would screen without the scene at Filmex, then with the scene elsewhere to big laughs. Neither Gilliam nor Jones could really remember why the scene had troubled them to begin with.[30]

DENNIS: "At least ours was committed. It wasn't just a string of pussy jokes"—Dennis is defending his scene as he reclines in the mud next to the Old Woman, just as the Three-Headed Knight defends his scene as being "visually" significant. The sexual ribaldry here and through the balance of the Castle Anthrax scene allies it with Middle Ages poets like François Villon (b. 1431), whose bawdy verse featured prostitutes and copulation and besottedness and dead men at the gallows, and whose work was likely known to the group's medievalist Jones, at least. This vulgarity runs through literature significant to the Pythons, including Chaucer's Miller, Reeve, and Wife of Bath from *Canterbury Tales*, Sidney's Ovidian fascination with Penelope,[31] Boccaccio's *Decameron*, and the works of John Wilmot, Earl of Rochester; Jonson, Jonathan Swift; Voltaire; and others. Villon's poem "For Fat Margot" is typically earthy:

> Then we make up in bed, and she, more bloated
> than a poisonous dung beetle, farts
> and laughs and claps me on the head,
> says I'm cute and whacks my thigh.
> When we awake, her belly starts to quiver
> and she mounts me, to spare love's fruit;
> I groan, squashed beneath her weight—
> this lechery of hers will ruin me,
> in this brothel where we ply our trade.[32]

Villon's work was quite popular by the later fifteenth century.

SOLDIERS: "Get on with it!"—Two things here. First, this "Get on with it!" shout is not part of the script as printed, and it's also not part of the finished film in every version (VHS, laser disc, DVD, etc.). There were versions of the film that played in screening settings prior to the film's initial release, and the Pythons used these screenings to gauge audience reaction to the film and tweak where necessary. The insertion of other commenting characters—Tim, Dennis and mother, the Three-Headed Knight, the serried line of pikemen, God—is yet another borrow from *Flying Circus*. In Ep. 12, as the show is wrapping up from "How Far Can a Minister Fall?," the host (Jones) asks if anyone has anything else to say. What follows is a quick montage of characters from Ep. 12 as well as previous episodes—in their places/costumes from those episodes—saying "no" (*MPFC: UC*, 1.195). In *Holy Grail*, neither Tim nor the row of pikemen have appeared to this point in the film, meaning this interstitial moment is a bit of an irruption into the smooth strata of the narrative by characters who, textually, don't yet exist.

This "Get on with it!" is almost a pantomime moment where the audience can participate vocally along with the staged performance. In most pantos the Pythons would have watched growing up, a character like the Principal Boy leads the audience in these retorts (as was seen in *MPFC* Ep. 30, the "*Puss in Boots*" adaptation), but here it's an assumed and collected desire for the plot to move forward that prompts the interjection. Panto audiences attend regularly for these very participatory moments, which remain a self-conscious part of the performances to this day.

DINGO: "The oral sex"—This is another of the "suggestions" made by the BBFC for excision to achieve the "A" rating. Clearly, the Pythons left the phrase in and cut other bits and pieces, instead.

Generally, any form of sexuality considered to be unproductive (meaning, no possibility of procreation) was "condemned as unnatural" by the church, according to Karras in *Sexuality in Medieval Europe* (92):

> Chastity was not the goal for most couples. Yet types of sexual activity that do not lead to conception—oral and anal sex, manual stimulation—were strictly forbidden. Unlike the female superior position [heterosexual coupling, woman on top], however, these practices are rarely mentioned (even to be censured) in the context of marriage. Early medieval penitentials are among the very few texts to condemn oral sex, and do not mention who the participants were (or even their gender). . . . We have no way of knowing whether this reflects an absence of the practices, or ignorance on the part of church authorities. . . . [O]ral sex seems a very obscure phenomenon in the Middle Ages. (107)

This last may be precisely why the Pythons would highlight the act—it seems out of place in this Castle of Maidens, in the Age of Chivalry, and especially in relation to Galahad the Chaste.

Ironically, though, the sin of sexual impropriety often took a back seat to the possibilities of unwanted, problematic illegitimate children. In Ep. 36 of *Flying Circus* the Pythons are crossing modern-day "porn merchants" with Elizabethans, and the arguments against uncontrolled sex were more political or even financial than spiritual or religious:

> The definition of pornography would have been quite different in Elizabethan times. According to Lynda Boose, pornography in the time of Shakespeare and Elizabeth was "a language not of lascivious delight but of sexual scatology—of slime, poison, garbage, vomit, clyster pipes, dung, and animality—that emerges connected to images of sexuality in the vocabulary" (193). The Pythons, then, have transposed the pornography of the twentieth century into Elizabethan times, an anachronistic incongruity common for the troupe. The fear of sexual license for Elizabeth's subjects was very real, of course, but only as it threatened to contaminate and confuse lineage lines with bastard children making inheritance claims. The homosexual (or "sodomitical," in the period terminology) exploits of men, especially, were less threatening—no procreation, simply recreation—so dallying with a catamite or ingle was frowned upon, but not often punished. See the author's chapter six in *MPSERD* for more. (*MPFC: UC*, 2.126)

The sexually active single female was societally unacceptable, but since she could engage in nonproductive sex and remain *virgo intacta*, her maidenhood secure, she was still a valuable commodity, and good marriage material. These maidens might be whispered about, but they could all still be maidens even after engaging with a willing Galahad.

It may even be the reason these maidens are together in this fortified location, according to Karras: "Stories about women's lust became not a means of recognizing women as sexual beings, but an excuse for denying women independence in other areas of life" (112). They are confined by their sexual appetites, which may be why Dingo is so frustrated as the very nearly willing Galahad is hustled out.

...there is a commotion behind and SIR LANCELOT and LIGHTNING *Concorde, possibly plus GAWAIN, burst into the bathing area with swords drawn . . .*—(PSC) This is one of those places in the script where the original name of Launcelot's horse (Idle), Lightning, was then changed to Concorde, which continued throughout. Launcelot's horse does not burst in with the rest of the group—there are only the three armed knights against these maidens.

Launcelot[33] does burst in, and he is leading two knights, one with a fish as a crest, and the other with a "Y" on his shield and tunic. Both knights following Launcelot are completely helmed, meaning their faces are obscured so that anyone can play the role in any scene. Gilliam will don a mustache and play a knight, in the background, when needed.

GIRLS: "Yes, let him handle us easily"—Again, these retorts are much like a pantomime audience responding to the principal's prompts in a *Jack and the Beanstalk* or *Dick Whittington's Cat*, meaning this scene would have had a fun additional level of reference for the acculturated English audience. The fact that many of the pantos featured careful *double entendres* and veiled sexual witticisms—most playing above the children's heads—would have been another point of identification for the "with it" audience as they watched this castle scene. The Pythons have used this nod and wink to the acculturated audience throughout *Flying Circus*, whether it's mentions or depictions of D. H. Lawrence works or classical scholars and philosophies, descriptions of character "types," or simple metatexts that cry out "Englishness" (like "Shakespeare"). Being "in" on the reference is a big part of the success (and cultural depth) of *Flying Circus*:

> The Pythons writing into the script "right out of D. H. Lawrence" obviates the need for a physical description of the set, for the production designers and viewers, and eventually taps into the acculturated viewer's knowledge of Lawrence, his tropes and characters/settings, and television and cinematic adaptations of his work. The viewer (or reader?) who understood these allusions could sport his/her "badge of acculturation," and "get" the in-jokes and allusions, just like one who "knows" Shakespeare can similarly claim acculturation (*MPSERD* 24–25). This is an example of the Pythons' trotting out their academic credentials, where the similarly educated viewer can appreciate the allusions on multiple levels. (*MPFC: UC*, 1.36)

And, in response to a character description in the script for *Flying Circus* Ep. 18:

> All this history and acculturation is summed up—for the Pythons and their viewers alike—with an iconic, recognizable shorthand description ("city of London ex-public school type") that is interpreted by the show's dressers into an equally recognizable costume. This level of cultural awareness would most certainly be missed by the unacculturated (non-English) viewer, and even the native viewer given sufficient passage of time. In fact, the brolly and trilby (or bowler hat) look was already dated by 1970, meaning the studio audience knew they were seeing a throwback reference to a bygone day, to the City Gent look of the Pythons' youth. (*MPFC: UC*, 1.279–80)

Even the almost immediate appropriation and repurposing of bits from the "Dead Parrot" sketch into and across English culture[34] signals the importance of this acculturation, and here it has carried across from the third season of *MPFC* and into this feature film.

LAUNCELOT: "Silence! Foul temptress!"—In *Vox clamantis*[35]—at least partly a response to the destructive Peasants' Revolt of 1381[36]—John Gower cautions the clergy (and especially monks, whose minds and spirits are supposed to be trained to higher things) of the mortal, eternal dangers posed by women:

> Shun a woman's conversation, O holy man; beware lest you entrust yourself to a passion raging beyond control. For the mind which is allured and bound over by a woman's love can never reach the pinnacle of virtue. Of what use is their prattling to you? If you come in as a monk, you will go away a foul adulterer. Unless you turn aside from the venomous serpent, you will be poisoned by her when you least expect. Every woman enkindles a flame of passion; if one touches her, he is burned instantly. If you ponder the books of the ancients and the writings of the Church Fathers, you may grieve that even holy men have met with ruin in this way. Did not woman expel man from the seat of Paradise? And was she not the source of our death? The man who is a good shepherd should therefore be vigilant, and he should everywhere drive these rapacious she-wolves away from the monastery.[37]

We'll revisit Gower and his ilk later, when we meet the moaning Roger the Shrubber.

GALAHAD: "Look, it's my duty as a knight to try and sample as much peril as I can"—The fact that Galahad is set to "sample" these perils, not "face" them, is likely why Launcelot describes the outcome as "too perilous" (*MPHGB*, 41). Remaining with these eager maidens might not only damage Galahad's purity as a noble and faithful warrior, as witnessed in the romance sources when ill choices were made by formerly "parfit" knights, but his participation in the promised sex act—a *dépit amoureux*, to be sure—could damage him in a very different way, according to von Ehrenkrook, who describes what constituted normal" sexual behavior in an ancient culture (read: Roman)—a culture thriving in Britain for several hundred years prior to Saxon incursions:

> "Normal" sexual behavior for a *vir* [a fully masculine male] encompassed three orifices: the *vir* who penetrates the vagina (*fututor*), the *vir* who penetrates the mouth (*irrumator*), and the *vir* who penetrates the anus (*pedicator/pedico*). That a *pedicator* might penetrate a male anus, or an *irrumator* a male mouth, was of no consequence to the penetrator's status as a *vir*. Conversely, the corresponding receptive behavior that did in fact compromise one's status as a *vir*, placing him into the category of gender deviant, *included performing oral sex on a female (cunnilinctor)* or male (*fellator*) and receiving anal intercourse (*pathicus* or *cinaedus*). (150)

The "peril," then, is that by participating with these maidens, Galahad might become less of a man, and thus not qualified to be a knight of the Round Table and to further God's quest for the Grail. The romance sources describe a seer who first praises Bors for his faithful achievements, then blasts Bors's cousin Launcelot for his knightly shortcomings. Launcelot might be the greatest warrior, and the one with the most promise, "but sin is so foul in him he may not achieve such holy deeds, for had not been his sin he had passed all the knights that ever were in his days," the old man tells Bors (*LMD'A*, 2.198). The wages of sin in *Le Morte D'Arthur* can be an inability to see holy things, including the Grail, and God hiding himself and his glory from his knights.[38]

These "penetrations" of all sorts are also depicted often in the margins of Gothic illuminated manuscripts, there labeled as "obscaena."[39]

LAUNCELOT: "No, no, we must find the Grail"—They've been off-task for a bit of screen time here, and Lancelot is attempting to right the ship as he saves Galahad, perhaps even reminding the audience, as well, of the true purpose of the film.

Here is a "show so far" pause in relation to the Grail quest.[40] Since the Gallic tongue-lashing the quest endured at the castle of Guy de Loimbard, the Grail itself has been: (a) mentioned emphatically by the Famous Historian; (b) *not* mentioned by Sir Robin or his minstrels (he would admit to being a Knight of the Round Table, which nearly cost him his head); (c) *mentioned* by Galahad but quickly forgotten and even pushed aside in favor of a promised sexual adventure; and (d) re-mentioned by Launcelot as a way to convince Galahad to avoid "almost certain temptation." Beyond this scene, the Soothsayer has nothing to say about the Grail, though Arthur will ask; the Knights Who Say Ni don't mention it, and neither do Arthur or Bedevere, as a shrubbery offering and arrangement takes precedence. In the printed script the Swamp Castle denizens and Launcelot and Concorde all ignore the quest, Launcelot even seeking a self-aggrandizing "daring, desperate adventure" instead[41]; finally, after the Knights Who Until Recently Said Ni are defeated, Robin admits that he is still looking for the Grail, though he's clearly just escaping the Three-Headed Knight. The quest is kick-started again as they gather together, and the following major scenes (Tim the Enchanter, the Cave of Caerbannog, the Bridge of Death, the Grail Castle) are fairly straightforward as they pursue the Grail.

LAUNCELOT: "**Quickly, the horses**"—This line is crossed-out. Launcelot and friends have hustled Galahad away from "almost certain temptation," they are outside the castle, and the script as printed directs them to their "horses": "*The thunderstorm is over. A bunch (sic) of PAGES are tethered to a tree with more men waiting.*" These kinds of group shots requiring multiple actors who often were double or triple cast anyway were a challenge, and in this case they obviously decided to do away with the scene altogether. The "(sic)" was part of the script, an insular joke (meaning, maybe it's more accurately a "gaggle," a "pod," or a "murder" of pages), something the Pythons had done during *Flying Circus*, in a scene description for Ep. 18, mentioning *Private Eye*'s use of the term as well (*MPFC: UC*, 1.287). In *Holy Grail*, the "(sic)" could also mean that "a bunch" is a serious overstatement during the film's production—they had to scrimp on everything—and they also knew it even before leaving London for the film location.

LAUNCELOT: "**No. It's unhealthy**"—Galahad is certain that he can face the peril of "a hundred and fifty" girls, but Launcelot isn't so sure. If, as Gawain and Lightning seem to think (see below), Launcelot is a closet homosexual, then this warning against heterosexual activity can be taken in a different context. If, however, Launcelot is simply concerned about sexual immoderation, which could be the case, given the number of potential partners for the innocent Galahad in Castle Anthrax, then he is echoing concerns of other medieval voices. From Karras:

> In the later Roman period, however, a number of writers suggested that sexual moderation was good for men both for health reasons and because it allowed them to focus on the life of the mind. [For Galahad, this means getting back on the Grail quest horse.] Pagan authors did not often go as far as Christians in suggesting total abstinence, but in their promotion of moderation they helped create a new ideal of masculinity based on self-control rather than on aggressive penetration of as many other people as possible. . . . Christianity fit well with this set of ideas. (44)

Both Galahad's and Lancelot's self-control—albeit, perhaps, for different reasons—will allow them to resume the Grail quest and complete that task, one set before them by the Christian God.

GALAHAD: "**. . . I bet you're gay**"—There were many medieval clerics and chroniclers who *did* believe that women were as close to an antichrist as could exist on earth, including the "moral Gower," who described the fairer sex as "venomous serpents" and "rapacious she-wolves."[42] It didn't mean that sodomitical pleasures were any more acceptable, of course. (Remember, any *nonreproductive* sexual relation would have been sinful, in the eyes of the

Church.) The concept of a "gay" man in this period, however, wasn't truly comprehended, according to Karras:

> Indeed, in some instances, the fact that the man was the active partner, the penetrator, made not only the consent of his partner but even the gender of his partner irrelevant. Medieval Europe did not exactly follow the ancient Greek pattern where as long as a man was the active partner, whether he penetrated a woman or a boy (or young man) was not a moral question but simply one of preferences. However, there were echoes or elements of such a pattern in medieval culture.
>
> It was possible for some medieval people to take the attitude that an active man was an active man, regardless of the gender of the passive partner, because there was no concept of a "homosexual identity" based on object choice. That is, men were not defined by the gender of the person they preferred, but rather by the role they played. Today we tend to label men who prefer to have sex with other men as "gay," regardless of the active/passive distinction. The Middle Ages did not have such a category. (166)

This is simply one of the more obvious anachronisms employed by the Pythons; it's used as a gag. It wouldn't be until *MPHG* is revisited in the Broadway play *Spamalot* in 2005 that the homosexual characters are identified and celebrated on this homosocial quest ("Find your male, that's your Grail").[43]

LAUNCELOT: "No I'm not"—This is a retort from Launcelot looped in after-the-fact, and it does not appear in the script as finished. Gay or not, Launcelot is a knight with his eye fixed on the Grail, but his unwillingness to dally with the maidens at Castle Anthrax casts suspicion, at least for Galahad. Edward II spent a good part of his life balancing on this razor's edge—between his obvious attraction to men, including Piers Gaveston and the younger Hugh Despenser, unnatural attractions that perplexed and annoyed his father Edward I, infuriated his wife, Isabella, and stirred his nobles into actions against him on several occasions—and his responsibilities as the virile leader and "father" of England.[44]

GAWAIN or LIGHTNING** **gives a knowing glance at LAUNCELOT—(PSC) In the finished film neither Gawain nor Lightning (Concorde) give any kind of "knowing glance," since they really cannot. The group has moved well away from the camera along the castle wall; they are almost out of earshot, and their backs are to us. Also, Launcelot's horse was never part of the rescue group. The "Lightning" gaffe wasn't caught here, as it has not been crossed out or changed in the script to "Concorde."

The implication of the glance, though, is that Launcelot may well be gay, and so his saving of Galahad from lustful women may not have been as noble as it appears.

VOICE OVER: "Sir Launcelot had saved . . ."—(PSC) Palin's narration elsewhere as "VOICE OVER" is often more conversational than the original script, and he digresses into "smashing" performances, and swallows and starlings, of course, prompting the collective rejoinder and some sort of physical assault.[45]

This particular voice-over is significantly padded out in the finished film, as the text from the script indicates: "Sir Launcelot had saved Galahad from almost certain temptation but they were still lost, far from the goal of their search for the Holy Grail. Only Bedevere and King Arthur himself, riding day and night, had made any progress" (*MPHGB*, 42). The voice-over narrator (Palin) goes on to mention the quality of the acting, how many laden or unladen swallows flights they'd traveled (or how far they'd traveled if the bird were walking), etc.

In one of the Pythons' most significant sources of both material and inspiration, *The Goon Show*, voice-overs like this one introduced and linked stories and story sections throughout the long-running BBC Home Service Radio series. Announcer Wallace Greenslade often performed the task, while bandleader Ray Ellington pinch-hit when necessary, and the various "Neddie" characterizations (all played by Harry Secombe) generally kept the outlandish narratives moving forward via pointed verbal prods and connective suturing. Example: In "The House of Teeth" episode, after a Ray Ellington song interlude, announcer Greenslade says "We return you now to Part Three, the Castle of the Missing Teeth," followed by a dramatic musical chord ("The House of Teeth," 31 January 1956).

SOLDIERS: "Get on with it!"—This line—where the row of pikemen seen later in the film all shout together—is not part of the finished script. This is a repeat from the Dingo section of the "Castle Anthrax" segment, and may have been included to take the place of the previous iteration, which didn't make it into the film as released into cinemas. These types of non sequitur-ish rejoinders, used often in *Flying Circus* ("Lemon curry"; the Knight and Rubber Chicken[46]), are largely avoided in *MPHG*, keeping the narrative body as sacrosanct as possible.

VOICE OVER: ". . . there aren't any swallows but I think you can hear a starling . . ."—This is the last line the narrator is able to utter before he is clobbered, offscreen. All irritating or even helpful narrators and transition types in *Holy Grail* tend to suffer similar fates. The woman turning the pages of "The Book of the Film" is snatched away by a beast, the Famous Historian is killed outright, and here the narrator is violently cut off in mid-explanation. These characters are set up to be omniscient, extra-diegetic influences that can act or comment upon the narrative being presented, but are also seemingly above the fray, so to speak. Not so, this moment of violence tells us. If there is a consistent trope or set of topoi the Pythons employ it is the fact that every presented reality can be undercut, reinformed and re-formed, leaving no stable narrative ground. This is actually what acculturated Python audiences have come to expect as they watched this film, as well. As will be seen, the end result is both a presentation and a world negated; the hand of the policeman covers the lens, the camera "falls," and by some fantastical linking of spatially and temporally distinct elements the projector for "us" also fails, and the film stock slips out of the gate.

In *The Goon Show* and *Flying Circus*, linkmen were particularly prone to abuse. There, such characters were punched, run over by cars, squashed by sixteen-ton weights or a giant hammer, blown up, or just shot dead.[47]

The starling—yet another bird in the Python bestiary—features prominently in *The Goon Show* episode "The Starlings" from 31 August 1954. This continuing character fascination with minutiae (birds, ants, termites) also comes from *Flying Circus*, where characters like Herbert Mental (Jones) collect bird watchers' eggs hoping for an appearance on *Man Alive* (Ep. 26), and well-regarded playwrights like Neville Shunte create murder mysteries based on hyperaccurate train timetables (Ep. 25).

Notes

1. The wolf is *not* included as part of the real or imagined bestiary described by Malory in *Le Morte D'Arthur*, meaning the knights weren't plagued by these creatures as they sought the Grail. Wolves are mentioned sparingly in the lengthy Malorian text, but only metaphorically ("I liken you to a wolf") or magically, as in a man turned into a "werewolf" for seven years. See *LMD'A*, 2.94 and 2.451, respectively.

2. The script sequence reads: *More louder closer howling. He grips his sword valiantly and as he glances around a flash of lightning reveals the silhouette of a huge terrifying castle, perhaps looking rather derelict. He makes up his mind in an instant and stumbles manfully towards it.* This castle, by the way, is not Doune (where most of the Castle Anthrax scene's interiors would be shot), or Stalker, where the final scenes of the film are set, but Bodiam Castle. Bodiam is the castle mentioned in the script early on as an example

of the type of castle the Pythons are thinking of when they call for a castle in the script. See the "Swallows" scene above for more on this castle, and how the Pythons had hoped to use it.

3. From a 5 December 2013 e-mail correspondence between the author and Doyle.

4. "Pledge by Mr Morley on 'Merrie England,'" *Times*, 11 December 1973: 8.

5. "Saxophonists in Contrast," *Times*, 10 August 1967: 5.

6. Another member of Grimms, poet/musician Roger McGough, had already been mentioned in the script for *MPFC* Ep. 37, as a character name for Idle (*MPFC: UC*, 2.136). It's likely Idle contributed the "Zoot" name to the script.

7. "Clowns on the Road," *Times*, 10 December 1974: 9.

8. Listen to the audio track for Palin, Cleese, and Idle in the 2001 DVD edition.

9. This same *Casino Royale* castle features a "lone Scots piper" on the battlements; the piper will reappear in Ep. 38's "The Kamikaze Highlanders" sketch, there played by Chapman.

10. "Organisms Sensitive to Penicillin," *Times*, 11 December 1943: 2. Pasteur had created inoculations for anthrax as early as 1881.

11. "House of Commons," *Times*, 5 December 1952: 2. The sitting minister was Sir Thomas Dugdale (1897–1977).

12. "Sheep Riddle Persists," *Times*, 4 April 1968: 4; "US Keeping Big Stocks of Biological Weapons," *Times*, 21 September 1970: 1. Nerve gas would leak again after an accident at Dugway in December 1969. All of these incidents—as well as the U.S. "assistance" to West Germany in the area of biological and chemical warfare—received significant coverage in British newspapers.

13. According to Palin, Jones and Palin started writing the script that would become *Holy Grail* on 20 March 1973 (*Diaries 1969–1979*, 111).

14. "Scientist Held in Germ Blackmail Case," *Times*, 23 November 1973: 6.

15. In *The Sword in the Stone*, alternately, it is the dreamy prospect of a soft feather bed—meant just for sleeping—that drives the fruitlessly questing King Pellinore.

16. Gilliam will use an image of Vincent de Beauvais in the "Tale of Sir Launcelot" animated section later. See that entry for more.

17. A monastery that houses both men and women.

18. The word *subtilioribus* in other editions translated as "fine" as opposed to "elaborate."

19. Tuchman, 106.

20. Tuchman, 101–7.

21. A character in Gilliam's *Time Bandits* is also named Winston. He is the shipmaster ogre played by Peter Vaughan.

22. In Ep. 23, "Fish Licence" and "Derby Council vs. All Blacks Rugby Match," the pomp and circumstance of the coronation is lampooned, as are the Dimbleby announcers. See *MPFC: UC*, 1.356. The Goons also have fun with the coronation and its stately gravitas.

23. Doyle does remember that "once settled in" at Doune, things got better, schedule-wise (e-mail correspondence with the author, 10 December, 2013). For him, the first days out at Castle Stalker were the "nightmare" days of the shoot. See those entries below.

24. They did these recordings with principal cast members as required in postproduction. The Black Knight, for example, needed to be almost completely dubbed by Cleese, and especially when the one-legged stand-in was in the costume. "All right, we'll call it a draw" is an ADR line, for example.

25. Listen to Jones's audio commentary on the DVD and Blu-ray editions of the film.

26. From Michael Billington's review of the play for the *Times*, dated 29 April 1967: 7. Wood was later profiled—and his work, including *Dingo*, discussed—in the *Times* on 8 March 1972 (page 13).

27. For coverage of this speech see the *Times* section on Parliament, 18 February 1966: 8.

28. Playwright Osborne (1929–1994) is discussed a number of times in *MPFC: UC*, as he was allied with the postwar "Angry Young Man" movement in the arts in Britain. See *MPFC: UC*, 1.35–38, 49, and 53.

29. The Theatres Act 1968 can be read at the National Archives, http://www.legislation.gov.uk/ukpga/1968/54.

30. Listen to the Jones and Gilliam audio comments on the 2012 Blu-ray edition of the film for more.

31. See *MPFC: UC*, 2.125, "morass of filth" entry, for more on Sidney's move away from Petrarchan "chaste love from afar" to the more Ovidian (earthy, lusty) descriptions of his Penelope, which is wryly ironic given Sidney's role in Ep. 36 as a "fighter of filth," an anti-pornography campaigner. This longer sketch, along with others including "*Njorl's Saga*" (Ep. 27) and "Dennis Moore" (Ep. 37) are tune-ups for *MPHG*.

32. From *The Complete Works of Francois Villon,* translated by Anthony Bonner, 107. Selections are also included in Bishop's *Horizon Book of the Middle Ages*, 294–95.

33. Launcelot, by the way, is spelled "Lancelot" and "Launcelot" on this same page. Again, this likely indicates several hands at the typewriter as the script was banged out.

34. See *MPFC: UC*, 1.134, the "irrelevant, isn't it" entry for examples of this almost instant appropriation.

35. What Barbara Tuchman calls "a jeremiad on the corruptions of the age" (509).

36. See the entry for John Gower in *The Cambridge History of English and American Literature*, Volume II, *The End of the Middle Ages*. http://www.bartleby.com/212/0601.html

37. Gower, *Vox Clamantis*, book 4, chapter 11, in Stockton, *The Major Latin Works of John Gower*, 176.

38. Bors himself is smitten temporarily blind just after this encounter with the old man, and a heavenly voice tells him: "Go hence, thou Sir Bors, for as yet thou art not worthy for to be in this place" (*LMD'A*, 198–99). Bors isn't sinful, but he also isn't spiritually ready for a higher glory.

39. Meaning "sexual" or "excretory things"; see Randall's *IMGM*, plates CIX through CXIII for examples, as well as entries for the "Title Sequence Animation" above (specifically, see notes on the "arse trumpeters").

40. In Ep. 33 of *MPFC*, a man (Jones) reads through the "show so far" to help viewers get up to speed (*JTW*, 2.131).

41. Though in the *film* as finished Launcelot—as his "*eyes light up with holy inspiration*"—mentions the potential rescue might be "the sign that leads" them to the Grail, which also serves to satisfy Launcelot's already-mentioned idiomatic needs.

42. Gower, *Vox Clamantis* book 4, chapter 11, in Stockton, *The Major Latin Works of John Gower*, 176. Chaucer had called his friend "moral Gower," affectionately and appropriately, in his dedication to *Troilus and Criseyde* (c. 1385).

43. *Spamalot* is also a return of the "multiple Grail" element found in Mitchison's 1955 novel *To the Chapel Perilous*, and which the original screenplay for *MPHG* embraced. With the exception of a Grail hinted at by the French Sentry (he's likely teasing), there is only one Grail being sought in the finished film.

44. For more on Edward II (and Gaveston) see Holmes, *The Later Middle Ages*, and McKisack, *The Fourteenth Century*.

45. For example, in the "Blind Soothsayer" scene that follows.

46. The "Lemon curry" interjections are discussed in *MPFC: UC*, 2.155, while the Knight and Rubber Chicken recurring motif—appearing in Eps. 2, 3, 5, 7, 9, and 13—in *MPFC: UC*, 1.23, 41, 153, and 206. There are myriad such time-and-space-fracturing interjections in *MPFC*; in *MPHG*, the modern world scenes/characters act in a similar capacity, and are likely less obtrusive, since they have their own narrative trajectory parallel to the quest. If the truly fractured structure of the original script had been kept—back and forth between medieval England, 1960s New York, Africa, modern England and Italy, and in and out of department stores—*Holy Grail* would have been a very different film indeed, and much akin to the *MPFC* series.

47. In "The White Neddie Trade" (3 February 1958), Neddie is shot by John Snagge as he tries to usurp Greenslade's announcing duties.

ANIMATION / LIVE ACTION SCENE 24

This transition to the Soothsayer scene looks as if it were planned for a mixture of live action and animation, but the animated portion either wasn't included or was never produced—likely the latter. Gilliam displays some bits of incomplete animation during his DVD commentary, including a castle being built, and there are semi-finished scenes of animation backgrounds illustrated in the "centerfold" color pages (between salmon pages 46 and 47) of *MPHGB*, but Gilliam provides no commentary or captioning on these works-in-progress. There is no description in the printed script as to what may have been included in this section, unless the entire Soothsayer scene was set to be a mix of live action and animation. See the entries for Facing Page 46 (a "centerfold" section) in appendix A ("Facing Pages") for discussions of these illustrations.

If the scene were truly to have been a mix of live action and animation, there were precedents for such work in *Flying Circus*, and the process—"colour separation"—is even commented upon by Mr. Praline (Cleese) in Ep. 18.[1] Moments in *MPFC* where either the Pythons enter the animated world or animated characters intrude on the real world (as will be seen later in *MPHG*, when the Legendary Beast appears), include the chase sequence in the "Escape (from Film)" section of the "Society for Putting Things on Top of Other Things" sketch (Ep. 18), where "live" versions of the Pythons interact (in a limited way) with an animated world. Earlier, in an animated sequence in Ep. 17, a "five frog curse" is cured by turning the animated frogs into Gumbies, who then announce the "Chemist Sketch"; in Ep. 26, a Babycham deer in an animated world appears with two live models (Gilliam and Cleveland) sporting "Hercules Hold-Em-In" trusses; and by Ep. 34, Gilliam is inserting animated dancing monsters into the live backgrounds of Mr. Pither's adventures in "The Cycling Tour."[2] In the latter example, the characters do not interact with the real world—they hide until it's safe to emerge.

"Sir Lancelot saves Sir Gallahad from almost certain temptation"—(PSC) On this "Book of the Film"–type page, both "Lancelot" and "Gallahad" are oddly spelled, at least compared to how the names generally appear in the printed script ("Launcelot" and "Galahad"). The "Galahad" name was also spelled with the double-l earlier, in the "Book of the Film" section, meaning Gilliam or his assistants (or Doyle) continued this different spelling.

Misspellings were part of the everyday production process during the run of *Flying Circus*. Personal names, geographical items, and brand names[3] could be misspelled, and those misspellings—though usually confined to internal BBC memos and records—also found their way into the weekly shows. In a sure sign the show was actually seen as "rubbish" through its first four episodes, Michael Palin's name is even misspelled in BBC memos for Ep. 2 (*MPFC: UC*, 1.32).

Scene 24—The illuminated manuscript version of the "Scene 24" page is fashioned after border designs in Evelyn Paul's work. See the entry above for the "Book of the Film" section for more on Paul's World War I–era retro manuscript styles. The leaf and vine patterns on the left leg of the design, including the curling tendril at the top left, are modeled after those found in the manuscript Royal 17 E.VII, which Randall includes several times in *IMGM*. Once again, as in the "Book of the Film" section earlier, Gilliam has used still photos (likely developed versions of screen or frame captures) in the illuminated manuscript's pages, which would be a rather startling anachronism if we weren't prepared for such things by this time in the film. The "beast" hand now turns the pages—no sign of the young woman.

Notes

1. *MPFC: UC*, 1.280.

2. See "*Animation: Bouncing on a naked lady, Jack and the Beanstalk, and Five Frog Curse*" in notes for Ep. 17, *MPFC: UC*, 1.264; see *MPFC: UC*, 1.386 for the Babycham animal; and view the final scene of Ep. 34 for more, respectively.

3. "Mrs. Korobro" should have been "Mrs. Korobko" (*MPFC: UC*, 1.245); it's "Hunslet" and not "Hunslett" (1.215); "Mary Bignall" should have been "Mary Bignal Rand" (1.174); throughout there are mistakes like "Coelocanth," "germoline," "Cincinnatti," "Bartcowicz," and "Anne Zeigler." "Cincinnatti" made it into Ep. 10 as part of a newspaper graphic—it was misspelled in the printed script and then on the newspaper prop. Some typist (maybe one of the Pythons) even managed to misspell "Magdalene" as "Madgalene," even though three of the Pythons attended Cambridge. See the *MPFC: UC* index for all these entries.

SCENE TWENTY
THE BLIND SOOTHSAYER OR "SCENE 24"

ARTHUR and BEDEVERE in the depths of a dark forest with an old blind Soothsayer—On the day scheduled to film this scene they were obviously far away from a suitable "dark forest" and had no inclination to return to one for a new camera setup. It looks as if they found instead an abandoned stone dwelling on the south shores of Loch Tay, north and east of where Castle Stalker is located.[1] This is also one of the myriad camera setups Jones had planned for the first days of shooting, a schedule that nearly broke the production's back, according to Doyle.[2] The dark, mysterious, gallimaufric interior is most likely created by one or two actual walls and then screens or drapes to block the light, accompanied by plenty of cluttered set dressing—if the interiors were shot on location at all.[3] In the Prince Valiant comic *The Prophecy* (first published in 1937), Horrit the Starving Witch brings Val into her hovel to tell his future. The light from a "peat ember" fire between Val and the witch is very similar to the firelit scene the Pythons create. The Soothsayer tells of an enchanter, a hidden cave, and the Bridge of Death; the cackling witch warns that Val will have to "confront the unicorn, the dragon and the griffon" soon, then orders him out of her sight. Arthur and Bedevere will finally be in the "dark forest" when they are somehow transported away from the Soothsayer's hut, part of the forest realm of the Knights Who Say Ni.

This scene between Arthur, Bedevere, and the blind Soothsayer is also reminiscent of the "witch" scenes from various *Macbeth* productions, including both Polanski's and Kurosawa's film versions. Polanski begins his film with images of the three weird sisters on a lonely beach in Wales and then introduces dozens of witches in the portentous cauldron scene later.[4] Kurosawa and his cowriters decided to reduce many seers to one. Washizu (Macbeth) and Miki (Banquo) meet this spectral figure as they wander through Spider's Web Forest looking for their lord's castle. The singular spirit turns a spinning wheel like a wheel of fortune as she prophesies.

(he stares into the blind eyes of the OLD MAN)—(PSC) This is a parenthetical in the script, sandwiched between spoken lines. In *Macbeth*, which the Pythons have clearly referenced in the look and "feel" of *Holy Grail*, the "lead" witch[5] has no eyes at all. Tiresias (of *Oedipus the King* and *Antigone* fame) was a blind seer, as is one of the characters from the film *The Seven Faces of Dr. Lao* (1964),[6] the painfully truthful soothsayer Apollonius of Tyana.

SOOTHSAYER: "He knows of a cave . . . a cave which no man has entered"—There is such a cave in the Hal Foster *Prince Valiant Fights Attila the Hun* comic (1939–1940), guarded by a witch and inside, by Father Time. The witch entices the headstrong young Val with a mocking challenge:

> "This is the Trophy-Room of Time. Here must all men and all things some day come, however unwillingly. Yet none dares enter it before his time."
>
> "I dare any adventure!" And the impulsive lad hitched up his sword belt and strode, somewhat unsteadily, into the deeps of the silent, gloomy cave. A cold, weird glow illuminated this mischancy place and he made out, at the far end, the bent figure of a frail old man seated forlornly on a throne. About him, in great crumbling heaps, lay the dusty wreckage of the treasures wrought by men. From ages beyond all remembering they were, worn and mouldering. Here lay the crowns of kings, mingled with the crutches of beggars and the loot of thieves, and all looked the same at last. Then Val shuddered, for a cold fear suddenly gripped him at the sight of all this hideous ruin. He stopped before the old man. (20–22)[7]

Val has met Father Time, and of course challenges him, only to lose years of his life with every attempted assault. Val will stagger away, his youth to reclaim as he drinks from a cup the witch gives him. "The next instant he rushed headlong from the cave, leaped upon his waiting horse and galloped away" (25).

SOOTHSAYER: "Gorge of Eternal Peril"—This naming (along with the "Bridge of Death") is again a direct borrow from the romances and the comic books inspired by them. In *Prince Valiant*, the sorceress Morgan Le Fey lives in the castle Dolorous Garde (from whence Val must rescue Gawain), while the Siege Perilous is the seat at the Round Table only one knight can fill—the knight who achieves the Grail—to all others the seat is fatal. In Malory's version can be found (or avoided) a Chapel Perilous, a Forest Perilous, a Port of Perilous Rock, a Pass Perilous, and all manner of diverse parlous passages and even "periloust" knights.

SOOTHSAYER: ". . .which no man has ever crossed"—When Macbeth hears that "None of woman born shall harm Macbeth," he naturally assumes this means he's virtually inviolate (he's not). These kinds of pronouncements in this genre generally mean someone's about to transcend the auguring—someone *will* sit in the Siege Perilous, somehow the Forest of Birnam *will* uproot itself and move, the Bridge of Death *will* be crossed, the Gorge of Eternal Peril *will* be transcended, etc. Both Macbeth and Arthur take these prophetic utterances of challenges seemingly insurmountable as surmountable, and press forward.

The OLD MAN laughs sinisterly and mockingly—The Soothsayer never answers any question directly, unlike the weird sisters in Polanski's (and Shakespeare's) *Macbeth*. The witches are evasive, cryptic, and allusive, yes, but they (or their "masters") will answer direct questions:

> Macbeth: I conjure you, by that which you profess, howe'er you come to know it, answer me to what I ask you!
>
> First Witch: Speak.
>
> Second Witch: Demand.
>
> Third Witch: We'll answer.[8]

The apparitions then tell Macbeth to be wary of Macduff, to not fear any man born of woman, and that he cannot fall unless the forest "come against him." Macbeth even asks what he should not (about Banquo's heir), is warned by the witches to stop asking, but they answer anyway. They're quite helpful after all. The Pythons' Soothsayer is never this directly helpful, though he offers valuable directions. In the *Dr. Lao* film[9] and book, Apollonius answers direct questions (When will I strike oil? When will I remarry?) with blunt directness—

"Never" to both—and then prophesies a miserable life of seclusion and loneliness followed by a nondescript death. In the film the woman who paid her nickel hustles out crying, as Apollonius apologizes wearily for being honest. In the book, the woman responds to the seer's dark prophesies by ignoring them almost entirely, and even tells him they would make a good couple:

> "We would get on splendidly, you and I; I am sure of it!"
> "I'm not. I told you there were no more men in your life. Don't try to make me eat my own words, please. The consultation is ended. Good afternoon."
> She started to say more, but there was no longer anyone to talk to. Apollonius had vanished with that suddenness commanded by only the most practiced magicians. (*The Circus of Dr. Lao*, 87–88)

The weird sisters also "laugh sinisterly and mockingly" in the Polanski film—"By the pricking of my thumbs, / Something wicked this way comes" (4.1.1572–73)—when Macbeth revisits their cavern, looking for confirmation of their earlier prophecies. In *Throne of Blood*, there is mocking laughter as Washizu and Miki ride through the forest—hopelessly lost, shooting arrows at laughing specters—and then singing from the witch.

As they touch the doorposts they just flake away into dust. The whole hut is rotten. It collapses—(PSC) The transition in the script is quite different from that as achieved in the finished film. The script called for the following after Arthur asks again about the Bridge leading to the Grail:

> The OLD MAN laughs sinisterly and mockingly. They look down and he is gone. They stand up. Suddenly behind them is a noise. They turn sharply. In the door of the little hut is a cat. It miaows and is gone.[10] They slowly back out of the hut. As they touch the doorposts. (*MPHGB*, 43)

This amount of set construction and destruction was clearly not in the film's meager budget, so the Soothsayer's hut merely disappears from around them—a cheap and age-old camera trick—and they appear in the forest where the next peril can begin almost immediately. Also, as this scene was noted in the final script as a combination of live action and animation, it may be that these effects were to be achieved with animation, and not with props and set-building. *The Quest of the Holy Grail* provided the literary precedent for this type of magical moment when Perceval nearly falls for a temptress but, espying the red cross on his sword, he comes to his senses: "He made the sign of the cross on his forehead and immediately the tent collapsed about him and he was shrouded in a cloud of blinding smoke, while so foul a stench pervaded everything that he thought he must be in hell" (*THG*, 155).[11]

And the witches from Polanski's version of *Macbeth*—a movie that had clearly influenced the look the Pythons were going for in this medieval story—have to be considered here. At the beginning of the film Banquo and Macbeth are accosted by these "weird sisters." Their stone dwelling is as ramshackle as the Soothsayer's, and as "imperfect speakers" they taunt and confuse Macbeth and Banquo ("Lesser than Macbeth, and greater"), just as the Soothsayer answers direct questions with sideways answers. Also, even though we and Macbeth see the ladies disappear through a closing door, Macbeth tells Banquo that the weird women vanished "into the air," causing Banquo to smile at the jest. Macbeth goes on, craftily: "And what seemed corporal melted, as breath into the wind." Banquo stops smiling, uncertain what to believe. In Scene 24, we don't see the Soothsayer vanish before us, nor do we see (as the script hints) that he's become a cat—he's gone, the hovel is gone, and Arthur and Bedevere are alone in a forest. The Soothsayer at least points Arthur and Bedevere toward the Enchanter and the Bridge of Death—and the knights will encounter both, eventually. The weird sisters prick Macbeth's mind, offering no ready answers, just the certainty that Macbeth will try them again.

In the door of the little hut is a cat. It miaows and is gone—(PSC) The intimation here is that the Soothsayer may have shape-shifted into feline form, which is another borrow from White's *The Sword in the Stone*. There, Wart is able to live as a fish, an ant, a merlin, an owl, a goose, and a badger, all thanks to Merlyn's magic. Merlyn accompanies him on some of these adventures, including into the moat. The Pythons have already borrowed mannerisms for Bedevere and a penchant for ant minutiae from this same book. Instead of having to wrangle a cat, though (an animal greatly mistreated in the Python world), a simple match cut takes Arthur and Bedevere from the Soothsayer's hovel to a forest setting.

The reliance on versions of the darkly magical *Macbeth* can be seen here as well, though this *Holy Grail* scene was not completed as written. In the first scene of the fourth act of Shakespeare's *Macbeth* the three Witches—not exiting, but entering—mark a cat's call: "Thrice the brinded cat hath mew'd" (4.1.1526). Macbeth will ask of and be shown his future (as will the unfortunate woman in *Dr. Lao*), and the witches will disappear as the vision ends, leaving him alone. In the *Dr. Lao* film, the crying old woman runs from the tent, only to stop and check her face in her "cruel" mirror.

Spooky music. They are thoroughly shaken, and they begin to hear noises of people moving in the forest around them—(PSC) For the medieval man the forest could indeed be a frightening place, though supposedly not so for a king. Washizu and Miki, for example, find a great deal to fear as they are lost in the great forest approaching Cobweb (or Forest) Castle. But first, the Wart. In *The Sword in the Stone*, the Wart becomes lost in the Forest Sauvage as he searches for Hob's hawk; there he encounters giants, fairies, a Questing Beast, and even Morgan Le Fay and the magical Merlyn before his adventures are complete. (Author T. H. White had described his approach to the book as a kind of wish fulfillment—a fantasy world he wished he could have experienced as a child, so fear didn't enter into it, instead wonder.[12]) According to Fossier, the average Middle Ages man, though, encountered the forest as an "overwhelming" and "sacred" place:

> The nearby forest weighed on the minds of the living; it was the indomitable domain of Nature, regenerated with every springtime, a place where certain trees grew whose life span was much longer than humans'. It was the sacred part of Creation, the part that could not be approached without a religious shudder because everything in it was strange and unknowable: its perfumes, its noises, the beasts who lived in it or who were thought to live in it. Along uncertain paths, thorns and barbs caught the traveler; fallen tree trunks hindered his progress; hidden quagmires lay in wait for him. These were the snares of the Evil One. (175–76)

And then there were the creatures, of course, and of all kinds, which Arthur and Bedevere obviously fear as they cast about in their own murky wood for:

> elves, goblins, trolls. . . . More to the south, they were called fairies, dragons, *tarasques*, and troops of fauns, sprites, and green dwarfs served Pan. All these were in league to bewitch and deceive credulous and fearful humans. One might stay in the forest for several days shaking with terror, as did a German emperor of the eleventh century, without finding a way out; the forest was where hated princes or lords were assassinated, where bandits lurked, and where one encountered such strange phenomena as pierced rocks, the remains of megaliths, and fairy circles. (176)

The forest could also be a source of wood for fires and for building homes and fences, a place for pigs to grow fat foraging for acorns, but also a hiding spot for bandit clans or the runaway serf; the forest helped define Britain, importantly, according to H. R. Loyn, who saw that "the story of Anglo-Saxon settlement, when looked at in depth, yields more of the saga of man against the forest than of Saxon against Celt. It was a colonizing movement in the true sense of the word" (quoted in Sawyer, 133). But, "[t]he lot of the forest dweller was a hard one," according to Poole (*DBMC*, 32). And though he might have the privilege (that he paid for) to "turn his pigs and cattle to graze" and "take dead wood for fuel and for the repair of his cottage," his access was greatly circumscribed and prey to his lord's whim: "At every turn he was subjected to harsh restrictions and petty annoyances" (32). Arthur's time in the forest is going to be no less discomfiting; not subjected to a lord's petty justice, but to the silly demands of powerful knights.

The forest might have been both frightening and fecund for the peasant, but in the early Middle Ages forests were the kings' pleasure domains, one royal benefit that seems to have eluded Arthur. By Henry II's reign, nearly one-third of all of southern England had been declared game-preserve lands, meaning the wood and animals and products of these vast stretches could be exploited solely by the king or with the king's permission (Poole, *DBMC*, 29). By the middle of the thirteenth century all of the sprawling county of Essex, for example, was considered royal forest (28, map). In the late twelfth-century "Dialogue of the Exchequer," Lord High Treasurer Richard Fitz Neal (d. 1198) describes the royal forests in majestic terms—they were the "sanctuary and special delight of kings, where, laying aside their cares, they withdraw to refresh themselves with a little hunting; there, away from the turmoils inherent in a court, they breathe the pleasure of natural freedom" (29). These would be the forests belonging to Henry II, of course, representing the *real* world of twelfth-century England. At this point in *Holy Grail*, however, Arthur and Bedevere happen to be traipsing through the *legendary* version of England, one where the forest isn't populated by roe or wild boar, but by lurking creatures of magic and malevolence, the kind of forest that Washizu and Miki fear they've entered, perhaps never to leave. They hear the cackling laughter of the "evil spirits" holding them there, and then they meet the spinning, soothsaying witch, who tells them of certain inevitabilities.

Scene to scene, Arthur's quest can't be certain which reality they'll encounter—the mythical, the Middle Ages, or the modern. In some scenes all three can be found. For Arthur and company, this forest will provide the Knights Who Say Ni, their powerful, charming words of force, and their demands for aligned shrubbery that both haunt them and successfully sidetrack their quest for a time.

Notes

1. This is where they will film the final scenes of the charge toward the Grail Castle, only to have the police arrest them. The Soothsayer's hovel and the hard rock mine doubling as the Cave of Caerbannog are in fairly close proximity here on the south side of Loch Tay, well north of Stirling.

2. From a 4 December 2013 e-mail correspondence with production manager/cameraman Doyle.

3. In the establishing shot (a slow zoom that shows the jumbled rock hovel—sans roof—smoke, a chicken, and the "horses" [servants] pawing around) the anachronistic wooden bureau that will be next to the Soothsayer inside the hut is here outside, against a stone wall. In the scene in *Macbeth* where the witches prophesy to Banquo and Macbeth, there is a goat wandering around the similarly jumbled, smoky cavern yard.

4. In the Shakespeare text, the first Polanski scene is also at the beginning, 1.1; the cauldron scene is 4.1 in Shakespeare.

5. In the film, Polanski gives many of the most portentous lines to this blind witch; Shakespeare had divvied them up a bit more fairly.

6. Directed by George Pal, and based on the book *The Circus of Dr. Lao* (1935) by Charles G. Finney.

7. Text from the 1952 book-form reprint.

8. In the *Riverside Shakespeare* (1974) this is found in 4.1.1579-1580 and 1590-1593. A good part of Macbeth's speech in between has been cut.

9. Pal's film *The Seven Faces of Dr. Lao* was appearing on British television as early as May 1972, and regularly thereafter through the mid-1970s.

10. See below for more on the mysterious cat.

11. In *Throne of Blood*, the film starts on the spot where the castle *used* to stand, grim markers left as warnings; then, pushing back time, the castle appears out of the mist, and the story is told.

12. Gallix, *Letters to a Friend*, 93–95.

THE KNIGHTS WHO SAY "NI"

TALL KNIGHT OF NI—There are quite a few giants in Malory's work, with most simply being nasty, thieving omnivores. There are a few, however, who manage to rate more characterization. Lamorak is stranded on the Isle of Servage, and the "lord of that isle hight Sir Nabon le Noire, [was] a great mighty giant" who also happened to nurture a hatred for "all the knights of King Arthur's" (*LMD'A*, 1.369–70). In Howard Pyle's illustrated version of this story, Tristram is told the familiar tale of this "black knight":

> The present lord of that island is *a very wicked and cruel knight, huge of frame and big of limb*, hight Sir Nabon surnamed le Noir. One time the noble and gentle knight who was my husband was the lord of that island and the castle thereon. . . . But one evil day when I and my lord were together upon that island, this Sir Nabon came thither by night, and with certain evil-disposed folk of the island he overcame my lord and slew him very treacherously. Me also he would have slain, or else have taken into shameful captivity, but, hearing the noise of that assault in which my lord was slain, I happily escaped, and so, when night had come, I got away from that island with several attendants who were faithful to me, and thus came to this castle where we are. Since that time Sir Nabon has held that castle as his own, ruling it in a very evil fashion. For you are to know that the castle sits very high upon the crags overlooking the sea, and whenever a vessel passeth by that way, *Sir Nabon goeth forth to meet it; and upon some of these crafts he levies toll*, and other ships he sinks after slaying the mariners and sailor-folk. . . . And if anyone is by chance cast ashore upon that island, that one he either slays or holds for ransom, or makes thereof a slave for to serve him.[1]

Like the Tall Knight of Ni, Nabon is not only large and frightening, he also demands payment (or simply takes it) of unfortunate travelers. With the help of Tristram, Nabon and his wicked son are eventually destroyed, and the wrongs righted.

As for the word "Ni," Palin, for example has mentioned this is a borrow from the Goons. This is true, in spirit, but in the one hundred sixty-odd surviving recorded *Goon Show* episodes, there is *no* utterance of the word "Ni" (pronounced "nee").[2] There are many, many nonsense words and sounds (and words that sound onomatopoeic) like "f'tang" (heard later in *MPHG*), or "hern," "fon," "spon," "plugee," "krurker," "sapristi," "plon," and the phrases "needle nardle noo" and "ying-tong-iddle-eye-po" that the Goons do employ—"ni" is not one of them.[3] In the episode "Quatermass OBE,"[4] for example, announcer Andrew Timothy soberly reads words like "ting-tong-billy-bong" and "f'tang" (the latter much like a Hollywood Western gunshot sound effect), followed by Wallace Greenslade intoning "the flin of the flongs, the clums the nib of the plume" (or very nearly that). And, the Pythons may actually have been reverencing the Goons but quoting themselves, since they had used "Ni" earlier in the second *MPFZ* episode (1972), produced for Bavarian television, as part of the song "Ya Tee Buckety." A portion of the chorus (sung by the townspeople with the king) is "Ni, ni, ni!" "F'tang" is also part of one of these nonsense songs.[5]

An extraordinary TALL KNIGHT in all black (possibly John with Mike on his shoulders)— (PSC) In the written script, the Tall Knight is to have walked up to them, his "heavy footfall" putting fear into their hearts. Palin does not stand on Cleese's shoulders, but on a platform built for the shot, meaning he can't move.[6] This character is one of a handful *seen* in the world of the film that may qualify as supernatural, or fantastical. Another is the Legendary Beast, discussed later. There are also two drawings of dragon figures, both used in relation to manuscript elements. The first is the feathered, long-necked dragon set in relation to "The Book of the Film" titles page, and the other is a version of this same dragon employed as an initial letter *R* for the "Tale of Sir Robin" frontispiece. Both of these are discussed in detail earlier.

Mentions in the film of such fantastical creatures include the dangerous "Chicken of Bristol" and the "Dragon of Angnor," both nearly foes of Sir Robin mentioned in the "Book of the Film" section. Together these are the kinds of creatures (some quasi-human, some animal, many hybrids) that occupy the margins of many Gothic illuminated manuscripts, as well as the wild horizon areas of *mappaemundi* like the Hereford Map, and the edges of the world.[7] From Camporesi:

> People's fears were exorcised by dumping them on those who inhabited the edges of the known world, who were lesser in some sense; whether troglodytes or pygmies. The centre (*Roma caput mundi*) could not tolerate the thought that the object of horror might not take root like nasty infection in the ghettos of the more distant suburbs of the world. Moreover, even nowadays, the *bidonvilles* of the outskirts are felt to be infected zones, where all kinds of monstrosities are possible, and where a different man is born, an aberrant from the prototype who inhabits the centre of things. (*The Incorruptible Flesh*, 79)

And while it's evident that the Grail quest itself is one that sends its adherents into unfamiliar and possibly dangerous corners of their "England," the fact that the British Isles are depicted on these maps as existing "within the liminal band at the edge of the *mappaemundi*"[8]—where these creatures were said to exist—the surprise might be in *not* encountering some of these fantastic creatures on this quest. The Legendary Beast is one such creature, perfectly at home in a dank cave at the edge of their travels, as well as in a Britain existing on the edge of the known world.

Salopian slang—(PSC) This is an odd aside meant for the reader of the script and no one else, and referring to Arthur and Patsy being shocked by the appearance of the giant knight. They are described as "*wazzing like mad*." The scene directions continue:

> *Salopian slang, meaning very scared, almost to the point of wetting oneself, e.g. before an important football match or prior to a postering. Salopian slang meaning a beating by the school praeposters. Sorry about the Salopian slant to this stage direction—Ed.* (43)

Arthur is then parenthetically described as being "*wazzed stiff*" as he is confronted by the looming knight who will say "Ni." Salopian is a name meaning "from or of Shropshire," according to the *OED*, and the praeposters would have been older boys in charge of younger boys at school. Discipline would have been part of the older boys' daily duties. Palin attended Shrewsbury School in Shrewsbury, Shropshire, and more than likely contributed this note. (*Private Eye* cofounders Christopher Booker and Richard Ingrams also attended Shrewsbury.)

TALL KNIGHT: ". . .Sacred Words. Ni . . . Peng . . . and Neee . . . Wom!"—Again, these are nonsense words that would seem to have no power or meaning, but this is the Pythons' world. Later, the seemingly harmless word "it" takes on powerful connotations against the Knights of Ni. In *MPFC*, simple words like "mattress" have power. In Ep. 8, a young couple has been warned to not say "mattress" to one of the salesmen—they slip and say it anyway, and the man immediately puts a bag over his head:

> The young married couple here have transgressed the laws of the sketch world—she's mentioned the unmentionable word—and all participants must endure even more elaborate rituals to set things right. This also exhibits once again the power of language and the presence of shibboleths in Python's *oeuvre*. Use (or abuse) of even a single word can send Python narratives off in wildly different directions, or can immediately "out" an interloper like a woman or anyone who doesn't understand the internal logic of the situation. In an animation for Ep. 2, for example, Rodin's "Thinker" disappears when his thought bubble ("I think, therefore I am") is popped—he can't exist without those words. See . . . Brian's badly memorized but beatific phrases in *Life of Brian*, or even the power of assuming Brian's name at the end of the film, when a man is saved from crucifixion just by saying, "I'm Brian!" (*MPFC: UC*, 1.135)

"Mattress" is a word of power, of course, while simple, recognizable idiomatic phrases such as "no time to lose" can be evacuated, emptied out, and purposely not refilled:

> In Ep. 8, the word "mattress" has been connected not to something to sleep on, but to a ritualized set of bizarre behaviors enacted by Mr. Lambert (Chapman) and counteracted by his coworkers, where the "something to sleep on" is to be known as a "dog kennel." Later, in Ep. 38, the phrase "No time to lose" will be worried over until it becomes meaninglessness, completely detached from its context, its connotative and denotative moorings, as Man (Palin) can't even figure out which word or syllable to stress, and the RSM (Jones) doesn't recognize the phrase at all. Successful communication, therefore, continues to evade most person-to-person transactions in the Python world.
>
> The Goons kick started this word-worrying in one of Milligan's more cerebral episodes, "Six Charlies in Search of an Author," where characters are controlled by and can control narrative trajectories simply by controlling the typewriter. In one exchange, the meaninglessness of word associations in a typical sentence is pointed up, as the speakers simply emphasize (put an accent on) different words:
>
> Ned (Secombe): (*gulps*) I haven't got any bones.
>
> Grytpype-Thynne (Sellers): Nonsense, nonsense, you'd fall down without them. You'd fall DOWN without them.
>
> Ned: You'd fall down without THEM.
>
> Grytpype-Thynne: YOU'D fall down without them.
>
> Peter (Sellers): Take yer choice. (*The Goon Show*, 26 December 1956)
>
> The concept is based, of course, on Pirandello's Modernist masterpiece play *Six Characters in Search of an Author*, from 1921, a reflexive work quite influential to the Pythons. (*MPFC: UC*, 1.254–55)

And in the *Goon Show* episode "The Chinese Legs," a new word is created:

> American Preacher (Sellers): . . . It is written in red, friends! Thou shalt not overdraw(er)! There is a new word—a new word of hope! And the word is . . .

Mueller (Milligan): (*quietly*) "Fon."

Preacher: Yes, "Fon!" This word "Fon" was invented by Mr. Tom Danglers of Quax!

Tom Danglers (Secombe): Yes, for many years now, I have felt the need for a new word in our language. For days and nights I lay awake thinking. Then suddenly, in a blinding flash of inspiration, I seen this word "Fon"! So up I got and wrote it down! It did look good, even in the dark! In the light of the morning it was still there, and I knew the word "Fon" was here to stay. I am very well pleased with it; thank you, and ta!

Preacher: Thank you sir! And now, my dear friends, Mr. Mueller, of the quarn hump, will now lead you all in saying "Fon!"

Mueller: After me now friends, *(ahem)—(sings)* "Fon". . .

Band (Omnes): "Fon." ("The Chinese Legs," 7 January 1960)

TALL KNIGHT: "We want . . . a shrubbery"—They demand a shrubbery, and then another shrubbery, thoughtfully arranged. This diminution—most tributes tend to be of some value—is yet another borrow from *Flying Circus*. In Ep. 13, "The Insurance Sketch" is one of the "japes" performed as they wait for the Queen to tune in:

Interior smooth-looking office. Mr Feldman behind a desk, Mr Martin in front of it. Both point to a sign on the desk: "Life Insurance Ltd."

Martin (Idle): Good morning. I've been in touch with you about the, er, life insurance . . .

Feldman (Cleese): Ah yes, did you bring the um . . . the specimen of your um . . . and so on, and so on?

Martin: Yes I did. It's in the car. There's rather a lot.

Feldman: Good, good.

Martin: Do you really need twelve gallons?

Feldman: No, no, not really.

Martin: Do you test it?

Feldman: No.

Martin: Well, why do you want it?

Feldman: Well, we do it to make sure you're serious about wanting life insurance I mean, if you're not, you won't spend a couple of months filling up that enormous churn with mmm, so on and so on . . .

Martin: Shall I bring it in?

Feldman: Good Lord no. Throw it away.

Martin: Throw it away? I was months filling that thing up.

The sound of the National Anthem starts. They stand to attention. (*JTW*, 2.36)

The demanding of feats and/or tributes can be found throughout the Arthurian literature, as well. In Malory's *LMD-WM*, Percival, Galahad, Bors, and Percival's sister are passing a castle when knights emerge demanding the "gentlewoman must yield . . . the custom of the castle," which happens to be rather more personal (and painful) than either a shrubbery or a felled tree: "'Sir,' said a knight, 'what maid passeth hereby should fill this dish full of blood of her right arm'" (384). Galahad and the others demur, of course, and successfully fight first ten and then sixty knights of the castle. At nightfall the castle's inhabitants convince the combatants to "take such harbour as here is," and during the sleepover tell the tale of the custom, which involves a leprous lady regenerated only by a maiden's pure blood. Moved, Percival's sister agrees to the sanguineous ministration (384–86).

Other yieldings in *Le Morte D'Arthur* include: the riches of Europe to the marauding, conquering Arthur from cities promising allegiance and future truage if Arthur leaves them be (*LMD'A*, 1.191); the yielding of pagan Saracen beliefs for enlightened Christianity (1.185–88); and the true knight must yield to God if he is to truly serve Him (2.309–10). There were also various instances of truage payments that Arthur reneged on once he defeated the continental armies.

Notes

1. From Pyle, *The Story of the Champions of the Round Table*, 199–200.
2. The author owns and has listened to, numerous times, all surviving episodes.
3. A handful of the printed scripts are collected in *The Goon Show Scripts* (1972), and many more are faithfully (though not terribly accurately) transcribed on many web pages.
4. *The Goon Show*, 2 February 1959.
5. The *FZ* episodes were recorded in 1971 and 1972, at the Munich Film Studio and in the Halblech, Germany region.
6. If they had decided to put Palin on Cleese's shoulders, this would have been inspired by part of the "*Archaeology Today*" sketch, where characters climb onto each other's shoulders to be taller, and therefore better archaeologists. See *MPFC: UC*, 1.332 for more.
7. See the "earth to be banana-shaped" entry in "Book of the Film" above.
8. Mittman, *Maps and Monsters in Medieval England*, 44.

SCENE TWENTY-TWO
DEAD HISTORIAN AND POLICE

CUT BACK TO the HISTORIAN lying in the glade—This scene is something of a rarity in
Holy Grail. It's a shot meant to display simultaneous action, which we've not seen in the first
forty-six or so minutes of the film. Prior to this "meanwhile" kind of shot, the narrative has
moved forward along first a single path, following Arthur and Patsy, then parallel plot lines
involving Arthur and Bedevere, Lancelot, Galahad, and Robin, each moving along their own
separate but equal narrative through lines. Now for the balance of the film, the specter of the
modern investigating police force dogging the main action of the quest will be everpresent,
without the two paths meeting until Launcelot is arrested late in the film. This crosscutting
is generally structured to build suspense, and has been part of narrative cinema since Porter's
The Great Train Robbery in 1903.

SCENE TWENTY-THREE
THE TALE OF SIR LAUNCELOT— "BLOODY WEATHER"

This animated sequence is prompted by these few words in the finished script: *CUT TO an animated title—"The Tale of Sir Launcelot."* There is no other indication that this title is supposed to be followed by anything other than the next scene (labeled in the script as scene 18). Earlier, script promises of other animated sequences didn't pan out, meaning long after the script was finished the final animation decisions were still being made. The individual shots as completed include: (1) Interior: Illuminated title card being drawn by a hand with a quill pen, then squiggled; (2) interior, a Monk in his study, jiggled; (3) interior, the Monk's multi-floor monastery, also jiggled; (4) exterior, monastery, distant forest and horizon, jiggled, then settled as Monk shoos away the weather. We will look at each of these shots in order.

Image 1—The illuminated title card features artwork (especially the elaborate *L*) fashioned after works like the *Book of the Kells* and especially the Lindisfarne Gospels, some of the "insular" illuminations from Britain and Ireland between about 600 and 900 CE (earlier than most of the other Gothic images Gilliam employs).[1] This one does feature some of the distinctive trademarks of the Celtic style, including the "trumpet spiral" and the triple-loop "triquetra" designs, both found in the vertical leg of the *l*, at the top and bottom.[2] Gilliam has included some kind of zoomorphic figure (it's too small to identify with any certainty) draped across the foot of the letter, as well, another feature of the Celtic style.

There are elaborate *L* initials elsewhere, in MS Burney 26 and in MS Ludwig 1, for example, but not so elaborate as Gilliam's version, which looks as if it may be fashioned for a psalter—though Gilliam constructed the letter from at least three separate sources. The vertical line of the *L* is possibly borrowed from a canon table page, or at least inspired by one. These can be seen in Brown's illuminated manuscript guide (33).

There is also a bird image much like the one standing on the *un* in *Launcelot* found on the "John" incipit page of the Lindisfarne Gospels, while the "Eagle of Mark" (f. 84v) in the *Book of Durrow* is also stylistically similar (as in many of the insular texts). There are a number of eagles associated with John in period illuminated manuscripts (from as early as the eleventh century), as well, and their poses are remarkably similar to Gilliam's version.

Image 2—In the next image, the monk figure is borrowed from a miniature of Vincent de Beauvais[3] (c. 1190–1264), a Dominican monk who wrote the *Speculum Maius*, a Middle Ages encyclopedia, to inspire "greater veneration and reverence" of the "magnitude and beauty and permanence of [God's] creation" (Bishop, *HBMA*, 277). The miniature—Vincent sitting at a desk and writing his book—is found at the beginning of Book 1 of *Speculum historiale*

(*Le miroir historial*), from the Netherlands (1478–1483). Gilliam has switched out the background (see below), Vincent's head, and the pen in his hand, replacing the pen with a feather quill. (Perhaps he wanted to link it better, visually, to the following scene in Prince Herbert's room in Swamp Castle, where a desk and quill pens are seen and used.) Bishop notes that this iconic scene was a particular favorite of Middle Ages artists, and Gilliam includes many of the semantic elements of such a scene:

> The writer, warmly gowned, sits at a sloping desk, with a stand above or at his side for reference books. Before him is a fair sheet of paper or parchment; at hand an inkhorn, a goose quill, and a penknife to keep it sharpened and to scrape out the inner fuzz; also a stick of lead and a ruler to make guidelines and margins for the page, a scraper for erasing errors and pumice to clean sheets and a bear's or goat's tooth to polish parchment; and wax and seal to attest genuineness, for a man's signature had then no legal standing; also perhaps an hourglass and a charcoal brazier for warming the fingers and drying ink. A dog or cat sits on the floor, watching with admiration.[4]

Gilliam also undercuts the idyll, of course, since this is a Python film.[5]

The new head (on Beauvais' cowled shoulders) is a recognizable borrow from Gilliam's *MPFC* animations. He has reappropriated an image of British General Charles Cornwallis (1738–1805), likely based on the Benjamin Smith (after John Singleton Copley) stipple engraving in the National Portrait Gallery collection.[6] The Cornwallis face is earlier seen in *MPFC* Ep. 13, where he comments on the poor quality of the first series' wrap-up ("What a terrible way to end the series") (*MPFC: UC*, 1.217). The original de Beauvais image is another one found in *FMA*,[7] where Gilliam borrowed a number of illustrations for these animations, as well as sketching material as he prepared for the animated sequences. See the entries in the "The Book of the Film" section for more, as well as appendix A, where the "Facing Pages" are annotated.

There is also a clear precedent for a scribe or illuminator to feature himself in relation to his own work. Gilliam appears a handful of times in *MPFC* in relation to his art (*MPFC: UC*, 1.94, 131–32). Most transcribers and especially illustrators labored in obscurity, only identifiable by academics much later, and then by similar style and time period, but almost never by name. Thankfully, that was not always the case. Gilliam shows us the monk at work here in his scriptorium, connecting him directly to his creation of the Launcelot illumination title; later, Gilliam himself will appear, only to die of a heart attack, ending the animated adventure. The manuscript painter Hugo the Painter, or "Master Hugo" (c. 1130–1160) fashioned an image of himself—dressed as a monk and dipping a pen in ink—in the pages of Jerome's *Commentary on Isaiah*, a portion of which is depicted in *FMA*,[8] one of Gilliam's known sources.[9] Hugo has written above him his name and the following: "*Imago pictoris et illuminatoris huius operis*" ("An image of the painter and illuminator of this work").[10] Brother Rufillus of Weissenau also proudly included himself in an inhabited *R* in a twelfth-century German manuscript, one that Gilliam found and used for the title sequence of the film.[11] See section eight of the "Title Sequence Animation" entry above for more. The monk Matthew Paris, who died c. 1259, also signed at least one of his works and included an image of himself prostrate at the feet of the Virgin and Child (*FMA*, 312). This Benedictine monk, based at St. Albans, was quite a character, and has been "described as a medieval Macaulay: robust, prejudiced, somewhat slipshod, but also, because of his very limitations, irresistibly readable" (Brown, *Understanding Illuminated Manuscripts*, 13). He seems just the type to include a large image of himself in *Historia Anglorum*. Another artist/monk, Eadmer of Canterbury—depicted with quill and sharpening knife—can be found in Ludwig XI 6;[12] and lastly, it's the illuminator Hildebertus who best fits Gilliam's depiction of the distracted scribe as presented in *Holy Grail*. In Hildebertus's rendering of his working space—he sits on a pedestal, an elaborate, lion-shaped desk before him, quill behind his ear and sharpening knife in hand, his assistant Everwinus working on floral designs at his feet. Surrounded by the tools of his work he is instead sidetracked—in his right hand he appears ready to throw something at a mouse nibbling on cheese and upsetting dishes on a nearby table. The text he's working on reads: "*Pessime mus, saepe me provocas ad iram: ut te deus perdat*" ("You lousy mouse, you often provoke me to anger; may God destroy you"[13]) (*FMA*, 310). Not the "bloody weather," but very nearly.

Gilliam also performed a bit of photographic legerdemain here—as was so often the case in his earlier contributions to *Flying Circus*. The *background* of this scribe scene is borrowed almost completely from an illustration of Jean Miélot (d. 1472), scribe/translator to Duke Philip the Good of Burgundy, found in his compilation of the *Miracles de Notre Dame*. Miélot produced twenty-two works for the Duke.[14] The image of the (likely) ducal library is laterally reversed for Gilliam's use. Just behind the monk at the foreground of the frame can be glimpsed the hands and arm of the original scribe in the red-colored background—the overlain writing desk and book obscure most of that background. Looking carefully, Miélot's chin can even be glimpsed under the center book, which had been partly obscured in the original work, but which Gilliam "drew out" for the new scene. Gilliam likely was certain the viewer wouldn't see the background figure, focusing instead on the large, bright, animated monk in the foreground.

Image 3—The third shot—the interior of what seems to be a vaulted palazzo—is actually a perspectival drawing that acts as the monk's multi-floor home/abbey. Idle calls it an "M. C. Escher"[15]—it isn't. It is actually a retouched version of Jan Vredeman de Vries's (1527–c. 1604) perspective series, specifically plate 39. Gilliam has done some touch up work to make the scene fit his monk's needs. The doorway at the left—where the monk emerges—featured visible stairs in the original work; those stairs have been removed for this animated sequence. The door at the right still features the matching stairs. Gilliam has blacked out the spaces between pillars and the floors in general, excepting the tiled floor far below. Looking closely, the labeling de Vries included for teaching purposes can be glimpsed, starting with *e* at the top center, then down through *d*, *c*, *b*, and *a*. De Vries's perspectival lines can also still be seen crossing the balustrades, and on the colored tiles. The lines meet at the vanishing point, which is bottom center, on a blue tile. The labels for the guidelines that cross from the four corners of the space are also still visible, labeled (from bottom left) *f*, *i*, *g*, and *h*. In the original drawing, the plate number label—39—was included just left of the *f*—this number has been blacked out.

The architect and painter de Vries's landmark book *Perspective* was republished in a Dover edition in 1968, and Gilliam borrowed all or parts of six de Vries plates for many *Flying Circus* animations (plates 7, 15, 24, 28, 42, and 47).[16] See "artworks" in the index and then assorted entries ("de Vries") in the author's *MPFC: UC* (2013) for more on Gilliam's magpie animation, and for the significance and usefulness of Jan de Vries's work.

Image 4—The fourth and final shot of this animated sequence is the payoff. The full sequence doesn't just connect or transition, it is a three-beat setup to a clever, even subtle gag. There is also a version of this setup and payoff, also involving weather, in Gilliam's *Animations of Mortality*. There, in a set of pages loosely labeled a "Sketch Book," dozens of fragmented sketches of creatures, hybrids, buildings, machines, etc. grace the pages, likely collected and thrown together from multiple sources. One of the pages features a sequence of eleven storyboards. In the first frame, a man stands outside his small home at night; from there he goes inside to bed, and the lights go out. Outside, cranes and rolling scaffolding haul in clouds and the sun through the next five or six frames. By the end, when the man awakes and goes back outside, it's a sunny day and the weather is in place.[17]

This monk may be a Benedictine-type whose "vow of *stabilitas loci*" (a vow not to travel) means he stays in his monastery and practices *ruminatio*—studying, contemplating, and writing—he takes "his pilgrimage without leaving home," a *peregrinatio in stabilitate* (Mittman, 31). Knowing this—that he's always working at home, and always needing complete focus to contemplate the will of God—it is easy to see he'd react quickly and decisively to shush outside disturbances, even if it's just the "bloody weather."

And as for the act of writing itself, during this period most written work was actually accomplished in Gilliam's depicted setting, according to Fossier:

> The men who wrote were sometimes laymen, like the Italian scriveners of the eighth century, or merchant accountants of the thirteenth century, when the economy demanded many more written documents. In the overwhelming majority, however, they were clerics, workers in the episcopal writing bureaus known as *officialités*, chaplains of princes or lords, monks above all, ten or twenty of them working under dictation in the *scriptoria* of monasteries to produce copies of works of piety. . . . (*AO*, 319)

The fact that Prince Herbert can write (and write well) and that Launcelot can read might be somewhat remarkable given the literacy rate of the period, even among those noble-born. Fossier earlier notes that the Merovingian King Chilperic I made up more letters than he actually knew, that Charlemagne "was never able to hold a pen," and that the Capetian Henry I signed his official acts "with an X" (315). That Brother Maynard and his young monkish assistant can both read (the scriptures and an Aramaic inscription, respectively) isn't out of order, of course, given their positions as members of the small percentage of the medieval population[18] trained in both reading and writing. These are the only instances in *Holy Grail* where characters display any kind of reading or writing literacy as we would describe it.[19]

SCRIBE: "And you, clear off! Bloody weather"—Not part of the printed script, the actions—a meticulous scribe being forced into error—can perhaps be attributed to the "patron demon of scribes" Titivillus, whose mission seems to have been the coaxing of scribal errors. Misspellings, lost lines, smudges, the lot; Titivillus was the copyist's personal demon.[20] Here it's the rambunctious weather acting the bothersome part, causing the scribe to foul his "Launcelot" illumination.

Notes

1. See Brown, *Understanding Illuminated Manuscripts*.

2. Brown, 36.

3. Beauvais has been mentioned earlier in relation to his scathing views on women—they are "a hindrance to devotion." See entries in the "Castle Anthrax" scene for more.

4. *HBMA*, 280. There is such an image, as described, on page 288 of *HBMA*. The image Gilliam used for reference didn't feature the homely touches of the admiring pets.

5. As will be seen below, some of the medieval scribe images also poke fun at the scribe's lot, just as the marginal illustrations can comment on and undercut the seriousness of written work in Gothic manuscripts.

6. Gilliam and the Pythons employed a number of paintings from both the NPG and National Gallery collections (along with the Tate museums, et al.) during the *MPFC* run, including *Cardinal de*

Richelieu (c. 1640), and works from Bronzino, Crivelli, Turner, and Constable, to mention just a few. See the index in *MPFC: UC* under "art galleries" for more.

7. *FMA*, 192.

8. *FMA*, 296.

9. The other identifiable sources being Randall, *IMGM*, Butterworth, *The Growth of Industrial Art*, De Vries, *Perspective*, and likely Bishop, *HBMA* (1968), as mentioned above. Gilliam utilized other texts—these are the ones that can be identified precisely.

10. Latin translation by Prof. Roger Macfarlane.

11. This *R* is reproduced in *FMA* on page 303.

12. Brown, 16.

13. Latin translations provided by Prof. Roger Macfarlane.

14. According to the *CE*; see the entry for "Lille, " http://www.catholic.org/encyclopedia/view .php?id=7108

15. Part of Idle's DVD commentary track for the Blu-ray edition of the film.

16. In the credit sequence for the first series of *MPFC* Gilliam places a wheeled Cardinal de Richelieu against the background of an abbey nave, the nave being de Vries's plate 47; in that same sequence a nude reclines against another de Vries background, plate 42, which is a perspectival street scene. Gilliam retouches these scenes as needed, adding color, removing buildings or fountains, and adding whatever silliness he may require. See *MPFC: UC*, 1.5.

17. There are no page numbers in *Animations of Mortality*, published by Methuen in 1978 and 1981.

18. Fossier estimates that in England in 1450 there were about twenty thousand clerics in a population of three million; clerics represented about 10 percent of the population of France at the same time (315).

19. There are signs (in triplicate) in the forest where Sir Robin meets the Three-Headed Knight—warning signs—though Robin and his men seem to take no notice of them. Perhaps, since he employs a minstrel, Robin cannot read or write, and assumes he has no need for those skills.

20. See *HBMA*, 283.

THE TALE OF SIR LAUNCELOT SCENE

EXTERIOR: SWAMP CASTLE—DAY—This exterior, establishing long shot is *not* accounted for in the printed script. The exterior shot is a filmed image of the castle at Bodiam,[1] mentioned earlier as the type of castle the Pythons were thinking of when they wrote "castle" in the script. Julian Doyle shot this footage separate from the days of the film's principal photography.[2] See the notes for scene 2, "Coconuts and Swallows," for more.

like a night shirt—(PSC) There are really no costume directions for the various knights, or for most of the characters in the film, likely because the Pythons knew they would be producing the film themselves, and didn't have to write for anyone else. Jones and Gilliam would have called for costumes befitting a thirteenth- or fourteenth-century setting, and it would have been Hazel Pethig's job to make up these costumes on the film's meager budget. For Herbert's father here, Palin is wearing a rough, fur-trimmed cloak, likely meant to underscore his "northernness" (his rusticity, even though he is wealthy). Farther south, in the more refined London of 1337, the newest batch of sumptuary laws forbade anyone wearing fur that could not prove "an annual income of £100 per year" (Mortimer, 104). The fact that Herbert's father appears to be wearing cheaper, coarser fur—not ermine or weasel, for example—it might even be horsehair, is likely an emblem of his "northern" wealth but lower status.

For Herbert, this *"long white undershirt (like a night shirt)"* direction is obviously meant to help define his character. The script has already called Herbert "quite embarrassingly unattractive," and in that he does resemble the feared result in medieval times of consanguineous relationships. This level of acceptable consanguinity often depended on how wealthy the applicants were, whether they were Jews, or other factors. The Church generally said "no" to any marriage within the fourth degree (Tuchman, 27, 47). Tuchman further describes one of many young princes born to a wealthy and ancient family, young Pierre d'Ailly, who, sounding like Herbert, doesn't want what most young men should want:

> Pierre had been orphaned at three and rather precociously renounced the flesh in an oath of perpetual chastity at six. . . . At eight he was an overgrown, hollow-chested ascetic, who was sent to study in Paris, where he practiced fasting and self-flagellation. . . . His life was "nothing but humility" and "always he fled from the vanities and superfluities of the world." [He would die] of consumption and self-imposed rigors in 1387. (465–66)

The only trait missing is Pierre's yearning to sing (and a father who forbids it), though he did perform constant oblations.

FATHER: "One day lad, all this will be yours . . ."—The rules of primogeniture didn't really solidify until the thirteenth century in England, but the value of a large, stable estate to both its lord and his sovereign were obvious: larger estates meant better protection, increased wealth, and more available knights and soldiers for a sovereign. Herbert's father doesn't mention a king, and when Launcelot eventually mentions "Arthur," Father can only think of Camelot as "good pig country," and not his place as a vassal to any king. In his own mind, at least, Herbert's father is separate from the demands of fealty.

There is also no sign in this scene of a mother figure, except where Herbert misspeaks in a moment, calling his father "Mother." It is a father and a single son as far as we know, and the plans are for a marriage to the lone daughter of another perhaps widowed father who also happens to be quite wealthy. The usual Middle Ages challenges of a widow inheriting at least one-third of her husband's estates upon his death are avoided here, as are the extra cast members (the latter being the more likely reason there are few mothers or spouses or children or even families depicted in *Holy Grail*).

PRINCE: "What—the curtains?"—This deflation is a borrow from the mock epics of history—the whole of *Don Quixote* (discussed earlier), or Pope's *Rape of the Lock*, where a bit of snipped hair is the cause of great turmoil, Swift's "Big-endian" civil war of *Gulliver's Travels*, and Dryden, Gay, and Fielding, et al.—and from their own sketches, including *"Njorl's Saga," "Restaurant Sketch,"* and thrilling introductions like the following, from Ep. 22:

Cut to stock film of battleships, steaming on the seas. Stirring music plays over.

Voice Over (Cleese): There have been many stirring tales told of the sea and also some fairly uninteresting ones only marginally connected with it, like this one. Sorry, this isn't a very good announcement. Sorry. (*JTW*, 1.301)

Herbert's father is talking grandly about lands and inheritances and the future, like any medieval lord; Herbert can only see the draperies.

PRINCE: "But, mother . . ."—This family's tenuous hold on gender appellations may also be attributable to swimming in the shallow end of the gene pool, like most European royalty across the Middle Ages. Tuchman often has to resort to words like "sickly," "sallow," and "slightly hunchbacked," as well as "pale and thin" and "weakling"[3] to describe the physical traits of the inbred nobility in fourteenth-century France and England. For the right money and often with a papal dispensation, degrees of consanguinity could be overlooked, and the resulting generations (if any survived) suffered the consequences. In the *Goon Show* episode "The Gold Plate Robbery," a wealthy family suffers these very same confusions:

Seagoon (Secombe): Oh, Ellington, how many times must I tell you not to stand in the shade, you'll ruin the colour scheme. Now, where's me Lady Lavinia Seagoon?

O'Blast (Ray Ellington): Well she's in the great granite baronial dining-hall.

Seagoon: What's she doing?

O'Blast: Eatin' chips.

Seagoon: Chips? Ah, ha ha, she must be practising for dinnertime. Drive me there.

Car starts up, then stops.

Seagoon: Thank you Ellington. Mother? Mother! Oh Mummy?

Lady Seagoon (Sellers): What is it Roger darling?

Seagoon: Oh, Daddy, what are you doing at home?

Lady Seagoon: I live here, and I'm Mummy not Daddy, you've just got to know the difference some time.

Seagoon: Gad, this revelation makes me a man of the world, no more short trousers for me.

Lady Seagoon: Eschewed shorts? Oh how proud your father would have been. Now tell me all about the foxhunt.

Seagoon: It was wonderful mummy. A beautiful spring morning, flowers blooming, and blood everywhere. It's grand to be in England.

Basil (Milligan): (*posh*) Hello mother, hello Roger . . . by Jove, I'm dashed hungry!

Lady Seagoon: Basil darling, where's your chin gone?

Basil: I've never had one Mummy.

Lady Seagoon: You poor thing.[4]

Also in *The Goon Show*, in "The MacReekie Rising of '74" episode, Bluebottle makes a similar mistake:

Seagoon (Secombe): Hah. Is Corporal Bluebottle's raiding party back yet?

Bluebottle (Sellers): Yes it is. And look here, I've got a hundred and ninety kilts.

Seagoon: Kilts? Those are skirts.

Bluebottle: Ooh, no wonder they put up such a fight. Yeeheheeee!

Seagoon: Bluebottle, you must learn to tell the difference![5]

Throughout both the *Goon Show* and *Flying Circus* episodes the female parts were almost always played by men, though textually, even though the depiction is an obvious one, the cross-dresser isn't acknowledged.[6]

FATHER: "I built this kingdom up from nothing . . ."—Not likely, especially during the period(s) depicted. During the Roman, Saxon, Danish, and Norman epochs in England, large landholders would have been subject to the political and/or military system in place above them, most getting their lands thanks to service to their lord, fortuitous marriages, or as an agreement to protect the flank of the kingdom (i.e., The Marches), etc. When the Normans arrived in 1066, for example, there followed a significant redistribution of wealth, out of Saxon hands and into the hands of those allied to William's administration; this "system" seems to have worked to solidify William's control:

> By the eleventh century a complex system of services and obligations had evolved. All land was regarded as belonging to the King under God. The tenants-in-chief, the greater nobles, held land from the King in return for stipulated military service. They, in turn, would sub-let to individuals who would serve in the quota of knights owed to the King. These tenants and sub-tenants had a duty to the peasants of administrating justice in the courts and of defending them in return for agricultural work and payment in food and produce. The essence of the system was protection in return for service. (Norman and Pottinger, 25)

The king of Swamp Castle doesn't seem to be aware of these commitments. He is aware of Camelot, though (he's heard it's good pig country), so he *should* know of King Arthur, but he's clearly not aware of the fealty obligations to that monarch. Norman and Pottinger go on, noting that William divided up his new kingdom—piecemeal, since it took time to "conquer" the whole country—"in a strict system, each of about 200 great nobles receiving a large number of manors scattered over the country in return for . . . service" (25). Estates like Swamp Castle might have escaped some of these demands and regular dynastic shufflings—it is located in a swampy place of fen-like liminality—meaning it was both less desirable and perhaps militarily less significant. (Vast marshy expanses often acted as natural protections from land-based invasion.) More likely, though, the Pythons are telescoping time, bringing characters or characteristics from the modern world into the medieval. Herbert's father is the contemporary self-made Englishman, akin to a successful merchant, or the owner of a northern textile mill or a tin or coal mine, someone not born into affluence or privilege, but who, through his own efforts and the changing world brought on by the Industrial Revolution, is able to amass wealth and, thereafter, even status and power.[7] This character is closer to a Dennis-type, meaning he's more of a modern construction, a new money northerner—a Bradford parvenu—not unlike the ur-Python "Four Yorkshire Gentlemen."[8]

Tuchman writes similarly of Wyclif's *heretical* (as opposed to feudal or manorial) assumptions in fourteenth-century England. Thanks to the schism created when competing popes—Urban and Clement—tried to wield "supreme executive power" in the name of God, Wyclif[9] in 1379 moved toward what would become known as protestantism, disacknowledging the religious power structure he was supposed to uphold:

> Wyclif was now prepared to sweep away the entire ecclesiastical superstructure—papacy, hierarchy, orders. Having rejected the divine authority of the Church, it was now that he came to his rejection of its essence—the power of the sacraments, specifically of the Eucharist. (338)

Tuchman goes on, noting that when Wyclif "transferred salvation from the agency of the Church to the individual," he had done nothing less than "start . . . the modern world" (339). Herbert's father seems to be doing his northerner's version of this same transition, from manorialism to democracy in one go.

The Father is a coarser man than Arthur or his knights—his is wealth newfound and *earned* by scheming and hard work, he wears animal skins, he worries about farming and livestock, his hair and beard are unkempt.[10] He is clearly a northerner as opposed to a southerner, meaning of London and its environs. The Pythons have already played on this identity via the father and son characters in the "Flying Sheep" and "Working-Class Playwright" sketches in *MPFC*.[11] In more contemporary accounts a northerner is known for his or her "down-to-earth attitude,"[12] they are "strong-minded" and "imperturbable in action,"[13] they are "friendlier to strangers" than those from the south[14]—the "salt of the earth" and "backbone of England" description isn't far afield, though all of these definitions are at some level pejorative, coming as they often do from more civilized, patronizing denizens of the south, where London just happens to be. Clive O'Brien writes of Birmingham, the "hard centre of England," a place even Jane Austen found "direful," and for whom the populace was

> summed up by what many people have felt about Birmingham folk in years since. . . . [They were] encumbered with many low connexions, but gave themselves immense airs, expecting to be on a footing with the old-established families. And how they got their fortunes nobody knew. . . . One of the figures on the city's coat of arms is a workman standing firmly on two solid legs and staring at the outside world in a belligerent way. He is wearing brown trousers and black boots. The symbolism is still superb. . . . The essence of Birmingham is knowing how to make things better while cutting 4d. off the wholesale price. Birmingham is listening to a long, long argument

and then saying, "Yes, but what are we actually doing about it?" Birmingham is tearing things down and putting things up.[15]

Even the Labour PM Wilson was more like Dennis and Herbert's father than the Heath-like Arthur, according to Sandbrook: "Wilson played up his humble roots and Yorkshire background, emphasizing to interviewers that he owed his success to plain living, hard work and ordinary values. . . . [H]e projected himself as a cheeky outsider with self-consciously 'ordinary' tastes" (*White Heat*, 5).

FATHER: ". . . other kings said I was daft"—In some Grail lore (from Boron, specifically), Glastonbury was the final resting place of Arthur, on the island known as Avalon. The abbey there was said by some to have been founded by Joseph of Arimathea, though it likely came to be in the seventh century. Glastonbury is a place of marshes and fens, and in ancient times, of trackless water and bogs. Building a castle in the midst of that fetid, seemingly bottomless expanse *would* have been daft, but easier to defend, and much more challenging to assault. In the twelfth century, Glastonbury monks announced the discovery of the burial places of both Arthur and Guinevere, likely as a good way to increase tourist and pilgrim interest in their waterlogged region.[16] Between the tenth and thirteenth centuries, according to W. G. Hoskins, improvements were made—many acres of land around the abbey were ditched, drained, and transitioned to "rich grazing land."[17] The Glastonbury Abbey burned and fell down in 1184 (just like the third iteration of Swamp Castle, which "burned down, fell over, then sank into the swamp"). The abbey was rebuilt and prospered, but after Henry VIII's dissolutive attentions the abbey was stripped of its valuables, and, over time, even of its building stone. It has been a ruin since the sixteenth century.

Swamp Castle would have to have been built *on* something. The transition between motte and bailey (primarily earthwork) castle structures and stone castles wasn't a smooth one, necessarily. The motte would have been created by piling excavated soil from the surrounding moat, and that soil could be moist and/or clayey, therefore unstable, prone to swelling and settling. Motte towers *were* built, but they were generally smaller and made of wood. Some local lords likely tried building stronger, stone fortifications on these mottes, only to discover the underlying soil's weaknesses:

> Once the earth [of the new motte] had been allowed to settle, some of these mottes were topped with a stone tower, which they could not have supported when the earth was newly dug. In one case the earth was held from sliding down by an overall coating of clay. At Farnham Castle there was a stone tower inside the mound to support the weight of the tower which originally stood on top. (Norman and Pottinger, 29)

It's likely that a fair number of these hill forts began as simple, heavy stone towers but were replaced by wood when the settling issue was discovered. The king of Swamp Castle could have learned from these earlier lessons in substructural work.

FATHER: "So I built another one . . . that fell over and then sank into the swamp"—In *Historia Brittonum*, the ill-fated Vortigern is tasked by his wise men to build a citadel on the edges of his lands where he can essentially hide from the "treacherous" people he has "received" (the invited Saxon hordes), as well as his own angry citizens:

> The king, pleased with this advice, departed with his wise men, and travelled through many parts of his territories, in search of a place convenient for the purpose of building a citadel. Having, to no purpose, travelled far and wide, they came at length to a province called Guenet; and having surveyed the mountains of Heremus, they discovered, on the summit of one of them, a situa-

tion, adapted to the construction of a citadel. Upon this, the wise men said to the king, "Build here a city; for, in this place, it will ever be secure against the barbarians." Then the king sent for artificers, carpenters, stone-masons, and collected all the materials requisite to building; but the whole of these disappeared in one night, so that nothing remained of what had been provided for the constructing of the citadel. Materials were, therefore, from all parts, procured a second and third time, and again vanished as before, leaving and rendering every effort ineffectual. Vortigern inquired of his wise men the cause of this opposition to his undertaking, and of so much useless expense of labour? They replied, "You must find a child born without a father, put him to death, and sprinkle with his blood the ground on which the citadel is to be built, or you will never accomplish your purpose."(*HB*, para. 40)

Vortigern's men then find the young Merlin (Myrddin Emrys), who tells him the dragons fighting beneath the castle's proposed foundations won't permit a fortress to be built. Just a bit later in the tale, the recalcitrant Vortigern's castle built on the River Towy is burned to the ground following three days of prayer led by St. Germanus (para. 47).

Geoffrey of Monmouth's version isn't all that different, but puts a finer point on the nightly results:

Howbeit, he at last took counsel of his wizards, and bade them tell him what he should do. They told him that he ought to build him a tower exceeding strong, as all his other castles he had lost. He sought accordingly in all manner of places to find one fit for such a purpose and came at last unto Mount Snowden, where, assembling a great gang of masons from divers countries, he bade them build the tower. The stonemasons, accordingly, came together and began to lay the foundations thereof, but whatsoever they wrought one day was all swallowed up by the soil the next, in such sort as that they knew not whither their work had vanished unto. (*HKB*, 132–33)

Beyond the mythical element, the political situation in Britain toward the end of the Roman presence in the early fifth century may have influenced this repetitive structure (building castles; castles falling; rebuilding of castles). Snyder (1998) notes: "So frequent were British usurpations in this brief four-year period [406–410] that the island earned a long-lasting reputation, throughout the once-Roman world, for political irregularity and vice" (18).

The combining of two unlikely images—a new building/home and a fetid swamp—is actually much aligned, according to William Miller in *Anatomy of Disgust*. After quoting *Macbeth*'s witches—"Fillet of a fenny snake, / Eye of newt, and toe of frog"—Miller makes the death/life medieval connection:

Here is our first view of a string of images that will form as consistent a theme as there is in the world of disgust. What disgusts, startlingly, is the capacity for life, and not just because life implies its correlative death and decay: for it is decay that seems to engender life. Images of decay seem to imperceptibly slide into images of fertility and out again. Death thus horrifies and disgusts not just because it smells revoltingly bad, but because it is not an end to the process of living but part of a cycle of eternal recurrence. (40)

Building and rebuilding a castle—signs of new, rejuvenating life, and in a swamp—representing fecund death and decay—is a juxtaposition very much at home in the medieval world, where science and magic, and for the Pythons, the ancient and the modern, can be so cousinly.

FATHER: "And that put the fear of God into everyone . . ."—An excised section. This line and the following—"They gave me lands . . . and they gave me fields and they gave me soldiers"—posit Herbert's father as a man made *by* others, actually contradicting his first line, that he built his empire on his own. The lines as printed paint him as more of a typical medieval

English lord or lay magnate—always beholden to someone above him, and dominating those below him—while the final version renders him more the self-made northerner whose swampy kingdom is self-contained, self-defined, and somehow separate from the feudal patronage structure of the Middle Ages.

HERBERT: "I'd rather . . . just . . . sing . . ."—This is a classic borrow from the 1927 Al Jolson film *The Jazz Singer*, where young Jakie Rabinowitz doesn't want to follow in his father's footsteps as a cantor—he yearns to tread the boards of the vulgar musical stage instead. This also may be the most obvious influence of the recent and very popular stage and film musical *Camelot* (1960 and 1967, respectively).

MUSIC INTRO—(PSC) This soupçon of introductory music—an upswell into a promised song that doesn't materialize—is some of the canned music purchased from DeWolfe. Neil Innes had worked on a score for the film, but in the end the bits and pieces of found music served the purpose better, and were likely cheaper.[18] The Pythons had accessed DeWolfe and the BBC music and sound collection throughout the run of *Flying Circus*.[19]

FATHER: "You're not going into a song while I'm here!"—Here, Herbert's father actually turns toward the camera, acknowledging that a recorded (or just witnessed) performance is in the offing, very nearly breaking the fourth wall in a way not seen since Dingo's direct address earlier. He doesn't directly acknowledge the camera, though, meaning the music is somehow diegetic, and somehow at the father's command. Again, in the musical genre these self-conscious moments are *contained* by the performance aspects of the characters and setting.

The soundtrack albums for the *Camelot* play and film were incredibly popular, as had been the LPs for *The Sound of Music* and *South Pacific*. The focus on Herbert's need "to sing" may be a result of this recent musical proliferation—it seemed like everyone was singing. In the mid-1960s, Cliff Richard and Engelbert Humperdinck[20] were enormously popular, as were the Beatles and the Rolling Stones, but they weren't at the top of the heap, according to Sandbrook:

> Even the appeal of Cliff, though, paled by comparison with one of the unlikeliest cultural success stories of the decade: the musical soundtrack. As one writer puts it, the most popular group of the sixties was not the Beatles or the Stones, but "Soundtrack, featuring Original Cast." The most popular Beatles' album, *Please Please Me*, spent forty-three weeks in the Top Ten. By comparison, the soundtrack of the American musical *South Pacific* spent forty-six weeks at *number one*, and more than three years in the Top Ten. Yet even this was dwarfed by the outstanding musical product of the sixties, Rodgers and Hammerstein's *The Sound of Music*. The two versions of the phenomenally successful musical—a Broadway recording from 1960 and the film soundtrack of 1965 [*sic*]—remained in the Top Ten of the album chart for more than five years, and the film soundtrack held the number one spot for a staggering 69 weeks. By October 1968, *The Sound of Music* had sold more than two million copies in Britain alone.[21] (*White Heat*, 412–13)

In the years leading up to the production of *Holy Grail*, music and songs had been belted out from myriad (and sometimes odd) locales in feature film musicals, including not just the wartime South Pacific and Nazi-controlled Austria, but Yonkers, New York (*Hello, Dolly!*), the Holy Land (*Jesus Christ Superstar*), West End and Broadway stages (*Star!*), dark, dank, and dance-friendly Dickensian London (*Oliver!*), WWI Europe (*Darling Lili*), California gold country (*Paint Your Wagon*), and even the mythical "Sea Star Island" (*Dr. Doolittle*) and "Missitucky" (*Finian's Rainbow*). Camelot has already been overrun by those who prefer to sing and dance, so it's no surprise there might be other would-be performers in this world like Herbert. For the record, the film manages to at last veer away from a full-blown musical eruption as Arthur, Herbert's father, and then even Launcelot pull the narrative into more sober, non-musical directions.

FATHER: ". . . biggest tracts of open land in Britain"—Princess Lucky's father might be an upper-crust landowner, the type of man in the type of social station that Herbert's father aspires to, with the effeminate Herbert being the only bump in the road to a successful "merger." The "up from nothing" northerner has done everything he sees necessary to make this social jump—built a series of impressive castles, made plans for fashionable alterations to the castle, and prepped his "son" for a marriage of convenience and necessity into the upper class. In this the social and class differences between the skinheads of Britain in the 1970s and many of their targets of violence split right along these same lines, with "the class division between killer and victim . . . typical of such violence" (Turner, 64). If Herbert won't give up his effeteness (fondness for vocal performance and musicals, for example), then the father is prepared to use violence—Launcelot's and his own—as a means of enabling his upward mobility, and replace Herbert with Launcelot.

FATHER: "Listen, Alice"—Herbert's father has recognized his child's effeminacy, and will treat him with all the scorn reserved for the son who fails to live up to a father's (and by association, medieval society's) expectations. During this exchange the Father hits Herbert on the back of the head (when Herbert asks about the curtains), he hits him on both arms to emphasize the strength of his kingdom, grabs him by the collar, and finally slaps him on the face. Herbert shies weakly—wetly—from each touch.

And since he's "Alice" *and* "Herbert" (and "embarrassingly unattractive") perhaps Herbert is one of the "abnormal people" who live on the edges of the world as depicted on the English Psalter world map[22] (c. 1260) or Hereford Mappaemundi (c. 1290). There, among the mermaids, minotaurs, and tigolopes, can be found human-like troglodytes (cave dwellers), marmini (four-eyed seamen), and hermaphrodites, the dual-sex aberrations. But Herbert also claims to be heterosexual, as he tries to define the "girl" he's to marry to his impatient father, who only wants to hear his son say he'll marry Princess Lucky and get his hands on her "huge tracts of land." Chaucer deals in a similarly cryptic way with his character the Pardoner, who has stringy hair, a weak voice, and no beard—a sallow figure indeed, as Elspeth Whitney notes:

> [T]he Prologue's detailed but inconclusive description of the Pardoner's physical characteristics suggests some form of more hidden deviancy, one unacknowledged by the Pardoner himself and not clearly identified by his fellow pilgrims. This physical anomaly, signaled most directly by the much-discussed line "I trowe he were a geldying or a mare" (I 691) points the reader toward a disjunction between the Pardoner's self-proclaimed gender identity as a young man planning on marriage who wishes to "enjoy a wench in every town" and his emasculated bodily condition. The complexities of Chaucer's portrait of the Pardoner have resulted in a proliferation of diagnoses, none of which has gained universal acceptance. Since Walter Curry's introduction of the topic in 1919, when he named the Pardoner as a eunuch *ex navitate*, the Pardoner has been categorized as a "normal" male, a congenital eunuch, a man who has been castrated, a man impotent but physically intact, a hermaphrodite, "a testicular pseudo-hermaphrodite of the feminine type," an oversexed womanizer, an alcoholic, a "drag queen," a cross-dressed woman, and, most resonantly, a homosexual. (Whitney, "What's Wrong with the Pardoner?," 357–58)

It won't be until Idle's later Python mash-up *Spamalot* that homosexuality will be acknowledged head on, as the Pythons don't really hint in *MPHG* that Herbert is anything but sallow and effeminate. Herbert just wants the girl that he marries to "have that certain, special something"—a something best described in song, which is of course endemic to the American film musical, especially of the 1950s.[23] Whitney goes on to describe the Pardoner as something of a "phlegmatic," with "strong indications of a cold and moist complexion" from Prologue's description; he is then "a male phlegmatic, that is, a man with a range of 'effeminate' or feminized characteristics, including various forms of nonreproductive sexuality" (360). Whitney continues: "Both Chaucer and his audience would have understood a phlegmatic complexion to indicate a degree of sexual ambiguity" (360). This seems to suit the spindly figure of Herbert quite well, with his drawn, ashen face, plentiful moles, stringy hair, and torpid physique and physicality.

FATHER: "We live in a bloody swamp, we need all the land we can get"—Swamp Castle may be situated in a fen region, like the sprawling Somerset Levels in the southwest, or the Fens in the northeast, near Lincoln and Peterborough, or Romney Marsh in the southeast. But the unmitigated fen wasn't always just a "bloody swamp," according to Raban. The wealthy Crowland Abbey is a case in point, appearing very much like the kind of operation Herbert's father owns and seeks to increase upon:

> A moderately well-endowed pre-Conquest Benedictine house set in the heart of undrained Lincolnshire fen, it owned properties in both the surrounding marshland and on higher ground in the nearby counties of Huntingdonshire, Northamptonshire, Cambridgeshire and Leicestershire. Some were fifty miles or more from the abbey but, despite this, by the end of the thirteenth century there was considerable specialization in production and a centralized accounting system. The upland manors of Northamptonshire, better suited to arable agriculture, supplied grain to the abbey, while the fenland granges with their rich grazing operated as cattle farms. Crops and livestock were exchanged as required between manors and via the centre. (Raban, 34)

Swamp Castle owns the marshy land on which it sits, and Herbert's father is looking to acquire a "stretch of farmland near the mountains" and Camelot. These swampy areas, though, have been problematic for centuries—for subsistence farmers, travelers, and law enforcement—and have been actively managed (canalized and drained) since at least Anglo-Saxon times. Herbert's father could perhaps have improved his lot with such drainages; these areas have also been and continue to be valuable agricultural (arable) and grazing land, as hinted at by Herbert's father. Over the centuries canals and windpumps had drained the marshes to reveal arable and pastoral land.[24] These windpumps appear many times in the margins of illuminated manuscripts; Randall's *IMGM* includes at least seventeen separate windmill images, one featuring prominently from the familiar Royal 10 E.IV manuscript.[25]

Historically, for example, a family like the de Clare clan (descended illegitimately from Richard I, Duke of Normandy) qualifies for this position, since by the thirteenth century their holdings included vast acreages in England, Ireland, and Wales.

Raban explains Herbert's father's fixation on property acquisition, and it's not just due to his own land's moisture levels:

> Another bond common to all ranks in rural society was dependence on land, not merely to support life, but for status and power at whatever level it was exercised. Although day-to-day agricultural activities were not usually at the forefront of the minds of those who fought or prayed, land—its acquisition and retention—was an overwhelming preoccupation. It is hard for us to appreciate this territorial drive and the dynastic ambitions flowing from it. Lords spent what appear to be huge sums on litigation in defence of their titles against rival claimants. Security of tenure was probably the most sensitive point at issue between crown and subjects. *At a personal level, choice of marriage partner whether for lord or peasant was largely governed by territorial considerations, the wishes of the individual subordinated to those of the family. Quite simply, land—getting it, keeping it and, for all but the richest, exploiting it—dominated the lives of perhaps ninety percent of the population.* (37; italics added)

Raban concludes: "England in the thirteenth and fourteenth centuries, and for centuries to come, was above all a land based society" (37). And so Herbert's father is obsessed with land. **FATHER: "Don't like her? What's wrong with her? She's beautiful . . . she's rich . . ."**—And she's got "huge tracts of land." Only the second two really matter in this list of the girl's qualities. The interfamily connections in Europe in the Middle Ages were a "crisscrossing network, in the making of which two things were never considered: the sentiments of the parties to the marriage, and the interest of the populations involved" (Tuchman, 47). As late as the fourteenth century marriages were still being carefully arranged between children of seven and eight, or between an older prince and a girl as young as six—though in that case the prospective groom had to agree to wait until the bride reached the age of twelve to actually consummate the marriage. Emperor Ludwig had promised his daughter in marriage before she had even learned to talk.[26] Beauty or even attractiveness didn't often enter into these mergers, and for good reason, according to Tuchman:

> Marriages were the fabric of international as well as inter-noble relations, the primary source of territory, sovereignty, and alliance, and the major business of medieval diplomacy. The relations of countries and rulers depended not at all on common borders or natural interest but on dynastic connections and fantastic cousinships which could make a prince of Hungary heir to the throne of Naples and an English prince claimant to Castile. (47)

Herbert and Lucky are simply being stitched into this interwoven fabric of relationships as any child of the "nobility"—by birth or otherwise—would have been during this period, and as mentioned by Raban above, neither of the betrothed had a real say in it, "the wishes of the individual subordinated to those of the family" (Raban, 37).

A useful case in point was the arranged union of Count Louis de Male and Isabella,[27] daughter of Edward III. Edward had been assured that a match between his daughter and the son of the Count of Flanders would allow Edward to regain control of those Flemish towns lost at the unprecipitated fall of the "great master of Flanders," Artevelde (Tuchman, 80). Like Herbert's father, Edward is looking to retain and increase his holdings beyond his own borders (via an alliance marriage), and in this case, on the Continent. Isabella was then thirteen, while Louis was fourteen. Even at this tender age, however, young Louis was an ardent friend of France, and looked on the potential match as an outright surrender to English authority in the Low Countries, and he determined to fight the match. Young Louis's father, Count Louis de Nevers, was subsequently killed at the Battle of Crécy, where Edward's forces carried the day, further complicating but not precluding the proposed alliance. Young Louis's devotion to the French firmed up significantly after his father's death, creating a sticky situation for those on both sides in favor of the alliance, and illustrating a choice our Princess Lucky and even Prince Herbert could have made, and with similar indignation:

> But fifteen-year-old Louis, "who had been ever nourished among the noble men of France," would not agree and, "ever said he would not wed her whose father had slain his, though he might have half the whole realm of England." When the Flemings saw that their lord was "too much French and evil counseled," they put him in "courteous prison" until he should agree to accept their counsel, which greatly annoyed him, so that after several months in prison he gave the required promise. Released, he was allowed to go hawking by the river, but kept under such close surveillance lest he should steal away "that he could not piss without their knowledge." Under this treatment he finally agreed to wed. (Tuchman, 90)

The marriage was scheduled, and Edward and his household (and young Isabella) came to Flanders with a baggage train of gifts and wedding preparations. That same week Louis and his minder went hawking, as had become his custom, and at some point Louis put spurs to his horse and didn't stop "until he was over the border with France" (90). Louis was then married to another noblewoman in a completely French arrangement, and Isabella wouldn't be married for another thirteen years.[28]

It's easy to see how this complicated arrangement influenced the Pythons as they arranged for Herbert and Lucky to wed, and how their situation fits into the historical fourteenth-century mold quite aptly. Just as Louis didn't want to marry Isabella, Herbert doesn't want to marry Princess Lucky. Louis wants to exact revenge for his father's death and to deny the Continental political machinations of his father's killer, Edward; Herbert refuses simply because Lucky doesn't have a "certain . . . special . . . something." Moreover, Princess Lucky isn't all that thrilled with the prospect of marrying Herbert, though it's not clear whether she'll cite the murder of her father in the house of her affianced as just cause, though she could. Suffice to say that even in a period of carefully arranged marriage alliances, there are a number of historical examples of one or the other participants finding a way to upset the match, and for a variety of reasons, none of which necessarily involving "like" or "dislike."

FATHER: ". . . Princess Lucky"—Another silly name, not unlike the Princess with wooden teeth in the second *MPFZ* episode—she was Princess Mitzi Gaynor (Connie Booth), and her mother was Queen Syllabub (Chapman). Princess Mitzi eventually meets Prince Walter (Palin), who is "rather thin and spotty with a long nose and bandy legs and nasty, unpolished plywood teeth"[29]—not far from Herbert, honestly—but a prince, and thus marriageable. "Princess Lucky" is likely a borrow from the Pythons' beloved pantomime tradition, where such whimsically named characters—like "Princess So Shy" or "Princess Lima"—can be found.

PRINCE: ". . . the girl that I marry"—Herbert clearly wants a spouse who is female, meaning he sees himself as the husband, and therefore male, but he also practices "transgressive gender behavior" (he wants to sing; he isn't acquisitive, etc.). He's not the son most wealthy medieval landholders would want. Herbert does seem somewhere between a man's man and a woman, the only question being his precise position along that "spectrum," according to Virginia Burrus:

> There is by now widespread scholarly agreement that gender in antiquity was mapped not as a binary of two fixed and "opposite" sexes (as is typical of our own modern western culture) but rather as a dynamic spectrum or gradient of relative masculinities. On the positively valorized end of the spectrum were "true men," fully masculine; on the negatively valorized end, "true women," lacking masculinity. For men, the challenge was to establish virility and to avoid sliding down the slippery slope of feminization. (von Ehrenkrook, 148)

Herbert can "establish virility" by marrying Princes Lucky and producing children, which would seem to fit into the typical demands of the 1950s Hollywood musical schema, where a heterosexual coupling was the ultimate goal of the world of the film (and was usually the end of the film, as well). The singing and dancing stood in for courtship (and for sexual activity), with the end result being a happy couple on the very brink of familyhood.[30] Herbert can claim a "relative" masculinity not only for creating offspring, but by accepting his father's view of the appropriate medieval worldview—accepting, maintaining, managing, and increasing the holdings and properties of the family. The man's man would likely have to fight for his sovereign and act in a more masculine, rumbustious way—like Herbert's brusque father—but "relative masculinities" could obviate the need for such extremes for Herbert the fecund husband, father, and landlord. Herbert's father seems to echo Galen, that "each man trembled forever on the brink of becoming 'womanish.'. . . It was never enough to be male: a man had to *strive* to remain 'virile'"—meaning Herbert's sitting alone in his tower, singing romantic, longing songs and writing dramatic notes isn't nearly enough work to fend off what Philo of Alexandria termed the "disease of effimination," at least in his father's estimation (von Ehrenkrook, 149). This is likely why Herbert's father tries to physically "buck up" his son, slapping him around a bit, to rouse him from his womanish stupor and toward his marital bed.

Incidentally, we never do get to hear what Herbert's "certain special something" might be, since Father cuts off the music intro again.

FATHER: "Make sure the Prince doesn't leave this room . . ."—This is one of the verbal sketches borrowed from the Goons and the traditions of the music hall—"verbal" in that it requires no visual element to accompany it. The Pythons have always drawn on a rich heritage of British radio shows from the late 1930s through the 1960s, including *It's That Man Again*, *Band Waggon*, *The Archers*, *Take It from Here*, and *ISIRTA* (starring Cleese and sometimes Idle).[31] Earlier exchanges similar to this include the "Swallows" discussion and the "Plague Cart" argument. This is a holdover from *MPFC*, where the Pythons had already given viewers the "Dead Parrot" exchange, the "Argument Clinic" interactions, and the "Cheese Shop" listings. These transferred to recorded versions (LPs, cassette tapes) easily, relying almost solely on verbal dexterity and, if necessary, some limited viewer imagination.[32] The camera can be static, as well, rendering this scene a well-framed two-shot with Father in between the guards—it's essentially a vaudeville bit as seen from the third row, center.

FIRST GUARD: "Oh, yes. That's quite clear. No problem"—In the Cast List at the end of the printed script, Idle's character is fittingly called "The Guard Who Doesn't Hiccough But Tries to Get Things Straight" (*MPHGB*, 90). There, "hiccough" is misspelled as "hicough," with the missing "c" penciled in. These credits were obviously intended for production, hence the corrections, but in postproduction Jones and Gilliam decided to get rid of these credits in favor of the "silly" credits at the beginning of the film.

wedding suit on a table or chair—(PSC) Though we don't see the clothing clearly, if this is the time period envisioned by Jones (thirteenth to fourteenth century), the wealthy bridegroom would likely be wearing bright colors and expensive fabrics; maybe tight hose as an undergarment, as well as a close-fitting *paltock* (shirt) tied to hose and sleeves, a formal hood, and a luxurious *houppelande*—a long fur-lined robe with dagged funnel sleeves and a standing collar.[33] Again, none of these or many other details are in sight as the "suit" lies draped across the bottom of the frame. What is visible in the bottom left of the frame is colorful fabric of some sort featuring browns, greens, whites, and reds, and what looks to be stitched flower, leaf, and tendril designs. There are also a number of multicolored ostrich feathers in the room that, though exotic, could easily have been acquired (along with silk) by the wealthy thanks to active maritime trading routes during the Middle Ages that opened the Far East and Africa (often thanks to the Crusades).

. . . crosses to his desk and scribbles a quick note and impales it on an arrow . . .—This is a moment right out of Prince Valiant or a Robin Hood-type comic book series, where an evil someone (stepfather, uncle, black-hearted villain) has imprisoned a defenseless someone (Valiant himself, one of Robin's men, or Maid Marion), and the call goes out for a dramatic rescue. In issue thirty-six of the *Young Heroes* comic series, "Roger of Sherwood Forest" is depicted saving a blonde damsel from a tall tower. Roger hangs from a rope *while* holding the girl (and the rope) *while* fighting a guard who reaches out the window, sword threatening. This comic appeared in April–May 1955, from American Comics. This precise set of events, excepting the bow and arrow, are depicted in the *Adventures of Robin Hood*[34] comic book. In issue six, Maid Marian[35] has been captured by Morla Le Fey and imprisoned in a tall tower. Once left alone, she "discovers a quill pen, an inkstand, and writing parchment," and writes

a note to Robin. She puts the notes in a "leather water bottle," and throws it out the window and into the stream below.[36] Robin of course discovers the note and soon rescues Marian, killing no one (very few die in these comics; they surrender or die out-of-panel).

As for the action (business) here, the script is quite on-the-nose, detailing the father leaving the room, the guards returning to the door, the son gazing out the window, etc., describing each and every action of the silent scene. The only bit left out of the finished film is the note being affixed to the arrow. During a reaction shot of the smiling guards Herbert is somehow able to use the red bookmark and tie the paper onto the arrow. This is a typical bit of cinematic sleight-of-hand, when a confusing or complicated task is accomplished off-camera, allowing the scene to flow more smoothly.

Finally, the quill Herbert uses appears to be a hawk feather as opposed to the more traditional goose feather preferred by many medieval scribes (Fossier, 320).

He looks wetly defiant at the GUARDS . . .—(PSC) Possibly here meaning he's looking at them defiantly through teary eyes, but there's no indication Herbert is actually crying or even close to it. He and his father have likely had this kind of encounter before. Another more likely usage of the term "wet" can mean wan or weak, which fits Herbert's pale, sickly demeanor aptly. In the audio commentary for the 2001 DVD, for example, Palin describes his own portrayal of Galahad as a "wet and completely ineffectual character."

Notes

1. In the audio commentary on the 2012 Blu-ray edition of the film Jones misidentifies this castle as "another castle in Wales," though it's clearly an image of Bodiam. Kidwelly is the only castle in Wales used in the film, and then only as an insert. Cameraman and production manager Doyle recorded this image on a return trip from the Isle of Wight and, without the requisite smoke machine, had his girlfriend burn wet leaves for the smoky effects (Doyle).

2. From a 20 November 2013 e-mail correspondence with the author.

3. Tuchman, *A Distant Mirror*, 156 and 307.

4. "The Gold Plate Robbery" (16 February 1959) audio transcription.

5. "The MacReekie Rising of '74" (25 October 1956) audio transcription.

6. Over the entire forty-five-episode run of *MPFC*, cross-dressing is only acknowledged once, in Ep. 14, where a character (played by Cleese) admits to being a female impersonator. See *MPFC: UC*, 1.55.

7. In this he is like Mr. Brown in *Room at the Top*, the local industrial magnate who's worked his way into regional respectability, and is willing to do virtually anything to stay there. There were many of these "types" and working-class-meets-society situations in the various "Angry Young Man" novels, plays, and films of the 1950s–1960s. See the various entries for "Angry Young Men" in *MPFC: UC*, see also Hewison, *In Anger*; Aldgate, *Censorship and the Permissive Society*, and Booker, *The Neophiliacs*.

8. This sketch originated on the *At Last the 1948 Show* (1967), and became a staple of live Python stage shows.

9. Also spelled "Wycliffe."

10. The only other moments where lead characters are really connected in this way to domestic (and not Grail-related) duties are found in the "Dennis" scene as well as the excised knight introduction section, where Galahad is tending chickens and mending a hen-house, and Launcelot is taking care of children and doing the wash. Those removed, Herbert's father is the only man of the people.

11. See the many entries for the "Working-Class Playwright" sketch in Ep. 2 (*MPFC: UC*, 1.26–49). The "Flying Sheep" sketch is also found in *MPFC* Ep. 2, and features the broad stereotypes of the "Rustic" and "City Gent," both Python stock characters.

12. *Times*, 21 March 1966: 13.

13. "New Postmaster General and B.B.C.," *Times*, 5 July 1966: 13.

14. "Watchdogs for the Housewife," *Times*, 19 June 1968: 7.

15. "Hard Centre of England," *Times*, 25 November 1968: 1. O'Brien wants to separate Birmingham from the north; it stands on its own. To London, it's all north.

16. See Ashe, *The Quest for Arthur's Britain*, 119–28.

17. Hoskins, "The English Landscape," 14–17.

18. In his audio commentary codirector Jones mentions that the original score as completed was simply too "right" for the medieval setting—it didn't help undercut, throw into relief, *or* hyperbolize the action, so it was replaced during postproduction. Just a handful of years earlier director Stanley Kubrick had performed a similar swap for his film *2001: A Space Odyssey*. While editing the film he'd become so fond of the temp tracks (including works by Strauss and Ligeti) that he completely replaced the Alex North score.

19. See the entries for "DeWolfe Music," "incidental music," and "light music" in *MPFC: UC* for more on this thrifty trend. Also, see the entirety of appendix B in that book for the music cues and composers/performers employed by the Pythons for *MPFC*.

20. Both Richard and Humperdinck are mentioned in Ep. 18 of *MPFC*, and the entire cast of *The Sound of Music* appears in Ep. 42, "The Show-Jumping Musical" sketch. *The Sound of Music* is also the film that pensioners are screening when fighting breaks out in "Hell's Grannies," Ep. 8.

21. The success of *The Sound of Music* feature musical film at the worldwide box office also almost single-handedly saved Twentieth-Century Fox from receivership in the late 1960s, when it over-stretched to try for the musical grand slam—the results being megaflop musicals like *Dr. Doolittle* (1967), *Star* (1968), and *Hello Dolly* (1969)—effectively killing the big screen musical and nearly killing Fox. See Schatz's "New Hollywood" article for more.

22. Camille, *Image on the Edge*, 15.

23. See Altman, *The American Film Musical*.

24. See also Rowley, *The High Middle Ages: 1200–1550*, 110–12. Such reclamations were often undertaken only when the increasing population put pressure on existing arable and pastoral land.

25. *IMGM*, plate 212. This scene—not used in the finished film—is discussed in appendix A, Facing Page 46.

26. She never did speak, remaining a mute for life, which some interpreted as divine retribution for her father's thoughtlessness (Tuchman, 47).

27. Isabella will be discussed at some length later, in relation to Princess Lucky's smiling response to the news of Herbert's death.

28. Isabella was jilted by Louis; she was later offered to another older man; and she even famously jilted another suitor, the Emperor-elect Charles IV, all discussed below. She would eventually marry Enguerrand de Coucy VII, the nominal subject of Tuchman's *A Distant Mirror*.

29. Audio transcription, *Fliegender Zirkus*, Ep. 2.

30. See Altman, *The American Film Musical*, for more.

31. See the entries in *MPFC: UC*, under "radio shows" for more.

32. The Pythons' side business during the run of *MPFC* included a number of recorded albums (separate from their BBC work). "Argument Clinic" appeared on *Monty Pythons' Previous Record* in 1972.

33. See Holkeboer, *Patterns for Theatrical Costumes*. Thanks to Dr. Mary Farahnakian, as well.

34. Its name now changed slightly to ally it with the popular British TV show, *The Adventures of Robin Hood* (1955–1957) starring Richard Greene, which appeared on ITA's Associated Rediffusion in September 1955.

35. The spelling can be either or both "Marian" and "Marion," changing sometimes within a single issue.

36. *The Adventures of Robin Hood* #6, June 1957, page 6 of 37.

SCENE TWENTY-FIVE
LAUNCELOT AND CONCORDE

CUT TO the middle of the forest—(PSC) This is another sequential shot, but one where continuous action from one location (the tower) is linked to another location (the forest) thanks to a linking device (the arrow). There is a significant lag, of course—either the weakly shot arrow travels very slowly or it somehow very accurately covers an incredible distance—which is part of the humor. There are few of these types of continuous transitions in the film.

SIR LAUNCELOT is riding along with his trusty servant, . . .—(PSC) In the printed script, it looks as if the line either trailed off and was never finished, since after the comma there is a blank space and no period, or someone used white-out to obscure the final word. It may be that "Lightning" was originally typed there and then whited out or obscured somehow, with the rest of the references to "Lightning" on the page simply penciled through, and "Concorde" written in by hand. "Concorde" is a carry-over reference from *Flying Circus*, and would have been just as *au courant* in 1975 as it was earlier. From the "Ep. 37" section of *MPFC: UC*:

> [The name "Concorde"] elicits a generous laugh from the studio audience, perhaps because the horse's namesake—the still new Concorde SST aircraft—was very much in the public's view and imagination. There are, for example, more than 300 political cartoons treating the subject (Concorde's noise levels, cost overruns, the challenges of cooperating with the French, the expense of operating even one plane, etc.) that appeared in English newspapers during the 1964–1972 period. Also, the significant experienced and projected costs (and cost overruns) for the cooperative program had many asking how such a boondoggle could be justified in times of inflation, and preservationists worried about the sonic booms' deleterious effect on fragile stone cathedrals and churches throughout the country (see *Private Eye*, 9 October 1970, 21–22). (*MPFC: UC*, 2.132)

In the final draft of the *MPHG* script, Concorde is known as "Lightning," with almost every incidence of the name penciled through and "Concorde" written in by hand. The earlier name may well come from the popular children's novel published in 1948 *A Pony Called Lightning*, by Miriam E. Mason. Also, in the *Goon Show* episode "The Case of the Missing CD Plates" (18 October 1955), Henry Crun's very slow horse is called "Lightning." The evergreen significance of treasured memories from the Pythons' youth has been revealed many times before, especially in the myriad appearances of pantomime characters like Long John Silver, Puss in Boots, and the Pantomime Horse throughout *Flying Circus*,[1] as well as the mentions of the ubiquitous Spam[2] and English school life.[3]

In the Middle Ages the naming of destriers (warhorses) wasn't quite so diminutive, or topical, for that matter. Warhorses trained for battle tended to be large and dearly expensive and therefore valuable, and they bore such high-sounding names as *Bayard Dieu*, *Morel de Francia*, and *Bauzan de Burgh*, these expensive animals, the best of which might cost well over £100, were carefully registered and valued; for though the knights now normally fought on foot, strong horses were indispensable for the great *chevauchées* and for the pursuit of a broken enemy. (McKisack, 239)

The destrier names tended to indicate the color of the horse and its "place of origin," according to McKisack (239n). "Concorde," "Lightning," and even "Patsy" don't quite measure up to this medieval standard.

CONCORDE: "Message for you sir"—In the script as printed Launcelot sees the arrow and actually reacts with fear: "*He realises he might be in danger and so starts to crawl off . . . when he notices the note*" (*MPHGB*, 51). The Launcelot who appears in the film knows no such fear, as will be seen later at the Bridge of Death.

He falls forward revealing the arrow . . .—Concorde survives this wound, as do many in the romance sources. For example, Sir Alisander, who was "assotted upon his lady" such that he couldn't stop another damosel from running him through with a sword (*LMD'A*, 2.78). The damosel ran away, and Alisander was healed.

LAUNCELOT (*reading*): ". . . imprisoned by my father who wishes me to marry against my will"—As mentioned earlier, the Middle Ages were a period of carefully arranged marriages (at least among the nobility, the influential), especially where acquisitive wealth and power were concerned, and the "will" of the betrothed had little to do with things.

Incidentally, as late as the fourteenth century this letter would have been more likely written in French or Latin than English: "[T]here are almost no extant English letters before 1400" (Hallam, 297).

LAUNCELOT (*reading*): "I am in the Tall Tower of Swamp Castle"—Coincidentally, an archivolt (a curved ornamental molding) in the Modena, Italy, cathedral, begun about 1099, depicts Arthur and knights rescuing a damsel Winlogee from a fortress, where she is being held prisoner by Mardoc. This is one of a number of *Continental* references to Arthur and his exploits dating from about the beginning of the twelfth century, as his fame spread through the Middle East and then Asia (*QAB*, 8–9).

The "damosel in distress" theme is also broached a number of times in the Grail romances, though more often by messenger than letter. Sir Lancelot responds to many of these, including one where a "lady [came] out of a castle and cried on high, 'Ah, Lancelot, Lancelot, as thou art a flower of all knights'" (*LMD-WM*, 116), while in "The Tale of Sir Gareth of Orkney," "there came a damosel unto the great hall and saluted the King [Arthur], and prayed him of succour" from the pillaging of the Red Knight (122). In another more immediate instance it is Launcelot and only Launcelot who can save the trapped, intensely suffering damosel:

[H]ere is within this tower a dolorous lady that hath been there in pains many winters and days, for ever she boileth in scalding water; and but late, said all the people, Sir Gawaine was here and he might not help her, and so he left her in pain. So may I, said Sir Launcelot, leave her in pain as well as Sir Gawaine did. Nay, said the people, we know well that it is Sir Launcelot that shall deliver her. Well, said Launcelot, then shew me what I shall do.

Then they brought Sir Launcelot into the tower; and when he came to the chamber thereas this lady was, the doors of iron unlocked and unbolted. And so Sir Launcelot went into the chamber that was as hot as any stew. And there Sir Launcelot took the fairest lady by the hand that ever he saw, and she was naked as a needle; and by enchantment Queen Morgan le Fay and the Queen of Northgales had put her there in that pains, because she was called the fairest lady of that country; and there she had been five years, and never might she be delivered out of her great pains unto the time the best knight of the world had taken her by the hand.

> Then the people brought her clothes. And when she was arrayed, Sir Launcelot thought she was the fairest lady of the world. (*LMD'A*, 2.189)

Here the lady's suffering is physical, even grotesque, not the emotional pain Herbert experiences in being forced into a marriage of dynastic convenience, and she is literally saved from distress. Generally, when the damosel is saved, she is revealed to be a beauty, so Launcelot's confusion in *Holy Grail* when he finally meets the prisoner is understandable; Herbert is no fair lady.

LAUNCELOT: ". . . you shall not have died in vain . . ."—Concorde is not dying, of course, but his master's duty to him if he were is clear. During the Anglo-Saxon period in England, the death of a comrade or trusted servant demanded retaliation, according to Norman and Pottinger: "[T]heir lord was expected to avenge the death of one of his men with the blood of the slayer, or with a payment, called the *wergild*, to the dead man's lord and next-of-kin, extracted from the slayer" (13). Launcelot would then storm Swamp Castle looking for the sender of the fatal arrow, and revenge Concorde. It doesn't quite work out that way.

As early as January 1974, the ballooning production costs, price of jet fuel, and diminished airline orders had pundits discussing the "bleak horizons ahead for the British aerospace industry"—the Concorde project was on life support, to many.[4] By February of the same year, airlines like Lufthansa were announcing they would never buy or fly the Concorde, as it "was impossible . . . to operate [the] aircraft economically."[5] Japan Airlines followed suit, and other dominoes fell in line. For all but four airlines (British Airways, Air France, and to a much lesser extent Braniff and Singapore airlines), Concorde *was* built in vain.

CONCORDE: "I'm not quite dead, sir . . ."—Yet another near-death moment, as seen earlier with the old man in the Plague Cart scene, and that will reappear soon in the aftermath of Launcelot's raid on the wedding guests at Swamp Castle. This redirection is a borrow from both *MPFC* and the Goons.[6]

LAUNCELOT: "I will send help, brave friend . . ."—This section is likely at least partly ad-libbed by both Idle and Cleese, including Launcelot searching for the word "idiom," which does not appear in the printed script, where, instead, he exits with "as soon as I have accomplished the most daring, desperate adventure in this genre" (*MPHGB*, 52). Incidentally, Launcelot doesn't send help; he assaults the castle instead. Concorde makes his way into the castle to help Launcelot escape in an appropriately idiomatic way, and just as the scene is naturally coming to a close.

On the DVD commentary Cleese discusses the Concorde injury scene, spending most of his time pointing out the overabundant smoke effects and how, in his opinion, the acting performances and the comedy are obscured by the effect.

Notes

1. See the index for *MPFC: UC* under "pantomime" for the dozens of mentions of and references to pantomimes and panto characters throughout *MPFC*. The Goons referenced the treasured panto tradition often, as well.

2. *MPFC: UC*, 1.323, 325, 371, 381, 412; and 2.132, 168, 228. The "Spam" episode is Ep. 25, incidentally.

3. *MPFC: UC*, 1.37 and 2.58, as well as the mention of grammar schools throughout.

4. *Times*, 7 January 1974: 15.

5. "Lufthansa Rules Out Concorde as 'Impossible to Fly Economically' with Increased Fuel Bills," *Times*, 25 February 1974: 15.

6. See entries above in scene 4, "Bring Out Your Dead," for more on these earlier iterations.

SCENE TWENTY-SIX
LAUNCELOT STORMS SWAMP CASTLE

EXTERIOR—CASTLE GATEWAY—In the printed script the directions take us to the gateway where the sentries greet wedding guests and wait to be killed by Launcelot. In the finished film, this is instead a cut to Princess Lucky being prepared for the wedding, followed by a handful of establishing shots in the castle as the wedding preparations are underway. The first room is, in fact, a redressed version of Herbert's earlier-viewed tower garret—there weren't many interiors available for filming, so creative geography was employed.

The shots continue into the courtyard below, where the festivities are being prepared. Music can be heard, and a four-man group performs under a small canopy. This so-called "low" music is melodic (composed by Neil Innes), and would have been at home "almost anywhere" in the fourteenth century, according to Mortimer, including a "nobleman's feast," the "knighting of the prince of Wales" in 1306, and even from shepherds "in the hills" (249). The musicians set up by the Pythons look to have been provided with suitable period instruments, including what seem to be (from left to right) a rebec (the fiddle-type instrument), a transverse flute, a lute (or gittern), and bagpipes.[1] (See the "*tambourine . . . tabor . . . pipes*" entry above in scene 16, "The Tale of Sir Robin," for other period musical instruments already used.) There are also dancers depicted in the courtyard, and they seem to be performing the appropriately medieval "caroling" dance:

> At a local event . . . you are likely to find the common folk taking to their feet. Most amateur dancing takes the form of "caroling" in which everyone holds hands or links arms in a big circle and skips to the left or the right around the leader, who stands in the middle singing the verses of the song. Everyone taking part in the dance then sings the chorus. (Mortimer, 251)

Two hanging banners one each side of the gate with the monogram: "H & L"—This is outside the castle, at the front gate. The type of lettering used on these banners, as well as the floral tendril designs, are borrowed from the illuminated manuscripts of the period. The *L* looks similar to the one used for the "The Tale of Sir Launcelot" animated sequence earlier, the insular style of the eleventh and twelfth centuries. The *H* is more reminiscent of initial letters found in the name "Henricus" ("Henry," as in Henry VIII) on various royal charters of the mid-sixteenth century.

The TWO SENTRIES are watching him—In the printed script this is a simple scene—the sentries stand and wait, one raises his hand and says "Halt, friend," then Launcelot leaps out of nowhere and kills the guard. There is no mention of the film's use of repetition as

Launcelot runs toward the castle gate. This may have been finally decided on as the film was being edited, or at least in the postproduction phase, since this repeating sequence is noted as having been captured after principal photography was completed, on Hampstead Heath.[2] The outtakes for the film appearing on the Blu-ray edition of the film include a version of Launcelot's repetitive run, but this one is different in two respects. First, the gait Launcelot employs is a "silly" one, limbs askew, not unlike the silly gaits seen often in the Keystone Kops films (and later *The Benny Hill Show*, etc.), and perhaps even somewhat expected of Cleese, whose "Ministry of Silly Walks" performance had become well known.[3] Second, the scene is shot on location, likely somewhere near Stirling or Appin, and not on Hampstead Heath, closer to home, where pickup shots were generally accomplished.

This repetition is a moment of self-conscious reflexivity, the film drawing attention to itself, which was a hallmark of many New Wave films (and much postmodern art and literature in general). The introductory shot of Judas (Carl Anderson) in Norman Jewison's *Jesus Christ Superstar* is a slow zoom toward a mountain crag, where Judas sits. The shot is done four times in succession before settling in on the red-clad figure.[4] Filmmaker Luis Buñuel also includes moments of obvious repetition in films like *Exterminating Angel* (1962) and *The Milky Way* (1969),[5] and repetition for purposeful effect has been part of film since at least 1925, when Eisenstein employed the repeated image of the dish smashing in *Battleship Potemkin*. In the case of *Holy Grail*, the silly or simply repetitive side of the images is closer to perhaps Resnais's use of slow, seemingly repetitive tracking shots in *Last Year at Marienbad* (1961), and are meant to be overtly self-conscious, reminding the audience that a film is being watched.

Swashbuckling music (perhaps)—This same DeWolfe music cue appears later in Gilliam's *Brazil*, heard for the first time when the lowly salarymen at the Ministry of Information tune in to an exciting TV show when their boss (Ian Holm) is tucked away in his office. Doyle[6] mentions that he already had this snippet of music in his possession when the film was being edited, and as he assisted Jones with the music choices and music edit, this generic "swash-buckling music" was used, mostly thanks to its being at hand.[7]

This scene description moment may as well have read "*Korngold music (perhaps)*," since the type of score the Pythons are imagining clearly emerged from the adventure pictures starring Errol Flynn—such as *The Sea Hawk*—with scoring by Erich Korngold (1897–1957). See the next entry.

hacking right and left à la Errol Flynn—(PSC) Flynn (1909–1959) was the star of many classic Hollywood swashbuckling films, including *The Adventures of Robin Hood* (1938), *Captain Blood* (1935), and *The Sea Hawk* (1940), all scored by Erich Korngold.[8] All these films had appeared in British cinemas as the Pythons grew up, and all were very popular with the general public, but especially youngsters.[9]

He fights his way through the COUNTRY DANCE—(PSC) The sheer brutality of Launcelot's attack and the variety of targets chosen render this assault more of a classic *chevauchée* than a rescue mission. The *chevauchée* was an incursion of extended havoc and mayhem where marauding troops burned homes and outbuildings; killed livestock; destroyed food, personal possessions, and even wells; and generally terrorized the countryside. These rampages often included the deaths of many peasants, even whole villages. Launcelot seems determined to kill as many harmless, gaumless (none try to flee) wedding guests as possible, as well. A *chevauchée* could occur as an invading force moves into a new territory—such as the Black Prince pillaging from Bordeaux in 1355[10]—or, after failing to take a besieged castle, for example, the retreating troops could take out their anger (and reap their rewards[11]) in the duchy around the castle and on anything found alive or of value on the way back to the sea. Scottish forces regularly crossed the border and raided the northern English lands with such assaults. The Black Prince could claim several thousand soldiers ready to plunder in France; Launcelot is a man alone as he attacks Swamp Castle. Launcelot attacks musicians and wedding guests, liveried servants and guards, the best man, someone's "auntie," and even the bride's family, none of whom are combatants, clearly; they're just in his way as he seeks the Tall Tower. He hacks at a small vase of flowers hanging on the castle wall, the musicians, and even manages to kick the bride in the chest. In this Launcelot is also reminiscent of the "berserker," Norse warriors who whipped themselves into a trance-like frenzy as they prepped for battle.[12] The killing frenzy would stop only at death or victory.

Bemused looks of GUESTS—not horror so much as uncomprehending surprise—(PSC) It's difficult to see anyone's actual expression during the rampage, since the camera is either set far away in a wide, establishing shot, or in quite close (*"fairly CLOSE-UP chaotic shots"*), and there's camera movement and swift editing employed. However, no one is trying to run away, even as Launcelot moves from person to person, clearly inflicting great bodily harm. This is a typical response to such absurdities in the Python world. In *MPFC*, "The Dull Life of a City Stockbroker" sketch depicts a man who wanders through a landscape featuring his wife's obvious infidelities, an African native attack in his front garden, the Frankenstein monster at a bus stop, a pitched World War II–era battle in the streets, a hanging dead man and a snogging couple on his own desk—the man with the dull life (Palin) is oblivious to all of it. Most absurdities and atrocities are enacted in *Flying Circus* without much onlooker interest.

In the background of one of these Launcelot attack shots (specifically where the guard on the stairs is stabbed and falls onto the barrels) can be glimpsed a man in a pillory. The prisoner seems as well dressed as anyone, and this image of corporal punishment and/or public humiliation is a throwaway gag—everyone celebrates Herbert and Lucky's happy day, clearly.[13]

One COUNTRY DANCER is left holding just a hand—(PSC) This grotesque image is not included in the final cut of the film, but there is plenty of destruction to spare. The amputation image can be connected to an early scene in Kurosawa's fallen samurai film *Yojimbo*, when a dog trots through a deserted main street (of a village beset by rival clan wars) with a severed hand in its mouth. Also, the first scene of Polanski's *Macbeth* features the three weird women burying, among other things, a severed hand clutching a knife. Gilliam's animations during the run of *Flying Circus* focused on similar body horrors—dismembering, re-membering, and so on. From *MPFC: UC*, Ep. 15:

> In this animation, Reg's (Chapman) head is removed and used for the setting, and his right iris is eventually "borrowed" (in the animated diegetic world) for use as a cannonball. . . . Recognizable faces from the world of politics (Nabarro, Heath), sport or entertainment (W. G. Grace, Greer Garson) are given new, often grotesque bodies and/or abilities in Gilliam's world, and normal, unknown folk from traditional family photos also appear. The wholeness of the human body is the expectation, and Gilliam takes every opportunity he can to dismember and make strange and monstrous that formerly sanctified figure. This "body horror" phenomenon isn't new to Gilliam or the Pythons, having crept into [animation (Bob Godfrey, Jan Lenica, Stan Vanderbeek, anime[14]),] feature films (Hammer horror, bloody Peckinpah Westerns, George Romero's *Night of the Living Dead*, etc.) and on the nightly news as the color images from the day's fighting in Vietnam [were presented]. (1.241)

Right and left the GUESTS crumple in pools of blood . . .—(PSC) This scene of slaughter is drawn both from Malory *and* films of the postwar period. From Malory, part of the second "*Sangrail*" section for Sir Lancelot, where he decides to join the fight "to help there the weaker party in increasing . . . his chivalry":

> And so Sir Lancelot thrust in among the party of the castle, and smote down a knight, horse and man, to the earth; and then he rushed here and there and did many marvelous deeds of arms. And

then he drew out his sword and struck many knights to the earth, that all that saw him marveled that ever one knight might do so great deeds of arms. (*LMD-WM*, 348).

The massacre is also immediately followed by Lancelot succumbing to sorrow and shame for such wanton destruction (348–49). As he rides away Lancelot is told (by another helpful, informative recluse) that the fight he saw was actually a fight between good and evil, white and black, and because of his own pride he'd joined the black, the sinners, and "madest great sorrow" (350). Our Launcelot will apologize profusely, twice, for wreaking such havoc.

Gawain is also blessed with this homicidal fecundity in the *Lancelot-Grail*, where Arthur "accuses him of murdering many of the fifty-four knights who had died in the search for the Grail" (*THG*, 203–4). Gawain will fess up to killing more than thirty of these knights, calling the whole bloody scenario a "misfortune" (204).

The more violent films of the Vietnam era—from Kurosawa's blood-geyser *Sanjuro* in 1962 through Peckinpah's *Bring Me the Head of Alfredo Garcia* (1974)—dole out violence and unreal-looking blood in generous portions. Peckinpah[15] especially explored the world of manly, retributive violence in *The Wild Bunch* and *Straw Dogs*, where theatrical blood sprayed and flowed from body after body. Elsewhere, the death of Duncan in Polanski's *Macbeth* is a clumsy, fumbling, bloody affair, with the relentless, on-camera stabbing—by Macbeth himself—creating a slippery mess as Duncan tries to scrabble in vain to safety. The Hammer horror film sets of this same period were equally spattered with Kensington Gore, and further engorged with a vampiric and leering Gothic sexuality. Hollywood's new rating system had emerged just recently in November 1968, with the "R" rating custom made for more "mature" films featuring heightened depictions of sex and violence. Dozens of cheaply produced exploitation films followed almost immediately, with alluring titles like *Ramrodder* and *Beyond the Valley of the Dolls*,[16] as well as low-budget imports from Italy, Spain, Sweden, and Hong Kong.[17] Part of this newfound fascination with violent and sexually "rough" images can also be attributed to the ongoing and very visible war in Vietnam, a war fought in color and depicted on the evening newscasts.[18] The Pythons have already poked fun at this sanguinary penchant in the "Scott of the Sahara" sketch, Ep. 23 of *Flying Circus*, when a dying lion spurts a graceful stream of blood,[19] and Ep. 33, the "Salad Days" sketch, where blood is everywhere and Peckinpah is lampooned by name.[20]

PRINCE: "You got my note?"—In the printed script, a confused Launcelot stammers out a "Well . . . yes . . ." to this, while in the film as finished he instead qualifies his answer on the fly—"Well, well I got, uh, *a* note"—since he already sees that this rescue isn't what he'd expected. This careful picking at nits was characteristic of Python characters like Dennis Moore (also Cleese) in *Flying Circus*, who can wax long about how many times a week he target practices (Ep. 37), or Helmut (Palin), who is constantly niggling his wife with the difference between a sitting room and a drawing room in Ep. 40.

The question does remain: What was Launcelot thinking qualified as a noble deed, "the sign" that would kickstart the Grail quest again? Obviously he had to not only save someone from an evil other, but that someone likely had to be a damosel, not an effeminate man. Nowhere else is Launcelot choosy about his head- and sword-first thrusting—he will attack the French castle walls, at sword point save Galahad from "almost certain temptation," carve his way through Swamp Castle, and finally offer to attack the Bridgekeeper to cross the Gorge of Eternal Peril. Into all these endeavors he leaps. Here, he pauses for the first time. If there was any thought that Galahad's muttered "Bet you're gay" had any validity, that might be laid to rest here, as he clearly has no attraction to Herbert.[21]

Music cuts out—(PSC) Again, Herbert's father is almost more concerned with the specter of a musical number irrupting into his carefully crafted diegetic world than his son's happiness or the slaughter that he's just passed through, though he'll get to the latter.

PRINCE: "I'm . . . your son . . ."—This was just "I'm" in the printed script, and was added to at some point during production. We've seen that the relationship between Herbert and his father has been in question from the beginning, when Father calls him "Alice" instead of Herbert, and Herbert calls his father "mother." Identities are often shifty in the Python world.

The "Who are you?"—Father asks this of his dangerous visitor Launcelot—that precedes this could also be a fair, leading question. Launcelot has killed both employees and guests of the castle, and could be liable for those deaths. By the mid-fourteenth century, however, it was possible for a layman to claim the protection of "benefit of clergy." This had applied to actual clergymen since at least the reign of Henry II and his famous disagreements with Thomas Becket,[22] but by the reign of Edward III requirements were relaxed to simply "literacy"—the claimant had to be able to read. Launcelot has already proved himself qualified: He'd read the note from Herbert, aloud, and even in the presence of a witness, Concorde. After being accused of killing "eight wedding guests and all" in front of numerous witnesses, Launcelot could have pleaded benefit of clergy and been tried before an ecclesiastical court rather than a traditional court of law, where demonstrating his ability to read the Bible, for example, would benefit him. In the world of Swamp Castle and its environs, though, there doesn't seem to be anyone willing to pursue such retributive actions against the "influential knight" Launcelot; instead, he is to be sentenced to become a son-in-law to this grasping father and the husband of Princess Lucky.

But the Goons also ventured here in their earlier episode "The Whistling Spy Enigma," when Neddie has been waiting for a promised super spy:

Bluebottle (Sellers): I heard you call me, my highly skilled mysterious cap-i-tain. Sorry I didn't hear you first time, but my Dan Dare super cut-out cardboard radio receiver failed at a crucial moment. Moves upstage, strikes heroic pose, but unstrikes it when trousers fall down. Hee-Hee. Your turn.

Seagoon (Secombe): Tell me, who are you, you dirty-nosed Goon?

Eccles (Milligan): Well I'm Eccles, I told you that . . .

Seagoon: (*to Eccles*) Not you! (*to Bluebottle*) You!

Bluebottle: I am secret agent Bluebottle. (28 September 1954)

FATHER: "They cost fifty pounds each!"—The ubiquitous pound has been around since Charlemagne's time, and survived through the Anglo-Saxon period virtually unchanged (except in value). The actual value of coinage changed over time, depending on the pressure it was under, but fifty pounds for a single guard in any of the times posited by the Pythons—the sixth, tenth, twelfth, thirteenth, or fourteenth centuries—is vastly overvalued.[23] By the mid-fourteenth century, for example, an "average mason" could expect to make about £7 1s 6d for the *year* (with no Sunday work and dozens of "holy days" off), while a "master mason" (or master carpenter) could make between £10 and £17 annually, "similar to highly educated lawyers and physicians," according to Mortimer (100–101). Fifty pounds would have been a true fortune, then.

Tuchman notes that in 1345, Edward demanded all landowners (meaning those generating rent roll incomes) either serve in the military campaigns in person or provide for a funded substitute, using the following schedule: "A man with £5 of income from land or rents was to supply an archer, a £10 income supplied a mounted spearman, £20 supplied two of these, income over £25 supplied a man-at-arms, meaning usually a squire or knight" (82). The *high* end of the income bracket here is £25, so being able to pay £50 for a single guard would have likely been impossible.[24] In France during this same period, the fee for a *mounted* squire was only 6–7 sous per day. A lowly guard, sans horse, who wasn't expected to travel, be bivouacked or fight—who might be asked to stand guard at a castle gate greeting wedding guests—would have cost significantly less (Tuchman, 83–85). Account ledgers from the late thirteenth century indicate that Henry de Bray spent £12 to completely build out a new "hall and north chamber," and that Geoffrey de Langley's quite massive estates in Warwickshire and Gloucestershire were valued at about £200 per annum in 1274.[25] Willis figures that de Bray collected annual rents on 250 acres of demesne land totaling "£11 16s. 10½d.,"[26] and paid out "per annum to Nicholas de Chaunceus four shillings and a penny; to the convent of St Leonards sixpence; to the lord of Neubottle nineteen shillings and fivepence."[27] In fact, with a thirteenth-century-era income that generated anything in excess of twenty pounds, according to Raban, a monarch's expectations for men like Herbert's father increased quite specifically: "During the course of the thirteenth century, the policy known as distraint of knighthood *required* those with lands worth more than £20 per annum to become knights" (103; italics added). Historically speaking, there's no way a man of Herbert's father's means could have escaped a sovereign's attentions—his wealth was just too valuable (meaning borrowable).

Finally, the lowly pound, shilling, and pence went much farther in the twelfth to fourteenth centuries, clearly, and since possession of such a period fortune would have demanded a great deal more of the king of Swamp Castle, the Pythons likely picked "fifty pounds" right out of the air.

PRINCE: "I've got a rope here all ready"—Herbert actually produces a sheet and ties it to the bed frame, preparing to climb out of the tall tower with his rescuer Launcelot. In Malory's *The Noble Tale of Sir Lancelot du Lake*, Lancelot witnesses one knight being set upon by three, and, determining to even the odds, climbs out of the garret window using a bed sheet (110). There are also myriad similar escapes from dungeons and towers in the pages of Robin Hood and Prince Valiant–type comics of the mid-1950s.

FATHER: "You killed eight wedding guests in all"—In *LMD-WM*, in *The Noble Tale of Sir Lancelot du Lake*, Malory's Lancelot is accosted as he crosses a bridge, and responds, of course, in his own idiom:

> So on the third day he rode on a long bridge, and there started upon him suddenly a passing foul churl; and he smote his horse on the nose that he turned about, and asked him why he rode over that bridge without licence.
>
> "Why should I not ride this way?" said Sir Lancelot. "I may not ride beside."
>
> "Thou shalt not choose," said the churl, and lashed at him with a great club shod with iron. Then Sir Lancelot drew his sword and put the stroke aback, and cleft his head unto the paps. At the end of the bridge was *a fair village, and all the people, men and women, cried on Sir Lancelot, and said, "Sir knight, a worse deed didst thou never for thyself, for thou hast slain the chief porter of our castle."*
>
> Sir Lancelot let them say what they would, and straight he rode into the castle. And when he came into the castle he alit, and tied his horse to a ring on the wall; and there he saw a fair green court, and thither he addressed him, for there him thought was a fair place to fight in. So he looked about him, and saw much people in doors and windows that said, "Fair knight, thou art unhappy to come here." (109; italics added)

The description of the castle interior is also quite reminiscent of the Pythons' version of Swamp Castle, where Launcelot has killed and maimed many.

LAUNCELOT: ". . . the thing is . . . I thought your son was a lady"—The specter of Holy Grail–era homosexuality won't be fully realized until much later, when some of the

Pythons create and stage the play *Spamalot*, but references to sodomitical behaviors and/or same-sex misunderstandings do appear in some of the Grail romances.[28] In Malory's *A Noble Tale of Sir Lancelot du Lake*, Lancelot finds shelter in an empty pavilion, only to have the knight-owner of that pavilion return during the night:

> Then within the hour came the knight that owned the pavilion; he weened that his [mistress] had lain in the bed, and so laid him down by Sir Lancelot and took him in his arms and began to kiss him. And when Sir Lancelot felt a rough beard kissing him, he started out of the bed lightly, and the other knight after him; and either of them got their swords in their hands, and out at the pavilion door went the knight of the pavilion. And Sir Lancelot followed him . . . and wounded him sore, nigh unto death. (*LMD-WM*, 100)

Quickly thereafter the misunderstanding is discovered, Lancelot apologizes profusely, then promises to not only heal the knight, but also assist in promoting him to Arthur as a potential knight of the Round Table.

FATHER: "You only killed the Bride's father—that's all"—This is actually quite advantageous, and Herbert's father realizes it after just a few moments. Marriages during this period were always undertaken to cement alliances, forge new relationships of power, and acquire more riches, security, and dynastic longevity. Herbert's father wants more land—additional acres that mean more crops, more livestock, and more regional power—as well as direct relations with Camelot, the seat of power. With Princess Lucky's father dead but the proposed match still intact, Swamp Castle can realize all the increase without the headache of new familial relationships (no in-laws, but much of their properties), and Herbert's father even tries to insinuate himself into line for direct control over both the Princess's dowry *and* estates—the clever, scheming northern businessman at work.

FATHER: "You put your sword right through his head!"—It's sweetly naive that Launcelot asks if the Bride's father is "all right" after this revelation, as if he truly doesn't understand the consequences of his idiomatic or generic actions.[29]

Scores of these grotesque descriptions and images can be found in the Pythons' various source materials. There are all sorts of violations in the films *Throne of Blood* and *Macbeth*, discussed elsewhere, but also in Shakespeare's *The Tragedy of Macbeth*, where the reporting Sergeant describes the rampaging Macbeth as "Valor's minion" as "he unseam'd [Macdonwald] from the nave to the chaps, / And fix'd his head upon our battlements" (1.1.19, 22–23). Choosing a literary inspiration, there is a *bas-de-page* image in the illuminated manuscript Royal 10 E.IV (used elsewhere and extensively by Gilliam)[30] of a castle under attack. A defender of the castle has put his sword right through the head of a helmetless attacker on a siege ladder (f. 18v). Randall includes twenty-six images from the Royal 10 manuscript in *IMGM*. Gilliam borrows one (plate 212) for the "centerfold" section of the *MPHG* book.

FATHER: "It's going to cost me a fortune!"—Herbert's father is the scrabbling, somewhat mean northern landowner for whom expense and income mean everything. In this, though, he is very much aligned with the nobility of the thirteenth and fourteenth centuries in England, since the power of the purse more often than not dictated the reach of governmental activities. Just prior to the outbreak of the Hundred Years War, Edward III was paying for "a series of costly and inconclusive campaigns" in the lowlands of Scotland, with soldiers' wages alone reaching £12,000 (McKisack, 118). This was money that couldn't be used to support the struggling English holdings in France. As the Scottish war continued in the mid-1330s, costs escalated, and France attempted to wrangle its way into the Scottish issue, supporting Scotland, of course, while Pope Benedict XII was faced with an all-out northern and western European war as well as the financing of a new crusade (121–22). Everywhere you turn in these histories the subject of finance rears its head—costs of maintaining the royal houses and lifestyles, funding domestic and foreign military actions, and sustaining a working government and legal system; the availability of increased taxes during times of plague and famine, especially; the selling of crown jewels for ready cash; and so on.[31] As mentioned earlier, Edward III's successes in Flanders in 1340 helped the bottom line, but his creditors still wanted to keep his wife and children "as hostages for the payment of his debts" (128). Edward III's son, the Black Prince, was a military marvel against the French, then set up a lavishly expensive court at Bordeaux in 1362 and funded it with very unpopular *fouages*, or hearth taxes (144). By 1368 the people of Gascony had paid enough, and in 1369 Charles V declared Edward III's French lands confiscate, and the Hundred Years War resumed (145).

At the most local level, finally, even the proper maintenance of a manor meant that a steady income was necessary, and those streams of money were choked considerably during times of war, times of increased ninths, tenths, and other taxations, and especially as the productivity of the land diminished prior to the privations of various plagues.

FATHER: "Camelot? Are you from Camelot?"—The Father is worried about the expense of Launcelot's visit, but the glancing mention of "Camelot" has caught his ear. Consider the last time Camelot was named, by Robin's minstrel, when the mention led to the Three-Headed Knight threatening to kill him. Now, the cachet of Camelot is its agricultural fecundity—it's a commercial prospect for an on-the-job merchant looking to improve his fortunes. For many in the film audience, Camelot had been eponymously attached to the glistening Kennedy administration just a decade before, meaning the film's connections to "Camelot"—a "silly place" of song and dance, a place that could produce a cowardly Sir Robin, that was a seat of porcine commercial wealth—may have produced an entirely different set of associations to children of the 1960s and 1970s. As early as November 1964, one year after Kennedy's death, British papers were talking about the idealized Camelot and, not unlike *New York Times* editor James B. Reston a year earlier, trying to sift the hyperbole from the actual, sorting the legend from the living.[32] The *Times*'s Washington correspondent said it best: "[Kennedy] was not, as has been suggested, a perfect knight who had wandered from Camelot."[33] By 1974, "Camelot" may have been as linked to the Kennedy administration and myth as to Arthur, for many.

FATHER: ". . . very nice castle, Camelot . . ."—Here the good-natured rapacity of this king emerges in full flower—it is the "impressive sight" of a northerner "on the make," to mangle Barrie's phrase.[34] The Camelot we've seen, though, looks as dank and dark as any, and "silly" to boot.[35] The glorious castles wouldn't appear until the French versions of the romances much later, likely modeled on castles like the Coucy stronghold, which Tuchman describes in awe-inspiring terms:

> Formidable and grand on a hilltop in Picardy, the five-towered castle of Coucy dominated the approach to Paris from the north, but whether as guardian or as challenger of the monarchy in the capital was an open question. Thrusting up from the castle's center, a gigantic cylinder rose to twice the height of the four corner towers. This was the donjon or central citadel, the largest in Europe, the mightiest of its kind ever built in the Middle Ages or thereafter. . . . Travelers coming from any direction could see this colossus of baronial power from miles away and, on approaching it, feel the awe of the traveler in infidel lands at first sight of the pyramids. (3)

This imposing castle is of a type depicted by Doré in his illustrations for Tennyson's 1868 *Idylls of the King*, including massive walls leading to towers with peaked, tiled roofs.[36]

FATHER: ". . . very good pig country"—"Good pig country" would have been anywhere near accessible oak forests for acorn forage, of course, and, due to regional climate considerations, the southeast of England continues to be "pig country." Fossier further describes the symbiosis of pigs and acorn-rich forests during the Middle Ages:

> [I]n September, when acorns were plentiful, pigs were let loose in the forest. They might even live in the woods all year long, with the result that until at least the tenth century, a forested stretch was measured "in pigs," or the "surface necessary to nourish one pig for one year," estimated to be about one hectare. (183)

Herbert's father's observation, then, seems perfectly apt. Pigs were also popular for peasant farmers since they could be fed almost entirely on waste products from homes and villages, "a highly economical source of meat" for medieval men like the denizens of Swamp Castle (*HBMA*, 260). These woodland resources seem to have been quite important during the Anglo-Saxon period, as they figure into estate plans and proper inheritances and charters throughout the period, as well as being jealously guarded by the lord who claims ownership (Sawyer, 147–49). Arthur has been perambulating through "his" England, seeking knights to join his cause; he could just as easily have been "tracing the boundaries" of his kingdom, as was the case for government officials throughout the Anglo-Saxon years, and even after, as Domesday Book was being compiled. See Sawyer's chapter "The Making of the Landscape" in *From Roman Britain to Norman England* for more.

Father nonchalantly cuts it with his knife—(PSC) This attempted homicide of the effeminate Herbert[37] may well be a reference to the fairly recent spate of "queer bashing" experienced across Britain just a few years earlier. In 1969–1970 there was a trial at the Old Bailey concerning the murder of Michael de Gruchy on Wimbledon Common by a gang of twelve youths. The group had armed themselves and then lay in wait, looking for a homosexual to attack, according to their own testimony. The youths were all found guilty and variously sentenced, one to a life sentence. Throughout the run of *MPFC*, obviously homosexual or even just effeminate characters, both live and animated, are regularly shot, impaled, or beaten.[38]

Also, Herbert is cut loose by his father just when the much more appealing Sir Launcelot appears. In the "Winchester Manuscript" version of Malory's *Le Morte Darthur*, Sir Bors is forced to choose between his promise to remain chaste and the life of not only one fair lady, but her attendants, as well, who wait in a tall tower:

> Then looked he upward and saw they seemed all ladies of great estate, and richly well beseen. Then he had of them great pity; not for that he was not uncounselled in himself that he had liever they all had lost their souls than he his soul. And with that they fell all at once unto the earth; and when he saw that, he was all abashed and had thereof great marvel. And with that he blessed his body and his visage. (*LMD-WM*, 365)

But there is also the general violence of the period to be reckoned, violence that would have been looked upon "nonchalantly" by the Middle Ages man. Tuchman writes that "[w]hile total absence of inhibition was characteristic of persons born to rule, bizarre bursts of violence were becoming more frequent in these years, perhaps as a legacy of the Black Death and a sense of the insecurity of life" (133–34). She goes on to mention two well-heeled men, one of Italian nobility the other French, who killed their own sons (and direct heirs) in "fits of ungovernable rage" (134). These men murdered their male offspring (and changed their dynastic fortunes) without rational thought; Herbert's father seems to be quite calculating as he cuts Herbert's bed sheet, then puts his arm around the "brave but dangerous Sir Launcelot."

There is no sound except after a pause a slight squeal from very far away as the PRINCE makes contact with the ground—(PSC) There *is* a slight sound accompanying the squeal, a squishing or "raspberry"-type sound. This rather rude sound is a borrow from *Flying Circus* episodes as well as the *Goon Show*. The squishy, nearly flatulent sound effect is similar to one used by Gilliam in an animated sequence in Ep. 29, "Bouncy Ball Woman" (*MPFC: UC*, 2.40). The sound can also be heard in the infamous Ep. 19 animated sequence "The Spot," where it serves as the sound the Spot makes as it moves from place to place.[39] In the *Goon Show*, Milligan asked for the raspberry sounds made by donkeys included in various episodes,[40] for bodily sound effects, often. For the Pythons, the legacy of radio continues to be an important source as they create their imagined world.

LAUNCELOT: "... when I'm in this idiom ..."—In the printed script Launcelot blames his "genre," not his idiom. Perhaps the Pythons wanted to break up the reference repetitiveness. Concorde reminds Launcelot that it's his "idiom" he's enacting moments earlier, while Launcelot is sure that slinking away isn't right for his idiom later.

FATHER: "... doesn't Camelot own that stretch of farmland ..."—This line was to have been delivered as they walked off together, likely fading into the distance as they moved down the stairs. It is not part of the finished film, but it does reinforce Herbert's father's fixation on arable land acquisition, so essential to the Middle Ages nobleman.

This character's careful focus on properties and alliances further connects him back to the historical Henry de Bray,[41] a landowner of some significance from Northants. De Bray was a Northamptonshire, East Midlands nobleman (yes, another northerner) who left an intricately detailed record of his estates. According to the editor of *The Estate Book of Henry de Bray*, Dorothy Willis, de Bray was a man of many talents and interests—he was a builder ready to DIY a castle, for example—and (like Herbert's father) his personal wealth seemed of particular interest to him:

> In 1323 our Henry de Bray was among the half-dozen good and legal men who asserted on their oath in reply to an inquisition *ad quod damnum* ["appropriate to the harm"] that the Castle of Northampton was greatly in need of repair, and the items of repair and cost are all enumerated. In the Estate Book there is much evidence as to Henry's experience in building. . . . It is possibly a tribute to his capacities in this direction that he should have had any part in this matter. It is clear that the absence of Henry's name from the public records except in these three instances probably proves that he was of no great account in the greater world of affairs, and his interest in political affairs cannot have been at all strong, or he would surely have made some allusion to the Scotch wars or to the agitations of the King's visit to Northampton in 1318. . . . Henry's absorption in his own affairs seems to have been largely due to inherited feuds about land ownership. (xii–xiii)

Herbert's father is also absorbed in his own interests, he has a focus on land and land acquisition, and he's clearly not connected to what's going on at the seat of power, Camelot, though he's attentive if such interests promise increase.

FATHER: "... have all this knocked through"—This small talk is *not* part of the finished script, but the subject matter was both historical and au courant. The process of castle demolition and rebuilding had been part of various English kings' "consolidation of power" agenda for many years, including Henry II (1133–1189), who, upon assuming the throne in 1154, immediately began pulling down "adulterine" castles (those constructed without license, or by the crown's enemies, or on disputed royal lands) built or populated during the Anarchy.[42] Henry would also see to the destruction of dozens of castles following the unsuccessful conclusion of his sons' (and his wife's and a number of barons') rebellion in 1173–1174:

But if [Henry] dealt leniently with the barons, he dealt ruthlessly with their castles. He was determined to remove from them the power of resistance. A clause in the Assize of Northampton issued in 1176 instructs the justices to see that the demolished castles are utterly demolished, and that those which ought to be demolished are levelled to the ground, and the official records prove that the king's orders were carried out. (Poole, *DBMC*, 338).

The surviving royal castles were just as assiduously "repaired and strengthened" in the rebellion's aftermath, as Henry refortified his position of power (338).

Mortimer calls the fourteenth century in England "the great age of castle *rebuilding*" (155). During the latter part of that century Richard II issued "dozens of new licenses to crenellate" (install battlements on castle walls), while significant renovations (often for comfort and ostentation, not fortification) were made on the castles at Okehampton, Wigmore, Ludlow, Warwick, Bamburgh and Raby, Kenilworth and Hertford, Fotheringay and Caldicott, and more (155). There were also a number of brand-new castles like Penrith and Bodiam[43] constructed late in the century. McKisack notes that just as "splendid living and lavish hospitality were expected of great lords in an age that admired ostentation," their lessers, like Herbert's father—a provincial magnate of a fetid swamp—emulated them, spending both money earned and money borrowed (263). The castle at Berkeley, for example, where Edward II was likely murdered in 1327, was improved by the addition of "a fine new hall," making life in the old castle more comfortable (263). Herbert's father seems more interested in creating a new castle that can "overawe and entertain" rather than act in defense of his family and lands—perhaps since he's in a swamp the castle is safe enough from full-scale assault.

But this "knocked through" phenomenon wasn't confined to the post-Norman invasion period or to efforts to give brick-and-mortar foundations to the fortifying of familial dynasties. By the late 1960s, hundreds of ancient structures (stately homes, government and religious buildings, etc.) in Britain had been razed for various reasons, including space needs, modernization demands, spiraling costs for upkeep and inheritance taxation, and many simply because they were just old and out of fashion. Between the end of World War II and 1974, about 250 architecturally and/or historically significant country homes were demolished.[44] In *The Destruction of the Country House*, Dr. Roy Strong describes the unsympathetic world these historic homes encountered in the late 1960s and early 1970s:

In many cases a new generation has inherited, often with less inclination than the post-war owners to dedicate their lives to the often thankless task of maintaining an historic building and caring for its contents, gardens and parkland. Sheer acreage alone can no longer be coped with in the face of no help. The disappearance of gardeners, of living-in staff, of the estate carpenter and the odd-job man often spells the end of a house as a practical place to live in. (8)

There are dozens of newspaper articles from this same period describing the decline of these homes and the fortunes of the families who try to keep them up, as well as upbeat but still sobering estate agent listings for available portions of many historic houses and outbuildings (ready to be "knocked through"), their lands, and chattel.

The significance of such country houses in the collective English psyche is obvious, and to Herbert's father, as well:

Thanks to primogeniture, British country houses have remained treasure chests, while those on the Continent have been ransacked not just by revolution, but by partible inheritance: with every new generation, there's been another division of the spoils. Equipped with bottomless fortunes—and the leisure to go on year-long Grand Tours—British aristocrats took their pick from European art collections and covered their walls back home with Rembrandts, Titians and Poussins.[45]

Quite coincidentally to the Pythons' creation of *Holy Grail*, there was a new exhibition—also in 1974—hosted by the V & A Museum called *Destruction of the Country House*, which featured photographs of dozens of demolished stately homes, gardens, and properties. A book of the same name emerged from the exhibition, where Roy Strong lays out the country homes' significance to Britain:

> The great houses of England and their occupants represent a continuity within our society. The British by nature have a powerful sense of their historic identity, never more forcefully expressed than in time of war. In time of peace it tends to wither. We have a democratic society and are governed constitutionally, but we love the pomp and ceremony, the dedication and giving that we find epitomized in the Crown. The House of Lords survives and burgeons on life peerages and the irony of socialist aristocrats. So the great house and its inmates, manacled by time and successive Chancellors of the Exchequer, are not such an anachronism within our society. Country house owners are the hereditary custodians of what was one of the most vital forces of cultural creation in our history. They deserve consideration and justice as much as any other group within our society as they struggle to preserve and share with us the creative richness of our heritage. (10)

This and other cris de coeur continued to fall on largely deaf ears. In that same year (1974) Lord Rosebery passed away, leaving his vast estates to his family, along with a host of inheritance problems, including a staggering death duty. A three-year window for the payment of that duty saw the home put on the shopping block (1974–1977), as the Rosebery ancestral estate and stud farm at Leighton Buzzard, known as "Mentmore," sought wealthy buyers or government intervention in vain. The Mentmore home,[46] according to the current Lord Rosebery, cost £20,000 a year to run properly, plus staff costs, and given its museum-like design, the home wasn't "suitable for conversion" (meaning, being "knocked through" for a bed and breakfast or the like). Rosebery wasn't optimistic about finding a buyer, either, and even offered the home, its complete furnishings and art collection to the beleaguered Callaghan government as a potential museum in lieu of death duty payments.[47] The government eventually declined the offer, fearing the price of upkeep in the throes of Britain's economic doldrums, but still demanded the death duty.[48]

But the fate of country houses, castles, abbeys, and even modest homes in Britain had been tenuous across time. Remember that as rewards for service in the Norman Conquest, dozens of estates had been wrested from English hands and gifted to military and religious supporters of the Norman William; and later Henry VIII would famously reassign many surviving Catholic holdings in Britain to those adhering to the new state church—former abbeys being the foundation on which many new manorial estates (and universities) were constructed. In a move of convenience, not dissolution, the lord for Wharram Percy had his tenants forcibly removed, then knocked down their homes for additional sheep pasturage in the sixteenth century (Campbell, 1991, 9). Those without political clout suffered the most in these bullying events. Later, the Victorian era saw a spate of remodels of ancient British castles. Many converted abbeys, for instance, were significantly added to for servants' quarters, outbuildings, and such; but most castles in continual usage were simply remodeled as tastes and occupant needs changed over the decades.[49] Also, many soaring castles began rather humbly as Romanage earthworks, only to be fortified and refortified and finally remodeled into comfortable Tudor mansions, like Laugharne Castle in Wales.

But the costs associated with maintaining the ancestral home, once gotten, continued to spiral as *MPHG* was brought to fruition. In 1983 Stephen Webbe would look closely at the perilous situation of the country home across Britain, as even the tourist pound began to disappear:

> "The tourist boom of the '70s is now sadly behind us," observed Lady Mansfield of Scotland's Scone Palace recently. "The downward trend of the early '80s is already obvious enough to make us tighten our seat belts and take alert and uneasy notice." Bluntly, visitors are not pouring into historic houses the way they used to.
>
> In 1972, for instance, 320,000 people trooped around Longleat House, the Marquess of Bath's ancestral home in Wiltshire. In 1981, the year that admissions to historic buildings in England fell by 10 percent, only 150,000 came to see it. Last year, Lord Tavistock's Woburn Abbey in Bedfordshire suffered an 8 percent reduction in visitors. . . . The destruction of Britain's historic houses, which some say peaked in 1955, did not appreciably abate until about 1969 [following the 1968 Town and County Planning Act], when government permission was first required to demolish a house of any consequence.
>
> "The tide of demolition has been very, very much slowed down," says Marcus Binney, architectural editor of *Country Life* and chairman of SAVE Britain's Heritage, a group that campaigns on behalf of endangered buildings.[50]

Demolition did slow appreciably in the late 1960s and early 1970s, as SAVE Britain's Binney mentions, but what followed were years of pain as surviving ancestral homes and lands fell prey to changing tourist tastes, stagnant economies, oil embargoes, and the inevitability of taxes and death duties.

The 1960s had wrought changes previously unthinkable, even to the more (and more abundant) middle-class homes and family prospects. With the rising consumer culture and seemingly endless discretionary income (at least compared to the years of austerity), as well as the explosion of the modish Op Art styles and affordable, modular home furnishings, Britons spent their money on transforming their stolid, Victorian and Edwardian-era homes and flats into colorful personal expressions—they were having things "knocked through," as well. From Sandbrook:

> One problem was that millions of people lived not in specially built open-plan villas but in flats, narrow terraces or semi-detached houses, so *the sixties were boom years for renovations, knocking down walls and generally bashing houses about.* One woman later recalled that her mother spent a fortune "stripping things out of [her Edwardian] house, and gradually painting nearly everywhere white with bits of pine and metal strips and bright-coloured plastic and *knocking down the odd wall for the new open-plan effect.*" (*White Heat,* 77; italics added)

And back finally to the actual "knocked through" comment from Herbert's father. Palin here sounds like any suburbanite, DIY Briton looking to improve the market value of his home, even an upward-looking, middle-class "Ideal Home" type.[51] Herbert's father is, finally, a nouveau riche, rent roll–type landlord, not unlike a Barnsley coal or textile millionaire of the Victorian age, and keen to look and act the more upper-class part—perhaps the antithesis of a Dennis.

With fearless abandon he throws himself into the CROWD and starts hacking and slashing—In Launcelot's single-minded devotion to his sword and its abilities to remake the world, two very different comparisons come to mind. First, a "renegade prior of the Knights of St. John," Fra Monreale, was a famous and even respected brigand who commanded men at arms and the fear of many towns, including Venice, Rimini, Pisa, and Siena—he demanded and received tens of thousands of gold florins from each for protection. Though admittedly a criminal, his devotion to his craft and its tools (attrition via the sword) is Launcelot-like, and is especially justifiable given the retrograde nature of the world in the mid-fourteenth century. Finally arrested in

1354 and found guilty of myriad crimes, he was sentenced to public beheading in Rome, but remained steadfast throughout, according to Tuchman: "Unrepentant at the end, he declared himself justified 'in carving his way with a sword through a false and miserable world'" (164).

Second, the reemergence of the samurai film in the decades after the war offered several types of subgenres, as well as types of swordsmen. The significance of postwar Japanese film to the Pythons has been established, and the subgenres within these films were likely not lost on them, either. David Desser[52] lists the following categories of samurai films, each placing different emphasis on the value of society versus the individual, and the significance (presence/absence) of nostalgia, both key elements in the Pythons' work. This discussion of Desser's findings is a bit lengthy, but important as we understand some of the changes postwar (Japanese) cinema endured in its depictions of heroes and the heroic, and how the Pythons reacted to those changes.

The "Nostalgic Samurai Drama" can be characterized by its films, according to Desser, including *Seven Samurai* (1954). In these films there exists a significant *mono no aware* approach, thematically and stylistically. *Mono no aware* is the "feeling of sweet sadness, an almost inexpressible sensation of life's mortality which is pleasantly painful, and is one of the foundations of traditional Japanese aesthetic theory" (Desser, 148). The Pythons' dealing with their own collective pasts can be similarly colored, as, throughout the run of *MPFC*, they wrestled with and wrote from the wellspring of "lower middle with pretensions to middle-middle" class, according to Cleese: "It is funny how the whole of the Monty Python crew came from exactly the same strata. I have a feeling it's a sort of floating group without any affiliation with any other class" (Nathan, 183). But the nostalgic sadness is tinged and conveyed with mirth in *MPHG*. In these nostalgic samurai films there is what Desser sees as an "overvaluation of society" and an "undervaluation of the individual";[53] the films portray a longing for the past (underscoring the Japanese postwar experiences of loss and lack); and the heroes are often linked with nature. *Seven Samurai* features several groups—villagers, bandits, former samurai—and the former samurai (ronin) embrace nobility and self-destruction, yielding to the new age of the rising peasantry.

The "Anti-Feudal Samurai Drama" (Masaki's *Hara-kiri* [1962] and *Samurai Rebellion* [1967]) is the subgenre where there is an "overvaluation of society," an "undervaluation of individual," and a move toward *anti-nostalgia* based on increasing U.S.-Japan relations (including the renewal of the Mutual Security Pact, 1960), especially militaristic relations, and these films came to treat the past in a more political way. During these years (early 1960s), the antimilitary, anti-aggression sentiment is rising. Some of these films serve as "reminders of the dangers of feudalism" (152). This subgenre also tends to rely on widescreen processes to isolate, de-emphasize, and "contextualize" the hero. Also, the heroes are linked with society (urban, manmade settings), and the sense of *mono no aware* is still prevalent as the hero is allowed to be a tragic figure—he can fail nobly.

In the "Zen Fighters" films, like Inagaki's *Samurai Trilogy* (1954–1956), we see an "undervaluation of society" and an "overvaluation of the individual"; they can ignore or transcend the social contexts of their time; and society becomes a mere backdrop for the Zen swordsman's "ethical, moral and 'duelistic' impulses" (Desser, 154). Launcelot fits here, to a great extent. In kneeling before the prisoner in the tall tower (who turns out to be the sallow Herbert), sword before him, he is pledging this most efficient weapon to the ideals of beauty and chivalry, both of which shudder to a stop when Launcelot realizes whose "cry of distress" he's answering. In these "Zen" films, sword skills are perfected as *Bushido* constraints are removed, and the hero must test his skills again and again for validation (154). (Launcelot actively seeks opportunities to prove himself and resume the Quest.) These films and characters "move away from nobility of failure" because Zen fighters often achieve success; caring little for any life, they survive anyway (155). (Two "classic Zen swordsmen"—Kambei and Kyuzo in *Seven Samurai*—illustrate the borrowing from subgenre to subgenre [155].) Launcelot keeps slashing forward until arrested by forces beyond his control, and even beyond his world.

And finally in "The Sword Film," including *Yojimbo* and *Sanjuro*, society is undervalued and the individual is undervalued; the films (and its "hero") betray "a kind of nihilism" (158). In these films heroism is ultimately meaningless, as is any search for self-perfection; these films tend to present "a very bleak . . . stylized, view of the human condition" (162).

It's easy to see that the Pythons have picked bits and pieces from *each* of these categories for their several armigerous "heroes," and that they were fully cognizant of the multiple threads running through the Japanese sword pictures of their day. In their version(s), the Pythons *seem* to overvalue the individual in relation to an undervalued society (Arthur on a God-given quest through a fallen world), but that binary is in flux throughout the film, and by the end, our key individuals—Arthur and Bedevere and knights—are either dead or under arrest, and the world itself is denied. *Holy Grail* is a film of nostalgia, of "sweet sadness" for a world long gone, but also of the ignobility of failure, and of nihilism, to a certain degree—"where heroism is ultimately meaningless, as is a search for self-perfection" (162)—all delivered with a collective tongue in cheek; all for a lark. Desser notes the cultural importance of the Samurai film, and points out functions that the Pythons had already been exploring in *Flying Circus* and their sort of ever-present approach to history: "Like the Western, though, the Samurai film served, and continues to serve, an important cultural function helping to merge the past and the present and alleviate cultural tensions" (162–63).[54] As we are finding, the Pythons' work plows this same field.

LAUNCELOT: "I just got excited again and started to swashbuckle . . ."—This line gets changed to "I get carried away" in the film as finished. It might be that the pirate movie term crossed the Rubicon for the referent-cognizant Pythons, and the "swashbuckling" music and actions—without on-the-nose mentions—were seen as reference enough.

GUEST: "He's killed the best man!"—A fairly recent term, "best man" is of Scottish origin, and simply means a groomsman. There is no indication in the film that Herbert has any friends, of course, so the best man may have been arranged for (even hired?) by Herbert's father.

Hostile shouts of "arrest him" "boom in shot" etc.—(PSC) There are hostile shouts, but none that can be actually heard legibly. The "boom in shot" was a typical result of the faster, less precise world of the independent film shoot—like *Holy Grail*—the kind of thing that would never have been tolerated in a Hollywood film of the Golden Age (or a British film of the same period, for that matter). This kind of mistake happened more often in films where location shooting and handheld cameras were employed. In the American film *Badlands* (1973), for example, written and directed by first-time director Terrence Malick (b. 1943), the boom mic drops into view in a scene between father and daughter (Warren Oates and Sissy Spacek) as he paints a sign in their backyard.[55] The Pythons had fairly recently made fun of the accidental viewing of the microphone in Ep. 23 of *Flying Circus*, specifically the "French Subtitled Film." Shot on a rubbish tip near Paignton, the film *Le Fromage Grand* features a self-styled "revolutionnaire" (Jones) who tries to seduce a winsome blonde (Cleveland) clutching a Webb's Wonder lettuce. Eventually, the Frenchman loses interest—she's not responding enthusiastically to his fumbling advances—then she and the lettuce explode. From an entry in *MPFC: UC*, for Ep. 23:

> One of the characteristics of the French New Wave . . . was a conscious move away from classical, prestige-film Hollywood [and "tradition of quality" French film] aesthetics in favor of more

genre-influenced styles. The manipulation of classical form included taking the camera off of the tripod and especially the dolly, where steady, beautiful shots had created a hallmark of Hollywood cinema. Hand-held camera work (inspired by documentary films and especially the combat footage of WWII), black-and-white film stock, elliptical editing and storytelling, sex and sexuality as integral to the narrative and characters, and topicality characterized the movement. Godard's 1959 film *Breathless* is a terrific example of these formal concerns. (1.353)

See the other entries for the "French Subtitled Film" in Ep. 23 for more on this more "realistic" aesthetic, the faults of which could have easily found their way into *Holy Grail*.

As for arresting Launcelot, the chances of such an outcome would have been slim in the thirteenth and fourteenth centuries, according to Hallam. Firstly, Launcelot is a respected, knighted man who would likely have to kill someone at or above his social level to be threatened with punishment. Even then, a fine or a temporary exile was often the consequence—he wouldn't likely have answered with his own life. Second, this kind of bloody mayhem was fairly common, even to the point of ignoring it as long as the fabric of society wasn't ripped too badly: "The 13th and 14th centuries were rich in spectacular and bloody crimes, often unpunished, and the society which provided the backcloth for the tales of Robin Hood is easily seen as virtually ungovernable" (Hallam, 214). Launcelot won't be arrested until the end of the film, just after he's crossed the Bridge of Death, and then by twentieth-century police officers.

SECOND GUEST (*holding a limp WOMAN***): "He's killed my auntie"**—"Auntie" Min (Milligan) was one of the recurring characters throughout the run of the *Goon Show*, and the Pythons had mentioned significantly another auntie, this one suffering from "possibly gastro-enteritis," and announced live on the air during the *Election Night Special* coverage (Ep. 19).[56] By Ep. 31, "Michael's Auntie Betty in Australia" is listed as one of the producers of the CinemaScope-formatted *Party Hints by Veronica*.

Murmurs from CROWD; the BRIDE smiles with relief, coughs—Though prospective brides during the Middle Ages often couldn't choose to whom they would be affianced, there are examples of wealthy girls and women exercising a modicum of free will in this essential cementing-of-alliances tradition. Isabella, daughter of King Edward and Queen Philippa, had been proposed for marriage at the age of three to the son of the King of Castile, though the arrangements to marry the man who would be known as "Pedro the Cruel" did not come to fruition (Tuchman, 205). A second match "was held up owing to consanguinity" (to the son of the Duke of Brabant), "and while the Pope was considering dispensation, she was betrothed instead to the reluctant Louis of Flanders," who backed out at the very last moment (205). Isabella's father also tried to set up a match between she and Charles IV of Bohemia, a widower who would become Holy Roman Emperor, but this match also fell through. Isabella got her chance to smile like Princess Lucky at the age of nineteen, when she was set to marry Bérard d'Albret, scion of a wealthy French family. Edward gave a £1,000 pension to the prospective groom's father to smooth the way, and another £1,000 to Isabella herself, which she was to keep even if the marriage fell through.[57] What followed seems right out of the scene presented in the lavish wedding preparations of Swamp Castle:

> To carry the princess and her retinue of knights and ladies to Bordeaux, five ships were ordered by the direct method of furnishing a royal officer with warrant to arrest five suitable vessels in "all ports and places" from the mouth of the Thames westward. The bride's trousseau included robes of cloth of gold and Tripoli silk and a mantle of Indian silk lined in ermine and embroidered all over with leaves, doves, bears, and other devices worked in silver and gold. For another robe of crimson velvet, the elaborate embroidery fashionable at the time required thirteen days' work by twenty men and nine women. For gifts, Isabella brought 119 chaplets made of silk entwined with pearls

surmounted by a golden Agnus Dei standing on a green velvet band wrought with flowers and leaves. But these marvelous contrivances were never to be worn—or at least not as intended. At the water's edge Isabella changed her mind and came home. Was it desire to jilt as she had been jilted? Or reluctance to assume a lower rank? Or perhaps memory of her sister's death on an earlier voyage to Bordeaux? Or was the whole affair a contrivance to acquire revenues and a new wardrobe? (206)

Once Launcelot declines the offer of Princess Lucky's hand and begins his dramatic exit, it's not certain what will happen; it seems Herbert's father will have to wait and see how the swelling musical number comes out before he knows if he has a new daughter-in-law, or his search for a suitable match for Herbert and more arable and pastoral land must start all over again.

FATHER: "I don't want to think I've lost a son . . . as much as gained a daughter . . ."—Herbert's father wants to turn his son's supposed (and hoped for) death to his advantage, of course, and the practice of the "widow's dower" during this period is worth mentioning. If Herbert and Lucky *had* married, Herbert's estates would have been intestate, to a certain extent, had he died from his injuries after they'd married:

> [The w]idow's dower was another heavy burden on landholders of all rank, but especially for those with the obligations, but not necessarily the means that accompanied high status. Although custom varied . . . and husbands were free to augment the amount of land dictated, *a widow could expect to hold for the rest of her life at least a third of the land in her husband's possession at the time of his death.* (Raban, 37; italics added)

If Herbert and Lucky *had* married, and then Herbert had died, Father could be looking at losing control over one-third of his properties almost immediately. Inveigling himself into Lucky's family and household as a kind of grafted *paterfamilias* could have borne fruit, interestingly, especially if Herbert's father had pursued a sort of backwards version of *mort d'ancestor*, wherein a rightful heir could sue for control of an inheritance after the death of an ancestor.[58] He'd be turning the assize on its ear, of course, attempting to "adopt" Lucky away from her family, but that wouldn't be an unusual assay for a man like Herbert's father.

The fact that the Pythons have offered the most spare versions of a nuclear family here—a father and a son, or a father and a daughter—means there are likely no mothers, siblings, cousins, uncles, etc. who could legally and historically challenge this transaction, where, according to Fossier, the Middle Ages Church wanted focus to remain on the new couple, while juridical and familial tradition thought otherwise:

> [T]he conjugal nucleus won over against all larger structures [meaning, extended families]; second, the Church, by invoking the first couple, quite naturally pushed in that direction. As early as the Carolingian age, this structure was presented as the rule in the Church's dogmatic works, but it was a rule by no means universally respected at the time. Until the end of the Middle Ages, families resisted Church pressure and relied on the broader kinship group. This was more the case within the aristocracy, to be sure, but it probably was elsewhere as well. Until the thirteenth century, there is no real estate transaction involving the patrimony that does not require approval of members of the larger kinship group, the *laudatio parentum*, and when that larger group did not exist, the reverse move, the "lineage retrieval" taking back goods in the name of the family, obstructed any transaction that threatened the basic foundation of family stability. (106)

Herbert's father clearly wants to avoid any familial entanglements, any "retrievals," any competing claims on his or Herbert's or even Lucky's estates—he'll remake the "conjugal nucleus" to involve Launcelot and Lucky, too—and we see that he's ready to finish off Lucky's father (ostensibly her only relative) to smooth the way.

SHOUT FROM THE BACK: "He's not quite dead!"—This same structure—and this same gag—was used by the Goons more than once, including a *Christmas Carol*–type episode:

Sound FX: *Scribbling under.*

Scrooge (Sellers): Over to you. Marley is dead. Marley is dead.

Marley (Milligan): (*from far off*) No I'm not . . .

Sound FX: *Pistol shot.*

Marley: Ohhh!

Scrooge: Yes you are.[59]

The Pythons continue to mine the radio quarry that the Goons provided, this time taking advantage of the offscreen (or off-microphone) character participation. Also, the calling from offscreen is heard elsewhere in the Pythons' work. As early as Ep. 2, an Announcer (Idle) introduces "a man with three noses," and a disgruntled viewer later calls for "a man with nine legs"—both of these mentions get responding shouts from offstage, the offscreen voice remaining anonymous (*JTW*, 1.18, 24). Spike Milligan is even in studio when they are recording Ep. 19, and is heard from briefly. In *Life of Brian*, the plaintive or incessant offscreen voice is heard several times, including at a meeting of the Peoples Front of Judea:

Brian and Judith have arrived, and Judith tells everyone that Brian has painted the "Romans Go Home" slogan successfully.

Reg (Cleese): Oh, great! Great! We . . . we need doers in our movement Brian, but . . . before you join us, know this: there is not one of us here who would not gladly suffer death to rid this country of the Romans once and for all.

Revolutionary: (*from offscreen*) Umm . . . well, one.

Reg: Oh, yeah, yeah, there's one.[60]

FATHER: ". . . suddenly felt the icy . . . hand of death upon him"—This vivid poetic imagery is borrowed from the future (in relation to Herbert's father, at least), actually, from dramatist James Shirley (1596–1666), and a poem called "Death the Leveller":

> The glories of our blood and state
> Are shadows, not substantial things;
> There is no armour against Fate;
> Death lays his icy hand on kings:
> Sceptre and Crown
> Must tumble down,
> And in the dust be equal made
> With the poor crooked scythe and spade.[61]

Throughout *Flying Circus* the Pythons either quoted or by association referenced dozens of poets and dramatists, including Shakespeare, Keats, Milton, and Wordsworth, and even the Liverpool Poets, the infamous William McGonagall, and playwrights from J. M. Barrie through Thornton Wilder. See the index entries for "playwrights" and "poets" in *MPFC: UC*.

SHOUT FROM BACK: "Oh, he's died!"—This is one of those Pythonesque moments where something absurd or atrocious happens and no one seems to react appropriately. Launcelot watches dimly as the soldier who's been nodded at "discreetly" by Herbert's father moves to the victim, sees the fatal blow delivered, yet still registers no disgust or alarm. He's an upper-class visitor watching the quaint ways of these indigenous peoples—like members of the royal family on tours of the Commonwealth countries—half-smiling, nodding and waving as all manner of exotic dances and bare-breasted natives are paraded before them. Those around the dying father here are equally unaffected by the violence. In Ep. 33, "Salad Days," the blood-soaked violence of the boater-and-flannel crowd doesn't seem to register on any of the attendees not directly affected—they continue to squat, recline, or kneel amid the carnage, smiling and laughing, as if posing for an interminable portrait. Onlookers in the Python world are most often bemused, not horrified, when senseless violence erupts around them. When, in Ep. 6, a husband and wife (Ian Davidson and Jones) read the newspaper accounts of an Indian massacre at a local theater—where survivors *were* able to get refunds—the husband's response is typical: "That's what live theatre needs, a few more massacres" (*JTW*, 1.75).

FATHER: ". . . to think of me as her old dad . . . in a very real and legally binding sense"—This isn't as simple as he hopes, of course. Under English Common Law, adoptions couldn't be legally recognized, even though under earlier (Roman) law, such adoptions occurred fairly regularly. Scoffield writes, "Although there are many reasons for this, there were two factors that arose most often. They were: 1) the extreme high regard for blood lineage and 2) established mechanisms which made adoption unnecessary" (7).

Scoffield goes on to describe circumstances where the purposes and situations of adoption are achieved without having to actually try and adopt legally. To avoid surrendering his fortunes to his brother after his death, a Lincolnshire knight (supported by his wife) claimed a child was his even though all were certain he was too old to father a child. Unable to *prove* the child wasn't his, and, since the old knight died just after the brouhaha erupted, the courts eventually ruled in his favor, since the knight had gone to his grave swearing the child was his. Another case from the reign of Edward I mentions a young woman who brought an assize of *mort d'ancestor* after it was argued she couldn't have been the dead man's child, having been both conceived and born while this man was out of the county. The "justices awarded that she should recover the land, for the privities of the husband and wife are not to be known, and he might have come by night and engendered the plaintiff" (8). Scoffield continues, "The foregoing examples illustrate that the English law was very hesitant to make 'any inquiry into the paternity of . . . [a] child.'" But "presumption of paternity" wasn't the only side door around adoption. Scoffield quotes Bracton to the effect that

> spurious offspring . . . are legitimated sometimes as it were by adoption and with the consent and goodwill of the relatives, as if any one's wife has conceived by another man than by her husband, and although this is ascertained in truth, *if the husband has taken the child into his house and has avowed and nourished it as his son, he will be his heir and legitimate*, or if he has not expressly avowed him, provided he has not sent him away . . . such a child will be adjudged to be the heir and to be legitimate. (8; italics added)

Herbert's father is certainly trying to fulfill the demands of this version of pseudo-adoption, by offering to take in Princess Lucky as his own, hoping to "legitimate" her and her fortune to him.

Toward the end of Edward III's reign, catastrophic events like Launcelot's rampage in Swamp Castle—where members of prominent families were killed and maimed—indicated that times were changing. "There was little to compensate for the toll taken of the nobility,"

401

McKisack writes, "by plague and disease, battles and tournaments, political misadventure, and the normal hazards of medieval daily life" (260). The number of landed nobility was diminishing, and Edward III wasn't creating new earldoms, for example, to fill the gap. But this, according to McKisack, would have been very good news for Herbert's father: "[F]or the man of property, great or small, who had children the prospects were brighter than ever before." He continues: "The legal practice of the fourteenth century was allowing the land-owner a new freedom of action in disposing of his land" (260–61). These relaxations would allow for such landlords to move beyond primogeniture, to endow a daughter or wife or at will, to arrange marriages on their own and in their best interests, and to leave wills (after 1380) with explicit instructions as to how lands and chattel were to be handled after his death (261). Herbert's father could have had a number of options with which to legally consolidate and increase his properties, whether his son died or not.

FATHER: "And I'm sure . . . that the merger . . . er . . . the union . . ."—This coerced/forced matrimony trope is earlier seen in *Prince Valiant*, when Morgan Le Fey captures Gawain to make the knight her husband. Valiant comes to his friend's rescue (just like Launcelot rescues Galahad from Castle Anthrax), much to Gawain's relief:

> "My priceless squire!" laughs the gratified Gawain, "you have saved me from prison; you have saved me from death and now, you have saved me from matrimony!"
> *(Gawain turns to Morgan Le Fey)*
> "Dear Lady, your interest in me is most flattering, but knowing the fate of all your husbands, I'd make a nervous bridegroom in this unwholesome place." ("The Fairy Morgana," *Prince Valiant*, 23 April 1938)

The "merger" and "union" aspects of Herbert's father's deal mark it as a potential for creating a new dynasty, one not based on divine providence or nobility, but on a man's hard work and business cunning. (This is a world Arthur, for example, wouldn't understand, so it's good he's elsewhere at the moment.) This "Third Estate"–type northerner mirrors the changing power structures in fourteenth-century France, according to Tuchman, who writes of Etienne Marcel, a "rich draper whose post was equivalent to that of Mayor of Paris":

> He had been the spokesman when the Estate of 1355 made manifest their mistrust of the royal government. Marcel represented the mercantile magnates of the Third Estate, the producers and businessmen of medieval society who over the last 200 years had achieved an influence, in practice if not in status, equal to that of the great prelates and nobles. (155)

Without saying so, Herbert's father clearly sees himself in these terms.

The problem of a "widow" finding a second husband was also present in Middle Ages life, according to Raban, but Herbert's father knows a fiscal opportunity when he sees it, and the medieval practice of second-husband-searching came with financial opportunities attached:

> In normal circumstances, widows were not regarded as prime marriage partners, as a later study from Cambridgeshire shows, but in this community peasant custom gave second husbands a life interest in widows' dower land after their death. . . . Accustomed as we are to the partnership of contemporaries chosen for love, it is easy to misconstrue a society in which the choice of a spouse was a matter of economic significance and family interest and where limited life expectancy made remarriage commonplace. (13)

Princess Lucky isn't technically a widow, nor has Launcelot expressed *any* interest in marrying anyone we've met, but clearly that doesn't hinder Herbert's father from treating Lucky as both a widow and a daughter, and Launcelot as all but affianced—again, the power of words and naming in the Python world can be significant.

PRINCE: "I feel much better now"—The Black Knight is de-limbed but only admits to a "flesh wound"; the Old Man draped over the Large Man's shoulders in the "Plague Cart" scene was certain he'd get better (from a bout with the plague); and the man turned into a newt in the "She's a Witch" scene also "got better." In *LB*, a leper will be healed by Christ but admits to pining for his condition—he can no longer beg for a living—and an old man shrugs off threatened crucifixion as "a doddle." There are many, many "not quite dead" characters and moments throughout the Python *oeuvre*.

FATHER: "... you creep!"—Another reach across time for verbiage, since "creep" in this sense is a late nineteenth-century term, according to the *OED*.

MUSIC INTRO to song—This is not the same sweeping introduction as heard earlier, in the Tall Tower. This is a composed bit for the film, likely from Innes and/or Idle, and becomes the "He's Going to Tell" number.

adopts cod "and now a number from my friend" pose—(PSC) "Cod" here likely means a burlesque or mock version of such a stance, borrowed from panto and music hall performances alike, where the audience is in on the fun (the Principal Boy, for example, playing to and with the audience). Introductions of alternating songs from Gilbert and Sullivan light opera performances likely also qualify for this very stylized, self-conscious bit of stage business. A fairly recent Hollywood film musical like Disney's *The Happiest Millionaire*, starring British import Tommy Steele,[62] features just such self-conscious, acknowledged performances throughout.

LAUNCELOT: "We must escape before the song"—This line is removed, as is Concorde's retort "Come with me, sir," to which Launcelot responds: "You're not right for this genre. . . . I must escape more dramatically" (*MPHGB*, 60). The replacement for this section, including Launcelot's concern with his "idiom" (as opposed to his "genre"), and the "dramatically" significant method, give Concorde more credit for helping his master. It seems that both Herbert *and* Launcelot want to avoid the musical's confining generic idioms.

LAUNCELOT: "No, it's not right for my idiom"—We need to look no further than Gawain as he appears in *Sir Gawain and the Green Knight* for a knight trapped by his idiom. In "The Idea of the Green Knight," Besserman lays out Gawain's situation in relation to unexpected proposals from the Green Knight himself:

> Besides being psychologically implausible, Gawain's return to Hautdesert would simply not "group together" with the rest of the poet's matter. Gawain instead must be getting back to Camelot for the conventionally conclusive, crucial romance scene of the hero's reception and recounting of his adventure at his home court—the scene that closes the outer ring of the poem's narrative structure: Camelot-Hautdesert-Green Chapel-Camelot. (Besserman, 225)

Launcelot's narrative structure *cannot* include a sidepath into domesticity; his narrative *cannot* be further reshaped—he must leave Swamp Castle. After Gawain successfully withstands the Green Knight's three axe swings at his neck (two stop short, one nicks him), rather than accept the Green Knight's hearty invitation to stay for "holiday feasting and a reconciliation with the lady of the castle," Gawain responds with a Launcelot-like "prompt and comically emphatic demurral" (225). (Our Launcelot's "emphatic demurral" moments involve saying "no thank you" to saving Herbert, as well as backpedaling from the hand of Princess Lucky.) Besserman argues that Gawain cannot escape the strictures of the poem's genre, just like Launcelot can't escape his idiom.

Further, it is Herbert's father acting as this version of the Green Knight (Bertilak de Haut-desert) as he attempts to sidetrack Launcelot from his quest for the Grail in order to marry Princess Lucky. Launcelot will not be diverted onto this alternate path, nor will Gawain:

> Because [Lord Bertilak] now *tries and fails* to shape the plot of the narrative by adding an anticli-mactic lap to Gawain's quest and creating an otiose Hautdesert-Green Chapel-Hautdesert symmetry, both his potency as Gawain's antagonist and his role as the moving force in the narrative are even further diminished. (225)

Herbert's father is unsuccessful at his matchmaking attempts, and the fact that the musical number begins and he cannot stop it signals finally his own loss of narrative power. Herbert's father (he never even gets a name) will not reappear in the film; and Launcelot escapes to continue the Grail quest.

. . . grabs a rope off the wall and swings out over the heads of the CROWD . . .—In the printed script, Concorde (still named "Lightning") leaves the room as Launcelot tries to swing away. It's made clear that Launcelot's swinging in a "swashbuckling manner toward a large window," though such windows do not exist in the Doune Castle set, so Launcelot's target has to be off-camera. Also, Launcelot is left "swinging pathetically" in the script—the quiet call for help is a line written in after the fact.

Notes

1. The Pythons had earlier hired a medieval music group, The Cittie Waites (a "Tudor minstrels" group), to play in the background of a scene in Ep. 36, "The Life of Sir Phillip Sidney." See *MPFC: UC*, 2.123, 125. The Cittie Waites continue to perform to this date, with these and other period instruments.

2. See the Blu-ray commentary for more. Several pickup shots were recorded after the fact in this urban green area. The "Book of the Film" sections were also photographed after principal photography was completed. Gilliam lived very near this park, according to period phone books.

3. Found in Ep. 14 of *MPFC*.

4. Here, in this filmed adaptation of a theatrical musical (a rock opera), this visual repetition is likely linked to the repeating guitar vamp that leads into Judas's first song, "Heaven on Their Minds." The Pythons' version seems unmotivated, except to be odd, then funny.

5. Buñuel's *Exterminating Angel* (1962) appeared in London in June 1966, at the Academy Cinema Two. The self-conscious repetition there involves a repeated toast, as well as the trapped people. His *Viridiana* appeared at the Curzon in April 1962. Buñuel's marvelous *The Milky Way* (1969) debuted in November 1969 at the Cameo Poly Cinema, also with purposeful repetitive sequences (feet, jump rope). Buñuel wasn't afraid to mix his aesthetics—in the neo-realist-type film *Los Olvidados*, the depictions of abject poverty in Mexico City are punctuated by a boy's surrealistic fever dream, for example.

6. Julian Doyle was film editor, second unit director, and model photographer on the Gilliam-helmed film *Brazil*.

7. Doyle mentions that music choices were made based on cost and availability factors, and since Doyle already possessed the music cue *and* it was already transferred to 35 mm mag (a costly process), the choice was easy. From a 16 December 2013 e-mail correspondence with the author.

8. The Pythons begin a pirate movie in Ep. 25, *The Black Eagle*, but undercut it before it gets very far (see entries in *MPFC: UC*, 2.373). Launcelot will here be interrupted, twice, as he tries to explore his "idiom."

9. Critics of the period were rather more circumspect about the films, acknowledging their entertainment value and production qualities, but little else:

[T]he characters are cardboard figures from the picturesque past, and their language the commonplaces of modern times rather casually sprinkled with fustian. . . . There may be nothing new or brilliant in the production, but it is excellent in detail, avoids many obvious opportunities for bathos with considerable tact, and moves at a reasonable speed. ("Captain Blood," *Times*, 17 February 1936: 10)

It's easy to see how these films made lasting impressions on the young Pythons' minds.

10. For more on this significant series of raids, see Holmes, 122–23, McKisack, 138, and Tuchman, 137–41.

11. One such *chevauchée* in 1386—a combined sea battle and coastal fortification attack near Brest, France—rescued thousands of bottles of wine from French control, which were then brought back to England and sold for a tidy profit. According to the period chronicler Thomas Walsingham, writes McKisack, this was "the one bright spot . . . in a gloomy year" (447).

12. Jones includes a berserker character—who is, of course, concerned about his inadequate berserking abilities—in his 1989 film *Erik the Viking*. The Pythons also availed themselves of Icelandic lore as they wrote the "*Njorl's Saga*" sketch for the third season of *Flying Circus*.

13. This moment also refers back to the prisoner hanging on the wall outside Camelot as everyone inside sings and dances. The constant, visible presence of excruciating physical punishment in the medieval world was key to controlling the often emotionally immature population (see Tuchman).

14. See Amidi, *Cartoon Modern*, and Napier, *From Akira to Howl's Moving Castle*.

15. Peckinpah will be cited by name ("Peckinpahish") in the script's scene description for the "Killer Rabbit" sequence later. See notes for that sequence below for more.

16. One of the few major Hollywood studio films actually distributed with an "X" rating, a short list including *Midnight Cowboy* and *A Clockwork Orange*. *Beyond the Valley of the Dolls*, which appeared at the Carlton in London in February 1971, was produced in 1970 by legendary softcore filmmaker Russ Meyer, with a screenplay cowritten by young film critic Roger Ebert, and distribution by Twentieth-Century Fox. *Ramrodder* was, essentially, a "nudie" western. *BVD* appeared at the Carlton in London in February 1971.

17. The movie industry's gentlemen's agreement had been that unrated films like *Faster, Pussycat! Kill! Kill!* (1965), and many foreign films not submitted for Production Code review would not appear in traditional movie theater chains. With the new rating system, many films that would have been screened only in art houses or grindhouse cinemas (and college classrooms) found their way onto local movie screens throughout the early 1970s.

18. See the "Black Knight" entries above for more on the presence of Vietnam in period film and television.

19. See "blood goes pssssssssshhh . . .," *MPFC: UC*, 1.350.

20. See *MPFC: UC*, 2.91–100 for discussion of this entire sketch.

21. To be fair, Launcelot also has no desire to marry Princess Lucky, either, which likely confirms his true commitment to chastity, celibacy, and the Grail quest.

22. Referenced significantly in Ep. 28 of *Flying Circus*, the "Trim-Jeans Theatre" section.

23. By way of comparison, in the first two years of Henry II's reign (1154–1155) the "average royal expenditure" *totaled* about £10,000 each year (*HBI*, 76). Could Henry have had much of a working administration if he profligately averaged one-half of one percent of his total expenditures on a single guard? Not likely. Also, just a few years later a sailor's average daily wage during the Third Crusade (1189–1192) only amounted to two pence (83). By the fourteenth century, when "high agriculture" was the way to enrich oneself, the Bishop of Ely was able to earn a respectable £80 a year in income from his manor at Shelford between 1319 and 1323, before it was cut in half thanks to an "agricultural recession" between 1325 and 1333, and then fell dramatically to about £10 per year between 1333 and 1346 (McKisack, 330).

24. Even the wealthiest of nobles in both England and France of the fourteenth century more often than not were obliged to *borrow* against their properties, promise payment in installments, or offer spoils to finance war actions. Edward III was even forced to leave "the queen, his children, and the earls of Derby and Salisbury" on the Continent (in the Low Countries) as collateral for a loan in 1340

(McKisack, 162). See Tuchman and McKisack for more on the credit risks of this period, especially during the Hundred Years War. Willis notes that in England of the late thirteenth century "the normal qualification for the status of a knight was a rent roll of £20 per annum" (Willis, *The Estate Book of Henry de Bray*, xv). This was more than the well-to-do Henry de Bray could claim (his rent roll came to less than £12), meaning that even to significant men of wealth, £50 would have been an enormous, even unattainable sum.

25. See Raban, *England under Edward I and Edward II*, 30–31. Langley had participated in the first crusade under Edward I, and lived approximately 1215–1274.

26. Incidentally, this figure would have been worth about £888 in 1974, according to the retail price index, and an impressive £12,800 in annual earnings. Fifty pounds in 1274–1974 value comes to about £3,750, or £53,800 in annual earnings. In any case, fifty pounds per guard is more than generous. See the values tables at www.measuringworth.com.

27. Willis, *The Estate Book of Henry De Bray*, xv.

28. The existence of same-sex attractions and relationships during the medieval period is acknowledged in many sources; it is condemned, of course, by the Church, but often tolerated in the secular world as long as it was fairly covert. And since no bastard offspring were produced as a result of these trysts, no inheritance claims could be muddied, which would have been the most serious secular consideration of the period.

29. Launcelot continues to be this focused on the quest throughout the film, so much so that he is able to successfully cross the Bridge of Death and be arrested by police on the other side.

30. See the entry "Facing page 46" in appendix A for much more on this manuscript and Gilliam's reworking of the image.

31. In the author's paperback copy of May McKisack's *The Fourteenth Century*, there are pound (£) and dollar ($) sign notations in red ink in the margins wherever costs are discussed—thumbing back through it, there are scant few pages without such markings, especially during sections discussing Edward III's reign. It was due to lack of sufficient funds, for example, that the simmering tensions over English duchies in France were kept from boiling over for many years.

32. See Reston, "Why America Weeps."

33. "Kennedy: The Myth and the Reality," *Times*, 19 November 1964: 13.

34. From J. M. Barrie's play, *What Every Woman Knows*. See the "Scotsman on a horse" entry in *MPFC: UC*, 1.44.

35. The castles in fourteenth-century Scotland, where the film was produced, have been described in dolorous terms by visiting French knights: "Castles were bare and gloomy with primitive conditions and few comforts in a miserable climate" (Tuchman, 420). Most of this is evident in the interior scenes of Doune Castle, including the bracing wind blowing through curtained windows.

36. The 1874-built headquarters of the South Yorkshire NUM more than faintly resembles this type of castle, on a reduced but still quite noble scale. See the "ARTHUR (*with thankful reverence*): 'Camelot!'" entry in "The Book of the Film" above for more. See the English Heritage website (http://www.english-heritage.org.uk/) for images of this still proud building.

37. Though this may be simply a belated infanticide Herbert's father wished he'd accomplished years earlier.

38. *MPFC: UC*, 1.7, 34–35. See the index for dozens of citations involving homosexuality in *MPFC*. In Ep. 37, during the "Prejudice" sketch, the viewers and audience are invited to "Shoot the Poof." A hairdresser and a "camp highwayman," wearing all pink, are both shot dead.

39. "Infamous" due to silly, clumsy BBC censorship. Complaints about a line indicating the Prince dies of "cancer" (after he neglected to have the spot looked at) led to a badly dubbed "gangrene" instead. See *MPFC: UC*, 1.290 for a discussion of the animated sequence and the BBC's reaction to it.

40. Listen to the Goon's "The Sinking of Westminster Pier" (15 February 1955), during the "oyster sexer" section, for an example of the sound effect.

41. De Bray lived c. 1289–1340.

42. Poole notes that Henry (of Blois, King Stephen's brother), the bishop of Winchester, left the country for Cluny in 1155. In his absence Henry tore down five of the bishop's castles (*DBMC*, 322).

Henry was likely trying to erase the confusion brought on by the anarchy, resetting the power and influence of the monarchy.

43. This castle is mentioned in the printed script. See the screen direction entry "*CUT TO shot from over his shoulder: castle e.g. Bodium*" in scene 2, "Coconuts and Swallows" above.

44. See Harry Mount, "How England's Country Houses Recovered Their Glory," *Telegraph*, 9 July 2011.

45. Mount, "How England's Country Houses Recovered Their Glory."

46. Coincidentally, Gilliam will use the Mentmore home as a location for a portion of his 1986 film *Brazil*. The "Save Mentmore" campaign occupied many column inches in most British newspapers throughout 1977.

47. The staggering placeholder Callaghan government was in no financial position to support such an estate, and would be unseated by the Tories and Margaret Thatcher less than two years later.

48. *Times*, 30 January 1975: 16. Lord Rosebery later estimated that the death duties for the estate would come to about £5 million (*Times*, 20 January 1977: 4).

49. By the 1960s, it was estimated that the costs associated with keeping up a fifteenth- or sixteenth-century country house "rocket at the rate of 15 to 25 per cent per annum" (Strong, 9). Herbert's father is perhaps trying to stay ahead of the inevitable decay and wear and tear, maybe "knocking through" some of the older portions of Swamp Castle.

50. Webbe, "What Is Happening to the Stately Homes of Britain?"

51. Presented by the conservative *Daily Mail*, the Ideal Home was the annual display of "new furniture, appliance, and decorating ideas" (*MPFC: UC*, 2.133, 135). The Pythons had already made fun of the annual Ideal Home Exhibition (calling it the "Ideal Loon Exhibition") in Ep. 37 of *MPFC*, likely thanks to the presence of PM Heath and the Queen at the 1972 opening.

52. This "poorer verse" summary is adapted from Desser's excellent chapter "Toward a Structural Analysis of the Postwar Samurai Film" in his *Reframing Japanese Cinema*, 147–62.

53. See Desser, *Reframing Japanese Cinema*, 162, where these over- and undervaluations (Desser's terminology) are described.

54. Again, see Desser, "Toward a Structural Analysis of Postwar Samurai Film" in his *Reframing Japanese Cinema* for his much more sensible and well-written chapter.

55. In the late 1960s Malick was a Harvard graduate and then Rhodes Scholar at Magdalen College, Oxford. Well-reviewed in British newspapers (screening at the London Film Festival in November 1974), *Badlands* made its debut in London-area cinemas in December 1974.

56. Likely the Pythons' hero (of all the Goons) since he did all the writing, Milligan will be called out to (he's offscreen) during *Flying Circus* Ep. 19 (*JTW*, 1.262), and will make a short appearance in *Life of Brian*.

57. Tuchman notes that this arrangement was "unusual," and might have been intended as "an inducement to her to change her mind" (206).

58. Unless Swamp Castle is found near Bristol or Shrewsbury where, according to Poole, "the assize of mort d'ancestor did not run" (*DBMC*, 75). See the *OED* for a precise definition of the term.

59. Audio transcription, "A Christmas Carol," 24 December 1959.

60. Audio transcription, *Life of Brian*.

61. Found in the Bartleby version of Arthur Quiller-Couch's *The Oxford Book of English Verse: 1250–1900* (1919), http://www.bartleby.com/101/288.html.

62. The film also stars fellow Brits Greer Garson, Gladys Cooper, and Hermione Baddeley. The musical play *The Happiest Millionaire* appeared in London in 1956 to generally favorable reviews, while the film opened there a bit more tepidly in April 1968 (at the Odeon, Haymarket).

SCENE TWENTY-SEVEN
TOOTHLESS OLD CRONE AND
ROGER THE SHRUBBER

Toothless old CRONE by the roadside—This is the same woman (Bee Duffell) who was beating the cat against a wall earlier in the "Plague Cart" scene, and this is likely the same "impoverished village," as well. (Inside the hovel at the beginning of this scene she continues to beat the cat.) If that's the case, then Arthur and Patsy haven't made much progress at all, having circled back around fruitlessly—an unspoken metaphor for the film itself.

OLD CRONE: "No. Never. No shrubberies"—Yet another in a long line of refusals heard by Arthur as he quests. The crone never does give up the information he demands, thanks to Roger the Shrubber's intervention.

In this, the optimism or even agathism of Arthur and his single-mindedness for forward progress still echoes Wilson and the Labour party of the 1960s, especially after successive election victories in 1965 and 1966. Wilson—if no one else in the center of the Labour hierarchy—was certain that a mandate for change had been granted by the voters of Britain, and he was keen to act on the mandate. But the realities of Britain's faltering economy, its intractable labor issues, the political realities of Northern Ireland and unsustainable international military commitments, and the coming global economic slowdown combined to bring Wilson's dreams to heel. With the success of a second election adding seats to Labour's majority in 1966, the pump seemed primed, and Wilson was chuffed—the rebuffs quickly piled up, however, according to C. J. Bartlett:

> Labour's electoral victory in 1966 was almost its only cause for satisfaction in the later 1960s before its own illusory political recovery in 1970 [when the Conservatives surprised everyone and won the election], based on a temporary strengthening of the British economy. Both at home and abroad the Wilson government suffered one blow after another to its ambitious hopes. Finally not even severe deflationary packages could ward off devaluation at the end of 1967, while these same economic constraints remorselessly compelled a reluctant ministry to abandon its pretensions to maintain a world role for Britain. A bid to join the EEC was also defeated by de Gaulle. It was a dismal record after the great expectations and grand promises of 1964. Labour charges of thirteen wasted years under the Conservatives from 1951 were beginning to rebound. . . . The government was in trouble from the moment of its electoral victory in 1966. (*A History of Postwar Britain*, 227)

Arthur was met by God and tasked with a glorious quest; the very next scene is his first major snubbing, at the walls of Loimbard's castle. It gets no easier from there.

ARTHUR restrains him from threatening the LADY—(PSC) After the Crone tells them there are no shrubberies to be had in her village, the finished film deviates significantly from the script as printed. Arthur doesn't have to hold Bedevere back from "threatening" the crone, as the crossed-through scene description (*"Arthur restrains . . ."*) above claims, and it is Arthur himself who presses forward with the threats of saying "Ni" to the Old Crone. In the printed script, a full-page conversation between Arthur and Bedevere concerning an effective approach against the crone follows, all of which disappears before the finished film. What's missing in the filmed sequence is the recognizable, comedic three-set of suggestions made by Bedevere, who thinks he knows how to frighten the crone into submission—they can send the crone "a letter from a long way away,"[1] "talk to her in funny voices" (see below), or even tie themselves to trees—all three involve a distancing between the knights and the crone, of course, meaning Bedevere doesn't want to confront her intimately; his attempts at communication will be either from a safe distance, or by assuming a different, safer identity. Lastly, after Arthur tries to help Bedevere clue in on the fact that the crone needs to be made "as afraid of us as she is of the awful Knights Who Say Ni," Bedevere *"sagely"* is wrong yet again: "Hit ourselves with a big rock." Arthur then stops trying to elicit the right answer from Bedevere (which Bedevere himself had been able to do so well earlier, with the villagers wanting to burn a witch), and tells him straight out that they must threaten her by saying "Ni." Bedevere, of course, is aghast at the thought, but they push on into the scene as filmed.

It's worth cross-referencing the problems of successful communication throughout *Flying Circus*, but specifically Ep. 12, when the policemen can only communicate using odd voices. It may be that Bedevere is certain these backward people can only be understood using odd versions of communication, as discussed in *MPFC: UC*, notes for Ep. 12:

> All these characters (Mr. Lambert, Mr. Verity, et al.) have learned to communicate among themselves, leaving only the Man (Jones) to get up to speed, like the audience. The importance (and, often, difficulty) of communication in *FC* is a significant trope. In Ep. 14, the Minister delivers his answer in his "normal voice, and then in a kind of silly, high-pitched whine." Other characters only speak parts of words, so that only in a group can they utter complete sentences; one character speaks in anagrams; one insults the listener with every other sentence, etc. In a nicely visual twist on the trope, in Ep. 30, gestures are offered to denote "pauses in televised talk." (*MPFC: UC*, 1.191)

And while this section would have been a fun aside, it does bring the narrative to a standstill, since the crone would have been left to simply stare at Arthur and Bedevere as they exchanged these ideas on effective minatory techniques. As it is filmed, the crone only has to gape at them as Arthur tries to improve Bedevere's "Ni" from a mispronounced "Noo" sound. Again, the talismanic word is "Ni," not "Noo"—saying "Noo" to the Old Crone has no effect on her.

ROGER: "Oh, what sad times are these . . ."—There were dozens of chroniclers who wrote jeremiads on the fallen condition of man during the oppressive, war- and plague-ridden Middle Ages. Man's hubris, his spiritual malaise, *folies de grandeur*, acquisitiveness, and lack of humility before God were the general conditions leading to this destruction, but the mistreatment of those less fortunate—ignoring the poor and the sick, and the levying of crippling taxes to support "vainglory" against other nations or even the infidel—was also a guarantee that God's vengeance would be forthcoming.[2] The collapse of the chivalric code—where knights became "passing ruffians"—rated many mentions. During the "Great Anarchy" following the death of Henry I in 1135 and lasting through 1153, a nearly countrywide breakdown of public order was experienced in England, with familial and civil "private" wars also wreaking havoc across much of Normandy. Henry's nephew Stephen could not consolidate his power effectively, and Robert of Gloucester, along with Henry's daughter Matilda, were leading the rebellion by 1139. Matilda would control the southwest, while Stephen held the southeast, and there were nasty skirmishes and sieges aplenty.[3] Powerful men like Rannulf of Chester ransacked Coventry and its surroundings in 1147, making life miserable for ordinary people caught in the middle of this dynastic squabble. Poole notes that "men took advantage of the disturbed state of the country to live lawlessly," including one "itinerant knight" named Warin of Walcote. Warin is said to have abducted a local man's daughter as he was returning from "the war," and that living in peacetime was no guarantee of this knight's honorable behavior: "After the death of Stephen when peace was restored he fell into poverty because he could not rob as he used to do, but he could not refrain from robbery and he went everywhere and robbed as he used" (*DBMC*, 153). He was chased, captured while hiding in a "reed-bed," and eventually died in the pillory[4] according to testimony given many years later (153). The normal knights' reward of living off the spoils of the land during wartime was called common robbery during time of peace, and many knights saw these as the "sad times." French chronicler Jean Froissart recorded bits of a conversation he'd had with an unnamed Englishman: "Where are the great enterprises and valiant men, the glorious battles and conquests? Where are the knights in England who could do such deeds now? . . . The times are changed for the worse. . . . Now felonies and hates are nourished here" (Tuchman, 375–76). In England the early part of the fourteenth century qualifies for Roger the Shrubber's admonishment, as "a period of marked civil lawlessness," according to Rowley (39): "The reign of Edward II . . . was marked by political unrest and rebellion, and it can be no coincidence that the resultant breakdown of law and order was reflected in one of the highest concentrations of licenses [for crenellation and fortification] taken out in the Middle Ages" (*The High Middle Ages*, 39). *All* of Arthur's exchanges with those in castles happen with Arthur on the ground, looking up, the inhabitants safely above on crenellated parapets and battlements. *All* of those encounters go badly for Arthur, as well.

These ruffians were on the roads, as well (Arthur and Bedevere encounter the crone as they pass through a noisome village). Writing of a group of clergymen's arduous, parlous winter trip from Wales to Westminster, the difficulties of Middle Ages travel in western Britain are outlined by Gerald de Barry[5]:

> I say nothing of the expense and inconvenience, or their little acquaintance with the language and manners of the country through which they had to pass. Inns and conveyances there were none; the roads apparently had never been repaired from the days of the Romans in the more neglected districts of the west. The *confusion on the borders had filled them with thieves and vagabonds, to whom Welsh and English were alike lawful plunder*. . . . (Shrewsbury, 20; italics added)

Roger himself sounds very much like Gildas, the Christian polemicist who laments the fallen people around him, and the dark times he sees in history. Gildas was denouncing the "latter-day decadence" of a land where the chastened peoples (harrowed up by "the disasters which they had undergone") had died, and the following generations knew peace, then prosperity, and then dissolution (Alcock, 1989, 114). "Gildas was, in short, writing a work of admonition," P.H. Sawyer, explains, "in the hope of waking the consciences of 'foolish apostates,' cruel tyrants and 'imperfect pastors'" (16). These same upsetting conditions could be found along the Scottish border, as well, with great stretches of borderland bereft of anything but criminality and avarice. "[Gildas] denounces their injustice, their perfidy, their wars against each other, their private crimes, their sexual misconduct, their patronage of self-seeking favourites and cacophonous bards, and their pretense of putting things right by almsgivings and pious gestures" (*QAB*, 227). Gildas may have included a Grail quest as one of these useless, even selfish "pious gestures." Gildas writes in his quasi-historical lamentation:

> In this letter I shall deplore rather than denounce; my style may be worthless, but my intentions are kindly. What I have to deplore with mournful complaint is a general loss of good, a heaping up of bad. But no one should think that anything I say is said out of scorn for humanity or from a conviction that I am superior to all men. No, I sympathise with my country's difficulties and troubles, and rejoice in remedies to relieve them. I had decided to speak of the dangers run not by brave soldiers in the stress of war but by the lazy.[6]

Also, there is much support for even Arthur's mistreatment (in songs, poems, etc.) by monkish authors in various saints' lives, for example, where Arthur is characterized quite ignobly, and in need of a good thrashing: "Arthur is a military despot who tries to plunder the monks" (Ashe, 62–64).

And it wasn't just chroniclers and their jeremiads against the fallen nature of humankind that waxed so depressing and judgmental, but pre-Conquest land grant charters, of all things, "formidable documents" replete with threats from Æthelstan's court to future meddlers:

> If. . .anyone puffed up with the pride of arrogance shall try to destroy or infringe this little document of my agreement and confirmation . . . let him know that on the last and fearful day of assembly, when the trumpet of the archangel is clanging the call and bodies are leaving the foul graveyards, he will burn with Judas the commitor of impious treachery and also with the miserable Jews, blaspheming with sacrilegious mouth Christ on the altar of the Cross, in eternal confusion in the devouring flames of blazing torments in punishment without end. (quoted in Brooke, *FAH*, 77)

Later, as the fourteenth century came to a close, then staggering through yet another winnowing visit of the Black Death, the medieval mood had not improved, according to Tuchman:

> The unknown author of another indictment entitled it "Vices of the Different Orders of Society," and found all equally at fault: the Church is sunk in schism and simony, clergy and monks are in darkness, *kings, nobles, and knights given over to indulgence and rapine*, merchants to usury and fraud; law is a creature of bribery; the [peasants] are plunged in ignorance and oppressed by robbers and murderers. (509; italics added)

Tuchman notes that such a "pessimistic view of man's fate" was not new to the plague years but had been trumpeted by the clergy—"in order to prove the need of salvation"—across the Dark and Middle Ages (508). One hundred years before Cardinal d'Ailly's remonstrance (that the time of the Anti-Christ was at hand) there had been Thomas Aquinas's lamentations; Roger Bacon might as well be Roger the Shrubber as he complained in 1271 of the triumph of sin and dissembling ("More sins reign in these days than in any past age. . . . [J]ustice perisheth, all peace is broken"); and "a monk of Cluny" decried it all in 1040: "For whensoever religion hath failed among the pontiffs . . . what can we think but that the whole human race, root and branch, is sliding willingly down again into the gulf of primeval chaos?" (Tuchman, 508–9). Roger the Shrubber was just one voice raised among many, then, and in this the Pythons aren't exaggerating at all.

ROGER: ". . . passing ruffians . . ."—Roger is speaking to two men who are clearly not typical highwaymen; he can't but notice their cleanliness, their knightly and even kingly apparel, etc. Still, he is speaking to them as if they were nothing more than common brigands, disdainful of their hectoring ways, pronouncing judgment on them. This is reminiscent of the eventual relationship between Henry II and his friend Thomas Becket, appointed Archbishop of Canterbury in 1162. Once Thomas became archbishop, he became more ascetic—like Shakespeare's Hal becoming Henry after his father's death, and shrugging off his old ways and low friends like Falstaff—and Thomas and Henry began to disagree mightily, especially as to the role and significance of the archbishopric in the kingdom. Thomas essentially stood up for the rights of the Church as Henry pushed back with the rights of the Crown, leading to Thomas being murdered in his cathedral after Henry wished aloud for an end to Becket's impertinence and influence.[7] Roger seems little afraid of the monarch who stands before him, and clearly isn't afraid to admonish this clean man wearing a sword and crown.

Roger holds firm as a marker of men's sins against one another. That is, until he realizes they are potential customers—after he announces his trade their interest is immediately sparked (though Bedevere tries with good intentions to say "Ni" to Roger, as well), and they clearly come to an arrangement, albeit off-camera. This financial transaction is one of the few such moments carried over from the first draft of the script. After misplacing the Grail somehow, the questers visit Merlin in his ramshackle workshop to try and buy another Grail cobbled together from bits of "scrap iron and spare parts":

MERLIN: I could spray this down, strengthen the base with a couple of wing-nuts and there you are.

ARTHUR: It . . . er . . . doesn't really . . . look . . .

MERLIN: Oh I'll clean it up. (*MPHGB*, 26)

It's also interesting that this deal is hidden by an age-old filmic transition, a wipe (the only such transition in the film), which takes them from the filthy village and back to the forest of the Knights Who Say Ni in an instant. More on this transition and the elision below.

Tuchman describes the similar state of knights and knighthood across France in the early 1360s, when chivalry and nobility gave way to brutal survival: "Whether employed or living by adventure, they made pillage pay the cost. Life by the sword became subordinate to its means; the means became the end; the climate of the 14th century succumbed to the brute triumph of the lawless" (222). The "they" Tuchman describes were members of so-called "Free Companies,"[8] loose assemblages of soldiers-turned-brigands whose actions "write sorrow on the bosom of the earth" (163). These English, Welsh, and Gascon soldiers had been released from military service by the Black Prince after Poitiers,[9] and to support themselves continued with their plundering ways, but on a freelance basis. Eventually French and German soldiers joined them, and the nationless bands of "twenty to fifty around a captain" set to work: "The refrain of the chronicles, *arser et piller* (burning and plundering), follows their kind down the century" (163). Their modus operandi is recognizable, and might have been the reason French soldiers occupied an English castle earlier in the film: "Seizing a castle, they would use it as a stronghold from which to exact tribute from every traveler and raid the countryside" (163). It's no wonder that Roger is shaken when he thinks he finds such men in his village; their rapacity knew no bounds:

They imposed ransoms on prosperous villages and burned the poor ones, robbed abbeys and monasteries of their stores and valuables, pillaged peasants' barns, killed and tortured those who hid their goods or resisted ransom, not sparing the clergy or the aged, violated virgins, nuns, and mothers, abducted women as enforced camp-followers and men as servants. As the addiction took hold, they wantonly burned harvests and farm equipment and cut down trees and vines, destroying what they lived by, in actions which seem inexplicable except as a fever of the time or an exaggeration of the chroniclers. (164)

ROGER: "Nothing is sacred. Even those who arrange. . ."—Roger has taken up John Gower's cross in his *Mirour de l'omme* rebuke of the ill manners of all men in this new, sacrilegious age:

So goes the world from bad to worse when they who guard sheep or the herdsmen in their places, demand to be rewarded more for their labour than the master-bailiff used to be. And on the other hand it may be seen that whatever the work may be the labourer is so expensive that whoever wants anything done must pay five or six shillings for what formerly cost two. (*Mirour de l'omme*, 293)

Gower (1330–1408) would pen the epic poem *Vox clamantis* as a response to the Peasants' Revolt of 1381, a lamentation that fits nicely with Roger's whingings. For Gower, as discussed earlier,[10] there are only three estates—the cleric, the knight (nobility), and the peasant. In *Holy Grail* all three are included, though we won't actually *meet* the men of God until later in the film (Brother Maynard, et al.). In *Vox clamantis*, Gower reveals the peasants' schemings, especially in the attempted destruction of their betters:

So when the peasantry had been bound in chains and lay patiently under our foot, the ox returned to its yoke, and the seed flourished beneath the plowed fields, and the villein ceased his warring. Similarly, Satan's power lay prostrate, overwhelmed by divine might; but nevertheless it lurked in hiding among the ungovernable peasantry. For the peasant always lay in wait [to see] whether he by chance could bring the noble class to destruction. For his rough, boorish nature was not tempered by any affection, but he always had bitterness in his hateful heart. In his subjection the lowly plowman did not love, but rather feared and reviled, the very man who provided for him. Their very peace and quiet stirred up these men, so that this goading fear became more sharply whetted in them and their burden weighed heavily upon them. The intelligent man who guards himself will not be deceived: because of past injuries he is wary of future misfortunes. Yet God's right hand performed a miracle in order that that wrathful day might pass me by.[11]

But it wasn't just lamenters like Gower who saw the times as dark and foreboding; older men who had lived most of their lives before Henry I's passing were also poignant *aide-mémoires* of better times.[12] One such man, a knight, gave testimony in 1148 as a sort of expert witness on local time's passage, of the way things were, in relation to a court case between the shire and the abbey of Bury St. Edmunds. This old knight was called to testify because he remembered a different, bygone world, where things used to be sacred:

I am, as you see, a very old man, and I remember many things which happened in King Henry's time and even before that, when right and justice, peace and loyalty flourished in England. But because in the stress of war, justice has fled and laws are silenced, the liberties of churches, like other good things, have in many places perished.[13]

It's clear Roger remembers better times, else he has nothing to compare to the current world, but he doesn't mention those halcyon days.

ROGER: ". . .considerable economic stress at this time"—It's appropriate that Roger has conflated the sacred and the worldly here, as many did during this period, blaming financial disaster on supernatural caprice, or as retribution from an angry Creator. Over and over again, as dynastic strife raked across England and Normandy, the complaint heard most often was the deleterious effect such fighting had on trade and production. Every producer or broker like Roger would have been subject to various tolls and taxes, as well, with such assessments rising and becoming more frequent whenever armies had to be raised, ransoms paid, or castles refortified. In 1096 William Rufus arranged for his brothers Robert and Henry to grant him the duchy of Normandy without a fight; William promised to raise a payment of 10,000 marks of silver for the duchy. "It is stated that the barons granted a geld of 4*s.* on the hide," Poole writes, which was higher than the normal 2*s.* rate, but lower than an earlier levy of 6*s.* (*DBMC*, 110). No matter the normality of the rate, "bitter complaints" were reported from those so taxed, leading to Poole's grim, Roger-like conclusion: "Under William Rufus Normandy, like England, was oppressed and downtrodden" (111).

This "economic stress" led to some unusual agreements during this period of anarchy, according to Poole. When two of the country's most powerful earls—the rapacious Rannulf, Earl of Chester and the equally avaricious Robert of Leicester—found their "territorial power[s]" coming into conflict, a "clash of interests was almost inevitable," and they looked to settle future problems well short of war:

> The way these two earls of Chester and Leicester handled this awkward situation illustrates better than anything *the condition of the times*. They made a treaty, an elaborate set of arrangements to govern their conduct towards each other: neither must attack the other unless a formal defiance has been given fifteen days previously; a belt of "no-man's land," as it might be called, in which neither might erect castles, is drawn in a parabolic curve round Leicester. . . . Two bishops, those of Chester and Lincoln, hold the stakes, two pledges, who shall be surrendered, in the event of the infringement of the agreement, to the injured party. One of the most remarkable features of this treaty is that the king is all but ignored; he is out of the picture; there is only a grudging permission that if the king (the liege lord) makes war on one of the earls the other may assist the king, but only with twenty knights, and if he takes any plunder, it must be returned in full. Nevertheless, although this convention emphasized above all things a condition of feudal independence and its corollary, *a complete lack of effective central government*, it also reveals a desire on the part of the great feudatories to restore some sort of order in the chaos. The feud could not be altogether abolished, but it could be regulated and restrained. It was by means such as this adopted by the earls of Chester and Leicester that the recovery of the country to a settled state slowly advanced. (*DBMC*, 159–60; italics added)

Later, as Henry II enjoyed an era of relative peace in England following the quashing of his sons' rebellion, the rebuilding of agriculture, industry, and trade could begin. Prosperous abbeys like St. Benet's in Holme had been badly damaged, meaning production of goods and jobs to create that production had disappeared; three full years of respite were granted to farms in the "most affected counties"; and even the weavers in cities like Nottingham and Huntingdon were unable to "make their annual payment to the exchequer for their gilds" thanks to the long war's privations (*DBMC*, 338). Poole concludes: "These examples were taken at random, but they indicate considerable dislocation of industry and revenue in the country" (338). Sad times, Q.E.D.

With Arthur wandering the country, failing to be recognized as liege lord except by a handful of like-minded knights who have no influence or fortunes—and with Arthur himself representing the ineffective central government—it's no wonder Roger is so down in the mouth. Things are likely to get worse before they can get better. Perhaps Roger's only good news is the fact that he *happens* to live near an enchanted forest where the magical denizens *happen* to demand tributes comprising the very product he shifts for a living. Again, chance is a fine thing.

ROGER: "My name is Roger the Shrubber"—There was a "Robert the Hermit" who appeared at the French king's court in about 1392. The hermit told the king that God had saved him from a storm, but with a caveat—he was to warn the king that the decades-long war[14] with England must end, and that "all who opposed [peace] would pay dearly" (Tuchman, 511). The Duke of Burgundy arranged for Robert to similarly entreat the English representative, the Duke of Gloucester.

And even though "Roger the Shrubber" sounds silly, it's quite appropriate for a period when the fixed patronym was yet scarce. Period records mention an "Abraham the tinner" as employing about three hundred workers in 1357, for example. The fixed last name began to be much more common among common people in the third and fourth quarters of the fourteenth century, thanks, in part, to the physically and socially dislocative effects of various plagues and famine (Mortimer, 86–87).

Incidentally, "Roger" is the name of the long-lost ox the moaning peasant seeks in the thirteenth-century song-story *Aucassin et Nicolette* (*HBMA*, 240).

Notes

1. Episode 3 of *Flying Circus* is entitled "How to Recognize Different Types of Tree from Quite a Long Way Away," incidentally.

2. For many, especially European chroniclers (like Froissart) of the fourteenth century, the massacre of Christian forces by the infidel at Nicopolis in 1396—along with the ransoming that followed—were proof that God had indeed seen enough of these "sad times." See Tuchman.

3. See Poole, *DBMC*, 151–66. These "private wars" were often waged from individual castles, and were particularly damaging to just the immediate surrounding homes and villages, according to Poole. There seemed to have been scores of such destructive actions.

4. A pillory was seen earlier in the courtyard of Swamp Castle, as Launcelot hacks his way toward the Tall Tower.

5. From Cardiff to Westminster the trip is about 131 miles. Gerald of Wales lived c. 1146–c. 1223.

6. See Gildas, *The Ruin of Britain*, sect. 1, p. 13.

7. What Henry said precisely, and to whom, has been argued over since then, but Frank Barlow's reporting of biographer Edward Grim's version will suffice: "What miserable drones and traitors have I nourished and promoted in my household, who let their lord be treated with such shameful contempt by a low-born clerk!" (Barlow, *Thomas Becket*, 235). Most scholars surveying the period (Brooke's *FAH*; Poole's *DBMC*) don't bother to include any of the contending quotes. Ultimately, four knights heard whatever the king said as he raged—set out for Canterbury, challenged, and killed Thomas in 1170 in the name of the king. Henry would spend the rest of his life essentially repenting for whatever sins he committed in relation to his friend and mentor (and father figure) Thomas's death.

8. Also known as "routiers"; see Pool, *DBMC*, 343, 372–73.

9. The major 1356 battle saw the capture of King Jean II, his son, and the capture or death of many French knights and noblemen. The battle is discussed in more detail above, in relation to Arthur's attempted assault on the French-held castle. See notes for "*ARTHUR leads a charge toward the castle*," in scene 13, "Taunting Frenchmen."

10. Cf. entries discussing Gower and his work earlier, in the "Dennis the Peasant" and "Castle Anthrax" scenes.

11. From *Vox Clamantis* (1.21); see also Stockton, *The Major Latin Works of John Gower*, 94–95.

12. Henry had died in 1135 without a legitimate heir, and the following years became known as the Great Anarchy.

13. Quoted in Poole, *DBMC*, 156.

14. Which came to be known as the Hundred Years War.

SCENE TWENTY-EIGHT
KNIGHTS OF NI GET THEIR SHRUBBERY

EXTERIOR—GLADE—DUSK—The transition to this scene is actually a wipe, and it's the only one in the film. The wipe had been a staple of scores of classic Hollywood films across the years,[1] and filmmakers like Kurosawa—a western-influenced director—employed the transition throughout films like *Seven Samurai* and *Hidden Fortress*. Transitional wipes can also be found in many WB and MGM cartoons of the 1940s and 1950s.

TALL KNIGHT: "We are now no longer the Knights who say Ni!"—The significance of this update is, simply, that the new iteration of this fearsome group doesn't recognize the tributes paid to its earlier incarnation. By saying "another shrubbery," though, they do acknowledge the earlier group and its demands; if they didn't, they could have asked for a shrubbery (as if they'd not asked for this before), or anything else, including the tree-cutting tribute. The joke is also a topicality, drawn right from the headlines of the early 1970s.

For their next film, *Life of Brian*, the Pythons will poke fun at then-current political groups like the PLO and the SLA,[2] creating their own radical groups the Judean People's Front, the People's Front of Judea, and the Judean Popular People's Front. In one *LB* scene, anti-Roman militants are a bit confused as to which acronym—JPF or PFJ—they're currently supporting ("I thought we were the Popular Front . . ."). Throughout the 1960s the newspapers were full of references to terrorist cells in Algeria, Israel, northern Africa, Central and South America, and the Middle East in general, as well as Great Britain's own thorns, including the IRA, the Provisional IRA, and the B-Specials operating in Northern Ireland. Groups like the PLO and the IRA also "splintered" more than once, with several factions claiming new or authentic authority—likely quite confusing to everyone outside of the organizations, and many within.

TALL KNIGHT: "We are now the Knights who go Neeeow . . . wum . . . ping!"—He actually says something close to "Icky, icky, icky, icky, ftang, zoot-boing . . ." before trailing off. The "icky" likely comes from *Flying Circus*, Ep. 31, the "Language Laboratory" sketch:

"Ee ecky thump. Put wood in 'ole muther" . . . traditional or stereotypical Yorkshire sayings and accent, as delivered by northerner Palin. "I'll go to the foot of our stairs" is a Northern exclamation of surprise, not unlike "Well I'll be," while "Put wood in 'ole, muther" means "shut the door, mother," both delivered in the heaviest of Yorkshire Dales dialect. "Thump" is a Yorkshire festival, but can also be a feast or wake, and "Eckythump" (Lancastrian martial arts) would become a classic Goodies episode (1970–1982). This phrase may have been borrowed from Python colleague Bill Oddie (b. 1941 in Lancashire), star of *The Goodies* (1970–1981). Oddie worked with several of the Pythons (Chapman, Cleese, Idle) on *At Last the 1948 Show* (1967), and attended Cambridge, knowing Chapman, Cleese, and Idle there. The phrase is also heard in *ISIRTA*, where both Oddie and Cleese wrote and performed, and Idle occasionally contributed. (*MPFC: UC*, 2.76)

TALL KNIGHT: "... f'tang ..."—This nonsense word isn't reproduced in the printed script but can be clearly heard as part of the film's soundtrack, and is another borrow from the Goons. "F'tang" can be heard in "Call of the West" and other *Goon Show* episodes, in Eps. 17 and 19 of *MPFC*, and was also used as a lyric by the King (Jones) in the second *MPFZ* episode, where "Ni" may have also made its debut.[3] The Goons imbued all sorts of words with meaning where none previously existed—real words like "thing" and "legs" were taken out of context and granted extra power or meaning, along with nonsense words like "fon" and "quarn hump," and sounds galore.[4]

TALL KNIGHT: "... another shrubbery!"—These types of requests (or "marvellous enquests") are also made in Malory's *Le Morte D'Arthur*. In book IX, chapter 2, a damosel comes to Camelot bearing a black shield and asking for anyone to step forward to finish an unfinished quest. Sir Breunor—also known as "La Cote Male Taile" ("of the poorly-fitting coat")—volunteers for the quest, and then has to tolerate all manner of rebuke from the damosel, but also successfully faces one hundred knights (1.382–84).

TALL KNIGHT: "... you must cut down the mightiest tree in the forest ... with a herring"—For the first time in his questing mode Arthur says "no" to a demand. He doesn't see the request as ridiculous or even dangerous, just impossible: "It can't be done."

Malory's Arthur threw a similar request back at Rome, just after putting his sword through Emperor Lucius' head in the vale of Sessione:

> So on the morn they found in the heath three senators of Rome. When they were brought to the King, he said these words:
>
> "Now to save your lives I take no great force, with that ye will move on my message unto great Rome and present these corpses unto the proud Potentate, and after them my letters and my whole intent. And tell them in haste they shall see me, and I trow they will beware how they bourde with me and my knights."
>
> Then the Emperor himself was dressed in a chariot, and every two knights in a chariot sued after other, and the senators came after by couples in accord.
>
> "Now ye say to the Potentate and all the lords after, that I send them the tribute that I owe to Rome; for this is the true tribute that I and mine elders have lost these ten score winters. And say them as me seems I have sent them the whole sum, and if they think it not enough, I shall amend it when that I come." (*LMD-WM*, 92)

Eighteen days later the senators delivered the grisly truage to the Potentate, telling him to never ask for tax or truage of Britain again, on "pain of [his] head" (92).

The Goons had earlier suggested the usefulness of fish in the episode "The Thing on the Mountain," when announcer Wallace Greenslade introduces the second half of the show: "Now, if any listener would care to tie a vintage haddock to the third finger of his left hand and swing it round his head he will be able to hear 'The Thing on the Mountain' part two."[5] In *Flying Circus*, fish are mentioned often. There are goldfish in Ep. 3, a "fish emporia" in Ep. 7, a fish tank and cuttlefish in Ep. 8, "fish terriers" in Ep. 10, a "fishy requisite-t-t-t-t-t" in Ep. 17, a "fish licence" in Ep. 23, a "Fish Club" in Ep. 28, and an ailing "rabbit fish" in Ep. 29, just to pick a few.

ARTHUR: "It can't be done"—Once again the talismanic power of the word in the Python world appears. Here it is a "sauce for the goose" structure, where knights who formerly used words of power as weapons are not so inoculated against words that can weaken them. Where or how the power of these words originates or is even manifested is never made clear, and it really doesn't matter, since the effects of the words are evidence enough of their potency. In the feature film *Brazil*, directed and cowritten by Gilliam (and costarring Palin), it's Sam's clothing—not his badge or his title—that act the phylacteric so that our hero can make it through the bureaucracy and to his beloved:

Sam takes the file and begins to leave.

Sam (Jonathan Pryce): Don't worry, I'll get to her.

Jack looks him up and down.

Jack (Palin): You'll never get anywhere in a suit like that.

Sam looks at his grey suit, confused. Jack goes to a cabinet and pulls out another grey suit. He hands it to Sam.

Sam: Here. Try this.[6]

The conservative double-breasted suit looks no different than the one he's wearing, than the ones everyone at the Ministry of Information have been wearing—but somehow this new suit (likely Jack's) is the emblem of authority Sam needs. In *Flying Circus* it was the word "mattress" (Ep. 8) or a request for hardcore pornography ("Raise high the drawbridge . . ."; Ep. 36) that triggered unconscious reactions and broke down time barriers.[7]

OTHER KNIGHTS *(they all recoil in horror)*: **"Oh!"**—Yet another magic word has been discovered, this one by accident, and which has a profoundly negative effect on the Knights Who Until Recently Said Ni. This same trope (a version of an Achilles Heel) can be found in earlier fantasy stories, including Lloyd Alexander's *Prydain* series, specifically the book *Taran Wanderer*, published in 1967. There, the enchanter Morda has removed and hidden a bone from his little finger, and he will be undefeatable as long as that bone remains undiscovered. Morda claims and wields great power:

"At my command this Fair Folk spy turned into a sightless, creeping mole. Yes," Morda hissed, "I had gained power even beyond what I sought. Who now would disobey me when I held the means to make men into the weak, groveling creatures they truly are! Did I seek only a gem? The whole kingdom of the Fair Folk was within my grasp. And all of Prydain! It was then I understood my true destiny. The race of men at last had found its master!" (94)

Morda is able to turn all of Taran's companions into animals, but Taran is protected by the sliver of bone he carries. It takes a bit of doing, but Taran eventually discovers the bone's charm-like power over Morda, and—when the bone snaps—Morda is destroyed, and his victims revert to their original forms. The Tall Knight and his Knights Who Say Ni have ruled the dark forest for a long while, it appears, and all seem to be truly afraid of them, but the simple, accidental discovery of their "life secret"[8] ends their domination. It might be, though, that things return to normal as soon as this band of interlopers is out of earshot—many of the film's scenes are ended or abandoned with questions unanswered.

SINGERS: ". . . and his kidneys burnt and his nipples skewered off . . ."—These tortures sound quite made up, but the medieval fascination with corporeal pain and suffering rendered all kinds of mutilation possible, as Tuchman has pointed out.[9] It has been reported that Edward II may have been tortured and killed by having a red hot poker inserted through a funnel into his rectum,[10] perhaps burning his kidneys, making what sounds like turgid drama into real life, where similar corporeal atrocities greeted the medieval man:

[E]very church [parishioner] saw pictures of saints undergoing varieties of atrocious martyr-dom—by arrows, spears, fire, cut-off breasts—usually dripping blood. The Crucifixion with its nails, spears, thorns, whips, and more dripping blood was inescapable. Blood and cruelty were ubiquitous in Christian art, indeed essential to it, for Christ became Redeemer, and the saints sanctified, only through suffering violence at the hands of their fellow men. (Tuchman, 135)

Tuchman goes on to note that on the rolls of criminality in England during the fourteenth century, "manslaughter [was] far ahead of accident as cause of death, and more often than not the offender escaped punishment by obtaining benefit of clergy through bribes or the right con-nections" (134). "If life was filled with bodily harm," Tuchman continues, "literature reflected it" (134). For Robin, the literature of song tells his merry tale of violence discreetly avoided.

SINGERS: ". . . he was throwing in the sponge"—A boxing euphemism for quitting the match, this is another anachronistic element. In the original, cobbled draft of the film's script, however, there is an extended section featuring a contemporary New York boxing match where the fighter loses his head, and not for the first time (*MPHGB*, 28–32). This sketch would even-tually appear in the final, part-season of *MPFC*, Ep. 43, "Boxing Match Aftermath."

The TALL KNIGHT remains standing, trying to control his MEN—Actually, the Tall Knight remains standing (while his men are rolling about, covering their ears) because he can-not move, given the constraints of the costume they created for him. He is standing on a ladder or platform, and can't move or he'll fall. The full helmet and the copious facial hair force Palin to act with his eyes, hands, and mouth, and he admits to feeling constrained throughout. This was one of the scenes the Pythons would later consider cutting from the film, as they felt it wasn't working. (Listen to Palin's audio commentary for more.) Clearly, though, this scene has entered the cultural lexicon. The Three-Headed Knight earlier was also anchored in place.

Notes

1. See, for example, *Citizen Kane* (1941).

2. The Palestine Liberation Organization (PLO) was founded in the mid-1960s in Ramallah, West Bank; the Symbionese Liberation Army (SLA) was an American group formed in 1973. The SLA was prominently in the news by mid-February 1974, after kidnapping newspaper heiress Patricia Hearst in California. This gets funnier as it's remembered just how many similar guerrilla-type political groups announced themselves in the turbulent years of decolonization, including the PFLP (Popular Front for the Liberation of Palestine, the DFLP (Democratic Front for the Liberation of Palestine), and the PLF (Palestine Liberation Front), all founded within a few years of one another in the 1960s.

3. See the entry "*TALL KNIGHT OF NI*" in scene 21 for more on this magical word.

4. "Fon" and "quarn hump" can both be heard in the *Goon Show* episode "The Chinese Legs," broadcast 7 January 1960.

5. "The Thing on the Mountain" (6 January 1958), audio transcription.

6. *Brazil*, audio transcription.

7. See *MPFC: UC* entries for Episode 36, especially "I think I will" (2.124). This has been discussed above, in the "Introduction" section.

8. See the introductory material in *Taran Wanderer* (ix) for some discussion of the appearance of this "life secret" in Welsh mythology, which Alexander mined for his fantasy world.

9. See the entry for "*Prisoner hanging on castle wall*" in scene 10.

10. This seems the case in the printed play *Edward II*, by Marlowe, where Matrevis enters carrying a "spit," and they put the king on a table and murder him, not wanting to leave any outwardly visible bruising (*Edward II*, 5.5). The enactment of this scene could be quite gruesome, given the producer's interpretation of the sparse scene directions. This manner of death, if true, may have been connected to the whisperings of Edward and favorite "night-grown mushroom" Gaveston's physical attraction to and interaction with one another.

SCENE TWENTY-NINE
THE DEAD HISTORIAN COVERED

EXTERIOR—HISTORIAN'S GLADE—DAY—(PSC) This cutaway scene is in the printed script but does not appear in the finished film. The script calls for a cut to "*an almost subliminal shot*" of the Historian's Wife and the police leaving the glade. Instead, the police are covering the dead Historian with a blue tarpaulin as the wife describes and the inspector questions—in mime, essentially—what happened to her husband. There will be a later, shorter version of this scene that appears in the film but not in the printed script—where the policemen are searching for clues in the enchanted forest where the Knights Who Say Ni used to be.

A second part of this excised scene (penciled through) are the "Knights Who Say Ni" preparing for another unwitting traveler. They want more shrubberies, clearly, and wonder whether they should call themselves the "Knights of Nicky-Nicky" (*MPHGB*, 67–68).

SCENE THIRTY
KING BRIAN THE WILD

EXTERIOR—DAY—*A small group of peasants are being shuffled into a group formation . . . they burst into pleasant (mellifluous) song . . . a hail of arrows hits them and they crumple up*—(PSC) Thus begins a ten-page scene (script pages 68–78) that is completely scratched through in the final version of the script—none of this scene was ever filmed, due to time and budgetary constraints, though versions of this scene have appeared in later Python-related films (see below).

The missing scene focuses on King Brian the Wild's court, where there are no women, and the men are all ragged and injured. King Brian enjoys killing close harmony groups as they perform for him, and responds to every request of him with a violent act.[1] Brian also has a series of advisors who get injured and die as the scene moves along, and a herald who repeats quite loudly every word the king utters, often adding editorial comments along the way. Doyle mentions that it has always been one of his favorite scenes, and he was quite sad to see it elided due to time and money:

> I wanted Brian and was sorry to see it go. [They then] added Robin into the Ni scene [to fix the continuity problems]. When we got back to London Terry G got rid of Robin's Minstrels [they'd been killed in the missing Brian scene]. Most obvious use of elements [occur later] in *Jabberwocky*. I suggested they use a version of "Brian the Wild" in the [2014] stage show.[2]

When all the kingdom's close harmony groups are dead, King Brian orders his disemboweled but willing mandarin to find more or else.[3] The advisor hears Arthur and knights from afar, singing the "Knights of the Round Table" song.[4] He tries to convince them to perform for Brian, but they are suspicious of Brian's penchant for "close harmony" singing, Galahad offering "one line of plainsong with a bit of straight choral work" (the parsing and minutiae have begun yet again). It's not until the adviser, with his dying breath, issues the call as a challenge from King Brian to sing close harmony that Arthur agrees. Arthur and his knights are ready to sing, but the nearby archers put them off, even when they're pretending to hide, and violence is about to erupt when Robin's minstrels' "beautiful close harmony singing" is heard, and the arrows fly that way instead. This is how Robin's minstrels are removed from the action in the "final" version of the script. After this scene was excised, Gilliam was forced to animate a scene where the minstrels could be eaten, instead. There, as will be seen, the consuming happens behind a snow-covered rock, and is narrated by Palin.

This "King Brian the Wild" scene may have been jettisoned for more than time and budgetary reasons, of course. It's rather a long scene at ten written pages, and quite dialogue-heavy, with doses of brutishness not really found in the rest of the film. Gilliam and Jones cut and cut the shorter "Three-Headed Knight" scene because it played overlong and underwhelming, in both comedic and narrative terms, leaving us to wonder how a finished "King Brian" scene would have been eventually received. Also, the facts that early in the film Arthur and his closest knights choose to avoid Camelot altogether and that they aren't the ones who sang the "Knights of the Round Table" song, anyway, means it's less likely that they'd be riding through the countryside singing the song now. In other words, this scene mightn't have connected to the earlier events in anything but a clumsy way, so it may have been fairly easy to dispense with mounting it during location shooting. At its heart the scene is also reflective of earlier pedantic moments, especially the "swallow" minutiae, and may have been removed due to its familiarity.

There are a number of characters in the Pythons' source material that prefigure a hyperviolent King Brian–type, including Sagramor the Wild, often included as one of Arthur's knights. In some versions of these stories Sagramor can slip into a sort of "berserker" rage when fighting. He appears by name in many of the romances, and his character can change from tale to tale (he's easily bested a number of times, for example, in Malory's work). "Sagramour" is mentioned in Adams's "The Vision of Sir Lamoracke" (1886), but there he's also known as "sweet Sir Sagramor," while in *Le Morte D'Arthur* he's "Sagramore le Desirous," and so on. Another Brian, called Brian of the Isles by Malory, enjoyed imprisoning folk (including Gawain) for his amusement at Dolorous Guard, and then at Pendragon Castle, and Launcelot is called to eventually stop him. This Brian and his wife thank Launcelot for freeing the prisoners and putting an end to the imprisonments, oddly. It turns out they are very pleased to have been beaten by the noblest of Arthur's knights, Launcelot (*LMD'A*, 1.391–92).

In history, there are also candidates for the Brian character. King Charles VI was described as mad, on and off, for the last thirty years of his life (d. 1422; Tuchman, 513). Pedro the Cruel (1334–1369) of Spain could be mentioned, though his "monstrous" reputation changed over time—and he eventually became known as "Pedro the Just." Or there is Wenceslas IV (1361–1419), whom Tuchman calls a

> tragic, ruined figure, [he] emerges from the chronicles a kind of Caliban, half clownish, half vicious, a composite of half-truths and legends reflecting the animosities of his various sets of enemies. Because his reign was the source of the Hussite revolt against the rising Czech nationalism hostile to the Germans, Wenceslas suffered posthumously from both clerical and German chroniclers. . . . Said by his partisans to be good-looking and well-mannered, he appears more generally as a "wild boar" who went on rampages at night with bad companions, burst into burghers' houses to rape their wives, shut up his own wife in a whorehouse, roasted a cook who served him a burned meal. . . . Wenceslas became a confirmed alcoholic. . . . He grew increasingly irritable and black-tempered and indolent as a sovereign . . . and succumbed to fits of savagery in which he was thought sometimes to have "lost command of his reason." (482–84)

Though history (written by his enemies) has likely been unkind to Wenceslas, he was clearly at least a suitable prototype for an over-the-top monarch like King Brian.

From *Flying Circus*, the Piranha brothers are certainly early Brian-types. The "friends" and competitors around these East End gangsters tend to get banged up, just like Brian's court. Doug and Dinsdale are accused of nailing people's heads to coffee tables, inserting floor lamps through torsos, inserting heads into concrete, screwing someone's pelvis to a cake stand, or taking them "for a scrape" behind a tank as a lark. They threaten with guns, knives, small artillery, nuclear weapons, and even "sarcasm" during their reign of terror (*JTW*, 1.187–91). This same protracted scene of regnal-inspired violence will be revisited in the "King Byron the Questionable" scene in *Jabberwocky*, Gilliam's 1977 follow-up to *MPHG* starring Palin, and written by Gilliam and Charles Alversen. These scenes of filth and maiming—which had to be dumped from *Holy Grail* for reasons of economy—found full flower in many of the separate Python films to come, including *Jabberwocky*, *Yellowbeard*, *Time Bandits*, and *Erik the Viking*.

In the end, the fortuitous arrival of Robin and his minstrels, who are singing and dancing, distract King Brian from Arthur and the rest of the quest, and the volley of arrows meant for Arthur hit the minstrels instead. Brian is beside himself with glee at the sight of the "suddenly pin-cushioned" singers (also the last image of Washizu from *Throne of Blood*, incidentally), and Robin is "surprised but relieved" that his minstrels are finally dead (*MPHGB*, 77).

Notes

1. This "senseless violence" trope will reappear over and over again in later Python-related projects, including Gilliam's *Time Bandits*, where Robin Hood's men sucker punch the poor as they receive their handouts.

2. From a 6 December 2013 e-mail correspondence with the author.

3. There is also a tiny insert scene missing here, which would have looked like this:

Scene: Policemen on the Hunt
EXTERIOR—DAY—(PSC) This is another *missing* scene, one not appearing in the printed script at all. It is simply a "meanwhile" cut back to the forest where the "Knights Who Say Ni" were seen earlier. Policemen—this time "*two PLAIN CLOTHES DETECTIVES and a CONSTABLE*"—get out of a police car and examine the scene, looking for clues, finding one of Patsy's shoes.

4. Unlikely, since it was this song and the frivolity that accompanied it which prompted Arthur to avoid Camelot in the first place.

SCENE THIRTY-ONE
"PASSING SEASONS" ANIMATION

EXTERIOR—BEYOND THE FOREST—DAY—*ANIMATION*—This page is also a page "68," matching the typed page 68 that started the "King Brian the Wild" section. At some point *before* the script was completed and finalized this short, animated section was proposed in place of the ten-page "King Brian" or "close harmony" sequence. Instead of Robin and his minstrels coming into the Brian scene, they enter into the Knights Who Until Recently Said Ni scene, for example.[1] The word "Animation" has been written into the script after-the-fact, meaning the Pythons either forgot to note that the scene was to be a cartoon with voice-over work, or it was originally planned to be at least partly filmed on location, in live action.

Shots of ARTHUR etc. riding out of the forest—(PSC) A decidedly dull and fairly uncinematic shot, to be sure, that is made watchable by conversion to animation. The animated figures are all made to look like Arthur, Patsy, the minstrels, etc., but their forms are faithful to the figures seen in the margins of period illuminated manuscripts, including some with arched backs and others perpetually stooped, as will be discussed below.

VOICE OVER: ". . . set out on their search to find the Enchanter of whom the old man had spoken in scene twenty-four"—This represents a major reminder to the audience who may have forgotten both Scene 24 *and* the promised Enchanter. The "Scene 24" sequence occurred well back in the script on pages 42–43, and moments later (page 44) Arthur is asking the Tall Knight for help finding this same enchanter. It won't be until this current animated scene—beginning on script page 68[2]—that the Enchanter is again mentioned, meaning the "Voice Over" is simply being courteous to his audience. After all, the Launcelot and Concorde business; the Swamp Castle events surrounding Herbert, his father, and Launcelot; Roger the Shrubber; and the return to the Knights Who Until Recently Said Ni have been experienced since the last mention of the Enchanter. None of these narrative culs-de-sac were helpful in forwarding the quest for the Grail, interestingly, which might be either the Pythons' comment on similar sidetrackings in the romance sources—of which there are many—or indicative of their own struggles to fashion a narratively fluid quest story from gag-rich material. One of the common complaints voiced in contemporary reviews of the film was the "sketch-y" nature of the narrative—funny but separate and discrete two-minute bits stitched together in a clumsy, amusing story; indeed, "the story becomes less an excuse than an obstacle to the gags."[3] Arthur earlier asks the Soothsayer about the Enchanter's whereabouts at approximately 43:44, then asks the Tall Knight at 45:36, and finally the voice-over mentions the Enchanter again at 64:31. Incidentally, this pregnant pause would have been even longer if the Pythons had decided to keep the "King Brian the Wild" scene—a full ten pages of additional, grotesque material to shoot.

These sidetrackings, or missed goals, can be found throughout the history, as well, with Richard I's crusading offering a prime example. In late 1187 Jerusalem had fallen to the Muslim Saladin's forces, and new Pope Gregory VIII called for a crusade not long after. Richard and Philip II of France agreed to stop fighting each other and join the holy cause. In 1189 Richard began raising funds, and by mid-1190 he and Philip were leaving Marseille for Sicily. The people of Messina were hostile to these crusading armies, and "Richard was compelled to take the city by storm" (Poole, *DBMC*, 359–60). Things only got more challenging from there. "The Sicilian government was also hostile," Poole goes on; Richard's sister Joan was taken captive, freed, and eventually a fine was paid, while throughout these negotiations Philip "secretly abetted Richard's enemies" and took spoils wherever he could (360). It wouldn't be until March 1191 that "difficulties were smoothed out at Messina"— they'd wasted the entire winter and were no closer to the Holy Land (360). Richard finally sailed out of Messina in April and reached Palestine by June. Richard would retake Acre by mid-July, but Philip went home, supplies were a continuing problem, and Richard was unable to take Jerusalem—he got within eyesight of the walls, but no closer. He was able to get along quite well with Saladin and his brother Safadin, and even tried to make dynastic marriages a possibility, but those ambitions fell through, as well. He would sail home in October 1192, only to be sidetracked, again, in a denouement that sounds perfectly Pythonesque:

> After many adventures with pirates, storms, and shipwreck, Richard was thrown ashore with a few companions on the coast of Istria; thence, after more adventures, he reached the neighbourhood of Vienna where he fell into the hands of Duke Leopold of Austria (December) whom he had insulted and quarrelled with during the crusade. In February 1193 it was arranged that he should be delivered over to the emperor Henry VI. (*DBMC*, 362)

Richard I was a prisoner, held for ransom, and his brother John was busy trying to secure his own seat on Richard's throne (unsuccessfully, as it turns out). By February 1194 Richard had agreed to pay the staggering ransom of 150,000 marks of silver, as well as portions of Normandy, and he was finally set free (363). In the end Richard's noble quest had cost his people dearly, and he had very little to show for it, something Arthur *may* begin to appreciate of his own situation as he and Bedevere are escorted into police custody later in the film.

VOICE OVER: "Beyond the forest they met Launcelot and Galahad . . ."—In the extended, elided King Brian sequence, the knights had already come back together—excepting Robin—when they encountered Brian, allowing for them to both sing and be mistaken for a "close harmony group" (*MPHGB*, 68–69). In this new scene, the voice-over simply notes their return, just as earlier narration by the Very Famous Historian had mentioned their separation. Due to time and budget constraints, the Pythons found it necessary to cut narrative corners, adding expository voice-overs on top of animated bits and the "Book of the Film" sequence. These postproduction elements papered over the clunky transitions affordably, as they had throughout *Flying Circus*, where the sharing/gathering of such information was always a challenge:

> Generally, the Python characters will push on through a scene—usually attempting some sort of communication or transaction—without mentioning the miscommunication at all (cf. the "Police Station" in Ep. 12). This may be an indication of the transition in various episodes during this series from the self-aware-but-silent Modernist approach (where Joycean dialogue, for example,

can be delivered and responded to without any character batting an eye) *toward the more brazen self-aware-and-trumpeting-the-fact Postmodernist approach to the artificiality of the constructed scene.* The fact that the oft-used "Women's Institute" film clip has already been mentioned by a character *acknowledges the artificiality* (the "television-ness") *of the setting.* (*MPFC: UC*, 1.379; italics added)

Finally, the presence of these self-aware, textually postmodern linking elements have become as identified with Monty Python as any silliness in between—and they are certainly found throughout *MPFC*—meaning the ends have justified the means, and the *formal constraints* of the film actually enable it as a Python work.

EXTERIOR—ANOTHER LANDSCAPE—DAY—ANIMATION—(Again, this "Exterior" shot was labeled as an "Animation" scene after the script was printed out.)

Neither the printed script nor the book it's found in (*MPHGB*) offer any conclusive evidence as to when or why the "King Brian the Wild" sequence was swapped out for this simple animated transition; the many comments from the Pythons regarding limited funds and cramped shooting schedules provide useful hints. The film's postproduction godsend, Julian Doyle, confirms that "scheduling" was the direct cause. Once they got to Scotland and experienced the first few awful days, they realized either the "Ni" or "Brian" scene would have to be removed from the shooting schedule if they were to finish on time and within budget, and they chose to keep the "Ni" scene.[4]

This cartoon sequence is the second animated "tracking" shot sequence of the film, the first being the introduction of the "Tale of Sir Galahad" earlier (where the monks queued up to use the diving board). As before, the camera[5] tracks from right to left, this time revealing a wider-than-expected *bas-de-page* forested scene. Michael Camille has identified the importance of this portion of the medieval manuscript page: "As in so many manuscripts, it is that which is found at the bottom of the page that is most significant" (*Image on the Edge*, 20). These twelfth- to fifteenth-century volumes would have been delivered from perhaps more pious scribes to illustrators with spaces left for decorated initials and marginal illuminations. The artists were then supposed to add ruminative gospel artwork accordingly. In practice, these artists would render either faithfully or ironically (ideally according to the text above), or obscene, scatological, and undercutting illustrations. Working alone after the film/episode had been "completed," Gilliam had been afforded the same freedom, though he clearly hews close to the anarchic spirit of the *Holy Grail*'s filmed world as he creates his interstitial animations.[6] The Galahad animation earlier was also a *bas-de-page* setup. Here the stylized trees the knights walk through are Gilliam re-creations, but they are clearly modeled carefully after those he found in *Flowering of the Middle Ages* (183), and they are scattered throughout the medieval illuminated manuscripts he used as source material, including those found in the *Rutland Psalter*, referenced by Randall more than a dozen times. On page 183 in *FMA* there is a large sketched image drawn from the *Psalter of Saint Louis and Blanche of Castille*, a thirteenth-century manuscript housed in the Bibliotheque Nationale (MS. 1186, f. IV). The primarily oak and sycamore (or maple) trees Gilliam has emulated and designed are highly stylized—reflective of the popular heightened medieval manuscript style.[7]

The tracking shot moves across forested sections—versions of the *Rutland* and *St. Louis* psalters–type trees[8]—past a cave in a hill hiding the creature of Caerbannog[9] (seen later), and to another, smaller hillock. The troupe passes behind the hill with the cave, giving the illusion of depth to the flat animated scene. This larger hill (with the cave) has been modeled after several appearing in the *Rutland* manuscript, rendered larger and covered with trees by Gilliam. The lower left corner of the hill, for example, is fashioned very much like a hillock in *Rutland* on which a man stands, conversing with an ape, who sits in a stylized tree (Randall, LXVI: 321). As the tracking shot continues, the figures of Launcelot and Galahad and a smaller hill are discovered. The smaller hill is modeled after a mountain scene depicted in manuscript fr. 12400, f. 94v, known as "Traite de fauconnerie," from the late thirteenth century (LXX: 337).[10] The trees on this hillock are actually intricate, tendriled tree decorations drawn from pages of the Winchester Bible manuscript (c. 1160), specifically the "Life of David" plate.[11]

Though Gilliam clearly drew and colored his knights, pages, and musicians for these miniatures—each is dressed/badged/helmed just as they are in the film—the model for the knights, at least, seems to have come from an image in the Verdun 107 manuscript (f. 149v), where a David and Goliath scene is depicted. On this page Goliath is dressed as a knight, with the only necessary difference being his hand, which is gripping a spear; the hand has to be turned around as if he's holding reins, and the spear removed by Gilliam to complete the "riding" look (Randall, XXXI: 142).

In this same animated scene Launcelot and Galahad stand in front of two tents—one red-and-white-striped, the other perhaps burgundy and white—both drawn by Gilliam, but inspired by very similar images in illuminated manuscripts like MS 229 (f. 168r), part of Yale University's collection.[12] This original illustration shows knights clustered around a red-and-white tent; Gilliam used an image from this same manuscript earlier in the introduction to Sir Galahad's tale (MS 229 f. 253r), and sketched images of similar tents in *MPHGB* (facing page 37). The minstrels are also drawn by Gilliam, even given the proper instruments as played by the minstrel actors in the film—meaning they weren't just copied out of *IMGM* source material. The sources for these traipsing characters can be found throughout Randall, but are also depicted in the introductory pages of *HBMA*. There, five morris dancers caper across a *bas-de-page* design, all borrowed from the *Romance of Alexander* (Ms. Bodl. 264, f. 78). In Randall, similar group dancing- or game-type events (bent over, legs askew) can be seen on plates XLII and XLIII.

A jump cut takes us to another animated setting. The sun is rising on a mixed landscape—part border and decoration adapted from illuminated manuscripts, and part hillock, also adapted. Arthur and his fellow questers will walk into the shot from the right, then disappear behind the hillock after winter sets in (where Robin's minstrels are consumed). The upper left image of a blustery and blue "Old Man Winter" is likely a Gilliam creation (pictorially it very much resembles his God figure in the title sequence to *Meaning of Life*), but there are also many instances in the illuminated manuscript tradition where the face of an old man (often an old, bearded man with some kind of hybridized body) is depicted as marginalia in a corner.[13] One such facial figure can be seen in the *Macclesfield Psalter* (f. 20, verso), labeled "Wizard." The man faces outward (to the left), and his arms grow from where his body should be.[14] Several such figures appear in the Douce 6 manuscript[15]—see folios 70v and 72v in Douce 6, for example. Gilliam has borrowed from Douce 6 already (including the memorable springboarding monks/nuns). There are also many period maps and cityscapes that feature personified wind figures, including a c. 1200 depiction of "Aer" controlling the four winds in *Flowering of the Middle Ages* (199).

The hillock is adapted from at least two sources. The base of the hillock resembles the sources Gilliam used for the two hills seen in the previous animated frame, borrowed from *Rutland*. The upper portion of the hillock is of a more recent design—less stylized, more realistic—and not unlike those similar rock structures found in both Bosch and Dürer works.[16]

The corner and *bas-de-page* border (on which the questers walk on the animation) are both borrowed and slightly retouched for this scene. Gilliam has taken a good portion of the bottom left corner of folio 28 of W. 104, a fourteenth-century Franco-Flemish Hours manuscript, and cropped, extended, and replaced elements, though the whole is still quite recognizable. He has kept about the lower one-third of the left frame, cropping at a leaf decoration, and then taken five-sixths of the extant *bas-de-page* decoration and doubled it. Curiously, he has removed one of the animal designs in the section and replaced it with a floral design. The third section from the left featured a rabbit and dog, *tête-à-tête*, possibly in confrontation, and the fourth section depicted a small, stylized dragon curled up to match the circular space. So the original six decorative settings were: floral pattern, floral pattern, rabbit and dog, dragon, floral pattern, and floral pattern. As reconfigured for the filmed scene, Gilliam laid them out this way: floral pattern, floral pattern, floral pattern, dragon, floral pattern, floral pattern, dragon, followed by three floral patterns. The newly inserted floral patterns were simply inverted versions of the initial floral decoration. The end of the decoration is a simple curlicue design. Evelyn Paul updated this very same border design in her illustrated collection *Clair de Lune* (25, 104). There's even a bit of a *fleur-de-lis* that pokes up in the original manuscript rendering, out of frame, and Gilliam keeps that in the final version. It looks like a little knob jutting up into the snowy mound behind which Robin's minstrels disappear. A full version of this folio (f. 28) can be seen on plate IV (image 11) of Randall's *IMGM*.

The border at the left is a composite of several portions of this same manuscript page, with the projecting flourish at the bottom right of the original being moved to the top left of the animated scene, while the next flower above that is actually in place from the original—the flowers in between have been cut out to create open space. Above that, several tendrils leading to smaller flowers are repositioned (from the left and right original border extrusions) after being cropped slightly. Gilliam did much more than cut and paste—he chose existing bits carefully and manipulated them to create his own animated world.

VOICE OVER: ". . . frozen land of Nador . . ."—Located in northeastern Morocco, Nador is not likely to have been frozen, even during one of the mini-Ice Ages of the Middle Ages. Nador is just across the small Alboran Sea from southern Spain (and coastal cities Malaga and Almeria), where millions of Britons have taken the infamous package tours (including the ranting Tourist in the *MPFC* sketch "Travel Agent," Ep. 31). Like the mention of "Gildor" during Idle's voice-over for "*Njorl's Saga*" in *MPFC* Ep. 27, "Nador" is likely a foreign-sounding word simply pulled from a hat. Given that Nador is found on the Mediterranean coast, there is also a possibility that it was "discovered" by Europeans on the way to or from various Crusades, meriting a mention in this quest tale.

Coincidentally, Gilliam already used a map image from the same area in Ep. 6 (*MPFC: UC*, 1.87), showing Malaga and part of the Alboran Sea. It might be that Nador was part of the troupe's lexicon given its proximity to Melilla, which is actually a Spanish city on the Moroccan coast, and just a twenty-minute train ride from Nador. Also, Nador found itself mentioned in British newspapers between 1956 and 1974 quite a number of times thanks to both the city's strategic position as a Spanish outpost in Africa, its role in testy Franco-Moroccan relations, and significant Spanish construction projects, some of them conducted by British contractors, including enormous antennae constructed in the early 1970s.

VOICE OVER: ". . . forced to eat Robin's minstrels"—This does get a hearty laugh from most audiences, Robin's minstrels having become somewhat irksome, admittedly. One harsh winter or one year of bad crops didn't usually spell disaster, rather a string of lean growing seasons compounded to devastating effect, often followed hard by disease that took advantage of the population's weakened condition. Chronicler Roger of Wendover (d. 1236) recorded the results of one particularly bad period: "In that same year [1234], which was the third barren year on end, fatal sickness and famine raged everywhere. These disasters arose, no doubt, as much from the price of sin as through the inclement weather and the widespread crop failure" (Hallam, 53). Cannibalism wasn't new in Europe, either. Paleontologists have discovered evidence of nearly modern humans consuming other nearly modern humans (Neanderthals) that dates back 100,000 years.[17] Much later, during the time of the first Crusade, "Christian soldiers ate the flesh of local Muslims" in the Syrian city of Ma'arra, presenting chroniclers with a prickly challenge as they attempted to write celebratory accounts of this great, spiritual event.[18] "Medicines" made from pieces of mummies and even disinterred corpses were available and popular in Europe through at least the sixteenth and seventeenth centuries.[19] Cannibalism, in several guises, was known and tolerated, though not validated.

Arthur and his questers do seem to be in the wilderness here, perhaps wandering as they recover from their collectively fruitless Grail-seeking performance. During a later Bruce attempt to overthrow all of Ireland in 1315–1318, the Great Famine afflicted much of Europe (between 1315 and 1317), and by 1317 Edward Bruce's (b. 1280) troops were having trouble feeding themselves and their horses off the land. Upon this Bruce's death at the Battle of Faughart, the *Annals of Ulster* soberly record that "there was not done from the beginning of the world a deed that was better for the Men of Ireland" than Edward Bruce's execution, since his deprivations had led to Irish men and women having to eat each other.[20] Adverse weather, insect and crop disease scourges, and soil fatigue could lead to crop loss and starvation rather quickly, as Bishop notes, with the (understandable) attendant consequences:

> When famine struck, it brought with it the excesses of desperation, resort to barks and grasses that merely exasperated hunger's pangs. A twelfth-century bishop of Trier was assailed by a starving crowd that refused his offer of useless money, seized his fat palfrey, tore it to pieces, and devoured it before his eyes. There are even reports of cannibalism; perhaps the folk tales of ogres, of Jack and the Beanstalk, have some basis in fact. (*HBMA*, 238)

Cannibalism and the dismemberment of the human body—body horror[21]—had become staples of the *MPFC* board, both live action and animated. In the "Restaurant Abuse/Cannibalism" sketch, Ep. 26, a waiter is on the menu while a vicar waits in a pot in the corner; sailors decide who will eat whom on a lifeboat; and the Argyll Regiment is said to have eaten each other in Aden—rather than eating Arabs (*MPFC: UC*, 1.385–94). In an extended animated sequence from this same episode, various Civil War generals eat people and are themselves eaten as popcorn and frozen treats (1.386).

Dismembering and eating people is funny, of course, though it likely would have meant something more to an audience in 1975. Near Christmas 1972 two emaciated, nearly dead men emerged from the high Andes, having survived a plane crash at 12,000 feet, a two-month stranding, and a ten-day trek down the mountains. Others were still alive at the crash site, and soon all were rescued. The fact that sixteen people had survived seventy days in the forbidding and barren mountains was sensational; the news that they'd had to resort to eating the bodies of fellow deceased passengers was immediately sensationalized. New reports from Chile trumpeted the "devouring" of the dead, and the ordeal stayed in international newspapers for weeks and months. But one local priest, Father Thomas Gonzales of Santiago, saw the other side of the survivors' plight, acknowledging the occasional necessity of such acts: "In the case of the dead on board the Uruguayan aircraft, the most useful thing for these human bodies was to nourish the survivors." Gonzales concluded: "The dead, therefore, accomplished their mission, and there is no theological opposition in this case."[22] Arthur and company could have easily justified their "communion-like"[23] eating of Robin's minstrels, especially given the presence in Malory's work of the regular necessity of such ordinances (attending mass and matins, receiving communion, breaking a fast) regularly, and prior to embarking on *any* Grail-related or providential journey.

And even though the plight of the doomed Uruguayan flight's passengers had ended in late 1972, the harrowing events were still very much in the news as the Pythons set about writing and even shooting *MPHG* in 1973–1974. In February 1974 the paperback rights to the Piers Paul Read story *Alive: The Story of the Andes Survivors* were auctioned off to Pan Books for £27,000, hardback rights already owned by Alison Press.[24] This was a first-ever auction of its type, and was covered by most news organizations. Less than three months later in May 1974 two of the survivors—Fernando Parrado and Roberto Canessa—spoke of the crash and their agonizing decision in a closely covered London press conference (timed with the hardback book's release). These survivors also then appeared on BBC 1's *Midweek*[25] on 7 May 1974. The Pythons were in Scotland shooting the film in May 1974, of course—where local papers, radio, and TV would have covered the goings-on—and the voice-overs would have been recorded (and animated sequences completed) sometime soon afterward, during postproduction.

VOICE OVER: ". . . and there was much rejoicing"—This sentence structure and cant are borrowed from popular "troubadour romances" including "The Lady and the Buttercup," wherein a poor girl has been making offerings of butter to an image of the Virgin (a May Altar in a field), and the Virgin eventually wishes to repay the devotion to both the image and the girl:

> And the Holy Virgin was pleased and she said,
> "Take it now, my image, and eat it, for I think she
> meant no ill in giving it thee, but rather to do me
> pleasure."
> And the image said, "Nay, but make it a buttercup
> to grow in my hand."
> And the image reached down its hand and took the
> butter, and it became a very fair flower, bigger than
> any buttercup that ever was, and it was called a
> Marigold, because it was like gold and grew in the
> Holy Mother Mary's hand.
> And the cow gave much milk, and never was there
> so rich a field in all the world, and they got back all
> the pigs and the goats that they had sold. (40–41)

Also, the sort of half-hearted "Yeah" chorused by the rest of the quest (after they've eaten Robin's minstrels) can be earlier heard in an episode of *The Goon Show*, "The House of Teeth":

Seagoon (Secombe): William? Lay out my evening dress.

William (Sellers): Cor strewth, you wearing evening dress in this rain and mud, mate?

Seagoon: Yes! Remember, all of you—we're British. Together—hip hip!

Cast: (*miserably*) Hooray. . . . (31 January 1956; audio transcription)

MONTAGE of shots of the KNIGHTS—(PSC) This is as detailed as the printed script gets here, since as they both wrote the script and then shot the film the Pythons (including, likely,

Gilliam) had no idea what the animated sequence was actually going to contain, or, indeed, if the scene would be animated at all.[26]

Following the *bas-de-page* scene described above, the next scene features a man and two sheep on a new, snow-covered hillock. This scene begins with a close-up of the hill and occupants, then pulls back to reveal yet another typical "footer" illustration (*bas-de-page*) as found in many illuminated manuscripts. This full frame reveals not only the small hill, single tree, shepherd, and two sheep (the same sheep from the much earlier title sequence[27]), but additionally to the left of the hill a birdhouse-sized building and add-on building, probably meant to imitate a kind of roadside shrine or May Altar. Both trees in this frame are modeled after the sinewy trees found in most of these manuscripts (see Rutland and Royal 10, for example); the hill is xerographed and enlarged (originally from the *Rutland Psalter*, see Randall, LXVI: 321); while the miniature buildings comprise a kind of altar. There is an image of one such altar in Evelyn Paul's much later "Our Lady of the Buttercups" illustrations in the *Clair De Lune* collection. A tiny Virgin statue stands in a shrine box atop a small tree trunk, just next to a short song:

> Sweet Mother Mary mine,
> Guardian of the sleepy kine
> Dwelling in the meadow wide,
> Pilot of the grasstop tide.
> Bid me tell this tale for thee,
> That good & pleasing it may be. (36)

The tiny altar therein (which Paul will use again in *Aucassin and Nicolete* [1917]) looks very much like Gilliam's version, but instead of cattle ("kine") he depicts sheep and a shepherd. Gilliam's "altar" is clearly xerographed and manipulated a bit, and borrowed from a footer marginal illustration in Stowe 17 *(The Maastricht Hours)*, produced in the Netherlands. The Maastricht illustration is labeled (by Randall) as "Samson tearing down house of Philistines" (CXXXIII: 633; f. 122v). In the original illumination, the add-on to the tiny castle tower (or altar) is supported by two marbled columns, and Samson is grasping the outward column. The tower is perspectively out of proportion and stylized—this happens a great deal in these marginal illustrations, and was the look of the Gothic period. Gilliam replaces both Samson and the columns with a small tree trunk, making it look much more like a happy May Altar.

VOICE OVER: "Autumn changed into Winter . . . Winter changed into Spring . . ."— Certainly inspired by the famous sequence at the start of the Second Fytte of *Sir Gawain and the Green Knight*:

And so this Yule went by, and the year after it, each season in turn following the other. After Christmas came the crabbed Lent, that tries the flesh with fish and more simple food. But then the weather of the world quarrels with winter, and though the cold still clings, the clouds lift; copiously descends the rain in warm showers, and falls upon the fair earth. Flowers show there; green are the garments both of fields and of groves; birds hurry to build, and lustily they sing for the solace of the soft summer, that follows thereafter. Blossoms swell into bloom in rows rich and rank; and lovely notes are heard in the beauteous wood.

After the season of summer with the soft winds, when Zephyrus blows on seeds and herbs, happy is the plant that waxes then, when the dank dew drops from the leaves, to await the blissful glance of the bright sun. But then harvest hastens and hardens it soon: warns it to wax full ripe against the winter. He drives with drought the dust to rise,—from the face of the earth to fly full high. The wild wind of the welkin wrestles with the sun. The leaves fall from the bough and light on the ground. The grass becomes all gray that erst was green. Then all ripes and rots that which formerly flourished; and thus runs the year in yesterdays many; and winter returns again without asking any man, till the Michelmas moon has come in wintry wise. Then thinks Gawain full soon of his anxious voyage.[28]

VOICE OVER: ". . . Autumn gave Winter and Spring a miss . . ."—This is meant to be silly, yes, but similar weather anomalies did appear scattered across the Dark and Middle Ages, and by definition most of them were catastrophic, even apocalyptic, to ordinary folk. In the second third of the sixth century (c. 535–536) some significant natural event (likely one or more massive volcanic eruptions in Indonesia and/or South America) led to worldwide unseasonably cool weather—snow in warmer zones, crop failures, and associated malnourishment, illness, and premature death. Cooler-than-expected temperatures or wetter-than-expected seasons could push already strained medieval farming and husbandry to its limits, meaning any unseasonal weather might be the difference between life and death for the medieval peasant, especially. The heavy rains of 1315 were described in biblical terms by medieval chroniclers, especially after "crops failed all over Europe, and famine, the dark horseman of the Apocalypse, became familiar to all" (Tuchman, 24).

In her book *A Distant Mirror*, Tuchman notes that the fourteenth century was a challenging time for peasants for many reasons—manorial obligations, inadequate sanitation, plague—and when the weather didn't cooperate, it all became much, much worse. By the fin de siècle the new "century was already in trouble," and blame could be squarely placed on unreliable seasons:

> A physical chill settled on the fourteenth century at its very start, initiating the miseries to come. The Baltic Sea froze over twice, in 1303 and 1306–07; years followed of unseasonable cold, storms and rains, and a rise in the level of the Caspian Sea. Contemporaries could not know it was the onset of what has since been recognized as the Little Ice Age, caused by an advance of polar and alpine glaciers and lasting until about 1700. Nor were they yet aware that, owing to the climatic change, communication with Greenland was gradually being lost, that the Norse settlements there were being extinguished, that cultivation of grain was disappearing from Iceland and being severely reduced in Scandinavia. But they could feel the colder weather, and mark with fear the result: a shorter growing season. (24)

At its most elemental, giving even "Winter . . . a miss" would mean those crops that need a dormancy period would be the first to suffer. For example, all the orchard tasks usually reserved for when a fruit tree is in a state of dormancy (and not susceptible to stress) would have to be accomplished anyway, likely damaging the tree. And without a spring, going "straight on into summer" would mean little or no harvest in the fall. Even in bad crop years the villein or peasant would still have to satisfy his master's livestock and produce quotas first before seeing to his own needs, meaning colder seasons promoted ever-restricting cycles of agricultural diminishment, reduced nutrition, and increased susceptibility to disease.

Notes

1. In the scripted version, the minstrels are killed by Brian's men rather than saved for eating later, in the winter.

2. Page 68 would also have been the first page of the lengthy but excised "King Brian the Wild" sequence.

3. David Robinson, *Times*, 4 April 1975: 9.

4. From a 5 December 2013 e-mail correspondence with the author.

5. In traditional animation using a typical Oxberry-type stand, the overhead camera remains static, while the platen beneath (on which the backgrounds and animation material are placed/manipulated) moves laterally. In most traditional animation, the camera is locked down, meaning there can be no camera "moves," per se.

6. For their 1983 film *The Meaning of Life*, singly directed by Jones, Gilliam was working *apart* from the balance of the troupe as he created the *Crimson Permanent Assurance* sequence—so much so that it had to be fashioned into a supporting, standalone featurette rather than a fellow canto in the film, as had been planned.

7. Oak trees and leaves were a popular decoration in the illuminated manuscripts (and in English engravings of all kinds), and can be seen in, for example, the *bas-de-page* scene of Arundel 83, f. 14, found in Randall (LXX: 338). This image is just below one featuring a hillock that Gilliam nearly copied for this same sequence (the "small hillock," fr. 12400, f. 94v). Larger versions of maple or sycamore leaves can be found in Randall, as well (CVII: 513; CIX: 528; CXXVI: 598). Some of the sycamore-type leaves look to have been traced directly from CXXXIX: 665, which is a line-drawn image, and not colored-in by its artist. Sir Bedevere's insignia also features a blasted oak tree, with leaves at its base.

8. There are also a handful of shorter, stylized trees (one just above the lurking Beast) inspired by other illuminated manuscript examples, including Troyes 1905, f. 171 (Randall, XIX: 89). The *Rutland*-type trees can be found throughout the *Rutland* manuscript, beginning with the "Kalendar" section, with renderings in the months of May, August, and November.

9. This image—a creature in a cave—is found in the *Rutland Psalter*, as well. On f. 84r, a *bas-de-page* image depicts a *Rutland*-type sinewy hillock with a cave. Inside the cave is a naked man being lectured by an ape-man.

10. In the original image, a man is being lowered by two other men down the steep hill toward a bird's nest, where he will likely gather either eggs or the birds. Gilliam has removed all these figures as he repurposed the hill for the animated scene.

11. The Winchester Bible "look," however, *can* be found in other Bibles produced at the same time and by several individuals connected to the Winchester school, according to Oakeshott. This influential atelier is discussed in Oakeshott's *The Artists of the Winchester Bible* (London: Faber and Faber, 1945).

12. Gilliam also sketched similar tents as he prepared for the animated sequences. These are found on the facing pages; see Facing Page 37 in appendix A for more. These same kinds of tents were seen earlier, in the "Black Knight" scene, as well as in one of the troupe's reference resources for the "look" of this martial, medieval period, Polanski's film version of *Macbeth*.

13. It is also one of the few animated elements in the film that is "modeled," or made to appear more three-dimensional through shape and shading; such modeling had been characteristic of Gilliam's *original* artwork for *MPFC*, which appeared more often as the series moved forward.

14. This c. 1330 manuscript is part of the Fitzwilliam Museum collection, and features dozens of animals (including a giant skate fish), hybrids, grotesques, and absurdities, including fox doctors, men astride birds, and a man fighting a giant snail being watched by a laughing squirrel.

15. Flemish, fourteenth century. See the "*Animation*" entry in scene 17, "The Tale of Sir Galahad," for more on this manuscript source.

16. Gilliam sketched and created considerably using both sources, and Dürer's influence especially can be seen in *MPFC* animations and in books like *The Complete Works of Shakespeare and Monty Python* and *Animations of Mortality*. In *MPFC*, Dürer's influence is seen, for example, in Ep. 23:

> [A]s the letter is being "undelivered," a tinted version of a portion of Albrecht Dürer's *Apocalypse of St. John, The Dragon with the Seven Heads* is seen. Dürer's St. Anthony will be part of an animated sequence in Ep. 35. Gilliam also sketches portions of Dürer's work in *The Brand New Monty Python Bok*, and the German artist will figure prominently in the first *Fliegender Zirkus* episode (1971). In Bavaria they were celebrating the 500th anniversary of Dürer's birth in 1971, and the Pythons became part of that remembrance. (*MPFC: UC*, 1.350)

17. Defleur, et al., "Neanderthal Cannibalism at Moula-Guercy, Ardèche, France."

18. From Everts, "Europe's Hypocritical History of Cannibalism."

19. Everts, 2.

20. From the *Annals of Ulster*, p. 433, quoted in McKisack, *The Fourteenth Century* (44). The Great Famine is discussed earlier in relation to the abandoned castle of scene 5, "Dennis the Peasant." See also McKisack, 49–50.

21. *MPFC: UC*, 1.106, 240.

22. "Andes Crash Survivors Ate Bodies of Companions," *Times*, 27 December 1972: 3.

23. A number of the survivors of this crash who did consume their mates' human flesh said over and over again they treated the act as absolutely necessary for survival and akin to communion, as did many Roman Catholic apologists of the same period.

24. "Andes Crash Paperback Rights to Bring £27,000 Bid," *Times*, 28 February 1974: 15.

25. Two of *Midweek*'s presenters—Ludovic Kennedy and Robin Day—had both been mentioned by (or referenced in relation to) the Pythons during the run of *Flying Circus*. Day is mentioned by name as early as Ep. 1, and there are scattered references thereafter, while Kennedy (called "Ludovic Ludovic" by the Pythons) is mentioned in Ep. 37 in the "TV4 or Not TV4 Discussion" sketch. See the index for *MPFC: UC* for the many mentions of Day and Kennedy.

26. Remember that "ANIMATION" had been handwritten into the script, twice, on this same page at some point in production or preproduction.

27. See "*New trumpets emerging (downward, towards the earth) from the clouds and blasting an unsuspecting shepherd off a hilltop*" (in scene 12, "Title Sequence Animation") above for their first appearance.

28. *Sir Gawain and the Green Knight*. Trans. W.A. Neilson. Cambridge, Ontario: Middle English Series, 1999.

TIM THE ENCHANTER

EXTERIOR—WASTES—DAY—(PSC) This scene is simply described as being shot at "the top of the ridge," and "wild and in hospitable" [*sic*]. Likely proving that the script printed in *MPHGB* is at best a working version of the final shooting script, some member of the troupe actually made a typo correction, adding the upper and lower crescent lines to pull together "in" and "hospitable" into "inhospitable" (*MPHGB*, 68).

The Knights are riding along the top of the ridge—(PSC) There is no mention here that at the back of the train are now several holy men; their cart (complete with decorative crosses on top) can be glimpsed behind Arthur and knights as they make their way through the slate quarry and encounter Tim for the first time. The clergymen weren't part of the previous animated scene, either. With this the Pythons are juxtaposing the occult and organized religion in the same scene, an arrangement a medieval man would have recognized. With Tim and his magic show followed immediately by religion and faith (and armaments), the Pythons are reflecting the views of the ancient world replete with such seeming paradoxes. According to Barber in *The Holy Grail*:

> The concept of the "occult" is one which arouses deep suspicion, if not outright hostility, but it was actually a respectable strand of Western philosophy for many centuries, and had its roots in the ideas put forward by admirers of Plato's thought in the late Greek civilization centred on Alexandria in the fourth century. . . . [Later Agrippa] argued that magic exploited the invisible links between matter and spirit, and that the spiritual powers could be invoked by means of their material counterparts, if the keys to these links were known. On this philosophical basis rested alchemy, astrology and divination or fortune-telling. (290–91)

Perhaps this is why the Holy Hand Grenade *could* work—it is the *material* counterpart to God's wrath (like his Ark of the Covenant)—and the Killer Rabbit is destroyed.

. . . they see an impressive WIZARD figure . . .—In the Malorian source material there are no wizards, by name or title,[1] but there are quite a number of malevolent sorceresses, including Hellawes the Sorceress, "Lady of the Castle Nigramous." There are also a smattering of enchanters, four sorceress queens who imprison Launcelot, and the infamous Morgan Le Fay ("as false a sorceress and witch as then was living").[2] Also included in these sources are women who *practice* "witchcrafts," though not the folkcraft (leading to *maleficium*) likely practiced by the witch "Miss Islington" weighed against the duck earlier.

The original draft of the script indicates that this wizard was actually going to be a Merlin character—by name—but Merlin and his actions were eventually removed from all following drafts.[3] This may have been due, at least initially, to the concept's indebtedness to White's *The Sword in the Stone* world, where the Merlin figure looms large. Somewhere in these earliest drafts, for example, Merlin was to accompany the knights as they traveled, hawking potions along the way. This may have been in relation to a sketch Gilliam made of an ancient apothecary from *FMA*, discussed on Facing Page 68 in appendix A.[4] In earlier drafts Merlin also provided a jerry-rigged Grail for the quest—one they could show the eager citizens of grateful "North Camelot" and "South Camelot"[5] who are clamoring for a look. The knights have somehow mislaid the actual Grail they found when they snuck into the French-held castle. They've asked God if he knows where it is, and God just gets angry. (It's at this point in the first draft that they abandon God, fittingly.) Merlin first appears on page 25 of the first draft of the script, and then he's gone for good.

. . . conjuring up fire from the ground . . .—Doyle notes that some of these shots simply don't match, especially the color and texture of the background sky scenes. Some of the shots were performed with the entire cast and crew, and were photographed by Terry Bedford, while others (featuring Tim alone) were pickup shots done later by Doyle, and on an obviously cloudier, grayer day.[6] Continuity can be sacrificed when time and money are short, and where it's unlikely that audiences will notice the inconsistencies.[7] Such bits of mismatching are typical of most feature film productions, irrespective of how large the film's budget might be, or how much attention is lavished on continuity.

. . . causing various bushes and branches to burst into flame—(PSC) There are a number of images in the period illuminated manuscripts depicting versions of Moses and the burning bush;[8] witchcraft and sorcery, however, aren't equally represented. Since the text of most of these illuminated manuscripts were religious (versions of the complete Bible, individual books of the Bible, psalters, devotional books of hours, etc.), there would have been little or no place for heretical illustrations, but plenty of space for obscaena and silliness.

ARTHUR: ". . . without flint or tinder?"—Striking flint to steel or even rocks of iron pyrite has started fires for centuries,[9] while the Chinese had been working with explosive materials since about the ninth century. The fact that Arthur in Britain—at the edges of Rome's empire—wouldn't have heard of or seen such combustibles isn't surprising.[10] He will, however, anachronistically mention "dynamite" just a few screen minutes later.

TIM: "There are some who call me Tim"—If, as Burrow observes—discussing the revelation that the Green Knight's name is actually Lord Bertilak—"proper names, in romance and other medieval writing, are instruments of knowledge and power," then this *should be* a very significant moment in the film.[11] It is not, of course, in the Pythons' world. The knights gain no new knowledge or realize any useful power from this revelation, and aside from being led by the sometimes-called "Tim" to the mouth of the rabbit's cave—where a slaughter ensues and Tim laughs—Tim the Enchanter is of little help.[12] "Timotheus" is an ancient Christian name, from the Greek Τιμόθεος, which means, ironically (when considering the dark arts magician so named), "honoring God" *(OED)*. Also, given Cleese's performance here with a pronounced Scottish accent, the fact that "Tim" is also a nickname for a Glasgow Celtic football club supporter might come into play. Most likely, the choice of this somewhat odd nickname for a traditional character was just a bit of silliness—like "Dennis" or "Roger," "Zoot" or "Dingo"—"Tim the tinker" happens to be one of those waiting for Glutton in the pub in Langland's *Piers Plowman*.

ARTHUR: "You know much that is hidden O Tim"—An old man who had seemed so kindly and wise to Sir Percivale turns out to be an enchanter of some power and subtlety, as the disinherited damosel related: "Ah, sir knight," said she, "that same man is an enchanter and a multiplier of words. For and ye believe him ye shall plainly be shamed, and die in this rock for pure hunger, and be eaten with wild beasts; and ye be a young man and a goodly knight, and I shall help you and ye will" (*LMD'A*, 2.287). The questers, then, have every right to be anxious about this magical man who may hold the information they need; but they follow him to the mouth of the cave, anyway. Their disbelief (or fear of Tim's supernatural power) is made obvious or perhaps underscored by the sudden appearance of the religious brethren, with their own trappings of power and authority (the scriptures, the chattel and muniments of the organized Church, the Holy Hand Grenade).

This type of scene—where Arthur and his knights cower at the power of another—can be connected to Arthur's encounters in several of the saints' Lives, including Cadog, where Arthur can be churlish and unpleasant before learning his lesson as he deals with various saints (Padel, "Arthur," 8).

TIM produces another fire trick producing several different colours—The effects are fairly even and colorless throughout—excepting the orange of any flame—the flashpots producing mostly smoke and some minor flame. The applause from the impressed onlookers follows an explosion on a nearby barren tree.

Murmur of astonishment from the KNIGHTS—This "astonied" response to such supernatural power is also seen in the Malory work. Prior to his final battle with Mordred, Arthur dreams he is on the wheel of fortune, "a wonderful dream" that soon breaks bad:

> [H]e sat upon a chaflet in a chair, and the chair was fast to a wheel, and thereupon sat King Arthur in the richest cloth of gold that might be made; and the king thought there was under him, far from him, an hideous deep black water, and therein were all manner of serpents, and worms, and wild beasts, foul and horrible; and suddenly the king thought the wheel turned up-so-down, and he fell among the serpents, and every beast took him by a limb; and then the king cried as he lay in his bed and slept, "Help."
> And then knights, squires, and yeomen, awaked the king. (*LMD'A*, 2.510–11)

When Arthur finally awakes he is so amazed that "he wist not where he was" (2.511). Earlier, when Bors raises his sword to defend himself against his brother Lionel, the fiery powers of God intervene:

> And then he heard a voice that said, "Flee Bors, and touch him not, or else thou shalt slay him."
> Right so alit a cloud betwixt them *in likeness of a fire and a marvellous flame, that both their two shields burnt*. Then were they sore afraid, that they fell both to the earth, and lay there a great while in a swoon. And when they came to themself, Bors saw that his brother had no harm; then he held up both his hands, for he dread God had taken vengeance upon him. (2.327; italics added)

Most of the "astonied" or "amazed" moments in Malory, however, occur just after two combatants meet head on, concussing each other, and have nothing to do with the supernatural. And just as Arthur's knights will be awed and then heed the advice of the wielder of such power, Bors listens to the instruction of God to leave his brother and go find Percivale at the coast.

GALAHAD: "Do you know where it . . ."—The enchanter here "does another fire trick," one that explodes at Galahad's feet, sending him scurrying back behind Arthur. Galahad has already been told to mind his own business by the French castle guard. There's no indication in the printed script as to Tim targeting Galahad, which he does, and no indication that Galahad had stepped out in front of Arthur to ask his question, which he did, as well. Tim is clearly warning Galahad back with his magic, though Galahad is unharmed (just as Bors and Lionel are unburnt by God's fire above); the actions as played out in the film make more sense of the written sequence. These scenes would have been rehearsed and shot multiple times per camera setup,[13] giving the editorial team a wide array of possible versions (angles, performances) from which to choose.

TIM: "To the north there lies a cave . . ."—Much like antiquary John Norden's poetic description of a grave found at Tintagel, c. 1600: "Ther is in this Castle a hole hewed out of a rocke, made in manner of a graue, which is sayde to haue bene done by an Herimite for his burial; and the graue will fit euerye stature, as is effabuled; but experience doth not so assure me" (quoted in Padel, "Nature of Arthur," 27).

Tim goes on to warn them of the dangers of their journey to the Cave, and specifically of the beast guarding it, prompting Arthur to comment on the enchanter's "eccentric performance." This comment signals doubt, certainly, doubt that echoes Norden's as he tries the magical grave for himself. Padel notes that this one-size-fits-all grave reportage and the accompanying credulity (a healthy skepticism) of visitors and recorders of these sometime-Arthurian wonders can be found in several Celtic folklores (28). Our Arthur is clearly not convinced that Tim is completely trustworthy or that the cave they approach is any more threatening than bloviating Black or "Ni"-saying Knights; his doubt is eventually overcome, of course.

TIM: ". . . the Cave of Caerbannog . . ."—"Caer" is a Welsh prefix that can mean castle or even an enclosed space, and is the equivalent of the English suffixes "-chester" and "-caster" (*OED*). It's only unusual here as the prefix is generally used to denote a constructed stronghold, like Caernarfon, an enormous castle built atop a much older motte and bailey site by Edward I. The imposing Caernarfon helped the English control most of north Wales.

TIM: ". . . carved in mystic runes . . ."—Letters from an ancient Germanic alphabet, the script has already mentioned "rune stones" in view leading up to the Black Knight scene, though the stones do not appear in the finished film.[14] Perhaps not coincidentally, in May 1973 a Viking exhibit was mounted in Greenwich, and one of the prizes of the installation was a runestone, its inscription described in quite recognizable and not so "mystic" terms:

> A rare rune-stone inscription from eastern Sweden in the exhibition refers to Thorkel the Tall.[15] Now Thorkel has been heard of in these parts before. He came to Greenwich with his friend Olaf the Stout about 950 years ago and obtained £21,000 from Ethelred the Unready as a price for keeping the peace. Then, having stowed the Danegeld in his beautifully carved travelling chest, he went straight off and fought extremely bloodily and effectively on the side of Canute the Great against the English.[16]

Also, in December 1973 the BBC 2 show *The World About Us* presented an episode titled *The Riddle of the Runestone*. Most surviving runic inscriptions found in England don't appear on stones (or cave walls), but on more portable items including sword pommels and knife handles, gold and silver plates, brooches, cremation urns, coins, and so forth, and tend to have been found in the east and southeast.

TIM: ". . . the last words of Olfin Bedwere of Rheged . . ."—Likely another mish-mash of Welsh and Scot-sounding names and places. "Rheged" is actually an ancient region, perhaps in Cumbria and reaching even to southern Scotland. There are definitely "Arthurian" connections to these names: "Bedwere" is simply a version of the Welsh "Bedwyr," which becomes "Bedevere" elsewhere (Barron, 3); while "Olfin" might well be another version of "Olwen," from *Culhwch ac Olwen*, the "earliest Welsh Arthurian prose tale" (6). As has been shown above, the Pythons possessed enough knowledge of the "Arthurian" sources to purposefully make these types of references.

It's also possible the Pythons have conflated Arthurian characters, in this case Ulfin of Ridcaradoch and Urien (or Urian) Rheged (or of Moray),[17] along with Bedevere, creating a sort of portmanteau man. Ulfin (and Merlin) had assisted Arthur's father, Uther, when Uther sought to lie with Ygrane. Both Bedevere and Urian are with Arthur at the plenary court in the City of Legions, where most of the world gathers to acknowledge Arthur as the high king. Ulfin, Urien, and Bedevere are all part of the Galfridian version of Arthur's world.

TIM: "Bones of full fifty men . . ."—There are a number of places in the Malorian source material where the fierceness of the creature or knight is trumpeted, often beyond the eventual effectiveness of the foe. Arthur hears of a giant who terrorizes the land, a "foul and cruel" giant

> which had slain, murdered and devoured much people of the country, and had been sustained seven year with the children of the commons of that land, 'insomuch that all the children be all slain and destroyed; and now late he hath taken the Duchess of Brittany as she rode with her meyne, and hath led her to his lodging which is in a mountain, for to ravish and lie by her to her life's end, and many people followed her, more than five hundred, but all they might not rescue her, but they left her shrieking and crying lamentably, wherefore I suppose that he hath slain her in fulfilling his foul lust of lechery. (*LMD'A*, 1.173–74)

The "careful widow" (1.174) who tells of the marauding giant echoes the "eccentric" Tim's fears: "Sir knight, speak soft, for yonder is a devil, if he hear thee speak he will come and destroy thee; I hold thee unhappy; what dost thou here in this mountain? For if ye were such fifty as ye be, ye were not able to make resistance against this devil" (1.175). As will be seen below, Malory's Arthur and companions—though tested by this giant—manage to gut, emasculate, and then behead him, binding his "head to a barbican" (1.175–76).[18]

Elsewhere, this description of a vicious, waiting destroyer can be found in sources from *Beowulf* to *The Hobbit*. In *Beowulf* there is first Grendel, then his mother, and finally the dragon to be bested (and which costs Beowulf his life, as well); in *The Hobbit* it's the dragon Smaug sitting on the dwarves' golden horde. Grendel's attack on Hrothgar's hall is described in fittingly bloodthirsty terms, and serves as a clear precedent for Tim's description of the rabbit's potential for violence:

> A throng of thanemen: then [Grendel's] thoughts were exultant,
> He minded to sunder from each of the thanemen
> The life from his body, horrible demon,
> Ere morning came, since fate had allowed him
> Fate has decreed that he shall devour no more heroes.
> The prospect of plenty. Providence willed not
> To permit him any more of men under heaven
> To eat in the night-time. Higelac's kinsman
> Great sorrow endured how the dire-mooded creature
> In unlooked-for assaults were likely to bear him.
> No thought had the monster of deferring the matter,
> But on earliest occasion he quickly laid hold of
> A soldier asleep, suddenly tore him,
> Bit his bone-prison, the blood drank in currents,
> Swallowed in mouthfuls: he soon had the dead man's
> Feet and hands, too, eaten entirely. (XII: 21–35)[19]

439

ARTHUR: "What an eccentric performance"—This line was written in after the shooting script was finished, and may have been an ad-lib on set.[20] There is a very similar moment and expression in *Casino Royale*, after Sir James Bond (David Niven) has watched an Indian temple worker bow and scrape, backwards, out of the bedchamber. Bond mutters, almost to himself: "What an extraordinary performance."

This over-the-top performance could have been Cleese's "outrageous" Scots accent of course, which will be discussed in a moment, but there might be something more subtle, as well. The significance of an "eccentric performance" for the transitional Dark Age Man is found in the move toward organized, state religion—the Church—in the tenth and eleventh centuries a more complex, centralized structuring that was mirrored by changing political organization over the same period. Instead of a strange but interesting enchanter as depicted by the Pythons, it was the rites and observances surrounding the Eucharist that gave the papacy, specifically, increasing dominion as more "local theologies" were replaced, according to Barber.[21] Arthur and the Grail companions take Tim's directions to heart, just as the people of the brightening Dark Ages began to look to the clergy and the Church as their source of knowledge and guidance, with the "reinvented" Mass illustrating these changes:

> [Mass] became the product of religious imagination; it was conceived as a theatrical occasion, with an emphasis on splendour, light and richness in the candles and robes which were an essential part of its setting, and on mystery, in the half-seen acts of the priest around the altar at the distant end of the apse. In a Romanesque church, this would have been lit almost entirely by candles; the new light of Gothic architecture was only just beginning to relieve the darkness in which much church ritual took place. Ceremonial gestures such as the raising of the Host after its consecration by the priest are mentioned for the first time at the end of the twelfth century, and the ringing of bells to emphasize the solemnity of the moment was also a relatively new practice. In *Perlesvaus*, when king Arthur witnesses the Mass of the Grail, he is not watching an age-old ceremony whose power lies in its customary reiteration of the familiar yet awesome mysteries, but a new and dramatic occasion, striking in its novelty: the emphasis is on the strangeness of bells and chalices, which are essential elements in the ritual. (*THG*, 137–138)

An "eccentric performance," certainly. This "most theatrical event which ordinary men and women would experience" (139) involving the consecrated Host is not part of the Pythons' world—their Dark Ages are still quite dark, magic lingers where Christianity should hold sway, and the unobtainable Grail is simply a handy symbol of God's diminished presence in such "sad times" (as Roger opines earlier). There is, however, the specter of the eccentric enchanter being replaced or augmented by representatives of the Church once they reach the mouth of the cave. Brother Maynard and his retinue bring to bear the scriptures and the weapons of the Church—"the Word . . . made *flash*"?[22]—to combat a "fierce-tempered rodent" the wizard cannot best.

As for Cleese's performance as the "manky Scots git," his Scottish accent isn't particularly regional—there are hints of Glasgow and Edinburgh as well as just Pythonesque caricature—but his attention seems to be focused on rolling every "r" with gusto, and little else.[23]

Notes

1. In these same sources Merlin, for example, is called a "witch."

2. In the 1969 Penguin version of *Le Morte D'Arthur*, these instances can be found on the following pages, all in volume one, respectively: 1.223, 1.229, and 1.364.

3. See the entry Facing Page 68 in appendix A for more on this missing aspect of the film.

4. *FMA* was one of the identifiable sources Gilliam used as he prepped for the animated sequences of *Holy Grail*. See appendix A for much more on these sources.

5. These types of signs are seen earlier during *Flying Circus* Ep. 27, "*Njorl's Saga.*"

6. Drawn from a 16 December 2013 e-mail correspondence with the author.

7. The classic example I give to my students is the "X marks the spot" scene in Spielberg's *Indiana Jones and the Last Crusade* (1989), where Indy, looking for a tomb in an old library/chapel, stands at the top of stairs and points to a large "X" on the tile floor. Behind him is the most obviously false bookcase imaginable—but most viewers have never seen it. Spielberg knew where his audience would be focusing their attention, and it wasn't on the backgrounds.

8. See Randall, CV: 507, "Moses before burning bush," in Y.T. 8, f. 214v.

9. There have been significant deposits of accessible flint and iron pyrite utilized in Britain for thousands of years, while steel was used in weaponry throughout the Crusades, for example.

10. See the entries in the "She's a Witch" section in scene 7 above for more on the availability and spread of knowledge during this period.

11. Burrow is quoted by Besserman in "The Idea of the Green Knight" (226), an article referenced earlier in the discussion of Launcelot's idiomatic challenges in Swamp Castle.

12. In fact, this is the scene where the catholic representatives of organized religion *replace* the representative of magic and the supernatural—the transition from old to new, from dark to light, from superstition to belief and so on. The relative *effectiveness* of either is debatable.

13. The Blu-ray extras for the film depict, for example, Jones and Palin vamping through the "Dennis the Peasant" scene over and over as the camera rolls, capturing everything. A camera setup is a complicated and time-consuming process involving setting and resetting the camera and all lighting and sound equipment, blocking out actor movements and distances from the camera, and struggles with continuity (clouds, rain, wind, daylight, wild sound, etc.). It's in the best interest of the film crew to do as much with a single setup as possible, before striking that setup and moving to the next one, which might be a (seemingly) simple reverse shot for that same scene.

14. See the entry "*They pass rune stones*" in scene 6 for these stones in popular culture during the 1960s and 1970s.

15. "Thorkell Braggart" is mentioned in Ep. 27 of *Flying Circus* (*MPFC: UC*, 2.6).

16. "Vikings Descend on Greenwich," *Times*, 16 May 1973: 5.

17. See *HKB*, 221, 227, and 258 for Urian mentions; 206 and 207 for Ulfin; and 225–57 for Bedevere.

18. Jeffrey Cohen gives credit for this oft-used scenario where credit is due: "Geoffrey of Monmouth's *History of the Kings of Britain* invented the matrix of gendered and monstrous 'historical' bodies that enabled the birth of romance" (66). These "narratives"—where knights are de-limbed or giant knights defeated—"are components of a larger cultural discourse of masculine maturation . . . and differentiation" (66). Arthur is dismembering and overcoming in the vein of David defeating Goliath, or Beowulf maiming and killing Grendel. The only real difference for Arthur is that he collects no grisly trophies; these are rites of passage nonetheless. See Cohen, *Of Giants: Sex, Monsters and the Middle Ages*.

19. From the 1897 J. L. Hall translation *Beowulf: An Anglo-Saxon Epic Poem*.

20. Looking at the outtakes available as part of the 2012 Blu-ray edition, there are many scenes ("Dennis," "Castle Anthrax," etc.) where bits of dialogue or exchanges are performed back-to-back, no "cut" being called by the directors, meaning the Pythons could choose the best performance later.

21. *The Holy Grail*, 137.

22. After John 1:14.

23. Thanks to my favorite Edinburgher, Andrew John Black, for his help here.

SCENE THIRTY-THREE
KILLER RABBIT, AND HOLY HAND GRENADE

CUT TO impressive rock face—(PSC) This "impressive" scene is another that the Pythons had to settle on, as there were few cave-like formations in the areas where they'd chosen to shoot (Appin, Argyll, and Bute, Scotland). The "cave" is an abandoned hard rock mining entrance near Loch Tay, and it isn't as deep or impressive as it purports to be. One of the core principles of moviemaking is the crafting of illusions, of course, and the Pythons have managed to accomplish this on a shoestring budget, employing careful camera angles and creative use of locations.[1]

The initial shot of this scene isn't the rock face, however, it's a low angle shot set up at the mouth of the cave (before the cave has been glimpsed by the viewer), looking up at the ridge where Arthur and his knights appear. In the immediate foreground is a skull, complete with a very obvious join where the skull was cut to access the brain, *post mortem*. This prop, then, is likely from a medical school or the like. The Enchanter and the knights "emerge" in the distance from behind the skull, crossing the ridge. Gilliam will use this same framing device in the later film *Time Bandits*, when the quest (there made up of dwarves and a young boy) reaches the wastelands at the frontier of the Time of Legends.

A foreboding atmosphere supervenes—(PSC) "Supervene" is an unusual word choice here, as it commonly means a change or interruption has occurred "to an existing situation" (*OED*). Here, the Grail questers are nervous before they even arrive, including the "horses" left on the ridge above.

TIM takes a strange look at them—(PSC) This after Arthur notes that the "horses" are nervous, and they should be left on the ridge. Looking carefully at the film, this moment can be glimpsed, but with no cut to a close-up, it's only noticeable thanks to the script prompt. They either didn't create the insert reaction shot, or they did, and weren't satisfied with it.

TIM: "Behold the Cave of Caerbannog!"—They are creeping up to a kind of precipice, and the camera is behind them, the shot meant to reveal the cave as they creep closer. The camera actually glides with them and then smoothly up, meaning this is a kind of crane or jib arm shot—the *only* use of that particular camera mount and movement in the entire film. Generally on wheels or, in many cases, mounted on a dolly and "train tracks," the jib mount is both expensive and somewhat cumbersome, especially in location shooting. When queried, Doyle remembers the day vividly, and he's worth quoting:

> The crane—ah the crane! We had what I think was called the "scorpion dolly" which had a large crane adjustment. We had it all the way through the location shoot. Loading and unloading it was a pain—it required lead weights to balance both the camera (which was heavy) and the op-

erator and the focus.[2] I helped get the crane up the hill to the cave—I can still remember it to this day. A few days later I remember standing watching a shot with my arms folded and suddenly noticed my biceps had grown. That episode was enough; the time taken to prepare—and as we were not on flat ground—we couldn't mount it for one shot and stay on it for the next. I don't think we ever got it off the lorry again. We probably would have been better off with a "jib arm" which only carried the camera not the operators.[3]

Other than for this shot, then, the camera stayed on a tripod (for smooth shots) or on the camera operator's shoulder (for the "handheld" look). Another one-off in the film was the use of a wipe as a transition.

CUT TO shot of cave—(PSC) The lairs of Grendel and the dragon as described in the epic saga *Beowulf* provide some reference here. As Wiglaf enters and searches the dragon's cave he sees the belongings of those warriors who have come before:

> Then the trusty retainer treasure-gems many
> Victorious saw, when the seat he came near to,
> Gold-treasure sparkling spread on the bottom,
> Wonder on the wall, and the worm-creature's cavern,
> The ancient dawn-flier's, vessels a-standing,
> Cups of the ancients of cleansers bereavèd,
> Robbed of their ornaments: there were helmets in numbers,
> Old and rust-eaten, arm-bracelets many,
> Artfully woven. (*Beowulf*, 38.5–13)

The Pythons' cave setting does feature bones strewn about and bits of armor here and there, but the following scenic description isn't as obvious: "*A little dry ice, glowing green can be seen at the entrance*" (*MPHGB*, 71). There is a bit of the beloved smoke drifting across the scene in two medium close-up shots (to show the rabbit), but it's gone again in the wide shots, and there's no green glow anywhere.

Suddenly we become aware of total silence—(PSC) This is a hoped-for effect, likely, but the finished film soundtrack has a kind of almost theremin-sounding drone beneath everything, as well as a "breathing" sound effect (likely meant to emanate from the cave), besides all the expected ambient noise. Any noises made by the knights were to "*sound very exaggerated*" due to the silence, as well. This conceit is a direct borrow from Bergman's *Seventh Seal*, which the Pythons have acknowledged as a significant source for the film. When the Knight is walking across the gravel beach, his footsteps and the crashing waves are quite loud. The chessboard comes into view, which the camera rests its gaze upon, and an optical transition dissolves first the chessboard—leaving the waves crashing behind—followed by a quicker dissolve to the figure of Death standing on the beach nearby. In this scene the sound has been reduced dramatically to near-silence—the Knight then looks up, espying the black-robed figure.[4]

Doyle reports that it was Gilliam who made a first pass at the sound edit (dubbing) of the film, featuring "lots of chinking armour," but that it didn't play well to the first group seeing the cut. Jones then did a "re-dub" and "lots of FXs were taken out."[5] It's not clear how this cave scene would have been affected in these dubbing runs, but it is clear that the Pythons were concerned about the sound and sound effects of their silly film, like any serious filmmaker.

ARTHUR: "Keep me covered"—This is a holdover from the many westerns and World War II pictures the Pythons would have grown up watching. If the quest had carried bows—which they do not, as will be mentioned—then they might have something with which to give Arthur "cover." This is historically curious, since the English forces had been known as accomplished bowmen, and during the Hundred Years War the English longbow would indeed be *very* effective against the French:

> Edward III's first campaign in France . . . was won by virtue of a military innovation that was to become the nemesis of France. . . . This was the longbow, derived from the Welsh and developed under Edward I for use against the Scots in the highlands. With a range reaching 300 yards and a rapidity, in skilled hands, of ten to twelve arrows a minute in comparison to the crossbow's two, the longbow represented a revolutionary delivery of military force. . . . [T]he longbow's fearful hail shattered and demoralized the enemy. (Tuchman, 70)

Images of these bows in use can be seen in the pages of the *Luttrell Psalter*. Arthur and company could have used these against the Killer Rabbit, clearly. The bow-and-arrow (though not necessarily the longbow) appears significantly in the elided "King Brian the Wild" scene. There, close harmony groups are gleefully porcupined with arrows, but those scenes remained unfilmed.

ARTHUR: "You silly sod"—Originally meaning one who practiced sodomy (though by the mid-1970s the usage had softened into a more generic insult), "sod" is one of the words the BBC censored during the early portions of the *MPFC* series run, but which would appear uncensored by the second series and beyond.[6] "Sod" was *not* one of the words mentioned for removal (to get an "A" rating or certificate) from the BBFC prior to the film's general release.[7]

TIM: ". . . not an ordinary rabbit . . . 'tis the most foul cruel"—From an entry for *MPFC* Ep. 32, where "the big bad rabbit" has appeared in a children's book:

> The "killer rabbit" character—as silly and absurd as it seems in the hearing—may be traced to [several progenitors, including the rabbit disease epidemic of the 1950s discussed earlier, the more vicious rabbits (e.g., General Woundwort) in Richard Adams' *Watership Down* (1972), or, here, from] a marvelous sequence in Modernist novelist D. H. Lawrence's *Women in Love* (1921), where a pet rabbit reacts to being handled by Winnie and Gudrun:
>
>> They unlocked the door of the hutch. Gudrun thrust in her arm and seized the great, lusty rabbit as it crouched still, she grasped its long ears. It set its four feet flat, and thrust back. There was a long scraping sound as it was hauled forward, and in another instant it was in midair, lunging wildly, its body flying like a spring coiled and released, as it lashed out, suspended from the ears. Gudrun held the black-and-white tempest at arms' length, averting her face. But the rabbit was magically strong, it was all she could do to keep her grasp. She almost lost her presence of mind. . . .
>> Gudrun stood for a moment astounded by the thunderstorm that had sprung into being in her grip. Then her colour came up, a heavy rage came over her like a cloud. She stood shaken as a house in a storm, and utterly overcome. Her heart was arrested with fury at the mindlessness and the bestial stupidity of this struggle, her wrists were badly scored by the claws of the beast, a heavy cruelty welled up in her. (Ch. 18 ["Rabbit"])
>
> As early as Ep. 2, in the "Working-Class Playwright" sketch the Pythons display their knowledge of the England of D. H. Lawrence. (*MPFC: UC*, 2.78)

Hares in illuminated manuscripts are often put into unusually aggressive positions, as well. In Randall's *IMGM*, there are more than two hundred such illustrations, including hares hunting, fighting, tilting, assaulting a castle, killing dogs, and driving a gallows cart, as well as several where the hare is carrying a dead and trussed up man over its shoulder, as if going home after a successful hunt (LXXIV: 356, 357). In these margins, the hare lives a very active, humorous, aggressive, even deadly life, often taking the position of an aggressive man in human activities.[8]

Later, as the sixteenth-century witch craze spread through England, the rabbit became one of the "familiar spirits" associated with consorting with the devil. During her initial confession for "carnally" consorting with the devil and siring his "imps," one Elizabeth Clarke introduced her examiners to her familiar spirits (and witness John Stearne[9] attests to actually seeing these creatures), excepting one, in Stearne's words:

> [T]hen I asked her if they were not all come, for there were more come than she spoke of, she answered that they came double in severall shapes, but said, one [called "Sack & Sugar"] was still to come, which was to teare mee in peeces, then I asked her why, she said, because I would have swome her.[10]

The black beast "Sack & Sugar" was to come last and rend Stearne for wanting to "swim" Elizabeth, to throw her into water and "test" her, just as the village mob wanted to test Miss Islington earlier. Gaskill relates the rest: "But when 'Sack & Sugar' finally arrived, it seemed to witnesses to be no more than a harmless rabbit. None the less, Clarke assured Stearne that he was lucky it had not leapt onto his face, squeezed itself down his throat, and deposited 'a feast of Toades' in his belly" (50–51).

ROBIN: "You tit!"—This was originally "You shit," and is one of the curse words removed to achieve the "A" certificate and therefore a broader possible audience. A "tit" is a fool or an idiot (which is also what "sod" has come to mean, often). The "Working Class Playwright" (Chapman) yells "Yer tit!" at his "laborer" son (Idle) in Ep. 2 of *MPFC*; he's discovered his son wants to work in the mines for a living, not write plays or attend "gala luncheons" (*JTW*, 1.23).

Also, this is the moment where Robin admits to soiling his own armor, which is the second time this problem has been mentioned. In the "Book of the Film" Robin is given credit for, among other nearly noble deeds, "personally wetting himself at the Battle of Badon Hill" (*MPHGB*, facing page 21). He will soil his armor yet again after watching Bors lose his head. This incontinence trope will be revisited in *Time Bandits*, when Vincent (Palin) is tied to a tree (with Pansy [Shelley Duvall]), and his "personal problem" begins to reemerge.

TIM: "That rabbit's got a vicious streak. It's a killer"—In Ep. 20 of *MPFC*, a couple call in the Council Ratcatcher (Chapman) to solve a "little rodental problem." Once there, the Ratcatcher discovers the house is infested with sheep, not rats, and he decides to "lay down some sheep poison":

He disappears into the hole. We hear:

Voice Over: Baa, baa, baa.

A gunshot. The Ratcatcher reappears clutching his arm.

Ratcatcher: Aargh! Ooh! It's got a gun!

Mrs. Concrete (Palin): Blimey.

Ratcatcher: No, normally a sheep is a placid, timid creature, but you've got a killer! ("Killer Sheep"; audio transcription)

The mutated sheep ("Arthur X") and his gang go on to rob banks, assault a farmer, and even raid Selfridges.

There are also dozens of WB cartoons featuring tiny, seemingly innocuous and harmless little characters—worms, fleas, tiny birds, kittens—who, when provoked, can explode into volcanic rages. Both the Pythons and before them the Goons were greatly influenced by these cartoon worlds.

GALAHAD: "Get stuffed!"—This was another change thanks to the censor's "request." Galahad originally tells Tim to "fuck off," but it's likely the Pythons would have had *no* chance at an "A" certificate if they kept this particularly harsh invective. It's also likely no accident that Galahad is given this line, as an ironic reminder of his reputation for chastity and reverence, and his status as the chosen one who eventually finds the Holy Grail. This line was clearly one re-dubbed later, inserting the "Get stuffed!" during the postproduction process.

Also, on the opposite page to this one in *MPHGB*, the Daily Continuity Report (discussed in detail in appendix A) lists a series of "Wildtrack" recordings, which are sound recordings performed at the site of film shooting (to take advantage of the ambient sound of the location). In this case, they are recording "charging" noises (shouts, footsteps, sword noises as the knights attack the rabbit) and variants for Galahad's swearing, including "fart off" and "piss off," and so on. This is generally much more natural than having to revisit the scene in postproduction and dub over the existing soundtrack, which always sounds clumsy. It's odd, then, that the original line was used, then re-dubbed; it must have been the best *performance* of the lot (the scene is quite long).

TIM: "He'll do you up a treat, mate"—Colloquial phrase meaning extreme violence, a variation of it—"slit you up a treat"—is heard earlier in *Flying Circus* (*MPFC: UC*, 1.213).

ROBIN: "You manky Scots git!"—This was printed in the script as "You turd!" but was ultimately swapped for the handwritten "mangy Scots git."[11] Robin (Idle) says "manky," instead, which means "festering" or "disgusting"—as used by Joyce in *Finnegan's Wake*, for example. A "git" is a fool or a "worthless person" (*OED*). For the appalling "Mr and Mrs Git," see Ep. 21 of *Flying Circus*.

Scotsmen by name, dress, and accent continue to take a drubbing in the Python world. Ireland and Irishmen rarely make appearances in *MPFC*—likely due to the politically dangerous "Troubles"—but Scotland and Scotsmen are fair game throughout. In a scene from the "Science Fiction Sketch" in Ep. 7, an interviewing police inspector questions a woman whose husband has been turned into a Scotsman by alien blancmanges from space:

Inspector (Jones): Mrs. Potter—you knew Mr. Potter quite well I believe?

Wife (Idle): Oh yes, quite well. He was me husband.

Inspector: Yes. And, uh, he never showed any inclination towards being a Scotsman before this happened?

Wife: No, no, not at all. He was not that sort of person . . .

Inspector: He didn't wear a kilt or play the bagpipes?

Wife: No, no, no.

Inspector: He never got drunk at night or brought home black puddings?

Wife: No, no. Not at all.

Inspector: He didn't have an inadequate brain capacity?

Wife: No, no. Not at all.

Inspector: I see. So by your account Harold Potter was a perfectly ordinary Englishman without any tendency towards being a Scotsman whatsoever? ("Science Fiction Sketch"; audio transcription)

It turns out that Mr. Potter's favorite show, *Dr. Finlay's Casebook* (about a Scottish doctor) was the gateway for him to be turned into a Scotsman.

ROBIN: "What's he do? Nibble your bum?"—Mortimer notes that during the Middle Ages sarcastic humor seems to have been very popular: "Sarcasm might be commonly referred to as the lowest form of wit in our time, but in the fourteenth century it is just about the highest" (63). In this scene Robin makes himself feel better in relation to both Tim and the rabbit, which of course will backfire on him rather quickly—Tim will get the last laugh after the rabbit decapitates Bors. Overall, though, there aren't knights in the quest who are particularly sarcastic or down-in-the-mouth; the noble and providential nature of the holy undertaking kind of precludes that. Even Dennis, who might have reasons to be sarcastic thanks to his station in life and being faced with the negligible chances of real "progress" remains optimistic. He simply points out the silliness of Arthur's stated mythology without pointing the finger at Arthur—he's raging against the system. There isn't even much sarcasm in the first draft of the script, with the exception of the more mean-spirited God character found there.

"Bum" is also one of the words the show would not be using again, according to the BBC Man in Ep. 17, the "Naughty Chemist Sketch." The other verboten words included "botty," "pox," "wee-wee," "Semprini," and "knockers":

> The Pythons resort to such bodily/schoolboy (or even "carnivalesque") humor as often as their lofty predecessors Jonson, Swift, and Voltaire (see *MPSERD*, ch. 2.) The Goons also employed vulgar euphemisms, but within the more restrained limitations imposed by the BBC ("Auntie Beeb") of the 1950s. In just moments, another word—"Semprini"— will also be banned based on an assumed sexual connotation. (*MPFC: UC*, 1.271–72)

ARTHUR: "Go on, Bors . . ."—One of Arthur's Round Table knights, Bors is featured in Gawain's dream as a spotted bull (otherwise white), "which trespassed but once in his virginity, but sithen he keepeth himself so well in chastity . . . all is forgiven him and his misdeeds" (*LMD-WM*, 355). Bors, Galahad, and Percival are together able to finally reach and be succored by the Grail, as well (*LMD'A*, 2.364–66). Clearly that level of purity does not, for the Pythons, preserve Bors from an ignominious fate here, where he is the first to be killed by the "killer" rabbit. Malory also mentions that, like Bors here at the cave, many of the Knights of the Round Table who sought the Grail did not return to Camelot, they were "slain and destroyed, more than half" (*LMD-WM*, 394).

It's also clear that Gilliam has stepped into a costume again, this time as Bors. In the unused credits for the printed script, however, he is listed as playing "Sir Gawain (The First To Be Killed By The Rabbit),"[12] and Bors isn't mentioned at all. Bors is clearly something of an afterthought, since the "Y" on his shield and the "Y" on his surcoat don't match, color-wise.

A quick CLOSE-UP of a savage RABBIT biting through tin and BORS' head flies off— (PSC) This body horror moment is yet another borrow from the well-remembered *Macbeth*:

> Then, as Macbeth climbs stairs to get to Macduff, Macduff's large and furious stroke severs Macbeth's head from his body. Polanski's camera follows the head as it leaves the body and rolls on the floor (reminding us of Duncan's crown), and then the camera cuts to the body, sans head, which balances for a second on the steps before it sways backward, crashing down the steps. A horrible, sordid, realistic sequence. (Berlin, 296–97)

These moments of violence have been part of the New Wave of films since at least 1961 and Kurosawa's *Yojimbo*. Following this movement, Hammer films and Hollywood itself upped depictions of sexuality and violence (often intertwined) beyond what could have been imagined just a generation earlier.

The RABBIT leaps back to the mouth of the cave and sits there looking in the KNIGHTS' direction and growling menacingly—(PSC) This doesn't happen as cleanly as described, since the rabbit never growls at all (it sort of chirps or squeaks), and only moves along a line or is a kind of hand puppet at the throats (and over the tops of shields) of various knights. There is actually no shot that precisely mimics this description, though the subsequent scene—the rabbit hopping over a dead body after three knights are slaughtered—is a fairly close rendering.

ARTHUR: "Je . . . sus Christ!"—The BBFC representative suggested that they consider taking "the odd Jesus Christ" out of the film to bring it closer to an "A" certification (*MPHGB*, 49). This is one of the two scenes where it remains, the other being found earlier as Arthur and his knights assault the French-held castle.

TIM: "Well it's always the same. I always tell them . . ."—This line seems to indicate that Tim has led questers here before, that this is part of his fate or role in this world, lending the tale a more mythological, even melancholic tinge, given the inescapability of the situation. Here and there this quest has taken on a Dantean flavor, now Tim assuming the Virgil role and Arthur and friends acting the wide-eyed Dante as they reach the mouth of this dark cavern. Later they will climb aboard a boat on a lake version of Acheron (the Charon-type character is still in the printed script, not the finished film) before reaching their own version of Hell—another French-occupied castle. Dante and Virgil do get to escape Hell, of course, climbing past Satan and through the Earth to freedom. We won't see Tim after the failed attack on the rabbit; Arthur and his knights will make it through the Legendary Beast's cave without their guide, sacrificing only Brother Maynard. Their "freedom" is reaching the Bridge of Death.

The printed script is similar: "It's always the same . . . if I've said it once" (*MPHGB*, 74). Most of this dialogue is lost in the excitement of the aftermath of Bors' death. Unlike the printed script, Tim is no longer in the scene once the knights run away from the rabbit en masse; he has disappeared without trace, and it's religion's turn at the wheel (meaning Brother Maynard and the Holy Hand Grenade).

Peckinpahish shots—(PSC) The climactic, suicidal gun battle sequence in *The Wild Bunch* (1969)[13] between the surviving gang (William Holden, Ernest Borgnine, Warren Oates, and Ben Johnson) and the Mexican forces is likely what the Pythons are thinking when calling for these shots. Peckinpah's style included myriad close-ups and medium close-ups, some in slow motion, some in frantic real-time, many handheld and some on tripods, alternating swish pans and crash zooms—the patchwork discretely separating but ultimately weaving together an overall canvas of mayhem and bloody death.[14]

But the Pythons could also be commenting on the Peckinpah world as depicted in his films, which, as American reviewers noted, "appears to be one of extraordinary, shocking, almost insupportable violence."[15] *Times* critic J. R. Taylor disagreed. Writing in 1969, he saw the violence as germane to the entire exercise, and he found it "difficult to fault Mr. Peckinpah":

> He is depicting, quite deliberately, a violent era and a society attuned to violence, in which no one, not even children,[16] can remain totally innocent. To do this he needs to show violence: but he never broods on it, never sensationalizes it, and certainly never milks it for some kind of sadistic kick. The violence is almost abstract, part of a larger pattern, and it is the pattern rather than any of its constituent parts which remains in the mind, and by which the film stands or falls.[17]

The Pythons are less interested in the reasons why, likely, and more in the clear enthusiasm with which Peckinpah pursues his violent stories full of violent men in violent times. And given the descriptions of life for most people who had the misfortune to be born poor in the fourteenth century offered by Tuchman, McKisack, Mortimer, and others, it was a violent, hard-scrabble time where the most "reasonably violent"[18] men could survive and even thrive. Taylor sees a narrative thread in *The Wild Bunch* that can easily be applied to *MPHG*—rigid men and their ways encountered at the end of an era:[19]

> The theme, one which fascinates Peckinpah, is the man of action at the end of the line, offered, or taking, his last chance. So it was in *Guns in the Afternoon*, so in *Major Dundee*, and now here we meet a group even more evidently fated, by the built-in tensions of their own relationships with each other, and by the inexorable advance of the modern world of motors and aeroplanes, where their opportunistic, buccaneering way of life on the borders of civilisations will no longer have its place.[20]

This film and others like it of the period are elegies, then, noting the passage of time, characters, and notions of the west in general—and in the case of *The Wild Bunch*, with sadness, but also the grim laughter of those who survive. Arthur, the man of action, is first taking and is then offered a chance for glory—the gathering to Camelot, and the search for the Holy Grail. His group is truly fated, however, by their inability to fit into the worlds they are presented with—including both the legendary and the "real" Middle Ages—and the steady pursuit of the third, "modern" world in the form of investigating and arresting police officers.[21] Arthur can't even experience the "joy" Camus grants Sisyphus, since his fate doesn't seem to belong to him, but to the worlds he doesn't understand.[22] It also doesn't reach the level of the "tragic," in Camus's terms, since Arthur, Bedevere, Launcelot, and Galahad aren't gifted with an appropriate level of consciousness of their absurd situation. Camus can leave Sisyphus "at the foot of the mountain," able to push the rock again and again and experience the joy and satisfaction of the labor; Arthur can't be "the absurd man," even though he "says yes and his effort [would be] henceforth . . . unceasing"[23]—his efforts *would be* "unceasing," but for the intrusion of the controlling modern world, a world he's not conscious of, which puts an end to such fantasies. Those who seek for even glorious ideals in a relentlessly fallen world[24] are bound to be disappointed, bound to be hustled into the back of a police van.

Lastly, a number of these more close-up, frenetic shots were completed much later by Julian Doyle in the backyard of his home at 3 Rona Road, near Hampstead Heath (9 December 2013 e-mail correspondence). These would have been shots not involving the faces of any of the knights, but gloved hands, gripped shields and swords, and the assaulting rabbit.

. . . Kung-fu and karate-type films . . .—(PSC) The Pythons could be referring to the many films of directors like King Hu and Chang Cheh, both very active in the mid- to late 1960s and early 1970s producing dozens of Hong Kong-based *wuxia* or "chop socky" pictures. Bruce Lee had led the charge into Western cinemas, however, with his exciting brand of fighting movie in the early 1970s. By 1974, and after Lee's untimely death, the genre had reached phenomena status, grossing more than $12 million[25] in the United States alone, and sparking dozens of first Hong Kong and then international (including Hollywood) knock-offs. Lee's films had cost little and made millions, from *Big Boss* and *Fist of Fury*[26] through his masterwork *Enter the Dragon* to *Way of the Dragon*. In London-area cinemas, audiences including the Pythons could have seen Yu Wang's *One-Armed Boxer* at the Carlton in October 1974; or Lee's *The Big Boss* also at the Carlton by November 1973, while *Enter the Dragon* appeared in January 1974 at the Oxford Circus, Bloomsbury, *and* Leicester Square cinemas.[27] In fact, in January 1974 *Enter the Dragon*

was playing simultaneously at more London and borough theaters than any other feature film. By February 1975 the Electric Cinema Club was showing King Hu's *The Fate of Lee Khan* (1973), uncut and with subtitles (as opposed to bad dubbing).[28]

As for the style they are calling for, in her chapter "Ornate Choreographies of Violence" Verina Glaessner describes the attractions of this frenetic cinema:

> The films all hinged on extremely skillfully shot, elongated fight sequences that opened up a whole new perspective on the term "balletic violence." Although the protagonist might use knives or swords, chains or even occasionally guns, such technology came a long way behind the visually-involving way they used their bodies in a series of nicely judged blocks, kicks, and jabs punctuated by massive leaps and backed by a soundtrack of shrieks and groans. The screen was alive with an ornate choreography of violence that exploited the dance-like postures of traditional Chinese martial arts—a mixture of boxing, wrestling and kick fighting. It was exotic.[29]

The "karate-type" (Japanese) films the Pythons may be referencing aren't likely Kurosawa's—his films were often more "western" in aesthetic and editorial fluidity[30]—they're more likely those from later Japanese filmmakers like Masaki Kobayashi (*Samurai Rebellion*; *Hara Kiri*), gangster/spy director Akira Kobayashi (*Three Seconds Before Explosion* [1967]), or even iconoclast Seijun Suzuki, whose *Tokyo Drifter* (1966) and *Branded to Kill* (1967) twisted the genre into noir-ish, nihilistic, and sexually charged contortions.[31]

. . . four knights are comprehensively killed—(PSC) These occur hard on Bors's decapitation (by the rabbit), which was a fairly standard method of finishing a knight or any foe according to the Grail romances. The specter of death in the source material during both the Grail quests and other romance adventures are acknowledged, and especially so when a tale is beginning or coming to an end. Vacant seats at the Round Table are also addressed during these introductions and conclusions. There are eight knights missing (dead) at the start of the fourth chapter of "From the Marriage of King Uther to King Arthur," called *Of Nenive and Morgan le Fay*, and "two sieges void, for two knights were slain that twelvemonth" at the close of this same section. The eight "voids" are filled by Uriens, the King of the Lake, Hervis de Revel, Galagars, Gawain, Griflet, Kay, and Tor (*LMD-WM*, 59–60). The other two seats are filled by Pelleas and Marhalt (80). Generally, knights are elevated to the Table after we've been witness to their exploits in service of Arthur or the Lord, or both.

TIM . . . is pointing at them and laughing derisively—(PSC) Laughing at others' misfortunes is also a staple of fourteenth-century humor. The cuckolded husband is ridiculous, as is the overambitious commoner, the worldly prelate, and the scolding wife who finally gets hers. Gallows humor is also prevalent in a world so beset with death and physical suffering: "In a violent society even the humor is violent" (Mortimer, 64). Mortimer goes on to note that painful practical jokes (see Chaucer's *The Miller's Tale*, for instance) and incidents where others injure themselves are rich sources of laughter in fourteenth century literature and life (64). Against this backdrop the "King Brian the Wild" sequence *could have* resonated and even been justified.

ARTHUR: "Who did we lose? Uther. Gorlois . . ."—The batch of knights sent off to be sacrificed are new to the quest, as far as we know, so they won't be missed by the audience. It won't be until the Bridge of Death that we begin to lose our principal knights (those played by the Pythons themselves).

"Uther," "Gorlois," "Urien," "Ector," and "Bors" are all mentioned here (in the printed script) as having been "comprehensively killed" by the rabbit, though after the slaughter there are only three bodies in view near the rabbit. In the film as shot, the three dead are announced as "Gawain," "Ector," and "Bors," though Arthur clearly keeps thinking five are dead.[32]

"Uther" is actually Arthur's father (in Geoffrey of Monmouth's *HKB*), and is discussed in some detail in the "Coconuts and Swallows" notes earlier. It's likely he was swapped out by the Pythons to simply avoid the strangeness of introducing the father-son relationship so late in the film.[33] Having Uther around with Gorlois, as will be mentioned next, would be equally awkward. There are also differing versions of Uther's life and accomplishments in other French and German romance sources.[34]

"Gorlois" isn't part of the quest (especially with Uther), since even though Gorlois was of great help to Uther in securing his kingship, being a trusted retainer (as the Duke of Cornwall), Uther would conspire with Merlin to trick Gorlois's wife, Ygerna—"the most beautiful woman in Britain"—into lying with Uther disguised, by Merlin's potions, as Gorlois.[35] Gorlois is killed the very night that Arthur is conceived, allowing Uther and Ygerna to marry, but precluding Gorlois from continuing in any meaningful way as Uther's vassal or comrade (so no Grail quest). The inclusion of either Gorlois or Uther in the assault on the Cave of Caerbannog, then, would have been narratively tricky for the Pythons, and they steered clear.

"Urien" is likely Urien Rheged, mentioned above when Tim cites "Olfin Bedwere of Rheged." Urien is a *historical* Welsh king (fl. late sixth century) who was incorporated into the Arthurian sagas by native taletellers. The Welsh Triads[36] proclaim Urien more than once, and he is one of the few historical figures mentioned in any way by the Pythons.

"Ector" and "Hector" have also been mentioned earlier. As "Sir Ector," he is generally cast in these tales as Arthur's foster father, raising him after Merlin removes Arthur from Uther's home, the boy's noble heritage kept a secret until the sword can be pulled from the stone.[37] Another Ector (or Hector de Maris) inhabits *Le Morte D'Arthur*, where he is a half-brother of Launcelot, and a sometime enemy to Arthur, since he is allied with Launcelot after the Guinevere affair. It's not clear which Ector the Pythons might be referring to here.

Finally, it's also entirely possible this is yet another moment where names were pulled out of a hat—a hat containing names of knights attached in some way to Arthur and the Round Table—with no thought to familial, dynastic, or source material connections.[38] In any case, none made it into the film in any meaningful way, except to die when needed for a more noticeable body count.

ARTHUR: "That rabbit's dynamite"—Another purposeful anachronism, but also a bit of a setup for the "Holy Hand Grenade of Antioch" moment which is coming soon.

LAUNCELOT: "Do we have any bows?"—A very interesting item to be missing, given the success the longbow brought to English forces, even "the principal agent of the English victories of the Hundred Years Wars" (Norman and Pottinger, 50). McKisack goes even further: "[T]he long bow, effectively used, was to render obsolete the methods of fighting which had been common in western Europe since the eleventh century" (39). See the entry for "Keep me covered" just above for much more on this game-changing weapon.

It may well be that the Pythons decided to not include bows in their quest for two simple reasons. One, the safety issues (for insurance liability, etc.) might have demanded significant on-set weapons personnel not accounted for in the meager budget, and two, handling a problem from a safe distance isn't nearly as funny or dangerous. Overcoming the Killer Rabbit from the protection of the rocks isn't terribly cinematic, and the Knights Who Say Ni could have been outmaneuvered after volleys of arrows, etc. In fact, the significant archery demands of the excised "King Brian" scene may have been one of the principal reasons it was never filmed.

During the run of *MPFC*, bows and arrows were used sparingly. They appear in Eps. 6, 30, and 38, for example, where theater announcers, Terrence Rattigan and Stanley Kramer are variously impaled. In the second *MPFZ* episode, the opening scene is a "William Tell" sketch, featuring William expertly shooting an apple atop a boy's head. The camera then pulls back to reveal dozens of arrows in the boy, the same kind of look called for in the opening moments of the missing "King Brian" sequence.

LAUNCELOT: "We have the Holy Hand Grenade"—This promised "religious" explosion is a curious, perhaps even insensitive (though pointed) inclusion, given the very recent history of bombings in relation to "The Troubles." The immediate months leading up to the creation of *Holy Grail* were the worst of times for the "Irish situation," during which intimidation and bombing increased markedly—in Northern Ireland, then England—and all manner of weapons of war were associated with this righteous and "holy" cause as Catholics and Protestants targeted each other.[39] On 30 January 1972, the "Bloody Sunday" killings of unarmed civilians in Londonderry by Parachute Regiment troops lit the fuse for the mayhem to follow. Following the expected reprisals and British government arrest sweeps, "[t]here was an immediate upsurge in violence, with twenty-one people being killed in three days. The bombings and shootings simply increased in intensity," Marr writes. "In the first eight weeks of 1972, forty-nine people were killed and more than 250 seriously injured" (*A History of Modern Britain*, 335). An IRA retaliation saw a bomb attack at Aldershot headquarters of the Parachute Regiment, killing seven.[40] The year 1972 turned out to be horrendous for the people of the Belfast region, according to Sandbrook:

> By the end of 1972, the bloody rampage had accounted for 2,000 bomb explosions, 2,000 armed robberies and more than 10,000 shooting incidents, while 5,000 people had been badly injured and 479 people killed—all in just twelve months. More than half of the people killed were not soldiers or paramilitaries but ordinary members of the public. (*State of Emergency*, 498)

The following year brought the suffering much closer to home for the English. There were multiple bombings in London throughout 1973, including Hampstead, West End, Chelsea, Marble Arch, and West London Air Terminal. There were car bombs in Westminster and parcel bombs in postal centers across London and the boroughs. Pubs in Birmingham and Guildford were bombed; in July 1973 alone twenty bombs exploded in Belfast, killing eleven (Marr, 335–36). Many bombs were discovered that did not detonate, as well. The Christmas season of 1973 was particularly somber, as news reports warned of many IRA letterbombs "lurking in the Christmas mail" for Londoners.[41]

Arthur and the quest turn to the Church for support at this point of standstill. He and his questers have been following God's direction for most of the film, seeking the Grail resolutely (with the exception, perhaps, of Robin's group), but the film hasn't presented us with earthly religious figures excepting the flagellating monks. In one of the film's sources, Bergman's *Seventh Seal*, the specter of the Church is apparent throughout, from flagellant processionals to monks to churches themselves to the church's punishments. In that medieval world there is no escaping the influences of the church, whether you are a knight asking somewhat heretical questions or you are an unfortunate, convicted follower of darker forces—an end is in sight for both. Brother Maynard and his retinue first appear in the previous scene with Tim the Enchanter, where magic and the supernatural are pitched as the place Arthur can find guidance. Once they've reached the cave, wherein lies the next clue for their quest, and they encounter the Killer Rabbit, the magician textually disappears—he's of no use here. It's Brother Maynard and his relics that step in to fill the void left by the supernatural's absence. This is a bit late in such a spiritual quest, it seems, to encounter God's helpful earthly representatives, especially considering the importance of religion in the later Middle Ages:

> Religion was a greater power in the minds of men and in their material society than it has ever been before or since. At the climax of its struggle to control the world by the spirit, the Church had succeeded astonishingly in embodying in massive institutions the elusive impulses of devoutness. (Holmes, 41–42)

It may well be that since the Pythons didn't have access to the earthly representations of these "institutions"—there are no Gothic cathedrals or sprawling abbeys or even country parish churches in sight in the finished film—they had to wait until inclusion of churchmen could be (economically) narratively justified, meaning when they needed an explosive relic like the Holy Hand Grenade. And once the proper authority is accessed and the scriptural instructions are followed, the church can be an effective tool against "foul-tempered" rodents like the Killer Rabbit, and the Lord's quest can move forward.

ARTHUR: "The Holy Hand Grenade of Antioch"—This is likely the Python version of the Ark of the Covenant described in the Book of Exodus. The wandering Children of Israel carried the Ark before them as they made their way through the wilderness. The construction of the Ark is detailed by the Lord to Moses in Exodus 25:10–22, and its powers of protection (parting waters) and destruction (assisting in the collapse of Jericho's walls) are related in Joshua, chapters 3 and 6.

And as anachronistic as it seems, explosive devices had been used in sieges and battles throughout the thirteenth and fourteenth centuries in Europe and even Britain. Edward had pressed his longbow advantage with another weapon, deploying primitive but effective (if only psychologically) small cannon at the Battle of Crécy, for example, a resounding English victory (*HBMA*, 384–85). If this *is* 932, however, such weapons would be out of place on English battlefields.

ARTHUR: ". . . of Antioch"—Most of these Holy Hand Grenade lines are spoken by Launcelot in the film, but were given to Bedevere in the script as finished.

Antioch is mentioned in passing by Geoffrey in *HKB*, as he is rehearsing his version of history in "The Coming of the Romans" section: "At that time Peter the Apostle founded the church at Antioch. Later he came to Rome and held the bishopric there . . ." (122). Antioch is no more, but is known as the "Cradle of Civilization," was a Crusader's target as early as 1098, and was besieged through at least the thirteenth century when it fell to the Mongols.

ARTHUR: ". . . one of the sacred relics . . ."—There were scores of relics for sale or on display during the Middle Ages, including all or parts of John the Baptist's head, the True Cross, the bones of various apostles and saints, and by the thirteenth and fourteenth centuries there were often tiny relics of saints "embedded in the hilt of the knight's sword so that upon clasping it as he took his oath, he caused [his] vow to be registered in Heaven" (Tuchman, 62). Abbeys and churches could do brisk pilgrim business with a tantalizing selection of ancient relics. There was a continuing need for relics, then, even knowingly fake ones, as the unctuous Pardoner boasts in his portion of *The Canterbury Tales*, mentioned earlier.[42]

. . .a small group of MONKS process forward . . .—This is the first time these religious figures have been introduced as part of the quest.[43] They replace Tim the Enchanter and the world of magic; Tim was able to lead them there, but his powers are not brought to bear on the Killer Rabbit. After the slaughter, we only witness his powers of derision, and he then disappears entirely. The only other appearance of religious types in the film is the line of "self-destructive" monks seen prior to the "She's a Witch" scene earlier, where they are just linking material. This absence is a choice made by the Pythons, since the Church would have been the center of most people's lives—pauper, priest, merchant, and nobleman alike—for centuries. As Tuchman notes, "an institution so in command of culture and so rooted in the structure of society" is anything but invisible, though the Pythons have pushed it aside in *Holy Grail* to focus on the Arthurian conceit and attendant silliness. The mendicant orders had become quite entrenched in English society since at least Edward I's time, and were often greatly admired for their devotion and industry, according to Holmes: "In both the universities, where they quickly penetrated and took the lead, and the ordinary urban parishes, they were easily the most vital force in the thirteenth-century Church" (46). With great thinkers like the Franciscans Roger Bacon and John Duns Scotus (1266–1308) shining brilliantly from the universities in the thirteenth century, it's no wonder a king like Arthur wants learned and pious "brothers" as part of his quest.

As for the relic, it's not made clear which saint or apostle—or even one of the Trinity—authorizes this hand grenade, or what it might have been used for before it became a relic. The hand grenade is made to resemble a *globus cruciger*, a symbol of both royal and heavenly authority. Many European emperors, kings, and queens have been portraited holding the orb and scepter, including Charlemagne, Charles IV, Wenceslaus III, and Fredericks I and V. (It resembles the orb of imperial Rome, visible in many portraits and sculptures of Charlemagne, for example. One such image can be found in *HBMA*, p. 21.) In Ep. 14 of *MPFC*, the "small ad" animation, Gilliam uses an image of a flying Elizabeth I bearing the orb and scepter (*MPFC: UC*, 1.235). In Ep. 17, "*The Bishop*," the Pythons have already made double use of a Church device. The Bishop is carrying an elaborate crosier that flashes and rings—it's also a phone, so he can get to the next crime scene faster (1.266).

The orb/grenade *is* able to overcome the rabbit sentinel, essentially, but the questers are quickly on their own again once inside the cave. In fact, it is the saintly, scholarly Brother Maynard who is able to translate the wall etchings, but he is also the first meal for the Legendary Beast, as will be discussed below. With that, the power of both the occult *and* the Church will come to an end in the world of the film, and the relentless approach of the modern world is reinforced.

***ornate golden reliquary* . . .**—(PSC) A reliquary is a box made specifically to hold relics. Most Middle Ages houses of religious worship, devotion, or study maintained a reliquary, while noble houses often collected them. King Charles[44] is a particularly good example of this religious acquisitiveness—he had an enviable collection, including

> precious objects and gem-studded reliquaries to house the piece of Moses' rod, the top of John the Baptist's head, the flask of Virgin's milk, Christ's swaddling clothes, and bits and pieces of various instruments of the crucifixion, including the crown of thorns and a fragment of the True Cross, all of which the royal chapel possessed. (Tuchman, 237–38)

The hand grenade is suffused with the holy glow—(PSC) This special effect is called for more than once in the film, and is generally missing.[45] The only truly "holy glow" moments are those where God appears to the knights, and later the "grail-shaped beacon" over the Castle Anthrax. Otherwise, the glow is hinted at by the way those around the object or person treat that object or person. This "holy glow" is likely a holdover from biblical films including *The Ten Commandments*, where God's fire and glory suffuse objects like The Burning Bush, the tablets, and even Moses himself. In later Passion films like *The Greatest Story Ever Told*, this suffused glow tends to remain on the faces of those around the Savior—Christ himself is generally kept a respectful distance from the camera. Fittingly, the same kind of glow is used in the less-than-sacred, pulpish noir picture *Kiss Me Deadly*,[46] though when the glow is finally witnessed, it destroys the viewer.[47]

ALL KNIGHTS: ". . . can I have a dekko . . ."—(PSC) Part of the group's mumbling omitted from the finished film, "dekko" is Army slang meaning to have a look around (*OED*). There is also no sign of the rhubarbing hinted at by the script. Instead, Arthur's question about how the grenade works is answered immediately by Launcelot's "I know not." (*MPHGB*, 75).

ARTHUR: "Consult the Book of Armaments"—There are dozens of bits of apocryphal scripture, many more of which would have been available for study and copying out during the Middle Ages. The Prayer of Manasses, the books of Esdras, Tobit, Judith, and the Maccabees among many others found their way in and out of canonicity over the ages. The Latin Vulgate would have been the Bible most Christians would have known[48] during the early Middle Ages, having been compiled and translated by Jerome in the early fifth century.

The recitation here sounds very much like the instructions given in both Numbers and Leviticus to the recalcitrant children of Israel, where the Lord has to be overtly unequivocal so His children don't wander into sin.

ANOTHER MONK: (*reading from Bible*)—This monk and Brother Maynard are two of the few in *MPHG* who exhibit the ability to read, an ability that wouldn't have found itself at home in much of the population outside the religious orders. Since he's reading from scripture, it's also more than likely that he'd be reading Latin, then translating into colloquial English for the laymen in his audience. That monks could read and write, according to Mortimer, "was true for England in about 1200: in those days the ability to read was legally synonymous with being a clergyman" (68). By the fourteenth century the proliferation of records and recordkeeping in relation to religious and secular affairs meant that more and more people of all types could both read and write. Mortimer goes on: "Villeins," however, "do not feature in such lists [of literate men in the fourteenth and fifteenth centuries], the majority being unable to recognize their own name, let alone write it" (68). In *MPHG* Launcelot *reads* aloud from Herbert's handwritten note, while Arthur *recites* his lineage and claim to kingship by rote, interestingly, and must turn to his "scholar" Brother Maynard to read the inscription (in Aramaic) in the cave of the Legendary Beast.

In the "Cast List" included as part of the printed script in *MPHGB*, Palin's monk character is known as "Brother Maynard's Roommate" (90). This hint at homosociality, or even homosexuality, isn't unusual for the Pythons. Throughout the run of *MPFC*, homoeroticism is displayed in the relationships between TV presenters and men who think they're mice (Eps. 1 and 2), university dons (Ep. 2), policemen (Ep. 6), hermits (Ep. 8), the Household Cavalry (Ep. 14), between doctor and patient (E. 22), and in gay men's pornographic literature (Ep. 36), to name just a handful. See the index entries under "homosexuality" in *MPFC: UC* for more. Additionally, such same-sex relationships in the Middle Ages monastic life may have been privately justified by the simple fact that the sexual relations were non-productive, meaning no children could be engendered; the monks in question might still be able to consider themselves, technically, "chaste."

ANOTHER MONK: "St. Attila . . ."—Attila the Hun appeared more than once during the run of *Flying Circus*. There is a "Mr Attila the Hun" sketch in Ep. 13, for example, and an "*Attila the Hun Show*" sitcom in Ep. 20.

ANOTHER MONK: "And the Lord did grin . . ."—A seventeenth-century usage of the term, according to the *OED*, and one that generally relates to licentiousness, anger, or idiocy (these grins tend to be "unlovely" and "ghastly"). But in the spirit of Idle's earlier "Wink wink, nudge, nudge,"[49] the Lord *can* be described more colloquially, sometimes. The God as depicted by the Pythons (to these knights) is often churlish and short, and was even mean-spirited and spiteful in the draft script, so a grin isn't out of the realm of possibility. Remember Acts 17:30—"And the times of this ignorance God winked at; but now commandeth all men every where to repent."

ANOTHER MONK: ". . . the lambs and sloths and carp and anchovies and orang-utangs[50] and breakfast cereals and fruit bats . . ."—Another litany modeled on Old Testament lists suited for the wandering, hard-headed Children of Israel. This menu consists of foods not readily available or known in tenth-century Britain, of course, nor even the period from which the Book of Armaments may represent, which is part of the joke. The "sloth" and "orang-utang" creatures wouldn't have been widely known in Europe until the sixteenth and seventeenth centuries, as explorers returned from excursions to tropical and subtropical lands. There are hundreds of "ape" illustrations in Gothic illuminated manuscripts, yes, though it wouldn't be until Indonesia and Malaysia became trading sources that orangutan images could have entered popular culture in the west. "Carp" and "anchovies" have been harvested, preserved, and eaten for thousands of years, and breakfast cereals (oats, wheat, corn, etc.) have also been part of the human diet for millennia.[51] It's likely, though, that the "breakfast cereals" the Pythons are talking about are of the packaged type, including Kellogg's Corn Flakes, mentioned (and displayed) prominently in *MPFC*, Eps. 6, 44, and 45. The fruit bat would also have been known once its habitats became associated with international trading networks, though not likely as a food source.

ANOTHER MONK: "First shalt thou take out the Holy Pin . . ."—Again, the very precise demands of Mosaic Law, which in the Torah was parsed out to the "613 Commandments," including not erecting a pillar in a place of public worship, not muttering incantations, and not walking outside the walls of the city on Shabbat, and so on. There are also both positive and negative commandments (shalt and shalt nots). The Book of Armaments actually provides useful instructions here, allowing for the proper use of the Hand Grenade.

The instructions found in Exodus from the Lord through Moses for the construction of the Ark of the Covenant are similarly detailed:

> And they shall make an ark of shittim wood: two cubits and a half shall be the length thereof, and a cubit and a half the breadth thereof, and a cubit and a half the height thereof.
>
> And thou shalt overlay it with pure gold, within and without shalt thou overlay it, and shalt make upon it a crown of gold round about.
>
> And thou shalt cast four rings of gold for it, and put them in the four corners thereof; and two rings shall be in the one side of it, and two rings in the other side of it.
>
> And thou shalt make staves of shittim wood, and overlay them with gold.
>
> And thou shalt put the staves into the rings by the sides of the ark, that the ark may be borne with them.
>
> The staves shall be in the rings of the ark: they shall not be taken from it.
>
> And thou shalt put into the ark the testimony which I shall give thee.
>
> And thou shalt make a mercy seat of pure gold: two cubits and a half shall be the length thereof, and a cubit and a half the breadth thereof.
>
> And thou shalt make two cherubims of gold, of beaten work shalt thou make them, in the two ends of the mercy seat.
>
> And make one cherub on the one end, and the other cherub on the other end: even of the mercy seat shall ye make the cherubims on the two ends thereof. (Exodus 25:10–19)

There is also the sort of chiasmic structure of the syntax in verses eleven and eighteen the Pythons have mimicked, with a "thou shalt" in the first clause, and a "shalt thou" in the second clause. Phrases like "in my sight" are also characteristic of the language of the Old Testament, found in Jeremiah, Psalms, Isaiah, and so on.

ANOTHER MONK: ". . . being naughty in my sight, shall snuff it"—This was originally to be "shall croak" in the script as printed (*MPHGB*, 76).

ARTHUR: (*quietly*) "One, two, three"—This is the way the line appears in the script, with the "three" crossed out and "five" written in by hand. Off to the right on the page, Galahad corrects Arthur, and Arthur says "Three." It may have been that this scene wasn't completed as we know it until they were out on location, shooting the scene.

The challenges with consecutive numbers Arthur seems to encounter throughout the film is likely just Python silliness, but there is a medieval precedent for such inconsistencies. According to Robert Fossier, medieval man did not fixate on numbers as we do today: "[I]n all of the centuries of the Middle Ages, figures were not given their real arithmetical values except in ecclesiastical computation" (28). This inexactitude has frustrated scholars for centuries, of course, but seems at home in turbulent times:

> That "turn of mind" probably had psychological causes, for example, a clear indifference to exactitude in accounting that is not found in other cultures, notably Oriental or Semitic. Figures had only symbolic value. One, three, seven, and twelve were God, the Trinity, or figures found in the Bible; and as for six and its multiples six times six, they were the sign of what cannot be counted with the fingers of one hand, thus, what surpasses immediate understanding, whether what was in question was the dead or the living, years of age, or degrees of kinship. (*AO*, 28)

Fossier goes on to note that most Middle Ages men did not know their own age, couldn't name or count their cousins, and many had no idea how many children they may have fathered—the specifics of numbering and counting just weren't as important to the common man (28). Arthur will struggle with a countdown, the number of knights lost in a battle, and the number of questions asked by the Bridgekeeper, exhibiting his own place in this medieval world where there is "a certain indifference with regard to the number of individuals"—his quest group fluctuates in number as needed for the script—the world described by Fossier and depicted by the Pythons (28).

ARTHUR throws the grenade at the RABBIT—(PSC) Just after the grenade explodes, there is a cutaway to the forest of the Knights Who Until Recently Said Ni. The policemen and inspector are there, in the midst of scattered shrubbery and small white fences. This quick simultaneous action scene is not accounted for in the script. There is also no celebrating, praising, or "huzzah-ing," as the script calls for; the scene is a simple cut to the following scene, an interior shot of the cave, looking out.

Notes

1. See the "*interior of medieval hall*" entry in "Camelot ('It Is a Silly Place')", scene 10, above for more, including mention of Hollywood's equivalent Bronson Cave in Griffith Park.

2. Camera operator Atherton and camera focus Wellard, listed in the credits section above.

3. From a delightful 4 January 2014 e-mail correspondence with the author.

4. Bergman also plays with his soundscape in the dream sequence from *Wild Strawberries*—exaggerating, manipulating, or removing sounds at will.

5. From an 18 December 2013 e-mail correspondence.

6. See *MPFC: UC*, 1.336 and 343, as well as 2.178, and *MPFC: UC*'s index (under "censorship") for more on these words in the Python *oeuvre*.

7. A copy of that memo is included in *MPHGB*, on about page 49 (most of the book is unpaginated), just after the first draft of the script.

8. See Randall's *IMGM*, "Index of Subjects," 105–10 for scores of "hare" entries.

9. See the entries in scene 7, "She's a Witch," above for earlier mentions of witchfinders Stearne and Hopkins.

10. From Stearne, *A Confirmation and Discovery of Witchcraft*. To "swome her" means testing her purity by water, throwing her in the pond.

11. "Turd" was *not* one of the words the censor's representative mentioned as a possibility for deletion.

12. *MPHGB*, 90.

13. *The Wild Bunch* opened in London in August 1969 at the Warner, just as the Pythons were working on the first series of *MPFC*; *Butch Cassidy and the Sundance Kid* appeared at the Carlton in February 1970.

14. Director Clint Eastwood would adopt elements of this same frenetic style for his fight sequences in a number of his early films, including *The Outlaw Josey Wales* (1976).

15. Taylor, "Violence in the Abstract."

16. This refers to the images at the beginning of the film—prior to the first bloody robbery—of a group of children watching ants swarm over trapped scorpions. Just after the robbery, as the gang rides past, the children place burning grass on top of the swarming heap, giggling all the while.

17. Taylor, "Violence in the Abstract."

18. Dialogue from *The Crimson Permanent Assurance*, Gilliam's featurette attached to *Meaning of Life*.

19. Seen also in many period westerns, including *Butch Cassidy and the Sundance Kid*, where there is no place for "old" west bandits anymore, and the future (in the guise of the Pinkertons), pursues Butch and Sundance into death and history.

20. Taylor, "Violence in the Abstract."

21. In this last instance (the "steady pursuit") *MPHG* is related to *Butch Cassidy and the Sundance Kid*, where a similar tracking by the forces of the law and the emerging modern world (the twentieth century) spell irrevocable doom for these larger-than-life characters of lore.

22. See Camus, *The Myth of Sisyphus and Other Essays*, 88–91.

23. Camus, 91.

24. These ideals are still found in Peckinpah's world, but they are homosociality, the value of a man's word (does it matter to whom?), and the inevitability of death—but perhaps on one's own terms. The western as a genre of white and black hats, of good guys fighting bad guys as the frontier is pushed back, is gone by 1969—emptied out, then refilled by Peckinpah with manly relationships and nihilism, but not outright parody. The Pythons take that next step into the parodic, along with filmmakers like Mel Brooks.

25. "Kung Fu's Last Fight," *Time*, 11 November 1974.

26. Lee's very popular films began appearing in London cinemas in July 1973, with *Fist of Fury* at the Rialto running continuously through October 1973.

27. See the "Entertainments" listings in the *Times* for 10 January 1974 (page 11), for example. Also playing in London-area theaters during this same period are the influential films *Canterbury Tales* and *Seven Samurai*, both discussed elsewhere in this study.

28. Robinson, "Kung Fu," 9.

29. Glaessner, *Kung Fu: Cinema of Vengeance*, 7.

30. And only *Sanshiro Sugata* (1943) featured hand-to-hand fighting (judo), really.

31. Many of these more nihilistic, violent Japanese films found their way to audiences via film festivals, not theatrical distribution.

32. This is also the first instance when Arthur confuses "five" for "three" in a counting—he'll do it again when they count before throwing the grenade, and again at the Bridge of Death, when faced with "questions three."

33. Especially since Arthur was declaring his kingship by paternal right in that same scene—it might be quite clumsy to then have that same father hanging about for the son's defining quest.

34. See Robert de Boron and Wolfram von Eschenbach, for instance, both sources mentioned earlier.

35. See *HKB*, 202–8.

36. See entries in scene 16, the "Three-Headed Knight" section above for more on the Welsh literary triads.

37. Sir Ector is mentioned often in relation to the Wart and his upbringing along with Kay in White's *The Sword in the Stone*.

38. As Gilliam and Palin wrote *Time Bandits* together just a few years later, at first they just picked historical events and settings out of memory—moments in history that simply stood out to them as cinematic and intriguing—then set about deciding which ones worked better than others as the script moved forward. This tossed-salad effort may be showing in this section of *MPHG*, where this later scene didn't jibe precisely with an earlier scene, and revisions were made after the fact. This is also likely why the Pythons often shot multiple, quick, subtly varied versions of the same scene as they went along. See *Interview with Michael Palin and Terry Gilliam*, BBC Channel 4, 1993.

39. Tendler, "Big Arms Discoveries in Army's First Raids on Orange Halls."

40. Palin soberly mentions this bombing by name, without editorial comment on his part—which is unusual—in his diaries (73).

41. *Times*, 18 December 1973: 1; Gilliam and Palin would revisit this scene of holy celebration and carnage in *Brazil*, where a terrorist bombing campaign disrupts Christmas in a future London. The film followed the wave of high-profile assassinations and kidnappings that also occurred in the mid- to late 1970s.

42. See the "He's already got one, you see" entry above, in scene 13, "Taunting by Frenchmen."

43. These monks wear brown cloaks (or supertunics) over white tunics, similar to the white-over-brown dress of Carmelite monks of the period. They are also tonsured (heads shaved to a bald pate) and wears no socks, which would have been historically accurate, according to Mortimer: "Friars never wear socks. Not wearing something is also a way of making a fashion statement" (115). Palin's monk is completely barefoot, as is the thurible-swinging monk, while Idle's Brother Maynard wears sandals, meaning costumers likely had just the one pair of sandals.

44. This is the Valois king Charles V (1338–1380). He is mentioned earlier in reference to Dennis's mother *not* voting for Arthur as king.

45. Like many optical special effects, this would have been done in postproduction, meaning the shortage of time or money could have eliminated the effect.

46. And later, *Raiders of the Lost Ark* (1981) and *Pulp Fiction* (1994), as well.

47. In this case, the glow is created by intense radiation, and the greedy character who releases that genie from its bottle is destroyed. This same destruction is likely what Arthur and knights want to avoid when God first appears to them, averting their eyes so as to not look on God's glory and die.

48. More precisely, most Christians would have never owned, read, or even touched a Bible during their lifetimes. They could have *glimpsed* them in church or abbey settings, but the illuminated versions of the Bible would have been far too valuable for most. The fact that the monks carry their copy of the Bible (or the scriptures) is still a bit surprising, given the expense, value, and cumbersome size of most Bibles.

49. See Ep. 3, *Flying Circus*, "Nudge, Nudge."

50. In the printed script, this word is edited. It was originally typed as "orangu-tans," and was changed by hand (the typo fixed by one of the more anal Pythons, likely) to "orangu-tangs," the "g" and "s" written into the word. The word is often spelled "orang outan," as well (sometimes with a hyphen).

51. And even if these foods weren't endemic to Britain, the Roman occupation facilitated the importation of all sorts of exotic foods and spices (and cloths and tools) from the far corners of the Roman Empire and its trading partners.

SCENE THIRTY-FOUR
THE CAVE OF CAERBANNOG

. . . we see in the darkness . . . a fearsome looking CREATURE . . .—(PSC) Not so. The "creature" isn't glimpsed for a few moments, *after* Brother Maynard attempts to translate the writing on the cave wall. We have seen an image of the creature before, of course, during the "Seasons" voice-over (an animated sequence). In the script, the creature is said to be watching them "*with some surprise.*" The description also makes it clear that Brother Maynard has come into the cave with them. Prior to this, these kinds of specifics weren't included in the script—characters appear and disappear often without comment.

writing carved on the back of the cave wall—(PSC) A small piece of etched slate, evidently used as a drain cover for many years, was discovered in 1998 in relation to "King Arthur's Castle," which is "actually Earl Richard of Cornwall's thirteenth-century fortress" at Tintagel (Gidlow, 202). Some of the researchers associated with the find wanted to translate the shallow etchings—*"Patern"* . . . *"Coliavificit"* . . . *"Artognov"* . . . *"Col"* . . . *"Ficit"*—as *"Artognou, father of a descendant of Coll has had this made,"*[1] with the "Artognou" being translated as "Arthur." Gidlow argues that there is no precedent for finding the name Arthur in variations other than "Arthur itself, or accepted Latin versions of the same" (203). "Artognou" is not our Arthur, he concludes. Gidlow finishes: "We have to remember that the connection between Arthur and Tintagel is hardly founded on historical material. There is nothing in all the sources before Geoffrey to lead us to suspect that Arthur was connected with Tintagel, and all the later references derive from Geoffrey" (204). The confusion experienced by Arthur and his knights and even their scholarly monk is not unlike the confusion surrounding this stone's "proper" translation by scholars in the twentieth century (202–3).

Further, the earlier alleged twelfth-century discovery of a burial slab and attached cross with an elaborate inscription also merits mention, as the monks of Glastonbury Abbey (who announced the discovery) claimed to have found Arthur's burial place. The Latin inscription—*"HIC IACET SEPULTUS INCLITUS REX ARTURIUS IN INSULA AVALONIA"* (*"Here lies buried the renowned King Arthur in the Isle of Avalon"*)—not only confirmed to the monks that they had indeed found Arthur's body, but the pilgrimage and tourist lifeblood of the Abbey—which needed significant restoration—could be assured. Most such inscriptions found over the years in Britain tend to be more tantalizing than telling, especially in relation to Arthuriana.

Christopher Snyder notes that epigraphy such as this is "[a]nother category of evidence, indeed a primary source for the period" ("The Age of Arthur"). He goes on to say that inscribed stones from the Roman period and to a lesser extent the Brittonic age can be found across the British Isles, with most inscriptions written in Latin. The Pythons are upholding the "Joseph-brought-the-Grail-to-Britain" school of thought, however (borrowed from Robert de Boron), so Aramaic is the language of choice.

ARTHUR: "Brother Maynard, you're our scholar"—Quite accurate, historically. As has been mentioned earlier, bastions of learning tended to be the universities and abbeys, with the monastic tradition of learning and even translation/publication stretching back for centuries. McKisack mentions that even though the wealth of the various religious orders prompted "envy and criticism," the "value of the religious life well lived" was apparent, and, ultimately, that "some of the greatest scholars of the age" were friars (311).

To this point the religious men have been fairly liminal, appearing in the background in the preceding "Tim the Enchanter" scene, and only now full face for the first time. Brother Maynard and friends joined the quest at some point, it's clear, but where and why aren't indicated, either in the finished film or the script as printed. Likely, they joined when it was narratively propitious—Arthur will need a miracle of sorts to overcome the Killer Rabbit, one that his quest companions cannot provide. Halsall notes that during the "Arthurian" time such associations were fairly common. Germanus, Bishop of Auxerre,[2] visited Britain perhaps twice, in 429 and sometime in the 440s, ostensibly to help solve the Pelagian[3] controversy and keep the church in Britain strong and united with Rome. Germanus was a respected outsider "invited in to resolve the dispute," according to Halsall, which connects us to Brother Maynard's role in *MPHG*:

> The Holy Man's role as an "outsider" was an important part of his mystique. Gildas' narrative shows a series of appeals to outsiders and, at the end of the fourth century, Bishop Victricius of Rouen was invited to Britain to resolve an unspecified theological dispute. (79–80)

Brother Maynard is a scholar and a man of God, and in his scholarly books and religious chattel can be found the means to keep the quest moving forward—the knights' swords will have no effect in any of the following scenes, as they've reached the "spiritual" or even divine part of the journey.

BROTHER MAYNARD: "It is Aramaic"—Family of languages that includes Hebrew.

GALAHAD: "Joseph of Arimathea!"—According to Ashe, Joseph—the Jew who arranged for the interment of Christ—first appeared in the Grail stories thanks to Robert de Boron in about 1200 (*QAB*, 22). Those stories give the Grail (with drops of the crucified Messiah's blood) into the hands of soldier Joseph (a "new Grail hero"), which Barber notes, and later versions of the story see the Grail safely to Glastonbury, where Arthur was also allegedly buried (*THG*, 41). Ashe goes on to say that Boron allows Perceval to actually complete the Grail quest, while Malory gives that honor to Galahad (*QAB*, 22). There is a fifteenth-century stained glass window image of Joseph of Arimathea at All Saints Church, Langport, Somerset (22). Barber includes a Crucifixion image from *The High Book of the Grail* (1405) depicting Joseph gathering Christ's blood (*The Holy Grail*, 48).

And rather than the possibility that Joseph spoke Aramaic, being from a city in Judea (Arimathea), the knights here seem to be making the connection between "Aramaic" and "Arimathea" based on the words' first three syllables' pseudo-homonymic relation more than anything else.

BROTHER MAYNARD: "That's what it says"—Brother Maynard *is* a scholar and he *can* read Aramaic, which is better than anyone else in the group, but he's also demonstrating his own deficiency: he doesn't know what the text *means*. This means he's reading without value, essentially, without production, almost onanistically, which can't benefit the quest.

His reading only leads others in the group to guess wrongly as to what the inscription refers to, distracting themselves as the Beast approaches from behind. Roger Bacon[4] was hard on such unproductive clergy, though, to be fair, he was talking specifically about those who were illiterate, who couldn't read at all (meaning they couldn't help their flocks) but still enjoyed the benefits of their sinecure: "[They] recite the words of others without knowing in the least what they mean, like parrots and magpies" (Holmes, 42–43). Brother Maynard can read the inscription, but he can't interpret it. Textually, he's punished for his overreach, as the Legendary Beast consumes him.

A slightly different but just as fatal bit of misreading appears in Marlowe's *Edward II*, and was enacted in real life as Edward's keepers waited for word on their ward's fate at Berkeley Castle in September 1327. In the play, Young Mortimer reads out a carefully written message from Bishop Hereford, lines that purposefully can be interpreted two ways. The cryptic message reads: *"Edwardum occidere nolite timere bonum est,"* which is translated once as "Fear not to kill the king, 'tis good he die," though immediately read out again as "Kill not the king, 'tis good to fear the worst" (*Edward II*, 5.4.8–12). Mortimer opts for the first reading, of course. Bishop Hereford (Adam Orleton) wanted the king dead, but also wanted to make sure he himself was never blamed, should Edward's son or surviving friends contemplate revenge, according to Marlowe's version of the shadowy events. Historians aren't certain what actually happened, or if Edward even died at Berkeley. The Pythons will revisit this misreading trope in their next feature film, *Life of Brian*, when the Centurion gives Brian an impromptu lesson in proper Latin ("People called Romanes they go the house?").

**ARTHUR: "But if he was dying he wouldn't bother to carve "Aaaaaarrrrrrggghhh."
He'd just say it"**—Perhaps so. But someone as significant as Joseph of Arimathea in the story of Christ could easily have been gifted with supernal powers as needed, including living long enough to jot down the exact moment of his own death. In discussing the Middle Ages views of the authenticity of the Bible, G. G. Coulton mentions a passage in *The Jewish Encyclopedia* that seemed to grant Moses this ability: "Moses wrote the whole Pentateuch at God's dictation, even, according to R. Simeon, the last eight verses, relating to his own death" (*Medieval Panorama*, 413).

BROTHER MAYNARD: "It's down there carved in stone"—As Maynard reads the inscription he follows the line with his eyes and head, dipping slightly, as if the inscription is trailing off. The knights are certain such a literal interpretation of Joseph's last words is impossible, given the challenge of stone carvings. This is yet another visitation from an earlier Python work. In *MPFC*, a letter writer created a similar letter of complaint to the BBC in Ep. 12, just after two office workers began betting on which coworker would next leap to his death:

Cut to letter.

Voice Over (Chapman): Dear Sir, I am writing to complain about that sketch about people falling out of a high building. I have worked all my life in such a building and have never once . . . arrgghhh! *(splat)*

Cut to film of man falling out of window. (*JTW*, 1.148)

On the letter itself—which is revealed as the camera pulls back slightly—the "fall" is illustrated similarly to Brother Maynard's depiction: legible writing leading to a downward scribble.

GALAHAD: "Perhaps he was dictating"—As mentioned just above, the image of God dictating to Moses so that the five books of the Old Testament can be written as God wants them written gives credence to this assumption, even though Arthur snaps this logical window shut.

And even though the "where" is missing (or mangled, as Joseph died and carved), the *authenticity* of the writing wouldn't have been in question to the godly Middle Ages scholar, as Coulton points out:

> So, again, according to St Thomas, the primary interpretation of Holy Writ must be historical or literal. In this sense one word may, indeed, have different significations according to different contexts. But the literal sense is that which the Author intends: *and the Author of Holy Writ is God. There can be no falsehood anywhere in the literal sense of Holy Scripture.* (*Medieval Panorama*, 413; italics added)

Thomas agrees that there may be language challenges, interpretation challenges given the abilities of so-called learned men, and that figurative language ("Aaaaaarrrrrrrgggghhh") can be misunderstood by the "hasty or ignorant" reader. But, the will of God must be acknowledged—His scripture will be made manifest and shared:

> [Thomas further] insists that, wherever the literal sense conveys a statement of fact, that fact must not be questioned. For instance: "Those things which are said of [the Earthly] Paradise in Scripture are put before us by the method of historical narration. But, in all things, which Scripture thus hands down, *we must hold to the truth of the story as our foundation, and fabricate our spiritual expositions upon that foundation.*" (*Medieval Panorama*, 413; italics added)

Arthur and his quest will try and make the most literal sense of this Writ of God, the markings on the cave wall, and then will attempt to follow the path dictated by this version of "scripture." They will "fabricate" their "spiritual expositions" (and expeditions) on the foundation of God's chiseled Word. In this, they seem to be following quite faithfully St. Thomas's guidelines for the blessed, devout reader of the Word and Will of God.

BEDEVERE: "Do you think he meant the Camargue"—Camargue *is* in France, actually, south, on the Mediterranean Sea. There was a big push in the early 1970s by the French government looking for foreign investment in the Camargue region. "We're bending over backwards to give away a gold mine!" screamed the advertising headline in the *Times* (11 October 1971), as British hotel builders were targeted for this new, government-subsidized investment opportunity. At this same time there were also movements afoot to *curb* development and *save* the wildness of the salty Camargue marshland areas, with donations from the World Wildlife Fund going right to French President Pompidou.[5] There was also a half-page feature article that ran in March 1972 in the *Times*—"The Original Wild West"—looking at romantic horse riding vacations in the Camargue's vastness.[6] The previously little-known and sparsely inhabited region was much in the news as the Pythons prepared to write *Holy Grail*.

ARTHUR: "No, that's St. Ives"—Launcelot's pronunciation—"St. Aaaaaarrrrrgggghh's"—of St. Ives is perhaps a comment on the somewhat unusual Cornish accent. Cornwall is referred to directly only three times in *MPFC*, in Ep. 3, in a news tidbit from the "Stolen Newsreader," in Ep. 6, in relation to a particular candy ingredient, and more significantly throughout Ep. 34, when Mr. Pither is on a bicycle tour of Devon and Cornwall.[7] St. Ives is a northern coastal port in Cornwall, and well down the coast from Tintagel.[8]

A muffled roar is heard—(PSC) This isn't clear at all, but in the script after this offscreen sound (from the Beast), Robin was to have said "Hey!" upon glimpsing the monster. This was to be followed by another version of the "St. Ives" gag, but involving Herefordshire. It should be clear why this setup had to be changed—Robin was being played by an extra hiding behind his shield[9] so that Idle could play Brother Maynard, meaning Robin couldn't speak.

There in the opening is a huge, unpleasant, fairly well drawn cartoon beast—(PSC) It's not clear at all that the Legendary Beast is anywhere near the cave's entrance, since no light frames him. The comment on the cartoon's aesthetic appeals—"fairly well drawn"—is typical of the Pythons' *MPFC* scripts, where there are many such comments available for the reader of the script only, and which were likely never intended for print publication of any kind. Comments would have been for the other Pythons and/or the production team, week to week. See the *"poorer verses"* entry above in the "Camelot is a Silly Place" section for more.

BROTHER MAYNARD: "It's the Legendary Black Beast of Arrrghhh . . ."—In the finished film Brother Maynard (Idle) speaks this line, and is then consumed by the creature. The style of the consuming (Idle approaching the subjective camera and ducking down) is borrowed directly from *MPFC* Ep. 7, the "Science Fiction Sketch," where the Detective Inspector (also Idle) is eaten whole by Riley, the "blanc mange impersonator and cannibal" (*JTW* 1.92).

In the prose romances such beast encounters are often alluded to rather than described, and for good reason: narrative economy. When Lancelot and his son Galahad have been reunited aboard the mysterious ship (in the final "Lancelot" chapter of *The Tale of the Sangrail*), much that doesn't involve the Grail quest directly is left to the reader's imagination:

> So dwelled Sir Lancelot and Sir Galahad within that ship half a year, and served God daily and nightly with all their power. And often they arrived in isles far from folk, where there repaired none but wild beasts, and there they found many strange adventures were with wild beasts, and not in the quest of the Sangrail, therefore the tale maketh here no mention thereof, for it would be too long to tell of all those adventures that befell them. (*LMD-WM*, 389)

There is also a beast encounter earlier in Arthur's reign, when, resting at a well as he pursues a hart deep into the forest, Arthur watches as "the strangest beast that ever he saw or heard of" approaches, making a noise like "thirty couple hounds." The beast pauses for a drink at the well, its noise quieting as it drinks, then departs "with a great noise" (*LMD-WM*, 21–22). Arthur will later tell Merlin that the beast was "the most marvellous sight" he ever saw (22). This is the same beast—the Questing Beast—that Pellinore is pursuing in vain at the beginning of White's *The Sword in the Stone*. Malory's Arthur would also dream of a marauding dragon and boar:

> And as the king lay in his cabin in the ship, he fell in a slumbering and dreamed a marvellous dream: him seemed that a dreadful dragon did drown much of his people, and he came flying out of the west, and his head was enamelled with azure, and his shoulders shone as gold, his belly like mails of a marvellous hue, his tail full of tatters, his feet full of fine sable, and his claws like fine gold; and an hideous flame of fire flew out of his mouth, like as the land and water had flamed all of fire. After, him seemed there came out of the orient, a grimly boar all black in a cloud, and his paws as big as a post; he was rugged looking roughly, he was the foulest beast that ever man saw, he roared and romed so hideously that it were marvel to hear. Then the dreadful dragon advanced him and came in the wind like a falcon giving great strokes on the boar, and the boar hit him again with his grizzly tusks that his breast was all bloody, and that the hot blood made all the sea red of his blood. Then the dragon flew away all on an height, and came down with such a swough, and smote the boar on the ridge, which was ten foot large from the head to the tail, and smote the boar all to powder both flesh and bones, that it flittered all abroad on the sea (*LMD'A*, 1.172–73)

Another instance where the beast encounter is carefully detailed can be found in the "Arthur and Lucius the Emperor of Rome" section of *Le Morte Darthur*. There, Arthur approaches a giant "gnawing on a limb of a large man," sees a skewer-full of children roasting over a bonfire, and then

the glutton glared, and grieved full foul. He had teeth like a greyhound; he was the foulest wight that ever man saw, and there was never such one formed on earth, for there was never devil in hell more horribly made, for he was from head to the foot five fathom long and large. (*LMD-WM*, 90)

In a blow-by-blow account, Malory details how Arthur stabs into its brain, cuts the giant's "genitals asunder," slices open the giant's belly (spilling foul "gore" on the grass), and breaks several ribs before the creature succumbs. The "foul carl's" head is then removed and sent to the city to be in public view (90–91).

Finally, Gilliam's version is a chimeric, scaly, dragon-like creature, loaded with eyes and teeth, horns but no forelimbs—a mixture of creatures and animals described in the source material. (There are several sketches of the versions he considered on the facing pages; see appendix A.) As for narrative economy—the Pythons "defeat" the monster by stopping and then "erasing" him from the film in less than two seconds—and the quest can continue.

. . .there is a yell and a scream OUT OF VISION. ARTHUR turns—(PSC) A large section is crossed-out here, where Sir Hector—described as "northern and helpful"—tells Arthur that Sir Alf has been eaten:

ARTHUR: (to LAUNCELOT) I didn't know we had a Sir Alf.

HECTOR: He was feeding it bread.

ARTHUR: (shouting back) Well, that was a very silly thing to do. Now the rest of you stand well back from the Black Beast of Arrrghhh!

HECTOR: Arrrghhh! (*MPHGB*, 79)

The creature eats Hector and turns on the rest of them, with Gawain saying "It's only a cartoon," and Arthur shushing him. There is no "Sir Alf" in the Malorian source, and this may be a throwaway name connected to two other contemporary sources. First, *Sir Alf* Ramsey (1920–1999) was the coach who famously took the English football team to a World Cup championship in 1966, and was knighted the following year. In early May 1974, just when the Pythons were beginning the location shoot for *MPHG* in Scotland, Sir Alf's contract to manage England was very publicly *not* renewed, and pundits traced the beginning of his end back to England's 1–1 draw with Poland, a tie that eliminated England from the 1974 Cup.[10] England earned the draw with Poland on 17 October,[11] just as the Pythons and potential producers were discussing a possible film project, and Sir Alf was in the headlines in a big, negative way.[12] Sandbrook notes that *Times* editor Green pointed out Alf's managerial actions (or inactions) and their effect on the depressing game:

"For Sir Alf I can find no excuse," wrote Geoffrey Green in *The Times*, for "as the minutes unwound, seemingly faster and faster, there he sat with his substitutes on the sidelines . . . immobile while his men on the field drained themselves of their last ounce of energy," like some sporting equivalent of the politicians who had fiddled as Britain's economic reputation went up in smoke.[13]

The Pythons' Sir Alf is obviously not paying attention to the seriousness of the situation they're in—feeding bread to the monster instead of fleeing—and football's Sir Alf sits stonily as England's Cup hopes slip away. Most British news and sport outlets spewed similarly. Sir Alf's fall from grace, then, unfolded in slow motion as the Pythons created and then shot *Holy Grail*.

Second, the popular and controversial character Alf Garnett (Warren Mitchell), who had been spewing racially insensitive talk on *Till Death Us Do Part* since 1965 is also a possible "Sir Alf." A number of racially insensitive characters and situations in *MPFC* can be laid on Garnett's doorstep, including (but certainly not limited to) Mr. Concrete (Jones) in Ep. 20, Mr. Entrail (also Jones) in Ep. 44, and most of Ep. 45.

They run off. Darkness. The MONSTER lumbering through on animation—The script simply called for the chase to end with a whimper as the knights escape back out the front of the cave. The voice-over intoning the sudden death of the animator is written onto the opposite blank page of the script (*MPHGB*, facing page 79), with the animator given his own "Aaaaagh!" to utter as he dies.

VOICE OVER: ". . . the animator suffered a fatal heart attack"—This *deus ex machina* moment was written into the printed script after the fact, likely on the back of the preceding page and with a hand-drawn arrow indicating where to insert it.[14] It's an easy fix, of course, since additional animation costs money as does staging a battle between knights and a cartoon beast—whether animated, live action, or a complicated mixture of both. The intrusions of the modern world have already been blessed with believability in the Python's Dark Ages, so a cartoony death (farcical, fast-motion) fits well. It's also likely that the Pythons were drawing on their medieval sources yet again, since Chrétien de Troye's masterful work *Perceval* also ends abruptly—in mid-sentence, even: "When the queen saw her she asked her what was the matter—", and scholars assume the author died before finishing, perhaps even as the sentence was being composed (*Arthurian Romances*, 494).

There are also myriad instances in medieval history where the death of someone seems to change the course of that history. Example: By 1120 Henry I had achieved the long-sought consolidation of his power both in England and Normandy, defeating (mostly outmaneuvering) Louis VI, imprisoning the tenacious Duke Robert, and assuring that the itinerant claimant William Clito remained unrecognized and adrift (Poole, *DBMC*, 124–25). Everything was in place for a smooth transition from Henry to his son and heir, William Ætheling, cementing Anglo-Norman leadership over much of England and western Europe for years to come. The "sudden" moment of change came on 25 November 1120, when the ship on which young William was returning to England hit rocks and sank, killing all aboard, including Henry's legitimate and illegitimate children, and much of the royal household. Henry would die in 1135, childless, and the squabbling for his throne thereafter became known as the Great Anarchy (126–36). William Ætheling's sudden death meant that the dreams of power harbored by William Clito, Henry's immediate family, and nephews including eventual king Stephen of Blois could begin in earnest. The animator's demise allows Arthur's quest to continue; though in the script as printed, the Beast simply chases the quest out of the cave, to the same end.

This type of abrupt ending isn't even new to the Pythons, having been toyed with in both Eps. 34 and 41. Toward the end of Ep. 34 of *MPFC*, Mr. Pither (Palin) and Gulliver (Jones) are just about to be executed by a Soviet firing squad, when a "Scene Missing" insert appears, and in the following shot both men are safely out of danger (*JTW*, 2.163–64). Another cinematic fiat, the "scene missing" is generally a part of a film during the rough cut process, when a particular action sequence or (more often) special effects shot isn't finished for the film's first rough screening.[15] Here, it's an artificial, obvious way to end a scene without the traditional climactic moment—offering a jump to the denouement, instead. This is also the same episode featuring the Gilliam animated monsters that peek into scenes occasionally, then jump out at the end (after Pither rides away) to dance to "Jack in a Box." Episode 34 was completed by May 1972, two years prior to the start of *MPHG* filming.

In Ep. 41, the second in the abbreviated six-episode series completed after *Holy Grail*—and including significant sketches first appearing in the first draft of the *Holy Grail* script—the department store customer asks a clerk about different possible endings. In turn they discuss and we see bits of a "chase" ending, a walk "into the sunset," a "happy ending," a "summing up from the panel"—where lounging footballers muse lazily about the show—and finally:

> *Cut back to the store.*
>
> Assistant (Jones): No? A slow fade?
>
> *The picture begins to fade.*
>
> Chris (Idle): Nnnnnno. . .
>
> Assistant: Well how about a sudden ending?
>
> *Immediate blackout. (JTW, 2.275–76)*

The episode ends abruptly at this point.

VOICE OVER: "The cartoon peril was no more . . . the quest for the Holy Grail could continue"—This section and the Palin narration just above are penciled into the script after the fact, replacing more complicated responses and repeats of gags, transitioning us from inside the cave being imperiled by the beast to safely outside the cave. The script had simply called for an "Animated Sequence" (*MPHGB*, 79) that takes the knights through the cave's darkness and out, the monster somewhere behind them. Killing the animator, then, is a neat transition—obvious and jilting, but effective and likely time saving.

SCENE: Cave of Caerbannog Aftermath—In a short cutaway scene not included in the script, the police inspector and two uniformed constables examine the evidence left at the scene where several knights and the Killer Rabbit died. Following this "meanwhile" scene is another where the knights emerge from the other cave entrance, near the Bridge of Death. The Cave location is much further east of the Glencoe area, at the location where the Bridge of Death sequences had been shot in the first days of the shoot.

Notes

1. This is Professor Charles Thomas's version of the translation (Gidlow, 202). Gidlow prefers Andrew Smith's translation.

2. Later Saint Germanus (c. 378–c. 448), born in Gaul.

3. Touching the British church, Pelagianism held that through good works "one could earn a passage to heaven," which was "clearly heretical," since it "denied God any role in deciding who got into heaven and who did not" (Halsall, *Worlds of Arthur*, 80).

4. The Ilchester-born Bacon is mentioned earlier in relation to Bedevere's learning and Roger the Shrubber's lamentations.

5. "World Wildlife Fund Aid to Save Camargue," *Times*, 21 December 1971: 3.

6. Carter, John. "The Original Wild West." *Times*, 4 March 1972: 11. Incidentally, the Duke of Edinburgh would visit the region this same month as the queen toured others parts of France. These visits received significant news coverage, as well.

7. Though the location is allegedly Cornwall, Mr. Pither's cycling scenes were all shot on the Isle of Jersey. See entries in *MPFC: UC*, volume two, Ep. 34.

8. The Goons dedicated an episode to things spookily Arthurian (via Tennyson), "The Spectre of Tintagel," with a "cherry-nosed Cornishman" uttering the obligatory "ooh arr, ooh arr" dialogue.

9. In the infamous Ed Wood film *Plan 9 from Outer Space* (1959), Wood inserted previously recorded footage of his friend Bela Lugosi—who'd died in 1956—to likely increase the movie's audience appeal. To fill in story gaps that the mismatched footage couldn't, Wood brought in another man to dress as Lugosi for additional scenes, instructing the awkward replacement (his head, for example, was shaped completely differently) to hide his face behind his cloak. See Peary, *Cult Movies*.

10. "Sad Timing of Sir Alf Ramsey's Departure," *Times*, 2 May 1974: 10.

11. There is an intriguing, juxtaposing article that examines this England football "loss" in October 1973 against a backdrop of the Yom Kippur war and the end of the economic "golden age" Britain may have experienced since World War II. See Larry Elliott, "Lessons from Yom Kippur," *Guardian*, 7 October 2013: 23.

12. "England Fail to Qualify for World Cup Finals," *Times*, 18 October 1973: 12.

13. Sandbrook, *State of Emergency*, 540–41.

14. This quick scene was shot in the rented studio space on Tasker Road, the space taken over by Doyle and the production team as the preproduction of the film got underway. Information from Doyle's 2012 "Witness Statement" as well as a 9 December 2013 e-mail to the author.

15. When *Star Wars* was first screened for Fox executives, for example, many of the special effects shots were not complete, and a number of "scene missing" inserts were included instead. It's reported that many of those watching nodded off, certain they had a flop on their hands.

SCENE THIRTY-FIVE
THE BRIDGE OF DEATH

The KNIGHTS emerge . . . in a breathtaking, barren landscape. Glencoe—The only quest members who emerge are Arthur, Galahad, Robin, Bedevere, and Launcelot. There is no Gawain, who is later mentioned as trying to make his way across the bridge—his unsuccessful attempt is given to Galahad, instead.

The Pythons had visited the Glencoe area three years earlier, shooting many wild exterior scenes for "*Njorl's Saga.*" This sequence was the first shot for *MPHG*, beginning in late April 1974. The fact that Glencoe is mentioned by name in the script is evidence the Pythons had either certainly planned on shooting at least some of the film in the wilds of Scotland (before losing access to English castles), or that Glencoe is included as a mock-"breathtaking" setting.[1]

Finally, the syntax of this description is borrowed right from the Goons, as well. The script's text—"*The KNIGHTS emerge from the mouth of the cave to find themselves in a breath-taking, barren landscape. Glencoe*"—reads as if the "Glencoe" is supposed to be interpreted as a mock-epic moment, a diminution, the dropping off of a dramatic precipice, of sorts. In "The First Albert Memorial to the Moon" episode, the Goons use this same deflation, where the famed Gothic Revival memorial is being turned into something more useful, and sent somewhere where it would be less visible:

Seagoon (Secombe): For three months we worked like Trojans, and as you know Trojans are a lazy lot. Like the story of the Trojan horse, but that's a horse of a different colour.

Sellers: The Albert Memorial finally converted into a rocket, was finally ready for launching in an outlandish spot where no human being ever visited . . . Glasgow. (23 March 1958)

The inclusion of the Trojan horse reference is a happy coincidence the Pythons may have remembered, as well.

ARTHUR: "The Bridge of Death!"—The explanation as to how the Bridge of Death can be crossed is handwritten into the script, the original page completely crossed out (see the following entry).[2]

In *Le Morte D'Arthur* there are a number of bridges (and other transitional settings, like fords and thresholds) where "none can pass"—several discussed earlier in the "Black Knight" section—but also including a fairly traditional challenge and skirmish:

Then King Mark and Sir Dinadan rode forth a four leagues English, till that they came to a bridge where hoved a knight on horseback, armed and ready to joust.

"Lo," said Sir Dinadan unto King Mark, "yonder hoveth a knight that will joust, for *there shall none pass this bridge* but he must joust with that knight."

"It is well," said King Mark, "for this jousts falleth with thee."

Sir Dinadan knew the knight well that he was a noble knight, and fain he would have jousted, but he had had lever King Mark had jousted with him, but by no mean King Mark would not joust. Then Sir Dinadan might not refuse him in no manner.

And then either dressed their spears and their shields, and smote together. (*LMD'A*, 2.21; italics added)

Also, when Merlin buries Balin and Balan: "Then Merlin let make a bridge of iron and of steel into that island, and it was but half a foot broad, and *there shall never man pass that bridge*, nor have hardiness to go over, but if he were a passing good man and a good knight without treachery or villainy" (*LMD'A*, 1.90; italics added).

. . . there is a sort of a milestone . . .—(PSC) An entire page of the script is crossed out here. The latter half is a version of Arthur explaining how the Bridge of Death works (there's no indication as to how he gained this information), though without Arthur saying "five" instead of "three." The first part of the elided section features images borrowed from cartoons, and even Kurosawa's *Throne of Blood*. They emerge from the cave and immediately see a "sort of milestone" which reads "Aaaaaarrrrrrgggghhh! 5 miles," moments later another that reads "Aaaaaarrrrrrgggghhh! 4 miles," and finally another that points in the opposite direction and reads "Ni! 82 miles." Warner Bros.' cartoonists used these signs often, and versions of them are also used at the beginning of *Throne of Blood*, where engraved markers indicate the former site of the doomed Cobweb Castle. *Throne of Blood* is discussed a number of times earlier, as it was quite influential to the Pythons for the look of this medieval film. See various entries in the "Swallows," "Black Knight," and "Taunting by Frenchman" scenes above for more. The influence of cartoons is also discussed in *MPFC: UC*; see the index there under "animation" for much more.

LAUNCELOT: "Let me. I will take it single-handed . . ."—Launcelot, here attempting to insert himself between his liege lord and certain peril, is a direct borrow from the very popular narrative poem *Sir Gawain and the Green Knight*. The Green Knight has challenged Arthur and Arthur is about to accept when Gawain steps in and accepts the challenge for his king:

> Gawain by Guenevere
> Toward the king doth now incline:
> "I beseech, before all here,
> That this melee may be mine."[3]

Also, Launcelot continues to be the embodiment of the Anglo-Saxon period warrior: "Let him who can, achieve glory before he die that will be best for the lifeless warrior afterwards," according to one Saxon poet (Norman and Pottinger, 13). This able warrior had a high, unshakeable purpose:

> The young warrior joined the war-band of the most successful and experienced warrior he could find and followed him devotedly, eager for the fighting, the booty, and above all the glory and renown that such a leader must surely bring. There was no tribal link between lord and warrior. (13)

It's never mentioned exactly why Launcelot follows Arthur, nor how he is convinced (Bedevere, remember, saw and appreciated Arthur's scientific wisdom); it may just be that since

Arthur is King and Launcelot is the Noble Warrior, Launcelot follows his liege and fights, period.

BRIDGEKEEPER: "Must answer me / These questions three!"—Rather than answering questions it can be that *unasked* questions have ramifications in Arthur's world, as seen earlier in *The High History of the Holy Graal* discussion in the "Black Knight" sequence. The triads appear here again, as well, and the magical number three reminding us of *Macbeth*'s witches.

ROBIN: "Ask me the questions, Bridgekeeper. I am not afraid"—The moment Robin assumes the role of a sort of *miles gloriosus*, he's certain to fail. Hubris isn't often rewarded in the Arthurian sources, nor is the pointing up of another's sense of self-importance. To make "bobaunce," "avaunt," or "boast" in Malory's work is to invite trouble, at the least an admonishment and a painful lesson. In *Le Morte D'Arthur*, one Sir Gainus, a cousin to the Emperor Lucius, mocked Sir Gawaine, saying: "Lo, how these Britons be full of pride and boast, and they brag as though they bare up all the world" (*LMD'A*, 1.177). Gawaine responds by lopping off the man's head. Sir Helius "for pride and orgulity . . . would not smite Sir Palomides," and would soon regret it, especially when Palomides eventually "departed his head from the body" (2.132–33). "Pride" being the "head of all deadly sins," Galahad is admonished by "the good man" to change his ways and seek the Grail (Sangreal) with a pure heart and pure intent (2.261). "Virtuous living" will see the Grail quest accomplished—there's no place for pride or boasting.

BRIDGEKEEPER: "What is the capital of Assyria?"—This reference may have come from the Pythons' (well, Jones, really) earlier reading of Montgomery's book on warfare, which includes a lengthy section on Assyria; its capital, Nineveh; and the advanced (and cruel) methods of warfare practiced by those peoples (*A History of Warfare*, 51–57).

CUT TO SIR LAUNCELOT . . .—(PSC) After successfully answering three questions, Launcelot crosses the bridge and, in the finished film, is next seen being patted down and arrested. In the script version, he crosses and waits, hearing the unsuccessful crossing attempt of Gawain, who has managed to survive this long in the script but not the film itself. Gawain is asked the same two initial questions as Launcelot and Robin, then must answer: "What goes: black white . . . black white . . . black white?" His answer is "Babylon," and he is hurled into the chasm. This may have been unanswerable, of course, since it is a well-known children's riddle with dozens of possible answers, from penguins to newspapers to chessboards to the particularly popular "a nun falling down stairs," and so on. This Gawain exchange is all shot from Launcelot's point of view, with the mist hiding the goings-on at the middle of the bridge.

Just after Gawain is hurled to his death, "*suddenly a hand lands on LAUNCELOT's shoulder*," and a Policeman's voice is heard: "Just want to ask you some questions, sir." Launcelot is then led away for questioning. This scene was shot, but not included in the final edit of the film.[4] This action is a carryover from *MPFC* where, at the end of Ep. 29, "The Argument Clinic" sketch is disturbed by a line of trench-coated detectives from Scotland Yard clapping hands on shoulders and making arrests.

GAWAIN: "Blue . . . no Yellooooooowww!"—In the script version, it is Gawain who is given these lines, later taken by Galahad as the film was shot. Remember that Gawain had been announced as one of three killed in the Killer Rabbit assaults, along with Ector and Bors, just a few scenes earlier. The "final" script wasn't updated completely to take into account all the changes decided upon during shooting or even postproduction, though it's clear that the Pythons knew only the five principals (Arthur, Robin, Launcelot, Galahad, and Bedevere) would emerge from the cave and come toward the Bridge of Death—even though this scene was accomplished in the first days of the shoot.

The Pythons' inclusion or exclusion of knights likely came down to both narrative expediency and production costs, but such replacements weren't new to the Grail sagas. Thanks to the shifting nature of stories passed on via an oral tradition, characters and their exploits changed over time. In Malory's *Le Morte D'Arthur* it is Sir Bedevere who is entrusted with Arthur's sword Excalibur and its journey back to the Lady of the Lake. In the earlier Lancelot-Grail cycle (c. early thirteenth century), that role was given to Girflet (Halsall, *Worlds of Arthur*, 138).

As for the colors themselves, Fossier reports that color preferences changed across time during the Middle Ages, with blue rising in popularity "in the twelfth and thirteenth centuries," followed by an increased interest in yellow (and green) as the Middle Ages ebbed into the Early Modern period (*AO*, 303). Galahad and Gawain seem to have found themselves on the cusp of this transition in taste, perhaps, hence the slip of the tongue.

ARTHUR and BEDEVERE step forward—This sequence, a repeat-with-variation of the previous several encounters, is *not* part of the shooting script. In the script, Launcelot makes it across, then Robin fails, Gawain fails, and Launcelot is arrested—by then Arthur, Galahad, and Bedevere are already on the opposite side of the gorge, *"struggling towards the lake"* (*MPHGB*, 83). They have bested the Bridgekeeper somehow, off-camera. The blanks are filled in by the following short exchange:

BEDEVERE: (to ARTHUR) How did you know how many wing-beats a swallow needs to maintain velocity?

ARTHUR: Uh . . . when you're king you know all these things." (*MPHGB*, 83–84)

The attempt at narrative economy is appreciated, but the scene as played out—with Arthur accidentally turning the tables on the Bridgekeeper, using the Bridgekeeper's own announced rules—is more clever, from a writing standpoint, and it also continues to allow Arthur to plunge headlong into every situation with the full, unshakeable knowledge that God will always provide.

BRIDGEKEEPER: "I don't know that!"—The Bridgekeeper is hoisted on his own petard. This may be an example of *lex talionis*, and a portion of medieval law that required the accuser to take the place of the accused if the accusations go wrong. The Bridgekeeper can't answer his own questions, and so he is vaulted into the Gorge of Eternal Peril.

Alternately, since this is God's mission they're on, this can also be seen as the Almighty finally stepping in to right a wrong. When the loathed William Rufus (William the Conqueror's less-than-noble scion) was mysteriously killed by an arrow fired by his own man, there was quiet speculation about the "accidental" nature of the act. Other aspirants to the throne were immediately (and perhaps legitimately) suspect, including William's brothers, Robert and Henry, as was the man who allegedly fired the arrow, Walter Tirel, but no real scandal developed, and Henry was crowned soon after (Poole, *DBMC*, 98–99). According to Brooke, the chroniclers *and* people of the period in general disliked this William—he is described as a profane, vulgar, frightful kind of man, a man who laughed at God. The friendly arrow, then, was heavenly comeuppance: "The stories which surrounded Rufus's death underline the fact that men regarded his end as divine judgement." (*SNK*, 165). The Bridgekeeper suffers the same fate, earning his reward for blocking Arthur on the Lord's errand.

EXTERIOR—BRIDGE OF DEATH—DAY—This isn't part of the script as written, though it's clear that the end of the film demanded quite a bit of careful editing and narrative juggling to get the knights successfully to the cave, through the cave, and to the edge of the lake—all the while keeping track of who does and does not survive, scene to scene. Arthur and Bedevere have completed the journey across the bridge, and they are immediately looking for Launcelot.

CUT TO SIR LAUNCELOT—(PSC) The last scene Launcelot appears in is somewhere well beyond the far side of the gorge. Arthur and Bedevere have emerged from the end of the Bridge of Death, looking for Launcelot, even calling for him, and he's obviously well out of earshot. As they call and search about, we cut to a quick shot of Launcelot being frisked by the policemen who've been following them. Gilliam notes in his audio commentary on the Blu-ray that this scene was actually shot on Hampstead Heath, likely after the film had finished principal photography. Several other scenes—including Launcelot charging Swamp Castle and tree shots behind God—were also shot on Hampstead Heath, not far from Gilliam's home at the time.

Notes

1. According to Doyle, the bridge was built in a small gorge just near central Glencoe (not far from the Glencoe Mountain Search and Rescue HQ), south of the A82.

2. Both Jones and Doyle mention that the sync camera (for shooting sound) had broken on this very first day—shearing its gears—and Doyle encouraged them to keep shooting but with the non-sync camera. This meant that virtually everything had to be dubbed later, which is why some of the voices sound a bit different from other sections of the film. The alternative would have meant losing several days of filming as a replacement camera was secured from London. Jones discusses this in his Blu-ray audio commentary track, while Doyle's version comes from e-mail correspondences with the author (dated 5 December 2013).

3. From *Sir Gawain and the Green Knight*, in *The Norton Anthology of World Masterpieces* (1985), 1373, lines 339–42.

4. The scene is part of the outtakes presented on the 2012 Blu-ray edition of the film.

SCENE THIRTY-SIX
THE WONDERFUL BARGE AND THE GRAIL CASTLE

EXTERIOR—LAKE—DAY: *They land and get out of the boat . . .*—This begins the penultimate scene after several pages of crossed out scenes and handwritten substitutions.[1] After the following similar slugline, someone has penned "*The boat carries them across the magical lake*," which helps cover the proposed but missing animated boat sequence, connecting the end of the Bridge of Death scene to the Grail Castle. The final third of the film features many of these substitutions, as characters and even entire scenes had to be removed and/or rewritten to finish the film properly.

It's also interesting that in these last handful of pages of the written screenplay the Grail Castle is barely mentioned. After the Cave, the Bridge of Death, the Gorge of Eternal Peril, and the lake and the barge, the distant castle in the middle of the lake won't be mentioned as their ultimate goal until (in the script) they are off the boat and kneeling on the island, heads bowed in the shadow of the castle.[2] The Grail Castle *has not* been mentioned as the resting place of the Grail in the film, though such castles are mentioned throughout Malory and other romance sources. The Soothsayer didn't mention the Grail Castle—his prognostications stop at the Bridge of Death—nor did Tim the Enchanter, as he can see only as far as the cave's inscription. It's not until Brother Maynard reads Joseph of Arimathea's inscription that we hear of the Grail's resting place being a castle at all, the "Castle of Aaaaaarrrrrrggghhh." In the finished film, we finally see the castle (Stalker) as the boat approaches the island, and Arthur announces that they've arrived, using lines not written into the script. Narrative fluidity or even common sense shouldn't bother us by this point, of course.

BOATKEEPER: "He who would cross the Sea of Fate . . ."—This moment is crossed out, and any boatman is kept silent and offscreen in the finished film. In the script he was "*the same as the BRIDGEKEEPER and the SOOTHSAYER*"—meaning Gilliam—and when he asks for answers to "*these questions twenty-eight*," Arthur and Bedevere, frustrated, throw him into the lake.[3] Perhaps Gilliam wasn't ready to be in the full costume (including painful eye prosthetics) in the early days of the shoot. Somehow, Galahad has disappeared from this scene, or he simply didn't want to assist in the ungallant action against the grotty old man.[4] Rough storyboards for this elided scene are included in appendix A, Facing Page 84.

. . . *out of the mist appears a wonderful barge . . .*—(PSC) At the water of Mortaise, Lancelot waits for God to send him an adventure, and so he naps. In a vision he receives a visitation, hearing a voice: "Sir Lancelot, arise up and take thine armour, and enter into the first ship that thou shalt find":

474

And when he heard these words he started up and saw great clearness about him; and then he lifted up his hand and blessed him. And so he took his arms and made him ready; and at the last he came by a strand, and found a ship without sail or oar.

And as soon as he was within the ship, there he had the most sweetness that ever he felt, and he was fulfilled with all things that he thought on or desired. (*LMD'A*, 1.352)

According to the printed script Arthur and Bedevere similarly experience "*wonder*," they are "*bewitched*," and their expressions are "*suffused with heavenly radiance*" as they encounter this magical boat and approach their ultimate destination, the Grail Castle.

(Julian Doyle reports that his wife, Valerie Charlton, can be credited with the impressive dragonhead prow of this ship.[5])

ANIMATION—*A wondrous journey in animation . . .*—This section is crossed out, along with the Boatkeeper section just above it. Gilliam had intended to accomplish this transition from the shore to the castle in animation, but at some point they opted for a bit of a boat ride, live action. The cast and crew knew this change was in the works, since a boat build in Scotland was ordered a full two weeks before shooting began, according to Doyle.[6] There are a couple of Gilliam sketches on Facing Page 86 (*MPHGB*) of versions of this proposed animated sequence; see appendix A.

***They bend their heads in prayer, before the castle . . .*—**(PSC) This is as close as Arthur and Bedevere will get to the Grail, assuming it's in this castle at all. Throughout this version of the story, the actual Grail isn't glimpsed by anyone, as far as can be proven, and there's no proof that it even exists, beyond God's assertions and the Frenchman's, earlier, saying his master's "already got one." Malory provides challenges and disappointments of equal dimension in *Le Morte D'Arthur*. Launcelot is also unable to commune with the Holy Grail, even though he makes it all the way to the Grail Castle, to the threshold of the Grail Chamber. Peering in he glimpses the silver table, the red samite-draped holy vessel, the angels and candles and crosses and altar—but a voice tells him to flee, for his own sake. He enters the room anyway, and is almost immediately struck by "a breath that him thought it was intermeddled with fire, which smote him so sore in the visage that him thought it burn his visage" (*LMD'A*, 2.355–56). He is overcome and unconscious for twenty-five days. Launcelot is later told he has been chastened by God a day for every year of his sinful life, and that he has come as close to the Grail as he ever will (2.357–58).

ARTHUR: "The Castle Aaaaaarrrrrrgggghhh. . .our quest is at an end!"—Lines spoken by Arthur as he and Bedevere land on the Grail Castle island. These lines are not part of the script, either typed or written in after the fact. Arthur has put the pieces together, to his credit. Hints were given along the way, from the Soothsayer and Tim and Brother Maynard's recitation—but the dots weren't connected until Arthur *decided* that "The Castle Aaaaaarrrrrrgggghhh" as read by Brother Maynard and inscribed by Joseph wasn't either a typo or a death rattle. Arthur also kneels, sword out, head bowed, and begins to give thanks: "God be praised! Almighty God, we thank thee that thou hast vouchsafed to us the most Holy—Jesus Christ!" The last invective comes as another animal is catapulted at them from the battlements.

***Suddenly a voice comes from the battlements*—**(PSC) Also not mentioned in the script is the animal that is catapulted from the battlements and onto Arthur and Bedevere. The "thwang" of the catapult[7] is quite recognizable from the earlier French castle scene, as is the "baa" of the distressed longhaired sheep,[8] and immediately lets Arthur, Bedevere, and the audience know that the Grail will not be so easily achieved. Doyle mentions that he was up that morning at 5 AM looking for a suitable dead sheep—they found one in a field nearby—and the gutted carcass was actually so foul that crew members became physically ill.[9] This was also the latter part of what Doyle remembers as the worst day of the shoot, when he was wearing myriad hats: "For me the first week was a nightmare. Sheep, boat, battle, Castle (Stalker)—worst day and longest for me."[10]

This is only the fourth appearance of the forgotten but strategically critical sheep in the film. Sheep seem to have been part of the initial catapult projectiles from the French-held castle, and they appear later in both the title animation sequence and then the "Seasons" animation, along with their shepherd.[11] Importation of English wool was critical to Flanders, for example, where the high-quality English wool was woven into exportable cloth, such that embargoes and seizures announced in the 1270s[12] by Edward I encouraged the more hardheaded Flemish merchants and leadership to treat with Edward, and bend to his customs policy terms (Powicke, 621–22). "Kings, magnates, merchants and all Englishmen" were affected by this vital industry: "I thank God and ever shall, / It is the sheep hath paid for all," a Nottingham stapler would write later (Holmes, *LMA*, 31). In summer 1274, after the French king Philip declared his hesitating vassal King Edward in default, essentially taking back Edward's French duchy, England went to a wartime footing immediately, and wool was on their minds:

> A great council of prelates, magnates and barons hurriedly gathered early in June—there was no time for formal summons to a parliament—gave the king authority to seize all the wool, fells and hides in England, and eagerly agreed to military action in Gascony. Collectors of the wool were appointed all over the land. (Powicke, 630)

Available wool stock meant ready cash, and leverage against a recalcitrant trading partner like Flanders. When these very significant everyday elements of Middle Ages Britain aren't apparent in *Holy Grail*, it's clear that the more fantastical Arthurian elements are the narrative focus. This balance—between the Middle Ages proper and Arthur's England—shifts back and forth throughout the film.

FROG: ". . . perfidious English mousedropping hoarders . . . how you say: 'Begorrah!'"—In this instance the French sentry (Cleese) has become a "Frog," a pejorative term for the French popularized during World War I, though in their first appearance he was known simply as "Man." Harking back to a Python influence, in *The Goon Show*, Grytpype-Thynne (Sellers) calls the scheming Frenchman Moriarty (Milligan) a "frog-eater" in several episodes.[13] The term has shown up in *MPFC*, of course, as early as Ep. 10, when a "filthy bally froggie" is making love to Ken Biggles' (Chapman) objet d'amour, Vera (Jones). There is also a small group of flag-waving "froggies" waiting at the terminus of a Cross-Channel Jump in this same episode. Later in the "*Prejudice*" episode (and game show; Ep. 37), "Froggies" are lumped in with "Nigs," "Eyeties," and "Chinks," among several other demeaning terms.

"Begorrah"[14] is the oft-mimicked Anglo-Irish version of "By God," heard in many Irish impersonations of wildly varying quality. A nationwide advertising campaign for Irish tourism in 1965 included "A Short Tall Story" of the "lies" Londoners may have heard about Ireland, which concluded with: "Begob, sure, and it's another wee drop of the hard stuff I'll be after taking, begorrah!' It's all lies! Come on over and see for yourself."[15] Five years later the BBC's *Me Mammy* series "bubbles with stage Irishisms" according to a contemporary review in the *Times*, with songs like "Sodom and Begorrah" an example of the overtly obvious Irish witticisms.[16] The hoary jokes weren't lost on this television critic, and so oft-used and broadcast any alert Frenchman could have heard these gems, as well. But the recognizability of the joke is also important here:

> But somehow it always fails. There seems nothing to it beyond the natural charm of the crude jests. What the comedy lacks is any real daring. It is too safe. It is well trod ground and ultimately cosy in spite of the bogus viciousness and sham irreverence.

> No doubt the old jokes make a lot of people feel good, but it is a reactionary, after dinner conservative laughter which comes from this gummy humour that gives only the superficial appearance of bite but has not a tooth in its head.[17]

The significance of such "affectionate nostalgia"[18] has been discussed in relation to the Pythons, as they mine their collective, treasured pasts for odds and ends that often include insults and thrice-told jokes, warmed-over caricatures and stereotypes, despised and still fondly remembered people of all stripes. This is how a nasty Frenchman can (and even should) bar the way for Arthur and England as they reach for the Grail. Building on Heidegger's claim that essence and existence *could* supplant any potential for boredom, the Pythons can create their contrarian world:

> Well, in the twentieth century—and especially in the Python world where "positive value and real content" are replaced with a postmodern pastiche of nostalgia and cultural malaise and television-encouraged consumerism—the simple joy of "mere existence" is *not* enough, and the Python character (and narrative) tends to be adaptative and elusive, to become and become and become, constantly undercutting and reinventing itself. (*MPFC: UC*, 1.298)

In this world, Arthur cannot achieve the Grail, and an ignominious arrest and detention is quite fitting, even expected and satisfying.

ARTHUR: "How dare you profane this place with your presence!"—In his admonishing letter to Æthelbald discussed earlier, St. Boniface particularly condemned several kings'[19] philanderings with likely willing nuns, denouncing the trysts, of course, but also mentioning that the monasteries themselves were being debauched by such wanton sinfulness, and that God would have His justice. The Grail Castle is, in many sources, a place where only the incorrupt can *visit*, but dwelling is another problem entirely. In the *History of the Holy Grail* (part of the *Lancelot-Grail*) Josephus dies and possession of the Grail falls to Alain. One of Alain's converts, Alphasan, builds a stronghold for the Grail, then sleeps at the castle. In a vision Alphasan is told of his mistake:

> King, no man should lie in this palace—neither you nor anyone else—for scarcely could any man, through a good life, be worthy of remaining in the place where the Holy Vessel was honoured as you saw. You did a very foolhardy thing in coming to sleep here; Our Lord wants vengeance taken. (*THG*, 71)

Alphasan is then wounded in the thigh (a very common wound in these romances), "as a warning that no one save those who will achieve the Grail should attempt to stay in the Palace of Adventures" (71).

In this speech Arthur is also echoing Pope Urban II, who, in 1095, called on Christians everywhere to take up a crusade to save Jerusalem from the unholy disseisin of the infidel. Urban's impassioned rhetoric is recognizable in Arthur's verbiage, as the pontiff calls the in situ invaders "a race from the kingdom of the Persians, an accursed race, a race wholly alienated from God"; they are "not steadfast with God" as they "invaded the lands of those Christians" with "pillage and fire," destroying "the altars, after having defiled them with their uncleanness":

> Let the holy sepulcher of our Lord and Saviour, which is possessed by the unclean nations, especially arouse you, and the holy places which are now treated with ignominy and irreverently polluted with the filth of the unclean. . .wrest that land from the wicked race, and subject it to yourselves. (*HBMA*, 210–11)

The pope promises temporal and spiritual booty from this venture, while the noble Arthur still seems to just want the Grail because the Lord desired it of him. When the invading Christian armies laid siege to and then entered the Holy City, according to Foucher of Chartres' contemporary *History of Jerusalem* (c. 1125), a slaughter ensued: "Not a single life was spared" (*HBMA*, 211). It's hard to know what Arthur would have done if he'd actually made it into the Grail Castle and found the Grail.

ARTHUR: "... to which God himself has guided us"—In the minds of medieval men this looming failure can't be assigned to Arthur or even the interloping Frenchmen, but Providence, according to Morris. Arthur has invoked God's will and admonition from the beginning of this quest—when he defended his ascension "by Divine Providence" to the skeptical Dennis and Old Woman, and subsequently thanked the Lord (on bended knee) for his victory over the Black Knight, for guiding them to the Grail Castle island, etc.—so his defeat here at the Grail Castle must be the will of God. Morris writes that *if* High King of Ireland Diarmait (d. 1072)

> had routed the combined armies of the north and west, and with them the greatest of the monks, then the authority of the king of all Ireland would have been firmly vindicated, the independence of provincial kings and lesser dynasts curbed, the political power of the monks broken. When he failed, it was not one king who fell, but the monarchy itself. In an age when all of Europe saw the hand of God in each earthly decision, victory could not be ascribed to . . . superior generalship. [Both sides] had . . . invoked God with conflicting prayers, and God had made a clear decision. (173)

Here the realities of the twentieth century intervene—when the police arrive and block the castle assault—and the medieval God who would have the Grail sought is put in his place, even denied, as the hand of civil, temporal authority covers the camera lens, and the film ends.

And invoking the hand of Providence isn't the purview of such knights alone, either. When William Caxton published Malory's work he was keen to credit both Malory and the Almighty:

> Wherefore, such as have late been drawn out briefly into English I have after the simple cunning that God hath sent to me, under the favour and correction of all noble lords and gentlemen, enprised to imprint a book of the noble histories of the said King Arthur, and of certain of his knights, after a copy unto me delivered, which copy Sir Thomas Malory did take out of certain books of French, and reduced it into English. (*LMD'A*, 1.5)

It was by "God's grace" that Caxton published the work, that Men could be enlightened by it, "and come unto everlasting bliss unto heaven" through its examples (1.6).

Lastly, it's clear that in the script as written there were to have been one or more additional knights around Arthur and Bedevere there on the island, since Arthur is to have turned "*to the KNIGHTS*" (perhaps just Galahad and Bedevere) after this speech, and told them to advance with him on the castle. As the film was completed on location, however, the number and even names of knights changed as the film required, and only Arthur and Bedevere survived the Bridge of Death. And given the fact that these scenes were actually shot in the first days of the location shoot, the balance of the knights were either dead (in the script) or just elsewhere, meaning Palin as Galahad, for example, or Cleese and Idle, simply weren't scheduled to be on set, yet.[20] By shooting these culminative scenes first, with only Arthur and Bedevere available, the Pythons' hands were tied as to just which knights survive the terrors of the quest.

FROG: "How you English say: I one more time, mac . . ."—He's careful to try and attempt a certain Englishness in his speech, using as many idioms as he can jumble together.

This version of "mac"—meaning an informal address to a male friend or even a stranger—seems to date from about World War I,[21] and is perhaps even a nod toward the influential W. E. Johns Biggles character and world, which the Pythons reference a number of times in *MPFC*.[22]

Syntactically, this sequence of the Frenchman's cursings is much more convoluted than the first iteration, as if he's regressed in his English skills since he was last seen onscreen. Phrases like "Yes, depart a lot at this time, and cut the approaching any more" are more reminiscent of the African Native (Jones) in *MPFC* Ep. 29, who has not only lost his page in the script, but is having trouble with his syntax:

> Native: *(speaking the lines over to himself)* "Come on, you dogs, we have far to go. We must lose no time." *(speaks lines with eyes shut)* "Come on, you dogs, we have far to go. We must lose no time.". . ."Come on you dogs." *(he tosses the script, starts to push them roughly)* Come on you dogs, we have time to lose, this has gone too far! ("The Lost World of Roiurama"; audio transcription)

In fact, Cleese's mangled syntax here is almost closer to his earnest but befuddled Hungarian in Ep. 25, whose phrasebook has been maliciously ("My hovercraft is full of eels") mistranslated.

FROG: ". . . you brightly-coloured, mealy-templed, cranberry-smelling, electric donkey-bottom biters"—Some of the Frog's more colorful aspersions don't survive into the finished film. There were likely several versions of each of these invective-laced scenes recorded at the time, each slightly different from the other, with the best delivery chosen in editing.

ARTHUR: ". . . in the name of our Lord"—Despite yet another unexpected hurdle, Arthur is still holding to his Old Testament-type courage, like David, unafraid in the face of the cursing Goliath: "Thou comest to me with a sword, and with a spear, and with a shield: but I come to thee in the name of the Lord of hosts, the God of the armies of Israel, whom thou hast defied" (1 Sam. 17:45). Arthur will gather his "armies" and attack.

Arthur has been flogging his version of muscular Christianity since God first appeared earlier in the film. Just a few lines earlier he has called to the French in the name of "the Knights of Camelot," then invoking God's support and guidance for his knightly adventures. That failing, he switches to invoking God directly, yoking the Almighty's will with his knights' physical or athletic prowess, just as had been done before, in the Age of Empire:

> We wish to see our sons walking in the old paths with a few stumbling blocks removed. To the philosopher of any nation (not excluding our own) the spectacle of the Englishman going through the world with rifle in one hand and Bible in the other is laughable; but to Englishmen who are neither logicians nor idealists it is not. We wish to see his skill with the one and his faith in the other strengthened and increased. If asked what our muscular Christianity has done, we point to the British Empire. (Minchin, *Our Public Schools*, 113)

Muscular Christianity's partner here is not cricket or rugby football, but the sword and the knowledge of the will of God. If *MPHG* is concerned at least partly with current events including the state of the fading Empire, as has been argued, then the Pauline admonition (in Philippians, 1 Corinthians, etc.) for volitional Christianity applies—armed with God's will and a sword, Arthur quests onward against these recalcitrant frogs.

Also, the image of Arthur entering the fray of battle with God on his side isn't new. The *Annales Cambriae* (c. 955) references Arthur carrying the cross of Christ on his shoulders into battle, if the Welsh translations can be trusted. The image created thanks to this description is a burdensome one, even laughable, since Arthur would have to have been a truly magnificent warrior to be able to fight with a large cross weighing him down. Perhaps, as Thomas Jones point out, this is the kind of detail that, if taken at face value, positions Arthur as a historical character with legendary skills and feats—a kind of transitional Arthur, or an Arthur who can have a foot in both realms ("Early Evolution of the Legend of Arthur," 6). (The *HB* mentions Arthur carrying the image of the Virgin Mary on his shoulder—an equally tricky feat.) Other versions have posited that a mistranslation of the Old Welsh *scuit* ("shield") for the Old Welsh *scuid* ("shoulder") can account for the confusion, meaning Arthur carries an image of Christ's cross on his shield (5). In the "It is I, Arthur" entry in scene 2 the significance of shields as means of identification is discussed in more detail. This type of misunderstanding and/or visual incongruity has fueled the Pythons' comedy since before *Flying Circus*.

Guided or not, God-assisted or not, fated or not, the force that Arthur gathers to assault the castle and rescue the Grail cannot overcome the reality that the French represent and that appears finally in the form of swarming police officers, bringing "that which God himself" has commanded to an abrupt end.

ARTHUR: "If you do not, open these doors, we will take the castle by force"—Parzival tells his companions that "no man could ever win the Grail by force, except the one who is summoned there by God" (*THG*, 84). Since Arthur continues to believe that he has been called of God, he feels justified in storming the castle, that such an assault can be effective given God's grace, and so quickly gathers his forces for the assault.

ARTHUR: "In the name of God . . ."—This phrase—sometimes altered to "In the name of Jesus Christ"—appears dozens of times and throughout *Le Morte D'Arthur*, most often uttered by knights as they swear to a course of action or affirm their support of Arthur and the nobility of the quest. The second part of the interrupted phrase—"and the glory of our . . ."— and specifically the word "glory," is one that does *not* appear in Malory, "glory" being reserved for the phrase "vain glory" throughout *LMD'A*, and always as a cautionary, negative usage.

human ordure—(PSC) Arthur and Bedevere are hit by "*a bucket of slops*," according to the script after the first dumping (*MPHGB*, 85). This is the twisted version of the unction or anointing of kings, not unlike Jesus being crowned with thorns instead of gold. Even the Old French word from which "anoint" emerged, *enoint*, means "smeared on," essentially. Anointing was a crucial part (to the Church) of the king's coronation ceremony in the medieval Frankish kingdom in Gaul, and also had a place in eighth- through tenth-century coronations in Britain (Sawyer, 186). Ecgfrith (d. 796), for example, had been *consecrated*[23] king of Mercia at the request of his father, Offa, in 787, but wouldn't rule as king until 796, when his father died in July (270). By December 796, Ecgfrith was dead, as well. When Edward II was in custody and on his way to Berkeley Castle, Geoffrey le Baker reports that guards along the way spoke to the deposed king mockingly, and more: "They led the exemplar of endurance through the granges belonging to the castle of Bristol, and there that villain Gournay made a crown of hay and, daring to touch the Lord's anointed, put it on the head which once had been consecrated with holy oil, while the knights mocked him" (le Baker, *Chronicle*, 29–30). Arthur likely doesn't appreciate the humor in this sort of "Feast of Fools" activity, and whether he's being consecrated, anointed, or just pranked, the smelly end result is the same.[24]

Arthur and Bedevere get off easier here, though, given the other possibilities for things to be dropped from castle walls. Castles under siege could use firepots (filled with flaming pitch, Greek fire), "along with javelins, stones, boiling oil, and what can only be described as boiling porridge, a scalding oatmeal mush, which stuck to besiegers' skins" (Hallam, 203). Stinking is better than being crushed or burned.

The leaders of contemporary Britain didn't have to endure excremental assaults (except by verbal and printed association), but Heath was famously attacked in January 1972 by a young woman in Brussels as he arrived to triumphantly sign the documents for entry into the EEC

(Common Market). A cartoon by Michael Cummings the following day fittingly suggested that the "ghost of de Gaulle" threw the ink at Heath as he signed the document.[25] Heath himself would later write that this symbolic attack "shattered" him, coming as he prepared to sign the singular political and economic agreement of his ministership.[26] Arthur's moment at the gates of the Grail Castle is equally ruined by his French antagonists. (The Pythons used footage of the Heath assault in Ep. 39 of *MPFC*.[27]) Another cartoon printed the same day, penned by Paul Rigby, depicts ink bottles (hundreds of them) being thrown at Heath by the unemployed and the miners' unions.[28] And in another (by Emmwood), Heath's ink stains are labeled with his party's current crop of headaches, including the unemployed, Ulster (Northern Ireland), pollution, the coal strike, and Malta (on its way to becoming a republic).[29]

Two other cartoons illustrate similar attacks, but with manure. One depicts a farmer and tractor—along with numerous protestors—delivering a load of manure to the Minister of Agriculture's office windows, representing angry members of the National Farmers Union (NFU) who had been demanding higher farm subsidies.[30] Another—from the *Daily Sketch*—shows a farmer using a "Lilley MK II Muckspreader" to fire a stream of manure into the window of No. 10 Downing Street.[31] In December 1969, farmers and farm equipment from Devon brought Newton Abbot to a standstill in protest over weak prices and failing NFU support.[32]

FROG: ". . . fire arrows into the tops of your heads and make castanets out of your testicles . . ."—The second half of this insult was one of the lines the BBFC representative (Tony Kerpel) suggested for removal, along with a number of other curse-words and crudities, if the Pythons wanted to achieve an "A" rating. The Pythons' respondent Terry Mosaic suggested changes, and the film did eventually qualify for an "A" certificate.

ARTHUR: "Walk away. Just ignore him"—Geoffrey le Baker wrote that even during the worst verbal and physical cuffings (on his way to an ignominious death) "Edward [II] was a model of patience amongst a rabble of hell-hounds on that journey to Berkeley," and "ever patient in the face of his misfortunes." To the sympathetic le Baker, Edward was a pillar of long suffering (Hallam, 217–18). His son Edward III's attempted all-out assault on France in 1338–1339 was also an ill-fated venture. The king was forced to borrow money from Italian banks and his nobles to keep the campaigns on the move, and after wintering in Antwerp he tried to set out again, but diminishing support made every action a challenge:

> In 1339 Edward was ready to move, but his expensive allies were not anxious to help and he got no further than a small campaign on the French border in the area of Cambrai. After returning to England in February 1340 to borrow more money, he went back to take advantage of the strongly pro-English feeling in Flanders. . . . [O]n the way back he won his only great victory in this period of the war, the shattering defeat of the French fleet, which had sought to prevent his return, in the battle of Sluys off the coast of Flanders. Once he was back on the Continent he could still get no further than trivial operations of the French border. He returned to England finally in November after concluding the Truce of Espléchin that autumn. . . . The immediate reason for the King's return was lack of money. (Holmes, 120)

It's easy to imagine the tired and exasperated Edward—like Arthur and Bedevere—stepping off his boat and trudging wearily through tidal mud, back from the Continent with little to show for it. According to Holmes, Edward learned from this lesson that "direct raiding into France from the coast"—as opposed to marching through the Low Countries or Germany first—and defeating and holding Brittany (in 1342) as an "important English foothold in France" made subsequent raids more successful (121). Building on these inroads, Edward would have his great success at Crécy in 1346. Arthur, instead, goes from asking politely to demanding to an attempted full-scale assault—none of these pan out.

If Arthur had followed his own "walk away" advice here in response to this *brute de l'école* he may yet have triumphed in the Grail quest, or at least kept himself in the running. But given the fact that the romance sources generally warn against the use of violence in securing the Grail, and that more often than not the Grail itself (with God's blessing) summons the worthy quester, the Pythons' Arthur likely surrenders his chance when he summons an army. The helpful hermit Trevrizent in *Parzival* tells Parzival as much: "[I]t has never been customary that anyone, at any time, might gain the grail by fighting. I would gladly have deflected you from that purpose" (*THG*, 186). Critics including Jessie L. Weston have written about the seeming contradiction in Parzival's actions—the claim that force will not avail him of the Grail (Book IX), while later in the work (Book XVI) Wolfram seems to counter that same claim. The result sounds like the special position Arthur guilelessly assumes he's occupied all along:

> By the time Wolfram had reached the end of the poem, he found that his interpretation had dominated that of Kiot,[33] he had practically made Parzival do that which Trevrizent says is impossible ("Wouldst thou force thy God with thine anger?" Book IX. p. 267. "Though by thy wrath hast won blessing"), and this passage seems to be an attempt to harmonise these two conflicting ideas. It is not easy of interpretation, for on the face of it, while Trevrezent is asserting the unchanging nature of God's decrees, as illustrated by the history of the rebel angels, he is also implying that Parzival himself has been the object of special and peculiar favor on the part of the Deity, and that the foreordained course of events has in this case at least been modified. (222)

Perhaps Arthur has been "the object of special and peculiar favour" on God's part—certainly he was chosen to represent God on the Grail quest (we were witness to that), and from that Arthur could naturally assume that God's grace would blaze the trail before him—just as the Almighty's Ark of the Covenant had led and protected the children of Israel. But when this cleared path became obstructed, Arthur was always willing to become the muscular Christian and draw his sword for the Lord. The introduction of such tensions fuels von Eschenbach's version of the Grail legend, a version that Barber describes as "an altogether bolder concept of the chivalric world than anything that has gone before," a boldness that wouldn't stand up to the filliping postmodernism of the Pythons:

> Wolfram . . . gives a picture of the development of the individual within society: Parzival's rebellion against God is also an unconscious rebellion against his destiny as Grail king, and a betrayal of the society to which he and his family belong. For Wolfram is deeply conscious of dynasty and heredity: Parzival can only find himself by achieving the task which has been laid before him from birth. If he can recognize his own true nature and be reconciled to God through confession and penance, he will come again to the Grail . . . and heaven and earth will move once more in harmony. (Barber, 186)

Arthur is not allowed to learn these lessons (he pulls his sword at every confrontation), nor does God reappear to prod Arthur along with words of support or caution—they are on their own after His initial appearance. Arthur is not able make use of "confession or penance"—he may not even know he needs to—and thus he will not, *cannot* achieve the Grail, at least according to the romance authors' terms.

A small hail of chickens, watercress, badgers and mattresses follows them—(PSC) As Arthur and Bedevere beat a dignified retreat, they were to have been barraged by the above menagerie. This continued assault appears cursorily in the finished film—plant material and some clothing seem to go over the battlements, along with bent-arm "up yours" gestures and more "raspberries"—the scope of the barrage was likely reduced after the unscripted sheep catapult at the beginning of the scene.

As for the menagerie, most are fairly familiar for the Pythons. In the second *MPFZ* episode, prospectors pan for chickens in chicken-rich mountain streams, miners dig for chickens, and the "Hühnerminen von Nord-Dakota" (Chicken Mines of North Dakota) are described thanks to a handy stratigraphic diagram. Eventually, an animated oil derrick bursts with chickens, and these treasured "hen resources" rain down.[34] A wooden badger would have been Bedevere's next idea for sneaking into the French-held castle earlier, and "mattress" was the word to be avoided in Ep. 8 of *MPFC*. When written, the list of catapulted items was likely just a suggested laundry list that could be filled out on location, and with whatever might be handy.

FROG: "... illegitimate-faced bugger-folk"—"Bugger" has a long and naughty history, as far as words go, as explained in an entry for *MPFC* Ep. 15, for the conclusion of "The Spanish Inquisition" sketch:

> A fascinating possibility arises from the inclusion of this invective, beyond its sodomitical context: "Bugger" was actually a specialized term used to describe an Albigenses heretic in the fourteenth century (*OED*). The Albigenses felt that marriage and procreation were grievous sins, meaning sexual intercourse where fertilization is impossible might be more acceptable—buggery, then, becoming the sin of choice, and one that might be on the lips of the Church's Inquisitors.
>
> ... Over and over again in the late 1950s the term "bugger" and its variations ("buggery," "bogger," etc.) were consistently penciled through by the British Board of Film Censors (BBFC) and the Master of Revels for deletion from films and plays, respectively. As late as 1966 and the "British New Wave" film *Saturday Night and Sunday Morning* and the swinging 1960s film *Alfie* (and subsequent staged plays for each) the term was being elided, no matter the eventual rating or venue. It wouldn't be until *Up the Junction* (1967) that the BBFC would allow the use of the term "bugger" in British film and, somewhat coincidentally, full frontal nudity the following year in Lindsay Anderson's *If.* (*MPFC: UC*, 1.242)

FROG: "... you ain't heard nothing yet ..."—Famous line spoken by the inimitable Al Jolson in one of the few sync-sound sequences of *The Jazz Singer* (1927), the first feature film "talkie." In Coffee Dan's club, Jolson has just finished singing "Dirty Hands, Dirty Face," and during the applause he announces his next number, "Toot, Toot, Tootsie," promising the audience a singular performance. *The Jazz Singer* reappeared regularly on British television between 1970 and 1974, and in October 1972 a significant biography of Jolson was reviewed positively in major British newspapers.[35] Even closer to the production of *MPHG*, the National Film Theatre sponsored a sixty-feature program of WB films, including *The Jazz Singer* and *The Adventures of Robin Hood*, the latter being discussed earlier as the "swashbuckler" the Pythons referenced for Launcelot's assault on Swamp Castle.

FROG: "... A. King Esquire"—The French sentry drifts between modes of address for this English king before him, from "silly King" to "so-called Arthur King"[36] and "Monsieur Arthur King," though "Esquire" at least sounds complimentary. It's also possible that the Frog is using the term "esquire" in its proper form, meaning one who is of noble birth but who ranks below a knight, and certainly below a king. Drawn from the Latin *"armiger,"* meaning "armor bearer," "Esquire" puts a fine point on it since Arthur does bear arms, but *not* for someone else ranked above him. Both the Goons and the Pythons (and Benny Hill, and so on) had employed over-the-top accents as easy identifiers of foreign-ness. Shakespeare would lampoon the French in similar ways in the nationalistic *Henry V*, betraying

Katherine's "foreigner-ness" by skewing her English, reducing her lines, often, to nearly baby-talk. She asks: "Is it possible dat I sould love de ennemie of / France?" (5.2.169–70). After Henry gives her his much longer response, she counters with "I cannot tell wat is dat" (5.2.177). Her last words in butchered English (she does have one more speech in French) come soon after: "Den it sall also content me" (5.2.250). Her woman Alice is painted with the same brush, and though Alice is able to translate Henry's English into French, her accented English is nearly indecipherable; "Oui , dat de tongeus of de mans is be full of deceits: dat is de Princess" (5.2.119–20). . . . The primacy of the English language is trumpeted here, as is English-ness. Marston performs the same lingual gymnastics in regard to a foreigner in *The Dutch Courtesan*, wherein Francischina can be heard to utter: "O mine aderliver love, vat sall me do to re- / quit dis your mush affection?" (1.2.87–88). Francischina's accent also seems to come and go as the play moves on, much like Python's characters can massacre some words and leave others alone. (*MPFC: UC*, 1.23)

CUT BACK TO ARTHUR still walking away—The forlorn shot of Arthur and Bedevere trudging out of the loch, bespattered with both mud and ordure, isn't specifically mentioned in the script, likely because the script only fleetingly allows for the water between the castle and Arthur (mentioning the boat, for example). Doyle mentions that they had shot all day at this site, and that this coming ashore scene was the final shot of the day as the light (it "stays longer in Scotland") was fading. He goes on to say that the grim resolve on Arthur's face is actually Chapman being "really fed up" by this time—tired, cold, wet, and smelly after a long, long day.[37] They still had a one-hundred-mile drive ahead of them, too.

CUT TO enormous army forming up—(PSC) This is the extreme long shot seen earlier when Dingo, Zoot's sister, going on too long during her scene with Galahad in the Castle Anthrax, is encouraged to "Get on with it!" At that earlier moment this scene would have been completely out of place and without textual foundation—and knowing the Pythons, there was no promise to the audience that the unfamiliar scene of armies would ever be located, narratively.

Trebuchets . . .—(PSC) The script mentions both "trebuchets" and "siege towers" being on this battlefield, but those were clearly wished for rather than realized, given the film's budget constraints.[38] They would have to have been built on location, not unlike the Wooden Rabbit, the fake castle wall the French sentries leaned over, the scale model of Camelot (a painted plywood façade), the boat, etc. A trebuchet uses a counterweight to create the momentum necessary to hurl a projectile in a sling, as opposed to a catapult's tightly twisted ropes, creating a torsion effect.[39] A working catapult was likely implied earlier (via a "boing" sound effect[40]), when the aggressively lowing cow came "flying over the battlements" and squashed Galahad's page in the "Taunting by Frenchmen" scene. Both trebuchets and siege towers were regular medieval battlefield materiel, especially when castles or similar fortifications were being assaulted. The Pythons may have been thinking of King Richard's trebuchet-assisted assault on the city of Acre as part of the Crusades in 1191, or Edward Longshanks's trebuchet assault at Caerlaverock, or his siege on nearby Stirling Castle, where Edward used thirteen of the machines (Prestwich, 239). Finally, Edward's "Warwolf" siege engine (thought to have been an especially large trebuchet) must have been frightening indeed, since "it terrified the Scots who offered surrender rather than submit to its attentions. Edward, however, did not let them leave the castle for 24 hours, so that the 'Warwolf' could be tried out."[41]

One of the Pythons' admitted sources for the film, Montgomery's *A History of Warfare*, discusses both siege towers and trebuchets and their usage across time. Of course, trebuchets *and* siege towers would have been rather less effective against a castle like Stalker, since it sits on a small, sloping island surrounded by water, necessitating some kind of amphibious assault. In the end, the army Arthur led near Stirling would have been charging across a large, sloping field towards ultimately, the camera and crew.

A battlefield trebuchet would also have represented yet another slightly anachronistic element, since it is dated in the west to about the twelfth century, though the Pythons' telescoping of time and history continues to be the rule of thumb—a trebuchet or a police car aren't so terribly out of place. Catapult-like machines continued to be used in warfare, including during World War I (for hurling grenades and even gas bombs from trench to trench), and well beyond as they were soon adapted for use on aircraft carriers. A visual example of a battlefield trebuchet was available for the Pythons in Randall's *IMGM*, where one of the scenes features hares attacking a castle; the hares are armed with a hatchet, a siege ladder, a crossbow, and a large, loaded trebuchet.[42] The castle is being defended by soldiers who are men.

PIKEMEN . . .—(PSC) Soldiers armed with long, wooden shafts topped with a steel head, according to Montgomery, again. Montgomery characterizes the pike as one of the key weapons, along with the longbow and field artillery, which ended the effective days of heavy cavalry in warfare (*HW*, 195, 209). Given this description, the pikemen would have been a poor choice by a field commander for a *castle* siege; Arthur and especially Launcelot had earlier attacked a stone castle's walls with just their swords, to no effect. Unlike the trebuchets and siege towers, pikes and pikemen were easier to come by, the latter filled out by willing University of Stirling volunteers (see below, and appendix B).

These battle prep sequences are borrowed from Polanski's *Macbeth*, as well. On the wet and muddy expanse of an early battle sequence can be seen small tents, piles of spears, a catapult, etc. The Grail Castle assault sequence is likely a scene that Jones was instrumental in prepping—the attention to medieval battlefield details, including tentpoles and coverings, working forges and weapon sharpeners (neither mentioned in the scenic details) is evident.

Traditional army build-up shots—(PSC) This is the scene that most Stirling undergrads remember filming. Extras in these scenes include the following: Iain Banks, Steve Bannell, Duncan MacAulay, Jim McIver, Nick Rowe, Alastair Scott, and Russell Walker. Some of these student participants' memories of the filming are gratefully included in appendix B.

The final shot in this sequence features a knight putting "his" helmet on his head. The knight was actually Valerie Charlton, Julian Doyle's then-girlfriend, and the shot was made by Doyle at their apartment at 3 Rona Road, London, just near Hampstead Heath, and not far from Gilliam's home.[43] Again, as with some of the other insert shots made in Doyle's backyard (the flying cow, the flying miniature Wooden Rabbit), shooting on the balcony provided a "plain sky" background, free from trees and buildings.

serried ranks . . .—(PSC) Likely borrowed from both the Montgomery book, where various rank formations are discussed (e.g., pages 60, 232, and 362), as well as multiple film sources, including Kurosawa's *Macbeth* adaptation *Throne of Blood*. As the forces of Scotland and England marshal toward the end of Polanski's *Macbeth*, these same shots—side angles on marching pikemen—are the shots of choice.

ARTHUR: "Who are they?"—In the script as finalized Arthur doesn't know where this enormous army comes from; he has to hear it from Bedevere that they're "just some friends" (*MPHGB*, 87). Arthur and Bedevere have been taking turns throughout as they display knowledge or ignorance of the world they're traipsing through. For example, Arthur didn't know about the efficaciousness of sheep's bladders, but he did somehow understand the dangers of the Knights Who Say Ni, as well as the silliness of Camelot; neither knew anything of the Holy Hand Grenade, but Arthur knew how the Bridge of Death operated, and so on. In the film as shot, both Arthur and Bedevere seem fascinated by the assembled army, Bedevere even awed, but neither bothers to ask where the "serried ranks" might have come from—they just prepare to charge the castle, to liberate the Grail from the "Frogs."

ARTHUR: "French persons! Today the blood of many valiant knights . . ."—The political and dynastic histories of England and France had been intertwined since William arrived, defeating Harold in 1066—well known "English" kings like Henry II, Richard I, and John were actually Frenchmen in every way.[44] The iconic Richard, once he came of age, was reported to have visited England only twice, "once for his coronation, and once to raise money," and disliked England so much that he is said to have offered to sell London if only there were a buyer.[45] To the Arthur of the fifth and sixth centuries, or even of the tenth century, as the film's titles tell us, the French would have been invaders not unlike the unwelcome Saxons the mythical Arthur had so soundly defeated at Badon Hill; by the thirteenth century, the intermarrying with the Normans would have changed perceptions dramatically.

This sincerely emotional pronouncement is an echo of a passage from Geoffrey's *HKB*. The Saxons had promised to leave Britain—without honor, tails between their legs—after Arthur defeated them, taking everything from them except their boats. Partway home the Saxons "repented them of the covenant" they'd made and doubled back, invading at Totnes and killing everyone in their way as they moved toward Bath (186). "When word of this was brought unto the King, astonied beyond measure at their wicked daring, he bade judgment be done," and executed all his Saxon hostages and immediately set off for Somerset, proclaiming upon arrival:

> For that these Saxons, of most impious and hateful name, have disdained to keep faith with me, I, keeping faith unto my God, will endeavor me this day to revenge upon them the blood of my countrymen. To arms, therefore, ye warriors, to arms, and fall upon yonder traitors like men, for, of a certainty, by Christ's succor, we cannot fail of victory! (187)

Arthur and his armies carried the day, unlike the Pythons' Arthur, who sees his battle charge end in an arrest.

The mighty ARMY charges—This charge down the hill was done again and again. The extras remember anywhere from seven to thirty tiring runs; extra Nick Rowe remembers being told to yell "Betty Marsden" as they charged.[46]

...a couple of police cars roar around in front...—The policeman driving this car is production manager (and special effects cameraman) Julian Doyle, who much later assists Jones and Palin as they reenact the arrest with local children in *The Quest for the Holy Grail Locations*. At this point (very early in the shoot), the assembled university hordes are not part of the shot, just a handful of hastily costumed extras and locals on the shores of the loch. Doyle remembers that this scene was not scheduled until later in the shoot, and that codirector Jones surprised him with the request to shoot at Castle Stalker in the film's first days.[47] Doyle had scheduled these costumes and weapons for the following week and at Doune, not Stalker, so he hurriedly had to "organise [two] lorries and drivers to bring them up—[calling] on a [2p] pay phone in the street by the Loch."[48]

This intersection of the world of the medieval or fantasy film and the real world isn't terribly startling, since we've been given glimpses of the Historian, his wife, police officers and their car, and we've very recently seen Launcelot being frisked and arrested—and it isn't just a Python conceit, either. Luis Buñuel's *Simon of the Desert* (1965) made its debut in London in April 1969 at the Academy Cinema Two, and it also later played at the Institute of the Contemporary Arts Mall Cinema (on the Mall) in October 1974.[49] Simon's temptress eventually transports him from his ascetic life atop a lonely pillar in the desert to a modern NYC dance hall—the transition of a passing jet making the sound bridge—where the kids are dancing the "last dance." Simon was a fifth-century saint.

TWO POLICEWOMEN and the HISTORIAN'S WIFE—(PSC) The script calls for policewomen to emerge from the cars, but there are none. There are several male police officers, the Inspector ("Inspector End of Film"), and the Historian's Wife. There are a handful of women in armor and costumes in the bewildered army, however.

HISTORIAN'S WIFE: "Yes they're the ones, I'm sure!"—In a fitting end to this unsuccessful quest, the Historian's Wife has made an inaccurate identification—neither Arthur or Bedevere (or any of the knights we know) rode by on a horse earlier and killed the Famous Historian. As far as we know she's never laid eyes on Arthur and his quest group. The offending knight was dressed *like* Arthur and company, so guilt by association clearly applies. Remember that the witch earlier was so accused because she "looks like one," and Arthur was likely a king because he was so clean—appearances matter in this world.

INSPECTOR END OF FILM: "Grab 'em!"—The aptly-named inspector is yet another borrow from the *MPFC* world. In Ep. 25, "Inspector Tiger" enters the living room of the "Agatha Christie Sketch":

> Almost certainly at least a reference to Scotland Yard inspectors in general (as visible authority figures), but may also be a nod to the many television and film iterations of "Inspector" and "Detective Inspector." For instance, see the cast of the 1962 British TV series *Z Cars*. . . . In the 1947 film *Whispering City* there is an "Inspector Renaud" (loosely translating to "fox"), giving rise to "Inspector Fox." (The instance of "Renaud" as an early variation of "Reynard" is taken from the fourteenth-century epic poem *Sir Gawain and the Green Knight*. See the *OED*.) Also, veteran English actor Michael Bates (*Patton*; *Battle of Britain*) played Inspector Mole in the 1964 TV series *Cluff*. . . . In Ep. 29, finally, Cleese plays Inspector Leopard (who has changed his name from "Panther"), and Idle plays both Inspector Thompson's Gazelle and Inspector Baboon, and Chapman plays Inspector Fox. (*MPFC: UC*, 1.176)

There has also been an Inspector Dim of the Yard (Ep. 3), and a series of inspectors making arrests of fraud filmmakers in Ep. 29, including Inspector Flying Fox of the Yard. "Inspector End of the Film" is only named as such in the script—the name is never spoken—meaning this is also another in-joke for the Pythons themselves.

The POLICE grab ARTHUR and bundle him into the maria—(PSC) This is precisely the way the Goons concluded their one Arthurian episode, "The Spectre of Tintagel" (1 November 1956):

> Seagoon (Secombe): Golden platters, this must be the lost treasure of Tintagel, revealed to me as a sign that I am a direct descendant of King Arthur.
>
> Grytpype (Sellers): Three months at the Palladium and he thinks he's the King of England.
>
> Seagoon: What what what what what what what what?
>
> *FX: Knocking on door. Door opens.*
>
> Inspector (Sellers): Oh, er, good evening sir.
>
> Seagoon: Good evening Inspector.
>
> Inspector: Are you the owner of this manor?
>
> Seagoon: That is correct.
>
> Inspector: I see. Then perhaps you could explain this gold plate here?
>
> Seagoon: Certainly. It's mine.
>
> Inspector: The stolen regimental plate of the Second Pune Horse is yours?
>
> Seagoon: Yes! By Royal Prerogative.
>
> Inspector: Royal Prerogative? I see, what did you say your name was, sir?

Seagoon: King Arthur.

Inspector: King Arthur?

Seagoon: That's right, yes.

Inspector: Well, you'd better come with me Your Majesty, there's a . . . plain van outside that all our King Arthurs and three Napoleons have ridden in.

Seagoon: Ha ha ha, that's good enough for me.

Inspector: Yes.

Seagoon: Of course, this means the end of the House of Windsor, of course.

Inspector: Yes.

Seagoon: Prince Philip will have to go you know.

Inspector: You come with me Your Majesty, it'll all be all right in a moment, you just come outside.

Seagoon: I think I'll make you Prime Minister, you've got the right build, you know.

Inspector: That's very kind of you, Your Majesty, just follow me outside.

Seagoon: Fancy Ireland? Wales is doing nothing at the moment . . .

FX: Door closes. Police van drives rapidly away, bell ringing, fades away. (audio transcription)

INSPECTOR END OF THE FILM: "Move along. There's nothing to see! Keep moving!"—The crowd (and the audience) are being treated as if they've just been witnessing some public nuisance or disturbing the peace arrest—like The Beatles performing on the roof of Abbey Records in 1970—and not as a rampaging army, armed to the teeth, which they still are. In Spike Milligan's play and film *The Bed Sitting Room*, the helpful Metropolitan police (all two of them) float around the devastation of postapocalyptic England calmly urging the handful of survivors to "move along," since staying in one place would give the enemy a chance at targeting the few remaining Britons. The student demonstrations in London and around, for example, the London School of Economics in 1968 and 1971 were often handled this way to begin with, though some demonstrations, like the Park Lane anti–Vietnam War protest in July 1968 escalated to vandalism and violence. Police reaction to the rampage was described in comically serious tones: "Police reinforcements gathered at the Hilton, and one or two batons were drawn."[50] Ignoring the swords and pikes, the policeman in *MPHG* reaches for "an offensive weapon, that is"[51]—a shield—and takes it from one knight, just before clobbering the camera. In the running fight along Park Lane toward the Hilton Hotel in 1968, it was reported that the "offensive weapons" used by protestors included bottles, cans, and anything they could pull from the garbage bins along the street.

In medieval Britain it was expected that most males of "fighting age" would have had several offensive and defensive skill sets and tools. Archery had become a national sport during Edward I's reign, of course, preparing a nation for possible warfront service. English men and boys (excepting clergy) were to

> have been not only armed, but trained in the use of arms. Under Edward I's Statute of Westminster (created and modified before 1331), laymen between the ages of fifteen and sixty were bound to possess arms, ranging from the helmet, hauberk, and sword of the knight down to the poor man's bow, arrows, and knife. The object of this legislation was, of course, the defence of the realm and the maintenance of the peace. (McKisack, 203)

And while the constable in *MPHG* actually disarms a man bearing a shield, in Edward's time the constables commanded these local (hundred) forces, the *posse comitatus*, while the sheriff commanded groups of forces. These men being so disarmed by representatives of the crown must have been quite confused, given their knowledge of their king's martial demands.

These kinds of images—uniformed authority figures fighting for order with massed others—were ubiquitous in the 1960s and early 1970s. The Pythons had employed them in the "French Subtitled Film" sketch in Ep. 23; such images were on news broadcasts regularly in this postcolonial, civil rights, antiwar era. In 1972, for example, thousands protested and fought with police regularly in the streets of Cairo, Delhi, and the townships of Rhodesia, while in Northern Ireland the local government's attempts to ban processional marches led to even more demonstrative outbursts.[52] In late April 1974, just as the Pythons were starting location shooting for *Holy Grail*, the surging hooliganism in English football crested with the forced abandonment of a match at Old Trafford, where Manchester City led Manchester United 1–0. Mobs had repeatedly stormed the pitch, even before the match began, though the "police [had] managed to clear them off."[53] As the match progressed, however, the crowd began throwing "projectiles" at players and onto the pitch, and the match was abruptly stopped.

As the black maria drives away QUICK SHOT through window . . .—(PSC) This shot, where the other knights as well as the Soothsayer can be glimpsed in the back of the van, also under arrest, is not part of the finished film. The mention of the Soothsayer is crossed out in the script, as well. As filmed it's impossible to see if there's anyone else in the back of the police van, though it's likely that most of the other Pythons (and especially Cleese) were not on set for this day of running and shouting. The fact that the Soothsayer is crossed out might be due not to Gilliam's absence, but to the fact that he wanted to avoid the full makeup needed for this simple shot, so his character—like Launcelot, Robin, Galahad, Patsy, and others—simply disappear from the film.

He walks over to it and puts his hand over the lens—(PSC) It should be no surprise by this point that *Holy Grail* ends this way. It cannot end with Arthur achieving the Grail and successfully gathering his knights and power to Camelot—that narrative thread has been frayed for some time. It also cannot end at the level of the Middle Ages story, with, perhaps, Dennis achieving his goals of a workers' paradise; those worlds can only be in contention. And even the twentieth-century setting, since it has been acknowledged, must also end, since films by design have beginnings, middles, and ends. The conclusion of Kurosawa's *Seven Samurai* may have set the tone for many films to follow. There, following the final battle between the villagers and the bandits, and the loss of four of the seven samurai, the villagers are immediately back to work in the rice paddies, celebrating their victory but more importantly the coming growing season—they've already forgotten their ronin deliverers. The film ends quietly on a forlorn image of the four graves against the sky.

For *MPHG* this end moment is the ultimate acknowledgment of the artificiality of this medieval exercise, since cameras didn't record historical events as they happened; events had to be recreated for the cameras. The knights have tiptoed along this line between blissful unawareness and self-knowledge from the first frame of the film, with the knights themselves fairly caught up in the nobility of the quest, and the put upon underlings—like Patsy—free to at least murmur their worldly skepticism before being shushed. The *Goon Show* character Bluebottle operated in much this same way, nearly week-to-week acknowledging his place in the show's structure as tenuous and often lamenting the "deading" he was about to experience. This absolute recognition of the camera lens as window on a forbidden world has been with us since at least the 1920s, when in *One Week* the ur-surrealist comedic filmmaker Buster Keaton covers the camera lens with a hand as his onscreen wife reaches out of the tub for her dropped soap. There the *voyeuristic* aspects of the lens are acknowledged; in *Holy Grail* it is the recording of police activities better left unrecorded that prompts the action.

This is also a neat underscoring of many contemporary cultural critics' assessments of the decade itself. In 1980 Christopher Booker would describe the 1970s as the "most dramatic dead end in the history of mankind" (*The Seventies*, 253), and it seems Arthur and his knights have run smack into that unforgiving cul-de-sac.

Notes

1. According to Doyle, these scenes were not only recorded in the first days of shooting, the decision to come to Stalker as opposed to remaining in Killin and Glencoe was a last-minute one made without the production manager, and one that led to a challenging first few days. Doyle arrived in Scotland expecting the Glencoe and Killin scenes, and codirector Jones announced he wanted to shoot some of the battle scenes, as well: "I had no weapons or costumes for such an event," Doyle remembers. "These were ready to come up to Doune for the second week." They shot the Bridge of Death scenes on the first day, followed by the "walking and arriving at the boat" scenes, with Doyle scrambling to gather local people as the needed extras for the end of the battle sequence (Doyle e-mail, 28 November 2013).

2. One of the crossed-out scene descriptions may hint at the characters' seemingly arbitrary but controlled trajectory: "*As if bewitched, they find themselves drawing closer to the boat*" (*MPHGB*, 84). They cross the bridge and immediately begin to wander, having lost Launcelot, Robin, Gawain, and Galahad in the crossing. Arthur and Bedevere don't remind us or each other that they're looking for a castle, as per Brother Maynard's readings.

3. In the 1981 film *Time Bandits*, the ogre Winston (Peter Vaughan) and his wife (Katherine Helmond; both actors also appearing in *Brazil*) are also tossed into the water when they become too challenging to deal with.

4. It's more likely, though, that during filming it was decided to streamline the quest and give Galahad the Gawain demise (misstating his favorite color and being thrown into the gorge), meaning the script as typed became outdated but not physically updated.

5. From assorted court documents prepared in 2012.

6. Doyle e-mail, 28 November 2013.

7. The Goons also employed this type of sound effect, and often, using both catapult and springboard, depending on the episode. For a springboard version, listen to "The Missing No. 10 Downing Street" (3 November 1957); for a brace catapult, listen to "The Thing on the Mountain" (6 January 1958).

8. These long-wool sheep were particularly valuable to weavers during the Middle Ages, given the length of the wool, and the versatility it allowed in cloth making.

9. Partly drawn from the 28 November 2013 e-mail correspondence with the author, as well as comments made by Doyle in *The Quest for the Holy Grail Locations*.

10. 10 December 2013 e-mail correspondence with the author.

11. A shepherd who was actually a dog handler in the original image Gilliam accessed. See entries in the "*Animation*: Film Titles" section above.

12. These embargoes would be exercised again, for example, in the mid-1330s, attesting to their effectiveness (McKisack, 367). English wool was much desired on the Continent, and various English monarchs could pit one trading partner against another with this one commodity.

13. Including "The Pevensey Bay Disaster," "The Mighty Wurlitzer," "King Solomon's Mines," and "The Lost Year." The preceding descriptive adjectives include "reeking" and "crazy-type," etc.

14. The Goons also employ this instantly recognizable stereotype in the episode "House of Teeth" (31 January 1956), where a stage driver O'Brien (Ellington) concludes that the slowing horse "must be tired": "He's got his pyjamas on, begorrah."

15. *Times*, 16 January 1965: 11. The advertisements were meant to increase motor and/or caravan holidays in Ireland, with special car ferries made available for English tourists.

16. Stanley Reynolds, "Toothless," *Times* 8 August 1970: 6.

17. Reynolds, "Toothless," 6.

18. *MPFC: UC*, 1.105, 356, and 2.80.

19. Including kings Ceolred, Osred, and Æthelbald. See the entry for "*ANIMATION*" in "The Tale of Sir Galahad" scene above for more.

20. Remember that the first days of the shoot were supposed to be utilizing multiple locations (up to ten castles) for multiple camera setups in the Killin and Glencoe areas, and after at least one miserable day Doyle and Jones realized there was no feasible way to make this overly ambitious schedule actually work. They then reworked the schedule.

21. See the *OED* under "Mac, *n.*" definition two.

22. See entries in *MPFC: UC*, specifically Ep. 33. Johns's earlier works (published in the 1930s) had been republished in the 1950s as the Pythons were growing up, reaching a new audience of primarily young boys.

23. S. E. Kelly notes that the specific differences between a consecration and an anointing aren't understood, but that Offa seemed to be emulating Charlemagne, who asked the pope to consecrate his sons to be kings. See the entry for Offa in *ODNB*, http://www.oxforddnb.com/index/101020567/Offa.

24. See also Brooke, *The Saxon and Norman Kings*, 35–39 for more on the anointing and consecration of kings during this period.

25. The Cummings cartoon panel originally appeared in the *Daily Express*, 24 January 1972. Viewable at the British Cartoon Archive Database.

26. Sandbrook, *State of Emergency*, 167–68; see also Heath, *The Course of My Life*, 381–82.

27. See *MPFC: UC*, 2.153.

28. *Sun*, 24 January 1972. See also the British Cartoon Archive.

29. *Daily Mail*, 24 January 1972. See also BCA.

30. See *MPFC: UC*, 1.293; also British Cartoon Archive, 21 March 1969, "Gus," http://www.cartoons.ac.uk/browse/cartoon_item/artist=Gus%20[George%20Smith]?page=117. In 1969, Cledwyn Hughes (1916–2001) was the Labour cabinet member in charge of the Ministry of Agriculture, Fisheries and Foods.

31. See the British Cartoon Archive, 27 January 1970, artist Stan McMurtry (Mac) http://www.cartoons.ac.uk/browse/cartoon_item/anytext=Mcmurtry%2027%20January%201970?page=1.

32. "Militant Farmers Give Notice of Tougher Action," *Times*, 15 December 1969: 3. These same farmers promised to do the same to London if their demands weren't heard.

33. The mysterious French poet Wolfram von Eschenbach credits as the source of the original *Parzival* poem "Kyot of Provençal," who was likely invented by Wolfram himself; his source is most likely Chrétien's *Perceval*. See Barber, 175–77.

34. See the second *FZ* episode. The only script versions of these episodes are in German, and can be found in Thomas Woitkewitsch's *Monty Python's Fliegender Zirkus: Sämtliche Deutschen Shows* (Zürich: Haffmans, 1993).

35. "Why the Applause for Al Jolson Goes On and On," *Times*, 14 October 1972: 16.

36. This was a written-in change from "so-called King Arthur" (*MPHGB*, 26).

37. From 28 November and 10 December 2013 e-mail correspondences with the author.

38. Both catapults and siege towers (and pikemen, medieval arms, etc.) are featured in the Hal Foster-penned *Prince Valiant Fights Attila the Hun*, produced as a handsome color comic in 1952. The battle sequence against the castle covers pages 36–39 in volume two.

39. For descriptions of these weapons, their mechanics and ammunitions, see Dougherty, *The Medieval Warrior*, 198–201. The practice of launching dead and/or diseased bodies of humans and animals is also discussed.

40. The cartoony sound perhaps borrowed from various Wile E. Coyote cartoons including *Zoom and Bored*, where an enormous catapult backfires on him (naturally). Smaller catapult-type devices are used in the Wile E. Coyote cartoons *Beep, Beep* (1952) and *Going! Going! Gosh!* (1952). Both the Goons and the Pythons acknowledge borrowing from the cartoon worlds they grew up watching.

41. Prestwich, "Edward I's Armies," 239. See also Dougherty, 202–5.

42. Plate LXXIV, fig. 354, from Fitz. 298, f. 41.

43. From a 9 December 2013 e-mail correspondence.

44. See Studd, "A Fragile Tenure: England and Gascony 1216–1337" for more, as well as McKisack, and Bishop's *HBMA*.

45. *HBMA*, 49; see also Brooke, *FAH*, 211. It's not clear whether this was intended as a rueful joke, or that his impecunity was getting the better of him.

46. See appendix B, letter from Nick Rowe. Marsden (1919–1998) was a British actress known for *Carry On* films, the radio show *Round the Horne* (1965–1968), and *Doctor in Charge* (1972–1973), cowritten by Graham Chapman.

47. This kind of pell-mell filming schedule involving multiple, far-flung castles and myriad camera setups "collapsed" the following day, the crew's first day in Killin, and Doyle's more streamlined schedule was followed thereafter.

48. From the 28 November 2013 e-mail correspondence with the author.

49. "Not So Artless as They Look," *Times*, 3 April 1969: 14; and *Times*, 19 October 1974: 17.

50. "London Marchers Run Riot in Park Lane," *Times*, 22 July 1968: 1.

51. This was production manager Julian Doyle, who had also been driving the police car he purchased for the shoot. This line was ad-libbed, according to Doyle.

52. "To March or to Conciliate," *Times*, 5 February 1972: 15.

53. Tom Freeman, "Sad End at Old Trafford When Mob Rule Takes Over," *Times*, 29 April 1974: 13.

SCENE THIRTY-SEVEN
STOP THE FILM

There is a blank screen for some fifteen seconds—(PSC) After the hand covers the lens and the film stock can be seen "exiting" the gate, the screen does go to black with "slushy organ music" as accompaniment. This was added to the script after the fact. In the script as finished there was to be a cut to "*suddenly jazzy music*" followed by "*A new film completely free with the Monty Python film*" that was to be animated (*MPHGB*, 88). As elsewhere in the film, it's likely that Gilliam found himself plenty busy with the postproduction efforts involving the live action portions of the film, and that an entirely new subfilm was out of the question. This featurette was to include all the closing credits, was to be "*mainly animated*," and was to be "*about the credits*." This may have been a well-intentioned bone thrown to Gilliam early in the process, before his responsibilities as codirector were better understood. In the additional scenes of animated material available on the Blu-ray edition of the film, there's no indication that this kind of "enriched credits" animated sequence was ever begun.

CAST LIST—(PSC) There are no closing credits included with the film itself, the credits at the beginning serving that purpose. The credits as listed in *MPHGB* were obviously designed for inclusion with the finished film, and simply name which main troupe members played which characters, for example:

MICHAEL PALIN PLAYED: 1ST SOLDIER WITH A KEEN INTEREST IN BIRDS, DENNIS, MR DUCK (A VILLAGE CARPENTER WHO IS ALMOST KEENER THAN ANYONE ELSE TO BURN WITCHES), THREE-HEADED KNIGHT, SIR GALAHAD, KING OF SWAMP CASTLE, BROTHER MAYNARD'S ROOMMATE (*MPHGB*, 90)

Typos have been corrected by hand, including missing commas and parentheses, etc. The others are similarly commented upon, including (in descending order) Chapman, Cleese, Gilliam, Idle, Neil Innes, Jones, Palin, Connie Booth, Carol Cleveland, Bee Duffell, John Young, Rita Davies, Sally Kinghorn ("Either Winston or Piglet"), and Avril Stewart ("Either Piglet or Winston").

APPENDIX A

MONTY PYTHON AND THE HOLY GRAIL (BOOK) FACING PAGES

These facing pages are designed and likely also compiled by Derek Birdsall (b. 1934), the book's designer. A handful of preproduction and production elements are typically included: sketches and filming/blocking notes by codirectors Terry Jones and Terry Gilliam; copies of production (on set) photographs; suggested hand-sketched storyboard layouts by/from both directors; copies of typed "Daily Continuity Reports" listing locations, shots recorded, and shots printed; and frame captures from filmed scenes. These artifacts were all cobbled together in 1977 after the film was released into theaters and had become something of a sensation in the UK and especially the United States. The running order (a sort of table of contents) for the major parts of the book would read as follows (blank pages not included):

1. Title Page: *Monty Python's Second Film: A First Draft*

2. Script: *Monty Python and the Holy Grail*, First Draft (hand-numbered 1–47)

3. Memo regarding BBFC censor's requests, 5 Aug. 1974

4. Film trailer notes and lobby posters

5. Title Music notes and cues

6. "Final" Script: *Monty Python and the Holy Grail* (green, peach, rose, and blue pages numbered 1–88)
   6a. Frame capture and animated layouts (eight pages) between script pages 46 and 47
   6b. Frame capture and animated layouts (sixteen pages) between script pages 74 and 75

7. "Cast List" page

8. Statement of Financial Position and Cost of Production Statement, 17 Sep. 1975 (four pages)

The book has no table of contents or index of its own, and it is not continuously paginated. This appendix will examine the "decorated" pages—those facing pages with images, sketches, and handwritten notes from Jones and Gilliam—and not the pages printed to scripts or memos.[1] The typed pages are primarily script pages, and are referenced in the body of this book, scene-by-scene, as necessary. A "facing page" is simply a page in the book (on the reader's left) opposite a page of typed script text. I have included the relevant scene in the film or script to which the facing page can be linked.

Finally, the *identifiable* source books Gilliam used for sketching and copying, and which are referenced many times in this appendix and in the body of this book, include: Lilian Randall, *Images in the Margins of Gothic Manuscripts* (*IMGM*, 1966), Joan Evans, *The Flowering of the Middle Ages* (*FMA*, 1966), Jan Vredeman de Vries, *Perspective* (1968), Butterworth, *The Growth of Industrial Art* (*IA*, 1892), and Bishop, *The Horizon Book of the Middle Ages* (*HBMA*, 1968).

Facing page 1—("Coconuts and Swallows" scene) There are seven hand-drawn storyboards on this page. They comprise the film's opening scenes laid out on the script's first page, and involve at least three camera setups: Arthur and Patsy appearing through the mist (a long shot), Arthur and Patsy "hallo-ing" up to the castle battlements (a close-up two-shot), and Arthur and Patsy at the foot of the castle wall (another long shot). One of the directors has also written "1167 AD" above the second storyboard, an indication that the stated time frame for the film's setting had yet to be settled on, even as principal photography was being mapped out.

Facing page 2—("Coconuts and Swallows") The first sketch section includes storyboard sketches for shots 1–3 (Arthur and Patsy at the castle wall), while the bottom left of the page features a bird and a man whose eyes are floating out of his skull, like tethered balloons. The bird—though likely just a quick drawing of a bird in some kind of distress—does look very much like Dr. Seuss's character Gertrude McFuzz from the classic children's book *Yertle the Turtle and Other Stories* (1958). There are also several bird sketches in the pages of Gilliam's *Animations of Mortality* that resemble this one, including one where the bird wears a similarly pained expression as it tries to lay an egg much larger than itself. (This image might be inspired by a scene in the 1942 Tex Avery cartoon *Blitz Wolf*, where one of the Three Little Pigs drops a similarly enlarged bomb from a too-small plane.) Neither the bird nor the man appear in the finished film, as is the case with many Gilliam sketches included in *Monty Python and the Holy Grail (Book)*.

The "floating eyes" look will be revisited later, in the color-spread section between script pages 46 and 47. On that page Gilliam has created a snail/man hybrid—much like those found in the margins of Gothic manuscripts—and the man/snail's eyes float, tethered, from his eye sockets, like a snail's. See the "Centerfold" section of the discussion of Facing Page 46 below for more on this image. There is also an animated character in *Flying Circus* Ep. 33 whose eyes come out of their sockets, assisted by a Gilliam-created machine (animated link "*TV is bad for your eyes*," in *MPFC* Ep. 33).

Facing Page 3—("Coconuts and Swallows") There are seven hand-sketched storyboards for shots labeled 4–7, and it looks as if they at some point planned on shooting a take or two actually up on the walls (meaning close-ups of the sentries), but those shots were either not recorded or simply did not make it into the finished film.

Facing Page 4—("Bring Out Your Dead") This page features a handful of storyboard sketches, which look to be for the "Bring Out Your Dead" sequence, and are labeled as shots 1–12. One of the shots toward the beginning of the sequence calls for a "*Gibbet with lower half*" to be seen in the upper-right corner of the shot—a gibbet was a cage used to hang the bodies of criminals for public display—though a gibbet isn't seen in the finished sequence, likely replaced by the Catherine wheel in two other scenes. Also, the description of the actions of the two "*fighting men*"—"*Popping up & down into & out of shot each time with more* *frightening weapons*"—is not followed in the finished scene. In the finished film the fight is reduced to background material, and the plague cart and accompanying action/dialogue occupy the scene's attention.

Facing Page 5—("Bring Out Your Dead") The drawing on this page is a Gilliam rendering of a small human body beneath a much larger skeletal skull and spine. The corpse-like image is one that appears often in Gothic manuscripts, where harbingers of death regularly haunt the margins. One such image can be found in Randall's *IMGM*, in figures 657–58 from Stowe 17, depicting "Three living and three dead" (pl. CXXXVIII, ff. 199v–200). Stowe 17 is also known as the *Maastricht Hours*, and is found in the BLCIM (Randall, 37). There are also deathly characters like this in the *Lisle Psalter* (BLCIM), as well as *La Grant Danse Macabre*, an early printed book (1499). Images from both latter texts are found in another source text Gilliam accessed, Evans's *FMA* (241).

Facing Page 6—("Bring Out Your Dead") This page is densely populated with Gilliam sketchings, most but not all inspired by images in the Randall book. Those drawn from *IMGM* are hand-numbered by Gilliam, as elsewhere, and obviously represent his musings as he prepared to create the introductory and interstitial animations.[2] (These images are likely to have been compiled from multiple pages by book designer, Birdsall.) The numbered drawings include the following, moving from the top of the page and downward, clockwise:

"638"—A teacher in a pulpit instructing seated or kneeling men and women, perhaps giving a sermon, according to Randall (pl. CXXXIV, fig. 638), which itself is drawn from folio 181 of Stowe 17 (Randall, 31).

"352"—A king at the door of his proportionally stylized castle, looking a bit like a cuckoo appearing from a clock. In the original rendering as presented in *IMGM* the king lays his arm on his son, who holds two hounds on a leash (pl. LXXIII, fig. 352). The source is the Douce 366 manuscript, f. 72, from the *Ormesby Psalter* in the Bodleian collection (Randall, 31).

"612"—This sketch is labeled *"Amazing Angel"*; it's more specifically a "seraph," a six-winged angel. In the original manuscript, St. Francis is kneeling beneath the angel in Stowe 17, f. 175. Figure 612 is found on pl. CXXIX in Randall. This manuscript is also from the British Library collection, from the same Hours (aka *Maastricht*) as "638" above (Randall 37).

"97"—The sketch underneath this number is of an elephant carrying a castle. The castle appears to be drawn from figure 97 in Randall (pl. XXI), while the "elephant and castle" motif can be found in figures 167 and 170 in the same book (pl. XXXVI). Figure 97 is from the Yale MS, f. 18, *Lancelot del Lac* (38); figure 167 is from the manuscript Latin 14284, f. 18, an Hours from the Bibliothèque Nationale (Randall, 34); and figure 170 is from Munich c.g. 16, f. 22, the *Psalter of Queen Isabella*, Bayerische Staatsbibliothek (35).

Occupying the balance of this page are many drawings (and penned notes) not numbered by Gilliam but findable in Randall, as well as Gilliam-provided numbers without associated sketches. All these follow, clockwise, from top to bottom of the page:

"Lots of Angels 675-676-677-679"—A penned note from Gilliam. These are figure numbers from Randall's book, found on a two-plate spread in *IMGM* (pls. CXLII and CXLIII). On the left page, figure 675 is a rendering of the Annunciation, and comes from Add. 42130, f. 86, the *Luttrell Psalter*, in the British Library (Randall, 28). Figures 676 and 677 are also images from a life of the Virgin series, featuring the "Death and Assumption" segment, as well as the book's patrons, and is from Stowe 17, ff. 270v and 271, the *Maastricht Hours* (Randall, 37). On the right page, figure 679 features a miracle of the Virgin—a "king's soul saved from the devil"—and is from Royal 10 E.IV, f. 266, the *Smithfield Decretals*, British Library (Randall, 36). Though not noted by Gilliam, figure 678 (left page) also depicts an angel in the "Virgin Miracle" series, also from the *Luttrell Psalter*, f. 104, (Randall, 28). And though

Gilliam employed four distinct Gothic manuscript angels in his film title animated sequence (some doubled), none of the angels from these pages (or the earlier seraphs) made the cut.

"Little building towed along on wheels"—This is a Gilliam note without an accompanying sketch (at least on this particular page), though the figure number "354" is just next to this note. There is no wheeled building on the plate displaying figure 354 (pl. LXXIV), but such sketches can be seen on Facing Pages 51, 67, and 88. The images of simple carts and wheel-barrows appear fairly often in the marginalia of illuminated manuscripts, and Gilliam could have seen them as he perused *IMGM* in figures 58, 58a, 127, 129, 217, 230, 274, 375, 403, 444, and 494. Gilliam has also jotted an arrow from this entry downward to the next penned note, meaning he was likely thinking these images might end up conflated—the building being towed might have been a telescoping castle, for instance.

"Castle telescoping open—lots of knights coming out"—This is a combined Gilliam note and accompanying figure number ("354") from the Randall text. The telescoping castle image is drawn from Randall figure 354 (pl. LXXIV), which depicts rabbits storming a turreted ("telescoping") castle. There are soldiers and a trumpeter in the castle, and the rabbits are using pole axes, crossbows, and even a large counterweight trebuchet to make their siege. The connection between these attacking rabbits and the Wooden Rabbit seen later in *Holy Grail* is perhaps more than coincidental. Figure 354 is from the Fitzwilliam 298 manuscript, f. 41, the *Metz Pontifical*, Cambridge University (Randall, 32). There is another telescoping-type castle in figure 136 (pl. XXIX), from Douce 131, f. 54, an English psalter held at the Bodleian (Randall, 31), as well as figure 156 (pl. XXXIV), from Verdun 107 (f. 137v), a Breviary from the Bibliothèque Nationale (Randall, 37).

Untitled "creature" storyboard—This is a framed drawing of four creature heads, likely dragons, grouped together, and all nimbed (wearing haloes). This image can be seen in/on most Apocalypse texts, including *Cloisters*, *Lambeth*, and *Angers* (a tapestry series), and images from these texts are scattered throughout art and medieval history books. In the Paris version of the *Cloisters Apocalypse*, for example, this multi-headed and nimbed dragon figure is on page 76 (and several other pages), and in the version held by the Metropolitan Museum of Art it's on page 20, and at least eight other pages following. Gilliam will use images borrowed/adapted from the *Angers Apocalypse* in the cloud depictions of his title sequence, which follows the scene where God appears to Arthur and initiates the quest, as well as two angels from the *Cloisters Apocalypse* in the "*Monty Python and the Holy Grail*" title animation. See those sections for more.

Untitled "knight" image—This appears to be a sketch of Arthur in "full horsed" pose—hand and arm up, hand bent forward at the wrist, as if holding reins. (Facing Page 38 features closer studies of the limp-wristed hands, as well.) There are two smaller, similarly posed sketches on the opposite side of this page. There are a number of characters in the Randall book depicted with this swayback pose, as such stylization was fairly typical for the period, including many on the pages Gilliam will use in gathering images for his animations (plates IV, V, and IX, among others, in Randall).

Untitled "mouth" image—Next to Arthur's face is a small drawing of an open mouth. There is no description provided, but similar drawings appear on Facing Page 24, where Gilliam was obviously trying to work out what his animated version of God might eventually look like—whether a giant mouth in the clouds, or a fiery-eyed face, or just a looming, bearded man in clouds. In the end he decided to use a cutout of cricketer W. G. Grace.

Untitled "beast" image—A single, unannotated image made to look very much like the dragon heads mentioned above is seen at Arthur's feet. There doesn't seem to be any situational or narrative relationship between these three (Arthur, the mouth, and the dragon head) untitled sketches, so this may have just been the first go at a dragon sketch that was quickly abandoned. (Again, the book designer Birdsall likely received boxes of material to include in the book; many of these pages may be assembled individual sketches.)

"Building a Cathedral?"—This is a penned note to himself, and there's no accompanying drawing. Gilliam was considering a cathedral-building sequence for part of the animations,[3] perhaps as part of the film's title sequence, or maybe just as a transition. There is a cathedral-building image in the Randall book, figure 430 (pl. XC), from the Douce 6 manuscript, f. 95, a Psalter (Randall, 31). There are also a handful of larger, more elaborate images of churches and cathedrals being built in *FMA*, which Gilliam cites several times on Facing Page 68. The building images in *FMA* can be found on pages 86–87, 111, and 114.

Untitled "beast" image—A fierce beast drawing straight from either the *Cloisters* or *Lambeth* apocalypse texts ("The Dragon and the Beasts Cast into Hell" plate) occupies the center of this facing page. These texts are laid out almost identically, so either could have been Gilliam's source, or any later book that reference the works. This image is on f. 35 in the (Normandy) *Cloisters* (MMA collection), and f. 36v in the *Lambeth*. The *angle* of the beast's head is borrowed from all these original texts, though the specific facial details (eyes and eyebrows, curve of mouth) favor the *Cloisters* version. Part of this drawing appears to be the fires from Heaven, also seen in the various Apocalypse pages for this image, situated in Gilliam's version just as they are in the originals.

"86 Trumpeting"—Likely a typo by Gilliam, or a mismatch by the book's designer, since figure 86 (pl. XIX) in Randall depicts a Bishop (or abbot) and a nun, from Add. 49622, f. 117, the *Gorleston Psalter* (Randall, 28). This image is reminiscent of the one used in the Galahad animated introduction, where a nun kneels with a seated monk giving confession (*HBMA*, 143). That image is also found in Randall (XXIII: 112).

"Trumpeting"—This is just a single word penned by Gilliam; no accompanying drawing or plate/figure number for this bit of text at the bottom of the page. There are dozens of trumpets and trumpeters included in the figures gathered by Randall for *IMGM*, they appear in all the Apocalypse versions, and in many Hieronymus Bosch works—all references by Gilliam for these animations and sketches. Most of his trumpets he gathered from the Apocalypse texts, though in Randall they can be seen in figures 11 (a portion of which Gilliam will use later), 316–17, 354 (a figure already cited by Gilliam), 398, 422, 508, 518, 542–43, and 719.

Untitled "beast" image—Gilliam took this unannotated image—a two-legged hybrid creature with a sort of litter on its back—from the Randall book (pl. XXXVI, fig. 168), from the same plate where the "elephant and castle" figures are found. The original image comes from Fitzwilliam 2-1954, folio 25v, the so-called *Bird Psalter*, Cambridge collection (Randall, 32).

Untitled "beast" image—This is a very recognizable hybrid image from the *Luttrell Psalter*, one that has appeared in many books examining the art and life of the Middle Ages. This hybrid creature *does not* appear in the Randall book, though she does include many other scenes from *Luttrell*, so Gilliam found some other source as he drew this sketch. This *Luttrell* image also does not appear in any of the other identified Gilliam source texts. This image is from folio 182r of Add. 42130, also known as the *Luttrell Psalter*, in the British Library collection. Some of the angels described earlier are also drawn from the *Luttrell Psalter*, as is a snail and a boat Gilliam will sketch later, and a sheep seen in the film's animated title sequence.

Untitled "knight" images—Gilliam has sketched two knights in "horsed" position (like the Arthur sketch above), and they seem to be drawn from images in the Randall book, specifically figures 108 and 142. Figure 108 (pl. XXIII) features a handful of knights and their activities—tilting, etc.—and includes a "knight with spear and shield" (from Rylands lat. R117, f. 9). Figure 142 (pl. XXXI) depicts a David and Goliath scene, with Goliath looking every bit the medieval soldier—shield, lance, etc. To get the limp-wristed look Gilliam needed for the knights pretending to hold reins he would have simply erased the lance in either original image and reversed the hand. These images likely helped Gilliam create the animated knights and pages for the cartoon sequences of the film, as well. Figure 108 is a Psalter and Hours from the John Rylands Library, Manchester, while Figure 142 is from the Verdun 107 manuscript, f. 149v, a Breviary from the Bibliothèque Municipale (both Randall, 37).

Untitled images—The remaining unannotated images are of a giant figure perhaps preparing to stomp on someone, and a tall, narrow castle. The stomping giant figure will appear later in an unused, extended storyboard sequence on Facing Page 60, as well as Gilliam's *Time Bandits* (1981), while the castle seems an early sketch for the castle seen in the "Bloody Weather" sequence. Giants won't appear in the finished film, of course, likely due to budgetary restraints, though in the Grail romances Lancelot fights two giants (*LMD-WM*, 108) and Arthur betters a hideous man-eating giant on the continent (90). Lastly, there is a quick profile drawing of a bald, double-chinned man, also without annotation.

Facing Page 7—("Dennis the Peasant") There is a single drawing in the bottom left corner of this facing page. The image is of a stooped man carrying a box loaded with small, circular objects, and it's obviously a heavy load. Gilliam has penned "68" next to the man. The image is yet another borrow from the Randall book; she describes the man as "baker carrying tray on back," and there's another bakery-related image on the same plate (*IMGM* XV: 68). The original manuscript figure is from the illuminated manuscript Add. 36684, f. 48, which is an "Hours" book of the British Library collection.

Facing Page 11—("Dennis the Peasant" and "Black Knight") This page features several drawings. None of these drawings found their way into the finished film, but that's true of most of the doodlings in the book.

Six separate hand drawings occupy most of the *haut de page*. There are three separate images of hands with heads for fingertips—i.e., a snake head, a dragon head, antlered heads, and various grotesques. There are three other hands sketched—two just splayed on a solid surface, and one fashioned into a catapult device, like some sort of enormous vaudeville stage prop. (A hand with wheels on the fingertips appears in Gilliam's *Animations of Mortality*.) The balance of the sketches include, *cap-à-pie* and clockwise: a mosquito-like aircraft, a bit of foliage (see below), a hunched man, a buck-toothed man, a nude man on a plinth preparing to dive into a hole (posed not unlike the arse trumpeters), a hedgehog-type creature, a naked kneeling man (see below), a man with a telescoping neck, and an angel (see below). Other foliage sketches can be found on Facing Pages 32, 36, 51, and 62, also unannotated. A similarly styled angel is found on Facing Page 32, there a borrow from the pages of *IMGM*. Most of these are not images borrowed from Randall's book, either. These are Gilliam's equivalent of gothic marginalia, and he likely had pages and pages of such sketches completed during and after the filming of *Holy Grail*. The plinth image can be seen in Randall's book, as well. In figure 279, plate LVIII, there are images of idols being cast down from their pedestals, from the "Flight into Egypt" story found in "*Cloisters* 54.1.2," f. 83, the *Hours of Jeanne d'Evreux* (Randall, 30–31). Lastly, the kneeling man is very likely connected to a drawing that appears later, on Facing Page 43, where Gilliam has sketched out his version of a sixteenth-century Bosch (c. 1450–1516) painting, "Ascent of the Blessed," and where he left a note to himself: "*DON'T FORGET*." This image would not appear in *Holy Grail*, but would be used later in *Meaning of Life*, as gormless suburbanites in their cars make their way to heaven.

Facing Page 12—("The Black Knight") The storyboards here cover much of the Black Knight fight sequences (labeled as shots 1–18), including an unfilmed scene where the Black

Knight gets sand from a nearby tent to soak up the blood from the recently deceased green knight (labeled as shot 15 in the scene).

Facing Page 13—("The Black Knight") Two Gilliam drawings based on images from Randall's book, as well as a couple of notes Gilliam made for himself. One of the sketches is of a stylized, full-body lion, and is based on an image found in figure 320 of Randall's *IMGM* (pl. LXVI). The original image is copied from the Christ Church E.II manuscript, f. 46v, found in the Oxford, Christ Church Library (Randall, 30). The complete original drawing (as appearing in the manuscript) appears to be a *bas-de-page* scene of a lion fighting a unicorn.

The second sketch is a proposed storyboard featuring an inhabited initial and Arthur's party asking for recruits ("Join our quest," the Arthur figure calls upward); Gilliam has sub-titled it: "*A[rthur] coming to ask knight in letter.*" The inhabited initial image is borrowed from Randall, this time figure 423 (pl. LXXXVIII), the Trinity B.11.22 manuscript, f. 179v, found in Cambridge's Trinity College Library (Randall, 37). In the original inhabited letter there appears to be a man (likely a scholar) holding a loaf of bread. Gilliam has also penned a rather lengthy note for the proposed action of the scene, wrapping around the bottom and left side of the storyboard: "*A[rthur] goes into castle comes out with knight they go a few paces knight gets killed go back to castle new knight they come out he gets killed repeat after knight gets killed A tries getting back into castle no dice.*" This cartoony scene did not make it into the film's animations.

Gilliam has also included an image number ("269") and the description of an image he found there: "*Devil loading bodies into Beast's mouth.*" This is a reference to *IMGM* figure 269 (pl. LVI), and is a xerographed version of folio 309 from the manuscript BBR 15001, part of the Bibliothèque Royale collection, Brussels (Randall, 30). This same small image also features a depiction of St. Michael taking a soul to heaven in a napkin, and escaping the jaws of Hell. There are other "mouth of Hell" and "St. Michael" images in *FMA*. A "consuming devil" image not unlike this has also appeared in *MPFC* Ep. 24, the "Cartoon Religions Ltd" animation.

The last entry on this page is a penned note by Gilliam, obviously as a bit of a reminder to himself: "*God caught nude quickly grabs cloud to cover himself.*" This "God caught in a compromising position" image is broached by Gilliam elsewhere, including Facing Page 67, where God is "*caught playing with himself.*" This and most of the coarser references to the Almighty are expunged by the final cut of the film. In Bosch's *The Prodigal Son* there is similar image of a man urinating against the wall of a public house (Tolnay, 283–84).

Facing Page 14—("The Black Knight") Rough storyboards for the "Black Knight" fight sequence (shots 20–29), and two sketched cylinders. Gilliam continues to doodle geometric shapes on nearly every page included here, most having no connection to the film project. Bosch includes cylinders in some of his work, including altarpiece depictions of St. Jerome (Linfert, 97, 99).

For shot 20 one director has noted "*Patsy scurrying off,*" and shot 21 is to be "*Hand held.*" Shots 26a, 27, and 28, for instance, depict the Black Knight losing his second arm.

Facing Page 15—("The Black Knight") More "Black Knight" fight sequence storyboards (shots 30–35), including the handful of close-ups of Patsy with a note: "*Close ups of Patsy!*" Gilliam likely mentions this (and excitedly) as it was rare that Gilliam's Patsy was given close-up shots. Gilliam also notes that the fighting characters are "*Circling*" in shot 30, and that shot 31 (a close up of Arthur) is "*as and of [shot] 2C,*" recorded earlier.

Facing Page 18—("She's a Witch!") These are a series of storyboard sketches for the "She's a Witch!" sequence, obviously done either with a pen that leaked or on paper that ab-sorbed the ink badly (there are smudges on each thick line). The shots here are unnumbered.

Facing Page 19—("She's a Witch!") A handful of additional storyboards (shots 12–17) from this same "witch" scene.

Facing Page 20—("She's a Witch!" and "The Book of the Film") This facing page features Gilliam sketches. From the top of the page to the bottom, and clockwise, they are:

handwritten note—Gilliam obviously used this drawing paper as a notepad, as well. In the upper left corner of the page is a quickly scrawled note: "Rehearsal Thurs Sat & Sun," followed by an illegible location word. For the various *MPFC* series rehearsals, the cast had gathered at BBC Television Centre, Golders Green, and the Old Oak Club, Acton.

Untitled "hopping snails" image—There are several snails drawn into storyboard-type scenes on this page (three sets at the top, and one at the bottom of the page), each hopping quite ably, and set to squash a small knight figure brandishing a sword. This may have been an early way to get rid of a knight or page (not unlike dropping a Wooden Rabbit on a page, or eating Robin's minstrels, or having a rabbit kill Bors) that *did not* make it into the final script.

Though Gilliam drew quite a few of these images as he planned his animations, no snails appear in the finished film. There are more than a dozen images of snails in *IMGM*, including figure 468 (pl. XCVII), borrowed from the *Luttrell Psalter*, and occupying the *bas-de-page* almost completely (Add. 42130, f. 160). In Randall's book there are additional images of fighting snails (figs. 158, 225, 241, 301, 384); snails perched on walls, stilts, ladders, and a crossbar; snails frightening knights (figs. 307, 308, 385); and a snail confronting an ape on horseback (f. 27), etc. (see Randall, 214 for a more complete list). There are also very large snails featured in a Bruegel work, *Desidia* (1557). Gilliam and the rest of the troupe mention "Bruegel prints" in the printed script, for an animated sequence never completed. The following scene, the "Bring Out Your Dead" scene, is populated very much like a Bruegel print, *Triumph of Death* (c. 1562).

Gilliam has also appended a handwritten note to these snail drawings, likely as a reminder to himself when he eventually animated the sequences: "*BKGRND MOVING UP & DOWN BEFORE WE SEE SNAIL IN LONG SHOT.*" This seems to mean that we are to be in a subjective position (the camera view being the snail's view) as the scene begins.

Numbered "hybrid creature" image—Numbered by Gilliam "383," this is a sketch based on an image Gilliam found in Randall, at the top of figure 383 (pl. LXXX). Characterized as a "grotesque," this fanciful margin-dweller seems part fish, bird, and goat, and is nuzzling a bird in the original illustration, just as Gilliam sketched. The figure is drawn from M. 729, f. 273, the *Psalter of Yolande de Soissons*, Pierpont Morgan Library (Randall, 34).

Labeled "*Heraldic Psychadelia*" storyboards—Gilliam has penned a note next to these storyboards: "*Heraldic Psychadelia [sic] leading to knights A[rthur] & B[edevere] on way.*" Obviously Gilliam was thinking of illustrators Peter Max or Heinz Edelmann for this animated sequence (*à la The Yellow Submarine*), but eventually settled on period images (angels, St. Michael, a Christ figure). It may also be no accident that Pink Floyd was touring with its *psychedelic* stage show during fall 1974, including multiple dates in the UK in November and December. (The band, with other British rock groups, had helped finance the film.)

Untitled "trumpet" sketches—These sketches feature a trumpeter with a telescoping trumpet—a sort of Tex Avery gag seen often in cartoons of the 1930s and 1940s, especially from Warner Bros. There are trumpeters blowing trumpets from which emerge smaller trumpeters blowing smaller trumpets, and on. Though there are almost a dozen trumpet images in Randall's book—including pious angels and less-pious arse trumpeters—none of the Gothic images feature "peopled" trumpet bells. The largest trumpet here is "screaming" into the ear of a woman, who's cringing away from the noise (she's drawn in a straightforward manner—not stylized). See the entry for "Trumpeting" in the Facing Page 6 section for more.

Untitled "monopod" (or "sciapod") creature sketch—These single-footed creatures are found throughout the margins of illuminated manuscripts, on Middle Ages maps, as well as in more contemporary animations like *Yellow Submarine*, where such creatures ("kinky boot beasts," Paul calls them) attempt to stomp the tiny submarine as it passes.[4] In Randall the creatures can be found in figures 643 (W. 45, f. 92) and 644 (G.K.S. 3384, f. 108v), both on plate CXXXV, drawn from the *Psalter for Leonardo de Fieschi*, Walters Art Gallery collection, and a Flemish Psalter from the Det Kongelige Bibliotek (Randall, 37 and 32, respectively). Gilliam sketches them here but does not include them in the finished animations. He has utilized these fantastic creatures in his *Flying Circus* work, as well (Ep. 18).

Untitled "telescoping man" sketch—This is another character type that does not appear in the finished film, and also does not appear in the Gothic manuscripts or in Bosch's works, though there are some characters in the Bosch *oeuvre* that resemble these odd creatures. This particular character type—enormous feet, smaller legs and hips, and even smaller trunk and head—is likely a variation of Gilliam sketches of similar characters for this book, for *Animations of Mortality*, as part of *Monty Python's Big Red Book*, among other places, but none found their way into the film.

Untitled "hooded monks" sketch—This is the largest set of figures on the page. One monk figure is facing another, and the first has obviously asked about someone else. The second monk responds: "I'll go see if he's in." He then (well, his face) disappears from the cowl opening, and in the next drawing another face appears in that same space and says, "Oh hello."

Untitled "fishing fish" sketch—Between doodles there is a fishing scene. The fish in the sketch is fishing for a man, a kind of turnabout that is seen often in the margins of Gothic manuscripts. It is difficult to determine what the bait is, but it may be a book. There are images of hares hunting, trapping, and even imprisoning men, animals teaching humans, monkeys doing very human things (including performing a bishop's oblations at the altar), etc., in the margins of Gothic manuscripts.

Facing Page 21—(original "gathering" scene; "Camelot") The handwritten "Book of the Film" dialogue occupies this page, which wasn't part of the finished script as printed on 20 March 1974, and was likely penned in for the release of this book. The accuracy of the text (it is word-for-word as performed in the finished film) indicates the text was copied from the film and into the script, and not part of the original shooting script.

Facing Page 23—("Camelot") On page 23 itself there are doodles of rough storyboards (in the margin) for shots 9, 10, and 11 of the appearance of God scene. Someone (perhaps codirector Jones) has written *All in front projection* in this area, as well. "Front projection" is a well-used production device that projects the filmed material over the performers (or in this case, scenery, the trees) in a particular shot. The first image of God in the clouds is a front projection shot, the following five shots of God involve the animated frame only, and are followed by another processed shot (again, front projection) as God concludes his announcement and the clouds close. The result is often more natural looking than the older rear projection process, which had been employed since the 1930s.

Facing Page 24—("God Announces the Quest") A doodle and sketch page. There are eleven sketched storyboards for the "appearance of God" scene, four of which are in a more "finished" state (shading, coloring, etc.). Several feature a looming God with penetrating eyes, others a God surrounded by tiny angels, one featuring a rough doodle of the Holy Grail in clouds and glory, and two where the clouds have lips.

The assorted sketches around the bottom of the page include the following:

Untitled "whiskered belly" sketch—This is a reclining, nude Magritte-like figure with breasts/eyes and a stomach/nose with whiskers, featuring a pose much like Magritte's 1937 work *La race blanche*.

Additionally, there is a cloud and sun with feet (likely sketches for the "Bloody weather" animated scene); several heads and faces featuring figures with a toothed mouth and a smaller mouth within (see below); then assorted sketches of human figures, a footed plant (a Bosch-like figure), and squiggles (as if Gilliam were testing his pen's nib).

The "toothed" sketches are reminiscent of a very similar character created by Gilliam for a comic book sketch "Hamsters: A Warning" in *The Brand New Monty Python Bok* (1973).

Facing Page 25—("Taunting Frenchmen") This page features sketches and storyboards from the film's animated title sequence. From top to bottom, clockwise, images and hand-written text include two storyboard panels for an unused transition featuring Galahad—along with the penned "*Sir Launcelot had saved Galahad from almost Click-Click-Clickety*"—first in a close-up, then in a medium shot where a goateed Galahad is clearly attempting to either create or reattach his left arm using crochet needles and yarn (hence the "*clickety*" sound effects).

What follow are three rows of storyboards and several peripheral sketches of the "arse trumpet" and "sunrise" sections of the animated title sequence. Many of the sketches are very similar to the final shots as constructed for the film, with a few notable exceptions. For example, instead of blasting the shepherd off the grassy hill as seen in the finished film, the trumpets here merely blast from the heavens and across a barren landscape. Gilliam has penciled in "*Organ Playing Monks Too*" underneath the sixth and seventh storyboards (which in the finished film include the twinned images of an angel with a portative organ and Michael carrying napkined souls to heaven, then the waving Christ), but the "organ playing monks" do not appear in the finished film. The images he's referring to can be found in Randall, figures 117 (pl. XXIV) and 118 (pl. XXV), both from BBR 9961–62 f. 66, part of the Bibliothèque Royale's *Trèsor des Sciences* manuscript (Randall, 29). The sketched "sunrise" frames are *almost* identical to the unrolling scroll-like effect of the sun's rays in the finished film, though the waving/blessing Christ figure is missing in these early renderings.

Two tiny, large-eared faces are sketched in the bottom left corner, seemingly disconnected from anything else on the page. Finally, there is also a thin, stenciled scroll sketched in by Gilliam that reads: "*Hi there I'm King Boffo and Co. What's Your Name Sailor?*" This sort of "Hello Sailor" joke had been a *Goon Show* staple, and had also been used in *FC* a number of times (*MPFC: UC*, 1.34, 162, and 230). "Boffo" may be a reference to the fairly new children's book character in Frank Dicken's *The Great Boffo* (1973).

Facing Page 27—("Taunting Frenchmen") Here there are sketched storyboards for shots 16–25 of the "French Taunting" scene, including penciled directions like "*Hand Held*" (shot 17), "*Animals flying thru air*" (shot 19), "*Same as 18*" (shot 24), and "*Bums over battlements on fart line*," the last of which, of course, did not make it to the finished film. There are also assorted doodles of keyholes, battlements, the number "4," and a geometric "box girder" doodle. The keyholes indicate the Pythons may have been considering a keyhole shot through which the French occupation of the castle becomes apparent.

Facing page 30—("The Tale of Sir Robin") The balance of this peach-orange page offers sketches from Gilliam of various grotesque human and hybrid figures. Only one of the sketched figures is recognizable (from the finished film)—it is a small but accurate sketch (sans bared teeth) of the Beast that later chases the knights through the Cave of Caerbannog. One other is similar to an image found in a Bosch work. This is a tiny storyboard image that simply features a character peering from either a very starched cowl or from some carved opening, like a round window. In Bosch's *The Garden of Earthly Delights*, there is a character, likely a man, peering out of a neat hole in a piece of oversized and decorated fruit in the central panel (Linfert, 111; Tolnay, 233). Gilliam sketched a great deal from several Bosch works, as has been demonstrated, even some of the smallest images in the "backgrounds" of these works. See entries for Facing Pages 37, 38, 43, and 67.

Other sketches include two duck-billed characters with particularly pained expressions, a caricature of a human (complete with wide tie and bellbottoms), two characters that look like lumps of flesh with facial features, a torso-less, two-legged creature (similar to those on Facing Pages 6 and 37), two creatures that are simply legs and a twisted snout. These last two seem more Edelman-inspired than Bosch, as there are no "featureless" creatures in the margins of Gothic manuscripts.

Facing page 32—("The Tale of Sir Robin") This facing page is covered with sketches Gilliam performed, drawn primarily from the pages of Randall's book. From top to bottom, clockwise, the figure numbers Gilliam noted include "*362*," "*149*," "*168*," "*158*," "*169*," "*395*," and "*453*." There is also one drawing that is traceable back to the Randall book, but is unnumbered here.

"*362*"—The first sketch is a stylized hillock and hare hole borrowed from the *bas-de-page* section of figure 362 in Randall (pl. LXXV). Randall describes the entire scene as "Man and hare, hunting with bow and arrow," and notes that it comes from the *Rutland Psalter*, f. 57v, Belvoir Castle, Duke of Rutland collection (Randall, 36). Gilliam has removed the hunter and his dog—as well as two creatures that look on from the decorated border—from the original drawing. (The inspiration for the arse trumpeters in the animated title sequence is also borrowed from the *Rutland Psalter* via Randall's book.) This same original hillock image will be reconfigured and used again by Gilliam in the later animated sequence where Robin's minstrels are eaten. This is also one of only two images on this page that actually made it into the finished animations, the other being figure "433" discussed below.

"*149*"—The next sketch is a grotesque from the *bas-de-page* section of the *Lambeth* 233 manuscript, f. 15, and listed in Randall as figure 149 (pl. XXXII). Part of the Lambeth Palace Library collection, this manuscript is known as the *Bardoulf-Vaux Psalter* (Randall, 33). The grotesque is a torso-less, legs-and-head human-like creature (with a tail) depicted in a "Life of David" setting. This legs-and-head creature is seen a number of times in Bosch's work, including the prominent "man" at the center of the center panel in *The Temptation of St. Anthony* (or *Triptych of the Temptation of St. Anthony*, c. 1501; Linfert, 79).

"*168*"—The third sketch is a marginal parody (Randall guesses) of the popular elephant-and-castle theme seen elsewhere on this same page and sketched earlier by Gilliam on Facing Page 6 (XXXVI: 168). The earlier sketch is a bit more cartoony and suggestive, while this version is slightly more finished (beard, shadows included, etc.), and they are clearly separate sketches. The creature appears to be another bipedal but un-armed man/lion hybrid (*sans queue*) carrying two birds in the litter on its back, and stands on the left side of the left page, looking off the page. The original, parodic image is found in Fitzwilliam 2-1954, f. 25v, the *Bird Psalter*, Cambridge collection (Randall, 32).

"*158*"—The sketch near the center of the page is a hybrid snail/man from figure 158 in Randall (pl. XXXIV). In the original manuscript the snail/man is acting as mount to a jousting hare, and is tilting with a dog astride another hare on a decorative border in the fanciful *bas-de-page* illustration. This "Dog and hare tilting" scene is drawn from Y.T. 8, f. 294, the Yates Thompson collection, British Library (Randall, 38). This sketch is noteworthy in that it is one of the few Gilliam sketches where he tweaks the pose of the original. In this case the man/snail is fully on the ground, snail-like, while in the original the creature is rearing up, horse-like. Most of Gilliam's sketches (at least those borrowed from *IMGM*, *FMA*, or from Bosch) are faithful to the original layouts.

"169"—This figure is found on the same plate in Randall as figure 168 above, and depicts an unusually long-nosed (and long-tailed) elephant carrying a telescoping castle and armed knight (pl. XXXVI). There are three separate elephant images on this plate. This elephant-and-castle figure is borrowed from "Fitzwilliam 298," f. 26, the *Metz Pontifical* from the Cambridge, Fitzwilliam Museum collection (Randall, 32). Departing slightly from the source, Gilliam has not included an archer in front of the elephant, ready to fire at the knight.

Just beneath this sketch is evidence that the book designer (Birdsall) laid these images one on top of the other when arranging the facing pages. There are three part-images—two disconnected feet (almost precisely like the feet on the creature above, from figure 149), the palm of an upraised, stylized hand (perhaps making the "peace" sign), and a vertical, nimbose cloud bank (or another hillock) drawing—all are demi-obscured by the invisible bottom edge of the page containing figure 169 (and perhaps including figures 149, 168, and 158). These three occluded images do not appear in their completeness anywhere else in the book.

"395"—The next sketch depicts Eros, and in the original he's just shot in the breast a kneeling man and woman (Randall, LXXXIII: 395). In the original figure—"Man and woman, before Eros, kneeling," from Arras 139, f. 8—Eros has no arrow in his bow (he's shot both), though Gilliam includes the arrow in his version, and removes the targeted lovers. The image comes from the Bibliothèque Municipale, *Chansonnier d'Arras* (Randall, 28).

"433"—This is the model for the arse trumpeters seen earlier in the title animations, and is labeled "Man (contortionist) with cymbals" by Randall (XC: 433). The original drawing is found in the *Rutland Psalter*, f. 73, a manuscript that also provided the original for the hillock Gilliam sketched at the top of this page, and that will appear in the "eating of Robin's minstrels" animation later in the film (36). This is one of the handful of Gilliam sketches (perhaps eleven total, not including storyboards) that made the clear transition from drawing board to finished film.

Untitled "costumed man" sketch—One additional sketch clearly drawn from the Randall book but unnumbered here is of a "mummer," or pantomime performer, in the original dressed as a stag (Randall, XCII: 446). The costume itself looks more like a tree trunk with a stag's antlered head on top—the performer peering out from a hole in mid-trunk—but it could be purposely stylized. By the way the character is drawn it appears that the stag's horns were penned by Gilliam and were then obscured during the layout work for the book, which might account for the missing enumeration, as well. The original manuscript is "fr. 95," f. 261, *L'Histoire du graal*, from the Bibliothèque Nationale (Randall, 32). Gilliam has not included a man with a bagpipe and an antlered grotesque, both of which appear in the same *bas-de-page* section of the original manuscript page.

The remaining sketches on this page seem to be freehand doodles—five faces (three cowled, as if they're nuns, and two ambiguous male caricatures), two plants, a turreted castle, several pen-test squiggles, and a bulbous and unfinished female figure. None of these sketches found their way into the finished animations. There are three cowled/hooded nuns on plate CIX in Randall, any of which may have served as Gilliam's reference for the nun sketches here.

Facing page 36—("The Tale of Sir Galahad") This is a page loaded with sketches and early storyboards, many of which did make it into the finished animations—though often after significant alterations. From top to bottom, and moving clockwise, the sketches are as follows, some numbered (by Gilliam), and some not:

Untitled "legs" sketches—The first three drawings are of men seemingly wearing pull-up legs that cinch at the waist, legs that are bigger than their own legs. There is also an incomplete doodle of a man's face.

Annotated "hair shield" sketch—The first recognizable drawing is of a knight (or infantryman of some kind) carrying a spear and a large shield, the shield being the focus of the drawing. The shield features a large man's face, bearded, the beard trailing below the pointed base of the shield. Though not numbered, the shield image is drawn from the Randall book, figure 212. Gilliam has labeled the sketch with the note "*Hair hanging off shield.*" Gilliam found the example on plate XLIII in *IMGM*, where it's described as "*Giant before castle.*" The manuscript is the Royal 10 E.IV, f. 89, *Smithfield Decretals*, part of the extensive British Library collection (Randall, 36). Much of this same *bas-de-page* sequence will appear later in this book, between pages 46 and 47, being nearly completed drawings for animations that did not make it into the final film.

Untitled "castle on a hillock" sketch—The next several images (a separate drawing and seven small storyboards) are of a home or castle on a small hill, as well as several figures approaching this structure. The castle doesn't seem to be closely modeled on anything from Randall's book. The proposed blocking and movement of the scene will be revisited later in the scene where Robin's minstrels are eaten, though the image in one of the storyboards of clean wash on a line reflects back to the excised scene where Launcelot is gathered into the quest (*MPHGB*, 21). With only three characters sketched into the scene, it looks very much like the sequence was to include Arthur, Patsy, and Bedevere on their first recruiting visit, likely to Launcelot's castle, where Launcelot leaves his family to accompany his liege.

Untitled "trees" sketches—A landscape featuring several stylized trees (as seen in the pages of period manuscripts) follows, and a face (likely Robin) peeks from the branches of one tree. Later on this same page Gilliam will note that he's thinking of having Robin hide in a tree whilst two "*beasties*" or "*giants*" fight it out. Robin will come down when the fight is over and it can appear—to the approaching Arthur and the other knights—as if he's bested the creatures. (The complete handwritten note is included below, under "Note 2.") On a plate Gilliam clearly referenced in the Randall book is such an image—a man hiding at the top of a small tree, having been treed by a hare (LXXIV: 356). Gilliam has already noted the "telescoping castle" (fig. 354) on the same plate for another animation idea, as well as the hillock with the hare hole for another (fig. 362). Figure 356 is from Bodley 264, f. 81v, the *Romance of Alexander*, part of the Bodleian Library collection (Randall, 30).

Annotated "number" notes—Below the landscape sketch can be seen one of Gilliam's most detailed sketches, one also accompanied by careful and precise notes for himself. There are several elements to this section. The first is a carefully drawn frame (storyboard) for the "frozen land of Nador" section of the animated film, where Robin's minstrels will be eaten. This storyboard sketch features at least four knights, two or three servants with baggage, the decorated border they walk upon, the sun, and the "old man" north wind figure blowing the sun away (Gilliam pens "*sun blown away*"). These are all drawn in significant detail. To the right of this frame are four detailed and annotated numbers (all fancy or block letters), which are obviously figure numbers from the Randall book: "*10*," "*71*," "*112*," and "*117*." None of these references are drawn up, just noted as significant, and are as follows:

"*10*"—Gilliam notes "good page shape." At some point Gilliam was obviously thinking of duplicating an entire page from an illuminated manuscript in his animations, and figure 10 is noted as a "good" possibility for reference. This is a complete verso (left) page from the Walters collection, W. 82, f. 75v, and features, according to Randall: "Ape and bird, snaring with clapnet; Ape with birdcage; Hybrid man with tabor; Physician and man; Initial supported by man" (Randall, III: 10). W. 82 is a Flemish Psalter and Hours, part of the Walters Art Gallery collection (Randall, 38).

The creative layout and interactions of the characters, as well as the attractive hybrid and animal figures all likely contributed to Gilliam's interest in the plate. Each of the characters interacts with the decorative border nearest him, sometimes even connected to that border, such as: (1) The elongated physician along the left side, whose body acts as a border; (2) the man supporting the inhabited letter on his back; (3) both the man who is a patient at the top, and (4) the man who is a hybrid at the right, both of whose lower bodies meld with the decorated borders. The closest Gilliam comes to actually replicating a folio from an illuminated manuscript might be toward the end of the film, when the "frozen land of Nador" animated sequence reveals an elaborate *bas-de-page* setting. Elsewise, the "Book of the Film" images are also potential "good page shape" moments, though the text on each page is quite limited, and the decorations, though recognizable from illuminated manuscripts, are fairly conservative.

"71"—Gilliam notes "good composition" for this source, which is a *bas-de-page* section from BBR 10228, f. 6, and features decorative borders with small characters playing a game called "bandyball" (Randall, XVI: 71). It's a balanced layout, its decorated borders symmetrical without being elaborate, which may have caught Gilliam's eye. The original is part of the Bibliothèque Royale collection, Brussels, *Trèsor des Sciences* (Randall, 29). See notes for Facing Pages 13 and 25, above, for more BBR appearances.

"112"—Gilliam notes "*Monk & Nun Confession.*" This is one of a handful (there are about eleven, total) of images that make it from the original source material and into the finished animated sequences. A rather famous and memorable scene in the film is the "monk and nun confession" image seen toward the end of the Sir Galahad animated introduction. In that setting, the nun is spun around by another vaulting nun, ending upside down and naked below the waist. (See the entry for "The Tale of Sir Galahad" for more.) The "Confession of cleric and nun" image appears in Randall on plate XXIII, figure 112, and is borrowed from Stowe 17, f. 191. In the original manuscript it appears to be a large *bas-de-page* setting. Stowe 17, also known as the *Maastricht Hours*, is part of the British Library collection. This same manuscript has earlier been referenced. See notes to Facing Pages 5 and 6 for more.

At the bottom of the page are three items—a sketch of heavenly fire descending from stylized clouds, and two lengthy notes written by Gilliam:

Untitled "heavenly fire" sketch—The heaven's fire is borrowed from myriad apocalypse texts, several of which have been mentioned earlier, including *Angers*, *Cloisters*, and Douce. The fire is seen most prominently in the upper corner (precisely where Gilliam places it) in images like the "first trumpet" series, and panels like "Dragon cast into the jaws of Hell" from the *Lambeth Apocalypse*, as well as the *Cloisters* text, ff. 24, 34, and 35. A sketch of a mustachioed man (face only) is basking in the glory descending from the heavens, as well, and looks a bit like an earlier sketch of Galahad on Facing Page 25.

"Monk giving confession" **note**—Gilliam has written: "*112 Monk hearing confession—gives absolution—doing sign of cross then on last movement kung fu's* [sic] *the lady.*" By the time Gilliam created the animated sequences—likely during postproduction—he had changed the monk and nun actions to an accidental jostle leading to a kind of "rectal exam" moment, as seen in the finished sequence. There are actually two mentions of kung fu–type movements or images in this book/script; see the "Killer Rabbit" scene for the other.

"fighting beasties" **note**—"*Great fight going on between two amazing beasties—or two giants—Robyn* [sic] *hiding in tree—beasties kill each other Robyn* [sic] *gets down out of tree just as A[rthur] & knights ride in.*" Gilliam would draw bits of this proposed sequence twice on this same page. The first has already been described, while the second is another storyboarded

sequence and will be mentioned just below. The two "amazing beasties" may have appeared earlier in *MPFC* Ep. 34, dancing at the end of Jeremy Pither's "Cycling Tour" adventures.

"600"—The next set of drawings is an early version of the "springboard nuns" seen in the "Sir Galahad" animations. Here they are moving left to right (reversing the direction of the finished scene) and diving from a florid decoration emerging from a pond, which Gilliam labels *"procession [. . .] procession of monks stopping and starting"* and *"they run down board."* Similar processions can be seen in *HBMA*, where queued students are checking out library books, and nuns and monks form a procession to a statue of the Virgin (266–67; *Ordonnances de l'Hotel du Roy*). Gilliam may have intended to use a monk (male) image here instead of a nun (female), but in the end both the proposed model for these characters (see "600" below) and the characters in the finished animation are nuns. The florid decoration appears to be a reverse *p* seen often in illuminated manuscripts, one in which the monk and nun will eventually be located in the finished film sequence. These *p* initials are found through the psalters of the Gothic period, for example, and Gilliam's inspiration likely came from figure 423 in Randall.

The "600" is a figure number from Randall's *IMGM*, again (pl. CXXVI). Here Gilliam is borrowing from Stowe 17 again, an image of a nun at the feet of St. Christopher, from f. 113v. Even though Gilliam lists "600" as his likely inspiration, he does not use that particular image in the finished "vaulting" animation, using Randall's figure 112 instead, also from Stowe 17.

Annotated "ladder angels" sketch—Just above the previous set of drawings is an elaborate rendering of a "Jacob's Ladder" scene—possibly adapted from page 236 in *FMA*. Gilliam gives no page or figure number for reference (and this type of image *does not* appear in Randall or Bosch), and he penned *"Angels going up & down ladder to heaven"* to accompany this drawing. There are a number of other ladder images in *FMA*, some depicting workers clambering up and down as they work on churches in a fifteenth-century French manuscript illustration (*FMA*, 87). There are also dozens of ladder images in Bosch's work, as well, generally associated with grotesques or devils performing all manner of unholy errands.

"Robyn climbing down tree" **storyboards**—The next drawings are a return to Sir Robin fleeing a fight up a tree, and Gilliam notes below the five separate storyboard drawings that the scene is *"even better with bendy tree."* This sequence did not appear in the finished film. In fact, with the exception of Bedevere being found in the course of his duties at the witch "trial," none of the knights were gathered from their former lives as the script originally called for—they are introduced into the narrative via Polaroid-type photos in "The Book of the Film."

Untitled ephemera—There are also three quick sketches of faces on this page, none clearly connected to the film, and an enigmatic, unexplained reminder note of sorts in the corner: "Up to 250."

Facing page 37—("The Tale of Sir Galahad") There are only a handful of drawings on the upper half of this page, none of which made it into the finished animations. He's sketched (but not numbered) a *"Woman tent luring knights,"* three versions of a living female tent that obviously seduces knights into her labial folds. There is a tent from a Gothic manuscript in Randall that looks very much like the one Gilliam's recreated. In figure 34 (a *bas-de-page* image) there is an "Ape as queen, in tent" borrowed from Y.T. 8, f. 296, a *Breviary* from the British Library collection (Randall, 38). The other drawings include a sketched sailboat, a head-only creature chasing two men, a very Bosch-inspired head-and-legs grotesque, and a cloven-hoofed modern woman hybrid. There are a number of sailboats depicted in Bosch's work, though Gilliam's doesn't appear to be fashioned especially after any of those. There are no "head-only" creatures in Bosch, since even his most odd grotesques are gifted with legs or arms or some appendages to assist in locomotion. (There are several decapitated heads in Bosch panels, though none still alive.) The "head-and-legs" grotesque is, however, a Boschian creature.[5] In the left panel of *Hermit Saints*, there is a nun figure consisting of head and feet alone (Linfert, 27; Tolnay, 174); while in the center panel of *The Temptation of St. Anthony* there is at least one character before the saint who has no arms or torso (Linfert, 89; Tolnay, 134–36, 138). Again, none of these creatures appear in the finished film.

Facing page 38—("The Tale of Sir Galahad") This page contains sketches and storyboards, some of which made it to the finished film:

Untitled "diving nuns" storyboards—At the top of this page an early, rough rendering of the diving nuns scene is apparent. There are seven storyboards drawn in simple detail, with the florid, decorated borders and diving board included. The first five boards have reversed the screen direction of the finished version, with the divers moving from left to right, while the final two boards appear to reverse that reversal, with the last figure misdiving from the right to left of the screen. This is the second set of storyboards devoted to this sequence, the others are sketched out on Facing Page 36, and are also blocked out moving screen left to right.

Untitled "doors" sketch—This is a simple, unannotated (meaning ambiguous) sketch of a series of doors in a perspectival hallway, the longer-than-usual doorknobs casting long shadows. (If resembling anything, the sketch looks a bit like the multi-door sequence in *Yellow Submarine*, where Young Fred, Ringo, and John find Paul and George.) It's not clear whether this was a sketch that may have (1) had a home in the earliest iteration of the script (where the modern world, including the Harrods, intruded on the medieval world with regularity), or (2) it is a random doodle, of which there are many in these pages, or, possibly, it's (3) somehow connected to the more modern, mechanical sketches covering Facing Pages 51 and 63.

Numbered "rowing boat" sketch—This boat (pictured from above, with four oarsmen) is one of the two sketches on the page drawn directly from figures in Randall's *IMGM*. Labeled "468," Gilliam has sketched this boat from figure 468 (pl. XCVII), a full folio facsimile from Add. 42130 (f. 160), also known as the *Luttrell Psalter*. In the original image, two men are pulling the rowboat with a long rope. The left side and top of the figure is decorated with a flowery border, and a large snail occupies the *bas-de-page*. Gilliam has sketched and copied from *Luttrell* before, notably for Facing Page 6, as well as the sheep appearing in the animated titles. See the second entry in the "Title Sequence Animation" section for more.

Annotated "limp-wristed hands" sketches—A bit of a curiosity are these hands. Gilliam's drawn six separate versions (and one incomplete version) of what he's labeled as "The Knights' Hand," and they are clearly the *appropriate* way Arthur and his knights are to hold their hands (as if holding reins, loosely) as they "ride." He's also written "734" and "735" near the hands, indicating he found examples in *IMGM*. The exemplar hands are both from Arras 47, ff. 32 and 208v respectively, and simply feature both male and female characters handling reels, distaffs, and spindles (weaving tools) across separate *bas-de-page* scenes (pl. CLVII). Arras 47 is from the *Musée Diocésain*, a Psalter and Hours, Saint-Omer calendar (Randall, 28).

It's possible Gilliam sketched the hands here as he prepared to create the tiny animated knight characters who appear later in the "Passing Seasons/Frozen Land of Nador" animations where Robin's minstrels are first welcomed, then eaten. One of the hands is also attached to a hulking, stooped character—not a knight, it seems, but almost a hunchback. Again, there's no explanation given for this character and the limp-wristed pose he holds. The attention to detail Gilliam paid to these hands seems to promise a more elaborate and significant animated character or sequence, however, one that may have been second-guessed and/or preempted as the animations were completed.

"Clerics 128 [and] 122"—This is a penned note from Gilliam, with no accompanying image. Both Randall figures are *bas-de-page* scenes of clerics (and nuns, in the first) playing a ball and club game and lecturing, respectively (plates XXVII and XXV). These images don't seem to have been used specifically anywhere in the animations, or even in the surviving sketches, but their mention here gives an idea as to what Gilliam saw in his mind as a representative church figure for the animations. Figure 128 is copied from Bodley 264, f. 22, the *Romance of Alexander*, Bodleian Library; figure 122 is from Hague 78.D.40, f. 41v, part of a Missal from the Meermanno-Westreenianum Museum collection (Randall, 30, 33).

Untitled "winged insects" sketch—Hard to tell what these are specifically, though one appears to be heralded (it's "painted" in a checkerboard pattern, as if a colorful shield or flag), and fly- or mosquito-like, while the other is a head-on view of same. Insecta are few and far between in Gilliam's source material. There are only three instances of fly images included in Randall, no locusts or mosquitoes, a handful of bees and beehives, a dragonfly, two ant images, and only one grasshopper. Bosch would sketch and paint scores of insects and insect-looking monsters, including insect-like demons fighting angels and saints in the left panel of Bosch's *Last Judgment* (Linfert, 32–33, 121; Tolnay, 168, 170). Bosch's influence on the Pythons, even beyond Gilliam, is evident. He enjoyed turning the affairs of men, the Church, and the world upside down, even inside-out: "Once he had ventured into this topsy-turvydom, Bosch was to remain there for many years to come" (Linfert, 18). They likely admired Bosch's "bizarre alterations of the usual dimensions of things" (19).

Assorted "human" figures sketches—At the bottom left of the page Gilliam has sketched four human figures: one incredibly fat and sitting on a tiny stool; one walking and with enormous ears; and one coughing up a wishbone while being watched by a fourth man. Near this last pair Gilliam has penned "*Something stuck in throat*." The character with the oversized ears is reminiscent of a character depicted in Randall, figure 547 (pl. CXIV), and labeled "Panatios" (*Rutland Psalter*, f. 88v).

Untitled "Legendary Black Beast" face—Just above the human figures is a version of the creature that will appear later in the Cave of Caerbannog, consuming Brother Maynard and chasing the knights (until the animator dies). Storyboards for a Beast scene are mentioned below.

Untitled "human and wheeled" figures sketches—Another series of human-type figures not appearing in the film. Four are different versions of a single man who pulls on "wheel-pants" and says "*I'm going out dear*"; another is a man sitting with his hands trapped at his sides (trapped inside his high pants); a third is a large, busty woman standing on a plinth; and a fourth is another large woman chasing a heart. As for Gilliam's possible inspiration, in Bosch's *Last Judgment* (central panel) there are several condemned men fashioned into axles and tongues for a hellish processional cart (Tolnay, 174, 322). There is also an armless character able to move around with the aid of a wheeled walker in the right panel of *The Temptation of St. Anthony* (135). No wheeled characters appear in the pages of Randall's book, though there are many carts and wheelbarrows. Wheeled (or mechanically altered in some way) characters appear in *Flying Circus* animations, but none such mechanical hybrids are included in *Holy Grail*, even though there is a later sketch page covered with more modern (nineteenth century) mechanical blueprint sketches. For more on that puzzlement see entries for Facing Page 63.

Untitled "Beast eating Bro. Maynard" storyboards—The final images on the page include three rough storyboards from a later scene, where Bro. Maynard is being consumed. In the first, Maynard's feet are disappearing into the Beast's maw; in the second, the Beast is approaching the camera, mouth agape; and in the third, darkness. This sequence is accurate to the finished film, missing only an insert (a reaction shot) of the knights screaming in fear, between the first and second storyboard images.

Facing page 39—("Castle Anthrax") There are several Gilliam sketches, three of a living (as in possessing eyes, legs, etc.) feather quill creature, and one of a naked nun tied to the ground, a single cloven hoof visible near her. None of these images are found in the finished film, though the nun could be an early or discarded portion of the "Castle Anthrax" scene. As for the feather quill, Herbert (Jones) has already used a very stylish one in the "Swamp Castle" sequence. More likely, though, there is a very similar drawing in a book Gilliam will reference significantly for mechanical-type drawings, and that will be discussed in detail in the Facing Page 63 entry. For now, drawing number four in Butterworth's *The Growth of Industrial Art* (on page 53) is Gilliam's likely source for this writing instrument.

Facing page 40—("Castle Anthrax") This page features a single Gilliam drawing of a string-vested bovver boy-type (or maybe even a nineteenth-century athlete) wearing lace-up monster feet.

Facing page 43—("The Knights Who Say 'Ni'") This page is covered with sketches and rough storyboards, only one of which will appear in *Holy Grail*, and another on hold until *The Meaning of Life* almost a decade later (1983). Gilliam has numbered one drawing, and annotated or labeled four others, as well. From top to bottom, clockwise, the images include the following:

Untitled "landscape" sketch—This looks like the beginning of an aerial view landscape scene, not unlike the views often seen of ancient archaeology sites in Britain, including Silbury Mound or any surviving "motte"-based structure of myriad ancient castles. The sketch isn't finished, and may have been a first go at an animated map sequence.

Untitled "faces" sketches—Five sketched faces, four of which are similarly long chinned and male, and none appearing medieval in the least. Again, there is no indication that the book's designer, Derek Birdsall, had access to Gilliam artwork done exclusively for *Holy Grail*. As will be seen later, there are dozens of drawings that connect more directly to *Marty Feldman's Comedy Machine* (1971–1972), later *Flying Circus* episodes (shot October–December 1974), and even *Meaning of Life* (1983).

The fifth face is strikingly different—a bulbous, turbaned (or cowled) baby face, cheeks puffed out, as if blowing—this is disturbingly similar to the baby masks Gilliam would later employ in the feature film *Brazil* (1985). It's likely, however, that Gilliam found inspiration for this sketch and then mask in paintings he'll use often for *Holy Grail* sketch work, Bosch's *The Temptation of St. Anthony* and *The Garden of Earthly Delights*. In *Temptation*, this character (a tailed, feathered, two-legged grotesque) can be seen in the left panel, blowing on a bagpipe, and is isolated and quite visible (Tolnay, 134–35). In *Earthly Delights*, the figure is part of a more crowded, hellish musician scene, and is blowing on a large oboe-like instrument (204, 240, 245, 247). This second iteration of the character is in the precise position (angle of face, etc.) as Gilliam's sketch. More images from these same Bosch works will be discussed later, on Facing Page 67.

Annotated "*Half skeleton faces*" sketches—These faces are reminiscent of the many images of death (especially in relation to myriad plagues) in medieval art. A prominent version of this "half skeleton" can be seen in Jan Provoost's *The Miser and Death* (c. 1515–1521), in the right wing of the triptych. Bosch presents many, with *Death and the Usurer*, for example—the left panel of an incomplete triptych—depicting a cadaverous part-corpse, part-skeleton representing Death entering the dying miser's bed chambers. Gilliam has already provided a similar image (there with an attached, non-skeletal body), back on Facing Page 5. The specter of looming, inevitable death is found throughout manuscripts and artwork of the medieval period. In *Holy Grail*, of course, death is everywhere, right from the opening scene: There is a body high on a Catherine wheel, later piles of bodies on a plague cart, a man clubbed to death so he can join the others on the cart, a green knight skewered through the head, a witch sentenced to burning, servants squashed by a cow and a wooden rabbit, a Famous Historian hacked to death, three knights impaled by a giant lance, a dozen or more castle sentries and party guests killed and maimed, minstrels killed and eaten over a cold winter, knights massacred by a rabbit, and knights thrown from the Bridge of Death. The Pythons are clearly mimicking more serious medieval films like *Seventh Seal*, as well, with grisly lives and deaths simply made more absurd.

"*625*"—This is the only numbered drawing on the page, and it comes from Valenciennes 838, f. 61v, originally, though Gilliam clearly found it in *IMGM* (CXXXI: 625). This particular figure (as found on plate CXXXI) is just below another Gilliam sketched from but did not cite, a tall figure with animals discussed below at "hairy figure." The sketch Gilliam rendered is a storyboard-type, showing stylized clouds pouring out rain or fire (or just heaven's glory?) on the upturned face of a man, and is not unlike earlier sketches he's made from apocalypse sources. The original image is of the conversion of St. Paul (he is horsed, and cowering as beams emerge from the heavens); it is a "Calendriere-Obituaire," and is from the Bibliothèque Municipale collection (Randall, 37). The original artist has cleverly attached the clouds to the decorative border overhang of the manuscript, making it look as if Paul is in a shower of sorts. This character interaction with the physical world of the decorations is mimicked by Gilliam in the animated titles, when the novitiates not only line up on a border, but use a part of it as a diving board into a pool also contained and defined by the borders.

Annotated "Strange flying beasties" sketch—Alongside this sketch Gilliam wrote: "*Strange flying beastie w/ladders flying to roofs putting ladders up to climb up higher silly.*" The sketch he provides depicts a larger and smaller house, side-by-side, perhaps a church with an anteroom, as well as four "beasties" variously flying and climbing with their ladders. There are no images precisely like this in *IMGM*, though there are about a dozen ladder references in the various figures. Gilliam may have drawn his inspiration from the Jacob's Ladder reference he sketched earlier (see Facing Page 36), and continued to wonder why winged creatures like angels would ever need "silly" ladders. In Bosch's *Haywain* a devilish creature climbs a ladder with his load of mortar, assisting in the building of a hellish afterlife. There is also the image in Randall from the story of Theophilus, who attempts to renounce his pact with the devil (fig. 680). In the small image from Royal 2 B.VII, f. 211, devils appears to be breaking the ladder Theophilus climbs toward the Virgin (pl. CXLIII). Royal 2, also known as the *Queen Mary's Psalter*, is part of the British Library collection (Randall, 36).

But it is in the dark, fiery background of the center panel of Bosch's *The Temptation of St. Anthony* where Gilliam's most likely source can be identified. In this deep background portion of the panel a devil flies across the smoky, lowering sky carrying a ladder. In his sketches Gilliam has very nearly copied this devil image—including the winged figure's flying angle, the angle and length of the ladder, the look and figuration of the demon's wings and trailing tail, and so on. Gilliam has even included a similar version of the building that—in the Bosch work, a church with collapsing spire—the devil approaches (Tolnay, 136, 140, 146).

Untitled "God in the clouds" storyboard—This inclusion is a bit out of place, at least given its location opposite a "Bridge of Death" page in the script. It is clearly an early drawing from the "appearance of God" sequence seen earlier, and discussed in the sections for Facing Pages 23 and 24. This one is a lone storyboard depicting clouds, God's light, and two of the knights looking on, all sketched very loosely. Again, book designer Birdsall likely cobbled together Gilliam's work with some order in mind (most images from the film do tend to appear on script pages facing their scenes in the film), but this isn't always the case. There are quite a few sketches in this book dedicated to the "God" scene, meaning Gilliam spent time considering how to best manage the appearance of the Almighty. In the finished film there is a fleeting image of one such finished drawing tacked to the wall of Gilliam's art workspace. It can be seen behind him as Gilliam—the "Animator" mentioned by the film's narrator—dies of a heart attack.

"Do Not Forget" **note**—Gilliam penned *"Do not forget"* next to a sketch he made of a portion of the Bosch painting *Ascent into Heavenly Paradise* (c. 1504), which depicts angels guiding kneeling aspirants into the light-filled afterlife (Linfert, 24; Tolnay, 111, 114–15). The image wouldn't appear until the end of *Meaning of Life*, when—just prior to the closing musical number in heaven—dinner guests and their cars are escorted into the afterlife in this precise way.

Untitled "slithering and beaked beasts" sketches—Eight sketches of hybrids or grotesques fill the bottom left corner and side of this page, from two "serpent in the Garden"–type creatures to one wheeled yet still slithering dinosaur hybrid to five beak-mouthed creatures all menacing us head on. The serpent in Eden image is clearly borrowed from Bosch's *Haywain* triptych (after 1510), specifically the left panel, where the human-torsoed serpent is entwined around the tree and offers Eve the forbidden fruit. Gilliam has again nearly copied the layout and figuration of this source, as he will many times when redrawing from Bosch.

The last (uppermost) creature resembles a giant owl with a trailing tail. Gilliam has obvious Bosch influences, as has been shown, and in preparation for the *Holy Grail* animations he will directly sketch characters from a number of Bosch's works. Several of these images on Facing Page 43 are clearly Boschian, though not attributable to a specific painting. The owl is a good example of this ranging influence. In *Temptation* Bosch has included a prominently placed owl at the center of the painting's focus, sitting on the head of another character Gilliam will sketch (also on Facing Page 67). Bosch also included owls in a number of his other works, including the center panel of *Earthly Delights*—the owl is staring directly at the viewer—and in the center panel of *Haywain*, where the owl looks over the sensual wine-and-song scene of the idle rich (Linfert, 57). There are also many owls in Bosch's sketch pages. (In the Tolnay book there are dozens of owl images from many Bosch works, meaning Gilliam would have seen them over and over again as he leafed through its pages.) And since the owl was a medieval image of devilishness and sin (the bird of prey always watching), Gilliam's snarling, monstrous owl is no stretch from the Bosch. None of these owls or the other "beasties" make it into the final animations, though the snarling creatures may have been early iterations of the Beast seen later, especially given their "direct address" poses, as if they're also ready to eat Brother Maynard before advancing on the party of knights.

Beneath (and partly overlapped by) these fantastical creatures is a rather pleasant and out-of-place sketch of a woman who appears to be the Queen, wearing a plastic rain cap.

Untitled "naked man" sketch—At the center of the page are three separated drawings, the first being a man seen from behind, clad only in a hood and cowl and shoes/garters, as if he's cross-dressing (partly) as a nun. The man appears to be covering his private parts as he scurries away. A very similar character can be seen at the immediate forefront (base) of the center panel of the Bosch triptych *Last Judgment* (Tolnay, 174). That man is naked except for his hood and boots, he is bleeding from a wound on his torso, and he is being accosted by a helmeted demon.

Unnumbered "hairy figure" sketch—The second of these drawings is a tall, hairy figure, unnumbered but clearly drawn from an image found in the Randall book. Figure 623—Gilliam's source—is actually an image of St. Mary of Egypt, who lived wild in the desert, covered in hair, and carrying only three loaves of bread. Gilliam sketches her in this instance holding a single loaf, while the original in *IMGM* (pl. CXXXI) depicts Mary holding two loaves and feeding the third to a lion (Royal 10 E.IV, f. 280v). This figure is found on the same plate in Randall as the conversion of St. Paul image, mentioned above. Gilliam has also sketched a less hirsute version of Mary's face just next to the full body sketch, as if he were comparing the two possibilities. This manuscript has already been accessed by Gilliam for "angels" on Facing Page 6, and will be again for the "color centerfold" in the book (see Facing Page 46).

Annotated "*solid black figure*" sketch—This is a kind of artful sketch of several interacting figures, and Gilliam has penned a subtitle: "*Solid black figure moving strangely thru fully round figures.*" In the sketch are two solid black figures and three "round" figures (meaning more three-dimensional), with the black figures appearing to dash around and through the others, perhaps impishly, though not unnoticed. This is very likely referencing another Bosch work, this time *The Garden of Earthly Delights*. In the center panel there are couples and groups of people, most very fair skinned, but there are also a handful of almost jet-black people mingling in these couplings—characters so dark that their features are almost invisible.

Facing page 44—("The Knights Who Say 'Ni'") A collection of twelve drawings, most hastily sketched, it appears, as well as a "film strip" series of discontinuous images from the "Knights Who Say 'Ni'" scene when they've received their shrubbery and the white fence. The drawings include at least two versions of the "Legendary Black Beast" seen later in the film, two long-faced male character sketches, a multi-eyed person (the eyes look like curlers on her head), a dragon-ish hybrid, and a hunched, big-footed man. There is also a structure of some sort, perhaps a tent, but it is obscured by overlaid photos.

There are also two sketches from earlier in the film sequence. One is of a cloudbank sprouting trumpets, and the other is a psychedelic blob. Both are from the animated film titles section, though only the trumpets made it into the finished film. See the entry for Facing Page 25 for more on these trumpets, and for the psychedelic clouds, entries for Facing Pages 20 and 51, as well as the "Title Sequence Animation" section above.

Facing page 45—("The Knights Who Say 'Ni'" and "Swamp Castle") Storyboards and sketches from the "Bloody Weather" sequence, adorn this facing page. At the top are two detailed storyboards showing the legged clouds jumping up and down, etc., and Gilliam's penned "*HUP OOF OH UNGH HUP HUP*" above the boards (the style very reminiscent of Gene Deitch's 1961 cartoon *Munro*). Below, Gilliam has penned two Boschian creatures—head, elongated necks, tiny torsos, legs, and one even has tiny wings—and then fourteen small storyboards comprising nearly all of the "Bloody Weather" animation. He notes near the third storyboard (the close-up of the scribe's hand finishing a letter *L*): "*Just finishing letter noise makes him slip & ruin it.*" Under the seventh storyboard (showing the building and the sun, clouds, and horizon) he has written: "*Shadow of bldg. getting longer & shorter.*" However, the shadows of the scribe and the building do not fluctuate in the finished animated sequence, meaning in the interest of time or energy Gilliam changed his mind about manipulating them. The layouts in most of these renderings are also precisely opposite of what they are in the finished animations. After the initial image where the scribe is finishing Launcelot's inked name, the shots beyond are almost mirror images of the original drawings, i.e., the house is at the left of the frame instead of the right. The scene is still a very effective, understated comic setup and payoff.

Facing page 46—("Swamp Castle") Here begin four sets of color pages, between pages 46 and 47, totaling eight pages. There are eighteen frame captures, three per page, covering the first, second, and third pages, a two-page centerfold spread of completed (but not used in the finished film) animated work—followed by three more pages of frame captures.

The "centerfold" section of the book is a full-color spread featuring a composite setting of a castle, a windmill with a perched rooster, and soldiers atop a decorated border, as well as a large, looming snail/man hybrid. The castle, windmill and rooster, and several trees and tendrils are borrowed and recolored from *IMGM*, plate XLIII, figure 212 (from Royal 10 E.IV), though the image is reversed for this spread. The bands of lance-toting soldiers and the two beardless faces peering from the turrets are *not* part of the original work, nor are they sourced from Randall, Bosch, or *FMA*.[6] Gilliam has also removed several prominent figures from the original rendering: a giant carrying a faced, bearded shield and large spear with flag, an archer, as well as some tendriled border work. The bearded shield was earlier sketched by Gilliam and included on Facing Page 36. The giant and archer are preparing to lay siege to the castle, and Gilliam has also removed and then replaced the castle's few visible occupants with new occupants. These two new faces peer out of high windows at the massed soldiers below, and one man appears to be praying. There are five faces—three bearded, two youths—in the original work, and all in lower windows or in the courtyard. (Remnants of some of these figures can still be seen in Gilliam's touched-up version.)

The snail/man hybrid is also not part of the original *bas-de-page* work found in the *IMGM* figure 212, but is likely inspired by the snail from figure 468, as well as the snail/man hybrid in figure 158, both discussed above (pls. XCVII and XXXIV, respectively). Snails have been sketched throughout by Gilliam, and are discussed in the notes for Facing Pages 20, 32, 38, 60, 77, and 86.

The decorated border all the figures stand upon is from a different manuscript entirely—W. 104, figure 11 in *IMGM* (plate IV). This same border will appear in the scene where the seasons are changing and Robin's minstrels are eaten, and is an interesting composite of borders from the W. 104 manuscript. See the "Passing Seasons Animation" section for a full discussion of this border.

Facing page 49—("Swamp Castle") There are three thick-penned sketches on this page. Importantly, this is the page where this researcher (finally) made the connection between the *Monty Python and the Holy Grail (Book)*, Gilliam, and the Randall book *Images in the Margins of Gothic Manuscripts*.

The rather bizarre, feathery-headed figures toward the left of this page—and especially the character at the middle of the page—sparked a connection for me, having just leafed through Randall's *IMGM* for the first time merely looking for images that might have resembled Gilliam's work. Gilliam did not number or annotate these particular images in any way—but he had rendered them precisely, and placed them on his drawing page in the same proximity they share on the Randall plate—offering the connecting clue. From there it was a quick matter of checking the handful of provided numbers originally assumed to be page numbers, proving they were in fact figure numbers on plates (pages), and the rest quickly fell into place. This same plate (CI) has been mentioned before in these Facing Page notes, and is where Gilliam found the images of some of the limp-wristed hands he wanted for the horseless knights. (See the entry for Facing Page 38 for more on that.) As for the seemingly feathered faces, the one at top of the page is sketched from plate CI in Randall, figure 487 (simply known as "Man with harp"), and is another borrow from Yale MS. (f. 209), also known as *Lancelot del Lac*, from Yale University (Randall, 38). The other figure is both a face and a body (and the beginnings of the decorated border he stands upon), and is sketched from the same Randall plate, figure 488. The "Man with head of leaves" is copied from Add. 38114 (f. 67v), a French-produced thirteenth-century Bible from the British Library collection (Randall, 27).

The largest sketched figure on this facing page occupies the right half of the page and appears to be a more original, freehand sketch, and not necessarily based on a character or image found in Randall, *FMA*, or a Bosch work. (The profiled figure appears to be a torso-less grotesque, which have appeared in Bosch paintings and Gothic manuscripts, and have been discussed above in the entries for Facing Pages 32, 37, and 45.)

On the page opposite page 49 in *MPHGB* there are three sketches Gilliam obviously doodled. One looks like a more modern, jowly woman with no body, while the other two sketches are images taken from illuminated manuscripts. These images are found on plate CI in *IMGM* (figures 488 and 487), and they're even laid out in the same way they appear in Randall's book. The lower-left image is known as "Man with head of leaves," and is from Add. 38114, f. 67v, and the upper-right image is known as "Man with harp," lifted from Yale MS., f. 209. These images made it clear that Gilliam had access to Randall's book as he drew inspiration for the animated portions of the film.

Facing page 50—("Swamp Castle") There are only three images on this page, all clustered in the bottom left corner. The images are rough storyboards depicting a scene not found in the finished film. Two characters—perhaps Arthur and Patsy—walk across a landscape of enormous eyes all staring upward. In a two-shot storyboard, one character says to the other: "*I think we're being watched.*"

A similar image will be used elsewhere by Gilliam. In the opening credits to the feature film *Meaning of Life* there is a similar landscape, though the upward-staring eyes are replaced by breasts and nipples. This is also reminiscent of a scene in *The Yellow Submarine*, when the Beatles and Jeremy are standing in "the foothills of the headlands" (psychedelic heads as far as the eye can see). The influence of artists Heinz Edelmann and Peter Max on Gilliam has been mentioned earlier.

Facing page 51—("The Tale of Sir Launcelot") There are at least thirty-five separate Gilliam drawings on this page, most of which appear to have at least some connection to *Holy Grail*, though none (in forms seen here) made it into the finished film.

From top to bottom, clockwise, the drawings include: A goose-stepping, mustachioed chicken; two houses on wheels, one being towed by a car (and storyboarded); clouds (storyboarded); a giant floating apple (storyboarded); a cube; a flying, flatulent cloud/bird; an early sketch of the Legendary Black Beast (storyboarded); a psychedelic cloud and head scene, likely from the title storyboard sequence; a two-headed man (storyboard); a knight's helmet being used as a cooking pot (storyboards with camera move indicated); sketches of knights, including knights on parade (storyboard); illuminated manuscript-type "weather" boards; flying *fleurs-de-lis* (two of them, both storyboarded); a rotund giant (two storyboards); a giant peering at a tree or the ground (storyboard); two cowled figures, another knight with elaborate ostrich feather headdress; the sun and two monks; a plant sprouting a man's head and a plant sprouting a baby; a knight at a cave mouth facing a tree (storyboard); a detailed, scudding cloud landscape; a frog/man trying to snare flying people with his tongue (storyboard); and a bird (the Hitler chicken or an unladen swallow?) flying over an early scene in the film (storyboarded; and the elevated Catherine wheel is visible). Significant sketches worth mentioning in better context include:

Untitled "mustachioed chicken" sketch—This is a detached drawing that could be a caricature more Stalinesque than Hitlerian, but that's just an impression, since it's not labeled or attached to any other drawing or scene from the film. Hitler and the Nazis had been fair game in British political satire since at least 1942, when the Ministry of Information edited footage from Nazi propaganda newsreels into a silly "Doing the Lambeth Walk" satire (infuriating the Nazis, allegedly), and the Pythons sported with them in several *Flying Circus* episodes, including Eps. 1, 11, 12, and 28. Gilliam does not use chickens in his *Holy Grail* bestiary, though they have appeared a number of times in *FC* and *FZ*.

Untitled "wheeled houses" sketches—These look like they could be medieval pageant wagons or caravans, the second one being towed behind an auto, like a modern-day caravan. The idea of a caravan is quite old, of course, originally referring to pilgrims or even merchants traveling together through lonely or hostile territory in Early Modern times. The continuing presence of modern-day contraptions in Gilliam's sketches—but the lack of such anachronistic devices in the finished film—likely point to the Pythons' decision to keep the film as medieval as possible, and find most of the humor in period situations peppered with bits of anachronistic or ironic dialogue and visuals. (Gilliam will remedy this in *Life of Brian*, when a spaceship inadvertently picks up Brian from ancient Judea and takes him for a short but eventful *Star Wars*–like ride.) The intrusion of the modern-day police and police vehicles as *Holy Grail* moves on is certainly more noteworthy this way, and indicates the film has moved a long way from its earliest iteration, where the modern world interrupted regularly, ending at the Harrods lunch counter and with a car chase.

Labeled "cloud" storyboards—These cloud storyboards are worth mentioning simply because Gilliam spent more time and energy on them than most quick sketches, including some shading and even labeling one with color suggestions ("*white*," "*blue*," and "*gray*" for various parts of the cloud). It might be that these were part of the early ruminations for the "Bloody Weather" sequence, along with the scudding cloud landscape drawn below and in sketches on Facing Page 45.

Untitled "apple" storyboard—This storyboard simply depicts a giant apple hovering above an awed man, likely just a Magrittian absurdity employed for its visual effect. No over-sized fruit make it into the finished film. There are a few sketches below that depict a giant, and it may be that this apple is actually falling from the sky after being dropped or heaved by the giant.

Untitled "Legendary Black Beast" storyboard—This storyboard appears to depict a version of the Black Beast as well as the rabbit, both looking threatening, while a crowned figure cowers in the background. This may have been a sketch connected to the scene where Arthur sends Bors and then others to take care of the rabbit, though the Beast does not actually appear (in the finished film) until after this scene.

Untitled "psychedelic cloud" storyboard—These seem to be connected to drawings already seen on Facing Page 20, drawings that were likely considered for the animated titles sequence, but were shelved. There Gilliam penned: "*Heraldic Psychedelia leading to knights A[rthur] & B[edevere] on way*," alongside fanciful, Edelmann-like drawings and peopled heraldic trumpets. See entries for Facing Page 20 for more. In the later "Passing Seasons" animation, an Old Man Winter (or North Wind) figurehead is similarly connected to the decorative bordering, and blows winter weather over the land.

Untitled "knights" sketches—These various knight sketches indicate Gilliam was vamping on the well-known knight image—the ostrich plume on the helmet is instead a smoke trail; knights marching in a parade; a floating, two-plumed knight figure; and perhaps an early *cap-à-pie* version of Galahad (he wears a cross on his chest) with helmet and plume.

The "plume" gag is meant to be just that—a sight gag revealed by a camera pullback. Gilliam has drawn two storyboards—one larger than the other, the smaller one above the larger. There are arrows leading from the lower corners of the smaller storyboard to the upper corners of the larger, indicating a backwards camera (or lens) move. In the smaller, initial frame, we see a close-up of the helmet and plume, and simply assume we are seeing a typical feather-plumed helmet. The pullback reveals the helmet atop a tripod, both straddling a campfire—the plume is actually smoke or steam coming from the helmet, which is being used as a cooking pot. There aren't many of these kinds of sight gags in the film—a few might include the woman banging a cat against a wall in the "Plague Cart" scene, the hanging man clapping during the "Knights of the Round Table" musical number, and the man "fishing" in a small stream with a stick (he's bashing the water).

The "knights on parade" is another odd duck image. This single storyboard depicts a line of knights and even cleric types goose-stepping along a raised, trellised parade route, as a small crowd looks on (one man in the crowd stares at us, incidentally). Later on Facing Page 63, a "parade" is mentioned again in a Gilliam note (this one perhaps featuring a *fantastic locomotive*), though no parade appears in the finished film.

The "floating" knight seems to be an unfinished sketch. It depicts a knight helmet very much like the ones mentioned above, but with two plumes sprouting like large antlers, while the unfinished body floats above a raised plinth.

Untitled "weather" storyboards—These two boards present what look to be natural images influenced by Apocalypse-type sources. The first is a stormy sea and sky scene, with two tiny boats riding the crests of two waves. The clouds and water are made to resemble the wavy, stylized Gothic mode seen already in the opening titles animations. The second board is a similar setting but without the sailing boats, and includes a large, flaming image of the sun (or God's wrath) emanating from the upper-left corner of the frame. These images would look right at home in the colorful, vibrant sequences of Apocalypse texts. See the entries for Facing Pages 6, 36, and 43 for more on these texts, and Gilliam's use of them.

Untitled "flying *fleurs-de-lis*" storyboards—These look as if they were to be part of the animated title credit sequence, but were excised at some point. There are two boards, one depicting large *fleurs-de-lis* figures (big enough that only portions of seven fit in the frame), with arrows indicating a "panning down" camera direction. The second storyboard seems to indicate that the *fleurs-de-lis* are behaving like birds, flitting against the open sky.

Untitled "giants" boards—These storyboards are sketched in such a way as to suggest Gilliam may have been thinking of using forced perspective in some of the live action scenes, which can make one character seem larger than another. He'll use this technique in both *Time Bandits* and *Brazil*. Otherwise, these are three vague "giant" sketches that don't explain themselves terribly well, though likely Arthur and his knights were to have an encounter with a giant on their way to the Grail.

knight at a cave mouth—This looks as if the knight has emerged from the cave and is facing off with a menacing tree, one that is borrowed from the stylized trees found in many Gothic manuscripts. That, or this may be the tree that Robin was to have fled to as the "beasties" fought to the death beneath him, before he climbed down and took credit for their demises. This scene did not make it into Robin's story in the film.

frog/man hybrid—This type of hybrid wouldn't have been out of place in the margins of Gothic manuscripts, though none appear in Randall's book—frogs are only depicted three times.

bird and Catherine wheel scene—This final storyboard looks like a return to one of the opening scenes: either Arthur and Patsy cresting the hill and seeing the first castle, or Arthur and Patsy encountering Dennis. Both scenes featured the Catherine wheel raised high in the background. There is no indication what this scene may have added to either of the above-mentioned scenes; perhaps it is an ominous carrion bird flying across the middle ground.

Facing page 60—("The Tale of Sir Launcelot" and "Toothless Old Crone") On this facing page are included two entire sketched storyboard scenes for Gilliam animations that never came to fruition. There are also a handful of mostly Boschian character drawings.

The first set of fourteen storyboards depicts a tailed, armless, and perhaps beaked Boschian giant chasing a man out of a decorative border. By the third frame the pursued has made it to a small home, maybe even a castle, but small still to the giant. The giant looks at us (frame four), and raises a foot to squash the dwelling in frame five. (There is a larger sketch of a scene just like this one—a giant ready to stamp a small man—on Facing Page 6.) Before this giant can bring his foot down the dwelling expands, growing twice as tall. It is now clearly a castle. It trebles in size by the seventh frame, and the giant looks at us again, perplexed. A cadre of spear-carrying soldiers emerges from the castle and surrounds the giant. In the tenth frame a large projectile is launched from the castle, striking the giant's head. By the eleventh frame the giant is down and obviously dead, and the castle is shrinking again. In frame twelve the man stands outside the small home, staring at the moldering giant. The man stands on top of the supine giant, a handful of onlookers watching. The last frame is difficult to interpret, but it looks as if tents and structures have been built on the giant's remains, and the decorative border has returned to adorn the left side of the frame. It may be that the man has cut up and is selling the parts of the giant, but it's not certain (there is a doodle of a partitioned figure on the ground just below frame eleven).

The second set of storyboards depicts an epic fight between Launcelot and a giant snail. (A Gilliam note at the base of the storyboard sequence identifies the scene: "*Mebbe snail jumps bkwrds onto Launcelot.*") At least five of the storyboards are obscured by a page of jumbled drawings laid on top of them, likely by the book's designer, but most or all of the remaining thirteen frames can be seen. In the first frame a snail moves across the scene on a beautiful sunny day. The second and third frames are obscured, and by the fourth the snail is leaping at Launcelot, who wields his sword. The snail is leaping over Launcelot in the fifth frame, and it's apparent that Launcelot has emerged from a small castle to confront the snail. By frame six the snail has leaped over Launcelot completely, and likely reverses the move, as by the next visible frame, the tenth, the snail is leaping at Launcelot again. By the thirteenth (or so) frame the snail finally lands on Launcelot, and by the penultimate frame the snail's shell is upended, and Launcelot is peering out from the opening. The final frame seems to show Launcelot and the snail zooming away into the sky, as a small crowd watches. An image of a snail and a knight fighting in an illuminated manuscript—BBR 9391, f. 39—likely inspired Gilliam for this storyboard sequence. The image is found on Plate XLIX in *IMGM.*

A single sheet of doodles/sketches has been placed on top of the second set of storyboards, obscuring five or six. The doodles include a number of rough cubes, buildings and propeller shapes, as well as "nib-test" scribbles. The sketches include men's caricatured faces and upper bodies, primarily, none of which make it into the finished animation sequences for the film. There is also what appears to be a rough version of an angel playing a portative organ, not unlike the figure Gilliam includes in the animated title sequence. See the entry above for "Title Sequence Animation," fourth entry, for more on that image.

In Gilliam's *bas-de-page* sequence are three figures—two nearly identical grotesques and a masked man. The grotesques are tailed, masked, and torsoless characters with enormous, pull-on feet, and are quite reminiscent of a blue-hooded grotesque appearing in Bosch's *Last Judgment*, specifically in the lower-left portion of the center panel (Linfert, 89). A copy of this very same grotesque (the version at the bottom right of this page) finds its way into Gilliam's *Animations of Mortality*, in the "Sketch Book" section. The long-masked man (the mask sporting curlicue horns) is another version of a character seen on the overlain page mentioned in the preceding paragraph.

Facing page 62—("The Toothless Crone" and "Roger the Shrubber") These rough drawings appear to be an early sketch of what Roger's horse and cart might look like, with Roger at the reins, and several three-dimensional cube and structural drawings. In the finished film Roger's cart is pulled by shabby men.

Facing page 63—("Roger the Shrubber" and "Knights of Ni Get Their Shrubbery") This is a curious page indeed. Most of the page is taken up with industrial drawings—machines, buildings, and characters *not* germane to the medieval setting of the film, or even the anachronistic or reflexive moments of the film. There's also no indication that these drawings were made in relation to the production of *Holy Grail*. They may also be holdovers from *Flying Circus* or even from Gilliam's contributions to *Marty Feldman's Comedy Machine* (1971–1972), for which he produced machine-rich opening and closing credit sequences. Bits and pieces of these kinds of schematic drawings can be found in both *The Complete Works of Shakespeare and Monty Python* and *Animations of Mortality*. Some of this work will also appear much later in *Meaning of Life*.

This is another page where Gilliam helpfully provided page numbers, hints at a book source title, and even most of that title in his marginal notes. A page number followed by "IA" appears seventeen times on the page, and one drawing is even labeled more precisely: "*124 Industrial Art amazing furnace!!*" After significant searching for variations on the book title "Industrial Art" (and there have been many published over the last 110 years), the large format *The Growth of Industrial Art*, first published in 1892 (and then republished later in 1972) was determined to be Gilliam's source for all of these labeled drawings. The drawings, from top to bottom, clockwise, are as follows:

"*106 IA*"—The first drawing Gilliam notes is a "Stove," which in its original form happens to look very much like a nineteenth-century apartment building, a brownstone. In Gilliam's sketched version, he's removed the feet and flue from the original rendering, and placed the apartment-looking stove in an urban street setting—a brownstone. According to *IA*, the stove is an 1880 heating unit and warming oven (Butterworth, 106, fig. 5).

"*99 IA*"—Gilliam notes this next image as a "*Good plunger machine*," and the Butterworth book identifies it as a press for "extracting cane juice" in the sugar-making process, c. 1884 (99, fig. 6).

"*95 IA*"—This is an oil and gas manufacture machine, a "gas generating apparatus" (c. 1884), which Gilliam has redrawn, complete "with shuffling feet," as if part of a mechanical parade (95, fig. 5). Under a later drawing he will mention a potential "*parade*," meaning he had in mind something for these mechanical images that never materialized for the finished animations. This likely means that these were never intended for inclusion in *Holy Grail*, but slipped in with the other Gilliam artwork as this book was being put together in 1977.

"*64 IA*"—Labeled by Gilliam "*Good townscape!!!*" and "*Bridges*," this page contains multiple versions of iron truss bridges, with the "townscape" referring to a rendering of the "East River Suspension Bridge" (64, fig. 8). This is just a Gilliam note; there is no drawing adjacent.

"*109 IA*"—Gilliam has enthusiastically labeled this "*FANTASTIC LOCOMOTIVES*," and identified figures four, six, and seven as worth remembering. He quickly sketched the first two—outlines really—and in more detail sketched (and shaded) "No 7 Extend Cab double length" (109, figs. 4, 6, and 7).

"*69*"—Labeled "*Good Mining Machine Poss[ible] for Parade*," there is no associated drawing with this note, and no figure number, either. There are two figures that seem to fit the "possible for parade" demand, figures eight and nine, both of which are mounted on tracks, and both designed for mining coal (69, figs. 8 and 9).

"*112 IA*"—Gilliam has simply noted "*Silly cyclist*" next to this drawing of a large wheeled bike and rider. The figure he's drawn is a two-wheeled bicycle dated 1880, including the hunched and hiked-knee rider (112, fig. 10). The page is subtitled "Velocipedes" by editor Butterworth.

"60 IA"—This modest dwelling is a typical Gilliam setting, seen a number of times during the run of *Flying Circus*. It's a simple setup of three walls, ceiling, and floor, with a window and door. In its original form it's found on the "Architecture" page in *IA*, and is included as an example of a cutting-edge "removable window sash" (60, fig. 8). Gilliam has tweaked the drawing slightly, as he often does, this time including a landscape, horizon, and clouds just visible on either side of the cutaway walls, as if he's already thinking how the figure will fit into the animated world he's creating. He's done this same kind of creative emendation in the "stove" and "shuffling feet" drawings already discussed, and will continue to do so in drawings discussed below.

walking forest—This storyboard frame seems separate and distinct from most else on the page. It's simply a two-part drawing, on the left a stand of trees, four trunks visible and intermingled canopy, and on the right, a "walking" version of that same drawing. There is no notation or page number attached to this drawing. This may be related to precedents as varied as the moving forest in *Macbeth*, the walking tree mentioned in *MPFC* Ep. 45, or even just the limbed clouds and sun in the "Bloody Weather" scene earlier in *Holy Grail*.

"54 IA"—"*Think about this page*," Gilliam notes to himself, indicating page 54 in the Butterworth book. He performs no drawings (at least recorded here) from this page, which is given over to sketches of "Electrical Illumination and Motors," but he was clearly excited about the possibilities, given his note.

train track storyboard—This sketch looks more modern than medieval. Two characters—both seemingly wearing baseball caps—look at each other in the foreground, and what appears to be a train track disappears into the background between them. It's not clear how this may have fit into the finished film, though if a parade had been in the offing (see mentions of the "parade" above), it may have been used there.

booted chicken—A quick sketch of a chicken strutting with hip-high boots. This looks very much like an Edelmann-inspired character a seen in *Yellow Submarine* and the children's book *Andromedar SR-1* (Facing Page 20). A more finished version of this character can be found in Gilliam's *Animations of Mortality* on the "Lesson No. 3" page of the "Wonderful World of Animation" section.

"151"—Labeling this sketch "*151 Indust. Art*," Gilliam sketches and augments his version of this trunk, specifically number eleven on the page, a wardrobe. He removes the clothing interior in favor of a one-up, one-down apartment popping out of the trunk base. The trunk is otherwise rather precisely rendered from the original.

"99 IA"—This is another mechanical sketch "finished" by Gilliam; he draws the machine, shades it, and then adds clouds, sky, and a landscape. He even labels the sky ("*Blue & fluffy*") and the building ("*Grey*") for later coloring. These are "sugar making" machines, and the one Gilliam chose is a "German Beet Sugar Machine," c. 1879. He has cropped a bit of the upper levels of the plant as he creates the storyboard, and the original artist even provided a hint of clouds in the background on this page. A rough sketch, Gilliam has removed much of the finer detail from the source, including images of at least six workers in the sugar making plant.

"117 IA"—Gilliam notes: "*Silly man & machine for turning out something*" with a rough sketch. This is a c. 1878 "Automatic Lasting Machine," and even when the descriptions provided by Butterworth are read it doesn't explain itself too well (it produces wooden models for feet used by shoe and boot makers).

"37 IA"—Gilliam note: "*Eggs & boxes & things*." This is simply a rectangular egg carton with a cutaway corner, from *IA* page 37, a page depicting various "Egg Carriers." The carton

Gilliam sketched is number five on the page. There is also the beginning of a sketch above this one—a line of eggs standing on end—but Gilliam penned through the drawing.

"116 IA"—Gilliam note: *"No. 7 ought to be coming out of water."* This original is on the same page spread as the "silly man" image noted above in "117 IA," its page depicting "Boot and Shoe Nailing and Pegging" equipment. The seventh image on the page is a "hand pegging" machine. In the original drawing the machine is mounted at the edge of a worktable; Gilliam may have decided it looked nautilus-like and therefore should be *"coming out of water."*

"Safes"—This drawing of an open safe is labeled (*"Safes"*) but not given a page number. The page number in the *IA* book is 150, and is opposite the page where Gilliam found the "apartment wardrobe" described above in *"151 Indust. Art."* This particular drawing appears to be a composite of figure numbers four and five, though the angle of the drawing is more like number six. All are types of safes, and all sit with doors opened in the original images.

"57 IA"—Gilliam note: *"Do something with lift."* Perhaps an error by Gilliam, since the elevators ("lifts") are actually on page 59 of *IA*, not 57. Page 57 is given over to "Grain Conveyors," which have some lifting abilities, but Gilliam is clearly sketching from the examples of page 59. He hasn't reproduced any of the elevators precisely enough to identify which was his target, but there are resemblances to figures one, two, and six on page 59, all passenger or freight elevators.

brick wall storyboard—This is an unlabeled drawing that depicts a man staring up at a brick wall, and a man staring back from the other side. There are dozens of such brick walls in *IA*, though none seem to have directly influenced this sketch.

"124 Industrial Art"—Gilliam note: *"Amazing furnace!"* Gilliam's version of this "amazing furnace" is rather small and unadorned, and even difficult to see very well on the page. The original is a "Bessemer Plant," c. 1884, and is figure seven on page 124.

various sketches—These sketches in the corner of the page include three flowers (two are dandelions), a mountainous landscape, two cubed figures, a face shaped like a hot iron, and the word "Leviticus." None of these appear in the finished film, though there are a number of flowers included by Gothic artists in illuminated manuscripts.

"174 Industrial Art"—This is another "finished" or augmented drawing. Gilliam has added to the original, sketching several trees into the scene, making the machine look more like a towering building. He's also added a man sitting on another man's shoulders, twice (an arrow between them), with an appended note: *"Why is this man [sta]nding on the others shoulders."* He doesn't answer his own question, of course. The bracketed letters were missing on the page, likely due to another page covering them up as the book was created. The original—"Levers to Lift Stitches Over Vertically Arranged Needles," c. 1854—is drawing number four on page 174.

"170 IA"—Another augmented drawing. The machine has been sketched into a landscape, and is depicted from above—as if an establishing helicopter shot[7]—complete with clouds, cast shadows, and the outlines of land parcels (hedgerows?). The original drawing is a "steam vacuum pump" (c. 1842) depicted on a brick surface.

"Terrace house" sketches—A terrace house neighborhood is one where high-density populations can be housed in identical, attached rows of houses. They are seen in rich and poor areas alike, but have most often been associated with the demands of the Industrial Revolution, housing factory workers in sooty, despoiled mill and mine towns as affordably as possible. (The Catholic and Protestant families depicted in "Every Sperm is Sacred" in *Meaning of Life* both live in row houses in Yorkshire.) These are the kinds of houses and neighborhoods and towns that characters in the "Angry Young Men" world (*Room at the Top, Saturday Night and Sunday Morning, This Sporting Life*, et al.) roil around in and rage against, and the kind we've seen in *Flying Circus* sketches like "The New Cooker Sketch" (Ep. 14).

There are two terrace house sketches here. The first is a simple sketch of a single terrace house that is labeled "*Terrace house missile launchers.*" There is no indication as to the missile portion of the house.[8] The second sketch is more recognizable. Labeled "*Terraced houses flying in—taking over landscape,*" this image of a line of incoming terraced house won't make it into *Holy Grail*, but will appear in both the Gilliam book *Animations of Mortality* and later in animated form for the title sequence of *Meaning of Life.*

Facing page 65—("The Knights of Ni Get Their Shrubbery") There is a single Boschian hybrid in the bottom left corner of this page, a cartoony, four-legged and even winged amphibian with a human face.

Facing page 67—("The Dead Historian Covered") This is another densely populated page of sketches and storyboards, including:

Untitled "parchments" sketches—These are simply eight separate, tiny drawings of rolled parchment.

handwritten notes—Gilliam penned notes to himself at the top of the page, including these separate entries: "*Rich Castle*"; "*Fighting Beast*"; "*Monastery or Town*"; "*Angels*"; and "*Windmill.*" Next to this list is a sentence: "*Animation starts in Medieval Style begins to be intruded by other elements,*" which actually describes the bulk of the film.

Untitled "firing squad" sketch—This is a sight gag image. Three men with rifles fire point blank at an upright coffin tied to a tree. It looks much more like a "marginal" cartoon from *Mad* magazine's Sergio Aragones (b. 1937) than anything found in the margins of a Gothic manuscript, though the twisted humor is similar.

"God caught playing with himself" storyboards—This is one of those more profane images of or references to God that Gilliam sketched but didn't include in the finished film. In both the earliest iteration of the script and Gilliam's sketches in these pages there were more offensive portrayals of God (He's angry, spiteful, crude), and those depictions eventually gave way to the slightly terse ("Course it's a good idea!") but still mostly dignified ("it is your sacred task") Lord of Arthur and his knights.

Untitled "giant head" storyboard—This is a small, odd sketch of a giant, beaked bird head flying across a landscape.

Untitled "wheeled cart with house" sketch—There are a handful of these kinds of drawings in *IMGM*, many looking like vendor carts with dwellings on top. See the notes to Facing Pages 6 and 51 for more.

Unnumbered "dragon" head sketch—This head is oddly set on the page—craning upward and disembodied, though that could have been the position chosen by the book's designer. With some research it turns out this isn't a dragon but a lion, and it is also borrowed from the Randall book, figure 632 (pl. CXXXIII). In the original image Samson sits astride the lion, pulling back on his head and jaw, hence the craned neck here. The image is drawn from Y.T. 13, the Taymouth Hours, British Library collection (Randall, 38).

Untitled "wheeled weather" sketch—This sketch of a large cloud erected on a scaffold and on wheels is perhaps one of the unused studies for the "Bloody Weather" scene.

Untitled "hybrid creature" sketch—This hybrid is a four-legged, tailed, long-necked creature that seems part amphibian and part mammal. There are similar creatures on Facing Page 43, another Bosch-inspired page of drawings.

Untitled "cartoony" sketches—A man with three plug-in noses (different-sized noses, all interchangeable); a goateed grotesque; three iterations of a big-hand man (variations on the harp player from Bosch's *Temptation*); a profile sketch of an odd-looking, Gene Deitch-like character; a bloated torso on wheels; and a pumpkin-shaped head.

Bosch drawings—There are seven drawings borrowed from *The Temptation of St. Anthony*, which has been used already by Gilliam (Facing Page 43). Several, including a version of St. Anthony himself, are from the central focus area of the center panel, and include the following:

Untitled "harp player" sketch—An animal skeleton-faced Bosch grotesque plays a harp very near the center of the action, and Gilliam has redrawn this character (or portions of it) several times, mostly the right arm and hand. He has also replaced the skeleton face with an open-mouthed, human face, partially shrouded by a cowl and hood. He drew the face twice, and the arm three times (Tolnay, 136, 144, 152).

Untitled "blessing" man sketch—This is St. Anthony, who kneels at the center of the center panel of the Bosch work (Linfert, 79). This is a rather careful character study, and Gilliam has clearly taken time and effort to create a lifelike rendering, which is likely why this drawing stands out from most others in these pages.

Untitled "masked" man sketch—This character carries a mandolin, and is likely wearing a mask. He stands behind St. Anthony, with an owl perching on his head (Tolnay, 136, 138, 142; Linfert, 79).

Untitled "nimbed" man sketch—This character has a nimb of light or flames emanating from his head, and looks very much like Bosch's two *sketch* versions of St. Anthony as he prepared for the ultimate painting *The Temptation of St. Anthony* (Tolnay, 319).

Untitled "bridge" sketch—Though not immediately apparent, the small bridge Gilliam has drawn into the upper-left corner of this page is also lifted directly from Bosch's work. In *The Temptation of St. Anthony* it's found in the upper-left corner of the center panel, precisely as it's positioned in Gilliam's version. In that Bosch panel a horsed rider is crossing the bridge (at the head of others), while Gilliam has drawn a single man crossing his version of the bridge on foot (Tolnay, 153). A very similar bridge can be seen in both the right panel of Bosch's *Garden of Earthly Delights*, there being crossed by an armed and horsed attacking force, as well as at the center of the center panel of Bosch's *Last Judgment*, where grotesques of all types are crossing (Tolnay, 240, 243). It seems that when a bridge is needed, Bosch paints the same, simple one, over and over again.

Photo inserts between (crossed-out) pages 74 and 75—Between the final dusty red page (74) and the first blue page (75)—both crossed-through "King Brian the Wild" pages—are sixteen pages of frame captures and unused (but seemingly finished) animation pages. The animated spread is a two-page composite of two separate scenes. The first scene is when all the animated knights are reunited, "and there was much rejoicing." The second scene is when they've entered "the frozen land of Nador," and the sun is blown away by Old Man Winter. In this composite, the Old Man Winter character has been integrated into the branches of the Winchester Bible-like tree (a scene from the life of David), and the sun sits low on the horizon. Both of these scenes are discussed in the "Passing Seasons" Animation section of the main part of this book.

Facing page 68—("Animation: The Passing Seasons") Here are seventeen storyboards and two annotated sketches. The storyboards are from the final animated sequences, when Robin and his minstrels return, and then when the man on the hillock enjoys the passing seasons.

The drawings are labeled "*183 F of MA*" (a stylized tree) and "*188 F of MA*" (a multi-storied, cutaway building), and are borrowed from *The Flowering of the Middle Ages*. The tree image comes from the *Psalter of Saint Louis and Blanche of Castille*, a thirteenth-century manuscript housed in the Bibliothèque Nationale (MS. 1186, f. IV), mentioned earlier. The cutaway building is actually a medieval apothecary. The latter image—the apothecary—is not found in the finished film, and likely disappeared when the script elements of Arthur and Merlin and friends trafficking in potions was deleted during the writing process.

Facing page 71—("Tim the Enchanter" and "The Cave of Caerbannog") The director (or directors) covered this page with storyboards and notes for the shooting of the Killer Rabbit scene. The storyboards include the establishing shots ("*skull*" and "*scarred tree*") to the peering at the harmless rabbit to the handheld mayhem of the attacks. There are almost *seventy* hastily sketched storyboards, many recognizable as part of the finished film. Accompanying notes include mentions of the actors/characters involved, perhaps paired ("*Patsy and an "x";* *Galahad—Neil; Robin—Old Man; Bed[evere]—Suko; Lancelot—Eric*"), camera directions ("*Ad lib hand held*" and "*Tighter for pin out*"), and effects possibilities ("*Try real rabbit on Bors dummy pointed in right direction so that it will hop back to cave*"). It looks like extra Mitsuko ("Suko") Forstater participated, as did Neil Innes. It may be that the principals like Palin (in costume as a monk), Cleese (in makeup as Tim), and director Jones were purposely doubled in this long fight sequence. There are also directions for how Bro. Maynard should enter shots and be photographed (before being consumed), a complete sketch of how a rabbit on a string could be pulled directly at a dummy's head (leading to a decapitation), and at some point the directors wonder where and how a "stuffed rabbit" should be employed. There are also dozens of doodles, including the word "Inspector" written out ten (and a half) times, as well as myriad geometric figures (see below). Lastly, there is a reminder that "*2 Clipboards*" are needed at some point.

The geometric sketches—often a cylinder mounted on a rectangular or "crossed" base, and all done in three dimensions—may actually have a basis in the historical sources Gilliam plundered for the film. A very recognizable cylinder (with vines crawling along it) emerges from a rectangular base in the jumbled area immediately around the prostrate St. Jerome in the Bosch painting of the same name (Tolnay, 264–65, 269, 270). More geometric sketches will appear on Facing Page 77.

Facing page 77—("The Black Beast of Arrrghhh") This is a sketch page, primarily made up of versions of the "Beast." There are also assorted faces, claws/hands, hooves, and more geometric designs. Some sketches worth noting include: a caricature that may be Richard Nixon; several more snails in and out of their shells (see Facing Pages 21, 31, 38, 46, and 60); more long-faced human caricatures; and more images of the Beast attacking (see Facing Page 38, as well) and even eating Bro. Maynard. There is also a hippo facing the viewer, mouth open.

Facing page 78—("The Black Beast of Arrrghhh") Four sketched cave storyboards and another rendering of the "Beast" occupy this page. The storyboards include shots of reading the cave wall and Brother Maynard being consumed.

Facing page 79—("The Black Beast of Arrrghhh") There are four more storyboards from the Black Beast attack scene, as well as five other sketches of versions of the Black Beast, and various hands, feet, and eyes and nose, and a quick sketch of the face of the Mona Lisa. There is a single sketch depicting a screen or storyboard mounted on two human feet, the drawing on the screen looking very much like a *Yellow Submarine* "foothills of the headlands" scene (giant torsos rising out of a landscape).

Facing page 80—("The Bridge of Death") Thirteen storyboards depict the knights' escape from the cave and their discovery of the Bridge of Death. This would have been one of the very first days of shooting.

Facing page 81—("The Bridge of Death") Twenty-six separate storyboards (including five boards with four inserts each) trace the action from leaving the Cave to discovering the Bridge of Death to successfully answering questions and crossing. One action that is different from the finished film is the "hand on the shoulder" moment (kind of a "That's a fair cop" iteration, seen several times in *MPFC* Ep. 29) as Launcelot is arrested just after stepping off the bridge. In the film the scene involves Launcelot being patted down after crossing.

Facing page 83—("The Bridge of Death") This facing page is covered with the hand-written version of the Bridgekeeper's demise, likely penned for the book's publication. (The giveaway is the absolute accuracy of the dialogue, including all the hemming and hawing found in the lines as delivered, which are generally left out of printed scripts.)

Facing page 84—("At the Grail Castle") Twenty-eight storyboards of the "dragon" boat and the approach to the Grail Castle. An elided scene—where the boatkeeper demands answers to twenty-eight questions and is summarily tossed overboard—is drawn here but not included in the finished film.

Facing page 85—("At the Grail Castle") Twenty-six sketched storyboards of the approach to Grail Castle and the resulting taunts from the French occupiers.

Facing page 86—("At the Grail Castle") Another significant sketch page, including the following, top to bottom, and clockwise:

lion—This is a somewhat caricatured lion, a bit tatty, and looks like animated characters as produced by the Jay Ward and Bill Scott productions—that is, *Rocky & Bullwinkle*.

legged eggs—Two walking eggs (or ovoids), each with an eye hole. A character like this appeared in a Warner Bros.' Foghorn Leghorn cartoon, and there are also Bosch creatures very similar to this.

annotated storyboards—There are two storyboards sketched here, one of which is partially obscured by the "legged eggs" sketches, with this note from Gilliam: "*OS. change they react to this—all before town comes into view.*" The storyboard shows a man standing by a road sign labeled "2 mi." In the clearly visible storyboard there is a building at the far left; in the partially obscured storyboard the buildings are much closer, and the sign's lettering seems to have changed. Apparently, the town is moving closer, and the sign changes to reflect that.

Bosch profile—This looks like another sketch influenced by Bosch, this one likely from *Christ Carrying the Cross* (c. 1490). Bosch-inspired sketches have appeared on facing pages 37, 38, 43, 45, 60, and 67.

"*Good Boat 140*"—This is another figure number from *IMGM*. In this figure are two images of Noah's ark, one as it is under construction, and one as it is being loaded with animals. The plate XXX image is a full page from Add. 39810, f. 7, the *St. Omer Psalter*, and part of the British Library collection (Randall 28).

"*water move towards castle*"—This seems a variation on the storyboard above, with the boat riding a wave closer to the castle. This is likely part of a proposed animated scene from the Grail Castle sequence, with Castle Stalker in mind.

three-hooved creature—A very rough sketch of a torso, legs and triple-hooved footed creature.

cubes—Several adorned cubes—one with a man on the side, one with a man inside, one with a door, and one with other rectilinear designs. These seem to be doodles.

"*silly beasties leaping about . . .*"—A Gilliam note to himself: "*Silly beasties leaping about suddenly they leap into hiding—just as knights ride thru then they hop out again.*" This won't make it into the finished *Holy Grail*, but has already appeared in *Flying Circus* Ep. 34. Two animated creatures—one resembling the "Beast" designed for *Holy Grail*—are glimpsed throughout the episode, then leap out and dance when the coast is clear.

lance fishing—A clever visual pun. It looks as if a man—who has bested a knight (he's dead on the ground, as is his horse)—sits at streamside fishing with the fallen knight's jousting lance. There is a smaller, separate drawing of a fishing lance as well as the dead knight, next to this main drawing.

character sketches—Various sketches, a few of which are recognizable, including an oft-drawn snail, a version of the Legendary Black Beast, as well as a man wearing a hair tie, a standing man, a robed man, building blocks, a hand holding cigarettes(?), a rolling pin kind of device, and a child.

Facing page 87—("At the Grail Castle" and "Stop the Film") A DCR (dated 25 May 1974), labeled "Battlefield" (shot above Stirling). The shot is recorded without sound, and is noted as being "handheld." There is also a note that an extra somehow put a "pike thru filter/scratching lens slightly," which extra Alastair Scott remembered fondly: "Then someone tripped in front of the camera and accidentally put the tip of his pike into the lens, breaking a filter which word went round cost £100. The film crew were deeply pissed off about this" (appendix B).

Facing page 88—("Stop the Film") This is the final facing page featuring additional artwork or production material, and it includes storyboards, sketches, and a director's note. There is a handwritten note at the top of the page, which reads like a camera direction: "*When A[rthur] & B[edevere] hear voices & walk away from camera next shot should just have smoke first before they appear.*" This may be from the end of the film as they seek the Grail Castle, but it reads very much like the scene where horsemen are riding in and out of the fog at the beginning of Kurosawa's *Throne of Blood*, and so could be from earlier. Other images here include:

title storyboards—There are seven completed storyboards (and one partly complete) from the first section of the titles animations—the trumpet sequence. This is a more freeform opening sequence than the finished version, with Gilliam drawing elaborate, columnal clouds and angels with festooned trumpets. These more elaborate clouds are also sketched on Facing Page 51. There's no indication yet of Gilliam considering making copies from Gothic manuscript images.

men singing—Two singing figures—one a full body drawing of a man, head high, and notes coming from his mouth, as well as simply a singing head emerging from the distance.

storyboard sketches for Grail Castle sequence—Two rough sketches illustrating an establishing shot of the castle in water, the approaching boat, as well as the surrounding landscape. As this likely would have involved a helicopter to realize, the shot does not appear in the finished film.

wooden legs—Three successive sketches of a man with a wooden leg. These are also Bosch-inspired images, from the center panel of *The Temptation of St. Anthony* Gilliam's already mined (Facing Page 67). One of the figures just behind Anthony at the center of the triptych is a crippled man wearing a prosthetic on his right leg, and leaning on a long cane with his left hand. This type of "knee-bent" prosthetic is just the type Gilliam sketched.

final assault sketches—There are four "marshaling and attack" storyboards, three of which show a horde of castle defenders streaming out of the castle as Arthur's army attacks. No castle defenders are used in the finished film (they would have added to the budget). The fourth storyboard sketch shows assembled banners (heralds), and Gilliam has labeled it: "*Banners pouring thru.*" In the end, the assault on the Grail Castle took place on Sheriffmuir near Stirling.

mustachioed man—The design of this man hearkens back to the proposed psychedelic version of the animated title credits. He is designed to be something of a man-wagon—his enormous mustache stretches along the ground and ends at two mounted wheels.

birds and frogs—Two large dodo-type birds and two top heavy frogs. One of the birds is pulling a church on a wagon, the other sports four legs, and one of the frogs is labeled with an *R*. It's not clear whether Gilliam started a more complete label for the frog and stopped, or whether the balance of the word was covered by another illustration.

the Holy Grail—A sketch of a shining grail that looks very much like the grail used in the eventual animations.

pear-shaped knight—This looks like Bedevere as performed by Jones, appearing large in the hips and waist. The insignia on this knight's tunic is a cross.

split-head man—This image of death—with the skull splitting open—was fairly common in artwork of the medieval period.

Notes

1. I will skip completely the frame captures and still photos—they are self-explanatory. Facing Pages that are blank or have photos only are not included hereafter.

2. The reader will have to take my word on this, but the connection between the many numbered drawings on Gilliam's sketch sheets and Randall's *IMGM* (1968) wasn't made by this researcher until early 2011. The Gilliam commentary on the 2012 Blu-ray edition of *MPHG* was the first confirmation. Gilliam misremembers the title, but it's clear the book he's talking about is Randall's. Gilliam *does not* mention the other books (*The Flowering of the Middle Ages* or *Industrial Art*) where he borrowed images and inspiration, or where the many Bosch drawings came from. This author also belatedly discovered (in 2013) pertinent articles from 1998 and 2004 by Dr. Martine Meuwese, Cambridge Illumination Project, where the Randall source was also identified and discussed. *C'est la vie.*

3. Some of the unfinished animated work for this castle sequence can be seen on the "special features" of the Blu-ray edition of the film.

4. These same types of creatures are found in one other Edelmann work, a children's book published in 1971 called *Andromedar SR-1*. Both book and film could have been influential for Gilliam as he worked on ideas for *Holy Grail*.

5. Gervase of Tilbury writes of similar creatures living in Egypt, considered the "wilds" surrounding the Holy Land (Oman, 4).

6. This may have been an animation intended for the final scene of the film, when Arthur and his warriors encounter the French-occupied island castle. There are later storyboard images that depict the ship carrying Arthur and Bedevere as it nears the castle, likely for possible animated scenes.

7. The first draft of the script called for at least two helicopter shots. No such shots were made for the finished film.

8. The British ICBM of the period was Blue Streak, a missile system with a checkered operational history, and perhaps, to Gilliam, an ideal missile to be launched from a terraced house. See notes for "Black Knight" earlier.

PERSONAL CORRESPONDENCE

From Alastair Scott:

My memory of the circumstances of Stirling University students being involved is that the 'normal' (Equity-card-holding?) extras had effectively gone on strike or were at least demanding to be paid £5 per day. The film producers considered this unreasonable and thought 'Let's get some students and offered us £2 a day! Notices went up about extras wanted and we students were only too thrilled to take a day off and be involved in a 'Monty Python' event of such proportions—to be in a major film! And it was £2 plus food! We were the nearest uni to the battle scene location which I can't remember where it was but presume it was north of the uni on Sheriffmuir. We were taken there in buses—I imagine there must have been about 100 of us but the battle scene will give a more exact impression. We were assessed for size and just handed bits of clothing to put on and whatever weapon an official thought appropriate. I remember thinking how clever the chain mail was as it was just wool sprayed with silver paint, and as light as a feather. It was a day of much waiting around and inactivity. Naturally it took ages for everyone to be dressed and armed. Mostly I remember hanging around not having a clue what was going on. It all seemed fairly disorganised and chaotic.

Eventually we were called to action. We had to gather uphill from the camera and then come charging down, brandishing our weapons and screaming. The centre of our phalanx had to peel either side of the camera so that it would see men rushing past very close-up. My other main memory of the day was endless trips up the slope to repeat the process—again and again and again. Did we have to do it 10, 20 or 30 times? . . . it seemed like 30! People kept on laughing so we had to reshoot repeatedly because of this, being yelled at by people with megaphones to keep serious, angry faces. Then people would trip over as the terrain was full of tussocks, so we had to reshoot as half the 'army' hadn't even made it to the 'enemy'. As we were meant to be shooting a battle scene and yet we were the only army attacking an empty hillside of film crew, it was hard to take it seriously and it was all very surreal. It was also very hard to maintain a serious expression as people in front of you performed spectacular collapses with arms legs and weapons sprawling, and then lay there helpless in hysterics. So it took forever. Then someone tripped in front of the camera and accidentally put the tip of his pike into the lens, breaking a filter which word went round cost £100. The film crew were deeply pissed off about this.

Then they went for a few close-ups of people. I remember a group of us were selected and the camera panned across our woollen-tight-clad legs, closely cropped on the legs only. I was thrilled and made a note that on the film mine would be third pair of legs from the left. When I saw the film I was disappointed that the legs shots were not used. The battle-scene seemed ridiculously short—was it only about 30 seconds?—when we had the impression it would be a major feature!! Yet I thought they had put it together very cleverly.

We had a ball—it was a great experience and one we brag about in a lighthearted way!

From Jim McIver:

It had been known for some time that the "Monty Python" team were filming in the Stirling area, as, not only had various members of the cast been seen in local restaurants, but also a number of local people had been given temporary employment with the crew. One of my flat mates, Steve Bannell, worked with them for several weeks, following the completion of his dissertation, serving as a general 'odd job' man and doubling for Eric Idle in those scenes where he played several characters at once. He would come back in the evening and tell us about his weird day—stuffing rotting sheep carcasses, building giant wooden rabbits, etc.

Then, one day, notices went up at the MacRobert box office, inviting students to come along to appear as extras. There was a mad rush for places on the morning of the filming, and I think around 120 were selected, based on height, build, etc., for the various positions in the invading army (I was a bowman).

On the day of the filming, we were kitted out with our tunics, chain mail (knitted from string and painted silver), helmets and weapons, and had various touches of make-up applied to make us look haggard and dirty (Stirling students—surely not!). We were then loaded onto a coach and driven up to Sheriffmuir, where a number of coloured tents were visible along the ridge of a low, sloping field, and smoke was rising from various machines to create the appearance of mist.

The different units were separated out and given a minimum of coaching, and various shots of pike-men, bowmen and knights were filmed, most of which were never used. The rest of the day was spent charging down the slope towards an imaginary French army.

Each time we reached the bottom of the hill, we turned and looked back at what was truly like the scene of some battle! The ground was so uneven (a sort of dried-up bog), that quite a few people had fallen, and the ground was covered in swords, pikes and bows, not to mention the 'walking wounded' picking themselves up to trudge down to join the rest of us. Then we had to haul ourselves back up the hill and do it all over again. We must have charged 7 or 8 times that day, and it is a miracle no one was hurt.

It should be noted that it was a beautiful summer's day, and, after a few charges, there was no longer any need for make-up to give us that haggard, dirty look.

During the lunch break, which, I seem to recollect, was some sort of "shepherd's pie" and a mug of tea, I found a space to sit with my back to a Land Rover wheel while I ate. I got chatting to the 'occupant' of the other wheel, who turned out to be Terry Gilliam, no less. He was extremely friendly, as were the other "Pythons" with whom we spent the day. The only exception was John Cleese, who arrived, went into Make-Up, did his scene in the back of the Police van and promptly left again, much to everyone's disappointment.

When the filming was over, we were all desperate for a drink, as it had been extremely thirsty work. Indeed, during the lunch break, a number of knights commandeered a car to the nearby 'Sher-iffmuir Inn' and brought back a 'carry out' of dozens of cans of beer. The sight of all these medieval soldiers lying in the sun, drinking cans of MacEwan's will stay with me for life! I don't know what the patrons of the Inn thought, but then, it wasn't unusual to see a bear drinking beer in the bar of that particular establishment ('Hercules' was a brown bear, raised from a cub by the bar's owner Andy Robbins, and the two even had a wrestling ring set up the car park at one time).

As we waited for the coach back to the Uni, we were all sitting on the grass on a bend in the road, near the entrance to the field. The looks on the faces of passing motorists were hilarious! With the coach delayed somewhere, a number of us managed to hitch a lift back to the 'Grange' in the back of the "Black Maria" in which John Cleese had been filmed earlier. I now know what the "Black Hole of Calcutta" must have felt like—the smell of dozens of tired, sweaty bodies crammed into the back of the van was almost overwhelming!!!

It was one of the most enjoyable and memorable days of my student life, rounded off nicely by being paid the handsome sum of £2.00 for a day's work. It may not seem much now, but £1.00 could buy 5 or 6 pints at the 'Grange', plus 20 cigarettes, AND still leave you with some change!!! (God, re-reading what I just wrote makes me feel very old indeed—I sound like my grandfather!)

I have watched the film dozens of times, and have even used 'freeze frame' on the DVD, but I have never been able to identify either myself or anyone else I knew. I recall that 2 of the knights who led the charge were Nick Rowe (from St Albans?) and Duncan MacAulay (from Perth), but I couldn't say which one was which.

I don't know if any of this is of use to you, but it has certainly brought back fond memories for myself.

Good luck with your project!
Jim McIver (BA English Studies 1973–1976)
3rd Bowman from the left . . . possibly!

From Nick Rowe (second-year undergrad):

Warm, sunny day, probably early Fall 1974. I was a second year undergrad at Stirling. I was at the pub, I think, and someone suggested we go to Doune castle to see Monty Python filming. I had a car, so drove a few of us there, for a picnic. The Pythons were milling around in costume. I think I remember seeing the Trojan rabbit. Some of us were a bit drunk. One of the Pythons came over and asked us to quiet down, since they were filming.

Some days later there was a call for extras at Stirling. I joined in, for 5 pounds I think (plus a free sausage sandwich lunch). I was taller than the average student, so was picked out, along with a half dozen of the taller guys, to be a knight. I was given a suit of chainmail (made of string, I think), a helmet (with golden eagle on top), and a sword (I think). They put us all on a bus and drove us up to Sheriffmuir (desolate moorland scene on the hills a couple of miles north of the campus). We formed up as the army. I was in the second row, near the front, along with the other knights. They had us all shout "Betty Marsden" (I think). Then we charged. It was hard to see wearing a full helmet, so I tripped on a bunch of heather and fell flat on my face. The rest of the army ran past me.

When the "police" told us to go home, some of the army didn't obey quickly enough. They told us to obey, and look sheepish about it.

BIBLIOGRAPHY

Aberth, John. *A Knight at the Movies: Medieval History on Film*. New York: Routledge, 2003.

Adamnani, Saint. *Adamnani Vita S. Colombae*. Ed. J. T. Fowler and William Reeves. Oxford: Clarendon Press, 1894.

Adams, Oscar Fay. *The Vision of Sir Lamoracke: Post-Laureate Idyls and Other Poems*. Boston: Lothrop, 1886.

Ainsworth, W. Harrison. "Old Saint Paul's: An Historical Romance." *Ainsworth's Magazine: A Miscellany of Romance, General Literature, and Art*. London: Chapman and Hall, 1846.

Alcock, Leslie. *Arthur's Britain*. London: Penguin, 1989 (orig. 1971).

———. *Kings and Warriors, Craftsmen and Priests in Northern Britain AD 550–850*. Edinburgh: Society of Antiquaries of Scotland, 2003.

———. *Was This Camelot? Excavations at Cadbury Castle, 1966–1970*. New York: Stein and Day, 1972.

Aldgate, Anthony. *Censorship and the Permissive Society: British Cinema and Theatre, 1955–1965*. Oxford: Oxford University Press, 1995.

Alexander, Jonathan, and Paul Binski, eds. *Age of Chivalry: Art in Plantagenet England 1200–1400*. London: Weidenfeld and Nicolson, 1987.

Alt, James, Ivor Crewe, and Bo Särlvik. "Angels in Plastic: The Liberal Surge in 1974." *Political Studies* 25, no. 3 (September 1977): 343–68.

Altman, Rick. *The American Film Musical*. Bloomington: Indiana University Press, 1989.

Amidi, Amid. *Cartoon Modern: Style and Design in Fifties Animation*. San Francisco, CA: Chronicle Books, 2006.

Anglo-Saxon Chronicle, The. Ed. Michael J. Swanton. London: Routledge, 1996.

The Anglo-Saxon Version of the Life of St. Guthlac, Hermit of Crowland. Trans. and Notes by Charles W. Goodwin. London: John Russell Smith, 1848.

Approved Judgment Between (1) Mark Forstater (2) Mark Forstater Productions Limited and (1) Python (Monty) Pictures Ltd (2) Freeway Cam (UK) Ltd. High Court of Justice Chancery Division, 5 July 2013. http://www.judiciary.gov.uk/judgments/forstater-v-python-monty-pictures-ltd-other/

Ardagh, John. "Filming *The Canterbury Tales*: Pier Paolo's Chaucer-alla Roma." *Times* (20 November 1971): 7.

Ashe, Geoffrey. *The Discovery of King Arthur*. Garden City, NY: Anchor Press/Doubleday, 1985.

———. *The Quest for Arthur's Britain*. New York: Praeger, 1968.

Ashley, Doris. *King Arthur and the Knights of the Round Table*. London: Raphael Tuck, 1922.

Ashley, W. J., ed. *Edward III and His Wars, 1327–1360*. London: David Nutt, 1887.

Austin, Greta. "Were the Peasants Really So Clean? The Middle Ages in Film." *Film History* 14, no. 2 (2002): 136–41.

BIBLIOGRAPHY

Bakhtin, Mikhail. *Rabelais and His World*. Trans. Helene Iswolsky. Bloomington: Indiana University Press, 1984.

Ballard, J. G. *Empire of the Sun*. New York: Simon & Schuster, 1984.

Barber, Richard. *The Holy Grail: Imagination and Belief*. Cambridge, MA: Harvard University Press, 2004.

———. "Looking for the Holy Grail." *History Today* 54, no. 3 (March 2004): 13–19.

Barlow, Frank. *Thomas Becket*. Berkeley: University of California Press, 1986.

Barnes, Clive. "Out of Season on Broadway." *Times: New York Notebook* (10 May 1975): 9.

Barron, W. R. J., ed. *The Arthur of the English*. Cardiff: University of Wales Press, 2001.

Bartlett, C. J. *A History of Postwar Britain 1945–1974*. London: Longman, 1977.

Bartlett, Robert. *Inside the Medieval Mind: Knowledge*. TV documentary. BBC Films. 2008.

Baugh, Albert C. *A History of the English Language*. New York: Appleton-Century-Crofts, 1963.

———, et al. *A Literary History of England*. 2nd ed. New York: Appleton-Century-Crofts, 1948.

Bax, D. *Hieronymus Bosch: His Picture-Writing Deciphered*. Trans. M. A. Bax-Botha. Rotterdam: A.A. Balkema, 1979.

Bearman, Jonathan. "Anatomy of the Bennite Left." *International Socialism* 2, no. 6 (Autumn 1979): 51–70.

Beck, Jerry, and Will Friedwald, eds. *Looney Tunes and Merrie Melodies*. New York: Henry Holt, 1989.

Beckett, Andy. "1970s: From *Life on Mars* to the Return of *The Goodies . . .*" *Guardian* 25 May 2007. http://www.theguardian.com/lifeandstyle/2007/may/26/weekend.andybeckett.

Bede. *Bede's Ecclesiastical History of the English People*. Ed. Bertram Colgrave and R. A. B. Mynors. Oxford: Clarendon Press, 1969.

———. *A History of the English Church and People*. Trans. and ed. Leo Shirley Price. Baltimore, MD: Penguin, 1964.

Bell, Patrick. *The Labour Party in Opposition, 1970–1974*. London: Routledge, 2004.

Bellamy, Frank. *King Arthur and His Knights*. London: Book Palace, 2008.

Benn, Anthony (Tony) Wedgwood. *Against the Tide: Diaries 1973–76*. London: Hutchinson, 1989.

———. *The New Politics: A Socialist Reconnaissance* ("Fabian Tract 402"). London: Fabian Society, 1970.

———. *Office without Power: Diaries 1968–72*. London: Hutchinson, 1988.

———. *Out of the Wilderness: Diaries 1963–67*. London: Hutchinson, 1987.

Bennett, Alan, Peter Cook, Jonathan Miller, and Dudley Moore. *Beyond the Fringe*. New York: Random House, 1963.

———. *Beyond the Fringe: A Revue*. New York: Samuel French, 1964.

Beresford, M. W. *The Lost Villages of England*. New York: Philosophical Library, 1954.

Berlin, Normand. "Macbeth: Polanski and Shakespeare." *Literature/Film Quarterly* 1, no. 4 (Fall 1973): 291–98.

Bernstein, George Lurcy. *The Myth of Decline: The Rise of Britain since 1945*. London: Pimlico, 2004.

Berthelot, Anne. *King Arthur and the Knights of the Round Table*. New York: Harry N. Abrams, 1997.

Besserman, Lawrence. "The Idea of the Green Knight." *ELH* 53, no. 2 (Summer 1986): 219–39.

Binski, Paul, and Patrick Zutshi. *Western Illuminated Manuscripts: A Catalogue of the Collection in Cambridge University Library*. Cambridge: Cambridge University Press, 2011.

Bishop, Ellen. "Bakhtin, Carnival and Comedy: The New Grotesque in *Monty Python and the Holy Grail*." *Film Criticism* 15 (1990): 49–64.

Bishop, Morris. *The Horizon Book of the Middle Ages*. Boston: Houghton Mifflin, 1968.

Black, Lawrence. *Redefining British Politics: Culture, Consumerism and Participation, 1954–70*. Basingstoke: Palgrave Macmillan, 2010.

Black, Lawrence, Hugh Pemberton, and Pat Thane, eds. *Reassessing 1970s Britain*. Manchester: Manchester University Press, 2013.

Bloom, Harold. Introduction. In *Don Quixote*, by Miguel de Cervantes. Translated by Edith Grossman. New York: HarperCollins, 2003.

Boccaccio, Giovanni. *The Decameron*. Trans. John Payne. New York: Walter J. Black, 1886.

Bodleian Library Illuminated Manuscript Collection. LUNA. http://bodley30.bodley.ox.ac.uk:8180/luna/servlet/ODLodl~1~1.

Bolle, Frank W. *Robin Hood* (1955–1957). Magazine Enterprises. Comic Book Plus. http://comicbook plus.com/?cid=1073.

Booker, Christopher. *The Neophiliacs*. Boston: Gambit, 1970.

———. *The Seventies: Portrait of a Decade*. London: Allen Lane, 1980.

Bordwell, David. "The Art Cinema as a Mode of Film Practice." *Film Criticism* 4, no. 1 (Fall 1979): 57–64.

Bordwell, David, Janet Staiger, and Kristin Thompson. *The Classical Hollywood Cinema*. London: Routledge and Kegan Paul, 1985.

Boswell, James. *The Life of Samuel Johnson*. Garden City, NY: Doubleday, 1946.

Bourke, Joanna. *Eyewitness 1900–1909*. CD. BBC Audiobooks, 2004.

———. *Eyewitness 1970–1979*. CD. BBC Audiobooks, 2004.

Braekman, W. L., ed. *Of Hawks and Horses: Four Late Middle English Prose Treaties*. Scripta 16 (1986).

Braswell, Mary Flowers. "The Search for the Holy Grail: Arthurian Lacunae in the England of Edward III." *Studies in Philology* 108, no. 4 (Fall 2011): 469–87.

British Cartoon Archive. University of Kent. http://www.cartoons.ac.uk/.

"British Economics and Trade Union Politics 1973–1974." The National Archives. http://www.nation alarchives.gov.uk/releases/2005/nyo/politics.htm.

British Library Catalog of Illuminated Manuscripts. British Library and Museum. http://www.bl.uk/catalogues/illuminatedmanuscripts/welcome.htm.

British Telephone Archives. "British Phone Books, 1880–1984." Ancestry.com. http://search.ancestry.com/search/db.aspx?dbid=1025.

Britnell, Richard. "The Black Death in English Towns." *Urban History* 21, no. 2 (October 1994): 195–210.

Bromwich, Rachel, A. O. H. Jarman, and Brynley F. Roberts, eds. *The Arthur of the Welsh: The Arthurian Legend in Medieval Welsh Literature*. Cardiff: University of Wales Press, 1991.

———. *Trioedd Ynys Prydein*. Cardiff: University of Wales Press, 1963.

Brooke, Christopher. *Europe in the Central Middle Ages, 962–1154*. London: Longman, 1987 and 1964.

———. *From Alfred to Henry III: 871–1272*. New York: Norton, 1969.

———. *The Saxon and Norman Kings*. London: Fontana Library, 1967 and 1963.

———. *The Twelfth Century Renaissance*. New York: Harcourt, Brace and World, 1969.

Brown, Michelle P. *Understanding Illuminated Manuscripts: A Guide to Technical Terms*. Malibu, CA: J. Paul Getty Museum, 1994.

Brown, Tom. "Story of the Syndicalist Workers' Federation: Born in Struggle." Libcom.org. https://libcom.org/history/story-syndicalist-workers-federation-born-struggle.

———. *What's Wrong with the Unions? A Syndicalist Response*. Direct Action Pamphlet No. 1. London: SWF, 1955 and 1962: 8.

———. "Workers' Control." *Direct Action Pamphlet No. 4*. Libcom.org. https://libcom.org/library/direct-action-0.

———. "Nationalisation and the New Boss Class." *Direct Action Pamphlet No. 3*. Libcom.org. https://libcom.org/library/direct-action-0.

Burrows, J. A. *Gestures and Looks in Medieval Narrative*. Cambridge: Cambridge University Press, 2002.

Butterworth, Benjamin. *The Growth of Industrial Art*. Washington, DC: Government Printing Office, 1892.

———. *The Growth of Industrial Art*. New York: Alfred A. Knopf, 1972.

"Cadbury Castle." PastScape. English Heritage. http://www.pastscape.org/hob.aspx?hob_id=199646.

Calvi, Giulia. *Histories of a Plague Year: The Social and the Imaginary in Baroque Florence*. Trans. Dario Biocca and Bryant T. Ragan Jr. Berkeley: University of California Press, 1989.

Câmara, Archbishop Hélder. *Spiral of Violence*. London: Sheed and Ward, 1971.

The Cambridge History of English and American Literature. Vol. 2. Ed. A. W. Ward and A. R. Waller. Putnam, 1907–1921. Bartleby.com. http://www.bartleby.com/212/ .

The Cambridge Medieval History. Ed. J. B. Bury. New York: Macmillan, 1911.

Camille, Michael. *Gothic Art: Glorious Visions*. New York: Harry N. Abrams, 1996.

———. *Image on the Edge: The Margins of Medieval Art*. London: Reaktion Books, 1992.

————. *Mirror in Parchment: The Luttrell Psalter and the Making of Medieval England.* London: Reaktion Books, 1998.

Campbell, James, ed. *The Anglo-Saxons.* London: Penguin, 1991.

————. *Essays in Anglo-Saxon History.* London: Hambledon Press, 1986.

Camporesi, Piero. *The Incorruptible Flesh: Bodily Mutation and Mortification in Religion and Folklore.* Cambridge: Cambridge University Press, 1988.

Camus, Albert. *The Myth of Sisyphus and Other Essays.* Trans. Justin O'Brien. New York: Vintage Books, 1955.

Capp, Al. *The Best of Li'l Abner.* New York: Holt, Rinehart and Winston, 1978.

Caradoc of Llangarfan. "The Life of Gildas." *Medieval Sourcebook.* Fordham University. 2001. http://www.fordham.edu/halsall/basis/1150-Caradoc-LifeofGildas.asp.

Carlyle, Thomas. *History of Friedrich II of Prussia, Frederick the Great.* 1858–1865. Project Gutenberg. http://www.gutenberg.org/ebooks/25808.

Carpenter, David. *The Struggle for Mastery: The Penguin History of Britain 1066–1284.* London: Penguin, 2003.

Carrel, Helen. "The Ideology of Punishment in Late Medieval English Towns." *Social History* 34, no. 3 (August 2009): 301–20.

Cervantes, Miguel de. *Don Quixote.* Trans. Edith Grossman. New York: Harper Collins, 2003.

Chapman, Graham, John Cleese, Terry Gilliam, Eric Idle, and Michael Palin. *The Complete Works of Shakespeare and Monty Python.* London: Eyre Methuen, 1981.

————. *The Brand New Monty Python Bok.* London: Eyre Methuen, 1973.

————. *Monty Python and the Holy Grail (Book).* New York: Methuen, 1977.

————. *Monty Pythons' Big Red Book.* London: Methuen, 1971.

————. *Monty Python's Flying Circus.* 45 eps. 1969–1974.

————. *Monty Python's Flying Circus: Just the Words, Vols. 1 and 2.* London: Methuen, 1989.

Charles-Edwards, Thomas. "The Arthur of History." In *The Arthur of the Welsh: The Arthurian Legend in Medieval Welsh Literature*, ed. Rachel Bromwich, et al., 15–32. Cardiff: University of Wales Press, 1991.

Chaucer, Geoffrey. *The Canterbury Tales. The Riverside Chaucer, 3rd ed.* Boston: Houghton Mifflin, 1987.

Child, Francis James. *English and Scottish Ballads*, 8 Vols. Boston: J.R. Osgood, 1877.

The Chronicle of John, Bishop of Nikiu. Trans. R. H. Charles. London and Oxford: Williams & Norgate, 1916.

Claessens, Bob, and Jeanne Rousseau, eds. *Our Bruegel.* Antwerp: Mercatorfonds, 1969.

Coen, Deborah R. "Introduction: Witness to Disaster: Comparative Histories of Earthquake Science and Response." *Science in Context* 25, no. 1 (2012): 1–15.

Cohen, Jeffrey. *Of Giants: Sex, Monsters and the Middle Ages.* Minneapolis: University of Minnesota Press, 1999.

Cohn, Norman. *Europe's Inner Demons: An Enquiry Inspired by the Great Witch-Hunt.* London: Sussex University Press, 1975.

Colgrave, Bertram, and R. A. B. Mynors, eds. *Bede's Ecclesiastical History of the English People.* Oxford: Clarendon Press, 1969.

Collingwood, R. G. and J. N. L. Myres. *Roman Britain and the English Settlements.* Oxford: Clarendon Press, 1937.

Connell, Joanne, and Denny Meyer. "'Balamory Revisited': An Evaluation of the Screen Tourism Destination-Tourist Nexus." *Tourism Management* 30, no. 2 (2009): 194–207.

Coopey, Richard, and Nicholas Woodward, eds. *Britain in the 1970s: The Troubled Economy.* New York: St. Martin's, 1996.

Cornforth, John. *Country Houses in Britain: Can They Survive?* Crawley, Sussex: British Tourist Authority, 1974.

Coulton, G. G. *Medieval Panorama: The English Scene from Conquest to Reformation.* Cambridge: Cambridge University Press, 1949.

"Countdown to Crisis: Eight Days That Shook Britain." BBC News. 14 September 2000. http://news
.bbc.co.uk/2/hi/uk_news/924574.stm.

Cross, Tom Peete, trans. *A Story of Trystan, How He Went with Esyllt, the Wife of March y Meirchion.*
Studies in Philology 17, University of North Carolina. *SEJH.* http://sejh.pagesperso-orange.fr/keltia/
prydain/trystan-en.html.

Crossman, R. H. S., Michael Foot, and Ian Mikardo. *Keep Left.* London: New Statesman and Nation,
1947.

Cumming, Robert. *Annotated Art.* New York: DK, 1995.

Cummings, Michael. "Caricature de Cummings sur De Gaulle et l'adhésion du Royaume-Uni à la
CEE." From *Paris-Presse-L'intransigeant* (8 February 1963). CVCE. http://www.cvce.eu/obj/cari
cature_de_cummings_sur_les_conditions_d_adhesion_du_royaume_uni_aux_ce-fr-7341df8d-e5ac
-42b2-96bb-eafcc6c58a97.html.

Cunningham, Kevin. *The Bubonic Plague.* Minneapolis, MN: ABDO, 2011.

Darlington, Ralph, and Dave Lyddon. *Glorious Summer: Class Struggle in Britain 1972.* London: Bookmark, 2001.

Dawnay, Kit. "A History of Sterling." *Telegraph* (8 October 2001). http://www.telegraph.co.uk/
news/1399693/A-history-of-sterling.html.

Day, David. "*Monty Python and the Holy Grail*: Madness with a Definite Method." In *Cinema Arthuriana*, ed. Kevin J. Harty, 127–35. Jefferson, NC: McFarland, 2002.

De Boron, Robert. "The History of the Holy Grail: Prologue and Introduction." In *Sources of the Grail:
An Anthology*, ed. John Matthews, 162–73. Hudson, NY: Lindisfarne Press, 1996.

Defleur, Alban, et al. "Neanderthal Cannibalism at Moula-Guercy, Ardêche, France." *Science* (1 October 1999): 128–31.

Defoe, Daniel. *A Journal of the Plague Year; or, Memorials of the Great Pestilence in London in 1665.* London: Brayley, 1839.

De Graaf, Mia. "Jewel-Encrusted Goblet Found Gathering Dust in Tiny Spanish Museum . . ." *Mail
Online*, 31 March 2014. http://www.dailymail.co.uk/news/article-2593336/Jewel-encrusted-goblet
-gathering-dust-tiny-Spanish-museum-touched-lips-Jesus-fact-HOLY-GRAIL-say-two-histori
ans-book-prove-it.html.

Dekker, Thomas. *The Shoemaker's Holiday.* In *Drama of the English Renaissance: The Tudor Period*, ed.
Russell A. Fraser and Norman Rabkin. New York: Macmillan, 1976.

Delasanta, Rodney. "Penance and Poetry in the Canterbury Tales." *PMLA* 93, no. 2 (March 1978): 240–47.

Desser, David. *Reframing Japanese Cinema: Authorship, Genre, History.* Bloomington: Indiana University
Press, 1992.

De Troyes, Chrétien. *Arthurian Romances.* London: Penguin Books, 1991.

———. *Four Arthurian Romances: Eric et Enide, Cliges, Evain, and Lancelot.* Trans. W. W. Comfort.
Gutenberg Project. http://www.gutenberg.org/files/831/831-h/831-h.htm.

De Vries, Jan Vredeman. *Perspective.* New York: Dover, 1968.

Deuchler, Florens, Jeffrey M. Hoffeld, and Helmut Nickel. *The Cloisters Apocalypse I: An Early Fourteenth-Century Manuscript in Facsimile.* New York: Metropolitan Museum of Art, 1971.

———. *The Cloisters Apocalypse II: Commentaries on an Early Fourteenth-Century Manuscript.* New York:
Metropolitan Museum of Art, 1971.

Dickens, Charles. *Oliver Twist.* London: Richard Bentley, 1839.

Dickens, Frank. *The Great Boffo.* London: Abelard-Schuman, 1973.

A Dictionary of the English Language: A Digital Edition of the 1755 Classic by Samuel Johnson. Ed. Brandi
Besalke. November 10, 2012. http://johnsonsdictionaryonline.com/.

The Digital Scriptorium. University of California–Berkeley. http://bancroft.berkeley.edu/digitalscrip
torium/.

Dillenberger, John. *Images and Relics: Theological Perceptions and Visual Images in Sixteenth-
Century Europe.* Oxford: Oxford University Press, 1999.

Dixon, Arthur A. *The Holy Vessel Appeared in Their Midst.* In *King Arthur and the Knights of the Round
Table.* Doris Ashley. London: Raphael Tuck, 1922.

BIBLIOGRAPHY

Do Not Adjust Your Set. Television series, 1967–1969. ITV.

Donovan, Claire. *The Winchester Bible*. Toronto: University of Toronto Press, 1993.

Dougherty, Martin. *The Medieval Warrior: Weapons, Technology, and Fighting Techniques AD 1000– 1500*. Guilford, CT: Lyons Press, 2008.

Douglas, James. "The Overloaded Crown." *British Journal of Political Science* 6: 483–505.

Doyle, Julian. "Letter to Ian Kirk." Unpublished. 26 November 2011.

———. "Letter to Matjin Meerstadt, Freeway CAM (UK) Ltd." Unpublished. 2 April 2012.

———. *The Life of Brian Jesus*. Leicester: Matador, 2011.

———. *My Work*. "Statement made by Mr Doyle about the work he did on the [MPHG] film." Unpublished. 1 October 2012.

———. "Re: *Holy Grail* film production." E-mail messages to the author. November 2013–June 2014.

———. *Witness Statement of Julian Doyle*. "Between Mark Forstater and Mark Forstater Productions Ltd, claimants, and Python (Monty) Pictures Limited and Freeway Cam (UK) Limited, defendants." High Court of Justice, Chancery Division. Not dated (probably 2012).

Dumville, David N. "'Nennius' and the *Historia Brittonum*. *Studia Celtica* 10–11 (1975/1976): 78–95.

———. "Sub-Roman Britain: History and Legend." *History* 62, no. 205 (1977): 173–92.

Dyer, Christopher. *Everyday Life in Medieval England*. London: Hambledon and London, 2000.

Ebert, Roger. "*Macbeth*." Film Review. RogerEbert.com. 1 January 1971. http://www.rogerebert.com/reviews/macbeth-1971.

Eco, Umberto. *Travels in Hyperreality*. Orlando, FL: HBJ, 1986.

"Edward III." *Encyclopedia Britannica 1911 Edition*. Online Encyclopedia. http://encyclopedia.jrank.org/.

Eliot, Thomas Stearns. *The Waste Land* (1922). In *The Norton Anthology of World Masterpieces, Vol. 2*. 5th ed., ed. Maynard Mack, et al., 1673–87. New York: Norton, 1985.

Elley, Derek. *The Epic Film: Myth and History*. London: Routledge and Kegan Paul, 1984.

Emery, Fred. "How the Bitterness Came Through in This Back to Front Campaign." *Times* 30 April 1979: 8.

Engels, Friedrich. "The Origin of the Family, Private Property, and the State," 1884. Part IX: §3-4. Marxists Internet Archive. https://www.marxists.org/archive/marx/works/1884/origin-family/ch09.htm.

English Heritage. http://www.english-heritage.org.uk.

Epitome of the Ecclesiastical History of Philostorgius, Compiled by Photius, Patriarch of Constantinople. Trans. Edward Walford. London: Henry G. Bohn, 1855.

Evans, G. Blakemore, ed. *The Riverside Shakespeare*. Boston: Houghton Mifflin, 1974.

Evans, Joan, ed. *The Flowering of the Middle Ages*. New York: McGraw-Hill, 1966.

———, ed. and trans. *The Unconquered Knight: A Chronicle of the Deeds of Don Pero Nino, Count of Buelna*. Woodbridge, UK: The Boydell Press, 2004.

Everts, Sarah. "Europe's Hypocritical History of Cannibalism." Smithsonian.com. 24 April 2013. http://www.smithsonianmag.com/history/europes-hypocritical-history-of-cannibalism-42642371/?no-ist.

Farmer, D. L. "Prices and Wages, 1350–1500." In *Agrarian History of England and Wales, Vol. 3, 1348–1500*, ed. E. Miller. Cambridge: Cambridge University Press, 1991.

"Fetid Streets and Fouled Rivers." *Time* (9 November 1970).

Ferris, Paul. *The New Militants: Crisis in the Trade Unions*. Harmondsworth, UK: Penguin, 1972.

Fielding, Henry. *Tom Jones*. Ed. John Bender and Simon Stern. Oxford: Oxford University Press, 1996.

"Forecast: Cold and Dark." *Time* (21 February 1972): 47.

Forstater v Python (Monty) Pictures Ltd. Case No. HC11C01394, Royal Courts of Justice. 5 July 2013.

Fossier, Robert. *The Axe and the Oath: Ordinary Life in the Middle Ages*. Princeton, NJ: Princeton University Press, 2010.

Foster, Harold. *Prince Valiant Fights Attila the Hun*. Vol. 2. New York: Nostalgia Press, 1976.

———. *Prince Valiant in the Days of King Arthur*. Vol. 1. New York: Nostalgia Press, 1974.

———. *Prince Valiant's Perilous Voyage*. Vol. 4. New York: Nostalgia Press, 1976.

———. *Prince Valiant Queen of the Misty Isles*. Vol. 3. New York: Nostalgia Press, 1978.

Fox-Davies, Arthur Charles. *A Complete Guide to Heraldry*. London: Thomas Nelson, 1955.

Freely, John. *Before Galileo: The Birth of Modern Science in Medieval Europe*. New York: Overlook Duckworth, 2012.

Freeman, E. A. *The History of the Norman Conquest of England*. Chicago: University of Chicago Press, 1974.

Freemantle, Anne. *Age of Faith*. New York: Time-Life Books, 1965.

Friedman, Jeremy, et al. "Forum: Mao, Khrushchev, and China's Split with the USSR: Perspectives on *The Sino-Soviet Split*." *Journal of Cold War Studies* 12, no. 1 (Winter 2010): 120–65.

Frisch, Max. *Homo Faber*. Trans. Michael Bullock. New York: HBJ, 1959 and 1987.

Gallix, François, ed. *Letters to a Friend: The Correspondence between T. H. White and L. J. Potts*. New York: G.P. Putnam's Sons, 1982.

Gaskill, Malcolm. *Witchfinders: A Seventeenth-Century English Tragedy*. London: John Murray, 2005.

Geoffrey of Monmouth. "'Arthurian Passages from *The History of the Kings of Britain*' by Geoffrey Monmouth." Ed. and trans. J. A. Giles, D.L.C. The Camelot Project, University of Rochester. http://d.lib.rochester.edu/camelot/text/geoffrey-of-monmouth-arthurian-passages-from-the-history-of-the-kings-of-britain.

———. *History of the Kings of Britain*. Trans. Sebastian Evans. Revised by Charles W. Dunn. New York: E.P. Dutton, 1958.

Geographers' A to Z Street Atlas of London. Seven Oaks, Kent: Geographers' Map Co., 1968.

German, Lindsey, and John Rees. *A People's History of London*. London and New York: Verso, 2012.

Gervase of Tilbury. *Otia Imperialia: Recreation for an Emperor*. Ed. and trans. S. E. Banks and J. W. Binns. Oxford: Clarendon Press, 2002.

Gibson, William Sidney. *On Some Ancient Modes of Trial, Especially the Ordeals of Water, Fire, and Other Judicia Dei: Communicated to the Society of Antiquaries*. London: J. B. Nichols and Son, 1848.

Gidlow, Christopher. *The Reign of Arthur: From History to Legend*. Gloucestershire: Sutton, 2004.

Gildas. *The Ruin of Britain*. Trans. Michael Winterbottom. London and Chichester: Phillimore, 1978.

———. *De Excidio Britanniae* (Latin text). "The Sources on Vortigern." Ed. Robert Vermaat. Reprint of a portion of Ed. and Trans. Hugh Williams's Gildas, The Ruin of Britain &c. (1899), Cymmrodorion Record Series, No. 3. Transcribed by Roger Pearse. Vortigern Studies: British History 400–600. http://www.vortigernstudies.org.uk/arthist/vortigernquotesgil.htm.

Gilliam, Terry. *Animations of Mortality*. London: Eyre Methuen, 1978.

———. *Gilliam on Gilliam*. Ed. Ian Christie. London, New York: Faber and Faber, 1999.

Gilmour, Ian. "Dingy Quadrilaterals." *London Review of Books* (19 October 2006): 19–21.

Glaessner, Verina. *Kung Fu: Cinema of Vengeance*. New York: Bounty Books, 1974.

The Goon Show. Spike Milligan, Peter Sellers, and Harry Secombe. BBC Home Service 1951–1960. "*The Goon Show* Old Time Radio MP3 Collection," 2007.

The Gough Map. "Linguistic Geographies: The Gough Map of Great Britain." Kings College London. 2011. http://www.goughmap.org/.

Gower, John. *Confessio Amantis or Tales of the Seven Deadly Sins*, c. 1390. Project Gutenberg EBook. 1990. http://www.gutenberg.org/files/266/266-h/266-h.htm.

Grant, Edward. "The Nature of Western European Science in the Late Middle Ages (1200–1500). Lecture for the Taejon Expo '93: International Symposium on Traditional Sciences (29–30 April 1993). Bloomington: Indiana University Scholar Works Repository, 1993.

Grant, R. G., et al. *History of Britain and Ireland*. New York: DK, 2011.

"Great Britain: A Fair Cop." *Time* (16 July 1965): 37.

"Great Britain: The Widening Channel." *Time* (23 November 1959): 30.

Green, Thomas. *Concepts of Arthur*. Gloucestershire, UK: Tempus, 2007.

———. "The History and Historicisation of Arthur." In *Arthuriana: Early Arthurian Tradition and the Origins of the Legend*, 3–46. Louth, UK: Lindes Press, 2009.

Green, Caitlin R. "The Monstrous Regiment of Arthurs." *Arthuriana: Studies in Early Medieval History and Legend*. http://www.arthuriana.co.uk/historicity/arthurappendix.htm.

BIBLIOGRAPHY

Gregory of Tours. *History of the Franks*. ed. Paul Halsall. Medieval Sourcebook. Fordham University. http://www.fordham.edu/halsall/basis/gregory-hist.asp.

———. *History of the Franks*, VI.21. Trans. O. M. Dalton. Oxford: Clarendon Press, 1927.

Gyllene Böcker: Illuminerade medeltida handskrifter I dansk och svensk ägo. Stockholm: Nationalmuseum, 1952.

"Hafliði's Code." The Árni Magnússon Institute for Icelandic Studies. http://www.arnastofnun.is/page/althjodlegt_islenskunamskeid_en.

Hall, J. Lesslie, ed. and trans. *Beowulf: An Anglo-Saxon Epic Poem*. Project Gutenberg. July 2005. http://www.gutenberg.org/files/16328/16328-h/16328-h.htm.

Hallam, Elizabeth. *Four Gothic Kings*. New York: Weidenfeld and Nicolson, 1987.

Hallas, Duncan. "Reforming the Labour Party?" *International Socialism* 58 (May 1975): 23–24.

Halsall, Guy. *Worlds of Arthur: Facts and Fictions of the Dark Ages*. Oxford: Oxford University Press, 2013.

Hansen, Roger D. "Water-Related Infrastructure in Medieval London." Waterhistory.org. http://www.waterhistory.org/histories/london/.

Harty, Kevin, ed. *Cinema Arthuriana: Twenty Essays*. Jefferson, NC: McFarland, 2002.

Harvey, Barbara. *The Twelfth and Thirteenth Centuries*. Oxford: Oxford University Press, 2001.

Hatcher, John. "England in the Aftermath of the Black Death." *Past and Present* 144 (August 1994): 3–35.

Hayes, Kevin J. *Sam Peckinpah: Interviews*. Jackson: University Press of Mississippi, 2008.

Heath, Edward. *The Course of My Life: The Autobiography of Edward Heath*. London: Hodder Stoughton, 1998.

Heath, Sidney. *Pilgrim Life in the Middle Ages*. London: Unwin, 1911.

"Heath Takes His Case to the Voters." *Time* (18 February 1974): 49.

Heptonstall, Geoffrey. "Britain's Forgotten Prime Minister." *Contemporary Review* (June 2012): 185–91.

Herbert, J. A. *Illuminated Manuscripts*. New York: Burt Franklin, 1911.

Hewison, Robert. *In Anger: Culture in the Cold War, 1945–60*. London: Weidenfeld and Nicolson, 1981.

———. *Monty Python: The Case Against*. New York: Grove Press, 1981.

The High History of the Holy Graal. Trans. Sebastian Evans. London: J.M. Dent, 1903.

Higham, N. J. "Britons in Northern England." *Northern History* 38, no. 1 (March 2001): 5–25.

———. *The Death of Anglo-Saxon England*. Phoenix Mill, UK: Sutton Publishing, 1997.

———. *King Arthur: Myth-Making and History*. London: Routledge, 2002.

Hird, Christopher. "The Crippled Giants." *New Internationalist* 106 (December 1981): 18–19.

"A History of Anarcho-Syndicalism, Units 1–24." SelfEd Collective. Solidarity Federation. http://www.selfed.org.uk/a-s-history/a-history-of-anarcho-syndicalism.

"The History of Ericsson." www.ericssonhistory.com.

Hoffman, Donald L. "*Monty Python and the Holy Grail* in the Twenty-First Century." In *Cinema Arthuriana*, ed. Kevin J. Harty, 136–48. Jefferson, NC: McFarland, 2002.

Holkeboer, Katherine Strand. *Patterns for Theatrical Costumes: Garments, Trims and Accessories from Ancient Egypt to 1915*. New York: Prentice Hall, 1984.

Holland, Norman N. "The Puzzling Movies: Three Analyses and a Guess at Their Appeal." *Journal of Social Issues* 20, no.1 (1964): 71–96.

Holland, Stephen, ed. *Frank Bellamy's "King Arthur and His Knights: The Complete Adventure."* London: Book Palace Books, 2008.

Holmes, George. *The Later Middle Ages: 1272–1485*. New York: Norton Library, 1966.

Hoskins, W. G. "The English Landscape." In *Medieval England, Vol. 1.*, ed. A. L. Poole, 1–36. Oxford: Oxford University Press, 1958.

———. *The Making of the English Landscape*. London: Hodder and Stoughton, 1955.

"Houses of Benedictine Monks: Abbey of Bury St. Edmunds." *A History of the County of Suffolk: Vol. 2* (1975), 56–72. British History Online. http://www.british-history.ac.uk/report.aspx?compid=37880.

Houston, Mary G. *Medieval Costume in England and France*. London: Adam and Charles Black, 1939.

"Hypatia." *Encyclopedia Romana.* University of Chicago. http://penelope.uchicago.edu/~grout/encyclo paedia_romana/greece/paganism/hypatia.html.

I'm Sorry I'll Read That Again. BBC Radio. 1964–1973.

Ingrams, Richard, ed. *The Life and Times of Private Eye: 1961–1971.* New York: McGraw-Hill, 1971.

Internet Medieval Sourcebook. Fordham University. http://www.fordham.edu/halsall/sbook.asp.

Internet Modern History Sourcebook. Fordham University. http://www.fordham.edu/halsall/mod/modsbook.asp.

Internet Movie Database (IMDb). www.imdb.com.

———. "IMDb Top 250." IMDb Charts. http://www.imdb.com/chart/top.

Interview with Michael Palin & Terry Gilliam. BBC Channel 4. 1993.

In the Dispute Between the Devil and Humanity. Woodcut. In *Laienspiegel,* by Ulrich Tengler. Augsburg, 1510.

"Islington: Growth." *A History of the County of Middlesex: Vol. 8: Islington and Stoke Newington Parishes.* British History Online. http://www.british-history.ac.uk/report.aspx?compid=6734.

Jabberwocky. Dir. Terry Gilliam. UK, Python Films, 1977.

Jackson, Thomas. Originall of Vnbeliefe. London: John Clarke, 1625.

Jackson, Kenneth. *Language and History in Early Britain.* Edinburgh: Edinburgh University Press, 1953.

———. "Once Again Arthur's Battles." *Modern Philology* 43, no. 1 (August 1945): 44–57.

———. "The Arthur of History." *Arthurian Literature in the Middle Ages.* Oxford: Clarendon Press, 1959.

James, Lawrence. *The Rise and Fall of the British Empire.* New York: St. Martin's Griffin, 1994.

Johns, W. E. *Biggles and the Black Raider.* London: Hodder and Stoughton, 1953.

———. *Biggles and the Leopards of Zinn.* Leicester: Brockhampton Press, 1960.

Johnson, Kim. *The First 20 Years of Monty Python.* New York: St. Martin's Press, 1989.

———. *The First 28 Years of Monty Python.* New York: St. Martin's Press, 1998.

Jones, Dan. "The Peasants' Revolt." *History Today* (June 2009): 33–39.

Jones, Malcolm. *The Secret Middle Ages: Discovering the Real Medieval World.* London: Praeger, 2002.

Jones, Terry. *Chaucer's Knight: The Portrait of a Medieval Mercenary.* London: Weidenfeld and Nicolson, 1980.

Jones, Terry, and Alan Ereira. *Crusades.* New York: Facts on File and BBC Books, 1995.

Jones, Terry, Robert Yeager, Alan Fletcher, Julie Dor, and Terry Dolan. *Who Murdered Chaucer? A Medieval Mystery.* London: Methuen, 2003.

Jones, Thomas. "The Early Evolution of the Legend of Arthur." *Nottingham Mediaeval Studies* 8 (1964): 3–21.

Jonson, Ben. *Volpone.* In *Drama of the English Renaissance II: The Stuart Period,* ed. Russell A. Fraser and Norman Rabkin. New York: Macmillan, 1976.

Judt, Tony. *Postwar: A History of Europe since 1945.* New York: Penguin, 2005.

Kantor, J. R. "Science Reenters European Culture." In *The Scientific Evolution of Psychology, Vol. 1,* 311–26. Bloomington, IN: Principia Press, 1963.

Karras, Ruth Mazo. *Sexuality in Medieval Europe: Doing unto Others.* New York: Routledge, 2012.

Kauffmann, C. M. *A Survey of Manuscripts Illuminated in the British Isles, Vol. 3: Romanesque Manuscripts 1066–1190.* London: Harvey Miller, 1975.

Keen, Maurice. *Medieval Europe.* London: Penguin Books, 1968.

Keppie, Lawrence. *Scotland's Roman Remains.* Edinburgh: John Donald, 1998.

Kirby, D.P. *The Earliest English Kings.* London: Routledge, 2000.

Kirby, D. P., and J. E. Caerwyn Williams. Review of "The Age of Arthur." *Studia Celtica* 10–11 (1975–1976): 454–86.

Kirk, Maria Louise. *And Down the Long Beam Stole the Holy Grail.* In *The Story of Idylls of the King, Adapted from Tennyson.* Ed. Inez N. McFee. New York: F.A. Stokes, 1912.

Klein, Norman M. *Seven Minutes: The Life and Death of the American Animated Cartoon.* London: Verso, 1993.

Koepnik, Lutz P. "Unsettling America: German Westerns and Modernity." *Modernism/Modernity* 2, no. 3 (1995): 1–22.

BIBLIOGRAPHY

Kohn, A. "Syndicalism: Its Cause and Cure." *Socialist Standard* 100, no. 9 (December 1912): 25–26.

Kohn, Georg Childs. *Encyclopedia of Plague and Pestilence: From Ancient Times to the Present*. New York: Facts On File, 2008.

Kolpacoff, Jennifer. *History of Medieval Heresy and Inquisition*. Blue Ridge Summit, PA: Rowman & Littlefield, 2011.

Kramer, Heinrich, and Jacob Sprenger. *The Malleus Maleficarum* (*The Hammer of Witches*). Escondido, CA: Book Tree, 2000.

The Lancelot Grail, Parts I and II. Ed. Norris J. Lacy. Trans. Samuel N. Rosenberg and Carleton W. Carroll. Cambridge: Brewer, 2010.

Landow, George. "Tom Brown at Oxford *on Muscular Christianity*." The Victorian Web. http://www .victorianweb.org/authors/hughes/muscular.html.

Landy, Marcia. *Monty Python's Flying Circus*. Detroit: Wayne State University Press, 2005.

Langland, William. *Piers Plowman: A New Translation of the B Text*. Oxford: Oxford University Press, 1992.

———. *Piers Plowman*. "The Geoffrey Chaucer Page." Harvard University. http://sites.fas.harvard .edu/~chaucer/special/authors/langland/pp-pro.html.

"L'Aquila Quake: Italy Scientists Guilty of Manslaughter." BBC News 22 October 2012. http://www .bbc.com/news/world-europe-20025626.

Larsen, Darl. "'Is Not the Truth the Truth?' or Rude Frenchman in English Castles: Shakespeare's and Monty Python's (Ab)Uses of History." *Journal of the Utah Academy of Sciences, Arts, and Letters* 76 (1999): 201–12.

———. *"Its . . ." Shakespeare: English Renaissance Drama and Monty Python*. Dissertation. Northern Illinois University, 2000.

———. *Monty Python, Shakespeare and English Renaissance Drama*. Jefferson, NC: McFarland, 2003.

———. *Monty Python's Flying Circus: An Utterly Complete, Thoroughly Unillustrated, Absolutely Unauthorized Guide to Possibly All the References from Arthur "Two Sheds" Jackson to Zambesi*. Lanham, MD: Scarecrow Press, 2008.

———. *Monty Python's Flying Circus: An Utterly Complete, Thoroughly Unillustrated, Absolutely Unauthorized Guide to Possibly All the References from Arthur "Two Sheds" Jackson to Zambesi*. Lanham, MD: Taylor Trade Press, 2013.

Latham, Baldwin. "The Climatic Conditions Necessary for the Propagation and Spread of Plague." *Quarterly Journal of the Royal Meteorological Society* 26–27 (1900): 37–94.

Lawrence, Pieter. "The Bishop of Woolwich Squares the Circle." *Socialist Standard* (August 1963): 124–25.

Le Baker, Geoffrey. *The Chronicle of Geoffrey le Baker*. Trans. David Preest. Martlesham: Boydell Press, 2012.

Ledwirth, Mario. "IRA Terrorists 'Plotted to Kill Prince Philip . . .'" *Mail Online* 10 March 2014. http:// www.dailymail.co.uk/news/article-2577219/IRA-terrorists-plotted-kill-Prince-Philip-two-bombs -targeting-Australian-motorcade-royal-visit.html.

Lee, Stan, ed. *Black Knight*. Atlas Comics. June 1955.

Le Goff, Jacques. *The Birth of Europe*. Malden, MA: Blackwell, 2005.

Lester, G. A. "Chaucer's Knight and the Medieval Tournament." *Neophilologus* (1 July 1982): 460–68.

"Let's Go with Labour for the New Britain: The Labour Party's Manifesto for the 1964 General Election." London: Labour Party, 1964.

Levack, Brian P. *The Witch-Hunt in Early Modern Europe*. London: Longman, 2006.

L'Histoire de Guillame Marechal. Ed. Paul Meyer. Paris: Societe de l'histoire de France, 1891–1901.

Lindberg, David C. *The Beginnings of Western Science*. Chicago: University of Chicago Press, 2007.

Lindley, Arthur. "The Ahistoricism of Medieval Film." *Screening the Past* (29 May 1998). La Trobe University. http://tlweb.latrobe.edu.au/humanities/screeningthepast/firstrelease/fir598/ALfr3a.htm.

Linfert, Carl. *Hieronymus Bosch*. New York: Abrams, 1971.

Loomis, Roger S., ed. *Arthurian Literature in the Middle Ages*. Oxford: Clarendon Press, 1959.

Lyly, John. *Complete Works of John Lyly*. Ed. R. Warwick Bond. Oxford: Clarendon Press, 1902.

MacColl, Alan. "King Arthur and the Making of an English Britain." *History Today* 49, no. 3 (March 1999): 7–13.

MacLellan, W. J., and W. I. Sellers. "Ageing through the Ages." *Proceedings of the Royal College of Physicians of Edinburgh* 29, no. 1 (January 1999): 71–75.

Maddicott, J. R. "Plague in Seventh-Century England." *Past and Present* 156 (August 1997): 7–54.

Maitland, F. W. *Domesday Book and Beyond*. Cambridge: Cambridge University Press, 1907.

Malik, Rex. *What's Wrong with British Industry?* Baltimore, MD: Penguin, 1964.

Malory, Thomas. *Le Morte D'Arthur: Vols. 1 and 2*. Ed. Janet Cowen. London: Penguin, 2004, 1969.

———. *Le Morte Darthur: The Winchester Manuscript*. Ed. Helen Cooper. Oxford: Oxford University Press, 2008, 1998.

———. *Works*. Ed. Eugene Vinaver. Oxford: Oxford University Press, 1971.

Mansfield, Nick. *Buildings of the Labour Movement*. London: English Heritage, 2013.

Manzoni, Alessandro. *The Betrothed*. Hollywood, FL: Simon & Brown, 2011.

Marlowe, Christopher. *Edward II*. In *Drama of the English Renaissance I: The Tudor Period*, ed. Russell A. Fraser and Norman Rabkin. New York: Macmillan, 1976.

Marr, Andrew. "Chaos, Rubbish and Revolution." BBC News. 5 June 2007. http://news.bbc.co.uk/2/hi/uk_news/magazine/6721709.stm.

———. *A History of Modern Britain*. London: Macmillan, 2007.

Marston, John. *The Dutch Courtesan*. In *Drama of the English Renaissance II: The Stuart Period*, ed. Russell A. Fraser and Norman Rabkin. New York: Macmillan, 1976.

Matthews, John, ed. *Sources of the Grail: An Anthology*. Edinburgh: Floris Books, 1996.

Meuwese, Martine. "The Animation of Marginal Decorations in *Monty Python and the Holy Grail*." *Arthuriana* 14, no. 4 (2004).

Marwick, Arthur. *British Society since 1945*. London: Penguin, 2003.

Maxwell, Gordon S. *The Romans in Scotland*. Edinburgh: The Mercat Press, 1989.

McCabe, Bob, ed. *The Pythons: Autobiography by the Pythons*. New York: St. Martin's Griffin, 2005.

McCormick, Michael. "Rats, Communications, and Plague: Toward an Ecological History." *Journal of Interdisciplinary History* 34, no. 1 (Summer 2003): 1–25.

McGillivray, David. "Leo Kharibian." Obituary. *Guardian*, 12 September 2001. http://www.theguardian.com/news/2001/sep/12/guardianobituaries.

McGlynn, Sean. "Violence and the Law in Medieval England." *History Today* (April 2008): 53–59.

McKisack, May. *The Fourteenth Century: 1307–1399*. Oxford: Clarendon Press, 1959.

McNeill, T. E. *English Heritage Book of Castles*. London: Batsford, 1992.

Melly, George. *Revolt into Style: The Pop Arts*. London: Penguin, 1970.

Mielot, Jean. *Miracles de Nostre Dame*. Reproduced in Facsimile from Douce 374 in the Bodleian Library for John Malcolm of Poltalloch. Ed. George F. Warner. London: Nichols, 1885.

Miller, William Ian. *Anatomy of Disgust*. Cambridge, MA: Harvard University Press, 1997.

Milligan, Spike. *The Goon Show Scripts*. New York: St. Martin's, 1972.

———, et al. *The Goon Show*. Radio episodes. BBC Home Service, 1951–1960.

Minchin, J. G. Cotton. *Our Public Schools: Their Influence on English History*. London: Swann Sonnenschein & Co., 1901.

Mitchison, Naomi. *To the Chapel Perilous*. London: George Allen & Unwin, 1955.

Mittman, Asa Simon. *Maps and Monsters in Medieval England*. New York and London: Routledge, 2006.

Montgomery of Alamein, Field-Marshal Viscount. *A History of Warfare*. New York: The World Publishing Co., 1968.

Monty Python's And Now for Something Completely Different. Dir. Ian MacNaughton. USA, Columbia Pictures, 1971.

Monty Python and the Holy Grail. Dirs. Terry Gilliam and Terry Jones. UK, Michael White Productions, 1974.

Monty Python's Fliegender Zirkus: Samtliche deutschen Shows. Eds. Alfred Biolek and Thomas Woitkewitsch. Zurich: Haffmans Verlag AG, 1998.

BIBLIOGRAPHY

Monty Python's Flying Circus. Dir. John Howard Davies and Ian MacNaughton. BBC, 1969–1974.

Monty Python's Flying Circus Euroshow 71—May Day Special. BBC, 1971.

Monty Python's Life of Brian. Dir. Terry Jones. UK, HandMade Films, 1979.

Monty Python's Spamalot!. Wr. Eric Idle, et al. 2005.

Monty Python's the Meaning of Life. Dir. Terry Jones. UK, Celandine Films, 1983.

Moorhouse, Geoffrey. *Britain in the Sixties: The Other England*. Baltimore, MD: Penguin, 1964.

Morgan, David. *Monty Python Speaks!* New York: Avon Books, 1999.

Morgan, Kenneth O. *Britain since 1945: The People's Peace*. Oxford: Oxford University Press, 2001.

———. *The Oxford History of Britain*. Oxford: Oxford University Press, 2001.

Morgan, Nigel. *A Survey of Manuscripts Illuminated in the British Isles, Vol. 4: Early Gothic Manuscripts (I), 1190–1250*. London: Harvey-Miller, Oxford University Press, 1982.

———. *A Survey of Manuscripts Illuminated in the British Isles, Vol. 4: Early Gothic Manuscripts (II), 1250–1285*. London: Harvey-Miller, 1988.

Morgan, Nigel, and Lucy Freeman Sandler. "Manuscript Illumination of the Thirteenth and Fourteenth Centuries." *Age of Chivalry: Art in Plantagenet England 1200–1400*. London: Weidenfeld and Nicolson, 1987: 148–57.

Morris, John. *The Age of Arthur: A History of the British Isles from 350 to 650*. London: Wiedenfeld and Nicolson, 1973.

Mortimer, Ian. *The Time Traveler's Guide to Medieval England: A Handbook for Visitors to the Fourteenth Century*. New York: Touchstone, 2008.

Muller, Robert. *The Lost Diaries of Albert Smith*. London: Jonathan Cape, 1965.

Munby, Julian, Richard Barber, and Richard Brown. *Edward III's Round Table at Windsor: The House of the Round Table and the Windsor Festival of 1344*. Woodbridge, UK: Boydell, 2008.

Murray, Alexander. "Medieval Origins of the Witch Hunt." *Cambridge Quarterly* 7, no. 1 (1976): 63–74.

Napier, Susan J. *From Akira to Howl's Moving Castle*. New York: Palgrave Macmillan, 2005.

Nathan, David. *The Laughtermakers: A Quest for Comedy*. London: Peter Owen, 1971.

National Archives. http://www.nationalarchives.gov.uk/.

The New Partridge Dictionary of Slang and Unconventional English. www.partridgeslangonline.com/.

Nietzsche, Friedrich. *Die fröhliche Wissenschaft*. Leipzig: Chemnitz, 1882.

Norman, A.V.B., and Don Pottinger. *English Weapons and Warfare 449–1660*. New York: B&N Books, 1992.

Oakeshott, Walter, ed. *The Artists of the Winchester Bible*. London: Faber and Faber, 1945.

Oborne, Peter. "The Duke of Edinburgh: At 90: Prince Philip's Exemplary Life Can Be an Inspiration to All of Us." *Telegraph* (2 June 2011). http://blogs.telegraph.co.uk/news/peteroborne/100090543/prince-philip%E2%80%99s-exemplary-life-can-be-an-inspiration-to-us-all/.

"Off the Beaten Track with Cyril Lord David Cecil B. De Mille." *Private Eye* (1 January 1971): 13.

O'Hara, Glen. *Governing Post-War Britain: The Paradoxes of Progress, 1951–1973*. Houndmills, UK: Palgrave Macmillan, 2012.

Olsson, Kurt. "John Gower's *Vox Clamantis* and the Medieval Idea of Place." *Studies in Philology* 84, no. 2 (1987): 134–58.

Oman, C. C. "The English Folklore of Gervase of Tilbury." *Folklore* 55, no. 1 (March 1944): 2–15.

Opie, Iona, and Moira Tatem, eds. *The Oxford Dictionary of Superstitions*. Oxford: Oxford University Press, 1996.

Orderic Vitalis. *The Ecclesiastical History of England and Normandy*. Ed. T. Forester. London: Henry Bohn, 1856.

Orent, Wendy. *Plague: The Mysterious Past and Terrifying Future of the World's Most Dangerous Disease*. New York: Free Press, 2004.

Ormrod, Mark. *Edward III*. New Haven, CT: Yale University Press, 2011.

Padel, Oliver. "Arthur (supp. fl. in or before 6th cent.)." *Oxford Dictionary of National Biography*. Oxford University Press, 2004. http://www.oxforddnb.com/.

———. "The Nature of Arthur." *Cambrian Medieval Celtic Studies* 27 (Summer 1994): 1–31.

———. "Recent Work on the Origins of the Arthurian Legend: A Comment." *Arthuriana* 5, no. 3 (Fall 1995): 103–14.

Palin, Michael. *Diaries 1969–1979: The Python Years*. London: Thomas Dunne Books, 2007.

"Party Support Handbook—*The Rule Book*—Section M—Model Rules for a Regional Co-operative Party." Co-Operative Party. September 2010. http://party.coop/files/2013/05/The-Rule-Book-Section-M-Model-Rules-for-a-Regional-Co-operative-Party.pdf.

Paterson, Peter. *Tired and Emotional: The Life of Lord George Brown*. London: Chatto & Windus, 1993.

Paul, Evelyn. *Clair de Lune and Other Troubadour Romances*. New York: Brentano's, 1921.

———. *Aucassin and Nicolete* and *Clair de Lune*. http://www.Illuminated Books.com.

Paying for Labour's Programme: A Background Document. London: The Labour Party, 1973.

Peary, Danny. *Cult Movies*. New York: Delacourt Press, 1981.

Percival: The Story of the Grail. In *Arthurian Romances: Chrétien de Troyes*. Trans. D. D. R. Owen. London: Dent, 1987.

Petrarch. *The Sonnets, Triumphs and Other Poems of Petrarch*. Ed. Thomas Campbell. Project Gutenberg. http://www.gutenberg.org/files/17650/17650-h/17650-h.htm.

PHS. "Monty Python Hunts the Holy Grail." *Times Diary* (10 May 1974): 22.

Planchenault, René, ed. *L'Apocalypse d'Angers*. Paris: Caisse Nationale des Monuments Historiques et des Sites, 1966.

Poole, Austin Lane. *From Domesday Book to Magna Carta: 1087–1216*. Oxford: Oxford University Press, 1993 (orig. 1951).

———, ed. *Medieval England, Vols. 1 and 2*. Oxford: Clarendon Press, 1958.

———. "Recreations." In *Medieval England, Vol. 2*, ed. A. L. Poole, 605–32. Oxford: Clarendon Press, 1958.

Pope, Alexander. *The Rape of the Lock*. In *The Poems of Alexander Pope*. Ed. John Butt. New Haven, CT: Yale University Press, 1963.

Powicke, Maurice. *The Thirteenth Century: 1216–1307*. Oxford: Oxford University Press 1991.

Prestwich, Michael. "Edward I's Armies." *Journal of Medieval History* 37, no. 3 (2011): 233–44.

Purcell, Henry. *King Arthur*. In *Henry Purcell's Operas: The Complete Texts*. Ed. Michael Burden. Oxford: Oxford University Press, 2000.

Pyle, Howard. *The Story of King Arthur and His Knights*. New York: Scribner's, 1984 (1903).

———. *The Story of the Champions of the Round Table*. New York: Scribner's, 1933.

"Pythonland." *The Life of Python, Vol. 1*. A&E Network, 2001.

"The Quest for the Holy Grail Locations." Dir. Julian Doyle. *Monty Python and the Holy Grail* Blu-ray special feature. UK, Python Pictures, 2001.

Quiller-Couch, Arthur Thomas, Sir. *The Oxford Book of English Verse*. Oxford: Clarendon Press, 1919 (c. 1901). http://www.bartleby.com/101/.

Raban, Sandra. *England under Edward I and Edward II 1259–1327*. Oxford: Blackwell, 2000.

Randall, Lilian M. C. *Images in the Margins of Gothic Manuscripts*. Berkeley: University of California Press, 1966.

———. *Medieval and Renaissance Manuscripts in the Walters Art Gallery, Vol. 1: France, 875–1420*. Baltimore: Johns Hopkins University Press, 1989.

Reece, Richard. "Town and Country: The End of Roman Britain." *World Archaeology* 12, no. 1 (June 1980): 77–92.

Reis, Elizabeth. "Confess or Deny: What's a 'Witch' to Do?" New Hampshire Public Radio Broadcast. 1 September 2012. http://nhpr.org/post/september-1-elizabeth-reis-confess-or-deny-whats-witch-do.

Rentoul, John. "40 Years after Dark Side: Never Underestimate the Power of 'The Dark Side' . . . ." *Independent* 24 March 2013. http://www.independent.co.uk/arts-entertainment/music/features/40-years-after-dark-side-never-underestimate-the-power-of-the-dark-side-8547012.html.

Reston, James. "Poll Where Winners May Envy Losers." *Times*, 20 February 1974: 4.

———. "Why America Weeps: Kennedy Victim of Violent Streak He Sought to Curb in the Nation." *New York Times* 23 November 1963: 1, 7. http://www.nytimes.com/1963/11/23/why-america-weeps-kennedy-victim-of-violent-streak-he-sought-to-curb-in-the-nation.html?_r=0

Rigg, A. G. *A History of Anglo-Latin Literature*. Cambridge: Cambridge University Press, 1992.

Robb, John. *Punk Rock: An Oral History*. London: Ebury Press, 2007.

Robert of Avesbury. "The Black Death." In *Edward III and His Wars: Extracts from the Chronicles of Froissart, Jehan le Bel, Knighton, Adam of Murimuth, Robert of Avesbury, the Chronicle of Lanercost, the State Papers, & Other Contemporary Records*. Ed. W. J. Ashley. London: David Nutt, 1887.

Roberts, Jeremy. *King Arthur*. Minneapolis, MN: Lerner, 2001.

Roberts, Priscilla. "Perspectives on Lorenz M. Lüthi's *The Sino-Soviet Split: Cold War in the Communist World*." (Forum: Mao, Khrushchev, and China's Split with the USSR). *Journal of Cold War Studies* 12, no. 1 (Winter 2010): 120–28.

Robinson, David. "Axel's Lonely Castle: *The Gambler* (x) Universal, *Monty Python and the Holy Grail* (a) Casino, *Occasional Work of a Female Slave* (x)." *Times* (4 April 1975): 9.

———. "Fox into *Jackal*." *Times*, 15 June 1973: 9.

———. "Kung Fu." *Times*, 13 February 1975: 9.

"Robinson, Robert." Obituary. *Telegraph* 14 August 2011. http://www.telegraph.co.uk/news/obituaries/culture-obituaries/books-obituaries/8700576/Robert-Robinson.html.

Rocker, Rudolf. *Anarcho-Syndicalism: Theory and Practice*. New York: Gordon Press, 1972.

Rosenbaum, Jonathan. "*What's Up Tiger Lily?*" Review. *Monthly Film Bulletin* (March 1976): 65–66.

Rothwell, Kenneth S. "Roman Polanski's *Macbeth*: Golgotha Triumphant." *Literature/Film Quarterly* 1, no. 1 (Winter 1973): 71–75.

Rowley, Trevor. *The High Middle Ages: 1200–1550*. London: Routledge & Kegan Paul, 1986.

"A Ruinous Dispute." *Times* 3 January 1974: 13.

Russell, Jeffrey Burton. *Witchcraft in the Middle Ages*. Ithaca, NY: Cornell University Press, 1972.

Rutland Psalter: A Manuscript in the Library of Belvoir Castle. Introduction and edited by Eric George Millar. Oxford: Oxford, 1937.

Ryan, Peter. *The National Trust and the National Trust for Scotland*. London: J.M. Dent, 1969.

Sabine, Ernest L. "Latrines and Cesspools of Mediaeval London." *Speculum: A Journal of Medieval Studies* 9, no. 3 (July 1934): 303–21.

Sacks, Sheldon. *Fiction and the Shape of Belief*. Berkeley: University of California Press, 1964.

Sandbrook, Dominic. *Never Had It So Good: A History of Britain from Suez to the Beatles*. London: Little Brown, 2005.

———. *State of Emergency: The Way We Were: Britain 1970–74*. London: Allen Lane, 2010.

———. *White Heat: A History of Britain in the Swinging Sixties*. London: Little Brown, 2006.

Saul, Nigel. "Britain 1400." *History Today* 50, no. 7 (July 2000): 38–43.

Sawyer, P. H. *From Roman Britain to Norman England*. New York: Routledge, 1998 (1978).

Scanlon, Hugh. "The Role of Militancy." Interview. *New Left Review* 1, no. 46 (December 1967): 3–15.

———. *The Way Forward for Workers' Control*. London: Institute for Workers' Control, 1968.

Schatz, Thomas. "The New Hollywood." In *Film Theory Goes to the Movies*, ed. Jim Collins, Hilary Radner, and Ava Collins, 8–36. New York: Routledge, 1993.

Scherer, Margaret. *About the Round Table*. New York: Metropolitan Museum of Art, 1945.

Scoffield, Kelly H. "Adoption during the Roman Civil Law, the English Common Law and Early America." Paper submitted for Anglo-American Legal History, Prof. Thomas. Provo, UT: BYU Law Library, 1983.

Scot, Reginald. *The Discoverie of Witchcraft*. Ed. Brinsley Nicholson. London: Elliot Stock, 1886.

The Seventh Seal. Dir. Ingmar Bergman. Sweden, Svensk Filmindustri, 1957.

Shakespeare, William. *The Comedy of Errors*. The Riverside Shakespeare. Ed. G. Blakemore Evans. Boston: Houghton Mifflin, 1974.

———. *Hamlet*. The Riverside Shakespeare. Ed. G. Blakemore Evans. Boston: Houghton Mifflin, 1974.

———. *Henry IV*. The Riverside Shakespeare. Ed. G. Blakemore Evans. Boston: Houghton Mifflin, 1974.

———. *Henry V*. The Riverside Shakespeare. Ed. G. Blakemore Evans. Boston: Houghton Mifflin, 1974.

———. *Henry VIII*. The Riverside Shakespeare. Ed. G. Blakemore Evans. Boston: Houghton Mifflin, 1974.

————. *Love's Labor's Lost.* The Riverside Shakespeare. Ed. G. Blakemore Evans. Boston: Houghton Mifflin, 1974.

————. *Macbeth.* The Riverside Shakespeare. Ed. G. Blakemore Evans. Boston: Houghton Mifflin, 1974.

————. *Much Ado about Nothing.* The Riverside Shakespeare. Ed. G. Blakemore Evans. Boston: Houghton Mifflin, 1974.

————. *Romeo and Juliet.* The Riverside Shakespeare. Ed. G. Blakemore Evans. Boston: Houghton Mifflin, 1974.

————. *The Taming of the Shrew.* The Riverside Shakespeare. Ed. G. Blakemore Evans. Boston: Houghton Mifflin, 1974.

————. *Troilus and Cressida.* The Riverside Shakespeare. Ed. G. Blakemore Evans. Boston: Houghton Mifflin, 1974.

Shanks, Michael. *The Stagnant Society.* London: Penguin, 1972.

Shaw, G. B. *The Future of Political Science in America.* New York: Dodd, Mead and Co., 1933.

Shrewsbury, J. F. D. "The Yellow Plague." *Allied Science* 4, no. 1 (Winter 1949): 5–47.

Silver, Larry. *Hieronymus Bosch.* New York: Abbeville, 2006.

Simon of the Desert. Dir. Luis Buñuel. Mexico, Sindicato de Trabajadores de la Producción Cinematográfica, 1965.

Sir Gawain and the Green Knight. In *The Norton Anthology of World Masterpieces, Vol. 1.* 5th ed. New York: W.W. Norton, 1985.

Snyder, Christopher. *An Age of Tyrants: Britain and the Britons A.D. 400–600.* University Park: Pennsylvania State University Press, 1998.

————. "The Age of Arthur: Some Historical and Archaeological Background." *The Heroic Age* 1 (Spring/Summer 1999). http://www.heroicage.org/issues/1/haage.htm.

————. *The Britons.* Malden, MA: Blackwell, 2003.

————. *The World of King Arthur.* New York: Thames & Hudson, 2000.

Snyder, James, Henry Luttikhuizen, and Dorothy Verkerk. *The Art of the Middle Ages.* Upper Saddle River, NJ: Prentice Hall, 2006.

Snyder, Robert Lance. "'Shadow of Abandonment': Graham Greene's The Confidential Agent." *Texas Studies in Literature and Language* 52, no. 2 (Summer 2010): 203–26.

The Song of Roland. Trans. Dorothy L. Sayers. Harmondsworth, UK: Penguin Books, 1957.

Sorlin, Pierre. *The Film in History: Restaging the Past.* Oxford: Basil Blackwell, 1980.

The Sound of Music. Dir. Robert Wise. USA, Robert Wise Productions, 1965.

Southern, R. W. *The Making of the Middle Ages.* New Haven, CT: Yale University Press, 1961.

Spenser, Edmund. *The Faerie Queene.* Ed. A. C. Hamilton. New York: Longman, 1977.

Sprague, Kurth. "A Further Note on the Time-Period and Anachronisms in T. H. White's *The Once and Future King.*" England Have My Bones: For the Readers of T.H. White. 1996. http://www2.netdoor.com/~moulder/thwhite/toafk_b.html.

Stearne, John. *A Confirmation and Discovery of Witchcraft.* London: William Wilson, 1648.

Stenton, F. W. *Anglo-Saxon England.* Oxford: Oxford University Press, 2001 (1943).

Sterne, Laurence. *The Life & Opinions of Tristram Shandy.* New York: Modern Library, 1950.

Stockton, Eric W. *The Major Latin Works of John Gower.* Seattle: University of Washington Press, 1962.

Strickland, Deborah Higgs. "Monsters and Christian Enemies." *History Today* (February 2000): 45–51.

Strong, Roy, et al. *The Destruction of the Country House 1875–1975.* London: Thames and Hudson, 1974.

Studd, Robin. "A Fragile Tenure: England & Gascony 1216–1337." *History Today* (April 1986): 36–42.

Summis Desideratnes Affectibus. In *Witchcraft in Europe, 400–1700: A Documentary History,* ed. Alan Charles Kors and Edward Peters, 2nd ed., 177–80. Philadelphia: University of Pennsylvania Press, 2001.

"Swedish Film of Medieval Fatalism." *Times,* 10 March 1958: 5.

"Swedish Telecom." Swedish Telecom History. Funding Universe. http://www.fundinguniverse.com/company-histories/swedish-telecom-history/.

BIBLIOGRAPHY

Taylor, John. "Thomas Walsingham." *Oxford Dictionary of National Biography*, Oxford University Press, 2004. http://www.oxforddnb.com/index/28/101028628/.

Taylor, John Russell. "A Camera in the Bed." *Times*, 31 May 1969: 19.

———. "Not So Artless as They Look." *Times*, 3 April 1969: 14.

———. "Splendour in the Murk." *Times*, 1 July 1971: 20.

———. "Violence in the Abstract," *Times*, 21 August 1969: 11.

Telotte, J. P., ed. *The Cult Film Experience: Beyond All Reason*. Austin: University of Texas Press, 1991.

Tendler, Stewart. "Big Arms Discoveries in Army's First Raids on Orange Halls." *Times* 13 June 1974: 2.

Tennyson, Alfred. *Idylls of the King*. Minneapolis, MN: Filiquarian, 2007.

"Theatres Act 1968." National Archives. http://www.legislation.gov.uk/ukpga/1968/54/contents.

Thimann, Heidi. "Marginal Beings: Hybrids as the Other in Late Medieval Manuscripts." *Hortulus* 5, no. 1 (2009). http://hortulus-journal.com/journal/volume-5-number-1-2009/thimann/.

Thomas, Charles. "Are These the Walls of Camelot?" *Antiquity* 43 (1969): 27–30.

———. *Tintagel, Arthur and Archaeology*. London: Batsford/English Heritage, 1993.

Thompson, James Westfall. *The Medieval Library*. New York: Hafner, 1957.

Thompson, John O. *Monty Python: Complete and Utter Theory of the Grotesque*. London: BFI, 1982.

Thorpe, Vanessa. "Black Death Was Not Spread by Rat Fleas, Say Researchers." *Observer* 29 March 2014.

Thurston, Herbert. "Witchcraft." *The Catholic Encyclopedia*. Vol. 15. New York: Robert Appleton Company, 1912. New Advent. http://www.newadvent.org/cathen/15674a.htm.

Time Out London. "The 100 Best British Films." February 2013. http://www.timeout.com/london/film/the-100-best-british-films-3.

Toke, Leslie. "Flagellants." *The Catholic Encyclopedia*. Vol. 6. New York: Robert Appleton Company, 1909. New Advent. http://www.newadvent.org/cathen/06089c.htm.

Tolkien, J. R. R. *The Hobbit*. New York: Prentice Hall, 1991 (George Allen & Unwin, 1937).

Tolnay, Charles de. *Hieronymus Bosch*. Baden-Baden: Holle Verlag GMBH, 1965.

Toman, Rolf, ed. *The Art of Gothic: Architecture, Sculpture, Painting*. Cologne: Könemann, 1998.

Totaro, Rebecca, and Ernest B. Gilman. *Representing the Plague in Early Modern England*. New York: Routledge, 2011.

Trevelyan, G. M. *History of England*. 2nd ed. New York: Longmans, Green and Co., 1926.

———. *History of England*. 3rd ed. New York: Longmans, Green and Co., 1952.

"Trojan Horse in the E.E.C." *Times*, 10 January 1963: 9.

Tuchman, Barbara. *A Distant Mirror: The Calamitous 14th Century*. New York: Alfred Knopf, 1978.

Turner, Alwyn W. *Crisis? What Crisis? Britain in the 1970s*. London: Aurum, 2008.

Umland, Rebecca A., and Samuel J. Umland. *The Use of Arthurian Legend in Hollywood Film: From Connecticut Yankees to Fisher Kings*. Westport, CT: Greenwood Press, 1996.

"U.S. School Yearbooks." Ancestry.com. Provo, UT. Abt. 1975.

Vietnam Chronicles: The Abrams Tapes, 1968–1972. Ed. Lewis Sorley. Lubbock: Texas Tech, 2004.

Villalon, J. Andrew. "Gutierre Diaz de Gamez." *De Re Militari* Book Review. December 2005. http://www.deremilitari.org/REVIEWS/Gamez_UnconqKnight.htm.

Villon, Francois. "For Fat Margot." Trans. Anthony Bonner. In *The Complete Works of Francois Villon*. New York: McKay, 1960.

Voltaire. *Candide*. In *The Norton Anthology of World Masterpieces, Vol. 2*. 5th ed., ed. Maynard Mack, et al., 334–410. New York: Norton, 1985.

von Ehrenkrook, Jason. "Effeminacy in the Shadow of Empire: The Politics of Transgressive Gender in Josephus's *Bellum Judaicum*." *Jewish Quarterly Review* 101, no. 2 (Spring 2011): 145–63.

Von Eschenbach, Wolfram. *Parzival*. London: Penguin Books, 2004.

———. *Parzival: A Knightly Epic*. Vol. 2. Trans. Jessie L. Weston. New York: Stechert & Co., 1912.

Wagner, Anthony R. "Heraldry." In *Medieval England, Vol. 1*, ed. A. L. Poole, 605–32. Oxford: Clarendon Press, 1958.

Webbe, Stephen. "What Is Happening to the Stately Homes of Britain?" *Christian Science Monitor* (25 November 1983): 32–33. http://www.csmonitor.com/1983/1125/112501.html.

Welch, Martin. *The English Heritage Book of Anglo-Saxon England*. London: Batsford, 1992.

Wells, Paul. *Understanding Animation*. London: Routledge, 1998.

West, Anthony. "McCarthy in Westminster." *Spectator* (5 July 1963): 8–9.

"Western Europe: The Lonely Dreamer." *Time* (3 October 1960).

White, Andrew Dickson. *A History of the Warfare of Science with Theology in Christendom*. New York: D. Appleton Co., 1898.

White, Hayden. "Historiography and Historiophoty." *The American Historical Review* 93, no. 5 (December 1988): 1193–99.

White, Michael. *Empty Seats*. London: Hamish Hamilton, 1984.

White, T. H. *The Once and Future King*. New York: Putnam, 1939.

———. *The Sword in the Stone*. New York: G.P. Putnam Son's, 1938.

Whitehead, Phillip. *The Writing on the Wall: Britain in the Seventies*. London: Michael Joseph, 1985.

Whitney, Elspeth. "What's Wrong with the Pardoner? Complexion Theory, the Phlegmatic Man, and Effeminacy." *Chaucer Review* 45, no. 4 (2011): 357–89.

Williams, David. "Medieval Movies." *Yearbook of English Studies* 20, Literature in the Modern Media: Radio, Film, and Television Special Number (1990): 1–32.

Williams, Jay. *Knights of the Crusades*. New York: American Heritage Publishing, 1962.

Williams, Raymond. "The Liberals Move Up Fast." *The Nation* 29 October 1973: 432–34.

Willis, Dorothy, ed. *The Estate Book of Henry de Bray*. London: Royal Historical Society, 1916.

Wilmut, Roger. *From Fringe to Flying Circus*. London: Methuen, 1987.

Wilson, Harold. "Labour Party Annual Conference Speech." *Report of the Sixty-Second Annual Conference of the Labour Party*. Scarborough: Labour Party, 1963.

Wiseman, Howard M. "The Historicity and Historiography of Arthur: A Critical Review of *King Arthur: Myth-Making and History* by N. Higham, and *The Reign of Arthur: From History to Legend* by C. Gidlow." *The Heroic Age* 10 (May 2007). http://www.heroicage.org/issues/10/forum.html.

Wood, Michael. *The Story of England*. London: Penguin, 2010.

Woods, David. "An 'Earthquake' in Britain in 664." *Peritia* 19 (2005): 256–62.

"World in Brief." *The Scroll*. Ricks College, ID. University PressI Wire. 14 December 1973.

Wright, Jonathan. *Heretics: The Creation of Christianity from the Gnostics to the Modern Church*. Boston: Houghton Mifflin Harcourt, 2011.

Wyman, Carolyn. *Spam: A Biography*. Orlando, FL: Harcourt Brace, 1999.

Yorke, Barbara. "Kings of Kent (act. c. 450–c. 590)." *ODNB*. Oxford: Oxford University Press, 2004. http://www.oxforddnb.com/templates/article.jsp?articleid=52343&back=.

Young, Hugo. *This Blessed Plot: Britain and Europe from Churchill to Blair*. New York: Overlook Press, 1999.

Zedong, Mao. Report on an Investigation of the Peasant Movement in Hunan, March 1927. Internet Modern History Sourcebook. Fordham University. http://www.fordham.edu/halsall/mod/1927mao.html.

Zguta, Russell. "The Ordeal by Water (Swimming of Witches) in the East Slavic World." *Slavic Review* 36, no. 2 (June 977): 220–30.

INDEX

INDEX

sixteenth century, xviii, 26, 56, 58–59, 118, 151, 204, 208, 210, 211, 227, 310, 331, 370, 383, 394, 407n49, 429, 445, 456, 500

sixth century, xi, xiii, 29, 30, 31, 32, 37, 42, 43, 44, 45, 53, 54, 56, 66n57, 76, 83, 89, 96, 113, 124, 125, 138, 152n10, 215, 220n11, 233, 236, 310, 432, 451, 486

"The Sixties" (1960s), xiii–xiv, xxix, 1, 13, 14, 15, 20, 21, 22n27, 29, 32, 41–42, 65n28, 84, 106, 119, 123, 127, 130, 132, 141, 142, 146, 148, 152n9, 152n16, 158n140, 167, 169, 175, 202, 215, 233, 234, 242n36, 252, 255, 258, 263n18, 270, 279, 280, 281, 282, 292, 302–3, 329, 346n46, 372, 377, 378n7, 379n21, 390, 393, 395, 396, 407n49, 408, 417, 419n2, 441n14, 449, 483, 489. *See also* "The Fifties"; "The Seventies"

sketches (and doodles), 33, 72, 80, 195, 205, 217, 241n9, 253n14, 256, 261, 263n25, 265, 266, 269n2–3, 284, 286, 315, 322, 325, 362, 363, 426–27, 433n12, 433n16, 436, 465, 475, 495–529 *passim*, 529n2,

sketches (film/TV), xi, xviii, xix, xxii, xxiii, xxvi, 1, 3, 4, 12, 14, 17, 20, 25n82, 38, 47, 54, 56, 57, 59, 62, 64, 65n27, 68n90, 69n97, 69n113, 72, 84, 102, 131, 144, 146, 153n30, 159n162–63, 159n169, 159n172, 177, 178, 179, 184n47, 185n77, 204, 214, 220n10, 243n47, 244, 246, 253, 253n5, 254n28, 256, 258, 263n22, 264n32, 281, 282, 286, 287n10, 301, 311, 319, 340, 345n9, 346n31, 347, 357, 358, 359n6, 367, 369, 377, 378n8, 378n11, 379n20, 385, 386, 405n12, 405n20, 406n38, 416, 419, 424, 428, 429, 434, 444, 446, 447, 452, 455, 462, 464, 467, 471, 483, 487, 489. *See also Monty Python's Flying Circus* (episodes)

Slade, Julian, 165

Slater-Walker Securities, 17, 19, 25n88

Sleuth, 3

Smith, Ian. *See* Rhodesia

Smollett, Tobias, 90

Sneddon, Tracy, 6

"snuff it," 457

Snyder, Christopher, 36, 40, 43, 83, 84, 264n37, 371, 460

Snyder, James, 324

socialism, xxviiin25, 18, 19, 25n86, 106, 107, 112, 119, 123, 126–28, 142–44, 148, 150, 156n101–2, 252, 257, 263n16, 318, 394

Socialist Standard, 127, 257

Socialist (parties), 123, 127, 143, 147–48, 156n101–2, 252

Socialist Workers Party (SWP), 126

"Society for Putting Things on Top of Other Things," 234, 347. *See also Monty Python's Flying Circus* (episodes)

sod, 89, 286, 339, 342–43, 388–89, 444, 445, 483

Solzhenitsyn, Aleksandr, 61

Somerset, 26, 41, 83, 137, 252, 253n11, 307, 374, 461, 486

The Song of Roland, 164, 182n18, 304, 311–12, 313, 320n22

sound effects, 8, 16, 33–34, 55, 62, 79, 177, 214, 284–85, 328, 335, 355, 392, 406n40, 443, 490n7; catapult, 214, 284–85, 295, 484; hooves, 28, 33, 49, 53, 55, 58, 62; raspberries, 286, 392, 482

soundtrack, 2, 16, 62, 291, 335, 417, 443, 446, 450

soundtrack albums. *See* albums

Sources of the Grail: An Anthology. See Matthews, John

South Saxons, 50

Southern, R. W., 140

Spain, 151, 157n113, 160n188, 235, 240, 241, 273, 285, 288n26, 331, 386, 422, 428. *See also* Europe

Spam, 247–48, 252, 254n17, 254n20, 254n22, 380, 382n2

"Spam," 382n2. *See also Monty Python's Flying Circus* (episodes)

"The Spanish Inquisition," 72, 178, 483. *See also Monty Python's Flying Circus* (episodes)

spear. *See* weapons

Speculum Maius. See de Beauvais, Vincent

Spenser, Edmund, xii, 223n79

"The Spot," 392. *See also Monty Python's Flying Circus* (episodes)

"Spot the Loony," 177. *See also Monty Python's Flying Circus* (episodes)

Sprague, Kurth, 193, 221n22

Squire, Romilly, 6

St. Aaaaaarrrrrggghhh. *See* castles

St. Abraham, 88

St. Albans, xxviiin23, 50–51, 362, 533

St. Anthony, 88, 205, 266, 433n16, 505, 510, 511, 512, 513, 525, 528. *See also* Bosch, Hieronymus

St. Athanasius, 88

St. Attila, 455. *See also* Attila the Hun

St. Augustine, 41, 166, 307

St. Benedict, 92n24, 192, 194, 220n11, 256, 362, 364, 374

St. Benet's, 414

St. Boniface, 322–23, 477

ABOUT THE AUTHOR

Darl Larsen was born and raised in central California and has been part of the film faculty at Brigham Young University since 1998. He took degrees at UC Santa Barbara, Brigham Young University, and Northern Illinois University. He is professor in both the Media Arts department and the Center for Animation at BYU, teaching film, animation, screenwriting, and popular culture studies. He has written extensively in the area of Monty Python studies. He lives in Provo, Utah, with his family.